Alternative Minimum Tax–2010

If AMTI minus the exemption is:		The Tax Is:	
Over—	But Not Over—		Of the Amount Over—
$0	$175,000*	26%	$0
175,000*		$45,500* – 28%	
175,000*			

*$87,500 and $22,750 for married taxpayers filing separately.

Social Security Tax–2010

Category	
OASDI	
Medicare	
Total	7.65%

Self-Employment Tax–2010

Category	Rate	Dollar Limit
OASDI	12.40%	$106,800
Medicare	2.90%	None
Total	15.30%	

STANDARD DEDUCTION

Filing Status	2010 Amount
Married individuals filing joint returns and surviving spouses	$11,400
Heads of households	8,400
Unmarried individuals (other than surviving spouses and heads of households)	5,700
Married individuals filing separate return	5,700
Additional standard deductions for the aged and the blind	
Individual who is married and surviving spouses	1,100*
Individual who is unmarried and not a surviving spouse	1,400*
Taxpayer claimed as dependent on another taxpayer's return	950

*These amounts are $2,200 and $2,800, respectively, for a taxpayer who is both aged and blind.

Personal Exemption 2010: $3,650 Prior to 2010, personal exemptions were subject to a reduction for higher income taxpayers. This reduction has been eliminated for 2010 and future years although there has been some discussion about bringing this provision back into the law to raise additional revenue for the government.

Itemized Deductions

Prior to 2010, total itemized deductions were subject to a reduction for higher income taxpayers. This reduction has been eliminated for 2010 and future years. Whether the elimination is permanent is uncertain.

PRENTICE HALL
FEDERAL TAXAT...
2011

Individuals

EDITORS

THOMAS R. POPE
University of Kentucky

KENNETH E. ANDERSON
University of Tennessee

JOHN L. KRAMER
University of Florida

CONTRIBUTING AUTHORS

D. DALE BANDY
University of Central Florida

N. ALLEN FORD
University of Kansas

ROBERT L. GARDNER
Brigham Young University

RICHARD J. JOSEPH
Hult International Business School

LEANN LUNA
University of Tennessee

MICHAEL S. SCHADEWALD
University of Wisconsin–Milwaukee

Prentice Hall

Boston Columbus Indianapolis New York San Francisco Upper Saddle River
Amsterdam Cape Town Dubai London Madrid Milan Munich Paris Montreal Toronto
Delhi Mexico City Sao Paulo Sydney Hong Kong Seoul Singapore Taipei Tokyo

VP, Editorial Director: Sally Yagan
AVP/Editor-in-Chief: Donna Battista
Acquisitions Editor: Julie Broich
AVP/Director of Product Development: Lisa Strite
Product Development Manager: Ashley Santora
Editorial Project Manager: Rebecca Knauer
Editorial Assistant: Christina Rumbaugh
Director of Marketing: Kate Valentine
VP/Director of Marketing: Patrice Lumumba Jones
Senior Marketing Manager: Elizabeth Averbeck
Marketing Assistant: Ian Gold
Senior Managing Editor: Cynthia Zonneveld
Senior Production Project Manager: Rhonda Aversa
Associate Director of Manufacturing: Alexis Heydt
Senior Operations Specialist: Diane Peirano
Cover Design: Black Horse Designs
Art Director: Jonathan Boylan
Cover Image: © iStockphoto LP
Manager, Rights and Permissions: Shannon Barbe
Manager, Cover Visual Research & Permissions: Karen Sanatar
Production Media Project Manager: John Cassar
Editorial Media Project Manager: Allison Longley
Full-Service Project Management: Diane Kohnen/S4Carlisle Publishing Services
Composition: S4Carlisle Publishing Services
Printer/Binder: Courier/Kendallville
Cover Printer: Lehigh-Phoenix Color/Hagerstown
Text Font: 10/12 Sabon

Prentice Hall
is an imprint of

10 9 8 7 6 5 4 3 2 1
ISBN-10: 0-13-213857-3
ISBN-13: 978-0-13-213857-4

www.pearsonhighered.com

CONTENTS

iii

CHAPTER 13
▶ PROPERTY TRANSACTIONS: SECTION 1231 AND RECAPTURE 13-1

CHAPTER 14
▶ SPECIAL TAX COMPUTATION METHODS, TAX CREDITS, AND PAYMENT OF TAX 14-1

ABOUT THE EDITORS

THOMAS R. POPE

Thomas R. Pope is the Ernst & Young Professor of Accounting at the University of Kentucky. He received a B.S. from the University of Louisville and an M.S. and D.B.A. in business administration from the University of Kentucky. He teaches international taxation, partnership and S corporation taxation, tax research and policy, and introductory taxation and has won outstanding teaching awards at the University, College, and School of Accountancy levels. He has published articles in *The Accounting Review*, the *Tax Adviser, Taxes, Tax Notes,* and a number of other journals. Professor Pope's extensive professional experience includes eight years with Big Four accounting firms. Five of those years were with Ernst & Whinney (now part of Ernst & Young), including two years with their National Tax Department in Washington, D.C. He subsequently held the position of Senior Manager in charge of the Tax Department in Lexington, Kentucky. Professor Pope also has been a leader and speaker at professional tax conferences all over the United States and is active as a tax consultant.

KENNETH E. ANDERSON

Kenneth E. Anderson is the Pugh & Company Professor of Accounting at the University of Tennessee. He earned a B.B.A. from the University of Wisconsin–Milwaukee and subsequently attained the level of tax manager with Ernst & Young. He then earned a Ph.D. from Indiana University. He teaches corporate taxation, partnership taxation, and tax strategy, and has three times won the Beta Alpha Psi Outstanding Educator Award. Professor Anderson also is the Director of the Master of Accountancy Program. He has published articles in *The Accounting Review, The Journal of the American Taxation Association, Advances in Taxation,* the *Journal of Accountancy,* the *Journal of Financial Service Professionals,* and a number of other journals.

JOHN L. KRAMER

John L. Kramer is a former Professor of Accounting at the University of Florida. He was a recipient of a Teaching Improvement Program award given by the University of Florida in 1994. He holds a Ph.D. in Business Administration and an M.B.A. from the University of Michigan (Ann Arbor), and a B.B.A. from the University of Michigan (Dearborn). He is a past president of the American Taxation Association and the Florida Association of Accounting Educators, as well as a past editor of *The Journal of the American Taxation Association.* In 2001, Professor Kramer received the Ray M. Sommerfeld Outstanding Tax Education Award, co-sponsored by the American Taxation Association and Ernst & Young. Professor Kramer has taught for the American Institute of CPAs, American Tax Institute of Europe, and a number of national and regional accounting firms. He has been a frequent speaker at academic and professional conferences, as well as having served as an expert witness in a number of court cases. He has published over 50 articles in *The Accounting Review, The Journal of the American Taxation Association,* the *Tax Adviser,* the *Journal of Taxation,* and other academic and professional journals. Professor Kramer has been an editor on *The Prentice Hall Federal Tax* series since 1989.

D. Dale Bandy is Professor Emeritus in the School of Accounting at the University of Central Florida. He received a B.S. from the University of Tulsa, an M.B.A. from the University of Arkansas, and a Ph.D. from the University of Texas at Austin. He helped to establish the Master of Science in Taxation programs at the University of Central Florida and California State University, Fullerton, where he previously taught. In 1985, he was selected by the California Society of Certified Public Accountants as the Accounting Educator of the year. Professor Bandy has published 8 books and more than 30 articles in accounting and taxation. His articles have appeared in the *Journal of Taxation,* the *Journal of Accountancy, Advances in Taxation,* the *Tax Adviser, The CPA Journal, Management Accounting,* and a number of other journals.

N. Allen Ford is the Larry D. Homer/KPMG Peat Marwick Distinguished Teaching Professor of Professional Accounting at the University of Kansas. He received an undergraduate degree from Centenary College in Shreveport, Louisiana, and both the M.B.A. and Ph.D. in Business from the University of Arkansas. He has published over 40 articles related to taxation, financial accounting, and accounting education in journals such as *The Accounting Review, The Journal of the American Taxation Association,* and *The Journal of Taxation.* He served as president of the American Taxation Association in 1979–80. Professor Ford has received numerous teaching awards at the college and university levels. In 1993, he received the Byron T. Shutz Award for Distinguished Teaching in Economics and Business. In 1996 he received the Ray M. Sommerfeld Outstanding Tax Educator Award, which is jointly sponsored by the American Taxation Association and Ernst & Young and in 1998 he received the Kansas Society of CPAs Outstanding Education Award.

Robert L. Gardner is the Robert J. Smith Professor of Accounting in the School of Accountancy at Brigham Young University (BYU). He received a B.S. and M.B.A. from the University of Utah and a Ph.D. from the University of Texas at Austin. He has authored or coauthored two books and over 25 articles in journals such as *The Tax Advisor, Journal of Corporate Taxation, Journal of Real Estate Taxation, Journal of Accounting Education, Journal of Taxation of S Corporations, and the International Tax Journal.* Professor Gardner has received several teaching awards. In 2001, he received the Outstanding Faculty Award in the Marriott School of Management at BYU. He has served on the Board of Trustees of the American Taxation Association and served as President of the ATA in 1999–2000.

Richard J. Joseph is the Provost of Hult International Business School in Cambridge, Massachusetts. He is a current member of the Hult Accounting Faculty and a former member of the tax faculty of The University of Texas at Austin. A graduate *magna cum laude* of Harvard College (B.A.), Oxford University (M.Litt.), and The University of Texas at Austin School of Law (J.D.), he has taught individual, corporate, international, state and local taxation, tax research methods, and the fundamentals of financial and managerial accounting. Before embarking on his academic career, Provost Joseph worked as an investment banker and securities trader on Wall Street and as a mergers and acquisitions lawyer in Texas. He is co-editor of the *Oxford Handbook on Mergers and Acquisitions* and has written numerous commentaries in the *Financial Times, The Christian Science Monitor, Tax Notes,* and *Tax Notes International.* His book, *The Origins of the American Income Tax,* explores the original intent, rationale, and effect of the early American income tax.

Michael S. Schadewald, Ph.D., CPA, is on the faculty of the University of Wisconsin-Milwaukee where he teaches graduate and undergraduate courses in business taxation. A graduate of the University of Minnesota, Professor Schadewald is a co-author of several books on multistate and international taxation and has published more than 40 articles in academic and professional journals, including *The Accounting Review, Journal of Accounting Research, Contemporary Accounting Research, The Journal of the American Taxation Association, CPA Journal, Journal of Taxation,* and *The Tax Adviser.* Professor Schadewald also has served on the editorial boards of *The Journal of the American Taxation Association, Journal of State Taxation, International Tax Journal, The International Journal of Accounting, Issues in Accounting Education,* and *Journal of Accounting Education.*

Why is the Pope/Anderson/Kramer series the best choice for your students?

The Pope/Anderson/Kramer 2011 Series in Federal Taxation is appropriate for use in any first course in federal taxation, and comes in a choice of three volumes:

Federal Taxation 2011: Individuals

Federal Taxation 2011: Corporations, Partnerships, Estates & Trusts
        (the companion book to *Individuals*)

Federal Taxation 2011: Comprehensive
        (includes 29 chapters; 14 chapters from *Individuals* and 15 chapters
        from *Corporations*)

- The *Corporations, Partnerships, Estates & Trusts* and *Comprehensive* volumes contain three comprehensive tax return problems whose data change with each edition, thereby keeping the problems fresh. Problem C:3-64 contains the comprehensive corporate tax return, Problem C:9-58 contains the comprehensive partnership tax return, and Problem C:11-64 contains the comprehensive S corporation tax return, which is based on the same facts as Problem C:9-58 so that students can compare the returns for these two entities.

- The *Corporations, Partnerships, Estates & Trusts* and *Comprehensive* volumes contain sections called Financial Statement Implications, which discuss the implications of Accounting Standards Codification (ASC) 740, formerly SFAS No. 109 and FIN 48. The main discussion of accounting for income taxes appears in Chapter C:3. The financial statement implications of other transactions appear in Chapters C5, C:7, C:8, and C:16 (*Corporations* volume only).

We want to stress that *all* entities are covered in the *Individuals* volume although the treatment is often briefer than in the *Corporations* and *Comprehensive* volumes. The *Individuals* volume, therefore, is appropriate for colleges and universities that require only one semester of taxation as well as those that require more than one semester of taxation. Further, this volume adapts the suggestions of the Model Tax Curriculum as promulgated by the American Institute of Certified Public Accountants.

Of course, this series retains core features popular with adopters and their students:

- **Blend of Technical Content and Readability**
  The Pope/Anderson/Kramer series is unsurpassed in blending the technical content of the tax law with a high level of readability for students. The authors continually refine this delicate balance to advance student learning.

- **Problem Materials**
  The problem materials in the series are continually praised for enabling students to apply the tax principles in the chapters to real-life situations. Learning is enhanced with challenging problem materials and the Pope/Anderson/Kramer series offer outstanding materials for classroom use.

- **JIT Custom Text**
  Now you can create your own tax book using content drawn from the Pope/Anderson/Kramer series. You can even include your own materials. Ask your Prentice Hall representative for specific information on custom text procedures and policies or log onto *www.pearsoncustom.com/custom-library* to learn more about your options.

- **NEW TaxACT 2009 Software Packaged with the Text for a Nominal Price**
  This user-friendly tax preparation program includes more than 80 tax forms, schedules, and worksheets. TaxACT calculates returns and alerts the user to possible errors or entries.

- **Commitment to Service**
  Faculty should log onto *www.pearsonhighered.com/replocator* to locate their Prentice Hall representative using our unique "Rep Locator" search feature.

Expert Insights—Unique Student Learning Features

What Would You Do in This Situation? Boxes

Unique to the Pope/Anderson/Kramer series, these boxes place students in a decision-making role. The boxes include many *current controversies* that are as yet unresolved or are currently being considered by the courts.

These boxes make extensive use of **Ethical Material** as they represent choices that may put the practitioner at odds with the client.

WHAT WOULD YOU DO IN THIS SITUATION?

INVENTORY VALUATION

Jack is a new tax client. He says he and his previous accountant did not get along very well. Jack owns an automobile dealership with sales of $12 million. He has provided you with most of the information you need to prepare his tax return, but he has not yet given you the year-end inventory value. You have completed much of the work on his return, but cannot complete it without the inventory figure. You have called Jack three times about the inventory. Each time he has interrupted, and asked you what his tax liability will be at alternative inventory levels. What problem do you see?

Stop & Think Boxes

These "speed bumps" encourage students to pause and apply what they have just learned. Solutions for each issue are provided in the box.

 STOP & THINK

Question: When one company purchases the assets of another company, the purchasing company may acquire goodwill. Since purchased goodwill is a Sec. 197 intangible asset and may be amortized over 15 years, the determination of the cost of goodwill is important. How is the "cost" of goodwill determined when the purchasing company purchases many assets in the acquisition?

Solution: The IRS requires that taxpayers use the "residual method" as prescribed in Sec. 1060. Under this method, all of the assets except for goodwill are valued. The total value of these assets is then subtracted from the total purchase price, and the residual is the amount of the purchase price allocated to goodwill.

Unique Margin Notes

These provide an extensive series of learning tips for students and faculty. No other text can match the quantity, quality, or variety of these resources:

- Additional Comment
- Key Points
- Real-World Examples
- Typical Misconceptions
- Ethical Points
- Self-Study Questions and Answers
- Book-to-Tax Accounting Comparisons
- Historical Notes
- Tax Strategy Tips
- New Tax Act
- Legislative Update

ETHICAL POINT

An employer must have a reasonable basis for treating a worker as an independent contractor or meet the general common law rules for determining whether an employer-employee relationship exists. Otherwise, the employer is liable for federal and state income tax withholding, FICA and FUTA taxes, interest, and penalties associated with the misclassification.

TAX STRATEGY TIP

Rather than having the corporation borrow money, an S corporation shareholder might consider borrowing money directly from the bank and then lending the loan proceeds to the corporation with the corporation guaranteeing the bank loan. In this way, the shareholder will obtain debt basis.

ADDITIONAL COMMENT

Stock purchased on which a dividend has been declared has an increased value. This value will drop when the corporation pays the dividend. If the dividend is eligible for a dividends-received deduction and the drop in value also creates a capital loss, corporate shareholders could use this event as a tax planning device. To avoid this result, no dividends-received deduction is available for stock held 45 days or less.

Innovative Technology and Supplements

FOR INSTRUCTORS

- *NEW TaxACT 2009 Software Packaged with the Text for a Nominal Price.* This user-friendly tax preparation program includes more than 80 tax forms, schedules, and worksheets. TaxACT calculates, returns, and alerts the user to possible errors or entries.

- *Instructor's Guide* contains sample syllabi, instructor outlines, and notes on the end-of-chapter problems. It also contains solutions to the tax form/tax return preparation problems. It is available as a password-protected download from the Instructor Resource Center on *www.pearsonhighered.com/accounting*. Ask your Prentice Hall representative for your password. It is also available in hard copy.

- *Solutions Manual* contains solutions to discussion questions, problems, and comprehensive and tax strategy problems. It also contains all solutions to the case study problems, research problems, and "What Would You Do in This Situation?" boxes. It is available as a password-protected download from the Instructor Resource Center on *www.pearsonhighered.com/accounting* and also in hard copy. Upon written request, Prentice Hall may grant permission for faculty to post solutions on a student-accessible site, provided that this is password-protected at the school.

- *Testing.* The **Test Item File** contains a wealth of true/false, multiple-choice, and calculative problems. A computerized program is available to adopters.

- *PowerPoint slides* include over 300 full-color electronic transparencies available for *Individuals* and *Corporations*. These are available for download on the Companion Website where students and faculty have access to them.

- *Some Instructor Resources* are available for platforms such as WebCT and Blackboard from our Instructor Resource Center.

Text Companion Website for Faculty and Students Available at *www.pearsonhighered.com/phtax*

The Web site provides a wealth of FREE material to help students study and help faculty prepare for class.

1. Student Resources include

- True/False and Multiple-Choice Questions
- Current Events
- Internet Resources
- Tax Law Updates
- PowerPoint Slides
- Multistate Income Taxation chapter with accompanying questions

2. Instructor Resources include

- An Instructor's guide, Solutions Manual, Testbank (both printed & computerized) and PowerPoint slides are available for instructors to download at *www.pearsonhighered.com/accounting*.
- Some Instructor Resources are available for platforms such as WebCT and Blackboard from our Instructor Resource Center.
- Additional Case Study problems, computational questions, and tax return problems appear in each chapter of the student site.

ACKNOWLEDGMENTS

Our policy is to provide annual editions and to prepare timely updated supplements when major tax revisions occur. We are most appreciative of the suggestions made by outside reviewers because these extensive review procedures have been valuable to the authors and editors during the revision process.

We are also grateful to the various graduate assistants, doctoral students, and colleagues who have reviewed the text and supplementary materials and checked solutions to maintain a high level of technical accuracy. In particular, we would like to acknowledge the following colleagues who assisted in the preparation of supplemental materials for this text:

Al Case	Southern Oregon University
Ann Burstein Cohen	SUNY at Buffalo
Arthur D. Cassill	Elon University
Craig J. Langstraat	University of Memphis
Kate Demarest	Carroll Community College
Richard Newmark	University of Northern Colorado
Susan Anderson	Appalachian State University

In addition, we want to thank Myron S. Scholes, Mark A. Wolfson, Merle Erickson, Edward L. Maydew, and Terry Shevlin for allowing us to use the model discussed in their text, *Taxes and Business Strategy: A Planning Approach*, as the basis for material in Chapter I:18.

Please send any comments to Kenneth E. Anderson or Thomas R. Pope.

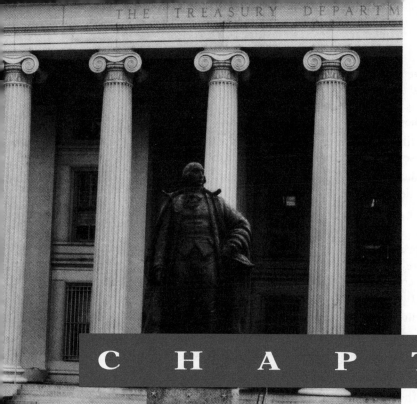

CHAPTER

1

AN INTRODUCTION TO TAXATION

LEARNING OBJECTIVES

After studying this chapter, you should be able to

1. ▶ Discuss the history of taxation in the United States

2. ▶ Differentiate between the three types of tax rate structures

3. ▶ Describe the various types of taxes

4. ▶ Discuss what constitutes a "good" tax structure, the objectives of the federal income tax law, and recent tax reform proposals

5. ▶ Describe the tax entities in the federal income tax system

6. ▶ Identify the various tax law sources and understand their implications for tax practice

7. ▶ Describe the legislative process for the enactment of the tax law

8. ▶ Describe the administrative procedures under the tax law

9. ▶ Describe the components of a tax practice and understand the importance of computer applications in taxation

KEY POINT

In many situations, the use of the tax laws to influence human behavior is deliberate. As will be seen later in this chapter, tax laws are often used to achieve social and economic objectives.

Federal income taxes have a significant effect on business, investor, and personal decisions in the United States. Because tax rates can be as high as 35% on corporations and individuals, virtually every transaction is impacted by income taxes. The following examples illustrate the impact of the tax law on various decisions in our society:

▶ Because of the deductibility of mortgage interest and real estate taxes, an individual may decide to purchase a home rather than to continue to rent an apartment.

▶ An investor may decide to delay selling some stock because of the significant taxes that may result from the sale.

▶ A corporation may get a larger tax deduction if it leases property rather than purchasing the property.

The purpose of this text is to provide an introduction to the study of federal income taxation. However, before discussing the specifics of the U.S. federal income tax law, it is helpful to have a broad conceptual understanding of the taxation process. This chapter provides an overview of the following topics:

▶ Historical developments of the federal tax system

▶ Types of taxes levied and structural considerations

▶ Objectives of the tax law, including a discussion of recent tax reform proposals

▶ Taxpaying entities in the federal income tax system

▶ Tax law sources and the legislative process

▶ Internal Revenue Service (IRS) collection, examination, and appeals processes

▶ The nature of tax practice, including computer applications and tax research

HISTORY OF TAXATION IN THE UNITED STATES

OBJECTIVE 1

Discuss the history of taxation in the United States

EARLY PERIODS

The federal income tax is the dominant form of taxation in the United States. In addition, most states and some cities and counties also impose an income tax. Both corporations and individuals are subject to such taxes.

Before 1913 (the date of enactment of the modern-day federal income tax), the federal government relied predominantly on customs duties and excise taxes to finance its operations. The first federal income tax on individuals was enacted in 1861 to finance the Civil War but was repealed after the war. The federal income tax was reinstated in 1894, however, that tax was challenged in the courts because the U.S. Constitution required that an income tax be apportioned among the states in proportion to their populations. This type of tax system, which would be both impractical and difficult to administer, would mean that different tax rates would apply to individual taxpayers depending on their states of residence.

In 1895, the Supreme Court ruled that the tax was in violation of the U.S. Constitution.[1] Therefore, it was necessary to amend the U.S. Constitution to permit the passage of a federal income tax law. This was accomplished by the Sixteenth Amendment, which was ratified in 1913. The Sixteenth Amendment, while being an extraordinarily important amendment, consists of one sentence.

HISTORICAL NOTE

The reinstatement of the income tax in 1894 was the subject of heated political controversy. In general, the representatives in Congress from the agricultural South and West favored the income tax in lieu of customs duties. Representatives from the industrial eastern states were against the income tax and favored protective tariff legislation.

Sixteenth Amendment to the Constitution of the United States

The Congress shall have the power to lay and collect taxes on incomes, from whatever source derived, without apportionment among the several States, and without regard to any census or enumeration.

---

[1] *Pollock v. Farmers' Loan & Trust Co.*, 3 AFTR 2602 (USSC, 1895). Note, however, that a federal income tax on corporations that was enacted in 1909 was held to be constitutional because it was treated as an excise tax. See *Flint v. Stone Tracy Co.*, 3 AFTR 2834 (USSC, 1911).

REVENUE ACTS FROM 1913 TO THE PRESENT

The Revenue Act of 1913 imposed a flat 1% tax (with no exemptions) on a corporation's net income. The rate varied from 1% to 7% for individuals, depending on the individual's income level. However, very few individuals paid federal income taxes because a $3,000 personal exemption ($4,000 for married individuals) was permitted as an offset to taxable income. These amounts were greater than the incomes of most individuals in 1913.

Various amendments to the original law were passed between 1913 and 1939 as separate revenue acts. For example, a deduction for dependency exemptions was provided in 1917. In 1939, the separate revenue acts were codified into the Internal Revenue Code of 1939. A similar codification was accomplished in 1954. The 1954 codification, which was known as the Internal Revenue Code of 1954, included the elimination of many "deadwood" provisions, a rearrangement and clarification of numerous code sections, and the addition of major tax law changes. Whenever changes to the Internal Revenue Code (IRC) are made, the old language is deleted and the new language added. Thus, the statutes are organized as a single document, and a tax advisor does not have to read through the applicable parts of all previous tax bills to find the most current law. In 1986, major changes were made to the tax law, and the basic tax law was redesignated as the Internal Revenue Code of 1986.

The federal income tax became a "mass tax" on individuals during the early 1940s. This change was deemed necessary to finance the revenue needs of the federal government during World War II. In 1939, less than 6% of the U.S. population was subject to the federal income tax; by 1945, 74% of the population was taxed.[2] To accommodate the broadened tax base and to avoid significant tax collection problems, Congress enacted pay-as-you-go withholding in 1943.

A major characteristic of the federal income tax since its inception to today is the manner in which the tax law is changed or modified. The federal income tax is changed on an **incremental** basis rather than a complete revision basis. Under so-called incrementalism, when a change in the tax law is deemed necessary by Congress, the entire law is not changed, but specific provisions of the tax law are added, changed, or deleted on an incremental basis. Thus, the federal income tax has been referred to as a "quiltwork" of tax laws, referring to the patchwork nature of the law. Without question, one of the principal reasons for the complexity of the federal income tax today is the incremental nature of tax legislation.

REVENUE SOURCES

As mentioned earlier, the largest source of federal revenues is individual income taxes. Other major revenue sources include Social Security (FICA) taxes and corporate income taxes (see Table I:1-1). Two notable trends from Table I:1-1 are (1) the gradual increase in social security taxes from 1960 to 2009 and (2) the gradual decrease in corporate income taxes for the same period. Individual income taxes have remained fairly stable during the past 40 years.

▼ TABLE I:1-1

Breakdown of Federal Revenues

	1960	1975	1994	2009
Individual income taxes	44%	45%	43%	47%
Social insurance taxes and contribution	16	32	37	35
Corporation income taxes	23	15	11	12
Other	17	8	9	6
Total	100%	100%	100%	100%

Source: Council of Economic Advisers, *Economic Indicators* (Washington, DC: U.S. Government Printing Office, 1967, 1977, 2009).

---

[2] Richard Goode, *The Individual Income Tax* (Washington, DC: The Brookings Institution, 1964), pp. 2–4.

Types of Tax Rate Structures

THE STRUCTURE OF INDIVIDUAL INCOME TAX RATES

Virtually all tax structures are comprised of two basic parts: the **tax base** and the **tax rate**. The tax base is the amount to which the tax rate is applied to determine the tax due. For example, an individual's tax base for the federal income tax is *taxable income*, as defined and determined by the income tax law. Similarly, the tax base for the property tax is generally the fair market value of property subject to the tax. The tax rate is merely the percentage rate applied to the tax base.

Tax rates may be progressive, proportional, or regressive. A **progressive rate** structure is one where the rate of tax increases as the tax base increases. The most notable tax that incorporates a progressive rate structure is the federal income tax. Thus, as a taxpayer's taxable income increases, a progressively higher rate of tax is applied. For 2010, the federal income tax rates for individuals begin at 10% and increase to 15%, 25%, 28%, 33%, and 35% as a taxpayer's taxable income increases.[3] Examples I:1-1 and I:1-2 show how the progressive rate structure of the federal income tax operates.

ADDITIONAL COMMENT

In the 1950s, the top marginal tax rate for individual taxpayers reached 92%. This astonishingly high rate only applied to taxpayers with very high taxable incomes but still is an extremely confiscatory tax rate.

EXAMPLE I:1-1 ▶ Alice, who is single, has $30,000 taxable income in 2010. Her federal income taxes for the year are $4,081, computed as follows: the first $8,375 of taxable income is taxed at 10% and the remaining $21,625 at 15%. (For tax rates, see the inside front cover.)

Allen, who is also single, has taxable income of $60,000. A 10% rate applies to the first $8,375 of taxable income, 15% on the next $25,625, and a 25% rate applies to the taxable income over $34,000. Thus, Allen's total tax is $11,181 [(0.10 × $8,375) + (0.15 × $25,625) + (0.25 × $26,000)].

If Allen's taxable income is $120,000, a 28% rate applies to $37,600 of his taxable income ($120,000 − $82,400) because the 28% rate applies to taxable income above $82,400 for a single individual and his total tax for the year is $27,309. Thus, the tax rates are progressive because the rate of tax increases as a taxpayer's taxable income increases. ◀

Notice in Example I:1-1 that taxable income has doubled in size in the three cases, but the income taxes have more than doubled (i.e., $4,081 to $11,181 to $27,309). This demonstrates how a progressive rate structure operates.

EXAMPLE I:1-2 ▶ Assume the same facts as in Example I:1-1 except that Alice has taxable income of $180,000. Of Alice's taxable income, $8,150 ($180,000 − $171,850) is subject to the 33% rate. Alternatively, if Allen has taxable income of $400,000, $26,350 ($400,000 − $373,650) is subject to the top marginal rate of 35%. ◀

A **proportional tax** rate, sometimes called a **flat tax**, is one where the rate of tax is the same for all taxpayers, regardless of the level of their tax base. This type of tax rate is generally used for real estate taxes, state and local sales taxes, personal property taxes, customs duties, and excise taxes. A flat tax has been the subject of considerable discussion over the past twenty years and promises to be a controversial topic as the debate on federal income tax reform continues into the future.

EXAMPLE I:1-3 ▶ Assume the same facts as in Example I:1-1, except that a 17% tax rate applies to all amounts of taxable income. Based on the assumed flat tax rate structure, Alice's federal income tax is $5,100 on $30,000 of taxable income; Allen's tax is $10,200 on $60,000 of taxable income and $20,400 on $120,000 of taxable income. The tax rate is proportional because the 17% rate applies to both taxpayers without regard to their income level. As you can see, a proportional tax rate results in substantially lower taxes for higher income taxpayers.[4] ◀

---

[3] See the inside front cover for the 2009 tax rates and Chapter I:2 for a discussion of the computation procedures. 2008 rate schedules and tax tables are located immediately before Appendix A.

[4] This example assumes the same tax base (taxable income) for the flat tax as with the current federal tax. Most flat tax proposals allow only a few deductions and, therefore, would generate higher taxes than in the example.

A **regressive tax** rate decreases with an increase in the tax base (e.g., income). Regressive taxes, while not consistent with the fairness of the income tax,[5] are found in the United States. The Social Security (FICA) tax is regressive because a fixed rate of tax of 6.20% for OASDI for both the employer and employee is levied up to a ceiling amount of $106,800 for 2009 and 2010. So, for example, assume Taxpayer A has income subject to Social Security of $80,000 and Taxpayer B income of $400,000. Taxpayer A's OASDI would be $4,960 ($80,000 × 0.062), Taxpayer B's OASDI would be $6,622 ($106,800 × 0.062). Taxpayer A's rate of tax is 6.2% while Taxpayer B's rate of tax is 1.7% ($6,622/$400,000). The employer and employee's Medicare tax rate is 1.45% for total wages earned, there is no ceiling amount for the Medicare portion of Social Security. The sales tax, which is levied by many states, is also regressive when measured against the income base.

THE STRUCTURE OF CORPORATE TAX RATES

Corporations are separate entities and are subject to income tax. The federal corporate income tax reflects a stair-step pattern of progression that tends to benefit small corporations. The corporate rates, which have not changed for several years, are as follows:[6]

Taxable Income[7]	Tax
First $50,000	15% of taxable income
Over $50,000 but not over $75,000	$7,500 + 25% of taxable income over $50,000
Over $75,000 but not over $100,000	$13,750 + 34% of taxable income over $75,000
Over $100,000 but not over $335,000	$22,250 + 39% of taxable income over $100,000
Over $335,000	34% of taxable income
Over $10,000,000 but not over $15,000,000	$3,400,000 + 35% of taxable income over $10,000,000
Over $15,000,000 but not over $18,333,333	$5,150,000 + 38% over $15,000,000
Over $18,333,333	35% of taxable income

MARGINAL, AVERAGE, AND EFFECTIVE TAX RATES FOR TAXPAYERS

A taxpayer's **marginal tax rate** is the tax rate applied to an incremental amount of taxable income that is added to the tax base. The marginal tax rate concept is useful for planning because it measures the tax effect of a proposed transaction.

EXAMPLE I:1-4 ▶

Tania, who is single, is considering the purchase of a personal residence that will provide a $20,000 tax deduction for interest expense and real estate taxes in 2010. Tania's taxable income would be reduced from $120,000 to $100,000 if she purchases the residence. Because a 28% tax rate applies to taxable income from $100,000 to $120,000, Tania's marginal tax rate is 28%. Thus, Tania's tax savings from purchasing the personal residence would be $5,600 (0.28 × $20,000). ◀

While the marginal tax rate measures the tax rate applicable to the next $1 of income or deduction for a taxpayer, there are two other tax rates that are used primarily by tax policymakers: average tax rate and effective tax rate. The **average tax rate** is computed by dividing the total tax liability by the amount of taxable income. This represents the average rate of tax for each dollar of taxable income. For example, a single taxpayer with taxable income of $400,000 in 2010 would incur a total tax liability of $117,644. The taxpayer's marginal tax rate is 35%, but his average tax rate is 29.4% ($117,644/$400,000).

---

[5] See the discussion of equity and fairness later in this chapter.
[6] For C corporations with taxable income over $100,000, the lower rates of tax on the first $75,000 of income are gradually phased out by applying a 5-percentage-point surtax on taxable income from $100,000 to $335,000 so that benefits of the favorable rates are eliminated once a corporation's taxable income reaches $335,000. Once taxable income exceeds $335,000 the tax equals 34% of taxable income. A 35% tax rate applies to taxable income in excess of $10 million. For corporations with taxable income in excess of $15 million, a 3 percentage-point-surtax applies to taxable income from $15 million to $18,333,333 to eliminate the lower 34% rate that applies to the first $10 million of taxable income.

[7] Also see the inside back cover for the corporation income tax rates.

The **effective tax rate** is the total tax liability divided by total economic income. **Total economic income** includes all types of economic income that a taxpayer has for the year. Thus, economic income is much broader than taxable income and includes most types of excludible income, such as tax-exempt bond interest, and generally permits business deductions but not personal-type deductions. It should be pointed out that economic income is *not* statutorily defined and experts may disagree on a precise calculation. The basic purpose of calculating the effective tax rate is to provide a broad measure of taxpayers' ability to pay taxes. Accordingly, the effective tax rate mainly is used by tax policymakers to determine the fairness of the income tax system.

EXAMPLE I:1-5 ▶ Amelia, who is single, has adjusted gross income of $140,000 and economic income of $175,000 in 2010. The difference is attributable to $35,000 of tax-exempt bond interest. If Amelia has deductions of $30,000, then her taxable income is $110,000, and her total tax is $24,509. Her average tax rate is 22.28% ($24,509 ÷ $110,000). Amelia's effective tax rate is 14.01% ($24,509 ÷ $175,000). Amelia's effective tax rate is considerably lower than her average tax rate because of her substantial amount of tax-exempt income. ◀

STOP & THINK

Question: Gwen, a single taxpayer, has seen her income climb to $200,000 in the current year. She wants a tax planner to help her reduce her tax liability. In planning for tax clients, tax professionals almost exclusively use the marginal tax rate in their analysis rather than the average tax rate. Why is the marginal tax rate much more important in the tax planning process than the average tax rate?

Solution: Because tax planning is done at the margin. A single taxpayer who has taxable income of $200,000 has a marginal tax rate of 33% (at 2010 rates), but an average tax rate of 25.57%, computed as follows:

Taxable income		$200,000
Tax on first $171,850 of taxable income		$41,827
Remaining taxable income	$28,150	
Times: Marginal tax rate	× 0.33	9,290
Total tax liability		$ 51,117

$$\text{Average tax rate} = \frac{\text{Total tax}}{\text{Taxable income}} = \frac{\$\,51,117}{\$200,000} = 25.56\%$$

If a tax planner could reduce Gwen's taxable income by $10,000, Gwen's tax liability would decrease by $3,333 ($10,000 × 0.33). When the taxpayer wants to know how much she can save through tax planning, the appropriate marginal tax rate yields the answer.

Overall, effective federal income tax rates for individuals have decreased slightly during the period 1993–2005,[8] amounting to 9.0% in 2005 as compared with 10.0% in 1993. For the highest 20% of households, the effective individual income tax rate declined to 14.1% in 2005 from 14.9% in 1993.

ADDITIONAL COMMENT

In the determination of tax rates, one should consider the incidence of taxation that involves the issue of who really bears the burden of the tax. If a city raises the real property tax but landlords simply raise rents to pass on the higher taxes, the tax burden is shifted to their tenants. The concept has important implications in determining any kind of average or effective tax rate.

DETERMINATION OF TAXABLE INCOME AND TAX DUE

As will be discussed in later chapters, the federal income taxes imposed on all taxpayers (individuals, corporations, estates, and trusts) are based on the determination of taxable income. In general, taxable income is computed as follows:

Total income (income from whatever source derived)	$xxx
Minus: Exclusions (specifically defined items, such as tax-exempt bond interest)	(xx)

[8] Congressional Budget Office, *Historical Effective Federal Tax Rates: 1979 to 2005* (Washington, DC: U.S. Government Printing Office, December, 2007), p. 4.

Gross income	$xxx
Minus: Deductions (business expenses and itemized deductions)	(xx)
Exemptions (not applicable for corporations)	(xx)
Taxable income	$xxx
Times: Applicable tax rate	× .xx
Income tax before credits	$xxx
Minus: Tax credits	(xx)
Total tax liability	$xxx
Minus: Prepayments	(xx)
Balance due or refund	$xxx

Each different type of taxpayer (individuals, corporations, etc.) computes taxable income in a slightly different manner, but all use the general framework above. An introductory discussion of the various types of taxpayers is provided later in this chapter. More detailed discussions of individual taxpayers (Chapter I:2) and corporation taxpayers (Chapter I:16) are examined in this *Individuals* book. Corporations, estates, and trusts are further examined in *Prentice Hall's Federal Taxation: Corporations, Partnerships, Estates, and Trusts.*

OTHER TYPES OF TAXES

STATE AND LOCAL INCOME AND FRANCHISE TAXES

In addition to federal income taxes, many states and local jurisdictions impose income taxes on individuals and businesses. These state and local taxes have gradually increased over the years and currently represent a significant source of revenue for state and local governments but also represent a significant tax burden on taxpayers.

State and local income taxes vary greatly in both form and rates.[9] Only seven states do not impose an individual income tax.[10] In most instances, state income tax rates are mildly progressive and are based on an individual's federal adjusted gross income (AGI), with minor adjustments.[11] For example, a typical adjustment to a state income tax return is interest income on federal government bonds, which is subject to tax on the federal return but is generally not subject to state income taxes. Some states also allow a deduction for federal income taxes in the computation of taxable income for state income tax purposes.

ADDITIONAL COMMENT

States that do not impose a state income tax depend on other taxes to support the government mission, principally sales taxes.

ADDITIONAL COMMENT

State income tax rates for individuals have increased significantly in the past twenty years. Thirty-three states now have marginal tax rates of 6% or higher.

States imposing a state income tax generally require the withholding of state income taxes and have established mandatory estimated tax payment procedures. The due date for filing state income tax returns generally coincides with the due date for the federal income tax returns (e.g., the fifteenth day of the fourth month following the close of the tax year for individuals).

Most states impose a corporate income tax, although in some instances the tax is called a **franchise tax**. Franchise taxes usually are based on a weighted-average formula consisting of net worth, income, and sales.

WEALTH TRANSFER TAXES

U.S. citizens are subject to taxation on certain transfers of property to another person. The tax law provides a unified transfer tax system that imposes a single tax on transfers of property taking place during an individual's lifetime (gifts) and at death (estates). (See the inside back cover of the text for the transfer tax rate schedules.) Formerly, the gift and estate tax laws were separate and distinct. The federal estate tax was initially enacted in 1916. The original gift tax law dates back to 1932. The gift tax was originally imposed to prevent widespread avoidance of the estate tax (e.g., taxpayers could make tax-free gifts of property

---

[9] For a thorough discussion of state and local taxes, see the chapter entitled *Multistate Income Taxation* that accompanies this textbook in electronic form on the Prentice Hall Federal Taxation 2011 Web page at www.prenhall.com/phtax.
[10] These states are Alaska, Florida, Nevada, South Dakota, Texas, Washing-

ton, and Wyoming. New Hampshire has an income tax that is levied only on dividend and interest income and Tennessee's income tax applies only to income from stocks and bonds.
[11] See Chapter I:2 for a discussion of the AGI computation.

before their death). Both the gift and estate taxes are wealth transfer taxes levied on the transfer of property and are based on the fair market value (FMV) of the transferred property on the date of the transfer. Following are brief descriptions of the gift tax and estate tax.

THE FEDERAL GIFT TAX. The **gift tax** is an excise tax that is imposed on the donor (not the donee) for transfers of property that are considered to be a taxable gift. A gift, generally speaking, is a transfer made gratuitously and with donative intent. However, the gift tax law has expanded the definition to include transfers that are not supported by full and adequate consideration.[12] To arrive at the amount of taxable gifts for the current year, a $13,000 annual exclusion is allowed per donee.[13] In addition, an unlimited marital deduction is allowed for transfers between spouses.[14] The formula for computing the gift tax is as follows:

KEY POINT

The $13,000 annual exclusion is an important tax-planning tool for wealthy parents who want to transfer assets to their children and thereby minimize their gift and estate taxes. A husband and wife who have three children could transfer a maximum of $78,000 [($13,000 × 2) × 3] to their children each year without incurring any gift tax.

FMV of all gifts made in the current year			$x,xxx
Minus:	Annual donee exclusions ($13,000 per donee)	$xx	
	Marital deduction for gifts to spouse	xx	
	Charitable contribution deduction	xx	(xxx)
Plus:	Taxable gifts for all prior years		xxx
Cumulative taxable gifts (tax base)			$x,xxx
Times:	Unified transfer tax rates		× .xx
Tentative tax on gift tax base			$ xxx
Minus:	Unified transfer taxes paid in prior years		(xx)
	Unified credit		(xx)
Unified transfer tax (gift tax) due in the current year			$ xx

Note that the gift tax is cumulative over the taxpayer's lifetime (i.e., the tax calculation for the current year includes the taxable gifts made in prior years). The detailed tax rules relating to the gift tax are covered in Chapter C:12 in both *Prentice Hall's Federal Taxation: Corporations, Partnerships, Estates, and Trusts* and the *Comprehensive* volume. The following general concepts and rules for the federal gift tax are presented as background material for other chapters of this text dealing with individual taxpayers:

ADDITIONAL COMMENT

The gift tax was enacted to make the estate tax more effective. Without a gift tax, estate taxes could be easily avoided by large gifts made before death.

▶ Gifts between spouses are exempted from the gift tax due to the operation of an unlimited marital deduction.

▶ The primary liability for payment of the gift tax is imposed on the **donor**. The donee is contingently liable for payment of the gift tax in the event of nonpayment by the donor.

▶ A donor is permitted a $13,000 annual exclusion for gifts of a present interest to each donee.[15]

▶ Charitable contributions are effectively exempted from the gift tax because an unlimited deduction is allowed.

▶ The tax basis of the property to the donee is generally the donor's cost. It is the lesser of the donor's cost and the property's FMV on the date of the gift if the property is sold by the donee at a loss. (See Chapter I:5 for a discussion of the gift tax basis rules.)

▶ A unified tax credit equivalent to a $1,000,000 deduction is available to offset any gift tax on taxable gifts that exceed the $13,000 annual exclusion.[16]

EXAMPLE I:1-6 ▶ Antonio makes the following gifts in the year 2010:

▶ $25,000 cash gift to his wife

▶ $15,000 contribution to the United Way

---

[12] Sec. 2512(b).

[13] Sec. 2503(b). The annual exclusion for gift tax purposes had been $10,000 for many years. However, for 2002–2005, the inflation adjustment increased the exclusion to $11,000, for 2006–2008, the exclusion was increased to $12,000. For 2009 and later years, the current exclusion has been increased to $13,000.

[14] Sec. 2523(a).

[15] A gift of a present interest is an interest that is already in existence and the donee is currently entitled to receive the income from the property. A gift of a future interest comes into being at some future date (e.g., property is transferred by gift to a trust in which the donee is not entitled to the income from the property until the donor dies) and is not eligible for the $13,000 annual exclusion.

[16] The applicable exclusion amount was $675,000 in 2000 and 2001 and was increased to the current $1,000,000 in 2002 and later years. For further details, see *Prentice Hall's Federal Taxation: Corporations, Partnerships, Estates and Trusts*, 2010 Edition, Chapters C:12 and C:13.

▶ Gift of a personal automobile valued at $40,000 to his adult son

▶ Gift of a personal computer valued at $4,000 to a friend

The $25,000 gift to his wife is not taxed because of a $13,000 annual exclusion and a $12,000 marital deduction. The $15,000 contribution to the United Way is also not taxed because of the unlimited deduction for charitable contributions. The $40,000 gift Antonio made to his son is reduced by the $13,000 annual exclusion to each donee, leaving a $27,000 taxable gift.[17] The $4,000 gift to the friend is not taxed because of the annual exclusion of up to $13,000 in gifts to a donee in a tax year. Thus, total taxable gifts for the current year subject to the unified transfer tax are $27,000. ◀

 STOP & THINK

Question: An important but frequently overlooked aspect of gift taxes is the interaction of gift taxes and income taxes. In many cases, gifts are made *primarily* for income tax purposes. Why would a gift be made for income tax purposes?

Solution: Gifts are frequently made to shift income from one family member to another family member who is in a lower marginal tax bracket. For example, assume Fran and Jan are married, have one 15-year-old son, earn $400,000 per year from their business, and generate $100,000 per year in dividends and interest from a substantial portfolio of stocks and bonds. With such a high level of income, Fran and Jan are in the 35% marginal tax bracket. If they make a gift of some of the stocks and bonds to their son, the dividends and interest attributable to the gift are taxed to the son at his marginal tax rate (maybe 10% or 15%). If the son's marginal tax rate is lower than 35%, the family unit reduces its overall income taxes.

THE FEDERAL ESTATE TAX. The **federal estate tax** is part of the unified transfer tax system that is based on the total property transfers an individual makes both during his or her lifetime and at death.

EXAMPLE I:1-7 ▶

TYPICAL MISCONCEPTION

It is sometimes thought that the federal estate tax raises significant amounts of revenue, but it has not been a significant revenue producer since World War II. Only 49,000 estate tax returns were filed in 2006 generating approximately $25 billion in tax revenues. This amount represents about 3% of revenues generated by income taxes on individuals.

SPECIAL NOTE

The unified credit equivalent amount of $3,500,000 has not been officially enacted for 2010 at the date of this writing. We expect the $3,500,000 to be enacted by Congress. See Chapters 12 and 13 of the *Corporations* volume for more details and discussion on page I1:10.

Amy dies during the current year. The formula for computing the estate tax on Amy's estate is as follows:

Gross estate (FMV of all property owned by the decedent at the date of death)		$xxx,xxx
Minus:	Deductions for funeral and administration expenses, debts of the decedent, charitable contributions, and the marital deduction for property transferred to a spouse	(x,xxx)
Taxable estate		$ x,xxx
Plus:	Taxable gifts made after 1976	xx
Tax base		$ x,xxx
Times:	Unified transfer tax rate(s)	× .xx
Tentative tax on estate tax base		$ xxx
Minus:	Tax credits (e.g., the unified tax credit equivalent to a $3,500,000 deduction in 2009 and 2010 (see note in left column), $2,000,000 deduction in 2006, 2007, and 2008, and $1,500,000 in 2004 and 2005)	(xx)
	Gift taxes paid after 1976	(xx)
Unified transfer tax (estate tax) due		$ xx	◀

The estate tax rules are discussed in more detail in Chapter C:13 in *Prentice Hall's Federal Taxation: Corporations, Partnerships, Estates, and Trusts* and in the *Comprehensive* volume. The following general rules are provided as background material for subsequent chapters of this text dealing with individual taxpayers:

▶ The decedent's property is valued at its FMV on the date of death unless the alternative valuation date (six months after the date of death) is elected. The alternative valuation date may be elected only if the aggregate value of the gross estate decreases during the

---

[17] This example assumes that the automobile is a gift rather than an obligation of support under state law and also assumes that Antonio's wife does not join with Antonio in electing to treat the gift to the son as having been made by both spouses (a gift-splitting election). In such event, donee exclusions of $26,000 (2 × $13,000) would be available, resulting in a taxable gift of only $14,000.

six-month period following the date of death and the election results in a lower estate tax liability.

▶ The basis of the property received by the estate and by the decedent's heirs is the property's FMV on the date of death (or the alternate valuation date if it is elected).

▶ Property transferred to the decedent's spouse is exempt from the estate tax because of the estate tax marital deduction provision.

EXAMPLE I:1-8 ▶ Barry died in 2010, leaving a $5,000,000 gross estate. In years prior to 2010 (but after 1976), Barry had made taxable gifts of $500,000. Of the $5,000,000 gross estate, one-half of the estate was transferred to his wife, administrative and funeral expenses are $30,000, Barry had debts of $170,000, and the remainder of the estate was transferred to his children. The estate tax due is computed as follows:

SPECIAL NOTE

The estate tax has been repealed effective January 1, 2010. However, it is widely expected that Congress will reinstate the estate tax at 2009 rates. The coverage in this chapter reflects the reinstatement of the estate tax. See Chapters 12 and 13 of the *Corporations* volume for more details.

Gross estate		$5,000,000
Minus:	Marital deduction	(2,500,000)
	Funeral and administrative expenses	(30,000)
	Decedent's debts	(170,000)
Taxable estate		$2,300,000
Plus:	Taxable gifts made after 1976	500,000
Tax base		$2,800,000
Tentative tax on estate tax base		$ 915,800[a]
Minus:	Tax credits (unified tax credit—see inside back cover for table)	(1,455,800)
	(See Special Note in left column.)	
Unified transfer tax due		$ —0— ◀

[a]$555,800 + (0.45 × $800,000)

Because of the generous credit and deduction provisions (e.g., the unified tax credit and the unlimited marital deduction), few estates are required to pay estate taxes. As can be seen above, the gross estate of the decedent was $2.5 million but no estate taxes were due primarily because of the large marital deduction and the unified credit. However, estate taxes rise quickly as is demonstrated below in Example I:1-9.

EXAMPLE I:1-9 ▶ Assume the same facts for Barry as in Example I:1-8 except that Barry's gross estate is $10,000,000 rather than $5,000,000. The estate tax due is computed as follows:

Gross estate		$10,000,000
Minus:	Marital deduction	(5,000,000)
	Funeral and administrative expenses	(30,000)
	Decedent's debts	(170,000)
Taxable estate		$ 4,800,000
Plus:	Taxable gifts made after 1976	500,000
Tax base		$ 5,300,000
Tentative tax on estate tax base		$ 2,265,800[b]
Minus:	Tax credits (unified tax credit)	(1,455,800)
	(See Special Note in left column.)	
Unified transfer tax due		$ 810,500 ◀

[b]$555,800 + (0.45 × $3,800,000)

The estate tax (not the gift tax) has been scheduled for repeal for the past nine years, effective January 1, 2010. However, most tax professionals had expected Congress to extend the estate tax prior to its repeal. The House of Representatives did pass a bill in December, 2009 to extend the estate tax. However, the Senate has yet to address this matter at the time of this writing. Therefore, technically, the estate tax has been repealed, although it is expected that the law will be reinstated retroactively to January 1, 2010 at 2009 rates and exemptions. By not providing some certainty to taxpayers in this area of the tax law, Congress has been irresponsible. For a more detailed discussion of the estate tax, see Chapters 12 and 13 of *Prentice Hall's Federal Taxation 2011 Corporations, Partnerships, Estates, and Trusts.*

OTHER TYPES OF TAXES

Although this text focuses primarily on the federal income tax, some mention should be made of the following other types of taxes levied by federal, state, and local governments.

▶ **Property taxes** are based on the value of a taxpayer's property, which may include both real estate and personal property. Real estate taxes are a major source of revenue for local governments. In addition, some state and local governments levy a personal property tax on intangibles such as securities and tangible personal property (e.g., the value of a personal automobile).

▶ **Federal excise taxes** and **customs duties** on imported goods have declined in relative importance over the years but remain significant sources of revenue. Federal excise taxes are imposed on alcohol, tobacco, gasoline, telephone usage, production of oil and gas, and many other types of goods. Many state and local governments impose similar excise taxes on goods and services.

▶ **Sales taxes** are a major source of revenue for state and local governments. Sales taxes are imposed on retail sales of tangible personal property (e.g., clothing and automobiles). Some states also impose a sales tax on personal services (e.g., accounting and legal fees). Certain items often are exempt from the sales tax levy (e.g., food items or medicines), and the rates vary widely between individual state and local governments. Sales taxes are not deductible for federal income tax purposes unless incurred in a trade or business.

▶ **Employment taxes** include Social Security (**FICA**) and federal and state unemployment compensation taxes. If an individual is classified as an employee, the FICA tax that is imposed on the employee is comprised of two parts, 6.2% for old-age, survivors, and disability insurance (OASDI) and 1.45% for hospital insurance (HI), for a total of 7.65%. The OASDI portion is imposed on the first $106,800 (2009 and 2010) of wages, whereas the HI portion has no ceiling. Both of these taxes are imposed on both the employer and employee. If an individual is self-employed, a self-employment tax is imposed at a 15.3% rate (12.4% for OASDI and 2.9% for HI) on the individual's self-employment income, with a ceiling on the OASDI portion of $106,800 (in 2009 and 2010).[18] Similar to employees, there is no ceiling on the HI portion for self-employed individuals.

▶ Employers are required to pay federal and state unemployment taxes to fund the payment of unemployment benefits to former employees. The federal rate is 6.2% on the first $7,000 of wages for each employee in 2009.[19] However, a credit is granted for up to 5.4% of wages for taxes paid to the state government so that the actual amount paid to the federal government may be as low as 0.8%.[20] The amount of tax paid to the state depends on the employer's prior experience with respect to the frequency and amount of unemployment claims. In Kentucky, for example, the highest rate of unemployment tax imposed is 3% and this rate is subsequently adjusted down if the employer has a small number of unemployment claims.

The types of taxes and structural considerations that were previously discussed are summarized in Topic Review I:1-1.

CRITERIA FOR A TAX STRUCTURE

Establishing criteria for a "good" tax structure was first attempted in 1776 by economist Adam Smith.[21] Smith's four "canons of taxation"—equity, certainty, convenience, and economy—are still used today when tax policy issues are discussed. Many have added a fifth canon of simplicity. Below is a discussion of these criteria and how they relate to income taxes as well as other taxes.

---

[18] Self-employed individuals receive an income tax deduction equal to 50% of taxes paid on their self-employment income and this deduction is also allowed to compute the amount of self-employment income (see Secs. 164(f) and 1402(a)(12) and Chapter I:14).
[19] Sec. 3301.

[20] Sec. 3302. State unemployment taxes in some states are levied on tax bases above $7,000. For example, the wage base ceiling in North Carolina is $12,500 in 2008.
[21] Adam Smith, *The Wealth of Nations* (New York: Random House, Modern Library, 1937), pp. 777–779.

Topic Review I:1-1

Types of Taxes and Tax Structure

TYPE OF TAX	TAX STRUCTURE	TAX BASE
Individuals:		
Federal income tax	Progressive	Gross income from all sources unless specifically excluded by law reduced by deductions and exemptions
State income tax	Progressive	Generally based on AGI for federal income tax purposes with adjustments
Federal gift tax	Progressive	FMV of all taxable gifts made during the tax year
Federal estate tax	Progressive	FMV of property owned at death plus taxable gifts made after 1976
Corporations:		
Federal corporate income tax	Progressive	Gross income from all sources unless specifically excluded by law reduced by deductions
State corporate income tax	Proportional or progressive	Federal corporate taxable income with adjustments
State franchise tax	Proportional	Usually based on a weighted-average formula consisting of net worth, income, and sales
Other Types of Taxes:		
Property taxes	Proportional	FMV of personal or real property
Excise taxes	Proportional	Customs and duties on imported and domestic goods from alcohol to telephone usage
Sales taxes	Proportional	Retail sales of tangible personal property or personal services
FICA and self-employment taxes	Regressive	Based on wages or self-employment income
Unemployment taxes	Regressive	Usually first $7,000 of an employee's wages

HISTORICAL COMMENT

The Revenue Reconciliation Act of 1993 followed through on President Clinton's campaign promise to increase taxes on high-income taxpayers to correct perceived inequities resulting from the lowering of the top tax rates in the Tax Reform Act of 1986.

KEY POINT

Using retroactive dates for changes in the tax law does not help to accomplish the objective of certainty. For example, the effective date of the increase in the top tax rate was made retroactive to January 1, 1993, in tax legislation signed by President Clinton on August 19, 1993. This retroactive tax increase was unpopular with high-income taxpayers.

EQUITY

A rather obvious criteria for a good tax is that the tax be equitable or fair to taxpayers. However, equity or fairness is elusive because of the subjectivity of the concept. What one person may conclude is fair in a particular situation may be considered totally unfair by another person. In other words, fairness is relative in nature and is extremely difficult to measure. For example, the deductibility of mortgage interest on a taxpayer's home certainly seems to be a fair provision for taxpayers. However, for taxpayers who do not own a home but live in a rental apartment, the deductibility of mortgage interest may not be considered as fair because the renter cannot deduct any portion of the rent paid. In other types of situations, the federal tax law includes various measures to ensure that taxpayers are treated fairly. For example, a foreign tax credit is available to minimize the double taxation that would otherwise occur when U.S. taxpayers earn income in a foreign country that is taxed by both the United States and the country in which it is earned. (See the glossary at the end of this volume for a definition of tax credits and Chapter I:14 for a discussion of the foreign tax credit.) Two aspects of equity are commonly discussed in the tax policy literature, **horizontal equity** and **vertical equity**. Horizontal equity refers to the notion that similarly situated taxpayers should be treated equally. Thus, two taxpayers who each have income of $50,000 should both pay the same amount of tax. Vertical equity, on the other hand, implies that taxpayers who are not similarly situated should be treated differently. Thus, if Taxpayer A has income of $50,000 and Taxpayer B has income of $20,000, Taxpayers A and B should not pay the same amount of income tax. Vertical equity provides that the incidence of taxation should be borne by those who have the **ability to pay** the tax, based on income or wealth. The progressive rate structure is founded on the vertical equity premise.

CERTAINTY

A certain tax (1) ensures a stable source of government operating revenues and (2) provides taxpayers with some degree of certainty concerning the amount of their annual tax

liability. A tax that is simple to understand and administer provides certainty for taxpayers. For many years, our income tax laws have been criticized as being overly complex and difficult to administer. Consider the remarks of a noted tax authority at a conference on federal income tax simplification:

> Tax advisers—at least some tax advisers—are saying that the income tax system is not working. They are saying that they don't know what the law provides, that the IRS does not know what the law provides, that taxpayers are not abiding by the law they don't know.[22]

While the above statement is over 30 years old, it is certainly still viable today. This uncertainty in the tax law causes frequent disputes between taxpayers and the IRS and has resulted in extensive litigation.

The federal tax system has made some attempts to provide certainty for taxpayers. For example, the IRS issues advance rulings to taxpayers, which provides some assurance concerning the tax consequences of a proposed transaction for the taxpayer who requests the ruling. The taxpayer may rely on the ruling if the transaction is completed in accordance with the terms of the ruling request. For example, if a merger of two corporations is being considered, the transaction can be structured so that the shareholders and the corporations do not recognize gain or loss. If a favorable ruling is received and the transaction is completed as planned, the IRS cannot later assert that the merger does not qualify for tax-free treatment.

CONVENIENCE

A tax law should be easily assessed, collected, and administered. Taxpayers should not be overly burdened with the maintenance of records and compliance considerations (preparation of their tax returns, payment of their taxes, and so on). One of the reasons that the sales tax is such a popular form of tax for state and local governments is that it is convenient for taxpayers to pay and for the government to collect. The consumer need not complete a tax return or keep detailed records.

ECONOMY

An economical tax structure should require only minimal compliance and administrative costs. The IRS collection costs, amounting to less than 0.5% of revenues, are minimal relative to the total collections of revenues from the federal income tax. Estimates of taxpayer compliance costs are less certain. One indicator of total compliance costs for taxpayers is the demand for tax professionals. Tax practice has been and continues to be one of the fastest growing areas in public accounting firms. Most large corporations also maintain sizable tax departments that engage in tax research, compliance, and planning activities. In addition, many commercial tax return preparer services are available to assist taxpayers who have relatively uncomplicated tax returns.

Complying with the tax laws is enormously expensive for both businesses and individuals in the United States. In 2005, businesses spent an estimated $148 billion to comply with the federal tax laws, while it cost individuals about $111 billion.[23] Compliance with state and local taxes costs another $80 billion. Clearly, the cost of complying with the nation's tax laws is significant, in terms of both money and time.

A more difficult question is whether the tax structure is economical in terms of taxpayer compliance. The issues of tax avoidance and tax evasion are becoming increasingly more important. The General Accounting Office (GAO) reported that two-thirds of tax returns are out of compliance, resulting in net income being underreported by 25%.[24]

SIMPLICITY

One of the important measures of any tax system is that of simplicity, or at least, not undue complexity. Taxpayers should be able to understand and comply with any tax system within reasonable boundaries. The sales tax is an example of a tax system that is relatively simple, although the sales tax as it applies to businesses can become fairly complex.

ADDITIONAL COMMENT

Humorist Jim Boren has proposed a constitutional amendment that would require any retroactive tax increases to be followed by retroactive elections for president, vice president, and all members of Congress.

ADDITIONAL COMMENT

For tax year 2007, 58% of all individual tax returns were prepared by paid tax-return preparers. This compares with 48% of returns prepared by paid return preparers in 1990. For taxpayers who file Form 1040 (as opposed to form 1040A and Form 1040EZ), 91% used paid preparers.

---

[22] Sidney L. Roberts, "The Viewpoint of the Tax Adviser: An Overview of Simplification," *Tax Adviser,* January 1979, p. 32.
[23] Scott A. Hodge, J. Scott Moody, and Wendy P. Warcholik, "The Rising Cost of Complying with the Federal Income Tax," Special Report No. 138, *Tax Foundation,* January, 2006, p. 1.

[24] News Report. "Compliance Said to Be Poor Among Sole Proprietorships," *Tax Notes,* December 12, 1994, p. 1328.

The federal income tax system in the United States has become inordinately complex over the years and complexity is one of the major criticisms of the income tax. The following is a quote from the report from the President's Advisory Panel on Federal Tax Reform:[25]

> In short, our current tax code is a complicated mess. Instead of clarity, we have opacity. Instead of simplicity, we have complexity. Instead of fair principles, we have seemingly arbitrary rules. Instead of contributing to economic growth, it detracts from growth. Time and time again, witnesses told the Panel about these failings in the tax code.

While simplicity is an admirable goal of any tax system, achieving this goal in the federal income tax system is difficult and involves the trade-off of other important objectives. For example, simplicity and fairness are almost impossible to achieve together. If the income tax law is extremely simple, like a flat tax rate on all income, the possible result is that many taxpayers will not be treated fairly. Consider this case, two taxpayers, A and B both earn $100,000 per year and we have a flat rate tax of 20% so that each taxpayer will pay $20,000 in income taxes for the year. However, assume that taxpayer B has a severe illness that requires him to pay medical expenses of $60,000 per year. Should both A and B pay the same income tax for the year? There is no absolute correct answer in this case, it depends on your definition of fairness. Thus, making the income tax law simple may not be the top priority in tax reform.

OBJECTIVES OF THE FEDERAL INCOME TAX LAW

The primary objective of the federal income tax law is to raise revenues for government operations. In recent years, the federal government has broadened its use of the tax laws to accomplish various economic and social policy objectives.

ECONOMIC OBJECTIVES

ADDITIONAL COMMENT

Among the provisions in the tax law that are designed to enhance the level of health care are the deductibility of medical expenses, deductibility of charitable contributions to hospitals, and exclusion of fringe benefits provided by employers for medical insurance premiums and medical care.

The federal income tax law is used as a fiscal policy tool to stimulate private investment, reduce unemployment, and mitigate the effects of inflation on the economy. Consider the following example: Tax credits for businesses operating in distressed urban and rural areas (empowerment zones) are allowed to provide economic revitalization of such areas. This is a clear example of using the federal income tax law to stimulate private investment in specific areas.

Many items in the tax law are adjusted for inflation by using the consumer price index, including the tax brackets, personal and dependency exemptions, and standard deduction amounts. These inflation adjustments provide relief for individual taxpayers who would otherwise be subject to increased taxes due to the effects of inflation. (See Chapter I:2 for a discussion of the tax computation for individuals.)

ENCOURAGEMENT OF CERTAIN ACTIVITIES AND INDUSTRIES

The federal income tax law also attempts to stimulate and encourage certain activities, specialized industries, and small businesses. One such example is the encouragement of research activities by permitting an immediate write-off of expenses and a special tax credit for increasing research and experimental costs. Special incentives are also provided to the oil and gas industry through percentage depletion allowances and an election to deduct intangible drilling costs.

Certain favorable tax provisions are provided for small businesses, including reduced corporate tax rates of 15% on the first $50,000 of taxable income and 25% for the next $25,000 of taxable income. Favorable ordinary loss (instead of capital

---

[25] Report of the President's Advisory Panel on Federal Tax Reform, *Simple, Fair, & Pro-Growth: Proposals to Fix America's Tax System*, November 2005, p. 2. See the discussion of tax reform in this chapter.

loss) deductions are granted to individual investors who sell their small business corporation stock at a loss, provided that certain requirements are met.[26] In addition, noncorporate investors may exclude up to 50% of the gain realized from the disposition of qualified small business stock if the stock is held for more than five years.[27]

SOCIAL OBJECTIVES

ADDITIONAL COMMENT

Deductible contributions made by self-employed individuals to their retirement plans (Keogh plans) totaled $22.2 billion in 2007. Charitable deductions totaled over $193 billion that same year.

The tax law attempts to encourage or discourage certain socially desirable or undersirable activities. For example:

▶ Special tax-favored pension and profit-sharing plans have been created for employees and self-employed individuals to supplement the social security retirement system.

▶ Charitable contributions are deductible to encourage individuals to contribute to charitable organizations.

▶ The claiming of a deduction for illegal bribes, fines, and penalties has been prohibited to discourage activities that are contrary to public policy.

EXAMPLE I:1-10 ▶ Able Corporation establishes a qualified pension plan for its employees whereby it makes all of the annual contributions to the plan. Able's contributions to the pension trust are currently deductible and not includible in the employees' gross income until the pension payments are distributed during their retirement years. Earnings on the contributed funds also are nontaxable until such amounts are distributed to the employees. ◀

EXAMPLE I:1-11 ▶ Anita contributes $10,000 annually to her church, which is a qualified charitable organization. Anita's marginal tax rate is 25%. Her after-tax cost of contributing to the church is only $7,500 [$10,000 − (0.25 × $10,000)]. ◀

EXAMPLE I:1-12 ▶ Ace Trucking Company incurs $10,000 in fines imposed by local and state governments for overloading its trucks during the current tax year. The fines are not deductible because the activity is contrary to public policy. ◀

The tax law objectives previously discussed are highlighted in Topic Review I:1-2.

INCOME TAX REFORM PROPOSALS

Tax reform has been a much debated topic over the years but has taken center stage recently. There has been a flurry of books, articles, and newspaper editorials that range from installing a completely new tax system to a partial revision of the current income

Topic Review I:1-2

Objectives of the Tax Law

OBJECTIVE	EXAMPLE
Stimulate investment	Provide a tax credit for the purchase of business equipment
Prevent taxpayers from paying a higher percentage of their income in personal income taxes due to inflation (bracket creep)	Index the tax rates, standard deduction, and personal and dependency exemptions for inflation
Encourage research activities that will in turn strengthen the competitiveness of U.S. companies	Allow research expenditures to be written off in the year incurred and offer a tax credit for increasing research and experimental costs
Encourage venture capital for small businesses	Reduce corporate income tax rates on the first $75,000 of taxable income. Allow businesses to immediately expense $134,000 (2010) of certain depreciable business assets acquired each year.
Encourage social objectives	Provide a tax deduction for charitable contributions; provide favorable tax treatment for contributions to qualified pension plans

---

[26] Sec. 1244. [27] Sec. 1202.

tax. Few people support keeping the income tax system as it currently stands. Some proponents of a new tax system advocate substituting a retail sales tax at the federal level for the income tax, others favor a value-added tax system (VAT tax) that is widely used in Europe. A partial revision of what we have now is also a popular option.

In early 2005, President George W. Bush appointed an advisory panel to completely study the current tax system and recommend options to the current tax system. The President allowed the panel great latitude in making recommendations except that the new system must raise the same amount of tax revenues as the current tax system. In November, 2005, the Panel issued its report entitled *Simple, Fair, & Pro-Growth: Proposals to Fix America's Tax System*.[28] Below is a brief summary of the report:

► The Panel proposed two options, (1) The Simplified Income Tax Plan (SITP), and (2) The Growth and Investment Tax Plan (GITP). The SITP uses the current income tax system as a starting point for reform whereas the GITP would shift the current system toward a consumption tax.

► The SITP widens the tax base by eliminating most deductions that are currently in place, moderately reduces tax rates to four brackets of 15%, 25%, 30%, and 33%, replaces the personal exemptions and standard deduction with a new Family Credit, changes the mortgage interest deduction to a 15% credit, and allows charitable contributions that are in excess of 1% of income. A major thrust of the proposal is to simplify and streamline the computation and filing of annual income tax returns. Finally, the alternative minimum tax (AMT) is repealed.

► The SITP increases incentives to save and invest. Several new tax-favored savings plans are proposed, 100% of dividends from U.S. corporations are excluded from taxation, and 75% of capital gains from U.S. corporation stock are excluded.

► The SITP dramatically changes the taxation of U.S. taxpayers operating outside the United States. The proposal would move to a territorial system which essentially means that U.S. businesses are not taxed on earnings earned outside the country.

► The GITP would be very similar to the SITP for individual taxpayers except that there would only be three rate brackets of 15%, 25%, and 30%. And dividends and capital gains would continue to be taxed at 15% as under current law.

► The principal differences between the GITP and the SITP are related to business. Principally, businesses would be permitted to expense all business investments, such as machinery and equipment, but not land and buildings. Large businesses would not be taxed on interest income but would also not be allowed to deduct interest expense. Small businesses would be permitted to use a simplified method of accounting, very similar to a cash-basis of accounting.

At present, it is unclear as to the impact of the Panel's recommendations. While the recommendations are well thought-out, there are other pressing matters facing Congress that may postpone implementation of tax reform in a comprehensive manner. Piecemeal changes to the tax code certainly may continue and this only ensures continued complexity in the tax law.

ENTITIES IN THE FEDERAL INCOME TAX SYSTEM

OBJECTIVE 5

Describe the tax entities in the federal income tax system

The federal income tax law levies taxes on taxpayers. However, not all entities that file income tax returns pay income taxes. For example, a partnership is required to file a tax return but does not pay any income tax because the income (or loss) of the partnership is allocated to the partners who report the income or loss on their individual tax returns. Therefore, the various entities in the federal income tax system may be classified into two

---

[28] Supra, note 25.

general categories, *taxpaying entities* and *flow-through entities*.[29] Taxpaying entities generally are required to pay income taxes on their taxable income. Flow-through entities, on the other hand, generally do not directly pay income taxes but merely pass the income on to a taxpaying entity. The major entities in each category are as follows:

Taxpaying Entities	*Flow-through Entities*
Individuals	Sole proprietorship
C corporations (regular corporations)	Partnerships
	S corporations
	Limited Liability Company (LLC) or Limited Liability Partnership (LLP)
	Trusts

Each of these entities is discussed below. The purpose of this section is to provide an overall picture of the various entities in the federal income tax system.

TAXPAYING ENTITIES

INDIVIDUALS. Individual taxpayers are the principal taxpaying entities in the federal income tax system. In 2009, income taxes paid by individual taxpayers comprised nearly 47% of total federal revenues. If Social Security taxes are included, individual taxpayers paid 82% of total federal revenues (see Table I:1-1 for details). Thus, the study of taxation of individuals is a very important topic and is discussed extensively in this *Individuals* textbook.

Individuals pay income taxes on all gross income minus allowable deductions. Gross income minus allowable deductions is referred to as *taxable income*. Gross income subject to taxation may be broadly classified into three categories:

▶ Earned income from sources such as salaries and wages, business income, and retirement income.

▶ Investment income, including interest income, dividends, capital gains, and rents and royalties.

▶ Flow-through income from partnerships, limited liability companies (LLCs), Subchapter S corporations, estates, and trusts.

Allowable deductions include expenses attributable to the gross income above and certain personal deductions and exemptions specifically allowed under the tax law. Gross income and allowable deductions and exemptions are discussed in detail later in this textbook.

Individual taxpayers use the tax formula below to compute their taxable income:

Total income, from whatever source derived	$xxx
Minus: Exclusions, as provided in the tax law	(xxx)
Gross income	xxx
Minus: Deductions for adjusted gross income	(xxx)
Adjusted gross income (AGI)	xxx
Minus: Deductions from AGI:	
Greater of itemized deductions or standard deduction	(xxx)
Personal and dependency exemptions	(xxx)
Taxable income	$xxx

Exclusions are items of income that the tax law specifically exempts from taxation. They include such items as gifts, inheritances, interest income from state and local bonds, loans, and life insurance proceeds. Exclusions are discussed in Chapter I:4.

Once an individual determines that an expenditure is allowed as a deduction for tax purposes, he or she must classify the deduction as *for AGI* or *from AGI*. This classification is very important and is discussed in Chapter I:6. Deductions *for AGI* basically are (1) expenses connected with a taxpayer's business or rental property, or (2) other specified

---

[29] Some entities have characteristics of both categories of entities, including certain types of trusts and S corporations.

deductions, such as moving expenses, contributions to an Individual Retirement Account (IRA), alimony, and a number of other specific items. Deductions *from* AGI are either itemized deductions or the standard deduction, whichever is greater, and personal and dependency exemptions. Itemized deductions primarily are personal-type deductions of the taxpayer, such as medical expenses, state and local taxes, mortgage interest, and charitable contributions. Itemized deductions are discussed in Chapter I:7. The standard deduction is a set amount that all taxpayers may deduct. For 2009 and 2010, the standard deduction is $5,700 ($11,400 for married couples filing a joint return) and is indexed annually for inflation. Thus, if a single taxpayer's itemized deductions for 2010 were $5,000, the taxpayer would deduct the standard deduction of $5,700 instead. On the other hand, if the taxpayer's itemized deductions were $6,000, the taxpayer would deduct $6,000 because that amount exceeds the standard deduction.

Personal and dependency exemptions also are specific deductions allowed to individuals. The personal exemption is for the taxpayer and spouse whereas dependency exemptions are for the taxpayer's children or other dependents. The personal and dependency exemption in 2009 and 2010 is $3,650. So, a husband and wife who have two dependent children would be entitled to a deduction of $14,600 ($3,650 × 4). This exemption amount is phased-out for higher income taxpayers and is indexed annually for inflation. Personal and dependency exemptions are discussed further in Chapter I:2.

Once taxable income is determined, tax rates are applied to this amount to arrive at the income tax liability for the year. Certain credits are allowed that reduce the income tax liability on a dollar-for-dollar basis. Individual income tax rates may be found inside the front cover of this textbook. Because individuals are subject to withholding and estimated tax payment rules, they may pay a balance due or receive a refund upon filing their tax return.

EXAMPLE I:1-13 ▶ Jeff Payne, a single taxpayer, is employed by a large corporation and has the following information for the current year of 2010:

INCOME AND OTHER RECEIPTS	
Salary from corporation	$120,000
Interest income from savings account	13,000
Interest on New York City bond	600
Loan from bank	20,000
Share of income from a partnership in which Jeff is a partner	8,600
Gift from Jeff's grandmother	11,000
Total	$173,200

DEDUCTIONS, EXEMPTIONS, AND PAYMENTS	
Itemized deductions	17,000
Personal exemption (2010)	3,650
Federal income taxes withheld from salary	30,000

Jeff's taxable income and income tax liability for 2010 would be computed as follows:

Total income			$173,200
Minus:	Exclusions:		
	Interest on New York City bond	$ 600	
	Loan from bank	20,000	
	Gift from Jeff's grandmother	$11,000	31,600
Gross income			141,600
Minus:	Deductions for AGI		0
Adjusted gross income (AGI)			141,600
Minus:	Deductions from AGI:		
	Itemized deductions	$17,000	
	Personal exemption	3,650	(20,650)
Taxable income			$120,950

The itemized deductions of $17,000 exceed Jeff's allowable standard deduction for 2010 of $5,700 and, therefore, are used to reduce taxable income.

To compute Jeff's income tax liability for the year, the rate schedules inside the front cover of the textbook are used. Jeff's income tax liability (using single taxpayer rates) would be $27,575 [$16,781 + 0.28($120,950 − $82,400)]. Since Jeff had $30,000 of federal income taxes

withheld from his salary, he would be entitled to a tax refund of $2,425 ($30,000.00 − $27,575). ◀

Individual taxpayers are required to file a tax return annually, Form 1040, which is due on or before April 15 of the year following the taxable year. As can be seen from the tax rate schedules located on the inside cover of this textbook, rates range from 10% to 35%. However, some types of income are taxed at lower rates. For example, dividends from most U.S. corporations are subject to a maximum rate of 15% (0% for lower income taxpayers after 2007 through 2010). This 15% rate (or 0% as above for qualified dividends) also applies to long-term capital gains, such as gains on the sale of stocks and bonds. With these lower rates, a high-income taxpayer in the 35% marginal tax bracket would only pay a maximum of 15% on any qualified dividends received or long-term capital gains. The remainder of the taxpayer's income would be subject to the higher rates.

C CORPORATIONS.   C corporations, many times referred to as regular corporations, also are taxpaying entities. These corporations, both publicly-held corporations traded on stock exchanges and privately-owned corporations, accounted for approximately 12% of total federal revenues in 2009. The percentage of federal revenues provided by C corporations has been steadily declining over the past 40 years, a concern of tax policymakers as more and more taxes are being shifted to individual taxpayers. A major disadvantage of C corporations is they are subject to so-called double taxation. Double taxation results from the corporation paying income tax on its taxable income and shareholders paying income tax on any dividends received from the corporation or on the gain from selling their stock in the corporation. Thus, the same corporate income is subjected to taxation twice—once at the corporate level and again at the shareholder level. For many years, much tax planning has been directed at trying to so arrange the tax affairs of a C corporation to avoid double taxation. This discussion of C corporations is divided into two parts, (1) taxation of C corporations and (2) the operation of double taxation.

Taxation of C corporations.   C corporations are taxed on their taxable income in a manner similar to individuals. The major difference between corporations and individuals is that corporations are not allowed personal exemptions and personal deductions. Thus, the concept of AGI does not pertain to corporations. Taxable income for corporations is computed as follows:

Total income, from whatever source derived	$xxx
Minus: Exclusions, as provided in the tax law	(xxx)
Gross income	xxx
Minus: Deductions (ordinary and necessary expenses related to the corporation's trade or business)	(xxx)
Taxable income	$xxx

This taxable income is subject to tax rates that range from 15% to 35% (see rate schedule in the inside rear cover of the textbook). A more detailed discussion of corporation taxation is contained in Chapter I:16 of this *Principles* textbook and Chapter C:3 of the *Corporations, Partnerships, Estates, and Trusts* volume.

EXAMPLE I:1-14 ▶ During the current taxable year, Crimson Corporation generated gross income of $1,500,000 and had ordinary and necessary deductions of $900,000, resulting in taxable income of $600,000. Based on the corporation rate schedules, Crimson would be subject to taxes of $204,000 [$113,900 + .34($600,000 − 335,000)]. ◀

C corporations are required to file tax returns annually using Form 1120, which is due on or after the 15th day of the third month after the close of the corporation's tax year (e.g., March 15 for calendar year taxpayers).

Double taxation of C corporation earnings.   As mentioned previously, C corporations are subject to double taxation. The corporation pays income tax on its taxable income

and then shareholders must pay income tax on any dividends paid by the corporation or on the sale of their stock. Tax legislation in 2003 substantially reduced the impact of double taxation by reducing to 15% the maximum tax rate on most corporate dividends received by individuals. This 15% rate is further reduced to 0% after 2007 (5% for tax years prior to 2008) for lower-income taxpayers in the 10% or 15% tax brackets. Prior to this reduction in tax rates on qualified dividends, dividends were subject to tax at regular tax rates. Thus, under current tax law, a taxpayer in the 35% marginal tax bracket (see tax rate schedules inside the front cover of this textbook) pays only a 15% tax rate on any dividends received. The same reduced tax rates apply to long-term capital gains on the sale of their corporate stock. These tax rates apply through 2010 unless Congress acts to make them permanent.

EXAMPLE I:1-15 ▶ Using the same facts for Crimson Corporation in Example I:1-14, assume the corporation paid dividends to shareholders during 2010 of $400,000. Further assume that the marginal tax bracket of the shareholders is 28%. The shareholders collectively would have to pay individual income taxes of $60,000 ($400,000 × 15%) as the maximum tax rate on qualified dividends is 15%. The total tax on the corporation's taxable income of $600,000, therefore, would be $264,000 ($204,000 paid by Crimson Corporation plus $60,000 paid by the shareholders), or an effective tax rate of 44% ($264,000/$600,000). The 44% is only federal income taxes and does not include any state or local income taxes that the corporation may have to pay. Under prior law, the shareholders would have had to pay tax on the dividends at a 28% rate, or $112,000 ($400,000 × 28%). ◀

While the reduced rate of tax on qualified dividends is certainly favorable to shareholders, the double taxation of C corporation earnings is still an onerous tax. A common method to avoid this double taxation by C corporations with a small number of shareholders is to payout the corporate earnings in the form of salary and bonuses, thereby making the payout deductible by the corporation and eliminating double taxation. The Internal Revenue Service (IRS), however, may attack this plan by asserting that the salary and bonuses are unreasonably large and, in fact, a disguised dividend.

EXAMPLE I:1-16 ▶ Assume in Example I:1-14 that Crimson had only one shareholder, Joe Bank, who also is the president of the corporation. The corporation paid the entire $600,000 to Mr. Bank in the form of a bonus rather than as a dividend. The corporation could deduct the $600,000, thereby reducing its taxable income to zero. Mr. Bank would have to include the $600,000 in his personal income and would pay taxes on this amount. If his average tax rate on the $600,000 was 30%, he would owe $180,000 on the $600,000. The $180,000 would represent the total taxes of both the corporation and shareholder and would save $84,000 ($264,000 − $180,000) from the previous example. The IRS may attack this plan by alleging that Mr. Bank's salary and bonus are unreasonably high and recharacterize part of the $600,000 as a dividend. Because dividends are not deductible by the corporation, the corporation would be subject to additional income taxes. At the same time, if the IRS is successful, the portion of the salary and bonus of Mr. Bank that is recharacterized as a dividend would be subject to the maximum 15% tax rate. ◀

FLOW-THROUGH ENTITIES

The simplest form of a flow-through entity is the sole proprietorship as there are no formal requirements to form such an entity. The net income earned by the proprietor is reported on Schedule C of Form 1040. Thus, the income of the sole proprietorship merely flows to the proprietor's individual tax return. The net income of the sole proprietorship is subject to income tax only once (at the individual level) but is also subject to self-employment tax (Social Security and Medicare taxes).

Flow-through entities, such as partnership, limited liability companies (LLCs), limited liability partnerships (LLPs), and S corporations have the major advantage of being subject to only one level of taxation. All of these entities file tax returns, but, in general, the entities do not pay any income taxes. The income earned by the entity is allocated to the owners based on their proportionate ownership or some other allocation arrangement. Thus, the entity income tax return is really just an information return. The income allocated to the owners is then reported on their own tax returns. The income of the entity, therefore, is subject to a single level of taxation. This single level of tax is a major advantage of the flow-through form over C corporations.

To ensure a single level of taxation for flow-through entities, the tax law employs a unique method of basis adjustments. Every owner of the entity has an *adjusted basis* (basis) in his or her ownership interest. An owner's basis in a flow-through entity is determined as follows:

▶ Each owner obtains an original basis in his or her ownership interest upon the formation of the entity (investment in the entity) or purchase of the interest.

▶ The owner's basis increases for any additional capital contributions to the entity in subsequent years.

▶ The owner's basis increases for the owner's share of income for tax purposes or decreases for losses.

▶ The owner's basis increases for the owner's share of entity liabilities. Differences exist between partnerships and S corporations as to which liabilities are added to an owner's basis. Details on this topic are covered in later chapters of this textbook.

▶ The owner's basis decreases for money or property distributed to the owner by the entity.

Without these basis adjustments, the owner could be subject to double taxation upon selling his or her interest or upon dissolution of the entity. Practitioners refer to this basis as "outside basis" as opposed to "inside basis," which is the entity's basis in its assets.

EXAMPLE I:1-17 ▶ Wildcat Company is a flow-through entity with two owners, Rich and Teresa. Each owner has a $10,000 original basis in the entity. In its first year of operations, Wildcat Company earns $50,000, which is allocated $25,000 to each owner. Thus, each owner reports $25,000 in his individual income tax return even though the entity does not distribute any of the earnings to the owners. At the beginning of the second year, Rich sells his interest to Steve for $35,000. If Rich did not get an increased basis adjustment for his $25,000 of earnings, he would recognize a $25,000 gain ($35,000 selling price − $10,000 basis in the entity) on the sale of his interest, which taxes him twice on the $25,000. However, both Rich and Teresa do increase their bases to $35,000 ($10,000 original basis + $25,000 share of entity earnings) at the end of the first tax year. Therefore, when Rich sells his interest for $35,000, he incurs no additional taxable gain ($35,000 selling price − $35,000 basis in the entity = $0 gain). ◀

Below is a brief description of the four basic types of flow-through business entities.

PARTNERSHIPS. A partnership is the classic flow-through entity as it has been around the longest. The Internal Revenue Code (IRC) defines a partnership as "a syndicate, group, pool, joint venture, or other incorporated organization" that carries on any business, financial operation, or venture.[30] Thus, if two or more individuals, corporations, trusts, or estates decide to operate a business or financial venture, the business or venture can be classified as a partnership. Unlike a corporation, which must file incorporation documents with the state, partnerships require no legal documentation. However, tax advisors strongly advise partnerships to have written agreements as to the operation of the partnership and how income, deductions, losses, and credits will be allocated to the partners. Most states have laws that govern the rights and restrictions of partnerships and their partners.

Partnerships file an annual income tax return which is just an information return because the partnership entity is not subject to taxation. The return, Form 1065 (U.S. Partnership Return of Income), reports the results of the partnership's operations. An accompanying form, Schedule K-1, reports the separate income, deductions, losses, and credits that flow through to the partners. The partners, in turn, take the information from their Schedule K-1 and report the various items on their individual returns.

EXAMPLE I:1-18 ▶ Donald and Minnie form a real estate company and decide to operate as a partnership, the DM Partnership. Donald is a 60% partner and Minnie is a 40% partner. Donald invests $60,000 into DM and Minnie contributes real estate with a basis and fair market value of $40,000. In its first year of operation, DM Partnership earns ordinary income of $150,000. The partnership files Form 1065 and reports the $150,000 but is not subject to any income taxation. Included in the

---

[30] Sec. 761(a).

partnership return are two Schedule K-1s that report $90,000 to Donald ($150,000 × 60%) and $60,000 ($150,000 × 40%) to Minnie. Donald reports $90,000 on his individual income tax return, Form 1040, and Minnie reports $60,000 on her individual return. If the partnership distributed $72,000 to Donald and $48,000 to Minnie during the year, the distributions are considered a return of capital and are not taxable to either partner. Donald's adjusted basis in his partnership interest would be $78,000 ($60,000 + $90,000 − $72,000) and Minnie's adjusted basis would be $52,000 ($40,000 + $60,000 − $48,000). ◀

S CORPORATIONS. S corporations are a special form of corporation treated by the tax laws as flow-through entities. They are incorporated under state law just as any other corporation but, if they so elect, are treated as flow-through entities for tax purposes. S corporations are so named because the rules pertaining to this type of entity are located in Subchapter S of the IRC. S corporations have been referred to as "corporations taxed like a partnership." Although this statement is partially true, important differences exist, such as a limitation on the number of shareholders, strict rules on allocation of income or losses, and several other differences. Similar to partnerships, S corporations are not taxed and income, deductions, losses, and credits flow through to its shareholders. Allocations of income, deductions, losses, and credits to shareholders are based on a per share-per day basis. Importantly, S corporation shareholders enjoy limited liability, as do C corporation shareholders.

To achieve S corporation status, the corporation must file an S election and all of its shareholders must consent to that election. S corporations annually file an information return, Form 1120S (U.S. Income Tax Return for an S Corporation), which reports the results of the corporation's operations and, like partnerships, also submits Schedule K-1 to each shareholder which reports the allocable share of income, deduction, loss, and credit that flow through to each shareholder.

Similar to partnerships, S corporations impose only a single level of taxation to its shareholders and the tax law uses basis adjustments to achieve this single level of taxation. The basis adjustments for S corporation shareholders are nearly identical to those for partnerships. The major difference is how liabilities affect the basis of S corporation shareholders. S corporation shareholders obtain basis only for *direct* loans to the corporation and they treat their debt basis separately from stock basis. Partners of a partnership generally increase their basis for all partnership liabilities.

EXAMPLE I:1-19 ▶ Paul and Peter form a corporation in Ohio as equal shareholders. Upon advice from their tax advisor, they decide to elect S corporation status for federal and state tax purposes and file the necessary forms. Both Paul and Peter invest $25,000 in the corporation and each receives 100 shares of common stock of the corporation. During the first year, the corporation reports net ordinary income of $62,000 and a long-term capital gain of $10,000 of Form 1120S. Each shareholder receives a $20,000 distribution from the corporation during the year. In Year 1, the corporation pays no federal or state income taxes, but both Paul and Peter report $31,000 of ordinary income and $5,000 of long-term capital gain on their individual returns. Since the shareholders have sufficient basis, the $20,000 distribution to each shareholder is not subject to taxation. Paul and Peter would each have a basis in their S corporation stock of $41,000 ($25,000 + $31,000 + $5,000 − $20,000) at the end of Year 1. ◀

EXAMPLE I:1-20 ▶ In Year 2, the corporation earns $74,000 of ordinary income and no capital gains. Also, on July 1 of Year 2, Peter sells one-half (50 shares) of his stock to Mary. So, from July 1 to December 31, Paul owns 50% of the corporate stock and Peter and Mary each own 25%. S corporation earnings must be allocated on a per share−per day basis, so the income of $74,000 is allocated to each shareholder as follows:

Paul	$74,000 × 365/365 × 50% = $37,000
Peter	($74,000 × 181/365 × 50%) + ($74,000 × 184/365 × 25%) = $27,674
Mary	$74,000 × 184/365 × 25% = $9,326)

◀

LIMITED LIABILITY COMPANIES. A limited liability company (LLC) is a legal entity under the laws of all 50 states and the District of Columbia and is a very popular organizational form. LLCs combine the best features of a partnership and a corporation by

being treated as a partnership while providing the limited liability protection of a corporation. Thus, LLC owners, called members, are subject to a single level of taxation and are not liable for the liabilties of the LLC.

An LLC is formed under state law similar to a corporation. After formed, the LLC elects whether to be taxed either as a partnership or a corporation.[31] Under Treasury Regulations, an LLC with more than one member is treated as a partnership unless the LLC affirmatively elects to be classified as a corporation. In most cases, LLCs will prefer to be classified as a partnership because of the tax advantages of a single level of taxation. If an LLC elects to be treated as a partnership, it files its tax return on Form 1065 (U.S. Partnership Return of Income). The LLC, however, is not legally a partnership; it is just treated as one for federal income tax purposes. A single member LLC is disregarded for tax purposes and the LLC income, deductions, etc. are reported directly on the member's Schedule C of Form 1040 as a sole proprietor. If an LLC elects to be taxed as a corporation under the Treasury Regulations, it would file Form 1120 (U.S. Corporation Income Tax Return). Further, S corporation status can be achieved by electing to be taxed as a corporation and then make an S election. Thus, the LLC would be considered an LLC for state law purposes but an S corporation for income tax purposes.

EXAMPLE I:1-21 ▶ Karen and David start a wholesale business and decide to operate the business as an LLC. They first must legally form the organization under state law. After the LLC is legally formed, they must decide how the LLC will be treated for income tax purposes. Because they want a single level of taxation, Karen and David elect to be treated as a partnership. Since being treated as a partnership is the default classification under Treasury Regulations, no forms need to be filed with the IRS. At the end of the first year, the LLC will file a Form 1065 and check the box indicating that the entity is an LLC filing as a partnership. All partner allocations, basis adjustments, and all other tax rules for the LLC are identical with partnership rules. ◀

LIMITED LIABILITY PARTNERSHIPS. All 50 states and the District of Columbia have statutes that allow a business to operate as a limited liability partnership (LLP). Basically, an LLP is similar to an LLC except that a partner of an LLP *is not* liable for any liability arising from acts of negligence or misconduct or similar acts of another partner of the LLP. Thus, an LLP is much more desirable than a general partnership where partners are liable for all partnership liabilities. Professional service organizations, such as many CPA firms, have adopted the LLP form, primarily to limit legal liability.

EXAMPLE I:1-22 ▶ The accounting firm of Gartman & Kuhn, CPAs, is operating as a general partnership and has 20 partners in the firm. The firm is concerned about the unlimited liability that exists for the partnership, especially in today's litigious environment. The firm decides to convert from a partnership to an LLP. The conversion is simple and tax-free,[32] and protects the partners of the new LLP entity against liabilities of the LLP arising from acts of negligence or misconduct of other partners or employees. ◀

OTHER ENTITIES

TRUSTS. Trusts are somewhat of a hybrid entity in that they may either be a taxpaying entity or flow-through entity. Also, there are a number of different types of trusts, so the discussion here is very general in nature. Trusts typically are subject to income taxation on all of its net income that is *not* distributed to the beneficiaries. The portion of net income that is distributed to beneficiaries is taxed to the beneficiaries. One drawback to the use of trusts is that the income tax rates are extremely progressive, reaching the 35% bracket when the taxable income of the trust reaches $11,200 in 2010. Trusts use Form 1041 to file its tax information.

EXAMPLE I:1-23 ▶ Ben establishes a trust for the benefit of his daughter. The principal amount of the trust is $500,000 and is projected to earn approximately 10% per year. In the current year, the trust earned $50,000 of investment income and had $5,000 of expenses. If the trust did not make any

---

[31] The LLC makes the election pursuant to the "check-the-box" Regulations, Reg. Secs. 301.7701-1 through -4.

[32] Rev. Rul. 95-37, 1995-1 C.B. 130.

distributions during the year to the daughter, the entire $45,000 (less a small exemption) would be subject to income taxation to the trust. Much of the taxable income would be subject to taxation at the 35% rate. Alternatively, if the trust distributed the entire $45,000 to the daughter, she would report the $45,000 on her individual tax return. Assuming she does not have significant other income, she would most likely be in the 25% marginal tax bracket. The trust's taxable income would be zero and would have no income tax liability. ◀

TAX LAW SOURCES

OBJECTIVE 6

Identify the various tax law sources and understand their implications for tax practice

The solution to any tax question may only be resolved by reference to tax law sources (also referred to as tax law authority). Tax law sources are generated from all three branches of the federal government, i.e., legislative, executive, and judicial. The principal sources of tax law are as follows:

Branch	*Tax Law Source*
Legislative	Internal Revenue Code
	Congressional Committee Reports
Executive (Administrative)	Income Tax Regulations
	Revenue Rulings
	Revenue Procedures
	Letter Rulings
Judicial	Court Decisions

ADDITIONAL COMMENT

Knowledge of tax law sources could be considered the most important topic in this book. It is similar to the old Chinese proverb that states that if you give a person a fish you have fed him for one day, but if you teach a person how to fish you have fed him for the rest of his life. By analogy, if a person has a knowledge of the tax law sources, he or she should be able to locate the answers to tax questions throughout his or her career.

A thorough knowledge of the various sources above as well as the relative weights attached to each source is vital to tax professionals. Because of the vast volume of tax law sources, the ability to "find the answer" to a tax question is of fundamental importance. In addition, the evaluation of the weight (or importance) of different sources of authority is also crucial in arriving at a proper conclusion. For example, a decision of the U.S. Supreme Court on a tax matter would certainly carry more weight than a Revenue Ruling issued by the Internal Revenue Service.

Clearly, the most authoritative source of tax law is the Internal Revenue Code, which is the tax law passed by Congress. However, Congress is not capable of anticipating every type of transaction that taxpayers might engage in, so most of the statutes in the Code contain very general language. Because of the general language contained in the Code, both administrative and judicial interpretations are necessary to apply the tax law to specific situations and transactions. Thus, the regulations and rulings of the IRS and the decisions of the courts are an integral part of the federal income tax law. For a detailed discussion of tax law sources, see Chapter I:15 (Chapter C:1 of the *Comprehensive* edition). Topic Review I:1-3 provides an overview of the tax law sources.

ENACTMENT OF A TAX LAW

OBJECTIVE 7

Describe the legislative process for the enactment of the tax law

Under the U.S. Constitution, the House of Representatives is responsible for initiating new tax legislation. However, tax bills may also originate in the Senate as riders to nontax legislative proposals. Often, major tax proposals are initiated by the President and accompanied by a Treasury Department study or proposal, and then introduced into Congress by one or more representatives from the President's political party.

STEPS IN THE LEGISLATIVE PROCESS

The specific steps in the legislative process are discussed below and are summarized in Table I:1-2. These steps typically include:

1. A tax bill is introduced in the House of Representatives and is referred to the House Ways and Means Committee.
2. The proposal is considered by the House Ways and Means Committee, and public hearings are held. Testimony may be given by members of professional groups such

Topic Review I:1-3

Tax Law Sources

SOURCE	KEY POINTS	WEIGHT OF AUTHORITY
LEGISLATIVE		
Internal Revenue Code	Contains provisions governing income, estate and gift, employment, alcohol, tobacco, and excise taxes.	Serves as the highest legislative authority for tax research, planning, and compliance activities.
ADMINISTRATIVE		
Treasury Regulations	Represents interpretations of the tax code by the Secretary of the Treasury. Regulations may be initially issued in proposed, temporary, and final form and are interpretative or legislative.	Legislative regulations have a higher degree of authority than interpretative regulations. Proposed regulations do not have authoritative weight.
IRS Rulings	The IRS issues Revenue Rulings (letter rulings or published rulings), Revenue Procedures, Information Releases, and Technical Advice Memoranda.	These pronouncements reflect the IRS's interpretation of the law and do not have the same level of scope and authority as Treasury Regulations.
JUDICIAL		
Judicial doctrines	Judicial doctrines are concepts that have evolved from Supreme Court cases that are used by the courts to decide tax issues. Examples include substance over form, tax benefit rule, and constructive receipt.	Judicial doctrines that evolve from Supreme Court cases have substantial weight of authority because they have the force and effect of law.
Judicial interpretations	Tax cases are initially considered by a trial court (i.e., the Tax Court, a Federal district court, or the U.S. Court of Federal Claims). Either the taxpayer or the IRS may appeal to an appeals court. A final appeal is to the U.S. Supreme Court.	A trial court must abide by the precedents set by the court of appeals of the same jurisdiction. An appeals court is not required to follow the decisions of another court of appeals. A Supreme Court decision is the "law of the land."

ADDITIONAL COMMENT

In 2009, the chairman of the House Ways and Means Committee was Rep. Charles Rangel of New York, and the chairman of the Senate Finance Committee was Sen. Max Baucus of Montana.

ADDITIONAL COMMENT

The corridors near Congress's tax-writing rooms are called "Gucci Gulch," so named for the designer clothing worn by many of the lobbyists who congregate there when a tax bill is being considered.

HISTORICAL NOTE

Few CPAs have been elected to Congress. Currently, the only CPA in Congress is John Campbell of California.

as the American Institute of CPAs and the American Bar Association and from various special-interest groups.

3. The tax bill is voted on by the House Ways and Means Committee and, if approved, is forwarded to the House of Representatives for a vote. Amendments to the bill from individual members of the House of Representatives are generally not allowed.

4. If passed by the House, the bill is forwarded to the Senate for consideration by the Senate Finance Committee, and public hearings are held.

5. The tax bill approved by the Senate Finance Committee may be substantially different from the House of Representatives' version.

6. The Senate Finance Committee reports the Senate bill to the Senate for consideration. The Senate generally permits amendments (e.g., new provisions) to be offered on the Senate floor.

7. If approved by the Senate, both the Senate and House bills are sent to a Joint Conference Committee consisting of an equal number of members from the Senate and the House of Representatives.

8. The Senate and House bills are reconciled in the Joint Conference Committee. This process of reconciliation generally involves substantial compromise if the provisions of both bills are different. A final bill is then resubmitted to the House and Senate for approval.

9. If the Joint Conference Committee bill is approved by the House and Senate, it is sent to the President for approval or veto.

10. A presidential veto may be overturned if a two-thirds majority vote is obtained in both the House and Senate.

▼ TABLE I:1-2

Steps in the Legislative Process

1. Treasury studies prepared on needed tax reform
2. President makes proposals to Congress
3. House Ways and Means Committee prepares House bill
4. Approval of House bill by the House of Representatives
5. Senate Finance Committee prepares Senate bill
6. Approval of Senate bill by the Senate
7. Compromise bill approved by a Joint Conference Committee
8. Approval of Joint Conference Committee bill by both the House and Senate
9. Approval or veto of legislation by the President
10. New tax law and amendments incorporated into the Code

11. Committee reports are prepared by the staffs of the House Ways and Means Committee, the Senate Finance Committee, and the Joint Conference Committee as the bill progresses through Congress. These reports help to explain the new law before the Treasury Department drafts regulations on the tax law changes as well as to explain the intent of Congress for passing the new law.

ADMINISTRATION OF THE TAX LAW AND TAX PRACTICE ISSUES

OBJECTIVE 8

Describe the administrative procedures under the tax law

ORGANIZATION OF THE INTERNAL REVENUE SERVICE

The **IRS** is the branch of the Treasury Department that is responsible for administering the federal tax law. It is organized on a national, regional, district, and service center basis. The responsibilities and functions of the various administrative branches include the following:

▶ The Commissioner of Internal Revenue, appointed by the President, is the chief officer of the IRS. This individual is supported by the Chief Counsel's office, which is responsible for preparing the government's case for litigation of tax disputes.

▶ The National Office includes a deputy commissioner, a series of assistants to the commissioner, a chief inspector, and a chief counsel. A significant responsibility of the National Office is to process ruling requests and to prepare revenue procedures that assist taxpayers with compliance matters.

▶ Four divisions, organized functionally, including (1) Wage and Investment Income, (2) Small Business and Self-Employed, (3) Large and Mid-size Business, and (4) Tax Exempt.

ADDITIONAL COMMENT

A survey of members of the American Institute of CPAs found that more than half of the 1,036 members who responded had an unfavorable opinion of the IRS. However, the accountants gave the IRS good marks for courtesy and a willingness to solve problems.

▶ District directors supervise the performance of IRS audits and collection of delinquent taxes in 33 districts.

▶ Ten service centers perform tax return processing work. They also select tax returns for audit.

▶ For the 2005 fiscal year, the IRS had approximately 94,000 employees and a budget of $10.027 billion.

In 1998, Congress enacted legislation with a major objective of reforming the manner in which the IRS administers the tax system. The taxpaying public has been increasingly critical of the IRS, especially with the allegedly insensitive and strong-arm tactics used against taxpayers. Therefore, the legislation placed a greater emphasis on serving the public and meeting taxpayer needs. While substantial organizational and operational changes to the IRS were mandated, only time will tell if this legislation will be successful. Details of the Act are outside the scope of this textbook.

ENFORCEMENT PROCEDURES

All tax returns are initially checked for mathematical accuracy and items that are clearly erroneous. The Form W-2 amounts (e.g., wages, and so on), Form 1099 information return amounts (e.g., relating to dividend and interest payments, and so on) and other forms filed with the IRS by the payer are checked against the amounts reported on the tax return. If differences are noted, the IRS Center merely sends the taxpayer a bill for the corrected amount of tax and a statement of the differences. In some instances, the difference is due to a classification error by the IRS, and the additional assessment can be resolved by written correspondence. A refund check may be sent to the taxpayer if an overpayment of tax has been made.

EXAMPLE I:1-24 ▶

ADDITIONAL COMMENT

Individuals may call 800-366-4484 to report misconduct of IRS employees.

Bart is an author of books and properly reports royalties on Schedule C (Profit or Loss from Business). The IRS computer matching of the Form 1099 information returns from the publishing companies incorrectly assumes that the royalties should be reported on Schedule E (Supplemental Income and Loss). If the IRS sends the taxpayer a statement of the difference and an adjusted tax bill, this matter (including the abatement of added tax, interest, and penalties) should be resolved by correspondence with the IRS. ◀

SELECTION OF RETURNS FOR AUDIT

ADDITIONAL COMMENT

A special task force has recommended that the percentage of returns audited be increased to 2.5%. Many individuals feel that the probability of being audited is so low as to be disregarded.

The U.S. tax system is based on self-assessment and voluntary compliance. However, enforcement by the IRS is essential to maintain the integrity of the tax system. The IRS uses both computers and experienced personnel to select returns for examination. With respect to the use of the computer, a **Discriminant Function System (DIF)** is used to classify returns to be selected for audit. The DIF system generates a "score" for a return based on the potential for the return to generate additional tax revenue. After returns are scored under the DIF system, the returns are manually screened by experienced IRS personnel who decide which returns warrant further examination. In the aggregate, less than 1% of all individual returns are selected for examination each year. Some examples of situations where individuals are more likely to be audited include the following:

ADDITIONAL COMMENT

In 2002, the IRS launched the National Research Program (NRP) to select returns for audit. The NRP will update data compiled in the old TCMP audits and develop new statistical models for identifying returns most likely to contain errors.

▶ Individuals who are sole proprietors and claim expenses in connection with their trade or businesses, especially if significant tax losses are incurred.

▶ Itemized deductions exceeding an average amount for the person's income level

▶ Filing of a refund claim by a taxpayer who has been previously audited, where substantial tax deficiencies have been assessed

▶ Individuals who are self-employed with substantial business income or income from a profession (e.g., a medical doctor)

ETHICAL POINT

A CPA should not recommend a position to a client that exploits the IRS audit selection process.

AUDIT PROCEDURES. Audits of most individuals are handled through an **office audit procedure** in an office of the IRS. In most cases, an individual is asked to substantiate a particular deduction, credit, or income item (e.g., charitable contributions that appear to be excessive). The office audit procedure does not involve a complete audit of all items on the return.

EXAMPLE I:1-25 ▶

Brad obtains a divorce during the current year and reports a $30,000 deduction for alimony. The IRS may conduct an office audit to ascertain whether the amount is properly deductible as alimony and does not represent a disguised property settlement to Brad's ex-wife. Brad may be asked to submit verification (e.g., a property settlement agreement between the spouses that designates the payments as alimony). ◀

KEY POINT

A taxpayer may appear on his or her own behalf before the IRS during an audit. An attorney or CPA in good standing is authorized to practice before the IRS upon the filing of a written statement that he or she is currently so qualified and is authorized to represent the taxpayer.

A **field audit procedure** often is used for corporations and individuals engaged in a trade or business. A field audit generally is broader in scope than the office audit (e.g., several items on the tax return may be reviewed). A field audit usually is conducted at the taxpayer's place of business or the office of his or her tax advisor.

Most large corporations are subject to annual audits. The year under audit may be several years prior to the current year because the corporation often will waive the statute of limitations pending the resolution of disputed issues.

STATUTE OF LIMITATIONS

Most taxpayers feel a sense of relief after they have prepared their income tax return and have mailed it to the IRS. However, the filing of the tax return is not necessarily the end of the story for that particular taxable year. It is possible, of course, that the IRS may select their tax return for audit after the return has been initially processed or a taxpayer may have filed an amended return to correct an error or omission.

REAL-WORLD EXAMPLE

Based on an IRS audit, the Mustang Ranch, Nevada's most famous legal bordello, was assessed some $13 million in taxes. When the amount owed could not be paid, the IRS sold the property to recoup the taxes.

Both the IRS and taxpayers can make corrections to a return after it has been originally filed. Fortunately, both only have a limited time period in which to make such corrections. This time period is called the **statute of limitations** and prevents either the taxpayer or the IRS from changing a filed tax return after the time period has expired. The general rule for the statute of limitations is three years from the later of the date the tax return was actually filed or its due date.[33] However, a six-year statute of limitations applies if the taxpayer omits items of gross income that in total exceed 25% of the gross income reported on the return.[34] The statute of limitations remains open indefinitely if a fraudulent return is filed or if no return is filed.[35]

EXAMPLE I:1-26 ▶ Betty, a calendar-year taxpayer, is audited by the IRS in February 2010 for the tax year 2008. During the course of the audit, the IRS proposes additional tax for 2008, because Betty failed to substantiate certain travel and entertainment expense deductions. During the course of the audit, the IRS discovers that Betty failed to file a tax return for 2003, and in 2007 an item of gross income amounting to $26,000 was not reported. Gross income reported on the 2007 return was $72,000. Assuming Betty's 2008 return was filed on or before its due date (April 15, 2009), the IRS may assess a deficiency for 2008 because the three-year statute of limitations will not expire until April 15, 2012. A deficiency also may be assessed for the 2007 return because a six-year statute of limitations applies since the omission is more than 25% of the gross income reported on the return. A deficiency also may be assessed for 2003 as there is no statute of limitations for fraud. ◀

ADDITIONAL COMMENT

More than 150 penalties can be imposed on taxpayers. In fact, applying the penalties has become so complicated that the IRS is currently considering ways to consolidate and simplify them.

INTEREST

Interest accrues on both assessments of additional tax due and on refunds that the taxpayer receives from the government.[36] No interest is paid on a tax refund if the amount is refunded by the IRS within 45 days of the day prescribed for filing the return (e.g., April 15) determined without regard to extensions.[37] If a return is filed after the filing date, no interest is paid if the refund is made within 45 days of the date the return was filed.

EXAMPLE I:1-27 ▶ Beverly, a calendar-year taxpayer, files her 2009 tax return on February 1, 2010, and requests a $500 refund. No interest accrues on the refund amount if the IRS sends the refund check to Beverly within 45 days of the April 15, 2010, due date. ◀

ADDITIONAL COMMENT

In addition to the penalties listed on this page, the government also assesses penalties for civil fraud and criminal fraud. Criminal fraud carries a maximum penalty of $100,000, a prison sentence of up to five years, or both.

PENALTIES

Various nondeductible penalties are imposed on the net tax due for failure to comply, including

▶ A penalty of 5% per month (or fraction thereof) subject to a maximum of 25% for failure to file a tax return[38]

---

[33] Secs. 6501(a) and (b)(1). Similar rules apply to claims for a refund filed by the taxpayer. Section 6511(a) requires that a refund claim be filed within three years of the date the return was filed or within two years of the date the tax was paid, whichever is later.

[34] Sec. 6501(e). See also *Stephen G. Colestock*, 102 T.C. 380 (1994), where the Tax Court ruled that the extended six-year limitation period applied to a married couple's entire tax liability for the tax year at issue, not just to items that constituted substantial omissions of gross income. Thus, the IRS was able to assert an increased deficiency and additional penalties attributable to a disallowed depreciation deduction.

[35] Sec. 6501(c).

[36] Sec. 6621(a). The rate is adjusted four times a year by the Treasury Department based on the current interest rate for short-term federal obliga-

tions. The interest rate individual taxpayers must pay to the IRS on underpayments of tax is the federal short-term rate plus three percentage points. The interest rate paid to taxpayers on overpayments of tax is the federal short-term rate plus two percentage points. The annual interest rate on noncorporate underpayments and overpayments for the period October 1, 2009, through December 31, 2009, was 4%.

[37] Sec. 6611(e).

[38] Sec. 6651(a)(1). The penalty assessed may be very small in some instances even though the taxpayer owes a large tax bill for the year because penalties are imposed on the net tax due. The percentages are increased to 15% per month (or fraction thereof) up to a maximum of 75% if the penalty is for fraudulent failure to file under Sec. 6651(f).

▶ A penalty of 0.5% per month (or fraction thereof) up to a maximum of 25% for failure to pay the tax that is due[39]

▶ An accuracy-related penalty of 20% of the underpayment for items such as negligence or disregard of rules or regulations, any substantial understatement of income tax, or any substantial misstatement of valuation[40]

▶ A 75% penalty for fraud[41]

▶ A penalty based on the current interest rate for underpayment of estimated taxes[42]

▶ Significant new penalties on tax return preparers have been enacted by Congress for taxable years 2007 and forward. In general, these new penalties are applicable for any position on a tax return where there is a "realistic possibility" (one-in-three chance) that the position would not be upheld in a court of law. The penalty is not assessed if the position is disclosed in the return.

ADDITIONAL COMMENT

Pete Rose, major league baseball's all-time hit leader, was sent to prison in 1990 for income tax evasion.

ADMINISTRATIVE APPEAL PROCEDURES

If an IRS agent issues a deficiency assessment, the taxpayer may make an appeal to the IRS Appeals Division. Some disputes involve a gray area (e.g., a situation where some courts have held for the IRS whereas other courts have held for the taxpayer on facts that are similar to the disputed issue). In such a case, the taxpayer may be able to negotiate a compromise settlement (e.g., a percentage of the disputed tax amount plus interest and penalties) with the Appeals Division based on the "hazards of litigation" (i.e., the probability of winning or losing the case if it is litigated).

Components OF A TAX PRACTICE

OBJECTIVE 9

Describe the components of a tax practice and understand the importance of computer applications in taxation

Tax practice is a rapidly growing field that provides substantial opportunities for tax specialists in public accounting, law, and industry. The tasks performed by a tax professional may range from the preparation of a simple Form 1040 for an individual to the conduct of tax research and planning for highly complex business situations. Tax practice consists of the following activities:

▶ Tax compliance and procedure (i.e., tax return preparation and representation of a client in administrative proceedings before the IRS)

▶ Tax research

▶ Tax planning and consulting

▶ Financial planning

TYPICAL MISCONCEPTION

Many people believe that a tax practitioner should serve in the capacity of a neutral, unbiased expert. They tend to forget that tax practitioners are being paid to represent their clients' interests. A tax practitioner may sometimes recommend a position that is defensible, but where the weight of authority is on the side of the IRS.

TAX COMPLIANCE AND PROCEDURE

Preparation of tax returns is a significant component of tax practice. Tax practitioners often prepare federal, state, and local tax returns for individuals, corporations, estates, trusts, and so on. In larger corporations, the tax return preparation (i.e., compliance) function usually is performed by a company's internal tax department staff. In such a case, a CPA or other tax practitioner may assist the client with the tax research and planning aspects of their tax practice, and may even review their return before it is filed.

An important part of tax practice consists of assisting the client in negotiations with the IRS. If a client is audited, the practitioner acts as the client's representative in discussions with the IRS agent. If a tax deficiency is assessed, the practitioner assists the client if

---

[39] Sec. 6651(a)(2). If the failure to file penalty (5%) and the failure to pay the tax penalty (0.5%) are both applicable, the failure to file penalty is reduced by the failure to pay penalty per Sec. 6651(c)(1). Further, the penalty is increased to 1% per month after the IRS notifies the taxpayer that it will levy on the taxpayer's assets.

[40] Sec. 6662.
[41] Sec. 6663.
[42] Sec. 6654.

an administrative appeal is contemplated with the IRS's Appellate Division. In most instances, an attorney is retained if litigation is being considered.

TAX RESEARCH

Tax research is the search for the best possible defensibly correct solution to a problem involving either a completed transaction (e.g., a sale of property) or a proposed transaction (e.g., a proposed merger of two corporations). Research involves each of the following steps:

▶ Determine the facts.

▶ Identify the issue(s).

▶ Identify and analyze the tax law sources (i.e., code provisions, Treasury Regulations, administrative rulings, and court cases).

▶ Evaluate nontax (e.g., business) implications.

▶ Solve the problem.

▶ Communicate the findings to the client.

Tax research may be conducted in connection with tax return preparation, tax planning, or procedural activities. A more thorough discussion of tax research is presented in Chapter I:15.

TAX PLANNING AND CONSULTING

Tax planning involves the process of structuring one's affairs so as to minimize the amount of taxes *and* maximize the after-tax return. Thus, optimal tax planning is *not* to just pay the least amount of tax but to maximize after-tax cash flows. A text on tax research and planning has delineated the following tax planning principles:[43]

▶ Keep sufficient records.

▶ Forecast the effect of future events.

▶ Support the plan with a sound business purpose.

▶ Base the plan on sound legal authorities.

▶ Do not carry a good plan too far.

▶ Make the plan flexible.

▶ Integrate the tax plan with other factors in decision making.

▶ Conduct research to learn whether a similar plan has previously proved unsuccessful (e.g., a court case involving similar facts may have upheld the IRS's position).

▶ Consider the "maximum" risk exposure of the client (e.g., if the plan is subsequently challenged by the IRS and the tax treatment is disallowed, what is the economic impact upon the taxpayer?).

▶ Consider the effect of timing (e.g., whether it is more beneficial to take a deduction in one year versus another).

▶ Shape the plan to the client's needs and desires.

CPAs and attorneys frequently are engaged by their clients to perform consulting services to optimize the client's tax situation. For example, a major corporation client is considering the acquisition of a major international corporation and wants to make sure that the tax implications of such an acquisition are properly managed. The CPA will be engaged to perform a thorough review of the transaction to ensure that the client is fully aware of the tax results of the acquisition, and possibly may request an advance ruling from the IRS.

Because of the importance of planning in tax practice, subsequent chapters in this text include a separate section on tax planning to discuss issues that are related to the topical coverage. These tax planning principles should be kept in mind when attempting to use the tax planning recommendations. Also, a systematic approach to tax planning devel-

SELF-STUDY QUESTION

Do large national CPA firms generally stress the importance of tax research in connection with tax-return preparation or tax planning?

ANSWER

The large CPA firms emphasize their skills in tax planning. Sometimes a slight alteration of a proposed transaction can save the client substantial tax dollars. This is high-value-added work and can be billed at premium rates.

ADDITIONAL COMMENT

Several national accounting firms have divided their tax departments into two basic groups, consulting and compliance. The tax consultants work with clients in tax planning and consulting matters and do not prepare tax returns. Tax returns are prepared by the compliance staff.

---

[43] Fred W. Norwood et al., *Federal Taxation: Research, Planning, and Procedures*, 2nd ed. (Englewood Cliffs, NJ: Prentice Hall, 1979), pp. 215–216.

oped by two noted tax academicians, Myron Scholes and Mark Wolfson, is discussed in Chapter I:18.

FINANCIAL PLANNING

A relatively new field for tax professionals is that of financial planning for individual clients. Since taxes are an integral part of any financial plan and since a tax specialist regularly meets with his or her clients (filing returns and other tax matters), the area of financial planning has become increasingly a part of tax practice. The typical steps in performing a financial planning engagement include the following steps:

▶ Determine the client's financial goals and objectives.

▶ Review the client's insurance coverage for adequacy and appropriateness.

▶ Recommend an investment strategy, including risk analysis and asset allocation.

▶ Review tax returns to ensure that, through proper tax planning, the client is maximizing his or her after-tax cash flow.

▶ Review the client's retirement plans to assure compliance with the law and possible new alternatives.

▶ Review all documents related to estate and gift planning and work with the client's attorney to minimize all transfer taxes and fulfill the client's objectives.

COMPUTER APPLICATIONS IN TAX PRACTICE

TAX RETURN PREPARATION

To prepare tax returns, most tax practitioners purchase tax preparation software from companies such as Commerce Clearing House or Intuit. This software allows the preparation of accurate and professional-looking tax returns. A word of caution, however, is in order. As with any computer software, the preparation of tax returns using the computer requires as much knowledge and expertise from the preparer as doing the returns by hand. A recent trend in tax return preparation is the **electronic filing** of tax returns, i.e., a "paperless" tax return. Taxpayers send their returns electronically to the IRS for processing, thereby saving enormous amounts of paper and, perhaps, reducing human error.

TAX PLANNING APPLICATIONS

Performing tax planning for clients involves the evaluation of alternative courses of action. This evaluation process can be very time-consuming because of the tax calculations necessary to arrive at an optimal solution. The computer has become an essential tool in this process because of the speed with which the tax calculations can be made. Many tax professionals now use sophisticated software to perform tax planning for their clients. A prime example of the use of the computer in tax planning has been in deciding whether a taxpayer should invest in a Roth Individual Retirement Account (Roth IRA) or a regular IRA (see Chapter I:9 for more details on IRAs). There are many factors to consider, including current and projected tax rates, current and projected level of income, etc. With the computer, a tax professional can vary the assumptions and create a number of alternatives within a relatively short period of time. To perform this task by hand would require an enormous commitment of time. As with most aspects of life, the impact of the computer on tax planning has been highly significant and will only increase in the future.

TAX RESEARCH APPLICATIONS

Computerized information-retrieval systems are used in tax research and are rapidly replacing books as the principal source of tax-related information. Most commercial research services are offered on the internet.[44] The principal Internet services are RIA's *Checkpoint*

---

[44] For a guide to tax information on the internet, link to the website of the American Taxation Association at www.atasection.org under Tax Directories.

and CCH's *Tax Research Network*. These commercial Internet services contain a wide range of materials available to tax researchers who subscribe to the service. In addition, the IRS has a home page (www.irs.gov) that taxpayers can access for forms, publications, and other related materials. All of the major accounting firms and many other tax organizations have home pages that allow users to access a myriad of tax information.

PROBLEM MATERIALS

DISCUSSION QUESTIONS

I:1-1 The Supreme Court in 1895 ruled that the income tax was unconstitutional because the tax needed to be apportioned among the states in proportion to their populations. Why would the requirement of proportionality be so difficult to administer?

I:1-2 Why was pay-as-you-go withholding needed in 1943?

I:1-3 Congressman Patrick indicates that he is opposed to new tax legislative proposals that call for a flat tax rate that are being considered by Congress because the new taxing structure would not be in accord with our traditional practice of taxing those who have the ability to pay the tax. Discuss the position of the congressman, giving consideration to tax rate structures (e.g., progressive, proportional, and regressive) and the concept of equity.

I:1-4 The governor of your state stated in a recent political speech that he has never supported any income tax increases as the tax rates have remained at the same level during his entire term of office. Yet, you believe that you are paying more tax this year than in previous years even though your income has not increased. How can both you and the governor be correct? In other words, is it possible for the government to raise taxes without raising tax rates?

I:1-5 Carmen has computed that her average tax rate is 16% and her marginal tax rate is 25% for the current year. She is considering whether to make a charitable contribution to her church before the end of the tax year. Which tax rate is of greater significance in measuring the tax effect for her decision? Explain.

I:1-6 Why are the gift and estate taxes called wealth transfer taxes? What is the tax base for computing each of these taxes?

I:1-7 Cathy, who is single, makes gifts of $50,000 to each of her two adult children.
a. Who is primarily liable for the gift tax on the two gifts, Cathy or the two children?
b. If Cathy has never made a taxable gift in prior years, is a gift tax due on the two gifts?

I:1-8 Carlos inherits 100 shares of Allied Corporation stock from his father. The stock cost his father $8,000 and had a $10,000 FMV on the date of his father's death. The alternate valuation date was not elected. What is Carlos's tax basis for the Allied stock when it is received from the estate?

I:1-9 Most estates are not subject to the federal estate tax.
a. Why is this the case?
b. Do you believe most estates should be subject to the federal estate tax?

I:1-10 Indicate which of the following taxes are generally progressive, proportional, or regressive:
a. State income taxes
b. Federal estate tax
c. Corporate state franchise tax
d. Property taxes
e. State sales taxes

I:1-11 Carolyn operates a consulting business as a sole proprietor (unincorporated). Carolyn has been approached by one of her major clients to become an employee. If she accepts the new job, she would no longer operate her consulting business. From the standpoint of paying Social Security taxes, would Carolyn's Social Security taxes increase or decrease if she becomes an employee? Why?

I:1-12 The three different levels of government (federal, state, and local) must impose taxes to carry out their functions. For each of the types of taxes below, discuss which level of government primarily uses that type of tax.
a. Property taxes
b. Excise taxes
c. Sales taxes
d. Income taxes
e. Employment taxes

I:1-13 A "good" tax structure has five characteristics.
a. Briefly discuss the five characteristics.
b. Using the five characteristics, evaluate the following tax structures:
   1. Federal income tax
   2. State sales tax
   3. Local ad valorem property tax

I:1-14 Two commonly-recognized measures of the fairness of an income tax structure are "horizontal equity" and "vertical equity."
a. Discuss what is meant by horizontal equity and vertical equity as it pertains to the income tax.

b. Why is it so difficult to design a "fair" tax structure?

I:1-15 The primary objective of the federal income tax law is to raise revenue. What are its secondary objectives?

I:1-16 If the objectives of the federal tax system are multifaceted and include raising revenues, providing investment incentives, encouraging certain industries, and meeting desired social objectives, is it possible to achieve a simplified tax system? Explain.

I:1-17 Distinguish between *taxpaying entities* and *flow-through entities* from the standpoint of the federal income tax law.

I:1-18 Sally and Tom are married, have three dependent children, and file a joint return in 2010. If they have adjusted gross income (AGI) of $90,000 and itemized deductions of $10,000, what is their taxable income for 2010?

I:1-19 The Bruin Corporation, a C corporation, is owned 100% by John Bean and had taxable income in 2010 of $500,000. In December 2010, the corporation has decided to distribute $400,000 to John and has asked you whether it would be better to distribute the money as a dividend or salary. John is in the 35% marginal tax bracket. How would you respond to Bruin Corporation?

I:1-20 Discuss what is meant by the term "double taxation" of corporations. Develop an example of double taxation using a corporation and shareholder.

I:1-21 Limited liability companies (LLCs) are very popular today as a form of organization. Assume a client asks you to explain what this type of organization is all about. Prepare a brief description of the federal income tax aspects of LLCs.

I:1-22 For flow-through entities, such as partnerships, how does the tax law use partner basis adjustments to prevent double taxation of partnership income?

I:1-23 Partnerships and S corporations are flow-through entities. In connection with filing annual tax returns, these entities must include Form K-1 in the returns. What is Form K-1, what is its purpose, and who receives the form?

I:1-24 The PDQ Partnership earned ordinary income of $150,000 in 2008. The partnership has three equal partners, Pete, Donald, and Quint. Quint, who is single, uses the standard deduction, and has other income of $15,000 (not connected with the partnership) in 2010. He receives a $30,000 distribution from the partnership during the year. What are the total tax consequences for Quint in 2010?

I:1-25 Why is a thorough knowledge of sources of tax law so important for a professional person who works in the tax area?

I:1-26 The Internal Revenue Code is the most authoritative source of income tax law. In trying to resolve an income tax question, however, a tax researcher also consults administrative rulings (Income Tax Regulations, Revenue Rulings, etc.) and court decisions. Why wouldn't the tax researcher just consult the Code since it is the highest authority? Similarly, why is there a need for administrative rulings and court decisions?

I:1-27 Congressional committee reports are an important source of information concerning the legislative enactment of tax law.
a. Name the three Congressional committee reports that are issued in connection with a new tax bill.
b. Of what importance are Congressional committee reports to tax practitioners?

I:1-28 What is the primary service function provided by the National Office of the IRS?

I:1-29 What types of taxpayers are more likely to be audited by the IRS?

I:1-30 Anya is concerned that she will be audited by the IRS.
a. Under what circumstances is it possible that the IRS will review each line item on her tax return?
b. Is it likely that all items on Anya's return will be audited?

I:1-31 **a.** What does the term "hazards of litigation" mean in the context of taxation?
b. Why would the IRS or a taxpayer settle or compromise a case based on the "hazards of litigation"?

I:1-32 If a taxpayer files his or her tax return and receives a tax refund from the IRS, does this mean that the IRS feels that the return is correct and will not be subject to a future audit.

I:1-33 State the statute of limitations for transactions involving:
a. Fraud (e.g., failure to file a tax return)
b. Disallowance of tax deduction items
c. The omission of rental income equal to greater than 25% of the taxpayer's reported gross income

I:1-34 In reference to tax research, what is meant by *the best possible defensibly correct solution*?

I:1-35 The profession of tax practice involves four principal areas of activity. Discuss these four areas.

I:1-36 Many tax professionals have moved into the field of financial planning for their clients.
a. How do taxes impact financial planning for a client?
b. Why do tax professionals have a perfect opportunity to perform financial planning for their clients?

I:1-37 Is the principal goal of tax planning to absolutely minimize the amount of taxes that a taxpayer must pay?

I:1-38 Explain how a computer can assist a tax practitioner in tax planning activities and making complex tax calculations.

PROBLEMS

I:1-39 *Tax Rates.* Latesha, a single taxpayer, had the following income and deductions for the tax year 2010:

INCOME:	Salary	$ 60,000
	Business Income	25,000
	Interest income from bonds	10,000
	Tax-exempt bond interest	5,000
	TOTAL INCOME	100,000
DEDUCTIONS:	Business expenses	$ 9,500
	Itemized deductions	20,000
	Personal exemption	3,650
	TOTAL DEDUCTIONS	33,150

a. Compute Latesha's taxable income and federal tax liability for 2010.
b. Compute Latesha's marginal, average, and effective tax rates.
c. For tax planning purposes, which of the three rates in Part b is the most important?

I:1-40 *Marginal Tax Rate.* Jill and George are married and file a joint return. They expect to have $400,000 of taxable income in the next year and are considering whether to purchase a personal residence that would provide additional tax deductions of $80,000 for mortgage interest and real estate taxes.
a. What is their marginal tax rate for purposes of making this decision? Ignore the effects of a phase-out of personal exemptions and itemized deductions (see Chapters I:2 and I:7, respectively).
b. What is the tax savings if the residence is acquired?

I:1-41 *Gift Tax.* Betsy, a married taxpayer, makes the following gifts during the current year (2010): $20,000 to her church, $30,000 to her daughter, and $25,000 to her husband.
a. What is the amount of Betsy's taxable gifts for the current year (assuming that she does not elect to split the gifts with her spouse)?
b. How would your answer to Part a change if a gift-splitting election were made?

I:1-42 *Estate Tax.* Clay dies in 2010 and has a gross estate valued at $4,800,000. Six months after his death, the gross assets are valued at $5,000,000. The estate incurs funeral and administration expenses of $125,000. Clay also had debts amounting to $75,000 and bequeathed $500,000 of the property to his wife. The remainder of his estate goes to his children. During his life, Clay made no taxable gifts. Assume the estate tax has been reinstated for 2010.
a. What is the amount of Clay's taxable estate?
b. What is the tax base for computing Clay's estate tax?
c. What is the amount of estate tax owed if the tentative estate tax (before credits) is $1,725,800?
d. Alternatively, if, six months after his death, the gross assets in Clay's estate declined in value to $3,500,000, can the administrator of Clay's estate elect the alternate valuation date? What are the important factors that the administrator should consider as to whether the alternate valuation date should be elected?

I:1-43 *Comparison of Tax Entities.*
a. Keith Thomas began a new consulting business on January 1, 2010. He organized the business as a C corporation, KT, Inc. During 2010, the corporation was reasonably successful and generated revenues of $1,050,000. KT had operating expenses of $800,000 before any payments to Keith. During 2010, KT paid dividends to Keith in the amount of $250,000. Assume that Keith had other ordinary taxable income of $120,000, itemized deductions of $40,000, is married (wife has no income), and has no children. Compute the total tax liability of KT and Keith for 2010. Ignore any phaseouts of itemized deductions or personal exemptions.
b. Instead of organizing the consulting business as a C corporation, assume Keith organized the business as a limited liability company, KT, LLC. KT made a distribution of $250,000 to Keith during 2010. Compute the total tax liability of KT and Keith for 2010. Ignore any phaseouts of itemized deductions or personal exemptions.

I:1-44 *Partnership Income.* Howard Gartman is a 40% partner in the Horton & Gartman Partnership. During 2010, the partnership reported the total items below (100%) on its Form 1065:

Ordinary income	$180,000
Qualified dividends	10,000
Long-term capital loss	(12,000)
Long-term capital gain	28,000
Charitable contributions	4,000
Cash distributions to partners	150,000

Howard and his wife Dawn, who file a joint return, also had the following income and deductions from sources not connected with the partnership:

Income

Dawn's salary	$40,000
Qualified dividends	3,000

Deductions

Mortgage interest	6,000
Real estate taxes	1,800
Charitable contributions	1,000

Howard and Dawn have two dependent children. During 2010, Dawn had $6,000 in federal income taxes withheld from her salary and Howard made four estimated tax payments of $3,000 each ($12,000 total). Compute Howard and Dawn's Federal income tax liability for 2010 and whether they have a balance due or a tax refund.

I:1-45   *Interest and Penalties.* In 2009, Paul, who is single, has a comfortable salary from his job as well as income from his investment portfolio. However, he is habitually late in filing his federal income tax return. He did not file his 2009 income tax return until November 30, 2010 (due date was April 15, 2010) and no extensions of time to file the return were filed. Below are amounts from his 2009 return:

Taxable income	$140,000
Total tax liability on taxable income	32,909
Total federal tax withheld from his salary	27,290

Paul sent a check with his return to the IRS for the balance due of $5,619. He is relieved that he has completed his filing requirement for 2009 *and* has met his financial obligation to the government for 2009.

Has Paul met *all* of his financial obligations to the IRS for 2009? If not, what additional amounts will Paul be liable to pay to the IRS?

I:1-46   *IRS Audits.* Which of the following individuals is most likely to be audited?
a. Connie has a $20,000 net loss from her unincorporated business (a cattle ranch). She also received a $200,000 salary as an executive of a corporation.
b. Craig has AGI of $20,000 from wages and uses the standard deduction.
c. Dale fails to report $120 of dividends from a stock investment. His taxable income is $40,000 and he has no other unusually large itemized deductions or business expenses. A Form 1099 is reported to the IRS.

I:1-47   *Statute of Limitations.* In April 2010, Dan is audited by the IRS for the year 2008. During the course of the audit, the agent discovers that Dan's deductions for business travel and entertainment are unsubstantiated and a $600 deficiency assessment is proposed for the tax year 2008. The agent also examined some prior year returns. The agent discovers that Dan failed to report $40,000 of gross business income on his 2006 return. Gross income of $60,000 was reported in 2006. The agent also discovers that Dan failed to file a tax return in 2001.

Will the statute of limitations prevent the IRS from issuing a deficiency assessment for 2008, 2006, or 2001? Explain.

TAX STRATEGY PROBLEM

I:1-48   Pedro Bourbone is the founder and owner of a highly successful small business and, over the past several years, has accumulated a significant amount of personal wealth. His portfolio of stocks and bonds is worth nearly $5,000,000 and generates income from dividends and interest of nearly $250,000 per year. With his salary from the business and his dividends and interest, Pedro has taxable income of approximately $600,000 per year and is clearly in the top individual marginal tax bracket. Pedro is married and has three

children, ages 16, 14, and 12. Neither his wife nor his children are employed and have no income. Pedro has come to you as his CPA to discuss ways to reduce his individual tax liability as well as to discuss the potential estate tax upon his death. You mention the possibility of making gifts each year to his children. Explain how annual gifts to his children will reduce both his income during lifetime and his estate tax at death.

CASE STUDY PROBLEM

I:1-49   John Gemstone, a wealthy client, has recently been audited by the IRS. The agent has questioned the following deduction items on Mr. Gemstone's tax return for the year under review:

- A $10,000 loss deduction on the rental of his beach cottage.
- A $20,000 charitable contribution deduction for the donation of a painting to a local art museum. The agent has questioned whether the painting is overvalued.
- A $15,000 loss deduction from the operation of a cattle breeding ranch. The agent is concerned that the ranch is not a legitimate business (i.e., is a hobby).

Your supervisor has requested that you represent Mr. Gemstone in his discussions with the IRS.

a. What additional questions should you ask Mr. Gemstone in an attempt to substantiate the deductibility of the above items?

b. What tax research procedures might be applied to build the best possible case for your client?

RESEARCH PROBLEM

I:1-50   Read the following two cases and explain why the Supreme Court reached different conclusions for cases involving similar facts and issues:

- *CIR v. Court Holding Co.,* 33 AFTR 593, 45-1 USTC ¶9215 (USSC, 1945)
- *U.S. v. Cumberland Public Service Co.,* 38 AFTR 978, 50-1 USTC ¶9129 (USSC, 1950)

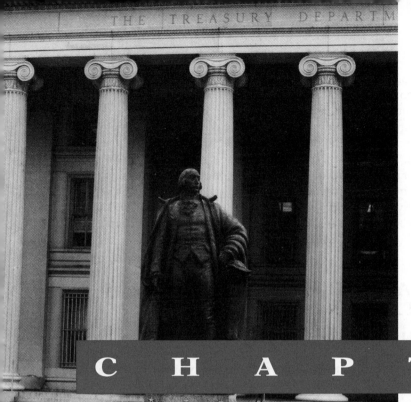

2

CHAPTER

DETERMINATION OF TAX

LEARNING OBJECTIVES

After studying this chapter, you should be able to

1. Use the tax formula to compute an individual's taxable income

2. Determine the amount allowable for the standard deduction

3. Determine the amount and the correct number of personal and dependency exemptions

4. Determine the amount of child credit

5. Determine the filing status of individuals

6. Explain the tax formula for corporations

7. Explain the basic concepts of property transactions

Each year, over 130 million individuals and married couples file tax forms on which they compute their federal income tax. The income tax is imposed "on the taxable income of every individual."[1] The amount of tax actually owed by an individual taxpayer is determined by applying a complex set of rules that together make up the income tax law. To understand the income tax, it is necessary to study the basic formula on which the income tax computation is based. Therefore, this chapter introduces the income tax formula and begins the development of its components. Because the income tax formula constitutes the basis of the income tax, most of the remainder of this book is an expansion of the formula. In addition to individual taxpayers, about 5 million corporations and 2 million partnerships file returns each year. These entities are also discussed in this chapter.

FORMULA FOR INDIVIDUAL INCOME TAX

BASIC FORMULA

Most individuals compute their income tax by using the formula illustrated in Table I:2-1. The formula itself appears rather simple. However, the complexity of the income tax results from the intricate rules that must be applied in order to arrive at the amounts that enter into the formula.

The tax formula is incorporated into the income tax form. The tax formula illustrated in Table I:2-1 can be compared with Form 1040, which is reproduced in Figure I:2-1. Some differences exist between the tax formula below and the tax form itself. For example, taxpayers generally are not required to report exclusions (nontaxable income) on their tax returns. One exception does require taxpayers to disclose tax-exempt interest income. A number of separate schedules are used to report various types of income. For example, income from a sole proprietorship is reported on Schedule C, where gross income from the business is reduced by related expenses that are deductions for adjusted gross income (AGI). Only the net income from the business actually appears on Form 1040. Also, Form 1040 is used to collect other taxes such as the self-employment tax. Hence, a line is provided for that tax on Form 1040. The main reason for differences between the formula and the form is administrative convenience. That is, there is no reason to require taxpayers to disclose income if the income is not subject to tax, it is more simple to report business income on a separate schedule, and it is convenient to collect other taxes on the same tax form.

ADDITIONAL COMMENT

"There is one difference between a tax collector and a taxidermist—the taxidermist leaves the hide." This is a quote from Mortimer Caplan, former Director of the Bureau of Internal Revenue, *Time,* Feb. 1, 1963.

ADDITIONAL COMMENT

The IRS estimates that the average taxpayer will spend 3 hours and 59 minutes in preparing just a Form 1040. When the estimated time for recordkeeping, learning about the law, and sending the form is added to the preparation time, the total time estimate jumps to 9 hours and 54 minutes. Each additional form and schedule adds even more time.

ADDITIONAL COMMENT

Comedian Jay Leno's explanation as to why the IRS calls it Form 1040 was, "For every $50 you earn, you get $10 and they get $40."

▼ **TABLE I:2-1**

Tax Formula for Individuals

Income from whatever source derived	$xxx,xxx
Minus: Exclusions	(xxx)
Gross income	$ xx,xxx
Minus: Deductions for adjusted gross income	(xxx)
Adjusted gross income	$ x,xxx
Minus: Deductions from adjusted gross income:	
Greater of itemized deductions or the standard deduction	(xx)
Personal and dependency exemptions	(xx)
Taxable income	$ x,xxx
Times: Tax rate or rates (from tax table or schedule)	× .xx
Gross tax	$ xx
Minus: Credits and prepayments	(x)
Net tax payable or refund due	$ xx

---

[1] Sec. 1.

Examination of the formula reveals terms such as *gross income, exclusions, adjusted gross income, exemptions, gross tax,* and *credits.* These terms and others that make up the formula are defined below.

DEFINITIONS

INCOME.   The term **income** includes both taxable and nontaxable income. Although the term is not specifically defined in the tax law, it does include income from any source.[2] Its meaning is close to that of the term **revenue.** However, it does not include a "return of capital." Thus, in the case of the sale of property, only the gain, not the entire sales proceeds, is viewed as income. This view extends to the sale of inventory, where gross profit is viewed as income, as opposed to the sale price.

EXCLUSION.   Not all income is taxable. An **exclusion** is any item of income that the tax law says is not taxable. Congress, over the years, has specifically excluded certain types of income from taxation for various social, economic, and political reasons. Chapter I:4 discusses specific exclusions and the reasons for their existence. Table I:2-2 contains a sample of the major exclusions from gross income.

GROSS INCOME.   **Gross income** is income reduced by exclusions. In other words, it is income from taxable sources and is reported on the return (excluded income need not be disclosed). Section 61(a) contains a partial list of items of gross income. The items listed in Sec. 61(a) are shown in Table I:2-3. Note, however, that Sec. 61(a) states that unless otherwise provided, "gross income means all income from whatever source derived, including (but not limited to)" the listed items of income. Thus, even though an item is omitted from the list does not necessarily mean that the item is excluded. For example, illegal income, although omitted from the list, is taxable.[3]

▼ TABLE I:2-2
Major Exclusions

Gifts and inheritances
Life insurance proceeds
Welfare and certain other transfer payments
Certain scholarships and fellowships
Certain payments for injury and sickness
   Personal physical injury settlements
   Worker's compensation
   Medical expense reimbursements
Certain employee fringe benefits
   Health plan premiums
   Group term life insurance premiums (limited)
   Meals and lodging
   Employee discounts
   Dependent care
Certain foreign-earned income
Interest on state and local government bonds
Certain interest of Series EE bonds
Certain improvements by lessee to lessor's property
Child support payments
Property settlements pursuant to a divorce
Gain from the sale of a personal residence (limited)

---

[2] Sec. 61(a).

[3] *U.S. v. Manley S. Sullivan,* 6 AFTR 6753, 1 USTC ¶236 (USSC, 1927).

▼ **TABLE I:2-3**
Gross Income Items Listed in Sec. 61(a)

Compensation for services, including fees, commissions, fringe benefits, and similar items
Gross income derived from business
Gains derived from dealings in property
Interest
Rents
Royalties
Dividends
Alimony and separate maintenance payments
Annuities
Income from life insurance and endowment contracts
Pensions
Income from the discharge of indebtedness
Distributive share of partnership gross income
Income in respect of a decedent
Income from an interest in an estate or trust

ADDITIONAL COMMENT

In 2007, there were a total of 143 million individual income tax returns filed. 93.8 million of these returns had AGI under $50,000, and 4.5 million returns filed with AGI over $200,000.

DEDUCTIONS FOR ADJUSTED GROSS INCOME. In general, taxpayers may deduct expenses that are specifically allowed by the tax law. Allowable deductions include business and investment expenses generally, along with personal expenses that are specifically provided for in the IRC, such as charitable contributions. Most purely personal expenses are not deductible.

Deductions fall into two categories for individual taxpayers: deductions *for* adjusted gross income and deductions *from* adjusted gross income. In general, **deductions for adjusted gross income** are expenses connected with a trade or business. For the most part, **deductions from adjusted gross income** are personal expenses that Congress has chosen to allow. This classification scheme, however, is not always followed. For example, alimony paid, which is not a business expense, is a deduction *for* adjusted gross income. Table I:2-4 contains a partial list of deductions *for* adjusted gross income that is taken from Sec. 62. Deductions for adjusted gross income are discussed further in Chapter I:6.

ADJUSTED GROSS INCOME. **Adjusted gross income (AGI)** is a measure of income that falls between gross income and taxable income. AGI is important because it is used in numerous other tax computations, especially to impose limitations. For example, AGI is used to establish floors for the medical deduction and casualty loss deduction and to establish a ceiling for the charitable contribution deduction.

DEDUCTIONS FROM ADJUSTED GROSS INCOME. Section 62 lists deductions *for* AGI (see Table I:2-4). Thus, any allowable deduction not listed in Sec. 62 is a deduction *from* AGI. The two categories of deductions *from* adjusted gross income are (1) itemized deductions or the standard deduction and (2) personal and dependency exemptions.[4] Deductions from AGI are discussed further in Chapter I:7 of this textbook.

ADDITIONAL COMMENT

Itemized deductions were claimed on 35.4% of all returns filed in 2007.

ITEMIZED DEDUCTIONS AND THE STANDARD DEDUCTION. As mentioned above, taxpayers generally cannot deduct personal expenses.[5] Congress, however, allows taxpayers to deduct specified personal expenses such as charitable contributions and medical expenses. In addition, taxpayers are allowed to itemize expenses related to the pro-

---

[4] Sec. 63.

[5] Sec. 262.

▼ TABLE I:2-4
Deductions for Adjusted Gross Income Listed in Sec. 62

Trade and business deductions
Reimbursed employee expenses and certain expenses of performing artists
Losses from the sale or exchange of property
Deductions attributable to rents and royalties
Certain deductions of life tenants and income beneficiaries of property
Contributions to retirement plans (Keoghs and IRAs)
Penalties forfeited because of premature withdrawal of funds from time savings accounts
*One-half of self-employment taxes paid
*Health insurance costs incurred by a self-employed person
Alimony
Moving expenses
Certain required repayments of supplemental unemployment compensation
Jury duty pay remitted to an individual's employer
Certain environmental expenditures (reforestation and clean fuel)
Interest on education loans
Contribution to medical savings account

*Though not actually mentioned in Sec. 62, self-employment taxes and health insurance costs of self-employed persons are defined by Secs. 164(f) and 162(l), respectively, as trade or business deductions thereby indirectly enabling taxpayers to deduct these amounts for AGI.

ADDITIONAL COMMENT

Tax rate schedules, the standard deduction, personal exemptions, and other amounts are adjusted annually for inflation. Because of "rounding conventions," not every amount changes each year.

HISTORICAL NOTE

In 1986, when parents were required merely to list the names of their children to claim them as a dependent, 77 million children were claimed. In 1987, when taxpayers were required to list children's Social Security numbers to prove that the exemptions were valid, the number of children claimed as dependents decreased to 70 million.

HISTORICAL NOTE

As recently as 1986, the highest marginal tax rate was 50%, and as recently as 1980, it was 70%.

duction or collection of income, the management of property held for the production of income, and the determination, collection, or refund of any tax.[6]

Taxpayers have the choice of claiming either itemized deductions or the standard deduction. The amount of the standard deduction varies depending on the taxpayer's filing status, age, and vision. As a practical matter, for most taxpayers the standard deduction is greater than the total itemized deductions. Taxpayers with small amounts of deductible expenses do not itemize and, in fact, do not have to keep records of medical expenses and other itemized deductions. The relationship between itemized deductions and the standard deduction is discussed later in this chapter.

PERSONAL AND DEPENDENCY EXEMPTIONS. A **personal exemption** generally is allowed for each taxpayer and his or her spouse and an additional dependency exemption is permitted for each dependent. Both personal and dependency exemptions are equal to $3,650 in 2009 and 2010. The amount of an exemption is adjusted annually for increases in the cost of living.

TAXABLE INCOME. **Taxable income** is adjusted gross income reduced by deductions *from* AGI. It is the amount of income that is taxed.

TAX RATES AND GROSS TAX. Tax rates are the percentage rates, set by Congress, at which income is taxed. Currently there are six tax rates that range from 10% to 35%.

Through 2010	10%, 15%, 25%, 28%, 33%, and 35%
2011 and later	15%, 28%, 31%, 36%, 39.6%

Taxpayers compute their tax by multiplying the percentage rates found in the tax rate schedules times taxable income. However, most taxpayers simply look in a tax table to find their gross tax. These two alternatives are discussed in more detail later in this chapter. The gross tax is the amount of tax determined by this process.

---

[6] Sec. 212.

▼ **TABLE I:2-5**
Partial List of Tax Credits

Refundable

    Withholding from wages and back-up withholding
    Estimated tax payments
    Overpayment of prior year's tax
    Excess Social Security taxes paid
    Nonhighway-use gasoline tax
    Earned income credit
    Regulated investment company credit
    Payments made with extension request
    Child credit (in some cases)
    Making work pay credit (2009 and 2010 only)

Nonrefundable

    Adoption expense credit
    Credit for the elderly and disabled
    Foreign tax credit
    Child and dependent care credit
    Business energy credit
    Qualified electric vehicle credit
    Research and experimentation credit
    Low-income housing credit
    Building rehabilitation credit
    Hope and lifetime learning credits

SELF-STUDY QUESTION

If a taxpayer is in the 25% marginal tax bracket, would he or she prefer $100 of tax credits or $300 of tax deductions?

ANSWER

The taxpayer would prefer the $100 of tax credits. The $300 of deductions will result in a tax savings of $75 ($300 × 0.25), whereas the $100 of credits would result in a tax savings of $100.

CREDITS AND PREPAYMENTS. **Tax credits**, which include prepayments, are amounts that can be subtracted from the gross tax to arrive at the net tax due or refund due. Credits may be classified as either refundable or nonrefundable tax credits. **Refundable tax credits** are allowed to reduce a taxpayer's tax liability to zero and, if some credit still remains, are refundable (paid) by the government to the taxpayer. Prepayments of tax, which are amounts paid to the government during the year through means such as withholding from wages, and selected other items are classified as **refundable tax credits. Nonrefundable tax credits** are allowances that have been created by Congress for various social, economic, and political reasons such as the child and dependent care credits. Nonrefundable tax credits can be subtracted from the tax and may reduce the tax liability to zero. However, if the nonrefundable credits exceed the tax liability, none of the excess will be paid to the taxpayer. A partial list of refundable and nonrefundable tax credits can be found in Table I:2-5 and are covered in detail in Chapter I:14.

TAX FORMULA ILLUSTRATED

The following example illustrates the tax formula and Form 1040.

EXAMPLE I:2-1 ▶ The following facts relate to Larry S. and Jane V. Lane, who are married and file a joint return in 2009. Betty is their 9-year-old dependent daughter.

Salary	$75,000
Interest Income:	
Taxable	4,000
Exempt	500
Individual Retirement Account (IRA) contribution	5,000
Itemized deductions	12,300
Personal and dependency exemptions (3 × $3,650)	10,950
Federal income taxes withheld from salary	6,000
Make work pay credit	800

Their tax is computed as follows:

Income:

	Salary	$75,000
	Taxable interest	4,000
	Tax-exempt interest	500
	Total	$79,500
Minus:	Exclusion:	
	Tax-exempt interest	(500)
Gross income		$79,000
Minus:	Deductions for AGI:	
	IRA contribution	(5,000)
Adjusted gross income		$74,000
Minus:	Deductions from AGI:	
	Itemized deductions	(12,300)
	Personal and dependency exemptions	(10,950)
Taxable income		$50,750

Gross tax (2009 tax table)			$ 6,781
Minus:	Credits and prepayments		
	Making work pay credit	(800)	
	Child credit	(1,000)	
	Federal income tax withheld	(6,000)	(7,800)
Tax refund			$ 1,019 ◄

This tax is also computed on Form 1040 (see Figure I:2-1). Note that certain additional information, such as the taxpayers' address and Social Security numbers, also is included on the return.

DEDUCTIONS FROM ADJUSTED GROSS INCOME

ITEMIZED DEDUCTIONS

Itemized deductions are claimed only if the total of such expenses exceeds the standard deduction. Here, consideration is given to which expenses may be itemized and the relationship between itemized deductions and the standard deduction.

ADDITIONAL COMMENT

Of the total itemized deductions reported in 2007, interest paid in the amount of $524.8 billion comprised the largest portion at 38.2%. Taxes paid came in second with 33.9% of total itemized deductions.

DEDUCTIBLE ITEMS. Congress allows taxpayers to itemize specified personal expenses. These specified expenses include medical expenses, taxes, investment and residential interest, charitable contributions, casualty and theft losses, and employee expenses. In addition, taxpayers are allowed to itemize expenses related to the production or collection of nonbusiness income, the management of property held for the production of income, and the determination, collection, or refund of any tax. A partial list of itemized deductions is found in Table I:2-6.

ITEMIZED DEDUCTION FLOORS. There are four adjusted gross income floors associated with itemized deductions. AGI floors represent amounts subtracted from deductions in arriving at allowable amounts. Three of the floors apply to specific categories of itemized deductions; the remaining floor applies to total itemized deductions. The floors based on AGI are as follows:

▶ Medical expenses: only medical expenses over 7.5% of AGI of are deductible.

▶ Casualty losses: only casualty losses in excess of 10% of AGI are deductible.

▶ Miscellaneous itemized deductions: only miscellaneous itemized deductions in excess of 2% of AGI are deductible.

Form 1040

Department of the Treasury—Internal Revenue Service

U.S. Individual Income Tax Return 2009

(99) IRS Use Only—Do not write or staple in this space.

For the year Jan. 1–Dec. 31, 2009, or other tax year beginning _____ , 2009, ending _____ , 20____

OMB No. 1545-0074

Label

(See instructions on page 14.)

Use the IRS label.

Otherwise, please print or type.

Presidential Election Campaign

Your first name and initial: **Larry S.** Last name: **Lane**

Your social security number: **123 45 6789**

If a joint return, spouse's first name and initial: **Jane V.** Last name: **Lane**

Spouse's social security number: **987 65 4321**

Home address (number and street). If you have a P.O. box, see page 14. **116 E. Edwards** Apt. no. ____

▲ You **must** enter your SSN(s) above. ▲

City, town or post office, state, and ZIP code. If you have a foreign address, see page 14. **Lubbock, Texas 40401**

Checking a box below will not change your tax or refund.

► Check here if you, or your spouse if filing jointly, want $3 to go to this fund (see page 14) ► ☐ You ☐ Spouse

Filing Status

Check only one box.

1. ☐ Single
2. ☒ Married filing jointly (even if only one had income)
3. ☐ Married filing separately. Enter spouse's SSN above and full name here. ►
4. ☐ Head of household (with qualifying person). (See page 15.) If the qualifying person is a child but not your dependent, enter this child's name here. ►
5. ☐ Qualifying widow(er) with dependent child (see page 16)

Exemptions

6a ☒ **Yourself.** If someone can claim you as a dependent, **do not** check box 6a . . . . . .

b ☒ **Spouse** . . . .

Boxes checked on 6a and 6b: **2**

c Dependents:

(1) First name Last name	(2) Dependent's social security number	(3) Dependent's relationship to you	(4) ✓ if qualifying child for child tax credit (see page 17)
Betty Lane	125 25 7774		☑
			☐
			☐
			☐

If more than four dependents, see page 17 and check here ► ☐

No. of children on 6c who:
- lived with you: **1**
- did not live with you due to divorce or separation (see page 18): ____
- Dependents on 6c not entered above: ____

d Total number of exemptions claimed . . . .

Add numbers on lines above ► **3**

Income

Attach Form(s) W-2 here. Also attach Forms W-2G and 1099-R if tax was withheld.

If you did not get a W-2, see page 22.

Enclose, but do not attach, any payment. Also, please use Form 1040-V.

7	Wages, salaries, tips, etc. Attach Form(s) W-2	**7**	75,000
8a	**Taxable** interest. Attach Schedule B if required	**8a**	4,000
b	**Tax-exempt** interest. **Do not** include on line 8a . .	**8b**	500	
9a	Ordinary dividends. Attach Schedule B if required	**9a**	
b	Qualified dividends (see page 22)	**9b**		
10	Taxable refunds, credits, or offsets of state and local income taxes (see page 23)	**10**	
11	Alimony received	**11**	
12	Business income or (loss). Attach Schedule C or C-EZ	**12**	
13	Capital gain or (loss). Attach Schedule D if required. If not required, check here ► ☐	**13**	
14	Other gains or (losses). Attach Form 4797	**14**	
15a	IRA distributions .	**15a**		**b** Taxable amount (see page 24)	**15b**	
16a	Pensions and annuities	**16a**		**b** Taxable amount (see page 25)	**16b**	
17	Rental real estate, royalties, partnerships, S corporations, trusts, etc. Attach Schedule E	**17**	
18	Farm income or (loss). Attach Schedule F	**18**	
19	Unemployment compensation in excess of $2,400 per recipient (see page 27) . . .	**19**	
20a	Social security benefits	**20a**		**b** Taxable amount (see page 27)	**20b**	
21	Other income. List type and amount (see page 29) _____	**21**	
22	Add the amounts in the far right column for lines 7 through 21. This is your **total income** ►	**22**	79,000

Adjusted Gross Income

23	Educator expenses (see page 29)	**23**	
24	Certain business expenses of reservists, performing artists, and fee-basis government officials. Attach Form 2106 or 2106-EZ	**24**	
25	Health savings account deduction. Attach Form 8889 .	**25**	
26	Moving expenses. Attach Form 3903	**26**	
27	One-half of self-employment tax. Attach Schedule SE .	**27**	
28	Self-employed SEP, SIMPLE, and qualified plans . .	**28**	
29	Self-employed health insurance deduction (see page 30)	**29**	
30	Penalty on early withdrawal of savings	**30**	
31a	Alimony paid **b** Recipient's SSN ►	**31a**	
32	IRA deduction (see page 31)	**32**	5,000
33	Student loan interest deduction (see page 34) . .	**33**	
34	Tuition and fees deduction. Attach Form 8917 . . .	**34**	
35	Domestic production activities deduction. Attach Form 8903	**35**	
36	Add lines 23 through 31a and 32 through 35	**36**	5,000
37	Subtract line 36 from line 22. This is your **adjusted gross income** . . . . . ►	**37**	74,000

For Disclosure, Privacy Act, and Paperwork Reduction Act Notice, see page 97. Cat. No. 11320B Form **1040** (2009)

FIGURE I:2-1 ► FORM 1040

Tax and Credits	38	Amount from line 37 (adjusted gross income)	38	74,000	
	39a	Check if: ☐ **You** were born before January 2, 1945, ☐ Blind. **Total boxes** ☐ **Spouse** was born before January 2, 1945, ☐ Blind. checked ▶ 39a			
Standard Deduction for— • People who check any box on line 39a, 39b, or 40b **or** who can be claimed as a dependent, see page 35. • All others: Single or Married filing separately, $5,700 Married filing jointly or Qualifying widow(er), $11,400 Head of household, $8,350	b	If your spouse itemizes on a separate return or you were a dual-status alien, see page 35 and check here ▶ 39b ☐			
	40a	**Itemized deductions** (from Schedule A) or your **standard deduction** (see left margin) . .	40a	12,300	
	b	If you are increasing your standard deduction by certain real estate taxes, new motor vehicle taxes, or a net disaster loss, attach Schedule L and check here (see page 35) . ▶ 40b ☐			
	41	Subtract line 40a from line 38	41	61,700	
	42	**Exemptions.** If line 38 is $125,100 or less and you did not provide housing to a Midwestern displaced individual, multiply $3,650 by the number on line 6d. Otherwise, see page 37 . .	42	10,950	
	43	**Taxable income.** Subtract line 42 from line 41. If line 42 is more than line 41, enter -0- . .	43	50,750	
	44	**Tax** (see page 37). Check if any tax is from: **a** ☐ Form(s) 8814 **b** ☐ Form 4972 .	44	6,781	
	45	**Alternative minimum tax** (see page 40). Attach Form 6251	45		
	46	Add lines 44 and 45 . . . . ▶	46	6,781	
	47	Foreign tax credit. Attach Form 1116 if required	47		
	48	Credit for child and dependent care expenses. Attach Form 2441	48		
	49	Education credits from Form 8863, line 29	49		
	50	Retirement savings contributions credit. Attach Form 8880	50		
	51	Child tax credit (see page 42)	51	1,000	
	52	Credits from Form: **a** ☐ 8396 **b** ☐ 8839 **c** ☐ 5695	52		
	53	Other credits from Form: **a** ☐ 3800 **b** ☐ 8801 **c** ☐	53		
	54	Add lines 47 through 53. These are your **total credits**	54	1,000	
	55	Subtract line 54 from line 46. If line 54 is more than line 46, enter -0- . . . . . ▶	55	5,781	
Other Taxes	56	Self-employment tax. Attach Schedule SE	56		
	57	Unreported social security and Medicare tax from Form: **a** ☐ 4137 **b** ☐ 8919 . .	57		
	58	Additional tax on IRAs, other qualified retirement plans, etc. Attach Form 5329 if required . .	58		
	59	Additional taxes: **a** ☐ AEIC payments **b** ☐ Household employment taxes. Attach Schedule H	59		
	60	Add lines 55 through 59. This is your **total tax** . . . . ▶	60	5,781	
Payments	61	Federal income tax withheld from Forms W-2 and 1099 . .	61	6,000	
	62	2009 estimated tax payments and amount applied from 2008 return	62		
If you have a qualifying child, attach Schedule EIC.	63	Making work pay and government retiree credits. Attach Schedule M	63	800	
	64a	**Earned income credit (EIC)**	64a		
	b	Nontaxable combat pay election 64b			
	65	Additional child tax credit. Attach Form 8812	65		
	66	Refundable education credit from Form 8863, line 16 . . .	66		
	67	First-time homebuyer credit. Attach Form 5405 . . .	67		
	68	Amount paid with request for extension to file (see page 72) .	68		
	69	Excess social security and tier 1 RRTA tax withheld (see page 72)	69		
	70	Credits from Form: **a** ☐ 2439 **b** ☐ 4136 **c** ☐ 8801 **d** ☐ 8885	70		
	71	Add lines 61, 62, 63, 64a, and 65 through 70. These are your **total payments** . . . . ▶	71	6,800	
Refund Direct deposit? See page 73 and fill in 73b, 73c, and 73d, or Form 8888.	72	If line 71 is more than line 60, subtract line 60 from line 71. This is the amount you **overpaid**	72	1,019	
	73a	Amount of line 72 you want **refunded to you.** If Form 8888 is attached, check here . ▶ ☐	73a	1,019	
	▶ b	Routing number _____ ▶ c Type: ☐ Checking ☐ Savings			
	▶ d	Account number _____			
	74	Amount of line 72 you want **applied to your 2010 estimated tax** ▶ 74			
Amount You Owe	75	**Amount you owe.** Subtract line 71 from line 60. For details on how to pay, see page 74 . ▶	75		
	76	Estimated tax penalty (see page 74) 76			

Third Party Designee

Do you want to allow another person to discuss this return with the IRS (see page 75)? ☐ **Yes.** Complete the following. ☐ **No**

Designee's name ▶	Phone no. ▶	Personal identification number (PIN) ▶

Sign Here

Joint return? See page 15. Keep a copy for your records.

Under penalties of perjury, I declare that I have examined this return and accompanying schedules and statements, and to the best of my knowledge and belief, they are true, correct, and complete. Declaration of preparer (other than taxpayer) is based on all information of which preparer has any knowledge.

Your signature	Date	Your occupation	Daytime phone number
Larry S. Lane	4/15/10	Attorney	555 555-1212
Spouse's signature. If a joint return, **both** must sign.	Date	Spouse's occupation	
Jane V. Lane	4/15/10	Student	

Paid Preparer's Use Only

Preparer's signature ▶		Date	Check if self-employed ☐	Preparer's SSN or PTIN
Firm's name (or yours if self-employed), address, and ZIP code	▶		EIN	
			Phone no.	

Form **1040** (2009)

FIGURE I:2-1 ▶ FORM 1040 (CONTINUED)

▼ **TABLE I:2-6**

Partial List of Itemized Deductions

Medical expenses (over 7.5% of adjusted gross income)
Certain taxes
   State, local, and foreign income and real property taxes
   State and local personal property taxes
Residential interest and investment interest (limited)
Charitable contributions (limited)
Casualty and theft losses (over 10% of adjusted gross income)
Miscellaneous deductions (over 2% of adjusted gross income)
   Employee expenses (e.g., professional and union dues, professional publications, travel,
      transportation, education, job hunting, office-in-home, special clothing, and 50% of
      entertainment expenses)
   Expenses for producing investment income (e.g., accounting and legal fees, safe deposit
      rental, fees paid to an IRA custodian)
   Tax advice and tax return preparation and related costs
Other miscellaneous deductions
   Federal estate tax attributable to income in respect of a decedent
   Gambling losses to the extent of winnings
   Amortization of bond premium
   Amounts restored under claim of right

These floors are discussed in more detail in Chapter I:7.[7]

EXAMPLE I:2-2 ▶ John and Jane file a joint tax return in 2010 and report AGI of $170,000. Their itemized deductions include $15,500 of medical expenses and home mortgage interest of $10,000. The AGI floor reduces the medical expense deduction to $2,750 [$15,500 − (0.075 × $170,000)]. Thus, the total itemized deductions allowed is $12,750. ◀

STANDARD DEDUCTION

OBJECTIVE 2

Determine the amount allowable for the standard deduction

Itemized deductions are claimed only if the total amount of such deductions exceeds the standard deduction. The **standard deduction** is an amount set by Congress. It varies from year to year depending on the taxpayer's filing status, age, and vision.

KEY POINT

The dollar amount of the standard deduction generally increases each year because it is indexed to the rate of inflation.

Filing Status	Standard Deduction 2009	Standard Deduction 2010
Single individual other than heads of households	$ 5,700	$ 5,700
Married couples filing joint returns and surviving spouses	11,400	11,400
Married people filing separate returns	5,700	5,700
Heads of households	8,350	8,400

The differences between the 2009 and 2010 amounts represent adjustments for the increase in the cost of living. As you can see, a very minor difference exists between 2009 and 2010.

---

[7] A temporary rule required higher income taxpayers to reduce total itemized deduction by 1% of AGI in excess of $166,800 in 2009. The provision does not apply to 2010 and later years.

In 2009 and 2010, a married taxpayer's standard deduction is increased by $1,100 if he or she is elderly or blind ($2,200 if the taxpayer is elderly *and* blind) or has a spouse who is elderly or blind (for a maximum possible increase of $4,400 for a married couple). If an unmarried taxpayer is elderly or blind, his or her standard deduction is increased by $1,400 and $2,800 if the taxpayer is elderly *and* blind. Thus, in 2009 or 2010, a single taxpayer, age 65 and not blind, is entitled to a $7,100 ($5,700 + $1,400) standard deduction. Two special rules relating to age and blindness are noted below.

ADDITIONAL COMMENT

Of all individual returns filed in 2006, 63.8% claimed the standard deduction.

▶ The increase in the standard deduction for elderly taxpayers is available if the taxpayer turns 65 during the tax year. For purposes of this requirement, a taxpayer is considered to be age 65 on the day before his or her sixty-fifth birthday. Thus, a taxpayer who reaches age 65 on January 1 of a year is deemed to have reached age 65 on December 31 of the preceding year. The adjustment is allowed on the final return of a deceased taxpayer only if he or she reached age 65 before death.

▶ The IRC defines blindness as corrected vision in the better eye of no better than 20/200 or a field of no greater than 20 degrees. Vision is determined as of the last day of the tax year or, in the case of a deceased taxpayer, as of the date of death.

The standard deduction simplifies the computation of taxable income. As previously noted, for most taxpayers the standard deduction is greater than total itemized deductions. Those taxpayers do not itemize and, in fact, do not even have to keep records of medical expenses and other itemized deductions.

Who actually itemizes and who does not? High-income taxpayers are more likely to itemize than low-income taxpayers simply because they incur more expenses that can be itemized. This is true even though the AGI floors (previously discussed) affect high-income taxpayers more than low-income taxpayers. Another characteristic of taxpayers who generally itemize their deductions are individuals who own their homes and incur home mortgage expenses and property taxes. These two expenses are deductible and alone often exceed the standard deduction.[8]

EXAMPLE I:2-3 ▶ In 2010, Joan is single and a homeowner who incurs property taxes on her home of $2,000, makes charitable contributions of $500, and pays mortgage interest of $6,000. Joan's adjusted gross income is $32,000. Her taxable income is computed as follows:

Adjusted gross income		$32,000
Minus: Itemized deductions:		
Charitable contributions	$ 500	
Property taxes	2,000	
Mortgage interest	6,000	(8,500)
Minus: Personal exemption		(3,650)
Taxable income		$19,850 ◀

Joan would itemize her deductions because they ($8,500) are greater than her standard deduction ($5,700).

EXAMPLE I:2-4 ▶ Assume the same facts as in Example I:2-3 except that Joan is not a homeowner. Thus, she has no property taxes or mortgage interest but does pay rent of $800 per month for an apartment. Her taxable income is computed as follows:

Adjusted gross income	$32,000
Minus: Standard deduction	(5,700)
Minus: Personal exemption	(3,650)
Taxable income	$22,650 ◀

---

[8] A temporary rule permitted taxpayers to increase their standard deduction by the amount of state and local real property taxes paid up to $500 ($1,000 on a joint return) in 2008 and 2009. In 2009, taxpayers could also increase the standard deduction by the amount and certain disaster losses and the amount of sales tax paid on the purchase of a new motor vehicle.

Joan would use the standard deduction of $5,700 because it is greater than her itemized deductions of $500. Rent paid for a personal apartment is not deductible.

LOSS OF THE STANDARD DEDUCTION. Congress decided that some taxpayers should not be permitted to use the standard deduction as they possibly would receive an unintended tax benefit.[9] The standard deduction is unavailable to three categories of taxpayers:

▶ An individual filing a return for a period less than twelve months because of a change in accounting period.

▶ A married taxpayer filing a separate return in instances where the other spouse itemizes.

▶ Nonresident aliens.

To illustrate why Congress does not permit certain taxpayers to claim the standard deduction, consider what could happen if a married couple files separate returns but only one spouse itemizes. On a separate return in 2010 when the standard deduction is $5,700, one spouse could claim all itemized deductions while the other uses the standard deduction.

EXAMPLE I:2-5 ▶ Clay and Joy, a married couple, have incomes of $35,000 and $34,000, respectively. Their itemized deductions total $9,000. They would claim a $11,400 standard deduction on a joint return. If Clay filed a separate return and claimed all of the deductions, his itemized deductions of $9,000 would be greater than the $5,700 standard deduction. If Joy could claim the standard deduction on her return, their total deductions would equal $14,700 ($9,000 + $5,700). The law, however, requires that either they both itemize or they both use the standard deduction. ◀

Limitation on the Standard Deduction. A special rule applies to any individual for whom the dependency exemption is allowable to another taxpayer. The standard deduction of the dependent is limited to the greater of (1) the dependent's earned income plus $300 or (2) $950 (in 2009 and 2010). The purpose of this limitation is to prevent parents from shifting unearned income, such as interest and dividends, to their children and avoid paying tax on such income. Without this rule, children could use the standard deduction to offset interest and dividends.

EXAMPLE I:2-6 ▶ Webb and Beth are married, in the 35% marginal tax rate bracket, and have one son, Vincent, age 15. Vincent has no income and is claimed as a dependent by his parents. Webb and Beth transfer stocks and bonds that earn $3,000 in dividends and interest to Vincent. Their goal is to shift the $3,000 of income to Vincent to utilize his standard deduction. However, since Vincent is claimed as a dependent by his parents on their return, Vincent's standard deduction is limited to $950, i.e., the *greater* of $950 or his earned income plus $300 ($0 + $300). ◀

EXAMPLE I:2-7 ▶ Assume the same facts as in Example I:2-6 except Vincent has a part-time job and earns $2,000 in wages. Vincent's standard deduction would be $2,300 ($2,000 + $300). Alternatively, if Vincent's wages were $6,000, his standard deduction would be $5,700 (the maximum for a single individual). ◀

OBJECTIVE 3

Determine the amount and the correct number of personal and dependency exemptions

PERSONAL EXEMPTIONS

Taxpayers cannot deduct personal expenses except for certain itemized deductions that are specifically authorized under the tax law. Congress has recognized the need to protect a small amount of income from tax in order to allow the taxpayer to meet personal expenses. Thus, almost every individual taxpayer is allowed a personal exemption of $3,650 (in 2009 and 2010). Because there are two taxpayers on a joint return filed by a married couple, they are allowed two personal exemptions. In addition, if a married person files a separate return, the taxpayer can claim a personal exemption for his or her spouse if the spouse has no gross income during the year and the spouse is not the dependent of another taxpayer.[10]

Only one personal exemption is allowed for each person. Therefore, an individual who is claimed as a dependent by another person is not entitled to a personal exemption on his

---

[9] Sec. 63(c)(6).

[10] Sec. 151(b).

or her own return. Despite the loss of the personal exemption, most dependents owe little or no tax because they can usually offset their small income by the standard deduction.

DEPENDENCY EXEMPTIONS

ADDITIONAL COMMENT

One should forsake any preconceived notions as to what constitutes a dependent before examining the dependency tests.

Virtually all taxpayers can claim a *personal exemption* for themselves. In addition, taxpayers may also claim a *dependency exemption* for each dependent.[11] To qualify as a dependent, an individual must meet the definition of either a *qualifying child* or a *qualifying relative*. All dependents must meet several requirements. Four requirements are common to all dependents. All dependents must:

▶ Have a qualifying identification number.

▶ Meet a citizenship test.

▶ Meet a separate return test.

▶ Not themselves claim another person as a dependent.

Additional requirements also must be met depending on whether the dependent is a qualifying child or a qualifying relative.

REQUIREMENTS FOR ALL DEPENDENTS. The requirements applicable to all dependents are:

Identification number. Every dependent must have a Social Security number, and that number must be reported on the return.[12]

Citizenship. Dependents must be U.S. citizens[13] or nationals,[14] or residents[15] of the U.S., Canada, or Mexico for some part of the year.

Joint return. Married dependents cannot file joint returns. However, a taxpayer is entitled to the exemption if the dependent files a joint return solely to claim a refund of tax withheld (i.e., there is no tax on the joint return and there would have been no tax on two separate returns).[16] Married dependents should weigh the taxes that would be saved by the family from an exemption against the taxes that would be saved by filing a joint return. Depending on the circumstances, either alternative may be more beneficial.

No dependent. Dependents who file tax returns may not claim personal or dependency exemptions on their returns.

ADDITIONAL REQUIREMENTS FOR QUALIFYING CHILDREN. To claim a dependency exemption for an individual who is considered a *qualifying child*, the following additional requirements must be met:

▶ A relationship test.

▶ An age test.

▶ An abode test.

▶ A support test.

Relationship test. Eligible children include the taxpayer's children (including natural, adopted, foster, and stepchildren) and the taxpayer's siblings (including half-siblings and step-siblings) along with descendants of any of the above. A child is adopted if the child has been legally adopted or has been legally placed in a home for adoption.

---

[11] Sec. 152.
[12] Sec. 151(e). The IRS has the authority to disallow dependency exemptions for otherwise qualified dependents without Social Ssecurity numbers and with incorrectly reported Social Security numbers. A missing or incorrectly reported Social Security number may also bar an otherwise eligible individual from claiming head-of-household filing status.
[13] U.S. citizens living in foreign countries can claim dependency exemptions for adopted children even if the children are not U.S. citizens.

[14] A U.S. national is an individual born in an outlying possession such as American Samoa.
[15] A resident is a person who is not a U.S. citizen and who is legally residing in the United States with intent to stay here permanently (see Sec. 7701(b)).
[16] Rev. Rul. 54-567, 1954-2 C.B. 108 and Rev. Rul 65-34, 1965-1 C.B. 86. The theory is that the taxpayer is filing a claim for refund and not actually filing a tax return.

Age test. A qualifying child must be under age 19, a full-time student under age 24, or a permanently and totally disabled child.[17] A child is considered to be a student if he or she is in full-time attendance at a qualified educational institution during at least five months of the year. To be full-time, a student must carry the number of hours or courses the educational institution requires a student to take to be considered full-time.

Abode test. A qualifying child must have the same principal abode as the taxpayer for more than half of the year. A noncustodial parent meets this requirement if the custodial parent agrees in writing.

Support test. A qualifying child may not provide more than one-half of his or her own support during the year. Support is defined below in connection with the discussion of other dependents. Unlike other dependents, there is no requirement that the taxpayer provide more than one-half of the qualifying child's support, only that the dependent cannot provide more than one-half of his or her own support. This can be important in situations such as divorces where one spouse provides support, but the other has custody.

EXAMPLE I:2-8 ▶ Keith and Barbara file a joint return and have one son, Jeff, age 28. Because of a temporary illness, Jeff had to quit his job in June and moved back home to live with his parents. Keith and Barbara provided 70% of Jeff's support. Jeff earned $18,000. Jeff is not a qualifying child for purposes of the dependency exemption. Although Jeff meets the relationship, abode, and support tests, he fails the age test. ◀

REQUIREMENTS FOR OTHER RELATIVES. A dependency exemption may also be claimed for a *qualifying relative*. To be eligible, dependents must meet the common requirements above and three additional requirements:

▶ Relationship test.

▶ Gross income test.

▶ Support test.

Relationship test. Other relatives must either be related to the taxpayer or reside in the taxpayer's household for the entire year. Although this group is referred to as "other qualifying relatives," that term is misleading because individuals who live with the taxpayer do not actually have to be related to the taxpayer. The relationship between the taxpayer and the dependent cannot violate local law.[18] Relatives who can be claimed as dependents even if they do not live with the taxpayer include the taxpayer's parents and their ancestors and siblings, the taxpayer's stepparents, and specified in-laws (mother, father, brother, sister, son, and daughter) along with qualifying children discussed above. As a result, a qualifying child may be claimed as a dependent if the child meets the tests described here even if the child fails the requirements for qualifying children. Thus, a son who is age 24 can be claimed as a dependent if the son meets the support and gross income tests discussed below even though that son could not be claimed as a dependent under the requirements for a qualifying child.

EXAMPLE I:2-9 ▶ Jesse supports three people, all of whom have gross income of less than $3,650, Tina, an unrelated child who lives with him; his cousin Judy, who lives in another state; and his daughter Vicki, who lives in her own home. Jesse can claim two dependency exemptions: one for Tina, who lives with him (a person who lives with the taxpayer need not be related) and one for his daughter. Jesse cannot claim a dependency exemption for Judy as cousins do not meet the relationship test. ◀

On a joint return the dependent needs to be related to only one spouse.[19] Once established, a relationship is not terminated by death or divorce.

---

[17] As noted, taxpayers attain the age 65, for purposes of the additional standard deduction, on the day before the anniversaries of their births. As a result, an individual whose birthday is January 1 is considered to be age 65 in the year prior to the individual's 65th birthday. A child whose 19th birthday is on January 1 is considered to be under the age 19 in the previous year. The rule also is followed for purposes of determining whether the child is

under age 24, and is used in connection with age 17 threshold associated with the child credit. Rev. Rul. 2003-72, 2003-2 C.B. 353.

[18] Sec. 152(f)(3). The exemption has been disallowed where the relationship constituted "cohabitation" and was illegal in the state (*Cassius L. Peacock, III*, PH T.C. Memo ¶78.030, 37 TCM 177).

[19] Reg. Sec. 1.152-2(d).

EXAMPLE I:2-10 ▶ Ken and Lisa support Lisa's mother and claim her as a dependent on a joint return. Following Lisa's death, Ken continues to support Lisa's mother. Lisa's mother continues to be Ken's mother-in-law and can be claimed as a dependent. ◀

Gross income test. The dependent's gross income must be less than the exemption amount for the year ($3,650 in 2009 and 2010). The statutory definition of gross income is used in applying this limitation. Therefore, nontaxable scholarships, tax-exempt bond interest, and nontaxable Social Security benefits are not considered, but salary, taxable interest, and rent are considered in deciding whether the person meets this test.

EXAMPLE I:2-11 ▶ Jim, age 22, a full-time college student, lives with his cousin who provides more than one-half of Jim's support. Jim earned $8,000 from a summer job. Even though Jim's cousin provided over one-half of his support, Jim cannot be claimed as a dependent as Jim does not meet the gross income test. Alternatively, if Jim lived with and were supported by his brother, he could be claimed as a dependent because, as a brother, Jim is a qualifying child and is exempt from the gross income test. ◀

Support test. The taxpayer must normally provide more than one-half of a dependent's financial support during the year. Support includes amounts spent by the taxpayer, the dependent, and other individuals. Welfare[20] and Social Security benefits[21] spent on support count even if they are excluded from gross income. Scholarships, however, do not count as support if the amounts are tax exempt.

EXAMPLE I:2-12 ▶ Tarer provided $3,000 of support for his mother, Mary. Tarer's sister provided $1,000. Mary spent $4,500 of her savings for her own support. Because Mary provided over one-half of her own support, she cannot be claimed as a dependent. ◀

EXAMPLE I:2-13

ADDITIONAL COMMENT

A TV set bought by a parent for his 12-year-old child and set up in her bedroom was considered support (Rev. Rul. 77-282, 1977-2 C.B. 52). A power lawn mower, however, bought by a parent of a 13-year-old child was not considered support. The parent had assigned the child the job of mowing the lawn, and the power mower was intended to make the job more palatable. The lawn mower was considered a family item that benefits all members of the household (Rev. Rul. 77-282, 1977-2 C.B. 52.)

▶ George's father received Social Security benefits of $6,600, of which $1,800 were deposited into a savings account. He spent the remaining $4,800 on food, clothing, and lodging. George spent $5,600 to support his father. George meets the support test because the amount saved is not counted in the support test. ◀

Support includes amounts spent for food, clothing, shelter, medical and dental care, education, and the like.[22] Support is not limited to these items.[23] Support does not include the value of services rendered by the taxpayer to the dependent.[24] Also, the IRS and the courts have excluded various other expenses from support.[25]

Generally, the amount of support equals the cost of the item, but in the case of support provided in a noncash form, such as lodging, the amount of support equals the fair market value or fair rental value. The cost of an item such as a television or an automobile is included in support if the item actually is support.[26]

EXAMPLE I:2-14 ▶ Vicki's mother lives with her. Vicki purchased clothing for her mother costing $800 and provided her with a room that Vicki estimates she could have rented for $2,800. Vicki spent $2,500 for groceries she shared with her mother and $1,200 for utilities. In addition, Vicki purchased a television for $750 that she placed in the living room. Vicki and her mother both used the television. Vicki's support for her mother, at a minimum, includes:

Clothing	$ 800
Rental value of room	2,800
Food	1,250
Total	$4,850

---

[20] Rev. Rul. 71-468, 1971-2 C.B. 115.
[21] Rev. Ruls. 57-344, 1957-2 C.B. 112, and 58-419, 1958-2 C.B. 57.
[22] Reg. Sec. 1.152-1(a)(2)(i).
[23] Examples of other items that have been held to be support include church contributions (Rev. Rul. 58-67, 1958-1 C.B. 62), telephone (*William K. Price, III*, 1961 PH T.C. Memo ¶61,173, 20 TCM 886), medical insurance premiums (*James Edward Parker*, 1959 PH T.C. Memo ¶52,182, 18 TCM 800), child care (*Marvin D. Tucker*, 1957 PH T.C. Memo ¶57,118, 16 TCM 488), toys (*Loren S. Brumber*, 1952 PH T.C. Memo ¶52,087, 11 TCM 289), and vacations (*George R. Melat*, 1953 PH T.C. Memo ¶53,141, 12 TCM 443).

[24] *Frank Markarian v. CIR.*, 16 AFTR 2d 5785, 65-2 USTC ¶9699 (7th Cir., 1965).
[25] Examples of items that have been excluded are funeral expenses (Rev. Rul. 65-307, 1965-2 C.B. 40), taxes (Rev. Rul. 58-67, 1958-1 C.B. 62), a rifle, lawn mower, boat insurance (*Harriet C. Flower v. U.S.*, 52 AFTR 1383, 57-1 USTC ¶9655 (D.C. Pa., 1957)), and life insurance premiums (*John F. Miller*, 1959 PH T.C. Memo ¶59,155, 18 TCM 673).
[26] Rev. Rul. 77-282, 1977-2 C.B. 52.

Whether a portion of the utilities could be included in support would depend on whether the rental rate for the room included utilities. The fact that the mother used the television set probably would not be sufficient to cause its cost to be viewed as support. On the other hand, if the television set was a gift to the mother, was placed in her room, and was used exclusively by her, the cost probably would qualify as support. ◄

If a taxpayer contributes a lump sum for the support of two or more individuals, the amount is allocated between the individuals on a pro rata basis unless proof exists to the contrary.[27]

EXAMPLE I:2-15 ▶ Jaime pays rent of $9,000 for an apartment occupied by his aunts Alice, Beth, and Cindy. Alice spends $4,000 toward her own support, Beth spends $2,000, and Cindy spends $2,500. Jaime is assumed to have provided $3,000 of support for each aunt. Thus, assuming the other tests are met, Jaime can claim exemptions for Beth and Cindy, but not for Alice. ◄

EXAMPLE I:2-16 ▶ Paul and Mary have three children and are unclear whether they can claim their children as dependents. Information on the children is as follows:

▶ Peter, age 25, who served in the military immediately after high school, is a college senior. He worked part-time earning $2,200 and provided 20% of his support.

▶ Mark, age 22, graduated from college in May (he was a full-time student for five months of the year), and accepted a job in June. He lived with his parents for the entire year, earned $28,000, and provided 70% of his own support.

▶ Ruth, age 18, graduated from high school in May, and moved into an apartment immediately after graduation. She earned $5,500 from a job and provided 30% of her own support for the year.

Assume Paul and Mary provide all the support not provided by the children. The first step is to determine whether any of the children are considered qualifying children. None of the children are qualifying children. Peter is over age 23. Mark provided more than 50% of his own support. Ruth did not live with her parents for more than one-half of the year. The second step is to determine whether any of the children are considered qualifying relatives. Peter is considered as a qualifying relative as he meets the relationship, gross income, and support tests. Mark fails both the gross income and support tests, and Ruth fails the gross income test. Thus, only Peter can be claimed as a dependency exemption. ◄

TIE-BREAKER RULES FOR DEPENDENCY EXEMPTIONS. More than one person can meet the requirements to claim someone as a dependent. Tie-breakers decide who receives the exemption in such situations, as follows:

▶ First, taxpayers who meet the requirements to claim the dependent under the qualifying child rules have priority over individuals who meet the requirements for other relatives.

▶ The next priority provides that parents have priority over other individuals.

▶ Finally, if neither of the first two tie-breakers apply, the third tie-breaker specifies that the exemption is awarded to the taxpayer with the highest AGI.

Consider a niece who lives with three aunts who contribute equal amounts to her support. Assuming other requirements are met, all three aunts satisfy the requirements to claim the niece as a dependent under the qualifying child rule. Taxpayers who meet the requirements to claim a dependent under the qualifying child rules have priority over individuals who meet the requirements for other relatives. This first tie-breaker would not determine which aunt receives the exemption as each meets the qualifying child requirement. Moving to the second tie-breaker, parents have priority over other individuals. Again, the tie-breaker will not determine which aunt receives the exemption as they are not the child's parent. Thus, in this case, the aunt with the greatest AGI would receive the exemption. In cases involving two parents, the exemption is awarded to the parent with whom the child resided for the longer period of time during the year, and if the child spent equal amounts of time with each parent, the exemption is awarded to the parent with the higher AGI.

---

[27] Rev. Rul. 64-222, 1964-2 C.B. 47.

Two provisions can override the normal operation of dependency exemption rules:

▶ A Multiple Support Declaration (Form 2120) can enable a taxpayer to claim a dependency exemption in situations where the taxpayer does not provide over one-half of the dependent's support. This can be very important when several individuals contribute to the support of an individual who is not a qualifying child.

▶ A Release of Claim to Exemption for Child of Divorced or Separated Parents (Form 8332) can enable a noncustodial parent to claim an exemption.

MULTIPLE SUPPORT AGREEMENTS.   Often several people contribute to the support of a dependent. When a group provides over one-half of the support of an individual but no one member of the group provides over one-half of the support, eligible members of the group are allowed to designate one group member to claim the exemption. Each eligible member (other than the taxpayer receiving the exemption) must agree in writing. The taxpayer claiming the exemption must complete a Multiple Support Declaration (Form 2120, shown on page I:2-18). An eligible member is one who contributes more than 10% of the dependent's support and meet all requirements for claiming a dependency exemption except the support requirement.[28]

EXAMPLE I:2-17 ▶ John T. Abel lives alone. His support comes from the following sources:

Andy (son)	$ 400
Gabe (son)	2,800
Mable (daughter)	2,000
Betty (friend)	2,800
Total	$8,000

Either Gabe or Mable can claim a dependency exemption if the other agrees in writing. Andy cannot claim the exemption because he did not provide over 10% of John's support. Betty cannot claim a dependency exemption because she is not related and John does not live with her. For this reason, Andy and Betty need not agree in writing. Form 2120 is included in the return of the taxpayer claiming the exemption. A completed Form 2120 is illustrated in Figure I:2-2. ◀

The Multiple Support Declaration can supercede the tie-breaker rules discussed above except that the agreement cannot be used to pass the exemption from a person who is entitled to claim the dependent under the qualifying child rules to a person who is entitled to claim the exemption under the other dependent's rule.[29]

ADDITIONAL COMMENT

Form 8332 may be completed each year by the custodial parent to relinquish the dependency exemption for only that year, or it may be completed once, relinquishing the exemption for all future years.

PARENTAL RELEASE.   In the case of divorced or separated parents, the dependency exemption of children generally is awarded to the custodial parent. However, the noncustodial parent may claim the dependency exemption if the divorce or separation instrument specifies so, or if the custodial parent agrees in writing. The signed statement must be attached to the noncustodial parent's return each year in which the exemption is claimed. Form 8332 may be used for this purpose. In the case of a divorce or separation, the custodial spouse probably would be reluctant to relinquish the dependency exemption for a child. A noncustodial parent, however, might be able to negotiate the exemption in exchange for increased child support payments.

EXAMPLE I:2-18 ▶ Hal and Pam obtain a divorce under the terms of which Pam receives custody of their son. Hal is ordered to pay $600 per month of child support. In absence of a written agreement to the contrary, Pam will receive the dependency exemption for the child. ◀

EXAMPLE I:2-19 ▶ Assume the same facts as in Example I:2-18 except that Pam negotiates child support payments of $800 per month and agrees in writing to allow Hal to claim the dependency exemption for the child. The written agreement will enable Hal to claim the dependency exemption for the child. ◀

---

[28] Sec. 152(c).

[29] Reg. Sec. 152(d)(1)(D).

Form **2120**
(Rev. October 2005)

Department of the Treasury
Internal Revenue Service

Multiple Support Declaration

▶ **Attach to Form 1040 or Form 1040A.**

OMB No. 1545-0074

Attachment
Sequence No. **114**

Name(s) shown on return

Gabe I. Abel

Your social security number

123 : 45 : 6789

During the calendar year _____ 2009 _____ , the eligible persons listed below each paid over 10% of the support of:

John T. Abel

Name of your qualifying relative

I have a signed statement from each eligible person waiving his or her right to claim this person as a dependent for any tax year that began in the above calendar year.

Mable B. Abel

Eligible person's name

222 : 11 : 0001

Social security number

402 N. Lable Lane Lawrence, NJ 08649

Address (number, street, apt. no., city, state, and ZIP code)

Eligible person's name

Social security number

Address (number, street, apt. no., city, state, and ZIP code)

Eligible person's name

Social security number

Address (number, street, apt. no., city, state, and ZIP code)

Eligible person's name

Social security number

Address (number, street, apt. no., city, state, and ZIP code)

FIGURE I:2-2 ▶ FORM 2120

EXAMPLE I:2-20 ▶ Andy and Beth obtain a divorce under the terms of which they share custody of their daughter. The divorce decree does not specify who is to receive the dependency exemption. Whoever has custody for the greater part of the year receives the dependency exemption for the daughter unless they agree otherwise in writing. If they share custody equally, the parent with the higher AGI receives the exemption. ◀

SELF-STUDY QUESTION

Beth's mother, who is a U.S. citizen, has moved to France to spend her retirement years. She has retained her U.S. citizenship, but she is now a resident of France. Is it possible for Beth to claim her mother as a dependent?

ANSWER

Yes, the mother need only be a U.S. citizen.

A temporary provision that phased-out personal and dependency exemptions for higher income taxpayers expired in 2009. In 2009, for example, the phase-out began at $166,801 of adjusted gross income for single taxpayers and ended at $289,301.

EXAMPLE I:2-21 ▶ In 2010, Lee, a single taxpayer with one dependent, reports AGI of $120,000. Her personal and dependency exemption amount is $7,300 ($3,650 × 2). ◀

The rules for deducting personal and dependency exemptions are summarized in Topic Review I:2-1.

OBJECTIVE 4

Determine the amount of child credit

ADDITIONAL COMMENT

There are now two credits that have similar names: the child tax credit and the child and dependent care credit. They are quite different in how the credit amounts are computed and which dependents qualify.

CHILD CREDIT

Under Sec. 24 of the IRC, individual taxpayers may claim a "child credit" of $1,000 for each qualifying child. The credit is reduced by $50 for each $1,000 (or fraction thereof) by which the taxpayer's modified adjusted gross income exceeds a threshold amount ($110,000 on joint returns, $75,000 for single taxpayers, and $55,000 for married persons filing separate returns). Neither the amount of the credit or the phase-out thresholds is indexed for inflation. Modified adjusted gross income is AGI plus any amounts excluded from gross income under Secs. 911, 931, and 933 which relate to certain foreign earned income and possession's income. To qualify for the credit, a child must be under the age of 17 and be a "qualifying child" as defined in the above discussion of dependency exemptions. See Chapter I:14 for more information regarding the child credit.

Topic Review I:2-1

Personal and Dependency Exemptions

EXEMPTIONS IN GENERAL

▶ One exemption is available for each taxpayer (except when the taxpayer is the dependent of another) and for each dependent.
▶ The amount of each exemption, which is adjusted annually for inflation, is $3,650 in 2009 and 2010.

DEPENDENCY EXEMPTIONS

▶ One exemption is allowed for each dependent. As noted above, the exemptions are phased out for higher-income taxpayers.
▶ Each dependent must meet multiple conditions. All dependents (1) must have Social Security numbers reported on the taxpayer's return, (2) must meet a citizenship test, (3) cannot normally file a joint return, and (4) cannot claim others as dependents. Qualifying children must (1) be the taxpayer's child or sibling, (2) be under 18, a full-time student under 24, or disabled, (3) live with the taxpayer, and (4) not be self-supporting. Other qualifying relatives must (1) be related to the taxpayer, (2) have gross income less than the amount of the personal exemption, and (3) receive over one-half of their support from the taxpayer.

EXAMPLE I:2-22 ▶ Jane and Bill have two eligible dependent children and a modified AGI of $120,300. They have excess AGI of $10,300 ($120,300 − $110,000) and are entitled to a credit of $1,450 [(2 × $1,000) − (11 × $50)]. ◀

The child credit is refundable to the extent of 15% of the taxpayer's earned income in excess of $3,000 in 2009 and 2010. The earned income threshold would have been $12,550 in 2009, but was temporarily changed by *The American Recovery and Reinvestment Act of 2009* in an effort to increase the credit's availability during the current period of high unemployment.

EXAMPLE I:2-23 ▶ Georgia's four dependent children entitle her to a child credit of $4,000. Assume her salary is $25,000 and her gross tax is $500. Her child credit exceeds her tax by $3,500. A portion of her child credit is refundable, but the refund is limited to $3,300 [15% × ($25,000 − $3,000)]. ◀

MAKING WORK PAY CREDIT

To attempt to stimulate the sagging U.S. economy, the American Recovery and Reinvestment Act of 2009 provides a new refundable credit for 2009 and 2010, the Making Work Pay Credit. The credit is equal to the *lesser* of:

1) 6.2% of the taxpayer's earned income, or
2) $400 ($800 for married taxpayers filing a joint return)

As with so many provisions in the tax law, this credit is also subject to an AGI phaseout. The credit is reduced by 2% of the taxpayer's modified AGI that exceeds $75,000 ($150,000 for joint filers) Modified AGI is AGI reduced by certain special exclusions of U.S. territories. Therefore, the $400 credit is phased out completely at a modified AGI of $95,000, the $800 credit is phased out at $190,000.

DETERMINING THE AMOUNT OF TAX

After taxable income is computed, the next step is to determine the gross tax. Most individuals determine the amount of gross tax by looking in the tax table. (See page T-2 after Chapter I:18 in *Individuals* volume or after Chapter C:15 in the *Comprehensive* volume.) This method allows the taxpayer to arrive at the gross tax without the need for multiplication and, therefore, simplifies the computation and reduces the number of errors. Individuals are required to use the tax table unless taxable income exceeds the maximum income in the table (currently $100,000), or if the taxpayer files a short period return on account of a change in the annual accounting period.

Taxpayers who cannot use the tax table instead use the tax rate schedule (located after Chapter I:18 and on the inside cover of the text). Taxpayers using the tax rate schedule must actually compute the tax.

EXAMPLE I:2-24 ▶ Liz is single and has taxable income of $48,210 in 2009. Liz's tax is determined by reference to the tax table for single taxpayers. (At the time of this writing, the 2009 tax table was the most recent available.) The tax from the table is $8,244. ◀

EXAMPLE I:2-25 ▶ Jack and Pam are married, file a joint tax return, and have taxable income of $105,000 in 2010. They will use the tax rate schedule to compute their tax. The tax is computed as follows:

Tax on $68,000	$ 9,362
Tax on remaining $37,000 at 25%	9,250
Gross tax	$18,612 ◀

FILING STATUS

OBJECTIVE 5

Determine the filing status of individuals

For 2010, there are six tax brackets applicable to individual taxpayers: 10%, 15%, 25%, 28%, 33%, and 35%. These rates are progressive in that as a taxpayer's income increases, the taxpayer moves into higher tax brackets. The income level at which higher tax brackets begin depends on the taxpayer's filing status. There are five different filing statuses but only

four rate schedules and/or tax tables because married couples filing jointly and certain surviving spouses use the same rate schedule or tax table. The five filing statuses are as follows:

KEY POINT

Currently the highest tax rates are those for married filing separately, and the lowest are those for married filing jointly.

▶ Married filing jointly

▶ Surviving spouse

▶ Head of household

▶ Single

▶ Married filing separately

Before 1948, one rate schedule was used by all taxpayers. If a husband and wife both had income, each filed a return. This treatment was deemed to be unfair because various states allocated income between spouses differently. Some states used a community property law system while other states used a common law system. Today, only a few states continue to use the community property law system.[30]

SELF-STUDY QUESTION

If Congress were to adopt a truly proportional tax system, would it be necessary to have the four different tax rate schedules?

ANSWER

No, in a proportional tax system, there is no need for different rate schedules because all taxable income would be taxed at the same rate.

In general, community property law allocates community income equally between a husband and wife, regardless of which spouse actually earns the income. In other states, income belongs to the spouse who produces the income. With a progressive tax system, placing income on one return instead of two can result in a much greater tax. For this reason, couples residing in noncommunity property states often paid more tax than their counterparts who resided in community property states. In 1948, Congress developed the joint-rate schedule to rectify this problem. Unmarried taxpayers who headed families felt they also should receive tax relief because they shared their incomes with their families. So, in 1957, Congress created a rate schedule for heads of households. Below is a discussion of who is covered by each filing status.

JOINT RETURN

A *joint return* can be filed by a man and woman if they meet certain tests.

▶ They must be legally married as of the last day of the tax year.[31] Whether a couple is married depends on the laws of the state of residence. The Federal *Defense of Marriage Act of 1996* (amending I USC 3) defines marriage as being between a man and a woman. As a result, joint Federal income tax returns by same sex couples are prohibited.[32] Couples in the process of a divorce are considered married until the date the divorce becomes final. A couple need not be living together in order to file a joint return. A joint return can be filed if one spouse dies during the year as long as the survivor does not remarry before the year-end. The executor of the estate must agree to the filing of a joint return.

▶ They must have the same tax year-end (except in the case of death).

▶ Both the husband and wife must be U.S. citizens or residents. An exception allows a joint return if the nonresident alien spouse agrees to report all of his or her income on the return.[33]

STOP & THINK

Question: Some higher income couples who marry find that their tax liabilities increase even if their combined incomes remain unchanged. Others find that their tax liabilities decrease. Explain why taxes increase for some couples, but decrease for others.

Solution: Couples who marry ordinarily move from two individual returns where incomes are taxed using the rate schedule for single individuals to one return where the combined incomes are taxed using the joint rate schedule. The less progressive joint rate schedule results in a lower tax when one spouse has most of the income because more of that spouse's income is taxed at lower rates. However, when a higher income husband and wife

---

[30] Several states had either adopted or had begun to adopt community property laws in order to reduce the federal taxes paid by their residents. After the joint rate schedule was created, states without a tradition of community property law returned to common law. For a more detailed discussion of community property states, see page I:3-6.

[31] Sec. 6013.

[32] See also *Robert D. Mueller*, RIA TC Memo ¶2001,274, 82 TCM 764. A few states, however, do recognize same-sex marriages and allow same-sex couples to file joint state income tax returns. Common law marriages

between a man and a woman recognized in the state of residence are considered valid. On the other hand, an annulled marriage is viewed as never having been valid. Such a couple cannot file a joint return.

[33] Nonresident aliens are taxed only on income earned in the United States. If a joint return is filed by a U.S. citizen and his or her foreign spouse, they would receive the benefit of the low rate schedule, even though only the U.S. citizen reported income on the return. Thus, to file a joint return, the couple must agree to report both incomes (Sec. 6013(g)).

ADDITIONAL COMMENT
Since marital status for the entire year is determined on the last day of the year, some couples actually plan for their wedding to occur on December 31 or January 1. In general, if only one person has income, the wedding should take place on December 31. If both have income, a January 1 wedding is better (for tax purposes).

have approximately equal incomes, their combined incomes are taxed at higher rates on one joint return. Even though the joint rate schedule is the least progressive, the combined tax for higher income couples is greater because the 25% and higher brackets in the joint rate schedule are less than twice as wide as the same brackets for single taxpayers. For example, two single individuals with $80,000 of taxable income each are in the 25% tax bracket, while a married couple with $160,000 of taxable income is in the 28% bracket. This results because the 28% bracket begins at $82,400 for single taxpayers, but at $137,300 for married couples. Assuming the taxable income on the joint return is $160,000, the so-called marriage penalty is $681 because $22,700 of income is taxed at 28% instead of 25%. The additional tax is even greater for taxpayers with higher incomes. Nevertheless, because the lower tax brackets were widened in 2003, the additional tax for married couples is considerably less than it has been in the past.

SURVIVING SPOUSE

A widow or widower can file a joint return for the year his or her spouse dies if the widow or widower does not remarry. For the two years after the year of death, the widow or widower can file as a surviving spouse only if he or she meets specific conditions. The **surviving spouse** (sometimes called a qualifying widow or widower) must[34]

▶ Have not remarried as of the year end in which surviving spouse status is claimed.

▶ Be a U.S. citizen or resident.

▶ Have qualified to file a joint return in the year of death.

▶ Have at least one son, stepson, daughter, or stepdaughter[35] living at home during the entire year and the taxpayer must pay over half of the expenses of the home.

KEY POINT
The surviving-spouse provision entitles the taxpayer to the lower joint return tax rate schedule and to the higher joint return standard deduction.

In the year of death, a joint return can be filed. On the joint return, the income of the deceased spouse (earned before death) and the survivor are both reported. Personal exemptions are allowed for both spouses. In the two years following death, surviving spouse status can be claimed only if the conditions outlined above are met. Only the surviving spouse's income is reported and, of course, no personal exemption is available for the deceased spouse. What the two situations have in common is that in both instances, the taxpayer can use the more favorable joint rate schedule and standard deduction amount.

EXAMPLE I:2-26 ▶ Connie and Carl are married and have no dependent children. Carl dies in 2010. Connie can file a joint return, even though her husband died before the end of the year. Alternatively, Connie can file as a married individual filing a separate return. In 2011, however, Connie must file as a single taxpayer since she has no dependent children who would qualify her as a surviving spouse or a head of household. Alternatively, if Connie and Carl had dependent children, Connie could file as a surviving spouse for 2011 and 2012 and use the joint return rate schedules. ◀

 STOP & THINK

Question: Most recently-widowed individuals do not qualify for surviving spouse status. Why?

Solution: Most individuals are widowed late in life after their children are grown and have left home. As having a dependent child is a requirement for surviving spouse status, these individuals do not qualify for the special lower tax rate. Such individuals may ordinarily file a joint return in the year of the spouse's death.

ADDITIONAL COMMENT
Due in part to the high divorce rate in this country, the number of head-of-household returns has increased. In 1975, only 6% of all returns had the filing status of head-of-household. In 1996, that number was 11.6%, or 12.0 million returns. By 2007, the number was 14.8% or 21.2 million returns.

HEAD OF HOUSEHOLD

A second rate schedule or tax table is available to a head of household. The head of household rates increase more rapidly than those applicable to married taxpayers filing jointly and surviving spouses, but more slowly than those applicable to other single taxpayers. To claim head-of-household status, a taxpayer must meet all of the following conditions:[36]

---

[34] Sec. 2(a).
[35] Includes an adopted child or a stepchild, but not a foster child.

[36] Sec. 2(b).

> ► Be unmarried as of the last day of the tax year. Exceptions apply to individuals married to nonresident aliens[37] and to abandoned spouses.[38] An individual cannot claim head-of-household status in the year his or her spouse died. Such individuals must file a joint return or a separate return.

> ► Not be a surviving spouse.

> ► Be a U.S. citizen or resident.

> ► Pay over half of the costs of maintaining as his or her home a household in which a dependent lives for more than half of the tax year. An exception permits a taxpayer who maintains a household in which a qualifying child[39] lives for more than half of the tax year to claim head-of-household status when the qualifying child is not the taxpayer's dependent. This comes into play in the case of divorced parents when the dependency exemption goes to the non-custodial parent as well as in the case of financially independent children. A second exception permits a taxpayer to claim head-of-household status if he or she maintains a separate household for a dependent parent. This enables the parent to continue living in his or her own home.

EXAMPLE I:2-27 ►

Brad and Ellen divorce. Ellen receives custody of their child, and Brad is ordered by the court to pay child support of $6,000 per year. Ellen agrees in writing to allow Brad to claim the dependency exemption for the child. If Ellen maintains the home in which she and her child live, she can claim head-of-household status even though the child is Brad's dependent. ◄

ADDITIONAL COMMENT

In 2007, approximately 20 married couples filed joint returns for every married couple that filed separately. 54 million married couples filed joint returns during the year.

As noted, the taxpayer must pay over half of the costs of maintaining the household. These expenses include property taxes, mortgage interest, rent, utility charges, upkeep and repairs, property insurance, and food consumed on the premises. Such costs do not include clothing, education, medical treatment, vacations, life insurance, transportation, or the value of services provided by the taxpayer.[40]

SINGLE TAXPAYER

An unmarried individual who does not qualify as a surviving spouse or a head of household must file as a single taxpayer. The tax rates progress more rapidly than those that apply to other unmarried taxpayers.

EXAMPLE I:2-28 ►

KEY POINT

Several disadvantages are associated with the filing of separate returns by married individuals. For example, a taxpayer may lose all or part of the benefits of the deduction for individual retirement accounts, the child care credit, and the earned income credit.

Becky, a single taxpayer with no dependents, files her first tax return. She will file as a single taxpayer. ◄

MARRIED FILING A SEPARATE RETURN

Married individuals who choose to file separate returns must use the separate rate schedule. The rates on this schedule increase more rapidly than other individual rate schedules. The implications of joint returns versus separate returns are discussed later in this chapter.

EXAMPLE I:2-29 ►

On December 31, Rose marries Joe. Because they were married before the year ended, they may elect to file jointly. Alternatively, they may file separate returns with each using the rate schedule applicable to separate returns. ◄

KEY POINT

When one thinks of a person who would qualify as an abandoned spouse, one thinks of a person in dire financial condition. If no relief were granted, this person would be required to use the married filing separately tax rate schedule, which contains the highest rates.

The filing requirements for individuals are summarized in Topic Review I:2-2.

ABANDONED SPOUSE

The particular rate schedule a taxpayer uses can have a great impact on the amount of tax. Without any special rule, an abandoned spouse would be required to file using the rate schedules for a married person filing separately. Congress has provided relief for taxpayers in this situation if they can meet certain conditions. A married individual can claim head-of-household status if[41]

---

[37] Specifically, this refers to an individual married to a nonresident alien if he or she meets the remaining head-of-household requirements.

[38] Abandoned spouse rules are discussed under a separate heading later in this chapter.

[39] Qualifying child has the same meaning as is associated with dependency exemptions except that the child cannot be married and must be a U.S. citizen, resident or national.

[40] Reg. Sec. 1.2-2(d).

[41] Sec. 2(c).

Topic Review I:2-2

Filing Status and Requirements

Filing Status	Must Maintain Household	Must Have Dependent	Marital Status	Must Be Citizen	Tax Rates
Joint	No requirement	No	Married	Yes	Lowest rates, but two incomes are combined
Surviving spouse	Yes	Yes, son or daughter	Widowed in prior or second prior year	Yes	Uses same schedule as married couple filing joint return
Head of household	Yes	Generally, yes	Generally, single	Yes	Intermediate tax rates
Single	No requirement	No	Single	No	Highest tax rates for unmarried taxpayers
Separate	No requirement	No	Married	No	Highest tax rates

▶ The taxpayer lived apart from his or her spouse for the last six months of the year.

▶ The taxpayer pays over half of the cost of maintaining a household in which the taxpayer and a dependent son or daughter live for over half of the year.[42]

▶ The taxpayer is a U.S. citizen or resident.

The requirement that the taxpayer have a dependent child is met if a taxpayer who is otherwise qualified to claim the child as a dependent signs an agreement that allows the child's noncustodial parent to claim the dependency exemption for the child.[43]

EXAMPLE I:2-30 ▶ In October, Bob and Gail decide to separate. Gail supports their children after the separation and pays the costs of maintaining their home. Gail cannot claim abandoned spouse status because Bob lived with her for over one-half of the year. If she had obtained a divorce before the end of the year, she could have filed as a head of household. In the absence of a divorce, Gail must file a separate return, unless both Bob and Gail agree to file a joint return. ◀

EXAMPLE I:2-31 ▶ Assume the same facts as in Example I:2-30 except that Gail continues to support her children and pay household expenses during the next year. She can file as a head of household even if she has not obtained a divorce. ◀

CHILDREN WITH UNEARNED INCOME

In the past, taxpayers in high tax brackets were able to reduce their tax liability by shifting income to children and other dependents. Under prior law, no tax was due if the income was less than the dependent's personal exemption and standard deduction. Even if the shifted income was greater than these amounts, there was a tax savings if the dependent was in a low tax bracket. Under current law, three rules curtail the advantages of shifting income to dependents:

▶ Dependents do not receive a personal exemption on their own returns.

▶ A dependent's standard deduction is reduced to the greater of $950 (in 2009 and 2010) or the dependent's earned income (such as salary) plus $300 (in 2009 and 2010).

▶ The tax on the net unearned income (such as dividends and interest) of a child under age 18 (under age 24 in certain instances described below) is figured by reference to the parents' tax rate if it is higher than the child's rate. This provision is often called the "kiddie tax".

The first two rules have been discussed previously in this chapter. How the "kiddie tax" is computed depends on the child's age.

KEY POINT

Children under the age of 18 will not have their net unearned income tax at their parents' tax rate until the children's unearned income exceeds $1,900.

---

[42] Includes adopted child, stepchild, and foster child.   [43] Sec. 152(e).

Prior to the year a child turns 18, the kiddie tax applies if the unearned income exceeds the $1,900 threshold. For the year the child turns 18 (and only that year), the kiddie tax applies if child's earned income is less than or equal to one-half of his or her support and unearned income exceeds the $1,900 threshold. From the year a child turns 19 up to and including the year the child turns 23, the kiddie tax applies only if the child is a full-time student, the child's earned income is less than or equal to one-half of his or her support, and unearned income exceeds the $1,900 threshold.

EXAMPLE I:2-32 ▶ In 2010, Tim is an 18-year-old who received $2,400 of interest income and $4,500 from a part-time job. His support, which he paid himself, totaled $8,000. As he is self-supporting, his parent's cannot claim him as a dependent. The kiddie tax does not apply as his earned income exceeds one-half of his support. He is entitled to the regular standard deduction and a personal exemption. He owes no tax as these deductions exceed his income. ◀

EXAMPLE I:2-33 ▶ Assume the same facts as in Example I:2-32 except that Tim's parents provided over one-half of his support. Tim saved his earnings for college. Because Tim is a dependent, he is not entitled to a personal exemption. Tim's standard deduction is limited to the greater of $950 or his earned income plus $300 (but not more than $5,700). Because his earned income is $4,500, the standard deduction is $4,800 ($4,500 + $300). Therefore, Tim's taxable income is $2,100 ($6,900 AGI − $4,800 standard deduction). The kiddie tax does not apply as his earned income $4,500 exceeds one-half of his support. The application of the kiddie tax is based on whether the child has earned income, not whether the child is self supporting. Tim's regular tax rate of 10% applies resulting in a tax of $210 (10% × $2,100). ◀

When the kiddie tax applies, part of the net unearned income of the child under age 24 is taxed at the child's rate, and part at the parents' marginal tax rate if that rate is higher than the child's rate. This tax can be computed following a three-step process:

1. Compute the child's taxable income in the normal fashion for dependents as discussed earlier in this chapter.

2. Compute the child's net unearned income:

Unearned income (described below)	$xxx
Less: Statutory deduction of $950	(xxx)
Less: Greater of	
a. $950 of standard deduction, or	
b. Itemized deductions directly connected with	
the production of the unearned income.	(xxx)
Equals: Net unearned income	$xxx

3. Compute the child's tax:

Net unearned income times parents' marginal tax rate	$xxx
Plus: Difference between taxable income and net	
unearned income times child's tax rate	xxx
Equals: Child's total tax	$xxx

Unearned income is the child's investment income including dividends, taxable interest, capital gains, rents, royalties and other income that is not earned income (such as salary).[44]

EXAMPLE I:2-34 ▶ Assume the same facts as in Example I:2-32 except that Tim is age 17. His standard deduction is still $4,800 and his taxable income is also $2,100. Since Tim is under age 18, a portion of his unearned income may be subject to tax at his parents' 28% rate. The computation of Tim's tax is as follows:

---

[44] Sec. 1(g)(4).

1. Compute Tim's taxable income:

Wages		$4,500
Interest income		2,400
Adjusted gross income		$6,900
Standard deduction	$4,800	
Personal exemption	0	4,800
Taxable income		$2,100

2. Compute Tim's net unearned income:

Unearned income: Interest income	$2,400
Statutory deduction	(950)
Portion of standard deduction	(950)
Net unearned income	$ 500

3. Compute Tim's tax

Tax on net unearned income: $500 × 28%	$ 140
Tax on taxable income minus net unearned income:	
($2,100 − $500) × 10%	160
Total income tax	$ 300 ◄

As discussed in more detail in Chapters I:3 and I:5, dividend income and capital gains are currently taxed at lower rates than other income. For example, the long-term capital gains and dividend income of individuals in the 25% and higher brackets are taxed 15%. In 2008 through 2010, individuals in the 10% and 15% tax brackets pay no tax on dividend income or long-term capital gains. These lower rates also apply to the kiddie tax calculation. In figuring the tax where the parents file separate returns, the tax rate of the parent with the greater taxable income is used. If the parents are divorced, the parent with custody is the relevant parent.

EXAMPLE I:2-35 ▶ Celeste, age 12 and a dependent of her parents, received $2,000 of dividend income. This was her sole source of income during the year. Her parents are in the 25% income tax bracket. Her taxable income is $1,050 ($2,000 dividend − $950 standard deduction) and her net unearned income is $100 ($2,000 − $950 − $950). Her tax is $15 ($950 × 0.00 + $100 × 0.15). The first $950 of taxable income is taxed at Celeste's rate for dividends, which is 0%, while the balance of her income is taxed at her parents' rate for dividends of 15%. ◄

Parents of a child subject to the kiddie tax may elect to include the child's dividend and interest income on their own return.[45] This rule eliminates the need to file a tax return for the child. To be eligible for the election, the child's gross income must come solely from dividends and interest, and such income must not exceed $9,500 (2009 and 2010). Furthermore, there can be no withholding or estimated payment using the child's Social Security number. Parents use Form 8814, Parents' Election to Report Child's Interest and Dividends.

 STOP & THINK *Question:* Jane and Bill have three dependent teen-age children. Jane operates a retail business and Bill farms. They earn over $200,000 each year. Can they use compensation paid to children as a tax saving device?

Solution: The so called "kiddie tax" does not apply to income earned by children. In many instances, parents can employ their children in family businesses and reduce the family's tax. Individual children may be able to perform a variety of services. They may be assigned chores on the farm such as feeding livestock, milking, gathering eggs, or operating equipment. In the retail business they can be assigned tasks such as filing, answering phones, stocking shelves, making deliveries, and operating cash registers.

Jane and Bill can deduct reasonable compensation paid to the children for the services they provide. The payments are deductible by the parents on their return where it would otherwise be taxed at a high rate. Assuming compensation paid to each child is less than

[45] Sec. 1(g)(7).

the amount of the standard deduction, no income tax is owed by them. Assuming the parents continue to provide over one-half of the children's support they remain entitled to dependency exemptions.

BUSINESS INCOME AND BUSINESS ENTITIES

OBJECTIVE 6

Explain the tax formula for corporations

ADDITIONAL COMMENT

In 2006, there were 5.8 million corporate tax returns filed.

KEY POINT

The tax formula for C corporations differs from the tax formula for individuals in several important respects. The corporate tax formula does not contain an adjusted gross income figure, personal and dependency exemptions, or the standard deduction.

How business income is reported depends on the type of entity. Proprietors report their business income on Schedule C of Form 1040 (Schedule F in the case of farmers). The income is taxed on the proprietor's Form 1040 along with the taxpayer's other income. Approximately 17 million taxpayers report income on Schedule C each year.

Corporations are divided into two groups: C corporations and S corporations. **C corporations**, also called **regular corporations**, are treated as separate entities for tax purposes and pay income taxes on the corporation's taxable income. Shareholders are taxed on dividends they receive from a C corporation but are not taxed on the corporation's undistributed income. Lower tax rates apply temporarily to dividends received by individual taxpayers. See Chapter I:3. Approximately 2 million corporations file the regular corporate return, Form 1120, each year.

The tax formula for C corporations is presented in Table I:2-7. The major difference between the formulas for individual and corporate taxpayers is the fact that there is only one category of deductions for corporations. Personal expenses do not come into consideration. Therefore, there are no itemized deductions, standard deductions, or personal exemptions. The tax rates applicable to C corporations are as follows:[46]

Taxable Income	*Tax*
First $50,000	15% of taxable income
Over $50,000, but not over $75,000	$7,500 + 25% of taxable income over $50,000
Over $75,000, but not over $100,000	$13,750 + 34% of taxable income over $75,000
Over $100,000, but not over $335,000	$22,250 + 39% of taxable income over $100,000
Over $335,000, but not over $10,000,000	$113,900 + 34% of taxable income over $335,000
Over $10,000,000, but not over $15,000,000	$3,400,000 + 35% of taxable income over $10,000,000
Over $15,000,000, but not over $18,333,333	$5,150,000 + 38% of taxable income over $15,000,000
Over $18,333,333	$6,416,667 + 35% of taxable income over $18,333,333

Note that the corporate tax rates reflect a stair-step pattern of progression, with the two highest rates of 39% and 38% in the middle of the progression. The benefits of the two lowest tax rates of 15% and 25% are completely eliminated by the application of the 39% tax rate to taxable income between $100,000 and $335,000. Likewise, the benefit of the 34% tax rate on taxable income between $335,000 and $10,000,000 is eliminated by the application of a 38% tax rate on taxable income between $15,000,000 and $18,333,333.

The second group of corporations, **S corporations**, generally are not treated as separate entities for tax purposes. They are referred to as flow-through entities. S corporation shareholders are required to report their respective shares of the S corporation's income on their individual tax returns even if the income is not distributed. All shareholders must agree to the S corporation election when it is made. S corporations must also meet a series of conditions, such as having no foreign shareholders. S corporations report ordinary

---

[46] Income of certain personal service corporations is taxed at a flat rate of 35%.

▼ **TABLE I:2-7**

Tax Formula for C Corporations

Income from whatever source derived	$xxx
Minus: Exclusions	(xxx)
Gross income	$xxx
Minus: Deductions	(xxx)
Taxable income	$xxx
Times: Tax rates	× .xx
Gross tax	$xxx
Minus: Credits and prepayments	(xxx)
Net tax payable or refund due	$xxx

income and special items separately and shareholders in turn report their respective shares of the ordinary income and of each special item. Approximately 3 million corporations file S corporation returns, Form 1120S, each year.

In one sense, there is no formula to compute an S corporation's taxable income because the corporation normally does not pay a tax. S corporations do file returns, but the returns are more informational in nature, much like the returns of a partnership. A residual income total, known as ordinary income, is computed on the return. Special items, such as capital gains and losses and charitable contributions, are kept separate from the ordinary income amount. This is because every item that would receive special treatment on a shareholder's return is passed through to the shareholder with its status intact. Each shareholder reports his or her share of the ordinary income and his or her share of each special item. Losses pass through and generally can be deducted by shareholders up to their respective bases in the corporation's stock. Losses are also subject to other rules, such as the at-risk and passive activity loss rules, and are covered in Chapter I:8.

Partnerships, like S corporations, are flow-through entities for tax purposes. Partners report their respective shares of the partnership's income on their tax returns even if the income is not distributed. Approximately 2 million partnerships file returns, Form 1065, each year. Like S corporations, partnerships report ordinary income and special items separately and the partners report their respective shares of the ordinary income and of each special item. Losses also pass through and generally can be deducted by partners on their returns.

EXAMPLE I:2-36 ▶ Jane is starting Jane's Computer Services and is considering alternative organizational forms. She anticipates the business will earn $100,000 from operations before compensating her for her services and before charitable contributions. Jane, who is single, has $3,000 of income from other sources and other itemized deductions of $11,000. Her compensation for services will be

WHAT WOULD YOU DO IN THIS SITUATION?

⚖ **CHOICE OF RATE SCHEDULES**

Jane Brown married Jim four years ago. Two years ago Jim lost his job. After looking for work for several months, Jim left town to look for work, and Jane has not heard from him. Jim's brother told Jane that he had heard that Jim lived in Texas, but a friend said he heard that Jim had been killed in an automobile accident. Jane went back to school and completed a program as a medical technician. She returned to work this year, and she earned $35,000. She has asked you to prepare her tax return this year. She has asked you whether she should file as a single taxpayer, married person filing separately, or as a married person filing jointly. Because she has had a low income until recently, she has taken no legal steps to resolve her status. What should she do?

$50,000. Charitable contributions to be made by the business are expected to be $4,000. Other distributions to her from the business are expected to be $15,000. Compare her income tax for 2009 assuming she operates the business as a proprietorship, an S corporation, and a C corporation. Ignore payroll and other taxes.

	Proprietorship	S Corporation	C Corporation
Business Income			
Operating income	$100,000	$100,000	$100,000
Compensation paid to Jane		(50,000)	(50,000)
Contributions			(4,000)
Net	$100,000	$ 50,000	$ 46,000
Corporate income tax			$ 6,900
Jane's Income			
Business income (above)	$100,000	$ 50,000	
Compensation (above)		50,000	$50,000
Dividends			15,000
Other income	3,000	3,000	3,000
Adjusted Gross Income	$103,000	$103,000	$68,000
Contributions	($ 4,000)	($ 4,000)	
Other itemized deductions	(11,000)	(11,000)	(11,000)
Personal exemption	(3,650)	(3,650)	(3,650)
Taxable income	$ 84,350	$ 84,350	$53,350
Individual income tax	$ 17,327	$ 17,327	$ 8,019
Total tax	$ 17,327	$ 17,327	$14,919

In each of the alternatives, Jane reports other income of $3,000 and other itemized deductions of $11,000 on her personal return.

No separate return is filed for the proprietorship. Jane reports the $100,000 income from her business on Schedule C of her Form 1040 and she claims the $4,000 charitable contribution as an itemized deduction on Schedule A along with the other itemized deductions. In this case, whether Jane considers part of the income from the business to be compensation for her services is irrelevant.

With an S election, two returns are filed, a Form 1120S for the corporation and a Form 1040 on Jane's behalf. Because of the S election, the corporation pays no tax. Items reported on the Form 1120S "pass through" the corporation and are reported by Jane on her own return. The $50,000 of compensation paid to Jane by the corporation is deducted by the corporation in computing its income and is taxable to Jane. Jane also reports the remaining $50,000 of the corporation's income on her return and claims the $4,000 charitable contribution as an itemized deduction.

The C corporation is taxed as a separate entity. The corporation files a Form 1120 on which it would deduct the $50,000 of compensation paid to Jane along with the $4,000 charitable contribution and pay a $6,900 (15% × $46,000) tax on the remaining income. Jane reports the $50,000 salary along with the $15,000 dividend distributed by the corporation. Note that the dividend of $15,000 paid by the corporation is not deductible by the corporation. A temporary provision reduces the "double tax" on the dividends Jane receives from the corporation by subjecting the dividends to a 15% tax rate instead of the 25% rate that would otherwise apply. (See Chapter I:3.) As a result, her tax on the dividends is $2,250 (15% × $15,000) and her tax on her remaining income of $38,350 ($53,350 − $15,000) is $5,769 (from the rate schedule). Her total tax is $8,019. The total tax for the corporation and Jane is $14,919.

As shown, Jane's total current income tax will be lower if she chooses to operate her business as a C corporation even though the $15,000 paid to her as a dividend is taxed twice—once inside the corporation when it is earned and again on Jane's return. The reason the total tax is lower is because the income retained by the corporation is taxed at the corporation's marginal tax rate of 15% instead of being taxed at Jane's marginal rates of 25% and 28%. The savings will be lost in the future if the corporation distributes the retained income as a dividend. Clearly, if the plans are to distribute the retained income in the near future, it is desirable to operate as a proprietorship or an S corporation so that the distribution can be made without any future tax.

Self-employment taxes and social security taxes would also be considered when an organizational form is selected for a new business. Although detailed consideration of these taxes is found in Chapter I:14, it is noted here that the self-employment tax, which generally applies to

the proprietorship and partnership forms of doing business, would be greater than the social security tax which would apply only to the wages paid to Jane by the S and C corporations. Given the facts in this case, Jane might judge the proprietorship organizational form less favorably when these taxes are taken into consideration. Jane should consider these taxes along with other taxes (e.g., state and local taxes) and other nontax factors such as liability protection before making a final decision. ◀

The detailed rules of C corporations are covered in Chapter I:16 while S corporations and partnerships are covered in Chapter I:17 of the *Individuals* volume. All three are covered more extensively in the *Corporations, Partnerships, Estates, and Trusts* volume and the *Comprehensive* volume.

TREATMENT OF CAPITAL GAINS AND LOSSES

OBJECTIVE 7

Explain the basic concepts of property transactions

Capital gains and losses have been accorded favored tax treatment since 1922. Favored tax treatment essentially means that capital gains are taxed at a lower rate than is ordinary income. A purpose of the special rules is to distinguish capital appreciation from gains attributable to ordinary business transactions and speculation. This goal is accomplished by defining capital assets to not include certain business property (e.g., inventory and trade receivables) and by requiring taxpayers to hold capital assets for minimum time periods in order to benefit from the lower rates that are available to capital gains.

The discussion below is intended as a brief introduction to capital gains and losses. A detailed discussion of this topic is contained in Chapter I:5.

HISTORICAL NOTE

Net capital gains reported on individual income tax returns dropped from nearly $300 billion in 1986 to about $133 billion in 1987. The latter amount was more in line with 1984 and 1985. The large amount reported in 1986 was due to the fact that a 60% long-term capital gain deduction was available to individuals in 1986 but was repealed as of December 31, 1986. Many taxpayers sold capital assets to take advantage of the lower effective rates that existed in 1986.

DEFINITION OF *CAPITAL ASSETS*

A **capital gain** or **loss** is the gain or loss from the sale or exchange of a capital asset. Unfortunately, the tax law merely states what is not a capital asset. In other words, **capital assets** are assets other than those listed in Sec. 1221. A detailed discussion is found in Chapter I:5. Here we simply note the categories of properties included on the list, which are thereby excluded from capital asset status are inventory, trade receivables, certain properties created by the efforts of the taxpayer (such as works of art), depreciable business property and business land, and certain government publications. All other assets are considered capital assets and include investment property (such as stocks and bonds) and personal-use property (such as personal residence or automobile). As noted, a purpose of the rules applicable to capital gains and losses is to distinguish capital appreciation from gains derived from ordinary business operations. The profit from the sale of inventory and trade receivables is viewed as business profit as opposed to capital appreciation. Thus, a gain realized by an artist on the sale of one of his or her own works is ordinary income from personal services. However, gain from the sale of artwork held as an investment or for personal use would be treated as a capital gain.

ADDITIONAL COMMENT

The amount of net capital gains reported on 2007 individual tax returns totaled $907.7 billion, and represented five years of double-digit growth in capital gains. This growth has surely diminished in 2008 and 2009, but figures on these years are not out yet.

TAX TREATMENT OF GAINS AND LOSSES

Capital gains and losses are divided into long-term (associated with property held over one year) and short-term (associated with property held one year or less). In 2009 and 2010, individual taxpayers pay a maximum 15% tax on a net long-term capital gain (no tax in the case of individuals who are in the 10% and/or 15% tax brackets). In 2011, the tax rate is scheduled to increase to 20% (or the taxpayer's regular tax rate if lower). A net short-term capital gain is taxed at the same rate as other income.

On the other hand, individuals who suffer net capital losses can deduct only up to $3,000 of the losses from other income. A net capital loss in excess of $3,000 can be carried over and offset against future capital gains or, subject to the $3,000 limitation, deducted from other income.

TAX PLANNING CONSIDERATIONS

SHIFTING INCOME BETWEEN FAMILY MEMBERS

Because of the progressive tax system, families often can reduce their taxes by **shifting income** to family members who are in lower tax brackets.

EXAMPLE I:2-37 ▶ Mary, who is in the 35% tax bracket, shifted $5,000 of income to her 25-year-old son, Steve, by making a gift of a 10%, $50,000 corporate bond. Steve had no income as he suffered a business loss. In absence of the shift, 35% of the income would have gone for taxes. There is no tax on Steve's return because the income is offset by his loss. ◀

EXAMPLE I:2-38 ▶ Farouk, who is in the 35% tax bracket, shifted $2,000 of interest income to his 25-year-old daughter, Dana, who is in the 10% tax bracket. The tax savings from the shift is $500 [(0.35 × $2,000) − (0.10 × $2,000)]. ◀

ADDITIONAL COMMENT

All 50 states have enacted laws that simplify the procedures for making gifts to minors. This type of law, which in most states is called the Uniform Gifts to Minors Act, is especially important when making gifts of securities.

As noted earlier in this chapter, the net unearned income of children under the age of 24 is taxed at their parents' tax rate. Hence, a shifting of income to young children is often an ineffective method of minimizing tax.

Shifting income must be distinguished from assigning income. Earned income is taxed to the person who produces it. Income from property is taxed to the person who owns the property. Ordering income to be paid to another is an assignment of income that does not change who is taxed on the income. Normally, in the case of income from property, ownership of the property must be transferred in order to shift the income.

EXAMPLE I:2-39 ▶ John owns stock in Valley Corporation. John orders the corporation to pay this year's dividends to his daughter. John will be taxed on the income even though he has assigned it to another person. ◀

EXAMPLE I:2-40 ▶ Kay owns stock in Valley Corporation. Kay gives the stock to her 25-year-old son. Future dividends on Valley stock will be taxed to the son instead of to Kay. ◀

Individuals often are unwilling to give property away completely. As a result, personal preference may limit the amount of tax planning that is possible.

SPLITTING INCOME

Splitting income consists of creating additional taxable entities, especially corporations, in order to reduce an individual's effective tax rate.

EXAMPLE I:2-41 ▶ Tom is a taxpayer in the 35% tax bracket and is involved in a variety of businesses. One business has been producing $20,000 of income per year for several years. Tom incorporates the business. The first $50,000 of a corporation's income is taxed at a 15% rate. Thus, the tax on the income is reduced by $4,000 [(0.35 × $20,000) − (0.15 × $20,000)]. ◀

The creation of a new corporate entity to split income is not always desirable because the corporation's income will be taxed to the shareholder as a dividend if it is distributed. In addition, if income is allowed to accumulate in a corporation indefinitely, it may be subject to the accumulated earnings tax.[47]

KEY POINT

The ability to maximize itemized deductions by the timing of expenditures is somewhat limited. The two most significant items that would lend themselves to such a strategy are property taxes and charitable contributions. Prepaid interest is not deductible until accrued.

MAXIMIZING ITEMIZED DEDUCTIONS

Timing expenditures properly often can increase deductions. In general, cash-basis taxpayers deduct expenses in the year paid. If itemized deductions are less than the standard deduction, the taxpayer will receive no tax benefit from the deductions. A taxpayer in that situation could defer some payments or accelerate others to maximize expenses in one year, thereby creating a sufficient amount of deductions in that year.

---

[47] Amounts accumulated in a corporation in excess of $250,000 may be subject to this tax. However, amounts accumulated for business purposes are exempt.

This subject is discussed briefly in Chapter I:16 and extensively in *Prentice Hall's Federal Taxation: Corporations, Partnerships, Estates and Trusts.*

EXAMPLE I:2-42 ▶ Jean's property taxes are due on January 1 of each year. Jean is a single, cash-basis, calendar-year taxpayer. Itemized deductions other than property taxes total $3,000 in each year. Jean pays the 2010 property taxes of $1,600 on January 1, 2010, and the 2011 property taxes of $1,600 on December 31, 2010. In the absence of doubling up, Jean would not be able to itemize in either year. The itemized deductions of $4,600 ($3,000 + $1,600) would be less than the standard deduction of $5,700. By doubling up, Jean has itemized deductions of $6,200 ($3,000 + $1,600 + $1,600) in 2010. (To simplify the illustration the $500 increase in the standard deduction available in 2010 is ignored.) ◀

Medical expenses are deductible only to the extent they exceed 7.5% of a taxpayer's AGI. In situations where medical expenses are just under 7.5% of AGI, taxpayers may be able to create a deduction by doubling up.

EXAMPLE I:2-43 ▶ Troy's AGI is $20,000. So far in 2010, Troy's medical expenses have totaled $1,300. Troy has received a bill from his dentist for $500 that is due January 15, 2011. By paying the bill in 2010, Troy will have a deduction for medical expenses of $300 [$1,300 + $500 − (0.075 × $20,000)]. This assumes that Troy's other itemized deductions exceed the standard deduction.[48] ◀

FILING JOINT OR SEPARATE RETURNS

FACTORS TO BE CONSIDERED. In general, married couples may file either joint or separate returns. As noted earlier, if one spouse has significantly more than half of their combined income, filing separately will increase the couple's total income tax. Because of the potential tax saving from a joint return and because it is simpler to prepare one return than two, most married couples file jointly.

It should be noted that the joint return is not always preferred. Separate returns may result in increased deductions. Because only one spouse's income is reported on a separate return, medical expenses are more likely to exceed the 7.5% of adjusted gross income floor if one spouse incurs most of the medical expenses. Similarly, casualty losses involving personal-use assets, which are allowable only to the extent that they exceed 10% of AGI, may be deductible on separate returns.

One significant impact of the joint return is the joint income tax liability. Both the husband and wife may be liable for taxes owed on a joint return. This could be a major problem if a couple separates or divorces after filing a return.

EXAMPLE I:2-44 ▶ Jim and Pat file a joint return. They are both informed as to the relevant information pertaining to the return. The next year they separate, and Jim moves out of town without leaving a forwarding address. The IRS audits their joint return and disallows $400 of charitable contributions deducted on the original return. Pat may be held responsible for the additional taxes owed. The IRS does not have to attempt to locate Jim in order to collect the tax. ◀

ETHICAL POINT

Because innocent spouse rules are strict, it may sometimes be safer to file a separate return than run the risk of being held responsible for the acts of another.

INNOCENT SPOUSE PROVISION. When married couples file a joint return, each spouse generally is liable for the entire tax and any penalties imposed.[49] This is the case even if all of the income was earned by one spouse. This rule could prove unfair in some instances, especially where one spouse concealed information from the other. For that reason, the Code contains an **innocent spouse** provision. An innocent spouse is relieved of the liability for tax on unreported income if:

▶ The amount is attributable to erroneous items of the other spouse.

▶ The innocent spouse did not know and had no reason to know that there was such an understatement of tax.

▶ Under the circumstances, it would be inequitable to hold the innocent spouse liable for the understatement.

▶ The innocent spouse elects relief within two years after the IRS begins collection activities.[50]

EXAMPLE I:2-45 ▶ Dan and Joy file a joint return. Dan traveled much of the time and Joy had little information as to his whereabouts or income. Joy worked and her own salary was the sole source of her sup-

---

[48] For a discussion of restrictions on the deductibility of prepaid medical expenses, see Chapter I:7.

[49] Sec. 6013(d)(3).
[50] Sec. 6015(b).

port. Their return was audited by the IRS. The audit disclosed that Dan had not reported income from a job he had held for several months during the year. In this situation, Joy may be able to use the innocent spouse provision in order to avoid being held liable for the tax on the unreported income. ◀

The election is permitted when the innocent spouse was aware of the understatement, but did not know or have reason to know the extent of the understatement. Relief is limited to the portion of the understatement attributable to the "unknown" amounts.

SEPARATE LIABILITY ELECTION. Couples who file joint returns and are subsequently divorced, widowed, or separated may make a separate liability election. An electing spouse is liable only for the portion of any understatement attributable to him or her.

EXAMPLE I:2-46 ▶ Al and Ann divorce after filing a joint return. An IRS examination of the return reveals $20,000 of unreported income attributable to Al and $10,000 of unallowable deductions attributable to Ann. Together, these amounts result in an understatement of their tax by $9,000. If Ann can establish that she was unaware of Al's unreported income, she can make a separate liability election. She will be liable only for $3,000 of tax as she is responsible for only one third of the understatement. The allocation would not be different because only part of the deductions were disallowed because of an AGI floor. ◀

The election must be made within two years after the IRS begins collections efforts. The election may be made by both spouses. The election is invalid if the spouse responsible for the errors transfers assets to the "innocent" spouse in an effort to avoid payment.

ELECTING TO CHANGE TO A JOINT RETURN. In general, a husband and wife who file separate returns for a given year may elect to change to a joint return by filing an amended joint return. This change is permitted after the due date but must occur within three years of the due date including extensions. Taxpayers may not change from a joint return to separate returns after the due date.[51]

COMPLIANCE AND PROCEDURAL CONSIDERATIONS

WHO MUST FILE

ADDITIONAL
COMMENT

The IRS is encouraging nonfilers (i.e., individuals and businesses who should have filed previous tax returns but did not) to come forward. The IRS estimates that approximately 10 million people fail to file their income tax returns each year.

ADDITIONAL
COMMENT

A file-by-telephone system has been tested in some states in the last few years. The filers dial a toll-free telephone number and enter tax return data with a touch-tone telephone. While the taxpayer is still on the line, the IRS calculates any refund or tax due. The taxpayers then mail a signed Form 1040-TEL.

Whether an individual must file a tax return is based on the amount of the individual's gross income.[52] The fact that the individual owes no tax does not mean that a return need not be filed. The gross income filing levels are as follows:[53]

	2009	2010
Single	$ 9,350	$ 9,350
Single (65 or over)	10,750	10,750
Married, filing jointly	18,700	18,700
Married, filing jointly (one spouse 65 or over)	19,800	19,800
Married, filing jointly (both 65 or over)	20,900	20,900
Surviving spouse	15,050	15,050
Surviving spouse (65 or over)	16,150	16,150
Married, filing separately	3,650	3,650
Married, living separately from spouse at year-end	3,650	3,650
Head of household	12,000	12,050
Head of household (65 or over)	13,400	13,450

---

[51] Reg. Sec. 1.6013-1(a). However, a couple who filed a joint return whose marriage is later annulled must file amended returns as singles (Rev. Rul. 76-255, 1976-2 C.B. 40).

[52] *Gross income* has its usual meaning except that the gain excluded from the sale of a personal residence and excluded foreign earned income are included (Sec. 6012(c)).

[53] Sec. 6012(a)(1).

ADDITIONAL COMMENT

The IRS is required to impound tax refunds to help other agencies collect overdue student loans, child support, etc. However, the IRS found that people whose refunds were offset in 1985 and 1986 were far more likely than others to file no returns in the next two years or to file returns without paying all they owed.

There are three situations where taxpayers must file even if the gross income is less than the amounts shown above:

▶ Taxpayers who receive advance payments of the earned income credit (see Chapter I:14) must file regardless of their income levels.

▶ Taxpayers with net self-employment income of $400 or more must file regardless of their total gross income.

▶ Taxpayers who can be claimed as a dependent by another must file if they have either unearned income over $950 or total gross income over the standard deduction.

In general, taxpayers must file if their gross income equals or exceeds the sum of the personal exemption and the standard deduction (including the additional standard deduction due to age but not blindness). The blindness allowance and dependency exemptions are not considered. If the disallowance of the standard deduction rules apply, the standard deduction is ignored in determining whether taxpayers must file.

EXAMPLE I:2-47 ▶

In 2010, Carol is a single, self-supporting taxpayer with no dependents. Carol must file if her gross income is $9,350 or greater ($5,700 + $3,650). ◀

KEY POINT

It is possible that a taxpayer may be required to file an income tax return but still have no tax liability.

DUE DATES AND EXTENSIONS

Returns for individuals and partnerships are due on the fifteenth day of the fourth month following the close of the tax year, which for calendar-year taxpayers is April 15.[54] Returns for C corporations and S corporations are due on the fifteenth day of the third month following the close of the tax year, which for calendar-year corporations is March 15.[55] A due date that falls on a Saturday, Sunday, or a holiday is automatically extended to the next day that is not a Saturday, Sunday, or holiday.[56] As noted, individuals are required to file only if their gross income exceeds prescribed thresholds. Partnerships and corporations, however, are required to file even if they have no gross income.

Individuals may obtain an automatic extension of six months by filing Form 4868 (Application for Automatic Extension of Time to File U.S. Individual Income Tax Return). C corporations and S corporations may obtain an automatic extension of six months by filing Form 7004. Partnerships may obtain a 5 month extension by filing Form 7004.

An extension to file a return is not an extension to pay any tax that is owed. Taxpayers must project their tax liability to the best of their ability and remit with the extension any amount that has not been prepaid through withholding or estimated payments. Interest and penalty may apply to amounts paid after the regular due date. See Chapter C:15 in the *Comprehensive* volume and the *Corporations, Partnerships, Estates, and Trusts* volume for more on payment requirements.

	Individuals	Partnerships	Corporations
Returns	Forms 1040, 1040A, 1040EZ	Form 1065	Forms 1120, 1120S
Return due date	15th day of 4th month	15th day of 4th month	15th day of 3rd month
Automatic extension	Form 4868 (6 months)	Form 7004 (5 months)	Form 7004 (6 months)

ADDITIONAL COMMENT

In 2006, of the 134 million returns filed, over 73 million returns were filed electronically, or 54.5%. This compares with 61 million electronic returns in 2003. The IRS goal was to have 80% of individual return filed electronically by 2007.

USE OF FORMS 1040, 1040EZ, AND 1040A

The primary individual tax return is Form 1040. Complicated returns often involve many additional forms and schedules. Two shorter forms are available to taxpayers with less-complicated tax returns. Form 1040EZ is available to single taxpayers and married individuals who file a joint return. Such taxpayers must have taxable income of less than $50,000 and claim no dependents. To use Form 1040EZ, the taxpayer's income must consist of salary and wages plus no more than $1,500 of taxable interest income. No deduc-

---

[54] Sec. 6072(a).
[55] Sec. 6072(b).
[56] Sec. 7503.

SELF-STUDY QUESTION

It is sometimes said that the hall-mark of the U.S. federal income tax system is voluntary compliance. With so much information being reported to the IRS, how voluntary is the system?

ANSWER

The system is not very voluntary with respect to income subject to reporting. But some sources of income, such as income from self-employment, are not subject to reporting by a third party. Also, the IRS would have to audit a tax return to verify most of the deductions.

tions (other than the standard deduction) or credits (other than withholding from salary and wages) can be taken on the return.

Form 1040A is available to taxpayers who have somewhat more involved returns. Form 1040A can be used by taxpayers claiming any number of exemptions or any filing status. Salary, wages, dividends, interest, pension and annuity income, and unemployment compensation can be reported on Form 1040A. Taxpayers may deduct IRA contributions. Taxpayers may also claim credits for withholding, child care, and earned income.

SYSTEM FOR REPORTING INCOME

There is a significant and expanding relationship between computers, tax returns, the tax-payer identification system, and information returns. The IRS keeps records based on tax-payer identification numbers. Individual taxpayers report information based on Social Security numbers, whereas employer identification numbers (EIN) are used by corporations, other taxpayers, and tax-exempt entities. Individuals who employ others have both a Social Security number and an employer identification number.

Employers, banks, stockbrokers, savings and loans, and so on report payments they make to others along with the payee's identification number. Today, the IRS computers match much of the reported information with tax returns, using the taxpayer identification number as the cross-reference. The need for accurate information returns is obvious. Some major information returns are listed below:

Basic Form	Type of Payment	Required if Amount Equals or Exceeds
1099-R	Pensions and annuities	$600
W-2	Salary, wages, etc.	600
1099-DIV	Dividends	10
1099-INT	Interest	600[57]
1099-B	Sale of a security	All
1099-G	Unemployment compensation, tax refunds, etc.	10
1099-MISC	Rent, royalties, etc.	600
1099-R	Total lump-sum distributions from retirement plans	600[58]

This information-reporting system makes it more difficult for taxpayers to avoid IRS detection if they omit income from their returns.

PROBLEM MATERIALS

DISCUSSION QUESTIONS

I:2-1 a. The tax law refers to gross income, yet the term gross income is not found on Form 1040. Explain.
b. Why is it important to understand the concept of gross income even though the term is not found on Form 1040?

I:2-2 Explain the distinction between income and gross income.

I:2-3 a. Explain the distinction between a deduction and a credit.
b. Which is worth more, a $10 deduction or a $10 credit?
c. Explain the difference between refundable and nonrefundable credits.

I:2-4 List the conditions that must be met in order to claim a dependency exemption for qualifying children and qualifying relatives. Briefly explain each one.

I:2-5 a. Briefly explain the concept of support.
b. If a taxpayer provides 50% or less of another person's support, is it possible for the taxpayer to claim a dependency exemption? Explain.
c. Does support include the value of an automobile? Explain.

I:2-6 Under what circumstances must a taxpayer use a rate schedule instead of a tax table?

I:2-7 a. What determines who must file a tax return?
b. Is an individual required to file a tax return if he or she owes no tax?

---

[57] For banks and corporations the amount is $10. [58] Except that all IRA distributions must be reported.

I:2-8 Many homeowners itemize deductions while many renters claim the standard deduction. Explain.

I:2-9 Tax rules are often very precise. For example, a taxpayer must ordinarily provide "over 50%" of another person's support in order to claim a dependency exemption. Why is the threshold "over 50%" as opposed to "50% or more?"

I:2-10 What is the normal due date for the tax return of calendar-year taxpayers? What happens to the due date if it falls on a Saturday, Sunday, or holiday?

I:2-11 Sometimes taxpayers may not be able to file their tax returns by the normal due date. Are extensions available? How long are the extensions? Do extensions enable taxpayers to delay paying the tax they owe?

I:2-12 Can tax-exempt income qualify as support? Explain.

I:2-13 Can a scholarship qualify as support?

I:2-14 Explain the purpose of the multiple support agreement.

I:2-15 Summarize the rules that explain which parent receives the dependency exemption for children in cases of divorce.

I:2-16 What conditions must be met by a married couple before they can file a joint return?

I:2-17 Explain what is meant by the phrase *maintain a household.*

I:2-18 Under what circumstances, if any, can a married person file as a head of household?

I:2-19 a. Explain the principal difference in the tax treatment of an S corporation and a C corporation.
b. Why would a C corporation be used if an S corporation is generally exempt from tax?

I:2-20 Income earned by C corporations is taxed twice, once when the income is earned and again when it is distributed. If so, how is it possible that operating a business as a C corporation can reduce taxes.

I:2-21 a. What assets are excluded from capital asset status?
b. Are capital gains given favorable tax treatment?
c. What is the significance of an asset being classified as a capital asset?
d. Are capital losses deductible?

I:2-22 Is there any tax advantage for an individual who has held an appreciated capital asset for eleven months to delay the sale of the asset? Explain.

I:2-23 a. Explain the difference between income splitting and income shifting.
b. Why are taxpayers interested in shifting income from one tax return to another within the same family or economic unit?
c. Is there a relationship between the tax on unearned income of a minor and taxpayers who attempt to shift income?

I:2-24 a. Who is liable for additional taxes on a joint return?
b. Why is this so important?

I:2-25 Can couples change from joint returns to separate returns? Separate to joint?

ISSUE IDENTIFICATION QUESTIONS

I:2-26 This year, Yung Tseng, a U.S. citizen, supported his nephew who is attending school in the United States. Yung is a U.S. citizen, but his nephew is a citizen of Hong Kong. The nephew has a student visa, but he hopes to become a permanent U. S. resident. Other family members hope to come to the U.S. What issues must be considered by Yung?

I:2-27 Carmen and Carlos, who have filed joint tax returns for several years, separated this year. Carlos works in construction and is often paid in cash. Carlos says he only worked a few weeks this year and made $11,000. In prior years he made approximately $35,000 per year, and Carmen is surprised that his income is so low this year. Carmen received a salary of $38,000 as a medical laboratory technician. They have no dependents and claim the standard deduction. What tax issues should Carmen and Carlos consider?

I:2-28 Jane and Bill have lived in a home Bill inherited from his parents. Their son Jim lives with them. Bill and Jane obtain a divorce during the current year. Under the terms of the divorce, Jane receives possession of the home for a period of five years and custody of Jim. Bill is obligated to furnish over one-half of the cost of the maintenance, taxes, and insurance on the home and pay $6,000 of child support per year. Bill lives in an apartment. What tax issues should Jane and Bill consider?

PROBLEMS

I:2-29 *Computation of Tax.* The following information relates to two married couples:

	Lanes	Waynes
Salary (earned by one spouse)	$32,000	$115,000
Interest income	1,000	10,000
Deductible IRA contribution	5,000	0
Itemized deductions	15,000	15,000
Exemptions	7,300	7,300
Withholding	700	18,700

Compute the 2010 tax due or refund due for each couple. Assume that the itemized deductions have been reduced by the applicable floors. Ignore credits.

I:2-30 *Computation of Taxable Income.* The following information for 2010 relates to Tom, a single taxpayer, age 18:

Salary	$1,800
Interest income	1,600
Itemized deductions	600

a. Compute Tom's taxable income assuming he is self-supporting.
b. Compute Tom's taxable income assuming he is a dependent of his parents.

I:2-31 *Joint Versus Separate Returns.* Carl and Carol have salaries of $14,000 and $22,000, respectively. Their itemized deductions total $6,000. They are married and both are under age 65.
a. Compute their taxable income assuming they file jointly.
b. Compute their taxable incomes assuming they file separate returns and that Carol claims all of the itemized deductions.

I:2-32 *Joint Versus Separate Returns.* Hal attended school much of 2010, during which time he was supported by his parents. Hal married Ruth in December 2010. Hal graduated and commenced work in 2011. Ruth worked during 2010 and earned $18,000. Hal's only income was $1,100 of interest. Hal's parents are in the 28% tax bracket. Thus, claiming Hal as a dependent would save them $1,022 (0.28 × $3,650) of taxes.
a. Compute Hal and Ruth's gross tax if they file a joint return.
b. Compute Ruth's gross tax if she files a separate return in order to allow Hal's parents to claim him as a dependent.
c. Which alternative would be better for the family? In other words, will filing a joint return save Hal and Ruth more than $1,022?

I:2-33 *Dependency Exemptions.* Wes and Tina are a married couple and provide financial assistance to several persons during the current year. For the situations below, determine whether the individuals qualify as dependency exemptions for Wes and Tina. In all of the situations below, assume that any dependency tests not mentioned have been met.
a. Brian is age 24 and Wes and Tina's son. He is a full-time student and lives in an apartment near campus. Wes and Tina provide over 50% of his support. Brian works as a waiter and earned $3,800.
b. Same as Part a except that Brian is a part-time student.
c. Sherry is age 22 and Wes and Tina's daughter. She is a full-time student and lives in the college dormitory. Wes and Tina provide over 50% of her support. Sherry works part-time as a bookkeeper and earned $3,800.
d. Same as Part c except that Sherry is a part-time student.
e. Granny, age 82, is Tina's grandmother and lives with Wes and Tina. During the current year, Granny's only sources of income were her Social Security of $4,800 and interest on U.S. bonds of $3,800. Granny uses her income to pay for 40% of her total support, Wes and Tina provide the remainder of Granny's support.

I:2-34 *Dependency Exemptions.* John and Carole file a joint return in 2010 and have three children: Jack, age 23; David, age 20; and Kristen, age 15. All three children live at home the entire year. Below is information about each of the children:
• Jack: graduated from college in December 2009 and is going to medical school beginning in July 2011. In 2010, Jack worked sparingly as he studied for the medical school entrance exam, but did earn $4,000. John and Carole provided 80% of Jack's support during the year.

- David: a full-time student at State U. in 2010, earned $6,400 from a part-time job, and provided 40% of his own support.
- Kristen: a full-time student in high school, had no gross income, and provided none of her own support.

a. Based on the above facts, which of the children can be claimed by John and Carole in 2009?

b. How would your answer to Part a change if Jack began medical school in July?

c. How would your answer to Part a change if Jack earned $3,000 rather than $4,000 in 2009?

d. How would your answer to Part a change if David was a part-time student rather than a full-time student in 2010?

e. How would your answer to Part a change if David provided 60% of his own support rather than 40%?

I:2-35 *Dependency Exemptions and Child Credit.* Robert provides much of the support for his daughter, Jane, and her two children. Jane earned $20,000. Robert, whose AGI is $350,000, paid the rent of $11,000 on Jane's apartment and provided an additional $15,000 support. Jane is age 30, and her children are age 7 and age 4.

a. Can Robert claim a dependency exemption for Jane?

b. Can Jane claim her children as dependents?

c. Who is entitled to the child credit?

I:2-36 *Dependency Exemptions.* Juan helps support his mother Maria, his son Jose, and a niece Norma. How many dependency exemptions can Juan claim given these additional facts?

Maria lives with Juan. She receives $12,000 of Social Security benefits which she uses to pay for food, clothing, medical expenses, and other living expenses. Juan provides Maria's room which has a rental value of $5,000 and pays an additional $4,000 toward her support.

Jose, age 12, lives with his mother, Linda. Juan pays $12,000 per year child support, and Linda provides an additional $4,000 of support.

Norma, age 20, is a part-time college student who lives in an apartment. She earned $6,000 working part-time and received a scholarship of $2,000. Norma's father provided $4,000 toward her support, and Juan provided $7,000.

I:2-37 *Dependency Exemptions.* Anna, age 65, who lives with her unmarried son, Mario, received $7,000, which was used for her support during the year. The sources of support were as follows:

Social Security benefits	$1,500
Mario	2,600
Caroline, an unrelated friend	800
Doug, Anna's son	500
Elaine, Anna's sister	1,600
Total	$7,000

a. Who is eligible to claim Anna as a dependent?

b. What must be done before Mario can claim the exemption?

c. Can anyone claim head-of-household status based on Anna's dependency exemption? Explain.

d. Can Mario claim an old age allowance for his mother? Explain.

I:2-38 *Dependency Exemption and Child Credit: Divorced Parents.* Joe and Joan divorce during the current year. Joan receives custody of their three children. Joe agrees to pay $5,000 of child support for each child.

a. Assuming no written agreement, who will receive the dependency exemption and child credit for the children? Explain.

b. Would it make any difference if Joe could prove that he provided over one-half of the support for each child?

I:2-39 *Filing Status, Dependency Exemptions, and Child Credit.* For the following taxpayers, indicate which tax form should be used, the applicable filing status, and the number of personal and dependency exemptions available, and the number of children who qualify for the child credit.

a. Arnie is a single college student who earned $7,700 working part-time. He had $200 of interest income and received $1,000 of support from his parents.

b. Buddy is a single college student who earned $7,700 working part-time. He had $1,600 of interest income and received $1,000 of support from his parents.

c. Cindy is divorced and received $6,000 of alimony from her former husband and earned $12,000 working as a secretary. She also received $1,800 of child support for her son who lives with her. According to a written agreement, her former husband is entitled to receive the dependency exemption.

d. Debbie is a widow, age 68, who receives a pension of $8,000, nontaxable social security benefits of $8,000, and interest of $4,000. She has no dependents.

e. Edith is married, but her husband left her two years ago and she has not seen him since. Edith supported herself and her daughter, age 6. She paid all household expenses. Her income of $16,000 consisted of a salary of $15,200 and interest of $800.

I:2-40 *Dependency Exemptions and Child Credit.* How many dependency exemptions are the following taxpayers entitled to, assuming the people involved are U.S. citizens? Which dependents qualify for the child credit?

a. Andrew supports his cousin Mary, who does not live with him. Mary has no income and is single.

b. Bob and Ann are filing a joint return. Bob provided over one-half of his father's support. The father received Social Security benefits of $6,000 and taxable interest income of $800. The father is single and does not live with them.

c. Clay provides 60% of his single daughter's support. She earned $3,000 while attending school during the year as a full-time student. She is 22 years old.

d. Dave provided 30% of his mother's support and she provided 55% of her own support. Dave's brother provided the remainder. The brother agreed to sign a multiple support agreement.

I:2-41 *Dependency Exemptions, Child Credits, Tax Rate Schedules, and Divorce.* Juan and Maria, who have two young children, are in the process of obtaining a divorce. Juan expects to have $200,000 of income each year while Maria expects to have $60,000 of income each year. Assume the children will live with Maria after the divorce and that Juan will pay child support.

a. What advice can you provide them regarding the dependency exemptions for the children?

b. What advice can you provide them regarding the child credit?

c. What advice can you provide regarding tax rate schedules?

I:2-42 *Marriage and Taxes.* Bill and Mary plan to marry in December 2010. Bill's salary is $32,000 and he owns his own residence. His itemized deductions total $12,000. Mary's salary is $39,000. Her itemized deductions total only $1,600 as she does not own her own residence. For purposes of this problem, assume 2011 tax rates, exemptions, and standard deductions are the same as 2010.

a. What will their tax be if they marry before year-end and file a joint return?

b. What will their combined taxes be for the year if they delay the marriage until 2011?

c. What factors contribute to the difference in taxes?

I:2-43 *Filing Requirement.* Which of the following taxpayers must file a 2010 return?

a. Amy, age 19 and single, has $8,050 of wages, $800 of interest, and $350 of self-employment income.

b. Betty, age 67 and single, has a taxable pension of $9,100 and Social Security benefits of $6,200.

c. Chris, age 15 and single, is a dependent of his parents. Chris has earned income of $1,600 and interest of $400.

d. Dawn, age 15 and single, is a dependent of her parents. She has earned income of $400 and interest of $1,600.

e. Doug, age 25, and his wife are separated. He earned $5,000 while attending school during the year.

I:2-44 *Head of Household.* In the following situations, indicate whether the taxpayer qualifies as a head of household.

a. Allen is divorced from his wife. He maintains a household for himself and his dependent mother.

b. Beth is divorced from her husband. She maintains a home for herself and supports an elderly aunt who lives in a retirement home.

c. Cindy was widowed last year. She maintains a household for herself and her dependent daughter, who lived with her during the year.

d. Dick is not divorced, but lived apart from his wife for the entire year. He maintains a household for himself and his dependent daughter. He does not receive any financial support from his wife.

I:2-45   *Filing Status.* For the following independent situations, determine the optimum filing status for the years in question.

   a. Wayne and Celia had been married for 24 years before Wayne died in an accident in October 2008. Celia and her son, Wally, age 21 in 2008, continued to live at home in 2008, 2009, 2010, and 2011. Wally worked part-time (earning $5,000 in each of the four years) and attended the university on a part-time basis. Celia provided more than 50% of Wally's support for all four years. What is Celia's filing status for 2008, 2009, 2010, and 2011?

   b. Juanita is a single parent who in 2010 maintained a household for her unmarried son Josh, age 19. Josh graduated from high school in 2009 and has not decided whether to attend college. Thus, in 2010, Josh worked full-time and earned $16,000. Juanita provided approximately 40% of Josh's support in 2010 but provided all the expenses of maintaining the household. What is Juanita's filing status for 2010?

   c. Gomer and Gertrude are married and have one dependent son in 2010. In April 2010, Gomer left Gertrude a note informing her that he needed his freedom and he was leaving her. As of December 31, 2010, Gertrude had not seen nor heard a word from Gomer since April. Gertrude fully supported her son and completely maintained the household. What is Gertrude's filing status in 2010 assuming she was still legally married at December 31, 2010?

I:2-46   *Computation of Taxable Income.* Jim and Pat are married and file jointly. In 2010, Jim earned a salary of $46,000. Pat is self-employed. Her gross business income was $49,000 and her business expenses totaled $24,000. Each contributed $5,000 to a deductible IRA. Their itemized deductions total $13,000. Compute Parts a, b, and c without regard to self-employment tax.

   a. Compute their gross income.

   b. Compute their adjusted gross income.

   c. Compute their taxable income assuming they have a dependent daughter.

I:2-47   *Itemized versus Standard Deduction.* Jan, a single taxpayer, has adjusted gross income of $250,000, medical expenses of $10,000, home mortgage interest of $3,000, property taxes of $2,000. and miscellaneous itemized deductions of $3,500. Should she itemize or claim the standard deduction?

I:2-48   *Kiddie Tax.* Debbie is 24 years old and a dependent of her parents. She earns $4,200 working part-time and receives $2,200 interest on savings. She saves both the salary and interest. What is her taxable income? Would her taxable income or tax be different if Debbie were 16 years old?

I:2-49   *Computation of Tax, Standard Deduction, and Kiddie Tax.* Anthony and Latrisha are married and have two sons, James, age 25, and Jonas, age 13. Both sons are properly claimed as dependents. Anthony and Latrisha's taxable income is $130,000 in 2010 and they file a joint return. Both James and Jonas had part-time jobs as well as some unearned income. Below is a summary of their total income.

	James	*Jonas*
Wages	$2,800	$ 400
Taxable interest	1,800	2,000

Compute the taxable income and tax liability for James and Jonas.

I:2-50   *Computation of Tax.* Georgia, a single taxpayer, operates a business that produces $100,000 of income before any amounts are paid to her. She has no dependents and no other income. She has itemized deductions of $18,000. Compute the *total* income tax that would be paid assuming the following additional facts. Ignore payroll taxes.

   a. Georgia operates the business as an S corporation receiving a salary from the corporation of $60,000. The corporation distributes all of its remaining income to the shareholders.

   b. She operates the business as a C corporation receiving a salary from the corporation of $60,000. The corporation distributes its *after* tax income to her as a dividend.

   c. How would the total tax change in each of the first two requirements if the corporation made no payments to the owner other than the salary?

I:2-51   *Child Credit.* In 2010, Lana, a single taxpayer with AGI of $85,400, claims exemptions for three dependent children, all under age 17. What is the amount of her child credit?

I:2-52 *Capital Gains and Losses.* Bob and Anna are in the 35% tax bracket for ordinary income and the 15% bracket for capital gains. They have owned several blocks of stock for many years. They are considering the sale of two blocks of stock. The sale of one block would produce a gain of $10,000. The sale of the other would produce a loss of $15,000. For purposes of this problem, ignore personal exemptions, itemized deductions and other phase-outs. They have no other gains or losses this year.
a. How much tax will they save if they sell the block of stock that produces a loss?
b. How much additional tax will they pay if they sell the block of stock that produces a gain?
c. What will be the impact on their taxes if they sell both blocks of stock?

I:2-53 *Timing of Deductions.* Virginia is a cash-basis, calendar-year taxpayer. Her salary is $20,000, and she is single. She plans to purchase a residence in 2011. She anticipates her property taxes and interest will total $7,200. Each year, Virginia contributes approximately $1,000 to charity. Her other itemized deductions total approximately $800. For purposes of this problem, assume 2011 tax rates, exemptions, and standard deductions are the same as 2010.
a. What will her gross tax be in 2010 and 2011 if she contributes $1,000 to charity in each year?
b. What will her gross tax be in 2010 and 2011 if she contributes $2,000 to charity in 2009 but makes no contribution in 2011?
c. What will her gross tax be in 2010 and 2011 if she makes no contribution in 2010 but contributes $2,000 in 2011?
d. Alternative c results in a lower tax than either a or b. Why?

I:2-54 *Tax Forms and Filing Status.* Which tax form is used by the following individuals?
a. Anita is single, age 68, and has a salary of $22,000 and interest of $300.
b. Betty owns an apartment complex that produced rental income of $36,000. Expenses totaled $38,500.
c. Clay's wife died last year. He qualifies as a surviving spouse. His salary is $24,000.
d. Donna is a head of household. Her salary is $27,000 and she has $200 of interest income.

I:2-55 *Computation of Tax.* Maria is a single taxpayer. Her salary is $51,000. Maria realized a short-term capital loss of $5,000. Her itemized deductions total $4,000.
a. Compute Maria's adjusted gross income.
b. Compute her taxable income.
c. Compute her tax liability.

I:2-56 *Kiddie Tax.* Ralph and Tina (husband and wife) transferred taxable bonds worth $30,000 to Pam, their 12-year-old daughter. Pam received $3,500 of interest on the bonds in the current year. Ralph and Tina have a combined taxable income of $83,000.
a. Compute Ralph and Tina's gross tax. Assume they do not include Pam's income on their return.
b. Can Ralph and Tina claim a child credit for Pam?
c. Compute Pam's taxable income and gross tax.
d. What would be Pam's tax if she were age 25?

I:2-57 *Filing Status.* Assume Gail is a wealthy widow whose husband died last year. Her dependent daughter lives with her for the entire year. Gail has interest income totaling $370,000 and she pays property taxes and home mortgage interest totaling $20,000.
a. What filing status applies to Gail?
b. Compute her taxable income and gross tax.
c. Assume that Gail does not have a daughter. What is Gail's filing status?
d. Compute Gail's taxable income and gross tax assuming she does not have a daughter.

TAX STRATEGY PROBLEMS

I:2-58 Jack is starting a business that he expects to produce $60,000 of income this year before compensating Jack for his services. He has $1,000 of other income and itemized deductions totaling $10,000. He wants to know whether he should incorporate or operate the business as a proprietorship. If a corporation is formed, he wants to know whether he should make an S election. If he incorporates, the corporation will pay Jack a salary of $40,000. He expects to distribute an additional $5,000 of corporate profits to himself each year. Jack is single.

Required: Which organizational form, proprietorship, S corporation, or C corporation, will produce the lowest total current income tax liability for Jack and his business? Ignore payroll and other taxes.

I:2-59   Andrea, who is in the 35% tax bracket, is interested in reducing her taxes. She is considering several alternatives. For each alternative listed below, indicate how much tax, if any, she would save?

a. Give $2,000 to a charity. Assume she itemizes.

b. Give $2,000 to a charity. Assume she does not itemize.

c. Make a gift of bonds valued at $8,000 yielding $600 of interest annually to her 15-year-old daughter who has no other income.

d. Sell the bonds from part c for $8,000 and buy tax exempt bonds yielding $300.

TAX FORM/RETURN PREPARATION PROBLEMS

I:2-60   Aida Petosa (SSN 123-45-6789) is the 12-year-old daughter of Alfredo Petosa (SSN 987-65-4321). Her only income is $2,800 of interest on savings. Alfredo qualifies as a head of household, and his taxable income is $52,000. Compute her tax using Form 8615.

I:2-61   James S. (SSN 123-45-6789) and Lulu B. Watson (SSN 987-65-4321) reside at 999 E. North Street, Richmond, Virginia 23174. They have one dependent child, Waldo, age 4 (SSN 123-45-4321) and they are both under 65 years old. They do not wish to take advantage of the presidential election campaign check-off. Other relevant information includes

James's salary as a mechanic	$19,000
Lulu's salary as a teacher	23,000
Interest (First National Bank)	2,100
Withholding	2,000

Complete their Form 1040A.

I:2-62   John R. Lane (SSN 123-44-6666) lives at 1010 Ipsen Street, Yorba Linda, California 90102. John, a single taxpayer, age 66, provided 100% of his cousin's support. The cousin lives in Arizona. He wants to take advantage of the presidential election campaign check-off. John is an accountant. Other relevant information includes

Salary	$20,000
Taxable pension	31,000
Interest income	300
IRA deduction	5,000
Itemized deductions (from Schedule A)	8,000
Withholding	6,000

Assume that Schedule A, if necessary, has already been completed. Complete Form 1040.

CASE STUDY PROBLEMS

I:2-63   Bala and Ann purchased as investments three identical parcels of land over a several-year period. Two years ago they gave one parcel to their daughter, Kim, who is now age 16. They have an offer from an investor who is interested in acquiring all three parcels. The buyer is able to purchase only two of the parcels now, but wants to purchase the third parcel two or three years from now, when he expects to have available funds to acquire the property. Because they paid different prices for the parcels, the sales will result in different amounts of gains and losses. The sale of one parcel owned by Bala and Ann will result in a $20,000 gain and the sale of the other parcel will result in a $28,000 loss. The sale of the parcel owned by Kim will result in a $19,000 gain. Kim has no other income and does not expect any significant income for several years. Bala and Ann, however, are in the 35% tax bracket. They do not have any other capital gains this year. Which two properties would you recommend that they sell this year? Why?

I:2-64   Larry and Sue separated at the end of the year. Larry has asked Sue to sign a joint income tax return for the year because he feels that the tax will be lower on a joint return. Larry and Sue both work. Sue received a salary of $25,000 and Larry's salary was $20,000. Larry works as a waiter at a local restaurant and received tips. The restaurant asked Larry

to indicate the amount of tips he received so that they could report the information to the IRS. Larry reported to the employer that the tips amounted to $3,000, but Sue believes that the amount was probably $6,000 to $10,000. They do not have enough expenses to itemize. Sue has asked you what are the advantages and risks of filing a joint return.

TAX RESEARCH PROBLEMS

I:2-65 Ed has supported his stepdaughter, her husband, and their child since his wife's death three years ago. Ed promised his late wife that he would support her daughter from a former marriage and her daughter's husband until they both finished college. They live in another state, and meet gross income filing requirements. Is Ed entitled to dependency exemptions for the three individuals?

A partial list of research sources is

- Sec. 152
- Reg. Sec. 1.152-2
- *Desio Barbetti*, 9 T.C. 1097 (1947)

I:2-66 Bob and Sue were expecting a baby in January, but Sue was rushed to the hospital in December. She delivered the baby but it died the first night. Are Bob and Sue entitled to a dependency exemption for the baby?

Research sources include Rev. Rul. 73-156, 1973-1 C.B. 58.

I:2-67 Larry has severe vision problems and, in the past, he has claimed the additional standard deduction available to blind taxpayers. This year Larry's doctor prescribed a new type of contact lens that greatly improved his vision. Naturally, Larry was elated, but unfortunately new problems developed. He suffered severe pain, infection, and ulcers from wearing the new lens. The doctor recommended that he remove the lens and after several weeks his eyes healed. The doctor told him that he could wear the contacts again, but only for brief time periods, or the problems would recur. Can Larry claim the additional standard deduction available to blind taxpayers?

Research sources include *Emanuel Hollman*, 38 T.C. 251 (1963).

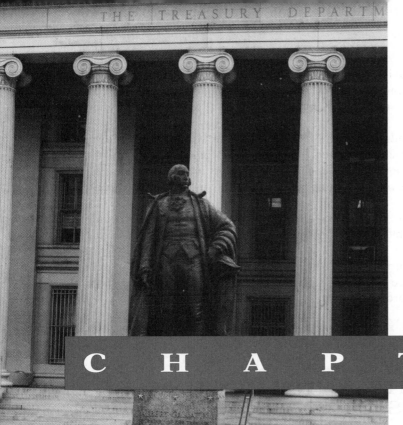

3

CHAPTER

GROSS INCOME: INCLUSIONS

LEARNING OBJECTIVES

After studying this chapter, you should be able to

1 ▸ Explain the difference between the economic, accounting, and tax concepts of income

2 ▸ Explain the principles used to determine who is taxed on a particular item of income

3 ▸ Determine when a particular item of income is taxable under both the cash and accrual methods of reporting

4 ▸ Apply the rules of Sec. 61(a) to determine whether items such as compensation, dividends, alimony, and pensions are taxable

Computation of an individual's income tax liability begins with the determination of income. Although the meaning of the term *income* has long been debated by economists, accountants, tax specialists, and politicians, no universally operational definition has been accepted.

The Sixteenth Amendment to the Constitution gave Congress the power to tax "income from whatever source derived." To ensure the constitutionality of the income tax, this phrase is incorporated in Sec. 61(a), where **gross income** is defined as follows: "Except as otherwise provided . . . gross income means all income from whatever source derived."

This chapter examines the concept of income for the purpose of determining what items of income are taxable. Chapter I:4 considers items of income that are excluded from gross income. As noted in Chapter I:2, many provisions in the tax law are created by a process of political compromise. Thus, there is no single explanation of why certain items are taxable and others are not. For this reason, determining whether a particular item of income is taxable often proves difficult.

Economic and accounting concepts of income

ECONOMIC CONCEPT

In economics, *income* is defined as the amount an individual could consume during a period and remain as well off at the end of the period as he or she was at the beginning of the period. To the economist, therefore, income includes both the wealth that flows to the individual and changes in the value of the individual's store of wealth. Or, more simply, income equals consumption plus the change in wealth.

EXAMPLE I:3-1 ▶

Alice earned a salary of $40,000. She consumed $30,000 of food, clothing, housing, medical care, and other goods and services. Assets owned by Alice were worth $100,000 at the beginning of the year. Her assets, including $10,000 of salary that was saved, were worth $115,000 at the end of the year. Her liabilities did not change during the year. Alice's economic income is $45,000 [$30,000 + ($115,000 − $100,000)]. ◀

Under the economist's definition, unrealized gains, as well as gifts and inheritances, are income. Furthermore, the economist adjusts for inflation in measuring income. An individual has no income to the extent that an increase in the measured value of property is caused by a decrease in the value of the measuring unit. In other words, inflation does not increase wealth and, therefore, does not cause an individual to be better off.

ACCOUNTING CONCEPT

In accounting, income is measured by a transaction approach. Accountants usually measure income when it is *realized* in a transaction. Values measured by transactions are relatively objective as accountants recognize (i.e., report) income, expenses, gains, and losses that have been realized as a result of a completed transaction. Accountants believe that the economic concept of income is too subjective to be used as a basis for financial reporting and, therefore, have traditionally used historical costs in measuring income instead of using unconfirmed estimates of changes in market value. In accounting, the meaning of the term *realization* is critical to the income measurement process. *Realization* generally results upon the occurrence of two events: (1) a change in the form or substance of a taxpayer's property (or phrased another way, a severance of the economic interest in the property) and (2) a transaction with a second party. Realization occurs when a taxpayer sells property. Conversely, the mere increase in value of property owned by a taxpayer will not result in the realization of income because there has been no change in the form of the property and no transaction with a second party.

EXAMPLE I:3-2 ▶ Assume the same facts as in Example I:3-1. The amount consumed by Alice, the increase in the value of the property owned by her, and inflation are all ignored by the accountant in measuring her income. Only when she sells or otherwise disposes of the assets that have increased in value will the accountant recognize the gain. Thus, Alice's accounting income is $40,000. ◀

TAX CONCEPT OF INCOME

The income tax law essentially has adopted the accountant's concept of income rather than the economist's. The reasons for this generally relate to matters of administrative convenience and the wherewithal-to-pay concept. However, as we will see later, there are many differences between income for tax purposes and accounting income.

In general, three conditions must be met for amounts to be taxable.

▶ There must be economic benefit. The economic benefit is not limited to cash payments. Employees who receive a company's stock, rather than cash, are receiving an economic benefit. Taxpayers benefit even if they direct that payments be made to other persons. As a result, employees cannot avoid being taxed on their earnings by ordering that their salaries be paid directly to creditors or family members.

▶ The income must be realized. In general, realization occurs when the earning process is complete and a transaction with another party takes place that permits an objective measure of the income. This objective measurement increases "administrative convenience" which is discussed below. Unlike financial accounting, there are many exceptions that result in income being reported when the taxpayer receives payment even if that is at a time other than when the earning process is complete. These exceptions result in taxes being owed when the taxpayer has the "wherewithal to pay" (see below). Taxpayers who use the "cash method" of reporting, discussed later in the chapter, are normally taxed when payment is received.

▶ The income must be recognized. Some items of income are not taxable because of special provisions in the tax law. For example, certain real estate exchanges and corporate reorganizations are not taxable because of statutory nonrecognition rules. In such cases, the taxpayer receives a lower basis in replacement property, and that often means the income is recognized when the replacement property is sold. The tax law also contains exclusions that exempt specific types of income such as scholarships, inheritances, and municipal bond interest. Within statutory limitations, taxpayers are never taxed on such items of income.

ADMINISTRATIVE CONVENIENCE

The economic concept of income is considered to be too subjective to be used in determining taxable income. The need for objectivity in taxation is evident. If taxpayers were required to report increases in value as income, some individuals would certainly understate values to reduce their tax liabilities. The IRS and even the most honest taxpayer often would disagree over values and, as a result, the tax system would be extremely difficult to administer. The disputes over valuation issues would be frequent and the courts would be burdened with added litigation. This problem is evidenced by the few situations where valuations are required in the determination of tax. For example, taxpayers who contribute property to charity usually can deduct the value of the property. The courts are continuously having to resolve disputes between taxpayers and the IRS over the value of such contributions. Furthermore, in the case of certain large contributions of property, taxpayers are required to attach to their returns appraisals of the contributed property. Penalties apply to taxpayers who substantially overvalue contributions.

In some instances, objectivity is achieved at the price of equity. For example, a taxpayer who owns land that has substantially declined in value generally cannot recognize the decline in value until it is realized through a disposition of the land. Similarly, an increase in value, no matter how large, is not taxed until a sale or exchange of the

property has occurred. A taxpayer with a modest salary may feel that it is unfair that he or she is taxed on the salary while another person is not taxed on unrealized gains amounting to millions of dollars. As noted above, however, it would be practically impossible to fairly and consistently administer an income tax law that was based on values.

WHEREWITHAL TO PAY

The wherewithal-to-pay concept holds that tax should be collected when the taxpayer is in the best position to pay the tax. A taxpayer who sells property and collects the cash is in a better position to pay the tax than a taxpayer who owns property that is merely increasing in value without a sale.

This concept is the rationale for several tax provisions. For example, the tax law allows a taxpayer who sells property on the installment basis to report the gain as the installment payments are collected, rather than at the time of the sale. Losses, on the other hand, cannot be reported on the installment basis, as the wherewithal-to-pay is not an issue. The concept is also used to justify differences between the tax law and financial accounting principles. Prepaid income is not income from an accounting standpoint until it is earned. The tax law, however, takes the position that prepaid income is subject to taxation at the time it is collected, rather than as it is earned. At the time of collection, the taxpayer clearly has the cash available to pay the tax. If the tax were deferred until the income is earned, the taxpayer may no longer have the cash.

GROSS INCOME DEFINED

Section 61(a) provides the following general definition and listing of income items:

General Definition.—Except as otherwise provided in this subtitle, gross income means all income from whatever source derived, including (but not limited to) the following items:

1. Compensation for services, including fees, commissions, fringe benefits, and similar items
2. Gross income derived from business
3. Gains derived from dealings in property
4. Interest
5. Rents
6. Royalties
7. Dividends
8. Alimony and separate maintenance payments
9. Annuities
10. Income from life insurance and endowment contracts
11. Pensions
12. Income from discharge of indebtedness
13. Distributive share of partnership gross income
14. Income in respect of a decedent
15. Income from an interest in an estate or trust

This definition certainly is not all-inclusive. For example, it does not indicate whether specific items of income such as property insurance settlements, gambling winnings, or illegal income are taxable. One point is apparent: The phrase *[e]xcept as otherwise provided* means that all sources of income are presumed to be taxable unless there is a specific exclusion in the income tax law. The IRS does not have to prove that an item of income is taxable. Rather, the taxpayer must prove that the item of income is excluded. Thus, gambling winnings and illegal income are taxable simply because no specific provisions in the tax law exclude such amounts from taxation. As we shall see, life insurance proceeds and certain other insurance proceeds are specifically excluded from gross income.

FORM OF RECEIPT. Gross income is not limited to amounts received in the form of cash. According to Reg. Sec. 1.61-1(a), income may be "realized in any form, whether in money, property, or services." The important question is whether the taxpayer receives an economic benefit. This rule covers barter transactions which are direct exchanges of property and services. Each party to the transaction is taxed on the value of the property or

services received in the exchange. In general, the cost basis of property given up in a barter transaction can be subtracted from the value of the property received in arriving at the taxable amount.

EXAMPLE I:3-3 ▶ King Corporation transfers 1,000 shares of its stock to its president. The stock has no restrictions and is part of the president's compensation. The president must include the value of the stock in gross income. ◀

EXAMPLE I:3-4 ▶ Ali, an attorney, performs legal services for Paul, a painter, in exchange for Paul's promise to paint Ali's residence. Each taxpayer realizes income equal to the value of services received. Thus, Ali must report income in an amount equal to the value of the painting services provided by Paul. Paul must report the value of Ali's legal services. These amounts, assuming an arm's-length transaction, should be the same. ◀

EXAMPLE I:3-5 ▶ USA Corporation distributes an automobile to Vicki, a shareholder, in lieu of a cash dividend. Vicki must report the value of the automobile as dividend income. ◀

EXAMPLE I:3-6 ▶ Len has fallen behind on loan payments due to a bank. The bank obtains a court order requiring Len's employer to pay part of Len's wages directly to the bank. Len will be taxed on the full wages even though a portion goes directly to the bank. ◀

EXAMPLE I:3-7 ▶ Wayne borrowed $3,000 from his employer. The employer awarded year-end bonuses to other employees but told Wayne that the debt was being forgiven in lieu of a bonus. Wayne must include the $3,000 in income. ◀

 STOP & THINK *Question:* As noted, income is taxable even if it is paid in a form other than cash. What problems does this produce for the IRS and taxpayers?

Solution: Two major problems are created: valuation and enforcement. First, it is necessary to determine the market value of property and services when income is received in a form other than cash. Determining values can be difficult. Second, enforcement by the IRS is made much more difficult because such income is not documented by canceled checks, credit card receipts, or other records. Thus, as demonstrated in Example I:3-4 above, many of these so-called traded services are not reported as income. This evasion of income represents billions of lost tax revenues to the government.

INDIRECT ECONOMIC BENEFIT. As indicated earlier, the taxability of income often depends on whether the taxpayer receives an economic benefit. In general, if a taxpayer benefits from an item, it is taxable. Frequently, however, an employer may make an expenditure in which its employees may incidentally or indirectly benefit. For example,

▶ Security guards patrol an employer's plant, protecting both the employer's property and the employees. The employees receive an indirect benefit for the protection provided by the security guards.

▶ An employer requires employees to undergo an annual checkup, the cost of which is paid by the employer.

▶ An employer provides protective clothing worn by employees while on the job.

▶ A shipping company provides sleeping accommodations to sailors while ships are at sea.

▶ A company requires certain employees to wear shoes manufactured by the company and provide regular reports on the quality of the shoes.

It is now well-established that taxpayers may exclude such indirect benefits from gross income. This judicially-developed rule holds that an expenditure is excludible if it is made in order to serve the business needs of the employer and any benefit to the employee is secondary and incidental.

Congress also has established rules dealing with situations where expenditures are made primarily to benefit employees. While expenditures made by employers that primarily benefit employees are generally taxable, there are instances whereby such

expenditures are not taxable. These rules, which are discussed in Chapters I:4 and I:9, permit employees to exclude certain fringe benefits (such as employee discounts) from gross income.

TO WHOM IS INCOME TAXABLE?

OBJECTIVE 2

Explain the principles used to determine who is taxed on a particular item of income

Once it is established that income is taxable, it is necessary to determine to whom it is taxable. Although such determinations are usually easy, there are circumstances where income is not necessarily taxed to the person who receives it. If physical receipt of income was the only test, a family might reduce or eliminate its income tax by having income paid to children and other members who are in low tax brackets or have no tax liability.

ASSIGNMENT OF INCOME

In 1930, the Supreme Court held in a landmark case, *Lucas v. Earl,* that an individual is taxed on the earnings from his or her personal services.[1] Specifically, the Supreme Court held that a husband was taxed on the earnings from his law practice, even though he had signed a legally enforceable agreement with his wife that the earnings would be shared equally. An agreement to assign income does not permit a person to avoid being taxed on the income. The Court used the previously developed analogy that likens income to the fruit and capital to the tree.[2] Accordingly, the fruit (income) could not be attributed to a tree other than the one on which it grew.

KEY POINT

The law makes a clear distinction between an assignment of income and an assignment of income-producing property. The income is taxable to the assignor in the former case, but where there is a bona fide gift of property the income is taxable to the assignee.

In 1940, the Supreme Court, in *Helvering v. Horst,* extended the assignment of income doctrine to income from property.[3] In this case, the taxpayer detached interest coupons from bonds and gave the coupons to his son. The son collected the interest and reported it on his own return. The Supreme Court held that the taxpayer was taxed on the interest income because he owned the bonds. This holding leads to a basic rule that the income from property is taxed to the owner of the property. To transfer the income from property, the taxpayer must transfer ownership of the property itself.[4]

ADDITIONAL COMMENT

The community property states are generally located in the western or southwestern United States. Generally these states were settled by immigrants from France and Spain, and their state laws reflect this fact. The common law is derived from English common law.

Although married couples may file joint returns today, this privilege did not become available until 1948. Assignment of income is an issue today when other individuals such as parents and children are involved, and it can still be an issue with married couples if they file separate returns.

ALLOCATING INCOME BETWEEN MARRIED PEOPLE

ADDITIONAL COMMENT

Community property laws are sometimes difficult to generalize. Depending on the specific law within a community property state, one-half of estimated taxes paid by one spouse may or may not be used by the other spouse on a separate return.

For federal income tax purposes, income is allocated between a husband and wife depending on the state of residence. Forty-one states follow a common law property system, whereas nine states[5] use a community property system. Under common law, income is generally taxed to the individual who earns the income, either through labor or capital. Thus, in the case of a married couple, if the wife owns stock in her separate name and receives dividends from such stock, the income is taxed entirely to the wife. Generally, the only **joint income** in a common law state is income from jointly owned property.[6]

In community property states, income may be either separate or community. **Community income** is considered to belong equally to the spouses. In all community property states, the income from the personal efforts of either spouse is considered to belong

---

[1] *Lucas v. Earl,* 8 AFTR 10287, 2 USTC ¶496 (USSC, 1930).
[2] The analogy had been used some ten years earlier in *Eisner v. Myrtle H. Macomber,* 3 AFTR 3020, 1 USTC ¶32 (USSC, 1920). The court originally used the analogy in efforts to distinguish income from capital.
[3] *Helvering v. Horst,* 24 AFTR 1058, 40-2 USTC ¶9787 (USSC, 1940).
[4] A series of rather specific rules allocates income between the former and current owner when income-producing property is transferred. For example, in the case of bonds transferred by gift, the IRS has ruled that interest must be allocated based on the number of days the bonds were held by each owner

during the interest period (Rev. Rul. 72-312, 1972-1 C.B. 22). A similar allocation must be made if bonds are sold (Rev. Rul. 72-224, 1972-1 C.B. 30).
[5] The states are Arizona, California, Idaho, Louisiana, Nevada, New Mexico, Texas, Washington, and Wisconsin. Residents of Alaska may elect to be subject to community property law.
[6] Historically, tenancy by the entirety, a form of joint ownership between spouses, allocated all income to the husband. Today, the laws of many states allocate income from property held in tenancy by the entirety equally between the spouses.

equally to the spouses. Furthermore, income from community property is considered to be community income. Thus, if a wife's salary is used to purchase stock, subsequent dividends are community income.

Couples can have separate property even in community property states. **Separate property** consists of all property owned before marriage and gifts and inheritances acquired after marriage. Whether income from separate property is community or separate depends on the state. In Idaho, Louisiana, Texas, and Wisconsin income from separate property is community income. In Arizona, California, Nevada, New Mexico, and Washington, such income is separate income.

EXAMPLE I:3-8 ▶ A husband and wife file separate returns. The husband's salary is $40,000 and the wife's salary is $48,000. The wife received $1,000 of dividends on stock she had inherited from her parents. Interest of $1,200 was received on bonds that were purchased from the husband's salary. They received $2,600 in rent from farm land that they purchased jointly. The income would be allocated, depending on the state of residence, as follows:

California (Community Property State)	Husband	Wife
Salary	$44,000	$44,000
Dividends		1,000
Interest	600	600
Rent	1,300	1,300
Total	$45,900	$46,900

Texas (Community Property State)	Husband	Wife
Salary	$44,000	$44,000
Dividends	500	500
Interest	600	600
Rent	1,300	1,300
Total	$46,400	$46,400

Pennsylvania (Common Law State)	Husband	Wife
Salary	$40,000	$48,000
Dividends		1,000
Interest	1,200	
Rent	1,300	1,300
Total	$42,500	$50,300 ◀

These rules are important when couples file separate returns. The community income rules can prove to be a problem if one spouse conceals income from the other. Normally, each spouse is expected to report one-half of all community income. This treatment is inequitable if one spouse is not aware that the community income was earned. Special rules excuse an innocent spouse who fails to report community income on a separate return, provided that the spouse had no knowledge or reason to know of the item and, as a result, the inclusion of the community income would be inequitable.[7] A corresponding provision permits the IRS to include the entire amount in the income of the other spouse.[8]

STOP & THINK *Question:* The tax treatment of income earned in a common law state versus a community property state can be very inconsistent. As noted, the Supreme Court, in *Lucas v. Earl*, decided that a husband was taxed on all his income even though he agreed to share that income with his wife. Nevertheless, community income in a community property state is divided equally between husbands and wives even if one spouse earned all of the income. Why the tax distinction?

Solution: Lucas v. Earl dealt with a case in a common law state where the husband was legally entitled to the income, but decided to divide it with his wife. In community property states, couples are legally obligated to share their incomes. The federal income tax law respects the different property law systems of the states and taxes the income of

[7] Sec. 66(b).   [8] Sec. 66(c).

persons based on state law. It would be unfairly burdensome to tax individuals on income to which they never had any legal right.

INCOME OF MINOR CHILDREN

As noted earlier, whether a husband or wife is taxed on income is determined by state law. However, earnings of a minor child are taxed to the child regardless of the state's property law system. Therefore, earnings of a child from either personal services (compensation) or from property (dividends, interest, rents, etc.) are taxed to the child, not the child's parents. As noted in Chapter I:2, the unearned income of a child under age 24 may be taxed at the parents' tax rate if it is higher than the child's rate. Alternatively, the parents may elect to include the child's unearned income on their return. In the case of spouses, the spouse who has a legal right to such income determines who is taxed on it. In the case of children, however, the individual who earns the income is the individual who is taxed on it.

WHEN IS INCOME TAXABLE?

OBJECTIVE 3

Determine when a particular item of income is taxable under both the cash and accrual methods of reporting

The year in which income is taxed depends on the taxpayer's accounting method. The three primary overall accounting methods are the **cash receipts and disbursements method,** the **accrual method,** and the **hybrid method.** While taxpayers have the right to choose a method of accounting, the chosen method still must clearly reflect income as determined by the IRS. The IRS has the power to change the accounting method used by a taxpayer if, in the opinion of the IRS, the method being used does not clearly reflect income. Further, the Regulations require taxpayers to use the accrual method for determining purchases and sales when a taxpayer maintains an inventory.[9] However, the IRS has ruled that taxpayers whose annual gross receipts for the three prior years do not exceed $1 million ($10 million if the taxpayer's principal business is not the sale of inventory) are exempt from the requirement and may use the cash method.[10] This exception for small taxpayers is discussed in more detail below.

Section 448 requires C corporations (and partnerships with corporate partners), tax shelters, and certain trusts to use the accrual method of accounting. Qualified personal service corporations, certain types of farms, and entities with average gross receipts under $5 million are exempt from the requirement.

KEY POINT

Neither the IRC nor the Regulations define the terms *accounting* and *accounting method.*

Once an accounting method has been adopted, it cannot be changed without permission of the IRS. See Chapter I:11.

CASH METHOD

ADDITIONAL COMMENT

Taxpayers engaged in more than one trade or business may use a different method of accounting for each separate trade or business.

The **cash receipts and disbursements method** of accounting is used by most individual taxpayers and many small businesses. (See Chapter I:11 for a more complete discussion of who is permitted to use the cash method.) Under this method, income is reported in the year the taxpayer actually or constructively receives the income rather than in the year the income is earned. The income can be received by the taxpayer or the taxpayer's agent and be in the form of cash, other property, or services.[11] In the case of property or services, the amount included in income is the value of the property or services. An accounts receivable or other unsupported promise to pay is considered to have no value under the cash method and, as a result, no income is recognized until the receivable is collected. Topic Review I:3-1 summarizes when various types of income are reported.

ADDITIONAL COMMENT

The use of the cash receipts and disbursements method of accounting gives the taxpayer some control over the timing of the recognition of income and deductions. It also has the advantage of simplicity.

The fact that prepaid income is usually taxed when received, rather than when earned, often results in a mismatching of income and expenses.

EXAMPLE I:3-9 ▶

In December of the current year, Troy, who owns an apartment building, collects the first and last months' rent from a new tenant. Troy must report two months' rent in the current year. The

---

[9] Reg. Sec. 1.446-1(c)(2)(i).
[10] Rev. Proc. 2001-10, 2001-1 C.B. 272, modifying and superseding Rev. Proc. 2000-22, 2000-01 C.B. 1008, Rev. Proc. 2002-1 C.B. 1, and Rev. Proc. 2002-28, 2002-1 C.B. 815.

[11] An agent can be an employee, relative, or other person authorized to receive the income.

Topic Review I:3-1

When Income Is Taxable

ITEM	CASH BASIS	ACCRUAL BASIS
Compensation	Year actually or constructively received.	Year earned or year received if prepaid.
Interest	Year actually or constructively received.	Year accrued or year received if prepaid.
Discount on Series E or EE Bonds	Choice of reporting interest as it accrues or at maturity.	Year accrued.
Dividends	Year actually or constructively received.	Year actually or constructively received.
Rent	Year actually or constructively received (does not apply to a deposit).	Year accrued or year received if prepaid (year accrued if services are associated, e.g., in a hotel or motel) (does not apply to a deposit).
Services (maintenance contracts, dance lessons, etc.)	Year actually or constructively received.	Year accrued or year received if prepaid except that a taxpayer may report the income as it accrues if all the services are to be performed by the end of the next tax year.
Sale of goods	Year actually or constructively received.	Year of sale or year cash is received if prepaid except may elect to report in year of sale if goods are not on hand, amount received is less than cost of item, and same accounting method is used for financial accounting.
Subscriptions (newspapers, magazines, etc.)	Year actually or constructively received.	Year earned or year cash is received, if prepaid, except may elect to report income as newspaper, etc., is published.
Memberships (automobile clubs, etc.)	Year actually or constructively received.	Year earned or year received if prepaid (certain nonstock corporations may elect to report prepaid amounts over the membership period, if the period covers three years or less).
Sale of property (other than stock)	Year actually or constructively received.	Year transaction is completed (e.g., the close of escrow in case of sale of real estate).
Sale of stock	Year transaction is executed.	Year transaction is executed.

actual expenses associated with the last month's rental are not incurred until the last month. However, Troy must report two months' income this year, but may only deduct one month's expenses. ◄

ADDITIONAL COMMENT

There is no recognized doctrine of constructive payment.

REAL-WORLD EXAMPLE

Paul Hornung, a former football player with the Green Bay Packers, was awarded an automobile in 1961 for being the outstanding player in the NFL championship game, but he did not actually receive it until 1962. He attempted to invoke the constructive receipt doctrine and report the income in 1961. The court held that he could not claim constructive receipt because the car was not set aside in the year of the award. *Paul V. Hornung,* 47 T.C. 428 (1967).

Reporting prepaid income can have harsh results because it is not offset by related deductions. If the income is taxed before the expenses are incurred, the taxpayer may not have enough cash to pay the expenses when they are incurred.[12] This burden is mitigated, in part, by Treasury Regulations and Revenue Procedures discussed in this chapter (e.g., the treatment of prepaid income, page I:3-11).

CONSTRUCTIVE RECEIPT. As noted, a cash-basis taxpayer must report income in the year in which it is actually or constructively received. Constructive receipt means that the income is made available to the taxpayer so that he may draw upon it at any time. However, income is not constructively received if the taxpayer's control of its receipt is subject to substantial limitations or restrictions. This rule prevents taxpayers from deferring income that is otherwise available by merely "turning their backs" on it. A taxpayer cannot defer income recognition by refusing to accept payment until a later taxable year.

Examples of constructive receipt where taxpayers are required to report taxable income even though no cash is actually received include:

---

[12] This mismatching of income and expenses affects both cash and accrual basis taxpayers.

▶ A check received after banking hours[13]

▶ Interest credited to a bank savings account[14]

▶ Bond interest coupons that have matured but have not been redeemed[15]

▶ Salary available to an employee who does not accept payment[16]

An amount is not considered to be constructively received if:

▶ It is subject to substantial limitations or restrictions.

▶ The payor does not have the funds necessary to make payment.

▶ The amount is unavailable to the taxpayer.

EXAMPLE I:3-10 ▶ Beth owns an ordinary life insurance policy with a cash surrender value. She need not report any income as the cash surrender value increases because the requirement that she cancel the policy in order to collect the cash surrender value constitutes a substantial restriction. If she cancels the policy, she reports as income the difference between the cash surrender value collected and net premiums paid. ◀

EXAMPLE I:3-11 ▶ Cathy has received a paycheck from her employer but has been told to hold the check until the employer has sufficient funds to cover the payroll. Cathy need not report the amount of the check as income until funds are deposited to the employer's account. ◀

EXAMPLE I:3-12 ▶ On December 2, 2010, Dan sold land for $100,000 with payment due on February 2, 2011. During the negotiations, the buyer offered to pay cash. Because the parties did not agree to a cash transaction, there was no constructive receipt in 2010. Under the terms of the sale, funds were not available at the time of sale. Thus, Dan is permitted to defer the recognition of income under the contract since the contract is made before the income is earned. ◀

EXCEPTIONS. There are exceptions to the basic rule that cash-basis taxpayers report income when it is actually or constructively received.

▶ The interest on Series E and Series EE U.S. savings bonds need not be reported until the final maturity date, which varies but may be as long as forty years after the date of issue, and can be deferred even longer if the bonds are exchanged within one year of the final maturity date for Series HH U.S. savings bonds.[17] Many taxpayers purchase bonds that mature after retirement when the taxpayers expect to be in a lower tax bracket.

EXAMPLE I:3-13 ▶ Tenisha purchases a Series EE U.S. savings bond for $2,500 that will mature in 10 years. The bond pays no interest until maturity when it will be worth $5,000. Tenisha is not required to report any interest income for tax purposes until the bond matures. At maturity, when Tenisha receives the $5,000, she will report $2,500 of interest income. If she desires to defer the interest further, she could exchange her Series EE bond for a Series HH bond within one year. ◀

▶ Special rules also apply to farmers and ranchers. Farmers may report crop insurance proceeds in the year following receipt if the crop would have ordinarily been sold in the following year. Ranchers who sell livestock on account of a drought, flood, or other weather related condition may delay reporting income until the following year if they can establish that the livestock sale would otherwise have taken place in a later tax year.[18] These rules help taxpayers avoid a bunching of income into one year.

▶ Small taxpayer exception for inventories. As noted above, taxpayers who have average annual gross receipts of $1 million or less for the prior three years ($10 million or less if the taxpayer's principal business is not the sale of inventory) are exempt from maintaining inventories and may use the cash method. The ruling was widely interpreted to

---

[13] *Charles F. Kahler*, 18 T.C. 31 (1952).
[14] Reg. Sec. 1.451-2(b).
[15] Ibid.
[16] *James J. Cooney*, 18 T.C. 883 (1952).
[17] Series E bonds were issued prior to 1980; Series EE bonds were issued after 1979. The interest on the Series HH bonds is taxable as received.

[18] Recognizing the volatile nature of farming and ranching, Congress established a special averaging technique for farmers and ranchers. Electing farmers and ranchers compute their tax on the average income for the current and three preceding years. Sec. 1301.

mean that small taxpayers did not need to account for inventories and could deduct the amount of their purchases in the year of payment. However, the IRS subsequently issued Rev. Proc. 2001-10, whereby it was clarified that the small taxpayer exception will only allow small taxpayers to deduct purchases of inventory in the year of purchase if (1) the inventory purchases are paid for by the end of the year and (2) the inventory is actually sold in such year. The effect of this new ruling basically is to eliminate the small taxpayer exception with respect to inventories.

EXAMPLE I:3-14 ▶ The Cheryl Corporation begins a new retail business in the current year and has sales of $400,000. The corporation has year-end accounts receivable of $15,000 and purchases $240,000 of merchandise during the year. At year-end, the corporation has not paid for $30,000 of the merchandise it had purchased and has $50,000 of inventory on hand. The corporation pays operating expenses of $140,000 during the year. As the average gross receipts are less than $1 million, the corporation can use either the cash or accrual method. The corporation's income computed under both methods is as follows:

		Accrual		Cash
Sales		$400,000		$385,000
Purchases	$240,000		$210,000	
Ending inventory	50,000		20,000*	
Cost of sales		190,000		190,000
Gross profit		210,000		195,000
Expenses		140,000		140,000
Net income		$ 70,000		$ 55,000

*$50,000 − $30,000 = $20,000

The difference between the accrual and cash methods is that the sales are not reported under the cash method until such sales are actually collected. Thus, the corporation does not include year-end receivables in this year's income. The year-end receivables will be reported when the receivables are collected in later taxable years.

As can be seen above, the cost of sales under both the accrual and cash methods are the same. This is because under Rev. Proc. 2001-10, taxpayers may not deduct inventory unless it is both paid for and sold. Since $30,000 was not paid for by year-end, it is not deductible and the purchases under the cash method are $30,000 less than under the accrual method. The ending inventory under the cash method is the physical inventory of $50,000 reduced by the $30,000 of inventory on hand that has not been paid for by year-end. ◀

REAL-WORLD EXAMPLE

The Ninth Circuit Court of Appeals has held that "markers" customers gave to a gambling casino to evidence their indebtedness to the casino required accrual even though the receivables were legally unenforceable under state law. The court found that there need only be a "reasonable expectancy" that payment would be made. *Flamingo Resort, Inc. v. U.S.*, 50 AFTR 2d 82-502, 82-1 USTC ¶9136 (9th Cir., 1982).

ACCRUAL METHOD

Taxpayers using the accrual method of accounting generally report income in the year it is earned. Income is considered to have been earned when all the events have occurred that fix the right to receive the income and when the amount of income can be determined with reasonable accuracy.[19] In the case of a sale of property, income normally accrues when title passes to the buyer.[20] Income from services accrues as the services are performed.

PREPAID INCOME. A major exception to the normal operation of the accrual method is the rules applicable to the receipt of prepaid income. Prepaid income is generally taxable in the year of receipt. For example, if a lender receives January interest in the preceding December, it is taxable in the year received, whether the lender uses the cash or accrual method. This treatment, of course, differs from financial accounting, where the interest would be reported as it accrues.

Two important exceptions to the general rule are worth noting. Accrual-basis taxpayers may defer recognizing income in the case of certain advance payments for *goods* and in the case of certain advance payments for *services* to be rendered. A taxpayer may defer advance payments for goods (inventory) if the taxpayer's method of accounting for the sale is the same for tax and financial accounting purposes.[21]

---

[19] Reg. Sec. 1.451-1(a).
[20] Regulation Sec. 1.446-1(c)(1)(ii), however, does permit taxpayers the right to accrue income from the sale of inventory when the goods are shipped, when the product is delivered or accepted, or when title passes, as long as the method is consistently used.
[21] Reg. Sec. 1.451-5.

Under Rev. Proc. 2004-34, taxpayers may defer payments for future services to the year following the year in which the payment is received.[22] Revenue relating to services provided in the year payment is received is reported currently. Revenue relating to future years is reported in the year following the year of receipt even if the payments relate to multiple future years. The rule can be applied to a variety of services such as Internet service, dance lessons, maintenance contracts (but not warranties included in the sales price of a product), membership fees, and rent (if services are associated with the rent, such as a hotel or motel). The procedure is available when service and products are provided together. The procedure does not apply to rent (if services are not associated with the rent), insurance premiums, interest, or warranty contracts included in the price of a product.

EXAMPLE I:3-15 ▶

REAL-WORLD EXAMPLE

A dance studio using the accrual method was required to include in taxable income all advance payments for lessons in the form of cash and negotiable notes, plus contract installments due but remaining unpaid at year end. *Mark E. Schlude v. CIR,* 11 AFTR 2d 751, 63-1 USTC ¶9284 (USSC, 1963).

Bear Corporation, a publicly held, accrual-basis taxpayer that uses the calendar year as its tax year, sells computer courses under contracts ranging from three months to two years. When income is reported depends on the length of the contract and the month in which the contract is sold. Assume that Bear sells three contracts in July 2010. One is for three months costing $90, a second is for one year costing $300, and the third for two years costing $500. The $90 charged for the three month contract is reported currently as all services are provided currently. One-half of $300 charged for the one year contract is reported in 2010 and one-half is reported in 2011 as one-half of the services are provided currently and one-half will be provided in 2011. One-fourth of the $500 charged for the two year contract is reported in 2010 and the balance is reported in 2011. This is because Rev. Proc. 2004-34 does not permit income to be deferred beyond the end of the year following the year in which payment is received.

Length of Contract	Year Includible in Gross Income	
	2010	2011
3 months	$ 90	
12 months	150	$150
24 months	125	375

◀

HYBRID METHOD

The **hybrid method** of accounting is a combination of the cash and accrual methods. Under the hybrid method, some items of income or expense are reported under the cash basis and others are reported under the accrual method. The method is most often encountered in small businesses that maintain inventories and are required to use the accrual method of accounting for purchases and sales of goods. Such businesses often prefer to use the cash method of reporting for other items because the cash method is simpler and may provide greater flexibility for tax planning. A taxpayer using the hybrid method of accounting would use the accrual method with respect to purchases and sales of goods but would use the cash method in computing all other items of income and expenses.

 STOP & THINK

Question: Taxpayers who are eligible to use the cash method often choose the cash method of reporting income over the accrual method. Why is the cash method generally more favorable for income tax purposes?

Solution: Taxpayers who have the option frequently choose the cash method over the accrual method because it is simpler, offers greater tax planning opportunity, and results in taxes being owed when income is actually received. The cash method is simpler because taxpayers are not required to make the complex accruals associated with the accrual method. Planning opportunities are greater because cash basis taxpayers can deduct expenses when paid, thereby allowing taxpayers to control their tax liability. Under the accrual method, prepaid expenses are not deductible when paid, but must be deducted over the periods benefitted. Finally, cash basis taxpayers do not have to pay taxes until they receive the money. Under the accrual method, income is reported when it is earned even if it has not been received. As a result, accrual basis taxpayers sometimes have to pay the tax before they actually receive the income they have earned.

---

[22] 2004-1 C.B. 991.

ITEMS OF GROSS INCOME: SEC. 61(a)

Section 61(a), quoted earlier in this chapter, states that gross income includes, but is not limited to, fifteen specifically listed types of income. Several of these items are discussed below.

COMPENSATION

Compensation is payment for personal services. It includes salaries, wages, fees, commissions, tips, bonuses, and specialized forms of compensation such as director's fees, jury fees, and marriage fees received by clergymen. What the compensation is called, how it is computed, the form and frequency of payment, and whether the compensation is subject to withholding is of little significance. Similarly, the fact that the services are part-time, one-time, seasonal, or temporary is immaterial.

There are exclusions, however, for a variety of employer-provided fringe benefits such as group term life insurance premiums, health and accident insurance premiums, employee discounts, contributions to retirement plans, and education benefits. In addition, there is a limited exclusion applicable to foreign-earned income. Both fringe benefits and the foreign-earned income exclusion are discussed in Chapter I:4.

BUSINESS INCOME

The term *gross income* usually refers to the total amount received from a particular source. In the case of businesses that provide services (e.g., accounting and law), the gross business income is the total amount received. In the case of manufacturing, merchandising, and mining, however, gross income is total sales less the cost of goods sold. Thus, gross income for tax purposes is comparable to gross profit for financial accounting purposes.

The cost of goods sold is, in effect, treated as a return of capital. Chapter I:4 discusses a well-established tax concept that a return of capital is not income and, therefore, cannot be subject to the income tax. Chapter I:11 discusses how inventories are valued.

GAINS FROM DEALINGS IN PROPERTY

Gains realized from property transactions are included in gross income unless a nonrecognition rule applies. As is true with business inventories, taxpayers may deduct the cost of property in order to arrive at the gain from a property transaction.[23] The tax law contains over 30 nonrecognition rules, which allow taxpayers to postpone the recognition of gains and losses from certain types of property transactions. In a few instances, these rules allow taxpayers to permanently exclude gains from gross income.[24]

Losses are not offset against gains in computing gross income. Rather, most losses are deductions *for* adjusted gross income. Furthermore, net capital losses for individuals are subject to provisions that limit the amount that can be deducted from other income to $3,000 per year. Losses from the sale or disposition of an asset held for personal use are not deductible.

INTEREST

Interest is compensation for the use of money. Taxable interest includes interest on bank deposits, corporate bonds, mortgages, life insurance policies, tax refunds, most U.S. government obligations,[25] and foreign government obligations.[26] Nontaxable interest is discussed below.

TAX-EXEMPT INTEREST. Since the inception of the federal income tax in 1913, interest on obligations of states, territories, and U.S. possessions and their political subdivisions has been tax exempt.[27] Bonds issued by school districts, port authorities, toll road commissions, counties, and fire districts have been held to be tax exempt. In addition, Sec. 501(c)(3) organizations may issue up to $225 million of tax-exempt bonds. Such organizations include private universities, hospitals, churches, and similar nonprofit organizations.

---

[23] Note that *business income* and *gains from dealings in property* are overlapping terms. The gross profit from the sale of inventory is actually both business income and a gain from a property transaction. Typically, however, the phrase *gains from dealings in property* may be assumed to mean gains from dealings in property other than inventory, so as to avoid confusion.

[24] For example, Sec. 121 allows taxpayers to exclude a limited amount of gain from a sale of a personal residence.

[25] The interest on many federal obligations issued before March 1, 1942 is tax exempt.

[26] Reg. Sec. 1.61-7.

As noted above, this exclusion does not extend to interest paid on most U.S. government obligations or foreign government obligations, nor does the exclusion exempt from taxation gains from the sale of state or local government bonds or interest on tax refunds paid by state and municipal governments.

There has always been some uncertainty as to whether the federal government could tax interest on state and local government obligations. The basic question is whether taxing these obligations would violate the doctrine of intergovernmental immunity in that the tax would reduce the ability of state and local governments to finance their operations because taxable bonds usually pay a higher rate of interest than tax-exempt bonds. The belief that taxing state and local government interest is unconstitutional is no longer widely held. While there have been efforts to tax interest on state and local bonds, the only changes have been to limit the use of bonds for private activities,[28] federally insured loans,[29] and arbitrage.[30]

In 2009 and 2010, state and local governments may elect to issue taxable bonds that are eligible for a tax credit of up to 35% of the interest paid. The state and local governments issuing such bonds may choose to receive the credit themselves or pass the credit on to investors. Obviously, issuing agencies that pass the credit to investors will be able to borrow at lower interest rates.

SERIES EE SAVINGS BOND EXCLUSION. Taxpayers may purchase and eventually redeem Series EE bonds tax-free if they use the proceeds to pay certain college expenses for themselves, a spouse, or dependents.[31]

To qualify for the exclusion:

▶ The bonds must be purchased after 1989 by an individual who is age 24 or older at the time of the purchase.

▶ The bonds must be purchased by the owner and cannot be a gift to the owner.

▶ The receipts from the bond redemption must be used for tuition and fees, which are first reduced by tax-exempt scholarships, veterans benefits, Hope and Lifetime Learning credits, and other similar amounts.[32]

▶ Married couples living together must file a joint return to obtain the exclusion.

The full amount of interest is excluded only if the combined amount of principal and interest received during the year does not exceed the net qualified educational expenses (tuition and fees reduced by exempt scholarships, etc.), and the taxpayer's 2010 modified adjusted gross income is not over $70,100 ($105,100 for married individuals filing a joint return). The exclusion is fully phased-out for taxpayers whose 2010 modified AGI is more than $85,100 ($135,100 for married individuals filing a joint return).[33]

If the net qualified education expenses are less than the total principal and interest, a portion of the interest is excluded based on the ratio of the qualified educational expenses to the total principal and interest. The tentative exclusion is equal to

$$\text{Series EE interest} \times \frac{\text{Net qualified educational expenses}}{\text{Series EE interest} + \text{Principal}}$$

EXAMPLE I:3-16 ▶ In 2010, Lois redeems Series EE bonds and receives $6,000, consisting of $1,875 of interest and $4,125 of principal. Assume that the net qualifying education expenses total $4,800. Lois's educational expenses equal 80% of the total amount received ($4,800 ÷ $6,000). Thus, her exclusion is limited to $1,500 (0.80 × $1,875). ◀

---

[27] Sec. 103(a)(1).

[28] Interest from state and local bonds issued for private activities such as the construction of sports facilities, convention centers, and industrial park sites is taxable. A limited amount of tax-exempt bonds can be issued each year by a state for "qualified" private activities such as airport construction, redevelopment, and student loans. The limit is the greater of $225 million or $75 per resident (Sec. 146(d)). Though exempt from regular income tax, interest from these "qualified" private activity bonds is subject to the alternative minimum tax (see Chapter I:14).

[29] Sec. 149(b).

[30] Sec. 148. Interest from state or local government bonds issued for the purpose of using the proceeds to buy higher-yield investments is taxable. Such bonds are called arbitrage bonds.

[31] Sec. 135(c).

[32] The exclusion is not permitted for amounts paid for sports, games, or hobbies unless they are part of a degree program (Sec. 135(c)(2)(B)).

[33] Each of these amounts is adjusted annually for inflation. In 2009, the phase-out started at $69,950 ($104,900 on joint returns) and ended at $84,950 ($134,900 on joint returns).

ADDITIONAL COMMENT
A child born today will require about $100,000 for a four-year college education. If interest rates are around 6%, one would have to save about $245 a month until the child entered school to be able to pay this amount.

As noted, the amount of the exclusion is further reduced if modified adjusted gross income exceeds a $70,100 threshold ($105,100 for married individuals filing a joint return). Modified adjusted gross income includes the interest from education savings bonds and certain otherwise excludable foreign income.[34] The reduction is computed as follows:

$$\text{Otherwise excludable amount} \times \frac{\text{Excess modified AGI}}{\$15,000 \ (\$30,000 \text{ for joint filers})}$$

EXAMPLE I:3-17 ▶ Assume the same facts as in Example I:3-16 and that Lois is single and has other adjusted gross income of $73,225, making her total AGI $75,100 ($73,225 + $1,875). Lois's otherwise available exclusion of $1,500 is reduced by $500 to $1,000. This reduction is computed by dividing the excess modified AGI of $5,000 ($73,225 + $1,875 − $70,100) by $15,000 and multiplying the result by $1,500. ◀

One difficulty with the rules is that the phase-out of the exclusion is based on income in the year the bonds are redeemed, not the year they are purchased. As a result, some taxpayers who purchase bonds anticipating an exclusion find they are ineligible for the exclusion when the bonds are redeemed.

RENTS AND ROYALTIES

Amounts received as rents or royalties are included in gross income. As noted earlier, prepaid rent is taxable when received. Security deposits, which are refundable to tenants upon the expiration of a lease, are not included in gross income. The deposit is included in gross income only if it is not refunded upon the expiration of the lease.

EXAMPLE I:3-18 ▶ In December 2010, Buddy rents an apartment to Gary. Buddy receives the first and last months' rent plus a security deposit of $500. Buddy must include in 2010 gross income both the first and last months' rent. Assume that Gary moves out of the apartment in 2012 and Buddy keeps $300 of the security deposit to cover repairs costing $200 and five days' unpaid rent, which amounts to $100. In 2012, Buddy would include the $300 in gross income and could deduct $200 for repairs. ◀

Royalties from copyrights, patents, and oil, gas, and mineral rights are all taxable as ordinary income. **Royalties** are proceeds paid to an owner by others who do business under some right belonging to the owner. Amounts received by a lessor to cancel, amend, or modify a lease also are taxable.

STOP & THINK *Question:* Financial accounting contains extensive rules distinguishing "operating leases" from "capital leases." The IRC has no such rules. While the tax law does require the capitalization of leases that are in substance a purchase of the asset, most authority relating to the distinction comes from court cases. Why doesn't the tax law include specific rules relating to leased property?

Solution: The financial accounting rules that require businesses to capitalize some leases were established because of concern that long-term lease commitments represented unrecorded liabilities. Unrecorded liabilities distort a company's balance sheet, but may not distort reported income. Since the tax law is concerned with the reporting of income rather than the balance sheet, neither Congress nor the Treasury Department has seen the need to adopt leasing rules like those in financial accounting.

IMPROVEMENTS BY LESSEES. Improvements made by a lessee that increase the value of leased property are included in the lessor's income only if the improvements are made in lieu of paying rent or if rent is reduced because of the improvements. In such situations,

---

[34] Specifically, modified adjusted gross income includes amounts that qualify for the foreign earned income exclusion (Sec. 911), the exclusion for possession's income (Sec. 931), and the exclusion for income from Puerto Rico (Sec. 933). The limitation is determined after taking the partial exclusion for Social Security benefits and railroad retirement (Sec. 86), claiming the allowable deduction for retirement contributions (Sec. 219), and applying the passive loss limitation (Sec. 469).

the lessor must include the fair market value (FMV) of the improvement in gross income when it is made to the property.[35]

EXAMPLE I:3-19 ▶ Rita rents an apartment to Anna. The apartment normally would rent for $1,000 per month, but Rita agrees to accept $400 per month for the first year if Anna builds a block wall around the property. Rita estimates that she would have to pay someone $6,000 to build the wall. Rita is accepting reduced rent and must report gross income of $6,000 when the wall is added to the property. The $6,000 could be added to Rita's basis in the property and should qualify as a depreciable asset. ◀

Improvements not made in lieu of rent are not income to the lessor. No adjustment is made to the lessor's basis in the property and, therefore, no depreciation is allowable. Gain or loss is recognized only when the property is disposed of.[36] Whether the improvements are in lieu of rent depends on the intent of the parties. This determination is based on the facts of the particular situation. The rental rate, the terms of the rental agreement, and whether the improvements have an estimated useful life exceeding the term of the lease may all be indications of intent.

DIVIDENDS

ADDITIONAL COMMENT

Shareholders of closely held corporations generally do not want to receive dividends from their corporations. The reason? They are taxed as ordinary income and the corporation does not receive a tax deduction for the payments.

Dividends are included in shareholder gross income. The result is a so-called double tax because corporations are taxed on income they earn, and shareholders are taxed when the income is distributed as dividends.

As noted in the previous chapter many corporations avoid the problem of "double taxation" by making S elections which result in the corporations and their shareholders being taxed much like partnerships. Two other important provisions reduce the tax burden on dividends:

▶ C Corporation receiving dividends from other C Corporations may claim a "dividends received deduction" that reduces, and in some cases eliminates, the second corporate tax on the income. The amount of the dividend received deduction is generally 70% of dividends received by a corporation owning less than 20% of the distributing corporation, 80% of dividends received by a corporation owning at least 20% but less than 80% of the distributing corporation, and 100% of the dividends received by a corporation owning 80% or more of the distributing corporation. This rule is discussed more in Chapter I:16 and in-depth in *Prentice Hall's Federal Taxation: Corporations, Partnerships, Estates & Trusts* text and the *Comprehensive* volume.

▶ Lower tax rates temporarily apply to qualified dividends received by individuals. In 2010, there is no tax on qualified dividends received by individuals in the 10% and 15% brackets. While dividends received by individuals in higher tax brackets are taxed at 15%. These lower tax rates on dividends only are available if the stock meets a special 60-day holding period. After 2010, dividends are scheduled to revert back and be taxed at the individual shareholder's regular tax rate.

In general, the above provisions apply to domestic corporations because foreign corporations are not automatically subject to the U.S. income tax. Only domestic corporations may make S elections. Dividends received from foreign corporations are generally ineligible for either the dividend received deduction or the lower tax rates discussed above.

EXAMPLE I:3-20 ▶ Georgia is in the 25% tax bracket. She owns 10% of Orange Corporation, an S corporation with $20,000 of income. The corporation distributes $1,000 to Georgia. She receives a $500 dividend from Red Corporation, a U.S. corporation, and $300 from Blue Corporation, a foreign corporation. Georgia will include $2,800 in gross income. This includes her share of Orange Corporation's income or $2,000 (10% × $20,000) along with $500 she received from Red Corporation and $300 she received from Blue Corporation. As Orange Corporation made an S election, she must include in gross income her share of the corporation's income even though only part of it is distributed. The tax rate that applies to the $2,000 depends on the nature of the income earned by Orange Corporation. For example, part or all of the income could be

---

[35] Reg. Sec. 1.109-1.

[36] Reg. Sec. 1.1019-1.

treated as capital gains or dividend income if Orange earned those types of income while income from operations would be taxed at Georgia's higher tax rate of 25%. The dividend from Red Corporation qualifies for the favorable 15% tax rate applicable to dividends. The dividend from Blue Corporation will be taxed at Georgia's regular tax rate of 25% as it was paid by a foreign corporation. ◄

EXAMPLE I:3-21 ►

Celeste is a single taxpayer with a salary of $43,000, qualified dividend income of $3,000, and itemized deductions of $8,000. Her taxable income is:

Adjusted gross income	$46,000
Itemized deductions	(8,000)
Personal exemption	(3,650)
Taxable income	$34,350

Her taxable income excluding dividends is $31,350 ($34,350 − $3,000), and is taxed at regular rates. The 15% tax bracket for single taxpayers ends at $34,000. As a result, $2,650 ($34,000 − $31,350) of Celeste's dividends are tax free, and the balance of the dividends or $350 ($3,000 − $2,650) is taxed at 15%.

Tax on ordinary income of $31,350 using rate schedule	$ 4,284
$2,650 of dividend income is tax free	–0–
Tax on $350 of dividend income at 15%	52
Taxable income	$ 4,336 ◄

DIVIDENDS DEFINED. Distributions to shareholders are taxable as dividends only to the extent they are made from either the corporation's current earnings and profits (a concept similar, although not identical, to current year's net income for financial accounting purposes) or accumulated earnings and profits (a concept similar, although not identical, to beginning of the year retained earnings).[37] Earnings and profits are discussed in Chapter I:16 and in greater depth in *Prentice Hall's Federal Taxation: Corporations, Partnerships, Estates, and Trusts* text and the *Comprehensive* volume. Distributions in excess of current and accumulated earnings and profits are treated as a nontaxable recovery of capital. Such distributions reduce the shareholder's basis in the stock. Distributions in excess of the basis of the stock are classified as capital gains.

EXAMPLE I:3-22 ►

Liz is the sole shareholder in Atlantic Corporation and has owned the stock for five years. The basis of her stock is $50,000. Atlantic distributes $40,000 to Liz. Accumulated earnings and profits at the beginning of the year equal $25,000, and current earnings and profits equal $10,000. Liz will report $35,000 of taxable dividend income and a nontaxable return of capital equal to $5,000. In addition, Liz must reduce her basis in the stock by $5,000. Alternatively, if the distribution to Liz were $100,000, she would report $35,000 of taxable dividend income, $50,000 as a nontaxable return of capital, and a $15,000 long-term capital gain. ◄

STOCK DIVIDENDS. A **stock dividend** is a distribution by a corporation to its shareholders of the corporation's own stock. In 1920, the Supreme Court held that simple stock dividends could not be taxed because they were not income.[38] More precisely, income had not been realized because there was no real change in the taxpayer's interest or the risks faced by the taxpayer. Over the years, however, the exclusion for stock dividends has been narrowed. If a shareholder has the option of receiving either cash or stock, the shareholder is taxed even if he or she opts to receive stock. The option to receive cash constitutes constructive receipt of the cash. Today, many other features of a stock dividend may cause it to be taxed. For example, a distribution in which preferred stock is distributed to some common shareholders and common stock is distributed to others is taxable.[39] The recipient of a taxable stock dividend includes the value of the stock received in gross income, and that amount becomes the basis of the shares received.

A nontaxable stock dividend has no effect on a shareholder's income in the year received. The basis of the old shares is allocated between the old shares and the new

ADDITIONAL COMMENT

Many mutual funds do not want their shareholders to have a large tax bill on the undistributed capital gains allocated among the shareholders. Some mutual funds will sell stocks in the portfolio that can be sold at a loss to offset gains incurred earlier in the year.

---

[37] Sec. 316(a). The federal income tax became effective on March 1, 1913. Thus, income accumulated before that date can still be distributed on a tax-exempt basis.

[38] *Eisner v. Myrtle H. Macomber*, 3 AFTR 3020, 1 USTC ¶32 (USSC, 1920).
[39] Reg. Sec. 1.305-4.

shares. Furthermore, the holding period for the new shares starts on the same date as the holding period of the old.

EXAMPLE I:3-23 ▶ Carol purchases 100 shares of Mesa Corporation stock for $1,100 (or $11 per share). Carol receives 10 shares of Mesa stock as a nontaxable stock dividend. After the dividend, Carol owns 110 shares of stock with a total basis of $1,100 (or $10 per share). All of the stock is assumed to have been acquired at the time of the original purchase. ◀

REAL-WORLD EXAMPLE

In the 1989 trial of Leona Helmsley, the billionaire hotel queen, it was disclosed that she had billed her companies for millions of dollars in personal items. The items ranged from a $12.99 girdle to a $1 million limestone-and-marble pool enclosure at her estate. She was sentenced to four years in prison and fined $7.1 million. The amounts paid to her by her companies represented constructive dividends.

CAPITAL GAIN DIVIDENDS. A **capital gain dividend** is a distribution by a regulated investment company (commonly called a *mutual fund*) of capital gains realized from the sale of investments in the fund. Such dividends also include any undistributed capital gains allocated to shareholders by such companies.[40] Capital gain dividends are long-term regardless of how long the shareholder has owned the stock of the regulated investment company.

CONSTRUCTIVE DIVIDENDS. In many corporations, the same individuals are both shareholders and employees. A corporation may not deduct dividends paid to shareholders but is permitted to deduct reasonable compensation. Questions are often raised as to whether amounts reported as compensation are really disguised dividends. If an amount called compensation is unreasonably high, it will be disallowed and reclassified as a dividend.[41] Often the reasonableness of compensation is determined by comparing the compensation paid to the employee-shareholders with amounts paid to others performing similar services.

EXAMPLE I:3-24 ▶ Carmen owns 100% of the stock in Florida Corporation and receives a $400,000 salary for serving as president. The corporation reports no taxable income and pays no dividends. Presidents of similar companies received salaries ranging from $75,000 to $160,000. The IRS probably would disallow a portion of Carmen's salary as unreasonable resulting in the corporation owing tax. The disallowed portion would be treated as a dividend. ◀

ADDITIONAL COMMENT

In one case, the taxpayer, who was also the president and principal shareholder, diverted cash from vending and pinball machines at his truck stops/restaurants to his personal use. The IRS's position was that these diverted cash amounts were a constructive dividend. *Hagaman v. CIR.*, 69 AFTR 2d 92-906 (6th Cir., 1992).

Constructive dividends are not limited to shareholder-employee compensation payments but may include situations where the shareholder also is a landlord (e.g., property is rented to the corporation at an amount greater than its fair rental value). A shareholder also may receive a constructive dividend because of a creditor or vendor relationship. It is not necessary that a dividend be formally declared or that distributions be in proportion to stock holdings. **Constructive dividends** are often distributions that are intended to result in a deduction to the corporation and taxable income (such as compensation) to the shareholder.[42] Other constructive dividends are intended to produce a nonreportable benefit to the shareholder,[43] or even result in a deduction to the corporation without income to the shareholder.[44]

ALIMONY AND SEPARATE MAINTENANCE PAYMENTS

Any payment pursuant to a divorce or legal separation must be classified as one of the following for tax purposes:

(1) Alimony;

(2) Child support; or

(3) Property settlement.

The treatment of a payment depends on its classification. Alimony is deductible by the payor spouse and taxable to the payee spouse. Neither child support payments nor property settlements have any tax ramifications, that is, they are not subject to tax to the payee spouse nor deductible by the payor spouse.

Example I:3-25 demonstrates the significant difference in taxation that can occur when a payment is classified as either alimony or a property settlement.

---

[40] Sec. 852(b).
[41] Sec. 162(a)(1).
[42] Other examples include excessive royalties (*Peterson & Pegau Baking Co.*, 2 B.T.A. 637 (1925)) and rent (*Limericks, Inc. v. CIR*, 36 AFTR 649, 48-1 USTC ¶9146 (5th Cir., 1948)).
[43] Examples include bargain sales of corporate assets to shareholders (*J. E. Timberlake v. CIR*, 30 AFTR 583, 42-2 USTC ¶9822 (4th Cir., 1942)),

redemptions of a shareholder's stock (Sec. 302), and loans to shareholders that are actually dividends (*George Blood Enterprises, Inc.*, 1976 PH T.C. Memo ¶76,102, 35 TCM 436).
[44] Examples include paying an employee's personal expenses (*The Lang Chevrolet Co.*, 1967 PH T.C. Memo ¶67,212, 26 TCM 1054) and purchasing assets for an employee's use (*Joseph Morgenstern*, 1955 PH T.C. Memo ¶55,086, 14 TCM 282).

EXAMPLE I:3-25 ▶
ADDITIONAL COMMENT

Child-support payments are not treated as alimony and are neither deductible by the payor spouse nor includible in income of the payee spouse.

ADDITIONAL COMMENT

If any amount specified in the divorce instrument will be reduced due to the happening of a contingency relating to a child or reduced at a time that can clearly be associated with such contingency, the amount of the reduction is treated as child support.

ETHICAL POINT

Tax consultants who advise divorcing couples may face an ethical dilemma because advice that benefits one spouse may be detrimental to the other, and because of the need to maintain confidential client relationships.

EXAMPLE I:3-26 ▶

Helen earns $500,000 and, as a result of her divorce, she is required to pay William $250,000. If the payment is a property settlement, Helen cannot deduct any of the $250,000 payment and William is not required to include the payment in his income. However, if the $250,000 is alimony, Helen can deduct the full amount in computing her adjusted gross income. William reports the $250,000 as alimony income. ◀

The tax law has rather specific rules that distinguish alimony, child support, and property settlements. Under current law, in order to be treated as **alimony**, payments must meet all of the following requirements:[45]

▶ Be made in cash (not property)

▶ Be made pursuant to a divorce, separation, or a written agreement between the spouses

▶ Terminate at the death of the payee

▶ Not be designated as being other than alimony (e.g., child support)

▶ Be made between people who are living in separate households

These rules are summarized in Topic Review I:3-2. Certain aspects of these rules will be discussed further.

A **property settlement** is a division of property pursuant to a divorce. In general, each spouse is entitled to the property brought into the marriage and a share of the property accumulated during marriage.[46] A division of property does not result in any income to either spouse, nor does either spouse receive a tax deduction. The basis of property received by either spouse as a result of the divorce or separation remains unchanged.

As a result of a divorce, Dawn receives stock that she purchased with her former husband during their marriage for $12,000. At the time of the divorce, the stock was worth $14,000. Neither Dawn nor her former husband reports income from the transfer of the stock because the stock was acquired as a property settlement. If Dawn subsequently sold the stock for $15,000, she would report a $3,000 gain. ◀

Topic Review I:3-2

Tax Rules for Alimony

TREATMENT OF RECIPIENT

The recipient of alimony must include the amounts received in gross income. Property settlements and child support payments are not taxable.

TREATMENT OF PAYOR

The payor of alimony may deduct amounts paid *for* adjusted gross income. Property settlements and child support payments are not deductible.

APPLICABLE TO

Payments must be pursuant to a divorce, separation, or a written agreement between spouses.

REQUIREMENTS

Spouses must be living in separate households. Payments must be in the form of cash paid to (or for the benefit of) a spouse or former spouse. Payments must terminate at the death of the payee. Payments may not be designated as being other than alimony (such as child support or a property settlement).

RECAPTURE

If the amount of payments declines in the second or third year, a portion of the early payments may have to be recaptured as income by the payor. The payee may deduct the same recaptured amount.

---

[45] Before 1942, alimony was not deductible (*Gould v. Gould*, 3 AFTR 2958, 1 USTC ¶13 (USSC, 1917)). The original rules were revised in 1984 and again in 1986. Prior rules apply to earlier divorces unless both spouses elect to apply current rules.

[46] How the property accumulated during marriage is divided may be determined by an agreement of the parties, or if they are unable to agree, on a basis of state law.

One unusual rule found in the current law that relates to alimony is the so-called **recapture provision.** This provision was established to prevent a large property settlement that might take place after a divorce from being treated as alimony so as to produce a deduction for the payor. In essence, the concept of recapture in connection with a divorce means that the payor of the alimony (who has taken a deduction for such amounts in prior years) must report the recapture amount in his or her income. The payee (who has reported the income in prior years) receives a deduction for the recaptured amount. This recapture occurs because the payments that originally were reported as alimony are being reclassified as property settlements.

Recapture occurs if payments decrease sharply in either the second or third year. Specifically, the amount of second-year alimony recaptured is equal to the second-year alimony reduced by the total of $15,000 plus the third-year alimony. The amount of first-year alimony recaptured is equal to the first-year alimony reduced by the total of $15,000 plus the average alimony paid in the second year (reduced by the recapture for that year) and the third year. The calculation of recapture for both the first and second years is shown below.

$$R_2 = A_2 - (\$15,000 + A_3)$$

$$R_1 = A_1 - [\$15,000 + (A_2 + A_3 - R_2)/2]$$

A_i = Alimony paid in first (A_1), second (A_2), and third year (A_3), respectively.

R_i = Recaptured alimony from the first (R_1) and second year (R_2), respectively.

Both first- and second-year amounts are recaptured by requiring the payor to report the excess as income (and allowing the payee to deduct the same amount) in the third year. Recapture is not required if payments cease because of the death of either spouse or remarriage of the recipient.

EXAMPLE I:3-27 ▶ As a result of their divorce, Hal is ordered to pay to Rose $100,000 alimony in 2010 and $20,000 per year thereafter until her death or remarriage. Hal must recapture the amount of the decrease that exceeds $35,000, or $65,000 ($100,000 − $20,000 − $15,000). The $65,000 of alimony in 2010 must be reported by Hal as income during 2012. Also, Rose may deduct the $65,000 *for* AGI in 2012. ◀

EXAMPLE I:3-28 ▶ As a result of their separation, Mary agrees to pay Tom $20,000 per year. The payments are to cease if Tom remarries. In the year after the agreement is reached, Tom remarries and Mary discontinues the payments. No recapture is required because the payments are contingent on the remarriage of the recipient and the payments have been discontinued because of the occurrence of this contingency. ◀

PENSIONS AND ANNUITIES

An **annuity** is a series of regular payments that will continue for a fixed period of time or until the death of the recipient. Taxpayers occasionally purchase annuities from insurance companies to provide a source of funds during retirement years. The insurance company may agree to make payments to the insured for the remainder of the insured's life. The retired individual is assured of a steady flow of funds for life. The price paid for the annuity represents its cost. The insured taxpayer is permitted to recover this cost tax-free.

Individuals receiving an annuity are permitted to exclude their cost, but are taxed on the remaining portion of the annuity. The following steps can be followed to determine the nontaxable portion of the annuity:

▶ Determine the **expected return multiple.** This multiple is the number of years that the annuity is expected to continue and may be a stated term, say ten years, or it may be for the remainder of the taxpayer's life. In the latter situation, the expected return multiple (life expectancy) is determined by referring to a table (see Table I:3-1) developed by the IRS.

▶ Determine the **expected return.** This return is computed by multiplying the amount of the annual payment by the expected return multiple.

ADDITIONAL COMMENT

The three largest sources of non-wage income in 2004, in rank order, were net capital gains, pensions and annuities, and business and professional net income.

ADDITIONAL COMMENT

The expected return is limited to amounts receivable as an annuity. It does not include amounts that may be paid after death, nor does it include anticipated dividends.

▼ TABLE I:3-1
Ordinary Life Annuities (One Life) Expected Return Multiple

Age	Multiple	Age	Multiple	Age	Multiple
5	76.6	42	40.6	79	10.0
6	75.6	43	39.6	80	9.5
7	74.7	44	38.7	81	8.9
8	73.7	45	37.7	82	8.4
9	72.7	46	36.8	83	7.9
10	71.7	47	35.9	84	7.4
11	70.7	48	34.9	85	6.9
12	69.7	49	34.0	86	6.5
13	68.8	50	33.1	87	6.1
14	67.8	51	32.2	88	5.7
15	66.8	52	31.3	89	5.3
16	65.8	53	30.4	90	5.0
17	64.8	54	29.5	91	4.7
18	63.9	55	28.6	92	4.4
19	62.9	56	27.7	93	4.1
20	61.9	57	26.8	94	3.9
21	60.9	58	25.9	95	3.7
22	59.9	59	25.0	96	3.4
23	59.0	60	24.2	97	3.2
24	58.0	61	23.3	98	3.0
25	57.0	62	22.5	99	2.8
26	56.0	63	21.6	100	2.7
27	55.1	64	20.8	101	2.5
28	54.1	65	20.0	102	2.3
29	53.1	66	19.2	103	2.1
30	52.2	67	18.4	104	1.9
31	51.2	68	17.6	105	1.8
32	50.2	69	16.8	106	1.6
33	49.3	70	16.0	107	1.4
34	48.3	71	15.3	108	1.3
35	47.3	72	14.6	109	1.1
36	46.4	73	13.9	110	1.0
37	45.4	74	13.2	111	.9
38	44.4	75	12.5	112	.8
39	43.5	76	11.9	113	.7
40	42.5	77	11.2	114	.6
41	41.5	78	10.6	115	.5

Source: Reg. Sec. 1.72-9, Table V.

Note: This table should be used if any or all investments were made on or after July 1, 1986. If all investments were made before July 1, 1986, use Reg. Sec. 1.72-9, Table I (not shown).

▶ Determine the **exclusion ratio.** This ratio is computed by dividing the investment in the contract (its cost) by the expected return (from above).

▶ Determine the **current year's exclusion.** This exclusion is computed by multiplying the exclusion ratio (from above) times the amount received during the year.

EXAMPLE I:3-29 ▶ David, age 65, purchases an annuity for $30,000. Under the terms of the annuity, David is to receive $300 per month ($3,600 per year) for the rest of his life.

▶ The expected return multiple is 20.0. The multiple is obtained from Table I:3-1.

▶ The expected return is $72,000 (20.0 × $3,600).

▶ The exclusion ratio is 0.417 ($30,000 ÷ $72,000).

▶ The exclusion is $1,500 (0.417 × $3,600). ◀

After the entire cost of an annuity has been recovered, the full amount of all future payments is taxable. On the other hand, if an individual dies before recovering the entire cost, the remaining unrecovered cost can be deducted as an itemized deduction on that individual's final return. Insurance companies and businesses with retirement plans compute the taxable portion of annuities and report the amounts to recipients on Form 1099.

KEY POINT

The simplified method is used only for annuity distributions from qualified retirement plans. All other annuity distributions are taxed in accordance with the general rules above.

SIMPLIFIED METHOD FOR QUALIFIED RETIREMENT PLAN ANNUITIES. Distributions from pensions and other qualified retirement plans are often paid in the form of an annuity. Both the employer and the employee often contribute funds to plans during the years of employment. When an employee retires, the amounts contributed and income accumulated thereon become available to the retired employee. In some cases, the retired employee has the option of receiving a lump-sum payment or an annuity. The employee's cost is limited to amounts contributed (usually through withholding) by the employee that were previously taxed to the employee. The employee may recover this cost tax-free. The employee's cost does not include employer contributions.

A simplified method is now used to determine the taxable portion of an annuity paid from a qualified retirement plan (such as a pension). Under the simplified method, the non-taxable portion of each annuity payment is equal to the employee's investment in the annuity divided by the number of anticipated payments as determined from the following table:

Age of Primary Annuitant on the Start Date	Number of Anticipated Payments
55 and under	360
56–60	310
61–65	260
66–70	210
71 and over	160

EXAMPLE I:3-30 ▶

Jack, age 62, retires, and receives a $1,000 per month annuity from his employer's qualified pension plan. Jack contributed $65,000 to the plan prior to his retirement. Under the simplified method, Jack would exclude $250 per month as a return of capital. This is calculated by dividing $65,000 by 260 anticipated payments. ◀

If payments are paid other than monthly, the number of anticipated payments is adjusted accordingly. Thus, if payments are made quarterly, the number from the table is divided by three.

KEY POINT

Under current law, a taxpayer must generally pay tax on a portion of each withdrawal made before the normal starting date of the annuity.

ADVANCE PAYMENTS. Many pensions contain provisions that allow taxpayers to withdraw amounts before the normal starting date. Under current law, an amount withdrawn from a pension before the starting date is considered to be in part a recovery of the employee's contributions and in part a recovery of the employer's contributions.[47] After all contributions have been withdrawn, additional withdrawals are fully taxable. In addition to being subject to the regular income tax, any amount withdrawn may also be subject to a 10% nondeductible penalty. The penalty is not applicable to taxpayers who are age 59½ or older. Other exceptions to the early withdrawal penalty are discussed in Chapter I:9.

EXAMPLE I:3-31 ▶

Dick, age 45 and in good health, withdrew $2,000 from a pension plan during the current year. No exception exempts Dick from the 10% penalty. Dick had made $40,000 of after-tax contributions to the plan, and his employer had contributed $60,000. Dick must include $1,200 (0.60 × $2,000) in income. Because no exception applies, Dick must also pay an additional penalty of $120 (0.10 × $1,200). The penalty is not deductible by Dick. ◀

INCOME FROM LIFE INSURANCE AND ENDOWMENT CONTRACTS

The face amount of life insurance received because of the death of the insured is not taxable. If the proceeds are left with the insurance company and as a result earn interest, the interest payments are taxable. (See Chapter I:4 for a detailed discussion of life insurance and endowment contracts.)

---

[47] Sec. 72(e).

INCOME FROM DISCHARGE OF INDEBTEDNESS

In general, the forgiveness of debt is a taxable event. The person who owed the money must report the amount forgiven as income unless one of several exceptions found in the tax law applies. These exceptions are discussed in Chapter I:4.

INCOME PASSED THROUGH TO TAXPAYER

Generally, entities are subject to income tax based on the amount of taxable income. Corporations, as an example, are subject to income taxation. As noted, certain types of entities are not subject to income taxation as their income is taxed directly to the owners of the entity rather than to the entities. Such entities are referred to as "flow-through entities." Section 61 specifically lists three such instances: the distributive share of a partnership's income, income in respect of a decedent, and income from an interest in an estate or trust. Though not mentioned in Sec. 61, similar treatment is accorded S corporation, Regulated Investment Company, and Real Estate Investment Trust income. In each case, the income that is produced by the entity merely flows through to the owner or beneficiary of such entity. The rules can be summarized as follows:

KEY POINT

The pass-through of income by a partnership can create a situation known as phantom income. In this situation, a partner is required to report income on his or her individual tax return, but the partner may not have received a cash distribution from the partnership.

▶ Each partner reports his or her share of the partnership's income. Each partner deducts his or her share of the partnership's expenses. The income and deductions are reported by the partners whether or not any amount is actually distributed by the partnership during the year.

▶ Income in respect of a decedent is income earned by an individual before death that is paid to another after the death. For example, salary earned by a husband before his death in an automobile accident may be paid to his widow. The recipient, in this case the widow, is taxed on the income if it has not been taxed to the decedent before his death.

▶ Income earned by estates and trusts is subject to taxation.[48] However, income distributions to beneficiaries are deductible by estates and trusts and are taxable to the beneficiaries. Thus, if a trust with $20,000 of income distributes $15,000 to its beneficiary, the trust is taxed on $5,000, and $15,000 is taxed to the beneficiary. Because of this approach estates and trusts are sometimes referred to as semi-flow-through or hybrid entities. The income taxation of estates and trusts is covered more fully in *Prentice Hall's Federal Taxation: Corporations, Partnerships, Estates, and Trusts*.

▶ S corporations are taxed much like partnerships. Each shareholder in the corporation is taxed on his or her proportionate share of the corporation's income whether or not the income is actually distributed.

▶ Regulated Investment Companies (RICs), often called mutual funds, and Real Estate Investment Trusts (REITs) are also flow through entities. RICs invest in securities and are required to distribute their income to shareholders who are taxed on the distributions. REITs invest in real estate and real estate loans. They too must distribute their income to investors who are taxed on the income. The distributions (dividends, interest, rents, and gains) retain their tax status when reported by the RIC and REIT investors.

OTHER ITEMS OF GROSS INCOME

The preceding discussions considered items of gross income specifically listed in Sec. 61(a). However, the fact that an item of income is listed in Sec. 61(a) does not necessarily cause it to be taxable. Rather, the condition that causes an item of income to be taxable is that it is not specifically excluded. Some items of gross income not mentioned in Sec. 61(a) are discussed below.

---

[48] Note the distinction between income in respect of a decedent and the income of an estate. Income in respect of a decedent is the income earned before death that was never taxed to the decedent. An example would be interest that was accrued but unpaid at death. Income of an estate is income earned after death that is paid to the estate. An example would be interest that accrues after the decedent's death.

PRIZES, AWARDS, GAMBLING WINNINGS, AND TREASURE FINDS

In general, prizes, awards, gambling winnings, and treasure finds are taxable.[49] Winnings in contests, competitions, and quiz shows as well as awards from an employer to an employee in recognition of some achievement in connection with his or her employment are taxable.[50] The amount to be included in gross income is the fair market value of the goods or services received. Total gambling winnings must be included in gross income.[51] This includes proceeds from lotteries, raffles, sweepstakes, and the like. Gambling losses (up to the amount of the current year's winnings) are allowable as an itemized deduction.[52] The Regulations state that a treasure find constitutes gross income to the extent of its value in the year in which it is reduced to undisputed possession.[53]

EXAMPLE I:3-32 ▶ Several years ago, Colleen purchased a used piano at an auction for $15. In the current year, she finds $4,500 of currency hidden in the piano. Colleen must report the $4,500 as income in the current year.[54] ◀

REAL-WORLD EXAMPLE

An accountant collected from a client money that was to be used to pay the client's taxes. Then the accountant appropriated the money for his own use. The accountant was held to have received unreported income. *Richard A. Reeves,* 1977 PH T.C. Memo ¶ 77,114, 36 TCM 500.

ILLEGAL INCOME

Income from illegal activities is taxable.[55] Some people find this part of the tax law surprising, but this fact serves as the basis for many criminal convictions given that few criminals report their illegal income. For example, Al Capone was convicted of income tax evasion, not bootlegging or other crimes. It is not necessary to prove that an individual had illegal income, but merely that the individual had income that was not reported.

Individuals have used varied defenses against this rule. One taxpayer was successful in convincing the Supreme Court that he should not be taxed on embezzlement gains because he had an unconditional obligation to repay the amount embezzled,[56] but the Supreme Court reversed this position in a later case.[57] The court concluded that although an obligation to repay existed, the taxpayer had no "consensual recognition" (intent) to repay. In addition to embezzlement of funds, the courts have held that a kidnapper's ransom was taxable,[58] along with profits from bookmaking,[59] card playing,[60] forgery,[61] stealing,[62] bank robbery,[63] sale of narcotics,[64] illegal sale of liquor,[65] and bribes.[66] (See Chapter I:6 for a discussion of related deductions.)

UNEMPLOYMENT COMPENSATION

ADDITIONAL COMMENT

Welfare payments are not normally required to be included in gross income. However, if the welfare payments are fraudulently received under state or federal assistance programs, they must be included in the recipient's gross income.

For many years, unemployment compensation was excluded from gross income. In 1978, Congress changed the law to fully tax unemployment compensation because these benefits are a substitute for taxable wages. However, pursuant to the American Recovery and Reinvestment Act of 2009, for tax years beginning in 2009, individuals may exclude up to $2,400 of unemployment benefits received during the year.

SOCIAL SECURITY BENEFITS

Social Security benefits were excluded from gross income until 1984. Between 1984 and 1993, up to 50% of Social Security benefits were taxable. Beginning in 1994, up to 85% of Social Security benefits may be taxable. Under Sec. 86, the portion of Social Security benefits that are taxable depends on the taxpayer's provisional income and filing status. *Provisional income* is computed using the following formula:

---

[49] Exclusions for scholarships and fellowships and a limited exclusion for prizes awarded for scientific, charitable, or similar meritorious achievements are discussed in Chapter I:4.
[50] Sec. 74 and Reg. Sec. 1.74-1.
[51] *U.S. v. Manley S. Sullivan,* 6 AFTR 6753, 1 USTC ¶236 (USSC, 1927).
[52] Sec. 165(d).
[53] Reg. Sec. 1.61-14(a).
[54] *Ermenegildo Cesarini v. U.S.,* 26 AFTR 2d 5107, 70-2 USTC ¶9509 (6th Cir., 1970).
[55] Reg. 1.61-14(a).
[56] *CIR v. Laird Wilcox,* 34 AFTR 811, 46-1 USTC ¶9188 (USSC, 1946).
[57] *Eugene C. James v. U.S.,* 7 AFTR 2d 1361, 61-1 USTC ¶9449 (USSC, 1961).

[58] *Murray Humphreys v. CIR,* 28 AFTR 1030, 42-1 USTC ¶9237 (7th Cir., 1942).
[59] *James P. McKenna,* 1 B.T.A. 326 (1925).
[60] *L. Weiner,* 10 B.T.A. 905 (1928).
[61] *Cass Sunstein,* 1966 PH T.C. Memo ¶66,043, 25 TCM 247.
[62] *Mathias Schira v. CIR,* 50 AFTR 1404, 57-1 USTC ¶9413 (6th Cir., 1957).
[63] *Gary Ayers,* 1978 PH T.C. Memo ¶78,341, 37 TCM 1415.
[64] *Antonino Farina v. McMahon,* 2 AFTR 2d 5918, 58-2 USTC ¶9938 (D.C. N.Y., 1958).
[65] *U.S. v. Manley S. Sullivan,* 6 AFTR 6753, 1 USTC ¶236 (USSC, 1927).
[66] *U.S. v. Patrick Commerford,* 12 AFTR 364, 1933 CCH ¶9255 (2nd Cir., 1933).

Adjusted gross income (excluding Social Security benefits)	$xx,xxx
Plus: Tax-exempt interest	x,xxx
Excluded foreign income	x,xxx
50% of Social Security benefits	x,xxx
Provisional income	$xx,xxx

MARRIED FILING SEPARATELY.   In the case of married couples who live together but file separately, taxable Social Security benefits are equal to the lesser of:

▶ 85% of Social Security benefits, or

▶ 85% of provisional income

MARRIED FILING JOINTLY.   For married couples filing jointly, the computation of the taxable portion of Social Security benefits is as follows:

▶ If provisional income is $32,000 or less, no Social Security benefits are taxable.

▶ If provisional income is over $32,000 (but not over $44,000), taxable Social Security benefits equal the lesser of:
    50% of the Social Security benefits, or
    50% of the excess of provisional income over $32,000

▶ If provisional income is over $44,000, taxable Social Security benefits are equal to the lesser of:
    85% of the Social Security benefits, or
    85% of provisional income over $44,000, plus the lesser of (1) $6,000 or (2) 50% of Social Security benefits

SINGLE TAXPAYERS.   For single taxpayers (and married persons living separately), the computation of the taxable portion of Social Security benefits is as follows:

▶ If provisional income is $25,000 or less, no Social Security benefits are taxable.

▶ If provisional income is over $25,000 (but not over $34,000), taxable Social Security benefits are equal to the lesser of:
    50% of the Social Security benefits, or
    50% of the excess of provisional income over $25,000

▶ If provisional income is over $34,000, taxable Social Security benefits are equal to the lesser of:
    85% of the Social Security benefits, or
    85% of provisional income over $34,000, plus the lesser of (1) $4,500 or (2) 50% of Social Security benefits

EXAMPLE I:3-33 ▶ Holly is a single taxpayer with a taxable pension of $22,000, tax-exempt interest of $10,000, and Social Security benefits of $8,000. Her provisional income is $36,000, determined as follows:

Adjusted gross income	$22,000
Plus: Tax-exempt interest	10,000
50% of Social Security benefits	4,000
Provisional income	$36,000

The taxable Social Security benefits are equal to $5,700, which is the lesser of $6,800 (0.85 × $8,000) or $5,700 ($1,700* + the lesser of $4,500 or $4,000**).

*($36,000 provisional income − $34,000 threshold) × 0.85.
**50% of the Social Security benefits. ◀

The result of the computation excludes from gross income the Social Security benefits received by lower-income individuals but taxes a portion (up to 85%) of the benefits received by taxpayers with higher incomes. As the thresholds are not adjusted for inflation, an increasing number of retirees are finding that a portion of their Social Security benefits is taxable.

The term **Social Security benefits** refers to basic monthly retirement and disability benefits paid under Social Security and also to tier-one railroad retirement benefits. It does

not include supplementary Medicare benefits that cover the cost of doctors' services and other medical benefits.

INSURANCE PROCEEDS AND COURT AWARDS

In general, insurance proceeds and court awards are taxable. Two exceptions are accident and health insurance benefits and the face amount of life insurance. (See Chapter I:4 for a discussion of these benefits.)

Insurance proceeds or court awards received because of the destruction of property are included in gross income only to the extent that the proceeds exceed the adjusted basis of the property. Involuntary conversion provisions permit taxpayers to avoid being taxed if they reinvest the proceeds in a qualified replacement property.[67] If the proceeds are less than the property's adjusted basis, they reduce the amount of any deductible loss. Proceeds of insurance guarding against loss of profits because of a casualty are taxable.[68] Similarly, if a taxpayer had to sue a customer to collect income owed to the taxpayer, the amount collected is taxable just as it would have been had the taxpayer collected the income without going to court.

EXAMPLE I:3-34 ▶ Gulf Corporation's factory was destroyed by fire. Gulf Corporation collected insurance of $400,000, which equaled the building's basis, and $250,000 for the profits lost during the time the company was rebuilding its factory. The $400,000 is not taxable because it constitutes a recovery of the basis of the factory. The $250,000 is taxable because it represents lost income. Recall that the income would have been taxable had it been earned by the company from regular operations. ◀

Although few exclusions are designed specifically for insurance proceeds or court awards, such amounts may be covered by other, more general exclusions. For example, Sec. 104(a)(2) excludes "damages (other than punitive damages) received . . . on account of personal physical injuries or sickness." Thus, amounts collected because of physical injury suffered in an automobile accident are excluded (see Chapter I:4).

RECOVERY OF PREVIOUSLY DEDUCTED AMOUNTS

On occasion, a taxpayer may deduct an amount in one year but recover the amount in a subsequent year. In general, the amount recovered must be included in the gross income in the year it is recovered. Cash-basis taxpayers encounter this situation more often than accrual-basis taxpayers because their expenses are generally deductible in the year they are paid. If the amount was overpaid, the taxpayer can anticipate a refund.

EXAMPLE I:3-35 ▶ During 2010, Cindy's employer withheld $1,000 from her wages for state income taxes. She claimed the $1,000 as an itemized deduction on her 2010 federal income tax return. Her itemized deductions totaled $12,000. On her 2010 state income tax return, her state income tax was only $800. As a result, Cindy received a $200 refund from the state in April 2011. Because Cindy deducted the full $1,000 in 2010, she must report the $200 refund as income on her 2011 federal income tax return. ◀

Any recovery of a previously deducted amount may lead to income recognition. Recovery, however, is often associated with expenses such as state income taxes or bad debts deducted in one year but recovered in a later year, medical expenses deducted in one year but reimbursed by insurance in a later year, casualty losses deducted in one year but reimbursed by court award or insurance in a later year, and deductions for amounts paid by check where the payee never cashed the check.

Several related rules should be noted:

▶ If the refund or other recovery occurs in the same year, the refund or recovery reduces the deduction and is not reported as income.

---

[67] The involuntary conversion provisions are discussed in Chapter I:12.
[68] *Oppenheim's Inc. v. Kavanagh*, 39 AFTR 468, 50-1 USTC ¶9249 (D.C.-Mich., 1950).

▶ Interest on the amount refunded is taxable and is not subject to the tax benefit rule (discussed below).

▶ The character of the income reported in the year of repayment is dependent on the type of deduction previously reported. For instance, if the taxpayer deducted a short-term capital loss in one year, the subsequent recovery would be a short-term capital gain.[69]

TAX BENEFIT RULE.   As noted above, a taxpayer who recovers an amount deducted in a previous year must report as gross income the amount recovered. The amount recovered need not be included in income, however, if the taxpayer received no tax benefit. A tax benefit occurs only if the deduction reduced the tax for the year.[70]

EXAMPLE I:3-36 ▶ In 2010, Jack's employer withheld $1,200 from his wages for state income tax. Jack claimed the $1,200 as an itemized deduction on his 2010 federal income tax return. Because of a variety of losses incurred by Jack, he reported a negative taxable income of $32,000 during 2010. The state refunded the $1,200 during 2011. Jack will not have to report the $1,200 as gross income on his federal return. He would have owed no federal income tax in 2010 even without the deduction for state income taxes. Therefore, Jack received no tax benefit from the deduction. ◀

Tax benefit may be absent in other situations. For example, a taxpayer's total itemized deductions may have been less than the standard deduction, or the expense may have been less than the applicable floor. To illustrate, medical expenses can be deducted only to the extent that they exceed 7.5% of adjusted gross income. If a taxpayer does not deduct medical expenses because they are less than the floor, the taxpayer does not have to report a subsequent reimbursement of the expense as income. If only a portion of an expense produces a tax benefit, only that portion has to be reported as income.

EXAMPLE I:3-37 ▶

REAL-WORLD EXAMPLE

An attorney collected fees from clients of his employer. Because the attorney and his employer were engaged in a dispute over ownership of the money, he deposited the disputed amount in a trust account. The attorney was taxable on the amounts in the year received because he had control over the funds under the claim of right doctrine. *Edward J. Costello, Jr.,* 1985 PH T.C. Memo ¶85,571, 50 TCM 1463.

In 2010, Chris, an unmarried individual, had $1,700 withheld from her wages for state income tax. Her itemized deductions consisted of state income taxes of $1,700 and charitable contributions of $4,150. Her itemized deductions exceed the standard deduction ($5,700 in 2010) by $150 ($1,700 + $4,150 − $5,700). If Chris received a state income tax refund of $200 in 2011 she must report only $150 as gross income in 2011. She benefited only from $150 of the deduction and so that is all she has to report as income. ◀

CLAIM OF RIGHT

Sometimes taxpayers receive disputed amounts. For example, a contractor may receive payment on a job when the quality of the work is being questioned by the customer, a salesperson may receive commissions when there is a question as to whether the sales are final, or a litigant may receive a court award even though the case is on appeal. Under the claim of right doctrine, the recipient of a disputed amount must include the amount received in gross income as long as the use of the funds is unrestricted.

EXAMPLE I:3-38 ▶ Jane wins a court case against a customer requiring the customer to pay her $10,000. The customer is unhappy with the result of the case and indicates that he plans to appeal, but pays the $10,000 to avoid interest on the amount in the event he loses the appeal. Jane must include the $10,000 in gross income even though she will have to repay the amount if she loses the appeal. ◀

EXAMPLE I:3-39 ▶ Assume the same facts as in Example I:3-38 except that the $10,000 is placed in escrow by the court awaiting the outcome of the appeal. Jane does not have to report the amount as she does not have use of the funds. ◀

Of course, taxpayers may be required to repay the disputed amount in a subsequent year. Such taxpayers may deduct the previously reported amount in the year of repayment. The taxes saved from such a deduction, however, may be considerably less than the

---

[69] *F. Donald Arrowsmith Exr. v. CIR,* 42 AFTR 649, 52-2 USTC ¶9527 (USSC, 1952).   [70] Sec. 111.

original tax. If the repayment is over $3,000, taxpayers have the option of reducing the current tax by the tax paid in the prior year or years on the repaid amount.[71]

EXAMPLE I:3-40 ▶ Assume the same facts as in Example I:3-38, except that after reporting the disputed $10,000 Jane loses the appeal and must repay the $10,000 to her customer. If Jane was in the 25% tax bracket when she reported the disputed amount, she would have paid a $2,500 (0.25 × $10,000) tax on the disputed amount. If she were in the 15% bracket when she made the repayment, she would recover only $1,500 by deducting the $10,000. Because the amount exceeds $3,000, Jane has the option of determining her current year's tax by deducting from the tax she would otherwise pay the $2,500 tax she paid in the earlier year. This credit is allowed in lieu of receiving a $10,000 deduction. ◀

TAX PLANNING CONSIDERATIONS

SHIFTING INCOME

A family can reduce its taxes by shifting income from family members who are in high tax brackets (e.g., parents) to family members who are in low tax brackets (e.g., children). Assignment of income rules prevent shifting from being done by merely redirecting the payment. Thus, a father cannot avoid a tax on his salary by ordering his employer to pay the salary to his daughter. Nevertheless, income can be shifted by transferring ownership of the property. For example, children may own stock in the family business. Dividends on the stock are taxed to the children. In the case of a child under age 24, however, the parents' (as opposed to the child's) tax rate often applies to unearned income in excess of $1,800. Series EE bonds may prove useful to avoid the kiddie tax because the interest is deferred until the bond is redeemed or matures. The maturity date, of course, may be after the child reaches age 24. Another shifting technique is for the child to work for the family business and be paid a reasonable salary. Such income is taxed at the child's tax rate, even if the child is under 24 years old, and can be offset by the child's own standard deduction.

Shifting of income is constrained by several factors. As noted, the assignment of income doctrine limits transfers. Reasonableness limitations constrain compensation and other payments. Furthermore, outright gifts of property are subject to gift taxes. Also, individuals are reluctant to transfer wealth to children for a variety of personal reasons. However, the tax saving potential of shifting income is often so great as to prompt many well-to-do families to use available shifting techniques.

ALIMONY

Whether payments made in connection with a divorce or separation are classified as alimony is of major tax significance. Such classification results in a deduction for the payor and income to the payee. Alimony is actually one way to shift income.

EXAMPLE I:3-41 ▶ Tony, who has a 35% marginal tax rate, makes payments of $40,000 to his former wife. If it is deductible as alimony, Tony will save $14,000 (0.35 × $40,000) a year in federal income taxes. The amount of tax that the former wife must pay depends on how much other income she has and whether she has deductions that reduce the tax. Her tax might be as high as her former husband's or as little as zero. ◀

ADDITIONAL COMMENT

In 2006, $9.1 billion of alimony paid was reported as a deduction, while only $8.1 billion was reported as taxable income.

Two points are clear. One is that both parties should understand the implication of having amounts treated as alimony. Second, the designation of the payments as alimony may be beneficial to both parties. The payor will, of course, benefit from a tax deduction. The payee may benefit because the payor may agree to make larger alimony payments since the payments are tax deductible.

---

[71] Sec. 1341.

PREPAID INCOME

As explained earlier in this chapter, prepaid income is generally taxable when received. This accelerated recognition of income may be a significant disadvantage to the taxpayer if the related expenses are incurred in a later tax year. Thus, tax planning for prepaid amounts is essential.

EXAMPLE I:3-42 ▶ Phil owns an apartment complex and requires tenants to pay the first and last months' rent before they move in. Rita, on the other hand, owns an apartment complex and requires tenants to pay the first month's rent and a refundable deposit (which equals one month's rent). Although the full amount received by Phil is taxable when it is received, only one-half of the amount received by Rita is taxable when it is received. Rita is required to refund the deposit, assuming the tenant vacates leaving the property in good condition and having paid all rent. Therefore, the deposit is not taxable. ◀

HISTORICAL NOTE

In 1954 Congress passed Sec. 452, allowing deferral of certain prepaid income, but in 1955 Congress retroactively repealed this section.

Taxpayers receiving advance payments in connection with services may be able to meet the requirements of Rev. Proc. 2004-34 (discussed earlier in the chapter); taxpayers receiving advance payments associated with the sale of merchandise may be able to meet the requirements of Reg. Sec. 1.451-5 (also discussed in this chapter). Also, special rules exist for subscription income, membership fees, crop insurance proceeds, and drought sales of livestock, all of which allow taxpayers to defer recognizing income.

TAXABLE, TAX-EXEMPT, OR TAX-DEFERRED BONDS

Which should a taxpayer choose: taxable bonds, tax-exempt bonds, or tax-deferred bonds? The answer depends on the relative interest rates and the taxpayer's current and future tax brackets. **Taxable bonds** yield the highest return, but the interest is taxable. **Tax-exempt bonds** yield a lower return. **Tax-deferred bonds** generally yield a return somewhere close to that of taxable bonds. Interest on U.S. Series EE savings bonds is tax exempt if it is used for educational purposes and if other requirements of Sec. 135 are met (see the discussion earlier in this chapter). If these conditions are not met, the tax is deferred until the bonds are redeemed. The taxpayer may be in a lower bracket when the tax is eventually paid, and in the meantime, the interest that will eventually go to pay taxes is earning additional income.

The decision between taxable and exempt bonds is a rather easy one if the risk of the investments is assumed to be approximately equal. A taxpayer should invest in exempt bonds instead of taxable bonds if the interest on the exempt bonds is greater than the interest on the taxable bonds multiplied by 1 minus the taxpayer's marginal tax bracket (expressed as a decimal). Stated in a formula, this means invest in tax-exempt bonds if

$$\text{Return on the tax-exempt bonds} > \text{Return on the taxable bonds} \times (1 - \text{Marginal tax bracket})$$

EXAMPLE I:3-43 ▶ Robert's marginal tax bracket is 35% and he is trying to decide between tax-exempt bonds, which pay 6% interest, and taxable bonds paying 8% interest. Robert should invest in the exempt bonds because 6% is greater than 5.2% [0.08 × (1 − 0.35)]. ◀

Comparison of taxable bonds or exempt bonds to tax-deferred bonds is more complicated. As noted, the advantages of the tax-deferred bonds are twofold. First, the taxpayer may be in a lower tax bracket when the tax is paid (e.g., taxpayers who plan to redeem the bonds after retirement). Second, the amount that will eventually go to pay the tax earns income until the tax must be paid. Although the computation is not covered here, it is noted that taxpayers who anticipate that they will be in lower tax brackets and who plan to leave funds invested for several years may benefit from choosing Series EE U.S. savings bonds over taxable bonds. See Chapter I:18 in the *Individuals* text for a further discussion of taxable, tax exempt, and tax deferred investments.

REPORTING SAVINGS BOND INTEREST

It may be desirable to purchase Series EE bonds in the child's name despite the fact that such interest is subject to the kiddie tax (see Chapter I:2). This is because there is no

income tax as long as the child's annual income is less than $900. However, even if a child is not otherwise required to file a return, it is necessary to report interest on Series EE bonds annually by filing a tax return.[72] Taxpayers who have not been reporting savings bond interest annually may change to annual reporting, but are required to report both current and previously accrued interest in the year of the change.[73]

Taxpayers who report savings bond interest annually are allowed to change to the deferral method without IRS approval.[74] This is particularly useful where the decision to report interest currently was made before the imposition of the kiddie tax. Taxpayers who make this election are bound by it for five years.

DEFERRED COMPENSATION ARRANGEMENTS

Deferred compensation plans can be used as a means of avoiding the constructive receipt of income. Although income is normally taxable when the funds become available to the taxpayer, an advance contractual agreement can produce different results. Corporate executives, professional athletes, and others often sign agreements providing for compensation to be paid at future dates. Such agreements can produce tax savings because the recipients expect to be in a lower tax bracket. Because the arrangements are advance contractual agreements, the deferral of income does not constitute taxpayers "turning their backs" on the income.

EXAMPLE I:3-44 ▶ Alonzo, a 35-year-old professional basketball player, signs a contract specifying that he will be paid $400,000 per year for ten years even if he does not play. Because of his age, both Alonzo and the team recognize that he will probably play for one or two more years. If the agreement had specified that he was to receive a salary of $1,300,000 per year for two years, most of the income would have been taxed at the highest rates. By spreading the amount over a longer period, Alonzo pays tax at lower rates on much of the income. Alonzo is compensated for the delayed payment by receiving a larger total amount [i.e., $4 million ($400,000 × 10 years) versus $2.6 million ($1.3 million × 2 years)]. ◀

COMPLIANCE AND PROCEDURAL CONSIDERATIONS

ADDITIONAL COMMENT

The dollar amount of tax-exempt interest income is recorded on Form 1040, line 8b, but is not included in the tax base. The IRS requires the reporting of this type of income probably because it may affect the taxability of Social Security benefits.

Form 1040 lists various types of income. Some items of income (wages, tax refunds, alimony, pensions and annuities, unemployment compensation, Social Security benefits, and other income) are listed directly on Form 1040. Most expenses related to these items of income are deducted as miscellaneous itemized deductions on Schedule A.

Most other types of income (and related deductions) are reported on special schedules.

Topic Review I:3-3 summarizes the procedures for reporting income and related deductions.

EXAMPLE I:3-45 ▶ John J. Alexander has several items of income and related deductions:

KEY POINT

The amount labeled "total income" on line 22 of Form 1040 is not gross income, adjusted gross income, or taxable income.

Salary		$40,000
Deductible alimony payments		6,000
Taxable interest		300
Dividends:	Ford Motor Co.	1,150
	Omaha Mutual Fund	430
	Capital Gain Distribution: Omaha Mutual Fund	50
Rent income (depreciation, interest, repairs, and other related expenses total $9,000)		11,000

The reporting of these items of income is illustrated on page 1 of Form 1040 (Figure I:3-1) and on Schedule B of Form 1040 (Figure I:3-2). Salary and interest (because the interest is less than $1,500) are entered directly on Form 1040. Rental income would be entered on Schedule E (not illustrated), and the net income after deducting related expenses is transferred to Form 1040. Alimony received and alimony payments are reported on page 1 of Form 1040. ◀

[72] *Philip Apkin*, 86 T.C. 692 (1986).
[73] Reg. Sec. 1.454-1(a)(4), Ex. (1).

[74] Rev. Proc. 89-46, 1989-2 C.B. 597.

Topic Review I:3-3

Reporting of Income

TYPE OF INCOME	REPORTED ON	RELATED DEDUCTIONS ARE CLAIMED ON
Wages, salaries, tips, etc.	Form 1040	Schedule A and various other forms: moving, Form 3903; travel, transportation, etc., Form 2106
Interest	Form 1040 (if less than $1,500), otherwise Schedule B	Schedule A (miscellaneous deductions if any, e.g., safe deposit box fees)
Dividends	Form 1040 (if less than $1,500), otherwise Schedule B	Schedule A (miscellaneous deductions if any, e.g., safe deposit box fees)
Refund of state or local income taxes	Form 1040 (instructions contain a worksheet)	Schedule A (miscellaneous deductions if any, e.g., fee paid for tax advice)
Alimony	Form 1040	Schedule A (miscellaneous deduction, if any, e.g., legal fee associated with alimony)
Business income	Schedule C or C-EZ (net income or loss is transferred to Form 1040)	Schedule C or C-EZ (e.g., depreciation, advertising, repairs)
Capital gains	Schedule D	Schedule D (capital losses) or Schedule A (investment expenses)
Supplemental gains	Form 4797	Form 4797 (e.g., ordinary losses)
Pensions and annuities	Form 1040 (instructions contain a worksheet)	Generally no related deductions
Rents, royalties, partnerships, S corporations, estates, trusts, etc.	Schedule E	Schedule E
Farm income	Schedule F	Schedule F
Unemployment compensation	Form 1040	Generally no related deductions
Social Security benefits	Form 1040 (instructions contain a worksheet)	Generally no related deductions
Other income	Form 1040	Schedule A (miscellaneous deductions, if any)

PROBLEM MATERIALS

DISCUSSION QUESTIONS

I:3-1 What phrase is found in both the Sixteenth Amendment to the Constitution and Sec. 61(a)? Why does the phrase appear in both locations?

I:3-2 Contrast the accounting and economic concepts of income.

I:3-3 Why does the tax concept of income more closely resemble the accounting concept of income than the economic concept?

I:3-4 Explain the meaning of the term *wherewithal to pay* as it applies to taxation.

I:3-5 If a loan is repaid, the lender does not have to include the repayment in gross income. There is no exclusion in the tax law that permits taxpayers to omit such amounts from gross income. How can this be explained?

I:3-6 A landlord who receives prepaid rent is required to report that amount as gross income when the payment is received. Why would Congress choose to do this? What problem does this create for the taxpayer?

I:3-7 Office space is often rented without carpet, wall covering, or window covering. Furthermore, many rental agreements specify that these improvements cannot be removed by a tenant if removal causes any damage to the property. What issue does this raise?

I:3-8 Does the fact that an item of income is paid in a form other than cash mean it is nontaxable? Explain.

I:3-9 Explain the significance of *Lucas v. Earl* and *Helvering v. Horst*.

I:3-10 Under present-day tax law, community property rules are followed in allocating income between husband and wife. Is this consistent with *Lucas v. Earl?* Explain.

Form 1040 — Department of the Treasury—Internal Revenue Service

U.S. Individual Income Tax Return 2009 (99) IRS Use Only—Do not write or staple in this space.

OMB No. 1545-0074

For the year Jan. 1–Dec. 31, 2009, or other tax year beginning _____, 2009, ending _____, 20___

Label

(See instructions on page 14.)

Use the IRS label.
Otherwise, please print or type.

Your first name and initial: **John J.** Last name: **Alexander**

Your social security number: **123 45 6789**

If a joint return, spouse's first name and initial: ___ Last name: ___

Spouse's social security number:

Home address (number and street). If you have a P.O. box, see page 14. **41 Oak St** Apt. no.: ___

▲ You **must** enter your SSN(s) above. ▲

City, town or post office, state, and ZIP code. If you have a foreign address, see page 14. **Orlando, Fl 32816**

Checking a box below will not change your tax or refund.

Presidential Election Campaign ▶ Check here if you, or your spouse if filing jointly, want $3 to go to this fund (see page 14) ▶ ☐ You ☐ Spouse

Filing Status

Check only one box.

1. ☒ Single
2. ☐ Married filing jointly (even if only one had income)
3. ☐ Married filing separately. Enter spouse's SSN above and full name here. ▶
4. ☐ Head of household (with qualifying person). (See page 15.) If the qualifying person is a child but not your dependent, enter this child's name here. ▶
5. ☐ Qualifying widow(er) with dependent child (see page 16)

Exemptions

6a ☒ **Yourself.** If someone can claim you as a dependent, **do not** check box 6a
b ☐ **Spouse**

c Dependents:

(1) First name Last name	(2) Dependent's social security number	(3) Dependent's relationship to you	(4) ✓ if qualifying child for child tax credit (see page 17)
			☐
			☐
			☐
			☐

If more than four dependents, see page 17 and check here ▶ ☐

d Total number of exemptions claimed

Boxes checked on 6a and 6b: **1**
No. of children on 6c who:
• lived with you
• did not live with you due to divorce or separation (see page 18)
Dependents on 6c not entered above
Add numbers on lines above ▶ **1**

Income

Attach Form(s) W-2 here. Also attach Forms W-2G and 1099-R if tax was withheld.

If you did not get a W-2, see page 22.

Enclose, but do not attach, any payment. Also, please use **Form 1040-V.**

7	Wages, salaries, tips, etc. Attach Form(s) W-2	7	40,000
8a	**Taxable** interest. Attach Schedule B if required	8a	300
b	**Tax-exempt** interest. **Do not** include on line 8a 8b		
9a	Ordinary dividends. Attach Schedule B if required	9a	1,580
b	Qualified dividends (see page 22) 9b		
10	Taxable refunds, credits, or offsets of state and local income taxes (see page 23)	10	
11	Alimony received	11	
12	Business income or (loss). Attach Schedule C or C-EZ	12	
13	Capital gain or (loss). Attach Schedule D if required. If not required, check here ▶ ☐	13	50
14	Other gains or (losses). Attach Form 4797	14	
15a	IRA distributions 15a b Taxable amount (see page 24)	15b	
16a	Pensions and annuities 16a b Taxable amount (see page 25)	16b	
17	Rental real estate, royalties, partnerships, S corporations, trusts, etc. Attach Schedule E	17	2,000
18	Farm income or (loss). Attach Schedule F	18	
19	Unemployment compensation in excess of $2,400 per recipient (see page 27)	19	
20a	Social security benefits 20a b Taxable amount (see page 27)	20b	
21	Other income. List type and amount (see page 29) _____	21	
22	Add the amounts in the far right column for lines 7 through 21. This is your **total income** ▶	22	43,930

Adjusted Gross Income

23	Educator expenses (see page 29) 23		
24	Certain business expenses of reservists, performing artists, and fee-basis government officials. Attach Form 2106 or 2106-EZ 24		
25	Health savings account deduction. Attach Form 8889 25		
26	Moving expenses. Attach Form 3903 26		
27	One-half of self-employment tax. Attach Schedule SE 27		
28	Self-employed SEP, SIMPLE, and qualified plans 28		
29	Self-employed health insurance deduction (see page 30) 29		
30	Penalty on early withdrawal of savings 30		
31a	Alimony paid b Recipient's SSN ▶ 987 65 4321 31a 6,000		
32	IRA deduction (see page 31) 32		
33	Student loan interest deduction (see page 34) 33		
34	Tuition and fees deduction. Attach Form 8917 34		
35	Domestic production activities deduction. Attach Form 8903 35		
36	Add lines 23 through 31a and 32 through 35	36	6,000
37	Subtract line 36 from line 22. This is your **adjusted gross income** ▶	37	37,930

For Disclosure, Privacy Act, and Paperwork Reduction Act Notice, see page 97. Cat. No. 11320B Form **1040** (2009)

FIGURE I:3-1 ▶ FORM 1040 (PAGE 1)

SCHEDULE B
(Form 1040A or 1040)

Department of the Treasury
Internal Revenue Service (99)

Interest and Ordinary Dividends

▶ Attach to Form 1040A or 1040.　　▶ See instructions on back.

OMB No. 1545-0074

2009

Attachment
Sequence No. **08**

Name(s) shown on return	Your social security number
John J. Alexander	123　45　6789

Part I
Interest

(See instructions on back and the instructions for Form 1040A, or Form 1040, line 8a.)

Note. If you received a Form 1099-INT, Form 1099-OID, or substitute statement from a brokerage firm, list the firm's name as the payer and enter the total interest shown on that form.

		Amount
1	List name of payer. If any interest is from a seller-financed mortgage and the buyer used the property as a personal residence, see instructions on back and list this interest first. Also, show that buyer's social security number and address ▶	**1**
2	Add the amounts on line 1	**2**
3	Excludable interest on series EE and I U.S. savings bonds issued after 1989. Attach Form 8815	**3**
4	Subtract line 3 from line 2. Enter the result here and on Form 1040A, or Form 1040, line 8a ▶	**4**

Note. If line 4 is over $1,500, you must complete Part III.

Part II
Ordinary Dividends

(See instructions on back and the instructions for Form 1040A, or Form 1040, line 9a.)

Note. If you received a Form 1099-DIV or substitute statement from a brokerage firm, list the firm's name as the payer and enter the ordinary dividends shown on that form.

		Amount
5	List name of payer ▶	**5**
	Ford Motor Company	1,150
	Omaha Mutual Fund	430
6	Add the amounts on line 5. Enter the total here and on Form 1040A, or Form 1040, line 9a ▶	**6**　1,580

Note. If line 6 is over $1,500, you must complete Part III.

Part III
Foreign Accounts and Trusts

(See instructions on back.)

You must complete this part if you **(a)** had over $1,500 of taxable interest or ordinary dividends; **(b)** had a foreign account; or **(c)** received a distribution from, or were a grantor of, or a transferor to, a foreign trust.

		Yes	No
7a	At any time during 2009, did you have an interest in or a signature or other authority over a financial account in a foreign country, such as a bank account, securities account, or other financial account? See instructions on back for exceptions and filing requirements for Form TD F 90-22.1		X
b	If "Yes," enter the name of the foreign country ▶		
8	During 2009, did you receive a distribution from, or were you the grantor of, or transferor to, a foreign trust? If "Yes," you may have to file Form 3520. See instructions on back		X

For Paperwork Reduction Act Notice, see Form 1040A or 1040 instructions.　　Cat. No. 17146N　　Schedule B (Form 1040A or 1040) 2009

FIGURE I:3-2　　▶　SCHEDULES A & B (PAGE 2)

I:3-11 Ricardo owns a small unincorporated business. His 15-year-old daughter Jane works in the business on a part-time basis and was paid wages of $3,000 during the current year. Who is taxed on the child's earnings: Jane or her father? Explain.

I:3-12 Define the term *constructive receipt*. Explain its importance.

I:3-13 Explain three restrictions on the concept of constructive receipt.

I:3-14 When is income considered to be earned by an accrual-basis taxpayer?

I:3-15 a. Explain the difference between the treatment of prepaid income under the tax law and under financial accounting.
b. Why are the two treatments so different?
c. What problem does this treatment create for taxpayers?

I:3-16 Under what conditions is an accrual-basis taxpayer allowed to defer reporting amounts received in the advance of the delivery of goods?

I:3-17 Under what conditions is an accrual-basis taxpayer allowed to defer reporting advance payments received for services?

I:3-18 a. Is the interest received from government obligations taxable? Explain.
b. What impact does the fact that some bond interest is tax exempt have on interest rates?
c. Is an investor always better off buying tax-exempt bonds? Explain.

I:3-19 Corporations are taxed on the income they earn, and shareholders are taxed on the dividends they receive. What provisions in the tax law reduce this "double tax" burden?

I:3-20 Explain the relationship between dividends and earnings and profits.

I:3-21 On what basis did the Supreme Court in *Eisner v. Macomber* decide that stock dividends are nontaxable?

I:3-22 What is the significance of a constructive dividend?

I:3-23 Explain the importance of the distinction between alimony and a property settlement.

I:3-24 a. Are items of income not listed in Sec. 61 taxable? Explain.
b. Because there is no specific exclusion for unrealized income, why is it not taxable?
c. Can income be realized even when a cash-method taxpayer does not receive cash?
d. Does a cash basis taxpayer realize income upon the receipt of a note?

I:3-25 a. Briefly explain the tax benefit rule.
b. Is a taxpayer required to report the reimbursement of a medical expense by insurance as income if the reimbursement is received in the year following the year of the expenditure?

I:3-26 What opportunities are available for a taxpayer to defer the recognition of certain types of prepaid income? That is, what advice could you give someone who wishes to defer the reporting of prepaid income?

I:3-27 Taxpayers who deduct an expense one year but recover it the next year are required to include the recovered amount in gross income. The tax benefit rule provides relief if the original deduction did not result in any tax savings. Does this rule provide relief to taxpayers who are in a higher tax bracket in the year they recover the previously deducted expense?

I:3-28 George, a wealthy investor, is uncertain whether he should invest in taxable or tax-exempt bonds. What tax and nontax factors should he consider?

I:3-29 Do you agree or disagree with the following statement: A taxpayer should not have to report income when debt is forgiven because the taxpayer receives nothing. Explain.

I:3-30 Jack and June are retired and receive $10,000 of social security benefits and taxable pensions totaling $25,000. They have been offered $20,000 for a automobile that they restored after they retired. They did most of the restoration work themselves and the sale will result in a gain of $12,000. What tax issues should Jack and June consider?

ISSUE IDENTIFICATION QUESTIONS

I:3-31 State Construction Company is owned equally by Andy, Bill, and Charlie. Andy works in the corporation full-time, and Bill and Charlie work elsewhere. When Andy left his previous job to work for State, he signed a contract specifying that he would receive a salary of $50,000 per year. This year, Andy felt that the company could expand if it purchased more equipment, and he offered to delay receiving $20,000 of his salary so the funds could be used to purchase the equipment. Bill and Charlie agreed, and the equipment was purchased. It is expected that State will have enough cash to pay Andy by early March of next year. What tax issues should Andy consider?

I:3-32 Lisa and her daughter Jane are equal shareholders in Lisa's Flooring, Inc. Lisa founded the corporation and was the sole owner for over twenty years. The company is very successful and Lisa has accumulated a fairly large estate. When Jane turned age twenty-five last year, Lisa gave her half of the corporation's stock. The gift was properly reported on Lisa's gift tax return. Both Lisa and Jane now work full-time for the corporation. Lisa received

a salary of $55,000 per year before Jane started working for the company. After Jane started working, Lisa reduced her salary to $15,000 and started paying Jane a salary of $50,000. Lisa indicates that she still makes most major decisions in the company, but she hopes that Jane will play a more important role as she becomes more familiar with the company. What tax issues should Lisa and the corporation consider?

I:3-33 Larry's Art Gallery sells oil paintings, lithographs, and bronzes to collectors and corporations. Customers often come to Larry looking for special pieces. In order to meet customer needs, Larry often accepts orders and then travels looking for the desired item, which he purchases and delivers to the customer. The pieces are expensive, and Larry requires customers to demonstrate their sincerity by providing deposits. If it turns out that the item costs more than expected, Larry contacts the buyer and asks for additional funds. If the item costs less than expected, Larry refunds the excess amount. Also, Larry sometimes returns amounts he received in advance because he is unable to find what the customer wants. What tax issues should Larry's Art Gallery consider?

PROBLEMS

I:3-34 *Noncash Compensation.* For each of the following items indicate, whether the individual taxpayer must include any amount in gross income.
a. Employees of Eastside Bookstore are given their birthdays off with pay.
b. Westside Hardware, Inc., gave each employee 10 shares of Westside stock worth $100 per share in lieu of a cash bonus.
c. Employees of Northside Manufacturing were allowed to take home the company's old computers when the company purchased new ones.

I:3-35 *Constructive Receipt.* Which of the following constitutes constructive receipt in the current year ended December 31?
a. A salary check received at 6:00 p.m. on December 31, after all the banks have closed.
b. A rent check received on December 30 by the manager of an apartment complex. The manager normally collects the rent for the owner. The owner was out of town.
c. A paycheck received on December 29 that was not honored by the bank because the employer's account did not have sufficient funds.
d. A check received on December 30. The check was postdated January 2 of the following year.
e. A check received on January 2. The check had been mailed on December 30.

I:3-36 *Cash and Accrual Methods.* Carmen opens a retail store. Her sales during the first year are $600,000, of which $30,000 has not been collected at year-end. Her purchases are $400,000. She still owes $20,000 to her suppliers, and at year-end she has $50,000 of inventory on hand. She incurred operating expenses of $160,000. At year-end she has not paid $15,000 of the expenses.
a. Compute her net income from the business assuming she elects the accrual method.
b. Compute her net income from the business assuming she elects the cash method.
c. Would paying the $15,000 she owes for operating expenses before year-end change her net income under accrual method of reporting? under the cash method?

I:3-37 *Series EE Bond Interest.* In 2006, Harry and Mary purchased Series EE bonds, and in 2010 redeemed the bonds, receiving $500 of interest and $1,500 of principal. Their income from other sources totaled $30,000. They paid $2,200 in tuition and fees for their dependent daughter. Their daughter is a qualified student at State University.
a. How much of the Series EE bond interest is excludable?
b. Assuming that the daughter received a $1,000 scholarship, how much of the interest is excludable? Ignore any tax credits that might be available.
c. Assuming the daughter received the $1,000 scholarship and that the parents' income from other sources is $110,600, how much of the interest is excludable?

I:3-38 *Alimony.* As a result of their divorce, Fred agrees to pay alimony to Tammy of $20,000 per year. The payments are to cease in the event of Fred's or Tammy's death or in the event of Tammy's remarriage. In addition, Tammy is to receive their residence, which cost them $100,000 but is worth $140,000.
a. Does the fact that Tammy receives the residence at the time of the divorce mean that there is a reduction in alimony, which will lead to Fred having to recapture an amount in the subsequent year?
b. How will the $20,000 payments be treated by Fred and Tammy?

c. Would recapture of the payments be necessary if payment ceased because of Tammy's remarriage?

d. What is Tammy's basis in the residence?

I:3-39   *Constructive Dividend.* Brad owns a successful corporation that has substantial earnings and profits. During the year, the following payments were made by the corporation:

a. Salary of $250,000 to Brad. Officers in other corporations performing similar services receive between $50,000 and $85,000.

b. Rent of $25,000 to Brad. The rent is paid in connection with an office building owned by Brad and used by the corporation. Similar buildings rent for about the same amount.

c. Salary of $5,000 to Brad's daughter, who worked for the company full-time during the summer and part-time during the rest of the year while she attended high school.

d. Alimony of $40,000 to Brad's former wife. Although Brad was personally obligated to make the payments, he used corporation funds to make the payments.

Discuss the likelihood of these payments being treated as constructive dividends. If a payment is deemed to be a constructive dividend, indicate how such a payment will be treated.

I:3-40   *Constructive Dividend.* Which of the following would likely be a constructive dividend?

a. An unreasonable salary paid to a shareholder.

b. An unreasonable salary paid to the daughter of a shareholder.

c. A sale of a corporation's asset to a shareholder at fair market value.

d. A payment by a corporation of a shareholder's debts.

e. A payment by a corporation of a shareholder's personal expenses.

I:3-41   *Prepaid Rent.* Stan rented an office building to Clay for $3,000 per month. On December 29, 2009, Stan received a deposit of $4,000 in addition to the first and last months' rent. Occupancy began on January 2, 2010. On July 15, 2010, Clay closed his business and filed for bankruptcy. Stan had collected rent for February, March, and April on the first of each month. Stan had received May rent on May 10, but collected no payments afterwards. Stan withheld $800 from the deposit because of damage to the property and $1,500 for unpaid rent. He refunded the balance of the deposit to Clay. What amount would Stan report as gross income for 2009? for 2010?

I:3-42   *Rental Income.* Ed owns Oak Knoll Apartments. During the year, Fred, a tenant, moved to another state. Fred paid Ed $1,000 to cancel the two-year lease he had signed. Ed subsequently rented the unit to Wayne. Wayne paid the first and last months' rents of $800 each and a security deposit of $500. Ed also owns a building that is used as a health club. The club has signed a fifteen-year lease at an annual rental of $17,000. The owner of the club requested that Ed install a swimming pool on the property. Ed declined to do so. The owner of the club finally constructed the pool himself at a cost of $15,000. What amount must Ed include in gross income?

I:3-43   *Gross Income.* Susan's salary is $44,000 and she received dividends of $600. She received a statement from SJ partnership indicating that her share of the partnership's income was $4,000. The partnership distributed $1,000 to her during the year and $600 after year-end. She won $2,000 in the state lottery and spent $50 on lottery tickets. Which amounts are taxable?

I:3-44   *Interest Income.* Holly inherited $10,000 of City of Atlanta bonds in February. In March, she received interest of $500, and in April she sold the bonds at a $200 gain. Holly redeemed Series EE U.S. savings bonds that she had purchased several years ago. The accumulated interest totaled $800. Holly received $300 of interest on bonds issued by the City of Quebec, Canada. What amount, if any, of gross income must Holly report?

I:3-45   *Annuity Income.* Tim retired during the current year at age 58. He purchased an annuity from American National Life Company for $40,000. The annuity pays Tim $500 per month for life.

a. Compute Tim's annual exclusion.

b. How much income will Tim report each year after reaching age 84?

I:3-46   *Pension Income.* Beth turns 65 and retires from her position as a garment worker. She immediately began receiving a monthly pension for the remainder of her life of $300 from a qualified retirement plan. Over the years she worked, Beth made $13,104 of nondeductible contributions to the pension fund through withholding. How much must Beth report as income from the pension during the current year assuming she received 12 monthly payments?

I:3-47 *Social Security Benefits.* Dan and Diana file a joint return. Dan earned $31,000 during the year before losing his job. Diana received Social Security benefits of $5,000.

    a. Determine the taxable portion of the Social Security benefits.

    b. What is the taxable portion of the Social Security benefits if Dan earned $45,000 before losing his job?

I:3-48 *Social Security Benefits.* Lucia is a 69-year-old single individual who receives a taxable pension of $10,000 per year and Social Security benefits of $7,000. Lucia is considering the possibility of selling stock she has owned for years and using the funds to purchase a summer home. She will realize a gain of $20,000 when she sells the stock, which has been paying $1,000 of dividends each year. Lucia says her brother recommended that she sell half of the stock this year and half next year because selling all of the stock at once would affect the tax treatment of her Social Security benefits.

    a. Compute her AGI under the assumption she sells all of the stock now after receiving $1,000 dividends from the stock.

    b. Repeat the computation under the assumption she sells only half of the stock this year and also receives $1,000 dividends from the stock.

I:3-49 *Social Security Benefits.* Bob is a single individual and received a salary of $27,000 before he retired in October of this year. After he retired, he received Social Security benefits of $3,000 during the year.

    a. What amount, if any, of the Social Security benefits are taxable for the year?

    b. Would the answer be different if Bob also had $1,000 of tax exempt interest?

    c. What if he had had $10,000 of tax exempt interest?

I:3-50 *Adjusted Gross Income.* Amir, who is single, retired from his job this year. He received a salary of $25,000 for the portion of the year that he worked, tax-exempt interest of $3,000, and dividends from domestic corporations of $2,700. On September 1, he began receiving monthly pension payments of $1,000 and Social Security payments of $600. Assume an exclusion ratio of 40% for the pension. Amir owns a duplex that he rents to others. He received rent of $12,000 and incurred $17,000 of expenses related to the duplex. He continued to actively manage the property after he retired from his job. Compute Amir's adjusted gross income.

I:3-51 *Recovery of Previously Deducted Expense.* In 2011, Fred received a $1,000 refund of state income taxes withheld from his salary during 2010. For each of the following cases, indicate whether Fred must include any portion of the refund in his 2011 gross income.

    a. Fred did not itemize during 2010.

    b. Fred does not itemize during 2011.

    c. Fred uses the accrual method for determining his deduction for state income taxes.

    d. Fred suffered a net loss during 2010 of $20,000.

    e. Fred suffered a net loss during 2011 of $20,000.

    f. Fred's itemized deductions during 2011 exceeded the standard deduction by $400.

I:3-52 *Recovery of Previously Deducted Expense.* As the result of unexpected surgery, Jan incurred $14,000 of medical expenses in 2010. At the end of 2010, her medical insurance had paid only $5,000. Jan anticipates that the company will eventually pay an additional $7,000 of the bill. Because her AGI is $30,000 and there is a 7.5% floor for medical deductions, Jan can deduct medical expenses over $2,250. Her other itemized deductions exceed the standard deduction.

    a. If Jan pays the balance of the $9,000 medical expenses before the end of the year, can she claim a deduction in 2010?

    b. If she is reimbursed $7,000 in 2011, how will the reimbursement be treated?

I:3-53 *Court Awards and Insurance Settlements.* What amount, if any, must be included in gross income by the following taxpayers?

    a. Ann received $2,000 from her insurance company when her automobile which cost $3,000 was stolen.

    b. Barry received $3,000 from his brother. Barry had initiated a lawsuit against his brother in an effort to recover $3,000 he had previously loaned to him. The brother paid Barry back before the case was tried, and Barry dropped the lawsuit.

    c. Carry, an accountant, sued a client in order to collect her fee for doing tax work. Would Carry's accounting method make any difference?

    d. Dave has incurred $6,000 of medical expenses so far this year. He paid $400 of the expenses himself. His insurance company paid $4,000 of the expenses. The hospital is suing Dave and the insurance company for the balance, $1,600.

I:3-54 *Claim of Right.* USA Corporation hired Jesse to install a computer system for the company and paid him $8,000 for the work. USA soon realized that there were problems with the system and asked Jesse to refund the payment. At the end of the year the dispute had not been resolved. Jesse is in the 25% tax bracket in the year he did the original work. During the next year, when he is in the 15% tax bracket, Jesse refunds the $8,000 to USA.
a. Is the original payment taxable to Jesse when he receives it?
b. What options are available to Jesse when he repays the $8,000?
c. What option would have been available to Jesse if he had been asked to repay only $2,000?

I:3-55 *Tax Planning.* Bart and Kesha are in the 35% tax bracket. They are interested in reducing the taxes they pay each year. They are currently considering several alternatives. For each of the following alternatives, indicate how much tax, if any, they would save.
a. Make a gift of bonds valued at $5,000 that yield $400 per year interest to their 24-year-old daughter, who has no other income.
b. Sell the bonds from Part a rather than give them to their daughter, and buy tax-exempt bonds that pay 6%. Assume the bonds can be sold for an amount equal to their basis of $5,000.
c. Give $1,000 cash to a charity. Assume they itemize deductions.
d. Pay their daughter a salary of $10,000 for services rendered in their unincorporated business.

I:3-56 *Series EE Bond Interest and Kiddie Tax.* In 2010, Ken and Lynn paid $5,000 to purchase Series EE bonds in the name of their 11-year-old son. The son has no other income, and they are in the 28% tax bracket. The taxable interest during the first year will be $400 if an election is made to accrue the interest on an annual basis.
a. Will the child owe any tax on the bond interest?
b. Does the son need to file a tax return?
c. What are the tax consequences in 2010 and subsequent years if annual gifts are made to their son?

COMPREHENSIVE PROBLEMS

I:3-57 Matt and Sandy reside in a community property state. Matt left home in April 2010 because of disputes with his wife, Sandy. Subsequently, Matt earned $15,000. Before leaving home in April, Matt earned $3,000. Sandy was unaware of Matt's whereabouts or his earnings after he left home. The $3,000 earned by Matt before he left home was spent on food, housing, and other items shared by Matt and Sandy. Matt and Sandy have one child, who lived with Sandy after the husband left home.
a. Is any portion of Matt's earnings after he left home taxable to Sandy?
b. What filing status is applicable to Sandy if she filed a return?
c. How much income would Sandy be required to report if she filed?
d. Is Sandy required to file?

I:3-58 During 2010, Gary earned $57,000 as an executive. Gary, who is single, supported his half sister, who lives in a nursing home. Gary received the following interest: $400 on City of Los Angeles bonds, $200 on a money market account, and $2,100 on a loan made to his brother.

Gary spent one week serving on a jury and received $50.

Gary received a refund of federal income taxes withheld during the prior year of $1,200 and a state income tax refund of $140. Gary had itemized deductions last year of $8,000.

Gary received qualified dividends on Ace Corporation of $1,000 and on Tray Corporation of $1,400. Gary's itemized deductions equal $9,000, and withholding for federal income taxes is $8,000. Compute Gary's tax due or refund due for 2010.

TAX STRATEGY PROBLEMS

I:3-59 Kamal is starting a new business in 2010 which will operate as an S corporation. This means that income earned by the corporation will be reported by shareholders even if they do not receive distributions. Kamal has $120,000 of income from other sources, and itemized deductions totaling $15,000. He expects that the new business will produce $30,000 of income each year. He is considering giving his son Rashid 20% of the

stock in the corporation. Rashid is age 24, and is Kamal's dependent. Rashid's only other income is $2,000 of interest. Neither Kamal nor Rashid will be employed by the corporation. Which alternative will produce a lower income tax liability—having all stock owned by Kamal or having Kamal own 80% of the stock and Rashid own 20%? Assume Kamal's filing status is head-of-household and Rashid is single. Ignore other taxes. How would the answer be different if Rashid were age 17? Ignore credits.

I:3-60 Assume that it is December 31, and that Jake is considering making a $1,000 charitable contribution. Jake currently is in the 35% tax bracket, but expects that his tax bracket will be 28% next year. How much more will the deduction for the contribution be worth if it is made today compared to next year?

TAX FORM/RETURN PREPARATION PROBLEMS

I:3-61 Sally W. Emanual had the following dividends and interest during the current year:

Acorn Corporation bond interest		$ 700
City of Boston bonds interest		1,000
Camp Bank interest		1,250
Jet Corporation dividend (qualified)		1,300
North Mutual fund		
Capital gain distribution	100	
Ordinary dividend (qualified)	150	
Nontaxable distribution	200	450
Blue Corporation foreign dividend		250

Additional information pertaining to Sally Emanual includes

Salary	$30,000
Rent income	12,000
Expenses related to rent income	14,000
Pension benefits	8,000
Alimony paid to Sally	4,000

The taxable portion of the pension is $7,000. Sally actively participates in the rental activity. Other relevant information includes

Address: 430 Rumsey Place, West Falls, California 92699
Occupation: Credit manager
Social Security number: 123-45-4321
Marital status: Single

Complete Sally's Schedule B and page 1 of her Form 1040. Assume Schedule E has already been prepared.

CASE STUDY PROBLEMS

I:3-62 Jim and Linda are your tax clients. They were divorced two years ago, and the divorce decree stated that Jim was to make monthly payments to Linda. The court designated $300 per month as alimony and $200 per month as child support, or a total of $6,000 per year. Jim has been unemployed for much of the year and paid Linda $2,000 that he said was for child support. In addition, Jim transferred the title to a three-year-old automobile with a $4,000 FMV and basis of $7,000 in exchange for her promise not to pursue any claim she has against him for the unpaid child support and alimony. Does Linda have to report any alimony and is Jim entitled to an alimony deduction? Draft a memo for the file that discusses the tax consequences for both Jim and Linda.

I:3-63 John and Mary (your clients) have two small children and are looking for ways to help fund the children's college education. They have heard that Series EE bonds are a tax-favored way of saving and have requested your opinion on the tax consequences. They have asked your opinion regarding the relative advantages of purchasing Series EE bonds in their names versus the children's names. John and Mary have indicated that they expect to have a high level of income in the future and that their children may receive other income sources from future inheritances. Prepare a client memo making recommendations about the tax consequences of Series EE bond investments for John and Mary.

I:3-64 Lee and Jane have been your firm's clients for most of the twenty years they have been married. Recently Lee came to you and said that he and Jane are obtaining a divorce, and he wants you to help him with some of the tax and financial issues that may come up during the divorce. The next day, Jane called asking you for the same assistance. What ethical issues do you see in this case? What possible conflicts may arise if you represent both Lee and Jane?

TAX RESEARCH PROBLEM

I:3-65 William owns a building that is leased to Lester's Machine Shop. Lester requests that William rewire the building for new equipment Lester plans to purchase. The wiring would cost about $4,000, but would not increase the value of the building because its only use is in connection with the specialized equipment. Rather than lose Lester as a lessee, William agrees to forgo one month's rent of $1,000 if Lester will pay for the wiring. Because Lester does not want to move, he agrees. What amount, if any, must William include in gross income?

A partial list of research sources is

- Sec. 109
- Reg. Sec. 1.109-1
- *CIR v. Grace H. Cunningham*, 2 AFTR 2d 5511, 58-2 USTC ¶9771 (9th Cir., 1958)

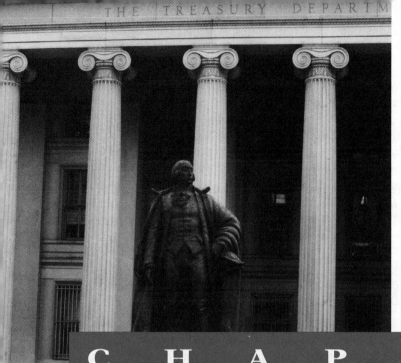

4

C H A P T E R

GROSS INCOME: EXCLUSIONS

LEARNING OBJECTIVES

After studying this chapter, you should be able to

1. ▶ Explain the conditions that must exist for an item to be excluded from gross income

2. ▶ Determine whether an item is income

3. ▶ Decide whether specific exclusions are available

4. ▶ Understand employment-related fringe benefit exclusion items

Chapter I:3 discussed items that must be included in gross income. This chapter considers items that are excluded from gross income. Under Sec. 61(a), all items of income are taxable unless specifically excluded. Taxpayers who wish to avoid being taxed have two basic alternatives. One approach is to establish that the item is not income. If an item is not income (e.g., if it is a return of capital), it is not subject to the income tax. The second approach is to establish that a specific exclusion applies to the item of income.

EXAMPLE I:4-1
KEY POINT

Given the sweeping definition of *income,* it is generally difficult to establish that an item is not income.

▶ Matt borrowed $10,000 from the bank. Although Matt received $10,000, it is not income because he is obligated to repay the amount borrowed. No specific statutory authority states that borrowed funds are excluded from taxation. Presumably, the fact that borrowed funds are not income is considered to be both fundamental and obvious. ◀

EXAMPLE I:4-2

▶ Sheila enrolled in State University. The university awarded her a $1,000 tuition scholarship because of her high admission test scores and grades. Section 117 excludes such scholarships from gross income. As a result, Sheila need not report the scholarship as income. ◀

OBJECTIVE 1

Explain the conditions that must exist for an item to be excluded from gross income

The major source of exclusions are those specific items contained in the IRC. These exclusions have evolved over the years and were enacted by Congress for a variety of reasons, including social and economic objectives.

Another source of exclusions are referred to as *administrative exclusions.* Exclusions exist because specific provisions in the Internal Revenue Code allow them. While the IRS has no authority to create exclusions, the IRS does have the authority to interpret the meaning of the Code. A liberal interpretation of the statute by the IRS may result in a broad definition of what constitutes an exclusion, and such a broad definition may reasonably be termed an administrative exclusion. For example, Sec. 102 excludes gifts received from gross income. The IRS has followed the practice of excluding certain welfare benefits from gross income, presumably because such benefits may be viewed as gifts.[1] The IRS could take the position that welfare benefits are not gifts. That position would no doubt be challenged in the courts.

REAL-WORLD EXAMPLE

Grants made to Native Americans by the federal government under the Indian Financing Act of 1974 to expand Native American–owned economic enterprises are excludable from gross income. Rev. Rul. 77-77, 1977-1 C.B. 11.

The term *judicial exclusions* should be considered in the same vein. Although the courts cannot create exclusions, they can interpret the statute and decide whether a particular item is covered by a statutory exclusion.

ITEMS THAT ARE NOT INCOME

OBJECTIVE 2

Determine whether an item is income

As noted above, some items are not income and, therefore, are not subject to the income tax. In addition to amounts obtained by a loan (discussed above), four other items are not considered income:

▶ Unrealized income
▶ Self-help income
▶ Rental value of personal-use property
▶ Gross selling price of property (as opposed to the profit or gain earned on the sale)

UNREALIZED INCOME

TYPICAL MISCONCEPTION

It is sometimes erroneously assumed that severance pay, embezzlement proceeds, gambling winnings, hobby income, prizes, rewards, and tips are not taxable.

Income that is not realized is not subject to income taxation. Thus, if a taxpayer owns stock in a company and the stock increases in value but the taxpayer does not sell the stock, no taxable income is realized.

This issue of the taxability of unrealized income was addressed over 80 years ago in *Eisner v. Macomber,* where the Supreme Court held that a stock dividend cannot be taxed

---

[1] For example, see Rev. Rul. 57-102, 1957-1 C.B. 26, which excludes from gross income public assistance payments to blind persons.

because the taxpayer had "received nothing that answers the definition of income within the meaning of the Sixteenth Amendment."[2] An ordinary stock dividend does not alter the existing proportionate ownership interest of any stockholder, nor does it increase the value of the individual's holdings. In effect, the Court concluded that realization must occur before income is recognized. Although narrowed by subsequent legislation and litigation, ordinary stock dividends continue to be excluded from gross income even today. Perhaps more important, *Eisner v. Macomber* established realization as a criterion for the recognition of income.

SELF-HELP INCOME

Although self-help income is considered as income by economists, it is not recognized as income by the IRS or by the courts. Taxpayers commonly benefit from activities such as painting their own homes or repairing their own automobiles. If a taxpayer hires someone else to do the work, the taxpayer has to earn income, pay tax on the income, and use the after-tax income to pay for the work. In either case, the taxpayer receives the same economic benefit, but the economic benefit derived from self-help is not included in the taxpayer's gross income.

This situation should be contrasted with taxable exchanges of services. A mechanic might agree to repair a painter's automobile in exchange for the painter's promise to paint the mechanic's home. In this instance, when the parties exchange services, each party realizes income equal to the value of the services received.

STOP & THINK

Question: The discussion of self-help income refers to an exchange of services between two individuals, such as a painter and a mechanic. How can a taxable barter transaction be distinguished from an act of friendship which is repaid?

Solution: When one person helps another without any promise of repayment, the act of kindness does not represent an exchange and is not taxable. Friends help one another from time to time without contractual reciprocity. As a result, such acts are not taxable. The distinction between a taxable barter exchange and acts of friendship is not always easy to make.

RENTAL VALUE OF PERSONAL-USE PROPERTY

Taxpayers are not taxed on the rental value of personally owned property. For example, taxpayers who own their own home receive the economic benefit of occupancy without being taxed on the rental value of the property. It would be very difficult to keep records and value benefits obtained from self-help and the personal use of property. For that reason, no significant effort has ever been made to tax such benefits.[3]

SELLING PRICE OF PROPERTY

If property is sold at a gain, the gain and not the entire sales price is taxable. Because the basic principle is almost universally accepted, the Supreme Court has never had to rule directly on whether the entire sale proceeds could be taxed. The IRS and the courts seemed to accept the basic principle even before the rule became part of the statute.[4] The primary reason for this principle (often referred to as the "recovery of capital" principle) is that a portion of the selling price represents a return of capital to the seller.

[2] 3 AFTR 3020, 1 USTC ¶32 (USSC, 1920).

[3] In 1928, the government tried unsuccessfully to tax the value of produce grown and consumed by a farmer (*Homer P. Morris*, 9 B.T.A. 1273 (1928)). The court stated, "To include the value of such products [would be to] in effect include in income something which Congress did not intend should be so regarded." The court did not explain how or why it reached this conclusion. In 1957, the IRS successfully disallowed the deduction of expenses incurred in raising such produce (*Robert L. Nowland v. CIR*, 51 AFTR 423, 57-1 USTC ¶9684 (4th Cir., 1957)).

[4] Section 202(a) of the Revenue Act of 1924 is the predecessor of current Sec. 1001(a), which states that only the gain portion of the sale proceeds is included in gross income. S. Rept. No. 398, 68th Cong., 1st Sess., p. 10 (1924) states that Sec. 202(a) sets forth general rules to be used in the computation of gain or loss. The Senate report further states that the provision "merely embodies in the law the present construction by the Department and the courts of the existing law."

MAJOR STATUTORY EXCLUSIONS

While Congress has created statutory exclusions for a variety of reasons, most exclusions have been enacted for reasons of social policy or reasons of incentive. The concept of social policy, that is, a concept of social generosity or benevolence, has prompted the government to exclude items such as:

▶ Gifts and inheritances (Sec. 102)

▶ Life insurance proceeds (Sec. 101)

▶ Public assistance payments

▶ Qualified adoption expenses (Sec. 137)

▶ Payments for personal physical sickness and injury (Sec. 104)

▶ Discharge of indebtedness during bankruptcy or insolvency (Sec. 108)

▶ Gain on sale of personal residence (Sec. 121)

▶ Partial exclusions for Social Security benefits (Sec. 86)

Other exclusions may be explained in terms of economic incentive, that is, the government's desire to encourage or reward a particular type of behavior.

▶ Awards for meritorious achievement (Sec. 74(b))

▶ Various employee fringe benefits (Secs. 79, 105, 106, 124, 125, 129, 132)

▶ Partial exclusion for scholarships (Sec. 117)

▶ Foreign-earned income (Sec. 911)

▶ Interest on state and local government obligations (Sec. 103)

Other reasons may exist for some of the exclusions listed above. For example, one reason income from the discharge of indebtedness during bankruptcy is excluded from gross income is the fact that such taxpayers would be unlikely to have the resources needed to pay the tax. (See Chapter I:3 for a discussion of tax-exempt interest and Social Security benefits, and Chapter I:12 for the treatment of gain on the sale of a personal residence.)

ADDITIONAL COMMENT

Tax expenditure estimates measure the decreases in individual and corporate income tax liabilities that result from provisions in income tax laws and regulations that provide economic incentives or tax relief to particular kinds of taxpayers.

GIFTS AND INHERITANCES

Congress has excluded the value of gifts and inheritances received from gross income since the inception of the income tax in 1913. Section 102 excludes the value of property received during the life of the donor (*inter vivos* **gifts**) and transfers at death (**testamentary transfers**—bequests, devises, and inheritances).[5] The recipient of such property is taxed on the income produced by the property after the transfer.[6] It should be noted that a donor, under the assignment of income doctrine, cannot avoid the income tax by making a gift of income. To avoid paying tax on income, a donor must make a gift of the underlying property.

TYPICAL MISCONCEPTION

Some people still believe that gifts above the gift exclusion amount of $13,000 are taxable to the donees. They are not since the Code specifically exempts all gifts, regardless of the amount. The donor may, however, depending on the circumstances, pay a gift tax.

EXAMPLE I:4-3 ▶ Stan owns stock in a corporation and orders the corporation to pay dividends on the stock to his daughter. Even though his daughter receives the dividends, Stan must include the dividends in his gross income. Stan could avoid being taxed on future dividends by making a gift of the stock to his daughter. ◀

It is often difficult to distinguish gifts, which are not included in the recipient's gross income, from other transfers, which are taxable. Gifts sometimes closely resemble prizes and awards.[7]

EXAMPLE I:4-4 ▶ Tina received a free automobile for being the ten millionth paying guest at an amusement park. The automobile is not considered a gift but a prize and is taxable to Tina. ◀

---

[5] Although excluded from gross income, such transfers may be subject to the gift tax or the estate tax which are imposed on the transferor.
[6] Reg. Sec. 1.102-1(b).

[7] Recall that under Sec. 74 (discussed in Chapter I:3) most prizes and awards are taxable.

Also, some payments made to employees by employers may resemble gifts.

EXAMPLE I:4-5 ▶ At Christmas, Red Corporation paid $500 to each employee who had been with the company for more than five years. These payments are not considered gifts for tax purposes and are taxable to the employees. ◀

REAL-WORLD EXAMPLE

Amounts received by a dealer from players in the operation of a gambling casino were not excludable as gifts even though impulsive generosity or superstition may be the dominant motive. The amounts were similar to tips, which are taxable. *Louis R. Tomburello,* 86 T.C. 540 (1986).

Whether a transfer is a gift depends on the intent of the donor. A donor is expected to be motivated by love, affection, kindness, sympathy, generosity, admiration, or similar emotions. In the two preceding examples, the transfers probably were made for business motives and not necessarily for donative reasons. Thus, the automobile is a taxable prize, and the amounts paid to employees represent taxable awards for services rendered, but see the discussion of Sec. 274 later in this chapter.

Transfers of money or property between family members frequently create problems of classification. For example, assume a father, who owns a business, hires his 10-year-old son to work in the business. Is the payment to the son a salary (and, therefore, deductible by the business) or is it really just a gift from the father to the son? The answer depends on the fair market value of the services performed by the son. If the son actually performs services that are commensurate with the salary paid, the payment may properly be classified as a salary. On the other hand, if the son is paid an amount that exceeds the value of the services, the excess amount will be treated as a gift.

LIFE INSURANCE PROCEEDS

Life insurance proceeds paid to a beneficiary because of the insured person's death are not taxable.[8] The exclusion applies whether the proceeds are paid in a lump sum or in installments. Amounts received in excess of the face amount of the policy usually are taxable as interest.

EXAMPLE I:4-6 ▶ Buddy is the beneficiary of a $100,000 insurance policy on his mother's life. Upon her death, he elects to receive $13,000 per year for ten years instead of the lump sum. He receives $10,000 per year tax-free ($100,000 ÷ 10), but the remaining $3,000 per year is taxable as interest. ◀

EXAMPLE I:4-7 ▶ Assume the same facts as in Example I:4-6, except that Buddy elects to receive the full $100,000 face amount upon his mother's death. None of the $100,000 is taxable. ◀

The exclusion exists because life insurance benefits closely resemble inheritances, which are not taxable.

There is one exception that may result in a portion of the face amount of a life insurance policy being included in gross income.[9] The life insurance exclusion generally is not available if the insurance policy is obtained by the beneficiary in exchange for valuable consideration from a person other than the insurance company. For example, an individual may purchase an existing life insurance policy for cash from another individual. In this situation, the exclusion for death benefits is limited to the consideration paid plus the premiums or other sums subsequently paid by the buyer.

EXAMPLE I:4-8 ▶

ADDITIONAL COMMENT

The proceeds of a life insurance policy payable to named beneficiaries can be excluded from the federal estate tax when the decedent does not possess any incidents of ownership. This provision and the exclusion from gross income of life insurance proceeds underscore the favored position of life insurance.

Kwame is the owner and beneficiary of a $100,000 policy on the life of his father. Kwame sells the policy to his brother Anwar for $10,000. Anwar subsequently pays premiums of $12,000. Upon his father's death, Anwar must include $78,000 [$100,000 − ($10,000 + $12,000)] in gross income. However, if Kwame gave the policy to his brother, all of the proceeds would be excluded from gross income because the gift of the policy does not constitute valuable consideration. ◀

The proceeds are excludable under the general exclusion for life insurance proceeds if the beneficiary's basis is found by reference to the transferor's basis (as would be true in the case of a gift), or if the policy is transferred to the insured, the insured's partner, a partnership that includes the insured, or a corporation in which the insured is a shareholder or officer.

---

[8] Sec. 101(a).

[9] Sec. 101(a)(2).

SURRENDER OR SALE OF POLICY. The exclusion for life insurance is available for amounts payable by reason of the death of the insured. In general, if a life policy is sold or surrendered for a lump sum before the death of the insured, the amount received is taxable to the extent that it exceeds the net premiums paid.[10] On the other hand, no loss is recognized if a life insurance policy is surrendered before maturity and premiums paid exceed the cash surrender value.[11]

"Accelerated death benefits" may be excluded from gross income. Accelerated death benefits include payments made to a terminally ill person and periodic payments made to a chronically ill person. A person is terminally ill if a physician certifies that he is reasonably likely to die within 24 months. A person is chronically ill if he has a disability requiring long-term care (e.g., nursing home care). In general, the exclusion for periodic payments made to a chronically ill person is limited to the greater of $290 per day ($280 per day in 2009), or the actual cost of such care. The exclusion covers amounts received from the insurance provider or from a "viatical settlement provider" (i.e., person in the business of providing accelerated death benefits).

EXAMPLE I:4-9 ▶ Harry has been diagnosed with advanced AIDS and is expected to live less than a year. Harry is covered by a life insurance policy with a $100,000 face amount. The insurance company offers terminally ill individuals the option of receiving 75% of the policy face amount. If Harry accepts the settlement, the amount he receives is excludable from gross income because he is terminally ill. ◀

EXAMPLE I:4-10 ▶ Mary suffered a severe stroke and has been admitted to a nursing home where she is expected to remain for the rest of her life. She is certified by a licensed health care practitioner as being a "chronically ill individual." Her nursing home expenses amount to $200 per day. Mary has elected to receive $225 per day from a $1,000,000 face amount life insurance policy as accelerated death benefits. Because she is a chronically ill individual, Mary may exclude the full amount she receives as it is less than the daily limitation of $290 established by law. ◀

DIVIDENDS ON LIFE INSURANCE AND ENDOWMENT POLICIES. Dividends on life insurance and endowment policies are normally not taxable because they are considered to be a partial return of premiums paid. The dividends are taxable to the extent that the total dividends received exceed the total premiums paid. Also, if dividends are left with the insurance company and earn interest, the interest is taxable.

ADOPTION EXPENSES

Congress provides tax benefits for qualified adoption expenses in the form of tax credits (see Chapter I:14) or an exclusion for amounts paid pursuant to an adoption assistance plan created by an employer. An employee is allowed a $12,170 ($12,150 in 2009) per child exclusion from gross income for qualified adoption expenses paid by an employer under an adoption assistance program.[12] The exclusion is phased-out ratably for taxpayers with modified adjusted gross income of $182,520 to $222,520 ($182,180 to $222,180 in 2009).

Qualified adoption expenses include adoption fees, court costs, attorney fees, and other expenses related to an adoption. An adoption assistance program is a separate written plan of an employer, exclusively for the benefit of its employees, to provide adoption assistance.

EXAMPLE I:4-11 ▶ Reggie and Rhonda are married, have AGI of $197,520, and adopt a child. Rhonda's employer maintains a written adoption assistance program. They spend $12,000 during the year in connection with the adoption, all of which is paid by Rhonda's employer pursuant to the plan. Reggie and Rhonda must include in their gross income an amount of $4,394, computed as follows:

---

[10] Sec. 72(e)(2). In some instances where distributions are made before the recipient reaches age 59½, a 10% penalty applies (see Sec. 72(q)).
[11] *London Shoe Co. v. CIR*, 16 AFTR 1398, 35-2 USTC ¶9664 (2nd Cir., 1935).

[12] Sec. 137.

Total adoption expenses paid from the plan	$12,000
Maximum exclusion	12,170
Phase-out percentage [($197,520 − $182,520)/($222,520 − $182,520)]	37.5%
Reduction in exclusion ($12,170 × 0.375)	4,564
Exclusion amount ($12,170 − $4,564)	7,606
Amount includible in gross income ($12,000 − $7,606)	4,394 ◀

In general, the exclusion cannot exceed the amount of qualified expenses. However, in the case of the adoption of a child with special needs, the exclusion is $12,170 (subject to the AGI phase-out). The exclusion is not limited to the actual expenses incurred.

EXAMPLE I:4-12 ▶ Assume the same facts as in the previous example except that the amount of adoption expenses paid totaled $4,000. The exclusion would be limited to $4,000 except in the case of an adoption of a child with special needs in which case the exclusion would be $7,606. ◀

AWARDS FOR MERITORIOUS ACHIEVEMENT

As noted in Chapter I:3, prizes and awards generally are taxable. An exception is applicable to awards and prizes made for religious, charitable, scientific, educational, artistic, literary, or civic achievement if the recipient:

▶ Was selected without action on his or her part to enter the contest or the proceeding,

▶ Does not have to perform substantial future services as a condition to receiving the prize or award, and

▶ Designates that the payor is to pay the amount of the award to either a government unit or a charitable organization.[13]

The recipient of such an award normally would owe no tax if he or she collected the proceeds and then contributed the proceeds to a charity because the gift would qualify as a deductible charitable contribution. However, the exclusion changes AGI and thereby affects other computations. Also, this rule is beneficial in situations where the taxpayer could not deduct the full amount of the award because of the limitation on the charitable contribution deduction (generally 50% of AGI; see Chapter I:7) or in the case of a small award to a taxpayer who does not itemize.

SCHOLARSHIPS AND FELLOWSHIPS

Subject to certain limitations, scholarships are excluded from gross income.[14] A scholarship is an amount paid or allowed to a student, whether an undergraduate or graduate, to aid degree-seeking individuals.

The exclusion for scholarships is limited to the amount of the scholarship used for *qualified tuition and related expenses*. Qualified tuition and related expenses typically include tuition and fees, books, supplies, and equipment required for courses of instruction at an educational organization. The value of services and accommodations supplied such as room, board, and laundry are not excluded. The exclusion for scholarships does not extend to salary paid for services even if all candidates for a particular degree are required to perform the services.[15]

EXAMPLE I:4-13 ▶ Becky is awarded a $5,000 per year scholarship by State University. Becky spends $3,000 of the scholarship for tuition, books, and supplies, and $2,000 for room and board. In addition, Becky works part-time on campus and earns $4,000, which covers the rest of her room and board and other expenses. Becky is taxed on the $2,000 of the scholarship spent for room and board and $4,000 of salary earned from her part-time job. ◀

[13] Sec. 74.
[14] Sec. 117.
[15] Scholarships may need to be reviewed to determine whether the amount constitutes compensation. A "scholarship" awarded to the winner of a televised beauty pageant by a profit-making corporation was ruled to be compensation for performing subsequent services for the corporation (Rev. Rul. 68-20, 1968-1 C.B. 55). An employer-paid "scholarship" was held to be compensation in a situation where the employee was on leave and was required to return to work after finishing the degree (*Richard E. Johnson v. Bingler*, 23 AFTR 2d 69-1212, 69-1 USTC ¶9348 (USSC, 1969)). However, in Ltr. Rul. 9526020 (September 10, 1995) the IRS ruled that grants to law students are not taxable even if they are conditioned upon the students agreeing to practice upon graduation in public, nonprofit, or other low paying sectors.

DISTRIBUTIONS FROM QUALIFIED TUITION PROGRAMS

To assist students (and/or their families) in meeting costs of higher education, Congress has expanded the income tax provisions dealing with *qualified tuition plans,* or so-called Section 529 plans. Basically, amounts are put into a qualified tuition plan (QTP) on behalf of a designated beneficiary and these amounts grow tax-free while in the QTP. The increase may be withdrawn tax-free by the beneficiary if the amounts are used for qualified higher education expenses, including tuition, books, fees, supplies, equipment, and room and board. Room and board is a qualified higher education expense only if the beneficiary is at least a half-time student. The principal reason that these plans are so useful is that there is no income limitation for such plans. Therefore, taxpayers who have very high incomes can invest amounts into a QTP for their children and obtain tax benefits.

QTP plans may be maintained either by state governments or private universities.[16] These plans are classified into two basic types, (1) plans where tuition credits are purchased today for future use, and (2) plans where amounts are invested in mutual funds or similar investments and used to pay the beneficiary's future education expenses. Private universities may only offer the second type of plan. A QTP, while typically set up by parents or grandparents, may be set up and funded by anyone interested in the child's college education.

Contributions to a QTP may be distributed tax-free. The amount that is treated as a distribution of the original contribution is determined under annuity rules discussed in Chapter I:13. In addition, distributions of income from QTPs may be excluded to the extent they are used for qualified higher education expenses. Any distribution of income not used to pay qualified expenses must be included in the beneficiary's gross income and is subject to a 10% penalty.

EXAMPLE I:4-14 ▶ David, a high income taxpayer, lives in Kentucky and has two children, ages 10 and 8. Kentucky offers a Qualified Tuition Program and David establishes a separate QTP for each of his children, investing $5,000 in each account. The money is invested by the state of Kentucky in a mutual fund. The $5,000 is considered as a gift by David to each child but since the annual gift tax exclusion is $12,000, no gift tax is due. David plans to put $5,000 into each child's account for the next several years. The amounts in the QTP grow tax-free. When the children begin attending college, distributions may be made to the children to pay for their college education expenses and no taxes will be due as long as the distributions do not exceed the amount of qualified higher education expenses. Any distribution of income not used for qualified education expenses must be included in the child's income and is subject to a 10% penalty. ◀

There are several other important considerations in QTPs, including:

▶ A valuable feature of QTPs is the ability to change beneficiaries in the future without any tax consequences as long as the new beneficiary is a member of the original beneficiary's family. Members of the family are very broadly defined and include all of the relationships for determining a dependency exemption as well as first cousins.

▶ The exclusion permitted under Sec. 529 must be reduced by any amounts used to claim the HOPE credit or the lifetime learning credit.[17]

▶ The amounts transferred into a QTP are treated as a gift by the transferor to the designated beneficiary and, when combined with other gifts, are generally limited to $12,000 per year for each beneficiary. Donors may elect to treat large gifts as having been made over five years.

PAYMENTS FOR INJURY AND SICKNESS

Sec. 104(a) excludes from gross income the "amount of any damages (other than punitive damages) . . . received . . . on account of personal physical injuries or physical sickness." Thus, for example, a taxpayer may exclude an insurance settlement for physical injury

---

[16] Under prior law, Section 529 plans could only be established and maintained by the states and by eligible private institutions.

[17] Sec. 529(c)(3)(B)(v). These credits are discussed in Chapter I:14 of this textbook.

that resulted from an automobile accident. Section 104(a) does not cover amounts awarded for nonphysical injuries (such as a damaged reputation or libel) except that taxpayers may exclude reimbursements for medical expenses related to nonphysical injuries.

An attempt to challenge the constitutionality of this provision in the Court of Appeals of the District of Columbia was successful initially, but the court subsequently reversed itself.[18]

EXAMPLE I:4-15 ▶ After she was denied a promotion, Jane sued her employer claiming sex discrimination. She was awarded $5,000 to cover the medical bills she incurred because of the related emotional distress, $20,000 to punish her employer for discrimination, and $10,000 to compensate her for lost wages. The $5,000 awarded to cover medical bills is excluded from gross income, but not the amounts awarded as punitive damages or lost wages. ◀

The exclusion under Sec. 104(a) applies to damages received because of emotional distress in only two situations: (1) when the payments are for medical expenses related to the emotional distress, and (2) when the payments are for emotional distress *attributable* to a physical injury (including physical injury suffered by another person).

Sometimes, victims are awarded amounts that are intended to punish the guilty party. These so-called punitive damages are taxable even when they are awarded for physical injuries.

EXAMPLE I:4-16 ▶ Mary was injured in an automobile accident caused by another driver. Mary's daughter, Sarah, was in the automobile, but she was not physically injured. The other driver's insurance company was required by a court to pay Mary $10,000 to cover medical bills relating to her injuries, $5,000 to compensate her for emotional distress caused by the injuries, and $15,000 of punitive damages. Sarah was paid $3,000 to compensate her for distress caused by her witnessing her mother's injuries. Only the $15,000 of punitive damages are taxable to Mary as the other amounts are compensatory damages related to her physical injuries. Sarah's damage award of $3,000 is also excludable. ◀

Sec. 104(a)(3) excludes from gross income amounts collected under an accident and health insurance policy purchased by the taxpayer, even if the benefits are a substitute for lost income. In addition, Sec. 101 specifies that benefits received under a qualified long-term care insurance contract may be excluded from gross income, but limits the exclusion to the greater of $290 per day ($280 per day in 2009) or the actual cost of such care. Such policies pay for nursing home and other types of long-term care. If the benefits exceed the actual cost of such care but are less than $290 per day, no portion of the benefits is taxable.

EXAMPLE I:4-17 ▶ Chuck purchased a disability income policy from an insurance company. Chuck subsequently suffered a heart attack. Under the terms of the policy, Chuck received $2,500 per month for the five months he was unable to work. The amounts received are not taxable, even though the payments are a substitute for the wages lost due to the illness. ◀

This exclusion is not applicable if the accident and health benefits are provided by the taxpayer's employer.[19]

EXAMPLE I:4-18 ▶ Assume the same facts as in Example I:4-17 except that Chuck's employer paid the premiums on the policy. The amounts received by Chuck are taxable. ◀

EXAMPLE I:4-19 ▶ Ruth suffered a serious stroke and was admitted to a nursing home. During the year, she was in a nursing home for 140 days. Nursing home charges, physician fees, and other related expenses totaled $29,000.

---

[18] *Marrita Murphy v. CIR*, 100 AFTR2d 2007-5075, 2007-2 USTC ¶50,531, (DC Cir., 2007) reversing *Marrita Murphy v. CIR*, 98 AFTR2d 2006-6088, 2006-2 USTC ¶50,476, (DC Cir., 2006).

[19] A limited credit is available to taxpayers who receive such benefits. See Chapter I:14 for a discussion of the credit for the elderly and disabled.

Under Ruth's long-term care insurance contract, she received reimbursements of $31,000. The reimbursements are not includible in Ruth's gross income because the amounts are less than the allowed exclusion amount of $40,600 (140 days × $290). This exclusion applies even though she was reimbursed more than her actual costs. Alternatively, if the reimbursements had been $44,000, she would be required to report $3,400 ($44,000 − $40,600) as gross income. ◀

If the cost of the coverage is shared by the employer and the taxpayer, a portion of the benefits is taxable. For example, if the employer paid one-half of the premiums, one-half of the benefits would be taxable. The principal reason for the different tax treatment is that employer-paid coverage represents a tax-free employee fringe benefit, whereas employee-paid premiums are from after-tax dollars.

In the case of an award intended to reimburse the taxpayer for medical expenses, it follows that the taxpayer cannot deduct the reimbursed medical expenses.[20] If the award exceeds the actual expense, it is not taxable except in the case of employer-financed accident and health insurance and in the case of excess long-term care discussed above.[21]

State worker's compensation laws establish fixed amounts to be paid to employees suffering specific job-related injuries. Section 104(a)(1) specifically excludes worker's compensation from gross income, even though the payments are intended, in part, to reimburse injured workers for loss of future income and even if the injuries are nonphysical.

OBJECTIVE 4

Understand employment-related fringe benefit exclusion items

EMPLOYEE FRINGE BENEFITS

In general, employee compensation is taxable regardless of the form it takes. Nevertheless, the tax law encourages certain types of fringe benefits by allowing an employer to deduct the cost of the benefit, by permitting the employee to exclude the benefit from gross income, or by permitting both the employer deduction and an employee exclusion. Employee fringe benefits subject to special rules include employee insurance, Sec. 132 benefits, meals and lodging, dependent care, and cafeteria plans. These fringe benefits are discussed below.

ADDITIONAL COMMENT

Many companies provide health care benefits to retired employees. However, due to mounting medical insurance bills, a rising retiree population, and an FASB rule that requires firms to recognize the associated liability, a number of companies are requiring retired workers to pick up a larger portion of their medical costs.

ADDITIONAL COMMENT

The tax expenditure estimate associated with the exclusion of contributions by employers for medical insurance premiums and medical care for the year 2006 is $125 billion. This is the largest tax expenditure in the U.S. budget.

KEY POINT

The nondiscrimination requirements for self-insured accident and health plans are designed to ensure that such plans do not discriminate against rank-and-file workers.

EMPLOYER-PAID INSURANCE. Employers commonly provide group insurance coverage for employees. In general, employers may deduct the premiums paid for life, health, accident, and disability insurance. Normally an employee does not have to include in gross income premiums paid on his or her behalf for health, accident, and disability insurance. Special rules applicable to life insurance premiums are discussed below.

Benefits received from medical, health, and group term life insurance coverage generally are excluded from an employee's gross income. Benefits received from a disability policy are normally taxable, but may qualify for the credit for the elderly and disabled (see Chapter I:14). The tax treatments of employer-financed and taxpayer-financed insurance coverage are compared in Topic Review I:4-1.

The rules relating to accident and health insurance are more generous than those for some other types of benefits. Under Sec. 106, employers can deduct insurance premiums and employees need not report the premiums as income. This is true even if the insurance is offered only to officers and other highly compensated employees.

Some employers provide self-insured accident and health plans to employees. Under such plans the employer pays employee medical expenses directly. Such plans are called Health Reimbursement Arrangements and often supplement health insurance. Such plans are subject to nondiscrimination requirements. *Discrimination* is defined in terms of an eligibility test (whether a sufficient number of non-highly compensated employees are covered) and benefits (whether non-highly compensated employees receive benefits comparable to highly compensated employees). Highly compensated employees include the five highest-paid officers, greater-than-10% shareholders, and highest-paid 25% of other employees.[22] If a plan discriminates in favor of highly compensated employees, these employees must include in gross income any medical reimbursements they receive that are not available to other employees.

---

[20] See Chapter I:3 for a discussion of the reimbursement of an expense deducted in a preceding year.

[21] Sec. 105(a).

[22] Sec. 105(h)(5).

Topic Review I:4-1

Treatment of Insurance

	PREMIUMS PAID BY	
	EMPLOYER	*EMPLOYEE*
Medical and health Premiums	Premiums not included in employee's gross income. Premiums deductible by employer.	Premiums deductible as medical expense subject to 7.5% of AGI limitation.
Benefits	Excluded from employee's gross income except when benefits exceed actual expenses.	Excluded from gross income.
Disability Premiums	Premiums not included in employee's gross income. Premiums deductible by employer.	Not deductible.
Benefits	Included in employee's gross income. May qualify for credit for elderly and disabled.	Excluded from gross income.
Life insurance Premiums	Included in employee's gross income (except for limited exclusion applicable to group term life insurance). Premiums deductible by employer (assuming employer is not the beneficiary).	Not deductible.
Benefits	Excluded from gross income.	Excluded from gross income.

In general, life insurance premiums paid by an employer on an employee's behalf are deductible by the employer and are includable in the employee's gross income.[23] A limited exception is applicable to group term life insurance coverage. In general, premiums attributable to the first $50,000 of group term life insurance coverage may be excluded from an employee's gross income.[24] To qualify group term life insurance premiums for the exclusion, broad coverage of employees is required. Though somewhat different, the rules may be compared to those associated with self-insurance coverage.[25] The amount of coverage can vary between employees as long as the coverage bears a uniform relationship to each employee's compensation.

EXAMPLE I:4-20 ▶

TYPICAL MISCONCEPTION

Many individuals erroneously believe that all life insurance coverage provided by employers is exempt from income.

Data Corporation provides group term life insurance coverage for each full-time employee. The coverage is equal to one year's compensation. The arrangement constitutes a qualified group term life insurance plan. ◀

In the case of coverage that exceeds $50,000, employees must include in gross income the amount established by the Regulations. (See Table I:4-1.)

EXAMPLE I:4-21 ▶

USA Corporation provides Joy, age 61, with $150,000 of group term life insurance coverage. Joy must include in gross income $792, an amount determined by reference to Table I:4-1 [($100,000/$1,000 × $.66) × 12 = $792]. ◀

The amount that must otherwise be included in an employee's gross income is reduced by any premiums paid by the employee.

If group term life insurance coverage discriminates in favor of key employees, each key employee must include in gross income the greater of the premiums paid on his or her behalf or the amount determined based on Table I:4-1 without any exclusion for the first $50,000 of coverage.

---

[23] If the employer is the beneficiary of the policy, the employee receives no economic benefit and, as a result, need not include the premiums in gross income. Such premium payments are not deductible by the employer. Subsequent benefits are not included in the employer's gross income.

[24] Sec. 79(a).
[25] For example, the rules refer to "key employees" as opposed to highly compensated employees. The term *key employee* is somewhat narrower in scope.

▼ TABLE I:4-1

Uniform One-Month Group Term Premiums for $1,000 of Life Insurance Coverage

Employee's age	Premiums
Under 25	$0.05
25 to 29	.06
30 to 34	.08
35 to 39	.09
40 to 44	.10
45 to 49	.15
50 to 54	.23
55 to 59	.43
60 to 64	.66
65 to 69	1.27
70 and above	2.06

STOP & THINK

Question: Does the fact that employers can provide health insurance and group term life insurance to employees on a tax-favored basis mean that such benefits should be provided to all employees? Explain.

Solution: No. Providing such benefits to all employees may be inefficient. Some employees have other health coverage (e.g., coverage through a spouse's employer). Employees with no dependents may not want life insurance coverage. As a result, employers who provide all employees with such benefits may be spending money on coverage that some employees neither want nor need. A cafeteria plan, discussed later in this chapter, is often a more efficient option. Such plans permit employees to choose either cash or from a menu of tax-favored benefits. This does have significant social and economic implications. As the cost of health insurance increases, more employees, especially those with lower incomes, choose cash salary over health insurance coverage. This contributes to the growing number of individuals who do not have health insurance.

NEW TAX ACT

The American Recovery and Reinvestment Act of 2009 temporarily increased the monthly exclusion for commuter highway vehicles and transit passes to $230 beginning on or after February 17, 2009. The monthly exclusion was previously set at $120 for 2009.

ADDITIONAL COMMENT

The nondiscrimination rules do not apply to working condition fringe benefits. For example, if a corporation makes bodyguards available only to key officers, the working condition fringe benefit exclusion would still apply.

SECTION 132 FRINGE BENEFITS. It has become common for employers to provide employees with such diverse benefits as free parking, membership in professional organizations, and small discounts on products sold by the employer. Section 132 was added to the IRC in 1984 to clarify whether certain types of benefits are taxable. Section 132 lists six types of fringe benefits that may be excluded from an employee's gross income (see Topic Review I:4-2). Any costs incurred by an employer to provide the specified benefits are deductible under Sec. 162 if they meet the "ordinary and necessary" test of that section.[26] Benefits covered by Sec. 132 include:

▶ No-additional-cost benefits (e.g., a hotel employee's use of a vacant hotel room)

▶ Qualified employee discounts (e.g., discounts on merchandise sold by the employer)

▶ Working condition benefits (e.g., membership fees in professional organizations paid by an employer)

▶ De minimis benefits (e.g., coffee provided by the employer)

▶ Qualified transportation benefits such as transit passes and tokens, parking fees for van and car pooling vehicles, and bicycle commuting expenses are excluded. The exclusion for transit passes and tokens is limited to $120 per month for January and February 2009 and $230 per month for March 2009 through December 2010. The increase is temporary and the amount is scheduled to return to $120 per month, adjusted for inflation, beginning in 2011. The exclusion for qualified parking is limited to $230 per

---

[26] See Chapter I:6 for a discussion of Sec. 162 and its requirements. Section 274 does provide one exception to the general rule. The costs of maintaining recreational facilities (such as swimming pools) are not deductible if the facilities are made available on a discriminatory basis (e.g., only officers may use the facilities).

Topic Review I:4-2

Summary of Sec. 132 Fringe Benefits

SECTION	BENEFIT	MAY BE MADE AVAILABLE TO	COMMENTS
132(b)	No-additional-cost (e.g., telephone, unused hotel rooms for hotel employees, unused airline seats for airline employees)	Employees, spouses, dependents, and retirees	The services must be of the same types that are sold to customers and in the line of business in which the employee works. Discrimination is prohibited.
132(c)	Qualified employee discounts	Employees, spouses, dependents, and retirees	Discounts on services limited to 20%. Discounts on merchandise are limited to the employer's gross profit percentage. No discount is permitted on real estate, stock, or other investment type property. Discrimination is prohibited.
132(d)	Working condition (e.g., free magazines, out-placement, and memberships)	Employees	Discrimination is permitted. Special rules apply to tuition reductions for employees of educational institutions and to an auto salesperson's demonstrator.
132(e)	De minimis (e.g., free coffee, holiday turkeys, or use of company eating facilities)	Employees	Eating facilities must be made available on a nondiscriminatory basis.
132(f)	Qualified transportation fringes (e.g., transit passes, tokens, and parking)	Employees	Limited in 2009 to $230 per month for parking and other transportation fringes. Discrimination is permitted.
132(j)(4)	Recreation and athletic facilities (e.g., gyms, pools, saunas, and tennis courts)	Employees, spouses, dependents, and retirees	If discrimination is present, employer loses deduction.

month in 2009 and 2010. The exclusion for qualified bicycle commuting expenses is limited to $20 per month in 2009 and 2010 and expires at the end of 2010.

► Athletic facilities (e.g., employer-owned tennis courts used by employees)

No-additional-cost benefits are limited to services, as opposed to property. Common examples of no-additional-cost benefits include the use of vacant hotel rooms by hotel employees and standby air flights provided to airline employees. The employer may not incur substantial additional costs, including forgone revenue, in providing the services to the employee. Thus, a hotel may allow employees to stay in vacant hotel rooms even though the hotel incurs additional utility and laundry costs as a result of the stay. However, the hotel cannot allow the employees to stay in lieu of paying guests. No-additional-cost benefits are limited to services provided to employees, their spouses, dependent children, and to retired and disabled employees. The term employee includes partners who perform services for a partnership. In addition, the benefits may be extended, on a reciprocal basis, to employees of other companies in the same line of business.

Employers may permit employees to purchase goods and services at a discount from the price charged regular customers. In the case of services, the discount is limited to 20% of the price charged regular customers. In the case of property, the discount is limited to the company's gross profit percent. No discounts are permitted on real property or invest-ment property (e.g., houses or stocks). Further, the discounts must be from the same line of business in which the employee works. The discounts may be provided to the same per-sons as no-additional-cost benefits except that the discounts may not be provided on a reciprocal basis to employees of companies in the same line of business.

Discrimination is prohibited with respect to certain benefits. The benefits must be made available to employees in general rather than to highly compensated employees only. (See Topic Review I:4-2 for specific rules.)

SELF-STUDY QUESTION

Western Airlines and Central Airlines have a reciprocal agreement that permits employees of the other airline to travel for free on a standby basis. Stan, an employee of Western Airlines, takes a free flight on Central Airlines that would have cost $800. What is Stan's income?

ANSWER

None, reciprocal agreements with regard to no-additional-cost services are permitted.

EMPLOYEE AWARDS. As noted earlier, it is often difficult to distinguish between gifts and awards. The de minimis rule mentioned above permits employers to make small gifts such as a holiday turkey or a watch at retirement without the employee having to include the value of the gift in gross income. The employer is entitled to a deduction for the cost of such gifts.

Section 74 provides a similar rule for **employee achievement awards** and **qualified plan awards**.[27] Such awards must be in the form of tangible personal property other than cash and must be based on safety records or length of service. Employee achievement awards are limited to $400 for any one employee during the year. Furthermore, the awards must be presented as part of a meaningful presentation and awarded under circumstances that do not create a significant likelihood of the payment being disguised compensation. Qualified plan awards must be granted under a written plan and may not discriminate in favor of highly compensated employees. The average cost of qualified plan awards is limited to $400, but individual awards can be as large as $1,600.

▶ An award for length of service cannot qualify under the IRC if it is received during the employee's first five years of employment or if the employee has received a length-of-service award during the year or any of the preceding four years.

▶ No more than 10% of an employer's eligible employees may receive an excludable safety achievement award during any year. Eligible employees are employees whose positions involve significant safety concerns.

EXAMPLE I:4-22 ▶

Each year, USA Corporation presents length-of-service awards to employees who have been with the company five, ten, fifteen, or twenty years. The presentations are made at a luncheon sponsored by the company and include gifts such as desk clocks, briefcases, and watches, none of which cost more than $400. The awards, which qualify as employee achievement awards, are deductible by USA Corporation and are not taxable as income to USA's employees. ◀

Gifts to employees that do not qualify as employee achievement awards or qualified plan awards can be excluded by the employee only if the awards can be excluded as de minimis amounts under Sec. 132(e).

MEALS AND LODGING. Section 119 provides a limited exclusion for the value of meals and lodging that are provided to employees at either no cost or a reduced cost.

REAL-WORLD EXAMPLE

Many university presidents are furnished with personal residences, the value of which they can generally exclude from gross income.

REAL-WORLD EXAMPLE

A brewery provided houses on the business premises to officers. The value of the houses was excludable because it was important to have the officers available for around-the-clock operations of the business. *Adolph Coors Co.,* 1968 PH T.C. Memo ¶68, 256, 27 TCM 1351.

▶ Meals provided by an employer may be excluded from an employee's gross income if they are furnished on the employer's premises and for the convenience of the employer.

▶ Lodging provided by an employer may be excluded from an employee's gross income if it is furnished on the employer's premises and for the convenience of the employer, and the employee is required to accept the lodging as a condition of employment.

The requirement that meals and lodging be furnished on the premises of the employer refers to the employee's place of employment.[28] In one case, the Tax Court held that the business premises requirement was met in a situation where a hotel manager lived in a residence across the street from the hotel he managed.[29]

The convenience of the employer test considers whether a substantial noncompensatory business reason exists for providing the meals or lodging. Thus, the test is met if the owner of an apartment complex furnishes a unit to the manager of the complex because it is necessary to have the manager present on the premises even when he or she is off duty.

The value of lodging cannot be excluded from gross income unless the employee is required to accept the lodging as a condition of employment. This requirement is not met

---

[27] Sec. 74(c). The definitions and requirements for employee achievement awards and qualified plan awards are contained in Sec. 274(j).

[28] Reg. Sec. 1.119-1(c)(1).
[29] *Jack B. Lindeman,* 60 T.C. 609 (1973).

if the employee has a choice of accepting the lodging or receiving a cash allowance. Furthermore, meal allowances do not qualify for the exclusion because the employer does not actually provide the meal.[30] Section 132 (discussed earlier in this chapter) provides a de minimis exception. Some employers provide supper money to employees who must work overtime. If such benefits are occasionally provided to employees, the amount is excludable from the employees' gross income.

EXAMPLE I:4-23 ▶ A hospital maintains a cafeteria that is used by employees, patients, and visitors. Employees are provided free meals while on duty in order to be available for emergency calls. Since the meals are provided on the employer's premises and for the convenience of the employer, the value of the meals is excluded from the employees' gross income. ◀

EXAMPLE I:4-24 ▶ A state highway patrol organization provides its officers with a daily meal allowance to compensate them for meals eaten while they are on duty. Officers typically eat their meals at the restaurant of their choice. Because the officers receive cash instead of meals, the amount provided must be included in the officers' gross income. ◀

EXAMPLE I:4-25 ▶ A large corporation requires five of its employees to work overtime two evenings each year when the company takes inventory. The corporation gives each of the employees a small amount to cover the cost of the dinner for the two evenings. The amounts constitute supper money and are excluded from the employees' gross income. ◀

Section 119 provides that if employees can exclude the value of meals from gross income, the employer can deduct the full cost of the meal. Further, if more than half of the employees who receive meals meet the "convenience of the employer" test, then all employees who receive meals can exclude the value from gross income.

MEALS AND ENTERTAINMENT. One obvious question is whether employees who are reimbursed by their employers when they entertain customers must include the reimbursement in gross income. If they must include the reimbursement in gross income, can they deduct the cost of the entertainment and meals? Assuming conditions for deductibility are met, the tax law clearly allows 50% of the cost of entertaining customers to be deducted (discussed in Chapter I:9). Can the employee deduct the meals and entertainment that he personally consumes?

EXAMPLE I:4-26 ▶ Joe is a sales representative for Zero Corporation. As a part of his regular duties, Joe buys lunch for Wayne, a Zero Corporation customer. Fifty percent of the cost of Wayne's meal is deductible either by Joe if he pays for the luncheon without being reimbursed by his employer, or by the Zero Corporation if it reimburses Joe for the cost. Can Joe deduct 50% of the cost of his own meal if he pays for it and is not reimbursed? If Zero pays for the meal, must Joe include in his gross income the cost of his own lunch? ◀

In the above question, Joe apparently can deduct the portion of the luncheon that applies to himself. While this issue is not clear-cut, the IRS has indicated in Rev. Rul. 63-144 that it will not pursue the issue except where taxpayers claim deductions for substantial amounts of personal expenses.[31] In any case, it is an accepted practice today for taxpayers to deduct 50% of the total cost of a meal (taxpayer and customer) unless the practice is considered abusive.[32]

EMPLOYEE DEATH BENEFITS. Occasionally, an employer may make payments to the family or friends of an employee who dies. In some instances, the payments might be viewed as a gift made for reasons such as the financial need of the family, kindness, or charity. Alternatively, the amount might constitute a payment of compensation based on

---

[30] *CIR v. Robert J. Kowalski*, 40 AFTR 2d 77-6128, 77-2 USTC ¶9748 (USSC, 1977).
[31] Rev. Rul. 63-144, 1963-2 C.B. 129.

[32] See, however, *Richard A. Sutter*, 21 T.C. 170 (1953), where the Tax Court ruled that business meals, entertainment, etc. for one's own self are inherently personal and nondeductible. *Sutter* has been cited and upheld some 50 times.

WHAT WOULD YOU DO IN THIS SITUATION?

FRINGE BENEFIT

National Boats manufactures pleasure boats sold to consumers. The boats range in price from $40,000 to $1,500,000. Jake is the president of National Boats. The company provides Jake with one of its more expensive boats. The company pays for fuel, insurance, and other costs and deducts these expenses along with depreciation on the boat. The company states that Jake is responsible for testing and for demonstrating the boat to possible customers. Jake has had the same boat for two years, and the company plans to provide him with a new boat next month.

You asked Jake how often he uses the boat. He indicated that he uses it once or twice each month on weekends, except during the winter. You asked him who accompanies him, and what types of testing he conducts. He seemed reluctant to answer the question, but acknowledged that his family often accompanies him on the boat, and said that he tests it during ordinary operations to determine how it performs. He added that potential customers who have also accompanied him included neighbors and friends. What tax issues do you see?

the past services of the deceased employee. Gifts are, of course, excluded from gross income, whereas compensation is taxable. The treatment of payments made to the family or other beneficiaries of the employee's estate is determined by the following rules:

▶ Payments for past services (such as bonuses, accrued wages, and unused vacation pay) are taxable as income to the family and are deductible by the employer. The important issue is whether the employee would have received this amount had he or she lived. If the employer was legally obligated to make the payment at the time of the employee's death, the payments are taxable to the recipient.

▶ Other amounts may be either taxable compensation or excludable gifts depending on the facts and circumstances. If the amount is a gift, it is not deductible by the employer. If the amount is taxable income to the deceased employee's family, it is deductible by the employer.

In determining whether the amount is taxable, the courts have considered such factors as whether the employer derived benefit from the payment, whether the employee had been fully compensated, and whether the payment was made to the family and not to the estate. The Supreme Court stated, "The most critical consideration [in determining whether a transfer is a gift] is the transferor's 'intention'."[33] Although the case did not deal with death benefits, it did establish the importance of motive in determining whether a payment is a gift. Thus, the transfer should be made for reasons such as kindness, sympathy, generosity, affection, or admiration.

It should be noted that it is more difficult to establish that a payment is a gift in situations where the payments are made to persons owning stock in the corporation making the payment. Such payments may be construed as constructive dividends, which are not deductible by the corporation but are taxable income to the recipients.[34]

ADDITIONAL COMMENT

The $5,000 limit was placed on the exclusion for dependent care assistance programs because it was thought to be inequitable to provide an unlimited dependent care exclusion but a limited child care credit for people who pay their own child care expenses.

DEPENDENT CARE. **Dependent care assistance programs** are employer-financed programs that provide care for an employee's children or other dependents. An employee may exclude up to $5,000 of assistance each year ($2,500 for a married individual filing a separate return). The care must be of a type that, if paid by the employee, would qualify for the dependent care credit. Furthermore, the credit is scaled down if the employee receives benefits under the employer's plan. (See Chapter I:14 for a discussion of the child and dependent care rules.) The program cannot discriminate in favor of highly compensated employees or their dependents.[35]

---

[33] *CIR v. Mose Duberstein*, 5 AFTR 2d 1626, 60-2 USTC ¶9515 (USSC, 1960).
[34] *Ernest L. Poyner v. CIR*, 9 AFTR 2d 1151, 62-1 USTC ¶9387 (4th Cir., 1962).

[35] Sec. 129.

EDUCATIONAL ASSISTANCE.   Under Sec. 127 educational assistance plans, employers pay employee educational costs. Employees may exclude from gross income annual payments of up to $5,250. The exclusion applies to payments for tuition and similar amounts, fees, books, supplies, and equipment.

CAFETERIA PLANS.   **Cafeteria plans**, also called flexible spending accounts, are plans that offer employees the option of choosing cash or statutory nontaxable fringe benefits (such as group term life insurance, medical insurance, adoption expenses, child care, etc.). If the employee chooses cash, the cash is taxable. However, if the employee chooses a statutory nontaxable fringe benefit, the value of the benefit is excluded from gross income.[36] In other words, the fact that the employee could have chosen cash does not cause the fringe benefit to be taxed. The plan cannot discriminate in favor of highly compensated employees or their dependents or spouses.[37] Employer plans may specify what benefits are offered and may limit the amount of benefits individual employees may receive.

Some plans supplement wages; others are wage reduction plans. In supplemental wage plans, employer funds are used to pay fringe benefits. In the case of wage reduction plans, employees elect to receive reduced wages in exchange for the fringe benefits. In both cases, employees receive benefits without being taxed on them.

Employers often allow employees to use such funds to pay medical expenses. Typically, the plans supplement medical insurance, and funds are used to pay dental bills and other medical expenses not covered by regular insurance. In general, employees annually elect to set aside funds to pay medical expenses, and the employer pays the expenses using the set-aside funds. One problem with the agreements is that they are binding for one year. As a result, the employee loses the funds if the actual medical expenses are less than the amount set aside. Employers, on the other hand, are obligated to pay expenses up to the agreed amount even if the full amount has not yet been withheld from the employee's wages. Thus, the employer may lose money if an employee terminates employment after incurring the designated amount of medical expenses but before the full amount is withheld.

INTEREST-FREE LOANS.   One benefit that was often used in the past was interest-free loans to employees. Under present law, interest must generally be imputed on interest-free loans. (See Chapter I:11 for a detailed discussion of rules applicable to interest-free loans.)

ADVANTAGE OF FRINGE BENEFITS.   The major advantage of taking fringe benefits (such as those described above) in lieu of a cash payment is the fact that employees do not have to use after-tax income to obtain the product or service.

EXAMPLE I:4-27 ▶ Dan, an employee of Central Corporation, has a $40,000 life insurance policy and pays the premiums out of his salary. Since his salary is taxable, the premiums are paid on an after-tax basis. Kay, an employee for Western Corporation, is covered by a $40,000 group term life insurance policy financed by Western Corporation. Western Corporation pays the premiums on the policy. Because the premiums are excludable, Kay does not have to report the premiums as income. ◀

EXAMPLE I:4-28 ▶ John's employer establishes a cafeteria plan which allows each employee to set aside up to $5,000 for health insurance premiums and medical reimbursements. John, whose salary has been $30,000, agrees to a salary reduction of $4,000, of which $2,500 is to cover his health insurance premiums and $1,500 is available to reimburse his medical expenses. Under the arrangement, John's salary is reduced to $26,000 for tax purposes. Neither the health insurance coverage nor the medical expense reimbursement is taxable. During the year, John incurs $1,400 of medical expenses not covered by insurance. He receives a reimbursement for all of the expenses. His employer retains the remaining $100. Alternatively, if the medical expenses were $1,800, John would receive a reimbursement of $1,500 and he must pay the remaining $300 of expenses out of after-tax salary dollars. ◀

---

[36] Long-term care insurance (sometimes called nursing home insurance) can be offered to employees on a tax-favored basis, but that benefit cannot be offered as part of a flexible spending account.

[37] Sec. 125.

STOP & THINK

Question: Employers and employees both pay FICA taxes on salaries. Fringe benefits such as health insurance are exempt from both income taxes and FICA taxes. What is the tax effect of an employee's decision to elect health insurance coverage in exchange for a reduced salary?

Solution: The employee's income and FICA taxes are both lowered. The employer is permitted an income tax deduction for either the salary payment or the payment of the health insurance premium. The employer's FICA tax is reduced because the health insurance benefit also is exempt from that tax.

AVAILABILITY OF TAX-FAVORED FRINGE BENEFITS. The exclusion for many fringe benefits is only available to employees (and in some cases spouses, dependents, and retirees). Many tax-favored fringe benefits are unavailable to proprietors and partners. As a result, a partnership can provide $50,000 of group-term life insurance to employees on a tax-favored basis, but cannot provide the benefit on a tax-favored basis to its partners. Other fringe benefits that cannot be offered to proprietors or partners on a tax-favored basis include achievement awards, adoptions assistance, on-premises lodging, moving expense, and commuting and parking benefits (other than de minimis).[38]

Special rules apply to health insurance premiums and retirement plan contributions for proprietors and partners. The owners deduct these payments for AGI. This results in a self-employment tax on the amounts, but no income tax.

Shareholders, as such, are ineligible for tax-favored fringe benefits. In most cases employees of C corporations are eligible for tax-favored fringe benefits based on their wages even if they own stock. This is not true, however, for S corporation employees who own more than 2% of the corporation's stock. They are treated much like partners and proprietors with respect to fringe benefits. Health insurance premiums and retirement plan contributions made for these S corporation employee-shareholders are wages for income tax purposes. Like partners and proprietors, these S corporation employees-shareholders can deduct the amounts for AGI. Unlike partners and proprietors, the amounts are not subject to FICA or self-employment taxes.

The fact that fringe benefits provided to employee-shareholders of C corporations are treated more favorably than benefits provided to the owners of other businesses is an incentive for businesses to operate as C corporations.

ADDITIONAL COMMENT

Many U.S. embassies and consulates in foreign countries provide income tax assistance.

ADDITIONAL COMMENT

Foreign-earned income does not include amounts paid to an employee of the U.S. government or any U.S. government agency or instrumentality.

FOREIGN-EARNED INCOME EXCLUSION

In general, the income of U.S. citizens is subject to the U.S. income tax even if the income is derived from sources outside the United States. The foreign income of U.S. citizens also may be taxed by the host country possibly leading to a substantial double tax on the same income. The double tax is mitigated by a **foreign tax credit**. Subject to limitations, U.S. citizens may subtract from their U.S. income tax liability the income taxes they pay to foreign countries. (See Chapter I:14 for a discussion of foreign tax credit.)

In the case of foreign-earned income, individuals have available the alternative option of excluding the first $91,500 in 2010 ($91,400 in 2009) of foreign-earned income from gross income.[39] The *exclusion* is available in lieu of the foreign tax credit. If both a husband and wife have foreign-earned income, each may claim an exclusion. Community property rules are ignored in determining the amount of the exclusion. Thus, if only one spouse has foreign-earned income, only one exclusion is available. The principal reasons for the exclusion are to encourage U.S. businesses to operate in foreign countries and to hire U.S. citizens and resident aliens to manage the businesses. The hope is that such operations will improve the balance of payments. Taxpayers who elect the exclusion in one year may switch to the foreign tax credit in any subsequent year. Taxpayers who change from the exclusion to the credit may not reelect the exclusion

---

[38] Benefits that can be offered to proprietors and partners on a tax-favored basis include athletic facilities, de minimis benefits, no additional cost fringe benefits, dependent care assistance, educational assistance, discounts, on-premises meals, and working condition fringes.

[39] Sec. 911(b)(2).

before the sixth tax year after the tax year in which the change was made.[40] The IRS can waive the six-year limitation in special situations (such as an individual employee changing the location of his or her foreign employment).

Foreign-earned income includes an individual's earnings from personal services rendered in a foreign country. The place where the services are performed determines whether earned income is foreign or U.S. source income. If an individual is engaged in a trade or business in which both personal services and capital are material income-producing factors, no more than 30% of the net profits from the business may be excluded.[41] Furthermore, pensions, annuities, salary paid by the U.S. government, and deferred compensation do not qualify for the exclusion.[42]

To qualify for the foreign-earned income exclusion, the taxpayer must either be a bona fide resident of one or more foreign countries for an entire taxable year, or be present in one or more foreign countries for 330 days during a period of 12 consecutive months.[43] The exclusion limitation for a year must be prorated if the taxpayer is not present in, or a resident of, a foreign country or countries for the entire year.

EXAMPLE I:4-29 ▶ Sondra is given a temporary assignment to work in foreign country T. She arrives in T on October 19, 2010, and leaves on October 1, 2011. Although Sondra does not establish a permanent residence in T, she is present in T for at least 330 days out of a twelve-month period beginning on October 20, 2010. Thus, 73 days fall in 2010 and the rest in 2011. Sondra's exclusion for 2010 is limited to $18,300 [(73 ÷ 365) × $91,500]. She may exclude $18,300 or the income she earns in foreign country T during 2010, whichever is less. Sondra also may claim the foreign earned income exclusion in 2011 for the number of qualified days during the year. ◀

Deductions directly attributable to the excluded foreign-earned income are disallowed. Expenses attributable to foreign-earned income must be allocated if foreign-earned income exceeds the exclusion. The disallowed portion is determined by multiplying the total amount of such expenses by the ratio of excluded earned income over total foreign-earned income.

EXAMPLE I:4-30 ▶ Connie earned $137,250 while employed in a foreign country for the entire year. She is entitled to an exclusion of $91,500. Connie incurred $12,000 of travel, transportation, and other deductible expenses attributable to the foreign-earned income. She may deduct only $4,000 of such expenses because $8,000 [($91,500 ÷ $137,250) × $12,000] is allocated to the excluded income and, therefore, not deductible. The $4,000 is classified as a miscellaneous itemized deduction and subject to the 2% of AGI floor associated with such deductions. ◀

Housing costs in foreign countries are often higher than in the United States. In such situations, individuals may be able to exclude from gross income a portion of housing costs if they are provided by their employer and may be able to deduct a portion of such costs if they pay the costs themselves. Specifically, the exclusion (deduction) is available for housing costs that exceed 16% of the foreign earned income exclusion limitation or $14,640 (0.16 × $91,500) in 2010 ($14,624 in 2009). Because the maximum housing cost exclusion is 30%, the amount that can be excluded for housing costs under this rule generally is limited to $12,810 (0.14 × $91,500) in 2010 ($12,796 in 2009). The IRS provides higher amounts for cities with high cost-of-living. Further, the housing exclusion must be reduced if the taxpayer does not incur cost for the entire year.

EXAMPLE I:4-31 ▶ Wayne is employed in Quebec City, Canada, and earns a salary of $120,000. His housing costs are $32,000 for the year. Wayne can exclude $104,310 ($91,500 + $12,810) from gross income. If the housing costs had been $24,000, Wayne's foreign earned income exclusion would have totaled $100,868 [$91,500 + ($24,000 − $14,640). ◀

Taxpayers who exclude a portion, but not all foreign earned income are subject to a special tax computation. The result of the computation is to apply higher tax rates to the taxable portion of the foreign earned income. (See *Prentice Hall's Federal Taxation: Corporations, Partnerships, Estates, and Trusts*, Chapter 16.)

[40] Sec. 911(e)(2).
[41] Sec. 911(d)(2)(B).
[42] Sec. 911(b)(1)(B).
[43] Sec. 911(d).

INCOME FROM THE DISCHARGE OF A DEBT

If debt of a taxpayer is cancelled or forgiven, the taxpayer may have to include the cancelled amount in gross income. It is important to distinguish a debt cancellation from a gift, a bequest, or a renegotiation of the purchase price.

EXAMPLE I:4-32 ▶ Farouk loaned his daughter $4,000 to help her purchase an automobile. Several months after she purchased the automobile, but before she repaid the $4,000, Farouk's daughter married. Farouk told his daughter that he was "tearing up" the $4,000 note as a wedding present. In this instance, the amount forgiven would constitute an excludable gift and would not be taxable as income to the daughter. ◀

EXAMPLE I:4-33 ▶ Clay purchased a used automobile from a dealer for $6,000. He paid $2,000 down and agreed to pay the balance of $4,000 over three years. After Clay purchased the automobile, he determined that it was defective. Clay tried to return the automobile, but the automobile dealer refused. Clay threatened to sue the dealer. To resolve the problem, the dealer offered to reduce the balance due on the purchase-money debt from $4,000 to $2,500. Clay agreed. The transaction constitutes a reduction in the purchase price of the automobile. Clay will not recognize any income, but must reduce the basis in his automobile from $6,000 to $4,500. ◀

EXAMPLE I:4-34 ▶ Blue Corporation issued bonds for $1,000 when interest rates were low. After a few years, interest rates increased and the bond value declined to $850. Blue Corporation purchased the bonds on the open market. Blue will recognize $150 of income from the discharge of indebtedness. ◀

EXAMPLE I:4-35 ▶ Indy Coal Company has seen its business decline during the past two years. The Company has a significant amount of bank debt that was incurred over the years to fund its coal operations. In order to maintain its operations, Indy entered into an agreement with the bank whereby the bank agreed to cancel 50% of Indy's debt. Assuming Indy was solvent at the time of the cancellation, Indy must report the discharge of indebtedness as gross income. ◀

STOP & THINK

Question: In Example I:4-35, the bank agreed to cancel 50% of Indy Coal Company's debt. Why would a lender agree to unilaterally cancel a borrower's debt?

Solution: A bank might cancel a portion of a borrower's debt in order to protect the remaining portion of the debt. If the debt forced the company into bankruptcy, the bank may be able to collect none or only a small percentage of the debt. If the cancellation would help stabilize Indy, the bank may be able to collect at least 50% of the debt. Further, if Indy becomes a viable company in the years ahead, the bank will have a good customer to earn profits in the future.

REAL-WORLD EXAMPLE

A taxpayer purchased and retired its own bonds. The purchase resulted in a gain because the bonds were payable in British pounds, which had been devalued. The gain was excludable. *Kentucky & Indiana Terminal Railroad Co. v. U.S.*, 13 AFTR 2d 1148, 64-1 USTC ¶9374 (6th Cir., 1964).

The enforceability of a debt under state law may also determine whether the forgiveness results in income. For example, one case held that the forgiveness of a gambling debt was not included in gross income where the debt was unenforceable under state law.[44]

DISCHARGE IN BANKRUPTCY AND INSOLVENCY. Section 61(a)(12) indicates that gross income includes income from the discharge of an indebtedness. Section 108, on the other hand, provides for the following exceptions where the discharge of an indebtedness is not taxable:

▶ The discharge occurs in bankruptcy.

▶ The discharge occurs when the taxpayer is insolvent.

These exceptions are intended to allow a "fresh start" for bankrupt and other financially troubled taxpayers. Since a taxpayer is not required to include the discharge in gross income, he is required to reduce certain tax attributes. For example, if the taxpayer has a net operating loss carryover, the NOL carryover must be reduced by the excluded discharge.

If a debt is reduced during bankruptcy proceedings, the taxpayer recognizes no income even if the reduction in debt exceeds the available tax attributes. In the case of an insol-

---

[44] *David Zarin v. CIR*, 66 AFTR 2d 90-5679, 90-2 USTC ¶50,530 (3rd Cir., 1990).

NEW TAX ACT

The American Recovery and Reinvestment Act of 2009 allows businesses to postpone cancellation of debt income if the income results from the reacquisition of business debt during 2009 or 2010. The deferred income is to be reported over a five year period, 2014 through 2018.

ADDITIONAL COMMENT

Also excludable is the income from the cancellation of a student loan pursuant to a provision under which part of the debt is discharged due to working for a period of time in certain professions for a broad class of employers.

vent taxpayer, no income is recognized as long as the taxpayer is insolvent after the reduction in debt takes place. A taxpayer is insolvent if the debts owed by the taxpayer exceed the FMV of assets owned. Thus, an insolvent taxpayer reduces the tax attributes to the point of solvency. From that point on, any reduction in debt results in the recognition of income even if all tax attributes have not been offset.

STUDENT LOAN FORGIVENESS. Under Sec. 108(f)(2), the discharge of certain student loans is excluded from gross income if the discharge is contingent on the individual's performing certain public services. The loans must have been made by governmental, educational, or charitable organizations, and the loan proceeds must have been used to pay the cost of attending an educational institution or used to refinance outstanding student loans. Further, the loan forgiveness must be contingent upon the individual's working for a specified time period in certain professions, and the services must normally be performed for someone other than the lender.

EXAMPLE I:4-36 ▶

Lee borrowed $60,000 from the federal government to attend medical school. Under the terms of the loan, $20,000 of debt is forgiven for each year she practices medicine in designated low-income neighborhoods. Lee does not have to include the debt forgiveness in gross income. ◀

HOME MORTGAGE FORGIVENESS. The *Mortgage Forgiveness Debt Relief Act of 2007* temporarily amends the law that requires homeowners to include forgiven mortgage debt in gross income. This provision provides relief to homeowners who have their home subjected to foreclosure. The Act adds Sec. 108(a)(1)(E) and excludes debt forgiveness of up to $2 million during 2007, 2008, and 2009. This provision applies only to mortgages acquired in connection with the acquisition or improvement of a taxpayer's principal residence. Taxpayers are required to reduce the basis of their residence by the amount of the exclusion.

EXCLUSION FOR GAIN FROM SMALL BUSINESS STOCK

Noncorporate taxpayers may exclude 50% of the gain realized on the disposition of qualified small business stock issued after August 10, 1993, if the stock is held for more than five year.[45] The remaining gain is taxed at a rate not greater than 28% resulting in a maximum effective rate of 7%. For each issuer of qualified small business stock, there is a limit on the amount of gain a taxpayer may exclude. The amount of gain eligible for the exclusion may not exceed the greater of $10 million, reduced by amounts previously excluded for gains on the company's stock, or ten times the taxpayer's aggregate adjusted basis of the stock disposed of during the year.[46] When measuring the taxpayer's aggregate basis for the stock to determine the maximum amount of gain to exclude, the fair market value of the assets contributed to the corporation is used.

EXAMPLE I:4-37 ▶

Dennis contributed property with a basis of $1,000,000 and a FMV of $4,000,000 to a qualified small business corporation for all of its common stock. If he sells one-half of the stock after five years for $14,000,000, he may exclude $6,750,000 of the $13,500,000 ($14,000,000 − $500,000) realized gain. The maximum gain eligible for the exclusion is the greater of $10,000,000 or $20,000,000 [10 times the $2,000,000 basis ($4,000,000 FMV × 0.50) of the stock sold]. Thus, none of the $13,500,000 realized gain is subject to the limitation. ◀

Moreover, taxpayers do not have to recognize any gain if they reinvest the proceeds from the sale of small business stock in other small business stock within 60 days of the sale. Gain is recognized only to the extent that the amount realized from the sale exceeds the cost of the replacement stock. The basis of the replacement stock is reduced by the amount of gain not recognized. To qualify for the replacement provision the original stock must have been held for over 6 months.

---

[45] Sec. 1202(a). There are two instances where the exclusion is larger. The exclusion is 75% for stock acquired after February 17, 2009 and before January 1, 2011. The exclusion is 60% in the case of empowerment zone stock (75% if acquired after February 17, 2009 and before January 1, 2011).

[46] Sec. 1202(b)(1).

EXAMPLE I:4-38 ▶ Assume the same facts as in Example I:4-37, except that Dennis purchases $13,000,000 of small business investment stock within 60 days. Dennis is taxed only on $1,000,000 ($14,000,000 – $13,000,000) of his $13,500,000 realized gain. Dennis' basis for the new stock, however, is $500,000 ($13,000,000 cost of the new stock – $12,500,000 portion of the gain that is not taxed). ◀

A corporation may issue qualified small business stock only if the corporation is a C corporation that is not an excluded corporation with an aggregate adjusted basis of not more than $50 million of gross assets, and at least 80% of the value of its assets must be used in the active conduct of one or more qualified trades or businesses.[47]

Currently the maximum tax rate applicable to long-term capital gains is 15%. As a result, the 7% maximum tax rate applicable to small business stock is positive advantage.

OTHER EXCLUSIONS

The tax law contains other exclusions that are either covered elsewhere in the text or are of limited application. Table I:4-2 lists several such exclusions.

▼ **TABLE I:4-2**
Other Exclusions

Section	Applies to	Comments
121	Gain from sale of personal residence	Taxpayers may exclude up to $250,000 ($500,000 in the case of a married couple filing a joint return) of gain from the sale of a personal residence. (See Chapter I:12 for a detailed discussion of this provision.)
101(h)	Annuities paid to survivors of public safety officers	Annuities paid to survivors of public safety officers, such as firefighters and police officers, killed in the line of duty are excluded.
104(a)	Military disability pay	Military personnel may exclude disability pay, combat pay (noncommissioned personnel only), and housing allowances.
112	Combat pay	
134	Military housing allowance	
107	Housing allowance for ministers	Ministers may exclude either the rental value of their homes or a rental allowance if provided in connection with their religious duties.
119	Campus housing	A limited exclusion is provided to employees of educational institutions when they are provided with on-campus housing.
131	Foster care payments	Certain allowances received by foster care providers are excluded from gross income.
162(o)	Rural letter carrier's allowance	Rural letter carriers may exclude the "equipment maintenance allowance" they receive for the use of their personal automobiles in delivering the mail. They receive no deduction for the use of their automobiles.
408A(d)	Roth IRA distributions	Qualified distributions from Roth IRAs are excluded from gross income (see Chapter I:9 for a detailed discussion of the provisions).
530(d)	Education IRA distributions	Qualified distributions from Coverdell Education Savings Account IRAs are excluded from gross income (see Chapter I:9 for a detailed discussion of this provision).
988(e)	Personal foreign currency gains	Individuals are excused from recognizing gain on the disposition of foreign currency in any personal transaction, provided that the gain does not exceed $200.

---

[47] Secs. 1202(d) and (e). Excluded corporations are those engaged in providing professional services (e.g., law and health), financial services (e.g., banking and insurance), hospitality (e.g., hotels and restaurants), farming, and mining and oil and gas production.

TAX PLANNING CONSIDERATIONS

EMPLOYEE FRINGE BENEFITS

ADDITIONAL COMMENT

A case can be made for the desirability of encouraging employers to provide health insurance and other fringe benefits. However, these provisions may contribute to increases in the cost of insurance and medical care.

The tax law encourages certain forms of fringe benefits by allowing an employer to deduct the cost of the benefit while permitting the employee to exclude the benefit from gross income. This deduction does not represent an income tax advantage to the employer because compensation, whether in the form of cash or nontaxable fringe benefits, is deductible if reasonable in amount. While employees receive the greatest income tax benefit from the exclusion of fringe benefits from gross income, employers receive a small benefit from the fact that fringe benefits are not subject to Social Security and Medicare taxes.

EXAMPLE I:4-39 ▶

USA Company has decided to offer $20,000 of group term life insurance coverage for each of its employees at an average annual premium cost of $100 per employee. Tim, an employee of USA Corporation, is in the 15% tax bracket. Because USA is offering a nontaxable fringe benefit, Tim will owe no additional income tax. If Tim had received a salary increase of $100, he would have had to pay an additional income tax of $15 (0.15 × $100). The remaining $85 of after-tax income would probably not have been sufficient to obtain the same amount of life insurance coverage. ◀

Excluding fringe benefits from gross income favors employees who are subject to higher tax rates.

EXAMPLE I:4-40 ▶

Assume the same facts as in Example I:4-39 except that Tim is in the 35% tax rate. Tim would save $35 (0.35 × $100) of taxes by receiving the group term life insurance coverage instead of the $100 salary increase. ◀

ADDITIONAL COMMENT

Fringe benefits offered by potential employers are important consideration factors when weighing total compensation packages.

It is not always desirable for employers to offer nontaxable fringe benefits. Some employees are not interested in certain benefits. For example, in the case of married couples where both spouses are employed, it is not necessary for both employers to provide medical insurance coverage for both spouses. Alternatively, single employees may not feel the need for group term life insurance and employees with no children are uninterested in employer-provided child care.

To avoid providing fringe benefits that are unneeded or unwanted, many employers have turned to cafeteria plans. Under cafeteria plans, employees may select from a list of nontaxable fringe benefits. On the other hand, employees who so choose may receive cash in lieu of some or all of the nontaxable benefits. Thus, each employee selects what he or she wants most. One common result is that high-tax-rate employees select the nontaxable fringe benefits, whereas other employees choose to receive cash.

SELF-HELP INCOME AND USE OF PERSONALLY OWNED PROPERTY

As noted earlier in this chapter, self-help income and income derived from the use of personal property are not taxable. Thus, self-help income and personal ownership of property are favored by the tax system. Taxpayers who rent their personal residences cannot deduct rental payments, but taxpayers who own their residences do not pay rent and may deduct interest and real estate taxes as itemized deductions. Thus, the tax law encourages ownership of personal residences.

Effective tax planning necessitates weighing the tax incentives with other nontax factors. Taxpayers with little accumulated funds may find it difficult to purchase a residence despite the availability of tax incentives. Taxpayers who move frequently may find that transaction costs such as real estate commissions and other closing costs are greater than the tax benefits obtained from home ownership. Other factors such as the personal preference of the taxpayer and anticipated inflation rates must also be considered.

Self-help income must be viewed in the same way. Taxpayers who are deciding whether to paint their own residences or hire someone else to do it must consider factors such as personal preference and the amount of income that could be produced if the time were spent working at an activity that produces taxable income.

COMPLIANCE AND PROCEDURAL CONSIDERATIONS

Taxpayers are usually not required to disclose excluded income on their tax returns. For example, a taxpayer who receives a tax-exempt scholarship need not disclose that income on his or her tax return. An exception is provided for tax-exempt interest and Social Security benefits, which must be disclosed on the tax return. If a taxpayer's only income is from tax-exempt sources, the taxpayer need not file a tax return. Whether an individual must file a return is based on the amount of the individual's gross income for the year (see Chapter I:2).

This chapter considers the taxability of various fringe benefits. The rules regarding the need for an employer to withhold federal income taxes or to report a payment on an employee's Form W-2 (Statement of Income Tax Withheld on Wages) closely parallel the gross income rules. (See Chapter I:14 for a discussion of these reporting requirements.) In general, if a fringe benefit is nontaxable, employers do not withhold from the benefit, nor do they report the benefit on the employee's W-2 at year-end. On the other hand, if the benefit is taxable, it is subject to withholding and is reported on the employee's W-2 at year-end. Thus, employers do not withhold for nontaxable meals and lodging provided to employees[48] or a moving expense reimbursement if the expenses are deductible.[49] Similarly, no withholding is required for the following fringe benefits if they are nontaxable: scholarships and fellowships covered by Sec. 117, dependent care covered by Sec. 129, and miscellaneous fringes covered by Sec. 132.

There are exceptions to this basic system. Certain fringe benefits are not subject to withholding even if the benefits are taxable. These include group term life insurance coverage and medical expense reimbursements.

In general, fringe benefits which are exempt from income tax are also exempt from Social Security and Medicare taxes. For example, medical insurance coverage and group term life coverage of up to $50,000 can be provided to employees without either the employer or the employee owing any Social Security or Medicare taxes on the premiums. This is true if the employee elects the benefits instead of cash salary under a cafeteria plan.

Employers who are obligated to withhold from employee wages are subject to penalty if they fail to withhold, fail to provide employees with correct W-2s, or fail to correctly report the compensation and withholding information to the IRS.[50] In general, the failure to report wages and withholding to either employees or the IRS is subject to penalty generally equal to $50 per failure. The failure to withhold can result in a penalty equal to 100% of the amount that should have been withheld. The penalty can be imposed on the employer and other people, such as officers or accountants, who are responsible for withholding.

Occasionally, employees do not want employers to withhold taxes from their wages. Officers or others who choose not to withhold from employee wages face an extremely burdensome penalty, particularly if a large number of employees are involved. Therefore, it is important that employers comply with withholding requirements. One closely related issue is whether an individual is an employee subject to withholding or an independent contractor, as only employee wages are subject to withholding (see Chapter I:14).

---

[48] Reg. Sec. 31.3401(a)-1(b)(9).
[49] See Sec. 3401 for withholding requirements for numerous special situations.
[50] Secs. 6672, 6674, and 6721, respectively.

PROBLEM MATERIALS

DISCUSSION QUESTIONS

I:4-1 What is meant by the terms *administrative exclusion* and *judicial exclusion*?

I:4-2 There is no specific statutory exclusion for welfare benefits. Nevertheless, the IRS has ruled that such benefits are not taxable. Is this within the authority of the IRS?

I:4-3 What was the issue in the tax case *Eisner v. Macomber*? Why is the case important?

I:4-4 Most exclusions exist for one of two reasons. What are those reasons? Give examples of exclusions that exist for each.

I:4-5 a. If a gift of property is made, who is taxed on income produced by the property?
b. How can interfamily gifts reduce a family's total tax liability?

I:4-6 a. What role does intent play in determining whether a transfer is a gift and therefore not subject to the income tax?
b. Are tips received by employees from customers excludable from gross income as gifts? Explain.

I:4-7 What is the tax significance of the face amount of a life insurance policy?

I:4-8 What conditions must be met for an award to qualify for an exclusion under Sec. 74?

I:4-9 Which of the requirements for the Sec. 74 awards exclusion most severely limits its use? Does the exclusion benefit taxpayers more if they itemize their deductions or use the standard deduction?

I:4-10 a. Define the term *scholarship* as it is used in Sec. 117.
b. If a scholarship covers room and board, is it excludable?
c. If an employer provides a scholarship to an employee who is on leave of absence, is that scholarship taxable?
d. Is the amount paid by a university to students for services excludable from the students' gross income?

I:4-11 What special rules are applicable to non-degree candidates who receive scholarships?

I:4-12 Is the personal injury exclusion found in Sec. 104 limited to physical injury? Explain.

I:4-13 Answer the following questions relative to employer-financed medical and health, disability, and life insurance plans.
a. May employers deduct premiums paid on employee insurance?
b. Do employees have to include such premiums in gross income?
c. Are benefits paid to the employee included in the employee's gross income?

I:4-14 Special rules are applicable in situations where group term life insurance coverage exceeds $50,000. How are key employees treated?

I:4-15 a. What are the six major types of fringe benefits covered by Sec. 132?
b. What tax advantage is offered relative to such benefits?
c. Are such benefits available to employees only or may the benefits also be offered to spouses, dependents, and retirees?
d. Is discrimination prohibited relative to Sec. 132 benefits?
e. What is the tax impact on the employer and employees if an employer's plan is discriminatory?

I:4-16 What conditions must be met if an employee is to exclude meals and lodging furnished by an employer?

I:4-17 The president and vice president of USA Corporation receive benefits that are unavailable to other employees. These benefits include free parking, payment of monthly expenses in a local club, discounts on products sold by the corporation, and payment of premiums on a whole life insurance policy. Which of the benefits must be included in the gross income of the president and vice president?

I:4-18 Are the same fringe benefits that are available to employees also available to self-employed individuals?

I:4-19 If an employee takes a customer to lunch and discusses business, can the employee deduct 50% of the meal for both the customer and himself? Explain.

I:4-20 Are income distributions from a qualified state tuition program taxable?

I:4-21 What types of income qualify for the foreign-earned income exclusion?

I:4-22 Are taxpayers who claim the foreign-earned income exclusion entitled to deduct expenses incurred in producing that income? Explain.

I:4-23 a. Why is it important to distinguish debt cancellation from a gift, bequest, or renegotiation of a purchase price?
b. What happens to the basis of an asset if the taxpayer renegotiates its purchase price?

I:4-24 a. Under what conditions is the discharge of indebtedness not taxable?
b. If a father forgives a daughter's debt to him, is she required to include such amount in her gross income?

I:4-25 Bankrupt and insolvent taxpayers do not recognize income if debt is discharged. They must, however, reduce specified tax attributes. What is involved?

I:4-26 Are partners and proprietors at a disadvantage with respect to fringe benefits? Explain.

I:4-27 Why are cafeteria plans helpful in the design of an employee benefit plan that provides nontaxable fringe benefits?

I:4-28 Both high-income and low-income employees are covered by cafeteria plans. Under such plans, all employees may select from a list of nontaxable fringe benefits or they may elect to receive cash in lieu of these benefits.
   a. Which group of employees is more likely to choose nontaxable fringe benefits in lieu of cash? Explain.
   b. Is this result desirable from a social or economic point of view? Explain.

ISSUE IDENTIFICATION QUESTIONS

I:4-29 Luke, who retired this year, lives in a four-plex owned by Julie. Luke's income decreased when he retired, and he now has difficulty paying his rent. Julie offered to reduce Luke's rent if he would agree to mow the lawn, wash windows, and provide other maintenance services. Luke accepted, and Julie reduced the monthly rental from $650 to $300. What are the tax issues that should be considered by Luke and Julie?

I:4-30 Mildred worked as a maid for 27 years in the home of Larry and Kay. When she retired, they presented her with a check for $25,000, indicating that it was a way of showing their appreciation for her years of loyal service. What tax issues should Mildred and her employer consider?

I:4-31 Troy Department Stores offers employees discounts on merchandise carried in the store. Newly hired employees receive a 10% discount. The discount rate increases 1% each year until employees have 20 years of service when the discount rate is capped at 30%. What tax issues should Troy and the employees consider?

I:4-32 Jerry works in the human resources department of Ajax Corporation. One of his responsibilities is to interview prospective employees. Two or three days each week, Jerry takes a prospective employee to lunch, and Ajax reimburses him for the cost of the meals. What tax issues should Jerry and Ajax Corporation consider?

PROBLEMS

I:4-33 *Self-Help Income.* In which of the following situations would the taxpayer realize taxable income?
   a. A mechanic performs work on his own automobile. The mechanic would have charged a customer $400 for doing the same work.
   b. A mechanic repairs his neighbor's personal automobile. In exchange, the neighbor, an accountant, agrees to prepare the mechanic's tax return. The services performed are each worth $200.
   c. A mechanic repairs his daughter's automobile without any charge.

I:4-34 *Excludable Gifts.* Which of the following would be includable in gross income?
   a. Alice appeared on a TV quiz show and received a prize of $5,000.
   b. Bart received $500 from his employer because he developed an idea that reduced the employer's production costs.
   c. Chuck borrowed $500 from his mother in order to finance his last year in college. Upon his graduation, Chuck's mother told him he did not have to repay the $500. She intended the $500 to be a graduation present.

I:4-35 *Life Insurance Proceeds.* Don is the beneficiary of a $50,000 insurance policy on the life of his mother, Anna. To date, Anna has paid premiums of $16,000. What amount of gross income must be reported in each of the following cases?
   a. Anna elects to cancel the policy and receives $20,000, the cash surrender value of the policy.
   b. Anna dies and Don receives the face amount of the policy, $50,000.
   c. Anna dies and Don elects to receive $15,000 per year for four years.

I:4-36 *Transfer of Life Insurance.* Ed is the beneficiary of a $20,000 insurance policy on the life of his mother. Because Ed needs funds, he sells the policy to his sister, Amy, for $6,000. Amy subsequently pays premiums of $9,000.

a. How much income must Amy report if she collects the face value of the policy upon the death of her mother?

b. Would Amy have to report any income if her brother had given her the policy? Assume the only payment she made was $9,000 for the premiums.

I:4-37 *Settlement of Life Insurance Policy.* Sue is age 73 and has a great deal of difficulty living independently as she suffers from severe rheumatoid arthritis. She is covered by a $400,000 life insurance policy, and her children are named as her beneficiaries. Because of her health, Sue decides to live in a nursing home, but she does not have enough income to pay her nursing home bills which are expected to total $42,000 per year. The insurance company offers disabled individuals the option of either a reduced settlement on their policies or an annuity. Given Sue's age and health she has the option of receiving $3,200 per month or a lump sum payment of $225,000. To date, Sue has paid $80,000 in premiums on the policy.

a. How much income must Sue report if she chooses the lump sum settlement?

b. How much income must Sue report if she elects the annuity?

c. How much income would Sue have to report if her nursing home bills amounted to only $36,000 per year?

I:4-38 *Insurance Policy Dividends.* Hank carries a $100,000 insurance policy on his life. Premiums paid over the years total $8,000. Dividends on the policy have totaled $6,000. Hank has left the dividends on the policy with the insurance company. During the current year, the insurance company credited $600 of interest on the accumulated dividends to Hank's account.

a. How much income is Hank obligated to report in connection with the policy?

b. Would it make any difference if the accumulated dividends equaled $9,000 instead of $6,000?

I:4-39 *Prizes and Awards.* For each of the following, indicate whether the amount is taxable:

a. Peggy won $4,000 in the state lottery.

b. Jane won a $500 prize for her entry in a poetry contest.

c. Linda was awarded $2,000 when she was selected as "Teacher of the Year" by the local school district.

I:4-40 *Scholarships.* For each of the following, indicate the amount that must be included in the taxpayer's gross income:

a. Larry was given a $1,500 tuition scholarship to attend Eastern Law School. In addition, Eastern paid Larry $4,000 per year to work part-time in the campus bookstore.

b. Marty received a $10,000 football scholarship for attending Northern University. The scholarship covered tuition, room and board, laundry, and books. Four thousand dollars of the scholarship was designated for room and board and laundry. It was understood that Marty would participate in the school's intercollegiate football program, but Marty was not required to do so.

c. Western School of Nursing requires all third-year students to work twenty hours per week at an affiliated hospital. Each student is paid $10 per hour. Nancy, a third-year student, earned $10,000 during the year.

I:4-41 *Research Grant.* Otto is a biology professor at State University. The university gave Otto a sabbatical leave to study the surface of the flatworm. During the year he received a salary of $50,000, which is less than his regular salary of $56,000. Otto also received a grant to cover expenses associated with the study. The grant was $2,000, as were his related expenses. Otto also incurred memberships and other employment related expenses totaling $1,000. How much must Otto include in gross income?

I:4-42 *Payments for Personal Injury.* Determine which of the following payments for sickness and injury must be included in the taxpayer's gross income.

a. Pat was injured in an automobile accident. The other driver's insurance company paid him $2,000 to cover medical expenses and a compensatory amount of $4,000 for pain and suffering.

b. A newspaper article stated that Quincy had been convicted of tax evasion. Quincy, in fact, had never been accused of tax evasion. He sued and won a compensatory settlement of $4,000 from the newspaper.

c. Rob, who pays the cost of a commercial disability income policy, fell and injured his back. He was unable to work for six months. The insurance company paid him $1,800 per month during the time he was unable to work.

d. Steve fell and injured his knee. He was unable to work for four months. His employer-financed disability income policy paid Steve $1,600 per month during the time he was unable to work.

e. Ted suffered a stroke. He was unable to work for five months. His employer continued to pay Ted his salary of $1,700 per month during the time he was unable to work.

I:4-43   *Employee Benefits.* Ursula is employed by USA Corporation. USA Corporation provides medical and health, disability, and group term life insurance coverage for its employees. Premiums attributable to Ursula were as follows:

Medical and health	$3,600
Disability	300
Group term life (face amount is $40,000)	200

During the year, Ursula suffered a heart attack and subsequently died. Before her death, Ursula collected $14,000 as a reimbursement for medical expenses and $5,000 of disability income. Upon her death, Ursula's husband collected the $40,000 face value of the life insurance policy.

a. What amount can USA Corporation deduct for premiums attributable to Ursula?
b. How much must Ursula include in income relative to the premiums paid?
c. How much must Ursula include in income relative to the insurance benefits?
d. How much must Ursula's widower include in income?

I:4-44   *Group Term Life Insurance.* Data Corporation has four employees and provides group term life insurance coverage for all four employees. Coverage is nondiscriminatory and is as follows:

Employee	Age	Key Employee	Coverage	Actual Premiums
Andy	62	yes	$200,000	$4,000
Bob	52	yes	40,000	700
Cindy	33	no	80,000	600
Damitria	33	no	40,000	300

a. How much may Data Corporation deduct for group term life insurance premiums?
b. How much income must be reported by each employee?

I:4-45   *Life Insurance Proceeds.* Joe is the beneficiary of a life insurance policy taken out by his father several years ago. Joe's father died this year and Joe has the option of receiving $100,000 cash or electing to receive $14,000 per year for the remainder of his life. Joe is now 65. Joe's father paid $32,000 in premiums over the years.

a. How much must Joe include in gross income this year if he elects to accept the $100,000 face amount?
b. How much must be included in Joe's gross income this year if he elects to receive installment payments?

I:4-46   *Employee Benefits.* Al flies for AAA Airlines. AAA provides its employees with several fringe benefits. Al and his family are allowed to fly on a space-available basis on AAA Airline. Tickets used by Al and his family during the year are worth $2,000. AAA paid for a subscription to two magazines published for pilots. The subscriptions totaled $80. The airline paid for Al's meals and lodging while he was away from home overnight in connection with his job. Such meals and lodging cost AAA $10,000. Although Al could not eat while flying, he was allowed to drink coffee provided by the airline. The coffee was worth about $50. AAA provided Al with free parking, which is valued at $100 per month. The airline treated Al and his family to a one-week all-expenses-paid vacation at a resort near his home. This benefit was awarded because of Al's outstanding safety record. The value of the vacation was $2,300. Which of these benefits are taxable to Al?

I:4-47   *Employee Benefits.* Jet Corporation is involved in the purchase and rental of several large apartment complexes. Questions have been raised about the treatment of several items pertaining to Jet Corporation and its employees. Jet Corporation employs a manager for each complex. The manager is required to occupy a unit in the complex in order to be available at all hours. The average rental value of the units is $12,000 per year. The corporation's president finds that it is beneficial to the corporation if he entertains bankers and others with whom Jet does business. He does such entertaining about once each month and the corporation pays the cost. Business is discussed at the meals. The cost for the year of such entertaining was $1,500, and about one-third of cost was attributable to meals consumed by the president.

Each year as the company closes its books, the controller and certain other members of the accounting staff must work overtime. The company pays each employee supper money totaling $25 during this period.

The corporation's vice president is expected to travel on business-related matters to visit various properties owned by the corporation. Because of the distances involved, the vice president must stay away from home several nights. Total meals and lodging incurred on the trips total $3,000, most of which is attributable to the vice president himself.

Which amounts are deductible by the corporation? Which are taxable to the employee?

I:4-48 *Death Benefits.* After a brief illness, Bill died. Bill's employer paid $20,000 to his widow. The corporation sent along a letter with the check indicating that $5,000 represented payment for Bill's accrued vacation days and back wages. The balance was being awarded in recognition of Bill's many years of loyal service. The company was obligated to pay the accrued vacation days and back wages, but the balance was discretionary.
a. Is the employer entitled to deduct the $20,000 paid to Bill's widow?
b. Is Bill's widow required to include the $20,000 in her gross income?

I:4-49 *Foreign-Earned Income Exclusion.* For each of the following cases, indicate the amount of the foreign-earned income exclusion. (Disregard the effect of exemptions for certain allowances under Sec. 912.)
a. Sam, a U.S. citizen, is an assistant to the ambassador to Spain. Sam lives and works in Spain. His salary of $90,000 is paid by the U.S. government.
b. Jim, a U.S. citizen, owns an unincorporated oil drilling company that operates in Argentina, where he resides. The business is heavily dependent on equipment owned by Jim. His profit for the year totaled $100,000.
c. Ken, a U.S. citizen, works for a large Japanese corporation. Ken is employed in the United States, but must travel to Japan several times each year. During the current year he spent sixty days in Japan. This is typical of most years. His salary is $95,000.

I:4-50 *Foreign-Earned Income Exclusion.* On January 5, 2010 Rita left the United States for Germany, where she had accepted an appointment as vice president of foreign operations. Her employer, USA Corporation, told her the assignment would last about two years. Rita decided not to establish a permanent residence in Germany because her assignment was for only two years. Her salary for the year is $274,500. Rita incurred travel, transportation, and other related expenses totaling $6,000, none of which are reimbursed.
a. What is Rita's foreign-earned income exclusion?
b. How much may she deduct for travel and transportation?

I:4-51 *Discharge of Debt.* During bankruptcy, USA Corporation debt was reduced from $780,000 to $400,000. USA Corporation's assets are valued at $500,000. USA's NOL carryover was $400,000.
a. Is USA Corporation required to report any income from the discharge of its debts?
b. Which tax attributes are reduced and by how much? Assume USA does not make any special elections when reducing its attributes.

I:4-52 *Discharge of Debt.* Old Corporation has suffered losses for several years, and its debts total $500,000; Old's assets are valued at only $380,000. Old's creditors agree to reduce Old's debts by one-half in order to permit the corporation to continue to operate. Old's NOL carryover is $150,000.
a. What impact does the reduction in debt have on Old's NOL?
b. Is Old required to report any income?

I:4-53 *Court and Insurance Awards.* Determine whether the following items represent taxable income.
a. As the result of an age discrimination suit, Pat received a cash settlement of $40,000. One-half of the settlement represented wages lost by Pat as a result of the discrimination and the balance represented an award based on personal injury.
b. Matt sued the local newspaper for a story that reported he was affiliated with organized crime. The court awarded him $50,000 of libel damages.
c. Pam was injured in an automobile accident and received $10,000 from an employer-sponsored disability policy. In addition, her employer-financed medical insurance policy reimbursed her for $15,000 of medical expenses.

I:4-54 *Cafeteria Plan.* Jangyoun is a married taxpayer with a dependent 4-year-old daughter. His employer offers a flexible spending account under which he can choose to receive cash or, alternatively, choose from certain fringe benefits. These benefits include health insurance that costs $9,000 and child care that costs $2,600. Assume Jangyoun is in the 28% tax bracket.

a. How much income tax will Jangyoun save if he chooses to participate in the employer's health insurance plan? Assume that he does not have sufficient medical expenses to itemize his deductions.

b. Would you recommend that Jangyoun participate in the employer's health insurance plan if his wife's employer already provides comparable health insurance coverage for the family?

c. Would you recommend that Jangyoun participate in the employer-provided child care option if he has the alternative option of claiming a child care credit of $480?

I:4-55 *Exclusion of Gain from Small Business Stock.* Jose acquired 1,000 shares of Acorn Corporation common stock by transferring property with an adjusted basis of $1,000,000 and fair market value of $4,000,000 for 100% of the stock. Acorn is a qualified small business corporation. After six years, on April 1, 2010, Jose sells all of the Acorn Corporation common stock for $16,000,000.

a. What is the amount of gain that may be excluded from Jose's gross income?

b. What would your answer be if the fair market value of the Acorn stock were only $800,000 upon its issue?

c. What would your answer be if the stock were sold after two years?

d. Can Jose avoid recognizing gain by purchasing replacement stock?

COMPREHENSIVE PROBLEM

I:4-56 Pat was divorced from her husband in 2005. During the current year she received alimony of $18,000 and child support of $4,000 for her 11-year-old son, who lives with her. Her former husband had asked her to sign an agreement giving him the dependency exemption for the child but she declined to do so. After the divorce she accepted a position as a teacher in the local school district. During the current year she received a salary of $32,000. The school district paid her medical insurance premiums of $6,900 and provided her with group term life insurance coverage of $40,000. The premiums attributable to her coverage equaled $160. During her marriage, Pat's parents loaned her $8,000 to help with the down payment on her home. Her parents told her this year that they understand her financial problems and that they were cancelling the balance on the loan, which was $5,000. They did so because they wanted to help their only daughter.

Pat received dividends from National Motor Company of $4,600 and interest on State of California bonds of $2,850.

Pat sold her personal automobile for $2,800 because she needed a larger car. The automobile had cost $8,000. She purchased a new auto for $11,000. Pat had itemized deductions of $8,600. Compute her taxable income.

TAX STRATEGY PROBLEMS

I:4-57 Sally owns a small C corporation that has provided health insurance coverage for Sally and the company's three other employees. The insurance coverage for Sally and the three employees is individual coverage, not family coverage. Sally's own family coverage is through a separate private policy. She pays the premiums out of after-tax dollars. Sally's salary is $40,000 and the salary for the other three employees averages $30,000. The premiums on the health insurance policy average $2,000 per employee per year. The provider recently informed Sally that the premiums will increase to $2,500 per employee. The spouses of her two married employees have coverage through their employers. The third employee has announced that he will marry soon and would very much like to have family health insurance coverage. The insurance provider says that family coverage will approximately double the premiums. Sally is finding the cost of providing medical insurance coverage particularly burdensome for her small business. What planning suggestions can you offer?

I:4-58 Maria was planning to paint the interior of her apartment over a three-day weekend. Her employer asked her to work all three days and will pay her $600 overtime. She called a professional painter who offered to do the job for $500. He is willing to use the paint she has already purchased. Maria is in the 28% tax bracket. Will she be better off financially to work the overtime and pay the painter or to turn down the overtime and do the work herself? What other factors should she consider?

TAX FORM/RETURN PREPARATION PROBLEMS

I:4-59 A. J. Paige, Social Security number 111-22-3333, is the vice president of marketing (Australia) for International Industries, Inc. (III). III is headquartered at 123 Main Street, Los Angeles, California 92601. A. J., who is single, accepted the position and became a resident of Australia on July 8 of last year. Her business address is 242 Main, Melbourne, Australia. A. J.'s visa permits her to stay in Australia indefinitely. Her only trips to the United States in the current year were for vacations (August 2 to 16 and December 21 to 28). A. J.'s contract specifies that her appointment is to last indefinitely, but states that III is to pay her $4,000 per year to cover the cost of two vacation trips to the United States. Her salary is $140,000, out of which she pays rent on an apartment of $28,000 per year. A. J. has no family or residence in the United States. She paid an income tax in Australia of $23,500. Complete a Form 2555.

I:4-60 Alice Johnson, Social Security number 222-23-3334, is a single taxpayer and is employed as a secretary by State University of Florida. She has the following items pertaining to her income tax return for the current year:

- Received a $20,000 salary from her employer, who withheld $3,000 federal income tax.
- Received a gift of 1,000 shares of Ace Corporation stock with a $100,000 FMV from her mother. She also received $4,000 of cash dividends from the Ace Corporation. The dividends are qualified dividends.
- Received $1,000 of interest income on bonds issued by the City of Tampa.
- Received a regular stock dividend (nontaxable under Sec. 305) of 50 shares of Ace Corporation stock with a $5,000 FMV.
- Alice's employer paid $2,000 of medical and health insurance premiums on her behalf.
- Received $12,000 alimony from her ex-husband.
- State University provided $60,000 of group term life insurance. Alice is 42 years old and is not a key employee. The table in the text is applicable.
- Received a $1,000 cash award from her employer for being designated the Secretary of the Year.
- Total itemized deductions are $8,000.

Complete Form 1040 and accompanying schedules for Alice Johnson's federal income tax return for the current year.

CASE STUDY PROBLEMS

I:4-61 Able Corporation is a closely held company engaged in the manufacture and retail sales of automotive parts. Able maintains a qualified pension plan for its employees but has not offered nontaxable fringe benefits.

You are a tax consultant for the company who has been asked to prepare suggestions for the adoption of an employee fringe benefit plan. Your discussions with the client's chief financial officer reveal the following:

- Employees currently pay their own premiums for medical and health insurance.
- No group term life insurance is provided.
- The company owns a vacant building that could easily be converted to a parking garage.
- Many of the employees purchase automobile parts from the company's retail outlets and pay retail price.
- The president of the corporation would like to provide a dependent care assistance program under Sec. 129 for its employees.

Required: Prepare a client memo that recommends the adoption of an employee fringe benefit program. Your recommendations should discuss the pros and cons of different types of nontaxable fringe benefits.

I:4-62 Jay Corporation owns several automobile dealerships. This year, the corporation initiated a policy of giving the top salesperson at each dealership a free vacation trip to Florida. The president believes that this is an effective sales incentive. The cost of the vacations is deductible by the corporation as compensation paid to employees, and is taxable to the recipients. Nevertheless, the president objects to reporting the value of the vacations as income on the W-2s of the recipients and to withholding taxes from wages for the value of

the trips. He feels that this undermines the effectiveness of the incentive. What are the implications of this behavior for the corporation and the president?

TAX RESEARCH PROBLEMS

I:4-63   Ann is a graduate economics student at State University. State University awarded her a $1,000 scholarship. In addition, Ann works as a half-time teaching assistant in the Economics Department at State University. She is paid $7,000 per year and her tuition is waived. The salary is equal to that paid other part-time instructors. Her tuition would be $8,000 were it not for the waiver. Ann paid $500 for her books and supplies and she incurred living expenses of $7,400. Determine how much gross income Ann must report.
   A partial list of research sources is

- Sec. 117(d)
- Prop. Reg. 1.117-6(d)(5)

I:4-64   Kim leased an office building to USA Corporation under a ten-year lease specifying that at the end of the lease USA had to return the building to its original condition if any modifications were made. USA changed the interior of the building, and at the end of the lease USA paid Kim $30,000 instead of making the required repairs. Does Kim have to include the payment in gross income?
   A partial list of research sources is

- Sec. 109
- *Boston Fish Market Corp.*, 57 T.C. 884 (1972)
- *Sirbo Holdings Inc. v. CIR*, 31 AFTR 2d 73-1005, 73-1 USTC ¶9312 (2nd Cir., 1973)

I:4-65   As a result of a fire damaging their residence, the Taylors must stay in a motel for three weeks while their home is being restored. They pay $2,000 for the room and $500 for meals. Their homeowner's policy pays $2,500 to reimburse them for the cost. They estimate that during the five-week period they would normally spend $300 for meals. Is the reimbursement taxable?
   A partial list of research sources is

- Sec. 123
- Reg. Sec. 1.123-1

I:4-66   Bold Corporation paid $25 to each full-time employee at year-end in recognition of the holidays. Bold Corporation is interested in whether the amounts are taxable income to its employees, and whether the company can deduct the amounts.
   A partial list of research sources is

- Secs. 74(c), 102, 132(c), and 274(b)
- Reg. Sec. 1.132-6(e)(1)
- *Hallmark Cards, Inc. v. U.S.*, 9 AFTR 2d 391, 62-1 USTC ¶9162 (DC-Mo, 1961).
- Rev. Rul. 59-58, 1959-1 CB 17.

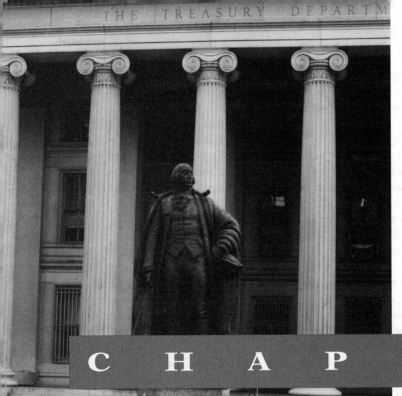

5

C H A P T E R

PROPERTY TRANSACTIONS: CAPITAL GAINS AND LOSSES

LEARNING OBJECTIVES

After studying this chapter, you should be able to

1 ▶ Determine the realized gain or loss from the sale or other disposition of property

2 ▶ Determine the amount realized from the sale or other disposition of property

3 ▶ Determine the basis of property

4 ▶ Distinguish between capital assets and other assets

5 ▶ Understand how capital gains and losses affect taxable income

6 ▶ Recognize when a sale or exchange has occurred

7 ▶ Determine the holding period for an asset when a sale or disposition occurs

HISTORICAL NOTE

A preferential tax rate on capital gains was included in the tax law from 1921 until 1987. A modest preferential rate was reintroduced in 1991, with capital gains for noncorporate taxpayers being subject to a maximum 28% tax rate and ordinary income being subject to a maximum tax rate of 31%. The rates were reduced in 1997 and reduced again in 2003.

ADDITIONAL COMMENT

For a discussion of the justification of preferential tax rates for LTCGs (see page I:5-30).

Gross income includes "gains derived from dealings in property,"[1] and certain "losses from sale or exchange of property"[2] are allowed as deductions from gross income to determine adjusted gross income. All recognized gains and losses must eventually be classified either as *capital* or *ordinary*. Except for a brief time in the mid-to-late 1980s, long-term capital gains (LTCGs) of individual taxpayers have consistently been taxed at lower rates than ordinary gains or short-term capital gains (STCGs).[3] This preferential treatment of capital gains, more precisely LTCGs, has been a much debated topic for many years. A discussion of the reasoning for imposing lower tax rates on LTCGs is provided near the end of this chapter.

The preferential treatment of capital gains has fluctuated widely over the years. For example, in the early 1980s, taxpayers were allowed to deduct 60% of the gain. In 1991, net capital gains were taxed at a maximum rate of 28%, then reduced to 20% for most taxpayers in 1997. Congress started applying different rates to different types of LTCG (i.e., a LTCG due to the sale of a collectible has a maximum rate of 28% while a LTCG due to the sale of stock has a maximum rate of 15%). Thus, depending on the political persuasion of the government, tax rates on net capital gains have yo-yoed up and down. A significant change in the rates for adjusted net capital gains occurred in 2003 when the rates were reduced from 20% to 15% for most taxpayers (5% for lower income taxpayers). For tax years beginning after 2007, the rate is zero instead of 5%.[4] With the maximum ordinary tax rate for individuals being 35% today, individuals can benefit by having a gain classified as a LTCG rather than as ordinary gain or STCG. Thus, much planning is performed to attempt to arrange one's affairs to take advantage of the lower capital gain rates.

As explained later, a LTCG may be subject to one of four different rates [0% (5% before 2008), 15%, 25% or 28%] depending on what type of asset is sold and the taxpayer's regular tax rate. The current rates are scheduled to expire for tax years beginning after December 31, 2010, unless the so-called "Bush tax cuts" are made permanent. If the rates are allowed to expire, the rates that were in effect for tax years ending before May 6, 2003, will apply. In most cases, those rates are higher than the current rates.

Capital losses must be offset against capital gains, and net capital losses are subjected to restrictions on their deductibility. Thus, most taxpayers prefer to have losses classified as ordinary instead of capital.

Most property transactions have tax consequences to the taxpayer. For example, when a sale, exchange, or abandonment occurs, the taxpayer must determine the realized gain or loss, the portion of the realized gain or loss that must be recognized (if any), and the character of the gain or loss. This chapter focuses on determining the realized gain or loss and the portion of the recognized gain or loss classified as capital or ordinary. When classifying a recognized gain or loss, (i.e., the gain or loss actually reported on the taxpayer's tax return) three important questions must be considered:

▶ What type of property has been sold or exchanged?

▶ When has a sale or exchange occurred?

▶ What is the holding period for the property?

In this chapter, these three questions are considered as well as difficulties associated with determining the basis of the property sold or exchanged and the amount of realized gains or losses.

---

[1] Sec. 61(a)(3).

[2] Sec. 62(a)(3).

[3] See page I:5-29 and below for a discussion of the holding period for capital assets. A capital gain or loss is long-term or short-term depending on the length of time the asset has been held by the taxpayer.

[4] Sec. 1(h)(1)(B).

DETERMINATION OF GAIN OR LOSS

OBJECTIVE 1

Determine the realized gain or loss from the sale or other disposition of property

REALIZED GAIN OR LOSS

To determine the **realized gain** or **loss**, the amount realized from the sale or exchange of property is compared with the adjusted basis of that property. A gain is realized when the amount realized is greater than the basis, and a loss is realized when the amount realized is less than the basis of the property.[5]

EXAMPLE I:5-1 ▶ Jack sells an asset with an adjusted basis of $10,000 to Judy for $14,000. Because the amount realized is greater than the basis, Jack has a realized gain of $4,000 ($14,000 − $10,000). ◀

Despite the fact that most transfers of property involve a sale, gains and losses may also be realized on certain other types of dispositions of property, such as exchanges, condemnations, casualties, thefts, bond retirements, and corporate distributions. However, gains and losses are generally not realized when property is disposed of by gift or bequest.

EXAMPLE I:5-2 ▶ Alice owns land held for investment with a basis of $20,000. The land is taken by the city by right of eminent domain, and she receives a payment of $30,000 for the land. This condemnation is treated as a sale or disposition for income tax purposes, and Alice's realized gain is $10,000 ($30,000 − $20,000). ◀

EXAMPLE I:5-3 ▶ Two years ago, Bob purchased stock of a newly formed corporation for $10,000. During the current year, he receives a $12,000 distribution, constituting a return of capital, from the corporation. This distribution is treated as a sale. Therefore, Bob has a realized gain of $2,000 ($12,000 − $10,000). Bob's basis for the stock is now zero because his basis of $10,000 has been recovered. ◀

There must be an identifiable event for a sale or other disposition to occur. Mere changes in the value of property are not normally recognized as a disposition for purposes of determining a realized gain or loss.

STUDY AID

Students should pay close attention to the technical terms used in tax law. For example, the similar sounding terms of "realized gain" and "recognized gain" are often different dollar amounts for the sale of an asset.

Many reasons exist for not taxing unrealized gains and losses that arise due to a mere change in value. The Treasury Regulations state that "A loss is not ordinarily sustained prior to the sale or other disposition of the property, for the reason that until such sale or other disposition occurs there remains the possibility that the taxpayer may recover or recoup the adjusted basis of the property."[6] Because of administrative difficulties associated with determining fair market value (FMV), disputes with the Internal Revenue Service (IRS) would be greatly increased if unrealized gains were taxed and unrealized losses were allowed as deductions. In addition, payment of tax on income is generally required only when a taxpayer has the wherewithal to pay the tax (e.g., the taxpayer has received cash from the sale or other disposition of property and can therefore pay the tax on the gain).

AMOUNT REALIZED. The **amount realized** from a sale or other disposition of property is the sum of any money received, the FMV of all other property received, and any debt assumed by the buyer.

EXAMPLE I:5-4 ▶ Tony sells land to Rita for $15,000 in cash and a machine having a $3,000 FMV. Tony's amount realized is $18,000 ($15,000 + $3,000). ◀

---

[5] Sec. 1001(a).

[6] Reg. Sec. 1.1001-1(c)(1).

OBJECTIVE 2

Determine the amount realized from the sale or other disposition of property

The determination of FMV is a question of fact and often creates considerable controversy between taxpayers and the IRS. **Fair market value (FMV)** is "the price at which property would change hands between a willing buyer and a willing seller, neither being under any compulsion to buy or sell."[7] The FMV of the asset given in the exchange may be easier to determine than the FMV of the property received. In those cases, the FMV of the property given may be used to measure the amount realized. If a buyer assumes the seller's liability or takes the property subject to the debt, the courts have included the amount of the liability when determining the amount realized.[8]

EXAMPLE I:5-5 ▶ Anna exchanges land subject to a liability of $20,000 for $35,000 of stock owned by Mario. Mario takes the property subject to the liability. The amount realized by Anna is $55,000 ($35,000 + $20,000 liability assumed by Mario). If Anna's adjusted basis for the land exchanged is $42,000, her realized gain is $13,000 ($55,000 − $42,000). ◀

In the above example, Anna receives stock with a $35,000 FMV and is relieved of a $20,000 debt. Mario's taking the property subject to the debt is equivalent to providing Anna with cash of $20,000. Thus, the amount realized by Anna is $55,000.

Generally, selling expenses such as sales commissions and advertising incurred in order to sell or dispose of the property reduce the amount realized.

EXAMPLE I:5-6 ▶ Doug sells stock of Briggs Corporation with a basis of $10,000, for $17,000. Doug pays a sales commission of $300. The amount realized by Doug is $16,700 ($17,000 − $300), and his realized gain is $6,700 ($16,700 − $10,000). ◀

TYPICAL MISCONCEPTION

The difference between the assumption of a liability and the taking of the property subject to the debt is sometimes confusing. The latter means that the lender can satisfy the debt only by repossessing the property. In the former case, where the buyer assumes the debt, the lender can satisfy the debt by repossessing the property and by going after other assets of the buyer.

ADJUSTED BASIS. The initial adjusted basis of property depends on how the property is acquired (e.g., by purchase, gift, or inheritance). Most property is acquired by purchase and therefore its initial basis is the cost of the property. However, if property is acquired from a decedent, its basis to the estate or heir is its FMV either at the date of death or, if the alternate valuation date is elected, six months from the date of death. The rules for determining the adjusted basis are discussed in subsequent sections of this chapter. Once the initial basis is determined, it may be adjusted upward or downward. Capital additions (also called capital expenditures) are expenditures that add to the value or prolong the life of property or adapt the property to a new or different use. Capital additions increase the basis. Capital recoveries, such as the deductions for casualty losses, cost recovery, and depreciation, reduce the basis. A property's adjusted basis can be determined by the following equation:

> Initial basis
> + Capital additions (e.g., new porch for a building)
> − Capital recoveries (e.g., depreciation deduction)
> = Adjusted basis

ETHICAL POINT

The taxpayer may have lost records relating to the basis of the assets acquired many years earlier. In that case, the CPA can accept estimates of the missing data made by the taxpayer.

Capital expenditures are distinguished from expenditures that are deductible as ordinary and necessary business expenses. For example, the cost of repairing a roof may be a deductible expense, whereas the cost of replacing a roof is a capital addition. It is sometimes difficult to determine whether an item is a capital expenditure or a business expense. Because of the preference for an immediate tax deduction, taxpayers normally prefer to classify expenditures as expenses rather than capital expenditures.

EXAMPLE I:5-7 ▶ Ellen pays $2,500 for a major overhaul of an automobile used in her trade or business. The $2,500 is capitalized as part of the automobile's cost rather than deducted as a repair expense. ◀

Capital recoveries reduce the adjusted basis. The most common form of capital recovery is the deduction for depreciation or cost recovery. As discussed in Chapter I:10, the modi-

---

[7] *CIR v. Homer H. Marshman*, 5 AFTR 2d 1528, 60-2 USTC ¶9484 (6th Cir., 1960).

[8] *Beulah B. Crane v. CIR*, 35 AFTR 776, 47-1 USTC ¶9217 (USSC, 1947).

fied accelerated cost recovery system (MACRS) is mandatory for most tangible depreciable property placed in service after 1986. The accelerated cost recovery system (ACRS) applies to most property placed in service after December 31, 1980, and before 1987.

EXAMPLE I:5-8 ▶

ADDITIONAL COMMENT

In addition to depreciation, other capital recoveries that reduce the adjusted basis of property include depletion, amortization, corporate distributions that are a return of basis, compensation or awards for involuntary conversions, deductible casualty losses, insurance reimbursements, and cash rebates received by a purchaser.

Jeremy paid $100,000 for equipment two years ago and has claimed depreciation deductions of $37,000 for the two years. The cost of repairs during the same period was $6,000. At the end of the two-year period, the property's adjusted basis is $63,000 ($100,000 − $37,000). The amount spent for repairs does not affect the basis. ◀

RECOVERY OF BASIS DOCTRINE. The **recovery of basis doctrine** states that taxpayers are allowed to recover the basis of an asset without being taxed because such amounts are a return of capital that the taxpayer has invested in the property. If a taxpayer receives a $12,000 return of capital distribution from a corporation when the taxpayer's basis for its investment in the corporation's stock is $10,000, the first $10,000 received represents a recovery of basis and the $2,000 excess amount is treated as a gain realized on a sale or exchange of the stock investment. In many cases, basis is recovered in the form of a deduction for depreciation, cost recovery, or a casualty loss.

TYPICAL MISCONCEPTION

It is sometimes incorrectly believed that all realized gains and losses are recognized for tax purposes. Although most realized gains are recognized, some realized losses are not. For example, losses on the sale or exchange of property held for personal use are not recognized.

RECOGNIZED GAIN OR LOSS

Realized gain or loss represents the difference between the amount realized and the adjusted basis when a sale or exchange occurs. The amount of gain or loss actually reported on the tax return is the **recognized gain or loss.** In some instances, gain or loss is not recognized due to special provisions in the tax law (e.g., a gain or loss may be deferred or a loss may be disallowed).

Losses are generally deductible if they are incurred in carrying on a trade or business, incurred in an activity engaged in for profit, and casualty and theft losses. Realized losses on the sale or exchange of assets held for personal use are not recognized for tax purposes. Therefore, a taxpayer who incurs a loss on the sale or exchange of a personal-use asset does not fully recover the basis. As explained in Chapter I:8, realized losses on personal-use assets may be recognized to some extent if the property is disposed of by casualty or theft.

EXAMPLE I:5-9 ▶

Ralph purchases a personal residence for $60,000. Deductions for depreciation are not allowed because the asset is not used in a trade or business or held for the production of income. If Ralph sells the house for $55,000, the realized loss of $5,000 is a capital loss but not deductible. He recovers only $55,000 of his original $60,000 basis. ◀

BASIS CONSIDERATIONS

OBJECTIVE 3

Determine the basis of property

COST OF ACQUIRED PROPERTY

In most cases, the basis of property is its cost. **Cost** is the amount paid for the property in cash or the FMV of other property given in the exchange. Any costs of acquiring the property and preparing the property for use are included in the cost of the property.

EXAMPLE I:5-10 ▶

Penny purchases equipment for $15,000, pays delivery costs of $300, and installation costs of $250. The cost of the equipment is $15,550. ◀

Funds borrowed and used to pay for an asset are included in the cost. Obligations of the seller that are assumed by the buyer increase the asset's cost.

EXAMPLE I:5-11 ▶

Peggy purchases an asset by paying cash of $40,000 and signs a note payable to the seller for $60,000. She also assumes a $2,000 lien against the property. Her basis for the asset is $102,000 and the amount realized by the seller is $102,000. ◀

UNIFORM CAPITALIZATION RULES. For financial accounting purposes, businesses must capitalize certain costs in connection with inventory, such as direct materials, direct labor, and overhead. For many years, businesses had a degree of flexibility with respect to capitalizing or expensing certain costs for tax purposes. However, the tax law now mandates one set of capitalization rules applicable to all taxpayers and all types of activities. These uniform capitalization rules, which apply principally to inventory, are provided in Sec. 263A and discussed in Chapter I:11.

The uniform capitalization rules also affect property other than inventory if the property is used in a taxpayer's trade or business or in an activity engaged in for profit. Taxes paid or accrued in connection with the acquisition of property are included as part of the cost of the acquired property. Taxes paid or accrued in connection with the disposition of property reduce the amount realized on the disposition.[9]

ADDITIONAL COMMENT

The sales tax is a good example of a tax that would be paid in connection with the acquisition of property.

EXAMPLE I:5-12 ▶ The Compact Corporation owns and operates a funeral home. The corporation purchases a hearse for $30,000 and pays sales taxes of $1,500. The cost basis for the hearse is $31,500. ◀

CAPITALIZATION OF INTEREST. Interest on debt paid or incurred during the production period to finance production expenditures incurred to construct, build, install, manufacture, develop, or improve real or tangible personal property must be capitalized.[10] The real or tangible personal property must have "a long useful life, an estimated production period exceeding two years, or an estimated production period exceeding one year and a cost exceeding $1,000,000."[11] Property has a long useful life if it is real property or property with a class life of at least 20 years. The production period starts when "production of the property begins and ends when the property is ready to be placed in service or is ready to be held for sale."[12]

EXAMPLE I:5-13 ▶ The Indiana Corporation started construction of a $3 million motel on July 1, 2009, and borrowed an amount equal to the motel's construction costs. The motel is completed and ready for service on October 1, 2010. Interest incurred for the construction loan for the period from July 1, 2009, through October 1, 2010, is included in the motel's cost. The capitalized interest cost is depreciated over the motel's thirty-nine year recovery period (see Chapter I:10). ◀

ADDITIONAL COMMENT

If a stockholder leaves his or her stock with a broker in street name, the stockholder can specifically identify the shares sold by simply informing the broker which shares he or she wishes to sell. The date basis of the shares sold should appear on the confirmation from the broker.

IDENTIFICATION PROBLEMS. In most cases, the adjusted basis of property sold is easily identified. However, problems arise when property is homogenous in nature such as when an investor owns several blocks of common stock of the same corporation purchased on different dates at different prices. The Regulations require the taxpayer to adequately identify the particular stock sold or exchanged.[13] Many investors allow brokers to hold their stock in street name (i.e., the brokerage firm holds title to the stock certificates) and thus do not make a physical transfer of securities. Such investors need to provide specific instructions to the broker as to which securities should be sold. If the stock sold or exchanged is not adequately identified, the first-in, first-out (FIFO) method must be used to identify the stock. With the FIFO method, the stock sold or exchanged is presumed to come from the first lot or lots acquired.

EXAMPLE I:5-14 ▶ Judy purchased 300 shares of the Gustavel Corporation stock last year:

Month Acquired	Size of Block	Basis
January	100 shares	$4,000
May	100	5,000
October	100	6,000

In March of the current year, Judy sells 120 shares of the stock for $5,160. If Judy specifically identifies the stock sold as being all of the stock purchased in October and 20 shares purchased in May, her realized loss is $1,840 [$5,160 − ($6,000 + $1,000)]. ◀

---

[9] Sec. 164(a).
[10] Sec. 263A(f).
[11] Sec. 263A(f)(1)(B).

[12] Sec. 263A(f)(4)(B).
[13] Reg. Sec. 1.1012-1(c)(1).

If Judy does not specifically identify the stock sold, the FIFO method is used, and her realized gain is $160 [$5,160 − ($4,000 + $1,000)].

Owners of shares of mutual funds have more choices when determining the basis of shares sold. In addition to FIFO and specific identification, they may use an average cost method.[14]

EXAMPLE I:5-15 ▶

ADDITIONAL COMMENT

Because of the difficulty and complexity of tracking basis of shares in a mutual fund, the average cost method is widely used by taxpayers.

Colin purchased 100 shares of Bluejay Mutual Fund on May 10, 2008, for $1,000, and has been reinvesting dividends. On December 20, 2010, he sells 115 shares.

	Amount	No. of Shares
Purchase May 10, 2008	$1,000	100
Reinvested Dividend Nov. 1, 2008	125	10
Reinvested Dividends Nov. 1, 2009	140	7
Reinvested Dividends Nov. 1, 2010	185	8
	1,450	125
		$11.60 Average Cost

His basis for the 115 shares sold is $1,225 with FIFO, $1,334 (115 × $11.60) with average cost and could be as high as $1,350 with specific identification. Note that if he sells the shares obtained with the reinvested dividends in 2010, part of the gain or loss is short-term. ◀

PROPERTY RECEIVED AS A GIFT: GIFTS AFTER 1921

The basis of property received as a gift is generally the same as the donor's basis.[15] If the FMV of the property at time of the gift is less than the donor's basis, the donee may have to use one basis if the property is subsequently disposed of at a gain and another if the property is disposed of at a loss. As discussed later in this chapter, the basis may be increased by a portion or all of the gift tax paid because of the transfer.

ADDITIONAL COMMENT

Upon receipt of property from a relative, one should inquire as to its basis at that time. It might be years later that the asset is sold and the information about the donor's basis may be lost or forgotten.

Current rules for determining the donee's basis for property received as a gift are a function of the relationship between the FMV of the property at the time the gift is made and the donor's basis. If the FMV is equal to or greater than the donor's basis, the donee's basis is the same as the donor's basis for all purposes. However, if the FMV is less than the donor's basis, the donee has a dual basis for the property, that is, a basis for loss and a basis for gain. If the donee later transfers the property at a loss, the donee's basis is the property's FMV at the time of the gift (basis for loss). However, if the donee transfers the property at a gain, the donee's basis is the same as the donor's basis (basis for gain).

EXAMPLE I:5-16 ▶

Kevin makes a gift of property with a basis of $350 to Janet when it has a $425 FMV. If Janet sells the property for $450, she has a realized gain of $100 ($450 − $350). If Janet sells the property for $330, she has a realized loss of $20 ($330 − $350). Because the FMV of the property at the time of the gift is more than the donor's basis, the donee's basis is $350 for determining both gain and loss. ◀

The following example illustrates the scenario when a taxpayer has a dual basis. The property is received as a gift when the FMV is less than the donor's basis, so the basis for determining a gain is different from the basis for determining a loss.

EXAMPLE I:5-17 ▶

Chuck makes a gift of property with a basis of $600 to Maggie when the property has a $500 FMV. Maggie's basis for the property is $600 if the property is sold at a gain (i.e., for more than $600), but the basis is $500 if the property is sold at a loss (i.e., for less than $500). If the property is sold for $500 or more but not more than $600, no gain or loss is recognized. ◀

The dual basis rules were designed to prevent tax-avoidance schemes. Taxpayers are prevented from shifting unrealized losses to another taxpayer by making gifts of such "loss"

---

[14] For mutual fund investors, the IRS has authorized the use of FIFO, specific identification, or two average cost basis methods if only a portion of the fund shares is redeemed or sold. (See Reg. Sec. 1.1012-1(e) and Chapter I:17.)

[15] Sec. 1015(a).

ADDITIONAL COMMENT

If Maggie in Example I:5-17 sells the land for $750, she has a $150 gain. If she sells the land for $400, she has a $100 loss, and there is no gain or loss if she sells the land for $560.

TAX STRATEGY TIP

Donors generally should not make gifts of property that have declined in value below original cost. Since the donee's basis will be the property's fair market value, the loss will never be recognized.

KEY POINT

No gift tax can be added to the basis of the property if the donor's basis is greater than the FMV of the property.

property. For example, a low-income taxpayer who owns property that has depreciated in value might transfer the property by gift to a high-income taxpayer who would receive greater tax benefit from the deduction of the loss upon the subsequent sale of the property. The loss basis rules prevent the donee from recognizing a loss on the sale of the property because the basis for loss is the lesser of the donor's basis or FMV on the date of the gift.

EFFECT OF GIFT TAX ON BASIS. If the donor pays a gift tax on the transfer of property, the donee's basis may be increased. This increase occurs only if the FMV of the property exceeds the donor's basis on the date of the gift. For taxable gifts after 1976, the increase in the donee's basis is equal to a pro rata portion of the gift tax attributable to the unrealized appreciation in the property. The amount of the addition to the donee's basis is determined as follows:[16]

$$\text{Gift tax paid} \times \frac{\text{FMV at time of the gift} - \text{Donor's basis}}{\text{Amount of the gift}}$$

The amount of the gift is the FMV of the property less the amount of the annual exclusion which is $13,000 starting in 2009.[17]

EXAMPLE I:5-18 ▶ During the current year, Cindy makes one gift of property with a $23,000 basis to Jessie when the property has a $63,000 FMV. Cindy pays a gift tax of $18,500. The amount of the gift is $50,000 ($63,000 − $13,000). Thus, 80% [($63,000 − $23,000)/$50,000] of the gift tax is added to Jessie's basis. Jessie's basis for the property for determining both gain and loss is $37,800 [$23,000 + (0.80 × $18,500)]. ◀

EXAMPLE I:5-19 ▶ During the current year, Sally makes a gift of property with a basis of $50,000 to Troy when the property has a $40,000 FMV. Sally pays a gift tax of $1,000. Troy's basis for the property is not affected by the gift tax paid by Sally because the FMV is less than the donor's basis at the time of the gift. Troy's basis for the property is $50,000 to determine gain and $40,000 to determine loss. ◀

STOP & THINK *Question:* Pete wants to make a gift of either ABC common stock (basis of $44,000 and FMV of $50,000) or XYZ common stock (basis of $73,000 and FMV of $50,000) to his nephew. Pete and his nephew have the same tax rate. Which stock should he give to his nephew?

Solution: Pete should give the ABC stock to his nephew because the nephew's basis for determining a gain or loss is $44,000 plus a portion of any gift tax Pete pays. The nephew's basis for XYZ common stock is $50,000 to determine a loss and $73,000 to determine a gain. If the nephew sells XYZ stock for less than $73,000, no loss is recognized and thus some of the basis is not used. Note that Pete would have a $23,000 loss if he sells the XYZ stock for $50,000. Furthermore, the nephew's basis for the XYZ stock is not increased if Pete has to pay a gift tax on the $38,000 taxable gift.

PROPERTY RECEIVED FROM A DECENT

The basis of property received from a decedent prior to 2010 is generally the FMV of the property at the date of the decedent's death or an alternate valuation date (AVD).[18] This can result in either a step up (increase) or step down (decrease) in basis.

EXAMPLE I:5-20 ▶ Patrick inherited property having an $8,000,000 FMV on the date of his sister's death in 2009. The decedent's basis in the property is $3,600,000. The executor of the estate does not elect the AVD. Patrick's basis for the property is $8,000,000. ◀

---

[16] Sec. 1015(d)(6).
[17] Sec. 1015(d)(2) and Sec. 2503(b). The annual exclusion for gifts was increased to $13,000 starting in 2009. From 2005–2008, an annual exclusion of $12,000 per year was allowed for each donee, from 2002–2004, the annual exclusion was $11,000. Prior to 2002, the annual exclusion was $10,000. See

Chapter I:1 for a limited discussion of the annual exclusion and Chapter C:12 of the *Corporations, Partnerships, Estates, and Trusts* and *Comprehensive* volumes for a more detailed discussion.
[18] Sec. 1014(a).

EXAMPLE I:5-21 ▶ Dianna inherited property having a $6,000,000 FMV at the date of the decedent's death in 2009. The decedent's basis in the property is $7,200,000. The AVD is not elected. Dianna's basis for the property is $6,000,000. ◀

REAL-WORLD EXAMPLE

The alternate valuation date was used in valuing the estates of many individuals owning large portfolios of common stocks who died shortly before the stock market crash in October 1987.

Instead of using the FMV on the date of death to determine the estate tax, the executor of the estate may elect to use the FMV on the AVD. The AVD is generally six months after the date of death. If the AVD is elected, the basis for all of the assets in the estate is their FMV on that date unless the property is distributed by the estate to the heirs or is sold before the AVD. If the AVD is used, property distributed or sold after the date of the decedent's death and before the AVD has a basis equal to its FMV on the date of distribution or the date of disposal.[19]

If the estate is small enough that an estate tax return is not required, the value of the property on the AVD may not be used.[20] An estate tax return must be filed if an individual dies in 2009 and the gross estate plus any previous taxable gifts exceeds $3,500,000.

EXAMPLE I:5-22 ▶ Marilyn inherited all of the property owned by an individual who died in April 2009, when the property had a $100,000 FMV. The value of the property six months later was $90,000. Because of the size of the estate, no estate tax was due. The AVD may not be used, and Marilyn's basis for the property is $100,000. Note that Marilyn does not want the AVD to be used because her basis would be $90,000 instead of $100,000. ◀

As noted above, the basis of the property to the estate and the heirs can be affected if the AVD is used to value the estate's assets. The AVD may be elected only if the value of the gross estate and the amount of estate tax after credits are reduced as a result of using the AVD.[21] This means that the aggregate value of the assets determined by using the AVD may be used only if the total value of the assets decreased during the six-month period.

EXAMPLE I:5-23 ▶ Helmut inherited all of the property owned by an individual who died in March 2009 when the FMV of the property was $3,800,000. Six months after the date of death, the property had a $3,950,000 FMV. The property is distributed to Helmut in December. Use of the AVD is not permitted because the value of the gross estate has increased. Therefore, his basis in the property is $3,800,000, the FMV on the date of death. ◀

An executor may elect to use the AVD to reduce the estate taxes owed by the estate. However, the income tax basis of the property included in the estate is also reduced for heirs who inherit the property.

EXAMPLE I:5-24 ▶ Michelle inherited property with a $4,200,000 FMV at the date of the decedent's death in 2009. The FMV of the property on the AVD (six months after the date of the decedent's death) is $3,740,000. The executor of the estate elects to use $3,740,000 to value the property for estate tax purposes, and Michelle's basis for the property is thus $3,740,000 instead of $4,200,000. ◀

In 2001, Congress eliminated the estate tax for individuals dying in 2010, however the estate tax will apply after 2010. Most tax professionals did not expect for the estate tax to actually be repealed for the year 2010, but Congress has not taken action to reinstate the estate tax as of early February of 2010.

The existence of the estate tax has implications for the basis of property received when one dies. For 2010, a modified carry over basis rule applies if there is no estate tax. A taxpayer will take the lesser of the decedent's basis or FMV at time of death, but the basis may be increased if the asset is appreciated. The basis may not be increased to more than the FMV, and the total amount of increase is limited to $1,300,000 plus any unused built-in loss or NOL carryover. A surviving spouse may receive an additional $3,000,000 adjustment.

If Patrick's sister in Example I:5-20 died in 2010 when there was no estate tax, Patrick's basis is $4,900,000 ($3,600,000 + $1,300,000). Patrick's basis is $7,900,000 if the decedent is his spouse ($3,600,000 + $1,300,000 + $3,000,000). Diana's basis in Example I:5-21 is $6,000,000 even if the death occurs in 2010.

---

[19] Sec. 2032(a).
[20] Rev. Rul. 56-60, 1956-1 C.B. 443. For a decedent dying in 2009, Sec. 6018(a) requires an estate tax return to be filed if the gross estate exceeds $3,500,000 ($2,000,000 in 2006–2008 and $1,500,000 for decedents dying in 2004 or 2005).

[21] Credits available include the unified transfer tax credit and possibly credits for gift taxes, foreign death taxes, and the credit for taxes on prior transfers.

COMMUNITY PROPERTY. If the decedent and the decedent's spouse own property under community property laws,[22] one-half of the property is included in the decedent's gross estate and its basis to the surviving spouse is its FMV.[23] The surviving spouse's one-half share of the community property is also adjusted to FMV.[24] In effect, the surviving spouse's share of the community property is considered to have passed from the decedent.

EXAMPLE I:5-25 ▶ Matt and Jane, a married couple, live in Texas, a community property state, and jointly own land as community property that cost $110,000. The land has an $800,000 FMV when Jane dies, leaving all of her property to Matt. His basis for the entire property is $800,000. ◀

In a common law state, only one-half of the jointly owned property is included in the decedent's estate and is adjusted to its FMV. The survivor's share of the jointly held property is not adjusted.

EXAMPLE I:5-26 ▶ Barry and Maria, a married couple, live in Iowa, a common law state, and jointly own land that cost $200,000. The property has a $700,000 FMV when Barry dies, leaving all of his property to Maria. Her basis for the land is $450,000 [$100,000 + (0.50 × $700,000)]. ◀

PROPERTY CONVERTED FROM PERSONAL USE TO BUSINESS USE

ADDITIONAL COMMENT

It is important to estimate the FMV of property at the time the property is converted from personal use to business use.

Often, taxpayers who own personal-use assets convert these assets to an income-producing use or for use in a trade or business. When this conversion occurs, the property's basis must be determined. The basis for computing depreciation is the lower of FMV or the adjusted basis of the property when the asset is transferred from personal use to an income-producing use or for use in a trade or business.[25] This rule prevents taxpayers from obtaining the benefits of depreciation to the extent that the property has declined in value during the period that it is held for personal use.

EXAMPLE I:5-27 ▶

REAL-WORLD EXAMPLE

A taxpayer sold a personal residence to a purchaser, and the purchaser rented the property from the taxpayer until financing could be secured. The rental agreement was executed simultaneously with the sales agreement and was incidental to the sale. The taxpayer was not permitted to recognize any loss on the sale because the property was never converted to rental property. *Henry B. Dawson*, 1972 PH T.C. Memo 31 TCM 5.

Olga owns a boat that cost $2,000 and is used for personal enjoyment. At a time when the boat has a $1,400 FMV, Olga transfers the boat to her business of operating a marina. The basis for depreciation is $1,400 because the FMV is less than Olga's adjusted basis at the time of conversion to business use. The $600 decline ($2,000 − $1,400) that occurred while Olga used the boat for personal use may not be deducted as depreciation. ◀

If the boat's FMV in Example I:5-27 is more than $2,000, the basis for depreciation is $2,000 because the FMV is higher than its adjusted basis at the time the asset is transferred to business use.

If a personal-use asset is transferred to business use when its FMV is less than its adjusted basis, the basis for determining a loss on a subsequent sale or disposition of the property is its FMV on the date of the conversion to business use less any depreciation taken after the transfer to business use.[26]

EXAMPLE I:5-28 ▶ Susanna purchased a personal residence in 1990 for $50,000 and converted the property to rental property in 1993 when its FMV was $46,000. Assume depreciation of $20,700 has been deducted after the conversion in 1993, and the property is sold for $21,000. The basis of the property is $25,300 ($46,000 − $20,700), and her loss on the sale is $4,300 ($21,000 − $25,300). ◀

The rule for determining basis, that is, lower of adjusted basis or FMV, applies only to the sale of converted property at a loss. The basis for determining gain is its adjusted basis when converted less depreciation taken after the transfer to business use.

EXAMPLE I:5-29 ▶ Assume the same facts as in Example I:5-28, except the property is sold for $31,000 instead of $21,000. The basis of the property is $29,300 ($50,000 − $20,700) and her gain is $1,700 ($31,000 − $29,300). ◀

Without the rule for determining basis of personal-use property converted to business property, taxpayers would have an incentive to convert nonbusiness assets that have declined in value to business use before selling the asset to convert nondeductible losses into deductible losses.

---

[22] Community property states are Arizona, California, Idaho, Louisiana, New Mexico, Nevada, Texas, and Washington. Wisconsin has a marital property law that is basically the same as community property.
[23] Sec. 1014(a).

[24] Sec. 1014(b)(6).
[25] Reg. Sec. 1.167(g)-1.
[26] Reg. Sec. 1.165-9(b)(2).

EXAMPLE I:5-30 ▶ Craig owns a personal-use asset with a basis of $80,000 and a $50,000 FMV. If he sells the asset for its FMV, the $30,000 loss ($50,000 − $80,000) is not deductible because losses on the sale of personal-use assets are not deductible. If Craig converts the asset to business use and then immediately sells the asset for $50,000, no loss is realized because the basis of the asset for purposes of determining loss is $50,000, the FMV when property was converted. ◀

ALLOCATION OF BASIS

REAL-WORLD EXAMPLE

A taxpayer purchased a group of lots and allocated the total cost evenly among the lots. The court, however, held that more cost should be allocated to the waterfront lots than to the interior lots. *Biscayne Bay Islands Co.,* 23 B.T.A. 731 (1931).

When property is obtained in one transaction and portions of the property are subsequently disposed of at different times, the basis of the property is allocated to the different portions of the property. Gain or loss is computed at the time of disposal for each portion. If one purchases a 20-acre tract of land and later sells the entire tract, an allocation of basis is not needed. However, if the taxpayer divides the property into smaller tracts of land for resale, the cost of the 20-acre tract must be allocated among the smaller tracts of land.

BASKET PURCHASE. If more than one asset is acquired in a single purchase transaction (i.e., a basket purchase), the cost must be apportioned to the various assets acquired. The allocation is based on the relative FMVs of the assets.

EXAMPLE I:5-31 ▶ Kelly purchases a duplex for $80,000 to use as a rental property. The land has a $15,000 FMV, and the building has a $65,000 FMV. Kelly's bases for the land and the building are $15,000 and $65,000, respectively. ◀

SELF-STUDY QUESTION

If Kelly in Example I:5-31 paid $2,000 for the cost of a title search and other costs that must be capitalized, what is the basis of the land and building?

ANSWER

Land $15,375
Building $66,625

Because no depreciation deduction is allowed for land, taxpayers tend to favor a liberal allocation of the total purchase price to the building. Appraisals or other measures of FMV may be used to make the allocation.

COMMON COSTS. As in the case of financial accounting, common costs incurred to obtain or prepare an asset for service must be capitalized and allocated to the basis of the individual assets.

EXAMPLE I:5-32 ▶ Priscilla acquires three machines for $60,000, which have FMVs of $30,000, $20,000, and $10,000, respectively. Costs of delivery amount to $2,000, and costs to install the three machines amount to $1,000. The total installation and delivery costs of $3,000 are allocated to the three machines based on their FMVs.

The allocation of the $3,000 of common costs occurs as follows:

$$\text{Machine No. 1:} \quad \frac{\$30,000 \text{ FMV}}{\$30,000 + \$20,000 + \$10,000} \times \$3,000 = \$1,500$$

$$\text{Machine No. 2:} \quad \frac{\$20,000 \text{ FMV}}{\$30,000 + \$20,000 + \$10,000} \times \$3,000 = \$1,000$$

$$\text{Machine No. 3:} \quad \frac{\$10,000 \text{ FMV}}{\$30,000 + \$20,000 + \$10,000} \times \$3,000 = \$500$$

The bases for each of the three machines are $31,500, $21,000, and $10,500, respectively. ◀

NONTAXABLE STOCK DIVIDENDS RECEIVED. If a nontaxable stock dividend is received, a portion of the basis of the stock on which the stock dividend is received is allocated to the new shares received from the stock dividend.[27] The cost basis of the previously acquired shares is reduced by the amount of basis allocated to the stock dividend shares. If the stock received as a stock dividend is the same type as the stock owned before the dividend, the total basis of the stock owned before the dividend is allocated equally to all shares now owned.

EXAMPLE I:5-33 ▶ Wayne owns 1,000 shares of Bell Corporation common stock with a $44,000 basis. Wayne receives a nontaxable 10% common stock dividend and now owns 1,100 shares of common stock. The basis for each share of common stock is now $40 ($44,000 ÷ 1,100). ◀

---

[27] Sec. 307(a).

If the stock received as a stock dividend is not the same type as the stock owned before the dividend, the allocation is based on relative FMVs.

EXAMPLE I:5-34 ▶ Stacey owns 500 shares of Montana Corporation common stock with a $60,000 basis. She receives a nontaxable stock dividend payable in 50 shares of preferred stock. At time of the distribution, the common stock has a $40,000 FMV ($80 × 500 shares), and the preferred stock has a $10,000 FMV ($200 × 50 shares). After the distribution, Stacey owns 50 shares of preferred stock with a basis of $12,000 [($10,000 ÷ $50,000) × $60,000]. Thus, $12,000 of the basis of the common stock is allocated to the preferred stock and the basis of the common stock is reduced from $60,000 to $48,000. ◀

KEY POINT

Corporations issue stock rights to shareholders so that the shareholders will be able to maintain their same proportional ownership in the corporation. This is called the preemptive right.

NONTAXABLE STOCK RIGHTS RECEIVED. Stock rights represent rights to acquire shares of a specified corporation's stock at a specific exercise price when certain conditions are met. The exercise price is usually less than the market price when the stock rights are issued. Stock rights may be distributed to employees as compensation, and they are often issued to shareholders to encourage them to purchase more stock, thereby providing more capital for the corporation.

If the FMV of nontaxable stock rights received is less than 15% of the FMV of the stock, the basis of the stock rights is zero unless the taxpayer elects to allocate the basis between the stock rights and the stock owned before distribution of the stock rights.[28]

EXAMPLE I:5-35 ▶ Tina owns 100 shares of Bear Corporation common stock with a $27,000 basis and a $50,000 FMV. She receives 100 nontaxable stock rights with a total FMV of $4,000. Because the FMV of the stock rights is less than 15% of the FMV of the stock (0.15 × $50,000 = $7,500), the basis of the stock rights is zero unless Tina elects to make an allocation. ◀

REAL-WORLD EXAMPLE

In 1993, United States Cellular Corporation issued one right for each common share held. Each whole right entitled the holder to buy one common share for $33.

If, Tina, in the example above, elects to allocate the basis of $27,000 between the stock rights and the stock, the basis of the rights is $2,000 ([$4,000 ÷ $54,000] × $27,000) and the basis of the stock is $25,000 ([$50,000 ÷ $54,000] × $27,000).

The decision to allocate the basis affects the gain or loss realized on the sale or disposition of the stock rights because the basis of the rights is zero unless an allocation is made. Furthermore, the basis of any stock acquired by exercising the rights is affected by whether or not a portion of the basis is allocated to the rights. The basis of stock acquired by exercising the stock rights is the amount paid plus the basis of the stock rights exercised.

EXAMPLE I:5-36 ▶ George receives 10 stock rights as a nontaxable distribution, and no basis is allocated to the stock rights. With each stock right, George may acquire one share of stock for $20. If he exercises all 10 stock rights, the new stock acquired has a basis of $200 ($20 × 10 shares). If George sells all 10 stock rights for $135, he has a realized gain of $135 ($135 − $0). ◀

If the FMV of a nontaxable stock right received is equal to or greater than 15% of the FMV of the stock, the basis of the stock owned before the distribution must be allocated between the stock and the stock rights.

EXAMPLE I:5-37 ▶ Helen owns 100 shares of NMO common stock with a $14,000 basis and a $30,000 FMV. She receives 100 stock rights with a total FMV of $5,000. Because the FMV of the stock rights is at least 15% of the FMV of the stock, the $14,000 basis must be allocated between the stock rights and the stock. The basis of the stock rights is $2,000 [($5,000 ÷ $35,000) × $14,000] and the basis of the stock is $12,000 [($30,000 ÷ $35,000) × $14,000]. ◀

A recipient of stock rights generally has three courses of action. The stock rights can be sold or exchanged, in which case the basis allocated to the stock rights, if any, is used to determine gain or loss. The stock rights may be exercised, and any basis allocated to the rights is added to the purchase price of the acquired stock. The stock rights may be allowed to expire, in which case no loss is recognized, and any basis allocated to the rights is reallocated back to the stock. If the stock rights received in the above example expire without being exercised, Helen does not recognize a loss and the basis of her 100 shares of common stock is $14,000.

Property basis rules are highlighted in Topic Review I:5-1.

---

[28] Sec. 307(b)(1).

Topic Review I:5-1

Property Basis Rules

METHOD ACQUIRED	BASIS OF THE ACQUIRED PROPERTY
1. Acquired by direct purchase	1. Basis includes the amount paid for the property, costs of preparing the property for use, obligations of the seller assumed by the buyer, and liabilities to which the property is subject.
2. Acquired as a gift. (a) FMV on the date of the gift is equal to or greater than the donor's basis (b) FMV on the date of the gift is less than the donor's basis	2. (a) The donee's basis is the same as the donor's basis plus a pro rata portion of the gift tax attributable to the property's unrealized appreciation at the time of the gift. (b) The donee's gain basis is the donor's basis and the loss basis is FMV. No increase for any gift tax paid.
3. Received from a decedent (a) AVD is not elected (b) AVD is elected	3. (a) The basis is its FMV on the date of death. (b) The basis of nondistributed property is its FMV on the AVD. If the property is distributed or sold before this date, its basis is FMV on the date of sale or distribution.
4. Converted from personal to business use	4. The basis for a loss (as well as for depreciation) is the lesser of its adjusted basis or FMV at date of conversion. The basis for a gain is its adjusted basis at date of conversion.
5. Nontaxable stock dividend	5. Basis of the stock dividend shares includes a pro rata portion of the adjusted basis of the underlying shares owned.
6. Nontaxable stock right	6. If the FMV of the rights is less than 15% of the stock's FMV, the basis of the rights is zero unless an election is made to allocate basis. Basis of the underlying stock is allocated to the rights based on the respective FMV's of the stock and rights.

DEFINITION OF A CAPITAL ASSET

OBJECTIVE 4

Distinguish between capital assets and other assets

TYPICAL MISCONCEPTION

It is common in financial accounting classes to include property used in a trade or business in the definition of a capital asset. For example, factory buildings, machinery, trucks, and office buildings would be defined as capital assets. However, such items are not capital assets for tax purposes.

Instead of defining capital assets, Sec. 1221 provides a list of properties that are **not** capital assets. Thus, a capital asset is any property owned by a taxpayer *other* than the types of property specified in Sec. 1221. Property that is not a capital asset includes the following:

1. Inventory or property held primarily for sale to customers in the ordinary course of a trade or business.
2. Property used in the trade or business and subject to the allowance for depreciation provided in Sec. 167 or real property used in a trade or business. (As explained in Chapter I:13, these properties are referred to as *Sec. 1231 assets* if held by the taxpayer more than one year.)
3. Accounts or notes receivable acquired in the ordinary course of a trade or business for services rendered or from the sale of property described in item 1.
4. Supplies of a type regularly used or consumed in the ordinary course of a trade or business.
5. Other assets including
   a. A letter, memorandum, or similar property held by a taxpayer for whom such property was prepared or produced.
   b. A copyright; a literary, musical, or artistic composition; a letter or memorandum; or similar property held by a taxpayer whose personal efforts created such property or whose basis in the property for determining a gain is determined by reference to the basis of such property in the hands of one who created the property or one for whom such property was prepared or produced.

c. A U.S. government publication held by a taxpayer who receives the publication by any means other than a purchase at the price the publication is offered for sale to the public.

d. A U.S. government publication held by a taxpayer whose basis in the property for determining a gain is determined by reference to the basis of such property in the hands of a taxpayer in item 5c (e.g., certain property received by gift).

EXAMPLE I:5-38 ▶ Maxine owns a building used in her business. Other business assets include equipment, inventory, and accounts receivable. None of the assets are classified as capital assets. ◀

Chapter I:13 provides an in-depth discussion of business assets such as buildings, land, and equipment. Although these items are not capital assets, Sec. 1231 provides in many cases that the gain on the sale or exchange of such an asset is eventually taxed as LTCG.

EXAMPLE I:5-39 ▶ Eric owns an automobile held for personal use and also owns a copyright for a book he has written. Because the copyright is held by the taxpayer whose personal efforts created the property, it is not a capital asset. The automobile held for personal use is a capital asset. ◀

By analyzing Examples I:5-38 and I:5-39, one can conclude that the classification of an asset is often determined by its use. An automobile used in a trade or business is not a capital asset but is a capital asset when held for personal use. Examples of assets that qualify as capital assets include a personal residence, land held for personal use, and investments in stocks and bonds. In addition, certain types of assets are specifically given capital asset status, such as patents, franchises, etc. These and other special assets are discussed later in this chapter.

Recently, Congress made a major change for self-created musical works. Pursuant to Sec. 1221(b)(3), a taxpayer whose personal efforts created such property may now make an election to treat the sale or exchange of musical compositions or copyrights in self-created musical works as a sale or exchange of a capital asset.

INFLUENCE OF THE COURTS

In *Corn Products Refining Co.*, the Supreme Court rendered a landmark decision when it determined that the sale of futures contracts related to the purchase of raw materials resulted in ordinary rather than capital gains and losses.[29] The Corn Products Company, a manufacturer of products made from grain corn, purchased futures contracts for corn to ensure an adequate supply of raw materials. Delivery of the corn was accepted when needed for manufacturing operations, and unneeded contracts were later sold. Corn Products contended that any gains or losses on the sale of the unneeded contracts should be capital gains and losses because futures contracts are customarily viewed as security investments, which qualify as capital assets. The Supreme Court held that these transactions represented an integral part of the business for the purpose of protecting the company's manufacturing operations and the gains and losses should, therefore, be ordinary in nature.

Although the *Corn Products* doctrine has been interpreted as creating a nonstatutory exception to the definition of a capital asset when the asset is purchased for business purposes, the Supreme Court ruled in the 1988 *Arkansas Best Corporation* case that the motivation for acquiring assets is irrelevant to the question of whether assets are capital assets. Arkansas Best, a bank holding company, sold shares of a bank's stock that had been acquired for the purpose of protecting its business reputation. Relying on the *Corn Products* doctrine, the company deducted the loss as ordinary. The Supreme Court ruled that the loss was a capital loss because the stock is within the broad definition of the term *capital asset* in Sec. 1221 and is outside the classes of property that are excluded from capital-asset status.[30] *Arkansas Best* apparently limits the application of *Corn Products* to hedging transactions that are an integral part of a taxpayer's system of acquiring inventory.

---

[29] *Corn Products Refining Co. v. CIR*, 47 AFTR 1789, 55-2 USTC ¶9746 (USSC, 1955).

[30] *Arkansas Best Corporation v. CIR*, 61 AFTR 2d 88-655, 88-1 USTC ¶9210 (USSC, 1988).

OTHER IRC PROVISIONS RELEVANT TO CAPITAL GAINS AND LOSSES

A number of IRC sections provide special treatment for certain types of assets and transactions. For example, loss on the sale or exchange of certain small business stock that qualifies as Sec. 1244 stock is treated as an ordinary loss rather than a capital loss to the extent of $50,000 per year ($100,000 if the taxpayer is married and files a joint return).[31]

DEALERS IN SECURITIES. Normally, a security dealer's gain on the sale or exchange of securities is ordinary income. Section 1236 provides an exception for dealers in securities if the dealer clearly identifies that the property is held for investment. This act of identification must occur before the close of the day on which the security is acquired, and the security must not be held primarily for sale to customers in the ordinary course of the dealer's trade or business at any time after the close of the day of purchase.

EXAMPLE I:5-40 ▶ Allyson, a dealer in securities, purchases Cook Corporation stock on April 8, and identifies the stock as being held for investment on that date. Four months later, Allyson sells the stock. Any gain or loss recognized due to the sale is capital gain or loss. ◀

Once a dealer clearly identifies a security as being held for investment, any loss on the sale or exchange of the security is treated as a capital loss.

EXAMPLE I:5-41 ▶ Kris, a dealer in securities, purchases Boston Corporation stock and clearly identifies the stock as being held for investment on the date of purchase. Eight months later, the security is removed from the investment account and held as inventory. If the security is later sold at a gain, the gain is an ordinary gain. However, if the stock is sold at a loss, the loss is a capital loss. ◀

Securities dealers must use the mark-to-market method for their inventory of securities. This method requires that securities be valued at FMV at the end of each taxable year. Dealers in securities recognize gain or loss each year as if the security is sold on the last day of the tax year. Gains and losses are generally treated as ordinary rather than capital. Gains or losses due to adjustments in subsequent years or resulting from the sale of the security must be adjusted to reflect gains and losses already taken into account when determining taxable income.[32]

EXAMPLE I:5-42 ▶ Jim Spikes, a dealer in securities and calendar-year taxpayer, purchases a security for inventory on October 10, 2010, for $10,000 and sells the security for $18,000 on July 1, 2011. The security's FMV on December 31, 2010, is $15,000. Jim recognizes $5,000 of ordinary income in 2010 and $3,000 of ordinary income in 2011. ◀

REAL PROPERTY SUBDIVIDED FOR SALE. A taxpayer who engages in regular sales of real estate is considered to be a dealer, and any gain or loss recognized is ordinary gain or loss rather than capital gain or loss. A special relief provision is provided in Sec. 1237 for nondealer, noncorporate taxpayers who subdivide a tract of real property into lots (two or more pieces of real property are considered to be a tract if they are contiguous). Part or all of the gain on the sale of the lots may be treated as a capital gain if the following provisions of Sec. 1237 are satisfied:

▶ During the year of sale, the noncorporate taxpayer must not hold any other real property primarily for sale in the ordinary course of business.

▶ Unless the property is acquired by inheritance or devise, the lots sold must be held by the taxpayer for a period of at least five years.

▶ No substantial improvement may be made by the taxpayer while holding the lots if the improvement substantially enhances the value of the lot.[33]

---

[31] Secs. 1244(a) and (b). (See Chapter I:8 for additional discussion on small business corporation stock losses.)

[32] Sec. 475. The mark-to-market rule also applies to some securities that are not inventory, but does not apply to any security that is held for investment and certain other transactions (see Sec. 475(b)).

[33] Certain improvements are not treated as substantial under Sec. 1237(b)(3) if the lot is held for at least ten years.

▶ The tract or any lot may not have been previously held primarily for sale to customers in the ordinary course of the taxpayer's trade or business unless such tract at that time was covered by Sec. 1237.

The primary advantage of Sec. 1237 is that potential controversy with the IRS is avoided as to whether a taxpayer who subdivides investment property is a dealer. Section 1237 does not apply to losses. Such losses are capital losses if the property is held for investment purposes, or ordinary losses if the taxpayer is a dealer.

If the Sec. 1237 requirements are satisfied, all gain on the sale of the first five lots may be capital gain. Starting in the tax year during which the sixth lot is sold, 5% of the selling price for all lots sold in that year and succeeding years is ordinary income.

EXAMPLE I:5-43 ▶ Jean subdivides a tract of land held as an investment into seven lots, and all requirements of Sec. 1237 are satisfied. The lots have a fair market value of $10,000 each and have a basis of $4,000. Jean incurs no selling expenses and sells four lots in 2010 and three lots in 2011. In 2010, all of the $24,000 [four lots × ($10,000 − $4,000)] gain is capital gain. In 2011, the year in which the sixth lot is sold, $1,500 of the gain is ordinary income [0.05 × ($10,000 × 3 lots)], and the remaining $16,500 {[three lots × ($10,000 − $4,000)] − $1,500} gain is capital gain. ◀

EXAMPLE I:5-44 ▶ Assume the same facts as in the above example, except that all seven lots are sold in 2010. The amount of ordinary income recognized is $3,500 [0.05 × ($10,000 × 7 lots)], and the remaining $38,500 {[seven lots × ($10,000 − $4,000)] − $3,500} gain is capital gain. ◀

ADDITIONAL COMMENT

If a taxpayer sells any lots from a tract and does not sell any others for a period of five years, the remaining property is considered a new tract.

Based on Examples I:5-43 and I:5-44, the advantage of selling no more than five lots in the first year should be apparent. Expenditures incurred to sell or exchange the lots are also treated favorably because they are first applied against the portion of the gain treated as ordinary income. Because selling expenses (e.g., commissions) are often equal to or greater than 5% of the selling price, this offset against ordinary income may result in the elimination of the ordinary income portion of the gain. Selling expenses in excess of the gain taxed as ordinary income reduce the amount realized on the sale or exchange.

NONBUSINESS BAD DEBT. Bad debt losses from nonbusiness debts are deductible only as short-term capital losses (STCLs),[34] regardless of when the debt occurred. A nonbusiness bad debt is deductible only in the year in which the debt becomes totally worthless.

EXAMPLE I:5-45 ▶ Two years ago, Alice loaned $4,000 to a friend. During the current year, the friend declares bankruptcy and the debt is entirely worthless. Assuming that Alice has no other gains and losses from the sale or exchange of capital assets during the year, she deducts $3,000 in determining adjusted gross income (AGI) and has a STCL carry forward of $1,000. ◀

$\mathbf{T}$AX TREATMENT FOR CAPITAL GAINS AND LOSSES OF NONCORPORATE TAXPAYERS

OBJECTIVE 5

Understand how capital gains and losses affect taxable income

To recognize capital gain or loss, it is necessary to have a sale or exchange of a capital asset. Once it is determined that a capital gain or loss has been realized and is to be recognized, it is necessary to classify the gains and losses as either short-term or long-term. If the asset is held for one year or less, the gain or loss is classified as a short-term capital gain (STCG) or a short-term capital loss (STCL). If the capital asset is held for more than one year, the gain or loss is classified as a long-term capital gain (LTCG) or long-term capital loss (LTCL).[35]

---

[34] Sec. 166(d)(1)(B). Also, see discussion of bad debts in Chapter I:8.
[35] While the Taxpayer Relief Act of 1997 reduced the rates for most LTCGs, it increased the required holding period to more than 18 months to be eligible for the lower rates of 10% and 20%. During the last few months of 1997, gain resulting from the sale of a capital asset might be taxed at many different rates depending on whether or not the holding period is one year or less, more

than one year but not more than 18 months, or more than 18 months. These changes in the law dramatically increased the complexity associated with the taxation of capital gains. The 1998 Restructuring and Reform Act eliminated the more than 18-month holding period requirement for tax years ending after 1997 and returned to the more than one year requirement to be LTCG.

CAPITAL GAINS

ADDITIONAL COMMENT

The rates for long-term capital gains have been lower than rates for ordinary income for many years. However, preferential rates for qualified dividends were enacted in 2003. Qualified dividends are now taxed at a maximum 15% rate, the same as for long-term capital gains which are ANCG.

The first step in determining the taxability of capital gains is to calculate *net capital gains* (NCG), which is defined as the excess of net long-term capital gain over net short-term capital loss.[36] All capital gains are not taxed at the same rate. So, depending on the type of property, NCG could be taxed at zero, 15%, 25%, or 28%. Prior to 2008, the zero rate was 5%. Once NCG has been determined, a portion of NCG may be classified as *adjusted net capital gain* (ANCG) which is subject to the lower rates of zero or 15%.

To compute NCG, first determine all STCGs, STCLs, LTCGs, LTCLs, and then net gains and losses as described below.

NET SHORT-TERM CAPITAL GAIN. If total STCGs for the tax year exceed total STCLs for that year, the excess is defined as net short-term capital gain (NSTCG). As discussed later, NSTCG may be offset by net long-term capital loss (NLTCL).

EXAMPLE I:5-46 ▶ Hal has two transactions involving the sale of capital assets during the year. As a result of those transactions, he has a STCG of $4,000 and a STCL of $3,000. Hal's NSTCG is $1,000 and his AGI increases by $1,000. His gross income increases by $4,000, and he is entitled to a $3,000 deduction for AGI. ◀

NET LONG-TERM CAPITAL GAIN. If the total LTCGs for the tax year exceed the total LTCLs for that year, the excess is defined as net long-term capital gain (NLTCG). As indicated earlier, a NCG exists when NLTCG exceeds net short-term capital loss (NSTCL).

EXAMPLE I:5-47 ▶ Clay has two transactions involving the sale of capital assets during the year. As a result of the transactions, he has a LTCG of $5,000 and a LTCL of $3,000. Clay has a NLTCG and a net capital gain of $2,000. His AGI increases by $2,000. ◀

EXAMPLE I:5-48 ▶ Linda has four transactions involving the sale of capital assets during the year. As a result of the transactions, she has a STCG of $5,000, a STCL of $7,000, a LTCG of $10,000, and a LTCL of $2,000. After the initial netting of short-term and long-term gains and losses, Linda has a NSTCL of $2,000 ($7,000 − $5,000) and a NLTCG of $8,000 ($10,000 − $2,000). Because the NLTCG exceeds the NSTCL by $6,000 ($8,000 − $2,000), her NCG is $6,000. ◀

LOWER RATES FOR ADJUSTED NET CAPITAL GAIN (ANCG). The rates of 15% and zero apply to ANCG and the rate to use depends upon the taxpayer's tax bracket. The maximum rate for ANCG recognized by noncorporate taxpayers (individuals, estates, and trusts) is 15%. The zero rate applies after 2007 to ANCG for taxpayers whose regular tax rate is 15% or less.[37]

EXAMPLE I:5-49 ▶ Sandy is single with taxable income of $100,000 without considering the sale of Merck stock during 2010 for $15,000. The stock was purchased four years earlier for $3,000. Sandy has $12,000 of NLTCG which is ANCG taxed at 15%. To compute her total tax for 2010, ordinary rates would be applied to the $100,000 and then the tax on ANCG (15% × $12,000) is added. ◀

EXAMPLE I:5-50 ▶ Assume the same facts as in Example I:5-49 except Sandy's taxable income without the capital gain is $11,400. The $12,000 ANCG is taxed at a rate of zero because her taxable income is less than $34,000. Taxable income up to $34,000 is subject to ordinary tax rates of no higher than 15%.

SELF-STUDY QUESTION

Mary sells common stock for a gain of $10,000 on December 29, 2010. The settlement date, or date that Mary will receive the proceeds from the stockbroker, is January 2, 2011. Will Mary report the gain on her 2010 or 2011 tax return?

ANSWER

Mary is required to report the gain in the year of the sale (2010). Losses are also recognized in the year of sale.

Computation of the tax becomes more complicated if the ANCG causes taxable income to exceed the $34,000 for a single taxpayer. If a single taxpayer has taxable income of $36,000 that includes $8,000 of ANCG, the taxpayer's tax is determined as follows:

Tax on $28,000 (taxable income without the ANCG)	$3,781.25	($837.50 + $19,625 × 15%)
+ Tax on $6,000 ($34,000 − $28,000) of the ANCG at zero	0	($6,000 × 0%)
+ Tax on $2,000 ($8,000 − $6,000) at 15% because the taxable income is greater than $34,000.	$ 300.00	($2,000 × 15%)
Total tax	$4,081.25	

◀

---

[36] Sec. 1222(11).　　　　[37] Sec. 1(h).

ADJUSTED NET CAPITAL GAINS (ANCG)

When computing ANCG, one has to consider that four different types of LTCGs may exist:

1. Collectibles gain
2. Part of the gain (generally 50%) resulting from the sale or exchange of qualified small business stock as defined in Sec. 1202
3. Unrecaptured Sec. 1250 gain[38]
4. All other LTCGs

It is the fourth group of LTCGs that receives the preferential rates of zero or 15%. The other three groups receive preferential treatment but not at the zero or 15% rate. The first two gains above are referred to as 28% rate gain because the maximum rate for those gains is 28%; the maximum rate for unrecaptured Sec. 1250 gain is 25%. Collectibles gain, as explained below, is the net of LTCG and LTCL from the sale of collectibles. Sec. 1202 stock is qualified small business stock designed to encourage investment in small businesses. Unrecaptured Sec. 1250 gain, which is taxed at a maximum 25% rate, generally occurs when a building is sold. For the second and third types of LTCG, the special provisions only apply to gains. Net losses from sale of Sec. 1202 stock are treated as normal LTCLs, and one cannot have a loss connected with an unrecaptured Sec. 1250 gain.

ANCG is defined as NCG less the first three gains listed above. However, the computation of ANCG is tricky because one has to consider the impact of net capital losses, both short-term and long-term. Taxpayers are permitted to offset capital losses against capital gains. But, as discussed above, there are four different types of LTCG. So, if a taxpayer has both LTCG and capital losses, the capital losses are first offset within the category (collectibles, Sec. 1202 stock, etc.), then any excess loss is offset against the highest rate LTCG category first and works down to the lowest rate category (i.e., 28% rate gain first, then 25%, then 15%). This topic is discussed in more detail on page I:5-19 below.

When a taxpayer has no capital losses and no qualified dividends, ANCG is NCG reduced by the first three types of LTCG listed above. Many taxpayers will not have the first three types of LTCG and therefore, NCG and ANCG will often be the same amount.

EXAMPLE I:5-51 ▶ During 2010, Charles sold two publicly-traded stocks. The first stock resulted in a LTCG of $10,000 while the second stock resulted in a LTCG of $15,000. These were his only transactions involving capital assets during the year. Charles' NCG and ANCG is $25,000 and this gain is subject to a maximum tax rate of 15%. ◀

EXAMPLE I:5-52 ▶ Assume in the example above that Charles also had a gain on the sale of a building that resulted in an unrecaptured Sec. 1250 gain of $50,000. Charles has NCG of $75,000 and ANCG of $25,000. The $50,000 gain is taxed at a maximum rate of 25% while the remaining $25,000 gain is taxed at a maximum rate of 15%. ◀

COLLECTIBLES GAIN. Gains resulting from the sale of collectibles such as artwork, rugs, antiques, stamps and most coins are taxed at a maximum rate of 28%.

EXAMPLE I:5-53 ▶ Danny, whose tax rate is 35%, purchased Bowling common stock and antique chairs for investment on March 10, 2008. He sells the assets in April 2010 and has a gain of $8,000 on the sale of the stock and $10,000 on the sale of the antique chairs. His NLTCG is $18,000, and his NCG is $18,000. His ANCG is $8,000 since $10,000 of the NCG is a collectibles gain. His tax on the capital gains is $4,000 [(15% × $8,000) + (28% × $10,000)]. ◀

SELF-STUDY QUESTION

Eliza, who is single, has taxable income of $60,000 including a $1,200 LTCG due to the sale of her baseball card collection. Does she receive preferential tax treatment?

SEC. 1202 GAIN. As explained in Chapter I:4, Sec. 1202 provides that noncorporate taxpayers may exclude 50% of the gain resulting from the sale or exchange of qualified small business stock (QSBS) issued after August 10, 1993, if the stock is held for more than five years. The exclusion for QSBS has been 50% for many years, but pursuant to the American Recovery and Reinvestment Act of 2009, the percentage has been increased to 75% for any QSBS acquired from February 18, 2009 through December 31, 2010. The 50% rate will still apply for stock acquired prior to February 18, 2009, and after December 31, 2010. Since the QSBS must be held for five years, it will be several years before the new and temporary 75% rate will take effect. A corporation may have QSBS only if the

---

[38] Sec. 1(h)(4).

ANSWER

No. Her marginal tax rate is 25% which is less than the maximum 28% rate that applies to collectibles gain. If her taxable income is $150,000, she saves $60 [(33% − 28%)($1,200)].

corporation is a C corporation and at least 80% of the value of its assets must be used in the active conduct of one or more qualified trades or businesses.[39]

Normally, the excluded gain is 50% of any gain resulting from the sale or exchange of QSBS held for more than five years and the remaining half of the gain is taxed at a maximum rate of 28%. However, the excluded gain may be less than 50% of the gain, because the amount of gain that may be excluded by a taxpayer for one corporation is 50% of the greater of $10,000,000 or ten times the aggregate basis of the qualified stock. If gain on the sale of QSBS is $11.4 million and $5 million of the gain is excluded, $5 million of the gain is taxed at 28% and the remaining $1.4 million gain is taxed at 15%.

EXAMPLE I:5-54 ▶

Raef purchased $200,000 of newly issued Monona common stock on October 1, 2005. On December 15, 2010, he sells the stock for $4 million, resulting in a $3.8 million gain. He excludes $1.9 million of the gain, and the remaining $1.9 million of gain is Sec. 1202 gain taxed at 28%. ◀

EXAMPLE I:5-55 ▶

ADDITIONAL COMMENT

If Raef's gain in Example I:5-54 is $12 million, he excludes $5 million, $5 million of the gain is taxed at 28%, and $2 million is taxed at 15%.

Matthew, whose tax rate is 33%, has the following capital gains this year:

STCG	$10,000
LTCG (artwork)	12,000
LTCG (stock of AT&T)	17,000
LTCG (QSBS held more than five years)	200,000

Matthew may exclude $100,000 of the $200,000 Sec. 1202 gain. His NCG is $129,000 ($12,000 + $17,000 + $100,000). His ANCG is $17,000. The increase in his tax is $37,210 [33%($10,000) + 28%($12,000) + 15%($17,000) + 28%($100,000)]. ◀

CAPITAL LOSSES

To have a capital loss, one must sell or exchange the capital asset for an amount less than its adjusted basis. As in the case of capital gains, the one-year period is used to determine whether the capital loss is short-term or long-term.

NET SHORT-TERM CAPITAL LOSS. If total STCLs exceed total STCGs for the tax year, the excess is defined as a net short-term capital loss (NSTCL). As indicated above, the NSTCL is first offset against any NLTCG to determine net capital gain. If NSTCL exceeds NLTCG, the capital loss may be offset, on a dollar-for-dollar basis, against a noncorporate taxpayer's ordinary income for amounts up to $3,000 in any one year.[40]

EXAMPLE I:5-56 ▶

ADDITIONAL COMMENT

A husband and wife filing a joint return may use capital losses carried forward from years when they were single. Also, a divorced couple may use capital losses carried forward from a joint return year to their single returns.

Bob has gross income of $60,000 before considering capital gains and losses. If Bob has a NLTCG of $10,000 and a NSTCL of $15,000, he has $5,000 of NSTCL in excess of NLTCG and may deduct $3,000 of the losses from gross income. Assuming no other deductions for AGI, Bob's AGI is $57,000 ($60,000 − $3,000). ◀

In the above example, $10,000 of Bob's NSTCL is used to offset the $10,000 of NLTCG, and $3,000 of the NSTCL is used to reduce ordinary income. However, $2,000 of the loss is not used. This net capital loss is carried forward for an indefinite number of years.[41] The loss retains its original character and will be treated as a STCL occurring in the subsequent year. If a taxpayer dies with an unused capital loss carryover, it expires.

EXAMPLE I:5-57 ▶

REAL-WORLD EXAMPLE

In 1975 an amendment was added to a tax bill in the House Ways and Means Committee that would have permitted individuals to take a three-year carryback for capital losses. When *The Wall Street Journal* published an article disclosing that the amendment would provide Ross Perot with a $15 million tax break, the amendment was defeated.

Last year, Milt had a NSTCL of $8,000 and a NLTCG of $2,600. The netting of short-term and long-term gains and losses resulted in a $5,400 excess of NSTCL over NLTCG, and $3,000 of this amount was offset against ordinary income. Milt's NSTCL carryforward is $2,400. During the current year he sells a capital asset and generates a STCG of $800. His NSTCL is $1,600 ($2,400 − $800), and the loss is offset against $1,600 of ordinary income. ◀

NET LONG-TERM CAPITAL LOSS. If total LTCLs for the tax year exceed total LTCGs for the year, the excess is defined as net long-term capital loss (NLTCL). If there is both a NSTCG and a NLTCL, the NLTCL is initially offset against the NSTCG on a dollar-for-dollar basis. If the NLTCL exceeds the NSTCG, the excess is offset against ordinary income on a dollar-for-dollar basis up to $3,000 per year.

---

[39] Sec. 1202.
[40] Sec. 1211(b). A $1,500 limitation applies to a married individual filing a separate return.

[41] Sec. 1212(b) and Reg. Sec. 1.1212-1(b).

EXAMPLE I:5-58 ▶ In the current year, Gordon has a NLTCL of $9,000 and a NSTCG of $2,000. He must use $2,000 of the NLTCL to offset the $2,000 NSTCG, and then use $3,000 of the $7,000 ($9,000 − $2,000) NLTCL to offset $3,000 of ordinary income. Gordon's carryforward of NLTCL is $4,000 [$9,000 − ($2,000 + $3,000)]. This amount is treated as a LTCL in subsequent years. ◀

If an individual has both NSTCL and NLTCL, the NSTCL is offset against ordinary income first, regardless of when the transactions occur during the year.

EXAMPLE I:5-59 ▶ In the current year, Beth has a NSTCL of $2,800 and a NLTCL of $2,000. The entire NSTCL is offset initially against $2,800 of ordinary income. Because capital losses may offset only $3,000 of ordinary income, $200 of NLTCL is used to offset $200 ($3,000 − $2,800) of ordinary income. The NLTCL carryover to the next year is $1,800 ($2,000 − $200). ◀

TAX STRATEGY TIP

Taxpayers who have realized capital gains during the tax year should consider selling securities with a loss during the same year. The losses can be offset against the gains and tax savings result.

CAPITAL LOSSES APPLIED TO CAPITAL GAINS BY GROUPS. Taxpayers separate their LTCGs and LTCLs into three tax rate groups: (1) 28% group, (2) 25% group, and (3) the 15% group. The 28% group includes capital gains and losses when the capital asset is a collectible held more than one year and part of the gain from the sale of QSBS held for more than five years. The 25% group consists of unrecaptured Sec. 1250 gain discussed in Chapter I:13, and there are no losses for this group. The 15% group includes capital gains and losses when the holding period is more than one year and the capital asset is not a collectible or Sec. 1202 small business stock.

When a taxpayer has NSTCL and NLTCG, the NSTCL is first offset against NLTCG from the 28% group, then the 25% group, and finally the 15% group. This treatment of NSTCL is favorable for taxpayers. Note that a taxpayer could have NLTCLs in one group, except the 25% group, and NLTCGs in another group. A net loss from the 28% group is first offset against gains in the 25% group then net gains in the 15% group. A net loss from the 15% group is first offset against net gains in the 28% group and then gains in the 25% group.[42]

EXAMPLE I:5-60 ▶ Leroy, whose tax rate is 35%, has NSTCL of $20,000, a $25,000 LTCG from the sale of a rare stamp held 16 months and an $18,000 LTCG from the sale of stock held for three years. The $20,000 NSTCL is offset against $20,000 of the collectibles gain in the 28% group. Leroy's NCG is $23,000 and his ANCG is $18,000. Leroy's tax liability increases by $4,100 [($5,000 × 28%) + ($18,000 × 15%)]. ◀

EXAMPLE I:5-61 ▶ Elizabeth, whose tax rate is 35%, has a $32,000 LTCL from the sale of stock held for four years and the following capital gains:

ADDITIONAL COMMENT

If Elizabeth in Example I:5-61 also had a $9,000 LTCG from the sale of stock held for two years, she would only be able to offset $23,000 of the LTCG in the 28% group.

NSTCG	$40,000
LTCG from sale of collectible	$30,000
LTCG in the 25% group (unrecaptured Sec. 1250 gain)	$10,000

The $32,000 LTCL is offset first against $30,000 of the LTCG in the 28% group (collectibles) and then $2,000 against the unrecaptured Sec. 1250 gain. Her NLTCG is $8,000 taxed at 25% while her $40,000 NSTCG is taxed at her ordinary income rate of 35%. ◀

STOP & THINK

Question: Srinija has a salary of $100,000. If she sells a non-personal use asset during the year and has a $40,000 loss, why is it important that the asset not be a capital asset?

Solution: Only $3,000 of a $40,000 capital loss is used as a deduction to reduce her gross income each year. Her AGI is $97,000 if the asset is a capital asset, and she has a $37,000 capital loss carryforward. All of the $40,000 loss is used to reduce her gross income if the asset is not a capital asset and her AGI is $60,000. It is possible that Srinija might not care whether or not the asset is a capital asset if she has capital gains that could be reduced by capital losses. If the asset is a personal-use asset, the loss is not deductible regardless of whether or not it is a capital asset.

TAX TREATMENT FOR NET CAPITAL GAIN. Congress eliminated preferential tax rates on NCG in 1986 by making the maximum ordinary income rate equal to the rate on net capital gains at 28%. However, this equality was short-lived as Congress, in 1991, increased the maximum ordinary income rate to 31% but left the NCG rate at 28%.[43] This newly-created preferential treatment for NCG's only applied to taxpayers whose tax rate exceeded 28%. The change in 1997 to rates as low as 10% benefited all noncorporate taxpayers if they held the capital asset for more than one year. The lower rates made taxpayers more interested in having capital gain income instead of ordinary income. Investors preferences for growth stocks as opposed to stocks with high dividends increased.

However, this preference was dramatically changed by the Jobs and Growth Tax Relief Reconciliation Act of 2003 which reduced the tax rate on qualified dividends to 5% (zero after 2007) and 15% as of January 1, 2003.[44] The rate on qualified dividends is 5% (zero after 2007) for a taxpayer with a regular tax rate of 15% or less, and 15% for a taxpayer with a regular tax rate greater than 15%. This significant reduction of tax rates for dividend income has resulted in an increased interest in stocks with high dividends.

Taxpayers who own mutual funds must recognize their share of capital gains even if no distributions are received. Many mutual fund shareholders reinvest their distributions instead of withdrawing assets from the mutual fund. Mutual funds must classify the gains as short-term or long-term, and long-term gains will need to be separated by rate groups. When shareholders of a mutual fund recognize their share of capital gains when no distribution is actually received, the basis for their shares is increased.

EXAMPLE I:5-62 ▶ Eunice, whose tax rate is 35%, is a shareholder of Canyon Mutual Fund. The basis for her shares is $23,000. At the end of the current year, she received a statement from Canyon indicating her share of the following: qualified dividend income, $200; STCG, $300; 28-percent rate gain, $1,000; and ANCG of $1,500. The increase in her taxes as a result of her ownership of the mutual shares is $640 [($200 × 15%) + ($300 × 35%) + ($1,000 × 28%) + ($1,500 × 15%)]. The basis for her shares of Canyon Mutual Fund is $26,000. ◀

TAX TREATMENT OF CAPITAL GAINS AND LOSSES: CORPORATE TAXPAYERS

Most topics covered in this chapter concerning capital gains and losses, including the classification of an asset as a capital asset, rules for determining holding periods, and the procedure for offsetting capital losses against capital gains, apply to both corporate and noncorporate taxpayers. However, a major difference is that the lower tax rates of 15%, 25%, and 28% on net capital gain for noncorporate taxpayers do not apply to corporations. A second significant difference relates to the treatment of capital losses: Unlike the noncorporate taxpayer who may deduct up to $3,000 of capital losses from ordinary income, corporations may offset capital losses only against capital gains. Corporate taxpayers may carry capital losses back to each of the three preceding tax years (the earliest of the three tax years first and then to the next two years) and forward for five years to offset capital gains in such years. When a corporate taxpayer carries a loss back to a preceding year or forward to a following year, the loss is treated as a STCL.[45]

EXAMPLE I:5-63 ▶

HISTORICAL NOTE

The House of Representatives proposed a reduction in corporate net capital gains in 1997, but the proposal was rejected.

The Peach Corporation has income from operations of $200,000, a NSTCG of $40,000, and a NLTCL of $56,000 during the current year. The $40,000 NSTCG is offset by $40,000 NLTCL. The remaining $16,000 of NSTCL may not be offset against the $200,000 of other income but may be carried back three years and then forward five years to offset capital gains arising in these years. If Peach has NLTCG and/or NSTCG in the previous three years, a refund of taxes paid during those years will be received during the current year. ◀

---

[43] For years prior to 1990, a myriad of rules have applied. Prior to 1987, noncorporate taxpayers received a deduction from gross income equal to 60% of the taxpayer's net capital gain. For years 1987–1990, net capital gains were subject to tax at ordinary income rates.

[44] Sec. 1(h)(11).
[45] Sec. 1212(a).

Topic Review I:5-2

Comparison of Corporate and Noncorporate Taxpayers: Capital Gains and Losses

	NONCORPORATE	CORPORATE
A statutory maximum tax rate applicable to net capital gain	Yes, 0% (5% if before 2008), 15%, 25%, and 28%	Yes, but rate is 35%
Offset of net capital losses against ordinary income	Yes, up to $3,000	No
Carryback of capital losses	No	Yes, three years as STCLs
Carryforward of capital losses	Yes, indefinitely	Yes, five years as STCLs

MAXIMUM RATE ON NET CAPITAL GAIN FOR CORPORATIONS. Unlike individual taxpayers, corporations do not receive any preferential rate reductions for net capital gains. Corporations apply a maximum rate of 35% to the corporation's net capital gain.[46] However, given the present tax rates for corporations, the existence of the 35% alternative rate for net capital gain has no benefit. A corporation subject to a rate of 39% because taxable income is greater than $100,000 but not more than $335,000 does not use the maximum 35% rate. In essence, therefore, corporations are taxed on capital gains at the same rates for ordinary income.

Topic Review I:5-2 summarizes the principal differences in the tax treatment of capital gains and losses for corporate and noncorporate taxpayers.

STOP & THINK

Question: Most taxpayers believe that if they have a LTCG, their income taxes will be less on the LTCG than on their other ordinary income. Explain why all taxpayers do not have a tax savings from a net capital gain.

Solution: Noncorporate taxpayers whose marginal tax rate is 28% or less will not have a reduction in taxes if the LTCG is gain from the sale of a collectible, or gain from the sale of qualified small business stock under Sec. 1202. Also, corporations are not eligible for the lower rates available to noncorporate taxpayers and pay taxes on NLTCG at the same rate as ordinary income.

SALE OR EXCHANGE

OBJECTIVE 6

Recognize when a sale or exchange has occurred

As previously indicated, capital gains and losses result from the sale or exchange of capital assets. Although Sec. 1222 does not define a sale or an exchange, a **sale** is generally considered to be a transaction where one receives cash or the equivalent of cash, including the assumption of one's debt. An **exchange** is a transaction where one receives a reciprocal transfer of property, as distinguished from a transaction where one receives only cash or a cash equivalent.[47]

EXAMPLE I:5-64 ▶

Two years ago, Bart acquired 100 shares of Alaska Corporation common stock for $12,000 to hold as an investment. Bart sells 50 shares of the stock to Sandy for $10,000 and transfers the other 50 shares to Gail in exchange for land that has a $10,000 FMV. In each transaction, Bart realizes a $4,000 ($10,000 − $6,000) LTCG due to the sale or exchange of a capital asset. The transfer to Sandy qualifies as a sale, and the transfer to Gail qualifies as an exchange. ◀

TYPICAL MISCONCEPTION

Because the carryover for net operating losses is 20 years, it is sometimes erroneously assumed that the carryover for corporate capital losses is also 20 years instead of five years.

To qualify as a sale or exchange, the transaction must be bona fide. Transactions between related parties such as family members are closely scrutinized. For example, a sale of property on credit to a relative may be a disguised gift if there is no intention of collecting the debt. If this is the case, a subsequent bad debt deduction due to the debt's

---

[46] Sec. 1201.

[47] Reg. Sec. 1.1002-1(d).

worthlessness is disallowed. In some instances, the Code specifically states that a particular transaction or event either qualifies or does not qualify for sale or exchange treatment. For example, the holder of an option who fails to exercise such an option treats the lapse of the option as a sale or exchange.[48] However, abandonment of property is generally not deemed to be a sale or exchange.[49]

WORTHLESS SECURITIES

ADDITIONAL COMMENT

The worthlessness of a security is treated as a sale or exchange so that the taxpayer is not forced to arrange for someone to buy the security for a token amount.

If a security that is a capital asset becomes worthless during the year, Sec. 165(g)(1) specifies that any loss is treated as a loss from the sale or exchange of a capital asset on the last day of the tax year. The term includes stock, a stock option, and "a bond, debenture, note or certificate, or other evidence of indebtedness, issued by a corporation or by a government or political division thereof, with interest coupons or in registered form."[50] Whether a security has become worthless during the year is a question of fact, and the taxpayer has the burden of proof to show evidence of worthlessness.[51]

EXAMPLE I:5-65 ▶

Charlotte purchased $40,000 of bonds issued by the Jet Corporation in March 2009. In February 2010, Jet is declared bankrupt, and its bonds are worthless. Charlotte has a LTCL of $40,000 because the bonds have become worthless and are deemed to have been sold on the last day of 2010. The more-than-one-year holding period requirement is satisfied by the last day of 2010. ◀

REAL-WORLD EXAMPLE

A corporation owned 76% of the stock of another company. The corporation later acquired the remaining 24% of the stock, allegedly for the purpose of avoiding interference by minority shareholders. Later the corporation claimed an ordinary loss on the worthless stock because it owned at least 80% of the stock. The Court treated the loss as a capital loss because the acquisition of the remaining stock was without a business purpose. *Hunter Mfg. Co.,* 21 T.C. 424 (1953).

SECURITIES IN AFFILIATED CORPORATIONS. If the security that becomes worthless is a security in a domestic affiliated corporation owned by a corporate taxpayer, the worthless security is not considered a capital asset. Thus, a corporate taxpayer's loss due to owning worthless securities in an affiliated corporation is treated as an ordinary loss. Because capital losses are of only limited benefit to corporate taxpayers, the classification of the loss as ordinary is preferable.

To qualify as an affiliated corporation, the parent corporation must own at least 80% of the voting power of all classes of stock and at least 80% of each class of nonvoting stock. The subsidiary corporation must be engaged in the active conduct of an operating business as opposed to being a passive investment company (i.e., more than 90% of its aggregate gross receipts must be from sources other than passive types of income such as royalties, dividends, and interest).[52]

EXAMPLE I:5-66 ▶

Ace Corporation owns 80% of all classes of stock issued by the same Jet Corporation described in Example I:5-65. Jet Corporation is actively engaged in an operating business and has no income from passive investments before being declared bankrupt. Ace's loss from its worthless stock investment is an ordinary loss instead of a capital loss because Jet is an affiliated corporation. Ace owns at least 80% of all classes of Jet's stock and more than 90% of Jet's gross receipts are from sources other than passive types of income. ◀

RETIREMENT OF DEBT INSTRUMENTS

Generally, the collection of a debt is not a sale or an exchange. However, if a debt instrument is retired, amounts received by the holder are treated as being received in an exchange.[53] Debt instruments include bonds, debentures, notes, certificates, and other evidences of indebtedness.

EXAMPLE I:5-67 ▶

In 2005 the Rocket Corporation issued $50,000 of five-year, interest-bearing bonds that were purchased by Elaine as an investment for $49,800. Elaine receives $50,000 at maturity in 2010. Retirement of the debt instrument is an exchange, and the $200 gain is a LTCG.[54] ◀

Although Congress has provided that retirements of debt instruments are treated as exchanges, Congress is not willing to allow taxpayers to convert large amounts of potential ordinary interest income into capital gain by purchasing debt instruments at a substantial

---

[48] Sec. 1234(b) and Reg. Sec. 1.1234-1(b).
[49] Reg. Secs. 1.165-2 and 1.167(a)-8.
[50] Sec. 165(g)(2).
[51] *Minnie K. Young v. CIR,* 28 AFTR 365, 41-2 USTC ¶9744 (2nd Cir., 1941).

[52] Sec. 165(g)(3).
[53] Sec. 1271(a).
[54] If Rocket Corporation issued the bonds with the intention of calling the bonds before maturity, Sec. 1271(a)(2) treats the gain as ordinary income.

discount. As illustrated in Example I:5-67, a small amount of bond discount is sometimes converted to capital gain. However, if the discount is large enough to be classified as original issue discount, the discount must be amortized and included in gross income for each day the debt instrument is held for both cash and accrual method taxpayer. Original issue discount (OID) is defined as "the excess (if any) of the stated redemption price at maturity over the issue price."[55]

EXAMPLE I:5-68 ▶

On January 1, 2010, Connie purchases $100,000 of the City Corporation's newly issued bonds for $85,000. The bonds mature in 20 years. In 2010 and in subsequent years Connie must annually recognize as interest income a portion of the $15,000 of OID. ◀

The OID is considered to be zero if the amount of discount "is less than ¼ of 1% of the stated redemption price at maturity, multiplied by the number of complete years to maturity."[56] In Example I:5-67, the $200 discount is not OID because it is less than $625 (0.0025 × $50,000 × 5 years). If Connie pays more than $95,000 for the bonds in Example I:5-68, the OID is zero.

ADDITIONAL COMMENT

Two different types of bonds are sold at a discount: original issue discount (OID) bonds and market discount bonds. OID bonds are issued at a discount, whereas market discount bonds have market discount resulting from a rise in interest rates after the issuance of the bonds.

ORIGINAL ISSUE DISCOUNT. Instead of spreading the OID ratably over the life of the bond, amortization of the discount is based on an interest amortization method called the **constant interest rate method**. The total amount of interest income is determined by multiplying the interest yield to maturity by the adjusted issue price. With this method of amortizing discount, the amount of OID amortized increases for each year the bond is held. In the above example, Connie recognizes a larger amount of interest income in 2011 than in 2010 due to amortization of the OID.

The daily portion of the OID for any accrual period is "determined by allocating to each day in any accrual period its ratable portion to the increase during such accrual period in the adjusted issue price of the debt instrument."[57] The increase in the adjusted issue price for any accrual period is shown below.

$$\text{Increase in the adjusted issue price} = \left[\begin{array}{c} \text{Adjusted issue} \\ \text{price at the} \\ \text{beginning of} \\ \text{the accrual} \\ \text{period} \end{array} \times \begin{array}{c} \text{Yield} \\ \text{to} \\ \text{maturity} \end{array} \right] - \begin{array}{c} \text{Interest} \\ \text{payments} \\ \text{during the} \\ \text{accrual} \\ \text{period} \end{array}$$

EXAMPLE I:5-69 ▶

KEY POINT

The owner of an OID bond is normally required to accrue interest income each year regardless of the owner's method of accounting.

On June 30, 2010, Fred purchases a 10%, $10,000 corporate bond for $9,264. The bond is issued on June 30, 2010, and matures in five years. Interest is paid semiannually, and the effective yield to maturity is 12% compounded semiannually. In 2010, Fred recognizes interest income of $556, as illustrated in Table I:5-1. The adjusted issue price as of January 1, 2011, is $9,320. This is the sum of the issue price plus any amounts of OID includible in the income of any holder since the date of issue. ◀

If a debt instrument is sold or exchanged before maturity, part of the OID is included in the seller's income. The amount to be included depends on the number of days the debt instrument is owned by the seller within the accrual period.

EXAMPLE I:5-70 ▶

Assume the same facts as in the above example, except that Fred sells the corporate bond to Carolyn on February 24, 2012 (the 55th day in the accrual period). Fred must include $20 [(55 days ÷ 182* days in the accrual period) × $67] of accrued interest for the period of January 1, 2012, to February 24, 2012, in income for 2012. Fred's basis for the bond increases by $20. Thus, his basis for determining a gain or loss is $9,462 ($9,442 + $20). ◀

*2012 is a leap year.

MARKET DISCOUNT BONDS PURCHASED AFTER APRIL 30, 1993. The sale or exchange of a market discount bond may result in part or all of the gain being classified

---

[55] Sec. 1273(a)(1).
[56] Sec. 1273(a)(3).

[57] Sec. 1272(a)(3).

▼ **TABLE I:5-1**

Computation for Interest Income in Examples I:5-69 and I:5-70

	Interest Received (1)	Amortization of Original Issue Discount (2)	Interest Income (3) = (1) + (2)	Taxpayer's Basis for the Bond
6-30-10				$ 9,264
12-31-10	$ 500	$ 56[a]	$ 556	9,320[b]
6-30-11	500	59	559	9,379
12-31-11	500	63	563	9,442
6-30-12	500	67	567	9,509
12-31-12	500	71	571	9,580
6-30-13	500	75	575	9,655
12-31-13	500	79	579	9,734
6-30-14	500	84	584	9,818
12-31-14	500	89	589	9,907
6-30-15	500	93[c]	593	10,000
	$5,000	$736	$5,736	

[a]6% × $9,264 − $500 = $56.
[b]$9,264 + $56 = $9,320.
[c]This figure is adjusted for rounding.

as ordinary income.[58] A market discount bond is a bond that is acquired in the bond market at a discount. Market discount is the excess of the stated redemption price of the bond at maturity over the taxpayer's basis for such bond immediately after it is acquired.

EXAMPLE I:5-71 ▶ On January 1, Stephano purchased $100,000 of 8%, 20-year bonds for $82,000. The bonds were issued at par by the Solar Corporation two years ago on January 1. The bonds are market discount bonds. ◀

Similar to OID, there is a de minimis rule for determining market discount. Market discount is zero if the discount is less than ¼ of 1% of the stated redemption price of the bond at maturity multiplied by the number of complete years to maturity.[59] If Stephano paid $95,500 or more for the Solar Corporation bonds in Example I:5-71, the bonds would not be market discount bonds.[60]

Gain realized on disposition of the market discount bond is ordinary income to the extent of the accrued market discount.[61] The ratable accrual method (straight line method computed on a daily basis) is used to determine the amount of the accrued market discount recognized as ordinary income.[62] The market discount is allocated on the basis of the number of days the taxpayer held the bond relative to the number of days between the acquisition date and maturity date.

EXAMPLE I:5-72 ▶ Assume the same facts as in Example I:5-71 except that Stephano sells the bonds to Kimberly three years later for $86,400 on January 1st. $3,000 (³⁄₁₈ × $18,000) of the $4,400 ($86,400 − $82,000) gain is ordinary income and the remaining gain is LTCG. If Stephano sold the bond for more than $82,000 but less than $85,000, all of the gain is ordinary income. The entire $18,000 gain is ordinary income if the bond is held to maturity. ◀

---

[58] Ordinary income treatment for accrued market discount does not apply to owners of taxable market discount bonds issued on or before July 18, 1984, if the bonds were acquired before May 1, 1993. Owners of tax-exempt bonds are not required to accrue market discount if the bonds were acquired before May 1, 1993 (regardless of the issue date).

[59] Sec. 1278(a)(2)(C).
[60] $100,000 × .25% × 18 years = $4,500.
[61] Sec. 1276(a)(1).
[62] Sec. 1276(b)(1). A taxpayer may elect to use the constant interest rate method (see Sec. 1276(b)(2)).

OPTIONS

The owner of an option to buy property may sell the option, exercise the option, or allow the option to expire. If the option is exercised, the amount paid for the option is added to the purchase price of the property acquired.[63]

EXAMPLE I:5-73 ▶

ADDITIONAL COMMENT

An option is a contract in which the owner of property agrees with a potential buyer that the potential buyer has the right to buy the property at a fixed price within a certain period of time.

On August 5, 2010, Len pays $600 for an option to acquire 100 shares of Hill Corporation common stock for $80 per share at any time before December 20, 2010. Len exercises the option on November 15, 2010, and pays $8,000 for the stock. Len's basis for the 100 shares of Hill is $8,600 ($8,000 + $600), and the stock's holding period begins on November 15, 2010. ◀

When an option is sold or allowed to expire, a sale or exchange has occurred and gain or loss is therefore recognized.[64] The character of the underlying property determines whether the gain or loss from the sale or expiration of the option is capital or ordinary in nature. If the optioned property is a capital asset, the option is treated as a capital asset and capital gain or loss is recognized on the sale or exchange.

EXAMPLE I:5-74 ▶

On March 2, 2010, Holly pays $270 for an option to acquire 100 shares of Arkansas Corporation stock for $30 per share at any time before December 10, 2010. As a result of an increase in the market value of the Arkansas stock, the market price of the option increases and Holly sells the option for $600 on August 2, 2010. Because the Arkansas stock is a capital asset in the hands of Holly, the option is a capital asset and she must recognize a STCG of $330 ($600 − $270). ◀

EXAMPLE I:5-75 ▶

On October 12, 2009, Mary paid $400 for an option to acquire 100 shares of Portland Corporation stock for $50 per share at any time before February 19, 2010. The price never exceeds $50 before February 19, 2010, and Mary does not exercise the option. Because the option expires, Mary recognizes a STCL of $400 in 2010. ◀

SELF-STUDY QUESTION

Marc writes a call option on stock owned by him and receives $800 on November 1, 2009. The value of the stock declines and the option is allowed to expire on February 15, 2010. When does Marc recognize the $800 gain?

ANSWER

Marc recognizes the gain in 2010 when the transaction is completed.

Transactions in which taxpayers purchase or write options to buy (calls) are quite common today. An investor who anticipates that the market value of a stock or security (e.g., common stock) will increase during the next few months may purchase a call option instead of actually buying the stock. As indicated above, the tax treatment for the option depends on whether the call is exercised, sold, or expires. Someone, however, must be willing to write a call on the stock. Typically an owner of the same stock will write a call option. The writer of the call receives a payment for granting the right to purchase the stock at a fixed price within a given period of time.

If the call is exercised, the writer of the call adds the amount received for the call to the sales price to determine the amount realized.[65] If the call is not exercised within the given time period and thus expires, the writer retains the amount received for the option and recognizes a STCG in the year the call expires. The gain is short-term even if the option is written and held for more than a year.

EXAMPLE I:5-76 ▶

Sam owns 100 shares of Madison Corporation common stock, which he purchased on May 1, 2003, for $4,000. On November 8, 2010, Sam writes a call that gives Joan, an investor, the option to purchase Sam's 100 shares of Madison stock at $60 per share any time before April 19, 2011. The current market price of Madison stock is $56 per share, and Sam receives $520 for writing the call. If the call is exercised, Sam has a LTCG of $2,520 [($6,000 + $520) − $4,000] in the year the call is exercised. If the call is not exercised and expires on April 19, 2011, Sam must recognize a STCG of $520 in 2011. ◀

EXAMPLE I:5-77
KEY POINT

Note that Sam in Example I:5-76 did not have to recognize gross income when he received $520 on November 8.

Assume the same facts as in Example I:5-76, and consider the tax treatment for Joan, the holder of the call. If Joan exercises the call, the basis of the stock is $6,520 ($6,000 + $520). If she does not exercise the call, a STCL of $520 is recognized. If Joan sells the call, the amount received is compared with her basis in the call ($520) to compute Joan's gain or loss. ◀

ʾul. 58-234, 1958-1 C.B. 279.
⁴(a).

[65] Rev. Rul. 58-234, 1958-1 C.B. 279.

PATENTS

To encourage technological progress and to clarify whether a transfer of rights to a patent is capital gain or ordinary income, Congress created Sec. 1235, which allows the holder of a patent to treat the gain resulting from the transfer of all substantial rights in a patent as LTCG. This tax treatment is more favorable than that accorded to producers of artistic and literary works, who receive ordinary rather than capital gain from the sale of their works.

KEY POINT

A copyright held by a taxpayer whose personal efforts created it is omitted from the definition of a capital asset. However, a patent can be considered a capital asset. In effect, the tax law could be said to favor individuals whose efforts lead to scientific or technological advancement.

REQUIREMENTS FOR CAPITAL GAIN TREATMENT. Section 1235 provides that the transfer of all substantial rights to a patent by the holder of the patent is treated as a sale or exchange of a capital asset that has been held long-term. Thus, LTCG is recognized on the transfer of a patent regardless of its holding period or the character of the asset. Favorable long-term capital gain treatment applies even if the transferor of the patent receives periodic payments contingent on the productivity, use, or disposition of the property transferred.[66]

EXAMPLE I:5-78 ▶ Clay invents a small utensil used to peel shrimp. He has a patent on the utensil and transfers all rights to the patent to a manufacturing company. Clay receives $100,000 plus 40 cents per utensil sold. Because Sec. 1235 applies, the total of the lump-sum payment and the royalty payments received less his cost basis for the patent is recognized as a LTCG. ◀

SUBSTANTIAL RIGHTS. The principal requirement in Sec. 1235 is that the holder must transfer all substantial rights to the patent. The Regulations state that the circumstances of the whole transaction should be considered in determining whether all substantial rights to a patent have been transferred.[67] All substantial rights have not been transferred if the patent rights of the purchaser are limited geographically within the country of issuance or the rights are for a period less than a patent's remaining life.

EXAMPLE I:5-79 ▶ Bruce, an inventor, transfers one of his U.S. patents on a manufacturing process to a manufacturer located in Utah. The manufacturer's rights to use the patent are limited to the state of Utah. Because the use of the patent is limited to a geographical area, all substantial rights have not been transferred, and Sec. 1235 does not apply. Payments received for the use of the patent are royalties and taxed as ordinary income. ◀

DEFINITION OF A HOLDER. Long-term capital gain treatment applies only to a holder of the patent rights. For purposes of Sec. 1235, a holder is an individual whose efforts created the property or an individual who acquires the patent rights from the creator for valuable consideration before the property covered by the patent is placed in service or used. Furthermore, the acquiring individual may not be related to the creator or be the creator's employer.

Section 1235 may not be used by corporate taxpayers because corporations are not permitted to be classified as holders. Although a partnership is not permitted to be a holder, individual partners may qualify as holders to the extent of the partner's interest in the patent owned by the partnership.

EXAMPLE I:5-80 ▶ Joy purchases a patent from Martin, whose efforts created the patent. The purchase occurs before the property is placed in service or used. Joy and Martin are unrelated individuals, and Joy is not Martin's employer. For purposes of Sec. 1235, both Joy and Martin qualify as holders. ◀

ADDITIONAL COMMENT

The scope of Sec. 1253 is very broad. A franchise "includes an agreement which gives one of the parties to the agreement the right to distribute, sell, or provide goods, services, or facilities within a specified area."

FRANCHISES, TRADEMARKS, AND TRADE NAMES

Before the enactment of Sec. 1253, significant uncertainty existed as to whether the transfer of a franchise, trademark, or trade name should be treated as a sale or exchange or as a licensing agreement. If the transfer is tantamount to a sale of the property, payments received should be treated by the transferor as a return of capital and capital gain, and the transferee should be required to capitalize and amortize such payments. However, if the

---

[66] Sec. 1235(a).

[67] Reg. Sec. 1.1235-2(b).

transfer represents a licensing agreement, the transferor should recognize ordinary income and the transferee should receive an ordinary deduction for such payments.

Section 1253, which applies to the granting of a franchise, trademark, or trade name, as well as renewals and transfers to third parties, attempts to resolve the uncertainty by stating, "A transfer of a franchise, trademark, or trade name shall not be treated as a sale or exchange of a capital asset if the transferor retains any significant power, right, or continuing interest with respect to the subject matter of the franchise, trademark, or trade name."[68]

Examples of some rights that are to be considered a "significant power, right, or continuing interest"[69] include the right to:

▶ Disapprove of any assignment.

▶ Terminate the agreement at will.

▶ Prescribe standards of quality for products, product services, and facilities.

▶ Require the exclusive selling or advertising of the transferor's products or services.

▶ Require the transferee to purchase substantially all of its supplies and equipment from the transferor.

If the transferor does not retain any significant power, right, or continuing interest in the property, the transferor treats the transfer as a sale of the franchise and has the benefits of capital gain treatment. However, any amounts received that are contingent on the productivity, use, or disposition of such property must be treated as ordinary income by the transferor.

EXAMPLE I:5-81 ▶ Rose, who owns a franchise with a basis of $100,000, transfers the franchise to Ruth and retains no significant power, right, or continuing interest. Rose receives a $250,000 down payment when the agreement is signed and annual payments for five years equal to 10% of all sales in excess of $2,000,000. Rose has a capital gain of $150,000 with respect to the initial payment, but all of the payments received during the next five years will be ordinary income because they are contingent payments. ◀

Under Sec. 1253, the transferee may deduct payments that are contingent on the productivity, use, or disposition of such property as business expenses. Generally, other payments are capitalized and amortized over a period of 15 years.[70] In practice, payments received for the transfer of a franchise are generally treated as ordinary income to the transferor and are deductible by the transferee because in most franchise agreements the transferor desires to maintain significant powers, rights, or continuing interests in the franchise operation. Also, in many instances the payments are, in part, predicated on the success of the franchised business and are, therefore, established as contingent payments.

LEASE CANCELLATION PAYMENTS

A lease arrangement may be terminated before the lease period expires, and a lease cancellation payment may be made as consideration for the other party's agreement to terminate the lease. Either a lessor or a lessee may receive such a payment because the payment is normally made by the person who wants to cancel the lease. The tax treatment may differ significantly depending on which party is the recipient.

PAYMENTS RECEIVED BY LESSOR. The Supreme Court has ruled that lease cancellation payments received by a lessor are treated as ordinary income on the basis that the payments represent a substitute for rent.[71] Lease cancellation payments are included in the lessor's income in the year received, even if the lessor uses an accrual method.[72]

PAYMENTS RECEIVED BY LESSEE. Payments received by a lessee for canceling a lease are considered amounts received in exchange for the lease.[73] If the lease is a capital asset, any gain or loss is a capital gain or loss.

---

[68] Sec. 1253(a). Section 1253(e) prevents the basic Sec. 1253 rules from applying to the transfer of a professional sports franchise.
[69] Sec. 1253(b)(2).
[70] Sec. 197(a).

[71] *Walter M. Hort v. CIR*, 25 AFTR 1207, 41-1 USTC ¶9354 (USSC, 1941).
[72] *Farrelly-Walsh, Inc.*, 13 B.T.A. 923 (1928).
[73] Sec. 1241.

EXAMPLE I:5-82 ▶ Jim has a three-year lease on a house used as his personal residence. The lessor has an opportunity to sell the house and has agreed to pay $1,000 to Jim to cancel the lease. Assuming that Jim has no basis in the lease, the gain of $1,000 is capital gain because the lease is a capital asset. ◀

HOLDING PERIOD

OBJECTIVE 7

Determine the holding period for an asset when a sale or disposition occurs

The length of time an asset is held before it is disposed of (i.e., the *holding period*) is an important factor in determining whether any gain or loss resulting from the disposition of a capital asset is treated as long-term or short-term. To be classified as a long-term capital gain or loss, the capital asset must be held more than one year.[74] To determine the holding period, the day of acquisition is excluded and the disposal date is included.[75]

If the date of disposition is the same date as the date of acquisition, but a year later, the asset is considered to have been held for only one year. If the property is held for an additional day, the holding period is more than one year.

EXAMPLE I:5-83 ▶ Arnie purchased a capital asset on April 20, 2009, and sells the asset at a gain on April 21, 2010. The gain is classified as a LTCG. If the asset is sold on or before April 20, 2010, the gain is a STCG. ◀

ADDITIONAL COMMENT

When determining the holding period for marketable securities, it is important to use the "trade" dates, not the "settlement" dates.

The fact that all months do not have the same number of days is not a factor in determining the one-year period. Acquisitions made on the last day of any month must be held until the first day of the thirteenth subsequent month in order to have been held for more than one year.

EXAMPLE I:5-84 ▶ Alford sells stock held as an investment and recognizes a gain. If the capital asset was purchased on May 31, 2009, the gain is LTCG subject to the 15% or zero rate if the asset is sold on or after June 1, 2010. If sold on or before May 31, 2010, the gain is STCG and the 15% and zero rates do not apply. ◀

ADDITIONAL COMMENT

On June 1, 1995, the Securities and Exchange Commission adopted a set of rules that requires investors who purchase or sell securities to deliver the funds to pay for the securities or deliver the certificates to be sold within three days of when the order is placed. Formerly, investors had five days to deliver funds or certificates.

PROPERTY RECEIVED AS A GIFT

If a person receives property as a gift and uses the donor's basis to determine the gain or loss from a sale or exchange, the donor's holding period is added to the donee's holding period.[76] In other words, the donee's holding period includes the donor's holding period. If, however, the donee's basis is the FMV of the property on the date of the gift, the donee's holding period starts on the day after the date of the gift. This situation occurs when the FMV is less than the donor's basis on the date of the gift and the property is subsequently sold at a loss.

EXAMPLE I:5-85 ▶ Cindy receives a capital asset as a gift from Marc on July 4, 2010, when the asset has a $4,000 FMV. Marc acquired the property on April 12, 2010, for $3,400. If Cindy sells the asset after April 12, 2011, any gain or loss is LTCG or LTCL. Cindy's basis is the donor's cost because the FMV of the property is higher than the donor's basis on the date of the gift. Because Cindy takes Marc's basis, Marc's holding period is included. ◀

EXAMPLE I:5-86 ▶ Roy receives a capital asset as a gift from Diane on September 12, 2010, when the asset has a $6,000 FMV. Diane acquired the asset on July 1, 2009, for $6,500. If the asset is sold at a gain (i.e., for more than $6,500), Roy's holding period starts on July 1, 2009, the date when Diane acquired the property, because the donor's basis of $6,500 is used by Roy to compute the gain. If the asset is sold at a loss (i.e., for less than $6,000), Roy's holding period does not start until the day after the date of the gift, September 13, 2010, because Roy's basis is the $6,000 FMV. The FMV is used to compute the loss because it is less than the donor's basis on the date of the gift. ◀

ADDITIONAL COMMENT

The provision permitting the holding period of property received from a decedent to be deemed to be long-term is a rule of convenience. It is not necessary to try to determine when the decedent actually acquired the property.

PROPERTY RECEIVED FROM A DECEDENT

The holding period of property received from a decedent is always deemed to be long-term. If the person who receives the property from the decedent sells the property within one year

---

[74] Sec. 1222. A six-month holding period was applied to property acquired after June 27, 1984 and before January 1, 1988.

[75] *H. M. Hooper*, 26 B.T.A. 758 (1932), and Rev. Rul. 70-598, 1970-2 C.B. 168.

[76] Sec. 1223(1) and Reg. Sec. 1.1223-1(b).

after the decedent's death, the property is considered to be held for more than one year regardless of how long the property is actually held.[77]

EXAMPLE I:5-87 ▶ The executor of Paul's estate sells certain securities for $41,000 on September 2, 2010, which are valued in the estate at their FMV of $40,000 on June 5, 2010, the date of Paul's death. The estate has a LTCG of $1,000 because the securities are considered to have been held long-term. ◀

NONTAXABLE EXCHANGES

In a nontaxable exchange, the basis of the property received is determined by taking into account the basis of the property given in the exchange. If the properties are capital assets or Sec. 1231 assets, the holding period of the property received includes the holding period of the surrendered property.[78] In essence, the holding period of the property given up in a tax-free exchange is tacked on to the holding period of the property received in the exchange.

RECEIPT OF NONTAXABLE STOCK DIVIDENDS AND STOCK RIGHTS

If a shareholder receives nontaxable stock dividends or stock rights, the holding period of the stock received as a dividend or the stock rights received includes the holding period for the stock owned by the shareholder.[79] However, if the stock rights are exercised, the holding period for the stock purchased begins with the date of exercise.

EXAMPLE I:5-88 ▶ As a result of owning Circle Corporation stock acquired three years ago, Paula receives nontaxable stock rights on June 5, 2010. Any gain or loss on the sale of the rights is long-term, regardless of whether any basis is allocated to the rights, because the holding period of the rights includes the holding period of the stock. ◀

EXAMPLE I:5-89 ▶ Assume the same facts as in the example above, except that the stock rights are exercised on August 20, 2010. The holding period for the newly acquired Circle stock begins on the date of exercise. ◀

STOP & THINK

Question: Carter owns 500 shares of Okoboji, Inc. (current market price of $310) with a basis of $101,500 acquired three years ago. In May of the current year, she receives 500 stock rights and exercises those rights that entitle her to purchase 500 shares of Okoboji at $300 per share. The current market price of the stock right is $40 per right. She plans to sell the 500 shares obtained by exercising the stock rights in January when she expects the market price to be $400 per share. Why should she elect to allocate basis to the stock rights?

Solution: If she does not allocate basis, her STCG will be $50,000 ($200,000 − $150,000). If she allocates basis to the stock rights, the basis of the 500 shares obtained when she exercises the rights is $161,600 ($150,000 + $11,600), and her STCG will be $38,400 ($200,000 − $161,600). Note that Carter might benefit by waiting a few months before selling because the gain might then be LTCG. She could sell the original 500 shares and have a LTCG.

JUSTIFICATION FOR PREFERENTIAL TREATMENT OF NET CAPITAL GAINS

Preferential treatment for capital gains was first created by the Revenue Act of 1921, which became effective on January 1, 1922. Despite almost continuous controversy concerning the need for preferential treatment, some form of preferential treatment for capital gains has existed since 1922. The range of controversy concerning the need for preferential tax treatment for capital gains is wide. Some maintain that capital gains do not

---

[77] Sec. 1223(11).
[78] Sec. 1223(1).

[79] Sec. 1223(5) and Reg. Sec. 1.1223-1(e).

HISTORICAL NOTE

In part the preferential treatment of net capital gains was repealed in the Tax Reform Act of 1986 because Congress believed that the reduction of individual tax rates on such forms of capital income as business profits, interest, dividends, and short-term capital gains eliminated the need for a reduced rate for net capital gains.

represent income and should not be taxed, whereas others maintain that capital gains are no different from any other type of income and should be taxed accordingly.[80] A few of the most common arguments are discussed below.

MOBILITY OF CAPITAL

Without some form of preferential treatment, taxpayers who own appreciated capital assets may be unwilling to sell or exchange the asset if high tax rates exist, despite the presence of more attractive investment opportunities. In essence, the taxpayer may be "locked in" to holding an appreciated capital asset instead of shifting resources to more profitable investments.

EXAMPLE I:5-90 ▶

Carmen owns Missouri Corporation stock with a $4,000 basis and a $20,000 FMV. She anticipates that the future after-tax annual return will be 10% on the Missouri stock and 12% on Kansas Corporation stock that has a similar level of risk. Assume her marginal tax rate is 35% (without consideration of favorable capital gain rates). Without preferential treatment of capital gains, Carmen will have to pay a tax of $5,600 ($16,000 × 0.35) on the sale of the Missouri stock and will have only $14,400 ($20,000 − $5,600) to invest in the Kansas stock. With a 12% return, she will receive an investment return of only $1,728 ($14,400 × 0.12), as compared with $2,000 ($20,000 × 0.10) if she maintains the investment in the Missouri stock. ◀

ADDITIONAL COMMENT

According to *The Wall Street Journal*, twelve industrialized nations impose a zero capital gains rate (10-15-07, p. A22).

While the payment of any tax due to the sale of an asset creates somewhat of a "locked-in" effect, the effect can be reduced by lowering the tax rate. The "locked-in" effect is even stronger for older taxpayers if the basis of inherited property is FMV at time of death. A lower tax rate on net capital gain should reduce the taxpayers unwillingness to sell the asset and allow for more mobility of capital. For a brief period in the 1990s, both the top ordinary income rate and the rate on net capital gain were 28%. Today, the top rate on ordinary income is 35% and 15% on adjusted net capital gain.

MITIGATION OF THE EFFECTS OF INFLATION AND THE PROGRESSIVE TAX SYSTEM

Because the tax laws do not generally reflect the effect of changes in purchasing power due to inflation, the sale or exchange of a capital asset may produce inequitable results. In fact, taxes may have to be paid even where a transaction results in an inflation-adjusted loss.

EXAMPLE I:5-91 ▶

Beverly purchased a capital asset nine years ago for $100,000. If the asset is sold today for $180,000 and the general price level has increased by 100% during the nine-year period, Beverly will have a taxable gain of $80,000, despite suffering an inflation-adjusted loss of $20,000 [$180,000 sale price − ($100,000 × 200%)]. ◀

ADDITIONAL COMMENT

The American Assembly at Columbia University, in its final report on *Reforming and Simplifying the Federal Tax System* issued in 1985, recommends that capital gains be taxed as ordinary income if they are adjusted for inflation.

With a progressive tax system, the failure to adjust for inflation creates an even greater distortion. However, it should be noted that this distortion applies to all assets, not just capital assets.

LOWERS THE COST OF CAPITAL

By reducing the tax rate on capital gains, investors are more willing to provide businesses with capital and the cost of capital is reduced. A lower cost of capital encourages capital formation to create more jobs and improve our competitive position in the global economy. Reducing the cost of capital is particularly important for the formation and growth of small business.

---

[80] Walter J. Blum, "A Handy Summary of the Capital Gains Argument," *Taxes—The Tax Magazine*, 35 (April 1957), pp. 247–66.

TAX PLANNING CONSIDERATIONS

SELECTION OF PROPERTY TO TRANSFER BY GIFT

Many tax reasons exist for making gifts of property, although the donor may incur a gift tax liability if the gift is a taxable gift. For example, taxpayers may give income-producing property to a taxpayer subject to a lower tax rate, or property expected to appreciate in the future may be given away to reduce estate taxes. Individuals may annually give property of $13,000[81] or less to a donee without making a taxable gift.[82]

EXAMPLE I:5-92 ▶ Maya, who is single, owns marketable securities with a $6,200 basis and $10,400 FMV. She makes gifts of the marketable securities to Phil and cash of $13,000 to Roy. Because of the $13,000 annual exclusion per donee, Maya's gifts are not taxable gifts. ◀

EXAMPLE I:5-93 ▶ Harry, who is single, makes a gift of land with a $313,000 basis and a $1,213,000 FMV to Rita. Harry's taxable gift is $1,200,000 ($1,213,000 − $13,000), and he incurs a gift tax liability. Rita's basis is $313,000 + 75% of the gift tax paid by Harry [($1,213,000 − $313,000)/$1,200,000 = 75%]. ◀

Individuals often reduce future estate taxes by making gifts. By using the annual exclusion, an individual may reduce future estate taxes and avoid the gift tax.

EXAMPLE I:5-94 ▶ Christine owns only one asset in 2009—cash of $4,200,000—and has no liabilities. In December of 2009, she gifted $13,000 to each of her five grandchildren. Because of the $13,000 annual exclusion per donee, Christine's gifts were not taxable gifts. By making the gifts, she reduced her potential gross estate by $65,000 (5 × $13,000). ◀

The selection of which property to give is important if one is attempting to reduce future estate taxes. It is generally preferable to make gifts of properties that are expected to significantly increase in value during the postgift period before the donor's death. Any increases in value after the date of the gift are not included in the donor's gross estate.

EXAMPLE I:5-95 ▶ In 1994, Hal owned Sun Corporation stock with a $100,000 FMV and Union Corporation stock with a $100,000 FMV. Hal expected the Sun stock to increase in value at a moderate rate and the Union stock to increase at a substantial rate. In 1994, Hal made a gift of the Union stock to Dana. Hal's taxable gift in 1994 was $90,000 ($100,000 − $10,000 annual exclusion in 1994). Hal dies in 2011 when the FMVs of the Sun and Union stocks are $180,000 and $425,000, respectively. The postgift appreciation of $325,000 ($425,000 − $100,000) is not included in Hal's gross estate. By giving the Union stock instead of the Sun stock in 1994, Hal reduces his gross estate by $245,000. ◀

Gifts are often made for income tax purposes to shift income to other family members who are in a lower income tax bracket than the donor.

EXAMPLE I:5-96 ▶ In 2010, Anne has a marginal tax rate of 33% and owns Atlantic Corporation bonds, which have a $5,000 basis and $8,000 FMV. The bonds pay interest of $1,000 per year. If Anne gives the bonds to her dependent child, the interest income is shifted to the child. If the child has no other income, the child's taxable income is $50 ($1,000 − $950 standard deduction), and the child's marginal tax rate is 10%. The gift results in an annual income tax savings to the family unit of $325 [(0.33 × $1,000) − (0.10 × $50)]. The rate of tax that is imposed may be the parent's rate (see Chapter I:2) if the child is less than 18 years old (possibly less than 24 years old after 2007) and has net unearned income in excess of $1,900.

In addition to shifting the interest income, Anne has also shifted a potential gain of $3,000. The child's basis for the bonds is $5,000 because the donee takes the donor's basis when the FMV of the property at the time of the gift is greater than the donor's basis. No gain is recog-

---

[81] In 2005–2008, the annual exclusion was $12,000.   [82] Sec. 2503(b).

nized by Anne when the gift is made, and a future sale of the property by the child may be taxed at a lower income tax rate. ◄

Although gifts of appreciated property may generate desirable income tax benefits, it is not usually advantageous to make a gift of property that has a basis greater than its FMV because the donee's basis for determining a loss is the FMV. The excess of the donor's basis over the FMV at the time of the gift may never generate any tax benefit for the donor or the donee. Therefore, the donor should sell the asset and make a gift of the proceeds if the loss on the sale is deductible.

EXAMPLE I:5-97 ▶ Bob owns Red Corporation stock with an $8,000 basis and $6,000 FMV, which is held as an investment. Bob wishes to make a graduation gift of the marketable securities to Angela, although he expects her to sell the stock and purchase a car. If Angela sells the stock for $6,000, no gain or loss is recognized because her loss basis for the stock is $6,000. In addition, no loss is recognized by Bob on the gift of the stock to Angela. Instead of giving the stock, Bob should sell it to recognize a $2,000 capital loss and then give the proceeds from the sale to Angela. ◄

The effect of gift taxes paid by the donor on the donee's basis for property received is another reason why it may be more advantageous to give appreciated property rather than property with a basis greater than its FMV. A portion of the gift taxes paid as a result of giving appreciated property is added to the property's basis. However, payment of gift taxes due to the gift of property that has a basis greater than its FMV does not result in an increase in the donee's basis.

SELECTION OF PROPERTY TO TRANSFER AT TIME OF DEATH

An integral part of gift and estate planning is the selection of property to be transferred to family members and others both during the taxpayer's lifetime and upon death. Usually, taxpayers find it advantageous to retain highly appreciated property in their estates and transfer such property at death to the taxpayer's heirs because the basis of the inherited property will be increased to its FMV at the date of death (or six months from the date of death if the alternate valuation date is elected). Of course, the impact of gift and estate taxes also play a major role in this planning process.

Investment and business assets that have declined in value (i.e., the FMV is less than the basis) should normally be sold before death to obtain an income tax deduction for the loss. If the property is not sold or otherwise disposed of before death, the basis of the inherited property is reduced to its FMV.

EXAMPLE I:5-98 ▶ Paul owns two farms of similar size and quality. Each farm has a $500,000 FMV. Paul's basis for the first farm is $100,000, and his basis for the second farm is $430,000. Eventually, Paul plans for both farms to be owned by Amy. However, he would like to transfer ownership of one farm now and retain the other farm until his death. Paul should make a gift of the second farm and transfer the first farm to Amy upon his death because the second farm has appreciated less in value. When Paul dies and devises the first farm to Amy, she will have a basis for the property equal to its FMV at the date of death even though Paul's basis is only $100,000. ◄

SELF-STUDY QUESTION

Doug owns IBM Corporation shares, which have a $50,000 FMV and basis of $75,000. Doug makes a deathbed telephone call to his stockbroker and sells the IBM shares. Assuming that Doug is in the 35% bracket and had no other capital gains or losses, calculate the tax savings associated with the sale.

ANSWER

Doug saves $1,050 ($3,000 × 0.35). It should be noted that the loss is limited to $3,000; if Doug dies, the unused capital loss of $22,000 is lost.

COMPLIANCE AND PROCEDURAL CONSIDERATIONS

DOCUMENTATION OF BASIS

KEY POINT

Many taxpayers do not maintain adequate records that can be used to document the basis of their most important asset, their personal residence. For example, taxpayers can increase the basis of their residence if they have the driveway paved or add a new room or porch.

The importance of being able to determine and document the basis of assets acquired by a taxpayer cannot be overemphasized. Accurate records of asset acquisitions, dispositions, and adjustments to basis are essential. When more than one asset is acquired at the same time, the amount paid must be allocated among the assets acquired based on their relative FMVs. Subsequent adjustments to basis, such as those due to capital improvements and depreciation deductions, must be documented.

Because the basis of property can be determined by reference to another person's basis for that asset (e.g., gifts), taxpayers should be particularly aware of obtaining documentation for that basis at the time of the transfer. In the case of a gift, the taxpayer's basis may be affected by any gift tax paid by the donor. A copy of the donor's gift tax return is useful in documenting the upward adjustment to the donor's basis in determining the donee's basis.

KEY POINT

Schedule D refers to 28% gain which is NCG taxed at a maximum rate of 28% (collectible gain and part of the Sec. 1202 gain).

Taxpayers who inherit property may use the decedent's federal Estate Tax Return (Form 706) to determine the FMV at the time of the decedent's death or FMV as of the alternate valuation date. However, the appraised value used for estate tax purposes is only presumptively correct for basis purposes. Although the FMVs used to determine the estate tax are typically used to determine basis, neither the taxpayer nor the IRS is barred from using an FMV for basis purposes that differs from the values used for the estate tax return.[83]

REAL-WORLD EXAMPLE

Artwork inherited by a married couple was originally valued at $12,000,000 for estate taxes based on a blockage discount. The IRS determined that the undiscounted value was $36,000,000 and the discounted value was $14,000,000. The taxpayers consented to the $14,000,000 value but later used $36,000,000 as the basis for the artwork after the statute of limitations had expired for the estate tax. The 9th Circuit Court of Appeals agreed with the IRS that the correct basis should be $14,000,000. *Janis v. Commissioner* 461 F.3d 1080 (CA-9, 2006)

REPORTING OF CAPITAL GAINS AND LOSSES ON SCHEDULE D

Capital gains and losses are reported by individuals on Schedule D, which is then attached to Form 1040. Part I is used to report short-term capital gains and losses, and Part II is used to report long-term capital gains and losses. Part III is a summary of Parts I and II.

Capital gains due to installment sales are first reported on a separate form before being included on Schedule D. The taxpayer's share of capital gains and losses from partnerships, S corporations, and fiduciaries is reported in Parts I and II on lines 5 and 12. The carryover of capital losses is also included in Parts I and II on lines 6 and 14.

A filled-in copy of Schedule D and a Qualified Dividends and Capital Gains Tax Worksheet are shown in Figure I:5-1. It includes computations relating to the information in Example I:5-99.

EXAMPLE I:5-99 ▶

Virgil Schmidt, a single taxpayer, uses the following information to prepare his Schedule D for 2009. Virgil received $8,000 of qualified dividends during the year. He sold 200 shares of Tennis Corporation stock for $13,000 on June 20, 2009. The shares were purchased on October 2, 2008, for $8,700. He has an STCL carryforward from 2008 of $8,200. He sold a piano for $4,000 on May 30, 2009. The piano was purchased on April 12, 1999, for $2,500 and used by his two sons. Virgil also sold 500 shares of Golf Corporation stock for $18,000 on November 30, 2009. He had purchased the stock on April 1, 2005, for $10,000.

Virgil has STCG of $4,300 that is offset by $8,200 of STCL carryforward on line 6. His NSTCL of $3,900 ($8,200 − $4,300) is shown on line 7. His $1,500 LTCG as a result of the sale of the piano (not a collectible) and his $8,000 LTCG from the sale of the Golf Corporation stock are on line 8. Thus, Virgil has a NLTCG of $9,500. He has ANCG of $5,600 ($9,500 − $3,900).

Because Virgil has ANCG of $5,600 and no 28% rate gains or unrecaptured Sec. 1250 gains, he computes his tax on the Qualified Dividends and Capital Gain Tax Worksheet. The preferential treatment for dividends and capital gains saves Virgil $1,768 of federal income taxes in 2009.

Virgil's taxable income including the above dividends and capital gains is $120,000. ◀

On the following pages are four worksheets that taxayers use to compute their tax if they have any 28% rate gains, unrecaptured Section 1250 gain or adjusted net capital gain (ANCG).

Taxpayers use the 28% Rate Gain Worksheet on page I:5-38 if they have gains from collectibles or Sec. 1202 stock.

---

[83] Rev. Rul. 54-97, 1954-1 C.B. 113 and *Achille F. Ford v. U.S.*, 5 AFTR 2d 1157, 60-1 USTC ¶9375 (Ct. Cls., 1960).

SCHEDULE D
(Form 1040)

Department of the Treasury
Internal Revenue Service (99)

Capital Gains and Losses

▶ Attach to Form 1040 or Form 1040NR. ▶ See Instructions for Schedule D (Form 1040).

▶ Use Schedule D-1 to list additional transactions for lines 1 and 8.

OMB No. 1545-0074

2009

Attachment Sequence No. **12**

Name(s) shown on return

Virgil Schmidt

Your social security number

Part I Short-Term Capital Gains and Losses—Assets Held One Year or Less

(a) Description of property (Example: 100 sh. XYZ Co.)	(b) Date acquired (Mo., day, yr.)	(c) Date sold (Mo., day, yr.)	(d) Sales price (see page D-7 of the instructions)	(e) Cost or other basis (see page D-7 of the instructions)	(f) Gain or (loss) Subtract (e) from (d)
1 200 sh. Tennis Corp.	10-2-08	6-20-09	13,000	8,700	4,300

2 Enter your short-term totals, if any, from Schedule D-1, line 2	**2**	
3 **Total short-term sales price amounts.** Add lines 1 and 2 in column (d)	**3** 13,000	

4 Short-term gain from Form 6252 and short-term gain or (loss) from Forms 4684, 6781, and 8824	**4**	
5 Net short-term gain or (loss) from partnerships, S corporations, estates, and trusts from Schedule(s) K-1	**5**	
6 Short-term capital loss carryover. Enter the amount, if any, from line 10 of your **Capital Loss Carryover Worksheet** on page D-7 of the instructions	**6** (8,200)
7 **Net short-term capital gain or (loss).** Combine lines 1 through 6 in column (f)	**7** (3,900)

Part II Long-Term Capital Gains and Losses—Assets Held More Than One Year

(a) Description of property (Example: 100 sh. XYZ Co.)	(b) Date acquired (Mo., day, yr.)	(c) Date sold (Mo., day, yr.)	(d) Sales price (see page D-7 of the instructions)	(e) Cost or other basis (see page D-7 of the instructions)	(f) Gain or (loss) Subtract (e) from (d)
8 Piano	4-12-99	5-3-09	4,000	2,500	1,500
500 sh. Golf Corporation	4-1-05	11-30-09	18,000	10,000	8,000

9 Enter your long-term totals, if any, from Schedule D-1, line 9	**9**	
10 **Total long-term sales price amounts.** Add lines 8 and 9 in column (d)	**10** 22,000	

11 Gain from Form 4797, Part I; long-term gain from Forms 2439 and 6252; and long-term gain or (loss) from Forms 4684, 6781, and 8824	**11**	
12 Net long-term gain or (loss) from partnerships, S corporations, estates, and trusts from Schedule(s) K-1	**12**	
13 Capital gain distributions. See page D-2 of the instructions	**13**	
14 Long-term capital loss carryover. Enter the amount, if any, from line 15 of your **Capital Loss Carryover Worksheet** on page D-7 of the instructions	**14** ( )
15 **Net long-term capital gain or (loss).** Combine lines 8 through 14 in column (f). Then go to Part III on the back	**15** 9,500

For Paperwork Reduction Act Notice, see Form 1040 or Form 1040NR instructions. Cat. No. 11338H Schedule D (Form 1040) 2009

FIGURE I:5-1 ▶ PARTS I–II OF SCHEDULE D FOR EXAMPLE I:5-99

Part III   **Summary**

16 Combine lines 7 and 15 and enter the result	**16**	5,600

If line 16 is:
- A **gain**, enter the amount from line 16 on Form 1040, line 13, or Form 1040NR, line 14. Then go to line 17 below.
- A **loss**, skip lines 17 through 20 below. Then go to line 21. Also be sure to complete line 22.
- **Zero**, skip lines 17 through 21 below and enter -0- on Form 1040, line 13, or Form 1040NR, line 14. Then go to line 22.

17   Are lines 15 and 16 **both** gains?
- ☑ **Yes.** Go to line 18.
- ☐ **No.** Skip lines 18 through 21, and go to line 22.

18 Enter the amount, if any, from line 7 of the **28% Rate Gain Worksheet** on page D-8 of the instructions . . . . ▶	**18**	

19 Enter the amount, if any, from line 18 of the **Unrecaptured Section 1250 Gain Worksheet** on page D-9 of the instructions . . . . ▶	**19**	

20   Are lines 18 and 19 **both** zero or blank?
- ☑ **Yes.** Complete Form 1040 through line 43, or Form 1040NR through line 40. Then complete the **Qualified Dividends and Capital Gain Tax Worksheet** on page 39 of the Instructions for Form 1040 (or in the Instructions for Form 1040NR). **Do not** complete lines 21 and 22 below.
- ☐ **No.** Complete Form 1040 through line 43, or Form 1040NR through line 40. Then complete the **Schedule D Tax Worksheet** on page D-10 of the instructions. **Do not** complete lines 21 and 22 below.

21   If line 16 is a loss, enter here and on Form 1040, line 13, or Form 1040NR, line 14, the **smaller** of:

- The loss on line 16 or
- ($3,000), or if married filing separately, ($1,500)

	21	( )

Note. When figuring which amount is smaller, treat both amounts as positive numbers.

22   Do you have qualified dividends on Form 1040, line 9b, or Form 1040NR, line 10b?

- ☐ **Yes.** Complete Form 1040 through line 43, or Form 1040NR through line 40. Then complete the **Qualified Dividends and Capital Gain Tax Worksheet** on page 39 of the Instructions for Form 1040 (or in the Instructions for Form 1040NR).
- ☑ **No.** Complete the rest of Form 1040 or Form 1040NR.

Schedule D (Form 1040) 2009

FIGURE I:5-1   ▶   PART III OF SCHEDULE D FOR EXAMPLE I:5-99

Qualified Dividends and Capital Gain Tax Worksheet—Line 44

Before you begin: √ See the instructions for line 44 that begin on page 37 to see if you can use this worksheet to figure your tax.

√ If you do not have to file Schedule D and you received capital gain distributions, be sure you checked the box on line 13 of Form 1040.

1. Enter the amount from Form 1040, line 43. However, if you are filing Form 2555 or 2555-EZ (relating to foreign earned income), enter the amount from line 3 of the worksheet on page 38 .... **1.** **120,000**

2. Enter the amount from Form 1040, line 9b* **2.** **8,000**

3. Are you filing Schedule D?*
   - ☑ **Yes.** Enter the **smaller** of line 15 or 16 of Schedule D. If either line 15 or line 16 is a loss, enter -0-
   - ☐ **No.** Enter the amount from Form 1040, line 13   **3.** **5,600**

4. Add lines 2 and 3 .... **4.** **13,600**

5. If you are claiming investment interest expense on Form 4952, enter the amount from line 4g of that form. Otherwise, enter -0- .... **5.** **-0-**

6. Subtract line 5 from line 4. If zero or less, enter -0- **6.** **13,600**

7. Subtract line 6 from line 1. If zero or less, enter -0- **7.** **106,400**

8. Enter the **smaller** of:
   - The amount on line 1, or
   - $33,950 if single or married filing separately, $67,900 if married filing jointly or qualifying widow(er), $45,500 if head of household. **8.** **33,950**

9. Is the amount on line 7 equal to or more than the amount on line 8?
   - ☑ **Yes.** Skip lines 9 and 10; go to line 11 and check the "No" box.
   - ☐ **No.** Enter the amount from line 7 .... **9.**

10. Subtract line 9 from line 8 .... **10.**

11. Are the amounts on lines 6 and 10 the same?
    - ☐ **Yes.** Skip lines 11 through 14; go to line 15.
    - ☑ **No.** Enter the **smaller** of line 1 or line 6 .... **11.** **13,600**

12. Enter the amount from line 10 (if line 10 is blank, enter -0-) .... **12.** **-0-**

13. Subtract line 12 from line 11 .... **13.** **13,600**

14. Multiply line 13 by 15% (.15) **14.** **2,040**

15. Figure the tax on the amount on line 7. Use the Tax Table or Tax Computation Worksheet, whichever applies **15.** **23,512**

16. Add lines 14 and 15 .... **16.** **25,552**

17. Figure the tax on the amount on line 1. Use the Tax Table or Tax Computation Worksheet, whichever applies **17.** **27,320**

18. **Tax on all taxable income.** Enter the **smaller** of line 16 or line 17. Also include this amount on Form 1040, line 44. If you are filing Form 2555 or 2555-EZ, do not enter this amount on Form 1040, line 44. Instead, enter it on line 4 of the worksheet on page 38 .... **18.** **25,552**

If you are filing Form 2555 or 2555-EZ, see the footnote in the worksheet on page 38 before completing this line.

FIGURE I:5-1 ▶ QUALIFIED DIVIDENDS AND CAPITAL GAIN TAX WORKSHEET–LINE 43 FOR EXAMPLE I:5-99

28% Rate Gain Worksheet—Line 18

 Keep for Your Records

1. Enter the total of all collectibles gain or (loss) from items you reported on line 8, column (f), of Schedules D and D-1 .... **1.** _____

2. Enter as a positive number the amount of any section 1202 exclusion you reported on line 8, column (f), of Schedules D and D-1, for which you excluded 50% of the gain, plus ⅔ of any section 1202 exclusion you reported on line 8, column (f), of Schedules D and D-1, for which you excluded 60% of the gain .... **2.** _____

3. Enter the total of all collectibles gain or (loss) from Form 4684, line 4 (but only if Form 4684, line 15, is more than zero); Form 6252; Form 6781, Part II; and Form 8824 .... **3.** _____

4. Enter the total of any collectibles gain reported to you on:
   - Form 1099-DIV, box 2d;
   - Form 2439, box 1d; and
   - Schedule K-1 from a partnership, S corporation, estate, or trust. } .... **4.** _____

5. Enter your long-term capital loss carryovers from Schedule D, line 14, and Schedule K-1 (Form 1041), box 11, code C .... **5.** (_____)

6. If Schedule D, line 7, is a (loss), enter that (loss) here. Otherwise, enter -0- .... **6.** (_____)

7. Combine lines 1 through 6. If zero or less, enter -0-. If more than zero, also enter this amount on Schedule D, line 18 .... **7.** _____

Taxpayers use the Unrecaptured Section 1250 Gain Worksheet below if they have gains from depreciable real estate.

Unrecaptured Section 1250 Gain Worksheet—Line 19

Keep for Your Records

If you are not reporting a gain on Form 4797, line 7, skip lines 1 through 9 and go to line 10.

1. If you have a section 1250 property in Part III of Form 4797 for which you made an entry in Part I of Form 4797 (but not on Form 6252), enter the **smaller** of line 22 or line 24 of Form 4797 for that property. If you did not have any such property, go to line 4. If you had more than one such property, see instructions .... **1.** _____

2. Enter the amount from Form 4797, line 26g, for the property for which you made an entry on line 1 .... **2.** _____

3. Subtract line 2 from line 1 .... **3.** _____

4. Enter the total unrecaptured section 1250 gain included on line 26 or line 37 of Form(s) 6252 from installment sales of trade or business property held more than 1 year (see instructions) .... **4.** _____

5. Enter the total of any amounts reported to you on a Schedule K-1 from a partnership or an S corporation as "unrecaptured section 1250 gain" .... **5.** _____

6. Add lines 3 through 5 .... **6.** _____

7. Enter the **smaller** of line 6 or the gain from Form 4797, line 7 .... **7.** _____

8. Enter the amount, if any, from Form 4797, line 8 .... **8.** _____

9. Subtract line 8 from line 7. If zero or less, enter -0- .... **9.** _____

10. Enter the amount of any gain from the sale or exchange of an interest in a partnership attributable to unrecaptured section 1250 gain (see instructions) .... **10.** _____

11. Enter the total of any amounts reported to you on a Schedule K-1, Form 1099-DIV, or Form 2439 as "unrecaptured section 1250 gain" from an estate, trust, real estate investment trust, or mutual fund (or other regulated investment company) .... **11.** _____

12. Enter the total of any unrecaptured section 1250 gain from sales (including installment sales) or other dispositions of section 1250 property held more than 1 year for which you did not make an entry in Part I of Form 4797 for the year of sale (see instructions) .... **12.** _____

13. Add lines 9 through 12 .... **13.** _____

14. If you had any section 1202 gain or collectibles gain or (loss), enter the total of lines 1 through 4 of the **28% Rate Gain Worksheet** on page D-8. Otherwise, enter -0- ...... **14.** _____

15. Enter the (loss), if any, from Schedule D, line 7. If Schedule D, line 7, is zero or a gain, enter -0- .... **15.** (_____)

16. Enter your long-term capital loss carryovers from Schedule D, line 14, and Schedule K-1 (Form 1041), box 11, code C* .... **16.** (_____)

17. Combine lines 14 through 16. If the result is a (loss), enter it as a positive amount. If the result is zero or a gain, enter -0- .... **17.** _____

18. **Unrecaptured section 1250 gain.** Subtract line 17 from line 13. If zero or less, enter -0-. If more than zero, enter the result here and on Schedule D, line 19 .... **18.** _____

*If you are filing Form 2555 or 2555-EZ (relating to foreign earned income), see the footnote in the Foreign Earned Income Tax Worksheet on page 38 of the Form 1040 instructions before completing this line.

Taxpayers such as Virgil in Example I:5-99 use the Qualified Dividends Capital Gain Tax Worksheet below if they either have qualified dividends or ANCG *and* do not have any 28% rate gain property or unrecaptured Section 1250 gain. This worksheet applies the lower preferential tax rates of zero or 15% for qualified dividends and ANCG.

Qualified Dividends and Capital Gain Tax Worksheet—Line 44

Form 1040—Line 44

Keep for Your Records

| **Before you begin:** | √ | See the instructions for line 44 that begin on page 37 to see if you can use this worksheet to figure your tax. |
| | √ | If you do not have to file Schedule D and you received capital gain distributions, be sure you checked the box on line 13 of Form 1040. |

1. Enter the amount from Form 1040, line 43. However, if you are filing Form 2555 or 2555-EZ (relating to foreign earned income), enter the amount from line 3 of the worksheet on page 38 .... **1.** _____

2. Enter the amount from Form 1040, line 9b* .... **2.** _____

3. Are you filing Schedule D?*

   ☐ **Yes.** Enter the **smaller** of line 15 or 16 of Schedule D. If either line 15 or line 16 is a loss, enter -0-

   ☐ **No.** Enter the amount from Form 1040, line 13 ⎫ **3.** _____

4. Add lines 2 and 3 .... **4.** _____

5. If you are claiming investment interest expense on Form 4952, enter the amount from line 4g of that form. Otherwise, enter -0- .... **5.** _____

6. Subtract line 5 from line 4. If zero or less, enter -0- .... **6.** _____

7. Subtract line 6 from line 1. If zero or less, enter -0- .... **7.** _____

8. Enter the **smaller** of:
   - The amount on line 1, or
   - $33,950 if single or married filing separately, $67,900 if married filing jointly or qualifying widow(er), $45,500 if head of household. ⎬ .... **8.** _____

9. Is the amount on line 7 equal to or more than the amount on line 8?

   ☐ **Yes.** Skip lines 9 and 10; go to line 11 and check the "No" box.

   ☐ **No.** Enter the amount from line 7 .... **9.** _____

10. Subtract line 9 from line 8 .... **10.** _____

11. Are the amounts on lines 6 and 10 the same?

    ☐ **Yes.** Skip lines 11 through 14; go to line 15.

    ☐ **No.** Enter the **smaller** of line 1 or line 6 .... **11.** _____

12. Enter the amount from line 10 (if line 10 is blank, enter -0-) .... **12.** _____

13. Subtract line 12 from line 11 .... **13.** _____

14. Multiply line 13 by 15% (.15) .... **14.** _____

15. Figure the tax on the amount on line 7. Use the Tax Table or Tax Computation Worksheet, whichever applies .... **15.** _____

16. Add lines 14 and 15 .... **16.** _____

17. Figure the tax on the amount on line 1. Use the Tax Table or Tax Computation Worksheet, whichever applies .... **17.** _____

18. **Tax on all taxable income.** Enter the **smaller** of line 16 or line 17. Also include this amount on Form 1040, line 44. If you are filing Form 2555 or 2555-EZ, do not enter this amount on Form 1040, line 44. Instead, enter it on line 4 of the worksheet on page 38 .... **18.** _____

If you are filing Form 2555 or 2555-EZ, see the footnote in the worksheet on page 38 before completing this line.

Taxpayers use the Schedule D Tax Workshop below if they have a 28% rate gain and/or unrecaptured Sec. 1250 gain.

Schedule D Tax Worksheet

Keep for Your Records

Complete this worksheet only if line 18 or line 19 of Schedule D is more than zero. Otherwise, complete the Qualified Dividends and Capital Gain Tax Worksheet on page 39 of the Instructions for Form 1040 (or in the Instructions for Form 1040NR) to figure your tax.

Exception: Do not use the Qualified Dividends and Capital Gain Tax Worksheet **or** this worksheet to figure your tax if:
- Line 15 or line 16 of Schedule D is zero or less **and** you have no qualified dividends on Form 1040, line 9b (or Form 1040NR, line 10b); **or**
- Form 1040, line 43 (or Form 1040NR, line 40) is zero or less.

Instead, see the instructions for Form 1040, line 44 (or Form 1040NR, line 41).

1. Enter your taxable income from Form 1040, line 43 (or Form 1040NR, line 40). (However, if you are filing Form 2555 or 2555-EZ (relating to foreign earned income), enter instead the amount from line 3 of the Foreign Earned Income Tax Worksheet on page 38 of the Form 1040 instructions) . . . . **1.** _____

2. Enter your qualified dividends from Form 1040, line 9b (or Form 1040NR, line 10b) . . . . **2.** _____

3. Enter the amount from Form 4952 (used to figure investment interest expense deduction), line 4g . . . . **3.** _____

4. Enter the amount from Form 4952, line 4e* . . **4.** _____

5. Subtract line 4 from line 3. If zero or less, enter -0- . . . . **5.** _____

6. Subtract line 5 from line 2. If zero or less, enter -0-** . . . . **6.** _____

7. Enter the **smaller** of line 15 or line 16 of Schedule D . . . . **7.** _____

8. Enter the **smaller** of line 3 or line 4 . . . . **8.** _____

9. Subtract line 8 from line 7. If zero or less, enter -0-** . . . . **9.** _____

10. Add lines 6 and 9 . . . . **10.** _____

11. Add lines 18 and 19 of Schedule D** . . . . **11.** _____

12. Enter the **smaller** of line 9 or line 11 . . . . **12.** _____

13. Subtract line 12 from line 10 . . . . **13.** _____

14. Subtract line 13 from line 1. If zero or less, enter -0- . . . . **14.** _____

15. Enter the **smaller** of:
   - The amount on line 1 **or**
   - $33,950 if single or married filing separately;
     $67,900 if married filing jointly or qualifying widow(er); or
     $45,500 if head of household
   } . . . . **15.** _____

16. Enter the **smaller** of line 14 or line 15 . . . . **16.** _____

17. Subtract line 10 from line 1. If zero or less, enter -0- . . . . **17.** _____

18. Enter the **larger** of line 16 or line 17 . . . . ▶ **18.** _____
   If lines 15 and 16 are the same, skip line 19 and go to line 20. Otherwise, go to line 19.

19. Subtract line 16 from line 15 . . . . ▶ **19.** _____
   If lines 1 and 15 are the same, skip lines 20 through 32 and go to line 33. Otherwise, go to line 20.

20. Enter the **smaller** of line 1 or line 13 . . . . **20.** _____

21. Enter the amount from line 19 (if line 19 is blank, enter -0-) . . . . **21.** _____

22. Subtract line 21 from line 20. If zero or less, enter -0- . . . . ▶ **22.** _____

23. Multiply line 22 by 15% (.15) . . . . **23.** _____
   If Schedule D, line 19, is zero or blank, skip lines 24 through 29 and go to line 30. Otherwise, go to line 24.

24. Enter the **smaller** of line 9 above or Schedule D, line 19 . . . . **24.** _____

25. Add lines 10 and 18 . . . . **25.** _____

26. Enter the amount from line 1 above . . . . **26.** _____

27. Subtract line 26 from line 25. If zero or less, enter -0- . . . . **27.** _____

28. Subtract line 27 from line 24. If zero or less, enter -0- . . . . ▶ **28.** _____

29. Multiply line 28 by 25% (.25) . . . . **29.** _____
   If Schedule D, line 18, is zero or blank, skip lines 30 through 32 and go to line 33. Otherwise, go to line 30.

30. Add lines 18, 19, 22, and 28 . . . . **30.** _____

31. Subtract line 30 from line 1 . . . . **31.** _____

32. Multiply line 31 by 28% (.28) . . . . **32.** _____

33. Figure the tax on the amount on **line 18**. Use the Tax Table or Tax Computation Worksheet, whichever applies . . . . **33.** _____

34. Add lines 23, 29, 32, and 33 . . . . **34.** _____

35. Figure the tax on the amount on **line 1**. Use the Tax Table or Tax Computation Worksheet, whichever applies . . . . **35.** _____

36. **Tax on all taxable income (including capital gains and qualified dividends).** Enter the **smaller** of line 34 or line 35. Also include this amount on Form 1040, line 44 (or Form 1040NR, line 41). (If you are filing Form 2555 or 2555-EZ, do not enter this amount on Form 1040, line 44. Instead, enter it on line 4 of the Foreign Earned Income Tax Worksheet in the Form 1040 instructions) . . . **36.** _____

*If applicable, enter instead the smaller amount you entered on the dotted line next to line 4e of Form 4952.

**If you are filing Form 2555 or 2555-EZ, see the footnote in the Foreign Earned Income Tax Worksheet on page 38 of the Form 1040 instructions before completing this line.

PROBLEM MATERIALS

DISCUSSION QUESTIONS

I:5-1 What problem may exist in determining the amount realized for an investor who exchanges common stock of a publicly traded corporation for a used building? How is the problem likely to be resolved?

I:5-2 In 1992, Ellen purchased a house for $60,000 to use as her personal residence. She paid $12,000 and borrowed $48,000 from the local savings and loan company. In 1995 she paid $10,000 to add a room to the house. In 1997 she paid $625 to have the house painted and $800 for built-in bookshelves. As of January 1 of the current year, she has reduced the $48,000 mortgage to $44,300. What is her basis for the house?

I:5-3 Vincent pays $20,000 for equipment to use in his trade or business. He pays sales tax of $800 as a result of the purchase. Must the $800 sales tax be capitalized as part of the purchase price?

I:5-4 Sergio owns 200 shares of Palm Corporation common stock, purchased during the prior year: 100 shares on July 5, for $9,000; and 100 shares on October 15, for $12,000. When Sergio sells 50 shares for $8,000 on July 18 of the current year, he does not identify the particular shares sold. Determine the amount and character of the gain.

I:5-5 On October 21 of the current year, David receives stock of Western Corporation as a gift from his grandfather, who acquired the stock on January 20, 1995. Under what conditions would David's holding period start on?
a. October 22 of the current year?
b. January 20, 1995?

I:5-6 Jim inherits stock (a capital asset) from his brother, who died in March of 2009, when the property had a $3,900,000 FMV. This property is the only property included in his brother's gross estate and there is a taxable estate. The FMV of the property as of the alternate valuation date was $3,700,000.
a. Why might the executor of the brother's estate elect to use the alternate valuation date to value the property?
b. Why might Jim prefer the executor to use FMV at time of the death to value the property?
c. If the marginal estate tax rate is 45% and Jim's marginal income tax rate is 25%, which value should the executor use?

I:5-7 Martha owns 500 shares of Columbus Corporation common stock at the beginning of the year with a basis of $82,500. During the year, Columbus declares and pays a 10% nontaxable stock dividend. What is her basis for each of the 50 shares received?

I:5-8 Mario owns 2,000 shares of Nevada Corporation common stock at the beginning of the year. His basis for the stock is $38,880. During the year, Nevada declares and pays a stock dividend. After the dividend, Mario's basis for each share of stock owned is $18. What is the percentage dividend paid by Nevada?

I:5-9 A corporate taxpayer plans to build a $6 million office building during the next 18 months. How must the corporation treat the interest on debt paid or incurred during the production period?

I:5-10 Andy owns an appliance store where he has merchandise such as refrigerators for sale. Roger, a bachelor, owns a refrigerator, which he uses in his apartment for personal use. For which individual is the refrigerator a capital asset?

I:5-11 Why did the Supreme Court rule in the *Corn Products* case that a gain due to the sale of futures contracts is ordinary income instead of capital gain?

I:5-12 When is the gain on the sale or exchange of securities by a dealer in securities classified as capital gain?

I:5-13 In 1982, Florence purchased 30 acres of land. She has not used the land for business purposes or made any substantial improvements to the property. During the current year, she subdivides the land into 15 lots and advertises the lots for sale. She sells four lots at a gain.
a. What is the character of the gain on the sale of the four lots?
b. Explain how the basis of each lot would be determined.

I:5-14 Amy has LTCGs that are taxed at different tax rates, 15%, 25% and 28%. She also has NSTCLs that amount to less than her NLTCG. The procedure for offsetting the NSTCL against the LTCGs is favorable to her. Explain.

I:5-15 Four years ago, Susan loaned $7,000 to her friend Joe. During the current year, the $7,000 loan is considered worthless. Explain how Susan should treat the worthless debt for tax purposes.

I:5-16 Why did the Supreme Court rule in *Arkansas Best* that the stock of a corporation purchased by the taxpayer to protect the taxpayer's business reputation was a capital asset?

I:5-17 The effective tax rate on gain of $1,000,000 resulting from the sale of qualified small business stock held more than five years is 14%. Do you agree or disagree? Explain.

I:5-18 Nancy and the Minor Corporation own bonds of the East Corporation. Minor Corporation owns 80% of the stock of East Corporation. East Corporation has declared bankruptcy this year, and bondholders will receive only 26% of the face value of the debt. Explain why the loss is a capital loss for Nancy but an ordinary loss for the Minor Corporation.

I:5-19 On January 1 of the current year, the Orange Corporation issues $500,000 of 11%, 20-year bonds for $480,000. Determine the amount of original issue discount, if any.

I:5-20 Today, Juanita purchases a 15-year, 7% bond of the Sunflower Corporation issued four years ago at par. She purchases the bond as an investment at a discount from the par value. If she sells the bonds two years from now, explain why some or all of the gain may be ordinary income.

I:5-21 Judy just obtained a patent on a new product she has developed. Bell Corporation wishes to market the product and will pay 12% of all future sales of the product to Judy. How can she be sure that the payments received will be treated as a long-term capital gain?

I:5-22 When is the transferor of a franchise unable to treat the transfer as a sale or an exchange of a capital asset?

I:5-23 How does a lessor treat payments received for canceling a lease?

I:5-24 What is the first day that an individual could sell a capital asset purchased on March 31, 2010 and have a holding period of more than one year?

I:5-25 Phil, a cash-basis taxpayer, sells the following marketable securities, which are capital assets during 2010. Determine whether the gains or losses are long-term or short-term. Also determine the net capital gain and adjusted net capital gain for 2010.

Capital Asset	Basis	Date Acquired	Trade Date in 2010	Sales Price
A	$40,000	Feb. 10, 2009	Aug. 12	$52,000
B	20,000	Dec. 5, 2009	May 2	17,000
C	30,000	Apr. 9, 2008	Dec. 10	37,400

I:5-26 How might the current treatment of capital losses discourage an individual investor from purchasing stock of a high-risk, start-up company?

I:5-27 An individual taxpayer has realized a $40,000 loss on the sale of an asset that had a holding period of eight months. Explain why the taxpayer may be indifferent as to whether the asset is a capital asset.

I:5-28 If Pam transfers an asset to Fred and the asset is subject to a liability that is assumed by Fred, how does Fred's assumption of the liability affect the amount realized by Pam? How does Fred's assumption of the liability affect his basis for the property?

ISSUE IDENTIFICATION QUESTIONS

I:5-29 Acorn Corporation, a company that purchases malt barley from farmers and sells it to brewers, is interested in determining whether a new variety of barley will grow successfully in the Pacific Northwest. The corporation has acquired the seed from Europe and will conduct the experiments with the cooperation of farmers in the area. If the experiments prove successful, Acorn will sell the remaining seed to the farmers. What tax issues should Acorn Corporation consider?

I:5-30 Lisa and John are in the business of breeding beavers to produce fur for sale. They recently purchased a pair of breeding beavers for $30,000 from XUN, Inc., and agreed to pay interest at 10% each year for five years. After the five-year period, they could pay the debt by delivering seven beavers to XUN, Inc., provided that each beaver was at least nine months old. Identify the tax issues involved in this situation.

I:5-31 Mike, a real estate broker in California, recently inherited a farm from his deceased uncle and plans to sell the farm to the first available buyer. His uncle purchased the property 12 years ago for $600,000. The FMV of the farm on the date of the uncle's death was $500,000. Mike sells the farm for $520,000 seven months after his uncle's death. What tax issues should Mike consider?

I:5-32 Sylvia, a dentist with excellent skills as a carpenter, started the construction of a house that she planned to give to her son as a surprise when he returned from Saudia Arabia, where he is serving in the military. She began construction on March 23, 2009, and finished the house on July 10, 2010, at a total cost of $70,000. Her son is expected to be home on September 1, 2010.

On July 30, 2010, Roscoe offered Sylvia $245,000 for the house and Sylvia considered the offer to be so attractive that she accepted it. She decided that she could purchase a suitable home for her son for about $200,000. What tax issues should Sylvia consider?

PROBLEMS

I:5-33 *Amount Realized.* Tracy owns a nondepreciable capital asset held for investment. The asset was purchased for $250,000 six years earlier and is now subject to a $75,000 liability. During the current year, Tracy transfers the asset to Tim in exchange for $94,000 cash and a new automobile with a $50,000 FMV to be used by Tracy for personal use; Tim assumes the $75,000 liability. Determine the amount of Tracy's LTCG or LTCL.

I:5-34 ***Basis of Property Received as a Gift.*** Doug receives a duplex as a gift from his uncle. The uncle's basis for the duplex and land is $90,000. At the time of the gift, the land and building have FMVs of $40,000 and $80,000, respectively. No gift tax is paid by Doug's uncle at the time of the gift.
  a. To determine gain, what is Doug's basis for the land?
  b. To determine gain, what is Doug's basis for the building?
  c. Will the basis of the land and building be the same as in Parts a and b for purposes of determining a loss?

I:5-35 ***Sale of Property Received as a Gift.*** During the current year, Stan sells a tract of land for $800,000. The property was received as a gift from Maxine on March 10, 1995, when the property had a $310,000 FMV. The taxable gift was $300,000 because the annual exclusion was $10,000 in 1995. Maxine purchased the property on April 12, 1980, for $110,000. At the time of the gift, Maxine paid a gift tax of $12,000. In order to sell the property, Stan paid a sales commission of $16,000.
  a. What is Stan's realized gain on the sale?
  b. How would your answer to Part a change, if at all, if the FMV of the gift property was $85,000 as of the date of the gift?

I:5-36 ***Sale of Asset Received as a Gift.*** Bud received 200 shares of Georgia Corporation stock from his uncle as a gift on July 20, 2009, when the stock had a $45,000 FMV. The uncle paid $30,000 for the stock on April 12, 1999. The taxable gift was $45,000, because his uncle made another gift to Bud for $20,000 in January. The uncle paid a gift tax of $1,500.
  Without considering the transactions below, Bud's AGI is $45,000 in 2010. No other transactions involving capital assets occur during the year. Analyze each transaction below, independent of the others, and determine Bud's AGI in each case.
  a. He sells the stock on October 12, 2010, for $48,000.
  b. He sells the stock on October 12, 2010, for $28,000.
  c. He sells the stock on December 16, 2010, for $42,000.

I:5-37 ***Basis of Property Converted from Personal Use.*** Irene owns a truck costing $15,000 and used for personal activities. The truck has a $9,600 FMV when it is transferred to her business, which is operated as a sole proprietorship.
  a. What is the basis of the truck for determining depreciation?
  b. What is Irene's realized gain or loss if the truck is sold for $5,000 after claiming depreciation of $4,000?

I:5-38 ***Sale of Assets Received as a Gift and Inherited.*** Daniel receives 400 shares of A&M Corporation stock from his aunt on May 20, 2010, as a gift when the stock has a $60,000 FMV. His aunt purchased the stock in 2003 for $42,000. The taxable gift is $60,000 because she made earlier gifts to Daniel during 2010 and used the annual exclusion. She paid a gift tax of $9,300 on the gift of A&M stock to Daniel.
  Daniel also inherited 300 shares of Longhorn Corporation preferred stock when his uncle died on November 12, 2009, when the stock's FMV was $30,000. His uncle purchased the stock in 1990 for $27,600. Determine the gain or loss on the sale of A&M and Longhorn stock on December 15, 2010, under each alternative situation below.
  a. A&M stock was sold for $62,600, and Longhorn stock was sold for $30,750.
  b. A&M stock was sold for $58,200, and Longhorn stock was sold for $28,650.
  c. Assume the same as in Part a except his aunt purchased A&M stock for $71,000 and his uncle purchased Longhorn stock for $31,200.

I:5-39 ***Personal-use Property Converted to Rental Property.*** Tally owns a house that she has been living in for eight years. She purchased the house in 1990 for $245,000 and the FMV today is $200,000. She is moving into her friend's house and has decided to convert her residence to rental property. Assume 20% of the property's value is allocated to land.
  a. What is the basis of the house for depreciation?
  b. If she claims depreciation of $15,000 and sells the property six years later for $260,000 (20% allocated to land), determine the gain on the sale of the building and gain on the sale of the land.
  c. How much of the gain is due to depreciation?
  d. If the FMV is $290,000 when she converts the house to rental property instead of $200,000, what is the basis of the house for depreciation?

I:5-40 ***Stock Rights.*** Kathleen owns 500 shares of Buda Corporation common stock which was purchased on March 20, 1999, for $48,000. On October 10 of the current year, she receives a distribution of 500 stock rights. Each stock right has a $20 FMV and the FMV of the Buda common stock is $100 per share. With each stock right, she may acquire one share of Buda common stock for $95.

a. How much gross income must Kathleen recognize?
b. What is the basis of each stock right received?
c. If she sells the 500 stock rights for $10,600, what is her gain?
d. If she exercises the 500 stock rights on November 10, what is the basis of the 500 shares she receives and when does the holding period for those shares start?

I:5-41 *Stock Rights.* Martha Lou owns 100 shares of Blain Corporation common stock. She purchased the stock on July 25, 1986, for $4,000. On May 2 of the current year, she receives a nontaxable distribution of 100 stock rights. Each stock right has a $10 FMV, and the FMV of the Blain common stock is $70 per share. With each stock right, Martha Lou may acquire one share of Blain common for $68 per share. Assuming that she elects to allocate basis to the stock rights, answer the following:
a. What is the basis allocated to the stock rights?
b. If she sells the stock rights on June 10 for $1,080, determine the amount and character of the recognized gain?
c. If she exercises the stock rights on May 14, what is the basis of the 100 shares purchased and when does the holding period start?
d. If she does not elect to allocate basis to the stock rights, determine the amount and character of the gain if she sells the stock rights on June 10 for $1,080?

I:5-42 *Real Property Subdivided for Sale.* Beth acquired only one tract of land seven years ago as an investment. In order to sell the land at a higher price, she decides to subdivide it into 20 lots. She pays for improvements such as clearing and leveling, but the improvements are not considered to be substantial. Each lot has a basis of $2,000, and a selling price of $6,000. Selling expenses of $480 were incurred to sell two lots last year. This year, ten lots are sold, and selling expenses amount to $1,900. How much ordinary income and capital gain must be recognized in the prior and current year?

I:5-43 *Marginal Tax Rates.* Mr. and Mrs. Dunbar have taxable income of $190,000 without considering the following sales. Consider the following independent cases where capital gains are recognized and determine the marginal tax rate for the capital gain in each case. Ignore the effect of increasing AGI on deductions.
    CASE A: $10,000 gain from sale of Storm Lake common stock held for seven months.
    CASE B: $10,000 gain from sale of antique clock held for six years.
    CASE C: $10,000 gain from sale of Ames preferred stock held for three years.

I:5-44 *Netting Gains and Losses* Trisha, whose tax rate is 35%, sells the following capital assets in 2010 with gains and losses as shown:

Asset	Gain or (Loss)	Holding Period
A	$15,000	15 months
B	7,000	20 months
C	(3,000)	14 months

a. Determine Trisha's increase in tax liability as a result of the three sales. All assets are stock held for investment. Ignore the effect of increasing AGI on deductions and phase-out amounts.
b. Determine her increase in tax liability if the holding period for asset B is 8 months.
c. Determine her increase in tax liability if the holding periods are the same as in Part a but asset B is an antique clock.

I:5-45 *Computing the Tax.* Donna files as a head of household in 2010 and has taxable income of $90,000, including the sale of a stock held as an investment for two years at a gain of $20,000. Only one asset was sold during the year and Donna does not have any capital loss carryovers.
a. What is the amount of Donna's tax liability?
b. What is the amount of Donna's tax liability if the stock is held for 11 months?

I:5-46 *Computing the Tax.* Wayne is single and has no dependents. Without considering his $11,000 adjusted net capital gain (ANCG), his taxable income in 2010 is as follows:

AGI		$166,800
Home mortgage interest	$22,150	
State and local income taxes	8,000	
Charitable contributions	7,000	
Personal exemption	3,650	40,800

Taxable income $126,000

a. What is Wayne's tax liability without the ANCG?

b. What is Wayne's tax liability with the ANCG?

I:5-47 *Computing the Sales Price.* An investor in a 28% tax bracket owns land that is a capital asset with a $50,000 basis and a holding period of three years. The investor wishes to sell the asset at a price high enough so that he will have $120,000 in cash after paying the taxes. What is the minimum price which the investor could accept?

I:5-48 *Capital Gains and Losses.* Consider the four independent situations below for an unmarried individual, and analyze the effects of the capital gains and losses on the individual's AGI. For each case, determine AGI after considering the capital gains and losses.

	Situation 1	Situation 2	Situation 3	Situation 4
AGI (excluding property transactions)	$40,000	$50,000	$60,000	$70,000
STCG	6,000	2,000	5,000	6,000
STCL	2,000	5,000	4,000	15,000
LTCG	3,500	15,000	10,000	9,000
LTCL	2,500	4,000	12,000	4,000

I:5-49 *Capital Losses.* To better understand the rules for offsetting capital losses and how to treat capital losses carried forward, analyze the following data for an unmarried individual for the period 2007 through 2010. No capital loss carryforwards are included in the figures. For each year, determine AGI and the capital losses to be carried forward to a later tax year.

	2007	2008	2009	2010
AGI (excluding property transactions)	$40,000	$50,000	$60,000	$70,000
STCG	4,000	5,000	7,000	10,000
STCL	9,000	3,000	5,000	12,000
LTCG	6,000	10,000	2,200	6,000
LTCL	5,000	21,000	1,000	9,500
AGI (including property transactions)	____	____	____	____
STCL to be carried forward	____	____	____	____
LTCL to be carried forward	____	____	____	____

I:5-50 *Character of Loss.* The Michigan Corporation owns 20% of the Wolverine Corporation. The Wolverine stock was acquired eight years ago to ensure a steady supply of raw materials. Michigan also owns 30% of Spartan Corporation and 85% of Huron Corporation. Stock in both corporations was acquired more than ten years ago for investment purposes. During the current year, Wolverine, Spartan, and Huron are deemed bankrupt, and the stocks are considered worthless. Describe how Michigan should treat its losses.

I:5-51 *Original Issue Discount.* On December 31, 2009, Phil purchased $20,000 of newly issued bonds of Texas Corporation for $16,568. The bonds are dated December 31, 2009. The bonds are 9%, 10-year bonds paying interest semiannually on June 30 and December 31. The bonds are priced to yield 12% compounded semiannually.

a. What is the amount of the original issue discount?

b. For the first semiannual period, what is the amount of the original issue discount Phil must recognize as ordinary income?

c. What is the total amount of interest income Phil must recognize in 2010?

d. What is Phil's basis for the bonds as of December 31, 2010?

I:5-52 On January 1, 2008, Swen paid $184,000 for $200,000 of the 8%, 20-year bonds of Penn Corporation, issued on January 1, 2004, at par. The bonds are held as an investment. Determine the gain and the character of the gain if the bonds are sold on January 1, 2010, for

a. $191,000

b. $185,750

c. $183,000

I:5-53 *Capital Gains and Losses.* During 2010, Gary receives a $50,000 salary and has no deductions for AGI. In 2009, Gary had a $5,000 STCL and no other capital losses or capital gains. Consider the following sales and determine Gary's AGI for 2010.

- An automobile purchased in 2005 for $10,800 and held for personal use is sold for $7,000.
- On April 10, 2010, stock held for investment is sold for $21,000. The stock was acquired on November 20, 2009, for $9,300.

I:5-54 *Call Options.* On February 10, 2010, Gail purchases 20 calls on Red Corporation for $250 per call. Each call represents an option to buy 100 shares of Red stock at $42 per share any time before November 25, 2010. Compute the gain or loss recognized, and determine whether the gain or loss is long-term or short-term for Gail in the following situations:
a. The 20 calls are sold on May 15, 2010, for $310 per call.
b. The calls are not exercised but allowed to expire.
c. The calls are exercised on July 15, 2010, and the 2,000 shares of Red Corporation stock are sold on July 20, 2011, for $50 per share.

I:5-55 *Call Writing.* Dan owns 500 shares of Rocket Corporation common stock. The stock was acquired two years ago for $30 per share. On October 2, 2010, Dan writes five calls on the stock, which represent options to buy the 500 shares of Rocket at $75 per share. For each call, Dan receives $210. The calls expire on June 22, 2011. Consider the following transactions and describe the tax treatment for Dan:
a. The five calls are exercised on December 4, 2010.
b. The calls are not exercised and allowed to expire.

I:5-56 *Corporate Capital Gains and Losses.* Determine the taxable income for the Columbia Corporation for the following independent cases:

Case	Income from Operations	STCG (NSTCL)	NLTCG (NLTCL)
A	$110,000	$30,000	$44,000
B	100,000	(50,000)	65,000
C	80,000	(37,000)	30,000
D	90,000	(15,000)	(9,000)

I:5-57 *Original Issue Discount.* On January 1, 2009, Sean purchased an 8%, $100,000 corporate bond for $92,277. The bond was issued on January 1, 2008, and matures on January 1, 2014. Interest is paid semiannually, and the effective yield to maturity is 10% compounded semiannually. On July 1, 2010, Sean sells the bond for $95,949. A schedule of interest amortization for the bond is shown in Table I:5-2.
a. How much interest income must Sean recognize in 2009?
b. How much interest income must Sean recognize in 2010?
c. How much gain must Sean recognize in 2010 on the sale of the bond?

▼ TABLE I:5-2
Interest Amortization for Problem I:5-57

	Interest Received (1)	Amortization of Discount (2)	Interest Income (3) = (1) + (2)
6-30-09	$4,000	$614	$4,614
12-31-09	4,000	645	4,645
6-30-10	4,000	677	4,677
12-31-10	4,000	711	4,711
6-30-11	4,000	747	4,747
12-31-11	4,000	783	4,783
6-30-12	4,000	823	4,823
12-31-12	4,000	864	4,864
6-30-13	4,000	907	4,907
12-31-13	4,000	952	4,952

I:5-58   *Capital Gains and Losses.* Martha has $40,000 AGI without considering the following information. During the year, she incurs a LTCL of $10,000 and has a gain of $14,000 due to the sale of a capital asset held for more than a year.

    a. If the $14,000 gain is not properly classified as a LTCG (i.e., is improperly treated as an ordinary gain), determine Martha's AGI.

    b. If the $14,000 gain is properly classified as a LTCG, determine her AGI.

    c. If Martha has a $2,500 STCL carryover from earlier years, how would the answers to Parts a and b be affected?

I:5-59   *Capital Gains and Losses.* Without considering the following capital gains and losses, Charlene, who is single, has taxable income of $400,000 and a marginal tax rate of 35%. During the year, she sold stock held for nine months at a gain of $10,000; stock held for three years at a gain of $15,000; and a collectible asset held for six years at a gain of $20,000. Ignore the effect of the gains on any threshold amounts and assume that her marginal tax rate of 35% does not change.

    a. What is her taxable income and the increase in her tax liability after considering the three gains?

    b. In addition to the above three sales, assume that she sells another asset and has a STCL of $14,000. What is her taxable income and the increase in her tax liability after considering the four transactions?

    c. In addition to the above three sales in Part a, assume that she sells another collectible asset held seven years as an investment and has a $27,000 capital loss. What is her taxable income and the increase in her tax liability after considering the four transactions?

I:5-60   *Corporate Capital Gains and Losses.* In 2005, the Ryan Corporation sold a capital asset and incurred a $40,000 LTCL that was carried forward to subsequent years. That sale was the only sale of a capital asset that Ryan made until 2010, when Ryan sells a capital asset and recognizes a STCG of $53,000. Without considering the STCG from the sale, Ryan's taxable income is $250,000.

    a. Determine the corporation's NSTCG for 2010.

    b. Determine the corporation's 2010 taxable income.

    c. If the sale of the asset in 2005 had occurred in 2004, determine the corporation's 2010 taxable income.

COMPREHENSIVE PROBLEM

I:5-61   Betty incurs the following transactions during the current year. Without considering the transactions, her 2010 AGI is $40,000. Analyze the transactions and answer the following questions:

    • On March 10, 2010, she sells a painting for $2,000. Betty is the artist, and she completed the painting in 2005. Her basis for the painting is $50.

    • On June 18, 2010, she receives $28,500 from the sale of stock purchased by her uncle in 1999 for $10,000, which she inherited on February 20, 2009, as a result of her uncle's death. The stock's FMV on that date is $30,000.

    • On July 30, 2010, she sells land for $25,000 that was received as a gift from her brother on April 8, 2010, when the land's FMV was $30,000. Her brother purchased the land for $43,000 on October 12, 2002. No gift tax was paid.

    a. What is her NSTCL or NSTCG?

    b. What is her NLTCL or NLTCG?

    c. What is the effect of capital gains and losses on her AGI?

    d. What is her capital loss carryforward to the next year?

TAX STRATEGY PROBLEMS

I:5-62   Dale purchased Blue Corporation stock four years ago for $1,000 as an investment. He intended to hold the stock until funds were needed to help pay for his daughter's college education. Today the stock has a $6,500 FMV and Dale decides to sell the stock and give the proceeds, less any taxes paid on the sale, to Tammy, his 25-year-old daughter. Dale's marginal tax rate is 30%. Tammy has no other gross income and receives more than half of her support from Dale.

a. What advice would you give to Dale?

b. What is the cash savings if Dale follows your advice?

c. What advice would you give Dale if Tammy is 17 years old?

I:5-63 Calvin, whose tax rate is 40% is considering two alternative investments on January 1, 20Y1. He can purchase $100,000 of 10% bonds due in five years or purchase $100,000 of Hobbes, Inc. common stock. The bonds are issued at par, pay interest annually on December 31, and mature at the end of five years. Interest received can be reinvested at 10%. Assume that he knows with relative certainty that the value of the stock will increase 8% each year (i.e., the value of the Hobbes stock will be $108,000 at the end of 20Y1) and the interest and principal for the bonds will be paid as scheduled. On December 31, 20Y5, he will sell the stock or receive the bond principal plus the last interest payment. Which alternative should Calvin select if he wants to have the greater amount of money as of January 1, 20Y6? Provide supporting information for your answer.

I:5-64 On December 20 of the current year, Winneld has decided to sell all of the stock that she owns and reinvest the proceeds in state of Minnesota bonds. Without considering the sales, her taxable income is expected to exceed $400,000 this year and in future years. Information about the stocks are provided below:

Corporation	FMV	Basis	Holding Period
Viking, Inc.	$190,000	$140,000	7 months
Twins, Inc.	200,000	255,000	4 years
Timberwolves, Inc.	382,000	300,000	3 years

She is willing to sell some of the stock this year and the remaining stock next year if it is more advantageous to spread the sales over two years. Assume that the FMV of the stock will not change during the next 30 days, her regular tax rate is 35% and ignore the effect of a sale on threshold amounts.

Determine the increase in her tax for each of the following alternatives and advise Winneld.

a. Sell all stock this year.

b. Sell Twins and Timberwolves this year and Viking in March of next year.

c. Sell Viking and Twins this year and Timberwolves in March of next year.

I:5-65 Dallas, whose tax rate is 35%, has recognized a STCL of $11,000 and a LTCG of $10,200 due to the sale of stock. In late December, he is considering the sale of an antique chair held for investment that would result in a LTCG of $5,000. If he sells the chair this year, what is the increase in his tax liability as a result of the sale? Ignore the phase out rules.

TAX FORM/RETURN PREPARATION PROBLEMS

I:5-66 Given the following information for Jane Cole, complete Schedule D of Form 1040 through Part III.

- Stock options, which she purchases on February 14 of the current year for $850, expire on October 1.

- On July 1, she sells for $1,500 her personal-use automobile acquired on March 31, 1990, for $8,000.

- On August 16, she sells for $3,100 her stock of York Corporation purchased as an investment on February 16, for $1,600.

- On March 15, she sells for $5,600 an antique ring, a gift from her grandmother on January 10, 1988, when its FMV was $1,600. The ring was purchased by her grand-mother on April 2, 1979, for $1,800.

- She has a STCL carryover of $250 from last year.

I:5-67 Spencer Duck (SSN 277-31-7264) is single and his eight-year-old son, Mitch, lives with him nine months of the year in a rented condominium at 321 Hickory Drive in Ames, Iowa. Mitch lives with his mother, Spencer's ex-wife, during the summer months. His mother provides more than half of Mitch's support and Spencer has agreed to allow her to claim Mitch as her dependent. Spencer has a salary of $39,000 and itemized deductions of $4,000. Taxes withheld during the year amount to $3,221. On July 14 of the current year, he sold the following assets:

- Spencer received a K-1 from a partnership indicating that his share of the partnership STCL is $200.

- Land was sold for $35,000. The land was received as a property settlement on January 10, 2001, when the land's FMV amounted to $30,000. His ex-wife's basis for the land, purchased on January 10, 1991, was $18,600.

- A personal-use computer acquired on March 2 last year for $4,000 was sold for $2,480.

- A membership card for a prestigious country club was sold for $8,500. The card was acquired on October 10, 1993, for $6,000.

- Marketable securities held as an investment were sold for $20,000. The securities were inherited from his uncle, who died on March 10 of the current year when FMV of the securities was $21,000. The uncle purchased the securities on May 10, 1990, for $10,700.

In addition to the above sales, Spencer received a $100 refund of state income taxes paid last year. Spencer used the standard deduction last year to compute his tax liability. Prepare Form 1040 and Schedule D for the current year.

CASE STUDY PROBLEMS

I:5-68 As a political consultant for an aspiring politician, you have been hired to evaluate the following statements that pertain to capital gains and losses. Evaluate the statement and provide at least a one-paragraph explanation of each statement. As you prepare your answer, consider the fact that the aspiring politician does not have much knowledge about taxation.

a. The tax on capital gains is considered a voluntary tax.

b. On October 22, 1986, the Tax Reform Act of 1986 was passed, which eliminated the 60% of net capital gain deduction (i.e., an individual taxpayer with $10,000 of net capital gain was entitled to a $6,000 deduction when computing AGI) before January 1, 1987. Many state governments enjoyed a substantial increase in 1986 tax revenue.

c. High-income taxpayers receive the most benefit from preferential treatment for capital gains.

I:5-69 Your client, Apex Corporation, entered into an agreement with an executive to purchase his personal residence at its current FMV in the event that his employment is terminated by the company during a five-year period. The executive's job was terminated before the end of the five-year period and Apex acquired the house for $500,000. Due to a downturn in the real estate market, a $200,000 loss was incurred by the company upon the resale of the house. The chief financial officer of Apex insists that the loss be characterized as ordinary, based on the *Corn Products* doctrine. Your research into this matter reveals that the weight of authority heavily favors capital loss treatment (i.e., case law based on facts identical to the above issue held that the loss was capital rather than ordinary). You therefore conclude that the client's position does not have a realistic possibility of being sustained administratively or judicially on its merits if challenged by the IRS. What responsibility do you have as a tax practitioner relative to preparing the client's tax return and rendering continuing tax consulting services to the client? (See the Section *Statements on Standards for Tax Services* in Chapter I:1 for a discussion of these issues.)

TAX RESEARCH PROBLEMS

I:5-70 Tom Williams is an equal partner in a partnership with the Kansas Corporation. Williams, an inventor, produced a new process while working for the partnership, which has been patented by the partnership. Before making any use of the patent, the partnership entered into a contract granting all rights to use the process for the life of the patent to the Mason Manufacturing Co.

The time between receiving the patent and entering into the contract with Mason amounted to eight months. Mason agreed to pay 0.3% of all sales revenue generated by products produced as a result of the process. If Mason fails to make payments on a timely basis, Mason's right to use the process is forfeited and the agreement between the partnership and Mason is canceled. Will any of the proceeds collected qualify as LTCG under Sec. 1235?

A partial list of research sources is

- Reg. Sec. 1.1235-2
- *George N. Soffron,* 35 T.C. 787 (1961)

I:5-71 Lynette, a famous basketball player, is considering the possibility of transferring the sole right to use her name to promote basketball shoes produced and sold by the NIK Corporation. NIK will pay $2 million to obtain the right to use Lynette's name for the

next 40 years. NIK may use the name on the shoes and as a part of any of the company's advertisements for basketball shoes. If Lynette signs the contract and receives the $2 million payment, will she have to recognize capital gain or ordinary income?

A partial list of research sources is

- Sec. 1221
- Rev. Rul. 65-261, 1965-2 C.B. 281

I:5-72   Jack, a tenured university professor, has been a malcontent for many years at Rockport University. The university has recently offered to pay $200,000 to Jack if he will relinquish his tenure position and resign. Jack is of the opinion that tenure is an intangible capital asset and the $200,000 received for release of the tenure should be a long-term capital gain. Explain why you agree or disagree.

A partial list of research sources is

- *Harry M. Flower,* 61 T.C. 140 (1973)
- *Estelle Goldman,* 1975 PH T.C. Memo ¶75,138, 34 TCM 639

I:5-73   Web Baker was hired three years ago by the Berry Corporation to serve as CEO for the company. As part of his employment contract, the corporation had agreed to purchase his residence at FMV in the event the company decided to fire him. Last year, Berry, unsatisfied with Web's performance, fired him and purchased the residence for $350,000. Berry immediately listed the house with a real estate agency. Soon after the purchase, the real estate market in the area experienced a serious decline, especially in higher-priced homes. Berry sold the house this year for $270,000 and paid selling expenses of $12,000. How should the Berry Corporation treat the $92,000 loss?

A partial list of research sources is

- Sec. 1221
- Rev. Rul. 82-204, 1982-2 C.B. 192
- *Azar Nut Co. v. CIR,* 67 AFTR 2d 91-987, 91-1 USTC ¶50,257 (5th Cir., 1991)

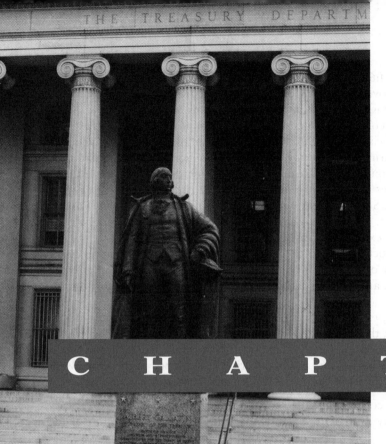

6

CHAPTER

DEDUCTIONS AND LOSSES

LEARNING OBJECTIVES

After studying this chapter, you should be able to

1. Distinguish between deductions *for* and *from* AGI

2. Discuss the criteria for deducting business and investment expenses

3. List the substantiation requirements for deducting travel and entertainment expenses

4. Explain the timing of deductions under both the cash and accrual methods of accounting

5. Explain the tax consequences of wash sales

6. Explain the tax consequences of transactions between related parties

7. Discuss the criteria for determining whether an activity is a hobby or a trade or business

8. Determine the tax consequences of vacation homes

The next five chapters (I:6–I:10) deal with deductions. As you recall from Chapters I:3 and I:4, the principles governing the reporting of income are based on an "all inclusive" system of taxation; that is, gross income includes all items of income unless specifically excluded by statute. In contrast, deductions or losses are not allowed for tax purposes unless the statute specifically provides for them. For example, a taxpayer who makes a donation to a charity during the year may deduct the donation because the statute specifically allows the deduction of charitable contributions under Sec. 170 of the IRC.

Chapter I:6 discusses the general requirements for the deductibility of taxpayer expenditures and losses. Some of these requirements apply to all taxpayers while others apply only to individuals. Chapter I:7 deals with itemized deductions for individual taxpayers, such as medical expenses, taxes, charitable contributions, interest expense, and other miscellaneous deductions. Chapter I:8 covers two major areas that apply to all taxpayers: the deductibility of losses and bad debts. Chapter I:9 discusses employee compensation and expenses, and Chapter I:10 discusses tax depreciation, amortization, and depletion.

As mentioned above, expenditures are deductible only if the IRC specifically allows the deduction. However, the IRC cannot possibly specify *every* deductible expense that a taxpayer might incur. Therefore, the IRC contains a framework for analyzing the nature of an expenditure. If the expenditure meets the criteria developed in the framework, the item is deductible. This framework provides three general categories of deductions:

(1) Expenses incurred in connection with a **trade or business** (Sec. 162);
(2) Expenses incurred by an individual in connection with the **production of income** (Sec. 212);
(3) Other types of expenses that fall within specific provisions of the IRC, such as certain types of interest expense, taxes, bad debts, and other expenditures by individuals for personal items such as medical expenses, alimony, and moving costs.

The first two categories of deductions, trade or business (Sec. 162) and production of income expenses (Sec. 212), are those incurred in connection with profit-motivated activities. The IRC does not attempt to specify every conceivable type of deductible expense included in these two categories. Rather, the IRC sets forth general guidelines for deductibility. Any expense incurred in connection with a trade or business or for the production of income is deductible if (1) it falls within the general guidelines and (2) the IRC does not specifically exclude it from deductibility. For example, although the IRC does not specifically provide for the deductibility of utilities or maintenance and repairs, these expenditures are deductible if incurred in a profit-motivated activity. These general guidelines are discussed later in this chapter.

For individuals, Sec. 212 allows a deduction for expenses related to the production of income expenses incurred for:

▶ Production or collection of income

▶ Management, conservation, or maintenance of property held for the production of income

▶ Determination, collection, or refund of any tax

As will be discussed later, for individuals, the distinction between a trade or business and the production of income is important because it can affect both the amount and type of the deduction. Expenses incurred in both types of activities must meet additional standards of deductibility; that is, they must also be ordinary, necessary, and reasonable in the context of the activity in which they are incurred. Losses incurred in either type of activity are deductible unless specifically limited.

Section 262 also provides, in general, that a deduction is not allowed for any personal, living, or family expenses. However, the tax law does specifically provide for the deductibility of certain personal expenditures or losses. For example, a taxpayer may deduct casualty losses (subject to certain limitations) for personal-use property. Taxpayers may also deduct personal expenditures for certain types of interest, taxes, medical expenses, alimony, and retirement savings if the expenditures meet strict requirements. Chapters I:7, I:8, and I:9 discuss deductions and losses for personal expenditures.

CLASSIFYING DEDUCTIONS AS FOR VERSUS FROM ADJUSTED GROSS INCOME (AGI)

OBJECTIVE 1

Distinguish between deductions for *and* from *AGI*

As mentioned in Chapter I:2, the tax formula for individuals divides all allowable business, investment, and personal deductions into the following two categories:

▶ Deductions subtracted from gross income in order to calculate adjusted gross income (*for* AGI deductions); and

▶ Deductions subtracted from AGI to calculate taxable income (*from* AGI deductions).

The concept of AGI applies only to individuals.

Section 62 specifically identifies deductions *for* AGI. All other deductions for individuals are deductions *from* AGI. The more common *for* AGI deductions include the following, subject to certain limitations:

▶ All allowable expenses incurred in an individual's trade or business, but not including an employee's unreimbursed business expenses

▶ Reimbursed employee business expenses

▶ Certain unreimbursed business expenses incurred by performing artists and employees of a state or a political subdivision thereof

▶ Losses from the sale or exchange of trade, business, or investment property

▶ Expenses attributable to the production of rent or royalty income

▶ Contributions to certain pension, profit-sharing, or retirement plan arrangements

▶ Penalties paid to a bank or other savings institution because of the early withdrawal of funds from a certificate of deposit or time savings account

▶ Alimony

▶ Moving expenses

▶ Cash payments made to a Health Savings Account

▶ Interest paid on qualified educational loans (student loan interest)

▶ Qualified tuition and related expenses for higher education up to $4,000

▶ One-half of the self-employment tax imposed on self-employed individuals and 100% of health insurance costs paid by such individuals (see Chapter I:14)[1]

KEY POINT

Many *for* AGI deductions are either expenses incurred in a trade or business or investment expenses or losses. Most of the deductible personal expenses are deductible *from* AGI.

NEW TAX ACT

The American Recovery and Reinvestment Act of 2009 allows taxpayers to deduct sales and excise taxes on the purchase of a new car as a deduction "for" AGI. This provision applies only in 2009.

For individuals, the distinction between deductions *for* AGI and *from* AGI is critical for two reasons. First, as explained in Chapter I:2, the tax formula allows individuals to deduct the greater of the standard deduction or the total of the *from* AGI (itemized) deductions in arriving at taxable income. Thus, a taxpayer does not benefit from these deductions if the total for the year does not exceed the standard deduction. Deductions *for* AGI, on the other hand, reduce AGI (and consequently taxable income) even if the standard deduction is used in computing taxable income.

EXAMPLE I:6-1 ▶

Brad, a single individual with no dependents, incurs $1,500 of deductible expenses and earns $50,000 in gross income during 2010. If the expenses are all deductions *from* AGI, Brad's taxable income is $40,650 (i.e., Brad receives a $3,650 deduction for his personal exemption and a $5,700 standard deduction). Brad receives no direct tax benefit from the expenses because they do not exceed the standard deduction. However, if the $1,500 of expenses are all deductions *for* AGI, Brad's taxable income is $39,150. In this latter case, Brad receives a full tax benefit from the expenses.

---

[1] Sections 62, 162(l) and 164(f). Other deductions *for* AGI include deductions for depreciation and depletion for life tenants and income beneficiaries of property, reforestation expenses, required repayments of supplemental unemployment compensation benefits, certain expenses incurred for clean-fuel vehicles and refueling property, jury duty pay that is remitted to an employer, attorney's fees paid out of awards in certain types of lawsuits, and certain trade or business expenses incurred by members of an Armed Forces unit when the individual is more than 100 miles away from home in connection with performing services as a member of that unit.

		Deductions *from AGI*	Deductions *for AGI*
Gross income		$50,000	$50,000
Minus:	*For AGI* deductions	0	(1,500)
AGI		$50,000	$48,500
Minus:	Standard deduction	(5,700)	(5,700)
	Personal exemption	(3,650)	(3,650)
Taxable income		$40,650	$39,150 ◀

The second important reason for the proper classification of deductions is that AGI acts as a limit on the amount of itemized deductions that can be taken. This limitation operates in three different ways:

▶ Certain itemized deductions such as medical expenses, casualty losses, and miscellaneous itemized deductions are only deductible to the extent they exceed a prescribed percentage of AGI. For example, an individual may deduct certain miscellaneous itemized deductions only to the extent that the sum of these deductions for the year exceeds 2% of the individual's AGI. These expenses include unreimbursed employee business expenses,[2] expenses incurred to produce investment income,[3] and the cost of tax advice and tax return preparation (see Chapter I:7). A taxpayer may deduct medical expenses only to the extent their total exceeds 7.5% of the individual's AGI for the year. Individual taxpayers must first reduce casualty losses on personal-use property by $100 per casualty event. After this reduction, casualty losses are deductible only to the extent that the sum exceeds 10% of the individual's AGI.

▶ AGI also acts as a limit on the deductibility of certain itemized deductions by placing a limit on the total amount of the deduction. For example, the deduction for charitable contributions may not exceed 50% of the taxpayer's AGI.

▶ Finally, under Sec. 68(f), total itemized deductions are subject to a 1% reduction in 2009 if the taxpayer's AGI exceeds $166,800 ($83,400 for married filing separately). This reduction of itemized deductions for higher income individuals is eliminated for tax years after 2009. The phaseout is scheduled to come back in 2011 at a 3% reduction rate. However, Congress may enact an extender bill that will cause the phaseout to apply to 2010 as well.

TAX LEGISLATION

As of early 2010, tax matters in many areas are highly uncertain, including the fate of these phaseouts.

Deductions *for* AGI are generally located in two places on the tax return. First, some deductions *for* AGI appear on the front page of Form 1040. These deductions include such items as moving expenses, alimony paid, one-half of self-employment taxes, and student loan interest. Second, other deductions appear on separate schedules, including Schedule C (Profit or Loss from Business), Schedule E (Supplemental Income or Loss), or Schedule F (Profit or Loss from Farming). The net profit or loss from these schedules carries over to the front page of Form 1040 as part of gross income. Thus, the deductions on these schedules are deductions *for* AGI. Figure P2-1 in Chapter I:2, contains the front page of Form 1040.

CRITERIA FOR DEDUCTING BUSINESS AND INVESTMENT EXPENSES

Business and investment expenses are deductible only if certain requirements are met. Thus, deductible business or investment expenses must be:

▶ Related to a profit-motivated activity of the taxpayer (i.e., a business or investment activity rather than a personal expenditure),

▶ Ordinary,

---

[2] These expenses include unreimbursed expenditures for travel and transportation, supplies, special clothing or uniforms, union dues, and subscriptions to trade journals. Reimbursed employee expenses are deductible *for* AGI and thus, are deductible in full. (See Chapter I:9.)

[3] These expenses include rental fees for safe deposit boxes used to hold investment property, subscriptions to investment journals, bank service charges on checking accounts used in an investment or income-producing activity, and fees paid for consulting advice. Expenses incurred in an investment or income-producing activity that generates either rental or royalty income are deductions *for* AGI.

OBJECTIVE 2

Discuss the criteria for deducting business and investment expenses

► Necessary,

► Reasonable in amount,

► Properly documented (discussed later in the chapter under the heading Proper Substantiation Requirement), and

► An expense of the taxpayer (not someone else's expense).

Furthermore, as discussed later in this chapter under the heading General Restrictions on the Deductibility of Expenses, even if the expense meets the requirements for deductibility above, taxpayers may not deduct expenditures meeting certain other criteria. Thus, an expenditure is not deductible if it is:

► A capital expenditure,

► An expense related to tax-exempt income,

► Illegal or in violation of public policy, or

► Specifically disallowed by the tax law.

Further discussion of these criteria and related matters follows.

BUSINESS OR INVESTMENT ACTIVITY

Deductible expenditures generally originate from a profit-motivated activity. Business expenses for all taxpayers are deductible under Sec. 162. Additionally, under Sec. 212, an individual may deduct an expense incurred for the production of income or for the maintenance and conservation of income-producing property (an investment activity). Thus, the requirement of an activity being profit-motivated is really two-pronged: (1) a determination of whether an expenditure originates from an activity engaged in for profit and (2) for individuals, a distinction between a trade or business and an investment activity.

REAL-WORLD EXAMPLE

A taxpayer attempted to deduct competitive bass fishing costs as a business expense, but the court concluded that there was no profit motive. Although the taxpayer maintained adequate business records, the taxpayer had a history of promptly ending unprofitable business ventures. His unwillingness to cease tournament bass fishing despite continued losses over several years suggested the lack of a profit motive. Moreover, the taxpayer's lifelong love of fishing suggested that the activity was engaged in for personal pleasure rather than for profit. *Thomas W. and Pamela A. Hill,* T.C. Summary Opinion 2006-120.

ACTIVITY ENGAGED IN FOR PROFIT.   This first part of the test classifies the expense as resulting from either a profit-motivated activity or a personal activity. For individuals, classifying expenses as either profit-motivated or personal can be quite difficult. For example, is the activity of coin collecting a hobby that is personal in nature, a profit-motivated business, or an investment activity? No single objective test is available. Rather, a tax advisor must examine all the facts and circumstances surrounding the activity in which the taxpayer incurs expenses in order to make this distinction. The section in this chapter entitled Hobby Losses discusses these factors in more detail, as well as other issues dealing with the determination of whether or not a particular activity is profit-motivated.

TRADE OR BUSINESS VERSUS INVESTMENT CLASSIFICATION.   The second part of the profit-motive test is the determination of whether a particular activity is a trade or business of the taxpayer or only an investment. This distinction generally is important only to individuals since corporations are assumed to be engaged in a business. It is important to individuals for several reasons. First, a loss on the sale of the assets used in the activity may be an ordinary loss if the activity is a trade or business.[4] If it is an investment activity, however, the loss is classified as a capital loss which, as explained in Chapter I:5, receives different treatment. Second, this distinction may control whether an expense of the activity is a deduction *for* AGI or a deduction *from* AGI. In general, expenses incurred in a trade or business are deductions *for* AGI whereas investment expenses, other than those incurred to produce rents and royalties, are deductions *from* AGI. Additionally, under Sec. 179, taxpayers may currently deduct a specified amount of tangible personal property placed into service during 2010 if the property is used in a trade or business. The deductible amount is phased out if the taxpayer places more than a specified amount of tangible personal property into service during the year. The amount of the current deduction and the threshold amount for the phase out are still in question for 2010 although it now appears that the current maximum $250,000 deduction will be extended for an additional year. However, taxpayers must capitalize and depreciate the same expenditures over several years if they are incurred in an investment activity rather than in a trade or business. (See Chapter I:10 for a discussion of the Sec. 179 current deduction for capital expenditures.)

---

[4] Under Sec. 1231, the exact treatment depends on the total gains and losses from such property for the year. See Chapter I:13 for a discussion of Sec. 1231.

EXAMPLE I:6-2 ▶ Robin is a self-employed financial consultant. She meets daily with a variety of clients to discuss their investments. Because she must keep abreast of the latest market quotes and strategies, Robin subscribes to several trade publications, newsletters, and quote services. During the year, Robin purchased a $4,000 computer to be used exclusively in her consulting business. Robin may deduct the expenses incurred for the publications and services as deductions for AGI because she incurred them in her consulting business. Furthermore, she can currently deduct the $4,000 paid for the computer under the special rules of Sec. 179 because it is a business asset, rather than an investment asset. ◀

Expenses incurred in an investment activity, other than those incurred to produce rents and royalties, are miscellaneous itemized deductions *from* AGI and are deductible only to the extent they exceed 2% of the taxpayer's AGI for the year (see Chapter I:7).

EXAMPLE I:6-3 ▶ Steve is a wealthy attorney who invests in the stock market and keeps abreast of the latest market quotes and strategies by subscribing to several trade publications and newsletters. This year he purchased a computer to use exclusively for tracking his investments. Steve generally spends a few hours each day studying this information and analyzing his portfolio. The subscription expenses are deductions *from* AGI because they are incurred in an investment (rather than a business) activity and do not relate to the production of rents and royalties. Steve cannot currently deduct the entire cost of the computer but must depreciate the cost over a period of five years. Furthermore, the deductibility of all of the above items depends on whether Steve's total miscellaneous itemized deductions exceed 2% of his AGI and whether Steve itemizes his deductions instead of using the standard deduction. ◀

ADDITIONAL COMMENT

A trade or business is an activity with a profit motive and some type of economic activity. An investment activity requires a profit motive but does not require economic activity.

Despite these important differences in treatment, the distinction between an investment activity and a trade or business is not always clear. The IRC and the Treasury Regulations do not provide a precise definition of what constitutes a trade or business. Judicial law, however, does provide some guidelines. In one of the first cases dealing with the issue, the Supreme Court stated that a trade or business involves "holding one's self out to others as engaged in the selling of goods or services."[5]

Later, another Supreme Court case emphasized that one must examine all the surrounding facts and circumstances to determine the underlying nature of an activity.[6] In that case, the taxpayer owned a large portfolio of stocks, bonds, and real estate. The taxpayer's holdings were so large that he rented offices and hired employees to help him manage the properties. The Court, however, regarded these activities as investment activities despite the size of the holdings and the amount of work and effort involved because the taxpayer merely kept records and collected interest and dividends from his securities. Other cases, however, indicate that a taxpayer who invests in stocks and bonds may be considered to be in a business if he or she frequently buys and sells securities in order to make a short-term profit on the daily swings in the market.

LEGAL AND ACCOUNTING FEES. Taxpayers may generally deduct legal and accounting fees incurred in the regular conduct of a trade or business or for the production of income. Taxpayers may also deduct fees incurred for the determination, collection, or refund of any tax. These deductions are *for* AGI if incurred in a trade or business or for the production of rents and royalties. Legal and accounting fees incurred in the determination or collection of taxes are also *for* AGI deductions if paid to prepare a taxpayer's Schedule C (Profit or Loss from Business), Part I of Schedule E (Supplemental Income and Loss, which is used to report rental and royalty income), and Schedule F (Farm Income and Expenses).[7] All other deductible legal and accounting fees incurred by the taxpayer are deductible *from* AGI as miscellaneous itemized deductions, subject to the 2% of AGI limitation. A filled-in Schedule C and copies of Schedule E and Schedule F are provided in Appendix B.

---

[5] *Deputy v. Pierre S. DuPont*, 23 AFTR 808, 40-1 USTC ¶9161 (USSC, 1940).
[6] *Eugene Higgins v. CIR*, 25 AFTR 1160, 41-1 USTC ¶9233 (USSC, 1941). See also *Chang H. Liang*, 23 T.C. 1040 (1955), and *Ralph E. Purvis v. CIR*,

37 AFTR 2d 76-968, 76-1 USTC ¶9270 (9th Cir., 1976); and *Samuel B. Levin v. U.S.*, 43 AFTR 2d 79-612, 79-1 USTC ¶9331 (Ct. Cls., 1979).
[7] Rev. Rul. 92-29, 1992-1 C.B. 20.

Taxpayers may not deduct legal fees incurred in the acquisition of property. Instead, taxpayers must capitalize these expenses and add them to the cost of the property. Likewise, taxpayers may not deduct legal expenses incurred for personal purposes.

EXAMPLE I:6-4 ▶ During the current year, Lia pays legal and accounting fees for the following:

Services rendered with regard to a contract dispute in Lia's business	$ 8,000
Services rendered in resolving a federal tax deficiency relating to Lia's business	2,500
Tax return preparation fees:	
Allocable to preparation of Schedule C	1,600
Allocable to preparation of Schedules A and B and to the remainder of	
Form 1040	400
Legal fees incident to a divorce	1,200
Total	$13,700

Lia may deduct $12,100 ($8,000 + $2,500 + $1,600) *for* AGI. The remaining $400 of tax preparation fees are deductible *from* AGI as a miscellaneous itemized deduction subject to the 2% of AGI limitation. The legal fees incident to the divorce are personal expenses and generally are not deductible. However, Lia could take a partial deduction *from* AGI as a miscellaneous itemized deduction to the extent these legal fees relate to giving tax advice incident to the divorce. ◀

ORDINARY EXPENSE

Another requirement for deductibility is that a business or investment expense must be **ordinary**. Although the IRC does not provide either a definition or an application of this requirement, the Treasury Regulations under Sec. 212 indicate that for an expense to be ordinary it must be reasonable in amount and it must bear a reasonable and proximate relationship to the income-producing activity or property. This means that more than a remote connection must exist between the expense and the anticipated income. It does not mean that the property must be producing income currently.

EXAMPLE I:6-5 ▶ Ahmed purchases a plot of land, on which there is an old vacant warehouse. Ahmed anticipates making a long-term profit from the investment because the value of the land is expected to appreciate eventually due to commercial development in the area. To help cover the costs of holding the property, Ahmed plans to rent storage space in the warehouse. During the current year, Ahmed incurs the following expenses, although he is unable to rent the warehouse:

ADDITIONAL COMMENT

A General Accounting Office report finds that tax cheating is widespread among self-employed taxpayers. These workers represent only 13% of all taxpayers, but account for approximately 40% of all underreported individual income. The report identified truckers as one of the least compliant groups.

Expenses	*Amount*
Property taxes	$1,000
Interest	4,000
Insurance	800
Utilities	200

All of these expenditures qualify as ordinary deductible expenses under Sec. 212 because they bear a reasonable and proximate relationship to the income Ahmed hopes to obtain, even though he generated no income from the property during the year. However, Ahmed might not be able to deduct them all in the current year because of the passive loss limitations explained in Chapter I:8. ◀

The Supreme Court has ruled that for an expense to be ordinary it must be customary or usual in the context of a particular industry or business community.[8] Thus, an expenditure may be ordinary in the context of one type of business, but not in the context of another.

EXAMPLE I:6-6 ▶ For many years, Hank has been an officer in Green Corporation, which is engaged in the grain business. Green Corporation purchases its grain from various suppliers. Last year, Green Corporation went bankrupt and was relieved from having to pay off its debts to its suppliers. In the current year, Hank enters into a contract to act as a commissioned agent to

---

[8] *Thomas H. Welch v. Helvering*, 12 AFTR 1456, 3 USTC ¶1164 (USSC, 1933) and *Deputy v. Pierre S. DuPont*, 23 AFTR 808, 40-1 USTC ¶9161 (USSC, 1940).

purchase grain for Green Corporation. To reestablish a relationship with suppliers whom Hank knew previously, Hank decides to pay off as many of Green Corporation's debts as he can. Hank is under no legal obligation to do so. Hank's payments are not ordinary. Rather, they are extraordinary expenditures made for goodwill to establish Hank in a new trade or business, and they must be capitalized. ◀

An expense may be ordinary with respect to a taxpayer even though that taxpayer encounters it only once.

EXAMPLE I:6-7 ▶ For several years, Health for You, Inc., has been engaged in the business of making and selling dietary supplements. Most of the advertisements, orders, and deliveries of the supplements are done through the mail. During the current year, the post office judged that some of the advertisements were false. As a result, a fraud order is issued under which the post office stamps "Fraudulent" on all letters addressed to Health for You, Inc., and then returns them to the senders. In an unsuccessful suit to prevent the post office from continuing this practice, Health for You expends $50,000 in lawyer's fees. These fees are ordinary business expenses because they are incurred in an action that normally or ordinarily would be taken under the circumstances. ◀

The Supreme Court has also indicated that the term *ordinary* in this context refers to an expenditure that is currently deductible rather than an expenditure that must be capitalized.[9]

NECESSARY EXPENSE

In addition to being ordinary, a deductible investment or business expense must also be **necessary**. The Supreme Court has indicated that an expense is considered necessary if it is "appropriate and helpful" in the taxpayer's business.[10] To meet this appropriate or helpful standard, an expenditure need not be necessary in the sense that it is indispensable. Rather, the test is whether a reasonable or prudent businessperson would incur the same expenditure under similar circumstances.

EXAMPLE I:6-8 ▶ The expenditures in Example I:6-6 (the payment of debts from a former business) and Example I:6-7 (the payment of legal fees) are both necessary because they are appropriate and helpful in each case. However, the expenditure in Example I:6-6 is not ordinary and, therefore, is not deductible. The expenditure in Example I:6-7 is deductible because it meets both tests. ◀

REASONABLE EXPENSE

Section 162 and Treasury Regulations under Sec. 212 provide that in order to be deductible the expense must be reasonable. Problems with meeting this standard can arise when a closely-held company pays a salary to an individual who is both a shareholder and an employee. In this situation, a controlling shareholder of a corporation may receive a payment, characterized as salary, that the IRS asserts is too large for the services rendered.

EXAMPLE I:6-9 ▶ Brian, the controlling shareholder and an employee of Central Corporation, receives an annual salary of $650,000. Based on several factors, such as the size of Central Corporation's total operations and a comparison of salary received by officers of comparably sized corporations, the IRS contends that Brian's salary should be no higher than $300,000. If Central successfully defends the $650,000 salary, the corporation is able to deduct the full amount as salary expense. If the defense is not successful, the excess $350,000 is considered a dividend to the extent of Central Corporation's earnings and profits, and no deduction is available to Central Corporation for this amount. In either event, Brian must take the full $650,000 into income. (See the Tax Planning Considerations section in this chapter for a discussion of the use of a payback agreement in these situations.) ◀

---

[9] *CIR v. S. B. Heininger,* 31 AFTR 783, 44-1 USTC ¶9109 (USSC, 1943). See also *CIR v. Walter F. Tellier,* 17 AFTR 2d 633, 66-1 USTC ¶9319 (USSC, 1966).

[10] *Thomas H. Welch v. Helvering,* 12 AFTR 1456, 3 USTC ¶1164 (USSC, 1933).

KEY POINT

Since the Sec. 162(m) compensation deduction limit applies only to publicly-held corporations, privately-held corporations are faced with the general reasonable standard which looks at the particular facts and circumstances.

In an attempt to link executive compensation to productivity and business performance and to discourage a common practice of increasing executive compensation despite declines in business performance, Congress enacted Sec. 162(m) that disallows a deduction for certain employee compensation that exceeds a yearly amount of $1 million. This limit applies to compensation payable by a publicly-held corporation to the corporation's chief executive officer and its four highest compensated officers for the taxable year. Compensation based on commissions or other performance goals is not subject to this limitation. Special rules and limitations apply to certain employers that are participating in the troubled assets relief program. (See Sec. 162(m)(5).)

The tests for determining whether a business or investment expense is deductible are summarized in Topic Review I:6-1.

EXPENSES AND LOSSES INCURRED DIRECTLY BY THE TAXPAYER

Generally, taxpayers may not take a deduction for a loss or expense of another person. This requirement attempts to prevent taxpayers from engaging in manipulative schemes.

EXAMPLE I:6-10 ▶ Juanita owns 60% of Hot Clothes, Inc. As CEO of Hot Clothes, Juanita is required to travel extensively. This year Hot Clothes purchases a business jet to facilitate Juanita's travel. In addition to her business travel, Juanita also uses the jet to take several family vacations. Hot Clothes may not take a deduction for Juanita's personal expenses. In order for the business to deduct these amounts, one of two procedures must be followed: (1) Juanita must report as additional compensation an amount that represents the use of the jet for her vacations, or (2) Juanita must reimburse Hot Clothes for the use of the jet for her vacations. ◀

This general rule applies to all types of expenditures, whether incurred in a trade or business, an investment activity, or a personal activity for which deductions are allowed. There is one exception: under Sec. 213 taxpayers may take a deduction for medical expenses paid on behalf of a dependent. Medical expenses are also deductible if paid for a person who would qualify as a dependent except for failing to meet certain other tests (see Chapter I:2). For example, under Sec. 152, the person's gross income must be less than the exemption amount to qualify as a qualifying relative, but for Sec. 213 this requirement is disregarded.

Topic Review I:6-1

Tests for Deductibility as a Business or Investment Expense	
TEST	**APPLICATION**
Ordinary	▶ Based on the facts and circumstances. ▶ Reasonable and proximate relationship to the activity. ▶ Customary or usual in context of the industry. ▶ Need not be encountered by the taxpayer more than once.
Necessary	▶ Based on the facts and circumstances. ▶ Appropriate and helpful. ▶ Need not be indispensable. ▶ Would a reasonable or prudent businessperson incur the same expense?
Reasonable	▶ Based on the facts and circumstances. ▶ Applies to all business and investment expenses. ▶ Compensation paid to an owner-employee of a small corporation is the most commonly contested area. ▶ Compensation in excess of $1 million payable by a publicly-held corporation to its key executives may not be deductible.

EXAMPLE I:6-11 ▶ During the current year, Dan incurs $3,400 in deductible medical expenses. Dan is supported by his father, Tom. Dan is 23 and is not a full-time student and therefore does not qualify as a dependent under the qualifying child rules of Sec. 152(c). Dan's gross income for the year is $15,000, which exceeds the exemption amount, and therefore Dan is not a qualifying relative of Tom under Sec. 152(d). If Tom pays Dan's medical expenses, Tom may deduct the expenses as an itemized deduction (subject to the 7.5% of AGI limitation) because of the modified test in Sec. 213 even though Tom may not take a dependency exemption for Dan. ◀

GENERAL RESTRICTIONS ON THE DEDUCTIBILITY OF EXPENSES

As mentioned earlier on page I:6-5, certain types of expenditures are not deductible. These types of expenditures fall within certain categories discussed below.

CAPITALIZATION VERSUS EXPENSE DEDUCTION

GENERAL CAPITALIZATION REQUIREMENTS. Under Sec. 263, a taxpayer may not take a current deduction for capital expenditures. Generally, expenses that add to the value of, substantially prolong the useful life of, or change the use of the property are considered **capital expenditures**. Thus, capital expenditures include the cost of acquiring or constructing buildings, machinery, equipment, furniture, and any similar property that has a useful life that extends substantially beyond the end of the tax year. Taxpayers must also capitalize the cost of goodwill purchased in connection with the acquisition of the assets of a going concern.[11] (See Chapter I:10 for a discussion of the amortization of goodwill.)

Some assets, such as buildings, machinery, equipment, furniture and fixtures, purchased goodwill, and customer lists are depreciable or amortizable and may provide deductions that spread over more than one tax year. Others, such as land, stock, and partnership interests, are neither depreciable nor amortizable and the taxpayer must wait until the taxpayer disposes of the asset to recover its cost. In some instances, it is difficult to ascertain whether an asset is eligible for depreciation or amortization. For example, the Tax Court has held that antique violin bows and an antique bass violin are depreciable property, overriding the IRS's arguments that they should not be depreciable because they were actually appreciating in value and it was impossible to determine their useful life.[12]

Maintenance and repair expenditures that only keep an asset in a normal operating condition are deductible if they do not increase the value or prolong the useful life of the asset. Distinguishing between a currently deductible expenditure and a capital expenditure can be difficult because expenditures for normal maintenance and repair can cost more than a capital improvement. Normal maintenance and repair may also increase the value of an asset. In one Tax Court case, the court held that expenditures incurred in replacing support beams and floor joists to shore up a sagging floor were deductible, whereas the court held that the cost of placing a new floor over an old one was a capital expenditure.[13] A tax advisor must examine all of the facts and circumstances to determine whether the expenditures constitute part of an overall plan of improvement or a change in use of the asset.

---

[11] Reg. Sec. 1.263(a)-2(h). See also *Indopco, Inc., v. CIR*, 69 AFTR 2d 92-694, 92-1 USTC ¶50,113 (USSC, 1992), where expenses incurred by a corporation that was the target of a "friendly" takeover were held to be nondeductible capital expenditures because they provided long-term benefits to the corporation. In this case, the Supreme Court held that these long-term benefits do not need to be associated with a specific identifiable asset.

[12] *Richard L. Simon*, 103 T.C. 247 (1994) and *Brian P. Liddle*, 76 AFTR 2d 95-6255, 95-2 USTC ¶50,488 (3rd Cir., 1959). The IRS has stated it will not follow these decisions. See AOD 96-9, 7/15/96.
[13] Reg. Sec. 1.162-4. See also *Standard Fruit Product Co.*, 1949 PH T.C. Memo ¶49,207, 8 TCM 733.

ADDITIONAL COMMENT

Some provisions permit taxpayers to depreciate or amortize capital expenditures over a relatively short period of time. For example, there is a rapid write-off available for pollution control facilities under Sec. 169 and for organization costs of corporations under Sec. 248.

BOOK-TAX COMPARISON

Although for tax purposes a taxpayer may elect to deduct these capital expenditures, for book purposes capital expenditures must still be capitalized and depreciated or amortized. This difference in treatment gives rise to a book-tax adjustment on Schedule M-1 or M-3 of a corporation's Form 1120.

ELECTION TO DEDUCT CURRENTLY. Taxpayers sometimes may elect a current deduction for certain capital expenditures. Taxpayers often prefer a current deduction over capitalizing and depreciating an asset because of the time value of money. Some expenditures that taxpayers may elect to deduct currently[14] include:

▶ Cost of fertilizers incurred by farmers

▶ Cost of soil and water conservation incurred by farmers

▶ Intangible drilling costs incurred in drilling oil and gas wells

▶ Costs for tertiary injectants

▶ Costs for certain mining development projects

▶ Costs incurred to remove architectural and transportation barriers to the handicapped and elderly

▶ Costs for certain qualified research and experimental expenditures

Taxpayers may also elect to deduct certain amounts each year for the purchase of qualified tangible personal property used in a trade or business instead of depreciating the property over its useful life. This deduction is subject to limitations in 2010. Chapter I:10 further examines the Sec. 179 election.

CAPITALIZATION OF DEDUCTION ITEMS. The exceptions mentioned above provide a current deduction for expenditures that are normally capital in nature. Conversely, Section 266 provides for the capitalization of certain expenses that are normally deductible. Section 266 is elective and applies to the following items:

▶ Annual property taxes, interest on a mortgage, and other carrying charges incurred on unimproved and unproductive real estate.

▶ Annual property taxes, interest, employment taxes, and other necessary expenses incurred for the development, improvement, or construction of real property, prior to the time construction is completed. For these expenses to be capitalized, the real property may be either improved or unimproved, productive or unproductive. After construction is completed, these types of expenses are fully deductible when incurred.

▶ Interest and employment taxes incurred in transporting and installing personalty (as opposed to realty) up to the time when the taxpayer first puts the property into use.

A taxpayer may make a new election to capitalize the expenses on unimproved and unproductive real estate each year.

EXAMPLE I:6-12 ▶ During 2010 and 2011, Nancy pays property taxes of $5,000 on a piece of land. During 2010, the land is vacant and unproductive. In 2011, Nancy uses the land as a parking lot, generating $7,000 in income. Nancy can elect to capitalize the taxes in 2010 because the property is both unimproved and unproductive. In 2011, however, the land is productive, and Nancy cannot elect to capitalize the taxes. Because the expenses relate to the production of rental income, they are deductible *for* AGI. If the land remains unproductive during 2011, Nancy can elect to capitalize the taxes paid in 2011. However, the election is optional and need not be made for 2011 merely because it is made in 2010. ◀

For the development or construction of real property, an election to capitalize the other expenses incurred during the development or construction period remains in effect for that year and for all subsequent years until the end of the construction period. However, a taxpayer may make the election on each new project separately.

EXAMPLE I:6-13 ▶ During the current year, Development, Inc. begins construction of an office building and a hotel. Development, Inc. incurs $20,000 in property taxes during the construction of the office building and $12,000 for the hotel. The election to capitalize the taxes on the office building does not bind Development, Inc. to make the same election with respect to the taxes on the hotel. ◀

---

[14] See Secs. 180, 175, 263(c), 193, 616, 190, and 174.

If a taxpayer elects to capitalize this type of expense under Sec. 266, the expense increases the basis of the property to which it pertains. If the property is depreciable, the taxpayer may deduct the expenses as depreciation deductions over a certain period. Taxpayers would want to make this election if they have large net operating loss (NOL) carryovers, or if they expect to be in a significantly higher tax bracket in future years and thus feel that the benefit of the deduction is greater in the future.

Under Sec. 263A, certain taxpayers must capitalize certain costs into inventory instead of taking a current deduction. (See Chapter I:11 for a discussion of inventories.)

EXPENSES RELATED TO EXEMPT INCOME

Under Sec. 265, taxpayers may not deduct any expense allocated or related to tax-exempt income. The purpose of this disallowance is to prevent the taxpayer from receiving a double tax benefit.

The IRC specifically disallows interest expense on debt the taxpayer incurs in order to purchase or hold tax-exempt securities. Thus, the disallowance depends on the taxpayer's intended use of the loan proceeds. Intent is generally determined by an examination of all the facts and circumstances surrounding the transaction. Intent to hold tax-exempt securities is shown if the tax-exempt securities are used as collateral in securing a loan.[15] If an individual who holds tax-exempt securities later incurs some debt, no disallowance will occur if the debt is incurred to finance personal items for which an interest deduction may be taken (e.g., a mortgage on a personal residence). However, if a taxpayer incurs the debt to finance an investment, a deduction for a portion of the interest is generally disallowed. Even though the debt is not incurred to hold tax-exempt securities, the deductibility of interest may still be limited. For example, if a taxpayer incurs interest on personal debt, this interest is not deductible unless the loan qualifies as home aquisition or home equity indebtedness. (See Chapter I:7 for a discussion of limitations on the deductibility of personal interest.)

SELF-STUDY QUESTION

Alpha, Inc., borrows $100,000 at a 10% rate of interest and invests the $100,000 in exempt bonds yielding 8%. Alpha is in the 35% tax bracket. Calculate what Alpha's cash flow on these transactions would be on an after-tax basis if expenses related to exempt income were deductible.

ANSWER

Alpha, Inc., has $8,000 of exempt income and $10,000 of interest expense. Cash flows would be equal to ($2,000) since there is no tax benefit for the interest. If the interest expense were deductible, its after-tax cost would be $6,500 ($10,000 − $3,500). Alpha's cash flow would be $1,500 ($8,000 − $6,500), allowing Alpha to make money on an unsound investment.

EXAMPLE I:6-14 ▶

BOOK-TAX COMPARISON

For book purposes, tax-exempt income and related expenses are included in the calculation of net income. For tax purposes, they are excluded from gross income resulting in a permanent book-tax difference that must be reported on schedule M-1 or M-3.

REAL-WORLD EXAMPLE

A subcontractor involved with the construction of a new shopping mall made kickbacks to the supervisor of the primary contractor. The kickbacks were deductible because they were not illegal, and the kickbacks were also ordinary and necessary because the subcontractor would not have been able to continue to work if the kickbacks had not been made. *Raymond Bertolini Trucking Co. v. CIR,* 54 AFTR 2d 84-5413, 1984-2 USTC ¶9591 (6th Cir., 1984).

Asian, Inc. has invested $80,000 in Gold Corporation stock, $120,000 in real estate, and $50,000 in tax-exempt municipal bonds. During the current year, Asian borrows $70,000 for the purpose of investing in a limited partnership. For the year, the company pays $6,000 interest on the loan. Under these circumstances, the IRS will presume that Asian, Inc. has incurred a portion of the debt in order to hold the tax-exempt securities and will disallow a portion of the deduction. Asian may overcome that presumption if it can show that it could not have sold the tax-exempt securities. Merely showing that the sale of the bonds would result in a loss will not overcome this presumption. ◀

EXPENDITURES CONTRARY TO PUBLIC POLICY

Certain expenditures, even though incurred in a profit-motivated activity, may not be deductible if the payment itself is illegal or if the payment is a penalty or fine resulting from an illegal act. These nondeductible expenses generally fall within one of the following categories:

▶ Illegal payments to government officials or employees

▶ Other illegal payments

▶ Kickbacks, rebates, and bribes under Medicare and Medicaid

▶ Payments of fines and penalties

▶ Payment of treble damages under the federal antitrust laws

BRIBES AND KICKBACKS. Under Sec. 162(c)(1), any illegal bribe or kickback made to any official or employee of a government is not deductible. This applies to payments made to:

▶ Federal officials and employees

▶ State, local, and foreign government officials and employees

▶ Officials and employees of an agency of a government

---

[15] Rev. Proc. 72-18, 1972-1 C.B. 740. See also *Wisconsin Cheeseman, Inc. v. U.S.,* 21 AFTR 2d 383, 68-1 USTC ¶9145 (7th Cir., 1968).

EXAMPLE I:6-15 ▶ During February of the current year, Road Corporation enters into a contract with the State of Iowa to construct a five-mile stretch of a new highway. Under the terms of the contract, Road Corporation must complete the project by October 22 of the current year. If it is not completed and accepted by Iowa on or before that date, Iowa will fine Road Corporation $5,000 per day for every day after October 22 until the project is accepted. By October 20, the project foreman realizes that the company will not make the deadline if it complies with all the requirements imposed by the state inspector assigned to the project. To avoid the fine, the foreman arranges for the inspector to "look the other way" on several of the requirements in exchange for a payment of $8,000. Because this payment constitutes an illegal bribe to a government official, the payment is not deductible. However, had they gone over budget, the $5,000 per day would have been a deductible expense. ◀

Taxpayers may not deduct illegal payments to officials or employees of a foreign government if the payment is unlawful under the Foreign Corrupt Practices Act of 1977, unless such payments constitute a normal way of doing business in that country. In all cases, the burden rests on the government to prove the illegality of the payment.

Illegal bribes, kickbacks, and other illegal payments made to people other than a government official or employee are nondeductible if they are illegal under a federal law that subjects the payor to a criminal penalty or loss of the privilege of doing business. In addition, illegal payments under a state law imposing the same penalties are nondeductible, but only if the state generally enforces its law. Here, the definition of a kickback includes a payment for referring a client, patient, or customer.

The courts and the IRS have made a distinction between an illegal nondeductible kickback and a rebate on the purchase of an item. If the seller pays a rebate directly to the purchaser, it is an adjustment to the selling price and, as such, is an *exclusion* (rather than a deduction) from gross income.[16] The distinction between the two payments seems to be that the seller and purchaser negotiate the rebate as part of the selling price.

Section 162(c)(3) specifically disallows a deduction for any kickback, rebate, or bribe under Medicare and Medicaid. Disallowed amounts include payments made by physicians or by suppliers and providers of goods and services who receive payment under the Social Security Act or a federally funded state plan. Unlike payments to foreign government or nongovernment employees and officials, these payments need not be illegal under federal or state law.

ETHICAL POINT

A CPA discovers that a client included fines and penalties in a miscellaneous expense section of a previously filed tax return. The CPA should recommend the filing of an amended return. However, the CPA is not obligated to inform the IRS, and the CPA may not do so without the client's permission, except where required by law.

STOP & THINK

Question: Queen, Inc., is engaged in the ship and boat repair business. Since the competition is very tough, Queen generally kicks back approximately 10% of any repair bill to any ship captain who brings the ship to Queen for repairs. Queen's customers include individual owners of large ocean-going yachts and fishing boats, as well as government vessels owned by state, federal, and foreign governments. During the current year, Queen paid $80,000 in kickbacks to the captains of privately-owned yachts and boats, $40,000 to the owners of privately-owned vessels, and $100,000 to the captains of state, federal, and foreign government vessels. The crews of these government vessels are government employees. What is the proper tax treatment of these payments?

Solution: The $40,000 in kickbacks paid directly to the owners of the privately-owned vessels are treated as merely a rebate in the price of the services and reduces Queen's gross income, unless the payments could result in the imposition of a criminal penalty or loss of the privilege of doing business. The kickbacks paid to the captains of the state and federal vessels are not deductible because they are paid to employees of state and federal governments. The kickbacks paid to the captains of the privately-owned vessels are not deductible if they are illegal and subject the payor to a criminal penalty or loss of the privilege to do business. Likewise, the payments to the captains of the foreign vessels are not deductible if the payments are unlawful under the Foreign Corrupt Practices Act.

---

[16] Rev. Rul. 82-149, 1982-2 C.B. 56.

FINES AND PENALTIES. Section 162(f) of the IRC also disallows a deduction for the payment of any fine or penalty paid to a government because of the violation of a law.

Furthermore, it disallows a deduction for two-thirds of any payment for damages made as a result of a conviction (or a guilty or no-contest plea) in an action regarding a criminal violation of the federal antitrust laws.[17]

EXAMPLE I:6-16 ▶ During the current year, the United States files criminal and civil actions against Allen, the president of Able Corporation, and Betty, the president of Bell Corporation, for conspiring to fix and maintain prices of electrical transformers. Both Allen and Betty enter pleas of no contest, and the appropriate judgments are entered. Subsequent to this action, Circle Corporation sues both Able and Bell Corporations for treble damages of $3,000,000. In settlement, Able and Bell Corporations each pay Circle Corporation $750,000. The maximum that Able and Bell Corporations may each deduct is $250,000 ($750,000 ÷ 3). ◀

EXPENSES RELATING TO AN ILLEGAL ACTIVITY. Interestingly, although the payment of an illegal bribe or kickback and the payment of a fine or penalty as the result of an illegal act are both nondeductible, expenses incurred in an illegal activity are generally deductible if they are ordinary, necessary, and reasonable and the taxpayer reports the income from the illegal activity.[18]

EXAMPLE I:6-17 ▶ Acme, Inc., owns and operates a small financial services business involved in the sale of securities and the lending of money. Acme often sells securities to customers in other states. However, because it has not registered the business with the appropriate state or federal authorities, the operation of the business is illegal. During the current year, Acme incurs the following expenses:

Interest	$ 20,000
Salaries	140,000
Depreciation	7,000
Printing	5,000
Bribe to employee of state securities commission	12,000
Total	$184,000

If Acme reports the income from this activity, the deductible expenses for the year total $172,000. The illegal payment of $12,000 to the government employee is not deductible. ◀

One exception to this general rule exists. Section 280E disallows a deduction for expenses incurred in an illegal business of trafficking or dealing in drugs.

OTHER EXPENDITURES SPECIFICALLY DISALLOWED

The IRC also specifically disallows deductions for certain other expenses, even though they might meet all the requirements mentioned previously. These include political contributions and lobbying expenses and, in certain situations, business start-up expenses.

POLITICAL CONTRIBUTIONS AND LOBBYING EXPENSES. Political contributions and lobbying expenses constitute one general category of disallowed expenses. Taxpayers may not deduct expenditures made in connection with the following:

▶ Influencing legislation

▶ Participating or intervening in any political campaign of any candidate for public office

▶ Attempting to influence the general public with respect to elections, legislative matters, or referendums

▶ Communicating directly with the President, Vice President, and certain other federal employees and officials

---

[17] Sec. 162(g).
[18] *CIR v. Neil Sullivan, et al.,* 1 AFTR 2d 1158, 58-1 USTC ¶9368 (USSC, 1958).

Sec. 162(e) also denies a deduction for contributions to tax-exempt organizations that carry on lobbying activities if a principal purpose of the contribution is to obtain a deduction for what otherwise would have been disallowed. Furthermore, the IRC disallows payments made for advertising in a convention or any other program if any part of the proceeds of the publication will directly or indirectly benefit a specific political party or candidate.[19]

Taxpayers may deduct lobbying expenses incurred to influence legislation on a local level if the legislation is of direct interest to the taxpayer's business. Local legislation includes actions by a legislative body of any political subdivision of a state (e.g., city or county council), but does not include any state or federal action. These deductible expenditures include expenses of communicating with or dues paid to an organization of which the taxpayer is a member. For administrative convenience, the deduction disallowance does not apply to any in-house expenditure attributable to such activities as long as the total of such expenditures for the taxable year does not exceed $2,000. In-house expenditures are expenses incurred directly by the taxpayer other than amounts paid to a professional lobbyist or dues that are allocable to lobbying. Additionally, the deduction disallowance does not apply to taxpayers engaged in the business of lobbying.

EXAMPLE I:6-18 ▶ Kensey & Associates is a large New York law firm. It is not in the lobbying business. During the year, the firm spends $6,000 to send some of its employees to Washington, D.C., to testify before a Congressional subcommittee with regard to proposed changes in the Social Security taxes imposed on employers. Such changes directly affect the firm's business because they affect the amount of taxes it must pay on behalf of its employees. The firm's ordinary and necessary expenses incurred with respect to the trip are not deductible because the expenses were incurred to influence federal rather than local legislation. ◀

If the legislation cannot reasonably be expected to directly affect the taxpayer's trade or business, the expenses are not deductible.

EXAMPLE I:6-19 ▶ Realty, LLC is a residential real estate company located in Chicago. The city of Chicago has proposed legislation to increase the hotel room tax. Realty spends time researching and traveling to speak to the Chicago City Council regarding this legislation. Although Realty, LLC incurs these expenses in an effort to influence legislation on the local level, it may not deduct these expenses because they are not of direct interest to its business. ◀

BUSINESS INVESTIGATION AND PREOPENING EXPENSES. At the election of the taxpayer, Section 195 of the IRC allows a current deduction in the year in which the business starts for business start-up expenditures. The current deduction amounts to the lesser of the amount of the start-up expenditures or $5,000, with a dollar for dollar phase-out for amounts incurred over $50,000. The remaining portion of start-up expenditures must be capitalized and amortized over a period of 180 months starting with the month in which the new business begins. Start-up expenditures specifically include three types of expenditures:

▶ *Business investigation expenses.* These expenses are costs a taxpayer incurs in reviewing and analyzing a prospective business before deciding whether to acquire or create it. The key here is that the taxpayer incurs the expenses before making a decision. These expenses include such items as analyses and surveys of markets, traffic patterns, products, labor supplies, and distribution facilities.

ADDITIONAL COMMENT

Costs incurred in connection with the issuance of stock or securities do not qualify as start-up costs. These costs are charged to Paid-in Capital.

▶ *Preopening or start-up costs.* Preopening or start-up costs are expenses incurred after a taxpayer decides to acquire or create a business but before the business activity itself has started. These costs include expenditures for training employees; advertising; securing supplies, distributors, and potential customers; and professional services in setting up the business' books and records. These costs must be incurred by a taxpayer not engaged in any existing business or engaged in a business unrelated to the business the taxpayer is acquiring or creating.

---

[19] Sec. 276(a). Nondeductible political contributions also include payments for admission to a dinner or program where the proceeds will benefit a party or candidate, or admission to an inaugural ball, party, or concert if the activity is identified with a political party or candidate.

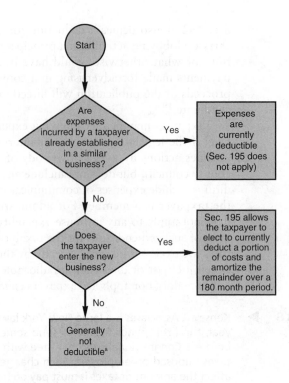

ª Rev. Rul. 57-418, 1957-2 C.B. 143 and Rev. Rul. 77-254, 1977-2 C.B. 63; *Morton Frank*, 20 T.C. 511 (1953).

FIGURE I:6-1 ▶ DEDUCTIBILITY OF BUSINESS INVESTIGATION AND START-UP COSTS

▶ *Expenses incurred in connection with an investment activity.* These expenses are costs incurred in connection with an investment activity that the taxpayer anticipates will become an active trade or business.

As defined by Sec. 195, start-up expenditures do not include these same types of expenses when incurred by a taxpayer already engaged in a business similar to the new one being created or acquired. In such a case, the taxpayer may deduct these expenditures currently because they originate in the taxpayer's existing business. Figure I:6-1 provides a flowchart to assist in properly classifying these types of expenditures.

STOP & THINK

Question: Shauna works in an automobile manufacturing plant in Detroit, Michigan. In January of the current year, she took a two-week vacation in order to fly to Orlando, Florida. While in Orlando, she spent some time investigating the possibility of opening a store in nearby Coco Beach. In total, she spent $800 on airfare, $1,500 on hotels and food, $300 on equipment rentals, and $300 on a car rental. In addition to spending time on the beach talking to people and checking out the rental equipment, she also spent some time talking to shop owners and real estate agents. After some analysis, however, Shauna has decided to keep her job in Detroit. What is the proper tax treatment for these expenditures?

Solution: In general, Sec. 162 of the IRC allows a deduction for expenses incurred in a business. Expenses incurred before the business starts are not incurred in a business and thus are not deductible under Sec. 162. However, under Sec. 195 a portion of certain expenditures such as business investigation expenses and start-up costs can be deducted currently while the remainder is capitalized and amortized over a 180-month period, beginning with the month in which the new business begins. Unfortunately Shauna did not open the new business. Thus, she may not deduct or amortize any of these expenses.

Topic Review I:6-2 summarizes the restrictions on the deductibility of these items.

Topic Review I:6-2

Restrictions on the Deductibility of Expense Items

ITEM	RESTRICTIONS IMPOSED
1. Capital expenditures	The general rule is that the expenditure is not currently deductible if its life extends beyond the end of the year. Special elections are available to currently deduct certain capital expenditures (e.g., research and experimental costs under Sec. 174; and limited amounts per year for acquisitions of tangible personal property used in a trade or business under Sec. 179).
2. Carrying charges	An election may be made under Sec. 266 to capitalize certain expenses that are normally deductible such as property and employment taxes, interest, and carrying charges on unimproved unproductive real estate.
3. Expenses related to tax-exempt income	Expenses such as interest incurred on debt used to purchase or carry tax-exempt securities are disallowed under Sec. 265.
4. Expenditures contrary to public policy	Such expenditures are generally not deductible. Examples include bribes and kickbacks, fines and penalties, and expenses of an illegal activity involved with trafficking or dealing in drugs.
5. Legal and accounting fees	Legal and accounting fees can be either *for* AGI deductible business expenses, nondeductible personal use expenditures, or *from* AGI fees incurred in the determination of any tax (e.g., tax return preparation fees).
6. Political contributions and lobby expenses	The general rule is that such items are not deductible (e.g., costs of influencing public opinion), but there are certain exceptions (e.g., costs of appearing before local legislative bodies on topics directly related to the taxpayer's business).
7. Business investigation and preopening expenses	The following rules apply: a. Currently deductible if the taxpayer is already engaged in a similar business. b. Not deductible if the taxpayer is not currently engaged in a similar business and does not enter the new business. c. An amount equal to the lesser of the amount of the expenses or $5,000 reduced by amounts incurred over $50,000 is currently deductible with the remainder to be capitalized and amortized over a 180 month period if the taxpayer enters the new business and makes an election. d. Deductible if expenditures constitute specific items such as legal expenses incurred in drafting purchase documents in an unsuccessful attempt to acquire a specific business. However, general investigation expenditures in search of a new business are not deductible.

PROPER SUBSTANTIATION REQUIREMENT

OBJECTIVE 3

List the substantiation requirements for deducting travel and entertainment expenses

Generally, the burden of proving the existence of a deduction or loss falls on the taxpayer. Thus, a taxpayer must properly substantiate all deductible expenses. Because the IRS may audit a return and request proof, taxpayers should retain items such as receipts, cancelled checks, and paid bills. Occasionally, the courts will allow a deduction that is not properly substantiated by the taxpayer if an expenditure clearly has been made. In these cases, the court estimates the amount of the deduction based on all the facts and circumstances. This procedure is known as the *Cohan* rule and derives its name from a court case in which the judge allowed a deduction for an estimated amount of certain expenses.[20] The most prudent course of action, of course, is to retain proper documentation rather than to rely upon the *Cohan* rule.

EXAMPLE I:6-20 ▶

In April of the current year, Terry took his tax records to a CPA to have his prior year's income tax return prepared. As part of the return, the CPA attached a supplemental schedule listing all of Terry's items of income and expense. After the return was prepared and filed, Terry's records

---

[20] *George M. Cohan v. CIR*, 8 AFTR 10552, 2 USTC ¶489 (2nd Cir., 1930). Interestingly, the *Cohan* case dealt with travel and entertainment expenses. Because of the subsequent enactment of Sec. 274(d), the *Cohan* rule may not be used to deduct entertainment expenses. It is still effective for other types of expenses.

were stolen. Upon audit two years later, the IRS disallowed Terry's deductions because he had no records to substantiate the expenses. When the case was litigated, the court allowed deductions for an estimated amount of expenses under the *Cohan* rule because of the list that was attached to Terry's return and because the court believed that Terry had testified honestly in his own behalf.[21] ◀

HISTORICAL NOTE

Justice Learned Hand, in permitting a deduction for unsubstantiated amounts in *George M. Cohan v. CIR*, 8 AFTR 10552, 2 USTC ¶489 (2nd Cir, 1930), wrote "absolute certainty in such matters is usually impossible and it is not necessary; the Board should make as close an approximation as it can, bearing heavily if it chooses on the taxpayer whose inexactitude is of his own making."

Additionally, Sections 274 and 280F provide specific and more stringent recordkeeping requirements for travel, entertainment, business gifts, computers, and vehicles used for transportation. In these cases, the taxpayer may not take a deduction unless the taxpayer substantiates the expenditure by either an adequate record or sufficient evidence that corroborates the taxpayer's statement. This substantiation may take the form of account books, diaries, logs, receipts and paid bills, trip sheets, expense reports, and statements of witnesses. The information that requires substantiation includes the following:

▶ Amount of the expense

▶ Time and place of the travel or entertainment

▶ Date and description of the gift

▶ Business purpose of the expenditure

▶ Business relationship to the taxpayer of the person entertained or of the person who received the gift

The *Cohan* rule does not apply to these types of expenses. (See Chapter I:9 for a more complete discussion regarding the deductibility of these types of expenses.)

WHEN AN EXPENSE IS DEDUCTIBLE

OBJECTIVE 4

Explain the timing of deductions under both the cash and accrual methods of accounting

Because the tax law generally requires calculating taxable income annually, the question of when a particular expense is deductible is especially important. The answer to this question largely depends on the taxpayer's method of accounting.[22] The most common methods include the following:

▶ Cash receipts and disbursements method (cash method)

▶ Accrual method

▶ Hybrid method (a combination of the cash and accrual methods where some items are accounted for on the cash method and other items are accounted for on the accrual method)

ADDITIONAL COMMENT

Section 446(b) provides that in cases where no method of accounting has been regularly used or if the method used does not clearly reflect income, then the computation of taxable income is to be made under a method that, in the opinion of the IRS, does clearly reflect income.

Taxpayers normally use the same method for computing taxable income that they use in keeping their financial accounting records. However, except for the use of the last-in, first-out (LIFO) method of accounting for inventory, the tax law does not generally require conformity. For example, many companies use the straight-line depreciation method for financial accounting purposes and the modified accelerated cost recovery system (MACRS) for tax purposes. This difference in depreciation methods, of course, results in a book-tax M-1 or M-3 adjustment.

CASH METHOD

Under the **cash method** of accounting, expenses are deductible when actually paid. The cash method considers payment by check a cash payment as long as the bank subsequently honors the check. This is the case even if the payee receives the check so late on the last day of the year that the payee could not have cashed it.[23] If the taxpayer mails the check near the end of the year, the taxpayer must have evidence that the mailing took place in the year

---

[21] *Layard M. White*, 1980 PH T.C. Memo ¶80,582, 41 TCM 671.

[22] Methods of accounting as they relate to the reporting of income are discussed in Chapter I:3. Methods of accounting as they relate to deductibility of expenses and losses are covered in this chapter. For an overall discussion of accounting methods, see Chapter I:11.

[23] *CIR v. Estate of M. A. Bradley*, 10 AFTR 1405, 3 USTC ¶904 (6th Cir., 1932) and *Charles F. Kahler*, 18 T.C. 31 (1952).

for which the taxpayer claims a deduction. Furthermore, the cash method considers payment by credit card a cash payment at the time of the charge rather than at the time the taxpayer pays for the charge.

A mere promise to pay, or the issuance of a note payable, does not constitute a payment under the cash method. Thus, a charge on an open account with a creditor is not deductible until an actual payment of cash satisfies the charge.

EXAMPLE I:6-21 ▶ Fox, Inc., a calendar-year taxpayer, is in the plumbing repair business. The business uses the cash method of accounting. Under an arrangement with one of its suppliers, Fox and its employees can pick up supplies at any time during the month by merely signing for them. At the end of the month, the supplier sends Fox a bill for the charges. Fox always pays the bill in full during the following month. In December of the current year, Fox charges $1,500 for supplies. During the same month Fox purchases a plumbing fixture for $250 from another supplier. Fox uses its charge card at the time of purchase. Fox may deduct the $250 during the current year. However, the $1,500 charged on the open account is deductible when paid in the following year. ◀

PREPAID EXPENSES. In general, a capital expenditure or the prepayment of expenses by a cash method taxpayer does not result in a current deduction if the expenditure creates an asset having a useful life that extends substantially beyond the close of the tax year. This can occur when a taxpayer makes expenditures for prepaid rent, services, or interest. However, in the case of prepaid rent, a circuit court of appeals decision has held that a taxpayer may take a current deduction for the entire amount of an expenditure if the period covered by the prepayment does not exceed one year and the rent agreement obligates the taxpayer to make the prepayment.[24]

EXAMPLE I:6-22 ▶ On November 1 of the current year, Twyla Corporation enters into a lease arrangement with Rashad to rent Rashad's office space for the following 36 months. By prepaying the rent for the entire 36-month period, Twyla Inc. is able to obtain a favorable monthly lease payment of $1,800. This prepayment creates an asset (a leasehold) with a useful life that extends substantially beyond the end of the taxable year. Thus, only $3,600 ($1,800 × 2 months) of the total payment is deductible in the current year. The rest must be capitalized and amortized over the life of the lease. However, assume that under the terms of the lease, Twyla Inc. is obligated to make three annual payments of $21,600 each November 1 for the subsequent 12 months. On November 1 of the current year, Twyla Inc. pays Rashad $21,600 for the first 12-month period. Because Twyla Inc. is obligated to make the prepayment and the period covered by the prepayment does not exceed one year, the entire $21,600 is deductible in the current year using the reasoning of the previously cited circuit court decision. ◀

PREPAID INTEREST. The IRC requires that prepaid interest expense be deducted over the period of the loan to which the interest charge is allocated.[25] Receipt of a discounted loan does not represent prepaid interest expense. Instead, the IRC deems the interest paid when the taxpayer repays the loan.

EXAMPLE I:6-23 ▶ During the current year, Richelle borrows $1,000 from the bank for use in her business. Richelle uses the cash method of accounting in her business. Under the terms of the loan, the bank discounts the loan by $80, issuing Richelle $920. When the loan comes due in the following year, however, Richelle is to repay the full $1,000. Richelle cannot deduct the $80 of interest expense until she repays the loan in the following year. ◀

REAL-WORLD EXAMPLE

A taxpayer made an overpayment of the federal income tax in 1975. In 1979, the IRS offset the overpayment against interest the taxpayer owed to the IRS. The Tax Court held that the interest expense was deductible in 1979 rather than in 1975. *Saverio Eboli*, 93 T.C. 123 (1989).

Taxpayers often prepay interest in the form of points. A point is one percent of the loan amount. Thus, the payment of two points on a $100,000 loan amounts to $2,000. While tax law generally requires the amortization of points over the life of the loan, points paid in connection with the purchase or improvement of a principal residence may be deductible when paid. Points paid in connection with the purchase (but not the

---

[24] *Martin J. Zaninovich v. CIR*, 45 AFTR 2d 80-1442, 80-1 USTC ¶9342 (9th Cir., 1980) and *Bonaire Development Co. v. CIR*, 50 AFTR 2d 82-5167, 82-2 USTC ¶9428 (9th Cir., 1982). See also *Stephen A. Keller v. CIR*, 53 AFTR 2d 84-663, 84-1 USTC ¶9194 (8th Cir., 1984).

[25] Sec. 461(g).

improvement) of a principal residence are automatically deductible in the year paid if they satisfy the following four requirements:

▶ the closing agreement clearly designates the amounts as points,

▶ the amount involves a computation as a percentage of the amount borrowed,

▶ the charging of points is an established business practice in the geographic area, and

▶ the points are paid in connection with the purchase of the taxpayer's principal residence which is used to secure the loan.[26]

REAL-WORLD EXAMPLE

The mortgage company will, at the end of the year, mail to the taxpayer a Form 1098 which shows the amount of interest and points paid.

Although points paid on loans incurred to *improve* the taxpayer's principal residence do not fall under this safe harbor rule, they still are currently deductible if the residence is collateral for the loan, the payment of points is an established business practice in the geographic area in which it is incurred, and the amount of the prepayment does not exceed the amount generally charged.

A taxpayer may not currently deduct points paid to refinance a mortgage on a principal residence because the points are not paid in connection with the purchase or improvement of the taxpayer's residence.[27]

EXAMPLE I:6-24 ▶ During the current year, Pam purchases a principal residence for $150,000, paying $50,000 down and financing the remainder with a 30-year mortgage secured by the property. Pam must make monthly payments on the mortgage. At the closing, Pam must pay three points as a loan origination fee. Because these points are paid in connection with the purchase of a principal residence, Pam may deduct $3,000 ($100,000 × 0.03) as interest expense during the current year. In addition, Pam may also deduct the interest portion of each monthly payment made during the year. On the other hand, assume that Pam takes out the $100,000 loan in order to refinance her home at a lower interest rate. The $3,000 prepaid interest is not currently deductible. Instead, Pam must deduct the interest ratably over the term of the loan. Thus, Pam may deduct an additional $8.33 ($3,000 ÷ 360 payments) interest expense for each payment that she makes during the year. ◀

If the taxpayer sells a home and pays off the refinanced mortgage, any unamortized portion of the points is deductible in the year of repayment. The tax law treats points paid by the seller as incurred by the purchaser and, therefore, the points are currently deductible by the purchaser if they meet the other requirements and are subtracted from the purchase price of the residence.[28]

The cash method of accounting provides some degree of flexibility to taxpayers because, under this method, taxpayers can generally deduct expenses when paid rather than when accrued. Thus, subject to the limitations mentioned above with regard to prepaid expenses, taxpayers may to some degree accelerate or defer deductions from one year to another by merely accelerating or deferring payment. However, the IRC imposes limitations on the use of the cash method. For example, taxpayers must account for inventories under the accrual method.[29] Furthermore, under Sec. 448, most C corporations (corporations that have not elected Subchapter S status), partnerships that have a C corporation as a partner, and tax shelters may not use the cash method. However, the IRC makes exceptions to this general rule for personal service corporations, small businesses with average annual gross receipts of $5 million or less, and businesses involved in the farming and timber businesses. (See Chapter I:11 for a complete discussion of the different accounting methods a taxpayer may use for computing taxable income.)

---

[26] Rev. Proc. 94-27, I.R.B. 94-15, 17. As explained in Chapter I:7, acquisition indebtedness incurred to acquire a personal residence is limited to $1,000,000. Hence, points that are allocated to the loan principal in excess of this limit are not deductible either.

[27] Rev. Rul. 87-22, 1987-1 C.B. 146, and Rev. Proc. 87-15, 1987-1 C.B. 624. However, the Eighth Circuit has allowed a current deduction for points paid upon the refinancing of a mortgage loan because the original loan was merely a "bridge" or temporary loan until permanent financing could be arranged.

See *James R. Huntsman v. CIR*, 66 AFTR 2d 90-5020, 90-2 USTC ¶50,340 (8th Cir., 1990).

[28] Rev. Proc. 94-27, I.R.B. 94-15, 17.

[29] Reg. §1.446-1(c)(2). However, most taxpayers with less than $1,000,000 of average annual gross receipts may use the cash method. See Rev. Proc. 2001-10, 2001-1 CB 272. The cash method may also be used by select taxpayers whose annual gross receipts do not exceed $10,000,000. See Rev. Proc. 2002-28, I.R.B. 2002-18, 815.

ACCRUAL METHOD

An **accrual method** taxpayer deducts expenses in the period in which they accrue. Generally, items accrue when the transaction meets both an **all-events test** and an economic performance test.[30]

ALL-EVENTS TEST. The all-events test is met when both of the following occur:

▶ The existence of a liability is established.

▶ The amount of the liability is determined with reasonable accuracy.

EXAMPLE I:6-25 ▶ During the current year, Phil provides services for Granite, Inc. Granite uses the accrual method of accounting. Phil claims that Granite owes $10,000 for the services. Granite admits owing Phil $6,000, but contests the remaining $4,000. Because the amount of the liability can be accurately established only with respect to $6,000, Granite can deduct only that amount. If Granite pays the full $10,000, it may deduct the full amount in the year of payment, even though the contested amount ($4,000) is not resolved until a subsequent taxable year.[31] If Phil loses the lawsuit and repays Granite the $4,000, Granite will include that amount in income in the year of repayment under the tax benefit rule (see Chapter I:11). ◀

Because of the all-events test, taxpayers may not deduct additions to reserves for estimated expenses such as warranty expenses. Instead, the taxpayer deducts the expenses in the year in which such work is actually performed.

EXAMPLE I:6-26 ▶ Best Corporation uses the accrual method of accounting and is engaged in the business of painting and rustproofing automobiles. Best Corporation provides a 5-year warranty for new vehicles and a 2-year warranty for used vehicles. Best Corp. extends the warranty only to the person who owns the car at the time the car is painted. Furthermore, in order to keep the warranty in force, the customer must present the vehicle to Best Corporation for inspection each year. The warranty is void if the vehicle is involved in an accident. Even though for financial accounting purposes Best Corporation may provide a reserve for estimated warranty expenses and deduct a reasonable addition to the reserve on an annual basis, no income tax deduction is allowed until the warranty work is actually done. ◀

ADDITIONAL COMMENT

Because of this difference between the tax treatment and the financial accounting treatment, an M-1 or M-3 adjustment must be made on a corporation's Form 1120.

ECONOMIC PERFORMANCE TEST. To be currently deductible under the accrual method, an expense must also meet an economic performance test. Exactly when economic performance occurs depends on the type of transaction. Table I:6-1 contains a listing of various types of transactions that may arise and identifies when economic performance is deemed to have occurred under Sec. 461(h).

EXAMPLE I:6-27 ▶ On December 20 of the current year, Pit Corporation, an accrual method taxpayer, enters into a binding contract with Pat to have Pat clean and paint the exterior of Pit's business building. Under the terms of the contract, Pat is to do the work in March of the following year. The total cost of the job is $4,000. Pit pays 10% down at the time the contract is signed. Because the job is not to be done until the following year, economic performance has not occurred in the current year and Pit may not deduct any portion of the expense in the current year. ◀

HISTORICAL NOTE

The economic performance test was added by Congress in the Tax Reform Act of 1984. Congress was concerned that in some situations taxpayers could deduct expenses currently, but the actual cash expenditure might not be made for several years. Taking a current deduction in such situations overstated the real cost because the time value of money was ignored.

An exception to the economic performance test provides that taxpayers may take a current deduction for recurring liabilities if all of the following occur:

▶ The item meets the all-events test during the year.

▶ Economic performance of the item occurs within the shorter of 8½ months after the close of the tax year or a reasonable period after the close of the tax year.

▶ The expense is recurring and the taxpayer consistently treats the item as incurred in the tax year.

▶ Either the item is not material or the accrual of the item in the tax year results in a more proper matching against income than accruing the item in the tax year in which economic performance occurs.

---

[30] Reg. Sec. 1.461-1(a)(2) and Sec. 461(h). [31] Reg. Sec. 1.461-2(a)(1).

▼ TABLE I:6-1

When Economic Performance Is Deemed to Have Occurred

Event That Gives Rise to Liability	When Economic Performance Is Deemed to Have Occurred (i.e., when the accrual method taxpayer may take the deduction)
Another person provides the taxpayer with property or services	When the person actually provides the services[a]
Taxpayer uses property	As the taxpayer uses the property[a]
Taxpayer must provide property or services to another person	As the taxpayer provides property or services to the other person[b]
Taxpayer must make payments to another, including payments for rebates and refunds, awards or prizes, insurance or service contracts, and taxes	As the taxpayer makes payments to the other person
Taxpayer must make payments to another person because of a tort, breach of contract, violation of law, or injury claim under a worker's compensation act	As the taxpayer makes payments to the other person

[a] Economic performance may be deemed to have occurred at the earlier date of payment if the taxpayer reasonably expects the property or services to be provided within 3½ months after the payment is made. Reg. Sec. 1.461-4(d)(6)(ii).
[b] Economic performance may also occur as the taxpayer incurs costs in connection with the obligation to provide the property or services. Reg. Sec. 1.461-4(d)(4)(i).

The recurring liability exception is available for the first four types of transactions identified in Table I:6-1, but it is not available for the last type of transaction in the table.

EXAMPLE I:6-28 ▶ Beta Inc. is a calendar-year, accrual method taxpayer. Every year at the end of October, Beta enters into a contract with Sam to provide snow removal services for the parking lots at Beta corporate offices. This contract extends for five months through the end of March of the following year. Because the all-events test is met (the liability is fixed), the expense recurs every year, economic performance occurs within the requisite period of time and the item is not material, Beta may deduct the entire expense in the year in which Beta and Sam enter into the contract. ◀

A special rule under Sec. 461(c) applies to real property taxes. Under this provision, a taxpayer may elect to accrue real property taxes ratably over the period to which the taxes relate. Once made, this election is irrevocable unless the taxpayer obtains permission from the IRS.

EXAMPLE I:6-29 ▶ Under the law of State X, the lien date for real property taxes for calendar year 2010 is January 1, 2010. The tax is payable in full on December 15, 2010. Alpha Corporation is an accrual method taxpayer that has a January 31 fiscal year-end. On January 1, 2010, real property taxes of $100,000 are assessed against a building Alpha owns. Alpha pays the taxes on December 15, 2010. If Alpha does not make the election to use the ratable accrual method, none of the payment is deductible in Alpha's fiscal year ending January 31, 2010, because the payment date is more than 8½ months after the January 31, 2010, year-end.

On the other hand, if Alpha makes the election, it may deduct $8,333 ($100,000 × $\frac{1}{12}$) in its fiscal year that ends January 31, 2010, and $91,667 ($100,000 × $\frac{11}{12}$) in its fiscal year that ends January 31, 2011.

If the taxes are paid on September 30, 2010, Alpha would be better off not making the ratable accrual election. In this case, the recurring item exception applies because the payment is made within 8½ months of Alpha's 2010 fiscal year-end. Thus, if Alpha does not make the election, all of the $100,000 is deductible in the fiscal year ending on January 31, 2010. ◀

Topic Review I:6-3 presents the rules for determining when an expense is deductible.

Topic Review I:6-3

When an Expense Is Deductible

CASH METHOD: DEDUCTIBLE WHEN PAID

Payment Is Made When
- ► Cash or other property is transferred.
- ► A check is delivered or mailed.
- ► An item is charged on a credit card.
  Note: A mere promise to pay or delivery of a note payable is not deductible under the cash method.

Prepaid Expenses
- ► Generally are deductible over the period covered.
- ► Deductible when paid if the period covered does not exceed one year.
- ► Prepaid interest is generally deductible ratably over the period covered by the loan.
- ► Points are deductible when paid if:
  —The loan is used to purchase or improve the taxpayer's principal residence.
  —The loan is secured by the residence.
  —Points are established business practice in the geographical area.
  —The points do not exceed the amount generally charged.
  —For points paid to purchase a principal residence, the closing agreement clearly designates the amount as points and the amount must be computed as a percentage of the amount borrowed.

ACCRUAL METHOD: DEDUCTIBLE WHEN ACCRUED

In General
- ► Taxpayers maintaining inventories must use the accrual method of accounting (except for taxpayers with average annual gross receipts of $10 million or less).
- ► Accrual occurs when the item satisfies both the all-events test and economic performance.

All-Events Test
- ► The existence of a liability is established and
- ► The amount of the liability is determined.

Economic Performance
- ► When economic performance occurs depends on the transaction involved (see Table I:6-1).
- ► Occurs in the year the item meets the all-events test and all of the following tests:
  —Actual economic performance occurs within the shorter of:
    8½ months after the taxable year or a reasonable period after the taxable year.
  —The expense is recurring and receives consistent treatment from year to year.
  —Either:
    The item is immaterial or
    Deducting the expense in the year it meets the all-events test results in a more proper matching of income and deductions.

SPECIAL DISALLOWANCE RULES

OBJECTIVE 5

Explain the tax consequences of wash sales

In addition to the general rules mentioned above, certain types of transactions are subject to further limitations and disallowances. These include wash sales, transactions between related persons, gambling losses, losses associated with an activity determined to be a hobby, expenses of renting a vacation home, and expenses of an office in the taxpayer's home. Further discussion of these special disallowance rules follows.

WASH SALES

Section 1091 disallows losses incurred on wash sales of stock or securities in the year of sale. For purposes of Sec. 1091, a **wash sale** occurs when:

- ► A taxpayer realizes a loss on the sale of stock or securities, and

▶ The taxpayer acquires "substantially identical" stock or securities within a 61-day period of time that extends from 30 days before the date of sale to 30 days after the date of sale.[32]

Thus, the purpose of the wash sale rule is to prevent taxpayers from generating artificial tax losses in situations where taxpayers do not intend to reduce their holdings in the stock or securities sold.

EXAMPLE I:6-30 ▶ Leslie realizes $10,000 in short-term capital gains (STCGs) through dealings in the stock market during the current year. Realizing that STCGs are fully includible in gross income and are taxed at ordinary rates unless they are offset against realized capital losses, Leslie analyzes her portfolio to determine whether she owns any stocks that have declined in value. She finds that the FMV of her Edison Corporation common stock is only $8,000, even though she originally purchased it for $16,000. Despite this paper loss on the stock, Leslie wants to retain the stock because she feels that Edison Corporation is still a good investment. If Leslie attempts to take advantage of the paper loss on the Edison stock by selling the stock she owns and repurchasing a similar number of shares of Edison common stock within the 61-day period, Sec. 1091 disallows the loss. ◀

At times, taxpayers may attempt to circumvent the wash sale provisions through either a sham transaction or an indirect repurchase of the securities. If this is the case, the wash sale provisions still prevent the recognition of the loss. The Supreme Court has held that losses on sales of stock by a husband were disallowed when the stockbroker was instructed to purchase the same number of shares in his wife's name.[33]

In some instances a taxpayer may attempt to circumvent the wash sale provisions by merely delaying the repurchase of the substantially identical stock. This tactic should work as long as a written agreement to repurchase the stock does not exist at the time of the sale or at any time within the 61-day period mandated by the Sec. 1091 wash sale provisions. If such an agreement exists, the courts will disallow the loss, even though the actual purchase does not occur within the 61-day period.[34]

In certain cases, taxpayers may still recognize losses on transactions that literally fall within the wash sale requirements. For example, a taxpayer may purchase stock and then sell a portion of those shares within 30 days where the intent is merely to reduce the stock holdings. Taken together, these two transactions meet the tests of Sec. 1091. However, because the purpose of the sale is to reduce the taxpayer's holdings rather than to generate an artificial tax loss, Sec. 1091 does not disallow the loss.[35] Section 1091 also does not apply to losses that a dealer in stock or securities realizes in the ordinary course of business.

If the taxpayer acquires fewer shares of stock within the 61-day period than the number of shares disposed of, Sec. 1091 disallows only a proportionate amount of the total loss.

EXAMPLE I:6-31 ▶ Several years ago, Henry purchased 100 shares of New Corporation common stock for $2,000 ($20 per share). On July 2 of the current year, Henry sells all 100 shares for $1,000. On July 30 of the current year, Henry purchases 75 shares (three-fourths of the original shares) of New Corporation common stock. As a result of the reacquisition, three-fourths of the total loss ($750) is disallowed. Henry recognizes the remaining $250 loss. ◀

SUBSTANTIALLY IDENTICAL STOCK OR SECURITIES. Only the acquisition of substantially identical stock or securities will cause a loss to be disallowed. The IRC and the Treasury Regulations do not define the term *substantially identical*. Judicial and administrative rulings have held that bonds issued by the same corporation generally are not substantially identical if they differ in terms (e.g., interest rate and term to maturity). However,

---

[32] Here the term *acquire* includes an acquisition of the stock either by purchase or in a taxable exchange. The term *stock or securities* includes contracts or options to acquire or sell stock or securities (see Sec. 1091(a)). The wash sale rules also apply to losses realized on the closing of a short sale of stock or securities if, within the 61-day period, substantially identical stock or securities were sold or another short sale of (or a securities futures contract to sell) substantially identical stock or securities was entered into.

[33] *John P. McWilliams v. CIR*, 35 AFTR 1184, 47-1 USTC ¶9289 (USSC, 1947).
[34] Rev. Rul. 72-225, 1972-1 C.B. 59, and *Frank Stein*, 1977 PH T.C. Memo ¶77,241, 36 TCM 992.
[35] Rev. Rul. 56-602, 1956-2 C.B. 527.

bonds of the same corporation that differ only in their maturity dates (e.g., the bonds do not come due for 16 years and mature within a few months of each other) have been held to be substantially identical. Generally, courts have not considered the preferred stock of a corporation to be substantially identical to the common stock of the same corporation.[36]

BASIS OF STOCK. If the wash sale provisions disallow a loss, then the disallowed loss increases the basis of the recently acquired stock. This increase in basis merely causes the disallowed loss to be deferred. The taxpayer will eventually recognize the loss upon the subsequent sale or disposition of the stock that causes the loss disallowance. If there has been more than one purchase of replacement stock and the amount of stock purchased within the 61-day period exceeds the stock that is sold, the stock that is deemed to have caused the loss to be disallowed is accounted for chronologically. The holding period of the replacement stock includes the period of time the taxpayer held the stock sold.

EXAMPLE I:6-32 ▶

Ingrid enters into the following transactions with regard to Pacific Corporation common stock:

Date	Transaction	Amount
January 4, 2004	Purchases 600 shares	$30,000
October 2, 2010	Purchases 400 shares	10,000
October 12, 2010	Sells original 600 shares	12,000
October 20, 2010	Purchases 200 shares	5,000
October 25, 2010	Purchases 300 shares	8,400

Because Ingrid purchases more than 600 shares within the 61-day period before and after the date of sale (the purchases made on October 2, 20, and 25), the recognition of the entire loss of $18,000 ($30,000 − $12,000) is postponed. Four hundred shares (two-thirds of the number of shares sold) are purchased on October 2 and 200 shares (one-third) are purchased on October 20. Thus, the basis of the 400 shares of stock purchased on October 2 is $22,000 [$10,000 purchase price + ($18,000 disallowed loss × 0.667)]. The basis of the 200 shares of stock purchased on October 20 is $11,000 [$5,000 + ($18,000 disallowed loss × 0.333)]. Both of these blocks of stock have a holding period that starts on January 4, 2004.[37] The basis of the 300 shares of stock purchased on October 25 is its purchase price of $8,400. Its holding period begins on October 25, 2010. ◀

STOP & THINK

Question: With regard to his investments in the stock market, the current year has been like a roller coaster ride for Doug. He now wants to do some year-end tax planning. For the year to date, he has realized a net gain of $12,000 on his stock investments. Although some of his current stock holdings have unrealized losses, he feels that they are excellent investments that will provide excellent returns in the next year or two. His stock broker has suggested that he sell enough of his holdings to realize a $12,000 loss (to offset the $12,000 capital gain) and then simply repurchase some of the stock. What advice would you give Doug as he discusses this strategy with his broker?

Solution: By realizing $12,000 in capital losses this year, Doug may be able to offset the capital gains he has already recognized. In order to recognize these losses, however, he must make sure that the wash sale provisions do not apply. Thus, he must either (1) purchase stock of different corporations or (2) delay the repurchase of the same issue of stock for at least 31 days after the date of sale. Since Doug is happy with his current investments, perhaps the second strategy is the best. Of course, other non-tax issues must also be considered. For example, does Doug think that the prices will go up quickly within the next 30 days? If so, he may lose out on some significant gains while he is waiting to repurchase the stock. Additionally, he must also consider the transaction costs (such as commissions).

---

[36] *Marie Hanlin, Executrix v. CIR,* 39-2 USTC ¶9783 (3d Cir., 1939). However, the IRS held in Rev. Rul. 77-201, 1977-1 C.B. 250, that the convertible preferred stock of a corporation is substantially identical to its common stock if the preferred stock has the same voting rights and is subject to the same dividend restrictions as the common stock, is unrestricted as to its convertibility, and sells at relatively the same price (taking into consideration the conversion ratio).

[37] An asset's holding period is important in determining whether subsequent gain or loss on the asset is long-term or short-term gain or loss. This is explained further in Chapter I:5.

TRANSACTIONS BETWEEN RELATED PARTIES

Section 267 places transactions between certain related parties under special scrutiny because of the potential for tax abuse. For example, a taxpayer could sell a piece of property at a loss to a wholly owned corporation. Without any restrictions on the deductibility of the loss, the individual could recognize the loss while still retaining effective control of the property. Under Sec. 267, related taxpayers may not take current deductions on two specific types of transactions. These transactions are:

▶ Losses on sales of property

▶ Accrued expenses that remain unpaid to the related cash method taxpayer at the end of the tax year

RELATED PARTIES DEFINED. Section 267 defines the following relationships as related parties:

▶ Individuals and their families. The term family includes an individual's spouse, brothers and sisters (including half-brothers and half-sisters), ancestors, and lineal descendants.

▶ An individual and a corporation in which the individual owns more than 50% of the value of the outstanding stock.

▶ Various relationships between grantors, beneficiaries, and fiduciaries of a trust or trusts, or between the fiduciary of a trust and a corporation if they meet certain ownership requirements.

▶ A corporation and a partnership if the same persons own more than 50% in value of the stock of the corporation and more than 50% of the partnership.

▶ Two corporations if the same persons own more than 50% in value of the outstanding stock of both corporations and at least one of the corporations is an S corporation.

▶ Other complex relationships involving trusts, corporations, and individuals.

Several of these relationships depend on an individual's ownership of a corporation. For example, if a taxpayer does not own more than 50% of a corporation's stock, the individual and the corporation are not related and a loss on the sale of business or investment property between the two is deductible. Occasionally, individuals might attempt to circumvent the related party rules by dispersing the ownership of a corporation (e.g., among close family members) while retaining economic control. To prevent these tactics, Sec. 267 contains constructive ownership rules whereby a taxpayer is deemed to own stock owned by certain other persons. These constructive ownership rules are as follows:

▶ Stock owned by an individual's family is treated as owned by the individual. Here the definition of *family* is the same as that of *related parties* (i.e., spouse, brothers and sisters, ancestors, and lineal descendants).

▶ Stock owned by a corporation, partnership, estate, or trust is treated as owned proportionately by the shareholders, partners, or beneficiaries.

▶ If an individual partner in a partnership owns (or is treated as owning) stock in a corporation, the individual is treated as owning any stock of that corporation owned by any other partner in the partnership. This does not occur, however, if the only stock the individual owns (or is considered to own) is through family attribution.[38]

▶ Stock ownership that is attributed to a shareholder or partner from an entity can be reattributed to another taxpayer under any of the constructive ownership rules. In other words, the same stock can be constructively owned by more than one person. However, stock ownership attributed to a taxpayer under the family or partner rules cannot be reattributed.

---

[38] Reg. Sec. 1.267(c)-1(b), Exs. (2) and (3).

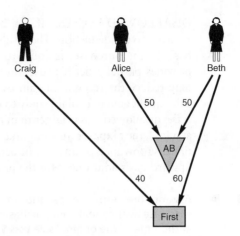

FIGURE I:6-2 ▶ ILLUSTRATION FOR EXAMPLE I:6-33

The following examples illustrate these rules.

EXAMPLE I:6-33 ▶ Alice and Beth are equal partners in the AB Partnership. Beth owns 60% of First Corporation's stock, and Craig, Alice's husband, owns the other 40%. The ownership of the partnership and the corporation is demonstrated in Figure I:6-2. Under the constructive ownership rules, Alice is considered to own Craig's 40% of the First Corporation stock. Alice is not considered to own the First Corporation stock owned by her partner, Beth, because the only First Corporation stock Alice owns (or is considered to own) is the stock owned by her husband. If Alice sells property at a loss to First Corporation, the loss is recognized because Alice does not directly or constructively own more than 50% of the First Corporation stock. ◀

EXAMPLE I:6-34 ▶ Assume the same facts as in Example I:6-33, except that the First Corporation stock is owned 50% by the AB Partnership and 25% each by Beth and Craig. The ownership of the partnership and the corporation is shown in Figure I:6-3. In addition to Craig's 25%, Alice is considered to own 50% of the stock owned by the AB Partnership because of her 50% ownership in AB. The other half of AB's stock ownership is attributed to her partner, Beth. However, Alice is also treated as owning the First Corporation stock Beth owns both actually and constructively (50%). Thus, Alice is treated as owning 100% of the First Corporation stock. In this case, Alice will not be able to recognize a loss on the sale of property to First Corporation. ◀

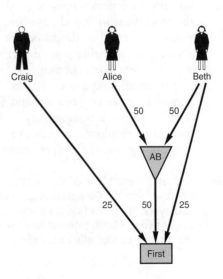

FIGURE I:6-3 ▶ ILLUSTRATION FOR EXAMPLE I:6-34

DISALLOWED LOSSES. If Sec. 267 disallows the loss, the original seller of the property receives no tax deduction. The disallowed loss has no effect on the purchaser's basis. The cost basis to the purchaser is equal to the amount paid for the property. However, Sec. 267 provides partial relief because, on a subsequent sale of the property, the related purchaser may reduce the recognized gain by the amount of the disallowed loss. This offsetting of a subsequent gain is available only to the related person who originally purchased the property. If the disallowed loss is larger than the subsequent gain, or if the purchaser sells the property at a loss, the taxpayer may not take a deduction for the unused loss. This may result in a partial disallowance of an overall economic loss for the related parties because there is no upward basis adjustment for the previously disallowed loss (as is the case for a wash sale).

EXAMPLE I:6-35 ▶ Assume three separate scenarios in which Sam sells a tract of land during the current year. In each case assume that Sam purchased the land from his father, Frank, for $10,000. Frank's basis at the time of the original sale was $15,000 in each case. Thus, Frank's $5,000 loss on each land sale was disallowed.

KEY POINT

The loss disallowance rule for related parties is more severe compared to the loss disallowance rule on wash sales. In a related party transaction, it is possible to lose the tax benefit of all or a portion of the economic loss.

	Scenario		
	1	2	3
Selling price	$17,000	$12,000	$ 8,000
Minus: Sam's basis	(10,000)	(10,000)	(10,000)
Sam's realized gain (loss)	$ 7,000	$ 2,000	$ (2,000)
Minus: Frank's disallowed loss (up to Sam's gain)	(5,000)	(2,000)	—0—
Sam's recognized gain (loss)	$2,000	—0—	($2,000)

In Scenario 1, Sam and Frank together have incurred an aggregate gain of $2,000 ($17,000 − $15,000). Thus, Frank's full disallowed loss reduces Sam's subsequent gain. In Scenario 2, the aggregate economic loss incurred by Sam and Frank is actually $3,000 ($12,000 − $15,000). However, the actual amount of the tax loss recognized by Sam and Frank is zero. In Scenario 3, the actual tax loss would have been $7,000 ($8,000 − $15,000) instead of $2,000 if Frank had held the land until its eventual sale. ◀

A similar rule found in Sec. 707(b)(1) disallows losses between a partner and a partnership in which the partner owns directly or indirectly over 50% of the partnership and between two partnerships in which the same people own directly or indirectly over 50% in each partnership. The constructive ownership rules of Sec. 267 apply here in determining ownership (see *Prentice Hall's Federal Taxation: Corporations, Partnerships, Estates, and Trusts* text or the *Comprehensive* volume).

KEY POINT

The effect of Sec. 267 with respect to unpaid expenses is to place an accrual method taxpayer on the cash method for amounts owed to a related cash method taxpayer.

UNPAID EXPENSES. Under Sec. 267, a related accrual-method obligor of any accrued but unpaid expenses must defer the deduction for those expenses until the year in which the related cash-method payee recognizes the amount as income. In effect, this rule prevents an accrual-method taxpayer (the payer) from taking a deduction for an unpaid expense in the earlier year of accrual while the related cash-method taxpayer (the payee) recognizes the payment as income in the subsequent year.

For unpaid expenses, Sec. 267 expands the definition of related parties to include a personal-service corporation and any employee-owner.[39] A personal-service corporation is one whose principal activity is the performance of personal services substantially performed by employee-owners. An employee-owner is an employee who owns any of the outstanding stock of the personal-service corporation.[40]

EXAMPLE I:6-36 ▶ Michelle owns 100% of the outstanding stock of Hill Corporation. Michelle is a cash-method taxpayer and Hill Corporation is an accrual-method taxpayer. Both taxpayers are calendar-year taxpayers. In a bona fide transaction, Hill borrows some funds from Michelle. By the end of the current year, $8,000 interest had accrued on the loan. However, Hill Corporation does not pay the interest to Michelle until February of the following year. Because Michelle is a cash-method

---

[39] Sec. 267(a)(2).
[40] Secs. 269A(b) and 441(i)(2). In determining the ownership of an employee-owner, the constructive ownership rules of Sec. 318 as modified by Sec.

441(i)(2) are used. These rules differ substantially from the constructive ownership rules of Sec. 267.

taxpayer, she reports the interest income when she receives it in the following year. Although Hill is an accrual-method taxpayer, it must defer the deduction for the interest expense until it pays the interest in February of the following year. The results are the same if Hill Corporation is a personal service corporation and Michelle is an employee and owns any amount of the Hill stock. ◄

For purposes of these unpaid expenses, the definition of *related parties* also includes various relationships involving partnerships or S corporations and any person who owns (either actually or constructively) any interest in these entities.[41]

<table>
<tr><td>

OBJECTIVE 7

Discuss the criteria for determining whether an activity is a hobby or a trade or business

</td></tr>
</table>

HOBBY LOSSES

Certain activities have both profit-motivated and personal attributes. In these cases, a tax advisor must examine all the relevant factors to determine the tax status of the activity since, in general, expenses incurred in a profit-motivated activity such as a business or investment are deductible, whereas most expenses associated with personal activities such as hobbies are not. Reg. Sec. 1.183-2(b) lists the factors the IRS uses to determine whether an activity is profit-motivated. These factors include the following:

▶ Whether the taxpayer conducts the activity in a businesslike manner.

▶ The expertise of the taxpayer or the taxpayer's advisors.

▶ The time and effort expended by the taxpayer in carrying on the activity.

▶ Whether the assets used in the activity are expected to appreciate in value.

▶ The taxpayer's success in carrying on other similar activities.

▶ The taxpayer's history of income or losses with respect to the activity.

▶ The amount of occasional profits earned, if any.

▶ The taxpayer's financial status.

▶ Any elements of personal pleasure or recreation the activity might involve.

No one of these factors is determinative. In fact, the IRS also may consider other factors not listed. Furthermore, the IRS does not make a determination by merely counting the number of factors that are present. Instead, the decision depends on an examination of all the factors together. The IRS can, therefore, make the decision on a more subjective basis than the taxpayer might like. If the IRS asserts that an activity is a personal one (i.e., a hobby) rather than a business or investment, the burden of proof rests on the taxpayer to prove otherwise.

ADDITIONAL COMMENT

Many of the court cases dealing with profit motive under Sec. 183 are ranch and farm cases. In fact, Sec. 183, now titled "Activities Not Engaged in for Profit" was originally titled "Farm Losses, etc." in the Tax Reform Act of 1969.

EXAMPLE I:6-37 ▶

Paula, a successful attorney with an annual income of $300,000, also enjoys raising and training quarter horses. She generally spends five to six hours each week training, showing, or racing the horses. Over the last four years her winnings from shows and races have amounted to $16,000. Over that same period, she has generated an additional $8,000 of income from stud fees and the sale of colts. Often the horses are used to take Paula's family or friends riding. In addition, Paula often participates in equestrian clinics and demonstrations for 4-H Clubs and other similar groups. Paula employs a high school student to feed the horses each day and clean the stalls weekly. Paula also hires a professional horse trainer for 4 hours each week to help her train the horses.

In this case, several factors such as the level of earnings, the hiring of professional help, and the amount of time spent in the activity might indicate that Paula is engaged in a business. Other factors, such as the time spent riding with family and friends, the voluntary clinics and demonstrations, and the small amount of revenue generated as compared with Paula's other income, support the position that Paula merely has a hobby of raising horses. ◄

In cases where a clear profit motive cannot be shown under the factors mentioned above, the Code provides a test whereby an activity may be presumed to be engaged in for profit. The activity meets the test if it shows a profit for any three years during a consecutive five-year period. The five-year period consists of the year in question plus the previous four years.[42] This presumption is rebuttable (i.e., if the taxpayer meets the test, the

---

[41] Sec. 267(e). A discussion of these modifications is beyond the scope of this book.
[42] Sec. 183(d). If the major part of the activity involves breeding, training,

showing, or racing horses, the five-year period is extended to a seven-year period, and a profit must be shown in only two, rather than three, of the years covered by that seven-year period.

IRS has the burden of proof to show that the activity *is not* profit motivated). However, if the taxpayer fails to meet this test, the taxpayer must prove that the activity *is* profit motivated.

If examination of the factors leads to the determination that the activity is a business, the taxpayer may deduct all qualified business expenses from the gross income, even if a net loss results.[43] However, if the factors lead to a determination that the activity is a hobby, the expenses are generally deductible as a miscellaneous itemized deduction but only to the extent of the gross income from the activity. A net loss may not be reported from the activity if it is a hobby.

EXAMPLE I:6-38 ▶

Lorenzo, a stockbroker, enjoys raising pedigreed poodles. Although he mainly raises them for recreation and relaxation after work, Lorenzo periodically sells some of his poodles. Lorenzo reports $850 in income and $2,900 in expenses from the activity on his 2010 tax return. Upon auditing Lorenzo's 2010 return, the IRS disallowed the expenses in excess of the income, arguing that the activity is a hobby rather than a business or investment. If Lorenzo can prove that he realized a profit from the poodle-raising operation for any three years from 2006 through 2010 inclusive, the presumption will be made that the poodles are raised for a profit and not for recreation. The IRS then has the burden of proof to show that the activity is really a hobby. If Lorenzo cannot show a profit for three years out of the five-year period, he must rely on the factors mentioned in the Treasury Regulations to convince the IRS and/or the courts that the activity is a business.

If Lorenzo's poodle-raising activity is determined to be a business, Lorenzo will report a net loss of $2,050 ($2,900 expenses − $850 income), assuming the loss is not incurred in a passive activity (see Chapter I:8). If the activity is determined to be a hobby, however, Lorenzo may deduct only $850 of the expenses (up to the amount of the gross income) as an itemized deduction. As explained later, these expenses must be deducted in a certain order. The remaining expenses are not allowed as tax deductions. ◀

DEDUCTIBLE EXPENSES. Some hobby activities generate gross income, even though profit is not a primary motive for the activity. In such situations, Sec. 183 allows the taxpayer to deduct the expenses related to the hobby, but only to the extent of the gross income from the hobby. Furthermore, a hobby-related expense is deductible only if it would have been deductible if incurred in a trade or business or an investment activity.

In essence, a taxpayer may deduct all the hobby-related expenses as long as there is enough gross income from the activity to cover the expenses. However, a taxpayer may not generate a tax loss from a hobby and then use it to offset the taxpayer's other types of income.

ORDER OF THE DEDUCTIONS. If the hobby expenses exceed the amount of gross income generated by the hobby, the expense deductions offset gross income in the following order:

▶ Tier 1: Expenses that are deductible even though not incurred in a trade or business (e.g., itemized deductions such as taxes, certain interest, and casualty losses)

▶ Tier 2: Other expenses of the hobby that could be deductible if incurred in a profit-motivated activity, but which do not reduce the tax basis of any of the assets used in the hobby (e.g., utilities and maintenance expenses)

▶ Tier 3: The expenses of the hobby that could be deductible if incurred in a profit-motivated activity and that reduce the basis of the hobby's assets (e.g., depreciation on fixed assets used in the hobby)[44]

To the extent that the expenses are deductible against the gross income of the activity, they are deductions *from* AGI and are deductible only if the taxpayer has itemized deductions in excess of the standard deduction. Form 1040 reports the tier 1 expenses in their respective sections on Schedule A. The tier 2 and tier 3 expenses allocated to the hobby are miscellaneous itemized deductions; therefore, these expenses are deductible only to the extent

---

[43] If the activity is a passive activity, however, the loss may be deferred or suspended. See Chapter I:8 for a discussion of the passive loss rules.

[44] Reg. Sec. 1.183-1(b).

they exceed 2% of AGI (see Chapter I:7). Form 1040 reports gross income from a hobby as other income. If gross income is not sufficient to cover all of the tier 1 expenses, the taxpayer may also deduct the excess tier 1 expenses as itemized deductions on Schedule A of Form 1040 because the tax law allows deductions for these expenses in any event. The tax law disallows deductions for any remaining expenses in the other two tiers, and the taxpayer may not carry them over to a subsequent year.

If depreciation expense is not deductible, the taxpayer does not need to reduce the cost basis of the asset by the amount of the disallowed depreciation expense.

EXAMPLE I:6-39 ▶

Lynn raises various plants and flowers in a small greenhouse constructed specifically for that purpose. During the current year, Lynn reports gross income from the greenhouse activities of $1,700. Lynn also incurs the following expenses:

Property taxes on the greenhouse	$1,150
Utilities	300
Depreciation (assuming the activity is considered a business)	800

If the greenhouse activity is considered to be a hobby rather than a business, the deductions Lynn may take are computed as follows:

Income From greenhouse		$1,700
Tier 1 Expenses:		
Property taxes	$1,150	
Tier 2 Expenses:		
Utilities	300	
Tier 3 Expenses:		
Depreciation[a]	250	$1,700
Total		$0

[a]Limited to greenhouse income remaining after accounting for the Tier 1 and Tier 2 expenses.   ◀

REAL-WORLD EXAMPLE

Good records are very important in establishing the existence of a business rather than a hobby. A taxpayer, who owned and operated an apple orchard, asserted that he maintained sufficient business records, consisting of bank deposit slips, check stubs, and tax forms. A separate bank account was also maintained. But the taxpayer did not present any production records for the apple orchard. In fact, at trial, the taxpayer was not even certain of the exact number of trees in the orchard. Thus, the court found that due to the limited records, the taxpayer's activity was considered to be a hobby rather than a business. *Zdun*, TC Memo 1998-296 (1998).

VACATION HOME

Because owning a second home or dwelling unit may have both personal and profit-motivated attributes, Sec. 280A may disallow or limit deductions for expenses related to the rental of a vacation home that is also used as a residence by the taxpayer.

OBJECTIVE 8

Determine the tax consequences of vacation homes

RESIDENCE DEFINED. For the restrictive rules of Sec. 280A to apply, the property must be a dwelling unit that qualifies as the taxpayer's residence. As used in this context, the term *dwelling unit* is quite expansive. The term dwelling unit may even include property such as boats and mobile homes. The determining factor is whether the property provides shelter and accommodations for eating and sleeping.[45] Thus, a mini-motorhome that contains the appropriate accommodations has been held to be a dwelling unit subject to the rules and limitations of Sec. 280A. The determination disregards the fact that the unit is small and cramped.

A dwelling unit qualifies as a residence if the number of days during which the taxpayer uses the property for personal use throughout the year exceeds the greater of the following:

▶ 14 days, or

▶ 10% of the number of days during the year that the property is rented at a fair rental.[46]

SELF-STUDY QUESTION

What is the maximum number of days during a year that a taxpayer may use a property for personal use and not have it considered to be used as a residence?

EXAMPLE I:6-40 ▶

ANSWER

If a property was rented for 332 days it could be used by the taxpayer for 33 days and not be considered a residence.

Sarah owns a houseboat on Lake Powell that she personally uses for 21 days out of the year. During the year she also rents out the boat for a total of 300 days. Even though Sarah's personal use exceeds 14 days during the year, the houseboat is not considered a residence under Sec. 280A because Sarah's personal use does not exceed 30 days during the year (10% of the 300 rental days for the year).   ◀

---

[45] *Ronald L. Haberkorn*, 75 T.C. 259 (1980), and *John O. Loughlin v. U.S.*, 50 AFTR 2d 82-5827, 82-2 USTC ¶9543 (D.C. Minn., 1982).

[46] Sec. 280A(d)(1). In certain cases, this residence test might be met when a taxpayer uses a property as his or her principal residence for part of the year and

rents the property for the rest of the year. This could occur, for example, when a taxpayer moves from his or her home and turns the old residence into a rental unit. In such a case, special rules prevent the home from being classified as a residence under Sec. 280A, thus preventing the application of the limitations.

For purposes of the residence test, a day of personal use includes any of the following:

▶ Any day the taxpayer or the taxpayer's family uses the property for personal purposes. Family is defined here as including taxpayer's spouse, brothers and sisters, ancestors, and lineal descendants.[47]

▶ Any day any individual uses the property under a reciprocal-use arrangement.[48]

▶ Any day any individual used the property and does not pay a fair rental for its use.[49]

Despite the family-use rule, if a taxpayer rents property at a fair rental to a family member who uses the property as a principal residence, such use does not constitute personal use by the taxpayer.

EXAMPLE I:6-41 ▶

During the current year, Peggy purchases a small house as an investment and rents the property to Stan, her married son, who uses the property as his principal residence. Peggy's son pays her a fair rental for the property. Because Stan uses the property as his principal residence and pays Peggy a fair rental for the property, Stan's personal use of the property does not constitute personal use by Peggy. Thus, the rules of Sec. 280A do not apply to limit the expenses that Peggy may deduct (although the passive loss rules may limit the deduction). ◀

KEY POINT

A second home is classified as either rental property, a residence, or some combination of the two. If it is classified as some combination of rental property and a residence, the expenses of the property must be allocated between the two categories.

ALLOCATION OF EXPENSES. The tax law requires allocation of the expenses related to the property between personal use and rental use. Generally, the tax law disallows a deduction for expenses allocable to personal use. However, qualified mortgage interest and real estate taxes are deductible even when allocated to personal use because such expenses are deductible on personal residences.[50] Expenses allocated to the rental use are deductible under Sec. 280A, but only to the extent of the gross income generated by the property. The property may not generate a loss used to reduce other income of the taxpayer. The taxpayer may carry over and deduct in a subsequent year expenses that are not currently deductible because they exceed the gross income from the property. However, the subsequent deduction may not exceed the gross income of the property for the subsequent year.[51] The order for deduction of the expenses allocated to the rental use of property is the same as the order for deduction of hobby losses under the rules of Sec. 183. Example I:6-40 illustrates these rules.

Allocation Formula. Sec. 280A uses the following formula to allocate expenses between the personal use and the rental use of the property:[52]

$$\text{Rental use expenses} = \frac{\text{Number of rental days}}{\text{Total number of days used}} \times \frac{\text{Total expenses}}{\text{for the year}}$$

The denominator of the allocation fraction is the sum of the days the property is rented plus the days the taxpayer uses it for personal purposes. The formula does not include the days that no one uses the property.

Some courts have modified the allocation formula by allowing the use of the total number of days in the year as the denominator for qualified residential interest and taxes.[53] Use of this ratio allocates less interest and taxes to the rental use, allowing more of the other expenses to be deducted against the rental income. Subject to limitations, the interest and taxes not allocated to the rental use are still deductible as itemized deductions. Example I:6-43 uses the allocation formula sanctioned by the courts.

---

[47] Sec. 280A(d)(2). A day during which the taxpayer spends substantially full time on repairs and maintenance does not count as a personal-use day.

[48] Sec. 280A(d)(2)(B). A reciprocal-use arrangement is one whereby another person uses the taxpayer's property in exchange for the taxpayer's use of the other person's property.

[49] Sec. 280A(d)(2)(C). Exactly what constitutes a fair rental must be determined by an examination of all the associated facts and circumstances.

[50] No deduction is allowed for interest incurred with respect to a personal residence if the debt on which the interest is paid is not secured by the property or the taxpayer has not chosen the property as a second residence for purposes of deducting the interest as qualified residential interest (see Chapter

I:7). For purposes of the discussion and examples used here, the assumption is made that the interest qualifies as qualified residential interest.

[51] Sec. 280A(c)(5)(B). The expenses that are carried over to the subsequent year are deductible to the extent of the property's gross income of that year, even though the property is not used by the taxpayer as a residence during that year.

[52] Sec. 280A(e)(1).

[53] *Dorance D. Bolton v. CIR*, 51 AFTR 2d 83-305, 82-2 USTC ¶9699 (9th Cir., 1982). See also *Edith G. McKinney v. CIR*, 52 AFTR 2d 83-6281, 83-2 USTC ¶9655 (10th Cir., 1983).

EXAMPLE I:6-42 ▶

Joan owns a cabin near the local ski resort. During the year, Joan and Joan's family use the cabin a total of 25 days. Joan also rents the cabin to out-of-state skiers for a total of 50 days during the year, generating rental income of $10,000. Joan incurs the following expenses:

Expense	Amount
Property taxes	$1,500
Interest on mortgage	3,000
Utilities	2,000
Insurance	1,500
Security and snow removal	2,500

Joan would have been entitled to $12,000 depreciation if the property had been entirely rental property held for investment. However, because the property is also used for personal purposes, the amount of deductions (for AGI) Joan may take with respect to the property during the year is as follows:

Item	Calculation	Amount
Rental income		$10,000
Interest and taxes	$4,500 \times \dfrac{50}{365}$	(616)[a]
All other expenses except depreciation	$6,000 \times \dfrac{50}{75}$	(4,000)
Depreciation	$12,000 \times \dfrac{50}{75}$	(5,384)[b]
Net income from property		$0

The income and these expenses are reported on Schedule E. Thus, the expenses allocated to the rental use are *for* AGI deductions. In addition to the deductions above, Joan may also deduct $3,884 ($4,500 − $616) interest and taxes as itemized deductions on Schedule A if the interest is qualified residence interest (see Chapter I:7) and her total itemized deductions exceed her standard deduction.

[a] Under the approach favored by the IRS, $3,000 ($4,500 × 50/75) of interest and taxes would be used to offset the gross income and only $3,000 of depreciation would be deductible.
[b] $8,000 of the depreciation is allocated to the rental use (50/75 × $12,000). Since the deduction for depreciation is limited to $5,384, the additional $2,616 ($8,000 − $5,384) can be carried over and deducted in the next year if the gross income of that year is sufficient to cover all the expenses allocable to the rental use. If there had been sufficient gross income, Joan could have taken $8,000 depreciation. ◀

NOMINAL NUMBER OF RENTAL DAYS. If a property qualifies as a taxpayer's residence under Sec. 280A and the taxpayer rents the property for less than 15 days during the year, the law takes the approach that the property is completely personal in nature. As such, the taxpayer does not have to report the rental income and cannot deduct any of the related expenses. However, expenses such as qualified residential interest and taxes may still be deductible as itemized deductions. (See Chapter I:7 for a discussion of the limitations on interest.)

EXAMPLE I:6-43
KEY POINT

Assume the same facts as in Example I:6-42, except that during the year Joan rents the cabin out for only 12 days and the amount of rental income is $2,400. The cabin qualifies as Joan's residence because her personal use exceeds 14 days. Because the cabin is rented for less than 15 days during the year, Joan may only take itemized deductions of $4,500 for the qualified residential interest and taxes. She may not deduct the other expenses. In addition, she does not include the $2,400 in gross income. ◀

NOMINAL NUMBER OF PERSONAL USE DAYS. If a taxpayer does not have enough personal use days during the year to qualify the property as a residence (i.e., the personal use is not more than the greater of 14 days or 10% of the rental days), the Sec. 280A rules and limitations do not apply. In such a case the taxpayer must still allocate the expenses of the property between the personal use and the rental use days. The taxpayer may deduct the taxes allocated to the personal use as an itemized deduction. However, since the property does not qualify as the taxpayer's residence, the taxpayer may not deduct any of the interest allocated to the personal use because the interest is not "qualified residential interest" (see Chapter I:7 for a discussion of the deductibility of personal interest and qualified residential

interest). The taxpayer may not deduct the tier 2 and 3 expenses allocated to the personal use. The income from the property and all of the expenses allocated to the rental use are reported on Schedule E of Form 1040. As such, the expenses are *for* AGI deductions. Any net income or loss from the property is subject to the Sec. 469 passive loss rules, which may limit the deductibility of any losses from the property (see Chapter I:8).

EXAMPLE I:6-44 ▶ Assume the same facts as in Example I:6-42 except that Joan and her family use the cabin only 10 days during the year and rent it out for 65 days of the year. Since Joan does not personally use the cabin for at least 14 days, the cabin is not considered her residence and the Sec. 280A rules do not apply. Instead, the interest allocated to the personal use is not deductible because it is not "qualified residential interest." Furthermore, the passive loss rules apply to the net income or loss from the property.

	Calculation	Amount
Rental income		$10,000
Interest	$ 3,000 × $\frac{65}{75}$	(2,600)[a]
Taxes	$ 1,500 × $\frac{65}{75}$	(1,300)[a]
Other expenses	$ 6,000 × $\frac{65}{75}$	(5,200)
Depreciation	$12,000 × $\frac{65}{75}$	(10,400)
	Total	$ (9,500)[b]

[a] Joan would treat the remaining $200 in taxes ($1,500 − $1,300) as an itemized deduction. However, Joan may not deduct the remaining $400 ($3,000 − $2,600) interest because it does not qualify as deductible residential interest.
[b] The deductibility of this $9,500 loss may be limited by the passive loss rules (see Chapter I:8). ◀

The rule of Sec. 280A regarding the rental of residential property is summarized in Figure I:6-4.

EXPENSES OF AN OFFICE IN THE HOME

Unless the taxpayer meets certain strictly imposed requirements, Sec. 280A disallows any deduction for home office expenses. In general, for a taxpayer to deduct office-in-home expenses, the taxpayer must use the office regularly and exclusively as either of the following:

▶ The principal place of business for a trade or business of the taxpayer, or

▶ A place where the taxpayer meets or deals with clients in the normal course of business.

The term "principal place of business" includes a home office used by the taxpayer for administrative or management activities of the business if no other fixed location exists where the taxpayer conducts these administrative or managerial activities.

For employees to take a deduction for home office expenses, the use must also have been for the convenience of the employer. In addition, a separate structure not attached to the taxpayer's house may qualify if regularly and exclusively used in connection with the taxpayer's business. (See Chapter I:9 for a comprehensive discussion of these rules.)

TAX PLANNING CONSIDERATIONS

HOBBY LOSSES

Deductions for expenses incurred in a hobby activity may not exceed the gross income generated by the hobby for the year. However, if the gross income exceeds the deductions from the activity in at least three out of five consecutive years (two out of seven for activities involving the breeding, training, showing, or racing of horses), tax law presumes the activity is a business, and the limits on the deductibility of expenses do not apply. Thus, if

(a) Personal use is more than the larger of (1) 14 days or (2) 10% of rental days.
(b) In order for the interest to be deductible, it must be "qualified residence interest" (see Chapter 7).
(c) In order for the interest to be deductible as qualified residence, the property must not have been rented at all during the year. If the property has been rented out, the interest allocated to personal use is not deductible (see Chapter 7).

FIGURE I:6-4 ▶ SECTION 280A: LIMITATION OF DEDUCTIONS ON RENTAL OF RESIDENTIAL PROPERTY

possible, taxpayers should use care in timing the realization of items of income and expense. For example, if an activity has shown a profit in only two out of the previous four years, a taxpayer may consider accelerating some of the income into the fifth year or deferring some of the expenses of the activity into the following year. Under the cash method of accounting, this can be done by delaying payment for some of the expenses or accelerating income-generating transactions. Note that meeting the three-out-of-five-year test does not automatically ensure the activity will be treated as a business. It merely compels the IRS to prove the activity is *not* a business. Under these circumstances, the IRS is less likely to challenge the deductions.

UNREASONABLE COMPENSATION

If the IRS feels that a salary payment to an officer of a corporation is excessive, it may recharacterize the excess portion as a dividend. If that happens, the corporation cannot deduct the full amount of the salary payment. To prevent a potential future disallowance, the parties may enter into a payback or hedge agreement, which provides that the employee must return to the corporation any payment held to be excessive. Under such an agreement, the employee receives a *for* AGI deduction for any amount he or she repays to the corporation. This deduction is available in the year of repayment. A payback agreement must meet the following requirements to be effective:

▶ The parties must enter into the agreement before actually making the payment.

▶ It must legally obligate the employee to repay the excess amount.[54]

[54] *Vincent E. Oswald*, 49 T.C. 645 (1968) and *J. G. Pahl*, 67 T.C. 286 (1976). See also *Ernest H. Berger*, 37 T.C. 1026 (1962).

WHAT WOULD YOU DO IN THIS SITUATION?

SERIOUS WINE OR HOBBY LOSS?

Mr. Bouteilles Gerbeuses has been your long-time tax client. He has amassed an impressive portfolio of real estate, securities, and joint venture investments. His net worth is substantial.

Despite all his material well-being, Mr. Gerbeuses wants to take on a new challenge—that of producing fine wines. He has not had any formal wine training but he has decided to start his own winery, named *Cuvée de Prestige.* He will pattern it after the great wine houses of Europe.

He already owns several hundred acres of agriculturally zoned land in the wine producing region of the Noir Valley. It happens to adjoin his home in the Wemadeit Country Club and Retirement Resort subdivision. He anticipates a life of semi-retirement by engaging in the art of malolactic fermentation and blending of his *blanc de blancs* and *pinot noir* grapes into his own estate wine. He expects his start-up capital investment to be over $5 million and does not expect the first harvest to take place for at least seven years after the initial planting of grape vines. He expects to offset any losses by his other income.

Assuming Mr. Gerbeuses comes to you for tax advice on his new wine venture, what tax and ethical issues should be considered?

The IRS may take the position that the existence of the payback agreement itself is evidence that the compensation is excessive. The corporation and employees can avoid this situation if they include the agreement in the general corporate bylaws rather than in a specific contract with a particular employee.[55]

TIMING OF DEDUCTIONS

Because of the time value of money, taxpayers generally prefer to deduct an expenditure as a current expense rather than capitalize it and spread the deductions over the next several years as depreciation or amortization. In addition, some capital expenditures (e.g., land) are not subject to depreciation or amortization. In some situations, however, the taxpayer may prefer to capitalize rather than expense a particular item. For example, if a taxpayer has net operating losses (NOLs) that are about to expire, a current deduction may prevent the use of these losses.[56]

In some cases it is difficult to determine whether an item should be treated as a capital expenditure or a deduction item (e.g., certain repairs may require capitalization). In addition, the taxpayer may elect to either capitalize or expense certain types of expenditures—such as those for research and experimentation. A tax practitioner should give consideration to the taxpayer's tax situation when making this decision. In making this decision, taxpayers and their advisors should consider NOL carryovers that might be expiring. They should also compare their current marginal tax rate with their anticipated future marginal tax rate.

COMPLIANCE AND PROCEDURAL CONSIDERATIONS

PROPER CLASSIFICATION OF DEDUCTIONS

Individuals report trade or business expenses on Schedule C (Profit or Loss from Business or Profession). It is similar to an income statement for business-related income and expenses. Income reported on Form 1040 includes the net income computed on Schedule C,

---

[55] *Charles Schneider and Co. v. CIR,* 34 AFTR 2d 74-5422, 74-2 USTC ¶9563 (8th Cir., 1974). See also *Plastics Universal Corp.,* 1979 PH T.C. Memo ¶79,355, 39 TCM 32. Additionally, some taxpayers have been successful in defending their current level of compensation where they proved that they had been undercompensated in prior years. See *Acme Construction Co., Inc.,* 1995 RIA T.C. Memo ¶95,600, 69 TCM 1596.

[56] A NOL arises when business expenses exceed business income for a year. This excess can be carried to another year (generally back two years and forward twenty years) and is deducted against the income of that year. If the years to which the NOL is carried do not have enough income, the NOL is lost when the carryover period expires. See Chapter I:8 for a discussion of NOLs.

SELF-STUDY
QUESTION
A professor in the Department of Accounting also teaches continuing education courses for the state CPA society as a sole proprietor. If she is a member of the state CPA society, are her dues deductible on Schedule C or as an itemized deduction?

ANSWER
Certainly, she would prefer to have the dues deductible on Schedule C so that they will not be subject to the 2% limit on miscellaneous itemized deductions. This question demonstrates the difficulty of classifying some deductions, and the answer probably depends on the primary reason for membership in the organization.

ADDITIONAL
COMMENT
When a taxpayer elects to defer the determination of whether a particular activity is engaged in for profit, the statute of limitations is automatically extended for all years in the postponement period. However, the automatic extension applies only to items that might be disallowed under the hobby loss rules.

because the process of arriving at the taxable income from the business involves deducting business-related expenses. Thus, these expenses are deductions *for* AGI. Similar treatment is given to expenses attributable to the production of rental and royalty income reported on Schedule E, which is an income statement. The other deductions *for* AGI have specific lines on Form 1040 itself.[57] All of these deductions appear before line 37 (where AGI appears) of Form 1040.

Deductions *from* AGI are reported on Schedule A, where they are totaled and then transferred to Line 40 of Form 1040.

A filled-in Schedule C is provided in Appendix B.

PROPER SUBSTANTIATION

The burden of proving the deductibility of any expense generally rests on the taxpayer. This has always been the case. However, in recent years Congress and the IRS have become increasingly concerned about the propriety of many deductions. In the case of travel and entertainment expenses, the Code states that taxpayers may not take a deduction for an improperly documented expense. This documentation must include the amount of the expense, the time and place of the travel or entertainment activity, the business purpose, and the business relationship of the people entertained.

BUSINESS VERSUS HOBBY

Self-employed individuals who claim a home office deduction on Schedule C must attach a Form 8829, used to allocate direct and indirect expenses to the appropriate use. Form 8829 need not be filed by employees who claim home office expenses on Form 2106.

When an activity has both profit-making and personal attributes, the burden is normally on the taxpayer to prove that the activity is a business. However, if a taxpayer can show that the activity has generated a profit in at least three out of five consecutive years (two out of seven for activities involving the breeding, training, showing, and racing of horses), the burden of proof shifts to the IRS. Because the statute of limitations generally runs three years after a return is filed for any particular year (i.e., for audit purposes the year closes and the IRS cannot assess any tax deficiency for that year), a potential problem exists for taxpayers who want to rely on this presumption during the first year or two of an activity's life. In these cases, the taxpayer may elect to defer the determination of whether the presumption applies until the fifth (seventh) year of operation. The election keeps the year in question open with respect to that activity until sufficient years have passed to allow for application of the presumptive test. If the taxpayer subsequently does not meet the presumptive test, the IRS can still assess a deficiency for that activity for the prior year, because the year is still open. A taxpayer makes the election by filing Form 5213 (Election to Postpone Determination as to Whether the Presumption That an Activity Is Engaged In for Profit Applies) within three years after the due date for the year in which the taxpayer first engages in the activity.

PROBLEM MATERIALS

DISCUSSION QUESTIONS

I:6-1 Why is the distinction between deductions *for* AGI and deductions *from* AGI important for individuals?

I:6-2 Sam owns a small house that he rents out to students attending the local university. Are the expenses associated with the rental unit deductions *for* or *from* AGI?

I:6-3 During the year, Sara sold a capital asset at a loss of $2,000. She had held the asset as an investment. This is the only capital asset she sold during the year. Is her deduction for this capital loss a deduction *for* or a deduction *from* AGI?

---

[57] Some of these expenses, such as employee business expenses (Form 2106) and moving expenses (Form 3903), are summarized on separate forms. These separate forms, however, are not net income statements in the same sense as Schedules C and E.

I:6-4   Discuss the difference in tax treatment between reimbursed employee business expenses and unreimbursed employee business expenses.

I:6-5   For the current year, Mario, a single individual with no dependents, receives income of $55,000 and incurs deductible expenses of $9,000.
   a. What is Mario's taxable income assuming that the expenses are deductions *for* AGI?
   b. What is Mario's taxable income assuming that the expenses are miscellaneous itemized deductions *from* AGI?

I:6-6   Deductible business or investment expenses must be related to a profit-motivated activity.
   a. What are the factors used in determining whether an activity is profit-motivated?
   b. Why are these factors so important in making this determination?

I:6-7   If an activity does not generate a profit in three out of five consecutive years, is it automatically deemed to be a hobby? Why or why not?

I:6-8   Because expenses incurred both in a business and for the production of investment income are deductible, why is it important to determine in which category a particular activity falls?

I:6-9   In order for a business expense to be deductible it must be *ordinary, necessary,* and *reasonable.* Explain what these terms mean.

I:6-10   What are the criteria for distinguishing between a deductible expense and a capital expenditure?

I:6-11   Why are expenses related to tax-exempt income disallowed?

I:6-12   Under what circumstances may a taxpayer deduct an illegal bribe or kickback?

I:6-13   Michelle pays a CPA $400 for the preparation of her federal income tax return. Michelle's only sources of income are her salary from employment and interest and dividends from her investments.
   a. Is this a deductible expense? If so, is it a deduction *for* or *from* AGI?
   b. Assume the same facts as in Part a except that in addition to her salary and investment and dividend income, Michelle also owns a small business. Of the $400 fee paid to the CPA, $250 is for the preparation of her Schedule C (Profit or Loss from Business). How much, if any, of the $400 is a deductible expense? Identify it as either *for* or *from* AGI.

I:6-14   Otter Corporation sends people to its state capital to lobby the legislature to build a proposed highway that is planned to run through the area where its business is located.
   a. If Otter Corp. incurs $3,200 of expenses, what part, if any, of its expenses are deductible?
   b. Would it make a difference if the proposed road were a city road rather than a state highway, and Otter lobbied its local government?
   c. Assume the same facts in Part a except that Otter's total expenses are $1,500. Are these expenses deductible?

I:6-15   During November and December of last year, Tommy's, Inc., incurred the following expenses in investigating the feasibility of opening a new restaurant in town:

Expenses to do a market survey	$3,800
Expenses to identify potential suppliers of goods	$2,000
Expenses to identify a proper location	$1,000

Explain the proper treatment of these expenses under the following scenarios:
   a. Tommy's, Inc., already owns another restaurant in town and is wanting to expand. Tommy's, Inc. opens the new restaurant in February of the current year.
   b. Assume that Tommy's, Inc. is in the book selling business and feels that its bookstore business is not making a high enough return and it wants to move into the restaurant business. It opens the restaurant in February of the current year.
   c. Same as Part b except Tommy's decides against opening a restaurant after getting back the results of the investigation.

I:6-16   What documentation is required in order for a travel or entertainment expense to be deductible?

I:6-17   Under what circumstances can prepaid expenses be deducted in the year of payment by a taxpayer using the cash method of accounting?

I:6-18   Under what circumstances would a taxpayer use both the cash method and the accrual method of accounting at the same time?

I:6-19   Whether the economic performance test is satisfied depends on the type of transaction and whether the transaction is recurring.
   a. When does economic performance occur for a taxpayer who must provide property or services to another person?
   b. When does economic performance occur when another person provides the taxpayer with property or services?
   c. Explain the exception to the economic performance test for recurring liabilities.

I:6-20   Why did Congress enact the wash sale provisions?

I:6-21   The wash sale rules disallow a loss in the year of sale when substantially identical stock or securities are acquired by the taxpayer within a 61-day period. What types of stock or securities are considered substantially identical?

I:6-22   Under Sec. 267, current deductions may not be taken for certain transactions between related parties.
   a. Who is considered a member of a taxpayer's family under the related party transaction rules of Sec. 267?
   b. Identify some of the other relationships that are considered related parties for purposes of

Sec. 267. Why are these other relationships included in the definition?

I:6-23   Under the related party rules of Sec. 267, why has Congress imposed the concept of constructive ownership?

I:6-24   If property is sold at a loss to a related taxpayer, under what circumstances can at least partial benefit be derived from the disallowed loss?

I:6-25   Assume that Jill is engaged in painting as a hobby. During the year, she earns $1,000 from sales of her paintings and incurs $1,300 expenses for supplies and lessons. Jill's salary from her job is $70,000. What is the tax treatment of the hobby income and expenses?

I:6-26   Under Sec. 280A, what constitutes personal use of a vacation home by the taxpayer?

I:6-27   Under Sec. 280A, how are expenses allocated to the rental use of a vacation home? In what order must the expenses be deducted against the gross income of the property?

I:6-28   Under Sec. 280A, how will a taxpayer report the income and expenses of a vacation home if it is rented out for only 12 days during the year?

ISSUE IDENTIFICATION QUESTIONS

I:6-29   David, a CPA for a large accounting firm, works 10- to 12-hour days. As a requirement for his position, he must attend social events to recruit new clients. In addition to his job with the accounting firm, he also has private clients in his unincorporated professional practice. David purchased exercise equipment for $3,000. He works out on the equipment to maintain his stamina and good health that enable him to carry such a heavy workload. What tax issues should David consider?

I:6-30   Gus, a football player who was renegotiating his contract with the Denver Broncos, paid his ex-girlfriend $25,000 to drop a sexual assault complaint against him and keep the matter confidential. The Broncos stated that if criminal charges were filed and made public, they would terminate his employment. What tax issues should Gus consider?

I:6-31   Kathleen pays $3,000 mortgage interest on the home that she and her husband live in. Kathleen and her husband live with Molly, Kathleen's mother. The title to the home is in Kathleen's name. However, the mortgage is Molly's obligation. Kathleen claims Molly as her dependent on her current tax return. What tax issues should Kathleen consider?

I:6-32   Katie and Alan are avid boaters and water skiers. They also enjoy parasailing. This year, they started a new parasailing venture to give rides to patrons. Katie and Alan are both employed full-time in other pursuits, but they take patrons out during the summer months, on weekends and holidays. Alan has attended classes on boat operation and parasailing instruction. Katie and Alan have owned a boat for four years, but because of the heavy usage this summer, they replaced their old boat in July. They plan on replacing their boat with a new one every two years now. They use their boat in the parasailing activity and for recreational purposes. This year, Katie and Alan earned $5,400 from chartering activities and incurred $11,600 of expenses associated with their boating and parasailing. What tax issues should Katie and Alan consider?

PROBLEMS

I:6-33   *For or From AGI Deductions.* Roberta is an accountant employed by a local firm. During the year, Roberta incurs the following unreimbursed expenses:

Item	Amount
Travel to client locations	$750
Subscriptions to professional journals	215
Taking potential clients to lunch	400
Photocopying	60

a. Identify which of these expenses are deductible and the amount that is deductible. Indicate whether they are deductible *for* or *from* AGI.

b. Would the answers to Part a change if the accounting firm reimburses Roberta for these expenses?

c. Assume all of the same facts as in Part a, except that Roberta is self-employed. Identify which of the expenses are deductible, and indicate whether they are deductions *for* or *from* AGI.

I:6-34   *For vs. from AGI.* During the current year, Kent, a single taxpayer, reports the following items of income and expense:

Income:	
Salary	$150,000
Dividends from Alta Corporation	800
Interest income from a savings account	1,500
Rental income from a small apartment he owns	8,000
Expenses:	
Medical	6,000
Interest on a principal residence	7,000
Real property taxes on the principal residence	4,300
Charitable contributions	4,000
Casualty loss—personal	6,100
Miscellaneous itemized deductions	1,200
Loss from the sale of Delta Corporation stock (held for two years)	2,000
Expenses incurred on the rental apartment:	
Maintenance	500
Property taxes	1,000
Utilities	2,400
Depreciation	1,700
Insurance	800
Alimony payments to former wife	10,000

Assuming all of these items are deductible and that the amounts are before any limitations, what is Kent's taxable income for the year?

I:6-35   *Capitalization vs. Expense.* Rentals R Us incurs the following expenditures on an apartment building it owns:

Item	Amount
Replace the roof	$25,000
Repaint the exterior	7,000
Install new locks	1,500
Replace broken windows	1,200
Replace crumbling sidewalks and stairs	7,000

Discuss the proper tax treatment for these expenditures.

I:6-36   *Political Contributions and Lobbying Expenses.* Eljay, LLP owns several apartment complexes and office buildings. The leasing and management of these buildings constitutes Eljay's only business activity. During the current year Eljay incurred the following:

- $900 in airfare and lodging incurred on a trip to Washington, D.C. The purpose of the trip was to protest proposed tax rate increases for individuals and corporations.

- $700 for renting space on billboards along the highway. The billboards express its concern regarding pending legislation that would significantly increase property taxes.

- $500 in airfare and hotel bills incurred on a trip to the state capital. The purpose of the trip was to meet with the legislative subcommittee on property taxation.

- $50 for a subscription to a political newsletter published by a national political party.

- $150 in making a presentation to the county council protesting a proposed increase in the property tax levy.

a. What is the total amount Eljay may deduct because of these expenditures?
b. Assume all the same facts as in Part a except that the expenses for the trip to the state capital are only $300 instead of $500. What amount may Eljay deduct because of these expenditures?

I:6-37   *Legal and Accounting Expenses.* Sam is a sole proprietor who owns, leases, and manages several apartment complexes and office buildings. During the current year, Sam incurs the following expenses. Which of these expenditures are deductible? Are they *for* or *from* AGI deductions?

a. $200 in attorney's fees for title searches on a new property Sam has acquired.
b. $450 in legal fees in an action brought to collect back rents.

c. $500 to his CPA for the preparation of his federal income tax return. $400 is for the preparation of Schedule C (Profit or Loss from Business).

d. $300 in attorney's fees for drafting a will.

e. $250 in attorney's fees in an unsuccessful attempt to prevent the city from rezoning the area of the city where several of his office buildings are located.

I:6-38   *Illegal Payments.* Damian Corporation is engaged in the business of purchasing and importing carpets from Iran. Importing these carpets from Iran is illegal. Following is a list of income and expense items for the year:

Item	Amount
Sales	$750,000
Cost of goods sold	270,000
Salaries	75,000
Freight	22,500
Bribes to customs officials	30,000
Lease payments on warehouses	15,000
Interest expense	12,000

a. What is the taxable income of Damian Corporation from the illegal business activity?

b. Assume the same facts as in Part a except that Damian's business consists of buying and selling marijuana and cocaine. What is Damian's taxable income from this illegal business activity?

I:6-39   *Illegal Payments.* Indicate whether Glenda can deduct the $5,000 payment in each of the following independent situations.

a. Glenda is a supplier of medical supplies. In order to secure a large sales contract to the regional Veterans Administration Hospital, Glenda makes a gift of $5,000 to the hospital's purchasing agent. The payment is illegal under state law.

b. Assume the same facts as in Part a, except that the payment is made to the purchasing agent of a government-owned hospital in Brazil.

c. Assume the same facts in Part a, except that the payment is made to the purchasing agent of a privately owned hospital in Idaho.

I:6-40   *Business Investigation Expenditures.* During January and February of the current year, Big Bang LLC incurs $3,000 in travel, feasibility studies, and legal expenses to investigate the feasibility of opening a new entertainment gallery in one of the new suburban malls in town. Big Bang already owns two other entertainment galleries in other malls in town.

a. What is the proper tax treatment of these expenses if Big Bang decides not to open the new gallery?

b. What is the proper tax treatment of these expenses if Big Bang decides to open the new gallery?

I:6-41   *Business Investigation Expenditures.* Assume the same facts as in Problem I:6-40, except that Big Bang LLC incurs $41,000 in expenses, it does *not* already own the other entertainment galleries and it does not own anything similar.

a. What is the proper tax treatment of these expenses if Big Bang does not open the new gallery?

b. What is the proper tax treatment of these expenses if Big Bang decides to open the new gallery on May 1 of the current year?

I:6-42   *Timing of Expense Recognition.* Solutions Corporation, a computer vendor and consulting company, uses the accrual method of accounting. Its tax year is the calendar year. The following are three of the corporation's transactions during the current year:

1. Solutions Corporation hired a contractor to remodel its sales floor. The contractor completed the remodeling on November 30. On December 15, Solutions received a $21,000 bill from the contractor. Solutions immediately contacted the contractor to contest the $8,000 labor charge included in the total bill, which Solutions claims should only be $7,000. Solutions made no payment on the bill.

2. Solutions offers a 2-year warranty on all of its computer systems. For sales of computers in the current year, it paid $11,500 to service warranties during the current tax year, and it expects to pay $12,000 to fulfill the remaining warranty obligations next year.

3. Every year, Solutions offers a series of six trade seminars from November 1 through March 31. It receives all registration fees from participants by October 1, before the

seminars begin. As of December 31, two of the six seminars are completed, and the next seminar is scheduled for January 14–15. The expenses incurred in performing the seminars are routine each year. On the first of each month from November through March, Solutions pays the $625 monthly rent for the seminar location. On September 16, Solutions signs a contract with the seminar teacher, a computers expert and excellent public speaker. The contract requires Solutions to pay the teacher $900 after each seminar, a total of $5,400. On October 3, Solutions signs a contract with a local printing company, which will provide text materials for the seminars. Solutions pays the printer $350 after each seminar's materials are delivered the day before the seminar.

Required:

a. How should Solutions Corporation treat these transactions? What rules apply?

b. How would your answer change if Solutions Corporation were a cash-method taxpayer?

I:6-43 *Prepaid Expenses.* Pamello, Inc., an engineering consulting firm, uses the cash method of accounting. Compute the amount of Pamello's current year deductions for the following transactions:

a. On November 1 of the current year, it entered into a lease to rent some office space for five years. The lease agreement states that the lease payments are $12,000 per year, payable in advance each November 1 for the following 12-month period. Under the terms of the lease, Pamello is required to pay a $5,000 deposit, refundable upon the termination of the lease.

b. On December 1 of the current year, Pamello also renewed its malpractice insurance, paying $18,000 for the three-year contract.

c. On December 31 of the current year, Pamello mailed out a check for $5,000 for drafting services performed for it by an individual who lives in another city.

d. On December 31, the firm received a shipment of $700 worth of stationery and other office supplies. Pamello has an open charge account with the office supply company, which bills the firm monthly for charges made during the year.

e. Finally, on December 31, Pamello picked up some work that a local printing company had done for it, which amounted to $1,000. The firm charged the $1,000 with its corporate credit card.

I:6-44 *Prepaid Interest.* During the current year, Richard and Alisha, a married couple who use the cash method of accounting, purchased a principal residence for $320,000. They paid $40,000 down and financed the remaining $280,000 of the purchase price with a 30-year mortgage. At the closing, they also paid $500 for an appraisal, $500 for a title search, and 1.5 points representing additional interest over the term of the loan. At the end of the year, Richard and Alisha received a statement from the mortgage company indicating that $12,000 of their total monthly payments made during the year represents interest and $1,000 is a reduction of the principal balance.

a. What is the total amount Richard and Alisha may deduct in the current year arising from the purchase and ownership of their home?

b. What is the treatment of the other items that are not deductible?

I:6-45 *Wash Sales.* Broward Corp. owns 1,500 shares of Silver Fox Corporation common stock. Broward Corp. purchased the 1,500 shares on April 17, 2006, for $20,000. On December 8, 2010, Broward sells 750 shares for $5,000. On January 2, 2011, Broward Corp. buys 250 shares of Silver Fox Corporation common stock for $1,750 and 50 shares of Silver Fox Corporation preferred stock for $1,000. The preferred stock is nonvoting, nonconvertible.

a. What is Broward's realized and recognized loss on the December 8 sale of stock?

b. What is Broward's basis and the holding periods of the stock?

I:6-46 *Wash Sales.* Cougar Corporation owns 1,000 shares of Western Corporation common stock, which it purchased on March 8, 2005, for $12,000. On October 3, 2010, Cougar purchases an additional 300 shares for $3,000. On October 12, 2010, it sells the original 1,000 shares for $8,500. On November 1, 2010, it purchases an additional 500 shares for $4,000.

a. What is Cougar's recognized gain or loss as a result of the sale on October 12, 2010?

b. What are the basis and the holding period of the stock Cougar continues to hold?

c. How would your answers to Parts a and b change if the stock Cougar purchases during 2010 is Western nonvoting, nonconvertible, preferred stock instead of Western common stock?

I:6-47   *Constructive Ownership.* During the current year, Troy sells land to Berry Corporation for $165,000. Troy purchased the land in 2000 for $170,000. The Berry Corporation is owned as follows:

Owner	Percentage Ownership
Tom (Troy's son)	20%
Jimmy (Troy's cousin)	15%
Jimmy's father (Troy's uncle)	30%
Angie (Troy's wife)	10%
Nicole (Angie's Sister)	25%

Troy and Jimmy are equal partners in a separate entity, TJ Partnership.
a. What is Troy's constructive ownership in Berry Corporation?
b. What is the amount of loss Troy may recognize?
c. How would your answers to Parts a and b change if TJ Partnership owned 25%, instead of Nicole?

I:6-48   *Constructive Ownership.* PIB Partnership is owned 20% by Shore, 40% by Steve, and 40% by Thann. Burnham, Inc. is owned 70% by PIB Partnership, 10% by Ralph, 10% by Thann, and 10% by Shore. Ralph and Thann are brothers. All other individuals are unrelated. During the current year, Ralph sold a piece of land to Burnham, Inc., for $90,000. Ralph originally purchased the land as an investment a few years ago for $100,000.
a. How much of the loss may Ralph recognize?
b. Now assume all the same facts except that the sale occurred between Thann and Burnham, Inc. How much of the loss may Thann recognize?
c. Now assume the same facts as in b except that Burnham, Inc., is owned 60% by Shore and 40% by Ralph. Thann sells the land to Burnham, Inc. How much of the loss may Thann recognize?

I:6-49   *Related Party Transactions.* Sally is an attorney who computes her taxable income using the cash method of accounting. Sage Corporation, owned 40% by Sally's brother, 40% by her cousin, and 20% by her grandmother, uses the accrual method of accounting. Sally is a calendar-year taxpayer, whereas Sage Corporation's fiscal year ends on January 31. During 2010, Sally does some consulting work for Sage Corporation for a fee of $10,000. The work is completed on December 15 and Sage receives Sally's invoice on that date. For each of the following assumptions, answer the following questions: During which tax year must Sally report the income? During which tax year must Sage Corporation deduct the expense?
a. The payment to Sally is made on December 27, 2010.
b. The payment to Sally is made on January 12, 2011.
c. The payment to Sally is made on February 3, 2011.

I:6-50   *Related Party Transactions.* During the current year, CVI Corporation sells a tract of land for $75,000. The sale is made to Sandi, CVI Corporation's sole shareholder. CVI Corporation originally purchased the land five years earlier for $98,000.
a. What is the amount of gain or loss that CVI Corporation will recognize on the sale during the current year?
b. Assume that in the following year, Sandi sells the land for $85,000. What is the amount of gain or loss Sandi will recognize? What are the tax consequences to CVI Corporation upon the subsequent sale by Sandi?
c. Assume that in the following year, Sandi sells the land for $70,000. What is the amount of gain or loss Sandi will recognize?
d. Assume that in the following year, Sandi sells the land for $105,000. What is the amount of gain or loss Sandi will recognize?

I:6-51   *Hobby Loss Presumptive Rule.* Rachel Schutz is a high school English teacher. In her spare time, she likes to make her own body lotion, lip-gloss, and bath and shower gel. She uses the bath products herself and gives them to her friends and relatives as gifts. In 2009, Rachel started attending arts and crafts festivals to sell her products three or four times a year, and she hands out her business card so her customers can buy directly from her by phone or email. In 2009, Rachel reported a net loss of $375 from the activity. In 2010, she reported a loss of $460. Rachel is audited for the year 2010, and the agent disallows the $460 loss. Rachel is pretty sure she will make a profit on her sales in 2011, and she

assumes she will continue to make a profit after 2011. Rachel is not sure that she can prove that her activity is not a hobby right now. What can she do to avoid proving that her loss is not a hobby loss?

I:6-52 *Hobby Loss Presumptive Rule.* Emily is an interior decorator who does consulting work for several furniture stores. Additionally, she has been designing and creating rubber stamps for the past several years. She sells the stamps to local stationary and novelty shops. Emily has reported the following net income or loss from the rubber stamp activity:

Year	Net Income (Loss)
2005	$ 300
2006	(900)
2007	(400)
2008	600
2009	(550)
2010	(800)

Emily is audited for the year 2010, and the agent disallows the $800 loss. Can Emily make an election for 2010 to keep the year open in anticipation of meeting the presumptive rule for the year? Why or why not?

I:6-53 *Hobby Losses.* Chuck, a dentist, raises prize rabbits for breeding and showing purposes. Assume that the activity is determined to be a hobby. During the year the activity generates the following items of income and expense:

Item	Amount
Sale of rabbits for breeding stock	$800
Prizes and awards	300
Property taxes on rabbit hutches	200
Feed	600
Veterinary fees	500
Depreciation on rabbit hutches	250

a. What is the total amount of deductions Chuck may take during the year with respect to the rabbit raising activities?
b. Identify which expenses may be deducted and indicate whether they are deductions *for* or *from* AGI.
c. By what amount is the cost basis of the rabbit hutches to be reduced for the year?

I:6-54 *Hobby Losses.* Assume the same facts as in Problem I:6-53, except that the income from the sale of rabbits is $1,200.
a. What is the total amount of deductions Chuck may take during the year with respect to the rabbit raising activities?
b. Identify which expenses may be deducted and indicate whether they are deductions *for* or *from* AGI.
c. By what amount is the cost basis of the rabbit hutches to be reduced for the year?

I:6-55 *Rental of Vacation Home.* During the current year, Kim incurs the following expenses with respect to her beachfront condominium in Hawaii:

Item	Amount
Insurance	$ 500
Repairs and maintenance	700
Interest on mortgage	3,000
Property taxes	1,000
Utilities	800

In addition to the expenses listed above, Kim could have deducted a total of $8,000 depreciation if the property had been acquired only for investment purposes. During the year, Kim uses the condominium 20 days for vacation. She also rented it out for a total of 60 days during the year, generating a total gross income of $9,000.
a. What is the total amount of deductions for and from AGI that Kim may take during the current year with respect to the condominium?
b. What is the effect on the basis of the condominium?

I:6-56 *Rental of Vacation Home.* Assume all of the same facts as in Problem I:6-55, except that during the year Kim rents the condominium a total of 14 days. How does Kim report the income and deductions from the property?

COMPREHENSIVE PROBLEMS

I:6-57 Bryce, a bank official, is married and files a joint return. During 2010 he engages in the following activities and transactions:

a. Being an avid fisherman, Bryce develops an expertise in tying flies. At times during the year, he is asked to conduct fly-tying demonstrations, for which he is paid a small fee. He also periodically sells flies that he makes. Income generated from these activities during the year is $2,500. The expenses for the year associated with Bryce's fly-tying activity include $125 personal property taxes on a small trailer that he uses exclusively for this purpose, $2,900 in supplies, $270 in repairs on the trailer, and $200 in gasoline for traveling to the demonstrations.

b. Bryce sells a small building lot to his brother for $40,000. Bryce purchased the lot four years ago for $47,000, hoping to make a profit.

c. Bryce enters into the following stock transactions: (None of the stock qualifies as small business stock.)

Date	Transaction
March 22	Purchases 100 shares of Silver Corporation common stock for $2,800.
April 5	Sells 200 shares of Gold Corporation common stock for $8,000. The stock was originally purchased two years ago for $5,000.
April 15	Sells 200 shares of Silver Corporation common stock for $5,400. The stock was originally purchased three years ago for $9,400.
May 20	Sells 100 shares of United Corporation common stock for $12,000. The stock was originally purchased five years ago for $10,000.

d. Bryce's salary for the year is $115,000. In addition to the items above, he also incurs $5,000 in other miscellaneous deductible itemized expenses.

Answer the following questions regarding Bryce's activities for the year.

1. Compute Bryce's taxable income for the year.
2. What is Bryce's basis in the Silver stock he continues to own?

I:6-58 Using the following facts, answer the questions below concerning Jaron's 2010 tax liability.

1. Two years ago, in November, 2008, when his wife died, Jaron left the CPA firm he was working for and started his own practice so he could have more time to spend with his four children. Jaron's children are 14, 16, 19, and 24 years old, respectively. The three youngest live at home with their father. Danny, Jaron's 19-year-old son, graduated from high school a year ago and is currently working at a local golf course. Danny earned $17,000 in the current year. Jaron's oldest daughter, Laura, is married and lives in town with her husband, Chad. Laura graduated from college two years ago and now works for a local advertising agency. What are Jaron's filing status and personal and dependency exemptions for 2010?

2. Jaron rents a small office downtown where he meets with clients and conducts business while his children are at school. He keeps all his client files and business records in this office. After school, he uses a converted bedroom in their home as his office. The following expenses are allocated to his home office (by square feet):

a. Depreciation $2,150
b. Taxes $1,500
c. Utilities $75

Can Jaron claim a deduction for his home office?

3. Jaron owns a condominium downtown. He rented it out 270 days during the year. He also allowed Laura and her husband to stay in the home rent-free for 24 days while they were looking for a place to stay. Fortunately, the condominium wasn't rented during the time they needed it. The following items of annual income and expense relate to the condominium:

a. Rental income $18,000
b. Interest $3,150
c. Taxes $1,700
d. Other expenses $6,000
e. Depreciation $7,090

What is the tax treatment of the condominium for Jaron in 2010?

4. On April 6, Jaron sold a parcel of land he had held for investment to a real estate development firm for $75,000. He purchased the land three years earlier from his brother for $70,000. His brother had originally purchased the land for $74,000. What is the amount and character of Jaron's gain or loss on the sale of the land?

5. On May 1, Jaron purchased 1,000 shares in Genomics Ltd. for $10 per share. In December he was forced to sell all 1,000 shares at $8 per share to avoid a conflict of interest. What is the amount and character of Jaron's gain or loss on the sale of the stock?

6. Jaron reported the following items of income and expense from his consulting practice:
   a. Consulting fees received $185,000
   b. Wages expense $47,400
   c. Rent expense $20,000
   d. Depreciation $2,100
   e. Other expenses $17,000
   What is Jaron's net income from his consulting practice?

7. When asked about potential itemized deductions, Jaron mentions that his house is fully paid-off and he paid off his student loans decades ago. He did pay, however, $2,100 in property taxes in the current year. Can Jaron deduct the property taxes paid in 2009?

8. Calculate Jaron's 2010 income tax liability. Ignore any available credits and self employment taxes.

TAX STRATEGY PROBLEMS

I:6-59 Danielle Anderson, your client and a cash method taxpayer, works full-time at a music store located in a mall. She assists the manager in buying decisions, serves customers on the sales floor, and plays music to draw in customers. On the weekends, she plays in various orchestras, working as an independent contractor. She does not work under a business name, maintain an office, or maintain a separate bank account for her performing activities. She always pays her bills as soon as possible, well before the bill due date. In prior years, she has taken every allowable deduction related to the performing activities. Prior year returns show the following taxable income on her Schedule C:

2006	$(5,000)
2007	2,100
2008	3,000
2009	(1,800)

Danielle has come to you on December 12, 2010. She understands that the IRS can deny losses generated by her performing business if it determines the business is actually a hobby. Because of the uncertainty of the entertainment industry, she will likely continue to generate profits in some years and losses in others. Still, she continues the activities with the intent to earn a profit.

Danielle routinely sends bills to orchestra clients at the end of the month for work she performed during the month. Most of her clients, including the Springville Orchestra, send payment within ten days of when they receive her bill.

The following is a summary of the business' financial position for 2010 as of 12/20/2010:

Income received to date	$9,000
General expenses paid to date	9,200

Other items:	
Bill for refurbishing work on cello, due 1/2/2011	$ 300
Newspaper bill for monthly advertisement, due 1/14/2011	200
Printer bill for business cards, due 1/5/2011	500
Meals eaten while in transit to performance locations	150
Income for 12/3/2010 performance with the Springville Orchestra	1,000

What will you recommend to your client? What issues must you address? What actions will you take to ensure the most favorable tax outcome possible? What advice, if any, will you give your client for the future?

I:6-60 Peter Baumann, your client, wants to sell a printing press to Chamberlain Corporation for $50,000. Pete has used the press in his business for two years and its adjusted basis is

$90,000. The Coxmann Partnership; Chloe International, Inc.; Watts, Inc., and Raleigh Corporation own Chamberlain Corporation equally. Pete and Emily Cox each own 50% of the Coxmann Partnership. Emily owns 70% of Chloe International, Inc., and Pete's sister Susan owns the other 30%. Pete's brother, Brian, owns 100% of Watts, Inc. Wade and Catherine Chamberlain, friends of Pete, own Raleigh Corporation equally. Peter wants to know what the tax consequences will be if he sells the printing press to Chamberlain Corporation. In a memo to Pete, explain any tax consequences of the proposed sale and any alternatives that would provide a better result.

TAX FORM/RETURN PREPARATION PROBLEMS

I:6-61   Dave Stevens, age 34, is a self-employed physical therapist. His wife Sarah, age 31, teaches English as a Second Language at a local language school. Dave's Social Security number is 417-46-9403. Sarah's Social Security number is 528-95-6271. Sarah and Dave have three children—Andrew, age 8; Isaac, age 6; and Mira, age 3. The children's Social Security numbers are, respectively, 377-83-2836, 377-64-7283, and 377-17-1415. They live at 12637 Pheasant Run, West Bend, Oregon 74658. They paid $8,900 in qualified residence interest and $2,400 in property taxes on their home. They had cash charitable contributions of $14,000. They also paid $180 to a CPA for preparing their federal and state income tax returns for the prior year, $100 of which was for the preparation of Dave's Schedule C. Sarah and Dave earned interest on CDs of $3,200. Sarah's salary for the year is $32,000, from which $9,600 in federal income tax and $1,400 in state income tax were withheld. Dave's office is located at Suite 402, 942 Woodview Drive, Portland, Oregon 74624, and his employer ID number is 22-7584904. Dave has been practicing for four years, and he uses the cash method of accounting. During the current year, Dave recorded the following items of income:

Revenue from patient visits	$300,000
Interest earned on the office checking balance	225

The following expenses were recorded on the office books:

Property taxes on the office	$ 4,500
Mortgage interest on the office	12,000
Depreciation on the office	4,500
Malpractice insurance	37,500
Utilities	3,750
Office staff salaries	51,000
Rent payments on equipment	15,000
Office magazine subscriptions	150
Office supplies	24,000
Medical journals	330

Dave pays $50 annually for use of a safety deposit box to store certain confidential documents related to his business. In addition to his medical practice, Dave spends 15 hours every week managing his real estate investments. To make sure he is aware of all current investment strategies and best practices, he subscribes to the following journals:

Wall Street Journal	$150
U.S. News & World Report	55
Money Magazine	45

Dave also paid $30,000 in estimated federal income taxes. Prepare Dave and Sarah's tax return (Form 1040, Schedules A, B, C, and SE) for the current year. Disregard any tax credits for which they may be eligible.

I:6-62   Lyle and Kaye James are married, have two minor children, Jessica, age 8 and Jerron, age 4, and are filing a joint tax return in the current year. They are both employed. Lyle and Kaye, ages 38 and 37, respectively, have combined salaries of $240,000, from which $46,000 of federal income tax and $10,000 of state income tax are withheld. Lyle and Kaye own two homes. Their primary residence is located at 11620 N. Mount Ave., New Haven, Connecticut 22222, and their vacation home is on the beach in Fort Lauderdale, Florida. They often rent their vacation home to supplement their income. The following items are related to the James' ownership of the two homes:

Item	New Haven	Fort Lauderdale
Rental income	$ —	$15,000
Qualified residence interest	7,200	5,000
Property taxes	1,400	1,000
Utilities	1,000	1,300
Repairs	200	300
Depreciation	0	3,500
Advertising	0	200
Insurance	1,500	1,500

The James family used their Fort Lauderdale home 20 days during the year. They rented the vacation home 60 days during the year. Lyle and Kaye jointly purchase stock in various corporations and make the following transactions in the current year. (None of the stock qualifies as small business stock.)

Date	Transaction	Price Paid/Sold
2/15	Bought 50 shares of Lake common stock (they own no other Lake stock)	$1,000
5/14	Bought 100 shares of Bass common stock (they own no other Bass stock)	3,000
5/24	Sold 25 shares of Lake common stock	250
5/27	Bought 50 shares of Lake common stock	900
	Sold 50 shares of Bass common stock	1,750
7/12	Bought 100 shares of Bass common stock	2,800

The James' have no other income or expense items. Lyle and Kaye's Social Security numbers are 111-22-3333 and 444-55-6666, respectively. Jessica and Jerron's Social Security numbers are 123-45-6789 and 888-99-1010. The James' use the IRS method of allocating all expenses between personal and rental use.

File the James' income tax return Form 1040, Schedules A, D, and E using the currently available forms and rates. Disregard any tax credits for which they may be eligible.

I:6-63 Scarlet Furniture Corporation, an accrual-method taxpayer, retails custom office furniture. On January 1 of the current year, Peter Marlin and John Tanner incorporated Scarlet Furniture Corporation. Peter transferred $350,000 cash for 70% of Scarlet's outstanding stock, and John transferred $150,000 cash for 30% of the outstanding stock. Scarlet generated the following financial statements at the end of its first year of operations:

Scarlet Corporation's Balance Sheet

Assets

Cash	$ 91,400
Inventory	48,000
Other Current Assets	50,000
Office Equipment	170,000
Building	250,000
Accumulated Depreciation	(20,000)
Land	550,000
Total Assets	$1,139,400

Liabilities and Owner's Equity

Accrued Expenses	$ 100,000
Long Term Debt	400,000
Common Stock	500,000
Retained Earnings	139,400
Total Liabilities and Owners' Equity	$1,139,400

Scarlet Corporation's Income Statement

Revenues	$650,000
Costs of Goods Sold	100,000
Gross Income	$550,000

Advertising Expense	40,000
Depreciation Expense	20,000*
Miscellaneous Expense	10,600**
Office Supplies	5,000
Property Tax Expense	60,000
Wages & Salaries Expense	135,000***
Warranty Expense	10,000****
Operating Income	$269,400
Interest Expense	30,000
Federal Income Tax Expense	100,000
Net Income	$139,400

*Depreciation expense for tax purposes was $120,441 because Scarlet made a Sec. 179 election to expense $105,000 of the cost of the equipment purchased this year.

**Miscellaneous expense relates to a $600 penalty fee as a result of a breached customer contract and a $10,000 fine assessed by OSHA for hazardous conditions in its storage facility.

***Wages and salary expense includes Peter's salary of $40,000 and the accrual of $15,000 of bonuses payable to Peter which Scarlet actually paid on February 10 of the following year.

****The actual expenditure paid for warranty repairs during the year is $2,000.

Scarlet does not make any sales or purchases on account. Scarlet's employer identification number is 12-34567. Its address is 789 Presidential Way, Seattle, Washington 54789. Peter Marlin's Social Security number is 555-66-8888. During the current year, the Corporation made federal estimated income tax payments of $50,000.

Prepare a Form 1120 for the initial return for Scarlet.

CASE STUDY PROBLEM

I:6-64 John and Kathy Brown have just been audited and the IRS agent disallowed the business loss they claimed in 2008. The agent asserted that the activity was a hobby, not a business.

John and Kathy live in Rochester, New York, near Lake Ontario. Kathy is a CPA, and John was formerly employed by an insurance firm. John's firm moved in 2003 and John resolved not to move to the firm's new location. Instead of seeking other employment John felt he could supplement his income by using his fishing expertise. He had been an avid fisherman for 15 years, and he owned a large Chris-Craft fly-bridge that he chartered to paying parties.

In 2004, Kathy and John developed a business plan, established a bank account for the charter activities, developed a bookkeeping system, and acquired insurance to cover the boat and the passengers. John fulfilled all the requirements to receive a U.S. Coast Guard operating license, a New York sport trolling license, and a seller's permit. These licenses and permits were necessary to legally operate a charter boat. The first year of their activity was 2004.

John advertised in local papers and regional sport fishing magazines. He usually had three or four half-day paying parties each week. John spent at least one day maintaining and repairing his boat. Kathy usually accompanied John on charters three or four times each year.

John's charter activity was unprofitable the first two years. In 2006, John and Kathy restructured the activity to improve profitability. The restructuring included increasing advertising, participating in outdoor shows, and negotiating small contracts with local businesses. After the restructuring, the activity provided a small profit in 2006 and 2007.

In 2008, John started working with another insurance company in the area on a full-time basis. Even though he returned to the insurance business, John normally took two paying parties and one nonpaying, promotional party each week throughout the fishing season. John's costs unexpectedly increased and he lost $8,000 in the activity during 2008. John and Kathy deducted the entire loss on Schedule C of their 2008 tax return.

Required: Prepare a memo to the Browns recommending what position they should take and why. Show the logic used in arriving at your recommendation.

TAX RESEARCH PROBLEM

I:6-65 Richard Penn lives in Harrisburg, Pennsylvania. Richard is the president of an architectural firm. Richard has become known throughout the community for excellent work and honesty in his business dealings. Richard believes his reputation is an integral part of the success of the firm.

Oil was found recently in the area around Harrisburg and some geologists believed the reserves were large. A few well-respected businesspeople organized Oil Company to develop a few wells. Although some oil was being extracted, the oil corporation lacked capital to develop the oil fields to their expected potential. After reading the geologists' report, Richard felt that Oil Company was a good investment; therefore, he acquired 25% of the company. A short time after Richard's acquisition, the price of foreign oil decreased sharply. The drop in foreign oil prices caused Oil Company to be unprofitable due to its high production costs. Three months later Oil Company filed bankruptcy.

The bankruptcy proceedings were reported in the local newspaper. Many of Oil Company's creditors were real estate developers that engaged Richard's architectural firm to provide designs. After Oil Company declared bankruptcy the architectural firm's business noticeably decreased.

Richard felt the decline in business was related to the bankruptcy of Oil Company. Richard convinced his partner to use the accumulated earnings of the firm to repay all the creditors of Oil Company.

Richard has asked you whether his firm can deduct the expenses of repaying Oil Company's creditors. After completing your research explain to Richard why the expenses are or are not deductible.

A partial list of research sources is as follows:

- Sec. 162
- *Thomas H. Welch v. Helvering,* 12 AFTR 1456, 3 USTC ¶1164 (USSC, 1933)
- *William A. Thompson, Jr.,* 1983 PH T.C. Memo ¶83,487, 46 TCM 1109

TAX RESEARCH CASE

I:6-66 Three years ago, Paul Wilde exercised all his stock options in the start up company he helped establish and walked away with over $100 million. Since that time, he has spent all his energy, time, and effort in managing his portfolio. His investment philosophy is one of steady, careful investment in a well-balanced portfolio. Thus, although each year he engages in several sales and purchases, he generally buys and holds the securities for both the dividends and the growth potential. Consequently, most of the stock sales he makes are of securities he has held for over one year. Because his investment activities have grown so large, this year he rented a suite of offices and hired two investment advisors and five secretaries to help him. He also purchased several new computers and some new office furniture for the office.

Paul has now come to you for some tax help. Specifically, he would like to know if his activities are considered a business or an investment activity. In your explanation, please include whether the expenses incurred in the activity are deductions *for* or *from* AGI.

A partial list of research sources is as follows:

- *Higgins v. CIR,* 25 AFTR 1160, 41-1 USTC §9233 (USSC, 1941)
- *Estate of Louis Yaeger, Deceased, Judith Winters, Ralph Meisels, Abraham J. Weber and the Bank of New York,* 889 F2d 29, 89-2 USTC ¶9633 (CA-2)
- *Frederick Mayer and Jan Perry Mayer,* 67 TCM 2949 (1994)
- *Rudolph W. and Abbie A. Steffler,* 69 TCM 2940 (1995)
- Sec. 179

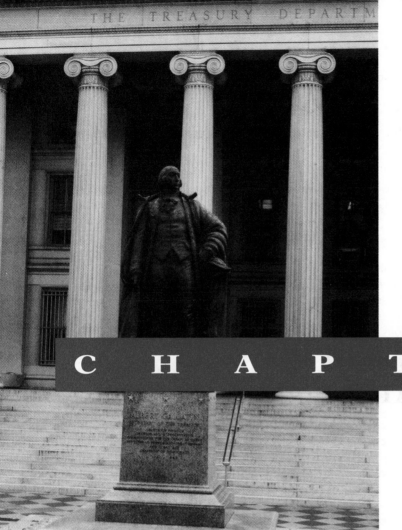

7

C H A P T E R

ITEMIZED DEDUCTIONS

LEARNING OBJECTIVES

After studying this chapter, you should be able to

▶ 1 Identify qualified medical expenses and compute the medical expense deduction

▶ 2 Determine the timing of a medical expense deduction and the effect of a reimbursement

▶ 3 Identify taxes that are deductible as itemized deductions

▶ 4 Identify different types of interest deductions

▶ 5 Compute the amount of investment interest deduction

▶ 6 Compute the deduction for qualified residence interest

▶ 7 Compute the amount of a charitable contribution deduction and identify limitations

▶ 8 Identify certain miscellaneous itemized deductions subject to the 2% of AGI limit

▶ 9 Compute total itemized deductions for a taxpayer who is subject to the itemized deduction phase-out.

As explained in Chapter I:6, most deductible expenses for individuals fit into three general categories:

▶ Expenses incurred in a trade or business

▶ Expenses incurred for the production of income (an investment activity) or for tax advice

▶ Certain specified personal expenses

If an expense is deductible based on the above categories, the expense must be classified as either *for* AGI or *from* AGI. The distinction between *for* and *from* AGI was discussed in Chapter I:6. This chapter focuses on deductions *from* AGI, also referred to as **itemized deductions**, which include medical expenses, taxes, interest, and charitable contributions. Chapter I:9 discusses other itemized deductions, such as employee business expenses, and Chapter I:8 discusses casualty losses on personal-use property.

In arriving at taxable income, individuals may subtract from AGI the larger of the standard deduction or the sum of all itemized deductions. However, as explained later in this chapter, unless Congress enacts a new law, for tax years beginning before or after 2010, certain itemized deductions for taxpayers with AGI in excess of certain limits will be reduced.

MEDICAL EXPENSES

Medical expenses, which comprise one category of deductible personal expenditures, are deductible because Congress felt that excessive medical expenses might ultimately affect a taxpayer's ability to pay his or her federal income tax. However, under Sec. 213, taxpayers may deduct medical expenses only to the extent the expenses exceed 7.5% of the taxpayer's AGI. To qualify as a medical expense deduction, the expenditure must be incurred for the medical care of a qualified individual. Taxpayers may not take a deduction for medical expenses to the extent the expenses are reimbursed (i.e., compensated for by insurance or otherwise).

QUALIFIED INDIVIDUALS

To deduct medical expenses, taxpayers must pay the expenses on behalf of themselves, their spouses, or their dependents.

TAXPAYER'S DEPENDENT. Deductible medical expenses include those paid on behalf of a taxpayer's dependent as well as on behalf of a person for whom the taxpayer could take a dependency exemption except for the failure to meet the gross income or joint return tests.[1]

EXAMPLE I:7-1 ▶

KEY POINT

Medical expenses are deductible for a person who satisfies only the support, relationship, and citizenship dependency tests.

In March of the current year, Jean's son, Steve, is involved in an automobile accident. Steve is 25 years old at the time of the accident and has worked full-time for part of the year, earning a total of $15,000. Because Steve has no medical insurance and cannot pay the medical bills or support himself as a result of the accident, Jean pays Steve's medical expenses and supports him for the rest of the year. Because Jean provides over one-half of Steve's support for the year and Steve, except for the gross income test, otherwise qualifies as Jean's dependent, (Steve is a qualifying relative rather than a qualifying child because he is over 19 and is not a full-time student) Jean may deduct the medical expenses she pays on his behalf. Jean may not claim a dependency exemption for Steve because the gross income test is not satisfied. ◀

CHILDREN OF DIVORCED PARENTS. As long as one divorced parent qualifies to claim the dependency exemption under Sec. 152(e), the parent who pays medical expenses on behalf of the children may deduct the expenses. The parent taking the medical expense deduction need not be the parent who may claim the dependency exemption.

---

[1] Sec. 152. See Chapter I:2 for the tests that must be met to claim a qualifying child or qualifying relative as a dependent.

QUALIFIED MEDICAL EXPENSES

OBJECTIVE 1

Identify qualified medical expenses and compute the medical expense deduction

The **medical expense deduction** is available only for expenditures paid for medical care. Section 213 defines *medical care* as amounts paid for

▶ The diagnosis, cure, mitigation, treatment, or prevention of disease

▶ The purpose of affecting any structure or function of the body

▶ Transportation primarily for and essential to the first two items listed above

▶ Qualified long-term care services

▶ Insurance covering all of the items listed above

ADDITIONAL COMMENT

In 2007, the deduction for medical expenses totaled over $76 billion, representing 5.5% of the total dollar amount of itemized deductions, making it the fifth largest itemized deduction.

DIAGNOSIS, CURE, MITIGATION, TREATMENT, OR PREVENTION OF DISEASE. Although the tax law does not precisely define the term *medical expense,* it is clear that medical expenses are deductible only if paid for procedures or treatments that are legal in the locality in which they are performed. For example, taxpayers may not deduct expenditures for controlled substances.[2] The definition of medical care includes preventive measures such as routine physical and dental examinations. However, other expenses should be "confined strictly to expenses incurred primarily for the prevention or alleviation of a physical or mental defect or illness." Thus, unless they are for routine physical or dental examinations, the expenditures must be for the purpose of curing a specific ailment rather than related to the general health of an individual. This determination is especially critical when the expenditures in question are for items such as vacations, weight loss programs, or stop smoking programs. The taxpayer may or may not incur such expenses for a specific ailment.

EXAMPLE I:7-2 ▶ Helmut is nervous and irritable because of pressures at work and begins to suffer angina symptoms. In order to relax and get away from it all, he takes an ocean cruise around the world. Helmut's angina symptoms ease while he is on the cruise. However, the Tax Court held that a cruise is not a proven medical necessity because Helmut's physician did not specifically prescribe it. Although the cruise was beneficial to Helmut's general health, it was not deductible.[3] ◀

EXAMPLE I:7-3 ▶ Dave enrolls in a weight reduction program on the advice of two doctors who prescribe the program as a means of relieving his obesity, hypertension, and certain hearing problems. These expenses qualify as deductible medical expenditures because they are incurred for specific medical conditions.[4] ◀

Although receipt of a doctor's recommendation for incurring the cost appears to lend a great deal of weight to deductibility, it is not always sufficient. For example, a taxpayer could not deduct the cost of dancing lessons for an emotionally disturbed child, even though the lessons proved to be beneficial and were recommended by a physician. Likewise, a taxpayer suffering from arthritis could not deduct the cost of ballroom dance lessons, even though a doctor recommended the lessons. On the other hand, the IRS has ruled that the cost of a clarinet and clarinet lessons was deductible when recommended by an orthodontist to correct a malocclusion of a child's teeth.[5] In short, determining the deductibility of certain expenditures can be difficult.

ADDITIONAL COMMENT

One cannot deduct the cost of nonprescription medicine (except insulin), toothpaste, toiletries, maternity clothes, diaper service, or funeral expenses.

Range of Deductible Medical Services. According to the Treasury Regulations, typical medical expenses include payments for a wide range of medical, dental, and other diagnostic and healing services. Thus, taxpayers may deduct payments to licensed or certified medical professionals such as general practitioners, obstetricians, surgeons, ophthalmologists, opticians, dentists, and orthodontists. Furthermore, deductible medical expenditures

---

[2] Reg. Sec. 1.213-1(e)(1)(ii). See also Rev. Rul. 97-9, 1997-1 C.B. 77 and IRS Publication 502 (2007) which contains the IRS's recommended treatment for a number of medical expenses.

[3] *Daniel E. Mizl,* 1980 PH T.C. Memo ¶80,227, 40 TCM 552. Even if the taxpayer's physician had prescribed the trip, it still may not have been deductible. See Reg. Sec. 1.213-1(e)(1)(ii).

[4] Rev. Rul. 2002-19, 2002-1 C.B. 778. However, the cost of diet foods or

weight loss programs directed at general health or appearance is not deductible. Furthermore, costs incurred for prescription drugs and programs to stop smoking are deductible but over-the-counter stop smoking aids are not. See Rev. Rul. 99-28, 1999-1 C.B. 1269.

[5] *John J. Thoene,* 33 T.C. 62 (1959), *Rose C. France v. CIR,* 50 AFTR 2d 82-5504, 1982-1 USTC ¶9225 (6th Cir., 1982), and Rev. Rul. 62-210, 1962-2 C.B. 89.

include payments for medical services rendered by individuals such as chiropractors, osteopaths, and psychotherapists who may or may not be required to be licensed or certified.[6] Taxpayers may deduct payments to Christian Science practitioners as well as acupuncture treatment if the taxpayer receives the treatment for a specific medical purpose.[7] Qualified medical expenses also include payment for hospital services, nursing services, laboratory fees, X-rays, artificial teeth or limbs, ambulance hire, eyeglasses, and prescribed medicines and insulin. Nondeductible expenses include expenditures for non-prescription medicines, drugs, vitamins, and other types of health foods that improve the individual's general health.

To deduct costs incurred for schools and camps, the taxpayer must show that the facility has the appropriate medical equipment and regularly engages in providing medical services. For example, a court held that expenses a taxpayer incurred to send his mentally handicapped son to a school with a special curriculum for such children were deductible. Similarly, another court allowed a taxpayer to deduct the cost of sending a child with psychiatric problems to a school specializing in learning disorders. However, taxpayers generally may not deduct the cost of sending children with special medical problems to schools or camps that do not have the proper equipment, facilities, or curriculum for such problems.

TYPICAL MISCONCEPTION

Taxpayers tend to define qualifying medical expenses too narrowly. This may be caused, in part, by comparison with expense reimbursement limitation policies of health insurance companies.

MEDICAL PROCEDURES AFFECTING ANY FUNCTION OR STRUCTURE OF THE BODY. Deductible medical expenditures also include payments for services affecting any function or structure of the body, even though no specific illness or disease exists. Thus, qualifying medical expenses include expenditures for such items as physical therapy, obstetrical services, eyeglasses, dental examinations and cleanings, and hearing aids. Under Sec. 213, cosmetic surgery or any other similar procedure does not qualify as a medical expense unless such surgery is necessary to correct a deformity arising from a congenital abnormality, a personal injury resulting from an accident or trauma, or a disfiguring disease. Cosmetic surgery is defined as any procedure undertaken to improve a person's appearance that does not meaningfully promote the proper function of the body or prevent or treat an illness or disease.

TRANSPORTATION ESSENTIAL TO MEDICAL CARE. Taxpayers may deduct transportation expenses that are essential to and incurred primarily for qualified medical care. Thus, taxpayers may deduct actual out-of-pocket automobile expenditures, taxis, airfare, ambulance fees, and other forms of transportation if the travel is for medical reasons. However, the tax law disallows a deduction if the travel is undertaken for recreational purposes or for the general improvement of the taxpayer's health.

ADDITIONAL COMMENT

In 2010 the standard mileage rate for business mileage is 50 cents, for medical and moving it is 16.5 cents, and for charitable purposes it is 14 cents.

In lieu of the actual cost of the use of an automobile, in 2010 the IRS allows a deduction of 16.5 cents for each mile that the automobile is driven for medical reasons. In addition to this standard mileage rate, taxpayers may also deduct the cost of tolls and parking.

Certain courts have held that the cost of meals and lodging while en route to a medical facility is part of deductible travel costs incurred for medical purposes. However, taxpayers may not deduct the cost of meals eaten on trips that are too short to warrant a stop for meals. Additionally, taxpayers may deduct only 50% of the cost of meals. (See Chapter I:9 for a discussion of the 50% disallowance rule for meals and entertainment.) The IRC limits the potential deduction for the cost of lodging to $50 per night. Furthermore, lodging expenses qualify as medical expenditures only if the travel is primarily for and essential to medical care, the medical care is provided in a licensed hospital (or a facility related or equivalent to a licensed hospital), and there is no significant element of personal pleasure or recreation in the travel. The tax law imposes the $50 limitation on lodging on a per-individual basis. Thus, if the patient is unable to travel alone, the taxpayer may deduct an additional $50 per night for the lodging costs of a nurse, parent, or spouse.

---

[6] Reg. Sec. 1.213-1(e)(1) and Rev. Rul. 63-91, 1963-1 C.B. 54. See also Ltr. Rul. 8919009 (February 6, 1989) where a pregnant woman was entitled to a deduction for the cost of childbirth classes to the extent that they prepared her for the childbirth. However, the cost of the classes where she received instructions on the care of the unborn child represented a flat fee that allowed a coach to attend the class with the taxpayer. Thus, one-half of the fee was deemed attributable to the coach and was not allowed as a qualified medical expense.
[7] Rev. Rul. 72-593, 1972-2 C.B. 180 and IRS Special Ruling, February 2, 1943.

QUALIFIED LONG-TERM CARE. Taxpayers may also deduct expenditures for qualified long-term care as medical expenses subject to the 7.5% of AGI limitation. Long-term care is defined as medical services required by a chronically ill individual which are provided under a prescribed plan of care. Under Sec. 7702B, such items include expenditures for diagnostic, preventive, therapeutic, curing, treating, mitigating, rehabilitative, and personal care services. A chronically ill individual generally is someone who, for a period of at least 90 days, cannot perform at least two daily living tasks such as eating, toileting (including continence), bathing, or dressing.

Expenditures for long-term care insurance premiums also qualify as medical deductions, subject to an annual limit based upon the age of an individual.[8]

CAPITAL EXPENDITURES FOR MEDICAL CARE. Generally, taxpayers may not currently deduct capital expenditures for federal income tax purposes. For assets used in a trade or business or held for the production of income, taxpayers must recover such costs through depreciation, cost recovery, or amortization. Capital expenditures incurred for personal medical purposes are not depreciable or amortizable. However, a current deduction is available when the capital expenditure is made to acquire an asset primarily for the medical care of the taxpayer, the taxpayer's spouse, or the taxpayer's dependents. To qualify as a deduction, the taxpayer must incur the expenditure as a medical necessity for primary use by the individual in need of medical treatment, and the expenditure must be reasonable in amount. The following are the three categories of deductible capital expenditures for medical care:[9]

▶ Expenditures that relate only to the sick or handicapped person, not to the permanent improvement or betterment of the taxpayer's property (e.g., eyeglasses, dogs or other animals that assist the blind or the deaf, artificial teeth and limbs, wheelchairs, crutches, and portable air conditioners purchased for the sole use of a sick person)

▶ Expenditures that permanently improve or better the taxpayer's residence as well as provide medical care (e.g., a swimming pool installed in the home of an individual suffering from arthritis)

▶ Expenditures to remove structural barriers in the home of a physically handicapped individual (e.g., costs of constructing entrance ramps, widening doorways and halls, lowering kitchen cabinets, and adding railings)

REAL-WORLD EXAMPLE

The cost of installing an elevator in the home upon the recommendation of a physician to help a patient with a heart condition was deductible to the extent that it did not increase the value of the home. *James E. Berry v. Wiseman*, 2 AFTR 2d 6015, 58-2 USTC ¶9870 (D.C. Okla., 1958).

Capital expenditures that relate only to the sick person (the first category) are fully deductible in the year paid. Expenditures that improve the residence (the second category) are deductible only to the extent that the amount of the expenditure exceeds the increase in the fair market value (FMV) of the residence brought about by the capital expenditure. Expenditures to remove physical barriers in the home of a physically handicapped individual (the third category) are deductible in full (i.e., the increase in the home's value is deemed to be zero). In addition, any costs of operating or maintaining the assets in all three categories are deductible as long as the medical reason for the capital expenditure continues to exist.[10] All of the above expenditures are subject to the 7.5% floor.

EXAMPLE I:7-4 ▶ During the current year, Rita is injured in an industrial accident. As a result, she sustains a chronic disabling leg injury, which requires her to spend much time in a wheelchair. Rita's physician recommends that a swimming pool be installed in her backyard and that she devote several hours each day to physical exercise. During the year, Rita makes the following expenditures:

Wheelchair	$ 2,500
Swimming pool	27,000
Operation and maintenance of the pool	1,800
Entrance ramp and door modification	5,000

---

[8] For 2010, if the individual is 40 years of age or less, the annual deductible limit for the premiums is $330. For individuals over 40 but less than 50 the limit is $620. For those over 50 but less than 60 the limit is $1,230; over 60 but less than 70 the limit is $3,290; and over 70 the limit is $4,110.

[9] Reg. Sec. 1.213-1(e)(1)(iii) and H. Rept. No. 99-841, 99th Cong., 2d Sess., p. II-22 (1986).
[10] Rev. Rul. 87-106, 1987-2 C.B. 67.

REAL-WORLD EXAMPLE

Taxpayers made nonrefundable advance payments required as a condition for an institution's future acceptance of their handicapped child for lifetime care in the event that taxpayers could not care for the child. The amounts paid were deductible as expenses for medical care in the year paid. Rev. Rul. 75-303, 1975-2 C.B. 87. This current deduction for prepaid amounts is only available for certain lifetime care expenditures incurred in situations described in this ruling. Rev. Rul. 93-72, I.R.B. 1993-34,7.

ADDITIONAL COMMENT

A taxpayer cannot deduct the 1.45% Medicare (hospital insurance benefits) tax that is withheld from wages as part of the Social Security tax.

A qualified appraiser estimates that the swimming pool increases the value of Rita's home by only $20,000. Rita's medical expenses for the year include $2,500 for the wheelchair, $7,000 for the swimming pool (the excess of the cost of the pool over the increase in the FMV of the home), $1,800 for the operation and maintenance of the pool, and $5,000 for the ramp and door modification.   ◀

COSTS OF LIVING IN INSTITUTIONS. The entire cost of in-patient hospital care, including meals and lodging, qualifies as a medical expense. However, if an individual is in an institution other than a hospital (e.g., a nursing home or a special school for the handicapped), the deductibility of the costs involved depends on the facts of the particular case. If the principal reason for the taxpayer's presence in an institution is the need for and availability of the medical care furnished by that institution, the qualified medical expenditures include the entire costs of meals, lodging, and other services necessary for furnishing the medical care.

MEDICAL INSURANCE PREMIUMS. Qualified medical expenses also include all premiums paid for medical insurance, including premiums paid for supplementary medical insurance for the aged under the Social Security Act and premiums paid for qualified long-term care insurance contracts. In many cases, taxpayers pay premiums for insurance coverage that extends beyond mere medical care. For example, in addition to the standard medical care coverage, an insurance policy may provide coverage for loss of income or loss of life, limb, or sight. In such cases, the tax law allows a deduction for the medical care portion of the premium only if the cost of each type of insurance is either separately stated in the contract or furnished to the policyholder by the insurance company in a separate statement.[11]

EXAMPLE I:7-5 ▶ Each month Malazia pays $300 for an insurance policy under which she is reimbursed for any doctor or hospital charges she incurs. In addition, the policy will pay two-thirds of her regular salary each month if she becomes disabled. Finally, the policy will pay her $10,000 for the loss of any limb. At the end of the year, her insurance company issues a statement that allocates two-thirds of the premiums to the medical insurance coverage. Malazia's medical care expenditure is $2,400 ($300 × 12 × 0.667).   ◀

If a taxpayer pays the premiums attributable to an individual or group medical insurance plan, the payments are deductible as medical expenses, which are itemized deductions in most cases. Self-employed individuals may deduct 100% of these amounts as deductions *for* AGI. Any amounts paid by the taxpayer's employer are excluded from the employee's gross income and are not includible in the taxpayer's medical expenses.[12]

Chapter I:9 discusses the deduction for medical savings accounts established for employees.

AMOUNT AND TIMING OF DEDUCTION

OBJECTIVE 2

Determine the timing of a medical expense deduction and the effect of a reimbursement

The amount and timing of the allowable medical expense deduction depend on when the taxpayer actually pays the medical expenses, the taxpayer's AGI, and whether the taxpayer receives any reimbursement for the medical expenses.

TIMING OF THE PAYMENT. In general, taxpayers may deduct medical expenses only in the year they actually pay the expenses. This rule applies regardless of the taxpayer's method of accounting or when the event that caused the expenditure occurs.[13] Thus, if taxpayers receive medical care during the year but have not paid for it as of the end of the year, taxpayers must defer the deduction for that care until the year they pay for the medical care. If the obligation is charged on a credit card, payment is deemed to have been

---

[11] Sec. 213(d). See also Rev. Ruls. 66-216, 1966-2 C.B. 100, and 79-175, 1979-1 C.B. 117.
[12] Sections 162 and 106.

[13] Reg. Sec. 1.213-1(a)(1). However, medical expenses paid within one year from the day following the taxpayer's death are treated as paid at the time they are incurred (see Sec. 213(c)).

made on the date of the charge, not on the later date when the taxpayer pays the credit card balance. Conversely, if medical care is prepaid, the deduction is deferred until the year the taxpayer receives the care unless there is a legal obligation to prepay or unless the prepayment is a requirement for the receipt of the medical care.[14]

LIMITATION ON AMOUNT DEDUCTIBLE. As previously noted, other than medical insurance premiums paid by self-exmployed individuals, the tax law allows a medical expense deduction only for the years in which the taxpayer itemizes his or her deductions and the taxpayer's expenditures for medical care exceed 7.5% of AGI.

EXAMPLE I:7-6 ▶ During the current year, Kelly incurs qualified medical expenditures of $3,000. Her AGI for the year is $30,000. After subtracting the floor, she has $750 ($3,000 − [0.075 × $30,000]) of deductible medical expenses. These medical expenses are added to Kelly's other itemized deductions to determine whether they exceed the standard deduction. ◀

SELF-STUDY QUESTION

Why does the IRS not require that the taxpayer file an amended return when a reimbursement is received in a later year?

ANSWER

The administrative burden on the IRS of processing additional returns would be too great.

MEDICAL INSURANCE REIMBURSEMENTS. Taxpayers may only deduct unreimbursed medical expenditures. It does not matter whether the reimbursement is from an insurance plan purchased from an insurance company, a medical reimbursement plan of an employer, or a payment resulting from litigation.

  If the taxpayer receives reimbursement in the same year he or she pays for the medical expenses, the amount of the reimbursement reduces the allowed deduction. If a taxpayer receives a reimbursement in a year subsequent to the year of payment, the taxpayer must include the reimbursement in gross income in the year of receipt to the extent that the taxpayer derived a tax benefit from the deduction in the previous year. If the taxpayer did not take a deduction in the prior year, the taxpayer doesn't need to report the reimbursement as income. This may occur because the taxpayer's total itemized deductions do not exceed the standard deduction or because the taxpayer's total medical expenses do not exceed 7.5% of AGI. If the taxpayer took a deduction in the prior year, however, the taxpayer must report as income the lesser of the amount of the reimbursement or the amount that medical expenses reduced the taxable income in the prior year.

EXAMPLE I:7-7 ▶ During 2010, Diane, a single taxpayer under age 65, reports the following items of income and expense:

AGI	$60,000
Total qualified medical expenses	6,500
Itemized deductions other than medical	3,900

Diane's taxable income for 2010 is calculated as follows:

AGI			$60,000
Reduction: Larger of itemized deductions or standard deduction			
Medical expenses	$6,500		
Minus: 7.5% of AGI	(4,500)	2,000	
Other itemized deductions		3,900	
Total itemized deductions		$5,900	
Greater of itemized deductions or standard deduction ($5,700)			(5,900)
Personal exemption			(3,650)
Taxable income			$50,450

  If during 2011 Diane receives a reimbursement of $1,500 for medical expenses incurred the prior year, she must include $200 ($5,900 − $5,700) in gross income for 2011, which is the amount of the tax benefit from the medical expense deduction for the prior year. This amount can be calculated by comparing the actual taxable income for 2010 with what would have been the 2010 taxable income if the reimbursement had been received that year.

---

[14] Rev. Rul. 78-39, 1978-1 C.B. 73 and *Robert M. Rose v. CIR*, 26 AFTR 2d 70-5653, 70-2 USTC ¶9646 (5th Cir., 1970). See also Rev. Rul. 93-72, Rev. Rul. 1993-2 C.B. 77, Rev. Rul. 75-302, 1975-2 C.B. 86, and Rev. Rul. 75-303, 1975-2 C.B. 87.

AGI		$60,000
Reduction: Larger of itemized		
deductions or standard deduction		
Medical expenses	$6,500	
Minus: Reimbursement	(1,500)	
7.5% of AGI	(4,500)	
Excess medical expenses		500
Plus: Other itemized deductions		3,900
Total itemized deductions		$4,400
Greater of itemized deductions		
or standard deduction ($5,700)		(5,700)
Personal exemption		(3,650)
Taxable income (assuming reimbursement		
was received in 2009)		$50,650
Minus: Actual 2009 taxable income		(50,450)
Tax benefit		$ 200 ◀

Topic Review I:7-1 highlights the principal requirements for the medical expense deduction previously discussed.

 STOP & THINK

Question: Vince and Diane are married and file a joint tax return. For the current year they estimate their AGI at $100,000. They also estimate their itemized deductions for taxes, interest, and charitable contributions total $9,000. Up to the current date they have incurred $7,000 in deductible medical expenses. For several months they have been considering laser surgery on Diane's eyes. The total expenditure for the operations will be $4,000 and is not covered by their medical insurance. Since they already have spent so much this year on medical expenses and they do not anticipate such large expenses next year, they are considering delaying the eye operation until next year. They estimate next year's AGI to be approximately $110,000. Does this decision make sense from a tax point of view?

Solution: From a tax point of view, Diane should consider having and paying for the operation this year. If so, $4,000 is added to the prior $7,000 medical expenditures for a total of $11,000 for the year. After applying the 7.5% of AGI limitation, $3,500 [$11,000 − ($100,000 × 0.075)] of the medical expenses is deductible. If they wait until next year and if their estimates are correct, none of the medical expenses in either year are deductible because of the 7.5% of AGI limitation.

Topic Review I:7-1

Medical Expense Deductions

ITEMS	DEDUCTION RULES AND LIMITATIONS
Qualifying expenditures	(a) Expenditures for the diagnosis, cure, mitigation, treatment, or prevention of disease and qualified long-term care.
	(b) Transportation at $16.5 per mile for 2010; lodging limited to $50 per night, per person; and 50% of meals.
	(c) Medical and qualified long-term care insurance premiums.
	(d) Capital expenditures (subject to specific limitations).
Qualifying individuals	Taxpayer, spouse, dependents, children of divorced parents even if not dependent, and persons who would qualify as dependent except for the failure to meet gross income or joint return tests.
Amount and timing of the deduction	Deduct in the year paid unless prepaid, then deductible when cost is incurred. If prepayment is required or there is a legal obligation to prepay, then deduct in year of prepayment. Medical expenses are subject to a 7.5% of AGI nondeductible limitation.
Treatment of insurance reimbursements	The deduction is reduced if the reimbursement is received in the year of payment. Reimbursements received in a subsequent year are included in gross income of the year received to the extent that a tax benefit was received in the earlier year.

TAXES

Section 164 provides taxpayers with a deduction for specifically listed taxes paid or accrued during the taxable year. Generally, cash-method taxpayers deduct the taxes when they pay for them, whereas taxpayers using the accrual method deduct taxes in the year the taxes accrue. The tax law specifically lists other taxes as nondeductible. To be deductible as a tax, the assessment in question must be a tax rather than a fee or charge imposed by a government for providing specific goods or services.

DEFINITION OF A TAX

A **tax** is a mandatory assessment levied under the authority of a political entity for the purpose of raising revenue to use for public or governmental purposes. Thus, fees, assessments, or fines imposed for specific privileges or services are not deductible as taxes under Sec. 164. These nontax items include:

▶ Vehicle registration and inspection fees

▶ Registration tags for pets

▶ Toll charges for highways and bridges

▶ Parking meter charges

▶ Charges for sewer, water, and other services

▶ Special assessments against real estate for items such as sidewalks, lighting, and streets

However, if taxpayers incur these nontax fees and charges in a business or income-producing activity, the taxpayers may either capitalize or deduct these items as ordinary and necessary business expenses or ordinary and necessary expenses incurred for the production of income.

DEDUCTIBLE TAXES

The following taxes are specifically deductible under Sec. 164:

▶ State, local, and foreign real property taxes

▶ State and local personal property taxes if based on value

▶ State, local, and foreign income, war profits, and excess profits taxes

▶ For tax years beginning before January 1, 2010, state and local sales taxes if the taxpayer makes an election to deduct these taxes instead of deducting state and local income taxes. Although under current law this election is no longer available for years beginning after December 31, 2009, it is widely expected that this election will be extended for one year through 2010. Likewise, under the new American Recovery and Reinvestment Act of 2009, taxpayers could deduct sales and excise taxes paid in 2009 as a deduction *for AGI* on new cars, light trucks, or motorcycles meeting certain requirements, such as only taxes related to the first $49,500 of the purchase price of the vehicle. This provision may also be extended through 2010.

▶ The environmental tax imposed by Section 59A

▶ Other state, local, and foreign taxes that are paid or incurred in either a trade or business or an income-producing activity

In general, taxes imposed by the federal government are not deductible in calculating a taxpayer's income tax.[15] However, federal customs and excise taxes incurred in the taxpayer's business or income-producing activity are deductible as ordinary and necessary expenses under Secs. 162 or 212. Furthermore, the *employer's* portion of federal Social Security taxes and federal and state unemployment taxes are deductible by the employer as ordinary and necessary business expenses if the employee works in the employer's business or income-producing activity and one-half of the self-employment tax imposed on a self-employed individual is deductible as a for AGI deduction.

---

[15] The generation-skipping transfer tax is imposed by the United States on certain distributions from a trust (see Sec. 2601) and is deductible for federal income tax purposes. Furthermore, under Sec. 691(c) a taxpayer who includes income in respect of a decedent in taxable income may deduct the estate tax attributable to that amount.

EXAMPLE I:7-8 ▶

ADDITIONAL COMMENT

Every state except Alaska, Florida, Nevada, New Hampshire, South Dakota, Tennessee, Texas, Washington, and Wyoming impose a personal income tax. Although New Hampshire and Tennessee do not impose a personal income tax, they do tax interest and dividends at the individual level.

STATE AND LOCAL INCOME TAXES

For individuals, state and local income taxes are normally an itemized (*from* AGI) deduction. Thus, a taxpayer does not receive any federal income tax benefit if these taxes, in addition to the other itemized deductions, do not exceed the standard deduction. Cash-method taxpayers deduct all state and local income taxes paid or withheld during the year even if the taxes are attributable to another tax year.

During 2010, Rita had $1,500 in state income taxes withheld from her salary. On April 15, 2011, Rita pays an additional $400 when she files her 2010 state income tax return. On her 2010 federal income tax return, Rita may deduct the $1,500 in state income taxes withheld from her salary during 2010 as an itemized deduction. The $400 that Rita pays on April 15, 2011, is deductible on her 2011 federal income tax return, even though the liability relates to her 2010 state income tax return. ◀

If a taxpayer receives a refund of state income taxes deducted in a prior year, the taxpayer must include the refund as income in the year of the refund to the extent the taxpayer received a tax benefit from the prior deduction. This calculation is similar to the calculation of the tax benefit from a medical expense reimbursement in Example I:7-7.

STATE AND LOCAL SALES TAXES

Taxpayers are allowed to deduct state and local sales taxes in lieu of state and local income taxes. This election is available for tax years beginning after December 31, 2003, and before January 1, 2011.[16] For those years, taxpayers electing to deduct state and local sales taxes had two options for determining the deductible amount. Taxpayers could deduct the actual amount of taxes paid by accumulating receipts showing the actual amount of taxes paid, or they could deduct the appropriate amount from tables provided by the Treasury Department. If a taxpayer used the amount from the tables, sales taxes paid on major purchases could be added to the table amount.

PERSONAL PROPERTY TAXES

Many state and local governments impose personal property taxes. For individuals, the key issue is whether the levy is a deductible tax under Sec. 164 or a nondeductible fee. To qualify as a deductible personal property tax, the levy must meet two basic tests:

▶ The tax must be an ad valorem tax on personal property. In other words, the property's value determines the amount of the tax rather than some other measure such as a vehicle's weight or model year.

▶ The tax must be imposed on an annual basis, even if not collected annually.[17]

If a personal property tax is based partly on value and partly on some other basis, only the ad valorem portion is deductible.

EXAMPLE I:7-9 ▶

ADDITIONAL COMMENT

Several states impose a tax on the value of a taxpayer's investment portfolio. This is an example of a deductible intangible personal property tax.

Banner County imposes on all passenger automobiles a property tax of 1% of value plus 20 cents per pound. Clay's automobile has a value of $20,000 and weighs 1,500 pounds. Clay may deduct $200 ($20,000 × 0.01) under Sec. 164. Clay may not deduct the remaining $300 (1,500 × 0.20) under Sec. 164; however, he may deduct it as an ordinary business expense if the automobile is used in his business. ◀

For individuals, personal property taxes are *from* AGI (itemized) deductions unless incurred in an individual's trade or business or for the production of rental income.

REAL ESTATE TAXES

Apportionment of Taxes. When real estate is sold during the year, the federal income tax deduction for property taxes imposed on that real estate is allocated between the seller and the purchaser based on the amount of time each taxpayer owns the property during the real property tax year. The real property tax year may or may not coincide with the taxpayer's tax year. The apportionment, based on the number of days each party holds the property during the real property tax year of sale, assumes that the purchaser owns the property on

---

[16] This provision has been extended by both the House and Senate at the time of publication of this textbook and is expected to be officially enacted for 2010.

[17] Reg. Sec. 1.164-3(c).

the date of the sale. This apportionment is mandatory for all taxpayers even though one of the parties (i.e., the purchaser or seller) may have actually paid the entire property tax bill. The party who actually pays the taxes (either the buyer or the seller) deducts his or her share of the taxes in the year he or she pays the taxes unless the taxpayer makes an election under Sec. 461(c) to accrue the taxes. The tax consequences do not depend on whether the agreement requires proration of the real estate taxes. Both the purchaser and the seller may deduct their apportioned share of the taxes, regardless of who actually pays the taxes. Generally the sales agreement provides for the proper apportionment of property taxes between the buyer and the seller and will state the amount of the taxes apportioned to each party separately from the selling price of the property. If the seller pays all of the taxes prior to the sale, at closing the buyer will reimburse the seller for the payment of these taxes in addition to paying the down payment. On the other hand, if the taxes are to be paid by the buyer after the purchase of the property, the amount collected from the buyer at closing is reduced by the amount of taxes allocated to the seller. This process does not impact the selling price of the property if properly allocated and accounted for at closing.[18]

ADDITIONAL COMMENT

Delinquent taxes of the seller that are paid by the buyer as part of the contract price are not deductible.

EXAMPLE I:7-10 ▶

The real property tax year for Bannock County is the calendar year. Property taxes for a particular real property tax year become a lien against the property as of June 30 of that year, and the owner of the property on that date becomes liable for the tax. However, the taxes are not payable until February 28 of the subsequent year. On May 30 of the current (non-leap) year, Sandy, a cash-method taxpayer, sells a building to Roger, who is also a cash-method taxpayer. The real estate taxes on the property for the current year are $1,095. Although Roger is liable for the payment of the tax, Sandy is treated as having paid $447 ($1,095 × 149/365 [the numerator of 149 is the number of days from January 1 through May 29 and the denominator is the entire real property tax year]) on the date of the sale. Roger may deduct his share of the taxes, equaling $648 ($1,095 × 216/365), in the subsequent year (i.e., the year during which Roger actually pays the full amount of property tax due of $1,095). On the other hand, if the taxes become a lien against the property on April 1, Sandy is the owner of the building on that date and, since she is liable for the tax, she will be the one who actually pays the tax. Under these circumstances, the result is the same (i.e., Sandy deducts $447 and Roger deducts $648) except that Roger may take the $648 deduction in the year of sale rather than in the year of payment and Sandy takes the $447 deduction in the year of payment rather than the year of sale. ◀

TYPICAL MISCONCEPTION

Taxpayers often fail to differentiate between assessments for new construction and for repairs. For example, an assessment for street repairs is deductible, but an assessment for the construction of a new street is not deductible.

REAL PROPERTY ASSESSMENTS FOR LOCAL BENEFITS. Local governments often make assessments against real estate for the purpose of funding local improvements. These assessments may be for such items as street improvements, sidewalks, lighting, drainage, and sewer improvements. If the tax assessment is only against the property that benefits from the improvement, it is not deductible, even though the general public may also incidentally benefit.[19] The tax law requires capitalization of such assessments as part of the property's adjusted basis.

Real property taxes incurred on personal-use assets, such as a personal residence, are deductible *from* AGI. Real property taxes incurred on business property or property held for the production of rental income are deductions *for* AGI.

ADDITIONAL STANDARD DEDUCTION FOR REAL PROPERTY TAXES. For tax years beginning in 2008 or 2009, homeowners who took the standard deduction rather than itemizing their deductions could claim an additional standard deduction for state and local real property taxes. The amount of this additional standard deduction was the lesser of (1) the amount that would have been deductible if the individual had itemized the deductions, or (2) $500 ($1,000 for married filing joint returns). Thus, the maximum additional standard deduction for 2008 and 2009 for real property taxes was $500 ($1,000 for joint filers). A proposal has been introduced in Congress to extend this additional standard deduction through 2010.

---

[18] However, if the agreement does not specifically provide and account for an apportionment of taxes, the apportionment of the taxes is still made and the seller's gain or loss on the sale (and the purchaser's basis in the property) must be adjusted either upward or downward, depending on which party actually pays the taxes.

[19] Reg. Sec. 1.164-4. However, if the assessment against the local benefits is made for maintenance, repair, or interest charges on the benefits, the assessment is deductible. The burden of proof to show how much of the assessment is deductible falls on the taxpayer (see Sec. 164(c)(1)).

SELF-EMPLOYMENT TAX

Self-employed individuals pay a tax on their self-employment income in lieu of the payment of a Social Security payroll tax on salary. The self-employment tax rate and total amount of tax are equal to the combined employee and employer Social Security tax (i.e., 12.4% with a ceiling of $106,800 in 2010 ($106,800 in 2009); and no ceiling for the 2.9% additional Medicare hospital insurance premium for self-employed individuals). Self-employed individuals may deduct one-half of the self-employment taxes paid as a *for* AGI deduction.[20]

NONDEDUCTIBLE TAXES

The following taxes are not deductible under Sec. 164:

▶ Federal income taxes

▶ Federal estate, inheritance, legacy, succession, and gift taxes

▶ Federal import or tariff duties and excise taxes unless incurred in the taxpayer's business or for the production of income

▶ Employee's portion of Social Security and other payroll taxes

▶ State and local sales taxes and state inheritance, legacy, succession, and gift taxes

▶ Foreign income taxes if the taxpayer elects to take the taxes as a credit against his or her federal income tax liability

▶ Property taxes on real estate to the extent treated as imposed on another taxpayer

SELF-STUDY QUESTION

Would a taxpayer normally prefer to deduct foreign taxes or take a foreign tax credit?

ANSWER

Normally the foreign tax credit is better because a credit provides a direct dollar-for-dollar reduction of the tax liability rather than a reduction of taxable income.

INTEREST

OBJECTIVE 4

Identify different types of interest deductions

In years past, taxpayers could deduct virtually all interest paid or accrued in the taxable year. Gradually, however, Congress has enacted numerous exceptions into the tax law rendering several types of interest nondeductible. For example, individuals may not deduct personal interest expense, such as interest paid on personal credit cards, automobile loans, etc. Interest incurred in connection with a trade or business is always deductible. Thus, to determine the amount of interest expense deduction, taxpayers must properly classify their interest expense for the year. The interest expense categories include the following:

▶ Active trade or business

▶ Passive activity

▶ Investment

▶ Personal

▶ Qualified residence

▶ Student loan

ADDITIONAL COMMENT

In 2007, the deduction for interest paid totaled $524.7 billion representing 38.25% of the total dollar amount of itemized deductions, making it the largest itemized deduction.

DEFINITION OF INTEREST

Interest is defined as "compensation for the use or forbearance of money."[21] Thus, finance charges, carrying charges, loan discounts, premiums, loan origination fees, and points are all considered interest if they represent a cost for the use of money.

CHARGE FOR SERVICES. In addition to interest, borrowers may incur other charges in connection with borrowing money. These service charges include fees for appraisals, title searches, bank service charges, and the annual service charge on credit cards. Unless incurred in a trade or business, these expenses are not deductible because they all represent nondeductible personal expenses. As explained in the section in this chapter entitled Personal Interest, although finance charges on credit cards represent interest rather than service costs (on page 7-16), they likewise are not deductible unless incurred in a trade or business.

BANK SERVICE CHARGES AND FINANCE CHARGES. Bank service charges on checking accounts are nondeductible expenses for services rendered rather than interest.

---

[20] Sec. 164(f). (See Chapter I:14 for a discussion of the self-employment tax.)   [21] *Deputy v. Pierre S. DuPont,* 23 AFTR 808, 40-1 USTC ¶9161 (USSC, 1940).

The annual service charge on credit cards is also a charge for services rather than interest. However, finance charges on credit cards are interest. Late payments charged by public utilities are interest expense because they do not relate to any specific service.[22] Of course, if taxpayers incur these expenses in a trade or business, they are deductible.

KEY POINT

In general, the classification of interest expense depends on the use to which the borrowed money is put, not on the nature of the property used to secure the loan.

CLASSIFICATION OF INTEREST EXPENSE

The deductibility of interest generally depends on the purpose for which the taxpayer incurs the indebtedness because interest incurred in certain activities is subject to limitation and disallowance. For example, interest expense incurred in the taxpayer's active business is deductible in full against the business income (a deduction *for* AGI, taken on Schedule C), whereas interest expense allocated to the purchase of the taxpayer's residence is subject to the limitations applicable to that type of interest and is an itemized deduction (a deduction *from* AGI). Except for certain student loan interest and certain interest on a personal residence, taxpayers may not deduct interest allocated to personal-use expenditures.

Pursuant to the Treasury Regulations, taxpayers must allocate interest expense to the different interest expense categories by identifying the use of the borrowed money. Property used as collateral in securing the debt normally has no bearing on the allocation of the interest expense.[23]

EXAMPLE I:7-11 ▶ Cathy pledges some stock and securities as collateral for a $30,000 loan. She then purchases an automobile with the proceeds of the loan. The automobile is used 100% of the time for personal use. Even though the collateral for the loan is investment property, the interest expense is allocated to a personal-use asset and is not deductible. ◀

If the taxpayer deposits borrowed funds in a bank rather than spending them immediately, the deposit is treated as an investment, and the interest on the loan is investment interest until the taxpayer withdraws or expends the funds. Then the taxpayer allocates the interest expense to a category based on the reason for making the expenditure, regardless of when the taxpayer actually pays the interest expense for the debt. This reallocation occurs as of the date the taxpayer writes the check on the account, as long as the delivery or mailing of the check occurs within a reasonable period of time.[24]

EXAMPLE I:7-12 ▶ On March 1 of the current year, José borrows $100,000 and immediately deposits the funds into an account that contains no other funds. José makes no additional deposits or payments. On May 1 of the current year, he withdraws $40,000 from the account and purchases a sailboat to be used for personal purposes. On July 1, José withdraws an additional $50,000 and purchases a passive activity. For the current year, the interest expense on the loan is categorized as follows: from March 1 through April 30, all of the expense is investment interest expense. 40% ($40,000/$100,000) of the interest expense attributable to the period May 1 through June 30 is classified as personal interest and the remainder is investment interest. The interest expense attributable to the period from July 1 to the end of the year is classified as 40% personal interest, 50% passive activity interest, and 10% investment interest. ◀

If both borrowed and personal funds are mingled in the same account, expenditures from that account are treated as coming first from the borrowed funds.[25]

EXAMPLE I:7-13 ▶ On April 1 of the current year, Diane borrows $30,000 and deposits it into a checking account that contains $10,000 of personal funds. On May 1 of the current year, Diane purchases a passive activity for $15,000, and on June 1 she purchases a personal automobile for $20,000. The $15,000 expended for the passive activity on May 1 is treated as coming from the borrowed funds. Thus, as of that date, one-half of the interest expense on the debt is reallocated from

---

[22] Rev. Rul. 73-136, 1973-1 C.B. 68 and Rev. Rul. 74-187, 1974-1 C.B. 48. However, interest on a credit card or interest charged by a public utility is not deductible if it is personal interest.

[23] Temp. Reg. Sec. 1.163-8T. The major exception to this rule deals with home equity loans where the funds borrowed may be used for any purpose. Home equity loans are discussed later in this chapter.

[24] Temp. Reg. Sec. 1.163-8T(c). If during any one month several expenditures are made from an account, the taxpayer may elect to treat all the expenditures as if made on the first day of the month. However, this election is made

on each account separately and is available only for accounts where the borrowed funds are already in the account as of the first day of the month. If the funds are not in the account as of the first day of the month, the expenditures may be treated as made on the date that the borrowed funds are deposited in the account. See Temp. Reg. Sec. 1.163-8T(c)(4)(iv).

[25] Temp. Reg. Sec. 1.163-8T(c)(4)(ii). However, if an expenditure is made out of the mingled funds within 15 days of the deposit of the borrowed funds into the account, the taxpayer may designate the expenditure to which the borrowed funds are allocated.

investment interest to passive activity interest. $15,000 of the funds expended for the personal automobile on June 1 is treated as coming from the borrowed funds, and the remaining $5,000 is treated as coming from the personal funds. Thus, as of June 1, the remaining interest expense on the debt is reallocated to personal interest. ◄

When the taxpayer repays the debt, the allocation of the repayment to the expenditures made with the borrowed funds occurs in the following order: (1) personal expenditures, (2) investment expenditures and passive activity expenditures other than rental real estate, (3) passive activity expenditures in rental real estate, and (4) trade or business expenditures.

ACTIVE TRADE OR BUSINESS. Generally, a taxpayer may deduct without limit any interest expense incurred in the taxpayer's active trade or business. As explained in Chapter I:6, the determination of whether a particular activity constitutes a trade or business or an investment depends on an examination of all the relevant facts and circumstances. For individuals, estates, trusts, and certain corporations, however, it is not sufficient that the taxpayer incur the interest in a trade or business. In addition, the taxpayer must *materially participate* in the business. If not, the activity is considered a passive activity, and losses from the activity (including the interest expense) are subject to the passive loss limitation rules (see Chapter I:8 for a discussion of these rules). Interest incurred in an active trade or business is a deduction *for AGI*.

PASSIVE ACTIVITY. Individuals, estates, trusts, and certain corporations that incur losses from passive activities are subject to the passive loss limitation rules explained in Chapter I:8. These rules prevent taxpayers from offsetting passive activity losses against other types of income such as salary, interest, dividends, and income from an active business. Taxpayers must include interest expense attributable to the passive activity in computing the net income or loss generated from the activity, and thus may not be able to deduct the interest under these limitation rules (see Chapter I:8 for a discussion of these rules).

OBJECTIVE 5

Compute the amount of investment interest deduction

INVESTMENT INTEREST. Individuals and other noncorporate taxpayers are limited on the deductibility of interest expense attributable to investments. Without any limitation, high-income taxpayers could realize significant tax savings by borrowing money to invest in assets that are appreciating in value but produce little or no current income. This would enable the taxpayer to offset current highly taxed income with a current interest deduction, while deferring the taxable income from the investment until it is sold at a later date. This technique also would enable taxpayers to increase their future capital gain income and reduce their current ordinary income. This procedure is favorable to individual and noncorporate taxpayers because the tax on capital gains is less than the tax on ordinary income.

Because of these concerns, Sec. 163(d) limits the current deduction for investment interest expense to the noncorporate taxpayer's net investment income for the taxable year. Any investment interest expense disallowed as a current deduction is carried over and treated as investment interest expense incurred in the following year.

EXAMPLE I:7-14 ▶ In the current year, Rita earns $27,000 in net investment income and incurs $40,000 of investment interest expense. Rita's interest expense deduction for the year is limited to $27,000, the amount of her net investment income.

The remaining investment interest expense of $13,000 ($40,000 − $27,000) may be carried over and deducted in a subsequent year. This carryover amount is treated as paid or accrued in the subsequent year and is subject to the disallowance rules that pertain to the subsequent year. ◄

Investment Interest. **Investment interest** is interest expense on indebtedness properly allocable to property held for investment. This includes property that generates portfolio types of income such as interest, dividends, annuities, and royalties. It does not include business interest, personal interest, qualified residence interest, or interest incurred in connection with any passive activity. Under Sec. 469, all rental activities are passive (see Chapter I:8 for a discussion of the passive loss limitation rules). Thus, interest incurred in owning and renting property is subject to the passive loss limitation rather than the investment interest limitation.

Investment interest also does not include interest expense incurred to purchase or hold tax-exempt securities. This interest is not deductible at all. Without this disallowance, a taxpayer could, in certain circumstances, actually borrow funds at a higher rate of interest than the rate at which they were reinvested, while still generating a positive net cash flow because the government would be subsidizing the transaction through the interest deduction on the borrowings.

Net Investment Income. For purposes of the investment interest limitation, the term **net investment income** means the excess of the taxpayer's investment income over investment expenses. Investment income is gross income from property held for investment, including items such as dividends, interest, annuities, net short-term capital gains, and royalties (if not earned in a trade or business), but excluding qualified dividends and net long-term capital gains taxed at the preferential 15% or lower rate.

As explained in earlier chapters, generally, the maximum tax rate on net capital gain and qualified dividends is 15%. Including either of these two items in the definition of investment income would increase the amount of deductible investment interest expense, which might offset other income that is taxed at higher rates. Thus, the definition of investment income generally excludes net capital gain attributable to the disposition of property held for investment and qualified dividends. However, at the election of the taxpayer, net capital gain from the disposition of investment property and qualified dividends can be included in investment income. To the extent the taxpayer elects to include gains from the disposition of investment property and qualified dividends in investment income, these items are taxed at the regular tax rates rather than at the preferential long-term capital gain rates.[26] The calculation of investment income does not include gains on business and personal-use property.

EXAMPLE I:7-15 ▶ During the current year, Michael incurs $15,000 investment interest expense, earns $7,000 of qualified dividends and $3,000 interest income. He also reports the following gains and losses from the sale of stocks and bonds during the year:

Short-term capital gains	$4,000
Short-term capital losses	(3,000)
Long-term capital gains	5,000
Long-term capital losses	(2,000)

Considering all of Michael's other income and deductions for the year, assume that he is subject to a 35% marginal tax rate. Michael's net capital gain is $3,000 (net long-term capital gain of $3,000 in excess of net short-term capital losses of $0). He also has a $1,000 ($4,000 − $3,000) net short-term capital gain. Thus, of his total capital gain of $4,000 ($9,000 of total gains − $5,000 of total losses), only $1,000 ($4,000 net gain − $3,000 net capital gain) is included in investment income. In addition, the $7,000 of qualified dividends also are not included in investment income. If Michael does not make an election, his investment income is $4,000 ($3,000 of interest plus $1,000 net short-term capital gain). He may deduct $4,000 of the investment interest expense in the current year. The excess investment interest for the current year of $11,000 ($15,000 − $4,000) is carried over to the next year. The $3,000 net capital gain and the qualified dividends are subject to the 15% ceiling tax rate on net capital gain. If Michael makes the election, his investment income is $14,000 (the $3,000 net capital gain and $7,000 of qualified dividends are included), and he may deduct $14,000 of the investment interest expense. Thus, only $1,000 ($15,000 − $14,000) of investment interest expense is not currently deductible and is carried over to the next year. However, his $3,000 net capital gain and $7,000 of qualified dividends are subject to the 35% ordinary income tax rate. ◀

ADDITIONAL COMMENT

Investment expenses are those which are deductible on the tax return, after the 2% limitation.

Investment expenses include all deductions (except interest) that are directly connected with the production of investment income. These expenses include rental fees for safe-deposit boxes, fees for investment counsel,[27] and subscriptions to investment and financial planning journals. As explained later in this chapter (see the section of this chapter titled Miscellaneous Itemized Deductions), these investment expenses are deductible only to the extent they exceed 2% of the taxpayer's AGI for the year. Only the investment

---

[26] Secs. 1(h)(3) and 163(d)(4)(B).
[27] Sec. 163(d)(4)(C). Commissions for the sale or purchase of investment property are not included here. A commission paid on the purchase of property is added to the purchase price (and the basis) of the property. A commission paid on the sale of property reduces the amount realized.

expenses remaining after application of this limitation are used in computing the net investment income. Furthermore, in computing the amount of the disallowed investment expenses, the 2% of AGI limitation applies to the noninvestment expenses first.[28] Any remaining 2% of AGI limitation then reduces the noninterest investment expenses.

EXAMPLE I:7-16 ▶ Kevin's AGI for the current year is $200,000. Included in his AGI is $175,000 salary and $25,000 of investment income. In earning the investment income, Kevin paid investment interest expense of $33,000. He also incurred the following expenditures subject to the 2% of AGI limitation:

Investment expenses:	
Subscriptions to investment journals	$ 700
Investment counseling	2,000
Safe-deposit box rental	300
Noninvestment expenses:	
Unreimbursed employee business expenses	1,500
Tax return preparation fees (non–business-related)	500

Kevin's investment interest expense deduction for the year is computed by first determining the deductible investment expenses (other than interest) and the net investment income.

Investment expenses:		
Subscriptions	$ 700	
Investment counseling	2,000	
Safe-deposit box rental	300	$3,000
Disallowed by the 2% limitation:		
2% of AGI ($200,000 × 0.02)	$4,000	
Unreimbursed employee expenses	(1,500)	
Tax return preparation fees	(500)	
Investment expenses (remainder of 2% limit allocated to investment expenses)		(2,000)
Deductible investment expenses		$1,000
Net investment income ($25,000 − $1,000)		$24,000

The investment interest expense deduction is limited to $24,000. The remaining investment interest of $9,000 ($33,000 − $24,000) is carried over and deducted in a subsequent year (subject to the disallowance rules that pertain to the subsequent year). ◀

PERSONAL INTEREST. In general, the tax law does not allow a deduction for interest expense on debt incurred for personal purposes. Thus, taxpayers may not deduct interest on credit cards, car loans, and consumer debt. However, taxpayers generally may deduct interest on debt to acquire a personal residence as well as interest on certain student loans.

QUALIFIED RESIDENCE INTEREST. Subject to certain limitations discussed below, individuals may deduct **qualified residence interest**. To be qualified residence interest, the interest payment must be either acquisition indebtedness or home equity indebtedness with respect to a qualified residence of the taxpayer. In all cases the residence must secure the debt.[29] A qualified residence (discussed below) may consist of the taxpayer's principal residence and a second residence.

ADDITIONAL COMMENT

Banks and other financial institutions that receive mortgage interest from homeowners are required to report interest of $600 or more to the IRS and to the homeowners on Form 1098.

Acquisition Indebtedness. Acquisition indebtedness is any debt secured by the residence and incurred in acquiring, constructing, or substantially improving the qualified residence. Debt may be treated as qualified acquisition indebtedness if the taxpayer acquires the

---

[28] H. Rept. No. 99-841, 99th Cong., 2d Sess., pp. II-153 and 154 (1986). The noninvestment expenses subject to the 2% of AGI limitation include unreimbursed employee business expenses, hobby expenses up to the income from the hobby, and tax return preparation fees.

[29] Sec. 163(h). If the loan is not secured by the residence, it does not qualify. In one instance the taxpayer agreed to purchase her ex-husband's interest in their residence. The terms of the sale were $10,000 down plus an unsecured $25,000 note. In a private ruling, the IRS ruled that because the note was not

secured by the residence, the interest on the note was not qualified residence interest. (See Ltr. Rul. 8752010 September 18, 1987.) However, if under any state or local homestead law the security interest is ineffective or unenforceable, the interest expense still qualifies as qualified residence interest. See Sec. 163(h)(4)(C). In another letter ruling the taxpayer borrowed money to purchase a residence securing the debt by pledging stock and bonds. Here also, the IRS denied the deduction because the loan was not secured by the residence. (See Ltr. Rul. 8906031 November 10, 1988.)

residence within 90 days before or after the date that the debt is incurred. In the case of the construction or substantial improvement of a residence, debt incurred before the completion of the construction or improvement can qualify as acquisition debt to the extent of construction expenditures that are made no more than 24 months before the date the debt is incurred. Furthermore, debt incurred after construction is complete and within 90 days of the completion date may qualify as acquisition indebtedness to the extent of any construction expenditures made within the 24-month period ending on the date the debt is incurred.[30] Making payments of principal on the loan reduces the amount of acquisition debt. The only way to increase the amount of acquisition debt is to make substantial improvements to the property. The taxpayer may refinance acquisition indebtedness (and therefore treat it as acquisition indebtedness) to the extent that the principal amount of the refinancing does not exceed the principal amount of the acquisition debt immediately before the refinancing.

EXAMPLE I:7-17 ▶ Kay acquired a personal residence in 1999 for $220,000 and borrowed $140,000 on a mortgage that was secured by the property. In the current year the principal balance of the mortgage has been reduced to $100,000. Kay's acquisition indebtedness in the current year is only $100,000 and cannot be increased above $100,000 (except by indebtedness incurred to substantially improve the residence). If she refinances the existing mortgage in the current year and the refinanced debt is $110,000, only $100,000 (the principal balance of the existing acquisition indebtedness) qualifies as acquisition indebtedness. ◀

The limitation for qualified acquisition indebtedness is $1,000,000 ($500,000 for a married individual filing a separate return). Qualified acquisition indebtedness incurred before October 13, 1987 (pre-October 13, 1987 indebtedness) is not subject to any limitation. However, the aggregate amount of pre-October 13, 1987 indebtedness reduces the $1,000,000 limitation on the indebtedness incurred after October 13, 1987.

ADDITIONAL COMMENT

Many banks, in attempting to generate new loan business, have heavily advertised the tax advantages of home equity indebtedness.

Home Equity Indebtedness. Taxpayers may also deduct interest incurred on home equity indebtedness (so-called home equity loans). Subject to certain limits, home equity indebtedness is any indebtedness (other than acquisition indebtedness) secured by a qualified residence of the taxpayer. The taxpayer may use the proceeds of the loan for any purpose (including purchasing or improving a qualified residence), as long as the taxpayer's qualified residence secures the loan. However, the tax law limits home equity indebtedness to the lesser of:

▶ The FMV of the qualified residence in excess of the acquisition indebtedness with respect to the residence, or

▶ $100,000 ($50,000 for a married individual filing a separate return)

The $1,000,000 limit on acquisition indebtedness and the $100,000 limit on home equity indebtedness are two separate limits. The maximum amount of indebtedness on which a taxpayer may deduct qualified residence interest is $1,100,000 if an individual has $100,000 or more equity in the property.

EXAMPLE I:7-18 ▶ On April 23 of the current year, Kesha borrows $125,000 to purchase a new sailboat. The loan is secured by her personal residence. On that date, the outstanding balance on the original debt Kesha incurred to purchase the residence is $400,000 and the FMV of the residence is $900,000. The original debt is also secured by Kesha's residence. Kesha may deduct the interest paid on the $400,000 of acquisition indebtedness, plus the interest paid on $100,000 of the home equity loan. The interest on $25,000 ($125,000 − $100,000) is treated as personal interest and is, therefore, not deductible. The home equity loan is limited to the lesser of $100,000 or the FMV of the residence in excess of the outstanding acquisition indebtedness (the lesser of $100,000 or $500,000 ($900,000 − $400,000)). ◀

Points Paid as Qualified Residence Interest. Often taxpayers must pay **points** on real estate debt. A point is equal to 1% of the loan amount. Thus, two points paid on a $120,000 mortgage equal $2,400 (120,000 × .02). Points often represent prepaid interest

---

[30] Notice 88-74, 1988-2 C.B. 385.

because the stated rate of interest for the loan is lower than the current rate of interest. Generally, prepaid interest paid in the form of points must be capitalized and amortized over the life of the loan. However, points paid on a loan incurred to purchase the taxpayer's principal residence (acquisition indebtedness) are automatically deductible when paid if certain requirements are met. The IRS has also indicated that points paid on Veteran Administration (VA) and Federal Home Administration (FHA) loans are also currently deductible as interest if clearly designated as points incurred in connection with the indebtedness.[31]

EXAMPLE I:7-19 ▶ During the current year, Kevin and Donna purchase a new home for $300,000, putting $100,000 down and borrowing $200,000. At the closing, they are required to pay one and one-half points as a loan discount in connection with the loan, which is secured by a mortgage against the home. The practice of charging points is an established business practice where they live.

These points represent prepaid interest on the purchase of a principal residence. Thus, in addition to the interest portion of every payment they make during the year, Kevin and Donna may also deduct $3,000 ($200,000 × 0.015) as interest paid during the year of purchase. ◀

Taxpayers must capitalize points paid on a loan to purchase property other than a principal residence or for refinancing a mortgage on a principal residence. If the property is used in a business, held as an investment, or a qualified residence (the taxpayer's principal residence and one other that the taxpayer chooses) the taxpayer may amortize the points over the life of the loan.[32]

In order for the points to be currently deductible, the purchaser of the principal residence (borrower) must have paid for them with unborrowed funds. However, amounts provided by the borrower as down payments, escrow deposits, earnest money, or other funds are treated as paid for the points. Furthermore, as long as the borrower provides sufficient funds in these other categories, he or she is treated as having paid the points even if the seller has paid for them on behalf of the borrower.[33]

Qualified Residence. For any tax year, a taxpayer may have two qualified residences:

▶ Taxpayer's principal residence

▶ One other residence selected by the taxpayer, with regard to which the taxpayer meets the residence test of Sec. 280A(d)(1).

In order to meet this residence test, the taxpayer must have personally used the property more than the greater of 14 days or 10% of any rental days during the year.[34]

EXAMPLE I:7-20
ADDITIONAL
COMMENT

Whether property is a residence for tax purposes is based on all the facts and circumstances, including the good faith of the taxpayer. A residence generally includes a house, condominium, mobile home, boat, or house trailer, that contains sleeping space and toilet and cooking facilities. Treas. Reg. § 1.163-10T(p)(3)(ii).

▶ Fred owns a lakeside cabin that he uses for vacations. He also rents the cabin out to others when he is not using it. During the year Fred rents the cabin out at a fair rental for 90 days. Fred personally uses the cabin for a total of 22 days. Because Fred's personal use for the year (22 days) exceeds 14 days [the greater of 14 days or 9 days (10% of the rental days)], the cabin qualifies as his residence for purposes of deducting qualified residence interest for the year. ◀

Despite the residence test, the taxpayer may select a property that has not been rented by the taxpayer at any time during the year as the second residence on which the taxpayer may deduct qualified residence interest.

---

[31] These requirements, mentioned in Chapter I:6, are as follows: The points must be paid in connection with the purchase (not the improvement) of the taxpayer's principal residence, the closing agreement must clearly designate the amounts as points paid in connection with the acquisition debt, the amount must be computed as a percentage of the amount borrowed, the points must conform with established business practices, and the loan must be secured by the residence. Rev. Proc. 94-27, 1994-1 C.B. 613. See also Rev. Proc. 92-12A, 1992-1 C.B. 664.

[32] Rev. Rul. 87-22, 1987-1 C.B. 146, and Rev. Proc. 87-15, 1987-1 C.B. 624. The 8th Circuit Court of Appeals has held in one case that points paid on refinancing a "bridge" or temporary loan are currently deductible. *James R. Huntsman v. CIR*, 66 AFTR 2d 90-5020, 90-2 USTC ¶ 50,340 (8th Cir., 1990), rev'g 91 TC 57 (1988). However, the IRS has announced that it will not follow *Huntsman* in circuits other than the circuit in which the case was decided (IRS Action on Decision CC-1991-02, Feb. 11, 1991).

[33] Reg. Sec. 1.6050H-1(f)(3). See also Rev. Proc. 94-27, 1994-1 C.B. 613.

[34] Sec. 280A(d)(1). Use by the taxpayer's family as defined in Sec. 267(c)(4), other individuals under a reciprocal-use arrangement, and anyone when a fair rental is not charged is counted as a day of personal use by the taxpayer (see Sec. 280A(d)(2) and Chapter I:6).

STOP & THINK

Question: Jana is about to purchase a new sport utility vehicle for $35,000. If she pays $5,000 down, the dealer is prepared to offer her a loan for the remaining $30,000 at 8% interest. In investigating other possible sources of funds, she found out that her brokerage firm would lend her the $30,000 at 9% interest if she pledged her stock as collateral. At her local credit union, she found that she could borrow the $30,000 at 10% interest if she took out a home equity loan by using her home as security. Jana is confused about which loan she should take.

Solution: The best way to analyze this problem is to compare the after-tax interest rates of the loans. Jana may not deduct the interest paid to the car dealer because it is personal interest. Thus, its after-tax interest rate remains at 8%. Furthermore, even though Jana uses her stock holdings as collateral, the interest on the loan from the brokerage firm is non-deductible personal interest because she uses the proceeds of the loan to purchase personal property rather than investment property. Its after-tax interest rate remains at 9%. Only the interest on the home equity loan from the credit union is potentially deductible. This depends, of course, on the amount of Jana's total itemized deductions. Assuming Jana's total itemized deductions exceed the standard deduction and Jana is in the 30% marginal tax bracket, the after-tax interest rate of the home equity loan drops from 10% to 7% [10% × (1 − 0.30)].

STUDENT LOAN INTEREST. If the loan meets certain requirements, individuals may take a *for* AGI deduction for interest paid on qualified education loans. The maximum annual interest deduction for qualified student loans is $2,500. Furthermore, for 2009 the deduction is phased out ratably for individuals with modified AGI of $60,000 to $75,000 ($120,000 to $150,000 for individuals filing joint returns).[35]

EXAMPLE I:7-21 ▶ During 2010, Ryan pays a total of $2,800 in interest on a loan incurred for qualified education expenses. Ryan is single and reports modified AGI of $69,000 for the year. Since his modified AGI of $69,000 is $9,000 greater than $60,000, the maximum deduction of $2,500 is reduced by 60% ($9,000/$15,000). Ryan may take a *for* AGI deduction of $1,000 [2,500 − (60% × 2,500)]. If Ryan pays only $1,800 of interest (rather than $2,800), the potential deduction of $1,800 would be reduced by 60% to $720 [$1,800 − (60% × $1,800)]. ◀

To qualify for this deduction, the interest must be payable on a loan incurred solely to pay for qualified higher education expenses. If a taxpayer takes out a loan to pay for higher education expenses and for other purposes, none of the interest on the loan qualifies. Higher education expenses include tuition, fees, books and equipment, and room and board incurred during a time the taxpayer, the taxpayer's spouse, or the taxpayer's dependent is a student at a qualified higher education institution on at least a half-time basis. However, these qualified expenditures do not include amounts excluded from income under an employer educational assistance program or from United States savings bonds, as well as any scholarship or allowance that is excluded from income. Furthermore, to prevent a double deduction, the tax law allows no deduction to an individual for whom a dependency exemption may be taken on another's tax return or for any amount that is deductible under any other provision of the Code.

TIMING OF THE INTEREST DEDUCTION

Under Sec. 163, deductible interest becomes deductible in the year the interest is paid or accrued. This generally means that cash method taxpayers deduct interest in the year paid, whereas accrual method taxpayers deduct interest as it accrues. However, the IRC makes exceptions to this general rule.

---

[35] The phase-out range is $15,000 ($30,000 for married filing jointly). Modified AGI includes certain excluded income from Guam, American Samoa, or Puerto Rico, as well as any income excluded under the foreign earned income provisions. Furthermore, the deduction for qualified tuition and related expenses is not allowed.

ADDITIONAL COMMENT

Points paid on the refinancing of an existing mortgage must be written off over the life of the new mortgage.

PREPAID INTEREST. If a cash method taxpayer prepays interest and the prepayment relates to a loan that extends beyond the end of the tax year, generally the taxpayer must capitalize the prepayment and amortize it over the periods to which the interest relates (i.e., the accrual method applies to cash method taxpayers in regards to prepaid interest). As previously discussed, the law makes one exception to this rule involving interest paid in the form of points charged in connection with the purchase or improvement of the taxpayer's principal residence. If these points represent prepaid interest, the taxpayer may deduct them in the year paid.[36]

INTEREST PAID WITH LOAN PROCEEDS. Assuming the interest is otherwise deductible, if an individual borrows money from a third party rather than from the original lending institution and uses the funds to make a payment on a previously outstanding loan, the individual generally may deduct the interest portion of the payment. However, if the taxpayer borrows the funds used to pay the interest on the first loan from the same lender to whom the interest is due, and either (1) the purpose of the second loan is to pay the interest on the first or (2) the borrower does not have unrestricted control of the funds, then the borrower may not deduct the interest.[37]

DISCOUNTED NOTES. Lending institutions often discount notes. In effect, the borrower pays the interest by repaying more money than is received when the note is signed. A cash method taxpayer can deduct this interest at the time of repayment, whereas an accrual method taxpayer must deduct the interest as it accrues over the term of the loan.

EXAMPLE I:7-22 ▶ On December 1, 2010, Stan borrows $1,000 from his credit union to use in his business. Under the terms of the contract, Stan actually receives $970 but is required to repay $1,000 on February 28, 2011 (three months later). Because Stan is a cash method taxpayer, he may deduct the full $30 interest in 2011 when the note is repaid. If he were an accrual method taxpayer, he could deduct $10 ($30 × 1/3) in 2010, and $20 ($30 × 2/3) in 2011. ◀

TYPICAL MISCONCEPTION

Taxpayers sometimes mistakenly assume that any business interest paid on loans between related taxpayers is not deductible. However, if the taxpayers are not governed by the Sec. 267 limitation and the interest is paid on a bona fide business loan, it is deductible.

INTEREST OWED TO A RELATED PARTY BY AN ACCRUAL METHOD TAXPAYER. One of the purposes of Sec. 267 is to require related cash method lenders and accrual method borrowers to report the results of their joint transaction in the same year. Thus, an accrual method taxpayer who is related to a cash method creditor must defer the deduction for any accrued expense (including interest) until the year in which the taxpayer actually pays the expense and the creditor reports the income. Section 267 also disallows losses on the sale of property between related parties. Disallowance of losses between related parties is discussed in Chapter I:6.

The relationships covered by this rule are quite extensive. Some of the more common relationships include the following:

▶ Members of a family (defined as an individual's brothers, sisters, spouse, ancestors, and lineal descendants)

▶ An individual and a C corporation in which the individual owns directly or indirectly more than 50% of the outstanding stock

▶ A corporation and a partnership which are both over 50% owned directly or indirectly by the same people

▶ A partnership and any partner of the partnership

▶ An S Corporation and any shareholder of the S Corporation[38]

---

[36] Sec. 461(g). In order for the exception to apply, the home must be used to secure the loan, and the charging of points must be an established business practice in the area where the loan is granted. (See the discussion of the deductibility of points in this chapter under the heading Definition of *Interest* as well as the discussion in Chapter I:6.)

[37] *H. C. Franklin v. CIR*, 50 AFTR 2d 82-5551, 82-2 USTC ¶9532 (5th Cir., 1982) and *Newton A. Burgess*, 8 T.C. 47 (1947). See also *Norman W. Menz*, 80 T.C. 1174 (1983). The IRS has also announced that it will disallow a deduction for interest paid with funds obtained through a second loan from the same lender (see IRS News Release 83-93, July 6, 1983).

[38] Secs. 267(b) and (e). The list of relationships is much more extensive than those mentioned. An S corporation is one that meets certain requirements and has made an election to have its income taxed directly to its shareholders. A C corporation is one that has not made an S election. (See Chapter C:11 of *Prentice Hall's Federal Taxation: Corporations, Partnerships, Estates, and Trusts* text or Chapter C:11 of *Prentice Hall's Federal Taxation: Comprehensive* text.)

EXAMPLE I:7-23 ▶ During the current year, Lisa, a cash method taxpayer, loans some money to her 100%-owned corporation, which uses the accrual method of accounting. As of December 31 of the current year, the corporation owes Lisa $3,000 in interest. However, because of a shortage of funds, the corporation does not actually pay the interest until February 15 of the following year. Despite the fact that the corporation uses the accrual method of accounting, the corporation cannot deduct the $3,000 until the corporation actually pays the interest to Lisa in the subsequent year. The result would be the same if the corporation were an S Corporation even if Lisa owned 50% or less of the outstanding stock. ◀

IMPUTED INTEREST. Under certain circumstances, if a taxpayer charges less than an adequate rate of interest, the IRS is authorized to impute an interest charge. This may cause the lender to have additional interest income and the borrower to have additional interest expense. The deductibility of this imputed interest expense depends on the classification of the expense (i.e. personal, investment, etc.). (See Chapter I:11 for a discussion of imputed interest.)

Topic Review I:7-2 summarizes the rules for deducting various types of interest.

Topic Review I:7-2

Deductibility of Interest Expense

TYPE OF INTEREST	RULES
Business	Deductible in full as a *for* AGI deduction.
Passive	Subject to the passive loss limits (see Chapter I:8).
Investment	Deductible as an itemized deduction to the extent of the taxpayer's net investment income for the year. Any amount not deductible is carried over to subsequent years.
Personal	Not deductible.
Qualified residence	(a) Must be attributable to debt secured by the taxpayer's principal residence and one other residence selected by the taxpayer. (b) Interest on up to $1,000,000 of home acquisition indebtedness is deductible as an itemized deduction. (c) Interest on home equity debt is deductible as an itemized deduction. Home equity debt is limited to the lesser of $100,000 or the excess of the FMV of the residence over the home acquisition indebtedness.
Student Loan Interest	(a) Payable on loan incurred to pay qualified higher education expenses. (b) Taken as a *for* AGI deduction. (c) Maximum deductible amount is $2,500. Deduction is phased out ratably for AGI between $60,000 to $75,000 ($120,000 to $150,000 for married filing jointly).

CHARITABLE CONTRIBUTIONS

OBJECTIVE 7

Compute the amount of a charitable contribution deduction and identify limitations

Under Sec. 170, individuals who itemize their deductions and corporations can deduct **charitable contributions** to qualified organizations. With the exception of certain contributions made by corporations (explained later in this chapter), a taxpayer takes the deduction in the year the contribution is made, regardless of the taxpayer's method of accounting. The amount of the deduction depends on the type of charity receiving the contribution, the type of property contributed, and the applicable limitations.

QUALIFYING ORGANIZATION

To deduct a contribution for federal income tax purposes, a taxpayer must make the contribution to or for the use of a qualified organization.[39] Contributions made directly to

---

[39] The Supreme Court has ruled that in order for a contribution to be for the use of a qualifying organization, the gift must be held either in a legally enforceable trust or in a similar legal arrangement. (See *U.S. v. Harold Davis*, 65 AFTR 2d 90-1051, 90-1 USTC ¶50,270 (USSC, 1990).)

ADDITIONAL
COMMENT

In 2007, the deduction for charitable contributions totaled $193.6 billion representing 14.11% of the total dollar amount of itemized deductions, making it the third largest itemized deduction.

individuals, even though the individuals may be needy, are generally not deductible.[40] Under Sec. 170, qualified organizations include the following:

▶ The United States, the District of Columbia, a state or possession of the United States, or a political subdivision of a state or possession

▶ A corporation, trust, community chest, fund or foundation created or organized under the laws of the United States, a state, possession, or the District of Columbia[41]

▶ A post or organization of war veterans

▶ A domestic fraternal society, order, or association[42]

▶ Certain cemetery companies

Because of the restrictions and limitations examined later in this chapter, these qualifying organizations are further classified into public charities and private nonoperating foundations. Different restrictions and limitations apply to each type of organization.

Public charities include:

REAL-WORLD
EXAMPLE

The American Red Cross, Boy Scouts of America, United Way, Goodwill, and Indiana University are examples of public charities.

▶ Churches or a convention or association of churches

▶ Educational institutions that normally maintain a regular faculty, curriculum, and regularly enrolled students

▶ Organizations such as hospitals and medical schools whose principal function is medical care or medical education and research

▶ Government-supported organizations that exist to receive, hold, invest, and administer property for the benefit of a college or university

▶ Any qualified governmental unit

▶ Organizations that normally receive a substantial part of their support from either a governmental unit or the general public

▶ Certain private operating foundations[43]

TYPE OF PROPERTY CONTRIBUTED

If a taxpayer makes a contribution in cash, the amount of the deduction is easily determinable. However, in order to assure that the contribution has been properly made to a qualified charity, the taxpayer is required to maintain a record of the contribution such as a bank record or a written communication from the donee.[44] If noncash property is donated, the amount of the contribution is not as easy to identify. In the case of noncash property, the amount of the donation depends on two factors: (1) the type of property donated and (2) the type of qualifying organization (public charity or private nonoperating foundation) to whom the property is given. Furthermore, a gift of property that consists of less than the donor's entire interest in the property is not usually considered a contribution of property. Thus, for example, no charitable contribution is allowed when an individual donates the use of a vacation home for a charitable fund-raising auction.[45]

SELF-STUDY
QUESTION

Doug purchases an item having a FMV of $75 for $100 in a charity auction. How much can he deduct?

ANSWER

Doug can deduct only $25 because the cash paid must be reduced by the value of the property received.

CONTRIBUTION OF LONG-TERM CAPITAL GAIN PROPERTY. In general, the amount of a donation of long-term capital gain property is its FMV. Regulation Sec. 1.170A-1(c)(2) defines a property's FMV as the price at which the property would change

---

[40] Under certain circumstances, a taxpayer may take a deduction (limited to $50 per month) for maintaining a student as a member of his or her household. The student may not be a dependent or relative of the taxpayer and must be placed in the taxpayer's home under an arrangement with a qualifying organization (see Sec. 170(g)).

[41] These organizations must be organized and operated exclusively for religious, charitable, scientific, literary, or educational purposes; to foster national or international amateur sports competition; or for the prevention of cruelty to children or animals.

[42] Furthermore, gifts to these organizations must be made by individuals and must be used exclusively for religious, charitable, scientific, literary, or educational purposes, or for the prevention of cruelty to children or animals.

[43] Sec. 170(b)(1)(E). The distinction between a private operating foundation

and a private nonoperating foundation generally depends on the way the foundation spends or distributes its income and contributions. The details of this distinction are beyond the scope of this text.

[44] Sec. 170(f)(17) and Notice 2008-16. This record must show (1) the name of the donee organization, (2) the date of the contribution, and (3) the amount of the contribution.

[45] Sec. 170(f)(3), Reg. Sec. 1.170A-7(a)(1) and Rev. Rul. 89-51, 1989-1 C.B. 89. Note, however, that certain transfers of partial interests in property do qualify (e.g., the contribution of certain remainder interests to a trust, the transfer of a remainder interest in a personal residence or a farm, or a contribution of an undivided interest in property). These exceptions are beyond the scope of this text.

ADDITIONAL COMMENT

The 2004 Jobs Act added new rules relating to the contribution of used vehicles and intellectual property. For a used vehicle donated to a charity, in most cases the deduction will be limited to the charity's gross proceeds on the subsequent sale of the vehicle. A taxpayer's deduction for the contribution of a patent or similar intellectual property is the taxpayer's basis in the property.

hands between a willing buyer and a willing seller, neither being under any compulsion to buy or sell and both having reasonable knowledge of relevant facts. For purposes of charitable contributions, **capital gain property** is property held over one year, on which the taxpayer would recognize a long-term capital gain if the taxpayer sold it at its FMV on the date of the contribution. If a capital loss or a short-term capital gain would be recognized on the sale of the capital asset, the property is considered to be ordinary income property for purposes of the charitable contribution deduction.

Contribution to a Private Nonoperating Foundation. The tax law provides an exception to this general rule for contributions of capital gain property to private nonoperating foundations. In general, a private nonoperating foundation is an organization that does not receive funding from the general public (e.g., the Carnegie Foundation). Private nonoperating foundations distribute funds to various charitable organizations that actually perform the charitable services. The amount of the contribution to a private nonoperating foundation is the property's FMV, reduced by the capital gain that would be recognized if the property were sold at its FMV on the date of the contribution. This means that generally the deductible amount of the contribution is the lesser of the property's adjusted basis or its FMV.[46]

EXAMPLE I:7-24 ▶ Betty purchased some land in 1991 for $10,000. In the current year, she contributes the land to the United Way. At the time of the contribution, the FMV of the property is $25,000. Because the land is long-term capital gain property donated to a public charity, the amount of the contribution is $25,000 (its FMV).

On the other hand, if Betty donates the land to Cherry Foundation, a private nonoperating foundation, the amount of the contribution is $10,000 ($25,000 − $15,000 capital gain that would be recognized if the land were sold). ◀

TYPICAL MISCONCEPTION

Many people do not understand that the unrelated use restriction applies only to tangible personal property. A gift of shares of stock (intangible property) would not be a gift of unrelated use property where the stock is sold by the donee.

Unrelated Use Property. A second exception applies to capital gain property (that is also tangible personal property) contributed to a public charity and used by the organization for purposes unrelated to the charity's function. In such cases, the amount of the contribution deduction is equal to the property's FMV minus the capital gain that would be recognized if the property were sold at its FMV. This amount generally is the property's adjusted basis. Tangible property is all property that is not intangible property (e.g., property other than stock, securities, copyrights, patents, and so on). Personal property is all property other than real estate. The taxpayer is responsible for proving that the property was not put to unrelated use. However, a taxpayer meets this burden of proof if, at the time of the contribution, the taxpayer reasonably anticipates that the property will not be put to unrelated use. The immediate sale of the property by the charitable organization is a use unrelated to its tax-exempt purpose.

EXAMPLE I:7-25 ▶ Laura purchases a painting for $3,000. Several years later she contributes the painting to a local college. The FMV of the painting is $5,000 at the time the property is contributed. The painting is both tangible personal property and capital gain property. The college places the painting in the library for display and study by art students. Because the college uses the painting for purposes related to its function as an educational institution, the amount of Laura's contribution is equal to its FMV ($5,000). On the other hand, if the college had sold the painting immediately after receiving it, the presumption is that the property's use was unrelated to the college's tax-exempt purpose. In this case, Laura's contribution is only $3,000. ◀

Certain Intangibles. Under Sec. 170(e)(1)(B), a third exception applies to the contribution of certain intangibles to a charitable organization. In this case, the amount of the charitable contribution is the FMV of the property, reduced by the amount of long-term capital gain that would have been recognized if the taxpayer had sold the property. These intangibles include patents, trademarks, a trade name or secret, know-how, a purchased copyright, and certain software.

---

[46] The amount of a contribution of appreciated stock made to a private nonoperating foundation remains at its FMV.

CONTRIBUTION OF ORDINARY INCOME PROPERTY

General Rule. If a taxpayer contributes ordinary income property to a charitable organization, the deduction is equal to the property's FMV minus the amount of gain that would be recognized if the taxpayer had sold the property at its FMV on the date of the contribution. In most cases, this deduction is equal to the property's adjusted basis. This rule applies regardless of the type of charitable organization to which the property is donated.

For this purpose, **ordinary income property** includes any property that would result in the recognition of income taxed at ordinary income rates if the taxpayer sold the property. Thus, ordinary income property includes inventory, works of art or manuscripts created by the taxpayer, capital assets that have been held for one year or less, and Sec. 1231 property to the extent a sale would result in the recognition of ordinary income due to depreciation recapture.[47]

EXAMPLE I:7-26 ▶ During the current year, Beta, Inc. purchases land as an investment for $10,000. Five months later, it contributes the land to the United Way. At the time of the contribution the property's FMV is $15,000. The amount of Beta's contribution is $10,000 ($15,000 − [$15,000 − $10,000]) because it held the land for less than one year. ◀

EXAMPLE I:7-27 ▶ Pork, Inc. purchased a machine a few years ago for $20,000 and used the machine in its business. During the current year, Pork, Inc. donates the machine to a local community college. At the time of the contribution, the machine's adjusted basis is $5,000 and its FMV is $8,000. Because Pork, Inc. would have recognized a $3,000 gain (all ordinary income under Sec. 1245) if the machine were sold at its FMV, the amount of the contribution is $5,000 ($8,000 − $3,000), which is equal to the machine's adjusted basis. ◀

Donation of Inventory by a Corporation. Under certain circumstances, a corporation's donation of inventory to certain public charities provides a larger charitable contribution deduction than the adjusted basis of the property. One such exception is available if the charity uses the inventory solely for the care of the ill, needy, or infants.[48] Another exception involves the donation of scientific equipment constructed by the taxpayer and donated to a college, university, or qualified research organization for use in research, experimentation, or research training in the physical or biological sciences. A third exception is available for contributions of computer technology and equipment donated to public libraries and elementary and secondary schools.[49] In all cases, the amount of the charitable contribution is the property's FMV, reduced by 50% (not 100%) of the ordinary income that the taxpayer would recognize if it had sold the property at its FMV. However, the amount of the contribution may not exceed twice the basis of the property.

EXAMPLE I:7-28 ▶ During the current year, Able Corporation, a manufacturer of medical supplies, donates some of its inventory to the American Red Cross. The Red Cross intends to use the inventory for the care of the needy and ill. At the time of the contribution, the FMV of the inventory is $10,000. Able's basis in the inventory is $3,000. Because this transaction qualifies under the exception, the amount of Able's contribution (before any limitations are applied) is $6,500 [$10,000 − (0.50 × $7,000)] but the actual amount of the contribution is limited to $6,000 (2 × the $3,000 basis in the property). ◀

CONTRIBUTION OF SERVICES. When a taxpayer renders services to a qualified charitable organization, the taxpayer may only deduct the unreimbursed expenses incurred incident to rendering the services. These items include out-of-pocket expenses, transportation expenses, the cost of lodging and 50% of the cost of meals while away from home, and the cost of a uniform that is required to be worn in performing the donated services but is not suitable for general wear. The out-of-pocket expenses are deductible only if incurred by the taxpayer who actually renders the services to the charity. Taxpayers cannot take a deduction for expenses while away from home unless they experience no

---

[47] Reg. Secs. 1.170A-4(b)(1) and 1.170A-4(d). Sec. 1231 property includes property used in a trade or business that is subject to depreciation. If it is sold at a gain, part or all of the gain is treated as ordinary income. Any remaining gain is subject to the Sec. 1231 rules. (See Chapter I:13 for an explanation of the depreciation recapture and Sec. 1231 rules.)

[48] Sec. 170(e). These charitable organizations are known as Sec. 501(c)(3) charities.

[49] Sec. 170(e)(6). This provision expires for contributions made after December 31, 2009.

significant element of personal pleasure, recreation, or vacation in such travel. Instead of the actual costs of operating an automobile while performing the donated services, the law permits a deduction of 14 cents per mile.[50]

EXAMPLE I:7-29 ▶

REAL-WORLD EXAMPLE

The cost of newspaper advertising, paper, pencils, and other supplies purchased by volunteers in connection with their involvement in the Volunteer Income Tax Assistance Program (VITA) is deductible. Rev. Rul. 80-45, 1980-1 C.B. 54.

During the current year, Tony spends a total of 100 hours developing an accounting system for the local council of the Boy Scouts of America. As an accountant, Tony earns $200 per hour. During the year, Tony also drives his car a total of 500 miles in performing the services for the Boy Scouts of America. If he uses the automatic mileage method to compute the amount of the charitable contribution, he can deduct $70 (0.14 × 500). No deduction is available for the value of 100 hours of Tony's contributed services. ◀

DEDUCTION LIMITATIONS

OVERALL 50% LIMITATION.   The charitable contribution deduction available for any tax year is subject to certain limitations. For individuals, the general overall limitation applicable to public charities is 50% of the taxpayer's AGI for the year. Any contributions in excess of the overall limitation may be carried forward and deducted in the subsequent five tax years. In addition, the tax law imposes further limitations on contributions of capital gain property to either a public charity or a private nonoperating foundation and all types of property contributions to private nonoperating foundations.

KEY POINT

The generosity of Congress in permitting individuals to use FMV is tempered by the 30% of AGI limitation.

30% LIMITATION.   Under certain circumstances, a special 30% of AGI limitation applies. Contributions of capital gain property (capital assets held over one year on which a gain would be realized if sold) to public charities are generally valued at the property's FMV, but the deduction may not exceed an overall limit of 30% of AGI instead of a 50% limit. This special 30% limit does not apply, however, in the following situations:

▶ Capital gain property (which is tangible personal property) donated to a public charity that does not put the property to its related use. In such cases, the amount of the contribution is reduced by the capital gain that would be recognized if the property were sold.

▶ The taxpayer elects to reduce the amount of the charitable contribution deduction by the capital gain that the taxpayer would recognize if he or she sold the property.

EXAMPLE I:7-30 ▶

Joy donates a painting to the local university during a year in which she has AGI of $50,000. The painting, which cost $10,000 several years before, is valued at $30,000 at the time of the contribution. The university exhibits the painting in its art gallery. Because the painting is put to a use related to the university's purpose, the amount of Joy's contribution is $30,000. The amount of Joy's charitable deduction for the year, however, is limited to $15,000 (0.30 × $50,000 AGI) unless she elects to reduce the amount of the contribution by the long-term capital gain. ◀

The overall deduction limitation of 30% of AGI also applies to the contribution of all types of property other than capital gain property (e.g., cash and ordinary income property) to a private nonoperating foundation. However, further restrictions may apply to the deductibility of certain contributions to this type of charity.

20% LIMITATION ON CAPITAL GAIN PROPERTY CONTRIBUTED TO PRIVATE NONOPERATING FOUNDATIONS.   Contributions of capital gain property to private nonoperating foundations may not exceed the lesser of (1) 20% of the taxpayer's AGI or (2) 30% of the taxpayer's AGI, reduced by any contributions of capital gain property donated to a public charity.

CONTRIBUTIONS FOR ATHLETIC EVENTS.   If a taxpayer makes a contribution to a college or university and in return receives the right to purchase tickets to athletic events, the taxpayer may deduct only 80% of the payment.

APPLYING THE DEDUCTION LIMITATIONS.   Contributions subject only to the 50% of AGI limitation are accounted for before the contributions subject to the 30% of AGI limitation.

---

[50] Sec. 170(i).

EXAMPLE I:7-31 ▶ During a year when Ted's AGI is $70,000, he donates $22,000 to his church and $18,000 to a private nonoperating charity. The church contribution is initially subject to the 50% limitation and is fully deductible because the $22,000 contribution is less than the limitation amount of $35,000 (0.50 × $70,000). Ted's deduction for the contribution to the private nonoperating charity (a 30% charity) is limited to $13,000 (the lesser of the following three amounts):

The actual contribution	$18,000
The remaining 50% limitation after the contribution to Ted's church [(0.50 × $70,000) − $22,000]	$13,000
30% of AGI (0.30 × $70,000)	$21,000 ◀

APPLICATION OF CARRYOVERS

As noted earlier, any contributions that exceed the 50% limitation may be carried over and deducted in the subsequent five years. These carryovers are subject to the limitations that apply in subsequent years. Thus, taxpayers may deduct carryovers only to the extent that the limitation of the subsequent year exceeds the contributions made during that year.

TAX PLANNING

If a taxpayer has contribution carryovers that are about to expire, the taxpayer should consider reducing the current year's contribution so that the carryovers can be deducted.

These general rules also apply with regard to the special limitations. For example, if the taxpayer donates property subject to the 30% limitation during the current year and the amount of the contribution exceeds the limitation, the excess may carry over to the five subsequent years subject to the 30% limitation in the carryover years. In the carryover year, a deduction may be taken for the excess contribution to the extent that the 30% limitation of the subsequent year exceeds the amount of the property donated during the subsequent year subject to the 30% limitation. Excess contributions of property subject to the 20% limitation may also carry over to the subsequent five years. This carryover is also subject to the special restrictions noted above for the 30% limitation. The carryovers are used in chronological order.

EXAMPLE I:7-32 ▶ Assume that for the years 2009 through 2011, Joan reports AGI and makes charitable contributions in the following amounts:

	2009	2010	2011
AGI	$40,000	$40,000	$60,000
Cash contributions subject to the 50% of AGI limitation	25,000	23,000	24,000
50% of AGI limitation	20,000	20,000	30,000

The amount of the charitable contribution deduction for each year and the order in which the deduction and carryovers are used are as follows:

	2009	2010	2011
Amount of deduction	$20,000	$20,000	$30,000
Amount of carryover			
From 2009	5,000	5,000	0
From 2010		3,000	2,000 ◀

SPECIAL RULES FOR CHARITABLE CONTRIBUTIONS MADE BY CORPORATIONS

The rules governing charitable contributions made by corporations are generally the same as those pertaining to contributions made by individuals. However, certain differences do exist.

PLEDGES MADE BY AN ACCRUAL METHOD CORPORATION. Generally, taxpayers may only deduct actual contributions (not pledges) made during the tax year. This rule applies to both cash and accrual method taxpayers. A major exception to this general rule exists for accrual method corporations. Such corporations may elect to claim a charitable deduction for the year in which the corporation makes a pledge as long as the actual contribution is made by the fifteenth day of the third month following the close of the year in which the pledge is made.

ETHICAL POINT

A tax practitioner should not be a party to the backdating of a Board of Director's authorization of a charitable contribution pledge so that the corporation may improperly deduct the contribution in the earlier year.

LIMITATION APPLICABLE TO CORPORATIONS. Corporate charitable deductions may not exceed 10% of the corporation's taxable income for the year. This amount is computed without regard to the dividends-received deduction, net operating loss or capital loss carrybacks, or any deduction for the charitable contribution itself. Excess contributions may be carried forward for five years and are deductible only if the current-year

contributions are less than the current year's 10% limitation. The corporation also uses the carryovers in chronological order.

SUMMARY OF DEDUCTION LIMITATIONS

Topic Review I:7-3 summarizes the rules governing the deduction for charitable contributions.

Topic Review I:7-3

Deduction Rules for Charitable Contributions

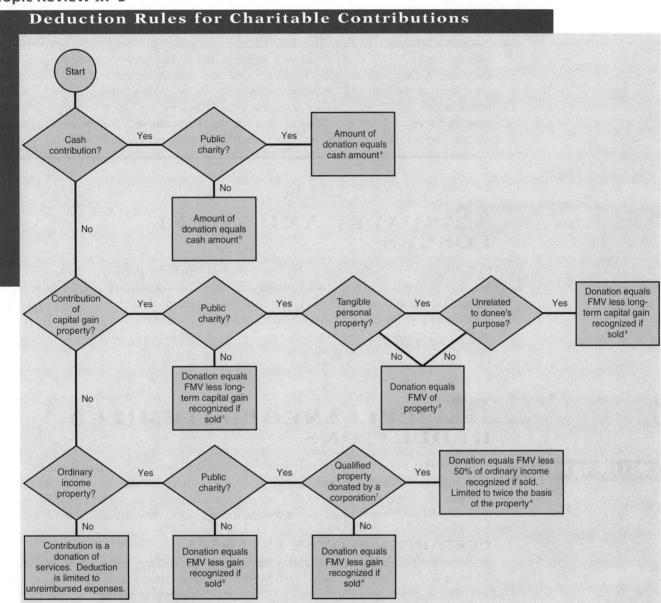

ᵃ Limited to 50% of AGI.
ᵇ Limited to lesser of (1) 30% of AGI or (2) remaining 50% of AGI after accounting for donations to public charities.
ᶜ Limited to lesser of (1) 20% of AGI or (2) 30% of AGI less capital gain contributions to public charities.
ᵈ Taxpayer may elect to scale down the amount of donation by long-term capital gain. If the election is made, limited to 50% of AGI. If no election is made, limited to 30% of AGI.
ᵉ Limited to 10% of the corporation's taxable income without regard to any deduction for charitable contributions, dividends received, a net operating loss carryback or a capital loss carryback.
ᶠ Qualified property consists of either (1) inventory or property used in a trade or business which will be used by a Sec. 501(c)(3) charity for the care of the ill, needy, or infants, (2) inventory constructed by the corporation which will be used by a qualified research institution in the physical or biological sciences, or (3) computer software and equipment donated to and used by elementary and secondary schools located in the United States and public libraries.

STOP & THINK

Question: During the current year, Kim pledges to contribute $10,000 to both the Boy Scouts of America (BSA) and to a private nonoperating foundation. She wants to satisfy those pledges before the end of the year in order to take a deduction this year. She has enough cash to satisfy one of the pledges, but must either sell or donate some land in order to satisfy the other. The land she has in mind has a fair market value of $10,000 and a cost basis of $2,000. She purchased the land four years ago. Kim estimates that she will have AGI of $500,000 and will be in the 35% marginal tax bracket. Assuming that both charities would gladly accept either contribution, how should Kim satisfy these pledges?

Solution: The amount of contribution of capital gain property to a public charity is the property's fair market value. The 30% of AGI limitation applies to such contributions. However, a contribution of capital gain property to a private non-operating foundation is the property's fair market value, reduced by the gain that the taxpayer would have recognized if he or she had sold the property (generally the property's basis). The 50% of AGI limitation applies to these contributions. Since Kim's AGI for the year is so high, the limitations do not apply. Thus, Kim should contribute the land to the BSA and the cash to the private non-operating foundation, for a total charitable contribution of $20,000.

CASUALTY AND THEFT LOSSES

Generally, taxpayers may not deduct losses on personal-use property. However, under Sec. 165 individuals may deduct a casualty or theft loss on personal-use property as an itemized deduction on Schedule A of Form 1040. Individuals deduct casualty losses on business and investment properties held for the production of rents or royalties in arriving at AGI. Other casualty losses on investment property are itemized deductions. Chapter I:8 discusses casualty losses in greater depth.

MISCELLANEOUS ITEMIZED DEDUCTIONS

OBJECTIVE 8

Identify certain miscellaneous itemized deductions subject to the 2% of AGI limit

Taxpayers may deduct various types of expenses as miscellaneous itemized deductions. These deductions include employment-related expenses of employees, certain investment-related expenses, and the cost of tax advice. However, as explained in Chapter I:9, these items generally are deductible only to the extent that, in the aggregate, they exceed 2% of AGI.

CERTAIN EMPLOYEE EXPENSES

Taxpayers may deduct certain employment-related expenses as itemized deductions on Schedule A. These expenses include *unreimbursed* expenditures for travel and transportation, dues to professional organizations, costs of job hunting, items of protective clothing or uniforms not suitable for everyday wear, union dues, subscriptions to trade journals, and so on. Chapter I:9 provides a more detailed discussion of this topic.

EXPENSES TO PRODUCE INVESTMENT INCOME

Under Sec. 212, individuals may deduct expenses incurred to produce income. If these expenses arise in an activity that produces either rental or royalty income, they are deductions *for* AGI (see the explanation in Chapter I:6). However, if a taxpayer incurs the expenses in generating other types of investment income, such as interest, dividends, etc., the individual taxpayer may deduct such expenses on Schedule A as itemized deductions. These investment-related expenditures include items such as rental fees for safe-deposit boxes used to hold investment property, subscriptions to investment and trade journals, bank service charges on

ETHICAL POINT

If a client furnishes a handwritten list of his or her miscellaneous itemized deductions to a CPA, the CPA may in good faith rely on the information without verification. However, the CPA should not ignore the implications of information that is provided and should make reasonable inquiries if the information furnished appears to be incorrect, incomplete, or inconsistent.

REAL-WORLD EXAMPLE

A taxpayer claimed that it was necessary to take a leave of absence from his job in order to appear before the Tax Court, to type various legal papers, and to take notes during the trial. He was not allowed to deduct the so-called lost wages representing the amount of vacation time spent in defending the suit. *James P. Stuart,* 1987 PH T.C. Memo ¶87,386, 54 TCM 70.

checking accounts used in an investment activity, and fees paid for consulting advice. These expenses are all subject to the 2% of AGI reduction. Flow-through entities (e.g., partnerships and S corporations) must report these types of investment expenses to their owners as separately stated items so that the 2% of AGI reduction may be applied.

COST OF TAX ADVICE

Section 212 provides individuals with a deduction for expenses incurred in connection with the determination, collection, or refund of any tax, including federal, state, local, and foreign income taxes as well as estate, gift, and inheritance taxes. These items include (1) tax return preparation fees, (2) appraisal fees incurred in determining the amount of a casualty loss, certain capital improvements for a medical deduction, or the FMV of property donated to a qualified charity, (3) fees paid to an accountant for representation in a tax audit, (4) long-distance telephone calls responding to IRS questions, (5) costs of tax return preparation materials and books, and (6) legal fees incurred in planning the tax consequences dealing with estate planning. If an individual incurs these items in connection with the taxpayer's (1) trade or business (reported on Schedule C), (2) farm income (reported on Schedule F), or (3) an activity which produces rents or royalties (reported on Part I of Schedule E), they are *for* AGI deductions.[51] All other expenses incurred for tax advice are miscellaneous itemized deductions subject to the 2% of AGI limitation.

Fees not directly connected with the determination, collection, or refund of a tax or with the taxpayer's trade or business are personal expenses and are not deductible. Thus, legal fees incurred for drafting wills generally are not deductible. However, legal expenses incurred in tax fraud cases in connection with the filing of a fraudulent return generally are deductible.[52] Legal fees relating to a divorce generally are not deductible, unless they deal with tax-related items such as determining who will receive the exemption for dependent children. Chapter I:3 discusses these fees in greater detail.

REDUCTION OF CERTAIN ITEMIZED DEDUCTIONS

OBJECTIVE 9

Compute total itemized deductions for a taxpayer who is subject to the itemized deduction phase-out

ADDITIONAL COMMENT

The reduction in itemized deductions obscures the true marginal tax rate applicable to high-income taxpayers and can be thought of as a hidden tax rate.

Because of concerns with the budget deficit, Congress enacted Sec. 68 several years ago which provides for a reduction in the total amount of certain itemized deductions for high-income taxpayers.[53] This reduction applies only to individuals with AGI in excess of a certain threshold amount. This AGI threshold amount for 2009 was $166,800 ($83,400 for married people filing separate returns). Starting in 2006, these phaseouts were gradually reduced and are completely eliminated by the year 2010. However, this elimination of the phaseout may be short-lived. If Congress does not pass another law changing the law as it now exists, the full reduction of these certain itemized deductions will again occur for tax years beginning in 2011 and beyond. Thus, if Congress doesn't take any action, the reduction in 2011 will be 3% of the amount that the individual's AGI for the year exceeds the threshold amount. However, two other limitations will apply. First, the reduction in the itemized deductions cannot exceed 80% of the total itemized deductions other than medical expenses, investment interest, casualty losses, and wagering losses. Second, the reduction is applied after taking into account the other limitations on itemized deductions (e.g., the 2% of AGI limitation on miscellaneous itemized deductions).

EXAMPLE I:7-33 ▶ During 2009, John and Sue (a married couple filing a joint return) reported AGI of $250,000. In addition, their itemized deductions consisted of $10,000 charitable contributions, $4,000 real property taxes, $8,000 state income taxes, and deductible investment interest expense of $5,000. Because their AGI exceeded $166,800, their itemized deductions for the year were limited to $26,168 ($27,000 − $832), computed as follows:

[51] Rev. Rul. 92-29, 1992-1 C.B. 20.
[52] Rev. Rul. 68-662, 1968-2 C.B. 69.
[53] In 2001, Congress authorized the elimination of this reduction of itemized deductions for high-income taxpayers. This elimination began in 2006 and by 2010 the reduction is completely eliminated. However, unless Congress changes the law, the phase out of the itemized deductions will apply again in 2011 and later years. Furthermore, Congress currently is considering a bill that would re-enact this reduction for 2010.

AGI	$250,000
Threshold	(166,800)
Excess	$ 83,200
Times: Reduction percentage (0.03 × ⅓)	× 0.01
Potential reduction	$832

Limit to reduction (not including investment interest):	
Charitable contributions	$ 10,000
Property taxes	4,000
State income taxes	8,000
Total	$ 22,000
Times: Limitation percentage	× 0.80
Overall limit on reduction	$ 17,600

The 80% limitation does not apply because the $832 reduction is less than $17,600. ◄

EXAMPLE I:7-34 ▶ Assume the same facts as Example I:7-33 except that John and Sue's AGI is $2,200,000. Now John and Sue's allowable itemized deductions for the year are $9,400 ($27,000 − 17,600), computed as follows:

AGI	$2,200,000
Threshold	(166,800)
Excess	$2,033,200
Times: Reduction percentage (0.03 × ⅓)	× 0.01
Potential reduction	$ 20,332

Limit to reduction (not including investment expense):	
Charitable contributions	$ 10,000
Property taxes	4,000
State income taxes	8,000
Total	$ 22,000
Times: Limitation percentage	× 0.80
Overall limit on reduction	$ 17,600

The 80% limitation applies in this case. Since the potential reduction of $20,332 is greater than 80% of the itemized deductions, other than investment interest expense, the total reduction is limited to $17,600. As can be seen from this example, the 80% limitation applies only to high income taxpayers with relatively small itemized deductions. ◄

STOP & THINK

Question: Joe is a general contractor who uses the cash method of accounting. He has been hired to do a job that will pay him $30,000. Under the terms of the agreement, Joe is to receive the full $30,000 when the job is complete. By December 15 of the current year, Joe estimates that the job can be completed with approximately seven more days of work. The person who hired Joe doesn't care if the job is completed in December of the current year or January of the subsequent year. Joe's AGI for the current year, excluding this job, will be $200,000. Joe and his wife, Kim, estimate that their state income taxes, residential interest, and charitable contributions for the current year total approximately $10,000. Because of a general economic slowdown, Joe estimates that his AGI for the subsequent year will be $90,000. What advice can you give Joe regarding when he should complete this job and collect the income?

Solution: For tax purposes, Joe should complete the job in January of the subsequent year for a couple of reasons. First, if their estimates are correct, Joe and Kim likely will be in the 28% marginal tax bracket for the current year and the 25% marginal tax bracket for the subsequent year. Second, Joe and Kim's AGI for the current year will exceed the threshold amount, thus causing a reduction in their itemized deductions. This reduction increases their effective tax rate. On the other hand, if Joe and Kim report the $30,000 in income in the subsequent year, they will not have to reduce their itemized deductions of that year. Finally, since there is only a delay of a few days between collecting the income in the current year and delaying the collection into the subsequent year, present value issues regarding the receipt of the income don't need to be addressed.

TAX PLANNING CONSIDERATIONS

MEDICAL EXPENSE DEDUCTION

WORKING WITH THE 7.5% OF AGI FLOOR. As explained previously, a deduction for medical expenses is available to individuals only to the extent that those expenditures exceed 7.5% of the taxpayer's AGI for the year. Thus, many individuals find that no deduction is available, even though their medical expenses are relatively high. In these cases, taxpayers may obtain some benefit if they can bunch the medical expenses into one year. Orthodontic work, certain orthopedic treatment, noncosmetic elective surgery, and new eyeglasses are all examples of medical expenditures that may be either accelerated or delayed into a year in which other medical expenses are high or AGI is lower.

Generally, a taxpayer may take a deduction for medical expenses only in the year in which the expense is actually paid. The mere prepayment of future expenses usually does not accelerate the deduction. However, taxpayers may take a deduction in the earlier year of payment if there is a legal obligation to pay or if the prepayment is a requirement for the receipt of the medical care.[54] If the taxpayer has already received the medical treatment, but the taxpayer does not have sufficient cash to pay the bill, the taxpayer may preserve a deduction for the current year by either borrowing the cash to satisfy the bill or by using a credit card.

EXAMPLE I:7-35 ▶

During the current year, Marty's estimated AGI is $50,000. Marty has already incurred $2,500 in medical expenses for himself and his family during the year. Because 7.5% of AGI for the year is $3,750, he receives no medical expense deduction. Marty plans to incur $3,500 in medical expenses for orthodontic work for his son next year. No other major medical expenses are anticipated, and Marty expects his AGI in the following year to remain the same. If these estimates are accurate, he will receive no medical deduction in either year. However, if the orthodontic work is started in the current year and Marty pays for the work, he will incur a total of $6,000 in medical expenses in the current year. Thus, $2,250 ($6,000 − $3,750) of the medical expenses may be deducted.

Mere prepayment in this case is not sufficient. Marty must have a portion of the orthodontic services performed in the earlier year. If he does not have sufficient cash to pay the bill in the current year, he could borrow the money or use a bank credit card. ◀

KEY POINT

Even if the medical expenses exceed 7.5% of AGI the taxpayer may not benefit from the deduction if the medical expenses in addition to the other itemized deductions do not exceed the standard deduction.

MULTIPLE SUPPORT AGREEMENTS. An individual may deduct medical expenses incurred for himself or herself, his or her spouse, dependents, children of divorced parents even if not a dependent, and persons who would qualify as a dependent except for the failure to meet the gross income or joint return test. In cases where a multiple support agreement has been filed, the tax law treats the individual who is the subject of the agreement as the dependent of the taxpayer entitled to the dependency exemption. Thus, to preserve the medical expense deduction, the taxpayer entitled to the dependency exemption should pay all medical expenditures for the dependent individual.

EXAMPLE I:7-36 ▶

Amy, Bart, Clay, and Donna each provide 25% of the support of their father, Eric. Under the terms of a multiple support agreement, Bart, Clay, and Donna all agree to allow Amy to claim the dependency exemption with respect to Eric. During the year, $3,000 in medical expenses are incurred on Eric's behalf. If Amy pays these expenses, she may deduct them (subject to limitations). However, if Bart, Clay, or Donna pays these expenses, no one may claim the medical expenses as a deduction. ◀

INTEREST EXPENSE DEDUCTION

A taxpayer may deduct qualified residence interest incurred on a principal residence and one other qualified residence that the taxpayer selects. The taxpayer makes this choice annually. The taxpayer may choose any residence that is not a rental property. Otherwise,

---

[54] *Robert M. Rose v. CIR*, 26 AFTR 2d 70-5653, 70-2 USTC ¶9646 (5th Cir., 1970). See also Rev. Ruls. 75-302, 1975-2 C.B. 86, and 75-303, 1975-2 C.B. 87, both clarified by Rev. Rul. 93-72, 1993-2 C.B. 77.

in order for the second residence to qualify, the taxpayer must use it personally for more than the greater of 14 days or 10% of the rental days during the year. If this test is met, however, the Sec. 280A limitations on the rental of vacation homes also apply. As explained in Chapter I:6, under these rules, taxpayers must allocate expenses between the rental use and the personal use of the property. Taxpayers may deduct the expenses allocated to the rental use only to the extent of the rental income. Of the expenses allocated to the personal use, only the taxes and interest (if the residence is selected and if the loan is secured by the residence) are deductible as itemized deductions.

If the personal use by the taxpayer does not meet the test mentioned above, the interest allocated to the personal use cannot qualify as residence interest and it becomes non-deductible personal interest. Furthermore, the passive loss rules apply to the rental income and expenses allocated to the rental use of the property (see Chapter I:8). Under these rules, individuals generally can deduct losses generated from a passive activity only to the extent of the individual's passive income. Certain individuals, however, may deduct up to $25,000 of losses from the rental of real estate. Thus, the two alternatives and their consequences are as follows:

▶ Meet the test. No loss from the rental portion of the property is deductible. However, the interest allocated to the personal use portion may be fully deductible as qualified residence interest.

▶ Do not meet the test. The interest allocated to the personal use portion is nondeductible personal interest. However, all of the passive loss from the rental portion is deductible against passive income. Furthermore, certain individuals may deduct up to $25,000 additional passive loss.

The alternative a taxpayer chooses depends on several factors, including the amount of the taxpayer's passive income, the total amount of itemized deductions, and whether the loan is secured by the vacation home.

DEDUCTION FOR CHARITABLE CONTRIBUTIONS

ELECTION TO REDUCE THE AMOUNT OF A CHARITABLE CONTRIBUTION. The election to reduce the contribution of capital gain property to public charities by the long-term capital gain that the taxpayer would recognize if he or she sold the property is an annual election that applies to all capital gain property donated to public charities during the year. Because the election increases the ceiling limitation from 30% to 50%, under certain circumstances a taxpayer may actually receive a larger deduction for the year than would normally be available if the taxpayer did not make the election.

SELF-STUDY QUESTION

What type of property lends itself to the "election to reduce"?

ANSWER

Property on which there is very little appreciation.

EXAMPLE I:7-37 ▶

During the current year, Jane has AGI of $50,000. She donates a painting to the local university during the same year. The painting, valued at $30,000 at the time of contribution, cost her $25,000 several years before. The university displays the painting in its art museum. If Jane does not make the election, the amount of the contribution is equal to its FMV ($30,000). However, Jane's charitable contribution deduction for the year is limited to $15,000 ($50,000 × 0.30). If Jane makes the election to reduce the contribution amount, the deduction is reduced to $25,000 ($30,000 − $5,000 LTCG). The deduction limitation, however, increases to $25,000 for the year because the limitation is now based on 50% of AGI instead of 30%. In this case, Jane will receive a larger deduction for the year by making the election. However, the cost associated with this election is the loss of $5,000 of deduction because the total deduction is reduced from $30,000 to $25,000 if she makes the election. ◀

Many tax practitioners make this election only when preparing the taxpayer's final tax return. The taxpayer makes the election at this time because charitable contribution carryovers to the decedent's estate are not permitted.

ADDITIONAL COMMENT

To help determine the FMV of contributed property, taxpayers can read IRS Pub. No. 561, Determining the Value of Donated Property.

DONATION OF APPRECIATED CAPITAL GAIN PROPERTY. Instead of selling substantially appreciated capital gain property and donating the cash proceeds, the taxpayer should donate the property directly to charity. If property is donated in this way, the donor receives a deduction equal to the FMV of the property and does not recognize any taxable gain on the disposition.

EXAMPLE I:7-38 ▶ Colleen wishes to satisfy a pledge of $100,000 made to a local university. She owns $100,000 worth of marketable securities purchased ten years ago for $30,000. Because the securities are marketable, the university is indifferent as to whether Colleen donates cash or the securities. Although her marginal tax rate is 35%, Colleen would be subject to a tax rate of 15% on the sale of the securities. She has enough AGI to be able to deduct the full contribution in the current year. The following chart summarizes the cash flows to Colleen under two different alternatives:

	Donate Securities	Sell Securities and Donate Cash
Proceeds of sale	0	$100,000
Tax on gain	0	(10,500)[a]
Cash payment to charity		(100,000)
Tax savings from the contribution deduction	$35,000[b]	35,000
Net cash flow	$35,000	$ 24,500

[a]($100,000 − $30,000) × 0.15 = $10,500.
[b]$100,000 × 0.35 = $35,000.

◀

In order to take a tax loss on business or investment property, a taxpayer should not donate property that has decreased in value. Rather, the taxpayer should sell the property, recognize the loss, and donate the cash proceeds.

COMPLIANCE AND PROCEDURAL CONSIDERATIONS

MEDICAL EXPENSES

In certain cases, expenditures qualify as both a medical care expense and a dependent care expense (i.e., expenses for household and dependent care services that the taxpayer must pay to be gainfully employed). A taxpayer who incurs an expense that qualifies under both provisions may choose to take either a medical expense deduction or a tax credit under Sec. 21.[55] However, if a taxpayer takes a credit for these expenses, they are not deductible as medical expenses.

EXAMPLE I:7-39 ▶ Joel's daughter, Debbie, is physically handicapped. As a result, Joel hires a nurse who provides daily care while he is at work. During the year, Joel pays the nurse a total of $3,000. This amount qualifies for both the dependent care credit and the medical expense deduction. If Joel takes the dependent care credit, the $3,000 may not be deducted as a medical expense. Because of the limitations imposed on each, the determination of which treatment is more advantageous depends on items such as the taxpayer's AGI, other medical expenses, and total itemized deductions. ◀

ADDITIONAL COMMENT

On Form 8283, the charitable organization is required to acknowledge receipt of the gift and to file an information return if the property is sold or disposed of within two years.

CHARITABLE CONTRIBUTIONS

Over the past several years, the IRS has significantly tightened the requirements needed to properly substantiate a charitable contribution in an attempt to prevent abuses in claiming inflated charitable contributions. In order for a taxpayer to take a deduction for a cash contribution of any amount, the taxpayer must be able to substantiate the contribution with either a bank record or a written receipt from the charity. Self-created documents are not sufficient. Previously, this requirement was imposed only on cash contributions of $250 or more. In addition, when a taxpayer donates property other than cash to a qualifying charity, proper determination of the property's FMV is a critical issue. Because of actual and perceived abuses in this area, the IRS often scrutinizes and, if necessary, challenges the valuation of contributed property. This is especially true for contributions of

---

[55] A credit of 35% of expenses for child and dependent care services is allowed if the dependent is under age 13 or a spouse or dependent who is mentally or physically incapable of caring for himself or herself. The credit is reduced 1% for every $2,000 (or portion thereof) of AGI over $15,000. However, the credit may not be reduced below 20%. (See the discussion on Personal Tax Credits in Chapter I:14 for a more detailed explanation of the child and dependent care credit.)

REAL-LIFE EXAMPLE

In one case the taxpayer, a CPA, failed to support a contribution with a qualified appraisal. As a result, his charitable deduction for art and printing supplies donated to a high school was denied. To substantiate the claimed $40,000 charitable deduction, the taxpayer submitted with Form 8283 an appraisal of the donated items made by the high school's principal. The principal, however, wasn't a "qualified appraiser." *D'Arcangelo,* TC Memo 1994-572 (1994).

ADDITIONAL COMMENT

If the taxpayer's total deduction for art is $20,000 or more, he or she must include an 8 × 10 inch color photograph or a color transparency no smaller than 4 × 5 inches.

property for which no published market quotes exist. Thus, the taxpayer must (1) properly substantiate the fact that the contribution has actually been made, and (2) in the case of the contribution of property, the taxpayer may be required to acquire and retain or provide to the IRS information documenting the property's FMV. As noted below, special detailed substantiation and documentation requirements apply to the contribution of used motor vehicles, boats, and airplanes.

PROPER SUBSTANTIATION. As mentioned above, if the contribution is made in cash, the taxpayer must retain evidence of the donation by keeping a cancelled check or other bank record or a receipt from the charitable organization. If the contribution is in the form of noncash property, the taxpayer must maintain records containing the following:

▶ Name and address of the charity to which the contribution was made

▶ Date and location of the contribution

▶ Description of the property

▶ FMV of the property

▶ Method of determining the property's FMV

▶ Signed copy of the appraisal report if an appraiser was used[56]

For charitable contributions of $250 or more, no deduction is allowed unless the contribution is substantiated by a contemporaneous, written acknowledgment (receipt) by the donee organization. This acknowledgment must contain the following information:

▶ The amount of cash and a description of any property contributed

▶ Whether or not the organization provided any goods or services in consideration for the cash or property received, including a description and good faith estimate of the value of any goods or services provided by the organization

The acknowledgment is contemporaneous if obtained by the earlier of the date the taxpayer files a return for the year in question or the extended due date for filing such a return. This substantiation requirement is waived if the donee organization files a return that contains the required information.[57] Additionally, no deduction is allowed for a contribution of clothing or household items unless the items are in "good" condition. Unfortunately, the law does not provide guidance as to what constitutes "good" condition.

DOCUMENTATION OF PROPERTY'S FMV. In addition to the substantiation requirement, in certain cases the taxpayer must also properly document the property's FMV. The specific documentation requirements depend upon the amount of the claimed deduction for the contributed property. If a claimed deduction for a contribution of property exceeds $500, noncorporate taxpayers (and closely held C corporations and personal service corporations) must include with their tax return a description of the property and any other information the IRS requires, including the type, location, holding period, basis, and FMV of the property. This information is reported on Form 8283 (see Appendix B). If the claimed deduction exceeds $5,000, in addition to the above requirements, all taxpayers must obtain a qualified appraisal of the property and must include with their tax return any additional information that the IRS requires. Finally, if the claimed deduction exceeds $500,000, all taxpayers are additionally required to obtain a qualified appraisal and actually attach the appraisal to their tax return. Because these documentation requirements are based on the amount of a claimed contribution, the donation of similar items of property donated to all charities will be treated as the donation of one property. This requirement prevents taxpayers from avoiding these documentation requirements by spreading out their contributions. If a partnership or an S corporation donates property, these documentation requirements are applied at the entity level. However, if the documentation requirements are not met, the deduction is denied at the partner or shareholder level. In general, these documentation rules do not apply to contributions of cash, certain intangibles, inventory, or publicly traded securities.

---

[56] Reg. Sec. 1.170A-13.

[57] Sec. 170(f)(8) and Reg. Sec. 1.170A-13(f).

CONTRIBUTION OF USED MOTOR VEHICLES, BOATS, AND AIRPLANES. Special documentation rules apply to contributions of motor vehicles, boats, and airplanes if the claimed value of the property exceeds $500. However, these rules do not apply if the contributed vehicle, boat, or airplane is inventory in the hands of the donor. If these special rules apply, the substantiation rules for a donation of property exceeding $250 are no longer applicable. Instead, the charity must give the taxpayer and the IRS a contemporaneous written acknowledgment of the contribution. This acknowledgment must be included with the taxpayer's tax return. The information included in the acknowledgment and the date by which the charity must give the acknowledgment to the taxpayer depend upon whether or not the charity sells the vehicle without any significant use or any material improvement of the vehicle. In either case, the acknowledgment must include the name and taxpayer identification number of the taxpayer who donated the vehicle, as well as the vehicle identification number. If the vehicle is sold by the charity before any significant use or material improvement, the acknowledgment must also include (1) a certification that the vehicle was sold in an arm's length transaction to an unrelated party, (2) the gross proceeds from the sale, and (3) a statement that the deductible amount may not exceed the amount of the gross proceeds. This acknowledgment must be given to the taxpayer within 30 days of the contribution of the vehicle to the charity, and, as mentioned earlier, the amount of the deduction for the vehicle is limited to the gross proceeds received from the sale. On the other hand, if the charity uses or improves the vehicle, the acknowledgment must also state: (1) the intended use or improvement and the intended duration of the use and (2) a certification that the vehicle will not be transferred or sold before completion of the intended use or improvement. This acknowledgment must be given to the taxpayer within 30 days of the sale of the vehicle.[58]

EXAMPLE I:7-40 ▶ During the current year, Peter Smith (SSN. 276-31-7242) reports AGI of $250,000. Smith also makes the following charitable contributions during the year:

▶ Smith performs voluntary dental work three days each month in rural areas of the state. Smith drives a total of 4,000 miles on these trips during the year.

▶ Smith makes the following contributions by cash or check: $750 to the city library, $2,000 to the United Way, $500 to a local community college, and $4,000 to his church.

▶ Smith contributes a tract of land to a small rural town. The town plans to erect a public library on the site. Smith purchased the land in 1997 for $5,000. Its appraised value at the time of the contribution is $8,000.

Smith's contributions are reported on the partially completed Schedule A shown in Figure I:7-1. The out-of-pocket expenses of $560 (4,000 miles × $0.14) and the contributions by cash or check of $7,250 (library, United Way, church, and community college) are totaled and reported on line 16. The property contribution of $8,000 is separately stated on line 17. Because Smith contributes property with a value exceeding $500, Form 8283, an appraisal summary, and signed statements by the qualified appraiser and an authorized official of the organization that received the property must be attached to the return. In addition, for the donations that separately exceed $250, Peter must obtain and retain written acknowledgments from the donee organizations in order for the contributions to be deductible. ◀

TAXES

Individuals generally report their deduction for property taxes on Schedule A of Form 1040. However, if the taxpayer incurs the taxes in his or her business, they are reported on Schedule C. Taxes incurred for the production of rents and royalties are reported on Schedule E. Taxes incurred in the taxpayer's farming business are reported on Schedule F. State and local income taxes imposed on individuals are always reported on Schedule A, even if the individual is self-employed.

Real estate brokers must report any real estate tax allocable to the purchaser of a residence. (See the discussion in this chapter regarding the allocation of real estate taxes between the seller and buyer of a residence.)[59] The broker reports this information on Form 1099-S (Proceeds from Real Estate Transactions).

---

[58] Sec. 170(f)(11) and (f)(12).

[59] Sec. 6045(e)(4) and Notice 93-4, 1993-1 C.B. 295.

SCHEDULE A (Form 1040)	Itemized Deductions	OMB No. 1545-0074
Department of the Treasury Internal Revenue Service (99)	▶ **Attach to Form 1040.** ▶ **See Instructions for Schedule A (Form 1040).**	20**09** Attachment Sequence No. **07**

Name(s) shown on Form 1040	Your social security number
Peter Smith	276 : 31 : 7242

Medical and Dental Expenses

Caution. Do not include expenses reimbursed or paid by others.

1	Medical and dental expenses (see page A-1)	1	
2	Enter amount from Form 1040, line 38 2		
3	Multiply line 2 by 7.5% (.075)	3	
4	Subtract line 3 from line 1. If line 3 is more than line 1, enter -0-		4

Taxes You Paid

(See page A-2.)

5	State and local **(check only one box):**	5	
	a ☐ Income taxes, **or**		
	b ☐ General sales taxes		
6	Real estate taxes (see page A-5)	6	
7	New motor vehicle taxes from line 11 of the worksheet on back. Skip this line if you checked box 5b	7	
8	Other taxes. List type and amount ▶ _____	8	
9	Add lines 5 through 8		9

Interest You Paid

(See page A-6.)

Note.
Personal interest is not deductible.

10	Home mortgage interest and points reported to you on Form 1098	10	
11	Home mortgage interest not reported to you on Form 1098. If paid to the person from whom you bought the home, see page A-7 and show that person's name, identifying no., and address ▶ _____ _____	11	
12	Points not reported to you on Form 1098. See page A-7 for special rules	12	
13	Qualified mortgage insurance premiums (see page A-7)	13	
14	Investment interest. Attach Form 4952 if required. (See page A-8.)	14	
15	Add lines 10 through 14		15

Gifts to Charity

If you made a gift and got a benefit for it, see page A-8.

16	Gifts by cash or check. If you made any gift of $250 or more, see page A-8	16	7,810
17	Other than by cash or check. If any gift of $250 or more, see page A-8. You **must** attach Form 8283 if over $500 . . .	17	8,000
18	Carryover from prior year	18	
19	Add lines 16 through 18		19 15,810

Casualty and Theft Losses

20	Casualty or theft loss(es). Attach Form 4684. (See page A-10.)		20

Job Expenses and Certain Miscellaneous Deductions

(See page A-10.)

21	Unreimbursed employee expenses—job travel, union dues, job education, etc. Attach Form 2106 or 2106-EZ if required. (See page A-10.) ▶ _____	21	
22	Tax preparation fees	22	
23	Other expenses—investment, safe deposit box, etc. List type and amount ▶ _____	23	
24	Add lines 21 through 23	24	
25	Enter amount from Form 1040, line 38 25		
26	Multiply line 25 by 2% (.02)	26	
27	Subtract line 26 from line 24. If line 26 is more than line 24, enter -0-		27

Other Miscellaneous Deductions

28	Other—from list on page A-11. List type and amount ▶ _____ _____		28

Total Itemized Deductions

29 Is Form 1040, line 38, over $166,800 (over $83,400 if married filing separately)?

☐ **No.** Your deduction is not limited. Add the amounts in the far right column for lines 4 through 28. Also, enter this amount on Form 1040, line 40a.   ▶   29

☑ **Yes.** Your deduction may be limited. See page A-11 for the amount to enter.

30 If you elect to itemize deductions even though they are less than your standard deduction, check here . . . . ▶ ☐

For Paperwork Reduction Act Notice, see Form 1040 instructions.   Cat. No. 17145C   Schedule A (Form 1040) 2009

FIGURE I:7-1   ▶   PARTIALLY COMPLETED SCHEDULE A

WHAT WOULD YOU DO IN THIS SITUATION?

GIVING TO BOTH: GOODWILL AND THE IRS

Much has been written about abusive practices concerning the valuation of noncash property donated to qualified charities. Under Sec. 170, both corporations and individuals may deduct the FMV of property contributed to charitable organizations. Of course, a number of valuation and percentage limitations and carryover rules are applicable to both individual and corporate taxpayers.

Assume your clients, Mr. and Mrs. Nicholas Nice, come into your office on December 27 for some year-end tax planning. Your review of their tax situation indicates that they have made substantial donations of clothing and household goods to Goodwill Industries. They have obtained proper documentation for donations made during the year but do not know how to qualify for taking a charitable deduction vis-à-vis valuation, forms, and the like. They do know that their original cost basis in the donated goods was $15,000 and that the goods were in good condition at the time of the donation. What tax and ethical issues should be considered?

EXAMPLE I:7-41 ▶ During the year, Andrea incurs $1,500 in property taxes on a two-family house. Andrea lives in one unit and rents out the other. She also pays $100 in registration fees and $600 in personal property taxes on her automobile, based on its value. Andrea uses the automobile 80% of the time in an unincorporated business. During the current year, she also pays $2,000 in state income taxes, all of which is attributable to her income of the prior year from the unincorporated business.

Because one-half of the real estate taxes are attributable to property used to produce rental income, $750 (0.50 × $1,500) is reported on Schedule E, and the remaining personal-use portion ($750) is reported on Schedule A. Because 80% of the use of the automobile is in Andrea's business, $80 (0.80 × $100) of the registration fee is deductible as a business expense on Schedule C. The remaining $20 is not deductible because the registration fee is not a tax. However, $480 (0.80 × $600) of the personal property tax on the automobile is deductible as a business expense on Schedule C. The remaining $120 is deductible as a tax on Schedule A. Finally, even though the tax is related to Andrea's business income, all $2,000 of the state income tax is reported on Schedule A. Because the state income tax is paid in the current year, it is deductible in the current year. ◀

PROBLEM MATERIALS

DISCUSSION QUESTIONS

I:7-1 a. For what persons may a taxpayer deduct medical expenses?
b. In the case of children of divorced parents, must the parent who is entitled to the dependency exemption pay the medical expenses of the child to ensure that the expenses are deductible? Explain.
c. Who should pay the medical expenses of an individual who is the subject of a multiple support agreement?

I:7-2 What is the definition of medical care for purposes of the medical care deduction?

I:7-3 a. What is the definition of cosmetic surgery under the Internal Revenue Code?
b. Is the cost of cosmetic surgery deductible as a medical expense? Explain.

I:7-4 a. If a taxpayer must travel away from his or her home in order to obtain medical care, which en route costs, if any, are deductible as medical expenses?
b. Are there any limits imposed on the deductibility of these expenses?

I:7-5 What are the rules dealing with the deductibility of the cost of meals and lodging incurred while away from home in order to receive medical treatment as an outpatient?

I:7-6 a. Which types of capital expenditures incurred specifically for medical purposes are deductible?
b. What limitations, if any, are imposed on the deductibility of these expenditures?

I:7-7 Bill, a plant manager, is suffering from a serious ulcer. Bill's doctor recommends that he spend

three weeks fishing and hunting in the Colorado Rockies. Can Bill deduct the costs of the trip as a medical expense?

I:7-8 In what cases are medical insurance premiums paid by an individual not deductible as qualified medical expenses?

I:7-9 What is the limit placed on medical expense deductions? When can a deduction be taken for medical care? What if the medical care is prepaid?

I:7-10 a. Which taxes are specifically deductible for federal income tax purposes under Sec. 164?
b. If a tax is not specifically listed in Sec. 164, under what circumstances may it still be deductible?

I:7-11 If Susan overpays her state income tax due to excess withholdings, can she deduct the entire amount in the year withheld? When Susan receives a refund from the state how must she treat that refund for tax purposes?

I:7-12 What is an ad valorem tax? If a tax that is levied on personal property is not an ad valorem tax, under what circumstances may it still be deductible?

I:7-13 When real estate is sold during a year, why is it necessary that the real estate taxes on the property be apportioned between the buyer and seller?

I:7-14 a. Identify the different categories of interest expense an individual may incur. How is the classification of the interest determined?
b. Are these different categories of interest deductible? If so, how?

I:7-15 At times, the term *points* is used to refer to different types of charges. Define the term and describe when points are deductible.

I:7-16 In which year or years are points (representing prepaid interest on a loan) deductible?

I:7-17 Why does Sec. 267 impose a restriction on the deductibility of expenses accrued and payable by an accrual method taxpayer to a related cash method taxpayer?

I:7-18 a. What is the amount of the annual limitation placed on the deductibility of investment interest expense?
b. Explain how net investment income is calculated.
c. Is any disallowed interest expense for the year allowable as a deduction in another year? If so, when?

I:7-19 Explain what acquisition indebtedness and home equity indebtedness are with respect to a qualified residence of a taxpayer. Identify any limitations on the deductibility of interest expense on this indebtedness.

I:7-20 Explain what a qualified residence is for purposes of qualified residence interest.

I:7-21 Why is interest expense disallowed if it is incurred to purchase or hold tax-exempt obligations?

I:7-22 When is interest generally deductible for cash-method taxpayers? Explain if the general rule applies to prepaid interest, interest paid with loan proceeds, discounted notes, and personal interest. If the general rule does not apply, explain when these interest expenses are deductible.

I:7-23 a. For purposes of the charitable contribution deduction, what is capital gain property? Ordinary income property?
b. What is the significance of classifying property as either capital gain property or ordinary income property?

I:7-24 How is the *amount* of a charitable contribution of capital gain property determined if it is donated to a private nonoperating foundation? How does this determination differ if capital gain property is donated to a public charity?

I:7-25 May an individual who is married and files a joint return deduct any charitable contributions if the itemized deductions total $7,000 (of which $3,000 are qualified charitable contributions)?

I:7-26 For individuals, what is the overall deduction limitation on charitable contributions? What is the limitation for corporations?

I:7-27 If a taxpayer's charitable contributions for any tax year exceed the deduction limitations, may the excess contributions be deducted in another year? If so, in which years may they be deducted?

I:7-28 How are charitable contribution deductions reported on the tax return for individuals? What reporting requirements must be met for the contribution of property?

I:7-29 List some of the more common miscellaneous itemized deductions and identify any limitations that are imposed on the deductibility of these items.

I:7-30 For 2009, certain itemized deductions of high-income taxpayers were reduced. Thus reduction may be re-enacted by Congress. Which itemized deductions were subject to this reduction and for 2009 when did the reduction apply?

ISSUE IDENTIFICATION QUESTIONS

I:7-31 Wayne and Maria file a joint tax return on which they itemize their deductions and report AGI of $50,000. During the year they incurred $1,500 of medical expenses when Maria broke her leg. Furthermore, their dentist informed them that their daughter, Alicia, needs $3,000 of orthodontic work to correct her overbite. Wayne also needs a new pair of eyeglasses that will cost $300. What tax issues should Wayne and Maria consider?

I:7-32 This year, Chuck took out a loan to purchase some raw land for investment. He paid $40,000 for the land, and he expects that within 5 years the land will be worth at least $75,000. Chuck is married, and his AGI for the year is $325,000. Chuck paid $4,300 in interest on the loan this year. Chuck has $2,600 in interest income and $1,300 in dividend income for the year. He plans to itemize his deductions so he can use the interest expense to offset his investment income. What tax issues should Chuck consider?

I:7-33 During the current year, George made contributions totaling $40,000 to an organization called the National Endowment for the Preservation of Liberty (NEPL). Later during the year, the NEPL started giving money to a political candidate to help with his campaign expenses. What tax issues should George consider?

I:7-34 During the current year, Bob has AGI of $100,000. He donates stock to his church that was purchased two years ago for $55,000. The FMV of the stock is $60,000. Bob has $5,000 of unused excess contributions from a prior year. What tax issues should Bob consider?

PROBLEMS

I:7-35 *Medical Expense Deduction.* During 2010, Angela sustains serious injuries from a snow-skiing accident. She incurs the following expenses:

Item	Amount
Doctor bills	$11,700
Hospital bills	9,400
Legal fees in suit against ski resort	3,000

Angela is single and has no dependents. During 2010, her salary is $58,000. She pays $600 in medical and dental insurance premiums, $2,750 in mortgage interest on her home, and $1,200 in interest on her car loan. Her health insurance provider reimburses her for $10,000 of the medical expenses. What is her 2010 taxable income?

I:7-36 *Reimbursement of Previously Deducted Medical Expenses.* Assume the same facts as in Problem I:7-35. In addition, assume that in 2011, Angela receives an additional $7,000 in a settlement of a lawsuit arising because of the snow-skiing accident. $4,000 of the settlement is to pay Angela's medical bills, and $3,000 is to reimburse her legal expenses. What is the proper tax treatment of this $7,000 settlement?

I:7-37 *Medical Expense Deduction.* Dan lives in Duncan, a small town in Arizona. Because of a rare blood disease, Dan is required to take special medical treatments once a month. The closest place these treatments are available to Dan is in Phoenix, 200 miles away. The treatments are provided on an outpatient basis but require him to stay overnight in Phoenix. During the year, Dan makes 12 trips to Phoenix by automobile to receive the treatments. The motel he always stays in charges $85 per night. For the year, Dan also spends a total of $250 for meals on these trips. $100 of this $250 is spent while en route to Phoenix. What is the amount of Dan's qualified medical expenses for 2010?

I:7-38 *Medical Expense Deduction.* Chad is divorced and has custody of Brett, his 14-year-old son. Chad's ex-wife has custody of their daughter, Sara. During the year, Chad incurs $3,000 for orthodontic work for Sara to correct a severe overbite and $2,000 in unreimbursed medical expenses associated with Brett's broken leg. Chad also pays $900 in health insurance premiums. Both Brett and Sara are covered under Chad's medical insurance plan. In addition, Chad incurs $400 for prescription drugs and $1,000 in doctor bills for himself. Chad's AGI is $40,000. What is Chad's medical expense deduction for the year assuming that his other itemized deductions exceed the standard deduction?

I:7-39 *Medical Expense Deduction.* In 2010, Charla, a single taxpayer with no dependents, was severely hurt in a farm accident. The accident left Charla's legs 85% paralyzed. After incurring $14,000 of medical expenses at the hospital, the doctor recommended that Charla install a pool at her home for therapy. The pool cost $25,000 to install and increased the value of her home by $22,000. She spent $930 maintaining the pool in 2010 and $1,060 in 2011. Charla also purchased a wheelchair on December 28, 2010, for $2,300, which she charged to her credit card. She paid her credit card bill on January 6, 2011. She also purchased a hospital bed for $3,800 but did not pay for the bed until 2011. Charla paid her physical therapist $4,000 for services performed in 2011. Charla paid $1,200 in medical insurance premiums in both 2010 and 2011. In 2011, the insurance company reimbursed Charla $9,000 for her hospital stay in 2010. Her AGI for

2010 and 2011 is $38,000 and $43,000, respectively, not considering any of the above items. Charla has no other itemized deductions in either year.

a. What is Charla's taxable income for 2010?

b. What is Charla's medical expense deduction for 2011? How does she treat the reimbursement?

I:7-40 *Deduction of Taxes.* Joyce is a single, cash-method taxpayer. On April 11, 2009, Joyce paid $120 with her 2008 state income tax return. During 2009, Joyce had $1,600 in state income taxes withheld. On April 13, 2010, Joyce paid $200 with her 2009 state tax return. During 2010, she had $2,100 in state income taxes withheld from her paycheck. Upon filing her 2010 tax return on April 15, 2011, she received a refund of $450 for excess state income taxes withheld. Joyce had total AGI in 2010 and 2011 of $51,000 and $53,500, respectively. In 2010, Joyce also paid $3,500 in qualified residence interest.

a. What is the amount of state income taxes Joyce may include as an itemized deduction for 2009?

b. What is the allowed itemized deduction for state income taxes for 2010?

c. What is her taxable income for 2010?

d. What is her AGI for 2011?

I:7-41 Assume the same facts as Problem I:7-40, but change the amount of Joyce's mortgage interest to $3,200.

a. What is her taxable income for 2010?

b. What is her AGI for 2011?

I:7-42 *Deduction of Taxes.* Dawn, a single, cash method taxpayer, paid the following taxes in 2010: Dawn's employer withheld $5,400 for federal income taxes, $2,000 for state income taxes, and $3,800 for FICA from her 2010 paychecks. Dawn purchased a new car and paid $600 in sales tax and $70 for the license. The car's FMV was $20,000 and it weighed 3,000 pounds. The county also assessed a property tax on the car. The tax was 2% of its value and $10 per hundredweight. The car is used 100% of the time for personal purposes. Dawn sold her house on April 15, 2010. The county's property tax on the home for 2010 is $1,850, payable on February 1, 2011. The county's real property tax year is the calendar year. Dawn's AGI for 2010 is $50,000 and her other itemized deductions exclusive of taxes are $4,000 (disregard any leap year).

a. What is Dawn's deduction for taxes in 2010?

b. Where on Dawn's tax return should she report her deduction for taxes?

I:7-43 *Apportionment of Real Estate Taxes.* On May 1 of the current year, Tara sells a building to Janet for $500,000. Tara's basis in the building is $300,000. The county in which the building is located has a real property tax year that ends on June 30. The taxes are payable by September 1 of that year. On September 1, Janet pays the annual property taxes of $6,000. Both Tara and Janet are calendar-year, cash method taxpayers. The closing agreement does not separately account for the property taxes. Disregard any leap year.

a. What amount of real property taxes may Janet deduct in the current year?

b. What amount of real property taxes may Tara deduct in the current year?

c. If no apportionment on the real property taxes is made in the sales agreement, what is Tara's total selling price of the building? Janet's basis for the building?

I:7-44 *Classification of Interest Expense.* On January 1 of the current year, Scott borrows $80,000, pledging the assets of his business as collateral. He immediately deposits the money in an interest-bearing checking account. Scott already had $20,000 in this account. On April 1, Scott invests $75,000 in a limited real estate partnership. On July 1, he buys a new ski boat for $12,000. On August 1, he makes a $10,000 capital contribution to his unincorporated business. Scott repays $50,000 of the loan on November 30 of the current year. Classify Scott's interest expense for the year.

I:7-45 *Investment Income and Deductions.* During 2010, Travis takes out a $40,000 loan, using stock he owns as collateral. He uses $10,000 to purchase a car, which he uses 100% for personal use. He uses the remaining funds to purchase stocks and bonds. He pays $3,200 interest on the loan. Travis also reports the following for the year:

AGI without any investment income	$130,000
State income taxes paid	8,400
Dividend income	10,000
Interest income	2,100

Investment expenses (exclusive of interest)	8,000
Net short term capital gains	7,300
Net long term capital gain	8,600

Travis is married and files a joint tax return. What is his net taxable income?

I:7-46   *Qualified Residence Interest.* During the current year, Tina purchases a beachfront condominium for $600,000, paying $150,000 down and taking out a $450,000 mortgage, secured by the property. At the time of the purchase, the outstanding mortgage on her principal residence is $700,000. This debt is secured by the residence and the FMV of the principal residence is $1,400,000. She purchased the principal residence in 1997. What is the amount of qualified indebtedness on which Tina may deduct the interest payments?

I:7-47   *Qualified Residence Interest.* Several years ago, Magdelena purchased a new residence for $300,000. Currently, the outstanding mortgage on the residence is $260,000. The current fair market value of the home is $330,000. Magdelena wants to borrow a sizable sum of money to pay for the college education costs of her two children and believes the interest would be deductible if she takes out a home equity loan. For each of the independent situations below, determine the amount of the loan on which Magdelena may deduct the interest as qualified residence interest.
a. Magdelena borrows $50,000 as a home equity loan.
b. Magdelena borrows $80,000 as a home equity loan.
c. Alternatively, assume the current fair market value of her residence is $410,000 and she borrows $110,000 as a home equity loan.
d. Alternatively, assume the current outstanding balance of the mortgage Magdelena incurred to purchase the home is $1,200,000, the home's fair market value is $1,400,000, and she borrows $80,000 as a home equity loan.

I:7-48   *Interest Between Related Parties.* Crown Corporation is an accrual method taxpayer owned 55% by Brett and 45% by Susie. Brett and Susie are good friends and have been business associates for several years. BJ Partnership is a cash method taxpayer, owned 40% by Brett and 60% by Jeremy, Brett's uncle. Both Crown Corporation and BJ Partnership are calendar year entities. On January 5 of the current year, Crown borrows $50,000 from BJ Partnership and pays 8% interest on the loan. Crown must pay the interest on January first of next year.
a. What amount of interest expense can Crown Corporation deduct in the current year?
b. How would your answer change if Jeremy were Brett's brother, instead of his uncle?

I:7-49   *Timing of Interest Deduction.* On April 1 of the current year, Henry borrows $12,000 from the bank for a year. Because the note is discounted for the interest charge and Henry receives proceeds of $10,200, he is required to repay the face amount of the loan ($12,000) in four equal quarterly payments beginning on July 1 of the current year. Henry is a cash method individual.
a. What is the amount of Henry's interest expense deduction in the current year with respect to this loan?
b. Assume the same facts except that the initial starting date when the repayments begin is April 1 of the following year. What is the amount of Henry's interest expense deduction in the current year?
c. Assume the same facts as in Part b, except that Henry is an accrual method taxpayer and the loan will be outstanding for one year. What is the amount of his interest expense deduction in the current year?

I:7-50   *Itemized Deductions.* During 2010, Doug incurs the following deductible expenses: $2,300 in state income taxes, $2,000 in local property taxes, $800 in medical expenses, and $1,500 in charitable contributions. He is single, has no dependents, and has $35,000 AGI for the year. What is the amount of Doug's taxable income?

I:7-51   *Computation of Taxable Income.* During 2010, James, a single, cash method taxpayer incurred the following expenditures:

Qualified medical expenses	$ 8,000
Investment interest expense	16,000
Other investment activity expenses	15,000
Qualified residence interest	12,000
Interest on loan on personal auto	2,000
Charitable contributions	3,000

State income tax paid	7,000
State sales tax paid	4,500
Property taxes	4,000
Tax return preparation and consulting fees	5,000

James' income consisted of the following items:

Salary	$70,000
Interest income	20,000
Long-term capital gains	23,000
Long-term capital losses	(15,000)

a. Compute James' taxable income for the year (assuming that he makes an election to have the net capital gain taxed at the regular tax rates).

b. What is James' investment interest carryover (if any)?

I:7-52 *Computation of Taxable Income.* Assume all the same facts as in Problem I:7-51 except that James' salary income is $130,000 instead of $70,000 and that he does not make the election. Compute James' taxable income for the year.

I:7-53 *Charitable Contributions: Services.* Donna is an attorney who renders volunteer legal services to a Legal Aid Society, which provides legal advice to low-income individuals. The Legal Aid Society is a qualified charitable organization. During the current year she spends a total of 200 hours in this volunteer work. Her regular billing rate is $150 per hour. In addition, she spends a total of $800 in out-of-pocket costs in providing these services. She receives no compensation and is not reimbursed for her out-of-pocket costs. What is Donna's charitable contribution for the year because of these activities?

I:7-54 *Charitable Contribution Limitations.* In each of the following independent cases, determine the amount of the charitable contribution and the limitation that would apply. In each case, assume that the donee is a qualified public charity.

a. Sharon donates a tract of land to a charitable organization. She has held the land for seven years. Her basis in the land is $10,000 and its FMV is $40,000.

b. Assume the same facts in Part a, except that Sharon has held the land for only 11 months and that its FMV is $23,000.

c. Jack purchases a historical document for $50,000. He donates the historical document to a charitable organization two years later. The organization plans to use it for research and study. Its FMV at the time of the donation is $100,000.

d. Assume the same facts in Part c, except that the organization plans to sell the document and put the money into an endowment fund.

e. Valerie donates some inventory to a charitable organization. The inventory is not food or clothing. The inventory is purchased for $500 and its FMV is $1,200 at the time of the donation. She held the inventory for seven months.

I:7-55 *Charitable Contributions to Private Nonoperating Foundations.* Assume the same facts as Problem I:7-54, except that the qualified organization is a private nonoperating foundation. Determine the amount of the charitable contribution for Parts a through e.

I:7-56 *Charitable Contribution Limitations.* During the current year, Helen donates stock worth $50,000 to her local community college. Two years ago the stock cost Helen $40,000. Her AGI for the current year is $100,000. Beginning next year, the bulk of her income will be from tax-exempt municipal securities. Thus, she is not interested in any carryover of excess charitable contribution. What is the maximum charitable contribution deduction Helen may take this year?

I:7-57 *Charitable Contribution Limitations.* During the current year, Melissa reports AGI of $200,000. As part of some estate planning, she donates $30,000 to her alma mater, Middle State University, and $65,000 to a private nonoperating foundation.

a. What is the amount of Melissa's charitable deduction for the current year?

b. Assume the same facts in Part a except that she donates $45,000 to Middle State University.

I:7-58 *Corporate Charitable Contributions.* Circle Corporation, an accrual method taxpayer, manufactures and sells mainframe computers. In January of the current year, Circle Corporation donates a mainframe that was part of its inventory to City College. City College will use the computer for physical science research. Circle's basis in the mainframe is $300,000. The computer's FMV is $650,000. On December 15 of the current year, Circle also pledged stock to the Red Cross and promised delivery of the stock by

March 1 of the following year. The stock's FMV is $100,000 and Circle's adjusted basis in the stock is $50,000. Circle has held the stock for over one year. Circle's taxable income (before deducting any charitable contributions) for the current year is $4,000,000.

a. What is the amount of Circle's charitable contribution for the current year?

b. How much of the contribution can Circle deduct in the current year and how much may be carried over, if any?

I:7-59 *Charitable Contribution Carryovers.* Bonnie's charitable contributions and AGI for the past four years were as follows:

	2007	2008	2009	2010
AGI	$50,000	$55,000	$58,000	$60,000
Contributions subject to the 50% limitation	40,000	29,000	25,000	10,000

What is the amount of the charitable deduction for each year and the order in which the deduction and carryovers are used?

COMPREHENSIVE PROBLEM

I:7-60 Tim and Monica Nelson are married, file a joint return, and are your newest tax clients. They provide you with the following information relating to their 2010 tax return:

1. Tim works as a pediatrician for the county hospital. The W-2 form he received from the hospital shows wages of $150,000 and state income tax withheld of $8,500.

2. Monica spends much of her time volunteering, but also works as a substitute teacher for the local schools. During the year, she spent 900 hours volunteering. When she doesn't volunteer, she earns $8.00 per hour working as a substitute. The W-2 form she received from the school district shows total wages of $3,888 and state income tax withheld of $85.

3. On April 13, the couple paid $250 in state taxes with their 2009 state income tax return. The Nelson's state and local sales taxes in 2010 were $5,500.

4. On December 18, the Nelsons donated a small building to the Boy Scouts of America. They purchased the building three years ago for $80,000. A professional appraiser determined the fair market value of the home was $96,000 on December 12.

5. Tim and Monica both received corrective eye surgery, at a total cost of $3,000. They also paid $1,900 in health insurance premiums.

6. On June 1, the couple bought a car for $16,000, paying $4,000 down and borrowing $12,000. They paid $750 total interest on the loan in 2010.

7. On June 10, the Nelsons took out a home equity loan of $20,000 to expand their home. They paid a total of $850 interest with their monthly payments on the loan.

8. The Nelsons paid a total of $2,300 interest on their original home loan.

9. They sold stock in Cabinets, Inc. for $5,200, which they purchased for $7,900 in March of the current year. They also sold stock in The Outdoor Corporation for $12,500, which they purchased several years ago for $8,600.

10. Tim incurred the following expenses related to his profession, none of which were reimbursed by his employer:

Item	Amount
Subscriptions to medical journals	$400
American Medical Association (AMA) annual membership fee	250

11. During the year, the couple paid their former tax advisor $700 to prepare their prior year tax return.

12. The Nelsons do not have children, and they do not provide significant financial support to any family members.

Required: Compute the Nelson's taxable income for 2010.

TAX STRATEGY PROBLEMS

I:7-61 Dean makes a pledge of $30,000 to a local college. The college is willing to accept either cash or marketable securities in fulfillment of the pledge. Dean owns stock in Ajax Corporation worth $30,000. The stock was purchased five years ago for $10,000. Dean's marginal tax rate is 35%. Should Dean sell the stock and then donate the cash, or should

he donate the stock directly? Compute the net tax benefit from each alternative and explain the difference.

I:7-62 On December 1, 2010, Rebecca Ward, a single taxpayer, comes to you for tax advice. At the end of every year, she donates $5,000 to charity. She has no other itemized deductions. This year, she plans to make her charitable donation with stock. She presents you with the following information relating to her stock investments:

Corporation	FMV on Dec. 1	Adjusted Basis	Date Purchased
Sycamore	9,600	7,800	5/22/05
Oak	2,900	3,800	9/10/06
Redwood	5,400	4,900	6/15/09

Which stock should Rebecca donate to charity? What other tax advice would you give her?

TAX FORM/RETURN PREPARATION PROBLEMS

I:7-63 Following is a list of information for Peter and Amy Jones for the current tax year. Peter and Amy are married and have three children, Aubrynne, Bryson, and Caden. They live at 1846 Joplin Way, Lakeville, MN 55022. Peter is a lawyer working for a Native American law firm. Amy works part-time in a genetic research lab. The Jones' Social Security numbers and ages are as follows:

Name	S.S. No.	Age
Peter	215-60-1989	32
Amy	301-60-2828	28
Aubrynne	713-84-5555	5
Bryson	714-87-2222	3
Caden	714-89-1684	1

Receipts

Peter's salary	$70,000
Amy's salary	32,000
Interest income on municipal bonds	2,400
Interest income on certificate of deposit (Universal Savings)	3,100
Dividends on GM stock	1,600

Disbursements

Eyeglasses and exam for Aubrynne	$ 600
Orthodontic work for Bryson to correct a congenital defect	2,500
Medical insurance premiums	1,800
Withholding for state income taxes	7,200
Withholding for federal income taxes	16,000
State income taxes paid with last year's tax return (paid when the return was filed in the current year)	500
Property taxes on home	1,100
Property taxes on automobile	300
Interest on home	9,700
Interest on credit cards	200
Cash contribution to church	3,900

In addition to the above, on September 17, Peter and Amy donate some Beta Trader, Inc. stock to Lakeville Community College. Beta Trader, Inc. is publicly traded. The FMV of the stock on the date of the contribution is $700. Peter and Amy had purchased the stock on November 7, 2003 for $300.

Compute Peter and Amy's income tax liability for the current year using Form 1040, Schedules A and B, and Form 8283, if necessary.

I:7-64 Kelly and Chanelle Chambers, ages 47 and 45, are married and live at 584 Thoreau Drive, Boston, MA 59483. Kelly's Social Security number is 254-93-9483 and Chanelle's is 374-48-2938. The Chambers have two children: Emma, age 23, and Chet, age 19. Their Social Security numbers are 385-64-8496 and 385-68-9462, respectively. Emma is a

single college student and earned $8,000 during the summer. Kelly and Chanelle help Emma through school by paying for her room, board, and tuition. Emma lives at home during the summer. Chet has a physical handicap and lives at home. He attends a local university and earned $4,000 working for a marketing firm. In sum, Kelly and Chanelle provide more than 50% of both Emma's and Chet's total support for the year.

Kelly is a commercial pilot for a small airline. His salary is $95,000, from which $19,000 of federal income tax and $8,000 of state income tax were withheld. Kelly also pays premiums for health, disability, and life insurance. $2,000 of the premium was for health insurance, $250 for disability, and $400 for life insurance.

Chanelle owns Alliance Networks, a proprietorship that does network consulting. During the year, Chanelle's gross revenues were $23,000. She incurred the following expenses in her business:

Liability insurance	$ 700
Software rental	5,400
Journals and magazines	150
Training seminars	1,200
Supplies	1,300
Donations to a political campaign fund	800

Kelly enjoys playing guitar and plays in a band. Kelly's band has developed a local following. This year, his gross revenues were $1,200 for playing shows and $700 on CD sales. He incurred the following expenses:

Studio rent expense	$1,300
Sound system repairs	200
CD production	500
New guitar and amplifier	800

Kelly's father passed away during the year. Kelly and Chanelle received $100,000 from the life insurance policy. Neither Kelly nor Chanelle paid any of the premiums.

Chanelle purchased 100 shares of Thurston Co. stock on May 1, 1991, for $1,000. Thurston Co. was declared bankrupt during the current year.

Chet's physician recommended that he see a physical therapist to help with his disability. Kelly paid the therapist $7,000 during the year because his insurance would not cover the bills.

Kelly and Chanelle went to Las Vegas and won $5,000 at the blackjack table. The next night, they lost $6,000.

Kelly and Chanelle gave $900 to their church and, during the year, they had the following other income and expenses:

Real estate taxes	$1,400
Property taxes on car (determined by value)	500
Home mortgage interest	9,000
Credit card finance charges	2,600
Tax return preparation fees ($600 is allocable to Chanelle's business)	1,000
Sales tax on purchases during the year	6,200
Interest from a savings account	800
Interest from City of Boston Bonds	700
Dividend from 3M stock	400

Prepare Kelly and Chanelle's tax return Form 1040 and Schedules A, B, C, D, and SE for the current year.

CASE STUDY PROBLEMS

I:7-65 Brian Brown, an executive at a manufacturing enterprise, comes to you on December 1 of the current year for tax advice. He has agreed to donate a small tract of land to the Rosepark Community College. The value of the land has been appraised at $58,000. Mr. Brown purchased the land 14 months ago for $50,000. Mr. Brown's estimated AGI for the current year is $100,000. He plans to retire next year and anticipates that his AGI will fall to $35,000 for all subsequent years. He does not anticipate making any additional large charitable contributions. He understands that there are special rules dealing with charitable contributions and wants your advice in order to get the maximum overall

tax benefit from his contribution. Because the college plans to use the property, selling the land is not an alternative. You are to prepare a letter to Mr. Brown explaining the tax consequences of the different alternatives. His address is 100 East Rosebrook, Mesa, Arizona 85203. For purposes of your analysis, assume that Mr. Brown is married and files a joint return. Also assume that Mr. Brown feels that an appropriate discount rate is 10%. In your analysis, use the tax rate schedules for the current year.

I:7-66　For several years, you have prepared the tax return for Alpha Corporation, a closely held corporation engaged in manufacturing garden tools. On February 20 of the current year, Bill Johnson, the president of Alpha Corporation, delivered to your office the files and information necessary for you to prepare Alpha's tax return for the immediately preceding tax year. Included in this information were the minutes of all meetings held by Alpha's Board of Directors during the year in question.

Then on February 27, Bill stops by your office and hands you an "addendum" to the minutes of the director's meeting held December 15 of the tax year for which you are preparing the tax return. The addendum is dated the same day as the director's meeting, and authorizes a charitable contribution pledge of $20,000 to the local community college. With a wink and a big smile, Bill explains that the addendum had been misplaced. In reviewing the original minutes, you find no mention of a charitable contribution pledge.

What should you do? [See Appendix E and the *Statements on Standards for Tax Services* section in Chapter I:15 (or C:1 of the *Comprehensive* volume) for a discussion of these issues.]

TAX RESEARCH PROBLEMS

I:7-67　Mark Hancock is a self-employed attorney who operates his law practice as an unincorporated sole proprietorship. In 2010, the IRS disallowed several business deductions he took in 2007 and 2008. In addition to paying the deficiency and assessed penalties, he also pays $18,000 in interest on the tax owed. Can he deduct that interest in the current year?

- Sec. 162, Sec. 163
- Reg. Sec. 1.163-9T
- *Kikalos v. Comm.*, 84 AFTR 2d 99-5933

I:7-68　Last year, Mr. Smith was involved in an automobile accident, severely injuring his legs. As part of a long-term rehabilitation process, his physician prescribes a daily routine of swimming. Because there is no readily available public facility nearby, Smith investigates the possibility of either building a pool in his own back yard or purchasing another home with a pool. In the current year he finds a new home with a pool and purchases it for $175,000. He then obtains some estimates and finds that it would cost approximately $20,000 to replace the pool in the home he has just purchased. He also obtains some real estate appraisals, which indicate that the existing pool increases the value of the home by only $8,000. During the current year, Smith also expends $500 in maintaining the pool and $1,800 in other medical expenses. What is the total amount of medical expenses he may claim in the current year? Smith's AGI for the year is $60,000.

- Sec. 213
- Reg. Sec. 1.213-1(e)(1)(iii)
- *Richard A. Polacsek*, 1981 PH T.C. Memo ¶81,569, 42 TCM 1289
- *Paul A. Lerew*, 1982 PH T.C. Memo ¶82,483, 44 TCM 918
- *Jacob H. Robbins*, 1982 PH T.C. Memo ¶82,565, 44 TCM 1254

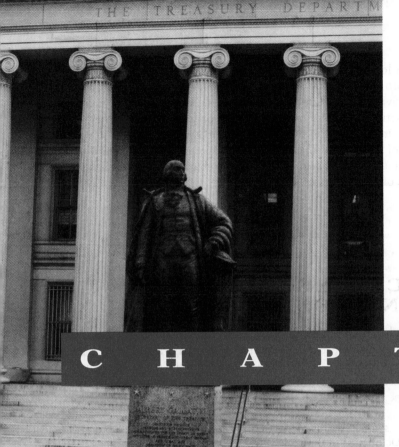

CHAPTER

8

LOSSES AND BAD DEBTS

LEARNING OBJECTIVES

After studying this chapter, you should be able to

1. Identify transactions that may result in losses

2. Determine the proper classification for losses

3. Calculate the suspended loss from passive activities

4. Identify what constitutes a passive activity loss

5. Determine when a taxpayer has materially participated in a passive activity

6. Identify and calculate the deduction for a casualty or theft loss

7. Compute the deduction for a bad debt

8. Compute a net operating loss deduction

Taxpayers often sustain losses on property sold, exchanged, or otherwise disposed of. If the taxpayer uses the property in a trade or business or holds the property for investment, the tax law generally provides a deduction for these losses. Noncorporate taxpayers may also take a limited deduction for losses on personal-use property that is either stolen or damaged in a casualty. Other losses on personal-use property (e.g., a sale of a personal residence at a loss) are not deductible. Taxpayers are also permitted a deduction for losses due to uncollectible business or nonbusiness debts. This chapter discusses the rules concerning the deductibility of these types of losses.

TRANSACTIONS THAT MAY RESULT IN LOSSES

OBJECTIVE 1

Identify transactions that may result in losses

For taxpayers to deduct a loss on property, the loss must be both realized and recognized for tax purposes. Generally, *realization* occurs in a completed (closed) transaction evidenced by an identifiable event. This is referred to as the closed transaction doctrine. As a general rule, taxpayers recognize realized losses on business or investment property unless a specific provision holds otherwise (see pages I:8-6 and I:8-7).

EXAMPLE I:8-1 ▶ Capital Corporation purchased 500 shares of Data Corporation stock for $10,000 on February 22 of the current year. By October 31 of the same year, the price of the stock declines to $8,000. Even though Capital has suffered an economic loss on the stock, no realization event has occurred, and the corporation may not deduct the $2,000 loss. However, if Capital sells the stock for $8,000 on October 31, it realizes the loss for tax purposes in the current year. ◀

ADDITIONAL COMMENT

If property is used partly for business and partly for personal use, the loss attributable to the business portion is deductible but the loss on the personal-use portion is not unless the loss was sustained in a casualty.

KEY POINT

Anticipated losses, including those for which reserves have been established, are not deductible.

Losses on property may arise in a variety of transactions, including:

▶ Sale or exchange of the property

▶ Expropriation, seizure, confiscation, or condemnation of the property by a government

▶ Abandonment of the property

▶ Worthlessness of stock or securities

▶ Planned demolition of the property in order to construct other property in its place

▶ Destruction of the property by fire, storm, or other casualty

▶ Theft

▶ Deductible business expenses exceeding business income, giving rise to a net operating loss (NOL)

SALE OR EXCHANGE OF PROPERTY

The amount of the loss a taxpayer incurs in a sale or exchange of property equals the excess of the property's adjusted basis over the amount realized for the property.[1] The amount realized for the property equals the sum of the money received plus the fair market value (FMV) of any other property received in the transaction. If the property sold or exchanged is subject to a mortgage or other liability, the amount realized also includes the amount of the liability transferred to the buyer.[2] The treatment of any selling costs depends on the type of property sold or exchanged. If the property is inventory (i.e., property normally held for sale in the taxpayer's business), the selling costs are generally deductible expenses in the year in which they are paid or incurred. However, if the sale involves property not normally held for sale by the taxpayer, the selling costs reduce the amount realized from the sale or exchange.

---

[1] Sec. 1001.
[2] *Beulah B. Crane v. CIR*, 35 AFTR 776, 47-1 USTC ¶9217 (USSC, 1947); and Reg. Sec. 1.1001-2. Under Sec. 108(a)(1)(E), for individuals, if the property transferred is a home and the debt discharged is qualified principal residence indebtedness, there is no gain on the transfer of the property and the taxpayer has no income from the discharge of the debt.

EXAMPLE I:8-2 ▶ Four years ago, Boyer Corporation purchased a plot of land as an investment for $50,000. Unfortunately, local economic conditions worsened after the land was purchased, and its value declined to $35,000. Boyer sells the property in the current year. At the time of the sale, the land is subject to a $10,000 mortgage. The terms of the sale are $25,000 paid in cash with the purchaser assuming the mortgage. Boyer also incurs $2,000 in sales commissions. The amount realized is $33,000 ($25,000 cash + $10,000 mortgage assumed by the buyer − $2,000 commissions). The loss on the sale is $17,000 ($50,000 basis − $33,000 amount realized). ◀

In general, taxpayers can only deduct losses they incur in the sale or exchange of property used in a trade or business or held for investment. Taxpayers cannot deduct losses they incur in the sale or exchange of personal-use property. Furthermore, the type of deduction a taxpayer may take for a loss realized on the sale or exchange of business or investment property depends on the type of property sold. For example, if inventory is sold, the loss is an ordinary loss. If the asset is a capital asset, the loss is a capital loss (see Chapter I:5). If the sale is of property used in a trade or business (a Sec. 1231 asset), the type of loss depends on the total net gain or loss realized on all the taxpayer's Sec. 1231 transactions during the year (see Chapter I:13).

EXPROPRIATED, SEIZED, CONFISCATED, OR CONDEMNED PROPERTY

A taxpayer may own property that the government expropriates, seizes, confiscates, or condemns. In these cases, the taxpayer incurs a deductible loss if the taxpayer used the property in a trade or business or held it for investment. However, the Tax Court has held that the confiscation, seizure, condemnation, or expropriation of property does not constitute a theft or a casualty. Rather, it is treated as a sale or exchange. Thus, no deductible loss arises if the seized property is personal-use property.[3] If the seized or condemned property is business or investment property, the classification of the loss depends on the type of property. (See the section in this chapter titled Classifying the Loss on the Taxpayer's Return.) A taxpayer may take the deduction only in the year in which the property is actually seized. Whether formal expropriation or nationalization occurs in a later year is irrelevant.[4] A taxpayer realizes gain if he or she receives compensation for the property in excess of its basis. Under certain circumstances, the taxpayer may defer this gain. (See Chapter I:12 for a discussion of the nonrecognition of gain in an involuntary conversion.)

ABANDONED PROPERTY

If a taxpayer's property becomes worthless or if it is not worth placing into a serviceable condition, the taxpayer may simply abandon the property. If the property still has basis, the taxpayer realizes a loss. The taxpayer may not deduct such losses if the property is personal-use property. However, the taxpayer may deduct losses on business or investment property. Furthermore, because the abandonment of property is not a sale or exchange, the loss is an ordinary loss. The amount of the loss is the property's adjusted basis on the date of abandonment. The taxpayer bears the burden of proof to show that the property was actually abandoned. If the property is depreciable (e.g., machinery and buildings), the taxpayer must actually physically abandon it to take the full amount of the loss.[5]

WORTHLESS SECURITIES

A taxpayer may take a deduction for securities that become completely worthless during the tax year.[6] Because the deduction is only available in the year the security actually becomes worthless, both the taxpayer and the IRS may have problems determining the year in which the security becomes worthless. A mere decline in value is not sufficient to create a deductible loss if the stock has any recognizable value. Furthermore, the sale of the stock for a nominal amount such as $1 does not necessarily establish that the stock became

---

[3] *William J. Powers*, 36 T.C. 1191 (1961).
[4] Rev. Rul. 62-197, 1962-2 C.B. 66 as modified by Rev. Rul. 69-498, 1969-2 C.B. 31. (See also *Estate of Frank Fuchs v. CIR*, 24 AFTR 2d 69-5077, 69-2 USTC ¶9505 (2nd Cir., 1969).)
[5] Reg. Sec. 1.167(a)-8(a)(4).

[6] For this purpose, a *security* is defined in Sec. 165(g)(2) as stock in a corporation, the right to subscribe for or receive a share of stock in a corporation, or a bond, debenture, note, or certificate of indebtedness issued by a corporation or a government either in registered form or with interest coupons. Promissory notes issued by a corporation are generally not securities.

worthless in the year of the sale. The taxpayer must show that the security is completely worthless and that the security became worthless during the year.

Under Sec. 165, once the taxpayer determines the year of worthlessness, the taxpayer treats the loss as a loss from the sale of a capital asset on the last day of the tax year. Although this provision does not help in determining the year of worthlessness, it does establish a definite date for purposes of measuring whether the loss is short- or long-term. In some cases, this provision causes the loss to be long-term because it extends the date of worthlessness to the end of the year.

EXAMPLE I:8-3 ▶ On February 20 of the current year, Control Corporation enters into bankruptcy with no possibility for the shareholders to receive anything of value. Because the amount of Control Corporation's outstanding liabilities exceeds the FMV of its assets on that date, the stock of the corporation becomes worthless. Janet, a calendar-year taxpayer, owns 500 shares of Control's common stock, which she had purchased for $10,000 through her broker on June 17 of the prior year. Under Sec. 165(g), she treats the loss as having arisen from the sale of a capital asset on the last day of the current year. Thus, Janet incurs a $10,000 long-term capital loss because the holding period for the stock is more than one year. On the other hand, if Janet had received the stock directly from Control Corporation in exchange for either money or other property, and if certain other requirements are met, the stock may qualify as Sec. 1244 stock. Individuals who sustain losses on Sec. 1244 stock receive a limited amount of ordinary loss treatment rather than capital loss treatment. (See the discussion in this chapter under the heading "Losses on Sec. 1244 Stock.") ◀

Under certain circumstances, if a domestic corporation owns worthless securities of an affiliated corporation, the domestic corporation treats the loss as having arisen from the sale of a noncapital asset. This allows the corporation to treat the loss as an ordinary loss rather than as a capital loss.[7] For this exception to apply, the corporation must meet the following requirements:

▶ The domestic corporation that is deducting the loss must own at least 80% of the voting power of all classes of the affiliated corporation's stock and 80% of the total value of the affiliated corporation stock.

▶ More than 90% of the affiliated corporation's gross receipts for all its taxable years must be from nonpassive income.[8]

DEMOLITION OF PROPERTY

At times, taxpayers, intent on building their own facilities, purchase land with an existing structure that must first be removed. Taxpayers may also demolish a structure they currently use to construct new facilities. In both cases, taxpayers may not deduct any demolition costs or any loss sustained on account of the demolition. Instead, under Sec. 280B, taxpayers must add these amounts to the basis of the land on which the demolished structure previously stood.

OBJECTIVE 2

Determine the proper classification for losses

CLASSIFYING THE LOSS ON THE TAXPAYER'S TAX RETURN

If a loss is deductible, the taxpayer must determine whether the loss is an ordinary loss or a capital loss. In addition, individual taxpayers must also identify the amount as either a deduction *for* or *from* AGI.

---

[7] As explained in Chapter I:5, the deductibility of capital losses is limited. For corporate taxpayers, capital losses must initially be offset against capital gains of the current year, and any excess loss is not deductible but must be carried back three years and forward for five years. Individuals may offset capital losses against capital gains and any excess loss is deductible up to $3,000 per year as an offset to ordinary income. Capital losses in excess of

this amount for an individual are carried forward for an indefinite period. Thus, taxpayers generally prefer ordinary losses rather than capital losses.
[8] Sec. 165(g)(3). *Nonpassive income* includes all income other than royalties, rents, dividends, interest, annuities, and gains from the sale or exchange of stocks and securities.

ORDINARY VERSUS CAPITAL LOSS

Whether a deductible loss is ordinary or capital depends on the type of property involved and the transaction in which the taxpayer sustains the loss. To incur a capital loss, a sale or exchange of a capital asset must occur. If both elements (i.e., a sale or exchange and a capital asset) are not present, the deduction is an ordinary loss. In general, all assets *except* inventory, notes and accounts receivable, and depreciable property and land used in a trade or business (i.e., property, plant, and machinery) are classified as **capital assets**.[9]

Because a casualty is not a sale or exchange, the destruction of a capital asset in a casualty creates an ordinary rather than a capital loss. Likewise, a deductible loss realized on the abandonment of property is an ordinary loss because an abandonment is not a sale or exchange.

EXAMPLE I:8-4 ▶

BOOK-TAX DIFFERENCE

For book purposes, it makes no difference if a gain or loss is ordinary or capital. The full amount of the loss is deductible. However, because corporations may not deduct a capital loss in excess of its capital gains for the year, a book-tax timing (temporary) difference may arise, making an M-1 or M-3 adjustment necessary.

On July 24 of the current year, Jermaine & Associates, LLP sells some investment property for $75,000. The property's adjusted basis is $85,000. The investment property is a capital asset. Jermaine realizes a $10,000 ($75,000 − $85,000) capital loss. If, instead, the property had been destroyed by fire and the partnership had received $75,000 in insurance proceeds, the $10,000 loss would have been an ordinary loss because a casualty is not a sale or exchange. ◀

Certain transactions, though not actually constituting a sale or exchange, receive sale or exchange treatment. For example, as mentioned previously, if a security owned by an individual investor becomes worthless during the year, the individual treats the loss as a loss from the sale of a capital asset on the last day of the tax year, even though no sale actually occurs. Thus, the loss is a capital loss. Likewise, the taxpayer will treat a seizure or condemnation of property as a sale or exchange.

SECTION 1231 PROPERTY. Whether a loss on a particular transaction is treated as a capital loss may also depend on the gains and losses reported from other property transactions for the tax year. For instance, under Sec. 1231, taxpayers must net certain gains and losses together. If the Sec. 1231 gains exceed the Sec. 1231 losses for the year, the taxpayer treats the net gain as a long-term capital gain. However, if the losses equal or exceed the gains, both the gains and the losses are treated as ordinary. **Section 1231 property** includes real or depreciable property used in a trade or business and held for more than one year. (See Chapter I:13 for a discussion of the netting procedure under Sec. 1231.)

LOSSES ON SEC. 1244 STOCK. Taxpayers generally recognize capital gain or loss on the sale of stock or securities. For individuals, the tax law provides an exception for losses from the sale or worthlessness of small business corporation (Sec. 1244) stock. Individuals may deduct these losses as ordinary losses up to a maximum of $50,000 per tax year ($100,000 for married taxpayers filing a joint return). Any remaining loss for the year is a capital loss.

To qualify the loss as ordinary under Sec. 1244, the following requirements must be met:

▶ The stock must be owned by an individual or a partnership.

▶ The stock must have been originally issued by the corporation to the individual or to a partnership in which an individual is a partner.[10]

▶ The stock must be stock in a domestic (U.S.) corporation.

▶ The stock must have been issued for cash or property other than stock or securities. Stock issued for services rendered is not eligible for Sec. 1244 treatment.

---

[9] Sec. 1221. Certain other exceptions also exist. The definition of a capital asset is more fully examined in Chapter I:5.

[10] Stock received in certain reorganizations of corporations in exchange for

Sec. 1244 stock is also considered Sec. 1244 stock. Section 1244 does not apply to stock that the individual has received through other means such as purchase in a secondary market, exchange, gift, or inheritance.

► The corporation must not have derived over 50% of its gross receipts from passive income sources during the five tax years immediately preceding the year of sale or worthlessness.[11]

► The amount of money and property contributed to both capital and paid-in surplus may not exceed $1 million at the time the corporation issues the stock.

Note that the last test listed above occurs when the corporation *actually issues the stock*. As long as the corporation's capital and paid-in surplus does not exceed $1 million at the time the stock was issued, the individual taxpayer may still report an ordinary loss on the stock even if the corporation has capital and paid-in surplus in excess of the $1 million limit at the time the loss is realized.

STOP & THINK

Question: Tony, a single taxpayer, incorporated Waffle, Inc. three years ago by contributing $70,000 in exchange for the stock. Waffle owns and operates a small restaurant. Unfortunately, Waffle's business never really became profitable. Tony has been trying to sell the Waffle stock since July of last year, but because the corporation had become insolvent, he couldn't find any buyers. In February of the current year, Waffle was judged to be bankrupt. Tony didn't receive anything for his stock. What issues should Tony's tax advisor address with regard to the Waffle, Inc. stock?

Solution: Tony's tax advisor must determine (1) the amount of any realized loss, (2) the year in which the loss is recognized, and (3) the character of the realized loss. The Waffle, Inc. stock is considered a security under Sec. 165. Whenever a security becomes completely worthless and it is determined that the owner will receive nothing for it, the owner realizes a loss to the extent of the security's basis ($70,000). The loss is deemed to be realized in the year in which the security becomes worthless. While the bankruptcy court ruled the stock to be worthless in February of the current year, the fact that Tony could not find any buyers last year because the corporation was insolvent may indicate that the stock really became worthless last year. This determination is important because Tony must recognize the loss in the year in which the stock becomes worthless. Furthermore, the stock is deemed to become worthless on the last day of that year. Since Tony received the stock directly from the corporation in exchange for contributed cash, Waffle, Inc.'s gross receipts are from business operations, and the capitalization at the time the stock is issued is less than $1 million, the stock qualifies as Sec. 1244 stock. Thus, $50,000 of the loss is characterized as ordinary loss. The remaining $20,000 is a long-term capital loss.

DISALLOWANCE POSSIBILITIES

The tax law may disallow or defer losses incurred in certain transactions and activities. Some of these transactions include:

► Transfers of property to a controlled corporation in exchange for stock of the corporation (see the discussion in Chapter C:2 of *Prentice Hall's Federal Taxation: Corporations, Partnerships, Estates, and Trusts* text and Chapter C:2 of the *Comprehensive* volume)

► Exchanges of property for other property considered to be like-kind to the property given up (see the discussion in Chapter I:12)

► Property sold to certain related parties (see the discussion in Chapter I:6)

► Wash sale transactions (see the discussion in Chapter I:6)

► Losses limited because the losses exceed the amount for which the taxpayer is at risk (see the discussion in Chapter C:9 of *Prentice Hall's Federal Taxation: Corporations, Partnerships, Estates, and Trusts* text and Chapter C:9 of the *Comprehensive* volume)

In addition, the passive loss rules discussed below may limit the amount of losses that individuals and certain corporations may deduct.

Topic Review I:8-1 contains a summary of loss transactions.

---

[11] For this purpose, passive income sources include royalties, rents, dividends, interest, annuities, and sales or exchanges of stocks and securities. If the corporation has not been in existence for a full five years, the gross receipts test is applied to the shorter period. If the corporation has not been in existence for an entire taxable year, the test is applied to the time period up to the date of the loss (see Sec. 1244(c)(2)).

Topic Review I:8-1

Transactions That May Result in Losses

TYPE OF TRANSACTION	RESULT
Sale or exchange	Taxpayers may not deduct a loss on personal-use property. The tax treatment of a loss on business or investment property depends on the type of property. Losses on capital assets result in capital losses. Losses on Sec. 1231 assets are subject to the Sec. 1231 netting rules discussed in Chapter I:13.
Seizure, expropriation, confiscation, or condemnation	Treated as a sale or exchange.
Abandonment	Not treated as a sale or exchange. No deduction is allowed for a loss on personal-use property. Business or investment property is given ordinary loss treatment.
Worthless securities	Treated as a loss from the sale of the securities on the last day of the year in which the securities become worthless. This generally will result in a capital loss. However, if the requirements of Sec. 1244 are met, at least part of the loss may be treated as an ordinary loss. (See Sec. 1244 stock below.) A loss realized by a corporation on worthless securities of an affiliated corporation results in an ordinary loss.
Demolition	No deductible loss is allowed. Instead, losses and costs of demolition are added to the basis of the land where the demolished structure was located.
Sec. 1244 stock	An ordinary loss is allowed for individuals up to $50,000 per year ($100,000 for married filing jointly). The remaining loss is capital. The stock must have been originally issued to the individual for property or cash, and the corporation must meet the requirements to be a small business corporation.

PASSIVE LOSSES

HISTORICAL NOTE

Before the passive activity loss limits became effective in 1987, most tax shelters were concentrated in the areas of real estate, oil and gas, equipment leasing, farming, motion pictures, timber, and research and development. Many tax shelters took advantage of liberal depreciation rules during the early 1980s such as the rapid depreciation of real estate over a 15-year period.

Before 1987, taxpayers were able to reduce their income tax liability on income from one business or investment activity with deductions, losses, and credits arising in another activity. Thus, taxpayers often invested in activities, called **tax shelters**, that would spin off tax deductions and credits. Many of these tax shelters were simply *passive investments* because they did not require the taxpayer's involvement or participation. In some situations, tax shelters had real economic substance, i.e., a taxpayer's economic return in this type of shelter was not based solely on the tax benefits that the activity generated. In many cases, however, tax shelters had no real economic substance other than the creation of deductions and credits that enabled taxpayers to reduce, and sometimes eliminate, the income tax liability from their other business activities. To prevent these perceived and real abuses, Congress enacted Sec. 469, which restricts the current use of losses and credits that arise in rental activities and in other activities in which the taxpayer does not materially participate. These activities constitute passive activities. (See the "Definition of a Passive Activity" section in this chapter for an extended discussion of what constitutes a passive activity.)

COMPUTATION OF PASSIVE LOSSES AND CREDITS

OBJECTIVE 3

Calculate the suspended loss from passive activities

In enacting the passive loss rules, Congress did not want to prevent taxpayers from currently deducting or using losses and credits generated in active business endeavors of the taxpayer. At the same time, Congress realized that certain investments (such as investments that generate interest or dividend income) normally give rise to taxable income, which could itself be sheltered by losses and credits that arise in other passive activities. Thus, Sec. 469 requires certain taxpayers to classify their income into three categories: *active income* (such as wages, salaries, and active business income), *portfolio (or investment) income,* and *passive income.* **Portfolio income** includes dividends, interest, annuities, and royalties (and allocable expenses and interest expense) not derived in the ordinary

course of a trade or business. Portfolio income also includes gains and losses on property that produces these types of income if the disposition of the property does not occur in the ordinary course of business.[12] Portfolio income becomes part of net investment income, which is used in computing the deduction limit for investment interest expense. (See Chapter I:7 for a discussion of the investment interest expense limitation.)

PASSIVE INCOME AND LOSSES. Taxpayers compute income and loss in the passive category separately for each passive activity in which they have invested. In general, for any tax year, a taxpayer may use losses generated in one passive activity to offset income from other passive activities, but may not use them to offset either active or portfolio income.

EXAMPLE I:8-5 ▶ During the year, Kasi, a CPA, reports $100,000 of active business income from his CPA practice. He also owns two passive activities. From activity A, he earns $10,000 of income, and from activity B, he incurs a $15,000 loss. Kasi may use $10,000 of the loss from activity B to offset the $10,000 of income from activity A. However, Kasi may not deduct the $5,000 excess loss from activity B in the current year, even though he has $100,000 of active business income. ◀

CARRYOVERS

KEY POINT

Excess passive activity losses are not "lost" because they can be carried over to future years.

A taxpayer carries over disallowed passive activity losses indefinitely and treats them as losses allocable to that specific passive activity in the following tax years. The taxpayer may use these losses, known as **suspended losses,** to offset passive activity income of the subsequent year, but generally may not offset other types of income. If a taxpayer has invested in several passive activities, and for the year some of the activities generate income while others generate losses, the loss carried over for each loss activity is a pro rata portion of the total passive loss for the year.

EXAMPLE I:8-6 ▶ Tammy reports the following income and loss for the year:

Salary	$200,000
Loss from activity X	(40,000)
Loss from activity Y	(10,000)
Income from activity Z	30,000

X, Y, and Z are all passive activities. The losses generated in activities X and Y offset the income from activity Z, but none of the salary income is offset. Thus, Tammy has a net passive loss for the year of $20,000 ($40,000 + $10,000 − $30,000), which must be carried over to subsequent years. The amount of the carryover attributable to each activity is as follows:

Activity X: $20,000 \times \dfrac{\$40,000}{\$50,000} = \$16,000$

Activity Y: $20,000 \times \dfrac{\$10,000}{\$50,000} = \$ 4,000$ ◀

TAXABLE DISPOSITION OF INTEREST IN A PASSIVE ACTIVITY. When a taxpayer disposes of a passive activity in a taxable transaction, the taxpayer can compute the economic gain or loss generated by the activity and can deduct the suspended losses of the activity against other income. However, the amount of the total net economic loss from the asset disposed of must first offset any passive income for the year from other passive activities.[13]

EXAMPLE I:8-7 ▶ During the current year, Pam realizes $6,000 of taxable income from activity A, $1,000 of loss from activity B, and $8,000 of taxable income from activity C. All three activities are passive activities with regard to Pam. In addition, $30,000 of passive losses from activity C are carried over from prior years. During the current year, Pam sells activity C for a $15,000 taxable gain. Pam reports salary income of $90,000 for the year. Because Pam sells activity C in a fully taxable transaction, Pam may deduct $2,000 of loss against the salary income:

---

[12] Sec. 469(e)(1). Gain or loss on property dispositions occurring in the ordinary course of business is either passive or active business income, depending on the taxpayer's level of involvement (i.e., material participation) in the activity.

[13] Sec. 469(g). Income from the activity for prior years may also be taken into account in arriving at the net income from all passive activities for the year if it is necessary to prevent avoidance of the passive loss rules.

Income for the year from C	$ 8,000	
Gain from the sale of C	15,000	
Suspended losses from C	(30,000)	
Total loss from C		($7,000)
Income for the year from A	$ 6,000	
Loss for the year from B	(1,000)	5,000
Pam's deduction against salary income		($2,000) ◄

BOOK-TAX DIFFERENCE

Since passive losses are not limited under financial accounting rules, the limitation and carryover of passive losses for tax purposes will create a timing (temporary) difference between book and tax. However, most taxpayers subject to the passive loss rules do not use financial accounting rules.

If the taxpayer sells the passive activity to a related party, he or she may not deduct the suspended loss until the related party sells the activity to a nonrelated person. The definition of *related persons* includes spouse, brothers and sisters, ancestors, lineal descendants, and corporations or partnerships in which the individual has a greater than 50% ownership.[14]

Although the death of a taxpayer is not a taxable disposition of the asset, some of the suspended losses may be deductible when a taxpayer dies. The amount of the deduction allowed is the amount by which the suspended losses exceed the increase in basis of the property. The decedent's final income tax return generally includes the deduction for these losses. Any suspended losses up to the amount of the increase in basis will never be deductible.[15]

EXAMPLE I:8-8 ▶

At the time that John died, he owned passive activity property with an adjusted basis of $20,000 and a FMV of $35,000. Suspended losses attributable to the property totaled $25,000. Because the increase in the basis of the property is $15,000 ($35,000 − $20,000), $15,000 of the suspended losses are lost. However, $10,000 ($25,000 suspended losses − $15,000 increase in basis) of the suspended losses are deductible on John's final income tax return. ◄

In general, the suspended losses of a passive activity become deductible only when the taxpayer completely disposes of his or her interest in the activity. However, in Treasury Reg. 1.469-4(g) the government has stated that taxpayers may treat the disposition of a substantial part of an activity as the disposition of a separate activity. This treatment is only available, however, if the taxpayer can establish with reasonable certainty the amount of income, deductions, credits, and suspended losses and credits that are allocable to that part of the activity.

CARRYOVERS FROM A FORMER PASSIVE ACTIVITY. The determination of whether an activity is passive with respect to a taxpayer must be made annually. Thus, an activity that was previously passive may not be passive with respect to the taxpayer for the current year. This is called a **former passive activity**. A taxpayer may deduct any loss carryover from a former passive activity against the current year's income of that activity even though the activity is not a passive activity in the current year. However, any suspended loss in excess of the activity's income for the year is still subject to the carryover limitations. Because the activity is no longer passive for the year, the current year's loss is deductible against active business income.

EXAMPLE I:8-9 ▶

Kris owns activity A, which, for the immediately preceding tax year, was considered a passive activity with regard to Kris. $10,000 in losses from activity A were disallowed and carried over to the current year. Because of Kris' increased involvement in activity A in the current year, it is not considered passive with regard to Kris for the current year. During the current year, activity A generates a $5,000 loss. During the current year, Kris also has an investment in activity B, a passive activity. Her share of activity B's income is $7,000. Kris reports $60,000 in salary. Because for the current year activity A is not a passive activity, the $5,000 current year loss is fully deductible against her salary. However, the $10,000 loss carryover from the prior year is deductible only against the $7,000 of income from passive activity B. The $3,000 ($10,000 − $7,000) excess is carried over to the subsequent year. ◄

---

[14] Other relationships described in Secs. 267(b) and 707(b) are also considered related parties for this purpose.

[15] Sec. 469(g)(2). Generally, the basis of inherited property is its FMV on the date of death (see Chapter I:5).

Credits. A taxpayer may only use tax credits generated in a passive activity against the portion of the tax liability that is attributable to passive income. The taxpayer determines this amount by comparing the tax liability on all income for the year with the tax liability on all income excluding the passive income.

EXAMPLE I:8-10 ▶ Dale invests in a passive activity. For the year, he must report $10,000 of taxable income from the passive activity. Dale's share of tax credits generated by the passive activity is $5,000. Assume Dale's precredit tax liability on all income (including the $10,000 from the passive activity) is $25,000, and his precredit tax liability on all income excluding the passive activity income is $22,000. He may use only $3,000 ($25,000 − $22,000) of the tax credits generated by the passive activity. The remaining $2,000 of tax credits is carried forward and may be used in a subsequent year against the portion of the tax liability attributable to passive activity income in that year. However, these credits may never offset any portion of the tax liability attributable to nonpassive activities. (See Chapter I:14 for a discussion of credits and their carryovers.) ◀

DEFINITION OF A PASSIVE ACTIVITY

OBJECTIVE 4

Identify what constitutes a passive activity loss

The term *passive activity* includes any trade or business in which the taxpayer does not materially participate as well as any rental activity. An important exception applies to a rental activity that is considered to be a *real property trade or business*. This exception is discussed below on page 8–14.[16] The definition of a passive activity is based on two critical elements: an identification of exactly what constitutes an activity and a determination of whether the taxpayer has materially participated in that activity.

IDENTIFICATION OF AN ACTIVITY. Identification of the activity becomes critical for several reasons. The determination of whether a taxpayer materially participates in an activity is determined separately for each activity. A taxpayer may deduct suspended losses of a passive activity when the taxpayer completely terminates his or her ownership of the activity. As explained in a subsequent section of this chapter, taxpayers may deduct currently up to $25,000 of passive losses from rental real estate activities. Thus, taxpayers must not combine losses from passive business and rental real estate activities into one activity.

The way taxpayers combine or separate operations into activities can significantly impact the deductibility of losses generated by the activities. Taxpayers may treat one or more activities as a single activity only if they constitute an "appropriate economic unit."[17] Although the taxpayer makes this determination by examining all the relevant facts and circumstances, the following factors receive the greatest weight:

▶ Similarities and differences in the types of business,

▶ The extent of common control,

▶ The extent of common ownership,

▶ The geographical location, and

▶ Any interdependencies between the operations (i.e., the extent to which they purchase or sell goods between the activities, have the same customers, are accounted for with a single set of books, etc.).

A taxpayer may treat more than one operation as a single activity, even if all of these factors do not apply. Furthermore, a taxpayer may use any reasonable method of applying the relevant facts and circumstances in grouping the activities.

EXAMPLE I:8-11 ▶ Carla owns a bakery and a movie theater in each of two different shopping malls, one located in Baltimore and the other in Philadelphia. Depending on other relevant facts and circumstances, a reasonable grouping of the operations may result in any of the following:

[16] Secs. 469(c)(1) and (c)(2). Sec. 469(c)(6) also includes investment (production of income) activities under Sec. 212 as a passive activity. Section 469(j)(8) defines the term *rental activity* as any activity where payments are principally for the use of tangible property. Pursuant to the Regulations, there are six exceptions to this general rule. These exceptions include (1) providing the use of tangible property where the average period of customer use is seven days or less, (2) the average period of customer use is 30 days or less and significant personal services are provided by the owner in conjunction with the use of the property, (3) extraordinary personal services are provided by the owner in conjunction with the use of the property, (4) the rental of the property is incidental to a nonrental activity of the taxpayer, (5) the property is customarily made available during defined business hours for nonexclusive use by various customers, or (6) the property is provided for use in a nonrental activity conducted by a partnership, S corporation, or joint venture in which the taxpayer owns an interest. The details of these exceptions are beyond the scope of this text. (See Reg. Sec. 1.469-1(e)(3)(iii).)

[17] Reg. Sec. 1.469-4.

> ► One activity involving all four operations
> ► Two activities: a bakery activity and a theater activity
> ► Two activities: a Baltimore activity and a Philadelphia activity
> ► Four activities ◄

Under the Treasury Regulations, taxpayers apparently have some degree of flexibility in determining the grouping into activities of different business operations. However, once taxpayers establish the activities, they must be consistent in grouping these activities in subsequent years unless material changes in the facts and circumstances clearly make the groupings inappropriate.

In identifying separate activities, taxpayers generally may not group rental operations with trade or business operations. However, a combination is allowed if either the rental operation is insubstantial in relation to the business operation or vice versa. Unfortunately, the Treasury Regulations do not give any guidance with regard to what is insubstantial. Furthermore, because of the special rules dealing with real estate rental activities (explained later in this chapter), the taxpayer may not combine rental activities involving real estate with rental activities involving personal property.

EXAMPLE I:8-12 ► Sandy owns a building in which she (1) operates a restaurant and (2) leases out apartments to tenants. Generally the tenants sign apartment leases of one year or longer. Of the total gross income derived from the building, 15% comes from the apartment rentals and 85% comes from the restaurant operation. If the apartment rental operation is insubstantial in relation to the restaurant operation, the taxpayer may combine the two into one activity. If it is not insubstantial, the two operations are considered two separate activities: a business activity and a rental real estate activity. ◄

Partnerships and S corporations (pass-through entities) must identify their business and rental activities by applying these rules at the partnership or S corporation level and then must report the results of their operations by activity to the partners or shareholders. Each partner or shareholder must then take the results from these activities and, using these same rules, combine them where appropriate with operations conducted either directly or through other pass-through entities. In fact, taxpayers hold many real estate passive activities as either partnerships or S corporations.

OBJECTIVE 5

Determine when a taxpayer has materially participated in a passive activity

MATERIAL PARTICIPATION. Once each activity is identified, taxpayers must determine whether the activity is passive or active. If the taxpayer does not **materially participate** in the activity, it is deemed to be a passive activity with respect to that taxpayer. Pursuant to the Treasury Regulations,[18] taxpayers materially participate in an activity if they meet at least one of the following tests:

> ► The individual participates in the activity for more than 500 hours during the year.
> ► The individual's participation in the activity for the year constitutes substantially all of the participation in the activity by all individuals, including individuals who do not own any interest in the activity.
> ► The individual participates in the activity for more than 100 hours during the year, and that participation is more than any other individual's participation for the year (including participation by individuals who do not own any interest in the activity).
> ► The individual participates in "significant participation activities" for an aggregate of more than 500 hours during the year.[19] Thus, an individual who spends over 100 hours each in several separate significant participation activities may aggregate the time spent in these activities in order to meet the 500-hour test.
> ► The individual materially participated in the activity in any five years during the immediately preceding ten taxable years. These five years need not be consecutive.

---

[18] Temp. Reg. Sec. 1.469-5T(a).
[19] A significant participation activity is a trade or business in which the individual participates for more than 100 hours during the year but for which the individual does not meet the material participation test alone (i.e., with respect to that activity, the individual does not meet one of the other material participation tests). (See Temp. Reg. Sec. 1.469-5T(c).)

▶ The individual materially participated in the activity for any three years preceding the year in question, and the activity is a personal service activity.[20]

▶ The individual participates in the activity on a regular, continuous, and substantial basis during the year, taking into account all the relevant facts and circumstances.

Note that the first four tests are based on the number of hours the taxpayer spent in the activity during the current year. The fifth and sixth tests are based on the material participation of the taxpayer in prior years and are designed to prevent taxpayers from asserting that retirement income is passive and offsetting it with passive losses from tax shelters. To determine whether a taxpayer materially participates in an activity, the participation of the taxpayer's spouse is also taken into account.

LIMITED PARTNERSHIPS. A limited partner has limited liability for his or her investment in the partnership and normally is not actively involved in the business of the partnership. As a consequence, a limited partner generally does not meet the material participation test and the limited partner's investment is treated as passive. Thus, most income and deductions passed through to a limited partner from a limited partnership are passive. However, a limited partner can meet the material participation test if the individual meets either the 500 hour test or the fifth and sixth tests above (prior year tests).

WORKING INTEREST IN AN OIL AND GAS PROPERTY. A working interest is an interest that is responsible for the cost of development or operation of the oil and gas property. This type of interest in an oil and gas property is not a passive activity as long as the taxpayer's liability in the interest is not a limited interest. Thus, even though a taxpayer may not materially participate in the activity, the passive loss rules do not apply. This is so even if the taxpayer holds the interest through an entity such as a partnership.

TAXPAYERS SUBJECT TO PASSIVE LOSS RULES

The passive loss limitation rules apply to:

▶ Individuals, estates, trusts

▶ Any closely held C corporation

▶ Any personal service corporation

▶ Certain publicly traded partnerships

Because the income and losses of partnerships and S corporations are taxed directly to the partners and shareholders, the passive loss rules do not apply to these entities.[21] Rather, the passive loss limitations apply directly at the partner or shareholder level. Thus, the situation may arise where one partner or shareholder is subject to the passive loss rules with regard to an activity conducted by the partnership or S corporation while other partners or shareholders are not.

Generally, regular corporations (i.e., C corporations) are not subject to the passive loss limitation rules. However, to prevent certain individuals from avoiding the passive loss rules through the use of a regular corporation, the rules do apply to closely held C corporations and personal service corporations.

CLOSELY HELD C CORPORATIONS. The passive loss rules apply to closely held C corporations but only on a limited basis. A **closely held C corporation** is a C corporation where more than 50% of the stock is owned by five or fewer individuals at any time during the last half of the corporation's taxable year.[22] Without this special rule involving

---

[20] A personal service activity involves rendering personal services in the fields of health, law, engineering, architecture, accounting, actuarial science, performing arts, or consulting. It also includes any other trade or business in which capital is not a material income-producing factor. (See Temp. Reg. Sec. 1.469-5T(d).)

[21] An S corporation is a corporation that has elected for federal income tax purposes to be treated basically like a partnership. Thus, the income or losses and separately stated items of an S corporation flow through to the shareholders and are reported on their individual tax returns.

[22] Secs. 469(j)(1), 465(a)(1)(B), and 542(a)(2).

closely held C corporations, taxpayers would be motivated to transfer their investments (both portfolio investments and passive activities) to a C corporation where the portfolio income could be offset by the corporation's passive losses. Thus, as applied to a closely held C corporation, the passive loss rules prevent passive activity losses from offsetting portfolio income. However, a closely held C corporation's passive losses may offset its income from active business operations.

EXAMPLE I:8-13 ▶

All of the outstanding stock of Delta Corporation is owned equally by individuals Allen and Beth. During the current year, Delta generates $15,000 taxable income from its active business operations. It also earns $10,000 of interest and dividends from investments and reports a $30,000 loss from a passive activity. Because Delta is a closely held C corporation, the $15,000 of taxable income from the active business is offset by $15,000 of the passive loss. However, the $10,000 of portfolio income may not be offset. Thus, for the current year, Delta reports $10,000 of taxable income from its portfolio income and has a $15,000 passive loss carryover. ◀

PERSONAL SERVICE CORPORATION. A **personal service corporation (PSC)** is a regular C corporation whose principal activity is the performance of personal services that are substantially performed by owner-employees.[23] However, a corporation is not a PSC unless owner-employees own more than 10% of the value of the stock. In contrast with a non-PSC closely held C corporation, the passive loss limitation rules apply in their entirety to a PSC. If a corporation is both a PSC and a closely held C corporation, the more restrictive rules for PSCs apply. Thus, passive losses of a PSC may not offset the PSC's active business income or portfolio income.

Material participation by PSCs and closely held C corporations. Special rules apply for determining whether closely held C corporations or PSCs materially participate in an activity. These corporations materially participate in an activity only if one or more shareholders who own more than 50% in value of the outstanding stock materially participate in the activity. In addition, a closely held C corporation (other than a PSC) materially participates in an activity if it meets *all* of the following tests with regard to an activity:

1. A substantial portion of the services of at least one full-time employee is in the active management of the activity.
2. A substantial portion of the services of at least three full-time nonowner employees is directly related to the activity.
3. The Sec. 162 business deductions of the activity exceed 15% of the activity's gross income for the period.[24]

PUBLICLY TRADED PARTNERSHIPS. In many cases, the tax law provisions for corporations apply to publicly traded partnerships (PTP). For purposes of the passive loss rules, a PTP is defined as any partnership if interests in the partnership are either traded on an established securities market or readily tradable on a secondary market.[25] If the corporate tax provisions apply to a PTP, the passive loss rules generally do not apply. However, if a PTP meets certain gross income requirements, the partnership tax provisions may still apply, causing its items of income, loss, and credit to flow through to the partners.[26] If this is the case, the passive loss rules apply at the partner level separately to the flow through items from each PTP. Thus, partners treat losses from a PTP as separate from any other type of income (passive, active business, or portfolio) and separate from

---

[23] Secs. 469(j)(2) and 269A(b)(1). For this purpose any employee who owns any stock of the corporation is an owner-employee. This stock ownership is determined by using the Sec. 318 constructive ownership rules as modified by Sec. 469(j)(2).

[24] Secs. 469(h)(4) and 465(c)(7). Tests 1 and 2 must be met for the 12-month period ending on the last day of the tax year. Test 3 must be met for the tax year. Furthermore, the Sec. 404 deductions are also included in the 15% of gross income test.

[25] Sec. 469(k)(2). (See Chapter C:10 of *Prentice Hall's Federal Taxation:*

Corporations, Partnerships, Estates, and Trusts and Chapter C:10 of the *Comprehensive* volume for a definition and discussion of publicly traded partnerships.)

[26] Sec. 7704(c). For the taxable year and all preceding years beginning after Dec. 31, 1987, at least 90% of the PTP's gross income consists of dividends, interest, real property rents, income from certain gas, oil, mineral or timber activities, and gains from the sale of real estate or certain capital assets. Furthermore, certain other PTPs may also elect to continue to be treated as a partnership rather than as a corporation.

any income from other PTPs. Partners can only carry these losses forward and offset them against income generated by that particular PTP in a subsequent year. Furthermore, a PTP loss may not offset any portfolio income that the PTP might generate. Any net income from PTPs is portfolio income.

EXAMPLE I:8-14 ▶ Mark owns interests in partnerships A and B, both of which are PTPs that are treated as partnerships. During the current year, Mark's share of the income from A is $2,000. Mark's share of B's loss is $1,200. B also generates some portfolio income. Mark's share of B's portfolio income is $800. The $1,200 loss from B may not offset any of B's $800 portfolio income. Furthermore, it may not offset any of the $2,000 income from A. The $2,000 income from A is treated as portfolio income. Thus, Mark reports $2,800 portfolio income and has a $1,200 suspended loss from B. In a subsequent year, Mark's share of any income from B can be offset by the $1,200 of suspended loss that is carried forward. ◀

Partners may deduct suspended losses from a PTP in the year the partner disposes of his or her interest in the PTP. Partners do not recognize a loss in the year that the PTP itself sells a passive activity.

REAL ESTATE BUSINESSES

In general, rental activities are considered passive activities. However, the passive activity loss rules do not apply to certain taxpayers who are involved in real property trades or businesses. Instead, these activities are treated as active businesses. A *real property trade or business* involves the development, redevelopment, construction, reconstruction, acquisition, conversion, rental, operation, management, leasing, or brokering of real property.

This exception only applies to a taxpayer if he or she meets both of the following requirements:

▶ More than one-half of the personal services the taxpayer performs in all trades or businesses during the year are in real property trades or businesses in which the taxpayer materially participates.

▶ The taxpayer performs more than 750 hours of work during the taxable year in real property trades or businesses in which the taxpayer materially participates.

In meeting these tests, personal services a taxpayer renders in his or her capacity as an employee are not treated as performed in real property trades or businesses unless the employee owns at least 5% of the employer. Furthermore, for married taxpayers filing a joint return, the exception applies only if one of the spouses separately meets both requirements. The time spent in the activity by both spouses counts toward the determination of whether or not the taxpayer meets the material participation test.

EXAMPLE I:8-15 ▶ Anwar and Anya are married and file a joint return. They own four large apartment complexes which they manage themselves. Neither is employed elsewhere. During the current year, Anya spent 500 hours keeping records and corresponding with tenants. Anwar spent 700 hours during the year maintaining and repairing the apartments. Even though all of Anya and Anwar's personal services are connected with a real property trade or business in which they materially participate, this rental activity is considered passive because neither Anwar nor Anya alone spends more than 750 hours doing services related to the rental activity. ◀

For a closely held C corporation to meet this rental real estate business exception, the corporation must derive more than one-half of its gross receipts from real property businesses in which it materially participates.

Any deduction allowed under the previously discussed exception for taxpayers involved in real property trades or businesses is not considered in determining the taxpayer's AGI for purposes of the phase-out of the $25,000 deduction available for taxpayers who actively participate in a rental real estate activity. (See the following section in this chapter for a discussion of the $25,000 active participation exception.)

OTHER RENTAL REAL ESTATE ACTIVITIES

Many rental real estate activities are not considered rental real estate businesses and are, therefore, subject to the passive loss rules. However, if an individual taxpayer meets certain requirements, the taxpayer still may deduct against other income up to $25,000 of annual losses from these passive rental real estate activities. To meet this exception, an individual must do both of the following:

▶ *Actively* participate in the activity

▶ Own at least 10% of the value of the activity for the entire tax year

Additionally, in order to take a deduction in the current year for a loss sustained in a prior year, Section 469(i) requires the taxpayer to actively participate in the activity during both years.

ACTIVE PARTICIPATION. A taxpayer can achieve *active participation*, as opposed to material participation, without regular, continuous, and material involvement in the activity and without meeting any of the material participation tests. However, the taxpayer still must participate in making management decisions or arranging for others to provide services in a significant and bona fide sense. This includes approving new tenants, deciding on rental terms, approving expenditures, and other similar decisions. Taxpayers may achieve active participation even if they hire a rental agent and others provide the services. However, a lessor under a net lease arrangement generally does not achieve active participation. Additionally, a limited partner generally cannot actively participate in any activity of a limited partnership.

LIMITATION ON DEDUCTION OF RENTAL REAL ESTATE LOSS. Taxpayers must first apply rental real estate losses against other net passive income for the year. Taxpayers may then reduce their portfolio or active business income by up to $25,000. However, the tax law requires reduction of the $25,000 amount by 50% of the taxpayer's AGI in excess of $100,000.[27] For this purpose, AGI does not include any passive activity loss or any loss allowable to taxpayers who materially participate in real property trades or businesses (e.g., a real estate developer). Thus, if a taxpayer has AGI of $150,000 or more, the rental real estate losses are not eligible for the $25,000 deduction and are aggregated with the taxpayer's other passive losses.

EXAMPLE I:8-16 ▶

During the current year, Penny, a married individual who files a joint return, reports the following items of income and loss:

Salary income	$120,000
Activity A (passive)	15,000
Activity B (nonbusiness rental real estate)	(50,000)

Penny owns over 10% and actively participates in activity B. Her AGI for the year is as follows:

Salary		$120,000
Passive income from activity A	$15,000	
Minus: Passive loss from activity B ($50,000, but limited to $15,000)	(15,000)	–0–
Minus: Maximum rental real estate loss (from activity B)	$25,000	
Reduced by phase-out: [($120,000 − $100,000) × 0.50]	(10,000)	
Deductible amount (but not to exceed actual loss)		(15,000)
AGI		$105,000

Penny may deduct $30,000 of the loss from activity B during the year ($15,000 as an offset to the passive income from activity A + $15,000 deductible against portfolio or active business income). Penny has $20,000 ($50,000 − $30,000) of suspended passive losses from activity B that are carried over to the following year. ◀

---

[27] This reduction does not apply to any portion of a passive activity loss attributable to the commercial revitalization deduction under Sec. 1400I. The com mercial revitalization deduction is beyond the scope of this discussion. Additionally, AGI is modified by certain items that are beyond this discussion.

The $25,000 limit applies to the sum of both deductions and credits. Thus, in order to properly apply the limit, taxpayers must convert the credits into deduction equivalents. A *deduction equivalent* is an amount that, if taken as a deduction, would reduce the tax liability by an amount equal to the credits. The amount of deduction equivalents can be computed by dividing the amount of the credit by the taxpayer's marginal tax rate. If the sum of the deductions and the deduction equivalents exceeds the $25,000 limit, the taxpayer must first use the deductions.

EXAMPLE I:8-17 ▶ Hal owns over 10% of activity A, in which he actively participates. Activity A is a passive real estate rental activity. Hal's marginal tax rate is 25% and he has AGI of less than $100,000. For the year, activity A generates a $20,000 net loss and $10,000 in tax credits, which amounts to $40,000 in deduction equivalent {$10,000/25%}. After deducting the $20,000 net loss against his active business and portfolio income, Hal has a remaining real estate deduction under the limit of $5,000 ($25,000 − $20,000). Thus, Hal may use $1,250 ($5,000 × 0.25) of the credits. The remaining $8,750 ($10,000 − $1,250) of tax credits must be carried over to subsequent years. ◀

If deductions and credits exceeding the $25,000 limit arise from more than one passive activity, the taxpayer must allocate the deductions and credits between the activities.[28]

EXAMPLE I:8-18 ▶ Mary has AGI of less than $100,000 and a 25% marginal tax rate. During the year she reports a $30,000 loss from activity A and a $10,000 loss from activity B, neither one of which involves a commercial revitalization deduction. Additionally, activity A generates $5,000 of tax credits. Both activities A and B are passive real estate rental activities in which Mary actively participates and owns over 10% of each activity. The $25,000 deduction is first allocated to the losses. Because the sum of the losses ($40,000) exceeds the limit, the deductible loss must be allocated ratably between the activities as follows:

Activity A: $25,000 × $30,000 ÷ $40,000 = $18,750
Activity B: $25,000 × $10,000 ÷ $40,000 = $6,250

Activity A has an $11,250 ($30,000 − $18,750) suspended loss, and activity B has a $3,750 ($10,000 − $6,250) suspended loss. In addition, activity A has $5,000 of suspended tax credits. ◀

Topic Review I:8-2 summarizes the passive activity loss rules.

STOP & THINK

Question: Jana is a businesswoman who has successfully invested in various stock and bond funds. Now she is considering diversifying her holdings by investing in real estate. One of the alternatives she is considering is purchasing an interest in a limited partnership that invests in real estate. A friend is also urging Jana to go into a partnership with him in order to purchase a small office building they would rent out. Assume that the size of Jana's investment in the two alternatives would be exactly the same and that Jana estimates the economic results to be equivalent (e.g., she expects both to spin off equivalent losses for the first few years and then begin turning a profit). What tax issues should Jana consider when making her investment decision?

Solution: In comparing alternatives such as these, of course, the most important considerations should be the non-tax factors such as cash flow from the investment, the capital appreciation of the assets, the marketability of the investment, and the risk. For example, as a limited partner, Jana will not personally be liable for debts of the partnership or lawsuits filed against the partnership. Purchase of the office building as a general partner with her friend will cause her to be personally liable unless it is done through an LLC or LLP. Additionally, in comparing these two alternatives, certain tax issues may come into play. Both alternatives are investments in rental real estate. However, Jana is not eligible to deduct up to $25,000 of the passive losses from the limited partnership because she will

---

[28] A taxpayer may earn different types of credits, based upon the different types of investments. Furthermore, the phase-out of the $25,000 limit is treated differently for different types of credits. For example, the phase-out for the rehabilitation credit only begins when the taxpayer's AGI exceeds $200,000. Additionally, there is no phase-out applied to the credit for low income housing. (See Sec. 469(e)(3) and Chapter I:14 for a discussion of these credits.) Thus, taxpayers are required to allocate the deductions and credits among the activities and account for them in a specific order. A complete analysis of these rules is beyond the scope of this discussion. Example I:8-18 assumes both activities earn the same type of credit and are subject to the $25,000 limit.

Topic Review I:8-2

Passive Losses

TOPIC	SUMMARY
Taxpayers covered	Individuals, estates, trusts, closely held C corporations, personal service corporations, certain publicly traded partnerships.
Passive activity	Any trade or business activity in which the taxpayer does not materially participate. Includes all rental activities except for certain rental real estate activities and exceptions contained in regulations. Does not include working interests in oil and gas property.
Limitation	Passive losses are deductible against passive income, but not against active or portfolio income. Disallowed losses are carried over to subsequent years (suspended losses). Losses must be accounted for separately by activity. Activities are identified by examining the taxpayer's undertakings.
Suspended losses	Must be allocated and attributed among the passive activities that generated the losses.
Disposition of interest	Suspended losses may be deducted in the year of a taxable disposition. For inherited property, suspended losses in excess of the increase in basis may be deducted on the final return of a decedent. Losses up to the amount of the basis increase are lost.
Material participation	Must be regular, continuous, and substantial. The regulations contain seven separate tests; four based on current-year participation; two based on participation in prior years; and one based on facts and circumstances.
Real property trades or businesses	Passive activity loss rules do not apply to taxpayers who materially participate in real property trade or business activities constituting more than 750 hours. Additionally, more than one-half of the taxpayer's personal services must be performed in real property trades or businesses in which the taxpayer materially participates.
Rental of real estate	Individuals may deduct losses up to $25,000 against active and portfolio income if they actively participate in the activity and own at least 10% of the value of the activity. Additionally, they may take certain credits generated in passive rental activities in which they actively participate. Active participation is a lesser standard than material participation, but the taxpayer must still participate in management decisions or arranging for others to provide services. The deduction and credits phase out at a 50% rate for AGI in excess of $100,000.

not actively participate in the partnership. On the other hand, if she is involved in management decisions regarding the office building held by the partnership, she will be actively participating and will be eligible for the $25,000 passive loss deduction exception. Of course, the benefit of this exception is phased out if her AGI exceeds $100,000.

CASUALTY AND THEFT LOSSES

OBJECTIVE 6

Identify and calculate the deduction for a casualty or theft loss

Taxpayers may deduct losses incurred in connection with business or investment property, but taxpayers generally are not allowed a deduction for losses on personal-use property. However, under Sec. 165, taxpayers may take a limited deduction if the loss on personal-use property arises from a fire, storm, shipwreck, other casualty, or theft. In other words, losses on personal-use property are deductible only if the loss results from a casualty. In order for an event to qualify as a casualty, the event must meet certain requirements.

CASUALTY DEFINED
According to the IRS, a deductible **casualty loss** is one that occurs in an identifiable event that is sudden, unexpected, or unusual.[29]

---

[29] IRS *Publication No. 547* (Nonbusiness Disasters, Casualties, and Thefts), 2009, p. 2.

IDENTIFIABLE EVENT.   Because the event that causes the loss must be *identifiable*, the act of losing or misplacing property is generally not considered a casualty.

However, in some cases, taxpayers have proven that the loss of property was the result of an identifiable event.

EXAMPLE I:8-19 ▶

One evening Troy and his wife, Lynn, go to the theater. Troy accidentally slams the car door on Lynn's hand. The impact breaks the flanges holding the diamond in her ring. As a result, the diamond falls from the ring and is lost. In this case, a deductible casualty loss has occurred.[30] ◀

KEY POINT

The taxpayer has the burden of proof to establish that a loss was caused by a casualty. The taxpayer should gather as much evidence as possible. Newspaper clippings, police reports, photographs, and insurance reports can be helpful in establishing the cause of the loss.

SUDDEN, UNEXPECTED, OR UNUSUAL EVENTS.   According to the IRS, a *sudden event* is one that is swift, not gradual or progressive. An *unexpected event* is one that is ordinarily unanticipated and not intended. An *unusual event* is one that is not a day-to-day occurrence and that is not typical of the activity.

Thus, the IRS has ruled that a deductible casualty loss occurred when a taxpayer went ice fishing and his automobile fell through the ice.[31] A taxpayer whose automobile was damaged as the result of an accident also sustained a deductible casualty loss. However, a taxpayer may not deduct losses incurred in an accident caused by the taxpayer's willful negligence or willful act.[32] Damage sustained as the result of an accident in an automobile race was held to be nondeductible because accidents occur often and are not unusual events in automobile races.[33]

ADDITIONAL COMMENT

Sudden, unexpected, or unusual events must also be accompanied by an external force. For example, a blown engine in an automobile is a sudden event but because no external force caused the event, the loss is not a casualty loss.

The following are a few examples of events that the courts have held to constitute a deductible casualty loss:

▶ Rust and water damage to furniture and carpets caused by the bursting of a water heater

▶ Damage to the exterior paint of a residence caused by a severe, sudden, and unexpected concentration of chemical fumes in the air

▶ Loss caused by fire (unless the taxpayer sets the fire, in which case no deduction is available)

▶ Damage to a building caused by an unusually large blast at a nearby quarry or a jet sonic boom[34]

▶ Death of trees just a few days after a sudden infestation of pine beetles[35]

The following are examples of events that the courts have held *not* to be a casualty:

▶ Water damage to the walls and ceiling of a taxpayer's personal residence as the result of the gradual deterioration of the roof[36]

▶ Trees dying because of gradual suffocation of the root systems

▶ The loss of trees and shrubs because of disease[37]

▶ Damage to carpet and clothing caused by moths and carpet beetles[38]

▶ Damage to a road due to freezing, thawing, and gradual deterioration[39]

▶ Damage to a residence caused by the gradual sinking of the land underneath the home[40]

▶ Damage caused by drought because it occurs through progressive deterioration

▶ The steady weakening of a building caused by normal wind and weather conditions

▶ The rusting and deterioration of a water heater[41]

ETHICAL POINT

A client loses his diamond ring while fishing and wants to deduct the loss as a casualty. The CPA should not sign the tax return unless he or she believes that the client's position has a realistic possibility of being sustained on its merits if challenged, which is doubtful in this situation.

[30] *John P. White*, 48 T.C. 430 (1967), *acq.* 1969-2 C.B. xxv. In another case, the taxpayer convinced the Tax Court to allow a deduction for a lost diamond, even though the taxpayer could not remember a specific blow to the ring. In this instance, the taxpayer obtained an expert witness to testify that the flanges of the ring were strong enough and in good enough repair that the loss of the diamond had to have been caused by a sudden, unexpected blow rather than by progressive deterioration.

[31] Rev. Rul. 69-88, 1969-1 C.B. 58.

[32] *Willie C. Robinson*, 1984 PH T.C. Memo ¶84,188, 47 TCM 1510 and Reg. Sec. 1.165-7(a)(3).

[33] Ltr. Rul. 8227010 (March 30, 1982) contains the above examples.

[34] *Ray Durden*, 3 T.C. 1 (1944), *acq.* 1944 C.B. 8 and Rev. Rul. 60-329, 1960-2 C.B. 67.

[35] Rev. Rul. 79-174, 1979-1 C.B. 99. See also *Charles A. Smithgall v. U.S.*, 47 AFTR 2d 81-695, 81-1 USTC ¶9121 (D.C.-Ga., 1980). However, the IRS has ruled in Ltr. Rul. 8544001 (July 12, 1985) that no casualty loss results when the time interval between the infestation and the death of the trees was too long.

[36] *Lauren Whiting*, 1975 PH T.C. Memo ¶75,038, 34 TCM 241.

[37] *William R. Miller*, 1970 PH T.C. Memo ¶70,167, 29 TCM 741 and Rev. Rul. 57-599, 1957-2 C.B. 142. (See also *Howard F. Burns v. U.S.*, 6 AFTR 2d 6036, 61-1 USTC ¶9127 (6th Cir., 1960).)

[38] Rev. Rul. 55-327, 1955-1 C.B. 25. (See also *J. P. Meersman v. U.S.*, 18 AFTR 2d 6152, 67-1 USTC ¶9125 (6th Cir., 1966).)

[39] *Howard Stacy*, 1970 PH T.C. Memo ¶70,127, 29 TCM 542. However, the breaking up of a road over a 4-month period because of extreme weather conditions was held to be a casualty. See *Emmett J. O'Connell v. U.S.*, 29 AFTR 2d 72-596, 72-1 USTC ¶9312, (D.C. Cal., 1972). (See also *Stephen L. Shaffer*, 1983 PH T.C. Memo ¶83,677, 47 TCM 285.)

[40] *Henry W. Berry*, 1969 PH T.C. Memo ¶69,162, 28 TCM 802. (See also *David McDaniel*, 1980 PH T.C. Memo ¶80,557, 41 TCM 563.)

[41] IRS *Publication No. 547* (Nonbusiness Disasters, Casualties, and Thefts), 2009, contains the above examples.

At times it is very difficult to determine under the particular facts whether the necessary requirements of suddenness, unexpectedness, or unusualness exist. For example, damage caused by the sudden infestation of pine beetles in some instances has been held to be a casualty, but in other instances it has not.[42]

THEFT DEFINED

Under Sec. 165, a taxpayer may also deduct a loss sustained as the result of a theft. This includes theft of business, investment, or personal-use property. The Treasury Regulations state that "the term theft shall be deemed to include, but shall not necessarily be limited to, larceny, embezzlement, and robbery."[43] A determination whether other actions also constitute theft often depends on whether the action involves criminal intent and is illegal under the state law where the action has occurred. Thus, the IRS has stated that blackmail, extortion, and kidnapping for ransom may also constitute theft.[44]

DEDUCTIBLE AMOUNT OF CASUALTY LOSS

The amount of a casualty loss deduction depends on the amount of the loss sustained, any insurance or other reimbursement received, and, in the case of personal-use property, the limitations imposed under the tax law.

MEASURING THE LOSS. In general, the amount of loss sustained in a casualty is the amount by which the casualty reduces the property's FMV. This is measured by comparing the property's FMV immediately before and immediately after the casualty.[45] The amount of the loss may not include any reduction in the FMV of the taxpayer's surrounding but undamaged property.

EXAMPLE I:8-20 ▶

ADDITIONAL COMMENT

Taxpayers cannot deduct a loss unless they own the damaged property. Therefore, a taxpayer cannot deduct amounts he or she paid to another individual for damage he or she caused to the other individual's property.

Gail purchased a vacation home for $310,000. Shortly after she purchased the property, a mudslide completely destroyed several neighboring cabins. Gail's cabin sustained no damage. After the slide, an appraisal reveals that the FMV of the cabin has declined to $250,000 because of fears that other mudslides might occur. The $60,000 reduction in the FMV of the cabin does not constitute a deductible casualty loss. ◀

The taxpayer must use actual market value, not sentimental value, to compute the reduction in the FMV. Additionally, the cost of protecting property to prevent damage from a casualty is not a deductible loss.

If the property involved in the casualty is only partially destroyed, the amount of the loss is the lesser of the reduction in the property's FMV or the taxpayer's adjusted basis in the property.

EXAMPLE I:8-21
TYPICAL MISCONCEPTION

Taxpayers sometimes think their loss should be based on the total economic loss rather than just the property's basis. Taxpayers should remember that they have not paid a tax on the appreciation in value and, therefore, should not be entitled to a deduction for a loss on the unrealized gain.

Troy purchased a home for $225,000 several years ago. Through the years, the value of the home appreciated until it was appraised at $325,000 in the current year. Shortly after the appraisal, a flood swept through the area and severely damaged Troy's home. After the flood, the value of the home declined to $90,000. Troy does not have any flood insurance. His loss is limited to the $225,000 basis in the home even though the economic loss is $235,000 ($325,000 − $90,000). ◀

If business or investment property is totally destroyed in a casualty, the amount of the loss is the taxpayer's adjusted basis in the property, even if it is greater than the property's FMV. However, if personal-use property is totally destroyed, the amount of the loss is limited to the lesser of the reduction in the property's FMV or the property's adjusted basis.

---

[42] Rev. Rul. 79-174, 1979-1 C.B. 99 and *George K. Notter*, 1985 PH T.C. Memo ¶85,391, 50 TCM 614. A graphic illustration of the controversy that may arise when determining whether an event is a casualty can be made by comparing the following two cases. In one case the taxpayer was washing dishes. Seeing a glass of water on the windowsill, he quickly dumped the contents down the drain and turned on the garbage disposal, not realizing that his wife's rings were in the glass. Damage to the rings in this case was deemed to be a casualty (*William H. Carpenter*, 1966 PH T.C. Memo ¶66,228, 25 TCM 1186). In the second case, the taxpayer gathered up some tissues

from the night stand and flushed them down the toilet, not knowing that his wife's rings were wrapped in one of them. This event was held not to be a casualty (*W.J. Keenan, Jr. v. Bowers*, 39 AFTR 849, 50-2 USTC ¶9444 (D.C.-S.C., 1950)).
[43] Reg. Sec. 1.165-8(d).
[44] Rev. Rul. 72-112, 1972-1 C.B. 60 and IRS *Publication No. 547* (Nonbusiness Disasters, Casualties, and Thefts), 2009, p. 1.
[45] Reg. Sec. 1.165-7(a)(2).

EXAMPLE I:8-22 ▶ A machine Beth uses in her business is completely destroyed by fire. At the time of the fire, the adjusted basis of the machine is $5,000 and its FMV is $3,000. Because the machine is business property, Beth's loss is $5,000. If the machine were a personal-use asset, the amount of the loss would be $3,000. ◀

Generally, taxpayers must establish the reduction in the FMV of the property by an appraisal. If an appraisal is difficult or impossible to obtain, the taxpayer may use the cost of the repairs instead. The repairs must meet all of the following requirements before the taxpayer may use this alternative:

▶ The repairs will bring the property back to its condition immediately before the casualty.

▶ The cost of the repairs is not excessive.

▶ The repairs do no more than repair the damage incurred in the casualty.

▶ The repairs do not increase the value of the property over its value immediately before the casualty.

If the same casualty destroys more than one property, the taxpayer calculates the loss on each property separately.[46] Thus, the taxpayer compares each property's basis with the reduction in the FMV of that property, rather than aggregating the basis and FMV amounts for all the properties destroyed in the casualty.

If the taxpayer receives insurance or any other type of recovery, the taxpayer must reduce the amount of the loss by these amounts. In some cases these payments may actually exceed the taxpayer's basis in the property, causing the realization of a gain. If certain requirements are met, taxpayers may defer or exclude the recognition of these gains. (See the detailed discussion of involuntary conversions in Chapter I:12.)

LIMITATIONS ON PERSONAL-USE PROPERTY

The amount an individual may deduct for a casualty loss on personal-use property is subject to two limitations: (1) losses sustained in each separate casualty must be reduced by $100, and (2) the total amount of all net casualty losses for personal-use property is reduced by 10% of the taxpayer's AGI for the year. For property destroyed in the same casualty, only $100 is deducted from all the properties (i.e., the taxpayer does not reduce the loss from each separate property by $100). For 2009, this $100 reduction for each casualty was $500. Under bills currently being considered by Congress this $500 reduction may be extended through 2010.

EXAMPLE I:8-23 ▶ During the year a windstorm blows over a large tree in front of Cathy's house, damaging the house and totally destroying her automobile. After the insurance reimbursement, the loss on the house amounts to $3,000, and the loss on the automobile is $2,500. Because the losses occur in the same casualty, the total amount of the loss is reduced to $5,400 ($3,000 + $2,500 − $100). If the damage to the car was sustained in a separate event such as an automobile accident, the total amount of the casualty losses incurred by Cathy during the year would have been $5,300 ($3,000 + $2,500 − $200). This $5,300 or $5,400 loss is then further reduced by 10% of Cathy's AGI for the year. ◀

EXAMPLE I:8-24 ▶ As the result of a storm, Liz incurs a $4,100 casualty loss on personal-use property during the year. She also sustains a $600 theft loss. Liz's AGI for the year is $50,000. She receives no tax deduction for the casualty and theft losses because they do not exceed the following limitations:

KEY POINT

Many taxpayers cannot deduct their casualty losses because of the $100 or $500 floor and 10% of AGI limitation.

	Storm	Theft	Total
Loss before limitations	$4,100	$600	$4,700
Minus: $100 floor	(100)	(100)	(200)
	$4,000	$500	$4,500
Minus: 10% of AGI (0.10 × $50,000)			(5,000)
Deductible loss			0 ◀

---

[46] Reg. Sec. 1.165-7(b)(2). For personal-use property, losses on real property and improvements to the property are computed in the aggregate. Thus, no separate basis need be apportioned to the improvements. (See Reg. Secs. 1.165-7(b)(2)(ii) and 1.165-7(b)(3) Example (3).)

Because of these limitations, many taxpayers who sustain casualty and theft losses on personal-use property do not receive a tax deduction. Furthermore, if the taxpayer's insurance covers the property, the taxpayer cannot take a casualty loss deduction unless he or she timely files an insurance claim for the loss. This disallowance relates only to the portion of the loss covered by the insurance.

Below is a summary of the rules concerning deductibility of casualty losses:

Result of Casualty		Business	Investment	Personal Use
Total Destruction	Amount of Casualty[a]	Basis	Basis	Lesser of: basis or decline in FMV, reduced by $100 and 10% of AGI
	Type	For AGI	From AGI (For AGI if Rental)	From AGI
Partial Destruction	Amount of Casualty[a]	Lesser of: basis or decline in FMV	Lesser of: basis or decline in FMV	Lesser of: basis or decline in FMV, reduced by $100 and 10% of AGI
	Type	For AGI	From AGI (For AGI if Rental)	From AGI

[a]All amounts are first reduced by any insurance reimbursement.

NETTING CASUALTY GAINS AND LOSSES ON PERSONAL-USE PROPERTY

Taxpayers must net casualty gains and losses incurred during the year on personal-use assets. They are not combined with casualty gains and losses on business and investment property. For purposes of the netting process, the losses should be reduced by any insurance reimbursements and the $100 limitation, but not the 10% of AGI floor. If the gains exceed the losses for the year, all the gains and losses are treated as capital gains and losses.

EXAMPLE I:8-25 ▶

During 2010, Pat incurs the following casualty gains and losses on personal-use assets. Assets W and X are destroyed in one casualty, and asset Y is destroyed in another. Pat acquired assets X and Y in the current year, whereas she acquired asset W several years ago.

Asset	Reduction in FMV	Adjusted Basis	Insurance	Holding Period
W	$10,000	$3,000	$10,000	More than 12 months
X	3,600	5,000	2,000	Less than one year
Y	1,600	3,000	0	Less than one year

Pat realizes a $7,000 ($10,000 − $3,000) gain on asset W because the insurance proceeds received for the asset exceed its basis. She realizes a $1,600 ($3,600 reduction in FMV − $2,000 insurance) loss on asset X. This loss is reduced to $1,500 because of the $100 reduction for personal casualty losses. She realizes a $1,600 loss on asset Y. Because this loss is realized as a result of the second casualty, the $100 limitation is deducted, resulting in a $1,500 loss from that casualty. Pat realizes a $4,000 [$7,000 − ($1,500 + $1,500)] net casualty gain for the year. Thus, the gain or loss on each asset is treated as a capital gain or loss. Pat must report a $7,000 long-term capital gain on asset W, a $1,500 short-term capital loss on asset X, and a $1,500 short-term capital loss on asset Y. ◀

If the casualty losses on personal-use property exceed the casualty gains for the year, the taxpayer must further reduce the net loss by 10% of AGI. The taxpayer performs all of these calculations (the netting process and reductions) on Form 4684. If any loss remains after the netting and reductions, the taxpayer reports the loss as an itemized deduction on Schedule A of Form 1040.

CASUALTY GAINS AND LOSSES ATTRIBUTABLE TO BUSINESS AND INVESTMENT PROPERTY

Taxpayers must net casualty gains and losses on business and investment property held over one year. (See Chapter I:13 for a discussion of the netting procedure under Sec. 1231.) If the losses exceed the gains, the business losses and losses on investment property that generate rents or royalties are *for* AGI deductions. Losses on other investment property (e.g., the theft of a security) are itemized deductions but are not subject to the 2% of AGI floor or the overall reduction of itemized deductions imposed if AGI exceeds certain limitation amounts.[47] The $100 or 10% of AGI limitations do not apply to losses on business and investment property. Casualty gains and losses on business and investment property held one year or less are all treated as ordinary.

TIMING OF CASUALTY LOSS DEDUCTION

In general, taxpayers must deduct casualty losses in the tax year in which the taxpayer sustains the loss. In the following instances, however, taxpayers may deduct the loss in another year:

▶ Theft losses

▶ Insurance or other reimbursements that the taxpayer can reasonably expect to receive in a subsequent year

▶ Certain disaster losses

THEFT. Taxpayers must deduct a theft loss in the tax year in which the taxpayer discovers the theft. This rule is equitable and practical because a taxpayer may not discover a theft until a subsequent year.

EXAMPLE I:8-26 ▶

REAL-WORLD EXAMPLE

A taxpayer had property confiscated by the Cuban government in 1960. The taxpayer left the country and could have filed for indemnity but did not because she expected to return. Later, the government took away the right of indemnity in 1961. Since she did not file for indemnity from the Cuban government when she had the chance, she was not allowed a casualty or theft loss. *Vila v. U.S.*, 23 AFTR 2d 69-1311 (1969).

Dale owns a hunting lodge in upstate New York. Sometime after his last trip to the lodge in November 2010, someone breaks into the lodge and steals several guns and paintings. Dale discovers the theft when he returns to the lodge on May 19, 2011. Dale's insurance does not cover the entire cost of the items. The loss is deductible in 2011, even though the theft may have occurred in 2010. ◀

INSURANCE AND OTHER REIMBURSEMENTS. Taxpayers must subtract any reimbursement received as compensation for a loss in arriving at the amount of the loss. This is necessary even when the taxpayer has not yet received the reimbursement, as long as there is a reasonable prospect that the taxpayer will receive it in the future. Thus, the taxpayer may not take a deduction in the year of loss if in that year a reasonable expectation of full recovery exists.[48] If no anticipation of full recovery exists, the taxpayer may deduct a loss in the year the casualty occurs for the estimated unrecovered amount. As previously mentioned, the taxpayer may not take a deduction to the extent the taxpayer has insured the personal-use property and the taxpayer does not file a timely insurance claim.

EXAMPLE I:8-27 ▶

In December of the current year, Andrea suffers a $10,000 casualty loss when her personal automobile is struck by a city bus. Although she does not receive any reimbursement from the insurance company by December 31, she reasonably expects to recover the full amount. Andrea may not deduct a casualty loss in the current year. ◀

EXAMPLE I:8-28 ▶

Assume the same facts as in Example I:8-27, except that Andrea reasonably anticipates her reimbursement from the insurance company will be only $7,000. In this case, her casualty loss in the current year is $3,000 (before reduction by the limitations). ◀

If the taxpayer does not receive the full amount of the anticipated recovery in the subsequent year, he or she may deduct the unrecovered portion. However, rather than filing an amended return for the year of loss, the taxpayer deducts the loss in the subsequent year. Thus in some cases, the taxpayer may spread the income tax consequences for a single casualty loss over two years.

---

[47] As explained in Chapter 6, the overall reduction of itemized deductions does not apply to 2010, but will apply to years after 2010 unless Congress changes the law.

[48] Reg. Sec. 1.165-1(d)(2)(i).

EXAMPLE I:8-29 ▶ During the current year, Javier's home is damaged by an exceptionally severe blast at a nearby stone quarry owned by Acme Corporation. Although the amount of the damage is properly appraised at $20,000, Javier can reasonably anticipate a recovery of only $15,000 from Acme Corporation at the end of the current year. He does not receive any recovery from Acme during the current year. Unfortunately, in the subsequent year Acme Corporation is declared bankrupt, and Javier does not receive any reimbursement. Javier's AGI is $40,000 in the current year and $45,000 in the subsequent year. During the current year, Javier may deduct $900 {$5,000 loss reasonably anticipated in the current year − [$100 limitation + (0.10 × $40,000)]}. In the subsequent year, Javier may deduct an additional casualty loss of $10,500 [$15,000 additional loss − (0.10 × $45,000)]. ◀

If a taxpayer receives a subsequent recovery for a previously deducted loss, the taxpayer includes the reimbursement in income in the year of recovery. The taxpayer does not file an amended return. However, the amount that the taxpayer must include in income is limited to the amount of tax benefit the taxpayer received for the previous deduction.

EXAMPLE I:8-30 ▶ During the current year, Becky's automobile sustains $5,000 in damages when it is struck by another automobile. The driver of the other automobile is at fault and is uninsured, and Becky does not reasonably expect to recover any of the loss. Becky's AGI for the current year is $35,000. Becky deducts $1,400 ($5,000 loss − [$100 + $3,500]). During the subsequent year, the other driver reimburses Becky for the full amount of the damage. Because Becky received a tax benefit of only $1,400 for the loss in the year of the accident, she must only include $1,400 in gross income in the subsequent year, even though she receives a $5,000 reimbursement. Becky does not file an amended return for the year of the accident. ◀

DISASTER LOSSES. Under certain circumstances, a taxpayer may elect to deduct a casualty loss in the year preceding the year in which the loss actually occurs. This election is available to taxpayers who suffer losses attributable to a disaster that occurs in an area subsequently declared by the President of the United States as a disaster area.[49] Thus, an individual can elect to deduct a disaster loss occurring in 2011 on his or her 2010 tax return or report it in the regular way on his or her 2011 return. The taxpayer must file an amended return (Form 1040X) unless he or she has not filed the prior year's return when the disaster is declared. This election allows taxpayers the possibility of receiving financial help sooner from potential tax refunds by filing an amendment to the prior year's return.

Topic Review I:8-3 summarizes the casualty loss deduction rules.

STOP & THINK

Question: Due to a series of hurricanes that hit Florida during the current year, many homes, roads, and other property are destroyed. Because of the tremendous destruction, the President of the United States declares the area a disaster area. One of the properties totally destroyed is Jack's vacation home in Miami. Jack uses the home exclusively for vacationing. The value of the home is $190,000. Unfortunately, Jack had not insured the home against a hurricane. What issues must Jack consider in determining the year in which to take the casualty loss?

Solution: Since the property was destroyed in a disaster and is located in an area which the President subsequently declared as a disaster area, Jack may take the casualty deduction either in the year of the casualty or in the previous year. The year which is most beneficial is based on several factors. The destroyed property was personal use property, so the deduction is an itemized deduction that would normally be subject to the 10% of AGI limitation. Thus, Jack should compare his estimated AGI for the current year with his AGI in the last year. He also should consider his other itemized deductions, including any other casualty losses that might be subject to the $100 or 10% of AGI limitation. In addition, he should compare his marginal tax rates in the two years. Jack should also consider the time value of money, since by taking the deduction on his prior year return, he will receive the tax benefit earlier than if he takes the deduction on the current year return.

[49] Sec. 165(i). Additionally, the same treatment may apply under Sec. 165 to taxpayers who live in a disaster area and who are ordered by a state or local government to move from or relocate their residence because the disaster caused the residence to be unsafe. In order to qualify for this treatment, the order to move must come from the state or local government within 120 days of the date that the President determines the area to be a disaster area. If the property destroyed in a presidentially declared disaster area is the taxpayer's principal residence and the casualty results in a gain, the taxpayer may exclude a portion of the gain if certain conditions are met (see Chapter I:12).

Topic Review I:8-3

Casualty Losses

TYPE OF PROPERTY	LIMITATION AND TREATMENT
Personal use	The amount of the loss is the lesser of the property's adjusted basis or the reduction of the asset's FMV. This amount is reduced by any insurance reimbursement. If the insurance reimbursement exceeds the property's basis, a gain is realized. To the extent the property is insured, a claim must be filed or the loss is disallowed.
	The amount of loss incurred in each separate casualty event during the year is reduced by $100. This $100 reduction was $500 in 2009 and may be changed to $500 for 2010 under a bill currently being considered by Congress.
	All casualty gains and losses for the year are netted. If the gains exceed the losses, all gains and losses are treated as capital gains and losses. If the losses exceed the gains, the net loss is reduced by 10% of AGI. Any remaining loss is an itemized deduction.
Business or investment	If the property is totally destroyed, the amount of the loss is the adjusted basis of the property. If only partially destroyed, the amount of the loss is the lesser of the property's adjusted basis or the reduction of the asset's FMV. This amount is reduced by any insurance reimbursement. A gain is realized if the insurance reimbursement exceeds the property's basis.
	For property held one year or less, the losses and gains are ordinary losses and gains. For property held over one year, the casualty gains and losses for the year are netted. The treatment depends on the total of the taxpayer's other Sec. 1231 transactions (see Chapter I:13). Business casualty losses and losses on investment property that generate rents or royalties are not subject to the $100 or 10% of AGI limitations.

BAD DEBTS

OBJECTIVE 7

Compute the deduction for a bad debt

In addition to losses on property, taxpayers may also sustain losses generated by uncollectible debts. In dealing with a deduction for **bad debts**, taxpayers must address the following requirements and issues:

▶ A bona fide debtor-creditor relationship must exist between the taxpayer and some other person or entity.

▶ The taxpayer must have basis in the debt.

▶ The debt must actually have become worthless during the year.

▶ The type and timing of a bad debt deduction depend on whether the debt is a business or nonbusiness bad debt.

ADDITIONAL COMMENT

The tax provisions that deal with deductions for losses and the tax provisions that deal with the deductions for bad debts are mutually exclusive, and an amount properly deductible as a loss cannot be deducted as a bad debt or vice versa.

Generally, taxpayers may use only the specific write-off method of accounting in deducting the bad debt. A partial or complete recovery of a debt that was previously deducted may occur. In many cases a recovery of this type causes income recognition in the year of the recovery.

BONA FIDE DEBTOR-CREDITOR RELATIONSHIP

Only items constituting bona fide debt are eligible to be deducted as a bad debt. A **bona fide debt** is one that arises from a valid and enforceable obligation to pay a fixed or determinable sum of money and results in a debtor-creditor relationship.[50]

KEY POINT

The fact that the debtor is a related party does not preclude deduction of a bad debt, but the taxpayer should be able to document the debt as being bona fide.

RELATED-PARTY TRANSACTIONS. Determining whether a bona fide loan transaction has actually taken place is especially critical when the transaction is between the taxpayer and a family member or other related party (e.g., a controlled corporation). The taxpayer must carefully examine all the facts and circumstances surrounding the transaction because a gift does not constitute a debt. The taxpayer's intent is critical. For example, if the taxpayer's intent is to provide property, cash, or services to someone else without receiving

[50] Reg. Sec. 1.166-1(c).

any consideration in return, a gift—not a loan—has been made. Some tests used to determine the taxpayer's intent include the following:

▶ Does a note or other written instrument exist which evidences an obligation to repay?[51]

▶ Have the parties established a definite schedule of repayment?

▶ Is a reasonable rate of interest stated?

▶ Would a person unrelated to the debtor make the loan?[52]

EXAMPLE I:8-31 ▶

REAL-WORLD EXAMPLE

A taxpayer advanced $8,500 to his son-in-law who operated a live-stock auction barn. The taxpayer was entitled to a bad debt deduction upon default because notations on the checks indicated that they were loans and undisputed testimony indicated that repayment was to be made within 90 days. *Giffin A. Andrew*, 54 T.C. 239 (1970).

During the current year Maria loaned $20,000 to her son Sam, who used the money in his business. Although they signed no written note or contract, Sam orally promised to repay Maria as soon as his business became profitable. No rate of interest was stated. Unfortunately, the business failed and Sam went out of business in the subsequent year. He never repaid the loan principal or interest.

In this case, no valid debt exists because the taxpayer did not establish an interest rate or a repayment schedule. An unrelated person would not have made a loan to Sam under these conditions. In addition, Maria does not receive any consideration in return for the "loan." Since the facts indicate that the transaction is actually a gift, Maria may not claim a bad debt deduction because of Sam's failure to repay. ◀

Tax advisors should also closely examine other related party transactions. For example, a loan from a shareholder to a controlled corporation may actually be an additional contribution to capital disguised as a loan. Thus, a transfer of cash by a shareholder who owns a controlling (i.e., more than 50%) interest in the stock of a corporation may indicate a capital contribution rather than a loan. Likewise, a "loan" from a corporation to a controlling shareholder may actually be a disguised dividend or a salary payment.

THIRD PARTY DEBT. Generally, a taxpayer may deduct a bad debt only when a debtor-creditor relationship exists. However, in some cases a taxpayer will guarantee or endorse someone else's obligation. If the terms of the guarantee force the taxpayer to pay the third party's debt, the guarantor may actually be the creditor. If the original debtor does not repay the taxpayer who guarantees and pays the debt, the guarantor may deduct the loss. Any accrued interest that the guarantor pays may also be deductible as a bad debt. However, the interest is not deductible as interest when paid by the guarantor because it accrued on someone else's debt. Here, too, the taxpayer's intent determines whether the guarantee and payment constitute a gift.

EXAMPLE I:8-32 ▶

Ron is the sole shareholder and a full-time employee of Zip Corporation. For Zip Corporation to obtain a bank loan, Ron personally signs a guarantee that the loan will be repaid. Unfortunately, Zip Corporation defaults on the loan and Ron must repay the loan. In this case, Ron signed the guarantee to preserve his job and enhance his investment in Zip Corporation. Although Ron receives no direct consideration for having signed the note, he does receive indirect consideration in the form of continued job security and protection of his investment. Because a business or investment purpose motivated Ron to sign the loan guarantee, Ron may deduct the bad debt. ◀

TAXPAYER'S BASIS IN THE DEBT

For a bad debt to be deductible, the creditor must have basis in the debt. The taxpayer may acquire this basis in different ways. If a taxpayer loans money, the taxpayer's basis in the debt is the amount loaned. If the debt arises because the taxpayer provides property or

---

[51] A written note or other instrument is an evidence of a bona fide debtor-creditor relationship. However, if the note or other instrument is registered or has interest coupons and is issued by a corporation or a government, the bad debt provisions of Sec. 166 do not apply. Instead, the worthless security provisions of Sec. 165 (previously discussed) apply.

[52] *Jean C. Tyler v. Tomlinson*, 24 AFTR 2d 69-5426, 69-2 USTC ¶9559 (5th Cir., 1969). (See also, *C. L. Hunt*, 1989 PH T.C. Memo ¶89,335, 57 TCM 919), where certain loans that the taxpayer made to his children were treated as bona fide loans, whereas others were treated as gifts. In that case, the

children had been trading in silver futures and were required to make margin calls. Because they could not make the calls, the children's positions were involuntarily liquidated. Up to the date of the liquidation, the taxpayer had made loans to the children that were payable on demand and were subject to the prime rate of interest. These loans were evidenced by promissory notes. After the liquidation, the taxpayer continued to make loans to the children. However, these loans were not evidenced by notes. The loans up to the time of the liquidation were treated as bona fide loans and the subsequent loans were treated as gifts.

services for the other party, basis is established only if the taxpayer has previously included the FMV of the property or services in income. This often depends on the taxpayer's method of accounting. An accrual method taxpayer generally reports income in the year the services are performed or the property is provided. (See the discussion in Chapter I:11.) Thus, an accrual method taxpayer has a basis in either a note receivable or an open account receivable equal to the amount included in gross income (i.e., the FMV of the services). A cash method taxpayer, however, reports income only in the year in which payment in the form of cash or property is received. Because a note constitutes the receipt of property, a cash method taxpayer reports income (and establishes basis) in the year the note is received. However, if the cash method taxpayer does not receive a note and the receivable is an open account item, the taxpayer reports no income until the receivable is collected. Thus, the taxpayer has no basis in the receivable and does not receive a bad debt deduction if the receivable is not collected.

EXAMPLE I:8-33 ▶

In October of the current year, Jim performs some legal services for Joy. Jim bills Joy for $10,000. Joy does not sign a note for the debt. As a cash method taxpayer, Jim does not include the $10,000 in his current year's income. After repeated efforts to collect the fee, Jim discovers in June of the subsequent year that Joy has left the city and cannot be found. Jim may not deduct a bad debt for the uncollected amount in the subsequent year because he has not taken the amount into income and he has no basis in the debt. If Joy had signed a note for the debt, Jim would have reported income in the current year in an amount equal to the note's FMV and could have deducted the loss when the note became uncollectible in the subsequent year. ◀

DEBT MUST BE WORTHLESS

To deduct a bad debt, the taxpayer must show that the debt is worthless. This determination is made by reference to all the pertinent evidence, including the general financial condition of the debtor and whether the debt is secured by collateral.

In proving the worthlessness of a debt, a taxpayer does not need to take legal action if the surrounding circumstances indicate that legal action probably would not result in the collection of the debt. By simply showing that legal action is not warranted, the taxpayer provides sufficient proof that the debt is worthless.[53] Indications that an unsecured debt is worthless include bankruptcy of the debtor, disappearance or death of a debtor, and repeated unsuccessful attempts at collection. Furthermore, if the surrounding circumstances warrant it, a taxpayer may deduct a worthless debt even before the debt comes due. As will be explained later in this chapter, a nonbusiness debt must be totally worthless before a deduction is allowed. However, a current deduction is allowed for a partially worthless business bad debt.

NONBUSINESS BAD DEBTS

The distinction between a business bad debt and a nonbusiness bad debt is important because the classification of the debt determines its tax treatment. A business bad debt gives rise to an ordinary deduction, whereas a taxpayer must treat a nonbusiness bad debt as a short-term capital loss. All loans made by a corporation are assumed to be associated with the corporation's business; therefore, the provisions for nonbusiness bad debts do not apply to corporations.

DEFINITION OF A NONBUSINESS BAD DEBT. A *nonbusiness debt* is defined as any debt other than (1) a debt created or acquired in connection with a trade or business of the taxpayer or (2) a debt the loss from the worthlessness of which is incurred in the taxpayer's trade or business. This determination depends on an examination of the facts and circumstances surrounding the debt in question.

A debt incurred in a taxpayer's business continues to be a business debt for that taxpayer even if, at the time the debt goes bad, the taxpayer has ceased conducting that particular business (situation (1) above). If another taxpayer acquires a business, any outstanding debt at the time the business is acquired continues to be business debt as long as the purchaser

---

[53] Reg. Sec. 1.166-2.

continues the business (situation (2) above). The debt is a nonbusiness debt if the person who owns the debt when it becomes worthless is not engaged in the business in which the debt is incurred either at the time the debt arose or when it becomes worthless.

EXAMPLE I:8-34 ▶ Matt, an individual who uses the accrual method of accounting, is engaged in the grocery business. During 2010, he extends credit to Jeff on an open account. In 2011, Matt sells his business to Joan, but retains Jeff's account. Jeff's account becomes worthless in 2011. Even though Matt is no longer engaged in the grocery business at the time the debt becomes worthless, he may deduct the loss as a business bad debt in 2011. If Joan purchases Jeff's account upon acquiring the grocery business, Joan is entitled to a business bad debt deduction in 2011 because the debt was incurred in the trade or business in which Joan is currently engaged. ◀

In addition, classification as a business debt requires a proximate relationship between the loan and the taxpayer's business.[54] According to the Supreme Court, this relationship exists if a business motive is the taxpayer's dominant motivation in making the loan. This determination must be made on a case-by-case basis. For example, when an individual stockholder who is also an employee of the corporation loans money to the corporation, is the loan a business or nonbusiness debt? Because an employee is considered to be engaged in the business of working for a corporation, a loan made to the corporation in an attempt to protect the employment relationship may be held to be a business debt. However, if the individual's dominant motive is to protect his or her stock investment, the loan is a nonbusiness debt.[55]

EXAMPLE I:8-35 ▶ Lisa is an individual engaged in the advertising business. If clients occasionally need additional funds to meet their cash-flow obligations, Lisa sometimes lends them money. Lisa's dominant motive for making the loans is to retain the clients. She has no ownership interests in these clients. Under these facts, if any of these loans becomes worthless, it would likely be considered a business bad debt.[56] ◀

TAX TREATMENT. Individuals deduct nonbusiness debts that become wholly worthless during the year as short-term capital losses. The length of time the debt is outstanding has no bearing on this treatment.

Individuals generally prefer an ordinary deduction over a short-term capital loss because the tax deduction attributable to net capital losses is limited to $3,000 each year. Any loss in excess of this limit is carried over to subsequent years to be included in the capital gain and loss netting process in those years (see Chapter I:5).

EXAMPLE I:8-36 ▶ During 2009, Kim loaned her friend $10,000. The friend used the funds to invest in commodities futures. The transaction had all the characteristics of a bona fide debt rather than a mere gift to a friend. Unfortunately, the commodities market prices declined, and Kim's friend incurred substantial losses. In 2010, Kim's friend declared personal bankruptcy and Kim was unable to collect any of the loan. Kim did not recognize any other capital gains or losses during 2010. The $10,000 bad debt loss recognized in 2010 is treated as a short-term capital loss. Thus, Kim may deduct only $3,000 in 2010. The remaining $7,000 is carried over indefinitely to 2011 and subsequent years. ◀

TYPICAL MISCONCEPTION

Partial worthlessness means that a debt is still partially recoverable. The term is sometimes erroneously applied to debt where there has been a partial recovery even though there is no prospect for further recovery.

PARTIAL WORTHLESSNESS. As previously noted, taxpayers may not deduct a partially worthless nonbusiness debt. Thus, a taxpayer cannot deduct a loss for a nonbusiness debt that is still partially recoverable during the year.

EXAMPLE I:8-37 ▶ Gordon, an individual, made a $5,000, five-year interest-bearing loan to a small company in 2009. Gordon was not in the trade or business of making commercial loans. In 2011, Gordon received word from the attorney who was appointed trustee of the company that bankruptcy proceedings had been filed. The trustee indicated that, although final disposition of the case will not occur until 2012, Gordon can reasonably expect to receive only 20 cents for every $1

[54] Reg. Sec. 1.166-5(b)(2).
[55] *John M. Trent v. CIR*, 7 AFTR 2d 1599, 61-2 USTC ¶9506 (2nd Cir., 1961). See also *Charles L. Hutchinson*, 1982 PH T.C. Memo ¶82,045, 43

TCM 440 and *U.S. v. Edna Generes*, 29 AFTR 2d 72-609, 72-1 USTC ¶9259 (USSC, 1972).
[56] *Stuart Bart*, 21 T.C. 880 (1954), *acq.* 1954-1 C.B. 3.

invested. Because this is a nonbusiness bad debt that is still partly recoverable in 2011, Gordon may not deduct the partial loss as a short-term capital loss in 2011. ◀

BUSINESS BAD DEBTS

The tax treatment of losses from business bad debts differs substantially from the treatment of nonbusiness bad debts. As previously discussed, a business bad debt provides an ordinary loss deduction. Furthermore, taxpayers may also deduct a business debt that has become only partially worthless during the year.

EXAMPLE I:8-38 ▶

Assume the same facts as in Example I:8-37 except that Gordon's loan is made for business reasons (e.g., to provide assistance to a customer in financial difficulty). Because 80% of the loan is reasonably expected to be unrecoverable during 2011, Gordon may deduct $4,000 (0.80 × $5,000) as an ordinary loss in 2011. If Gordon receives only $600 in 2012 as a settlement, he may deduct an additional $400 of ordinary loss for the year. ◀

BOOK-TAX DIFFERENCES

In general, for tax purposes, taxpayers can use only the specific write-off method of accounting for bad debts. However, a corporation or other taxpayer would probably be required to use the reserve method for financial reporting purposes. This book-tax difference is one of the most common M-1 or M-3 adjustments in filing a Form 1120 for corporate taxpayers.

ACCOUNTING FOR THE BUSINESS BAD DEBT. In general, two basic methods are available to account for business bad debts: the specific write-off method and the reserve method. Except for certain specialized industries, however, taxpayers can use only the specific write-off method for tax purposes. Under the **specific write-off method**, the taxpayer deducts each bad debt individually as it becomes worthless and writes it off as an expense. Taxpayers use this method for (1) business bad debts that are either totally or partially worthless and (2) nonbusiness bad debts that are totally worthless. However, as previously noted, taxpayers take no deduction for partially worthless nonbusiness bad debts.

In the case of a partially worthless business bad debt, taxpayers may only deduct the worthless part of the debt. The taxpayer must prove to the satisfaction of the IRS the amount of the debt that has become worthless.

RECOVERY OF BAD DEBTS. A taxpayer may collect a debt that was previously written off for tax purposes. Since the taxpayer previously deducted the uncollectible debt, the taxpayer must report the recovery as income in the year it is collected. The amount of the income that must be reported depends on the tax benefit rule discussed in Chapter I:4.

DEPOSITS IN INSOLVENT FINANCIAL INSTITUTIONS

At their election, qualified individuals may treat a loss on deposits in qualified bankrupt or insolvent financial institutions as a personal casualty loss in the year in which the individual can reasonably estimate the loss. The recognized loss is the difference between the taxpayer's basis in the deposit and a reasonable estimate of the amount that the taxpayer will receive. This treatment allows the individual an ordinary loss deduction, but subjects the loss to the personal casualty loss limitations. In lieu of this election, qualified individuals may elect to treat these losses as if they were incurred in a transaction entered into for profit (but not connected with a trade or business). This election is available only with respect to deposits that are not insured under federal law, and is limited to $20,000 ($10,000 if married and filing separately) per institution per year. This limitation is reduced by any insurance proceeds expected to be received under state law. This election also allows the individual an ordinary loss deduction but subjects the loss to the $20,000 limitation as well as the 2% of AGI floor on miscellaneous itemized deductions. If the taxpayer makes neither of these elections, the taxpayer may claim the loss as a nonbusiness bad debt (a short-term capital loss) in the year of worthlessness or partial recovery, whichever comes last.

KEY POINT

If a loss is treated as a casualty loss, it is subject to a $100 floor, and total net casualty losses for the year are deductible only to the extent that they exceed 10% of AGI.

A qualified individual is any individual *except* one who:

▶ Owns at least 1% of the outstanding stock of the financial institution

▶ Is an officer of the financial institution

▶ Is a relative of an officer or a 1% owner of the financial institution[57]

---

[57] Sec. 165(l). A *relative* is defined as a sibling, spouse, aunt, uncle, nephew, niece, ancestor, or lineal descendant.

Qualified financial institutions include banks, federal or state chartered savings and loans and thrift institutions, and federal or state insured credit unions.

This election applies to all losses sustained by the individual in the same institution and cannot be revoked unless the taxpayer receives IRS permission.[58]

The treatment of business and nonbusiness bad debts is summarized in Topic Review I:8-4.

Topic Review I:8-4

Bad Debts

TYPE OF DEBT	RESULTS
Nonbusiness	Deductible as a short-term capital loss.
	Deductible only when the debt is totally worthless.
	The taxpayer must have basis in the debt.
Business	Deductible as an ordinary loss.
	Except for certain specialized exceptions, the specific write-off method must be used. The reserve method is not available.
	May deduct partial worthlessness.
	Must have basis in the debt.

NET OPERATING LOSSES

OBJECTIVE 8

Compute a net operating loss deduction

A **net operating loss** (**NOL**) under Sec. 172 generally involves only business income and expenses. An NOL occurs when taxable income for any year is negative because business expenses exceed business income. A deduction for the NOL arises when a taxpayer carries the NOL to a year in which the taxpayer has taxable income. Thus, an NOL for one year becomes a deduction against taxable income of another year. This is accomplished in one of two ways:

▶ The year's NOL is carried back and deducted from the income of a previous year. This procedure provides for a refund of some of the taxes previously paid for the prior year.

▶ The year's NOL is carried forward and deducted from the income of a subsequent year. This procedure provides a reduction in the taxable income of the subsequent year, thus reducing the tax liability associated with that year.

The NOL deduction is intended to mitigate the inequity caused by the interaction of the progressive rate structure and the requirement to report income on an annual basis. This inequity arises between taxpayers whose business income fluctuates widely from year to year and those whose business income remains relatively constant.

KEY POINT

If taxpayers were not entitled to a deduction for net operating losses, taxpayers would actually pay a tax on an amount that exceeded their economic income over a period of time. The NOL deduction permits taxpayers to offset taxable income with losses incurred in other years.

EXAMPLE I:8-39 ▶

John and Julie Jones and Ken and Karen Smith are both married couples and file joint returns. Over a two-year period they both report a total of $140,000 in taxable income. However, John and Julie report $70,000 of taxable income each year; Ken and Karen report $200,000 of taxable income in the first year and a $60,000 loss in the second year. Without the NOL provisions, Mr. and Mrs. Jones would report a $19,726 ($9,863 + $9,863) total tax liability for the two years, whereas Mr. and Mrs. Smith would report a total tax liability of $44,244 (taxable income of $200,000).[59] However, Ken and Karen can carry back the $60,000 loss to recover a portion of the taxes paid on the $200,000 in the prior year. Based on 2010 rates, they would recover $16,800 of the $44,244 paid, resulting in a net tax liability for both years of $27,444 ($44,244 − $16,800). Although the total tax liability over the two years for the two couples is still unequal, the ability to carryover NOL's provides some degree of fairness. ◀

---

[58] The rules dealing with this special election are found in Notice 89-28, (1989-1 C.B. 667).

[59] Using the 2010 tax rate schedules.

COMPUTING THE NET OPERATING LOSS FOR INDIVIDUALS

The starting point in calculating an individual's NOL is generally taxable income. As mentioned earlier in this chapter, individuals may deduct three basic types of expenses to arrive at the amount of taxable income: business-related expenses, investment-related expenses, and certain personal expenses. The NOL, however, generally attempts to measure only the economic loss that occurs when business expenses exceed business income. Thus, individual taxpayers must make several adjustments to taxable income to arrive at the amount of the NOL for any particular year. These include adjustments for an NOL deduction, a capital loss deduction, the deduction for personal exemptions, and the excess of nonbusiness deductions over nonbusiness income.

ADD BACK ANY NOL DEDUCTION. Under certain circumstances, a taxpayer might have taken a deduction for an NOL arising from another tax year in computing the taxable loss for the current loss year. To allow this deduction to create or increase the NOL of the current loss year would provide an unwarranted benefit. Thus, taxable income for the current loss year must be increased for this deduction.

ADD BACK ANY CAPITAL LOSS DEDUCTION. To compute taxable income, individuals may deduct up to a maximum of $3,000 capital losses in excess of capital gains in any year. Any capital loss in excess of this limit can be carried over and deducted in a subsequent tax year, subject to the same limitation. Because capital losses have their separate carryover provisions, taxpayers must add back any deduction associated with these losses to taxable income to arrive at the NOL for the current loss year. To make this adjustment, the taxpayer must follow several steps:

Step 1: A taxpayer must separate nonbusiness capital gains and losses from business capital gains and losses. The nonbusiness gains and losses are then netted, while the business gains and losses are netted separately.

Step 2: If the nonbusiness capital gains exceed the nonbusiness capital losses, the excess, along with other types of nonbusiness income, is first used to offset any nonbusiness ordinary deductions. Any nonbusiness capital gain remaining is then used to offset any business capital loss in excess of the business capital gain for the year.[60]

Step 3: If both groups of transactions result in net losses, the capital loss deduction provided by these transactions must be added back. For purposes of the NOL, no deduction is allowed for either business or nonbusiness net capital losses.

Step 4: If the taxpayer's nonbusiness capital losses exceed the nonbusiness capital gains, the losses may not be offset against the taxpayer's excess business capital gains. Allowing this offset would provide an indirect deduction for a nonbusiness economic loss.[61]

EXAMPLE I:8-40 ▶ During the current year, Nils recognizes a short-term capital loss of $10,000 on the sale of an investment capital asset. He also recognizes a $5,000 long-term capital gain on the sale of a business capital asset. For taxable income purposes, the loss is netted against the gain, leaving a $5,000 net short-term capital loss. This loss provides a $3,000 deduction from taxable income, with the remaining $2,000 being carried forward to the following year. To compute the NOL, however, none of the $10,000 nonbusiness capital loss is deductible. Thus, the $3,000 deduction as well as the $5,000 loss that offset the business capital gain must be added back because in computing taxable income the taxpayer, in essence, has received a total $8,000 reduction from the nonbusiness capital loss. ◀

ADD BACK THE DEDUCTION FOR PERSONAL EXEMPTIONS. Because the deduction for personal and dependency exemptions is strictly a personal deduction, it must be added back to arrive at the year's NOL.

---

[60] Reg. Sec. 1.172-3. If the nonbusiness deductions exceed the nonbusiness income, the excess is added back. This adjustment is discussed later in the chapter.

[61] Sec. 172(d)(2). Note that all deductible nonbusiness capital losses involve investment property because capital losses on personal-use assets are not deductible in arriving at taxable income. To make the adjustment for any capital loss, the exclusion under Sec. 1202 for gains from small business stock is not allowed (see Chapter I:5).

ADDITIONAL COMMENT

An excess of nonbusiness deductions over nonbusiness income cannot increase the NOL. However, an excess of nonbusiness income over nonbusiness expenses can reduce the NOL.

ADD BACK EXCESS OF NONBUSINESS DEDUCTIONS OVER NONBUSINESS INCOME. Because nonbusiness deductions do not reflect an economic loss from business, they are not deductible in arriving at the NOL. However, these deductions do offset any nonbusiness income reported during the year. Nonbusiness income includes sources of income such as dividends and interest, as well as nonbusiness capital gains in excess of non-business capital losses. Wages and salary, even if they are earned in part-time employment, are considered business income. Nonbusiness deductions include itemized deductions such as charitable contributions, medical expenses, and nonbusiness interest and taxes. Casualty losses on personal-use assets, however, are treated as business losses and are excluded from this adjustment.[62] If a taxpayer does not have itemized deductions in excess of the standard deduction, the standard deduction is used as the amount of the nonbusiness deductions.

Following are several independent examples demonstrating these required adjustments. In each case, assume that Nancy is a single taxpayer.

EXAMPLE I:8-41 ▶ During 2010, Nancy, who is single, reports the following taxable income:

Gross income from business			$123,000	
Minus:	Business expenses		(147,000)	($24,000)
Plus:	Interest income			700
	Dividend income			400
AGI				($22,900)
Minus:	Greater of itemized deductions or standard deduction:			
	Interest expense	$ 6,000		
	Taxes	4,000		
	Casualty loss (reduced by the $100 floor)	1,000		
	Total itemized deductions	$ 11,000		
		or		
	Standard deduction	5,700		(11,000)
Minus:	Personal exemption			(3,650)
Taxable income				($37,550)

Nancy's NOL for the year is computed as follows:

Taxable income				($37,550)
Nonbusiness deductions:				
Itemized deductions		$11,000		
Minus:	Casualty loss	(1,000)	$ 10,000	
Minus:	Nonbusiness income:			
	Interest	$700		
	Dividends	400	(1,100)	
Plus:	Excess of nonbusiness deductions over nonbusiness income			8,900
Plus:	Personal exemption			3,650
Net operating loss				($25,000)[a] ◀

[a]Note that the NOL equals the total of the $24,000 net business loss and the $1,000 casualty loss.

EXAMPLE I:8-42 ▶ During 2010, Betsy, who is single, reports the following taxable income:

Gross income from business			$123,000	
Minus:	Business expenses		(147,000)	($24,000)
Plus:	Interest income			700
	Dividend income			400
AGI				($22,900)
Minus:	Greater of itemized deductions or standard deduction:			
	Interest expense		$ 2,000	
			or	
	Standard deduction		5,700	(5,700)
Minus:	Personal exemption			(3,650)
Taxable income				($32,250)

---

[62] Sec. 172(d)(4)(C).

Betsy's NOL for the year is computed as follows:

Taxable income		($32,250)
Nonbusiness deductions:		
Standard deduction	$ 5,700	
Minus: Nonbusiness income:		
Interest	$700	
Dividends	400	(1,100)
Plus: Excess of nonbusiness deductions over nonbusiness income		4,600
Plus: Personal exemption		3,650
Net operating loss		($24,000)[a] ◄

[a]Note that the NOL equals the net business loss for the year.

EXAMPLE I:8-43 ▶ During 2010, Rachael, who is single, reports the following taxable income:

Gross income from business		$123,000	
Minus Business expenses		(147,000)	($24,000)
Plus:	Interest income		700
	Dividend income		400
	Salary		6,000
	Nonbusiness LTCG		10,000
AGI			($6,900)
Minus:	Greater of itemized deductions or standard deduction:		
	Interest expense	$ 6,000	
	Taxes	4,000	
	Casualty (reduced by the $100 floor)	1,000	
Total itemized deductions		$ 11,000	
		or	
Standard deduction		5,700	(11,000)
Minus: Personal exemption			(3,650)
Taxable income			($21,550)

Rachael's NOL for the year is computed as follows:

Taxable income			($21,550)
Plus:	Nonbusiness deductions:		
	Itemized deductions	$11,000	
Minus: Casualty loss		(1,000)	$ 10,000
Minus:	Nonbusiness income:		
	Interest	$700	
	Dividends	400	
	LTCG	10,000	(11,100)
Excess of nonbusiness deductions over nonbusiness income			0
Plus:	Personal exemption		3,650
Net operating loss			($17,900)[a] ◄

[a]Note that the NOL can also be calculated as follows:

Loss from business	($24,000)
Salary	6,000
Casualty loss	(1,000)
Excess of nonbusiness income ($11,100) over nonbusiness deductions ($10,000)	1,100
NOL	($17,900)

CARRYBACK AND CARRYOVER PERIODS

Under Sec. 172, an NOL is initially carried back for two years and is deductible as an offset to the taxable income of the carryback years. Except as noted below, taxpayers must carry the loss back first. If any loss remains, taxpayers may then carry it forward for a period of 20 years.[63] Furthermore, in both the carryback and carryforward periods, the loss must be deducted from the years in chronological order. Thus, if an NOL is sustained

---

[63] For NOLs arising in a farming business, in a qualified small business attributable to a Presidentially declared disaster, or in a casualty or theft sustained by an individual, the carryback period is extended to three years.

These NOLs are taken after the regular NOL. Certain "specified liability losses" are entitled to a 10-year carryback. Sec. 172(b)(1)(C) and (f).

ADDITIONAL COMMENT

For NOLs incurred in a tax year that either begins or ends in 2008 or 2009, a special provision allows a taxpayer to elect to carry the loss back to the 5th, 4th, or 3rd prior years. This election applies to only one of the eligible NOL years and is subject to detailed requirements. The purpose of this election is to enable taxpayers to receive a tax refund sooner in order to help them weather the economic downturn that occurred in 2008 and 2009.

ADDITIONAL COMMENT

An election to forgo the carryback period for the NOL of any year is irrevocable.

in 2010, it first must be carried back to 2008, then to 2009, followed by 2011, 2012, and so on until the loss is completely used. Any NOL that is not used during the carryover period expires and is of no further tax benefit.

If the NOL is carried back to a prior year, the taxpayer must file for a refund of taxes previously paid. If the NOL deduction is carried forward, it reduces the taxable income and the tax liability for the carryover year.

ELECTION TO FORGO CARRYBACK PERIOD. A taxpayer may elect not to carry back the NOL, but to carry the loss forward. This election, which is made with respect to the entire carryback period, does not extend the carryforward period beyond 20 years. This allows a taxpayer some degree of flexibility in using the NOL deduction to the greatest advantage. (See the Tax Planning Considerations section in this chapter for a discussion of this topic.)

LOSS CARRYOVERS FROM TWO OR MORE YEARS. At times, a taxpayer might have NOL carryovers that are incurred in two or more taxable years. Often these losses are carried to the same years in the carryover period. If such is the case, the loss of the earliest year is always completely used first before deducting any of the loss incurred in a subsequent year. Because of the limited carryover period, this rule is beneficial to the taxpayer.

RECOMPUTATION OF TAXABLE INCOME IN THE CARRYOVER YEAR

When the taxpayer carries back the NOL deduction to a prior year, the taxpayer must recompute that year's taxable income. Because the NOL is attributable to a taxpayer's trade or business, it is deductible *for* AGI. As a result, the recomputation of taxable income for the carryback year may affect the deductible amount of certain itemized deductions because some of the deductions (e.g., the deductions for medical expenses, charitable contributions, and casualty losses) are limited or measured by reference to the taxpayer's AGI. All of these deductions except the deduction for charitable contributions must be recomputed using the reduced AGI amount.[64]

Once the taxpayer determines the tax refund for the carryback year, the taxpayer must calculate the amount of the NOL available to be deducted in subsequent carryover years. This is done by adjusting the recomputed income of the prior carryover year. Although certain differences exist, these adjustments are similar to those mentioned above.

The rules for computing and deducting NOLs are presented in Topic Review I:8-5.

Topic Review I:8-5

Net Operating Losses	
ITEM	**RULES**
Computation of NOL (adjustments to taxable income)	Add back any NOL deduction carried to the current year. Add back any capital loss deduction. Add back the deduction for personal and dependency exemptions. Add back the excess of nonbusiness deductions over nonbusiness income. For this purpose, casualty losses on personal-use property are treated as business losses.
Carryover period	May be carried back two years and forward twenty years (certain exceptions apply). Must be carried to the carryover years in chronological order: first carried back to the second prior year, then to the first prior year, then to the first succeeding year, etc. An election may be made to forgo the carryback. This does not extend the carryforward period. If losses from two or more years are carried to the same year, the losses from the earliest year are completely used first.

[64] Reg. Sec. 1.172-5(a)(2)(ii).

TAX PLANNING CONSIDERATIONS

BAD DEBTS

To deduct a bad debt, a taxpayer must show that the debt is worthless. At times the IRS might assert that the debt being written off is either not yet worthless or that it became worthless in a previous year. If the taxpayer is unable to overcome the IRS's assertion concerning the year of worthlessness, the taxpayer might be barred from filing an amended return for the prior year because of the statute of limitations.[65] Thus, taxpayers should carefully document all efforts at collection and other facts that show the debt is worthless.

As previously mentioned, a third-party guarantor of a loan who is required to repay the debt may, under certain circumstances, be entitled to a bad debt deduction. The guarantor must demonstrate that he or she received reasonable consideration in the form of cash or property in exchange for guaranteeing the debt. If the taxpayer does not receive proper consideration, the guarantee and subsequent payment of the loan by the guarantor is considered to be a gift rather than a loan. Reasonable consideration is also deemed to be received if the taxpayer enters into the agreement for a good faith business purpose or in accordance with normal business practice. However, if the taxpayer guarantees the debt of a spouse or a relative, the taxpayer must receive the consideration in the form of cash or property.

In the case of an outright loan between related taxpayers, the lender should always make sure to retain proper documentation to substantiate the fact that the transaction is a loan. If the taxpayer does not keep such documentation, the IRS may assert that the transaction is a gift.

CASUALTIES

A deduction is allowed for stolen property, but no deduction is allowed for lost property. Thus, taxpayers should always carefully document losses of property through theft (e.g., the filing of police reports or claims with the taxpayer's insurance company). In addition, pictures and written appraisals may be helpful to prove the amount of the loss.

NET OPERATING LOSSES

If a taxpayer incurs a net operating loss, the taxpayer should carefully analyze whether to elect to forgo the carryback period. Situations under which a taxpayer might elect to only carry the loss deduction forward include the following:

▶ A taxpayer might anticipate being in a higher marginal tax rate in future years than in the carryback years. If such is the case, the value of the deduction is higher in the carryforward years than in the carryback years. Taxpayers should consider, however, cash flows and the time value of money (e.g., the tax benefits from a refund of taxes are immediately available only if the NOL is carried back).

▶ General business and other tax credits that are nonrefundable (i.e., the credits are limited to the tax liability or some percentage thereof) may be reduced or eliminated for the carryback years because these credits must be recomputed based on the adjusted tax liability after applying the NOL carryback. (See Chapter I:14 for a discussion of tax credits.)

COMPLIANCE AND PROCEDURAL CONSIDERATIONS

CASUALTY LOSSES

If a taxpayer sustains a casualty loss in a location that the President of the United States declares a disaster area, he or she may make an election to deduct the loss in the year preceding the year in which the loss occurred. A taxpayer makes this election by either filing

---

[65] However, the statute of limitations for claims for a refund or credit because of a bad debt is extended from three years to seven years under Sec. 6511(d)(1), thus giving the taxpayer additional time if this is the case.

ADDITIONAL COMMENT

Instant access for downloading federal income tax forms, instructions, publications, etc. is available on the Internet (http://www.irs.gov).

the return for the previous year and including the loss in that year (if the return has not already been filed) or filing an amended return or claim for refund for that year.[66] The return should clearly include all the following information:

▶ That the election is being made

▶ The date of the disaster giving rise to the loss

▶ The city, county, and state in which the damaged property is located

The taxpayer must make the election before the due date of the return for the year in which the disaster actually occurs. Although the Regulations state that the election may not be revoked more than 90 days after it is made, the Tax Court has held that this part of the Regulation is invalid.[67]

NET OPERATING LOSSES

When an individual taxpayer carries an NOL deduction back to a prior year, the taxpayer claims a refund of taxes by either filing an amended return on Form 1040X or filing for a quick refund on Form 1045. Corporations use Form 1139. If the taxpayer uses Form 1045, the IRS must act on the application for refund within 90 days of the later of the date of the application or the last day of the month in which the return of the loss year must be filed.[68] A taxpayer must file Form 1045 within one year after the end of the year in which the NOL arose. The taxpayer must attach additional information such as pages 1 and 2 of Form 1040 for the year of loss, a copy of the application for an extension of time to file the return for the year of loss, and copies of forms or schedules for items refigured in the carryback years.

WORTHLESS SECURITIES

As explained earlier in this chapter, securities that become worthless during the taxable year are deemed to have become worthless on the last day of the year. In many cases, this treatment causes the loss to be treated as a long-term capital loss. If the loss from the worthless security is long term, the taxpayer reports it in Part II of Schedule D (Form 1040) along with the other long-term gains and losses for the year. The taxpayer reports short-term capital losses in Part I of Schedule D.

WHAT WOULD YOU DO IN THIS SITUATION?

A client comes to you with an idea to treat a loan that he made to one of his children two years ago as a bad debt. The loan is evidenced by a properly executed note with stated interest and payment dates. However, the client has not collected any loan payments or interest during the two-year period.

The child is insolvent and has declared bankruptcy. Before leaving your office, the client also mentions in passing that the child is in London on vacation with other members of the family and will stay in Europe for six weeks. What would you do about classifying this loan as a bad debt?

PROBLEM MATERIALS

DISCUSSION QUESTIONS

I:8-1 What is the closed transaction doctrine, and why does it exist for purposes of recognizing a loss realized on holding property?

I:8-2 When property is disposed of, what factors influence the amount of the deductible loss?

I:8-3 Describe the usual tax consequences that apply to a worthless security.

I:8-4 Under what circumstances will a loss that is realized on a worthless security not be treated as a capital loss?

---

[66] Reg. Sec. 1.165-11(e).
[67] *Chester Matheson*, 74 T.C. 836 (1980), *acq.* 1981-2 C.B. 2.

[68] IRS, 2008 *Instructions for Filing Form 1045*.

I:8-5 What two general requirements must be met for a transaction to result in a capital loss?

I:8-6 What requirements must be met for stock to be considered Sec. 1244 stock?

I:8-7 What tax treatment applies to gains and losses on Sec. 1244 stock?

I:8-8 Describe a situation where a loss on the sale of business or investment property is not currently deductible, and explain why.

I:8-9 a. What is a passive activity?
b. Who is subject to the passive loss limitation rules?

I:8-10 a. For purposes of the passive loss rules, what is a closely held C corporation?
b. In what way do the passive loss rules differ from the regular passive loss rules when applied to closely held C corporations?

I:8-11 Why is it important to identify exactly what constitutes an activity for purposes of the passive activity rules?

I:8-12 a. If a taxpayer is involved in several different business operations during the year, how is the determination made as to how many activities these operations constitute for purposes of the passive activity loss rules?
b. Can a business operation and a rental operation ever be combined into one activity? Explain.

I:8-13 Which of the following activities are considered passive for the year? Explain. Consider each situation independently.
a. Laura owns a rental unit that she rents out to students. The rental unit is Laura's only business and she spends approximately 875 hours per year managing, collecting the rent, advertising, and performing minor repairs. At times she must hire professionals such as plumbers to do the maintenance. Is the rental unit a passive activity with respect to Laura?
b. Kami is a medical doctor who works four days a week in a medical practice that she and five other doctors formed. Last year she and her partners formed another partnership that owns and operates a medical lab. The lab employs ten technicians, one of whom also acts as manager. During the year Kami spent 120 hours in meetings, reviewing records, etc., for the lab. Is the lab a passive activity with respect to Kami?
c. Assume the same facts in part b. In addition, assume that the same group of doctors have formed two other partnerships. One is a medical supply partnership. Kami spent 150 hours working for this partnership. The medical supply partnership has five full-time employees. Kami also spent 250 hours during the year working for the other partnership. This partnership specializes in providing medical services to individuals from out of town who are staying at local hotels and motels. This part-

nership hires two full-time and six part-time nurses. Are the lab and the two other partnerships passive activities with respect to Kami?

I:8-14 Explain the difference between materially participating and actively participating in an activity. When is the active participation test used?

I:8-15 a. What requirements must be met in order for a taxpayer to deduct up to $25,000 of passive losses from rental real estate activities against active and portfolio income?
b. What requirements must be met in order for a real estate rental activity to be considered a real estate business that is not subject to the passive loss rules?

I:8-16 Are the losses suspended under the passive loss rules lost forever? Explain.

I:8-17 What tests must be met to qualify a loss as deductible under the casualty loss provisions? Discuss the application of each of these tests.

I:8-18 Explain how a taxable gain on property can be realized because of a casualty event such as a fire or theft. How are these gains treated?

I:8-19 During the current year, Rulon's toilet overflowed because of a mechanical problem. Rulon was outside playing croquet, and by the time he returned, the water had flooded the basement, causing damage to the carpet, walls, and ceiling. The cost of repairing the damage was $9,000. Rulon has homeowners insurance that will cover half of the damage. However, because he has already had claims this year, Rulon does not want to report the incident to his insurance company for fear of a large increase in insurance rates. Instead, Rulon wants to deduct the loss as a casualty loss on his tax return. His AGI for this year is $50,000, and he has other itemized deductions of $6,000. Rulon is single. What amount of the casualty loss may he deduct?

I:8-20 Compare and contrast the computational rules for deducting casualty losses on personal-use property with casualty losses incurred on business or investment property.

I:8-21 Under what circumstances may a loss arising from a casualty or theft be deducted in a year other than the year in which the loss occurs?

I:8-22 For individuals, how are casualty losses on personal-use property reported on the tax return? How are casualty losses on business property reported?

I:8-23 Is the $100 floor on personal-use casualty losses imposed on each individual loss item if more than one item of property is destroyed in a single casualty? Is the floor imposed before or after the casualty gains are netted against the casualty losses?

I:8-24 Sarah loans $50,000 to her best friend, John. John uses the money to open a pizza parlor next to the local high school. Three years later, when John still owed Sarah $15,000, John closed the pizza parlor and declared bankruptcy. Discuss the appropriate tax treatment for Sarah.

I:8-25   Dana is an attorney who specializes in family law. She uses the cash method of accounting and is a calendar-year taxpayer. Last year, she represented a client in a lawsuit and billed the client $5,000 for her services. Although she made repeated attempts, Dana was unable to collect the outstanding receivable. Finally, in November of the current year, she finds out that the individual has moved without leaving any forwarding address. Dana's attempts to locate the individual are futile. What is the amount of deduction that Dana may take with respect to this bad debt?

I:8-26   Under what circumstances may a taxpayer deduct a bad debt even though another party to the transaction is the creditor?

I:8-27   What is the definition of a nonbusiness debt? What is the character of the deduction for a nonbusiness bad debt?

I:8-28   **a.** What alternatives do individuals have in deducting a loss on a deposit in a qualified financial institution?
      b. Explain when it might be better to elect one over the other.

I:8-29   A taxpayer collects a debt that was previously written off as a bad debt. What tax consequences arise if the recovery is received in a subsequent tax year?

I:8-30   What is an NOL deduction, and why is it allowed?

I:8-31   List the adjustments to an individual taxpayer's negative taxable income amount that must be made in computing an NOL for the year. What is the underlying rationale for requiring these adjustments for individuals?

I:8-32   **a.** What is the NOL carryback and carryover period?
      b. Does a taxpayer have any choice in deciding the years to which the NOL should be carried?
      c. Explain the circumstances under which a taxpayer might elect not to use the regular carryback or carryover period.

I:8-33   Can a casualty loss on a personal-use asset create or increase an NOL? Explain.

I:8-34   If an NOL is carried back to a prior year, what adjustments must be made to the prior year's taxable income? What are the possible results of the adjustments?

ISSUE IDENTIFICATION QUESTIONS

I:8-35   On January 12 of the current year, Barney Corporation, a publicly-held corporation, files for bankruptcy. During the bankruptcy proceedings it is determined that creditors will only receive 10% of what they are owed and that the shareholders will receive nothing. Sheryl, a calendar-year taxpayer, purchased 1,000 shares of Barney Corporation common stock for $7,000 on February 22 of the prior year. What tax issues should Sheryl consider?

I:8-36   Five years ago, Cora incorporated Gold, Inc., by contributing $80,000 and receiving 100% of the Gold common stock. Cora is single. Gold experienced financial difficulties. On December 22 of the current year, Cora sold all of her Gold stock for $5,000. What tax issues should Cora consider?

I:8-37   In a rage because of personal difficulties, Evan drove recklessly and crashed his automobile, doing $8,000 worth of damage. Fortunately, no one was injured. Since Evan received two speeding tickets during the past year, he is concerned about losing his insurance if he files an insurance claim. What tax issues should Evan consider?

I:8-38   Dan, a full-time employee of Beta, Inc., also owns 10% of its outstanding stock. The other 90% is owned by his three brothers. During the year, the president of Beta came to Dan, expressing grave concern about whether the company had the financial resources to remain in business. He mentioned specifically that a bank was threatening to force Beta to file bankruptcy if it didn't repay its $100,000 loan in full. After some negotiation, Dan agreed to loan Beta the $100,000 for one year until permanent financing could be obtained. A reasonable interest rate was set and a payment schedule was documented. Unfortunately, business did not improve, and Beta discontinued its business and did not repay the loan. What tax issues should Dan consider?

PROBLEMS

I:8-39   *Section 1244 Losses.* During the current year, Karen sells her entire interest in Central Corporation common stock for $22,000. She is the sole shareholder, and originally organized the corporation several years ago by contributing $89,000 in exchange for her stock, which qualifies as Sec. 1244 stock. Since its incorporation, Central has been involved in the manufacture of items that protect personal computers from static electricity. Unfortunately, this market is extremely competitive, and Central Corporation incurs substantial losses throughout its existence.
      a. Assuming Karen is single, what are the amount and the character of the loss recognized on the sale of the Central Corporation stock?

b. Assuming Karen is married and files a joint return, what are the amount and the character of the loss recognized on the sale of the Central Corporation stock?

c. How would your answer to Part a change if Karen had originally purchased the stock from another shareholder rather than organizing the corporation?

d. How might Karen have structured the transaction in Part a to receive a greater tax advantage?

I:8-40 *Amount and Character of Loss Transactions.* On September 30 of the current year, Silver Fox Corporation files for bankruptcy. At the time, it estimates that the total FMV of its assets is $725,000, whereas the total amount of its outstanding debt amounts to $950,000. Silver Fox Corporation has been engaged in the resale of tax preparation and tax research-related books and software for several years.

a. At the time of the bankruptcy, Silver Fox is owned by Randall, who purchased the stock from an investor for $250,000 several years ago. Randall is single. What are the amount and character of the loss sustained by Randall upon Silver Fox's bankruptcy?

b. How would your answer to part a change if Randall originally organized Silver Fox Corporation, capitalizing it with $250,000 of cash and assuming Silver Fox qualifies as a small business corporation?

c. How would your answer to Part a change if Randall were a corporation instead of an individual?

d. How would your answer to Part b change if Randall were a corporation instead of an individual?

I:8-41 *Amount and Character of Loss Transactions.* Five years ago, Brian and his brother Boyd formed Stewart Corp., a golf apparel manufacturing corporation. At that time, Brian contributed $300,000 to the corporation in exchange for 50% of its stock. During the current year, Brian needed some cash to purchase a golf course so he sold a third of his interest in Stewart Corp. for $85,000. He also sold stock in the following companies for the amounts indicated:

Corporation	Sales Proceeds	Adjusted Basis	When Acquired
IBM	$15,000	$10,000	52 months ago
Microsoft	25,000	45,000	18 months ago
Tidal Radio	32,000	12,000	7 months ago
Wavetable	20,000	26,000	4 months ago

During the year Brian hired a collection agency to collect a $14,000 loan he made to an old friend, which was due in full on January 1 of the current year. The agency found no trace of his friend. Also during the year, BTR Corporation, in which he owns stock, went bankrupt. His investment was worth $94,000 on January 1, he purchased it six years ago for $100,000, and he expects to receive only $8,000 in redemption of his stock. Finally, Brian's salary for the year was $114,000 for his work as an associate professor.

a. What are the net gains and losses from the above items and their character?

b. What is Brian's AGI for the year assuming he has no other items of income or deduction?

I:8-42 *Passive Losses.* In the current year Alice reports $150,000 of salary income, $20,000 of income from activity X, and $35,000 and $15,000 losses from activities Y and Z, respectively. All three activities are passive with respect to Alice and are purchased during the current year. What is the amount of loss that may be deducted with respect to each of these activities? Also compute the amount of loss that must be carried over for each activity.

I:8-43 *Passive Losses.* In the current year Clay reports income and losses from the following activities:

Activity X	$ 28,000
Activity Y	(10,000)
Activity Z	(20,000)
Salary	100,000

Activities X, Y, and Z are all passive with respect to Clay. Activity Z has $40,000 in passive losses which are carried over from the prior year. In the current year Clay sells activity Z for a taxable gain of $30,000.

a. What is the amount of loss that Clay may deduct and what is the amount that must be carried over in the current year?

b. Based solely on the amounts above, compute Clay's AGI for the current year.

I:8-44 ***Passive Losses: Rental Real Estate.*** During the current year, Irene, a married individual who files a joint return, reports the following items of income and loss:

Salary	$130,000
Activity X (passive)	10,000
Activity Y (rental real estate, nontrade or business)	(30,000)
Activity Z (rental real estate, nontrade or business)	(20,000)

Irene actively participates in activities Y and Z and owns 100% of both Y and Z.

a. What is Irene's AGI for the year?

b. What is the amount of suspended losses (if any) that may be carried over with respect to each activity?

I:8-45 ***Passive Losses.*** In 2009, Mark purchased two separate activities. Information regarding these activities for 2009 and 2010 is as follows:

	2009			2010	
Activity	*Status*	*Income (Loss)*	*Activity*	*Status*	*Income (Loss)*
A	Passive	($24,000)	A	Active	$10,000
B	Passive	(8,000)	B	Passive	20,000

The 2009 losses were suspended losses for that year. During 2010, Mark also reports salary income of $120,000 and interest and dividend income of $20,000. Compute the amount (if any) of losses attributable to activities A and B that are deductible in 2010 and any suspended losses carried to 2011.

I:8-46 ***Passive Losses.*** During the current year, Juan, a single individual, has AGI of $124,000 before taking into account any passive activity losses. He also actively participates and owns 100% of activity A, which is a real estate rental activity. For the year, activity A generates a net loss of $6,000 and $3,000 in tax credits. Juan is in the 28% tax bracket. What is the amount of suspended loss and credit from activity A that must be carried to subsequent years?

I:8-47 ***Passive Losses.*** In 2010, Julie, a single individual, reported the following items of income and deduction:

Salary	$166,000
Interest income	14,000
Long-term capital gain from sales of stock	22,000
Short-term capital losses from sales of stock	(17,000)
Loss from a passive rental real estate activity	(20,000)
Interest expense on loan to purchase stock	(21,000)
Qualified residence interest on residence	(12,000)
Charitable contributions	(8,000)
Property taxes on residence	(5,000)
Tax return preparation fees	(2,500)
Unreimbursed employee business expenses	(2,000)

Julie owns 100% and is an active participant in the rental real estate activity. What is Julie's taxable income in 2010?

I:8-48 ***Casualty Losses.*** Tony is a carpenter who owns his own furniture manufacturing business. During 2010, vandals broke into the workshop, damaged several pieces of equipment, stole his delivery truck, and also stole his personal automobile, which he often kept in the workshop garage. The asset descriptions and related values are as follows:

Asset	FMV Before Casualty	FMV After Casualty	Cost to Repair/Replace	Adjusted Basis	Insurance Proceeds
Equipment A	$12,300	$4,000	$ 8,700	$ 9,000	$ 3,700
Equipment B	8,100	0	9,000	3,000	7,800
Equipment C	Not Available	Not Available	13,800	15,300	11,400
Delivery Truck	18,000	0	32,000	17,500	16,000
Automobile	15,000	0	12,000	28,000	12,000

Although he could not obtain its fair market value after the casualties, Troy decided to repair rather than replace Equipment C.

Before considering any deductions because of these casualties, Troy's AGI is $80,000. What deductions may Tony take relating to the vandalism?

I:8-49   *Theft Losses.* On December 17, 2010, Kelly's business office safe is burglarized. The theft is discovered a few days after the burglary. $3,000 cash from the cash registers is stolen. A diamond necklace and a ring that Kelly frequently wore are also stolen. The necklace cost Kelly $2,300 many years ago and is insured for its $6,000 FMV. Kelly purchased the ring for $3,000 just two weeks before the burglary. Unfortunately, the ring and the cash are not insured. Kelly's AGI for the year, not including the items noted above, is $70,000.

     a. What is Kelly's deductible theft loss in the current year?

     b. What is Kelly's deductible theft loss in the current year if the theft is not discovered until January of the following year?

I:8-50   *Casualty Losses: Year of Deduction.* Jerry sprayed all of the landscaping around his house with a pesticide in June 2010. Shortly thereafter, all of the trees and shrubs unaccountably died. The FMV and the adjusted basis of the plants were $15,000. Later that year, the pesticide manufacturer announced a recall of the particular batch of pesticide that Jerry used. It also announced a program whereby consumers would be repaid for any damage caused by the improper mixture. Jerry is single and reports $38,000 AGI in 2010 and $42,000 in 2011.

     a. Assume that in 2010 Jerry files a claim for his losses and receives notification that payment of $15,000 will be received in 2011. Jerry receives full payment for the damage in 2010. How should the loss and the reimbursement be reported?

     b. How will your answer to Part a change if in 2011 the manufacturer files bankruptcy and Jerry receives $1,500 in total and final payment for his claim?

     c. How will your answer to Part a change if the announcement and the reimbursement do not occur until late in 2011, after Jerry has already filed his tax return for 2010?

I:8-51   *Personal-Use Casualty Losses.* In 2010 Ned completely destroys his personal automobile (purchased two years earlier for $28,000) in a traffic accident. Fortunately none of the occupants are injured. The FMV of the car before the accident is $18,000; after the accident it is worthless. Ned receives a $14,000 settlement from the insurance company. Later in the same year his house is burglarized and several antiques are stolen. The antiques were purchased a number of years earlier for $8,000. Their value at the time of the theft is estimated at $12,000. They are not insured. Ned's AGI for the current year is $60,000. What is the amount of Ned's deductible casualty loss in the current year, assuming the thefts are discovered in the same year?

I:8-52   *Casualty Losses.* During 2010, Pam incurred the following casualty losses:

Asset	FMV Before	FMV After	Basis	Insurance
Business 1	$18,000	$ 0	$15,000	$ 4,000
Business 2	25,000	10,000	8,000	3,000
Business 3	20,000	0	18,000	19,000
Personal 1	12,000	0	20,000	2,000
Personal 2	8,000	5,000	10,000	0
Personal 3	9,000	0	6,000	8,000

All of the items were destroyed in the same casualty. Before considering the casualty items, Pam reports business income of $80,000, qualified residential interest of $6,000, property taxes on her personal residence of $2,000, and charitable contributions of $4,000. Compute Pam's taxable income for 2010. Pam is single.

I:8-53   *Business Bad Debt.* Elaine is a physician who uses the cash method of accounting for tax purposes. During the current year, Elaine bills Ralph $1,200 for office visits and outpatient surgery. Unfortunately, unknown to Elaine, Ralph moves away leaving no payment and no forwarding address. What is the amount of Elaine's bad debt deduction with respect to Ralph's debt?

I:8-54   *Nonbusiness Bad Debt.* During 2009, Becky loans her brother Ken $5,000, which he intends to use to establish a small business. Because Ken has no other assets and needs cash to expand the business, the agreement provides that Ken will repay the debt if (and when) sufficient funds are generated from the business. No interest rate is agreed upon. The business is unsuccessful, and Ken is forced to file for bankruptcy in 2010. By the end of 2010, it is estimated that the creditors will receive only 20% of the amount owed. In 2011 the bankruptcy proceedings are closed, and the creditors receive 10% of the amount due on the debt. What is Becky's bad debt deduction for 2010? For 2011?

I:8-55   *Bad Debt Deduction.* Assume the same facts as in Problem I:8-54, except that Becky and Ken are not related and that under the terms of the loan Ken agrees to repay Becky the $5,000 plus interest (at a reasonable stated rate) over a five-year period. What is Becky's bad debt deduction for 2010? For 2011?

I:8-56 *Net Operating Loss Deduction.* Michelle and Mark are married and file a joint return. Michelle owns an unincorporated dental practice. Mark works part-time as a high school math teacher, and spends the remainder of his time caring for their daughter. During the current year, they report the following items:

Mark's salary	$18,000
Interest earned on savings account	1,200
Interest paid on personal residence	7,100
Itemized deductions for state and local taxes	3,400
Items relating to Michelle's dental practice	
Revenues	65,000
Payroll and salary expense	49,000
Supplies	17,000
Rent	16,400
Advertising	4,600
Depreciation	8,100

a. What is Michelle and Mark's taxable income or loss for the year?
b. What is Michelle and Mark's NOL for the year?

I:8-57 *Net Operating Loss Deduction.* Assume the same facts as in Problem I:8-56, except in addition to the other itemized deductions Michelle and Mark suffer a $4,500 deductible personal casualty loss (after limitations).
a. What is Michelle and Mark's taxable income or loss for the year?
b. What is Michelle and Mark's NOL for the year?

I:8-58 *Net Operating Loss Deduction.* Assume the same facts as in Problem I:8-56, except instead of a $3,400 itemized deduction for state and local taxes, Michelle and Mark have a $3,400 deductible casualty loss (after limitations).
a. What is Michelle and Mark's taxable income or loss for the year?
b. What is Michelle and Mark's NOL for the year?

I:8-59 *Net Operating Loss.* During the year, Karen, a single taxpayer, reports the following income and expense items relating to her interior design business:

Revenues	$52,000
Cost of goods sold	41,000
Advertising	3,300
Office supplies	1,700
Rent	13,800
Contract labor	28,000

Karen also worked part-time during the year, earning $13,500. She reports a long-term capital gain of $4,200, and a short-term capital loss of $3,800. Her itemized deductions total $5,200.
a. What is Karen's taxable income or loss for the year?
b. What is Karen's NOL for the year?

TAX STRATEGY PROBLEMS

I:8-60 In 2007, Annie Cook and several family members formed Treehouse Rentals, Inc., in Denver, Colorado. Treehouse is a closely-held C corporation engaged in the rental real estate business. Treehouse properly classifies its activities as passive. In 2007, 2008, and 2009, the corporation generated net passive losses of $380,000, $145,000, and $194,000, respectively, all of which were properly suspended.

Effective January 2010, Treehouse elected to be taxed as an S Corporation. Also during 2010, Treehouse sold two pieces of rental real estate property. The suspended losses related to these properties were $63,000 and $112,000.

How should Treehouse treat the disposition of the rental properties in 2010?

- Sec. 469, Sec. 1371
- TAM 9628002
- *St. Charles Investment Co. v. Comm.,* 86 AFTR 2d 2000-6882

I:8-61 Jace Seaton is a single taxpayer living in Eugene, Oregon. From 2006 to 2009, he worked as the CEO of Wengren & Jeffers, a local architectural firm. In 2010, he left the firm to start his own company. On October 25, 2010, he formed Seaton & Associates, a Limited Liability Company (LLC) under Oregon law.

Upon forming the LLC, Jace received an 80% interest in the company. Two other architects, Maria Juarez and Jaman Turhoon, each received a 10% interest in the company. Jace provided all necessary capital, whereas Maria and Jamal provided experience and a commitment to work for the company. Seaton & Associates chose to be taxed as a partnership for federal income tax purposes.

During 2010, Jace worked approximately 215 hours for Seaton & Associates, and received compensation of $7,200. Maria and Jamal each worked approximately 600 hours, and each received compensation of $16,000. In 2010, the company generated a net loss of $530,000.

How should the LLC members, particularly Jace, treat the loss generated in 2010?

- Reg. 1.469-5T
- *Gregg v. U.S.*, 87 AFTR 2d 2001-337

I:8-62 On November 15, Alex and Deanna Kent come to you for tax advice. The Kents, a married couple that files a joint tax return, own a rental home in Southern California. From January to November 1 of the current year, they rented out the home for 210 days. Since they live in Minnesota, they are considering staying in their rental home from December 10 to 31. If they do not stay in the home during that period, it will sit vacant. They ask you if this decision would have any tax consequences. They also provide you with the following information for the year:

Rental home income and expenses:

Rental income	$16,000
Mortgage interest	12,400
Property taxes	4,300
Homeowners Assoc. Fees	3,500
Depreciation	18,000

Other income and expenses:

Deanna's salary	75,000
Alex's salary	65,000
Passive income (from an investment in a limited partnership)	1,000
Mortgage interest	7,800
Charitable contributions	14,200
Medical expenses	8,100
Property taxes	2,900
State income taxes	9,700

What do you recommend to the Kents?

I:8-63 Jim had $100,000 in deposits in a savings account at a bank in Page, Arizona. The bank collapsed and Jim did not receive anything for his deposits. The bank was chartered by the state of Arizona and was not insured by federal law. Jim is not sure what his options are in deducting this loss on his tax return. What can Jim do to take advantage of this loss on his tax return? He has an AGI of $110,000 and no capital gains for the current year.

TAX FORM/RETURN PREPARATION PROBLEMS

I:8-64 Heather and Nikolay Laubert are married and file a joint income tax return. Their address is 3847 Jackdaw Path, Madison, WI 58493. Nikolay's Social Security number is 968-84-8532, and Heather's is 498-65-5432. Nikolay is a mechanical engineer, and Heather is a highly renowned speech therapist. She is self-employed. They report all their income and expenses on the cash method. For 2009, they report the following items of income and expense:

Gross receipts from Heather's business	$110,000
Rent on Heather's office	12,000
Receivables written off during the year (received in Heather's business)	1,300
Subscriptions to linguistic journals for Heather	250
Salary for Heather's secretary-receptionist	22,000
Nikolay's salary	78,000
Qualified medical expenses	12,000
Property taxes on their personal residence	4,200
State income tax refund received this year (the tax benefit was received in the prior year from the state income tax deduction)	400

State income taxes withheld on Nikolay's salary	4,600
Federal income taxes withheld on Nikolay's salary	12,000
Heather's estimated tax payments	20,000
Interest paid on residence	11,000
Income tax preparation fee for the prior year's return paid this year ($500 is allocated to preparation of Schedule C)	$940

Heather and Nikolay sold the following assets:

Asset	Acquired	Sold	Sales Price	Cost
KNA stock	2/12/08	3/13/09	$14,000	$ 8,000
AEN stock	3/2/09	7/7/09	20,000	22,000
KLN stock	6/8/04	4/10/09	13,000	17,000
Motorcycle	5/3/01	9/12/09	2,500	6,000

Heather owned the KLN stock and sold it to her brother, Jacob. Heather and Nikolay used the motorcycle for personal recreation.

In addition to the items above, they donate Miner Corporation stock to their community church. The FMV of the stock on the date it is donated (8/18/09) is $6,200. It cost $2,700 when purchased on 3/12/91. Heather and Nikolay's home is burglarized during the year. The burglar stole an entertainment system (FMV $3,500; cost $5,000), an antique diamond ring and pendant (FMV $12,000; cost $10,000), and a painting (FMV $1,500; cost $1,300). The insurance company pays $1,500 for the entertainment system, $4,000 for the jewelry, and $500 for the painting. Complete Heather and Nikolay's Form 1040, Schedules A, C, D, and SE, Form 4684, and Form 8283.

I:8-65 Kara and Brandon Arnold are married and file a joint return. Their Social Security numbers are 587-64-5235 and 588-54-8623, respectively. Kara and Brandon have one son, Henry, age 3. His Social Security number is 587-45-3197. They live at 356 Welcome Lane, Woodbury, WA 84653. They report their income on the cash method. During 2009, they report the following items:

Salary	$103,000
Interest income from money market accounts	600
Dividend income from Davis Corp. stock	700
Cash contributions to church	6,000
Rental of a condominium in Lutsen:	
Rental income (30 days)	12,000
Interest expense	7,000
Property taxes	3,200
Maintenance	1,700
Depreciation (entire year)	7,500
Insurance	2,000
Days of personal use	16

During the year the following events also occur:

a. In 2005, Brandon had loaned a friend $3,000 to help pay medical bills. During 2009, he discovers that his "friend" has skipped town.

b. On June 20, 2009, Brandon sells Kim Corporation stock for $16,000. He purchased the stock on December 12, 2004 for $22,000.

c. On September 19, 2009, Kara discovers that the penny stock of Roberts, Inc. she purchased on January 2 of the prior year is completely worthless. She paid $5,000 for the stock.

d. Instead of accepting the $60 the utility store offers for their old dishwasher, they donate it to Goodwill on November 21, 2009. They purchased the dishwasher for $750 on March 30, 2003. The new dishwasher cost $900.

e. Kara and Brandon purchased a new residence for $250,000. As part of the closing costs, they pay two points, or $3,800, on the mortgage, which is interest rather than loan processing fees. This payment enables them to obtain a more favorable interest rate for the term of the loan. They also paid $8,400 in interest on their mortgage on their personal residence.

f. They pay $4,100 in property taxes on their residence and $7,500 in state income taxes.

g. On July 20, 2009, Kara and Brandon donate 1,000 shares of Anton, Inc. stock to the local community college. The value of the stock on that date is $10,200. Anton, Inc. is a listed stock. They had purchased the stock on November 10, 2004 for $1,000.

h. $16,450 in federal income tax was withheld during the year.

Complete Kara and Brandon's Form 1040, Schedules A, B, D, and E, and Form 8283. For purposes of this problem, disregard the alternative minimum tax.

CASE STUDY PROBLEMS

I:8-66

Dr. John Brown is a physician who expects to make $150,000 this year from his medical practice. In addition, Dr. Brown expects to receive $10,000 dividends and interest income.

Last year, on the advice of a friend, Dr. Brown invested $100,000 in Limited, a limited partnership. He spends no time working for Limited. Limited's operations did not turn out exactly as planned, and Dr. Brown's share of Limited's losses last year amounted to $15,000. Dr. Brown has already been informed that his share of Limited's losses this year will be $10,000.

In January of the current year, Dr. Brown set up his own laboratory. Originally he intended to have the lab only do the work for his own practice, but other physicians in the area were impressed with the quick turnaround and convenience that the lab provided and began sending their work. This year, Dr. Brown estimates that the lab will generate $30,000 of taxable income. The work in the lab is done by two full-time qualified laboratory technicians. A part-time bookkeeper is hired to keep the books. Dr. Brown has spent 320 hours to date establishing and managing the lab. He plans to hire another technician who will also manage the lab so that it can operate on its own.

In November, Dr. Brown calls you requesting some tax advice. Specifically, he would like to know what actions he should take before the end of the year in order to reduce his tax liability for the current year.

Write a memo to Dr. Brown, detailing your suggestions. His address is: Dr. John Brown, 444 Physicians Drive, Suite 100, Anytown, USA 88888.

I:8-67

In preparing the tax return for one of your clients, Jack Johnson, you notice that he has listed a deduction for a large business bad debt. Jack explains that the loan was made to his corporate employer when the corporation was experiencing extreme cash flow difficulties. In fact, Jack was very concerned at the time he made the loan that the corporation would go bankrupt. This would have been extremely bad, because not only would he have lost his job, but he also would have lost the $80,000 he had invested in the common stock of the corporation.

You know that if the loan is a business loan Jack will receive an ordinary deduction. However, if the loan is a nonbusiness debt, it becomes a short-term capital loss (and Jack can only currently deduct $3,000).

After thoroughly reviewing all of the facts, you do a complete search of the relevant judicial and administrative authority. There you find that the courts are split as to whether under these circumstances the loan should be treated as a business or nonbusiness bad debt.

What position should you take on Jack's federal income tax return? (See the *Statements on Standards for Tax Services* section in Chapter I:15 and Appendix E for a discussion of this issue.)

TAX RESEARCH PROBLEM

I:8-68

Early in 2010, Kay meets Dan through a business associate. Dan tells Kay that he is directing a business venture that purchases poorly managed restaurants in order to turn them around and make them profitable. Dan mentions that he is currently involved in acquiring a real "gold mine" but needs to raise additional cash in order to purchase it. On the strength of Dan's representations, Kay loans Dan $30,000 for the venture. An agreement is written up between Kay and Dan, wherein Dan agrees to repay Kay the entire amount over a 5-year period plus 14% interest per annum on the unpaid balance. Later in the year, however, Kay discovers that Dan had never intended to purchase the restaurant and, in fact, had used most of the money for his own benefit. Upon making this discovery, Kay sues Dan for recovery of the money, alleging that Dan falsely, fraudulently, and deceitfully represented that the money would be invested and repaid, in order to cheat and defraud Kay out of her money. Unfortunately for Kay, she is never able to recover any amount of the loan. Discuss the tax treatment that Kay may claim with regard to the loss.

A partial list of research sources is:

- *Robert S. Gerstell*, 46 T.C. 161 (1966)
- *Michele Monteleone*, 34 T.C. 688 (1960)

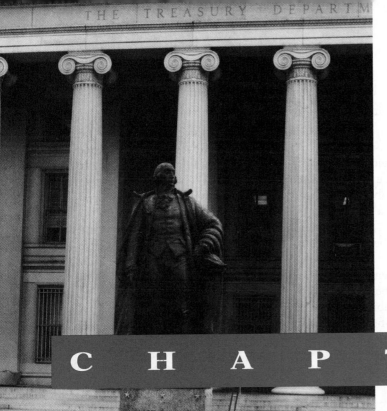

CHAPTER

9

EMPLOYEE EXPENSES AND DEFERRED COMPENSATION

LEARNING OBJECTIVES

After studying this chapter, you should be able to

▶ **1** Determine the proper classification and deductibility of travel and transportation expenses

▶ **2** Determine the proper deductible amount for entertainment expenses under the 50% disallowance rule

▶ **3** Identify deductible moving expenses and determine the amount and year of deductibility

▶ **4** Describe the requirements for deducting education expenses

▶ **5** Determine whether the expenses of an office in home meet the requirements for deductibility and apply the gross income limitations

▶ **6** Discuss the tax treatment and requirements for various deferred compensation arrangements

This chapter discusses the tax consequences from two types of expenditures:

▶ Expenditures incurred by an employee in connection with his or her job

▶ Deferred compensation payments made to employees

Employees routinely incur expenses in connection with their jobs, such as travel, entertainment, professional journals, etc. The tax law considers **employee expenses** to be incurred in connection with a trade or business and, therefore are deductible under Sec. 162. However, employee expenses are subject to a myriad of special rules and limitations. Because of the large number of taxpayers who are employees and the importance of the topic, this chapter discusses the rules as well as tax planning opportunities.

Deferred compensation refers to methods of compensating employees that are based on their current service, but the actual payments are deferred until future periods. Deferred compensation arrangements are very popular and widely used in business. The two principal types of deferred compensation methods are qualified plans and nonqualified plans. Qualified plans, such as pension and profit-sharing plans, have very favorable tax benefits but also impose strict eligibility and coverage requirements. Nonqualified plans, while not as tax advantageous as qualified plans, are very useful for highly compensated employees. Both of these types of deferred compensation arrangements are discussed later in this chapter.

CLASSIFICATION AND LIMITATIONS OF EMPLOYEE EXPENSES

Employee expenses, for purposes of the tax law, are divided into two classifications: *reimbursed* employee expenses and *unreimbursed* employee expenses. Reimbursed employee expenses are expenses incurred by the employee that are reimbursed by the employer. IRC Section 62(a)(2) provides that an employee may deduct reimbursed employee expenses *for* AGI. This presumes, of course, that the employee has included the reimbursement in his gross income. Unreimbursed employee expenses are generally deductible by employees, but are deductible *from* AGI. A more detailed discussion of the proper treatment of employee expenses under accountable and nonaccountable plans is presented later in this chapter.

Some of the more frequently encountered employee expenses discussed in this chapter include:

▶ Travel

▶ Transportation

▶ Moving

▶ Entertainment

▶ Education

▶ Office in home

Each of these types of employee expenses are discussed later in this chapter.

NATURE OF THE EMPLOYMENT RELATIONSHIP

An individual who provides services for another person or entity may be classified either as an employee or as a self-employed individual (also referred to as an independent contractor). If the individual is classified as self-employed, expenses are deductible *for* AGI under Sec. 162, and are reported on Schedule C of Form 1040. Conversely, expenses of employees are deductible either *for* or *from* AGI depending on whether such expenses are reimbursed or unreimbursed. In addition to the deductibility of expenses, the proper classification is also important due to employment taxes, such as Social Security taxes. As is discussed below, self-employed taxpayers must pay both the employee's and employer's shares of Social Security taxes.

EMPLOYER-EMPLOYEE RELATIONSHIP DEFINED. The Treasury Regulations provide that an employer-employee relationship generally exists where the employer has the

right to control and direct the individual who provides services with regard to the end result and the means by which the result is accomplished.[1]

EXAMPLE I:9-1 ▶ Carmen is a nurse who assists a group of doctors in a clinic. Carmen is under the direct supervision of the doctors and is told what procedures to perform and when to perform them. Therefore, Carmen is classified as an employee. ◀

EXAMPLE I:9-2 ▶ Carol is a registered nurse who provides in-home services to several elderly patients. She receives instructions from the patients' doctors regarding such items as medications and diet. Carol is directly responsible for the delivery of nursing care and is in control of the end result. Thus, Carol is self-employed. ◀

ADDITIONAL COMMENT

Anyone in a trade or business making payments of $600 or more to an independent contractor during a year must file Form 1099-MISC.

IMPORTANCE OF PROPER CLASSIFICATION. As mentioned above, proper classification is important both to employers and employees. If an individual is classified as an employee, the employer must match the Social Security and Medicare taxes that are paid by the employee. In addition, employers are generally liable for unemployment taxes for their employees. Thus, an employer must pay these employment taxes to the federal and/or state governments in addition to the wages, which means that the cost of an employee generally is higher than for a non-employee. If an individual is determined to *not* be an employee, the individual is considered to be self-employed (also called an independent contractor). Amounts paid to a self-employed individual are not considered to be wages and the payor is not responsible for any employment taxes. However, the self-employed individual must pay both the employee and employer portions *of Social Security* and Medicare taxes. This tax is referred to as the *self-employment tax*. As can be seen from the above discussion, employment taxes are shifted from the employer to the self-employed individual if the individual is not considered to be an employee.

Individuals may prefer to be classified as employees because the employee portion of the Social Security and Medicare taxes (7.65%) is only one-half of the self-employment tax rate (15.3%). Of the 7.65%, 6.2% (12.4% for self-employed individuals) is for the old age, survivors and disability insurance (OASDI) portion of the FICA tax and is assessed on a maximum income amount of $106,800 (2009 and 2010). The remaining 1.45% (2.9% for self-employed individuals) portion of the FICA tax is for hospital insurance and has no ceiling limitation.[2]

LITIGATION ISSUES AND ADMINISTRATIVE ENFORCEMENT. The determination as to whether an individual who performs services is either an employee or an independent contractor has been a major ongoing area of contention between the IRS and taxpayers. In determining whether a worker is an employee or independent contractor, the facts of the situation must be analyzed and divided into three main categories: behavioral control, financial control, and relationship of the parties. No one factor is necessarily determinative, the totality of the situation must be considered. The first category, behavioral control, entails whether the payor has the right to control how the individual does the work. *Behavioral control* is characterized by the amount of instruction as to how the work is to be done as well as the level of training that is provided to the individual. As to *financial control*, an independent contractor has a significant investment in his or her work, is not reimbursed for expenses, and has the opportunity for profit or loss. An employee generally would not have these characteristics in their role as an employee. The third category is that the *relationship of the parties* and looks at employee benefits and explicit written contracts that show the type of relationship intended. These three categories of tests are an outgrowth of the so-called "20 factor test" that was used for many years to determine whether an individual was considered an employee or independent contractor. Under either system, the determination is still a very difficult and uncertain determination.

Substantial litigation has occurred in the interpretation of these factors. For example, truck drivers who were owner-operators and were engaged under contract by an interstate

---

[1] Reg. Sec. 31.3401(c)-1(b).

[2] For a more detailed discussion of the self-employment tax, (see Chapter I:14).

trucking company were considered independent contractors because they selected their own routes and were paid a percentage of the company's receipts for shipment.[3] However, drivers for a moving van company were considered employees because the company exercised control over their assignments.[4]

LIMITATIONS ON UNREIMBURSED EMPLOYEE EXPENSES

2% NONDEDUCTIBLE FLOOR. Section 67 imposes a nondeductible floor of 2% of AGI to the following types of itemized deductions:

1) Unreimbursed employee business expenses,
2) Investment expenses,
3) Fees paid for tax advice and/or tax return preparation, and
4) Expenses allowed in connection with a hobby activity (see Chapter I:6 for details on hobby loss activities).

All of these types of expenses are referred to as **miscellaneous itemized deductions** in Sec. 67.[5] Unreimbursed employee expenses that are classified as miscellaneous itemized deductions include:

▶ Professional journals, professional dues, union dues, small tools and supplies
▶ Job-hunting expenses for seeking employment in the same trade or business (e.g., employment agency fees)
▶ The cost and maintenance of special clothing (e.g., uniforms for an airline pilot)

Investment expenses include expenses connected with the earning of investment income, such as publications and safe deposit box rentals. Other miscellaneous itemized deductions include items such as fees for tax return preparation and appraisal fees for charitable contributions.

EXAMPLE I:9-3 ▶

In 2010, Charles incurs and pays $3,000 of unreimbursed employee expenses, $1,000 of investment counseling fees, and $500 for the preparation of his 2009 income tax return. Charles's AGI is $100,000. The total miscellaneous itemized deductions are $4,500 ($3,000 + $1,000 + $500). Charles is limited to a $2,500 deduction ($4,500 − $2,000) because of the application of the 2% nondeductible floor (0.02 × $100,000 AGI = $2,000). ◀

EXCEPTIONS TO THE 2% FLOOR. The 2% floor applies to most miscellaneous itemized deductions. However, some miscellaneous itemized deductions, such as gambling losses (see footnote 5 below), are not subject to the 2% floor. Further, itemized deductions, such as charitable contributions, mortgage interest and real estate taxes on a principal residence, are not considered miscellaneous itemized deductions and therefore not subject to the 2% nondeductible floor.

EXAMPLE I:9-4 ▶

In the current year Carmelia, who is single, incurs $1,500 of unreimbursed employee expenses, $3,000 of charitable contributions, and $4,000 of mortgage interest and real estate taxes on her principal residence. She has no other miscellaneous itemized deductions or investment expenses, and her AGI is $100,000. The $1,500 of employee expenses are not deductible because the 2% nondeductible floor ($2,000 in this case) is higher than the $1,500 of expenses. The $3,000 of charitable contributions and $4,000 of mortgage interest and real estate taxes are fully deductible as itemized deductions because Carmelia's total itemized deductions of $7,000 exceed the standard deduction amount ($5,700 for a single taxpayer in 2010). The charitable contributions, mortgage interest, and real estate taxes are not subject to the 2% nondeductible floor. ◀

---

[3] Rev. Rul. 76-226, 1976-1 CB 332
[4] *R. N. Smith v. U.S.*, 78-1 USTC ¶9263 (CA-5, 1978).
[5] The 2% floor does not apply to certain other miscellaneous itemized deductions, including impairment-related work expenses for handicapped employees, amortizable bond premiums, certain short sale expenses, terminated annuity payments, and gambling losses to the extent of winnings.

TRAVEL EXPENSES

DEDUCTIBILITY OF TRAVEL EXPENSES

The deductibility of travel expenses depends on the nature of the expenditure and whether the employee receives a reimbursement from the employer. The following rules apply to the deductibility of travel expenses.

▶ If the taxpayer is engaged in a trade or business as a self-employed individual or is engaged in an activity for the production of rental and royalty income, the travel-related expenditures are deductible *for* AGI and the 2% nondeductible floor is not applicable.

▶ If the taxpayer is an employee and incurs travel expenses in connection with his job, the expenses are deductible either *for* AGI or *from* AGI depending on whether the expenses are reimbursed by the employer.

▶ Personal travel expenses are not deductible.

REIMBURSED EXPENSES. If business travel expenses are reimbursed and the reimbursement is included in the employee's gross income, the expenses are deductible *for* AGI.

UNREIMBURSED EXPENSES. Generally, if business travel expenses are not reimbursed by the taxpayer's employer, the expenses are a deduction *from* AGI subject to the 2% floor.

The tax rules for reporting reimbursed and unreimbursed employee business expenses are discussed in more detail later in this chapter. Table I:9-1 illustrates how travel expenses are reported.

DEFINITION OF TRAVEL EXPENSES

Travel expenses include transportation, meals, lodging, and other reasonable and necessary expenses incurred by a taxpayer while "away from home" in the pursuit of a trade or business or an employment-related activity. The term *travel expense* is more broadly defined in the IRC than is the term **transportation expense**. If an individual is not away from home, expenses related to local transportation are classified as transportation expenses rather than travel expenses. Transportation expenses for employees are deductible under certain conditions and are discussed later in this chapter.

▼ **TABLE I:9-1**
Classification of Travel Expenses

Situation Facts	TAX TREATMENT		
	Deductible *for* AGI	Deductible *from* AGI	Not Deductible
1. Cindy is a self-employed attorney who incurs travel expenses related to her business.	X[a]		
2. Jose, who lives in Dallas, is the owner of several apartment buildings in Denver. Periodically he travels to Denver to inspect and manage the properties.	X[a]		
3. Clay is an employee who is required to travel to company facilities throughout the U.S. in the conduct of his management responsibilities. Clay is not reimbursed by his employer.		X[b]	
4. Same as Situation 3, except that Clay is fully reimbursed by his employer and includes the reimbursement in his gross income.	X[a]		
5. Colleen works in New York City and travels to her parents' home in Dallas during the holidays.			X

[a] The 2% nondeductible floor is not applicable.
[b] The 2% nondeductible floor is applicable and the expenses are only deductible if in excess of the floor.

EXAMPLE I:9-5 ▶ Ahmed is away from home overnight on a job-related business trip and incurs airfare, hotel, and taxi fares amounting to $800. Because Ahmed is away from home, the $800 is treated as travel expenses. ◀

EXAMPLE I:9-6 ▶ Charlotte uses her personal automobile to make deliveries of company products to customers in the same local area of her employer's place of business. Charlotte's automobile expenses are classified as transportation expenses (rather than travel expenses) because she was not away from home when they were incurred. As is discussed later in this chapter, transportation expenses are deductible but are subject to strict recordkeeping rules. If Charlotte stopped to eat lunch alone during her delivery activities, the meals are not deductible as they are neither travel nor transportation expenses. ◀

HISTORICAL NOTE

The partial disallowance of business meals (and entertainment) of 50% was enacted because Congress believed that prior law had not focused sufficiently on the personal consumption element of deductible business meal and entertainment expenses. Congress felt that taxpayers who could arrange business settings for personal consumption were unfairly receiving a federal tax subsidy for such consumption.

TYPICAL MISCONCEPTION

There is a tendency to erroneously assume that a taxpayer's tax home is the location of his or her primary personal residence.

REAL-WORLD EXAMPLE

A taxpayer was employed by a traveling circus with headquarters in Chicago. The Tax Court held that the taxpayer's home was wherever he happened to be with the circus. Therefore, the cost of his meals and lodging was not deductible. *Nat Lewis*, 1954 PH T.C. Memo ¶54,233, 13 TCM 1167.

GENERAL QUALIFICATION REQUIREMENTS

To qualify as a travel expense deduction, the following requirements must be met:

▶ The purpose of the trip must be connected with a trade or business or be employment-related (e.g., personal vacation trips or commuting to and from a job location are nondeductible personal expenses).[6]

▶ The taxpayer must be away from his tax home overnight or for a sufficient duration to require sleep or rest before returning home.

AWAY-FROM-TAX-HOME REQUIREMENT. Travel expenses are deductible if the taxpayer is temporarily away from his tax home overnight. While this seems simple enough, there has been considerable debate as to what the words actually mean. There are three important aspects of this requirement: (1) where is the taxpayer's home, (2) how is *temporarily* distinguished from *indefinite* or *permanent*, and (3) how is the term *overnight* interpreted.

Taxpayer's home: The IRS's position is that a person's tax home is the location of his principal place of employment regardless of where the family residence is maintained. Thus, a taxpayer who works permanently or for an indefinite period of time away from his or her family residence is *not* considered to be away from home and, therefore, travel expenses are not deductible. In this situation, the taxpayer's *tax home* is considered to be his work location.

Temporary vs. Indefinite: To meet the away from home requirement, a taxpayer must be away from home on a temporary basis. Thus, an employee who travels out of town on a three-day business trip clearly meets this requirement. However, an employee whose primary residence is in one location but works on a permanent basis during the week at another location, and possibly has an apartment at the work location, is not considered away from home at the *work location*. In this case, the work location is considered his tax home for income tax purposes, and he is not considered to be away from home.

The determination of whether a taxpayer is away from home temporarily or indefinitely is based upon the length of time the taxpayer is at such location. Work assignments of more than one year are treated as indefinite.[7] Work assignments for one year or less are classified as either temporary or indefinite depending on the facts and circumstances of each case. If an employee is reassigned only for a temporary period, then his tax home does not change and the travel expenses are deductible. However, if the assignment is for an indefinite period, the individual's tax home shifts to the new location. The following bulleted items and examples are taken from Rev. Rul. 93-86[8] and are used to illustrate the IRS's position concerning whether a taxpayer is away from home temporarily for purposes of deducting travel expenses:

▶ A taxpayer accepts away from home employment where it is realistically expected that the work will be completed in six months. The actual employment period lasts ten months. Because the employment period is realistically expected to last (and does in fact last) for one year or less, the IRS's position is that the employment is temporary and the taxpayer's travel expenses are deductible.

---

[6] Travel expenses incurred in the production or collection of income are also deductible from AGI under Sec. 212(1), even though the travel is not connected with employment or with the conduct of a trade or business. See Rev. Rul. 84-113, 1984-2 C.B. 60.

[7] Sec. 162(a). See also Rev. Rul. 99-7, 1999-1 C.B. 361.

[8] Rev. Rul. 93-86, 1993-2 C.B. 71.

▶ A taxpayer accepts away from home employment where it is realistically expected that the work will be completed in 18 months but the work is actually completed in ten months. In such case the IRS's position is that the employment is treated as indefinite, regardless of whether it actually exceeds one year or not.

▶ A taxpayer accepts away from home employment where it is realistically expected that the work will be completed in nine months. After eight months the taxpayer is asked to remain for seven more months or a total period of more than one year. Based on these facts, the IRS's position is that the employment is temporary for eight months and the travel expenses are deductible for the eight-month period. The job is considered indefinite for the remaining seven months and no travel expense deduction is allowed for the travel expenses during this period.

Overnight test: To satisfy the overnight test, a taxpayer must show that it was reasonable for him to need to obtain sleep or rest during release time on such trips in order to meet the demands of his job.[9] Generally, costs of meals on one-day business trips are not deductible since the taxpayer was not away from home overnight. The Supreme Court held that a taxpayer who took short rest stops on long one-day business trips was not allowed to deduct his meals.[10] However, whether it is reasonable to need sleep or rest depends on the specific circumstances. A railroad conductor was allowed to deduct lodging, meals, and tips incurred during a six-hour layover on a total trip of 16 hours.[11]

EXAMPLE I:9-7 ▶ Roberto lives and works in Baltimore. He occasionally travels to New York City on business and stays overnight for two or three days at a time. Roberto clearly meets the away from home test and all of his travel expenses, including airfare, lodging, tips, taxi, and food (subject to the 50% disallowance) are deductible as travel expenses. ◀

EXAMPLE I:9-8 ▶ Tom lives with his family in Baltimore. In 2010, Tom loses his job in Baltimore and accepts a new full-time position in New York City. However, he decides not to move his family to New York but to rent an apartment and stay there during the week and return home on weekends. Tom's work assignment would be considered indefinite and the cost of his apartment, food, and other incidental expenses would not be deductible travel expenses because his tax home is New York and he is not considered to be away from home. ◀

EXAMPLE I:9-9 ▶ Gunther lives and works in Baltimore. Gunther's employer asks him to accept a temporary assignment in New York City for approximately seven months to work on a special project. Gunther rents an apartment in New York for the seven months, then returns to his regular office in Baltimore. Gunther's work assignment in New York is considered temporary because it is less than one year, and therefore, all of his apartment rent, food, laundry, and other incidental costs are deductible as travel expenses. Because apartments and food are expensive in New York, his travel expense deduction will be substantial. Good records to substantiate the work assignment and the expenses are very important in this case. ◀

SELF-STUDY QUESTION

A student accepts employment in another state during his summer vacation. Would the cost of his meals and lodging at the job location be deductible?

ANSWER

No, the student did not travel to the job because of the employer's business needs. *Peter F. Janss v. CIR*, 2 AFTR 2d 5927, 58-2 USTC ¶9873 (8th Cir., 1958).

BUSINESS VERSUS PLEASURE

Travel expenses are deductible only if they are incurred in the pursuit of a trade or business activity or are related to the taxpayer's employment. Thus, if a taxpayer takes a trip that is primarily personal in nature but some business is transacted, the only deductions allowed are those that are directly related to the business activity.[12] In such event, all of the traveling expenses to and from the destination are treated as nondeductible personal expenditures. However, if the trip is *primarily related* to business or employment, all of the traveling expenses to and from the destination are deductible, and meals and lodging, local transportation, and incidental expenses are allocated to the business and personal activities, respectively. In effect, an all-or-nothing approach is applied to the deductibility of traveling expenses to and from the destination depending upon the primary purpose for making the trip.

---

[9] Rev. Rul. 75-168, 1975-1 C.B. 58.
[10] *Correll v. U.S.*, 389 F2d 299 (1968).
[11] *Williams v. Patterson*, 286 F2d 333 (5th Cir. 1961) and Rev. Rul. 75-170, 1975-1 C.B. 60. See also *Marc G. Bisonnette*, 127 T.C. 124 (October 23,

2006), where a six-hour layover on 15-17 hour days for a ferry boat captain was held to be "away from home."
[12] Reg. Sec. 1.162-2(b)(1).

In determining the primary purpose for a trip, the amount of time spent on personal activities compared to the time spent on business activities is an important factor. However, the fact that a taxpayer may spend slightly more time on personal activities than business activities will not automatically prohibit the deductibility of the transportation expenses to and from the destination. The taxpayer must clearly show that the purpose of the trip was *primarily business*.

EXAMPLE I:9-10 ▶ Dana travels to New York on a business trip for her employer and spends $500 for a roundtrip airline ticket and $200 per day for hotel, meals, and incidental expenses. She is not reimbursed for the travel expenses. Dana spends three days in business meetings and vacations for two days. Because the trip is primarily business, the traveling expenses to and from the destination (e.g., airfare) of $500 are fully deductible by Dana. Dana's meals, lodging, and incidental expenses amount to $1,000 (5 days × $200), but only $600 ($200 × 3 business days) of such travel expenses is deductible. The deductible business meal expenses are reduced by 50%, and the total amount of deductible travel expenses are subject to the nondeductible 2% floor on miscellaneous itemized deductions. A proration of the meals, lodging, and incidental expenses based on the number of days may not be appropriate if the expenses are uneven or are directly related to either business or personal activities. ◀

EXAMPLE I:9-11 ▶ Assume that the facts in Example I:9-10 are reversed (i.e., that two days are employment-related and three days are personal). Because more time was spent on personal activities, the general rule would hold that the trip is primarily personal and the traveling expenses to and from the destination of $500 are not deductible. Thus, only $400 ($200 × two business days) of travel expenses related to meals, lodging, and incidental expenses are deductible (subject to the limitations previously discussed). ◀

EXAMPLE I:9-12 ▶ Carroll, who lives and works in St. Louis, is required by his employer to attend a sales meeting in San Francisco. The meeting lasts two days. Carroll decides to take three days of vacation and sightsee in the San Francisco area. Even though Carroll spent more days on personal activities than business activities, Carroll's airfare would be deductible if he can clearly show that the primary purpose of the trip was business. ◀

REAL-WORLD EXAMPLE

It is very difficult to deduct expenses of a spouse who accompanies his or her spouse to a business meeting or convention. The accompanying spouse not only must be an employee of the corporation but the reason for accompanying his or her spouse must be for bona fide business purpose.

The IRS has ruled that the incremental expenses of an additional night's lodging and an additional day's meals that are incurred to obtain "excursion" airfare rates with respect to employees whose business travel extends over Saturday night are deductible business expenses.[13] The reimbursement for these expenses is deductible by the employer (subject to the 50% disallowance for meals). The employer is not required to report the reimbursement on the employee's Form W-2 as gross income or withhold employment taxes.

Stringent rules are applied if the taxpayer is accompanied by family members because of the likelihood that the trip is primarily for personal reasons. No deduction is permitted for travel expenses of a spouse or dependent (or other person accompanying the taxpayer) unless the person is an employee, the travel is for a bona fide business purpose, and the expenses would be otherwise deductible.[14]

FOREIGN TRAVEL

Due to the potential for abuse, special rules apply to foreign travel and foreign convention expenses.[15] Travel expenses related to foreign conventions, seminars, or similar types of meetings are disallowed unless it can be shown that the meeting is directly related to the taxpayer's trade or business (including employment) activity and that it is reasonable for the meeting to be held outside North America. In addition, complex expense allocation rules are applied to business trips made outside the United States.[16]

---

[13] Ltr. Rul. 9237014 (June 10, 1992).
[14] Sec. 274(m)(3).
[15] Secs. 274(c) and (h).
[16] Reg. Sec. 1.274-4. No allocation of total expenses is made to the personal-use (nondeductible) element if an individual is away from home for seven

days or less or if less than 25% of the time is devoted to personal purposes. In all other cases, all of the foreign travel expenses (including transportation costs) must be apportioned between business and personal activities based on the relative percentage of time devoted to each activity.

SELF-STUDY QUESTION

Would the cost of going on a safari in Africa be deductible if the taxpayer were in the business of selling guns?

ANSWER

In an actual case, the Court held that the safari expenses were not sufficiently connected to the taxpayer's gun-selling business. Therefore, the safari costs were not deductible. *Vincent W. Eckel*, 1974 PH T.C. Memo ¶74,033, 33 TCM 147.

ADDITIONAL LIMITATIONS ON TRAVEL EXPENSES

IRC Section 274 also provides several limitations on the deductibility of certain types of travel expenses, including the following:

▶ Travel deductions are disallowed if the expenses are deductible only as a form of education. For example, a French language professor cannot deduct travel expenses to France if the purpose of the trip is to maintain a general familiarity with the French language and customs.

▶ Deductions allowed for luxury water travel (i.e., ocean liners, cruise ships, or other forms of water transportation) are limited to twice the highest per diem amount allowable for a day of domestic travel by employees in the executive branch of the federal government.

▶ Travel deductions to attend a convention, seminar, or meeting are not allowed if they are related to income-producing activities coming under Sec. 212. Expenses to attend a convention, seminar, or meeting are deductible if directly connected with a taxpayer's trade or business. However, expenses to attend such meetings on a U.S. cruise ship are deductible but only to a maximum amount of $2,000.

EXAMPLE I:9-13 ▶ Dawn travels on a cruise ship to attend a business meeting in Bermuda. The round-trip cost of the cruise is $4,000, and the travel is for a period of four days. If the daily per diem amount is $150 for a government employee, the travel expenses related to the cruise ship are limited to $1,200 ($300 per day × 4 days travel). ◀

EXAMPLE I:9-14 ▶ Danielle is an investor in the stock market who attends investment counseling seminars. During the current year, she incurs $4,000 in travel expenses and $1,000 in registration fees to attend the seminars. None of the travel expenses are deductible because the expenses are related to income-producing activities coming under Sec. 212. The registration fees are deductible as an investment expense. If Danielle was employed as a stockbroker (rather than an investor) and attended investment seminars, her travel expenses would be deductible as well as the registration fee. ◀

TRANSPORTATION EXPENSES

The deductibility and classification of transportation expenses also depends on the nature of the expenditure, as follows:

▶ Trade or business-related transportation expenses are deductible *for* AGI and are not subject to specific limitations.

▶ Transportation expenses related to the production of rental and royalty income (e.g., an owner-investor in rental properties) are deductible *for* AGI and are not subject to specific limitations.

▶ Reimbursed employee transportation expenses are deductible *for* AGI (assuming that an adequate accounting is made to the employer; see discussion of reimbursed employee business expenses on page I:9-17).

▶ Unreimbursed employee transportation expenses are deductible *from* AGI as itemized deductions subject to the 2% nondeductible floor for miscellaneous itemized deductions.

▶ Commuting expenses are nondeductible personal expenses.

DEFINITION AND CLASSIFICATION

KEY POINT

The primary difference between travel expenses and transportation expenses for tax purposes is that travel expenses are broad in nature and include transportation, lodging, meals, and other necessary expenses, whereas transportation expenses include only the cost of transportation.

Transportation expenses include such items as taxi fares, automobile expenses, airfares, tolls, and parking fees incurred in a trade or business or employment-related activity. Generally speaking, transportation expenses are those incurred for "local transportation" and are not treated as travel expenses because the away from home requirements have not been met. The cost of commuting to and from an employee's job location are nondeductible personal expenditures regardless of the length of the trip. Both unreimbursed employment-related travel and transportation expenses for employees are subject to the

2% floor on miscellaneous itemized deductions. If a reimbursement is received, such expenses would be deductible *for* AGI.

EXAMPLE I:9-15 ▶ Eurie's employer requires her to call on several customers at different locations in the metropolitan area during the course of the workday. Her transportation expenses (e.g., auto expenses, tolls, and parking) are deductible as transportation expenses because they are related to providing services as an employee. If Eurie is required to travel away from home overnight, the transportation costs are included with meals and lodging and deducted as a travel expense. In either situation, the unreimbursed employment-related expenses are treated as miscellaneous itemized deductions and are subject to the 2% nondeductible floor limitation. If the expenses were reimbursed by Eurie's employer and an adequate accounting is made to the employer, the expenses would be deductible *for* AGI. ◀

EXAMPLE I:9-16 ▶ David accepts a permanent job with a company located 80 miles from his principal residence. He decides not to move to the new location and drives the 160-mile roundtrip each day. None of David's transportation expenses are deductible because they are personal commuting expenses. (Note: Because the job is a permanent assignment, it is for an indefinite period rather than a temporary period and the transportation expenses are not deductible as travel expenses.) ◀

ADDITIONAL COMMENT

The IRS takes the position that the hauling of equipment, tools, etc., in an automobile for business purposes does not make the commuting expenses deductible. This position is based on the Supreme Court's decision in *Donald W. Fausner v. CIR,* 32 AFTR 2d 73-5202, 73-2 USTC ¶9515 (USSC, 1973). The Court held that it was not possible to allocate the automobile expenses between nondeductible commuting expenses and deductible business expenses. However, if the taxpayer incurs additional costs, such as in renting a trailer, these additional costs are deductible.

The following exceptions or unusual circumstances should be noted:

▶ Transportation expenses incurred to go from one job to another are deductible if an employee has more than one job. If the employee goes home between jobs, the deduction is only the amount it would have cost him to go directly from the first location to the second.[17]

▶ Certain transportation expenses related to income-producing activities are deductible under Sec. 212. Expenses are deductible *for* AGI if they are related to the production of rental or royalty income whereas expenses connected with other investment-related activities are deductible as miscellaneous itemized deductions subject to the 2% floor.

▶ Transportation expenses related to medical treatment may be deductible from AGI as a medical expense (subject to the limitations on the deductibility of medical expenses discussed in Chapter I:7).

▶ Transportation expenses related to charitable activities may be deductible as a charitable contribution (subject to the limitations on the deductibility of charitable contributions discussed in Chapter I:7).

▶ Transportation expenses incurred in going between the taxpayer's residence and a temporary work location outside the metropolitan area are deductible.[18] Further, assuming a taxpayer has at least one regular work location (such as his primary office location), transportation expenses are deductible in going between the taxpayer's residence and a temporary work location, regardless of the distance.[19] Thus, a CPA who is employed by a CPA firm and who maintains a regular work location (e.g., an office is provided at the CPA firm's work location) may deduct transportation expenses for trips from home to clients in the metropolitan area. Unreimbursed transportation costs for an employee are deductible *from* AGI as unreimbursed employee expenses that are subject to the 2% nondeductible floor. Transportation expenses for a self-employed individual are deductible *for* AGI.

EXAMPLE I:9-17 ▶ As shown in Figure I:9-1, Dick has two jobs that are 10 miles apart. Dick lives 5 miles from the first job site and 8 miles from the second job site. If Dick drives directly from Job 1 to Job 2, he may deduct the automobile costs associated with the 10-mile trip. If he goes home from the first job before driving to the second job, the deduction is still limited to 10 miles, even though he actually travels 13 miles. ◀

EXAMPLE I:9-18 ▶ Diana owns a duplex, which she rents to tenants. She periodically drives from her place of business to this income-producing property to collect the rents and to inspect the property. The transportation expenses are deductible *for* AGI as an expense related to the production of rental income under Sec. 212. ◀

---

[17] IRS, *Publication No. 463* (Travel, Entertainment, Gift, and Car Expenses), 2008.

[18] Rev. Rul. 99-7, 1999-1 C.B. 361.

[19] Ibid.

FIGURE I:9-1 ▶ ILLUSTRATION FOR EXAMPLE I:9-17

EXAMPLE I:9-19 ▶ Donna, an accountant who is employed by a CPA firm, travels from her home to an audit client located in the local metropolitan area. The firm maintains an office for Donna at their business location. She is not reimbursed for her transportation costs. The transportation costs are deductible *from* AGI as unreimbursed employee expenses that are subject to the 2% nondeductible floor. If Donna were instead a self-employed CPA operating a business from her home, her transportation expenses would be deductible *for* AGI. ◀

TREATMENT OF AUTOMOBILE EXPENSES

An employee or self-employed person may use either of two methods to deduct allowable automobile expenses. First, actual automobile expenses, including gas, oil, repairs, depreciation, interest, property taxes, license fees, and insurance are deductible based on the percentage of business miles to total miles. Detailed records to support the expenses are necessary in order to properly claim the deduction. To help reduce the burden of detailed recordkeeping, a second method, the standard mileage rate method, is available to taxpayers.

The standard mileage rate method permits a deduction based on a mileage rate of 50 cents per mile for the year 2010.[20] Parking and tolls for business purposes are allowed as an addition to this deduction as well as interest expense on an automobile loan and personal property taxes on the automobile. The following restrictions apply when the standard mileage rate is used:

▶ The standard mileage rate method cannot be used if two or more automobiles are used simultaneously for business purposes.

ADDITIONAL COMMENT

It should be remembered that in many cases the taxpayer can choose between the automatic mileage method and calculating the actual costs of operating the car. Although the automatic mileage method has the advantage of convenience, a calculation of the actual costs might produce a larger deduction.

▶ If a taxpayer changes from the standard mileage rate method rate in one year to the actual expense method in a later year, the basis of the used automobile must be reduced by 23 cents per mile for 2010, 21 cents per mile for 2008 and 2009, 19 cents per mile for 2007, 17 cents per mile for 2005 and 2006, and 16 cents per mile for 2003 and 2004, for any year or years in which the standard mileage rate method was used. The modified accelerated cost-recovery system (MACRS) rules (discussed in Chapter I:10) cannot be used for computing depreciation in the year of the change and for the remaining useful life of the automobile. In such case, only the straight-line method under the alternative depreciation system (ADS) may be used (see Chapter I:10).

▶ A change to the standard mileage rate method is not allowed for an automobile that was previously depreciated under the MACRS rules or where an election was made under Sec. 179 to expense part or all of the automobile's cost in the year of acquisition. (See Chapter I:10 for a discussion of the Sec. 179 election.)

▶ The actual expense method is based on the ratio of business or employment-related miles to total miles. (See Chapter I:10 for a discussion of specific restrictions on the computation of depreciation where mixed business- and personal-use automobiles are acquired.)

---

[20] Rev. Proc. 2009-54. For the taxable year 2009, the standard mileage rate was 55 cents per mile.

STOP & THINK

Question: Assume a taxpayer uses his car (original cost, $20,000) in his business, drives a total of 25,000 miles per year, and can substantiate 80% of the mileage as business use. In general, will the taxpayer benefit more from the standard mileage method of deducting automobile expenses or from the actual expenses method?

Solution: In general, the actual expenses method will yield a higher deduction. The AAA (American Automobile Association) estimates that it costs approximately $0.60 per mile or more (depending on the size of the car) to operate a car in the United States in 2010. Therefore, the actual cost of operating the automobile would be approximately $15,000 (25,000 miles × $0.60). The deductible amount for tax purposes would be 80% of $15,000, or $12,000 for the actual expense method. Compare this amount with the standard mileage amount of $10,000 (25,000 miles × 80% business usage × .50/mile) and the actual expenses method yields a higher deduction. Of course, each individual situation is different and the actual results can vary based on circumstances, such as the amount of repairs, depreciation, and so on.

EXAMPLE I:9-20 ▶

Danielle owns two automobiles that are used at the same time in her small unincorporated business. One automobile is driven by an employee of the business, and Danielle drives the other vehicle for business use. Danielle cannot use the standard mileage rate method for either automobile because both cars are used in the business simultaneously. ◀

EXAMPLE I:9-21 ▶

Doug acquired an automobile for use in his unincorporated business in 2007 and used the standard mileage rate method in 2007–2009. If the actual expense method is used for 2009 and later years, the automobile's adjusted basis (for depreciation purposes) must be reduced by 19 cents per mile for 2007 business usage, and 21 cents for 2008 and 2009. Thus, if the automobile originally cost $20,000 in 2007 and was used 10,000 miles for business purposes during the initial year and 15,000 miles each in 2008 and 2009, the adjusted basis for computing depreciation in 2010 is reduced to $11,800 {$20,000 − [(0.19 × 10,000) + (0.21 × 15,000) + (0.21 × 15,000)]}. The remaining $11,800 basis must be depreciated using straight-line depreciation over the automobile's estimated useful life if the actual expense method is used. ◀

EXAMPLE I:9-22 ▶

HISTORICAL NOTE

Congress enacted a "contemporaneous" records test in 1984 for substantiating expenses for automobiles and certain other activities. Public outcry caused Congress to repeal this requirement in 1985. Now the business use of an automobile can be substantiated either by keeping adequate records or by sufficient corroborating evidence, oral or written.

Edith uses her automobile 50% of the time for business and employment-related use and 50% for personal use. These percentages are substantiated by records that document the total usage for the automobile. During 2010, Edith drives 3,000 miles per month or a total of 36,000 miles for the year. If the standard mileage rate method is used, she can deduct $9,000 [(0.50 × 36,000 miles) × 50%] for the business and employment-related use. Additionally, Edith may deduct any business-related parking fees and tolls. ◀

REIMBURSEMENT OF AUTOMOBILE EXPENSES

An employee is entitled to deduct actual automobile expenses (or amounts derived under the standard mileage rate method if applicable) in excess of reimbursed amounts received from the employer. The computation is made on Form 2106 (Employee Business Expenses) and is reported on Schedule A of Form 1040.

EXAMPLE I:9-23 ▶

ADDITIONAL COMMENT

The kind of written record that could corroborate the business use of an automobile would include account books, diaries, logs, trip sheets, expense reports, or written statements from witnesses.

Elizabeth, who makes an adequate accounting to her employer, receives a $6,000 (20,000 miles at 30 cents per mile) reimbursement in 2010 for employment-related business miles. She incurs the following expenses related to both business and personal use:

Gas and oil	$ 4,500
Repairs and maintenance	2,700
Depreciation	3,000
Insurance	1,900
Total	$12,100

Elizabeth also spent $100 on parking fees and tolls that were all related to business. Elizabeth drives a total of 32,000 miles during the year. Thus, she uses her car 62.5% (20,000 miles ÷ 32,000 miles) for business use. After subtracting the employer's $6,000 reimbursement and adding the parking fees and tolls, Elizabeth may deduct $1,663 [($12,100 × 0.625) + $100 − $6,000] as a miscellaneous itemized deduction (subject to the 2% nondeductible floor) in 2010. Alternatively, if 2010 is the first year she used the car in her business, she could have claimed a deduction using the standard mileage rate method. In this case, before the reim-

bursement, the $7,663 ($7,563 + $100) of actual expenses is less than the $10,100 ($10,000 + $100) permitted under the standard mileage rate method [(32,000 miles × 62.5% × $0.50) + $100 business-related fees and tolls]. ◄

ENTERTAINMENT EXPENSES

Determine the proper deductible amount for entertainment expenses under the 50% disallowance rule

Entertainment of business customers and clients is a routine and, in many cases, an essential practice in business. Because entertainment expenses are considered ordinary and necessary practices of a business, they are deductible under either Sec. 162 or Sec. 212. However, the nature of entertainment expenses lend themselves to abuse by taxpayers. There certainly is an element of personal pleasure in taking a client or customer to a hockey game or a Philharmonic orchestra performance and allowing taxpayers to deduct such expenses creates serious enforcement problems for the IRS.

For the reasons above, Congress enacted Sec. 274, which is strictly a disallowance section and contains classification rules, restrictive tests, and specific recordkeeping requirements. To deduct entertainment expenses, taxpayers must first show that the expenditure qualifies for a deduction under Sec. 162 (trade or business expense) or Sec. 212 (investment-type expense). Then the various requirements of Sec. 274 must be adhered to in order for an entertainment expense to be deductible. Over the years, Congress has continued to tighten the rules for the deductibility of entertainment expenses.

50% DISALLOWANCE FOR MEAL AND ENTERTAINMENT EXPENSES

Section 274(n) provides that any expense incurred for either business meals or entertainment must be reduced by 50%.[21] Business meals may be deductible either as travel expenses or as entertainment, depending on the nature of the expenditure. In either case, the 50% limit applies to the cost of food and beverages including tips and taxes but is not applicable to transportation expenses incurred going to and from a business meal. Further, any portion of a business meal that is considered lavish or extravagant is disallowed.[22] In such a situation, the 50% reduction rule is applied to the allowable portion of the business meal.

EXAMPLE I:9-24 ► Krishna, a self-employed individual, pays $80 for a business meal plus $4 sales tax and a $16 tip. The total cost of the meal is $100. If $40 of the meal is considered lavish or extravagant, Krishna could deduct $30 ($60 × 0.50). ◄

If an employee incurs entertainment or business meal expenses that are fully reimbursed by the employer, it is the employer rather than the employee who is limited to a deduction for 50% of the expenses. Assuming the reimbursement is made pursuant to an accountable plan (see discussion later in this chapter), the employee would not include the reimbursement in income and would not be allowed a deduction.

EXAMPLE I:9-25 ► Gordon incurs employment-related entertainment expenses of $1,000 and is fully reimbursed by his employer pursuant to an accountable plan. The employer may deduct $500 [$1,000 − ($1,000 × 0.50)] of entertainment expenses. Gordon would not include the $1,000 reimbursement in gross income and would not be allowed to deduct the $1,000 as a deduction. Thus, there is no overall tax effect to Gordon. ◄

ADDITIONAL COMMENT

Entertainment expenses are not considered "directly related" if there are substantial distractions. Therefore, if a meeting takes place at a sporting event, theater, or night club, the entertainment cannot be "directly related." This type of entertainment could qualify as an "associated with" expense. An example of a "directly related" expense would be the costs related to a hospitality room at a convention.

Certain meals are not subject to the 50% disallowance, including meals that are treated as compensation to employees, employee picnics or other social gatherings primarily for the benefit of employees, or infrequent meals that would qualify as a de minimus fringe benefit.

CLASSIFICATION OF EXPENSES

If an individual is engaged in a trade or business (but not as an employee), allowable entertainment expenses are deductible *for* AGI. Employees, however, may deduct entertainment expenses only as a miscellaneous itemized deduction (subject to the 2% nondeductible

---

[21] For pre-1994 tax years, the disallowance was 20%. [22] Sec. 274(k).

floor) unless the expenses are reimbursed. The tax rules for reimbursements of employee business expenses are discussed more fully later in this chapter.

EXAMPLE I:9-26 ▶ Helen is a self-employed attorney who entertains clients and prospective clients. To the extent that these expenditures meet the Sec. 274 requirements, they are deductible by Helen as a *for AGI* expense on Schedule C of Form 1040 because Helen is engaged in a trade or business activity. The entertainment expenses are subject to the 50% limit but are not subject to the 2% nondeductible floor because the entertainment is deductible when determining AGI as a trade or business expense. ◀

CRITERIA FOR DEDUCTION. To be deductible as an entertainment expense, an expenditure must be either **directly related** to the active conduct of a trade or business or **associated with** the active conduct of a trade or business. Different restrictions apply to each of these categories. The Regulations under Sec. 274 provide the substantive rules for the two types of entertainment expenses.

"Directly Related" Expenses. To meet the requirements for a "directly related" **entertainment expense**, some business benefit must be expected from the business conducted other than goodwill and the expense must be incurred in a clear business setting (i.e., where there are no substantial distractions). In other words, business in anticipation of a business benefit must actually be conducted during the entertainment period.

"Associated With" Expenses. To qualify an expense as an "associated with" entertainment expenditure, the taxpayer must show a clear business purpose, such as obtaining new business or encouraging the continuation of an existing business relationship. An added restriction is placed on "associated with" entertainment in that the entertainment must directly precede or follow a bona fide business discussion. This means that the entertainment generally must occur on the same day that business is discussed.

EXAMPLE I:9-27 ▶ Holly is a lawyer who hosts a birthday party in her home. Most of the guests are law partners or clients. No formal business discussions are conducted either before or immediately following the party. The expenditures for the birthday party are not deductible because they do not meet either the "directly related" or "associated with" tests. ◀

Substantiation Requirements. In addition to both the directly related and associated with requirements, Sec. 274 imposes stringent substantiation requirements for entertainment expenses. In order to deduct entertainment expenses, taxpayers are required to substantiate each expenditure for which a deduction is claimed. Lack of documentation alone will cause the disallowance of a deduction.

BUSINESS MEALS

Business meals related to travel or entertainment activities are subject to the same business-connection requirements as other types of entertainment expenses. Thus, an entertainment deduction is allowed only if the meal meets the "directly related" or "associated with" tests previously discussed. In addition, the expense must not be lavish or extravagant under the circumstances, and the taxpayer (or an employee of the taxpayer) must generally be present when the food or beverages are furnished. These requirements do not apply to a business meal associated with travel where the taxpayer claims a deduction only for his or her own expenses.

EXAMPLE I:9-28 ▶ Hank is a salesman for a manufacturing supply company. Hank meets Harold, a purchasing agent who is an important customer, for lunch during a normal business day. Business is actually conducted during the lunch, and the lunch expenses are not lavish or extravagant under the circumstances. Hank is fully reimbursed by his employer for the $30 lunch expenses after an adequate accounting of the expenses is submitted. The business meal qualifies as "directly related" entertainment because the entertainment involved the actual conduct of business where some business benefit is reasonably expected and a business discussion was conducted during the meal. Hank's employer may deduct $15 ($30 × 0.50) of entertainment expenses. ◀

WHAT WOULD YOU DO IN THIS SITUATION?

You have recently acquired a new individual tax client, Joe Windsack, who is a manufacturer's representative for a local tool and die company. You have been engaged by Windsack to prepare his individual income tax return for the current year. Before the current tax year is over, you are at a party where Windsack is also a guest. You overhear Windsack bragging to a group of people that he substantially reduces his income tax liability by overstating meal and entertainment expenses. He indicated that he overstates the deductions in several ways: (1) when he goes out to lunch or dinner that is personal in nature, such as with his family, he always uses a credit card and fictitiously writes the name

of a client or prospective client on the charge card receipt, (2) when he goes out to lunch with several colleagues from his office (not business related), he charges the entire amount on his credit card (for everyone at the table), collects the cash from his colleagues for the cost of their meals, and then writes the entire amount off as a business-related meal, and (3) whenever he goes to any entertainment event, such as a ballgame, he always says that he took a client to the game with him and deducts the cost of the ticket as a business expense. When Windsack brings his tax information to you a couple of months later and you see a substantial amount of meal and entertainment expenses, what should you do?

EXAMPLE I:9-29 ▶ Assume the same facts as in Example I:9-28, except that the purchasing agent is a prospective customer and no business is actually discussed either during, directly preceding, or immediately following the meal. Thus, no deduction is allowed because no business is discussed either before, during, or after the meal. ◀

The Regulations provide that the surroundings in which food or beverages are furnished must be in an atmosphere where there are no substantial distractions to the discussion (e.g., a floor show).[23]

EXAMPLE I:9-30 ▶ Harry is a salesman who takes a customer to a local nightclub to watch a floor show and to have a few drinks. No business is discussed either before, during, or after the entertainment. The expenses for the beverages and floor show are not deductible because neither of the business meal requirements are met (i.e., the floor show produced substantial distractions, and no business was discussed). Even if business was actually discussed, no deduction would be allowed because there were substantial distractions. ◀

ENTERTAINMENT FACILITIES AND CLUB DUES

KEY POINT

Subject to a very few exceptions, no deduction is permitted for costs related to yachts, swimming pools, fishing camps, tennis courts, bowling alleys, vacation resorts, etc. This highly visible type of entertainment contributed to the public perception that the tax system was unfair.

No deduction is permitted for costs (e.g., depreciation, maintenance, repairs, and so on) related to the maintenance of facilities that are used for entertainment, amusement, or recreation. Facilities include yachts, hunting lodges, beach cottages, and so on.

No deduction is permitted for any type of club dues (including business, social, athletic, luncheon, and sporting clubs, as well as airline and hotel clubs).[24] Professional, civic and public service organizations (e.g., business leagues, trade associations, chambers of commerce, boards of trade, and real estate boards) are generally not subject to the dues disallowance rules. Initiation fees that are paid only upon joining a club are treated as nondeductible capital expenditures. While club dues are not deductible, other business expenses (e.g., business meals) are deductible if the general requirements for entertainment deductions are met.

EXAMPLE I:9-31 ▶ Heidi is a self-employed CPA who entertains clients at her country club. Her club expenses include the following:

Annual dues	$ 4,000
Meal and entertainment charges related to business use	3,000
Personal-use meal charges	2,500
Initiation fee	10,000
Total expenses	$19,500

---

[23] Reg. Sec. 1.274-2(f)(2)(i)(b).   [24] Sec. 274(a)(3).

The only expense that is deductible is 50% of the specific business charges relating to the meals and entertainment. Thus, Heidi may deduct $1,500 ($3,000 × 0.50) *for* AGI as a business expense because she is a self-employed CPA. ◄

BUSINESS GIFTS

Business gifts are subject to an annual ceiling amount of $25 per donee.[25] Amounts in excess of the $25 limit per donee are disallowed. The following rules and exceptions apply to determine the business gift deduction:

▶ Multiple gifts to each donee are aggregated for purposes of applying the $25 per donee annual limitation. Husbands and wives and other family members are treated as a single donee.

▶ Husbands and wives who make gifts to a particular donee are treated as a single taxpayer and are subject to a single $25 limit.

▶ Incidental costs such as gift wrapping, mailing, and delivery of gifts and certain imprinted gift items costing $4 or less are excluded.

▶ Employee achievement awards made for length of service or safety that are under $400 per individual are excluded.[26]

▶ A gift from an employee to his or her supervisor does not qualify as a business gift because such gifts are personal rather than business related and are, therefore, not deductible.

EXAMPLE I:9-32 ▶

REAL-WORLD EXAMPLE

A taxpayer who had deducted the full cost of two wedding gifts, both of which were in excess of $25 apiece, was able to deduct only $25 for each gift. *Jack R. Howard,* 1981 PH T.C. Memo ¶81,250, 41 TCM 1554.

Jack, an employee, makes the following gifts during the year, none of which are reimbursed by his employer:

Jack's immediate supervisor	$20
Jack's secretary	15
Jeff (a customer of Jack's)	24
Jeff's wife (a noncustomer)	26
Gift-wrapping for the gift to Jeff	4
Total	$89

Jack's total deduction for business gifts is $44 ($15 + $25 + $4) and is classified as a miscellaneous itemized deduction subject to the 2% nondeductible floor as an employee business expense. The $20 gift to Jack's immediate supervisor is not deductible. The gifts of $24 and $26 to Jeff and Jeff's wife must be aggregated and are limited to $25. The gift-wrapping charge is fully deductible because it is an incidental cost. ◄

LIMITATIONS ON ENTERTAINMENT TICKETS

In addition to the general 50% meals and entertainment limitation, the cost of a ticket for any entertainment activity or facility is limited to the ticket's face value. Thus, the 50% limit applies to the face value of the ticket. Further restrictions are placed on the rental of skyboxes that are leased for more than one event.[27]

EXAMPLE I:9-33 ▶

Able Corporation acquires four tickets to a football game for $500 that are used for entertaining customers. The face amount of the four tickets is only $100 in total. Able's deduction for entertainment is initially limited to the $100 face value of the tickets. The deductible amount is $50 ($100 × 0.50) after applying the 50% limit on entertainment expenses. ◄

---

[25] Sec. 274(b)(1).
[26] Sec. 274(j). The total limit including both qualified and nonqualified plan awards is $1,600 per individual (see Chapter I:4).
[27] Sec. 274(l)(2). The cost of a skybox is disallowed to the extent that it exceeds the cost of the highest-priced nonluxury box seat tickets multiplied

by the number of seats in the skybox (e.g., if a skybox contains 30 seats and the cost of the highest-priced nonluxury box seat for a particular event is $40, the deduction for the skybox is limited to $1,200 ($40 × 30). The deduction would be also reduced by the 50% limitation applicable to entertainment expenses.

REIMBURSED EMPLOYEE BUSINESS EXPENSES

The tax treatment of reimbursements received by an employee from his employer for employment-related expenses depends upon whether the reimbursement is made pursuant to an **accountable** or **nonaccountable** plan. An accountable plan is a reimbursement arrangement that meets both of the following two tests.[28]

1. Substantiation—the employee must make an adequate accounting of expenses to his employer, which means that each business expense must be substantiated (an expense report, for example); and
2. Return of excess reimbursement—within a reasonable period of time, the employee is required to return to the employer any portion of the reimbursement in excess of the substantiated expenses.

If both of these tests are not met, amounts paid to an employee generally are treated as paid under a nonaccountable plan. However, a special rule in Reg. Sec. 1.62-2(c) provides that if an employee does not return the excess reimbursement within a reasonable time period, only the portion of the reimbursement in excess of substantiated expenses is considered as being paid under a nonaccountable plan. The portion of the reimbursement for substantiated expenses is considered as being paid under an accountable plan.

ACCOUNTABLE PLAN. Under an accountable plan, reimbursements are included in gross income and expenses are deductible *for* AGI. Therefore, a taxpayer's AGI will not increase if employee business expenses are reimbursed under an accountable plan. Because reimbursements and expenses offset each other, when expenses are reimbursed under an accountable plan, taxpayers do not report the reimbursement or the expenses on their tax return. However, if an excess reimbursement is not returned to the employer, the excess reimbursement is included in the employee's gross income.[29]

EXAMPLE I:9-34 ▶ Antoine is an employee of the Bluechip Corporation, which maintains an accountable plan for purposes of reimbursing employee expenses. During the current year, Antoine went on a business trip and incurred $1,500 of expenses as follows: airfare, $800; lodging, $450; meals, $200; and tips, $50. Bluechip reimbursed him $1,500. Technically speaking, Antoine does have gross income of $1,500 and a deduction for AGI of $1,500. But, because the reimbursement is pursuant to an accountable plan, Antoine will not report the $1,500 reimbursement in his gross income and will not deduct any of the business expenses on his tax return. ◀

EXAMPLE I:9-35 ▶ Assume the same facts as in Example I:9-34 except that Bluechip advanced Antoine $1,800, rather than $1,500, for his business trip and his expenses were the same as above. If Antoine returned the excess $300 to Bluechip within a reasonable period of time, the result would be the same as in Example I:9-34. However, if Antoine did not return the excess reimbursement (even though he is required to under the terms of the plan), Antoine must include the $300 in his gross income. The portion of the $1,800 reimbursement that pertains to the substantiated expenses, $1,500, is treated as being paid under an accountable plan. Thus, $1,500 of the reimbursement and the $1,500 of substantiated expenses are netted together and not reported. However, the excess $300 reimbursement is treated as being paid under a nonaccountable plan and, therefore, includible in Antoine's gross income. ◀

If an employee receives a reimbursement that is not as much as his expenses, a proration is required.

---

[28] Reg. Sec. 1.62-2(c).
[29] In Rev. Rul. 2006-56, 2006-2 C.B. 874, the IRS warned taxpayers that reimbursements from accountable plans must be properly substantiated and excess amounts must be returned to the employer. An accountable plan that reaches the level of a "pattern of abuse" will be reclassified as a nonaccountable plan.

EXAMPLE I:9-36 ▶ Fred, an employee, incurs employment-related expenses of $4,500 consisting of $1,200 business meals, $1,800 local transportation, and $1,500 entertainment of customers. He is only reimbursed $3,000 from his employer. Since the reimbursement is less than the amount of expenses, Fred must prorate the expenses as follows:

Expense	Total Amount	Reimbursed Expense[a]	Unreimbursed Expense
Business meals	$1,200	$ 800	$ 400
Local transportation	1,800	1,200	600
Entertainment	1,500	1,000	500
Total	$4,500	$3,000	$1,500

The reimbursed expenses of $3,000 are not reported by Fred and the $3,000 reimbursement is not reportable as income. The $1,500 of unreimbursed expenses are deductible *from* AGI (subject to 2% of AGI) as follows:

Business meals ($400 × 50%)	$ 200
Local transportation	600
Entertainment ($500 × 50%)	250
	$1,050

[a]Reimbursements are allocated to each expense category on a prorata basis. For example, the $800 for business meals is computed, $\frac{\$1,200}{\$4,500} \times \$3,000$. ◀

KEY POINT

Why does the government require reimbursements from nonaccountable plans to be included in the employee's gross income? Because these types of plans are often referred to as "expense accounts paid to employees as additional compensation."

NONACCOUNTABLE PLAN. Under a nonaccountable plan, reimbursements are included in the employee's gross income and the expenses are deductible by the employee as miscellaneous itemized deductions, subject to the 2% of AGI floor and the 50% disallowance for meals and entertainment expenses.

EXAMPLE I:9-37 ▶ Use the same facts as in Example I:9-34 except that Bluechip does not require its employees to submit an accounting of expenses incurred. Bluechip's plan is a nonaccountable plan. Antoine must include the $1,500 in his gross income and may deduct the expenses as miscellaneous itemized deductions, subject to the 2% of AGI floor, in the amount of $1,400 [$800 + 450 + (200 × 50%) + 50]. ◀

PER DIEM ALLOWANCES FOR MEALS AND LODGING. The IRS permits employers and employees to use optional "per diem allowances" for meals and lodging expenses in lieu of actual expenses. The use of per diem allowances is intended to simplify the burden of keeping detailed records for taxpayers who incur significant travel expenses. Special tables have been issued by the IRS that provide fixed per diem amounts for lodging as well as meals and incidental expenses (M&IE). The per diem allowances vary in amount depending on the city in which the travel took place. The tables list many cities in the United States as well as many cities in foreign countries. Thus, a taxpayer must only substantiate the time, place, and business purpose of the trip and then is permitted to use the per diem allowances. The per diem system is permitted only for payments under an accountable plan, the expenses must be reasonably expected to be incurred, and the amount of expenses should be in reasonable proximity to the expected actual expense amount.[30] A full discussion of this topic is outside the scope of this textbook.

EXAMPLE I:9-38 ▶ Peyton Boying is an employee of UT, Inc. UT maintains an accountable plan for reimbursing employees for their business expenses. Peyton travels extensively in the United States for business purposes. Instead of requiring Peyton to keep actual records of his travel expenses, UT reimburses Peyton the per diem amounts as allowed by the IRS. Assuming Peyton traveled exclusively in low-cost localities (see footnote below) and was away from home for 100 days, UT could reimburse Peyton in the amount of $16,300 (100 days × $163) without the necessity

---

[30] The IRS tables for per diem allowances paid on or after October 1, 2009, may be found in Rev. Proc. 2009-47 I.R.B. 2009-42 (September 30, 2009) or IRS Publication 1542, which is periodically updated. The rate for travel on or after October 1, 2009 for high-cost localities (specifically identified by the

IRS) is $256 per day (including $58 for M&IE); low-cost localities are $158 per day (including $45 for M&IE). Further, self-employed individuals who are not reimbursed for their travel expenses may use the M&IE rate, but must substantiate lodging with actual receipts.

of Peyton keeping detailed records of his actual travel expenses. The amount that Peyton actually spent is irrelevant as the IRS will accept the per diem amounts.   ◄

Table I:9-2 summarizes the concepts relating to employee business expenses and reimbursements.

▼ **TABLE I:9-2**
Treatment of Employee Reimbursements

TYPE OF PLAN	TAX EFFECT
ACCOUNTABLE PLAN	
Reimbursement = Expense	No effect, amounts are netted and not reported on employee's return.
Reimbursement > Expense	Not permissible under plan, but should it occur, excess reimbursement is included in employee's gross income.
Reimbursement < Expense	Expenses are prorated to amount of reimbursement. Reimbursed expenses—no effect; unreimbursed expenses are deductible as miscellaneous itemized deductions subject to 2% of AGI "floor" or nondeductible amount.
NONACCOUNTABLE PLAN	
Reimbursements	Always included in employee's gross income.
Expenses	Deductible as miscellaneous itemized deductions subject to 2% of AGI "floor" or nondeductible amount.

Moving Expenses

ADDITIONAL COMMENT

In 2006, moving expenses deducted on tax returns totaled $3.2 billion.

Moving expenses are generally nondeductible personal expenditures. However, Sec. 217 allows a limited deduction for moving expenses for employees and self-employed people. The underlying rationale for this deduction is that such moves are similar to business expenditures because they are either employment-related or connected with a trade or business.

EXAMPLE I:9-39 ►

Ken retires from his job and moves from Tennessee to Arizona. His moving expenses are nondeductible personal expenditures because the move is not employment-related and he is not moving to look for a new job.   ◄

OBJECTIVE 3

Identify deductible moving expenses and determine the amount and year of deductibility

ADDITIONAL COMMENT

The time requirement test ensures that taxpayers cannot use temporary jobs as a pretext for deducting the cost of moving for personal reasons.

Two conditions must be met for a moving expense to be deductible:[31]

► *Distance requirement.* The new job location must be at least 50 miles farther from the taxpayer's old residence than the old residence was from the former place of employment. If an individual has no former place of employment, the new job must be at least 50 miles from the old residence.

► *Time requirement.* A new or transferred employee must be employed on a full-time basis at the new location for at least 39 weeks during the 12-month period immediately following the move. More stringent requirements must be met by self-employed people who either work as an employee at the new location or continue to be self-employed. Such individuals are subject to a 78-week minimum work period during the first two years following the move. At least 39 of the 78 weeks must be in the first 12-month period. A waiver of the time requirements is permitted for both employees and self-employed individuals if the taxpayer becomes disabled, dies, or is

---

[31] The requirements for deducting moving expenses are contained in Sec. 217 and the Treasury Regulations thereunder.

involuntarily terminated (other than for willful misconduct). Unemployed or retired individuals are generally not able to deduct moving expenses because they do not meet the 39- or 78-week test.

EXAMPLE I:9-40 ▶

Ellen is employed by the Able Company in Dallas, Texas. She lives 30 miles from her place of employment in Dallas. If Ellen accepts a new job in Houston, the new job location is 270 miles from her former residence in Dallas. The 50-mile distance requirement is satisfied because the distance from her old residence to her new job in Houston exceeds the distance from her old residence to her old job by 240 miles (270 − 30). In addition, to meet the time requirement, Ellen must be employed on a full-time basis in Houston for at least 39 weeks during the 12-month period immediately following the move. ◀

EXAMPLE I:9-41 ▶

ADDITIONAL COMMENT

The individual need not be employed at the location that he or she is leaving. For example, a graduating college student who has not been employed for the most recent four years could deduct moving costs if the distance requirement is satisfied and if he or she has been employed at the *new* location for the minimum time period.

Assume the same facts as in Example I:9-40, except that Ellen accepts a new job and moves to a new residence in a small town outside of Dallas. Her new job location is 55 miles from her former residence. The 50-mile distance requirement is not met because the distance from her old residence to her new job is 55 miles and the distance from her old residence to her old job is 30 miles; thus, the excess distance is only 25 miles. ◀

EXPENSE CLASSIFICATION

Moving expenses of an employee or a self-employed individual are deductible *for* AGI.[32] Thus, a taxpayer may receive a tax benefit from the deduction of moving expenses even if the standard deduction is used in lieu of itemizing deductions.

DEFINITION OF MOVING EXPENSES

DIRECT MOVING EXPENSES. Only direct moving expenses are deductible. These expenses are deductible without limit as long as they are reasonable in amount and include:

▶ The cost of moving household goods and personal effects from the former residence to the new residence (e.g., moving van).

KEY POINT

The standard mileage rate for purposes of the moving expense deduction is only 16.5 cents per mile, compared to the 2010 standard business mileage rate of 50 cents per mile.

▶ The cost of traveling (including lodging but excluding meals) from the former residence to the new residence. If the trip is by personal automobile, a deduction of 16.5 cents per mile (or actual expenses) is allowed for each automobile that is driven in 2010 (24 cents per mile in 2009).

The expenses of moving household goods and personal effects do not include storage charges in excess of 30 days, penalties for breaking leases, mortgage penalties, expenses of refitting drapes, or losses on deposits and club memberships.[33]

EXAMPLE I:9-42 ▶

Gail, a resident of California and a college student in that state, graduates from college and accepts a new position with an accounting firm in Atlanta. Thus, Gail is an employee of the Atlanta firm. Because the move meets the distance requirement (i.e., more than 50 miles), Gail qualifies for the deduction if she also meets the 39-week time requirement. Gail incurs the following expenses pursuant to the move: moving van, $1,200; lodging en route, $400; automobile expenses, $429 (2,600 miles × $0.165 cents per mile); and tolls and parking, $25. Assuming these expenses are reasonable, they qualify as direct moving expenses and are deductible without limitation. The cost of any meals incurred by Gail en route is not deductible. ◀

Otherwise allowable expenses of any individual other than the taxpayer are taken into account only if the individual has both the former residence and the new residence as his principal place of abode and is a member of the taxpayer's household.

EXAMPLE I:9-43 ▶

Assume the same facts as in Example I:9-42 except that Gail's son Paul is a member of her household. Additional automobile expenses (including tolls and parking) of $275 are incurred during the move because Paul owns an automobile which is driven to the new location. The $275 of additional automobile expenses are deductible as moving expenses because Paul is a member of Gail's household and his principal place of abode includes both the former and the new residences. ◀

---

[32] Sec. 62(a)(15). For years before 1994 moving expenses were deductible *from* AGI as an itemized deduction (not subject to the 2% nondeductible floor).

[33] Reg. Sec. 1.217-2(b)(3). In-transit storage charges for up to 30 consecutive days are allowable moving expenses.

HISTORICAL NOTE

Indirect moving expenses are not deductible after December 31, 1993. In the Revenue Reconciliation Act of 1993, Congress eliminated the deduction for costs associated with pre-move househunting trips, temporary quarters, and selling the old residence. Congress felt that a deduction was not justified for expenses that were not directly related to the move.

NONDEDUCTIBLE INDIRECT MOVING EXPENSES. In addition to the disallowed moving expenses previously discussed (e.g., meals en route, storage charges, etc.), the following indirect or moving-related expense items are not deductible:

▶ Househunting trips including meals, lodging, and transportation

▶ Temporary living expenses at the new job location

▶ Qualified expenses related to a sale, purchase, or lease of a residence (e.g., attorney's fees, points, or payments to a lessor to cancel a lease)

TREATMENT OF EMPLOYER REIMBURSEMENTS

Moving expense reimbursements made by an employer, either paid directly or through reimbursement, are excluded from the employee's gross income as a qualified fringe benefit under Sec. 132 to the extent that the expenses meet the requirements for deductibility (i.e., the reimbursement is for moving expenses that are otherwise deductible under Sec. 217). Moving expense reimbursements must be included in gross income if the employee actually deducted the expenses in a prior tax year or if the expenses are otherwise not deductible under Sec. 217.[34]

EXAMPLE I:9-44 ▶

In 2010, Ralph incurs $2,400 of moving expenses related to moving household effects and traveling to his new residence. He also incurs $2,600 of nondeductible moving-related expenses (e.g., househunting trips and temporary living expenses). Ralph receives a $5,000 reimbursement from his employer. Of the total reimbursement, $2,400 is excluded from gross income as a Sec. 132 fringe benefit. However, the $2,600 reimbursement for nondeductible moving-related expenses is included in Ralph's gross income under Sec. 82. None of the $2,400 of moving expenses may be deducted by Ralph because they were reimbursed by his employer and were not included in Ralph's gross income. ◀

EDUCATION EXPENSES

OBJECTIVE 4

Describe the requirements for deducting education expenses

Generally, education expenses are considered personal expenses and, therefore, are not deductible despite the obvious benefits that accrue to society from the pursuit of such activities. However, education expenses that are necessary in the pursuit of an employment-related or trade or business activity are deductible. It would be inequitable if such educational expenditures were not deductible because they are incurred to produce income from employment or business activities. The education expenses discussed in this chapter pertain to expenses that are related to an individual's trade or business, such as a job in the case of an employee or the business of a self-employed individual. However, there are a number of other provisions in the tax law that provide favorable tax advantages for education expenses. Most of these rules are covered elsewhere in this textbook; however, the major tax provisions dealing with education are summarized below.

▶ Tax credits—two important provisions benefiting education are the HOPE scholarship credit and the lifetime learning credit. Both of these items are credits and are available for the taxpayer and his dependents and are discussed in Chapter I:14.

▶ Exclusion for scholarships—scholarships received by students are generally excludable from gross income under Sec. 117. See the discussion of scholarships in Chapter I:4.

▶ Educational assistance for employees—if an employer maintains an educational assistance plan, amounts received by the employee for tuition and other expenses are excludable from the employee's gross income under Sec. 127. This exclusion is also discussed in Chapter I:4.

▶ Student loan interest—a *for* AGI deduction is permitted for certain student loan interest under Sec. 221. (See Chapter I:6 for a further discussion of this topic.)

ADDITIONAL COMMENT

Attendance at a convention or professional meeting is one of the most common deductible education expenses. Almost every profession or occupation has its own society or association. Often these organizations sponsor local, regional, or national meetings. Training sessions or other types of educational activities are normally included on the program.

[34] Sec. 82 and Sec. 132(g).

▶ Deduction for higher education expenses—for tax years 2004–2010, taxpayers may deduct up to $4,000 *for* AGI for tuition and related expenses under Sec. 222.[35] This deduction, as is the case for the tax credits and the student loan interest, is subject to a phase-out based on AGI. If a taxpayer's AGI does not exceed $65,000 ($130,000 on a joint return), the taxpayer may deduct up to $4,000. However, taxpayer's with AGI exceeding $65,000 but not exceeding $80,000 may deduct up to $2,000 in qualified expenses. No deduction is permitted for taxpayers with AGI in excess of $80,000 ($160,000 on a joint return). Further, taxpayers are not permitted to claim this deduction and also claim one of the tax credits above using the same expenses.

▶ Qualified state tuition programs—a very popular program for higher income taxpayers is the use of so-called Section 529 plans. These plans allow taxpayers to invest funds to be used for education and the income earned on such funds is not subject to tax. When amounts are withdrawn from the plan, the amounts are also not taxable if used for qualified education expenses. These plans are discussed in Chapter I:4.

▶ Coverdell Education IRA—these special IRAs are discussed later in this chapter and enable a taxpayer to invest up to $2,000 per year in a tax-deferred IRA.

CLASSIFICATION OF EDUCATION EXPENSES

Depending on the nature of the education-related activity, educational expenses may be either personal and nondeductible, deductible *for* AGI, deductible *from* AGI (as a miscellaneous itemized deduction), or reimbursed by an employer and excluded from gross income. Table I:9-3 illustrates the tax consequences that are accorded to various types of education expenses depending on the facts and circumstances and the type of expenditure for each case.

The discussion below focuses on the deductibility of education expenses that are related to a taxpayer's trade or business.

▼ **TABLE I:9-3**
Classification and Tax Treatment of Educational Expenses

Situation Facts	Classification and Tax Treatment
▶ Jeremy is a college student who is not classified as an employee and is pursuing a general course of study.	▶ The expenses are nondeductible personal expenditures regardless of whether Jeremy or his parents pay them.
▶ Irene is an employee who incurs certain employment-related educational expenses including travel, transportation, tuition, and books. Her expenses are not reimbursed by her employer.	▶ If the expenses meet the two general deduction requirements, the education expenses are deductible *from* AGI as a miscellaneous itemized deduction (subject to the 2% nondeductible floor).
▶ Jesse is an employee who receives educational assistance payments from his employer to reimburse him for certain educational expenses incurred in attending college at the undergraduate level.	▶ Educational assistance payments up to $5,250 per excluded from Jesse's gross income and are deductible by the employer as trade or business expenses if the requirements of Sec. 127 are met.[36]
▶ Jackie is a self-employed CPA who incurs education expenses including travel, transportation, books, registration fees, and so on to attend a continuing education conference.	▶ All of the education expenses are deductible *for* AGI as trade or business expenses.
▶ Jim is an employee who incurs education expenses for a continuing education course related to his employment, and the expenses are reimbursed by the employer.	▶ The reimbursement is deductible by the employer as a trade or business expense. There is no tax effect to the employee because the education expenses are offset by the reimbursement.

---

[35] This deduction was scheduled to expire after 2009. However, Congress extended this provision through December 31, 2010 in the Tax Extenders Act of 2009.

[36] The Sec. 127 exclusion is applicable for expenses paid by an employer for courses taken by employees. Qualified expenses include tuition, fees, and related expenses. Both undergraduate and graduate-level courses qualify for the exclusion.

GENERAL REQUIREMENTS FOR A DEDUCTION

TYPICAL MISCONCEPTION

Education costs include more than the cost of books, tuition, registration fees, and supplies. Transportation costs and travel costs are also included.

An employee generally may deduct education expenses if either of the following two requirements are met:[37]

▶ The expenditure is incurred to maintain or improve skills required by the individual in his or her employment, trade, or business; or

▶ The expenditure is incurred to meet requirements imposed by law or by the employer for retention of employment, rank, or compensation rate.

Even if one of the two requirements above are met, education expenses are not deductible if:

▶ The education is required to meet minimum educational requirements for qualification in the taxpayer's employment; or

▶ The education qualifies the taxpayer for a new trade or business (or employment activity).

ETHICAL POINT

A client asks advice from his CPA as to whether certain educational expenses are deductible. The CPA should inform the client that the advice reflects professional judgment based on an existing situation. The CPA should use cautionary language to the effect that the advice is based on facts as stated and authorities that are subject to change.

The deductibility of education expenses has been a frequent source of controversy and litigation because of the uncertainty in interpreting the above Regulations. The principal area of disagreement has been the interpretation of the term "qualifies the taxpayer for a new trade or business." If a taxpayer undertakes education and that education will *qualify* her for a new trade or business, then her expenses will not be deductible. For example, several courts have disallowed deductions to IRS agents and accountants for educational expenses incurred in obtaining a law degree, even though such training would be helpful in the taxpayer's employment.[38] The courts reasoned that the taxpayers were qualifying for a new profession (i.e., the practice of law). However, the IRS has ruled that a practicing dentist may deduct educational expenses in becoming an orthodontist under the theory that a dentist becoming an orthodontist is not entering a new trade or business.[39]

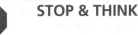 **STOP & THINK**

Question: The Regulations clearly provide that if the education "qualifies" a taxpayer for a new trade or business, the cost of such education is not deductible. If taken to the extreme, could the IRS argue that *any* course would qualify an individual for a new trade or business? For example, if a person took a basket weaving course, could not the IRS argue that the person is now qualified for the new trade or business of basket weaving? How can a taxpayer support his position that the education does not qualify him for a new trade or business in order to meet the deductibility requirements?

ADDITIONAL COMMENT

The same course could be deductible as a qualified educational expense or not depending on the particular situation of the student. For example, a CPA enrolled in a taxation course to update his or her tax knowledge could deduct the expense. On the other hand, a non-CPA taking the course as part of a series of courses meeting the requirements to sit for the CPA exam could not deduct the expense. The CPA has already met the minimum education requirements for the profession and the non-CPA has not.

Solution: This is a difficult question and many commentators have written that the Regulations are unfairly harsh toward taxpayers. The courts have required that the IRS be "reasonable" in its interpretations of qualification of a new trade or business. The best way for a taxpayer to support his position is to find a case where the facts are approximately the same as the taxpayer's and where the court has upheld the taxpayer's position in that case.

Generally, a taxpayer must be employed or self-employed to be eligible for an education expense deduction. However, some courts have permitted individuals to qualify if they are unemployed for a temporary period.[40] School teachers have generally qualified for an education expense deduction in situations where the public school system requires advanced education courses as a condition for retention of employment or renewal of a teaching certificate or where state law imposes similar requirements. However, college instructors who are working on a doctorate in a college where the Ph.D. is the minimum degree for holding a permanent position generally have not been permitted to deduct the expenditures made to obtain the degree.[41] The Tax Court recently allowed a taxpayer to deduct the cost of earning an M.B.A. because the education merely enhanced and maintained the skills he already had and did not qualify him for a new trade or business.[42]

[37] Reg. Sec. 1.162-5.

[38] *Jeffry L. Weiler,* 54 T.C. 398 (1970).

[39] Rev. Rul. 74-78, 1974-1 C.B. 44.

[40] *Robert J. Picknally,* 1977 PH T.C. Memo ¶77,321, 36 TCM 1292. The IRS has conceded that a deduction may be warranted in periods where the cessa-

tion of business activity was for periods of a year or less (Rev. Rul. 68-591, 1968-2 C.B. 73).

[41] *Kenneth C. Davis,* 65 T.C. 1014 (1976).

[42] *Daniel R. Allmeier, Jr.,* 90 TCM 197 (2005).

EXAMPLE I:9-45 ▶ Jane is a self-employed dentist who incurs education expenses attending a continuing education conference on new techniques in her field. Such expenditures are incurred to maintain or improve her skills as a practicing dentist (a trade or business activity). All of her educational expenses are deductible *for* AGI because Jane is currently engaged in a trade or business activity. ◀

EXAMPLE I:9-46 ▶ Juan is a business executive who incurs education expenses in the pursuit of an MBA degree in management. None of the expenses are reimbursed by Juan's employer. The expenses are deductible because they are incurred to maintain or improve Juan's skills as a manager and do not qualify Juan for a new trade or business. All of Juan's education expenses (e.g., travel, transportation, tuition, books, and word processing) are deductible *from* AGI as a miscellaneous itemized deduction (subject to the 2% nondeductible floor). ◀

EXAMPLE I:9-47 ▶ Janet is a high school teacher who is required by state law to complete a specified number of additional graduate courses to renew her provisional teaching certificate. None of the expenses are reimbursed by Janet's employer. The educational expenses are deductible *from* AGI as a miscellaneous itemized deduction (subject to the 2% nondeductible floor) because the expenditures are incurred to meet the requirements imposed by law to retain her job and do not qualify her for a new trade or business. ◀

EXAMPLE I:9-48 ▶ Jean is an accountant with a public accounting firm who incurs expenses in connection with taking the CPA examination (e.g., CPA review course fees, travel, and transportation). None of the expenses are reimbursed by Jean's employer. Even though the expenditures may improve her employment-related skills, they are not deductible because they are incurred to meet the minimum educational standards for qualification in Jean's accounting position.[43] ◀

EXAMPLE I:9-49 ▶ Joy is a tax accountant who incurs expenses to obtain a law degree. Despite the fact that the law school courses may be helpful to Joy to maintain or improve her skills as a tax practitioner, such expenses are not deductible because the taxpayer is qualifying for a new trade or business. If Joy were not a degree candidate at the law school and merely took a few tax law courses for continuing education, the educational expenses would be deductible because they are incurred to maintain or improve Joy's skills as a tax specialist and do not qualify her for a new trade or business. In such a case, the expenses are deductible *for* AGI if Joy is self-employed and *from* AGI as a miscellaneous itemized deduction (subject to the 2% nondeductible floor) if Joy is an employee. ◀

KEY POINT

The deduction for travel expenses is not permitted if the travel itself is the educational activity. Therefore, a high school teacher who teaches Spanish cannot deduct expenses incurred in living in Madrid during the summer.

OFFICE IN HOME EXPENSES

OBJECTIVE 5

Determine whether the expenses of an office in home meet the requirements for deductibility and apply the gross income limitations

Employees or self-employed individuals who use a portion of their home for trade or business or employment-related activities should be entitled to a deduction because the property is used for trade or business or employment-related activities. However, it is often difficult to determine whether a taxpayer is using a portion of the home for business or personal use.

For over twenty years, there has been an ongoing controversy in the tax law as to the deductibility of office in home expenses. Because of the possibility of abuse by taxpayers, the IRC, Treasury Regulations, and the courts[44] have been extremely strict as to who qualifies to deduct office in home expenses. In order to promote fairness and consistency in the tax law, Congress, effective for tax years beginning after December 31, 1998, liberalized the definition of an office in home that qualifies for a tax deduction.

ADDITIONAL COMMENT

Approximately 24 million individuals, or 23% of the work force, work at least part-time at home.

GENERAL REQUIREMENTS FOR A DEDUCTION

Employees and self-employed individuals are permitted to deduct office in home expenses only if the office is exclusively used on a regular basis under any of the following conditions:

▶ The office is used as the principal place of business for *any* trade or business of the taxpayer;

---

[43] Rev. Rul. 69-292, 1969-1 C.B. 84.

[44] See, for example, *CIR v. Nader E. Soliman*, 71 AFTR 2d 93-463, 93-1 USTC 50,014 (USSC, 1993).

REAL-WORLD EXAMPLE

Most teachers have been denied a home office deduction because the home office is not the principal place of business. Also, most teachers cannot demonstrate that their office in the home is for the convenience of the employer because the employer typically provides an office at the school.

▶ The office is used as a place for meeting or dealing with patients, clients, or customers in the normal course of business; or

▶ If the office in home is located in a separate structure which is not attached to the dwelling unit, the office is used exclusively and regularly in connection with the taxpayer's trade or business.[45]

In addition to meeting any of these tests, an employee further must prove that the exclusive use is for the convenience of the *employer*. It is not enough that it is merely appropriate or helpful to the employee.

The first condition above has caused the major controversy in this area. Taxpayers are required to prove that the office is used exclusively as the "principal place of business." Under prior law, the principal place of business was interpreted to mean the "most important or significant place for the business," or more precisely, where the primary services were performed. Thus, a physician who performed medical services at a hospital but maintained an office in home to perform administrative duties was not allowed a deduction for the office because the principal place of business was interpreted to be the hospital.

EXAMPLE I:9-50 ▶ In the *Soliman* case, Dr. Soliman was a self-employed anesthesiologist who performed medical services at three hospitals, none of which provided him with an office. He spent approximately two hours per day in his office in home where he maintained patient records and correspondence and he performed billing procedures. The office was not used as a place for meeting with or dealing with patients, clients, or customers in the normal course of his business. The U.S. Supreme Court denied a deduction for Dr. Soliman's office in home because it concluded that the essence of professional service rendered by the doctor was the actual medical treatment in the hospitals. A second factor considered by the court was the amount of time spent at the office relative to the total work effort. The effect of this case was to deny a deduction for an office in home for any type of taxpayer in a trade or business where the primary services were performed outside of the office (such as plumbers, electricians). This case was highly criticized. ◀

To combat the perceived unfairness of the *Soliman* case, Congress expanded the definition of "principal place of business" for tax years beginning after December 31, 1998. An office in home now qualifies as a taxpayer's principal place of business if:

1. the office is used by the taxpayer for *administrative or management* activities of the taxpayer's trade or business, and
2. there is no other fixed location of the trade or business where the taxpayer conducts substantial administrative or management activities of the trade or business.[46]

KEY POINT

The office-in-home deduction is available only where the office is being used for trade or business purposes. No deduction is permitted if the office is used to carry on investment activities.

Thus, the law essentially allows a deduction for an office in home even though the taxpayer provides his primary service away from the office. The above tests are clearly intended for self-employed taxpayers. However, they also apply to employees except that the additional "convenience of the employer" test will still apply.

EXAMPLE I:9-51 ▶ David is a self-employed electrician who performs his electrical services at the location of his customers. He also maintains an office where he does his administrative and management duties. David is permitted a deduction for an office in home even though his primary duties of providing electrical services are performed away from his office. ◀

EXAMPLE I:9-52 ▶ Barbara is an employee of DRK, Inc., and is provided with an office on DRK's premises. However, Barbara's job requires significant administrative work after normal working hours and she prefers to perform these duties in her office at home. Barbara may not deduct the costs of her office in home because she uses her office at home for *her* convenience, not her employer's convenience. ◀

As can be seen from the discussion above, the deduction for an office in home is generally restricted to self-employed taxpayers and employees who are not provided with an office by their employer. If a self-employed taxpayer maintains an office in home, the expenses are deductible *for* AGI. Employees must deduct the office in home expenses as miscellaneous itemized deductions, subject to the 2% nondeductible floor.

---

[45] Sec. 280A(c)(1).
[46] Ibid. For years before 1999, this new definition of principal place of business does not apply. Thus, the restrictive rules promulgated by *Soliman* apply to these years.

DEDUCTION AND LIMITATIONS

The deduction for home office expenses is computed using the following two categories of expenses:

1. Expenses directly related to the office, and
2. Expenses indirectly related to the office.

Direct expenses include operating expenses (supplies, etc.) that are used in the business as well as other expenses that relate solely to the office, such as painting and decorating just the office. Indirect expenses are the pro rata share of expenses that benefit the entire house or apartment, such as mortgage interest (or rent), real estate taxes, insurance, utilities, and maintenance. The office in the home expense is the sum of the direct expenses plus the pro rata share (generally based on square footage) of indirect expenses.

To compute the office in home deduction, taxpayers first subtract all expenses not connected with the office from the income generated by the business. Then, 100% of the direct expenses of the office and the percentage of indirect expenses based on the pro rata share of the house are deducted. The total of the office in home expenses cannot create a loss.

EXAMPLE I:9-53 ▶

TAX STRATEGY TIP

When a taxpayer depreciates his office in the home, the office becomes business property. Upon the sale of the residence, the portion of the sale price attributable to the office will not be eligible for the sale of principal residence exclusion. Therefore, taxpayers might consider only deducting direct expenses of an in-home office to preserve the exclusion.

Julie works as a full-time employee for a local company. She also operates a mail order business out of her home and maintains an office in her home that is used exclusively for business. The size of her home in total is 2,400 square feet and her office is 300 square feet. During the current year, she generated gross income of $18,000 and had $6,000 of business expenses, such as supplies and shipping charges. She also had the following expenses in connection with the office in her home:

Painting of office	$ 600
Decorations in office	900
Mortgage interest (total)	3,200
Real estate taxes (total)	1,800
Insurance (total)	600
Utilities (total)	2,400
Depreciation (total)	800

Julie's home office expense for the current year would be computed as follows:

Direct expenses:		
Painting	$ 600	
Decorations	900	$1,500
Indirect expenses:		
Mortgage interest	3,200	
Real estate taxes	1,800	
Insurance	600	
Utilities	2,400	
Depreciation	800	
	8,800	
Business percentage (300/2,400)	×12.5%	1,100
Total expense for office in home		$2,600

Julie would be allowed to deduct the $2,600 of office in home expenses as they do not exceed the $12,000 ($18,000 − $6,000) of income from the business. If Julie only had $8,000 of gross income and $6,000 of business expenses, her office in home expenses of $2,600 would be limited to $2,000. ◀

TYPICAL MISCONCEPTION

Where a taxpayer is not entitled to an office-in-home deduction, the taxpayer can still deduct directly related business expenses (e.g., the cost of office supplies, and a MACRS deduction on filing cabinets and other equipment).

As mentioned above, the total allowable office in home expenses may not exceed the taxpayer's gross income from the business (or rental) activity.[47] This ceiling limitation on office in home deductions is intended to prevent taxpayers from recognizing tax losses if the business (or rental) activity does not produce sufficient amounts of gross income. Expenses disallowed because of the gross income limitation can be carried forward but are subject to the gross income limitation in the later year and are subject to specific ordering rules.[48]

---

[47] Sec. 280A(c)(5).

[48] See Prop. Reg. Sec. 1.280A-2 for the ordering rules. These rules are similar, but not identical to the ordering rules for hobby losses under Sec. 183.

Employee expense classifications and deduction limitations are summarized in Topic Review I:9-1.

Topic Review I:9-1

Classification and Deductibility of Employee Expenses

Type of Expenditure	50% Disallowance	For or From AGI	Other Limitations
Miscellaneous itemized deductions	Applies to unreimbursed meals and entertainment	*From* AGI	Subject to 2% of AGI nondeductible floor.
Reimbursed travel expenses (adequate accounting is made)	Applies to the employer for meals portion of the travel only	*For* AGI	2% of AGI nondeductible floor applies only to employee expenses that exceed the reimbursement.
Unreimbursed travel expenses	Applies to meals portion of travel only	*From* AGI	Subject to the 2% of AGI nondeductible floor. Employee must be away from his or her tax home overnight.
Automobile expenses	Not applicable	*From* AGI	Subject to the 2% of AGI nondeductible floor. Actual costs or the standard mileage rate method may be used.
Moving expenses	Not applicable because meals are not deductible	*For* AGI	Indirect moving-related expenses are not deductible.
Entertainment expenses	Applies to all entertainment expenses	*From* AGI	Subject to the 2% of AGI nondeductible floor. Club dues and initiation fees are not deductible.
Education expenses deductible per Reg. Sec. 1.162-5	Applies to meal portion of education expenses	*From* AGI	Qualifying expenses are subject to the 2% of AGI nondeductible floor.
Office-in-home	Not applicable	*From* AGI; If trade- or business- related, the expenses are for AGI	Employment-related expenses (other than real estate taxes and interest) are subject to the 2% of AGI nondeductible floor. Gross income limitations apply to allowable expenses.

DEFERRED COMPENSATION

OBJECTIVE 6

Discuss the tax treatment and requirements for various deferred compensation arrangements

Various types of benefit plans providing favorable tax treatment are available to employees and self-employed individuals. These tax benefits are provided to stimulate savings accumulations necessary for retirement. Private retirement plans should be the primary source of retirement with the Social Security system as a supplement. Favorable tax consequences generally include the following benefits:

▶ Deferral of taxes on amounts contributed to retirement plans until the individual retires or receives a distribution from the plan

▶ An immediate deduction for contributions to qualified retirement plans for the employer or self-employed individual

▶ Deferral of taxation on income earned on retirement plan assets

The following types of *deferred compensation arrangements* are discussed here:

▶ Qualified pension and profit-sharing plans

▶ Nonqualified deferred compensation arrangements, including restricted property and employee stock option plans

▶ Self-employed retirement plans and individual retirement accounts (IRAs)

QUALIFIED PENSION AND PROFIT-SHARING PLANS

ADDITIONAL COMMENT

The Staff of the Joint Committee on Taxation estimates the revenue loss resulting from the deferral of taxes on contributions and earnings for qualified employer plans, individual retirement plans, and Keogh plans for 2008 will approximate $141 billion. This provision represents one of the largest tax expenditures of the federal government and is designed to encourage employers to establish pension plans for their employees.

The federal tax law provides favorable tax benefits for *qualified* pension and profit-sharing plans. A **qualified plan** is one that must meet strict requirements, such as not discriminating in favor of highly compensated individuals, be formed and operated for the exclusive benefit of employees, and meet specified vesting and funding requirements. In a qualified plan, both the employer and employee receive significant tax benefits, as follows:

EMPLOYER: receives an immediate tax deduction for pension and profit-sharing contributions made on behalf of employees.

EMPLOYEE: is not taxed on either employer or employee contributions or earnings of the plan assets until funds are withdrawn from the plan at retirement.[49] Thus, funds invested in a qualified plan grow tax-free during an employee's working years.

TYPES OF PLANS. Qualified plans[50] include:

▶ Pension plans

▶ Profit-sharing plans (including Sec. 401(k) plans)

▶ Stock bonus plans, including employee stock ownership plans (ESOPs)

Pension Plans. The features that distinguish a *qualified pension plan* include the following:

▶ Systematic and definite payments are made to a pension trust (without regard to profits) based on formulas or actuarial methods.

▶ A pension plan may provide for incidental benefits such as disability, death, or medical insurance benefits.

A pension plan may be either contributory or noncontributory. Under a **noncontributory pension plan,** the contributions are made solely by the employer. Under a **contributory pension plan,** the employee makes voluntary contributions into the plan that supplement any contributions made by the employer.

Pension plans also may be either defined contribution plans or defined benefit plans. In a **defined contribution pension plan,** a separate account is established for each participant and certain amounts are contributed based on a specific formula (e.g., a specified percentage of compensation). The benefits payable to the participant at retirement are based on the value of the participant's account (including the amount of earnings that accrue to the account) at the time of retirement.

EXAMPLE I:9-54 ▶

Alabama Corporation establishes a qualified pension plan for its employees that provides for employer contributions equal to 8% of each participant's salary. Retirement payments to each participant are based on the amount of accumulated benefits in the employee's account at the retirement date. The pension plan is a defined contribution plan, because the contribution rate is based on a specific and fixed percentage of compensation. ◀

KEY POINT

All qualified plans can be classified into two broad categories. They are either defined contribution plans or defined benefit plans. An understanding of the distinction between these two broad categories is important because some rules will apply to one type of plan but not the other.

Defined benefit plans establish a contribution formula based on actuarial techniques that are sufficient to fund a fixed benefit amount to be paid upon retirement. For example, a defined benefit plan might provide fixed retirement benefits equal to 40% of an employee's average salary for the five years before retirement.

A distinguishing feature of a defined benefit plan is that forfeitures of unvested amounts (e.g., due to employee resignations) must be used to reduce the employer contributions that would otherwise be made under the plan. In a defined contribution plan, however, the forfeitures related to unvested amounts may either be reallocated to the other participants in a nondiscriminatory manner or used to reduce future employer contributions.

---

[49] An employee may not be liable for federal income taxes but may be subject to Social Security taxes and possibly local or city income taxes.

[50] Qualified plans are generally covered in Secs. 401-416 of the IRC.

Profit-Sharing Plans. A qualified **profit-sharing plan** also may be established by an employer in addition to, or in lieu of, a qualified pension plan arrangement. Profit-sharing plans include the following distinguishing features:

▶ A definite, predetermined formula must be used to allocate employer contributions to individual employees and to establish benefit payments.

▶ Annual employer contributions are not required, but substantial and recurring contributions must be made to satisfy the requirement that the plan be permanent.

▶ Employees may be given the option to receive cash that is fully taxable as current compensation or to defer taxation on employer contributions by having such amounts contributed to the profit-sharing trust. Plans of this type are called Sec. 401(k) plans.[51]

▶ Forfeitures arising under the plan may be reallocated to the remaining participants to increase their profit-sharing benefits, provided that certain nondiscrimination requirements are met.

▶ Lump-sum payments made to an employee before retirement may be provided following a prescribed period for the vesting of such amounts.

▶ Incidental benefits such as disability, death, or medical insurance may also be provided in a profit-sharing arrangement.

Stock Bonus Plan. A **stock bonus plan** is a special type of defined contribution plan whereby the investments of the plan are in the employer-company's own stock. The employer makes its contribution to the trust either in cash or in stock. If in cash, the amounts are invested in the company's stock. The stock is allocated and subsequently distributed to the participants. Stock bonus plan requirements are similar to profit-sharing plans. An **employee stock ownership plan (ESOP)** is a type of qualified stock bonus plan.[52] An ESOP, funded by a combination of employer and employee contributions and plan loans, invest primarily in employer stock. The stock is held for the benefit of the employees. ESOPs are attractive because the employer is allowed to reduce taxable income by deducting any dividends that are paid to the participants (or their beneficiaries) in the year such amounts are paid and are taxable to the participant. For employer securities acquired by the ESOP, the dividends-paid deduction is limited to dividends paid on employer stock acquired with an ESOP loan.

QUALIFICATION REQUIREMENTS FOR A QUALIFIED PLAN

Qualified pension, profit-sharing, and stock bonus plans must meet complex qualification rules and requirements to achieve and maintain their favored qualifying status. A summary of the important requirements are discussed below.

▶ Section 401(a) requires that the plan must be for the employee's exclusive benefit. For example, the trust must follow prudent investment rules to ensure that the pension benefits will accrue for the employees' benefit.

▶ The plan may not discriminate in favor of highly compensated employees. Highly compensated employees are employees who meet either of two tests: (1) own more than 5% of the corporation's stock in either the current or prior year or (2) receive compensation of greater than $110,000 in the prior year.[53]

▶ Contributions and plan benefits must bear a uniform relationship to the compensation payments made to covered employees. For example, if contributions for the benefit of the participants are based on a fixed percentage of the employee's compensation (e.g., 4%), the plan should not be disqualified despite the fact that the contributions for highly-compensated employees are greater on an actual dollar basis than those for lower paid individuals.

---

[51] Sec. 401(k).
[52] Secs. 409(a) and 4975(e)(7).
[53] Sec. 414(q). The $110,000 applicable in 2010 amount is subject to annual indexing for inflation. The amount for 2009 was also $110,000 and for 2009

was $105,000. Alternatively, an employer may elect to define a highly-compensated group as employees earning more than $110,000 *and* the top 20% group of employees based on compensation.

> ▶ Certain coverage requirements that are expressed in terms of a portion of the employees covered by the plan must be met.

> ▶ An employee's right to receive benefits from the employer's contributions must vest (i.e., become nonforfeitable) after a certain period or number of years of employment. The vesting requirement is intended to ensure that a significant percentage of employees will eventually receive retirement benefits. Employer-provided benefits must be 100% vested after 5 years of service.[54] In all cases, any employee contributions to the plan must vest immediately.

EXAMPLE I:9-55 ▶ Ken is a participant in a noncontributory qualified pension plan that provides for no vesting until an employee completes three years of service. Ken terminates his employment with the company after two years of service. Because Ken has not met the minimum vesting requirements, he is not entitled to receive any of the employer contributions that are made on his behalf. ◀

ADDITIONAL COMMENT

Most employees choose to contribute amounts to their qualified retirement plans on a pre-tax basis because of the time value of money. A current deduction (and the related tax savings) is more valuable than a deduction at retirement.

TAX TREATMENT TO EMPLOYEES AND EMPLOYERS

Employer contributions to a qualified plan are immediately deductible (subject to specific limitations on contribution amounts), and earnings on pension fund investments are tax-exempt to the plan. Amounts paid into a plan by or for an employee are not taxable until the pension payments are received, normally at retirement. At the election of the employee, amounts may be treated as having been made from either pre-tax or after-tax earnings. If amounts contributed to a qualified plan by an employee are made on a pre-tax basis, the taxable portion of the employee's earnings is reduced by the contribution amount. This has the effect of permitting a deduction for the contribution amount. When amounts are withdrawn at retirement, the entire distribution is subject to taxation.

EXAMPLE I:9-56 ▶ Larry is an employee of Cisco Corporation, which maintains a Sec. 401(k) plan. Larry contributes 5% of his gross salary into the plan on a pre-tax basis. During the current year, Larry's gross salary is $80,000 so his Sec. 401(k) contribution is $4,000. Since Larry's contribution is made on a pre-tax basis, his taxable salary for the current year will be $76,000. In effect, Larry is able to deduct the $4,000 from his salary in the current year. When Larry retires and begins withdrawing amounts from the plan, the entire amount withdrawn will be subject to income taxation. ◀

Conversely, an employee may elect to contribute to a qualified plan on an after-tax basis. If, in Example I:9-56, Larry contributed to the Sec. 401(k) plan on an after-tax basis, his taxable salary would have been $80,000. The $4,000 contributed to the plan is treated as an investment in the plan and is considered a tax-free return of capital when this amount is withdrawn at retirement.[55]

EMPLOYEE RETIREMENT PAYMENTS. An employee's retirement benefits are generally taxed under the Sec. 72 annuity rules (see Chapter I:3). If the plan is noncontributory (i.e., no employee contributions are made to the plan), all of the pension benefits when received by the employee are fully taxable. If the plan is contributory, the taxability depends on whether the employee's contributions were made on a pre-tax or after-tax basis. If the contributions were made on a pre-tax basis, *all* retirement payments received by the employee are taxable. Alternatively, if the contributions were made on an after-tax basis, each payment is treated, in part, as a tax-free return of the employee's contributions and the remainder is taxable. The excluded portion is based on the ratio of the employee's investment in the contract to the expected return under the contract. However, the total amount that may be excluded is limited to the amount of the employee's contributions to the plan. If the employee dies before the entire investment in the contract is recovered, the unrecovered amount is allowed as an itemized deduction in the year of death.

---

[54] Sec. 411(a)(2)(A). An alternative vesting schedule may also be used that provides for 20% vesting each year beginning in the third year of service, Sec. 411(a)(2)(B). Thus, after a total of seven years of service, an employee would be 100% vested. In addition, a faster vesting schedule is provided in Sec. 411(a)(12) whereby the vesting begins after two years of service and increases at a rate of 20% per year to 100% after six years.

[55] Amounts contributed to a qualified plan on an after-tax basis are treated as an investment in the contract under the annuity rules of Sec. 72. Amounts withdrawn during retirement are taxed under the general rules of Sec. 72. (See Chapter I:3 for a discussion of taxation of annuities.)

EXAMPLE I:9-57 ▶ Kevin retires in 2010 at age 64 and will receive monthly annuity payments of $2,000 for life from his employer's qualified pension plan beginning in 2011. Kevin's investment in the contract (represented by his contributions made on an after-tax basis) is $100,000. Kevin's life expectancy per Sec. 72 is 260 months from the annuity starting date. So, for the next 260 months, Kevin can exclude $384.62 ($100,000/260 months). In 2011, Kevin would exclude $4,615.44 ($384.62 × 12 months) and $19,384.56 ($24,000.00 − $4,615.44) would be taxable. After Kevin receives payments for 260 months and his $100,000 investment in the contract is recovered, all subsequent payments are fully taxable. (See Chapter I:3 for a discussion of the annuity formula and related rules.) ◀

EXAMPLE I:9-58 ▶ Assume the same facts as in Example I:9-57 except that Kevin made all of his contributions to the plan on a pre-tax basis. In other words, the amount that he contributed to the plan was subtracted from his salary each year. When Kevin starts receiving payments from the plan, all amounts received will be taxable. Therefore, in 2011, Kevin will include $24,000 in his gross income. Most employees elect to "tax defer" their contributions into retirement plans in order to reduce their current year taxable income and take advantage of the time value of money principle. ◀

ADDITIONAL COMMENT

Many individuals have the option of taking their retirement savings from traditional pensions, profit-sharing plans, and 401(k)s as a lump sum or an annuity. Those who want to take a lump-sum distribution can delay taxes by transferring the money directly into a tax-deferred IRA.

If an employee age 59½ or older receives a lump-sum distribution from a qualified plan, a five-year forward income-averaging technique was generally available through 1999 to mitigate the effects of receiving a large amount of income in the year of the distribution.[56] Special tax treatment for lump-sum distributions is now available only for employees born before 1936. However, all taxpayers are eligible to make nontaxable rollovers of distributions from one qualified plan to another. Special rules apply to such rollovers.

LIMITATION ON EMPLOYER CONTRIBUTIONS. The Code places limitations on (1) amounts an employer may contribute to qualified pension, profit-sharing, and stock bonus plans and (2) amounts that the employer may deduct:

KEY POINT

For purposes of the limitation on employer contributions, all defined contribution plans maintained by one employer are treated as a single defined contribution plan. Furthermore, under some circumstances a group of employers can be treated as a single employer.

▶ Defined contribution plan contributions in 2010 are limited to the lesser of $49,000 or 100% of the employee's compensation.[57]

▶ Defined benefit plans are restricted to an annual benefit to an employee equal to the lesser of $195,000 for 2010 or 100% of the participant's average compensation for the highest three years.[58]

▶ An overall maximum annual employer deduction of 25% of compensation paid or accrued to plan participants is placed on defined contribution, profit-sharing, and stock bonus plans.[59] If an employer has more than one type of qualified plan (e.g., a defined benefit pension plan and a profit-sharing plan), a maximum deduction of 25% of compensation is allowed.

The distinguishing features and major requirements for qualified pension and profit-sharing plans are summarized in Topic Review I:9-2.

KEY POINT

Because nonqualified plans are not subject to the same restrictions as imposed upon qualified plans, they do not receive the same tax benefits that are available under qualified plans. For example, the employer may not be able to deduct amounts that are set aside for employees.

NONQUALIFIED PLANS

Nonqualified deferred compensation plans are often used by employers to provide incentives or supplementary retirement benefits for executives. Common forms of nonqualified plans include the following:

▶ An unfunded, nonforfeitable promise to pay fixed amounts of compensation in future periods.[60]

▶ Restricted property plans involving property transfers (usually in the form of the employer-company stock), where the property transferred is subject to a substantial risk of forfeiture and is nontransferable.[61]

---

[56] Sec. 402(e). The five-year forward averaging provision was repealed for tax years beginning after December 31, 1999.
[57] Sec. 415(c). The deduction limit for 2009 was also $49,000. In addition, individuals over 50 years of age are now eligible to contribute extra amounts into their plans. The amount of the so-called catch-up contributions depend on the type of plan.
[58] Sec. 415(b)(1). The benefit amount for 2009 was also $195,000. These

amounts are subject to indexing each year. For participants who separated from service before January 1, 2010, the 100% average is computed by multiplying the participant's compensation limitation by 1.053.
[59] Sec. 404(a)(3)(A).
[60] Rev. Rul. 60-31, 1960-1 C.B. 174.
[61] Sec. 83.

Topic Review I:9-2

Qualified Pension and Profit-Sharing Plans

DISTINGUISHING FEATURES AND MAJOR REQUIREMENTS

▶ Employer contributions and earnings on contributed amounts are not taxed to employees until distributed or made available. The contributions are immediately deductible by the employer.

▶ Pension plans can be established as either defined contribution or defined benefit plans in which systematic and definite payments are made to a pension trust. Incidental benefits (e.g., death and disability payments) can be provided under the plan.

▶ Profit-sharing plans require the use of a predetermined allocation formula and substantial and recurring contributions must be made although annual employer contributions are not required and the contributions need not be based on profits. Section 401(k) plans can be established where employees have the option to receive cash or to have such amounts contributed to the profit-sharing trust. The employer may also establish an ESOP where the plan is funded by a contribution of the employer's stock.

▶ Qualified plans must be created for the employees' exclusive benefit.

▶ The plans may not discriminate in favor of highly compensated employees.

▶ Contributions and plan benefits must bear a uniform relationship to the compensation of covered employees.

▶ Minimum vesting requirements must be met (e.g., 100% vesting after five years).

▶ Employee benefits are taxed under the Sec. 72 annuity rules.

▶ Total employer contributions to the plan are subject to specific ceiling limitations.

DISTINGUISHING CHARACTERISTICS OF NONQUALIFIED PLANS. Nonqualified plans are not subject to the same restrictions imposed on qualified plans (such as the nondiscrimination and vesting rules), although nonqualified plans may have some vesting rules. Thus, such plans are particularly suitable for use in executive compensation planning. In general, nonqualified plans impose certain restrictions on the outright transfer of the plan's benefits to the employee. This avoids immediate taxation under the constructive receipt doctrine, which does not apply if the benefits are not yet credited, set apart, or made available so that the employee may draw on them. The amount is taxed to the employee upon the lapse of such restrictions, and the employer receives a corresponding deduction in the same year.

UNFUNDED DEFERRED COMPENSATION PLANS. **Unfunded deferred compensation plans** are often used to compensate highly compensated employees who desire to defer the recognition of income until future periods (e.g., a professional athlete or a business executive who receives a signing bonus may prefer to defer the recognition of income from the bonus). In general, if the promise to make the compensation payment in a future period is nonforfeitable, the agreement must not be funded (e.g., the transfer of assets to a trust for the employee's benefit) or evidenced by a negotiable note. The employer, however, may establish an *escrow account* on behalf of the employee. Such an account is used to accumulate and invest the deferred compensation amounts. If the requirements for deferral are met, the employee is taxed when the amounts are actually paid or made available, and the employer receives a corresponding deduction in the same year.[62]

EXAMPLE I:9-59 ▶ In 2009, Kelly signs an employment contract to play professional football for the Chicago Skyhawks. The contract includes a $500,000 signing bonus that is payable in five annual installments beginning in 2015. The bonus agreement is nonforfeitable and is unfunded. The Skyhawks have agreed to place sufficient amounts of money into an escrow account to fund the future payments to Kelly. None of the $500,000 bonus is deductible by the employer or taxable to Kelly when the agreement is signed in 2009. The Skyhawks do not receive a deduction for any amounts that are deposited into the escrow account during the 2009–2014 period. In 2015, Kelly receives $100,000 taxable compensation (interest, if any, that accrued and was paid to Kelly is also taxable) upon receipt of the initial payment, and the Skyhawks receive a corresponding tax deduction. ◀

---

[62] Reg. Sec. 1.451-2(a).

New requirements were enacted in 2005 for nonqualified deferred compensation plans effective for amounts deferred in tax years beginning after December 31, 2004.[63] While a detailed examination of these new rules is outside the scope of this textbook, some major features of the new law are as follows:

▶ The new rules apply to any plan by which executive employees are permitted to defer the receipt and taxability of compensation from the current year to a future year. In prior years, the tax laws in this area were a wide range of cases and rulings.

▶ If deferred amounts under a plan fail to satisfy the new requirements at any time during the tax year, the recipient must pay the tax on the deferred compensation plus interest and an additional 20% excise tax.

▶ Distributions from the plan to recipients are subject to strict rules. Deferrals may be distributed to participants no earlier than the time of separation of service, pursuant to a fixed schedule in the plan, death, disability, an unforeseeable emergency, or upon a change in control of the company. Thus, early distributions are not generally permitted. In addition, acceleration of payment amounts are severely curtailed.

▶ Funding rules essentially have remained the same except that employers generally may no longer use offshore trusts.

Because of the complexity of the new rules in this area, taxpayers are strongly urged to look closely at their nonqualified deferred compensation plans to ensure that they comply with the new rules for 2005 and later years.

RESTRICTED PROPERTY PLANS. **Restricted property plans** are used to attract and retain key executives. Under such arrangements, the executive generally obtains an ownership interest (i.e., stock) in the corporation. Restricted property plans are governed by the income recognition rules contained in Sec. 83. Under these rules, the receipt of restricted property in exchange for services rendered is not taxable if the property is nontransferable and subject to a substantial risk of forfeiture.

The employee is treated as receiving taxable compensation based on the amount of the property's fair market value (FMV) (less any amount paid for the property) at the earlier of the time the property is no longer subject to a substantial risk of forfeiture or is transferable. The employer receives a corresponding compensation deduction at the same time the income is taxed to the employee.

EXAMPLE I:9-60 ▶ In 2010, Allied Corporation transfers 1,000 shares of its common stock to employee Karen as compensation pursuant to a restricted property plan. The FMV of the Allied stock is $10 per share on the transfer date. The restricted property agreement provides that the stock is nontransferable by Karen until the year 2012 (i.e., Karen cannot sell the stock to outsiders until year 2012). The stock is also subject to the restriction that if Karen voluntarily leaves the company before the year 2012, she must transfer the shares back to the company and will receive no benefit from the stock other than from the receipt of dividends. The FMV of the stock is $100 per share in year 2012 when the forfeiture and nontransferability restrictions lapse. Because the stock is both nontransferable and subject to a substantial risk of forfeiture from the issue date to year 2012, the tax consequences from the stock transfer are deferred for both Karen and Allied Corporation until the lapse of the nontransferability or forfeiture restrictions in year 2012. Thus, no tax consequences result in 2010 or 2011. In year 2012, Karen must report ordinary (compensation) income of $100,000 ($100 × 1,000 shares), and Allied Corporation is entitled to a corresponding compensation deduction of the same amount. Karen is taxed currently on the dividends she receives because they are not subject to any restrictions. ◀

KEY POINT

If an employee makes the election to be taxed immediately, he or she should be aware of the adverse consequences of leaving the company before the forfeiture restrictions lapse. The employee will not receive the property, and no deduction is allowed on the forfeiture.

Election to Be Taxed Immediately. An exception which permits an employee to elect (within 30 days after the receipt of restricted property) to recognize income immediately upon receipt of the restricted property is provided in Sec. 83(b). If the election is made, the employer is entitled to a corresponding deduction at the time the income is taxed to the employee. This election is frequently made when the fair market value of the restricted property is expected to increase significantly in the future and the future gain would be

---

[63] Sec. 409A.

taxed as long-term capital gain. Because the current rate of tax on long-term capital gains has been reduced to 15%, one would expect that more taxpayers will now make the Sec. 83(b) election.

EXAMPLE I:9-61 ▶

Assume the same facts as Example I:9-60, except that Karen elects to recognize income in 2010 (i.e., the transfer date). Karen must include $10,000 ($10 × 1,000 shares) in gross income as compensation in the current year and Allied Corporation is entitled to a corresponding deduction in the same year. Karen will report no income in 2012 when the restrictions lapse and her basis in the Allied Corporation stock remains at $10,000. If Karen sells the stock for $100,000 in the year 2012 after the restrictions lapse, Karen reports a $90,000 ($100,000 − $10,000) long-term capital gain on the sale.[64] If Karen voluntarily leaves the company before the forfeiture restrictions lapse, no deduction is allowed when the forfeiture occurs, despite the fact that Karen is previously taxed on the stock's value on the transfer date (i.e., $10,000 of income is recognized by Karen in the current year). In such event, Allied Corporation must include $10,000 in gross income in the year of the forfeiture (i.e., the amount of the deduction that is taken in the year of the transfer to the extent of any previous tax benefit). ◀

Nonqualified plan features and requirements are summarized in Topic Review I:9-3.

EMPLOYEE STOCK OPTIONS

Stock option plans are used by corporate employers to attract and retain key management employees. Both stock option and restricted property arrangements using the employer's stock permit the executive to receive a proprietary interest in the corporation. Thus, an executive may identify more closely with shareholder interests and the firm's long-run profit-maximization goals. The tax law currently includes two types of stock-option arrangements: the incentive stock option and the nonqualified stock option.[65] Each type is treated differently for tax purposes.

As will be seen in the discussions below, both types of plans have their respective advantages and disadvantages. Incentive stock option arrangements generally are preferred when long-term capital gain rates are low as compared to ordinary income rates. Thus, because long-term capital gain rates are 15% and marginal tax rates for ordinary income are rather high (35%), interest should continue in incentive stock option arrangements. However, an employer is more favorably treated under the nonqualified stock-option rules (i.e., the employer receives a tax deduction for the compensation related to a nonqualified stock option but does not receive a corresponding deduction if an incentive stock-option plan is adopted) and may therefore still prefer to continue to use nonqualified stock options.

REAL-WORLD EXAMPLE

The use of employee stock options has come under criticism recently in the financial press. The pressure to increase earnings has been a major issue in recent corporate scandals. Further, the Financial Accounting Standards Board has issued a statement requiring the current expensing of stock options in certain circumstances.

Topic Review I:9-3

Nonqualified Plans

DISTINGUISHING FEATURES AND MAJOR REQUIREMENTS

1. The employee is taxed upon the lapse of restrictions imposed on the availability or withdrawal of funds and the employer receives a corresponding deduction in the same year.
2. Nonqualified plans may discriminate in favor of highly compensated employees and no minimum vesting rules are required.
3. Restricted property (usually employer stock) may be offered to executives where the incidents of taxation are deferred if the property is nontransferable and subject to a substantial risk of forfeiture. An election may be made under Sec. 83(b) to recognize income immediately upon the receipt of the restricted property.
4. Restrictions must be imposed to avoid immediate taxation to the employee under the constructive receipt doctrine.
5. To avoid immediate taxation, restricted property plans must be both nonforfeitable and subject to a substantial risk of forfeiture.

---

[64] Sec. 1223. The holding period originates on the day following the transfer date because Karen made the election to be taxed immediately under Sec. 83(b).

[65] The incentive stock option rules are provided in Sec. 422, whereas the rules governing nonqualified stock options are contained in Reg. Sec. 1.83-7.

INCENTIVE STOCK OPTION PLANS.

Employer Requirements. An **incentive stock option (ISO)** must meet the following plan or employer requirements:[66]

KEY POINT

Incentive stock options have the disadvantage of not providing a compensation deduction for the employer.

▶ The option price must be equal to or greater than the stock's FMV on the option's grant date.

▶ The option must be granted within ten years of the date the plan is adopted, and the employee must exercise the option within ten years of the grant date.

▶ The option must be both exercisable only by the employee and nontransferable except in the event of death.

▶ The employee cannot own more than 10% of the voting power of the employer corporation's stock immediately before the option's grant date.

▶ The total FMV of the stock options that become exercisable to an employee in any given year may not exceed $100,000 (e.g., an employee can be granted ISOs to acquire $200,000 of stock in one year, provided that no more than $100,000 is exercisable in any given year).

▶ Other procedural requirements must be met (e.g., shareholder approval of the plan).

KEY POINT

Incentive stock options can be a valuable tax planning tool because the earliest that they are generally taxed is when they are exercised. Also, when an employee realizes profits from stock options, those profits in certain cases may qualify as capital gains.

Employee Requirements. In addition to the above plan requirements, the employee must meet the following requirements:

▶ The employee must not dispose of the stock within two years of the option's grant date nor within one year after the option's exercise date.

▶ The employee must be employed by the issuing company on the grant date and continue such employment until within three months before the exercise date.

If an employee meets the requirements listed above, no tax consequences occur on the grant date or the exercise date. However, the excess of the FMV over the option price on the exercise date is an adjustment for purposes of the alternative minimum tax (see Chapter I:14). When the employee sells the optioned stock, a long-term capital gain or loss is recognized. If the employee meets the two requirements, the employer does not receive a corresponding compensation deduction. If the requirements are not met, the option is treated as a nonqualified stock option.

EXAMPLE I:9-62 ▶

American Corporation grants an incentive stock option to Kay, an employee, on January 1, 2010. The option price is $100, and the FMV of the American stock is also $100 on the grant date. The option permits Kay to purchase 100 shares of American stock. Kay exercises the option on June 30, 2012, when the stock's FMV is $400. Kay sells the 100 shares of American stock on January 1, 2014, for $500 per share. Because Kay holds the stock for the required period (at least two years from the grant date and one year from the exercise date) and because Kay is employed by American Corporation on the grant date and within three months before the exercise date, all of the requirements for an ISO have been met. No income is recognized on the grant date or the exercise date, although $30,000 [($400 − $100) × 100 shares] is a tax preference item for the alternative minimum tax in 2012. Kay recognizes a $40,000 [($500 − $100) × 100 shares] long-term capital gain on the sale date in 2014. American Corporation is not entitled to a compensation deduction in any year. ◀

EXAMPLE I:9-63 ▶

KEY POINT

With ISOs, the employee does not recognize income when the option is exercised; income is recognized only when the stock is sold. With nonqualified stock options, income is recognized when the option is exercised or on the grant date and when the stock is sold at a gain.

Assume the same facts as Example I:9-62, except that Kay disposes of the stock on August 1, 2012, thus violating the one-year minimum holding period requirement after the exercise date. Kay must recognize ordinary income on the sale date equal to the spread between the option price and the exercise price, or $30,000 [($400 − $100) × 100 shares]. The $30,000 spread between the FMV and the option price is no longer a tax preference item because the option ceases to qualify as an ISO. American Corporation can claim a $30,000 compensation deduction in 2012. Kay also recognizes a $10,000 [($500 − $400 adjusted basis) × 100 shares] short-term capital gain on the sale date, which represents the appreciation of the stock from the exercise date to the sale date. The gain is short-term because the holding period from the exercise date to the sale date does not exceed one year. ◀

---

[66] Sec. 422.

NONQUALIFIED STOCK OPTION PLANS. Stock options that do not meet the plan requirements for incentive stock options are referred to as **nonqualified stock options**. The tax treatment of nonqualified stock options depends on whether the option has a **readily ascertainable fair market value** (e.g., whether the option is traded on an established options exchange).

Readily Ascertainable Fair Market Value. If a nonqualified stock option has a readily ascertainable FMV (e.g., the option is traded on an established options exchange), the employee recognizes ordinary income on the grant date equal to the difference between the stock's FMV and the option's exercise price. The employer receives a compensation deduction on the grant date equal to the same amount of income that is recognized by the employee. In such case, no tax consequences occur on the date the option is exercised, and the employee recognizes capital gain or loss upon the sale or disposition of the stock.

No Readily Ascertainable Fair Market Value. If a nonqualified stock option has no readily ascertainable FMV, no tax consequences occur on the grant date. On the exercise date the employee recognizes ordinary income equal to the spread between the FMV of the stock and the option price, and the employer receives a corresponding compensation deduction. When the stock option is exercised, the employee's basis in the stock is equal to the option price plus the amount reported as ordinary income on the exercise date. Capital gain or loss is recognized upon the subsequent sale of the stock by the employee.

The alternative minimum tax does not apply to nonqualified stock options regardless of whether the option has a readily ascertainable FMV. Table I:9-4 illustrates the tax consequences to employees and employers for such options.

As illustrated in Table I:9-4, Kim reports a total gain of $11,000 from the nonqualified stock option transaction under both circumstances. However, the character of her profit (i.e., ordinary income or capital gain) and the timing of the profit recognition (i.e., grant date or exercise date) depends on whether the option's FMV is readily ascertainable.

The distinguishing features and major requirements for employee stock options are summarized in Topic Review I:9-4.

▼ TABLE I:9-4
Taxation of Nonqualified Stock Options

Situation Facts	Readily Ascertainable FMV	No Readily Ascertainable FMV
Grant date: On January 1, 2008, Kim is granted a nonqualified stock option to purchase 100 shares of stock from Apple Corporation (Kim's employer) at $90 per share. The stock's FMV is $100 on the grant date.	Ordinary income of $1,000 is recognized [($100 − $90) × 100 shares] by Kim in 2008. Apple Corporation receives a corresponding $1,000 compensation deduction in 2008.	No tax consequences to Kim or Apple Corporation.
Exercise date: On January 31, 2010, Kim exercises the option and acquires the 100 shares of Apple Corporation stock for the $90 option price when the FMV is $190.	No tax consequences to Kim or Apple Corporation.	Kim recognizes ordinary income in 2010 of $10,000 [($190 − $90) × 100 shares], and Apple Corporation receives a $10,000 compensation deduction.
Sale date: On February 1, 2011, Kim sells the stock for $200 per share and realizes $20,000 ($200 × 100 shares).	Kim recognizes a $10,000 ($20,000 − $10,000 basis) long-term capital gain.[a]	Kim recognizes a $1,000 ($20,000 − $19,000 basis) long-term capital gain on the sale.[b]

[a] Kim's basis includes the amount paid for the optioned stock of $9,000 plus ordinary income of $1,000 recognized on the grant date. Kim's holding period commences on the January 1, 2008, grant date for determining whether the gain is long-term.

[b] Kim's basis includes the $9,000 paid for the option stock plus the $10,000 ordinary income recognized on the exercise date. Kim's holding period commences on the January 31, 2010, exercise date for determining whether the gain is long-term.

Topic Review I:9-4

Employee Stock Options

DISTINGUISHING FEATURES AND MAJOR REQUIREMENTS

▶ For an incentive stock option (ISO) plan no tax consequences occur on the grant or the exercise date (except for the recognition of a tax preference item under the AMT provisions on the exercise date). Capital gain or loss is recognized by the employee upon the sale or exchange of the stock. No deduction is allowed to the employer.

▶ ISOs and nonqualified stock options may be issued to highly-compensated employees without regard to nondiscrimination rules.

▶ If a nonqualified stock option has a readily ascertainable FMV, the employee recognizes ordinary income equal to the spread between the FMV of the stock and the option price on the grant date and the employer receives a corresponding deduction. If the option has no readily ascertainable FMV, income is recognized on the exercise date equal to the spread between the FMV of the stock and the option price and a corresponding deduction is available to the employer.

▶ For an ISO, the option price must be equal to or greater than the FMV of the stock on the grant date, employees cannot own more than 10% of the voting power of the employer's stock, and restrictions are placed on the total FMV of stock options that may be issued.

▶ To qualify under the ISO rules, a two-year holding period from the grant date is required (and at least one year after the exercise date) and the employee must continue to be employed by the company until within three months of the exercise date.

ADDITIONAL COMMENT

If you are self-employed and establish a Keogh plan, you must include any full-time employees in the plan.

PLANS FOR SELF-EMPLOYED INDIVIDUALS

Self-employed individuals, such as sole proprietors and partners who practice a trade or business, are not classified as employees and are subject to special retirement plan rules known as **H.R. 10 plans** (also called **Keogh plans**). Retirement plans of self-employed people are generally subject to the same contribution and benefit limitations as other qualified corporate plans. An employee who is covered under a qualified pension or profit-sharing plan for wages earned as an employee and who is also self-employed may establish an H.R. 10 plan for earned income derived from self-employment activities.

KEY POINT

Keogh plans can be either defined benefit or defined contribution plans. Many individuals avoid the defined benefit type of Keogh plan due to the extra paperwork and administrative costs.

For a **defined contribution H.R. 10 plan**, a self-employed individual in 2010 may contribute the smaller of $49,000 or 25% of earned income from the self-employment activity.[67] *Earned income* refers to net earnings from self-employment. However, for purposes of computing the maximum amount that may be contributed to a Keogh plan by a self-employed individual, earned income must be reduced by two amounts: (1) the 50% deduction for self-employment taxes and (2) the Keogh contribution itself. Since the contribution is based on earned income *after* the contribution, the 25% contribution percentage must be reduced to 20%.[68] To compute the limitations for 2010, a maximum of $245,000 of earned income may be taken into account for any one individual.[69]

EXAMPLE I:9-64 ▶ Larry is a self-employed CPA whose 2010 net earnings from his trade or business (before the H.R. 10 plan contribution but after the deduction for one-half of the self-employment taxes paid under Sec. 164(f) [see Chapter I:14]) is $100,000. Larry may contribute $20,000 to the plan for 2010. Larry must also provide coverage for all of his eligible full-time employees under the general rules provided in the law for qualified plans (e.g., nondiscrimination, vesting, and so on).[70] ◀

EXAMPLE I:9-65 ▶ Assume the same facts as in Example I:9-64 except that Larry's earnings from his trade or business (before the H.R. 10 plan contribution but after the deduction for one-half of the self-employment (taxes) is $300,000. The maximum contribution that Larry can make on his behalf in 2010 is $49,000 ($245,000 × 0.20). Even though his earnings were $300,000, the maximum compensation that can be used to calculate the H.R. 10 plan contribution in 2010 is $245,000. ◀

---

[67] Sec. 415(c)(1). Prior to 2002, the limitations were considerably lower. In 2001, for example, a self-employed individual could only contribute 25% of earned income to a maximum of $35,000.

[68] This reduction in contribution percentage is computed as follows: 0.25/1.00 + 0.25 = 0.20. If the Keogh contribution rate is 15% rather than 25%, the deductible percentage would be 13.0435%, computed as above, 0.15/1.00 + 0.15 = 0.130435. Other percentages can be calculated accordingly.

[69] Secs. 401(a)(17) and 404(l). The ceiling in 2009 was also $245,000.

[70] Sec. 401(d).

KEY POINT

A Keogh plan must be created no later than the last day of your tax year.

An H.R. 10 plan must be established before the end of the tax year, but contributions may be made up to the due date for the tax return (including extensions). All H.R. 10 pension contributions made by a self-employed individual for *employees* are deductible for AGI on Schedule C. The H.R. 10 contribution for the self-employed individual is deductible *for* AGI on page 1 of Form 1040.

INDIVIDUAL RETIREMENT ACCOUNTS (IRAs)

HISTORICAL NOTE

The IRA savings provisions were originally enacted in 1974 to provide a tax-favored retirement savings arrangement to individuals who were not covered under a qualified plan. Beginning in 1982, Congress extended IRA availability to all taxpayers. It was hoped that the extended availability would increase the level of savings and provide a discretionary retirement savings plan that was uniformly available. However, Congress in the Tax Reform Act of 1986 restricted the availability of IRAs because there was no discernible impact on aggregate personal savings.

Under current law, there are three types of IRAs that are available to taxpayers:

▶ Traditional IRA

▶ Roth IRA

▶ Coverdell Education Savings Account IRA[71]

Each of these three types of IRAs is discussed below.

TRADITIONAL IRA

Traditional IRAs have been in the law for about 30 years and taxpayers may make either deductible or nondeductible contributions to the IRA. A contribution to a traditional IRA that is deductible has two principal benefits: (1) the amount contributed to the IRA (maximum $5,000 per year for years 2008 and 2009) is deductible on the taxpayer's return[72] and (2) the income earned on the investments in the IRA is not subject to current taxation. However, when amounts are withdrawn from the IRA at retirement, such amounts are fully subject to taxation. Nondeductible contributions to a traditional IRA may not be deducted on the taxpayer's return, but such contributions are not subject to taxation when withdrawn from the IRA. While contributions are not subject to taxation, any earnings are subject to taxation when withdrawn.

Individuals may make deductible contributions equal to the lesser of $5,000 or 100% of compensation only if either of the following conditions exists:

▶ The individual is *not* an active participant in an employer-sponsored retirement plan, including tax-sheltered annuities, government plans, simplified employee pension plans, and H.R. 10 plans; or

▶ Individuals who are active participants in an employer-sponsored retirement plan must have an AGI equal to or below the following applicable dollar limits for 2010:[73] $56,000 ($55,000 in 2009) for an unmarried taxpayer; $89,000 (no change from 2009) for a married couple filing a joint return; zero for a married individual filing separately. If an individual has AGI above these amounts, the deductible IRA contribution amounts are phased out on a pro rata basis as AGI increases from $56,000 to $66,000 for unmarried taxpayers and from $89,000 to $109,000 for married taxpayers filing a joint return.

EXAMPLE I:9-66 ▶ Laura is an unmarried taxpayer who is not an active participant in an employer-sponsored retirement plan or other qualified plan. In 2010, Laura's AGI is $75,000, consisting of earned income from wages. Laura is not subject to the dollar limitation because she is not an active participant in a qualified plan and may, therefore, contribute and deduct up to $5,000 to a traditional IRA. Laura's AGI is reduced to $70,000 ($75,000 − $5,000) because the amount is deductible *for* AGI. ◀

EXAMPLE I:9-67 ▶ Judy is an unmarried taxpayer and an active participant in her employer's qualified retirement plan. In 2010, Judy's AGI is $60,000, consisting of earned income from wages of $57,000 and interest and dividends of $3,000. Since she is an active participant in a qualified plan and her AGI is over $56,000, her deductible contribution to a traditional IRA is subject to the phaseout. Since the ceiling amount is exceeded by $4,000 ($60,000 − $56,000), the maximum IRA contribution is reduced by 40% ($4,000/$10,000), or $2,000. Thus, the maximum that Judy can contribute and deduct to her IRA in 2010 is $3,000 ($5,000 − $2,000). ◀

---

[71] The Coverdell Education Savings Account was named after the late Senator Paul Coverdell of Georgia.

[72] The deductible amount to an IRA was increased from $2,000 prior to 2002 to $3,000 for 2002–2004, $4,000 for 2005–2007, and $5,000 in 2008 and future years. See Sec. 219 (b)(5). After 2008, the deductible amount will be indexed for inflation. Prior to 2002, the deductible amount was $2,000. In addition, individuals over 50 years of age are now eligible to contribute an extra $500 into their IRA in years 2002–2005 (increasing to $1,000 in 2006 and future years). These extra amounts are referred to as "catch-up contributions."

[73] Sec. 219(g).

ADDITIONAL COMMENT

Banks, savings and loan associations, insurance companies, and stock brokerage firms make IRAs available to taxpayers. Usually, the amounts are invested in long-term investment accounts. However, self-directed plans are offered by some stock brokerage firms. In this type of IRA, the taxpayer can specify how the contributions will be invested.

If a taxpayer's AGI exceeds the above limits, the taxpayer may make a nondeductible contribution of up to $5,000 to a traditional IRA. The benefit of making a nondeductible contribution to an IRA is that the earnings of the IRA investments grow tax-free. Thus, even though the *earnings* of the nondeductible IRA will be taxed when distributed, the ability to allow investments to compound before-tax is a major advantage for taxpayers. However, as will be seen in the discussion of Roth IRAs below, if a taxpayer can qualify for a Roth IRA rather than a traditional nondeductible IRA, the choice clearly favors a Roth IRA. The maximum amount of a nondeductible contribution that may be made to a traditional IRA is $5,000 minus the amount that is allowed as a deduction. Also, a taxpayer may elect for all of his contributions to be nondeductible even though the contributions are otherwise eligible to be deducted.

EXAMPLE I:9-68 ▶ Using the same facts as in Example I:9-67, Judy is permitted to make a nondeductible contribution to her IRA of $2,000 ($5,000 − $3,000). She also could elect to designate all $5,000 as a nondeductible contribution even though she is eligible to deduct the $3,000. ◀

Two special rules apply to married couples relative to traditional IRAs. First, if only one spouse is employed and this working spouse is otherwise eligible to make IRA contributions, the nonworking spouse may contribute up to $5,000 per year to an IRA (a so-called spousal IRA). Thus, a total of $10,000 may be deductible by a married couple ($5,000 to each spouse's IRA) even though only one spouse has earned income. It should be noted that even though only the working spouse must have earned income, such working spouse must have at least $10,000 of earned income in order to contribute $10,000 to the two IRAs. Second, if one spouse is covered under a qualified retirement plan but the other spouse is not covered, the non-covered spouse may contribute to a traditional deductible IRA. However, for 2010, the contribution to a traditional deductible IRA is phased out at adjusted gross incomes between $167,000 and $177,000.

EXAMPLE I:9-69 ▶ Gary and Babs are a married couple. Gary is covered under a qualified retirement plan at his job and earned $160,000 in 2010. Babs is employed as a secretary and earned $20,000 but is not covered under a qualified retirement plan. They file a joint return, have interest and dividend income of $20,000, and their AGI, therefore, is $200,000. Neither Gary nor Babs is entitled to deduct contributions to a traditional IRA. Gary cannot contribute and deduct any amount to an IRA because he is covered under another qualified plan and their AGI exceeds $109,000. Babs is also not eligible because their AGI exceeds $177,000. However, both Gary and Babs are allowed to make nondeductible contributions of $5,000 each to the IRA. ◀

EXAMPLE I:9-70 ▶ Assume the same facts as in Example I:9-69 but that Gary's income is $100,000 and their AGI is $130,000. Babs may contribute and deduct $5,000 to a traditional IRA because their AGI is less than $167,000. However, Gary may not make a deductible contribution because he is covered under a qualified plan and their AGI exceeds $109,000. Gary is permitted to make a $5,000 contribution to a nondeductible IRA. ◀

ADDITIONAL COMMENT

A contribution to an IRA for the year 2010 can be made as late as the due date for filing the 2010 return, or April 15, 2011.

The following significant tax rules apply to traditional IRAs:

▶ An IRA plan may be established between the end of the tax year and the due date for the tax return (not including any extensions that are permitted). Any deductible contributions made during this time are treated as a deduction for the prior year. Contributions are deductible if made by the due date for the tax return (i.e., contributions for 2010 must be made no later than April 15, 2011. Contributions to nondeductible IRAs also must be made by April 15 of the following year.

▶ Taxpayers who are 50 years of age or older by the end of the taxable year may contribute an additional $1,000 per year (or a total of $6,000 in 2010).

▶ Distributions from a traditional IRA are taxed under the annuity rules in Sec. 72. Normally distributions from an IRA are fully subject to taxation. However, if nondeductible contributions are made to an IRA, these amounts would represent the investment in the contract in calculating the exclusion ratio.

▶ Withdrawals by a participant before age 59½ are both includible in income and subject to a nondeductible 10% penalty tax.[74]

---

[74] Sec. 72(t). The amount subject to the 10% penalty is the portion of the amount that must be included in gross income. Exceptions to the 10% penalty are provided in the event of death, disability, and certain non-lump-sum distributions.

Two additional exceptions also apply: (1) withdrawals used to pay qualified higher education costs for taxpayer, spouse, children or grandchildren and (2) up to $10,000 to buy or build the principal residence for a "first time homebuyer."

▶ Withdrawals must begin no later than April 1 of the year following the end of the tax year in which the individual reaches age 70½. IRA contributions that were deducted over the years on the taxpayer's returns are fully taxable as ordinary income when the amounts are distributed.

▶ A nondeductible 6% penalty is levied on excess contributions to an IRA.[75]

ROTH IRA

The Roth IRA[76] is a relatively new type of IRA that is a so-called "backloaded IRA" because the tax benefits come at the end, not at the beginning, of the IRA. Contributions to a Roth IRA are nondeductible but all distributions from the IRA, including earnings, are nontaxable. The maximum amount that may be contributed to a Roth IRA is $5,000. However, taxpayers who are eligible for both a Roth IRA and a traditional IRA may only contribute a total of $5,000 to both types of IRAs. As with traditional IRAs, Roth IRAs are also subject to AGI phaseout limitations, although the limitation amounts are higher than with traditional IRAs.

All taxpayers may contribute up to the lesser of (1) $5,000 or (2) 100% of the taxpayer's compensation, to a Roth IRA; however, for 2010, this amount is phased-out for single taxpayers if their AGI is between $105,000 (also $105,000 in 2009) and $120,000 ($167,000 and $177,000 for married couples filing a joint return and $0 for married individuals filing separate returns). The principal advantage of the Roth IRA is the nontaxability of qualified distributions. One requirement of a qualified distribution is that the distribution must meet a five-year holding period. More specifically, the distribution may not be made before the end of the five-tax-year period beginning with the first tax year for which a contribution was made to the Roth IRA. The first tax year begins on the first day of the tax year (i.e., January 1 in most cases) in which a contribution was made even though such contribution may have been made later in such tax year. In addition to satisfying the five-year test, a qualifying distribution must also meet one of the following:

▶ made on or after the date on which the individual attains age 59½,

▶ made to a beneficiary (or the individual's estate) on or after the individual's death,

▶ attributable to the individual being disabled, or

▶ a distribution for first-time homebuyer expenses (maximum of $10,000).

An important aspect of distributions from a Roth IRA is a special ordering rule for determining the taxability of nonqualifying withdrawals. Under this rule, distributions are treated as being made from contributions first and, thus, are nontaxable. After all contributions have been withdrawn, any remaining amounts are considered taxable and subject to the 10% penalty.

EXAMPLE I:9-71 ▶ Ray and Sandy are married and Ray is covered under his employer's qualified retirement plan. Their AGI on a joint return is $130,000. Ray can contribute $5,000 to a Roth IRA. Alternatively, however, if their AGI was $173,000, Ray would be limited to a maximum contribution of $2,000. Since their AGI exceeds the threshold of $167,000 by $6,000, the $5,000 contribution is reduced by 60% ($6000/$10,000), or $3,000. ◀

EXAMPLE I:9-72 ▶ Bob, age 60 in 2009, contributes $5,000 each year to a Roth IRA in 2010, 2011, and 2012. On November 30, 2014, the value of the Roth IRA is $18,000. Bob has experienced some financial setbacks and needs to withdraw the money from the Roth IRA. If Bob withdraws $15,000 in 2014 and waits until January 2015 to withdraw the remaining $3,000, none of the distributions are taxable. This result occurs because the first $15,000 is treated as coming from contributions. The remaining $3,000 is nontaxable because Bob has met the five-year test and is over age 59½. Conversely, if Bob withdraws the entire $18,000 in 2014, $3,000 must be included in his income because the five-year test was not met. No penalty will be imposed because he is over age 59½. ◀

A final aspect of Roth IRAs is the ability to "rollover" funds from an existing traditional IRA into a Roth IRA. Since the taxpayer received a deduction for the contribution into the traditional IRA, any rollover amount must be included in gross income in the year the rollover occurred, but is not subject to the 10% penalty for early withdrawals. For years prior to 2010,

---

[75] Sec. 4973(b).

[76] Sec. 408A.

only taxpayers with AGI of $100,000 or less were eligible to rollover amounts from a traditional IRA to a Roth IRA. However, for tax years beginning in 2010, the $100,000 income limit has been repealed and permits all taxpayers to convert traditional IRAs to Roth IRAs. There is considerable interest in this option for taxpayers. The essential question is whether a taxpayer should convert his or her traditional IRA to a Roth IRA and pay the tax currently or keep the traditional IRA and pay the tax on a current basis as the amounts are withdrawn? The key variable in this analysis is the taxpayer's age. Younger taxpayers would definitely benefit with a Roth IRA as the amounts in the Roth IRA have years to accumulate and compound and such amounts will never be subject to taxation. Other important variables include the taxpayer's assessment of his or her future marginal tax rate and the ability to pay the tax on the rollover out of private funds. One further feature of a 2010 rollover of a traditional IRA to a Roth IRA is the option to pay the 2010 income tax in equal installments in 2011 and 2012. This spreading out the tax does not apply to rollovers in future years after 2010.

EXAMPLE I:9-73 ▶ Mikael has a traditional IRA that has a balance of $60,000 on June 30, 2009. He is single and has AGI of $80,000. Mikael is eligible to rollover the $60,000 to a Roth IRA. If he completes the rollover in 2009, he will be required to include the $60,000 in his gross income for 2009. He is not subject to the 10% early withdrawal penalty on the rollover. ◀

EXAMPLE I:9-74 ▶ John has a traditional IRA that has a balance of $250,000 on June 30, 2010. He is single and has AGI of $180,000. John would like to rollover the $250,000 to a Roth IRA. In 2009, John would not be eligible to do the rollover because his AGI exceeded $100,000. However, in 2010 and later years, the $100,000 AGI limitation does not apply. So, John is permitted to rollover the $250,000 from his traditional IRA to a Roth IRA in 2010. He must include the $250,000 in his gross income in 2010 but no penalty is imposed. John may also elect to include $125,000 in his gross income in 2011 and 2012. ◀

Below is a discussion of some of the important tax rules for Roth IRAs:

▶ Like traditional IRAs, Roth IRAs must be established by the due date of the tax return (not including extensions). Similarly, contributions to a Roth IRA also must be made by the due date of the return (i.e., April 15, 2011, for 2010 contributions).

▶ Contributions to a Roth IRA are never deductible.

▶ Contributions to a Roth IRA are subject to special modified AGI limitations.

▶ Contributions to a Roth IRA can be made after the owner has reached age 70½. Similarly, no distributions are required at any age from a Roth IRA. (Remember: owners of traditional IRAs must begin taking distributions in the year after the taxpayer has reached age 70½).

▶ Taxpayers who are 50 years or older by the end of the taxable year may contribute an additional $1,000 per year (or a total of $6,000 in 2010).

▶ Withdrawals from a Roth IRA are not taxable if such withdrawals are "qualified distributions." If a withdrawal is not a qualified distribution, the amount is taxed under special ordering rules and subject to the 10% penalty.

STOP & THINK *Question:* Both nondeductible contributions to a traditional IRA and contributions to a Roth IRA are similar in the sense that neither provides a tax deduction at the date of contribution. Which of the two types would be most advantageous to taxpayers?

Solution: Clearly, if a taxpayer qualifies for a Roth IRA, that type of IRA is superior to a nondeductible contribution to a traditional IRA. The reason is that distributions from a Roth IRA are totally excluded from gross income while only the principal portion of nondeductible contributions to a traditional IRA are excludable. In other words, the earnings generated in a Roth IRA are excluded from gross income whereas earnings associated with nondeductible contributions to a traditional IRA are subject to taxation. Generally, a nondeductible contribution to a traditional IRA will not be advantageous unless the taxpayer's AGI exceeds $177,000.

For a discussion of the decision whether to invest in a traditional deductible IRA or a Roth IRA, see the Tax Planning Considerations later in this chapter. Also, for a more detailed analysis including computations, see Chapter I:18 of the *Individuals* textbook.

Topic Review I:9-5

Traditional and Roth IRAs—Eligibility

If 2010 AGI Is	Eligible for IRA (Joint Returns)				
	Traditional IRA (Deductible)			Roth IRA	Traditional IRA (Nondeductible)*
	A	B	C		
Up to $89,000	Yes	Yes	Yes	Yes	Yes
$89,000–$109,000	Yes	Partially	Yes	Yes	Yes
$109,000–$167,000	Yes	No	Yes	Yes	Yes
$167,000–$177,000	Yes	No	Partially	Partially	Yes
Over $177,000	Yes	No	No	No	Yes

A   If neither spouse is an active participant in an employer-sponsored plan
B   For the IRA of a spouse who is an active participant in an employer-sponsored plan
C   For the IRA of a spouse who is not an active participant in an employer-sponsored plan

* If AGI is not above $177,000, a nondeductible IRA will not be advantageous.

Topic Review I:9-5 contains a table which summarizes the eligibility rules for traditional and Roth IRAs.

COVERDELL EDUCATION SAVINGS ACCOUNT

A special type of IRA, referred to as an Education IRA, was established to specifically assist low- and middle-income taxpayers with higher education expenses. The Education IRA was renamed the Coverdell Education Savings Account (CESA) in 2001. CESAs have a number of attractive features:

▶ The maximum annual contribution into such plan is $2,000.

▶ CESAs may be used for elementary and secondary education expenses as well as for higher education expenses, and

▶ Taxpayers can claim either the HOPE scholarship credit or lifetime learning credit as well as excluding distributions from a CESA in the same year.

A contributor can make a *nondeductible* contribution of up to $2,000 per year into a CESA for a designated beneficiary until the beneficiary reaches age 18.[77] The contributor need not be related to the beneficiary and there is no limit on the number of CESAs that can be set up by a contributor. Distributions to the beneficiary are excluded from gross income provided the distribution does not exceed the *qualified education expenses* of the designated beneficiary during the taxable year. Qualified education expenses include tuition, fees, books, supplies, equipment, and room and board. In the case of elementary and secondary education expenses, qualified education expenses include academic tutoring and Internet access fees. Distributions in any tax year in excess of qualified education expenses are includible in the gross income of the beneficiary and subject to a 10% penalty.

Similar to other IRA-type accounts, there are phaseout limits based on the contributor's AGI. The $2,000 annual contribution is phased out for married taxpayers filing joint returns with AGI from $190,000 to $220,000 ($95,000 to $110,000 for other taxpayers). In addition, if the taxpayer claims either the HOPE scholarship credit or the lifetime learning credit, the education expenses used for these credits must reduce the qualified expenses for exclusion from a CESA.

EXAMPLE I:9-75 ▶ Lee and Patsy are married and have two young grandchildren. To assist the grandchildren with their future education expenses, they set up a CESA for each child in 2010 and plan to deposit $2,000 in both accounts. Their AGI for 2010 is $202,000. Because their AGI exceeds $190,000, they are limited to putting $1,200 [$2,000 − $2,000($202,000 − $190,000)/$30,000)] into the accounts in 2010. In the future, the children can withdraw amounts tax-free from their CESA to pay for qualified education expenses for elementary, secondary, or higher education. ◀

---

[77] Sec. 530. Contributions are allowed to continue past age 18 for a special-needs beneficiary, Sec. 530(b)(1).

EXAMPLE I:9-76 ▶ Craig Shaw is about to enter State University as a freshman and plans to withdraw amounts from his CESA to help pay his expenses. His expenses for the Fall Semester 2010 are as follows:

Tuition and fees	$2,200
Books	500
Supplies	300
Room and board	2,400
Total	$5,400

Craig's parents plan on paying Craig's tuition and fees, and Craig will pay the remaining $3,200 from his CESA. Craig qualifies as a dependent of his parents for the tax year. Craig's parents plan on claiming the HOPE scholarship credit. Craig is not required to include the $3,200 in his gross income in 2010 as his qualified education expenses are at least $3,200. Craig's parents will use $2,200 to claim the HOPE credit. ◀

HEALTH SAVINGS ACCOUNTS

Health Savings Accounts (HSAs) were established by Congress for eligible individuals for taxable years beginning after December 31, 2003.[78] The purpose of HSAs is to enable individuals to accumulate funds on a tax-free basis to pay qualified medical expenses currently or in the future. In summary, HSAs operate as follows:

▶ The individual must be covered by a high-deductible health plan and not covered under any other health plan that is not a high-deductible health plan.

▶ Taxpayer contributes money into an HSA with a qualified trustee or custodian (much like an IRA). The taxpayer must be an eligible individual and the contributions are subject to limitations. These detailed issues are discussed below.

▶ The taxpayer is allowed a *for* AGI deduction in the year the contributions are made.

▶ Distributions from the HSA that are used exclusively to pay for qualified medical expenses (medical expenses as defined in Sec. 213(d), but not health insurance premiums) are excludable from gross income. However, any amount of the distribution that is not used to pay for qualified medical expenses is includable in the gross income of the taxpayer and subject to an additional 10% penalty. The 10% penalty is waived if the beneficiary/taxpayer is age 65 or older.

HSAs are only available to eligible individuals. An eligible individual is any individual who (1) is covered under a high-deductible health plan (HDHP), (2) is not also covered by any other health plan that is not an HDHP, (3) is not entitled to benefits under Medicare (i.e., generally, has not reached age 65), and (4) may not be claimed as a dependent on another person's tax return. An HDHP is a plan with an annual deductible in 2010 of at least $1,200 and annual out-of-pocket expenses (other than premiums) required to be paid not exceeding $5,950. For family coverage, these amounts are $2,400 and $11,900, respectively.

Annual contributions to an HSA are determined separately for each month the plan is in effect and is $1/12$ of the *lesser* of (1) 100% of the annual deductible under the HDHP ($1,200) or (2) $3,050. For individuals with family coverage under an HDHP, the amounts are (1) 100% of the annual deductible under the HDHP (minimum of $2,400) or (2) $6,150. Catch-up contributions are permitted for individuals age 55 to 64.

EXAMPLE I:9-77 ▶ Roy, age 45, established an HDHP for his family with a $3,600 annual deductible on May 1, 2010. Roy is eligible to put $2,400 (8 months × $300) into an HSA for the calendar year 2010. The purpose of the fund is to pay for medical expenses for himself and his family. In 2010, Roy is allowed to deduct the $2,400 as a deduction for AGI. Any earnings of the fund investments are not subject to tax if the distribution is used to pay qualified medical expenses. ◀

EXAMPLE I:9-78 ▶ In 2014, Roy takes a $5,000 distribution from the HSA to make a down payment on a new automobile. Since the distribution was not used to pay qualified medical expenses, Roy must include the $5,000 in his income and pay a $500 ($5,000 × 10%) penalty in 2014. ◀

---

[78] Sec. 223. Archer Medical Savings Accounts are similar to HSAs but cannot be established after 12/31/05. MSAs have a more restrictive definition of HDHP so there is little incentive to use them.

SIMPLIFIED EMPLOYEE PENSIONS

Due to the administrative complexity associated with qualified pension and profit-sharing plans, small businesses often establish simplified employee pension (SEP) plans for their employees. In a SEP, the employer makes contributions to the IRAs of its employees.[79] The following is a summary of the tax rules that apply to a SEP:

▶ The employer receives an immediate tax deduction for contributions made under the plan. The annual deductible contributions for each participant are limited to the lesser of 25% of the participant's compensation (up to a ceiling of $245,000 for 2010) and the dollar limitations for defined contribution plans.[80] The maximum amount for 2010 is $49,000.

▶ Contributions are treated as being made on the last day of the tax year if they are made by the due date of the tax return (including extensions).

▶ Employer contributions must be nondiscriminatory.

▶ Distributions from a SEP are subject to taxation based on the IRA rules (previously discussed) including the penalty tax for premature distributions.

▶ A self-employed person (i.e., a partner or sole proprietor) may establish a SEP rather than using an H.R. 10 plan arrangement because of reduced administrative complexity associated with a SEP.

SIMPLE RETIREMENT PLANS

Another more recent type of retirement savings plan for small businesses is called the savings incentive match plan for employees (SIMPLE).[81] This type of plan can be adopted by employers who have 100 or fewer employees who received at least $5,000 in compensation from the employer in the preceding year. A SIMPLE plan may be set up either as an IRA for each employee or part of a qualified cash or deferred arrangement (401(k) plan). Essentially, employees are allowed to make elective contributions in 2010 of up to $11,500 per year and employers are required to make matching contributions.

The unique features of the SIMPLE plans are (1) that elective contributions by employees must be matched by the employer or the employer has the option of making nonelective contributions, (2) that all contributions to an employee's SIMPLE account must be fully vested, and (3) the SIMPLE plans are not subject to the special nondiscrimination rules generally applicable to qualified plans. This last feature is important in that there is no requirement that a set number of employees *participate* in the plan, the only requirement is that all employees who had $5,000 in compensation in the previous year and are reasonably expected to have $5,000 in compensation in the current year must be eligible to participate.

TAX PLANNING CONSIDERATIONS

MOVING EXPENSES

To be eligible for the moving expense deduction, the moving expenses must be paid in connection with the commencement of work by the taxpayer as a full-time employee or self-employed individual. Therefore, it is important to secure full-time employment or to carry on a trade or business as a self-employed individual at the new location. Taxpayers who are approaching retirement are eligible for a moving expense deduction only if they continue to work in the new location before their actual retirement (e.g., 39 weeks in the 12-month period following the move).

EXAMPLE I:9-79 ▶ Louis decides to quit his job and return to school as a full-time graduate student. Louis incurs substantial long-distance moving expenses that would otherwise be deductible to relocate to the university where the education is to be taken. No deduction is allowed unless Louis is employed on a full-time basis or is engaged in a self-employment activity at the new location. ◀

REIMBURSED AMOUNTS. Moving expense reimbursements are often greater than the amounts allowable as a deduction. This is caused by the common practice of reimbursing

---

[79] Sec. 408(k).
[80] Sec. 404(h)(1).

[81] Sec. 408(p).

nondeductible items (e.g., an employer may reimburse an employee for the cost of certain indirect moving expenses such as househunting trips, which do not qualify as deductible moving expenses). This results in an increase in the employee's gross income to the extent of the excess reimbursement. From a tax planning standpoint, the employer may provide an additional payment to compensate the employee for the additional tax cost associated with the move (commonly referred to as a "gross-up").

EXAMPLE I:9-80 ▶ Austin Corporation has a policy of reimbursing transferred employees for 30% of their moving reimbursement that exceeds their deductible expenses to cover the federal and state tax costs associated with the excess reimbursement. Kathy, an employee, is transferred by the company to a new job location and incurs $6,000 of deductible moving expenses and receives an $8,000 reimbursement. Austin also will make an additional payment to Kathy of $600 (0.30 × $2,000) to cover the additional federal and state income tax costs. Kathy must include $2,600 ($2,000 + $600) of the reimbursement in gross income. ◀

PROVIDING NONTAXABLE COMPENSATION TO EMPLOYEES

Employers should consider the tax consequences to employees when changes in fringe benefit and deferred compensation arrangements are evaluated. For example, it is preferable for an employer to pay for fringe benefit items such as group term life insurance (up to $50,000 in coverage), health and accident insurance, employee parking, and so on rather than to give cash raises of a comparable amount. Such payments are nontaxable to the employee up to certain limits, whereas a comparable salary increase is fully taxable. Both types of payments are deductible by the employer.

Consideration should also be given to increased deferred compensation benefit programs for employees, particularly highly-compensated individuals. The use of nonqualified deferred compensation plans, restricted property, and stock options result in tax deferrals and may result in the eventual recognition of capital gains that may be used to offset capital losses or that are taxed at a maximum 15% marginal tax rate.

All eligible employees should consider establishing an individual retirement account (IRA) because of the available tax deferral benefits. Even if a premature withdrawal (i.e., before age 59½ occurs), the time value of the deferred benefits for the plan contributions and the earnings may be greater than the penalty tax imposed.

ROLLOVER OF TRADITIONAL IRA TO ROTH IRA

Taxpayers have the ability to rollover amounts from a traditional IRA to a Roth IRA. However, if such a rollover is made, the taxpayer must include the rollover amount in gross income in the year of the rollover. The principal benefit of the rollover is that once the amounts are in the Roth IRA, no further taxes are due on these amounts upon distribution (assuming the five-year test is met). The essential question, therefore, is whether it is advantageous to rollover amounts from a traditional IRA to a Roth IRA and pay the tax now or keep the traditional IRA intact and pay the tax when regular distributions are made.

The decision rests on several factors, including (1) the marginal tax rate at retirement, (2) age of taxpayer, and (3) payment of tax from rollover from post-tax funds. First, if a taxpayer's marginal tax rate at retirement is expected to be lower than the current tax rate, a rollover may not be advantageous. Second, younger taxpayers are more likely to benefit from a rollover because they have more years to accumulate earnings tax-free and may be in a lower tax bracket today than at retirement. Finally, if the taxes that accrue from the rollover must be paid from the rollover funds, a rollover will probably not be in the taxpayer's favor. In other words, taxpayers should have sufficient funds from other sources to pay the tax, then the entire amount of rollover into the Roth IRA will have maximum ability to grow on a tax-free basis.

Each case must be analyzed based on the unique factors of that particular situation. However, for most taxpayers, it is generally advantageous to rollover funds from a traditional IRA to a Roth IRA. For tax years beginning before January 1, 2010, as is pointed out earlier in this chapter, the individual must have AGI of $100,000 or less (before the rollover distribution) to qualify for the rollover. For tax years beginning after December 31, 2009, the $100,000 AGI limitation is repealed. Thus, higher income taxpayers will be able to rollover traditional IRAs to Roth IRAs beginning in 2010. These rollovers, of course, must be included in the gross income of the taxpayer.

COMPLIANCE AND PROCEDURAL CONSIDERATIONS

KEY POINT

It is extremely important to be able to substantiate travel and entertainment expenses. The *Cohan* Rule that permits a reasonable deduction when substantiation is lacking does not apply to travel and entertainment expenses (see Chapter I:6).

SUBSTANTIATING TRAVEL AND ENTERTAINMENT EXPENSES

Travel and entertainment expenses are disallowed if the taxpayer does not maintain adequate records or documentary proof of the expenditures.[82] Normally, documentation includes expense statements (diary or account book) and proof of the amount, time, place, and business purpose. Strict substantiation rules are enacted in the law to curb widespread abuses in the so-called expense account living practices engaged in by some taxpayers.

To make compliance easier, the IRS formulated the following administrative procedural rules:

▶ If an employee makes an adequate accounting of the expenditures to the employer, it is not necessary to submit a detailed statement on the employee's tax return unless the expenses exceed the reimbursements.

▶ The standard mileage rate may be used to compute automobile expenses in lieu of actual expenses and is reported on Form 2106 (Employee Business Expenses).

▶ Taxpayers may elect an optional method for computing deductions for business travel and meal expenses in lieu of using actual costs. If a per diem allowance is paid by an employer in lieu of reimbursing actual expenses, the reimbursement is deemed to be substantiated if it does not exceed a federal per diem rate for the travel locality. In lieu of using actual expenses an employee or self-employed individual may use the applicable federal per diem rate. The taxpayer must still provide documentation of time, place, and business purpose for the expenditures.

ETHICAL POINT

The CPA has a responsibility to make sure that proper documentation has been furnished by the taxpayer to substantiate travel and entertainment expenses according to the provisions in Sec. 274(d). The CPA cannot rely on the use of estimates for these expenses despite the fact that the *AICPA's Statements on Standards for Tax Services No. 4* (see Appendix E) permits the use of estimates if it is impractical to obtain exact data and the estimated amounts appear to be reasonable.

REPORTING EMPLOYEE BUSINESS EXPENSES

Form 2106 (Employee Business Expenses) is used to report employee business expenses (see Appendix B). Part I of Form 2106 is a recap of travel and transportation expenses. Part II includes a computation of automobile expenses using either actual expenses or the standard rate mileage method. Employer reimbursements must be included in the employee's wages on Form W-2 if an adequate accounting of the expenses is not made. Employer withholding of federal income tax is also required for nonaccountable plan reimbursements. Form 2106-EZ may be used by employees who do not receive an employer reimbursement, and where the standard mileage rate is used for the current year and for the year the taxpayer's automobile was first placed in service.

Moving expenses are reported on Form 3903 (Moving Expenses) instead of Form 2106 because they are treated differently from other employee expenses (e.g., unreimbursed moving expenses are deductible *for* AGI). Expenses such as entertainment, union dues, business gifts, and education expenses are reported on Schedule A of Form 1040 as itemized deductions (see Appendix B).

A filled-in copy of Form 2106 is shown in Figure I:9-2. It includes the computations relating to the information in Example I:9-81.

EXAMPLE I:9-81 ▶

ADDITIONAL COMMENT

Many of the provisions related to employee business expenses are very complex. It has been said of the general complexity of the tax law that "If Patrick Henry thought taxation without representation was bad, he should have seen taxation with representation."

Eric Graber, SSN 231-54-9876, is single and employed as a salesman by the Houston Corporation in 2009. Eric is required to use his personal automobile for employment-related business and placed the current automobile in service in 2006. He uses only one automobile for business purposes and has elected to use the mileage method for deducting expenses. During 2009, Eric drives his automobile 80% of the time for business use and incurs the following total expenses:

Gas and oil	$ 7,000
Repairs	600
Depreciation	1,675
Insurance	1,400
Parking and tolls (all business related)	250
Total	$10,925

---

[82] Sec. 274(d).

Form **2106**

Department of the Treasury
Internal Revenue Service (99)

Employee Business Expenses

▶ See separate instructions.

▶ **Attach to Form 1040 or Form 1040NR.**

OMB No. 1545-0074

20**09**

Attachment
Sequence No. **129**

Your name	Occupation in which you incurred expenses	Social security number
Eric Grabar	Sales	231 54 9876

Part I   Employee Business Expenses and Reimbursements

Step 1   Enter Your Expenses

			Column A Other Than Meals and Entertainment	Column B Meals and Entertainment
1	Vehicle expense from line 22 or line 29. (Rural mail carriers: See instructions.)	1	13,200	
2	Parking fees, tolls, and transportation, including train, bus, etc., that **did not** involve overnight travel or commuting to and from work .	2	250	
3	Travel expense while away from home overnight, including lodging, airplane, car rental, etc. **Do not** include meals and entertainment .	3	3,050	
4	Business expenses not included on lines 1 through 3. **Do not** include meals and entertainment	4		
5	Meals and entertainment expenses (see instructions)	5		950
6	**Total expenses.** In Column A, add lines 1 through 4 and enter the result. In Column B, enter the amount from line 5	6	16,500	950

Note: *If you were not reimbursed for any expenses in Step 1, skip line 7 and enter the amount from line 6 on line 8.*

Step 2   Enter Reimbursements Received From Your Employer for Expenses Listed in Step 1

7	Enter reimbursements received from your employer that were **not** reported to you in box 1 of Form W-2. Include any reimbursements reported under code "L" in box 12 of your Form W-2 (see instructions)	7	7,200	-0-

Step 3   Figure Expenses To Deduct on Schedule A (Form 1040 or Form 1040NR)

8	Subtract line 7 from line 6. If zero or less, enter -0-. However, if line 7 is greater than line 6 in Column A, report the excess as income on Form 1040, line 7 (or on Form 1040NR, line 8)	8	9,300	950

Note: If **both columns** of line 8 are zero, you cannot deduct employee business expenses. Stop here and attach Form 2106 to your return.

9	In Column A, enter the amount from line 8. In Column B, multiply line 8 by 50% (.50). (Employees subject to Department of Transportation (DOT) hours of service limits: Multiply meal expenses incurred while away from home on business by 80% (.80) instead of 50%. For details, see instructions.)	9	9,300	475
10	Add the amounts on line 9 of both columns and enter the total here. **Also, enter the total on Schedule A (Form 1040), line 21** (or on **Schedule A (Form 1040NR), line 9**). (Armed Forces reservists, qualified performing artists, fee-basis state or local government officials, and individuals with disabilities: See the instructions for special rules on where to enter the total.) ▶	10		9,775

For Paperwork Reduction Act Notice, see instructions.   Cat. No. 11700N   Form **2106** (2009)

FIGURE I:9-2   ▶   PAGE 1 OF FORM 2106 FOR EXAMPLE I:9-81

Part II	Vehicle Expenses

Section A—General Information (You must complete this section if you are claiming vehicle expenses.)

			(a) Vehicle 1	**(b)** Vehicle 2
11	Enter the date the vehicle was placed in service	11	7/ 1 /06	/ /
12	Total miles the vehicle was driven during 2009	12	30,000 miles	miles
13	Business miles included on line 12	13	24,000 miles	miles
14	Percent of business use. Divide line 13 by line 12	14	80 %	%
15	Average daily roundtrip commuting distance	15	8 miles	miles
16	Commuting miles included on line 12	16	2,000 miles	miles
17	Other miles. Add lines 13 and 16 and subtract the total from line 12 . .	17	4,000 miles	miles

		Yes	No
18	Was your vehicle available for personal use during off-duty hours?	☐ Yes	☐ No
19	Do you (or your spouse) have another vehicle available for personal use?	☐ Yes	☐ No
20	Do you have evidence to support your deduction?	☐ Yes	☐ No
21	If "Yes," is the evidence written?	☐ Yes	☐ No

Section B—Standard Mileage Rate (See the instructions for Part II to find out whether to complete this section or Section C.)

22	Multiply line 13 by 55¢ (.55). Enter the result here and on line 1	22	13,200

Section C—Actual Expenses

			(a) Vehicle 1		**(b)** Vehicle 2	
23	Gasoline, oil, repairs, vehicle insurance, etc.	23				
24a	Vehicle rentals	24a				
b	Inclusion amount (see instructions) .	24b				
c	Subtract line 24b from line 24a .	24c				
25	Value of employer-provided vehicle (applies only if 100% of annual lease value was included on Form W-2—see instructions)	25				
26	Add lines 23, 24c, and 25. . .	26				
27	Multiply line 26 by the percentage on line 14	27				
28	Depreciation (see instructions) .	28				
29	Add lines 27 and 28. Enter total here and on line 1	29				

Section D—Depreciation of Vehicles (Use this section only if you owned the vehicle and are completing Section C for the vehicle.)

			(a) Vehicle 1		**(b)** Vehicle 2	
30	Enter cost or other basis (see instructions)	30				
31	Enter section 179 deduction and special allowance (see instructions)	31				
32	Multiply line 30 by line 14 (see instructions if you claimed the section 179 deduction or special allowance)	32				
33	Enter depreciation method and percentage (see instructions) .	33				
34	Multiply line 32 by the percentage on line 33 (see instructions)	34				
35	Add lines 31 and 34	35				
36	Enter the applicable limit explained in the line 36 instructions . . .	36				
37	Multiply line 36 by the percentage on line 14	37				
38	Enter the **smaller** of line 35 or line 37. If you skipped lines 36 and 37, enter the amount from line 35. Also enter this amount on line 28 above.	38				

Form **2106** (2009)

FIGURE I:9-2 ▶ PAGE 2 OF FORM 2106 FOR EXAMPLE I:9-81

During the year, Eric drives a total of 30,000 miles throughout the year, of which 24,000 are business miles. Of the 6,000 personal miles, 2,000 miles are commuting to and from work. Eric receives a reimbursement of 30 cents per business mile from his employer. Eric also incurred $4,000 of unreimbursed employment-related travel and entertainment expenses. These expenses include the following:

Airfare	$ 2,500
Car rental	250
Business meals at which business was discussed	150
Laundry	100
Lodging	200
Entertainment of customers	800
Total	$ 4,000
Step 1, line 1: Vehicle expense (24,000 × $0.55)	$13,200
Step 2, line 7: (24,000 miles × $0.30)	$7,200
Section C, line 23: Actual expenses:	
Gas and oil	$7,000
Repairs	600
Insurance	1,400
Total	$ 9,000
Section C, line 28: Depreciation ($1,675 × .80)	$ 1,340

As can be seen from the completed Form 2106, Eric receives a larger deduction from the mileage method. This method has been elected by Eric. ◀

REPORTING MOVING EXPENSES

Employer reimbursements for qualifying moving expenses reduce the otherwise deductible amount for the employee. Reimbursements for nondeductible moving expenses are included in gross income and should be included in total wages on the employee's Form W-2 and reported on page 1 (line 7) of Form 1040. Employers should complete Form 4782 (Employee Moving Expense Information) which summarizes the moving expense payments made to the employee and to third parties. The form is provided to an employee to properly report his moving expenses and reimbursements. Form 3903 (Moving Expenses) is used to compute the allowable moving expenses and is attached to the employee's tax return (see Appendix B). Moving expenses are deductible *for* AGI on line 26 of page 1 of the 2009 Form 1040. Moving expenses are not subject to federal income tax withholding if it is reasonable to believe that an employee will be entitled to a deduction for such amounts. Reimbursements in excess of the deductible amounts, however, are subject to the withholding of income and social security taxes.

A taxpayer may deduct moving expenses, even though the tests for qualification have not been met (e.g., the 39-week test). If the individual subsequently fails to satisfy the requirements, gross income for the subsequent year must be increased by the previous tax benefit.[83] Another alternative is to wait until the tests have been met and then file an amended return (Form 1040X–see Appendix B) for the prior year.

KEY POINT

If a taxpayer who is an employee moves in early December, the earliest that the 39-week test could be met would be early September of the following year. This is well after the April 15 due date for the individual return. The taxpayer may nevertheless deduct the moving expenses in the earlier year.

REPORTING OFFICE IN HOME EXPENSES

Form 8829 (Expenses for Business Use of Your Home) must be used to figure the allowable expenses for business use that are reported on Schedule C (Profit or Loss from Business) and the carryover of any nondeductible amounts from prior years. Form 4562 (Depreciation and Amortization) must also be used to compute depreciation on the office portion of the residence. These tax forms are reproduced in Appendix B.

---

[83] Secs. 217(d)(2) and (3).

QUALIFICATION OF PENSION AND PROFIT-SHARING PLANS

The reporting requirements to establish and maintain a qualified pension or profit-sharing plan are too complex for this text. However, it should be noted that it is generally advisable for a taxpayer to obtain advance approval of the plan from the district director of the IRS by requesting a determination letter that all requirements for qualification have been met. A new determination letter should generally be requested when any material (e.g., substantial) modification is made to a plan. Material changes are frequently required when major tax legislation is enacted. In addition, several reports must be filed with the IRS and the U.S. Department of Labor.

PROBLEM MATERIALS

DISCUSSION QUESTIONS

I:9-1 Why is it important to distinguish whether an individual is an employee or an independent contractor (self-employed)?

I:9-2 Matt, a CPA, is employed full-time as a tax accountant for a major company. He also operates a small tax practice in his spare time. Matt incurs local transportation and unreimbursed travel expenses for both his employment and business activities. How does Matt report these expenses on his tax return?

I:9-3 Determine whether the following expenses are either deductible *for* AGI or *from* AGI or nondeductible on an employee's return. Indicate whether the expenses are subject to the 2% nondeductible floor for miscellaneous itemized deductions and whether the 50% meals and entertainment deduction limit applies.

a. Business meals that were reimbursed by the employer (an adequate accounting is made to the employer and any excess reimbursement must be repaid)

b. Automobile expenses associated with commuting to and from work

c. Legal expenses incurred to prepare the taxpayer's income tax return

d. Unreimbursed travel and transportation expenses (including meals)

e. Unreimbursed entertainment expenses

f. Qualified moving expenses of an employee

g. Education-related expenses involving tuition and books

I:9-4 Which of the following deduction items are subject to the 2% nondeductible floor applicable to miscellaneous itemized deductions?

a. Investment counseling fees

b. Fees for tax return preparation

c. Unreimbursed professional dues for an employee

d. Gambling losses

e. Interest on a personal residence

f. Unreimbursed employee travel expenses

g. Reimbursed employee travel expenses (an adequate accounting is made to the employer and any excess reimbursement must be repaid)

h. Safe deposit box rental expenses for an investor

I:9-5 In each of the following cases involving travel expenses, indicate how each item is reported on the taxpayer's tax return. Include any limitations that might affect its deductibility.

a. Marilyn, who lives in Houston, owns several apartments in Denver. To supervise the management of these properties, Marilyn incurs travel expenses including airfare, lodging, and meals while traveling to and from the apartment site.

b. Marc is an employee who incurs travel expenses as a salesperson. The expenses are fully reimbursed by his employer after an adequate accounting has been made.

c. Assume the same facts as in Part b, except that the expenses are not reimbursed.

d. Kay is a self-employed attorney who incurs travel expenses (including meals) to prepare a court case in a nearby city where she spends the night.

I:9-6 Kelly is an employee who incurs $2,000 of business meal expenses in connection with business entertainment and travel, none of which are reimbursed by her employer. $500 of the business meal costs are considered to be lavish or extravagant. How much can Kelly deduct before applying the 2% nondeductible floor on miscellaneous itemized deductions?

I:9-7 Latoya is a college professor who takes a nine-month leave of absence from her employment at a college in Ohio and accepts a visiting professorship (temporary assignment) at a college in Texas. Latoya leaves her husband and children in Ohio and incurs the following expenses in connection with the temporary assignment:

Airfare to and from the temporary assignment	$ 1,000
Living expenses in the new location (including meals of $1,000)	8,000
Personal clothing	1,500
Total	$10,500

a. Which (if any) of these items can Latoya deduct?

b. Would your answer to Part a change if Latoya, after completing the nine month assignment, resigned her position in Ohio and accepted a full-time assignment with the college in Texas?

I:9-8 Louie is a full-time employee for a retail company and also an investor in rental real estate in his spare time. In the current year, Louie incurs $2,500 of travel expenses and $1,000 in registration fees related to attending real estate investment seminars. He deducts the expenses on his income tax return as a *for* AGI expense related to the production of income. Are the travel expenses and registration fees deductible? Should they be classified as *for* AGI or *from* AGI?

I:9-9 If an employee receives a specific monthly amount from his or her employer as a reimbursement for employment-related entertainment, travel, and transportation expenses, why is it necessary to allocate a portion of the total reimbursement to each expense category?

I:9-10 If an employee receives a reimbursement of 40 cents a mile from her employer for employment-related transportation expenses, is the employee permitted to deduct the difference between the standard mileage rate and the reimbursement rate as an unreimbursed employee expense? What other alternative is available for claiming the transportation deduction?

I:9-11 If an employee (or self-employed individual) uses the standard mileage rate method for the year in which an automobile is acquired, may the actual expense method be used in a subsequent year? If so, what restrictions are imposed (if any) on depreciation methods? What adjustments to basis are required?

I:9-12 If an employee or self-employed individual uses the actual method of deducting automobile expenses and claims depreciation for the first two years of business use, can the individual switch to the standard mileage rate method for the third year and beyond?

I:9-13 Discuss the reporting procedures that should be followed by an employee to report employment-related expenses on his or her tax return under the following conditions:

a. Expenses are less than reimbursements, and no accounting is made to the employer.

b. Expenses equal reimbursements, and an adequate accounting is made to the employer.

c. Expenses exceed reimbursements, and an adequate accounting is made to the employer.

d. Expenses are less than reimbursements. An adequate accounting is made to the employer and the employee is required to repay any excess amount.

I:9-14 Why were distance and time requirements legislated as conditions for eligibility for a moving expense deduction?

I:9-15 Does it matter whether a moving expense is incurred by an employee, a self-employed individual, or an unemployed person?

I:9-16 Len incurs $2,000 of deductible moving expenses in the current year and is fully reimbursed by his employer in the same year.

a. How are the expense deduction and the reimbursement reported on Len's tax return if he uses the standard deduction?

b. What tax consequences occur if the reimbursement is $2,000 but only $1,200 of the $2,000 of moving expenses are tax deductible?

I:9-17 Why are strict recordkeeping requirements required for the deduction of entertainment expenses?

I:9-18 Louis incurs "directly related" entertainment expenses of $4,000, but he is reimbursed by his employer for only $3,000 after an adequate accounting is made.

a. How are these amounts reported on Louis's tax return?

b. What are the tax consequences if Louis is unable to provide adequate documentation of the expenditures during the course of an IRS audit of his tax return?

I:9-19 Latasha is a self-employed attorney who entertains clients and potential clients in her home.

a. What requirements must be met to qualify the outlays as deductible entertainment expenses?

b. What is the difference between "directly related" and "associated with" entertainment?

I:9-20 Liz is an employee who regularly entertains customers in connection with her job. In the current year, Liz incurs $6,000 in business meal expenses that are connected with entertainment. Liz's expenses are not lavish or extravagant. She itemizes her deductions in the current year.

a. If none of these expenses are reimbursed by Liz's employer, what amounts are deductible and how are they classified?

b. How are these amounts reported by Liz and her employer if all of her expenses are reimbursed and an adequate accounting is made by Liz?

I:9-21 Atlantic Corporation provides a cafeteria for its employees. The meal charges are set at a sufficiently high level that the employees are not taxed on the subsidized eating facilities. Are Atlantic's cafeteria-related costs subject to the 50% disallowance for business meals?

I:9-22 Lynn is a salesperson who entertains clients at business luncheons. A business relationship exists

for the entertainment, and there is a reasonable expectation of business benefit. However, no business discussions are generally conducted before, during, or immediately following the meals. Do the business meal expenditures qualify as entertainment expenses?

I:9-23 If an individual belongs to a country club and uses the facility primarily for business entertainment of customers, what portion of the club dues is deductible?

I:9-24 Bass Corporation purchases 10 tickets to the Super Bowl in January 2010 for entertaining its customers. Due to unusually high demand, the tickets have to be purchased from scalpers for $6,000 (10 × $600). The face value of the tickets is only $900 (10 × $90). What amount is deductible by Bass in 2010?

I:9-25 a. Discuss the two requirements for an employee expense reimbursement plan to be treated as an accountable plan.
b. How are expenses and reimbursements treated under an accountable plan?
c. How are expenses and reimbursements treated under a nonaccountable plan?

I:9-26 Martin is a tax accountant employed by a public accounting firm. He incurs the following expenses:

CPA review course	$ 400
Law school tuition and books	4,000
Accounting continuing education course (travel, fees, and transportation (including meals of $200)	600
Total	$5,000

Martin is a degree candidate at the law school. Which (if any) of these expenditures qualify as deductible education expenses? How are they reported?

I:9-27 Why are public school teachers generally allowed a deduction for education expenses related to graduate school or advanced courses?

I:9-28 Discuss whether any of the following individuals are entitled to an office-in-home deduction:
a. Maggie is a self-employed management consultant who maintains an office in her home exclusively used for client meetings and other business-related activities. Maggie has no other place of business and her office is the most significant place for her business. She has substantial income from the consulting practice.
b. Marty is a college professor who writes research papers for academic journals in his office at home which is used exclusively for this purpose. Although Marty has an office at his place of employment, he finds it very convenient to maintain an office at home to avoid distractions from students and colleagues. Marty receives no income from the publication of the research articles for the year in question.

c. Bobby operates his own sole proprietorship as an electrician. He maintains an office at home where he keeps his books, takes phone calls from customers, and does the payroll for his five employees. All of his electrical work is done at the location of his customers.

I:9-29 Compare and contrast the tax advantages accruing to employers and employees from the establishment of a qualified pension or profit-sharing plan versus a nonqualified deferred compensation arrangement (e.g., a restricted property plan).

I:9-30 What is the difference between a defined benefit pension plan and a defined contribution pension plan?

I:9-31 Austin Corporation is proposing the establishment of a pension plan that will cover only employees with salaries in excess of $110,000. No other employees are covered under comparable qualified plans. What problems (if any) do you envision regarding the plan's qualification with the IRS?

I:9-32 Babson Corporation is proposing the creation of a qualified profit-sharing plan for its employees. The proposed plan provides for vesting of employer contributions after 20 years because the company wants to discourage employee turnover and does not feel that short-term employees should qualify for benefits. Will this plan qualify? Why or why not?

I:9-33 Explain how distributions from a qualified pension plan, which are made in the form of annuity payments, are reported by an employee under the following circumstances:
a. No employee contributions are made to the plan.
b. The pension plan provides for matching employee contributions.

I:9-34 Discuss the limitations and restrictions that the Internal Revenue Code places on employer contributions to qualified pension and profit-sharing plans.

I:9-35 Why are nonqualified deferred compensation plans particularly well-suited for use in executive compensation arrangements?

I:9-36 If a newly-formed corporation is considering going public and anticipates substantial future appreciation in its stock, would it be advisable for an executive receiving restricted property to elect to recognize income immediately under Sec. 83(b)? Contrast the tax consequences of a restricted property arrangement for both the employer and employee when this election is made versus when it is not made. Consider the effect of the subsequent lapsing of the restrictions and the employee's sale of the stock.

I:9-37 List and discuss the qualification requirements for an incentive stock option plan (ISO). Describe the advantages and disadvantages of ISOs compared to nonqualified stock option plans.

I:9-38   What difference does it make if a nonqualified stock option has a readily ascertainable FMV on the grant date?

I:9-39   Is a self-employed individual, who is also employed and covered by an employer's qualified pension plan, eligible to establish an H.R. 10 or an SEP plan on his or her self-employment income?

I:9-40   What limitations are placed on self-employed individuals for contributions made to defined contribution H.R. 10 plans? Must self-employed individuals cover their full-time employees if an H.R. 10 plan is established?

I:9-41   Would you be more favorably inclined to advise a 50-year-old individual or a 30-year-old individual to establish a traditional deductible IRA? Why? A traditional nondeductible IRA? Why? Consider any tax problems involved if the IRA funds are needed before age 59½.

I:9-42   Discuss the essential differences between a traditional IRA and a Roth IRA.

I:9-43   Would it generally be advisable for a 30-year-old individual to invest in a traditional deductible IRA or a Roth IRA?

I:9-44   Your client, Charley Long, age 40, has requested your advice with respect to his IRA. He has a traditional IRA with a balance of $150,000 and his current AGI is $75,000. He expects his income to increase slightly when he retires at age 65. Charley has been reading about Roth IRAs and wants your advice as to whether he should rollover the $150,000 from his traditional IRA into a Roth IRA. He has sufficient outside money to pay any taxes due on the rollover. What advice would you give Charley?

I:9-45   Sally, who is single and age 40, made deductible IRA contributions in several early years, but has not been eligible to make deductible IRA contributions for the last 5 years because she is covered under her employer's plan. Her AGI is $70,000. She is interested in making IRA contributions in the current year. What advice would you give her?

I:9-46   Discuss the major features of a Coverdell Education Savings Account (CESA).

I:9-47   The owner of an unincorporated small business is considering whether to establish a simplified employee pension (SEP) plan for its employees.
  a. What nontax factors might make an SEP attractive as an alternative to establishing a qualified pension or profit-sharing plan?
  b. Is the owner of the small business eligible to make contributions on his or her behalf to the SEP?

ISSUE IDENTIFICATION QUESTIONS

I:9-48   Georgia is an executive who recently completed an assignment with her employer at an away-from-home location. It was realistically expected that the assignment would be completed in 15 months but the actual time period was only 11 months. Georgia incurred $15,000 of away-from-home expenses during the 11-month period, none of which were reimbursed by her employer. What tax issues should Georgia consider?

I:9-49   Jeremy is an executive for Columbia Corporation, which is going through a restructuring of its corporate headquarters operations. Columbia has offered to relocate Jeremy from its New York headquarters to its divisional operation in South Carolina and will reimburse him for both direct and indirect moving expenses. What tax issues should Jeremy consider?

I:9-50   Juan, a self-employed medical doctor, maintains an office in his home where he maintains patient records and performs billing procedures. Most of his time is spent visiting patients and performing surgical procedures in the operating room at several local hospitals. Juan intends to deduct his expenses of his office in his home. What tax issues should Juan consider?

I:9-51   David is on the audit staff of a national accounting firm. He has been with the firm for three years and is a CPA. David has applied and been accepted into a prestigious MBA program. The program is two years in duration. David has decided to resign from the accounting firm even though the firm has indicated that it would very much like David to return to work for the firm after he receives his MBA degree. David is somewhat interested in returning to public accounting but will certainly look at all of his options when he completes the program. David wants to deduct his education expenses. What are the relevant tax issues in this case?

PROBLEMS

I:9-52   *Employment-Related Expenses.* Mike incurs the following employment-related expenses in the current year:

Actual automobile expenses	$ 2,500
Moving expenses (deductible under Sec. 217)	4,000
Entertainment expenses	1,500
Travel expenses (including $500 of business meals)	2,500
Professional dues and subscriptions	500
Total	$11,000

Mike's AGI is $120,000 before any of the above expenses are deducted. None of the expenses listed above are reimbursed by Mike's employer. He has no other miscellaneous itemized deductions and does not use the standard deduction.

a. What is the amount of Mike's deduction for employment-related expenses?

b. How are these items reported in Mike's tax return?

I:9-53 *Travel and Entertainment.* Monique is a self-employed manufacturer's representative who solicits business for clients and receives a commission based on sales. She incurs the following expenditures during the current year:

Airfare and lodging while away from home overnight	$ 4,000
Business meals while traveling at which business is discussed	1,000
Local transportation costs for automobile, parking, tolls, etc. (business-related)	2,000
Commuting expenses	1,000
Local entertainment of customers	2,000
Total	$10,000

a. Which of the expenditures listed above (if any) are deductible by Monique?

b. Are each of these items classified as *for* AGI or *from* AGI deductions?

c. How would your answers to Parts a and b change if Monique were an employee rather than self-employed and none of the expenses were reimbursed by her employer?

I:9-54 *Unreimbursed Employee Expenses.* In the current year, Mary incurs $3,600 of unreimbursed employment-related travel and entertainment expenses. These expenses include the following:

Airfare	$1,500
Taxi fare	100
Meals eaten alone while away from home on business	300
Laundry	50
Lodging	650
Business meals with customers at which business is discussed	500
Entertainment of customers	500
Total	$3,600

Mary also pays $1,000 of investment counseling fees and $500 of tax return preparation fees in the current year. Mary's AGI is $70,000.

a. What is the total amount of Mary's deductible expenses?

b. Are the deductible expenses classified as *for* AGI or *from* AGI?

I:9-55 *Travel Expenses.* Marilyn, a business executive who lives and works in Cleveland, accepts a temporary out-of-town assignment in Atlanta for a period of ten months. Marilyn leaves her husband and children in Cleveland and rents an apartment in Atlanta during the ten-month period. Marilyn incurs the following expenses, none of which are reimbursed by her employer:

Airfare to and from Atlanta	$ 800
Airfare for weekend trips to visit her family	8,000
Apartment rent	10,000
Meals in Atlanta	8,500
Entertainment of customers	2,000
Total	$29,300

a. Which of the expenditures listed above (if any) are deductible by Marilyn (before any limitations are applied)?

b. Are each of these expenditures classified as *for* AGI or *from* AGI deductions?

c. If Marilyn's AGI is $120,000, what is the amount of the deduction for the expenditures?

d. Do the tax consequences change if Marilyn's assignment is for a period of more than one year and is for an indefinite period rather than a temporary period?

e. Do the tax consequences in Parts a through c change if it was realistically expected that the work would be completed in ten months but after the ten-month period Marilyn is asked to continue for seven more months and if an additional $10,000 of travel expenses are incurred during the extended period?

I:9-56 *Business/Personal Travel Expenses.* In the current year, Mike's AGI is $50,000. Mike has no miscellaneous itemized deductions other than the employment-related expenses listed below. Mike attends a professional trade association convention in Los Angeles. He spends three days at the meeting and two days vacationing before the meeting. Mike was unable to obtain excursion airfare rates (i.e., staying over a Saturday night) despite the fact that he was on vacation immediately before the meeting. Mike's total expenses include the following:

Airfare	$ 450
Meals ($50 per day)	250
Hotel ($100 per day)	500
Entertainment of customers (business is discussed)	500
Total	$1,700

Mike's employer reimburses him for the business-related expenses and, accordingly, Mike receives a reimbursement of $1,400 ($450 + 150 + 300 + 500).

a. How much can Mike deduct for employment-related expenses?

b. How is the reimbursement reported on Mike's tax return?

c. How much of the reimbursement may Mike's employer deduct?

I:9-57 *Employment-Related Expenses and Reimbursements.* Maxine incurs the following employment-related business expenses in the current year:

Professional dues and subscriptions	$1,000
Airfare and lodging	2,000
Local transportation for employment-related business activities	1,000
Customer entertainment (business lunches where business is discussed)	1,000
Total	$5,000

After making an adequate accounting of the expenses, Maxine receives a reimbursement of $3,000 from her employer. Assume that Maxine's AGI is $60,000, she has other miscellaneous itemized deductions of $1,000, and she does not use the standard deduction.

a. What amount of the expenses are deductible by Maxine?

b. Are each of these expenditures classified as *for* AGI or *from* AGI deductions?

c. How would your answers to Parts a and b change if Maxine instead received a $6,000 reimbursement?

I:9-58 *Miscellaneous Itemized Deductions.* In the current year, Melissa, a single employee whose AGI is $100,000 before any of the items below, incurs the following expenses:

Safe deposit box rental for investments	$ 100
Tax return preparation fees	500
Moving expenses (deductible under Sec. 217)	2,000
Mortgage interest on Melissa's principal residence	12,000
Real estate taxes on Melissa's principal residence	1,800
Unreimbursed employment-related expenses (other than business meals and entertainment)	6,000
Unreimbursed employment-related expenses for business meals and entertainment (business is discussed)	1,200
Total	$23,600

a. What is the amount of Melissa's total miscellaneous itemized deductions (after deducting the 2% floor)?

b. What is the amount of Melissa's total itemized deductions?

c. What is the amount of Melissa's total itemized deductions if her AGI, after all adjustments above, is $190,000?

I:9-59 *Transportation Expenses.* Cassady, an employee of a law firm, maintains an office at the principal business location of her firm. She frequently travels directly from her home to client locations within and outside the metropolitan area. Cassady is not reimbursed for her transportation expenses and has incurred the following:

Transportation expenses associated with trips to clients within the metropolitan area	$2,000
Transportation expenses associated with trips to clients located outside the metropolitan area	3,000
Total	$5,000

a. What is the amount of Cassady's deduction for transportation expenses?

b. How is the deduction reported on Cassady's tax return?

c. What is the amount of Cassady's deduction for transportation expenses and its classification if she is self-employed and operates her office from her home? Assume that the requirements of Sec. 280A are satisfied.

I:9-60 *Auto Expenses.* Michelle is an employee who must use her personal automobile for employment-related business trips. During 2010, Michelle drives her car 60% for business use and incurs the following total expenses (100% use of car):

Gas and oil	$ 9,000
Repairs	1,400
Depreciation	4,700
Insurance and license fees	1,300
Parking and tolls (business related)	100
Total	$16,500

Michelle drives 24,000 business miles during 2010 and receives a reimbursement of 40 cents per mile from her employer. Assume that an adequate accounting is made to Michelle's employer.

a. What amount is deductible (before the 2% nondeductible floor) if Michelle elects to use the standard mileage method?

b. What amount is deductible (before the 2% nondeductible floor) if Michelle uses the actual cost method?

c. Can taxpayers switch back and forth between the mileage and actual methods each year?

I:9-61 *Entertainment Expenses.* Milt, a self-employed attorney, incurs the following expenses in the current year:

Dues paid to the local chamber of commerce	$ 1,000
Business lunches for clients and prospective clients (Milt does not believe in conducting business discussions during lunch)	4,000
Entertainment of professional associates in his home (immediately following business meetings)	2,000
Country club dues (the club is used exclusively for business)	2,500
Entertainment of clients and prospective clients at the country club (meals and drinks)	1,500
Total	$11,000

a. Which of the expenditures listed above (if any) are deductible by Milt?

b. Are each of these items classified as *for* AGI or *from* AGI deductions?

I:9-62 *Entertainment Expenses.* Beach Corporation purchases tickets to sporting events and uses them to entertain customers. In the current year Beach Corporation purchases the following tickets:

100 tickets to football games (face value of the tickets is $3,600)	$ 6,000
A skybox rented for six NFL football games (seating capacity of the skybox is 20, and the highest price of a nonluxury box seat is $60)	18,000

What amount of the entertainment expenses is deductible in the current year?

I:9-63 *Reimbursed Employee Expenses.* Latrisha is an employee of the Cooper Company and incurs significant employment-related expenses. During the current year, she incurred the following expenses in connection with her job:

Travel: Airfare	$ 5,850
Lodging	1,800
Meals	1,200
Entertainment of customers	2,400
Total	$11,250

a. Determine the amount of deductible expenses for both Latrisha and the Cooper Company and, for Latrisha, whether they are deductible *for* AGI or *from* AGI assuming Cooper Company maintains an accountable plan for employee expense reimbursements, if the reimbursements are alternatively:

1. $11,250
2. $9,000
3. $14,000

b. What would be the result in Part a for each of the three situations if the plan was a nonaccountable plan?

I:9-64 *Moving Expenses.* Michael graduates from New York University and on February 1, 2010, accepts a position with a public accounting firm in Chicago. Michael is a resident of New York. In March, Michael travels to Chicago to locate a house and starts to work in June. He incurs the following expenses, none of which are reimbursed by the public accounting firm:

Automobile expense enroute	
(1,000 miles at 16.5 cents per mile—standard mileage rate)	$ 165
Cost of meals en route	100
Househunting trip travel expenses	1,400
Moving van expenses	3,970
Commission on the sale of	
Michael's New York condominium	3,500
Points paid to acquire a mortgage on	
Michael's new residence in Chicago	1,000
Temporary living expenses for one week	
in Chicago (hotel and $100 in meals)	400
Expenses incurred in decorating the new residence	500
Total expenses	$10,985

a. What is Michael's moving expense deduction?
b. How are the deductible expenses classified on Michael's tax return?
c. How would your answer to Part a change if all of Michael's expenses were reimbursed by his employer and he received a check for $10,985?

I:9-65 *Education Expenses.* For each of the following independent situations, determine whether any of the expenditures qualify as deductible education expenses in connection with a trade or business (Reg. Sec. 1.162-5). Are the expenditures classified as *for* AGI or *from* AGI deductions?
a. Law school tuition and books for an IRS agent who is pursuing a law degree: $2,000.
b. Continuing professional accounting education expenses of $1,900 for a self-employed CPA: travel, $1,000 (including $200 meals); registration fees, $800; books, $100.
c. MBA education expenses totaling $5,000 for a business executive of a major corporation: tuition, $4,000; transportation, $800; and books, $200.
d. Tuition and books acquired for graduate education courses required under state law for a schoolteacher in order to renew a provisional certificate: $1,000.
e. Bar review courses for a recent law school graduate: $1,000.

I:9-66 *Education Expenses.* Anne works for a CPA firm as a secretary/receptionist and earns approximately $27,000 per year. About five years earlier, she had completed 70 credit hours at State U. To increase her career potential, she decided to enroll at the local university to continue her college education and get an undergraduate degree in accounting with the ultimate goal of obtaining her CPA certificate. During 2010, she incurred the following education expenses:

Tuition and fees	$3,500
Books and supplies	800

What are Anne's options as to the deductibility of the above expenses?

I:9-67 *Office in Home.* Nancy is a self-employed artist who uses 10% of her residence as a studio. The studio portion is used exclusively for business and is frequented by customers on a regular basis. Nancy also uses her den as an office (10% of the total floor space of her home) to prepare bills and keep records. However, the den is also used by her children as a TV room. Nancy's income from the sale of the artwork amounts to $40,000 in the current year. She also incurs $2,000 of expenses directly related to the business other than home office expenses (e.g., art supplies and selling expenses). Nancy incurs the following expenses in the current year related to her residence:

Real estate taxes	$ 2,000
Mortgage interest	5,000
Insurance	500
Depreciation	3,500
Repairs and utilities	1,000
Total	$12,000

a. Which of the expenditures above (if any) are deductible? Are they *for* AGI or *from* AGI deductions?
b. Would your answer to Part a change if Nancy's income from painting were only $2,500 for the year? What is the amount of the office-in-home deduction and the amount of the carryover (if any) of the unused deductions? (Assume that Nancy is not subject to the hobby loss restrictions.)

I:9-68 *Office in Home.* Darrell is a self-employed consultant who uses 15% of his home exclusively as an office. Darrell operates completely out of his home office and makes all of his appointments from the office as well as keeping his books and records in the office. Darrell's gross income from his consulting business is $60,000 in 2010. He incurs $6,000 of expenses that are directly related to his business, such as computer and office supplies. Below are expenses that relate to Darrell's residence for 2010:

Real estate taxes	$ 4,000
Mortgage interest	8,000
Insurance	1,000
Depreciation	4,000
Repairs and utilities	1,000
Total	$18,000

a. Which of the above expenditures (if any) are deductible? Are they *for* AGI or *from* AGI deductions?
b. How would your answer change if Darrell was an employee of a consulting company and maintained an office at home in order to take work home with him so he did not have to spend so many hours at his consulting company office?

I:9-69 *Deferred Compensation Plan Requirements.* Identify whether each of the following plan features is associated with a qualified pension plan, a qualified profit-sharing plan, an employee stock ownership plan, a nonqualifed plan, or none of these plans.
a. Annual employer contributions are not required, but substantial and recurring contributions must be made based on a predetermined formula.
b. Annual, systematic, and definite employer contributions are required without regard to profits but based on actuarial methods.
c. Forfeitures must be used to reduce contributions that would otherwise be made under the plan.
d. The plan may discriminate in favor of highly compensated individuals.
e. The trust is funded with the contribution of employer stock, which is subsequently distributed to employees.

I:9-70 *Taxability of Pension Payments.* Pat is a participant in a qualified pension plan. She retires on January 1, 2010, at age 63, and receives pension payments beginning in January 2010. Her pension payments, which will be received monthly for life, amount to $1,000 per month. Pat contributed $30,000 to the pension plan on a pre-tax (or tax-deferred)

basis, and the number of anticipated payments based on Pat's age of 63 years is 260 months (see IRS table in Chapter I:3) from the date she starts receiving payments.

a. What gross income will Pat recognize in 2010 and each year thereafter?

b. How would your answer to Part a change if Pat made contributions to the plan on an after-tax basis?

c. If, in Part b, Pat dies in December 2011 after receiving pension payments for two full years, what tax consequences occur in the year of death?

I:9-71 *Restricted Property.* In 2010, Bear Corporation transfers 100 shares of its stock to its employee Patrick. The stock is valued at $10 per share on the issue date. The stock is subject to the following restrictions:

- Patrick cannot transfer the stock by sale or other disposition (except in the event of death) for a five-year period.

- The stock must be forfeited to Bear Corporation if Patrick voluntarily terminates his employment with the company within a five-year period.

In the year 2015, the Bear stock is worth $100 per share when the restrictions expire.

a. Assuming that no Sec. 83(b) election is made, what are the tax consequences to Patrick and Bear Corporation in 2010?

b. What are the tax consequences to Patrick and Bear Corporation if Patrick makes a valid Sec. 83(b) election in 2010?

c. What are the tax consequences to Patrick and Bear Corporation if Patrick forfeits the stock back to the company in 2011 when the stock is worth $20 per share if an election was made under Sec. 83(b)? What would happen if no Sec. 83(b) election were made?

d. What are the tax consequences to Patrick and Bear Corporation upon the lapse of the restrictions in the year 2015 if an election has been made under Sec. 83(b)? What would the results be if no Sec. 83(b) election were made?

e. What are the tax consequences to Patrick and Bear Corporation if Patrick sells the Bear stock in the year 2016 for $120 per share if a Sec. 83(b) election is made? if no Sec. 83(b) election is made?

I:9-72 *IRAs.* On February 15, 2011, Jamal, who is single and age 30, establishes an IRA and contributes $5,000 to the account. Jamal's adjusted gross income is $62,000 in 2010 and $57,000 in 2011. Jamal is an active participant in an employer-sponsored retirement plan.

a. What amount of the contribution is deductible? In what year is it deductible?

b. How is the deduction (if any) reported (i.e., *for* AGI or *from* AGI)?

c. How would your answer to Part a change, if at all, if Jamal were not an active participant in an employer-sponsored retirement plan?

d. How would your answer to Part a change if Jamal were married and files a joint return with his spouse, who has no earned income? (Assume their combined AGI is $85,000.)

I:9-73 *IRAs.* Phil, age 30, is married and files a joint return with his spouse. On February 15, 2011, Phil establishes an IRA for himself and a spousal IRA for his spouse with an $10,000 contribution, $5,000 for himself and $5,000 for his wife. Phil's spouse earned $1,000 in 2010 from a part-time job, and their combined AGI is $70,000. Neither Phil nor his spouse is an active participant in an employer-sponsored retirement plan.

a. What amount of the contribution is deductible?

b. To what year does the contribution apply? (Assume that an election is made to treat Phil's spouse as having no compensation.)

c. Is the deduction reported as *for* AGI or *from* AGI?

d. How would your answer to Part a change, if at all, if Phil and his spouse were active participants in an employer-sponsored retirement plan?

e. If a portion of the contribution is nondeductible in Part d, is it possible for Phil to make a deductible and a nondeductible contribution in the same year? Explain.

f. How would your answer to Part a change if Phil and his spouse's combined AGI were $120,000 in 2010 and Phil was an active participant in an employer-sponsored retirement plan?

I:9-74 *Roth IRA.* Chatham Mae is single, age 35, and wants to make a contribution to an IRA for the year ended December 31, 2010. She is an active participant in a qualified retirement plan sponsored by her employer. Her AGI for 2010 is $111,000 before considering any IRA contribution.

a. What type of IRA, if any, is Chatham Mae eligible to make a contribution to for 2010? If she is eligible to contribute to an IRA, what is the maximum amount that she can contribute to the IRA?

b. Assume Chatham Mae makes contributions of $12,000 over six years to a Roth IRA. In 2016, she withdraws $15,000 to pay off her car loan. Her financial advisor suggested she withdraw the money from the IRA for two major reasons: (1) to eliminate her debt and (2) no tax would be due on distributions from a Roth IRA after five years. Chatham Mae wants to verify the accuracy of her advisor's advice. What would be the tax consequences of this withdrawal? Alternatively, what if Chatham Mae withdrew the $15,000 to purchase a house (she is a first-time homebuyer)?

c. Alternatively to Part b above, assume Chatham Mae has a traditional deductible IRA that has a balance of $50,000. She has been able to deduct all of her contributions to the IRA in prior years. Her financial advisor has recommended that she rollover the funds from her traditional IRA to a Roth IRA in 2010. What are the tax consequences of this rollover in 2010?

I:9-75   *Coverdell Education Savings Accounts.* Jack and Katie have five grandchildren, ages 19, 16, 15, 12, and 10. They have established Coverdell Education Savings Accounts (CESA) for each of the grandchildren and would like to contribute the maximum amount allowable to each CESA for the 2010 taxable year. Jack and Katie's AGI for 2010 is $196,000.

a. How much can Jack and Katie contribute to each grandchild's CESA in 2010?

b. Assume that the 19-year-old granddaughter is a freshman in college and makes a withdrawal of $7,000 from her CESA during the year 2010. Her college expenses for 2010 were as follows:

Tuition	$1,500
Room and board	2,500
Books and supplies	500

The extra amount withdrawn was used a down payment on a car that the granddaughter purchased during the year. She needed the car in order to drive to school rather than having to either ride the bus or ride with a friend. What are the tax consequences of the $7,000 distribution to the granddaughter?

I:9-76   *H.R. 10 Plans.* Paula is a self-employed doctor who is considering whether to establish a defined contribution H.R. 10 plan. Paula's only employee is a full-time nurse who has been employed by Paula for seven years. Paula's net earnings from self-employment (before the H.R. 10 plan contribution but after the deduction for one-half of self-employment taxes paid) is expected to be $100,000 during the current year and in future years.

a. If the H.R. 10 plan is established, what is the maximum amount Paula can contribute for the nurse's benefit?

b. What is the maximum amount Paula can contribute for herself? Is the amount reported as a *for* AGI or *from* AGI deduction?

c. Is Paula's nurse required to be included in the plan?

d. What are the tax consequences if Paula makes a premature withdrawal from the plan before reaching age 59½?

I:9-77   *Stock Options.* Bell Corporation grants an incentive stock option to Peggy, an employee, on January 1, 2010, when the option price and FMV of the Bell stock is $80. The option entitles Peggy to buy 10 shares of Bell stock. Peggy exercises the option and acquires the stock on April 1, 2012, when the stock's FMV is $100. Peggy, while still employed by the Bell Corporation, sells the stock on May 1, 2014, for $120 per share.

a. What are the tax consequences to Peggy and Bell Corporation on the following dates: January 1, 2010; April 1, 2012; and May 1, 2014? (Assume all incentive stock option qualification requirements are met.)

b. How would your answer to Part a change if Peggy instead sold the Bell stock for $130 per share on May 1, 2012?

I:9-78   *Stock Options.* Bender Corporation grants a nonqualified stock option to Penny, an employee, on January 1, 2010, that entitled Penny to acquire 1,000 shares of Bender stock at $80 per share. On this date, the stock has a $100 FMV and the option has a readily ascertainable FMV. Penny exercises the option on January 1, 2011 (when the FMV of the stock is $150), and acquires 1,000 shares of the stock for $80 per share. Penny later sells the Bender stock on January 1, 2013, for $200 per share.

a. What are the tax consequences to Penny and Bender Corporation on the following dates: January 1, 2010; January 1, 2011; and January 1, 2013?

b. How would your answer to Part a change if the Bender stock were instead closely-held and the option had no readily ascertainable FMV?

COMPREHENSIVE PROBLEM

I:9-79   Dan and Cheryl are married, file a joint return, and have no children. Dan is a pharmaceutical salesman and Cheryl is a nurse at a local hospital. Dan's SSN is 400-20-1000 and Cheryl's SSN is 200-40-8000 and they reside at 2033 Palmetto Drive, Nashville, TN 28034. Dan is paid according to commissions from sales; however, his compensation is subject to withholding of income and payroll taxes. He also maintains an office in his home as the pharmaceutical company does not have an office in Nashville and when he is not traveling, Dan operates his business from his home office. During 2010, Dan earned total compensation from his job of $125,000, on which $20,000 of federal income taxes were withheld, $6,622 of OASDI, and $1,813 of Medicare taxes. No state income taxes were withheld. Cheryl earned a salary during 2010 of $45,400, on which federal taxes withheld were $5,000, OASDI of $2,815, and Medicare taxes of $658.

During 2010, Dan and Cheryl had interest income from corporate bonds and bank accounts of $1,450 and qualified dividends from stocks of $5,950. Dan also actively trades stocks and had the following results for 2010:

LTCG	$4,900
LTCL	(3,200)
STCG	0
STCL	(7,800)

He had no capital loss carryovers from previous years.

Dan does a considerable amount of travel in connection with his job. He uses his own car and is reimbursed $0.30 per business mile. During 2010, Dan drove his car a total of 38,000 miles, of which 32,000 were business related. He also had parking fees and tolls during the year of $280. Dan uses the mileage method for deducting auto expenses. Dan also had the following travel expenses while away from home during the year:

Hotel	$4,200
Meals	820
Entertainment of customers	1,080
Tips	100
Laundry and cleaning	150
Total	$6,350

Dan was reimbursed for the travel expenses by his employer, pursuant to an accountable plan, in the amount of $5,080.

Dan's expenses in connection with his office in the home were as follows:

Office supplies	$ 290
Telephone (separate line)	1,100
Utilities (entire house)	3,400
Homeowners insurance	600
Interest and property taxes (see below for totals)	
Repairs and maintenance (entire house)	800

Dan's office is 300 square feet and the total square footage of the house is 3,000 square feet. Dan and Cheryl purchased the house on June 12, 1997, for $280,000, of which $40,000 is attributable to the land.

Cheryl incurred several expenses in connection with her nursing job. She paid $450 in professional dues, $200 in professional journals, and $350 for uniforms.

Dan and Cheryl had the following other expenditures during the year:

Health insurance premiums (after-tax)		$ 4,400
Doctor bills		470
Real estate taxes on home		2,200
Personal property taxes		400
Mortgage interest		15,600
Charitable contributions—cash		9,000
Charitable contributions—GE stock		
FMV	$12,000	
Adjusted basis	2,000	
Tax preparation fees		750

Compute Dan and Cheryl's income tax liability for 2010.

TAX STRATEGY PROBLEM

I:9-80 Paul Price is the president and majority stockholder of Lightmore Communications, Inc. Lightmore is a C corporation and has been extremely successful over the past 20 years. Paul travels extensively in connection with the business to meet with existing and prospective clients. Paul's wife, Laura, would be helpful to Paul in his business entertaining if she could accompany him on many of his business trips and, furthermore, she was unable to go on these trips in the past because of their children at home. Their youngest child is now in college, and Laura's duties at home have diminished. During the current year, Laura has made a number of trips with Paul, but after conferring with the company's tax advisor, had been informed that Laura's expenses would not be deductible for tax purposes. The tax advisor suggested the possibility of putting Laura on the Lightmore payroll as an employee.

a. Would Laura's travel expenses be deductible if she was an employee of the corporation?

b. What other benefits would be available to Laura if she was an employee of the corporation?

c. Are there any detriments to putting Laura on the payroll?

TAX FORM/RETURN PREPARATION PROBLEMS

I:9-81 In 2009, Micah Johnson (SSN 277-33-7263) incurs the following unreimbursed employee business expenses:

Airplane and taxi fares	$ 4,000
Lodging away from home	5,000
Meals while away from home	1,000
Automobile expenses (related to 100% of the use of his personal automobile):	
Gasoline and oil	7,500
Repairs	1,000
Insurance	900
Depreciation	1,775
Parking and tolls (includes only business use)	100
Total	$21,275

Johnson receives a $7,800 reimbursement for the travel expenses. He did not receive any reimbursement for the auto expenses. He uses his personal automobile 80% for business use and placed his current automobile in service on October 1, 2006. Total business miles driven during the year amount to 26,400, his commuting miles in 2009 amount to 2,000, and other personal miles amount to 4,600 miles. Johnson's AGI is $60,000, and he has no other miscellaneous itemized deductions. Assume his business miles were driven equally during the year.

a. Calculate Johnson's expense deduction using the 2009 Form 2106 (Employee Business Expenses) based on actual automobile expenses and other employee business expenses.

b. Calculate Johnson's expense deduction for 2009 using the standard mileage rate method and other employee business expenses. (Assume that none of the restrictions on the use of the standard mileage rate method are applicable.)

I:9-82 George Large (SSN 414-33-5688) and his wife Marge Large (SSN 555-81-9495), who live at 2000 Lakeview Drive, Cleveland, OH 49001, want you to prepare their 2009 income tax return based on the information below:

George Large worked as a salesman for Toyboat, Inc. He received a salary of $80,000 ($8,500 of federal income taxes withheld and $1,800 of state income taxes withheld) plus an expense reimbursement from Toyboat of $5,000 to cover his employee business expenses. George must make an adequate accounting to his employer and return any excess reimbursement. Additionally, Toyboat provides George with medical insurance worth $7,200 per year. George drove his car 24,000 miles during the year. His log indicates that 18,000 miles were for sales calls to customers at the customers' offices and the remainder was personal mileage. George uses the standard mileage rate method. Assume his business miles were driven equally during the year. George is a professional basketball fan. He purchased two season tickets for a total of $4,000. He takes a customer to every game, and they discuss a little business at the games. George also takes clients to business lunches. His log indicates that he spent $1,500 on these business meals. George also took a five-day trip to the Toyboat headquarters in Musty, Ohio. He was so well-prepared that

he finished his business in three days, so he spent the other two days sightseeing. He had the following expenses during each of the five days of his trip:

Airfare	$200
Lodging	$85/day
Meals	$50/day
Taxicabs	$20/day

Marge Large is self-employed. She repairs rubber toy boats in the basement of their home, which is 25% of the house's square footage. She had the following income and expenses:

Income from rubber toy boat repairs	$12,000
Cost of supplies	5,000
Contract labor	3,500
Long-distance phone calls (business)	500

The Large's home cost a total of $150,000, of which the cost of the land was $20,000. The FMV of the house is $225,000. The house is depreciable over a 39-year recovery period. The Larges incurred other expenses:

Utility bills for the house	$2,000
Real estate taxes	2,500
Mortgage interest	4,500
Cash charitable contributions	3,500

Prepare Form 1040, Schedules A and C for Form 1040, and Forms 2106 and 8829 for the 2009 year. (Assume no depreciation for this problem and that no estimated taxes were paid by the Larges.)

CASE STUDY PROBLEMS

I:9-83   Ajax Corporation is a young high-growth company engaged in the manufacture and distribution of automotive parts. Its common stock has doubled in value since the company was listed on the NASDAQ exchange about two years ago. Ajax currently has a high debt/equity ratio due to the issuance of debt to finance its capital expansion needs. Despite rapid growth in assets and profitability, Ajax has severe cash flow problems and a poor working capital ratio. The company urgently needs to attract new executives to the organization and to provide financial incentives to existing top management because of recent turnover and high growth. Approximately 55% of the common stock is owned by Andrew Ajax, who is the CEO, and his immediate family. None of the other officers own stock in the company.

You are a tax consultant for the company who has been asked to prepare suggestions after reviewing the compensation system. Your discussions with several top management individuals reveal the following aspects of corporate strategy and philosophy:

- The company needs to expand the equity capital base because of its concern for the high risk caused by large amounts of debt.
- Improvement in cash flow and liquidity would enhance its stock price and enable the company to continue its high growth rate.
- Top management feels that employee loyalty and productivity would be improved if all employees owned some stock in the company. The company currently offers a qualified pension plan to its employees and executives that provides only minimal pension benefits. No other deferred compensation or bonus arrangements are currently being offered.
- Andrew Ajax feels that the top management group should own a substantial amount of Ajax stock to ensure that the interests of management correspond with the shareholder interests (i.e., the maximization of shareholder wealth).

The following four types of executive compensation arrangements have been discussed:

- Sec. 401(k) and ESOP plans for employees.
- Encourage all employees and executives to independently fund their retirement needs beyond any Social Security benefits by establishing IRA plans.
- Provide restricted property arrangements (using Ajax stock) to attract new top level executives and to retain existing executives.
- Offer nonqualified or incentive stock options to existing and new executives.

Required: Prepare a client memo that recommends revisions to Ajax Corporation's existing compensation system for both its employee and executive groups. Your recommendations should discuss the pros and cons of different deferred compensation arrangements and should consider both tax and nontax factors.

I:9-84 Steve is part owner and manager of a small manufacturing company that makes keypads for alarm systems. The keypads are sold to several different alarm companies throughout the country. Steve must travel to several cities each year to meet with current customers and to attract new business. When you meet with Steve to obtain information to prepare his current year tax return, he tells you that he has spent about $5,000 during the current year on airfare and taking his customers out to dinner to discuss business. Because he took most of his trips in the summer and fall, and it is now April of the following year, Steve cannot remember the exact time and places of the business dinners and did not retain any receipts for the cash used to pay the bills. However, he remembers the names of the customers he went to see, the business topics that were discussed, and the restaurants where he had his meals. As Steve's tax consultant, what is your responsibility regarding the treatment of the travel and entertainment expenses under the mandates of the AICPA's *Statements on Standards for Tax Services*? Prepare a client letter explaining to Steve the requirements under Sec. 274(d) for sufficient substantiation of travel and entertainment expenses. (See the *Statements on Standards for Tax Services* section in Chapter I:15 for a discussion of these issues and Appendix E.)

TAX RESEARCH PROBLEM

I:9-85 Charley Long is a truck driver, the 18-wheeler variety. He works for Fishy Co., a seafood company in Mobile, Alabama, and drives a company truck. Charley's job entails leaving Mobile at 4:00 PM each day (five days per week) and delivering fresh fish to restaurants and wholesale fish distributors in Mississippi and Louisiana. His last stop, in Lafayette, Louisiana, is generally around 12:00 midnight. It normally takes Charley about five hours to get back to Mobile.

Charley's routine is varied. Sometimes, he drives straight back to Mobile from Lafayette. On other occasions, he will pull off at a truck stop and sleep in his cab before returning to Mobile. His cab is equipped with sleeping facilities, although small and sparse. Finally, on other occasions, Charley will spend the night in a motel along the road. The Fishy Co. has no preference as to what Charley does and has given him permission to either drive back or stay overnight. However, the company does not reimburse him for his food and lodging expenses.

When Charley drives straight back to Mobile, Charley will eat one meal. When he sleeps overnight (either in his cab or in a motel), he will eat two meals, a late dinner and breakfast. He spends an average of $6.00 for dinner and $4.00 for breakfast. The cost of his motel averages $50.00 per night. When Charley sleeps in the cab, he generally sleeps about 4–5 hours and then drives on to Mobile.

During the current year, Charley incurred the following expenses:

Meals incurred on nonstop trips	$1,000
Meals incurred when: slept in cab	600
slept in motel	400
Lodging	2,300
Total	$4,300

The IRS has disallowed all of the above expenses on the grounds that they are not bona fide travel expenses but personal expenses. Would you advise Charley to contest this issue? A partial list of research sources is:

- Sec. 162(a)(2) and Reg. Sec. 1.162-2(a)
- *U.S. v. Correll*, 389 U.S. 299 (1967)
- *Williams v. Patterson*, 286 F.2d 333 (5th Cir. 1961)
- Rev. Rul. 75-168, 1975-1 C.B. 58 and Rev. Rul. 75-432, 1975-2 C.B. 60

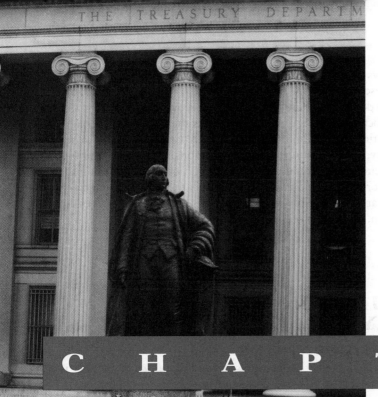

10

CHAPTER

DEPRECIATION, COST RECOVERY, AMORTIZATION, AND DEPLETION

LEARNING OBJECTIVES

After studying this chapter, you should be able to

▶ **1** Understand the general concepts of tax depreciation

▶ **2** Classify property and calculate depreciation under the MACRS rules

▶ **3** Calculate amortization for intangible assets and understand the difference between amortizable and non-amortizable assets

▶ **4** Apply cost and percentage depletion methods and understand the treatment for intangible drilling costs

CHAPTER OUTLINE

The income tax law allows taxpayers to deduct a reasonable allowance for the exhaustion, wear and tear, and obsolescence of property used in a trade or business or held for the production of income.[1] Such deductions enable taxpayers to recover the cost of an asset under the "return of capital" doctrine. Depreciation, therefore, is the systematic allocation of the cost of an asset over its estimated economic life. The term *depreciation* relates to deductions for most tangible property; *amortization* relates to deductions for intangible property; and *depletion* relates to deductions for natural resources (oil and gas, coal, etc.) While the concepts of depreciation, amortization, and depletion are similar to those in financial accounting, the income tax rules are unique. This chapter discusses the income tax rules relating to depreciation, amortization, and depletion.

DEPRECIATION AND COST RECOVERY

GENERAL CONSIDERATIONS

TYPICAL MISCONCEPTION

It is easy to forget that the depreciation or cost-recovery system that applies to any one asset is the system that was in effect when the property was placed in service. Property acquired in 1986 is not affected by the MACRS rules that became effective in 1987.

Taxpayers must use specific depreciation methods depending on *when* an asset is placed in service. Three separate depreciation and cost recovery systems are currently in place. These three distinct systems are the result of tax law changes in 1981 and 1986. The systems that taxpayers must use are as follows:

▶ Property placed in service after December 31, 1986. Taxpayers must use the Modified Accelerated Cost Recovery System (MACRS) as provided in Sec. 168.

▶ Property placed in service after December 31, 1980 and before January 1, 1987. Taxpayers must use the Accelerated Cost Recovery System (ACRS) as provided in Sec. 168.

▶ Property placed in service prior to 1981. Taxpayers must use the rules contained in Sec. 167. These rules basically follow financial accounting principles.

In this chapter, we emphasize the MACRS rules because most assets placed in service before 1987 are now fully depreciated.

The terms *depreciation* and *cost recovery* are used interchangeably in this text. The rules in Sec. 167 (or pre-ACRS) and the MACRS rules under Sec. 168 both refer to depreciation. However, the deduction under ACRS is referred to as cost recovery. In 1981, Congress initiated the original ACRS system to achieve a number of objectives, including a stimulus for private investment, improving business productivity, simplifying taxpayer compliance, and facilitating IRS administration of the tax law. Therefore, less importance was placed on the financial accounting concept of matching costs and revenues, which is the primary theory that governed the Sec. 167 depreciation rules. Congress' primary objective in 1981 was to allow businesses and investors to recover the cost of capitalized expenditures over a period of time that is substantially shorter than the property's economic useful life. Thus, the term *cost recovery* rather than *depreciation* was used under the ACRS system. The post-1986 MACRS rules more closely follow the concept of economic useful life and, therefore, the MACRS rules refer to depreciation rather than cost recovery.

HISTORICAL NOTE

Before 1954, except for the limited use of a declining-balance method, taxpayers were required to use the straight-line method.

COMMON RULES OF ALL SYSTEMS. Regardless of the particular system of depreciation required (i.e., MACRS, ACRS, etc.), certain rules are common to all systems of depreciation. These common rules are discussed below.

ADDITIONAL COMMENT

Property is considered to be "placed in service" when it is in a condition or state of readiness and is available for a specifically assigned function. This can be important in attempting to determine the first year that a depreciation deduction is available.

▶ Depreciation may be claimed only on property used in a trade or business or for the production of income. Thus, personal-use assets, such as a personal-use automobile or the taxpayer's personal residence, are not depreciable.

▶ No depreciation is permitted for land or other assets that have an indefinite life. Assets such as works of art are generally not depreciable.

---

[1] Sec. 167(a).

▶ First-year depreciation is permitted only in the year the asset is placed in service. For example, a taxpayer may purchase a depreciable asset in December 2010 but not place it in service until January 2011. In this case, depreciation is not allowed until 2011.

▶ Regardless of the depreciation system, consistency is required. Taxpayers must consistently use the method selected in the year the asset was placed in service unless a change of accounting method is requested from the IRS.

▶ The basis of property being depreciated must be reduced by the amount of depreciation that is allowable for each taxable year. An important aspect of depreciation is determining the amount of depreciation that is *allowed* and *allowable*. The depreciation allowed is the actual depreciation claimed by the taxpayer for a particular taxable year. Allowable depreciation is the amount of depreciation to be claimed under the tax law by using the slowest possible method (i.e., straight-line using the longest permissible recovery period). If a taxpayer does not take any depreciation during a particular year, the basis of property must be reduced by the amount of depreciation that should have been taken during the year (i.e., the allowable depreciation).

EXAMPLE I:10-1 ▶

Maria acquires and places in service a machine (7-year property) for $50,000 to be used in her business. She elects straight-line depreciation under MACRS. Maria properly takes depreciation in the first two years in the amount of $10,714 ($3,571 in Year 1 and $7,143 in Year 2, assuming the half-year convention). However, because of a net operating loss in Year 3, Maria did not take any depreciation on the tax return. The allowable depreciation in Year 3 was $7,143. Even though Maria did not claim the $7,143 in Year 3, the basis of the machine must still be reduced by that amount. Thus, at the end of Year 3, the basis of the machine would be $32,143 ($50,000 minus the allowable accumulated depreciation of $17,857). Obviously, Maria should amend her tax return for Year 3 and deduct the allowable depreciation. This would increase her net operating loss for Year 3, which either can be carried back two years or forward 20 years. ◀

TYPES OF PROPERTY. For both property law and income tax purposes, there are two basic types of property, tangible and intangible. **Tangible property** refers to property that has physical substance, such as land, buildings, natural resources, equipment, etc. **Intangible property** refers to property that does not have physical substance, such as goodwill, patents, and stocks and bonds. The cost of tangible property (other than land, of course) is systematically written off through depreciation or depletion. Natural resources, such as oil and gas reserves, are recovered through depletion. Intangible property is written off through amortization.

Tangible property is further classified as either real property or personal property. **Real property** (often referred to as real estate or realty) is defined as land or any structure permanently attached to the land, such as buildings. **Personal property** is any tangible property that is not real property, and includes items such as equipment, vehicles, furniture, etc. It is important to distinguish between personal property and personal-use property. **Personal-use property** is any property, tangible or intangible, real or personal, that is used by the taxpayer for his own personal use rather than in a trade or business or for the production of income.

CAPITALIZATION VERSUS EXPENSE. A frequent dilemma for taxpayers is whether an expenditure should be capitalized and expensed through depreciation, or expensed entirely in the current year. As discussed in Chapter I:6, if an expenditure either improves the efficiency of an asset or extends the life of an asset beyond the end of the year, the expenditure should generally be capitalized. However, most taxpayers have established materiality limits to justify the expensing of small expenditures that technically should be considered capital expenditures. Since capitalization-expense decisions are frequently subjective in nature, disputes between the IRS and taxpayers are common.

CONVERSION OF PERSONAL-USE PROPERTY. If personal-use property is either converted to business-use or held for the production of income (e.g., a principal residence converted to a rental house), the property's basis for depreciation purposes is the lesser of its adjusted basis or its fair market value (FMV) determined as of the conversion date.[2]

---

[2] Reg. Sec. 1.168(i)-4(b)(1).

This lower of cost or market rule prevents taxpayers from depreciating the portion of the cost that represents a nondeductible loss on a personal-use asset. Chapter I:5 discusses the disposition of personal-use property.

EXAMPLE I:10-2 ▶ Marty acquired a principal residence for $115,000 in 2005. In 2010, he converts the property to rental use because he is unable to sell the house due to a depressed local real estate market. The property's FMV is only $100,000 when it is converted to rental status in 2010. The $15,000 ($115,000 − $100,000) decline in value represents a nondeductible personal loss and is not depreciable. The depreciable basis of the rental property is $100,000 (minus the portion of the property's FMV that represents land, which is not depreciable). ◀

OBJECTIVE 1

Classify property and calculate depreciation under the MACRS rules

DEPRECIATION METHODS

As mentioned previously, the depreciation method required for income tax purposes depends on the date the asset was placed in service. Assets placed in service prior to 1987 must use the old depreciation methods that were in effect during those years.[3] Under current law, for assets placed in service after 1986, the MACRS system of depreciation is required for most assets. MACRS is different from depreciation methods used for financial accounting purposes in several ways, including the following:

▶ MACRS does not consider salvage value in the computation of the depreciation amount.

▶ MACRS uses specific asset classes. Both tangible personal property and real property must be placed into specific asset classes, based on the type of property. Asset classes refer to the number of years over which the asset must be depreciated, such as 5-year property, 7-year property, etc.

▶ MACRS uses fewer depreciation methods, and the methods are built into the MACRS tables. Both accelerated and straight-line methods are used in MACRS, but accelerated methods are not permissible for real property. The MACRS tables are summarized in Appendix C.

▶ MACRS uses assumptions about when assets are either placed in service or disposed of rather than using actual dates. The applicable assumption is called a *convention*. The **half-year convention** is generally required for all tangible personal property. It assumes that all asset acquisitions or dispositions are made at the midpoint of the tax year. A special convention that may apply to tangible personal property is the **mid-quarter convention**, discussed later in this chapter. For real estate, the **mid-month convention** is used. It assumes that all asset acquisitions or dispositions are made at the midpoint of the month in which the transaction occurs.

EXAMPLE I:10-3 ▶ Golden Corporation, a calendar year taxpayer, purchases a business-use machine on March 10, 2010. For depreciation purposes, under the half-year convention, the machine is treated as if it were placed in service on July 1, 2010, and one-half year's depreciation is allowable in 2010. The half-year convention assumes all asset acquisitions and dispositions occur at the midpoint of the tax year. ◀

EXAMPLE I:10-4 ▶ Assume that Golden Corporation, in Example I:10-3 above, uses the machine for several years and decides to sell the machine on October 30, 2013. To compute the depreciation deduction for the year 2013, under the half-year convention, Golden is permitted one-half year's depreciation. This one-half year's depreciation is required even though the actual sale occurred on October 30. ◀

EXAMPLE I:10-5 ▶ Silver, Inc., a calendar year taxpayer, purchases a business-use building on March 5, 2010. For depreciation purposes, under the mid-month convention, the building is treated as if it were placed in service on March 15, 2010, and 9½ months of depreciation is allowable in 2010 (one-half of a month for March plus nine full months). ◀

---

[3] For assets placed into service between 1981 and 1986, taxpayers were required to use the ACRS method; for assets placed into service before 1981, a pre-ACRS method was required. Pre-ACRS methods more closely resemble depreciation methods used for financial statement purposes.

CALCULATION OF DEPRECIATION

The annual depreciation deduction involves a number of variables. Below is a discussion of these variables in connection with the two principal types of depreciable property: tangible personal property and real property.

TANGIBLE PERSONAL PROPERTY: CLASSIFICATION AND RECOVERY RATES. Tangible personal property, such as equipment, furniture, computers, etc., is depreciable under MACRS if used in a trade or business or held for the production of income. Each piece of tangible personal property acquired must be classified into one of six asset classes.[4] Depreciation is computed using the percentages contained in Table 1 in Appendix C.

The MACRS recovery periods that apply to tangible personal property placed in service after December 31, 1986 are as follows:[5]

ADDITIONAL COMMENT

Most depreciable personal property is classified as 7-year property under MACRS.

KEY POINT

Notice that the recovery period for tax purposes is not necessarily dependent upon the asset's actual economic life. A property's class life and its actual economic life may be different.

▶ 3-Year   Property with a class life of 4 years or less. This category includes property such as tractor units, race horses over 12 years old, and special tools.

▶ 5-Year   Property with a a class life of more than 4 years but less than 10 years. This category includes property such as automobiles, light and heavy-duty general purpose trucks, computers, and research and experimental (R&E) equipment.

▶ 7-Year   Property with a class life of 10 years or more but less than 16 years. This category includes property such as office furniture and equipment, horses, single-purpose agricultural or horticultural structures, and property with no class life and not classified elsewhere. Most types of machinery are included in this class.

▶ 10-Year Property with a class life of more than 16 years, but less than 20 years. This category includes property such as barges, vessels, and petroleum and food processing equipment.

▶ 15-Year Property with a class life of more than 20 years, but less than 25 years. This category includes property such as billboards, service station buildings, and land improvements.

▶ 20-Year Property with a class life of 25 or more years, including property such as utilities and sewers.

KEY POINT

Remember that salvage value is not taken into consideration under the MACRS system.

Depreciation rates for the 3-year, 5-year, and 7-year recovery classes are provided in Table I:10-1. (See Table 1 in Appendix C for depreciation rates for all classes of property.) The rates are based on the 200% DB method switching to straight-line when it yields a larger amount. A half-year convention is used in the year of acquisition and zero salvage value is assumed. To properly apply the half-year convention when property is disposed of in a year before the final table year, the amount calculated from the table must be multiplied by one-half.

EXAMPLE I:10-6 ▶

In March 2010, Mary acquires and places in service a business machine which costs $20,000 and has a 7-year recovery period under MACRS rules. Assuming no Sec. 179 expensing (discussed later), the depreciation deduction for 2010 is $2,858 ($20,000 × 0.1429). MACRS depreciation deduction for the year placed in service also can be computed by applying the accelerated depreciation rate (using the half-year convention) to the basis of the assets. Thus the depreciation deduction for 2010 is $2,857 ($20,000 ÷ 7 years × 200% DB × 0.50 year). Minor differences between the two calculations are due to rounding. ◀

Certain types of property are *excluded* from MACRS depreciation, including:[6]

▶ Property depreciated under a method not expressed in terms of years, such as the units of production method, where the taxpayer elects to not depreciate the property under MACRS;

▶ Intangible assets, such as goodwill or copyrights;

▶ Films, videotapes, or sound recordings.

---

[4] To determine the class life of assets, see Rev. Proc. 87-56, modified by Rev. Proc. 88-22, which sets forth the class life of property for depreciation purposes.

[5] Sec. 168(e)(1).
[6] Sec. 168(f).

▼ **TABLE I:10-1 (a Portion of Table 1 in Appendix C)**

MACRS Percentage Rates for Tangible Personal Property (Using Half-Year Convention)

Recovery Year	Recovery Period		
	3-Year	5-Year	7-Year
1	33.33	20.00	14.29
2	44.45	32.00	24.49
3	14.81	19.20	17.49
4	7.41	11.52	12.49
5	—	11.52	8.93
6	—	5.76	8.92
7	—	—	8.93
8	—	—	4.46

Source: Table 1 of Rev. Proc. 87-57, 1987-2 C.B. 674.

Section 179 Expensing Election. In lieu of depreciating the cost of new or used tangible personal business property under the regular MACRS methods discussed above, taxpayers may elect to expense up to $250,000 (in 2010) of the acquisition cost as an ordinary deduction in the year the property is placed in service.[7] The immediate expensing election is not applicable to real estate. The election is made on an annual basis, and the taxpayer must select the assets to which the deduction applies. MACRS rules apply to any amount of an asset's cost not expensed under Sec. 179 or claimed as bonus depreciation (for years bonus is in effect).

The maximum Sec. 179 expense amount (ceiling) has been increasing over the past several years, as shown in Table I:10-2.

EXAMPLE I:10-7 ▶ In July 2010, Tanya acquires and places in service equipment costing $292,000 with a 7-year MACRS recovery period for 100% business use in her sole proprietorship. Tanya elects to

▼ **TABLE I:10-2**

Section 179 Expense Amounts

Tax Year Beginning In	Maximum Sec. 179 Expense (Ceiling)
2010 (see Legislative Update)	$250,000
2009	250,000
2008	250,000
2007	125,000
2006	108,000
2005	105,000
2004	102,000
2003	100,000

---

[7] Sec. 179. The Tax Increase Prevention and Reconciliation Act of 2005 extended the $100,000 base amount to 2008 and 2009 (inflation adjusted), and the Small Business and Work Opportunity Tax Act of 2007 extended it through 2010. The Economic Stimulus Act of 2008 increased the normal inflation-adjusted amount to $250,000 for 2008, the American Recovery and Reinvestment Act of 2009 extended the $250,000 into 2009, and the Hiring Incentives to Restore Employment (HIRE) Act of 2010 extends it into 2010.

expense $250,000 of the cost under Sec. 179 but elects out of bonus depreciation. Tanya's basis for MACRS depreciation is $42,000 ($292,000 − $250,000). Using the half-year convention (Table 1 of Appendix C), MACRS depreciation is $6,002 ($42,000 × 0.1429). Tanya's total 2010 depreciation is $256,002 ($250,000 + $6,002). ◀

The following limitations and special rules apply to the Sec. 179 election:

▶ The property must be purchased for use in an active trade or business (more than 50% business-use) as distinguished from property that is acquired for the production of income (e.g., personal property used in a rental activity held by an investor does not qualify).

▶ While qualified property is generally tangible personal property, off-the-shelf computer software that is placed in service after 2002 may be expensed under Sec. 179. This is software that is readily available for purchase by the general public, is subject to a nonexclusive license, and has not been substantially modified.

▶ The property cannot be acquired from a related party under Sec. 267 or by gift or inheritance.

ADDITIONAL COMMENT

Married taxpayers who file separate tax returns are each entitled to a maximum of half the regular limitation under Sec. 179.

▶ The Sec. 179 tax benefits are recaptured if the property is no longer predominantly used in a trade or business (e.g., the property is converted to personal use) at any time.[8] In the year of recapture, the taxpayer must include in gross income the amount previously expensed reduced by the amount of depreciation that would have been allowed for the period the property was held for business use.[9]

SELF-STUDY QUESTION

Are corporations entitled to the election to expense up to $250,000 under Sec. 179?

ANSWER

Yes, but larger corporations will not receive the benefit from it because the Sec. 179 deduction is reduced when the cost of qualified property exceeds $800,000.

▶ If the total cost of qualified property placed into service during the year is more than $800,000 (in 2008–2010), the $250,000 ceiling is reduced on a dollar-for-dollar basis by the excess amount. Thus, no deduction is permitted for the 2010 tax year if $1,050,000 or more of Sec. 179 property is placed in service. No carryovers of Sec. 179 depreciation under this provision are permitted. However, the portion of cost not expensed remains in the property's basis subject to MACRS depreciation.

▶ A second limitation on the total Sec. 179 deduction is that it cannot exceed the taxpayer's taxable income (before deducting the Sec. 179 expense) from the trade or business.[10] Any acquisition cost that cannot be deducted because of the limitation based on taxable income is carried forward for an unlimited number of years and is added to the other amounts eligible for the Sec. 179 deduction in the future year. Such carryover amount will be subject to the taxable income limitation in the carryover year.

EXAMPLE I:10-8 ▶ Pam owns an unincorporated manufacturing business. In 2010, she purchases and places in service $830,000 of qualifying equipment for use in her business. Pam's taxable income from the business (before deducting any Sec. 179 expense) is $28,000. The maximum Sec. 179 deduction of $250,000 is initially reduced by $30,000 ($830,000 − $800,000) because the total cost of qualified property placed in service during the year exceeds $800,000. Pam is allowed no carryover of the $30,000 reduced by this limitation. However, the $30,000 remains part of the equipment's basis subject to MACRS depreciation.

The remaining $220,000 ($250,000 − $30,000) Sec. 179 expense is further limited to business taxable income, so Pam's Sec. 179 deduction in 2010 will be $28,000. She may carry over $192,000 ($220,000 − $28,000) to 2011 as Sec. 179 depreciation in that year. Even though only $28,000 is deductible under Sec. 179, Pam must reduce the cost basis of the equipment by $220,000 to prevent double deduction of the Sec. 179 expense caused by the carryover. Thus, she will depreciate $610,000 ($830,000 − $220,000) using MACRS. ◀

Bonus Depreciation. In response to the terrorist attacks on September 11, 2001, Congress enacted special bonus depreciation for new qualified property placed in service after September 10, 2001 and before January 1, 2005. These special depreciation provisions were

---

[8] Sec. 179(d)(10).
[9] Reg. Sec. 1.179-1(e).
[10] Sec. 179(b)(3). Under Reg. Sec. 1.179-2(c)(5)(iv), employees are considered to be engaged in the active conduct of the trade or business from their employment. Thus, a small business person who is also an employee may include wages and salary derived from employment in determining taxable income for purposes of this limitation. Such amounts are considered derived from the conduct of a trade or business. For an individual, taxable income is also computed without regard to the deduction for one-half of self-employment taxes paid under Sec. 164(f) (see Chapter I:14).

effective in encouraging taxpayers to continue to invest in tangible personal property during that trying period of time. The original bonus depreciation provisions expired after December 31, 2004. However, the Economic Stimulus Act of 2008 together with the American Recovery and Reinvestment Act of 2009 reinstated 50% bonus depreciation for qualified property placed in service in 2008 and 2009 (See Legislative Update in the margin).

LEGISLATIVE UPDATE

At the time this textbook went to press, Congress had not extended bonus depreciation into 2010, nor do any bills currently under consideration contain an extension.

Original bonus depreciation was an additional 30% first-year depreciation for qualified property. This rate was in effect from September 11, 2001 to May 5, 2003. In 2003, the 30% first-year bonus depreciation was increased to 50% for qualified property placed in service after May 5, 2003 and before January 1, 2005. The 2008 and 2009 bonus depreciation percentage also is 50%. The specific rules discussed below are the same for both 30% and 50% bonus depreciation property. Bonus depreciation is automatically deductible for both the regular income tax and the alternative minimum tax (AMT). Taxpayers must elect *out* of bonus depreciation if they do not wish to claim the deduction.

Qualified property (generally non-real estate) includes: (1) MACRS property with a recovery period of 20 years or less; (2) computer software (other than computer software that must be amortized under Sec. 197); or (3) qualified leasehold improvement property (see discussion of qualified leasehold improvement property later in this chapter in connection with real property). To qualify, the property must be new property and original use of the property must begin with the taxpayer. Used property does not qualify for bonus depreciation.

The remaining basis of qualified property is depreciated under the usual rules for depreciating such property. If the taxpayer elects to expense property under Sec. 179, the Sec. 179 expense is deducted first, then the additional first-year bonus depreciation and, third, regular MACRS depreciation.[11] In years after the first year, regular MACRS depreciation is allowable under normal rules.

EXAMPLE I:10-9 ▶ On March 25, 2004, Wildcat Corporation, a calendar year taxpayer, purchased and placed in service machinery costing $252,000. The machinery was 7-year MACRS property and the half-year convention applied. Wildcat was eligible to expense $102,000 (the 2004 ceiling) of the cost of the machinery under Sec. 179. Wildcat also claimed bonus depreciation of $75,000 [($252,000 − $102,000) × 0.50]. In addition to Sec. 179 depreciation and bonus depreciation, Wildcat also claimed regular depreciation of $10,718 [($252,000 − $102,000 − $75,000) × 0.1429]. For 2010 (Year 7), Wildcat's allowable depreciation is $6,698 ($75,000 × 0.0893). The $75,000 is the remaining basis after the Sec. 179 and bonus depreciation claimed in 2004. ◀

EXAMPLE I:10-10 ▶ On February 10, 2009, Polar Corporation, a calendar year taxpayer, purchased and placed in service equipment costing $375,000. The equipment was 7-year MACRS property and the half-year convention applies. Polar was eligible to expense $250,000 of the cost of the equipment under Sec. 179. Polar also claimed bonus depreciation of $62,500 [($375,000 − $250,000) × 0.50]. MACRS depreciation for 2009 was $8,931 [($375,000 − $250,000 − $62,500) × 0.1429]. Thus, Polar's total 2009 depreciation on the equipment was $321,431. Polar's 2010 depreciation is $15,306 ($62,500 × 0.2449). ◀

KEY POINT

Remember, the mid-quarter convention does *not* apply to real property.

Use of the Mid-Quarter Convention. As mentioned previously, the MACRS system generally uses the half-year convention. However, the MACRS system requires the use of the **mid-quarter convention** if the aggregate basis of all *personal property* placed in service during the last three months of the year exceeds 40% of the cost of all personal property placed in service during the tax year.[12] The 40% test is applied after reducing the property's basis by Sec. 179 expensing, if elected, but not by bonus depreciation, if claimed. If the test is met, the mid-quarter convention must be used instead of the half-year convention, and special mid-quarter tables must be used to compute depreciation under this convention. (See Tables 2 through 5 in Appendix C.) Property placed in service and disposed of during the same tax year is not taken into account for purposes of the mid-quarter test,[13] nor is property expensed under Sec. 179.[14]

---

[11]Temp. Reg. 1.168(k)-1T(d)(3) Example 2.
[12] Sec. 168(d)(3).

[13] Sec. 168(d)(3)(B) and Reg. Sec. 1.168(d)-1(b)(3).
[14] PLR 9126014 (March 29, 1991).

The 40% rule prevents taxpayers from using the half-year convention and thereby obtaining one-half year's depreciation in the year of acquisition when a substantial portion of the assets are placed in service during the last quarter of the tax year.

EXAMPLE I:10-11 ▶ Michael, a calendar year taxpayer, acquires 5-year tangible personal property in 2010, does not elect Sec. 179, and places the properties in service as follows:

Date Placed in Service	Acquisition Cost
January 20	$ 80,000
April 18	100,000
November 5	252,000
Total	$432,000

Because more than 40% of the property acquired during the year is placed in service in the last three months ($252,000 ÷ $432,000 = 58.3%), the mid-quarter convention applies for all property placed in service during the year. Depreciation for 2010 is computed as follows:

Property Placed in Service	Year 1 MACRS Depreciation	Appendix C Table
January 20	$ 80,000 × 0.35 = $28,000	Table 2
April 18	100,000 × 0.25 = 25,000	Table 3
November 5	252,000 × 0.05 = 12,600	Table 5
Total	$65,600	

◀

EXAMPLE I:10-12 ▶ Assume the same facts as in Example I:10-11 except Michael elects to expense $250,000 under Sec. 179 and selects the property placed in service on November 5. Michael still elects out of bonus depreciation. In this case, the mid-quarter convention would not apply because not more than 40% of property (after the Sec. 179 deduction) was placed in service in the last quarter of the year [($252,000 − $250,000) ÷ $(432,000 − $250,000) = 1.1%]. Therefore, Michael uses the half-year convention, and his depreciation for 2010 is computed using Table 1 in Appendix C as follows:

Date Placed in Service	Year 1 MACRS Depreciation	Sec. 179 Depreciation	Total 2010 Depreciation
January 20	$ 80,000 × 0.20 = $16,000	–0–	$ 16,000
April 18	100,000 × 0.20 = 20,000	–0–	20,000
November 5	2,000* × 0.20 = 400	$250,000	250,400
Total			$286,400

* After Sec. 179 depreciation ($252,000 − $250,000)

In this case, the half-year convention yields larger depreciation in the first year. In some cases, the mid-quarter convention can yield a larger depreciation deduction. This situation occurs only when a large amount of property is placed in service in the first quarter of the year, yet enough property is placed in service in the fourth quarter to require the mid-quarter convention. ◀

ADDITIONAL POINT

To reflect the applicable convention, the taxpayer must manually adjust the depreciation factor found in the MACRS table for assets disposed of during the year.

Year of Disposition. The MACRS system requires that depreciation be taken in the year of disposition using the same convention that applied on acquisition (e.g., half-year, mid-month, or mid-quarter convention). Therefore, if property is disposed of during any year in which the half-year convention is applicable, the depreciation for the year of disposition will be one-half of the amount computed by using the table percentages.

EXAMPLE I:10-13 ▶ Michelle acquired machinery in March 2006 that qualified as 7-year MACRS property and had a $100,000 basis for depreciation. The half-year convention applied in the year of acquisition, and Michelle claimed no Sec. 179 depreciation on the machinery. In December 2010, Michelle sells the machinery. Michelle's depreciation deduction in 2010 is $4,465 ($100,000 × 0.0893 × 0.50). See Table 1 in Appendix C. ◀

If property is subject to the mid-quarter convention, it is treated as being disposed of at the midpoint of the quarter.

EXAMPLE I:10-14 ▶ In addition to other property acquired in the last quarter of 2006, Jason acquired $200,000 of 5-year property in May 2006 (second quarter). He depreciated all property acquired in 2006 using the mid-quarter convention. He claimed no Sec. 179 expense. If Jason sells the 5-year property on July 14, 2010 (third quarter), the property will be treated as if it were sold on August 15, 2010, which is the midpoint of the third quarter. Thus, using Table 3 in Appendix C, Jason claims $14,213 of depreciation in 2010 [($200,000 × 0.1137) × (2.5 ÷ 4)]. ◀

KEY POINT

Depreciable real property placed in service after 1986 must be depreciated using the straight-line method.

ADDITIONAL COMMENT

For purposes of determining whether at least 80% of the gross rental income is rental income from dwelling units, a taxpayer living in any part of the building includes the fair rental value of his unit in the gross rental income.

Real property falls into two categories: residential rental property and nonresidential real property. **Residential rental property** is defined as property from which at least 80% of the gross rental income is rental income from dwelling units.[15] Dwelling units include houses, apartments, and manufactured homes that are used for residential purposes but not hotels, motels, or other establishments for transient use. **Nonresidential real property** is any real property other than residential rental property.

REAL PROPERTY: CLASSIFICATION AND RECOVERY RATES. The MACRS recovery periods that apply to real property placed in service in years after 1986 are:

▶ Residential rental property: 27.5 years (Table 7 in Appendix C)

▶ Nonresidential real property: 39 years[16] (Tables 8 and 9 in Appendix C)

Straight-line depreciation must be used and is reflected in the tables. A mid-month convention is used in the year of acquisition and in the year of disposition.

EXAMPLE I:10-15 ▶

HISTORICAL NOTE

The recovery period for nonresidential real property was extended from 31.5 years to 39 years in 1993 to offset the revenue loss from liberalizing the passive activity loss rules affecting real estate.

On October 4, 2010, Husker, Inc., acquired an office building to relocate its rapidly-growing staff. The property was purchased for $1,500,000, of which $200,000 was allocated to the underlying land. Because the property is nonresidential real property, it is classified as 39-year property. Depreciation is computed using Table 9 in Appendix C (mid-month convention), totaling $6,955 ($1,300,000 × .00535). In 2011, depreciation on the building will be $33,332 ($1,300,000 × .02564). ◀

Taxpayers owning buildings must depreciate subsequent capital improvements. Capital improvements are depreciated over the full MACRS recovery period of the improvement, not over the remaining life or recovery period of the building. Thus, the cost of a new roof on an office building must be depreciated over 39 years, even though the building may have been placed in service several years ago.

QUALIFIED LEASEHOLD IMPROVEMENT PROPERTY. Qualified leasehold improvement property (QLIP) is defined as any improvement to an interior portion of nonresidential real property made by either a lessee or a lessor pursuant to a lease. The QLIP must have been placed in service more than three years after the date the building was first placed in service. Expenditures that enlarge a building or expenditures such as an elevator, an escalator, or a structural component that benefits either a common area or the internal structural framework of a building are not considered QLIP.

LEGISLATIVE UPDATE

At the time this textbook went to press, Congress had not extended bonus depreciation. However, one of the extenders bills currently under consideration would extend the 15-year recovery period into 2010 if passed.

As discussed previously, bonus depreciation (50% or 30%) was allowed for QLIP placed in service after September 10, 2001 and before January 1, 2005. The 50% bonus depreciation was again allowed for QLIP placed in service in 2008 and 2009. In recent tax legislation, Congress gave special treatment to QLIP by allowing a 15-year recovery period instead of the 39-year recovery period allowed for nonresidential real property. The shorter recovery period was effective for QLIP placed in service after December 31, 2005 and before January 1, 2010, and required straight-line depreciation with the half-year or midquarter convention, whichever was applicable.[17]

EXAMPLE I:10-16 ▶ Shaheen Corporation leased office space to operate its business in a 20-year-old building. In early 2009, the corporation made some major leasehold improvements, such as changing the size of offices by rearranging the walls, new ductwork, and other similar capital improvements to the office. The overall size of the office did not change. The leasehold improvements were

---

[15] Secs. 168(e)(2)(A).
[16] Sec. 168(c)(1). A 31.5-year recovery period applied to nonresidential real property placed in service on or after January 1, 1987, and before May 13, 1993.

[17] The shorter recovery period was instituted by the 2004 Jobs Act and extended by the Tax Relief and Health Care Act of 2006 and the Tax Extenders Act of 2008 to QLIP placed in service before January 1, 2010.

completed and placed in service on July 15, 2009, at a total cost of $120,000 and were considered qualified leasehold improvement property. Normally, leasehold improvements must be depreciated over 39 years. For 2009, however, Shaheen Corporation was permitted to take both 50% bonus depreciation and 15-year straight line MACRS depreciation on the leasehold improvements. Thus, in 2009, the depreciation deduction was:

Cost of qualified leasehold improvements	$120,000
Minus: Bonus depreciation	(60,000)
Depreciable basis	60,000
Times: Depreciation rate ($\frac{1}{15} \times \frac{1}{2}$)	0.03333
Depreciation on balance	$ 2,000
Total depreciation for 2009	$ 62,000

◀

STRAIGHT-LINE (METHOD) ELECTION UNDER MACRS. Instead of using the accelerated methods previously described under the MACRS rules, taxpayers may elect to use the straight-line method for tangible personal property. If the straight-line election is made, the taxpayer must use either the same depreciation period or an extended period based on the alternative depreciation system, as discussed below.[18]

EXAMPLE I:10-17 ▶ In early 2010, Delta Corporation places in service equipment costing $100,000. Delta does not elect Sec. 179 expensing and elects the straight line method under MACRS. Using a 7-year recovery period and half-year convention, Delta'a depreciation for 2010 is $7,143 [($100,000 ÷ 7 years) × 0.50]. ◀

ALTERNATIVE DEPRECIATION SYSTEM. The MACRS system provides an alternative depreciation system (ADS) that is required for certain property and is also available for all other depreciable assets if the taxpayer so elects.[19] The election is made on a year-by-year basis. Once the election is made for specified property, it is irrevocable. For personal property, the ADS election applies to all property within a class (all 5-year property, for example); for real property, the ADS election may be made on an individual property basis. The principal type of property for which the ADS is *required* is tangible property used predominantly outside the United States. ADS recovery periods are generally longer than recovery periods under MACRS, and ADS requires the use of the straight-line method with a half-year, mid-quarter, or mid-month convention, whichever is applicable. Thus, the ADS election is generally made by taxpayers who want to use the straight-line method over a longer recovery period. These taxpayers frequently have net operating losses or are subject to the alternative minimum tax (see Chapter I:14 for a discussion of the alternative minimum tax).

EXAMPLE I:10-18 ▶ In May 2010, Bob Roaster purchases an office building for $300,000 ($50,000 allocated to the land) as rental property. Because he has substantial net operating losses from other business ventures, Roaster elects to depreciate the building using ADS. Depreciation expense for 2010, using the mid-month convention and a 40-year life is $3,908 [$250,000 × .01563 (Table 12, Appendix C)]. If Roaster had not elected ADS, his depreciation would have been $4,013 [$250,000 × .01605 (Table 9, Appendix C)]. The difference is small because the recovery period is 39 years under regular MACRS and 40 years under ADS. ◀

If the taxpayer *elected* ADS, he or she also could use the bonus depreciation allowed in 2001-2004, 2008, and 2009. For property *required* to be depreciated under ADS, however, bonus depreciation was not permitted.

The alternative depreciation system also is used to compute earnings and profits (E&P) for a corporation and to compute the alternative minimum tax for both individuals and corporations (see Chapter I:14).

Topic Review I:10-1 presents a comparison of the MACRS and ADS rules.

---

[18] Sec. 168(g)(7).

[19] Sec. 168(g). (See Tables 10–12 in Appendix C.)

Topic Review I:10-1

Comparison of MACRS and ADS

	MACRS	ADS
Recovery Periods:		
Automobiles	5 years	5 years
Computers	5 years	5 years
Office machinery	5 years	6 years
Office furniture and equipment	7 years	10 years
Residential rental property	27.5 years	40 years
Nonresidential real property	39 years[b]	40 years
Personal property with no specified class life	7 years	12 years
Conventions:		
Personal property	Half-year or mid-quarter[a]	Half-year or mid-quarter[a]
Real property	Mid-month	Mid-month
Depreciation in year of sale:		
Personal property	Yes	Yes
Real property	Yes	Yes

[a] If more than 40% of the cost of personal property (after Sec. 179 expensing) is placed in service during the last quarter of year.
[b] For property placed in service prior to May 13, 1993, the recovery period is 31.5 years.

MACRS RESTRICTIONS

PERSONAL-USE ASSETS. The personal-use portion of an asset's cost is not depreciable. For example, if a taxpayer owns a duplex and uses one unit as a personal residence, only the unit that is rented to tenants qualifies for depreciation.

LISTED PROPERTY RULES. Because Congress was concerned about taxpayers claiming large depreciation deductions (using accelerated methods) on certain types of assets that are conducive to mixed business/personal use, it placed restrictions on assets that are classified as *listed property*. Listed property includes automobiles, computers and peripheral equipment, cellular telephones, and property generally used for purposes of entertainment, recreation, or amusement (for example, a video recorder). If a listed property's business use is greater than 50% of its total use, the taxpayer may elect Sec. 179 expensing for the business portion and may use regular MACRS tables for the remaining business portion of the asset's cost, including bonus depreciation where applicable. However, if the business use is 50% or less, the taxpayer may not elect Sec. 179 expensing, must use ADS (e.g., 5-year straight-line cost recovery for automobiles and computers), and may not use bonus depreciation (because ADS is required).

EXAMPLE I:10-19 ▶ In June 2010, Patrick acquires an automobile at a cost of $10,000. He uses it 60% for business. Assuming no Sec. 179 election, the depreciation deduction on the business-use portion of the automobile's cost is based on the MACRS system and 5-year recovery class because the automobile is predominantly used in business (i.e., more than 50%). The MACRS depreciation allowance in 2010 is $1,200 [($10,000 × 0.20) × 60% business use percentage]. (Table 1 in Appendix C.) ◀

EXAMPLE I:10-20 ▶

ADDITIONAL COMMENT

Congress enacted the restrictions on automobiles in 1984 because of a concern that the tax system was underwriting the acquisition of automobiles whose cost and luxury far exceeded what was required for business needs.

In June 2010, Paula acquires an automobile at a cost of $10,000. She uses it only 40% for business. Paula must use ADS to depreciate the business portion of the automobile, and Sec. 179 expensing is not allowed. The business portion is $4,000 ($10,000 × 0.40). Paula's depreciation allowance in 2010 using the straight-line method and the half-year convention is $400 [($4,000 ÷ 5 years) × 0.50]. ◀

Additional restrictions apply to employees who acquire listed property (e.g., an automobile, personal computer, etc.) for use in employment-related activities. In

addition to the "more than 50% test," such use must be for the convenience of the *employer* and be required as a condition of employment.[20] This rule is strictly interpreted by the IRS.

EXAMPLE I:10-21 ▶ Raul, a college professor, acquired a personal computer for use at home. He used the computer 60% of the time on teaching- and research-related activities associated with his job. The remaining usage was for personal activities. Raul's employer finds that it is helpful for employees to own a personal computer but does not require them to purchase a computer as a condition of employment. Raul meets the first requirement (i.e., the 60% business usage is greater than the 50% threshold). However, the second requirement for employees (that the use must be for the convenience of the employer and required as a condition of employment) is not met. Thus, no depreciation may be taken because the employment-related use is not deemed to be business use. ◀

RECAPTURE OF EXCESS COST RECOVERY DEDUCTIONS. Taxpayers are subject to depreciation recapture on listed property if MACRS rules were used originally and the property's business-use percentage decreases to 50% or less in a subsequent year. Depreciation deductions for all years are recomputed using ADS. The excess depreciation deducted, including any Sec. 179 expense and bonus depreciation, is recaptured as ordinary income by including it in the taxpayer's gross income in the year the business-use percentage first falls to 50% or below.[21] Once the business use falls to 50% or below, ADS must be used for the current year and for all subsequent years, even if the business-use percentage increases to more than 50% in a subsequent year.

EXAMPLE I:10-22 ▶ Paul, a self-employed attorney, acquired an automobile in June 2008 for $12,000. In both 2008 and 2009, Paul's business-use percentage was 60%. Depreciation under MACRS in 2008 and 2009 were as follows:

2008: Regular MACRS depreciation assuming 100% business use ($12,000 × 0.20)		2,400
Times: Business-use percentage		0.60
Depreciation for 60% business use		$1,440
2009: Regular MACRS depreciation assuming 100% business use ($12,000 × 0.32)		$3,840
Times: Business-use percentage		0.60
Depreciation for 60% business use		$2,304

In 2010, Paul's business-use percentage declines to 40%. Therefore, he must use ADS for 2010 and also recapture the excess depreciation taken in 2008 and 2009. The recapture is computed as follows:

MACRS depreciation taken in 2008 and 2009 ($1,440 + $2,304)		$3,744
2008: Recomputed ADS depreciation ($12,000 × 0.60 × 0.10)	$ 720	
2009: Recomputed ADS depreciation ($12,000 × 0.60 × 0.20)	1,440	(2,160)
Recapture of excess depreciation in 2010 (ordinary income)		$1,584

Paul must use ADS to compute depreciation in 2010 and all subsequent years. His 2010 deduction will be $960 ($12,000 × 0.40 × 0.20). ◀

LIMITATIONS ON LUXURY AUTOMOBILES. Because Congress believed that the normal MACRS depreciation deduction for automobiles used for business was too generous, it placed ceilings on deductions related to luxury passenger automobiles. A passenger automobile is defined as a 4-wheeled vehicle which is manufactured primarily for use on public streets, roads, and highways and which is rated at 6,000 pounds or less unloaded gross vehicle weight rating (GVWR).[22] In essence, taxpayers are still allowed to fully depreciate luxury cars, but must depreciate them over longer than the normal five-year recovery period.

---

[20] Sec. 280F(d)(3). Any other property used for transportation (e.g., a pickup truck) qualifies as listed property if the nature of the property lends itself to personal use. (See Sec. 280F(b)(4).)

[21] Sec. 280F(b).
[22] Sec. 280F(d)(5)(A).

EXAMPLE I:10-23 ▶ In 2010, Joe purchases a $60,000 automobile that he uses 100% for business purposes. Under normal MACRS rules and without considering Sec. 179, Joe could deduct depreciation of $12,000 in the first year ($60,000 × 0.20) and $19,000 ($60,000 × 0.32) in the second year. Thus, Joe could deduct 52% ($31,000 ÷ $60,000) of the cost of his automobile in the first two years, creating considerable tax savings.

To prevent such perceived abuse, Congress has implemented the following ceiling limitations for MACRS depreciation on passenger automobiles placed in service in 2010 (based on 100% business-use):

Year 1 (2010)	$3,060
Year 2 (2011)	4,900
Year 3 (2012)	2,950
Year 4 (2013 and subsequent years)	1,775

(For automobiles placed in service in prior years, see Table 6 in Appendix C.)

ADDITIONAL COMMENT

The limitations on luxury automobiles mean that the depreciation deductions are limited during the normal 5-year recovery period on business automobiles costing more than $15,300 for 2010 ($3,060 ÷ 0.20).

To compute the maximum MACRS depreciation deduction for a passenger automobile for any year, taxpayers must first compute depreciation under normal MACRS rules, including Sec. 179, and then compare this amount to the ceiling limitation for that year.[23] The maximum depreciation deduction allowed for any year cannot exceed the ceiling limitation amount. Due to the ceiling limitation, taxpayers usually do not elect Sec. 179 expensing on passenger automobiles.

EXAMPLE I:10-24 ▶ Amy purchases a $60,000 automobile in 2010 that she uses 100% for business purposes. She is limited to $3,060 of depreciation, as this ceiling amount is less than regular MACRS depreciation ($60,000 × 0.20 = $12,000).

After the first year, the procedure is the same as above. The regular MACRS deduction is computed and compared with the appropriate year of the ceiling limitation and the deduction allowed cannot exceed the ceiling amount. As Table I:10-3 shows, after the regular recovery period ends for passenger automobiles placed in service in 2010, the taxpayer would be entitled to a deduction of $1,775 per year until the automobile is fully depreciated. ◀

DEPRECIATING MIXED-USE AUTOMOBILES. Taxpayers who use passenger automobiles less than 100% for business must compute the regular MACRS depreciation amount, identify the ceiling amount, and then reduce each one by the percentage of personal use. The actual depreciation deduction for the year will be the lesser of the two reduced amounts. Complicating the matter, the taxpayer's basis in the automobile will decrease by the lesser of the *unreduced* amounts, even though that was not the amount allowed as a deduction.[24] Example 10-25 and Table 10-3 demonstrate this rule.

EXAMPLE I:10-25 ▶ Phil acquires an automobile for $50,000 in April 2010. He uses the automobile 80% for business and 20% for personal activities during 2010 and all succeeding years. Table I:10-3 lists the depreciation amounts, assuming that the 80% business use continues for the life of the automobile and that no amount is expensed under Sec. 179. At the end of the regular MACRS recovery period, the unrecovered cost of the business-use portion of the automobile may be recovered at an annual rate not to exceed $1,420 ($1,775 × 0.80). ◀

TYPICAL MISCONCEPTION

It is sometimes mistakenly believed that the Sec. 179 expensing allowance can be used to boost the first-year depreciation of luxury automobiles.

TRUCKS, VANS, AND SUVs. As mentioned previously, limitations are placed on "passenger automobiles" that have a gross vehicle weight rating (GVWR) of 6,000 pounds or less. SUVs rated at a GVWR exceeding 6,000 pounds were not subject to the ceiling limitations, so taxpayers could expense up to $100,000 (adjusted for inflation) under Sec. 179, thus creating a major tax planning opportunity. Pursuant to the 2004 Jobs Act, this controversial provision has been curtailed. For SUVs placed into service after October 22, 2004, the maximum Sec. 179 expense amount is $25,000,[25] rather than $250,000 (in 2008–2010).

---

[23] Bonus depreciation also applied to property placed in service from September 11, 2001 through December 31, 2004, in 2008, and in 2009 and was reflected in the limitations for those years.

[24] Sec. 280F(d)(8).

[25] Sec. 179(b)(6). Vehicles with a GVWR of more than 14,000 pounds are not considered SUVs and are not subject to the $25,000 limitation.

▼ TABLE I:10-3

Depreciation Amounts for Example I:10-25 (80% Business-Use Automobile)

	(A) MACRS Deduction: 100% Business Use (Table 1)	(B) Ceiling Limit: 100% Business Use (Table 6)	Deduction Allowed: 80% of Lesser of MACRS or ceiling	Unrecovered Basis
2010				
Regular MACRS calculation ($50,000 × 0.20)	$10,000	$ 3,060	$ 2,448	$46,940*
2011				
Regular MACRS calculation ($50,000 × 0.32)	$16,000	$ 4,900	$ 3,920	$42,040
2012				
Regular MACRS calculation ($50,000 × 0.192)	$ 9,600	$ 2,950	$ 2,360	$39,090
2013				
Regular MACRS calculation ($50,000 × 0.1152)	$ 5,760	$ 1,775	$ 1,420	$37,315
2014				
Regular MACRS calculation ($50,000 × 0.1152)	$ 5,760	$ 1,775	$ 1,420	$35,540
2015				
Regular MACRS calculation ($50,000 × 0.0576)	$ 2,880	$ 1,775	$ 1,420	$33,765
Total through 2015	$50,000	$16,235	$12,988	

2016 and subsequent years until fully depreciated

Ceiling limit		$ 1,775	$ 1,420	

* Unrecovered basis equals original basis minus the lesser of A or B [($50,000 − $3,060) in 2010] even though the annual deduction is limited to business usage.

Note: Based on the unrecovered basis of $33,765 at December 31, 2015, it would take Phil another 13.4 years to fully depreciate the automobile ($23,765 ÷ $1,775 = 13.4 years). The personal-use portion of the automobile's cost, $10,000 ($50,000 × 0.20), will never be depreciated and will be recovered only upon disposition.

However, SUVs with a GVWR of greater than 6,000 pounds will continue to have significant depreciation advantages over other vehicles because the ceiling limitations do not apply.

To qualify for the truck and van depreciation deduction, a vehicle must be a passenger vehicle built on a truck chassis with an unloaded gross weight of over 6,000 pounds. A vehicle buillt on an automobile chassis is classified as an automobile regardless of weight, even if its manufacturer calls it an SUV.

EXAMPLE I:10-26 ▶

ADDITIONAL COMMENT

Many SUVs have a rated GVWR of greater than 6,000 pounds, such as the Chevrolet Suburban, Dodge Durango, Hummer H1 and H2, and Toyota Sequoia. For a more complete list, go to www.carsdirect.com/home.

Two taxpayers purchase vehicles used 100% for business in July 2010, at a cost of $60,000 each. Taxpayer A purchases a BMW sedan that is considered a passenger automobile for tax purposes. Taxpayer B purchases a Ford Expedition which is rated at over 6,000 GVWR and, therefore, is not considered a passenger automobile and not subject to the ceiling limitations. Taxpayer B elects Sec. 179 expensing. The first-year depreciation for each vehicle for 2010 is computed below.

BMW: Regular MACRS depreciation from Table 1 ($60,000 × 0.20)	$12,000
Ceiling limitation	3,060

In this case, the maximum depreciation deduction on the vehicle for 2010 is $3,060

Ford Expedition: Section 179 depreciation (maximum)	$25,000

Regular MACRS depreciation from Table 1 [($60,000 − $25,000) × .020]   7,000
Total depreciation for 2010 $32,000

The Table 6 ceiling limitations do not apply because the vehicle has a GVWR of more than 6,000 pounds. ◄

This example shows the significant tax savings from buying a passenger vehicle on a truck chassis that has a GVWR of more than 6,000 pounds. It should be noted that any vehicle that avoids the ceiling limitations must be used more than 50% for business, under the general listed property rules.

Although some taxpayers avoid the ceiling limitations by purchasing heavy vehicles, other taxpayers who use light trucks and vans (6,000 GVWR or less) in their businesses are hurt by the ceiling limitations. In response to small business concerns, two recent exceptions to the ceiling limitations have been issued: (1) exemption from the ceiling limitations for vehicles that clearly are not for personal use and (2) higher ceiling limitation amounts for other light trucks and vans.

▶ Exemption from ceiling limitations: Certain "nonpersonal use" vehicles are completely exempt from the ceiling limitations.[26] These vehicles must be specifically modified so that they are not likely to be used more than a de minimis amount for personal purposes. This somewhat vague definition is explained further in the regulations as a van that only has a front bench for seating, has permanent shelving that fills most of the cargo area, or has been painted with advertising or the company's logo.

▶ Higher ceiling limitations: Even if a light truck or van does not meet the nonpersonal use criteria above, higher ceiling limitations have been issued for vehicles on a truck chassis.[27] For trucks and vans on a truck chassis that have a GVWR of 6,000 pounds or less, the ceiling amounts for 2010 (Table 6) are as follows:

	Annual Ceiling Limitations
Year 1 (2010)	$3,160
Year 2 (2011)	5,100
Year 3 (2012)	3,050
Year 4 (2013 and subsequent years)	1,875

ADDITIONAL COMMENT

The amount that can be deducted for leased automobiles is also limited.

ADDITIONAL COMPUTATIONS FOR LEASED VEHICLES. If a taxpayer leases an automobile or light truck or van for business purposes, the deduction for rental payments is reduced to reflect the luxury auto depreciation limits imposed on purchased vehicles. If these restrictions were not applied to leased automobiles, the ceiling limitations could be avoided by leasing instead of purchasing an automobile. The leasing restriction is accomplished by requiring taxpayers to reduce their deduction by an "inclusion amount" obtained from an IRS table.[28] This amount is based on the automobile's FMV and the tax year in which the lease commences, and is prorated for the percentage of business use and number of days used during the year. Partial lease inclusion tables are provided in Tables 13 and 14 in Appendix C.

EXAMPLE I:10-27 ▶

On January 1, 2009, Jim leased and placed in service an automobile with a $39,500 FMV and annual lease payments of $7,200. Jim uses the automobile 80% for business purposes. Jim can deduct 80% of the lease payments ($7,200 × 0.80 = $5,760) but must reduce his deduction by 80% of the inclusion amount from Table 13 to reflect the luxury auto depreciation limitation. For 2009, this reduction was $45 ($56 × 0.80). Thus, Jim's auto lease deduction for 2009 was $5,715 ($5,760 − $45). For 2010, the second year, Jim's auto lease deduction is $5,662 [$5,760 − ($122 × 0.80)]. ◄

Topic Review I:10-2 summarizes the special depreciation elections and restrictions.

---

[26] Temp. Reg. Sec. 1.274-5T(k), T.D. 9064 (6-30-2003) amending T.D. 8061.
[27] Rev. Proc. 2003-75, 2003-2 C.B. 1018.

[28] The latest lease inclusion table is contained in Rev. Proc. 2009-24, I.R.B. 2009-16.

Topic Review I:10-2

Special Depreciation Elections and Restrictions

SECTION 179 EXPENSING ELECTION

Maximum deduction: $250,000 (in 2008–2010) of the total cost of qualified property placed in service during the year.

Qualified property: New or used tangible personal business-use property.

Limitations on deduction:
1. Cost limitation: The maximum Sec. 179 expense is reduced dollar-for-dollar by the excess of total qualified property cost over $800,000 (in 2008–2010). Taxpayers may not carry forward amounts reduced by this limitation. However, the cost not expensed because of this limitation remains as basis subject to MACRS depreciation,
2. Taxable income limitation: The Sec. 179 expense after cost limitation is further limited to taxable income before the deduction. Taxpayers may carry forward amounts lost because of this limitation.

Basis reduction: The basis of qualified property for MACRS depreciation is reduced by the Sec. 179 expense (after the cost limitation reduction).

BUSINESS USE RESTRICTION

Listed property: If business use of listed property (defined on Page I:10-12) exceeds 50% of total use, taxpayers may elect Sec. 179 expensing for the business portion and may depreciate the remaining business-use portion using MACRS rules. If business use is 50% or less of total use, taxpayers may not elect Sec. 179 expensing and must depreciate listed property using ADS rules.

AUTOMOBILES, TRUCKS, AND VANS

Table 6 in Appendix C provides annual ceiling amounts for depreciation on 100% buiness-use automobiles and on 100% business-use trucks and vans with a GVWR of 6,000 pounds or less. The taxpayer computes regular depreciation under MACRS, including Sec. 179 expensing, and then compares that figure to the Table 6 ceiling figure. The deduction is the lesser of these two. If business-use is less than 100%, both figures must be reduced by the personal-use percentage. Basis nevertheless is adjusted by the unreduced figure. Business-use trucks and vans with a GVWR of more than 6,000 pounds are not subject to these limitations.

LEASED VEHICLES

Taxpayers who lease vehicles must subtract from their otherwise deductible lease payments as "inclusion amount" (see Tables 13 and 14 in Appendix C) to adjust the lease expense deduction for the luxury auto depreciation limitations imposed on purchased vehicles. This rule prevents individuals from avoiding the luxury auto depreciation limits by leasing vehicles.

AMORTIZATION

OBJECTIVE 2

Calculate amortization for intangible assets and understand the difference between amortizable and non-amortizable assets

Amortization deductions are allowed for a variety of intangible assets. Although amortization periods vary greatly depending on the type of asset, all intangible assets are amortized on a *straight-line basis*. The major intangible assets that may be amortized are as follows:

▶ Goodwill and Other Purchased Intangibles, Sec. 197
▶ Research and Experimental Expenditures, Sec. 174
▶ Computer software
▶ Start-up Expenditures, Sec. 195
▶ Organizational Expenditures, Sec. 248
▶ Pollution Control Facilities, Sec. 169

Several of the above intangibles are discussed below.

HISTORICAL NOTE

Prior to the tax change in 1993, no amortization for goodwill was allowed. So, in business acquisitions, the purchaser typically tried to allocate as little of the purchase price as possible to goodwill. These allocations frequently caused disputes with the IRS. Under current law, these disputes have lessened for purchased goodwill.

SEC. 197 INTANGIBLES

Sec. 197 allows a deduction for the amortization of certain acquired intangible assets. The amortization is deducted on a ratable basis (straight-line) over a 15-year period beginning with the month of acquisition.[29] In general, Sec. 197 applies only to intangible assets that

---

[29] Sec. 197(a).

are acquired in connection with the conduct of a trade or business or an activity engaged in for the production of income. Sec. 197 does not apply to an intangible asset that is internally created by the taxpayer, such as a patent resulting from the taxpayer's research and development lab. Internally-created patents and copyrights have definite and limited lives and are therefore amortizable over the defined period.[30] Internally created patents are generally amortized over 17 years; internally created copyrights over 28 years.

EXAMPLE I:10-28 ▶ On January 1, 2010, Central Corporation receives patent approval on an internally created process improvement. Legal costs associated with the patent are $100,000 and the patent has a legal life of 17 years. The patent does not qualify as a Sec. 197 intangible. The patent has a definite and limited life and is amortizable ratably over its legal life of 17 years beginning with the month of its creation. ◀

BOOK-TO-TAX ACCOUNTING COMPARISON

For financial statement reporting, a firm reduces goodwill by an impairment amount rather than by amortization.

DEFINITION OF A SEC. 197 INTANGIBLE ASSET. Sec. 197 intangibles (i.e., intangible assets that are subject to 15-year ratable amortization) include the following:

▶ Goodwill and going concern value. Conceptually, goodwill is an intangible asset that is neither separately identified or valued but possesses characteristics that allow a business to earn greater returns than would be possible without such characteristics. These characteristics include valued employees, superior management team, loyal customer base, strategic location, etc. For income tax purposes, however, goodwill is determined in a much more practical manner. **Goodwill** is defined as the value of a trade or business that is attributable to the expectation of continued customer patronage, whether due to the name or reputation of the trade or business or to any other factor.[31] Going concern value is the added value that attaches to acquired property because it is an integral part of a going concern.

▶ Intangible assets relating to the workforce, such as an information base (e.g., a customer list), know-how, customers, suppliers, or similar items (e.g., the portion of the purchase price of an acquired business that is attributable to an existing employment contract for a key employee.) Know-how related intangibles include patents, copyrights, formulas, and processes.

▶ Licenses, permits, or other rights granted by a governmental unit or agency (e.g., the capitalized cost of acquiring a radio broadcasting license).

▶ Covenants not to compete. A covenant not to compete represents an agreement between a buyer and seller of a business that the seller (i.e., the selling corporation and/or its shareholders) will not compete with the buyer for a limited period. The covenant may also be limited to a geographic area. A covenant not to compete must be amortized over 15 years even though the agreement was only for five years.[32]

▶ Franchises, trademarks, and trade names. A franchise includes any agreement that gives one of the parties the right to distribute, sell, or provide goods, services, or facilities, within a specified area.

EXAMPLE I:10-29 ▶ In January of the current year, Chicago Corporation acquires all the net assets of Coastal Corporation for $1 million. The following intangible assets are included in the purchase agreement:

Assets	Acquisition Cost
Goodwill and going concern value	$100,000
Licenses	55,000
Patents	45,000
Covenant not to compete for five years	90,000

All the intangible assets above qualify as Sec. 197 intangible assets and are amortizable on a ratable basis (straight-line) over 15 years beginning with the month of acquisition. This 15-year amortization period applies to the convenant not to compete even though the convenant is only for five years. ◀

---

[30] Reg. Sec. 1.167(a)-3.
[31] Reg. Sec. 1.197-2(b)(1).

[32] Frontier Chevrolet Co., 2003-1 USTC ¶50,490 (9th Cir., 2003) aff'g 116 T.C. 289 (2001).

STOP & THINK

Question: When one company purchases the assets of another company, the purchasing company may acquire goodwill. Because purchased goodwill is a Sec. 197 intangible asset and may be amortized over 15 years, determining the cost of goodwill is important. How is the "cost" of goodwill determined in an acquisition?

Solution: The IRS requires that taxpayers use the "residual method" as prescribed in Sec. 1060. Under this method, all of the assets except for goodwill are valued. The total value of these assets is then subtracted from the total purchase price, and the residual is the amount of the purchase price allocated to goodwill.

ADDITIONAL COMMENT

Sec. 1231 generally allows gains to be treated as long-term capital gains and losses to be deducted as ordinary losses. Sec. 1245 requires that gains be classified as ordinary income to the extent depreciation, amortization or depletion was claimed as an ordinary deduction in prior periods (see Chapter I:13).

CLASSIFICATION AND DISPOSITION OF INTANGIBLE ASSETS. A Sec. 197 intangible asset is treated as depreciable property. Thus, a disposition is given Sec. 1231 treatment if the intangible asset is held for more than one year.[33] Gain on disposition of a Sec. 197 intangible is subject to depreciation recapture under Sec. 1245 (see Chapter I:13).[34] Loss on disposition of a Sec. 197 intangible asset, however, is not deductible if other intangibles acquired in the same acquisition of a trade or business are retained. In such case, the bases of the retained Sec. 197 intangibles are increased by the disallowed loss.[35]

EXAMPLE I:10-30 ▶

Assume the same facts as in Example I:10-29. After five years, the covenant not to compete expires. Its adjusted basis is $60,000 [$90,000 − (5/15 × $90,000)]. The $60,000 loss is not deductible, and the disallowed loss is allocated to the retained Sec. 197 assets based on their respective FMVs. ◀

EXAMPLE I:10-31 ▶

Assume the same facts as in Example I:10-29. After one year the *patent* is sold for $50,000. In the initial year, $3,000 ($45,000 ÷ 15) of amortization was deducted. The recognized gain on the sale is $8,000 ($50,000 − $42,000). Of the gain, $3,000 is recaptured as ordinary income under Sec. 1245, and $5,000 is classified as Sec. 1231 gain. ◀

RESEARCH AND EXPERIMENTAL EXPENDITURES

TYPICAL MISCONCEPTION

It is sometimes mistakenly believed that if a company constructs a new building to be used entirely as a research facility, the entire cost of the building can be expensed. However, the expensing election applies only to the depreciation allowances on the building.

In general, research and experimental (R&E) expenditures include experimental and laboratory costs incidental to the development of a product.[36] Section 174 was enacted to clarify the income tax treatment of R&E expenditures. Treasury Regulations define items that do and do not qualify as R&E expenditures. These items are summarized in Table I:10-4. For income tax purposes, the following alternatives are available for qualified R&E expenditures:

▶ Expense in the year paid or incurred.

▶ Defer (capitalize as deferred expenses) and amortize the costs as a ratable deduction over a period of 60 months or more beginning with the month in which benefits are first realized.

▶ Capitalize and write off the costs only when the research project is abandoned or is worthless.[37]

A taxpayer must make an election to either expense or defer and amortize the costs in the initial year the R&E expenditures are incurred. If no election is made, the costs must be capitalized. The taxpayer must continue to use the same accounting method for the R&E expenditures unless IRS approval to change methods is obtained.

Below are some important points regarding R&E expenditures:

▶ Most taxpayers elect to expense the R&E expenditures because they prefer the immediate tax benefit.

▶ The deferral and amortization method is desirable if the taxpayer is currently in a low tax rate situation or expects initial NOLs during a start-up period.

▶ If the deferral and amortization method is used, the amortization period of 60 or more months commences with the month in which the benefits from the expenditures are first realized.

---

[33] Sec. 197(f)(7).
[34] Sec. 1245(a)(2)(C).
[35] Sec. 197(f)(1).

[36] Reg. Sec. 1.174-2(a)(2). The Regulations define the term *product* to include any pilot model, formula, invention, technique, patent, or similar product.
[37] Sec. 174.

▼ **TABLE I:10-4**
Research and Experimental Expenditures

Items That Qualify	Items That Do Not Qualify[a]
▶ Costs incident to the development of an experimental or pilot model, a plant process, a product, a formula, an invention	▶ Expenditures for ordinary testing or inspection of materials or products for quality control purposes
▶ Costs associated with product improvements	▶ Efficiency surveys and management studies
▶ Costs of obtaining a patent, such as attorney fees	▶ Marketing research, advertising, etc.
▶ Research contracted to others	▶ Cost of acquiring another person's patent, model, production, or process
▶ Depreciation or cost-recovery amounts attributable to capitalized R&E items (e.g., research laboratory and equipment)	▶ Research incurred in connection with literary, historical, or similar projects

[a] Certain of these expenses may be deductible as trade or business expenses under Sec. 162, subject to amortization under Sec. 197, or treated as start-up expenditures under Sec. 195.

▶ R&E expenses include depreciation allowances related to capitalized expenditures. Thus, if the deferral and amortization method is used, depreciation allowances are deferred as part of the R&E expenditures that are amortized over a period of at least 60 months. Capital expenditures made in connection with R&E activities cannot be expensed when they are incurred merely because an election to expense R&E costs are made.

▶ A tax credit may apply to certain research expenditures. (See Chapter I:14 for a discussion of the research activities credit.) Taxpayers must reduce any R&E expense deduction by the amount of the credit claimed.

EXAMPLE I:10-32 ▶ In 2010, Control Corporation leases a research laboratory to develop new products and to improve existing products. Control Corporation, a calendar year taxpayer that uses the accrual method of accounting, incurs the following expenditures during 2010:

Laboratory supplies and materials	$ 40,000
Laboratory equipment	60,000[a]
Utilities and rent	50,000
Salaries	50,000
Total expenditures	$200,000

[a] The MACRS recovery period is 5 years at a 20% rate for the initial year.

REAL-WORLD EXAMPLE

An airline company made payments to an aircraft manufacturer to help defray the cost of designing, developing, producing, and testing a supersonic transport prototype aircraft. These payments were considered R&E expenditures. Rev. Rul. 69-484, 1969-2 C.B. 38.

Assume the benefits from the R&E expenditures are first realized in January 2011. If Control Corporation elects to expense the R&E expenditures, the deduction in 2010 is $152,000 ($40,000 laboratory supplies and materials + $12,000 depreciation on the equipment + $50,000 utilities and rent + $50,000 salaries). If the deferral and amortization method is elected, none of the expenditures above are deductible in 2010 because the benefits of the R&E activities are not first realized until January 2011. If the 60-month minimum amortization period is elected, the monthly amortization commencing in January 2011 is $2,533 ($152,000 ÷ 60 months). The $48,000 ($60,000 − $12,000) of laboratory equipment cost is depreciated over the remaining MACRS recovery period beginning in 2011. ◀

COMPUTER SOFTWARE

The amortization or depreciation of computer software depends on the nature of the software and how it is acquired. Basically, computer software is either developed by the taxpayer or acquired (purchased or leased) from an outside party.

DEVELOPED COMPUTER SOFTWARE. The cost of developing computer software that is considered R&E may either be expensed in the year the costs are incurred or, if the taxpayer so elects, capitalized and amortized over 60 months beginning with the month in

which the taxpayer first realizes benefits from such expenditures, per Sec. 174. If the costs incurred to develop the software are not considered R&E costs (e.g., the software is not in the experimental stage), such costs should be depreciated on a straight line basis over 36 months beginning with the date the software is placed in service.[38]

PURCHASED COMPUTER SOFTWARE. Purchased computer software generally may be depreciated in two alternative ways: (1) if the software is included in the cost of the computer hardware, the software does not have to be separately stated as long as the taxpayer consistently follows this treatment. Therefore, the computer and software would be depreciated together under MACRS over five years; or (2) if the software is purchased separately, the software must be depreciated on a straight-line basis over 36 months. An exception to these rules occurs if computer software is purchased in connection with the acquisition of a number of assets of an existing trade or business. In this case, the computer software is considered to be a Sec. 197 intangible and must be amortized over a period of 15 years.[39]

EXAMPLE I:10-33 ▶ Morris Corporation purchased all the assets of an existing business on April 1, 2010 for $1,000,000. Included in the assets was some computer software that the corporation intends to use in its business. The software is specialized for use by Morris Corporation. Based on relative fair market values, the computer software is allocated a cost of $63,000. The software is considered a Sec. 197 intangible and would be amortized over 15 years beginning in the month of acquisition. For the eight-month period in calendar year 2010, Morris Corporation's amortization deduction would be $2,800 [($63,000 ÷ 15 years) × 8/12]. ◀

EXAMPLE I:10-34 ▶ Using the same facts as in Example I:10-33, if Morris Corporation had purchased computer software on April 1, 2010 (not in connection with an asset acquisition) for $63,000, the software would not be considered a Sec. 197 intangible and would be depreciable under Sec. 167(f) on a straight-line basis over a period of 36 months. Therefore, in 2010, Morris Corporation's depreciation deduction would be $14,000 [($63,000 ÷ 36) × 8 months]. ◀

Off-the-shelf computer software is now eligible for first-year expensing under Sec. 179. Off-the-shelf computer software is defined as software that is readily available for purchase by the general public, is subject to a nonexclusive license, and has not been substantially modified.

LEASED OR LICENSED COMPUTER SOFTWARE. Computer software that is leased or licensed for use in the taxpayer's trade or business generally is deductible in full in the year paid.[40]

DEPLETION, INTANGIBLE DRILLING AND DEVELOPMENT COSTS

OBJECTIVE 3

Apply cost and percentage depletion methods and understand the treatment for intangible drilling costs

The taxation of natural resources, such as oil and gas, coal, iron ore, etc. has many of its own specific rules. This section of the text discusses some of the concepts that apply to the oil and gas industry. Other natural resources have slightly different rules, but the oil and gas industry demonstrates the normal taxation of natural resources.

The exploration, development, and operation of oil and gas properties require an outlay of various types of expenditures. Below are the four major types of oil and gas property expenditures and their income tax treatment.

▶ Payments for the mineral interest. These costs are capitalized and recovered through depletion.

---

[38] Sec. 167(f)(1) and Rev. Proc. 2007-16, 2007-14 I.R.B. 358.

[39] Sec. 197(e)(3)(A). If the computer software acquired in an asset acquisition is software that is readily available for purchase by the general public, such software would not be considered a Sec. 197 intangible. (See Sec. 197(e)(3)(A)(i).)

[40] Reg. Sec. 1.162-11 and Rev. Proc. 2007-16, 2007-14 I.R.B. 358.

▶ Intangible drilling and development costs (e.g., labor and other operating costs to clear land, erect a derrick, and drill the well). Taxpayers elect to either capitalize or immediately expense these expenditures.

▶ Tangible asset costs (e.g., machinery, pipe). These expenditures must be capitalized and depreciated under the MACRS rules.

▶ Operating costs after the well is producing. These expenditures are deductible under Sec. 162 as ordinary and necessary business expenses.

DEPLETION METHODS

Depletion, similar to depreciation, is the using up of natural resources by the process of mining (coal, for example) or drilling (oil and gas). It is calculated under the **cost depletion method** or the **percentage depletion method** for each period. The method used in any year is the one that results in the largest deduction. Thus, percentage depletion may be used in one year and cost depletion may be used in the following year.

Depletion is allowed to the taxpayer who has an **economic interest** in the property. The person who typically has an economic interest in the property is the owner of the natural resource (i.e., the oil, gas, coal, etc.). Thus, depletion may be claimed by the persons who either own the natural resource property or retain a royalty interest. A mining company that only mines coal from a property and does not own (or lease) the underlying coal is not considered to hold an economic interest and, therefore, is not allowed a depletion deduction. The landowner who owns the coal would be entitled to the depletion deduction.

COST DEPLETION METHOD. The cost depletion method is similar to the units-of-production method of depreciation. The adjusted basis of the asset is divided by the estimated recoverable units to arrive at a per-unit depletion cost. This per-unit cost is then multiplied by the number of units sold to determine the cost depletion deduction.[41] If the original estimate of recoverable units is subsequently determined to be incorrect, the per-unit cost depletion rate must be revised and used on a prospective basis to determine cost depletion in future years.[42] It is not proper to file an amended return for the years in which the incorrect estimated unit cost was used.

EXAMPLE I:10-35 ▶

Ralph acquires an oil and gas property interest for $100,000 in 2010. The estimate of recoverable units is 10,000 barrels of oil. The per-unit cost depletion amount is $10 ($100,000 ÷ 10,000). If 3,000 units are produced and 2,000 units are sold in 2010, the cost depletion amount is $20,000 (2,000 units × $10 per unit). If cost depletion is used because it exceeds the percentage depletion amount, the cost basis of the property is reduced to $80,000 ($100,000 − $20,000) at the beginning of 2011. If the estimate of remaining recoverable units is revised downward from 8,000 units in 2011 (10,000 − 2,000 units sold in 2010) to 5,000 units (including the 1,000 barrels produced but not sold in 2010), the property's $80,000 adjusted basis is divided by 5,000 units to arrive at a new per-unit cost depletion amount of $16 for 2011. This process is continued each year until the cost of the oil and gas property interest is fully depleted. ◀

PERCENTAGE DEPLETION METHOD. Percentage depletion generally offers substantial tax benefits for taxpayers in the natural resources industry. The purpose of allowing percentage depletion is to encourage persons to invest and/or operate in an industry that is both capital intensive and high risk but is also vital to our national interests. Percentage depletion may be used by taxpayers for a wide variety of natural resources, such as oil and gas, coal, gold, etc. The percentage depletion method has not been available to *large* oil and gas producers since 1974; but it is still available to *small* oil and gas producers and royalty owners under a specific exemption in the law.[43] Percentage depletion is computed by multiplying the percentage depletion rate times the gross income from the property. However, the depletion amount may not exceed 50% of the taxable income from the property before depletion is deducted (100% for oil and gas properties).[44] Percentage depletion may not be calculated on any lease bonus, advance royalty, or other amount payable without regard to production from the property.

[41] Sec. 612.
[42] Sec. 611(a).
[43] Sec. 613A(c). To be classified as a small oil and gas producer or royalty owner, the maximum depletable quantity is based on average daily production of not more than 1,000 barrels of oil or 6 million cubic feet of natural gas.
[44] Sec. 613(a).

Whether the taxpayer uses cost depletion or percentage depletion, the amount of the depletion deduction reduces the basis of the natural resource property. Once the basis of depletable property has been reduced to zero, a taxpayer may no longer claim depletion using the cost depletion method. However, the taxpayer may continue to claim percentage depletion. Subsequent percentage depletion will not reduce the basis of the property below zero. It should be apparent that percentage depletion is a very advantageous method because the total depletion allowed over the life of the property may exceed the property's cost.[45]

Percentage depletion rates vary by the type of mineral. Depletion rates for selected minerals are as follows:

Mineral	Depletion Rate
Oil and gas	15%[46]
Coal, asbestos	10%
Gold, silver, copper, iron ore	15%
Sulphur and uranium	22%
Gravel, stone	5%
All other minerals	14%

EXAMPLE I:10-36 ▶

In the current year, Carmen acquires for $400,000 an oil and gas property interest with 200,000 barrels of estimated recoverable oil. During the year, 10,000 barrels of oil are sold for $250,000. Intangible drilling and development costs (IDCs) amount to $100,000 and are expensed in the current year. Other expenses are $50,000. Cost depletion is $20,000 [(10,000 barrels sold × ($400,000/200,000 barrels)] in the current year. The computation of percentage depletion is as follows:

HISTORICAL NOTE

An Arab oil embargo to the United States in 1973 created a situation where oil prices increased significantly. Consequently, most domestic U.S. oil producers reported huge profits. This situation contributed to the repeal of the percentage depletion allowance for large oil and gas producers.

(1) Percentage depletion before taxable income limitation ($250,000 × 0.15)	$ 37,500
(2) Taxable income ceiling:	
Gross income	$250,000
Minus: Intangible drilling costs (IDCs) expensed	(100,000)
Other expenses	(50,000)
Taxable income before depletion	$100,000
(3) Percentage depletion (lesser of (1) or (2))	$ 37,500

KEY POINT

The use of the percentage depletion method permits recovery of more than the cost of the property.

Carmen's depletion deduction is $37,500 because the percentage depletion amount is greater than the $20,000 of cost depletion. The adjusted basis of the property is reduced by $37,500, the amount of depletion actually claimed. ◀

TREATMENT OF INTANGIBLE DRILLING AND DEVELOPMENT COSTS

Intangible drilling and development costs (IDCs) may either be deducted as an expense or capitalized.[47] IDCs apply only to oil, gas, and geothermal wells and basically include all expenditures, other than the acquisition costs of the underlying property, that are incurred for the drilling and preparation of wells. If the IDCs are capitalized, the amounts are added to the property's basis for determining cost depletion, and the costs are expensed through cost depletion. For a well that is nonproductive (i.e., a dry hole), an ordinary loss is allowed for any IDC costs that have been capitalized and not recovered through depletion. The amount of depletion claimed in a tax year equals the greater of the percentage depletion and cost depletion amounts. If IDCs are capitalized and cost depletion is thereby increased, little or no tax benefit may result because the percentage depletion may still produce a greater deduction than cost depletion. Therefore, it is generally preferable to expense the IDCs if the percentage depletion is expected to be more than the cost depletion and is used to compute the depletion allowance.

---

[45] Depletion in excess of the adjusted basis of the property is a tax preference item under Sec. 57(a)(1).

[46] For small producers and royalty owners of oil and gas properties, there is a further limitation: the percentage depletion deduction may not exceed 65%

of taxable income from all sources before the depletion deduction. Sec. 613A(d)(1).

[47] Sec. 263(c).

EXAMPLE I:10-37 ▶ In the current year, Penny acquires certain rights to oil and gas property for $1,000,000, incurring $300,000 of IDCs. If the IDCs are capitalized, the basis for cost depletion purposes is $1,300,000. Assume that the cost depletion amounts are $100,000 in the current year if the IDCs are expensed and $130,000 if IDCs are capitalized. If the percentage depletion amount is $150,000, percentage depletion will be used because it is greater than either of the cost depletion amounts. Thus, expensing the IDCs permits Penny to deduct the entire $300,000 of IDCs in the current year plus $150,000 of percentage depletion. ◀

TAX PLANNING CONSIDERATIONS

ALTERNATIVE DEPRECIATION SYSTEM UNDER MACRS

ADDITIONAL COMMENT

A taxpayer who is attempting to report a profit in three out of five years in an attempt to avoid the hobby loss rules might want to use the alternative depreciation system.

In some instances, it may be preferable to elect to use the alternative depreciation system (ADS) rather than the regular MACRS rules. For example, a taxpayer who anticipates losses during the next few years or who currently has NOL carryovers may elect to use ADS, which employs the straight-line method of depreciation over a longer recovery period.

EXAMPLE I:10-38 ▶ Delta Corporation has substantial NOL carryovers that will expire if not used during the next few years. Delta anticipates it will not have taxable income for each of the next seven years if the regular MACRS rules are used to depreciate its fixed asset additions. In the current year, Delta acquires new machinery and equipment at a cost of $100,000. Assuming no Sec. 179 election and no bonus depreciation, depreciation deductions using the MACRS rules and a 7-year recovery period are $14,290 (0.1429 × $100,000). Depreciation deductions under the straight-line method using ADS with a 12-year recovery period and the half-year convention are only $4,167 [($100,000 ÷ 12 years) × 0.50 year]. The ADS election increases taxable income in the current year by $10,123 and allows Delta to offset additional loss carryovers (which might otherwise expire) against this income amount. ◀

USE OF UNITS OF PRODUCTION DEPRECIATION

Many times, the MACRS depreciation system requires taxpayers to use a recovery period that is much longer than the actual useful life of the asset. For example, assume a taxpayer uses a machine in his or her business that is classified as 7-year property under MACRS. However, the machine is operated 24 hours a day, seven days a week and will completely wear out in two years. The use of the 7-year recovery period substantially understates depreciation for the machine in the two years of actual use. Under Sec. 168(f), taxpayers may exclude property from the MACRS system if the property is depreciated under the unit-of-production method or any other method not expressed in terms of years. Therefore, if the taxpayer can express the useful life of the machine in terms of some base other than years (such as machine hours, units produced, etc.), it may be possible to depreciate the machine over a much shorter period than the seven years required under MACRS.

STRUCTURING A BUSINESS COMBINATION

REAL-WORLD EXAMPLE

A taxpayer purchased a business that owned retail franchises. The IRS determined that amounts paid in excess of the value of the net assets represented a nondepreciable "indivisible asset." However, the taxpayer was able to show that retail franchises have limited useful lives, and was able to amortize the excess costs. *Super Food Services, Inc. v. U.S.*, 24 AFTR 2d 69-5309, 69-2 USTC ¶9558 (7th Cir., 1969).

When a company purchases the assets of another business, the agreement must specify the amounts paid for the tangible depreciable, nondepreciable, and intangible assets. Also, the company must comply with the reporting requirements of Sec. 1060, which states that both the transferor and the transferee are bound by their written agreement as to the allocation of the purchase price to individual assets unless the IRS determines that such allocation is not appropriate. Amounts paid for tangible assets should be documented by appraisals and evidence of negotiations between the buyer and seller. Within reason, the purchaser should attempt to allocate as much of the total price to tangible depreciable assets, such as machinery and equipment. The purchaser also should consider allocating part of the purchase price to amortizable Sec. 197 intangible assets such as goodwill, covenants not to compete, patents, copyrights, licenses, and customer lists because such asset costs are recovered over a 15-year period. This is preferable to allocating the purchase price to depreciable real estate because such property must be depreciated over 39 years.

WHAT WOULD YOU DO IN THIS SITUATION?

Your CPA firm has a long-standing tax client named Widgets R Us, Incorporated (WRU). WRU has been a worldwide leader in widget technology for years and continues to expand its global market share through a substantial program of basic research and development of widget crystallization processes. You have advised WRU as to which of these expenditures qualify as research and experimental (R&E) expenditures. In addition, you have given timely advice as to when to expense rather than capitalize these expenditures.

You are having your monthly tax conference with Ms. Ima Worthmore, president of WRU, and Mr. Stan Cunning, tax counsel of WMU. Ms. Worthmore relates to you a conversation she had with the local manager of a competitor CPA firm, Ms. Ruth Less. Ms. Less told Ms. Worthmore that she had discovered that WRU was one of the top spenders on research and development

in the area and that her firm was "certified" to practice before the IRS and had experienced great success in gaining R&E write-offs for comparable firms. Ms. Less went on to say that, "For you, for this one year only, we offer to prepare your tax returns on a contingent basis. We promise to save you at least $1 million from what you are now paying the IRS through our better use of R&E write-offs, and our fee will only be 30% of the tax savings!"

Ms. Worthmore was excited that WRU might be able to pay considerably lower taxes and is somewhat perturbed because you had not brought this tax opportunity to her attention. She wants your firm to provide her with a counteroffer. How do you ethically respond to your client's request to match or better Ms. Ruth Less' proposal?

COMPLIANCE AND PROCEDURAL CONSIDERATIONS

REPORTING COST RECOVERY, DEPRECIATION, DEPLETION, AND AMORTIZATION DEDUCTIONS

Form 4562 is the primary reporting device for depreciation (cost recovery), depletion, and amortization. Individual taxpayers engaged in trade or business complete Form 4562 and carry the total to Schedule C of their Form 1040, using a separate 4562 for each enterprise. Corporate and other non-corporate taxpayers also use Form 4562, carrying the total to their specific returns. Individuals with rental property complete a 4562 and carry the total to Schedule E of their Form 1040.

Two exceptions to the use of Form 4562: (1) Depreciation on property used by an employee for business purposes is computed along with other employee business expenses on Form 2106, with the total carried to Schedule A of the Form 1040; (2) If a taxpayer computes depreciation only on property placed in service before the current year, Form 4562 is not required. Depreciation totals are entered directly on the applicable primary form. Taxpayers must still maintain detailed depreciation records to support the deduction.

EXAMPLE I:10-39 ▶ Form 4562 for 2009: George Jones, SSN 277-32-6542, is a building contractor who owns the following 100% business-use properties:

- ▶ Specialized utility repair truck (5-year property that is not listed property), costing $40,000, placed in service on February 15, 2009.
- ▶ Machinery and equipment (7-year property), costing $285,000, placed in service on June 10, 2009.
- ▶ Patent, costing $17,000, that was developed and placed in service on June 1, 2009, when it had a remaining legal life of 17 years.
- ▶ MACRS deduction for assets placed in service before 2009 is $66,000.

Jones had 2009 taxable income of $460,000 (before the Sec. 179 deduction and the deduction for one-half of self-employment taxes). George elected Sec. 179 expensing on the machinery and equipment, and claimed bonus depreciation on all qualifying property. Depreciation and amortization amounts are reported on Form 4562 and are shown in Figures I:10-1 and I:10-2. ◀

Form 4562

Department of the Treasury
Internal Revenue Service (99)

Depreciation and Amortization
(Including Information on Listed Property)

▶ See separate instructions.   ▶ Attach to your tax return.

OMB No. 1545-0172

2009

Attachment Sequence No. **67**

Name(s) shown on return: **George Jones**

Business or activity to which this form relates: **Building Contractor**

Identifying number: **277-32-6542**

Part I — Election To Expense Certain Property Under Section 179

Note: *If you have any listed property, complete Part V before you complete Part I.*

1	Maximum amount. See the instructions for a higher limit for certain businesses	1	$250,000
2	Total cost of section 179 property placed in service (see instructions)	2	$325,000
3	Threshold cost of section 179 property before reduction in limitation (see instructions)	3	$800,000
4	Reduction in limitation. Subtract line 3 from line 2. If zero or less, enter -0-	4	-0-
5	Dollar limitation for tax year. Subtract line 4 from line 1. If zero or less, enter -0-. If married filing separately, see instructions	5	$250,000

6	(a) Description of property	(b) Cost (business use only)	(c) Elected cost
	Truck	40,000	-0-
	Machinery and Equipment	285,000	250,000

7	Listed property. Enter the amount from line 29	7	-0-
8	Total elected cost of section 179 property. Add amounts in column (c), lines 6 and 7	8	250,000
9	Tentative deduction. Enter the **smaller** of line 5 or line 8	9	250,000
10	Carryover of disallowed deduction from line 13 of your 2008 Form 4562	10	
11	Business income limitation. Enter the smaller of business income (not less than zero) or line 5 (see instructions)	11	250,000
12	Section 179 expense deduction. Add lines 9 and 10, but do not enter more than line 11	12	250,000
13	Carryover of disallowed deduction to 2010. Add lines 9 and 10, less line 12 ▶	13	-0-

Note: *Do not use Part II or Part III below for listed property. Instead, use Part V.*

Part II — Special Depreciation Allowance and Other Depreciation (Do not include listed property.) (See instructions.)

14	Special depreciation allowance for qualified property (other than listed property) placed in service during the tax year (see instructions)	14	*37,500
15	Property subject to section 168(f)(1) election	15	
16	Other depreciation (including ACRS)	16	

Part III — MACRS Depreciation (Do not include listed property.) (See instructions.)

Section A

17	MACRS deductions for assets placed in service in tax years beginning before 2009	17	66,000
18	If you are electing to group any assets placed in service during the tax year into one or more general asset accounts, check here ▶ ☐		

Section B—Assets Placed in Service During 2009 Tax Year Using the General Depreciation System

(a) Classification of property	(b) Month and year placed in service	(c) Basis for depreciation (business/investment use only—see instructions)	(d) Recovery period	(e) Convention	(f) Method	(g) Depreciation deduction
19a 3-year property						
b 5-year property		**20,000	5 yrs.	HY	MACRS	4,000
c 7-year property		***17,500	7 yrs.	HY	MACRS	2,501
d 10-year property						
e 15-year property						
f 20-year property						
g 25-year property			25 yrs.		S/L	
h Residential rental property			27.5 yrs.	MM	S/L	
			27.5 yrs.	MM	S/L	
i Nonresidential real property			39 yrs.	MM	S/L	
				MM	S/L	

Section C—Assets Placed in Service During 2009 Tax Year Using the Alternative Depreciation System

20a Class life					S/L	
b 12-year			12 yrs.		S/L	
c 40-year			40 yrs.	MM	S/L	

Part IV — Summary (See instructions.)

21	Listed property. Enter amount from line 28	21	-0-
22	**Total.** Add amounts from line 12, lines 14 through 17, lines 19 and 20 in column (g), and line 21. Enter here and on the appropriate lines of your return. Partnerships and S corporations—see instructions	22	360,001
23	For assets shown above and placed in service during the current year, enter the portion of the basis attributable to section 263A costs	23	

For Paperwork Reduction Act Notice, see separate instructions.   Cat. No. 12906N   Form **4562** (2009)

*Line 14: Bonus = ($40,000 x 0.50) + [($285,000 − $250,000) x 0.50]

**Line 19b: $40,000 − $20,000

***Line 19c: $285,000 − $250,000 − $17,500

FIGURE I:10-1   ▶   FORM 4562

Form 4562 (2009)   Page **2**

Part V **Listed Property** (Include automobiles, certain other vehicles, cellular telephones, certain computers, and property used for entertainment, recreation, or amusement.)

Note: *For any vehicle for which you are using the standard mileage rate or deducting lease expense, complete* **only** *24a, 24b, columns (a) through (c) of Section A, all of Section B, and Section C if applicable.*

Section A—Depreciation and Other Information (Caution: *See the instructions for limits for passenger automobiles.*)

24a Do you have evidence to support the business/investment use claimed? ☐ **Yes** ☐ **No** **24b** If "Yes," is the evidence written? ☐ **Yes** ☐ **No**

(a) Type of property (list vehicles first)	(b) Date placed in service	(c) Business/ investment use percentage	(d) Cost or other basis	(e) Basis for depreciation (business/investment use only)	(f) Recovery period	(g) Method/ Convention	(h) Depreciation deduction	(i) Elected section 179 cost
25 Special depreciation allowance for qualified listed property placed in service during the tax year and used more than 50% in a qualified business use (see instructions)						**25**	-0-	
26 Property used more than 50% in a qualified business use:								
		%						
		%						
		%						
27 Property used 50% or less in a qualified business use:								
		%			S/L –			
		%			S/L –			
		%			S/L –			
28 Add amounts in column (h), lines 25 through 27. Enter here and on line 21, page 1 . . .						**28**		
29 Add amounts in column (i), line 26. Enter here and on line 7, page 1							**29**	-0-

Section B—Information on Use of Vehicles

Complete this section for vehicles used by a sole proprietor, partner, or other "more than 5% owner," or related person. If you provided vehicles to your employees, first answer the questions in Section C to see if you meet an exception to completing this section for those vehicles.

	(a) Vehicle 1		(b) Vehicle 2		(c) Vehicle 3		(d) Vehicle 4		(e) Vehicle 5		(f) Vehicle 6	
30 Total business/investment miles driven during the year (**do not** include commuting miles)												
31 Total commuting miles driven during the year												
32 Total other personal (noncommuting) miles driven												
33 Total miles driven during the year. Add lines 30 through 32												
	Yes	No	Yes	No	Yes	No	Yes	No	Yes	No	Yes	No
34 Was the vehicle available for personal use during off-duty hours?												
35 Was the vehicle used primarily by a more than 5% owner or related person?												
36 Is another vehicle available for personal use?												

Section C—Questions for Employers Who Provide Vehicles for Use by Their Employees

Answer these questions to determine if you meet an exception to completing Section B for vehicles used by employees who **are not** more than 5% owners or related persons (see instructions).

		Yes	No
37	Do you maintain a written policy statement that prohibits all personal use of vehicles, including commuting, by your employees?		
38	Do you maintain a written policy statement that prohibits personal use of vehicles, except commuting, by your employees? See the instructions for vehicles used by corporate officers, directors, or 1% or more owners . . .		
39	Do you treat all use of vehicles by employees as personal use?		
40	Do you provide more than five vehicles to your employees, obtain information from your employees about the use of the vehicles, and retain the information received?		
41	Do you meet the requirements concerning qualified automobile demonstration use? (See instructions.) . .		

Note: *If your answer to 37, 38, 39, 40, or 41 is "Yes," do not complete Section B for the covered vehicles.*

Part VI **Amortization**

(a) Description of costs	(b) Date amortization begins	(c) Amortizable amount	(d) Code section	(e) Amortization period or percentage	(f) Amortization for this year
42 Amortization of costs that begins during your 2009 tax year (see instructions):					
Patent	6-01-09	17,000	167	17 yrs.	*583
43 Amortization of costs that began before your 2009 tax year **43**					
44 Total. Add amounts in column (f). See the instructions for where to report **44**					583

Form **4562** (2009)

*($17,000 ÷ 17 yrs.) = $1,000 x 7/12 = $583

FIGURE I:10-2 ▶ FORM 4562 (CONTINUED)

PROBLEM MATERIALS

DISCUSSION QUESTIONS

I:10-1 Which of the following assets are subject to either amortization, depreciation, or cost recovery? Explain.
   a. An automobile held for personal use.
   b. Excess amounts paid in a business combination that are attributable to goodwill.
   c. Excess amounts paid in a business combination that are attributable to customer lists that have a limited useful life.
   d. A patent created internally which has a legal life of 17 years.
   e. Land held for investment purposes.
   f. A covenant not to compete which is entered into by the buyer and seller of a business.

I:10-2 Rick is a sole proprietor who has a small business currently operating at a loss. He would like to discontinue depreciating the fixed assets of the business for the next few years and to carry the deductions over to a future period. What tax consequences would result if Rick implements the plan to discontinue depreciation and then sells some of the depreciable assets several years later?

I:10-3 Rita acquired a personal residence two years ago for $120,000. In the current year, she purchases another residence and attempts to sell her former residence. Due to depressed housing conditions in the town where she used to live, Rita is unable to sell the house. Her former residence is now being offered for sale at $100,000 (its current FMV according to real estate appraisal experts). Rita has decided to rent the house rather than "give it away." She believes that renting the house on a permanent basis will permit her to write off the original $120,000 investment over its useful life and thus recoup her investment. What restrictions in the tax law may prevent her from accomplishing this objective? Explain.

I:10-4 Daytona Corporation, a manufacturing corporation, acquires the following business assets in the current year:
   • Furniture
   • Plumbing fixtures
   • Land
   • Goodwill and a trademark acquired in the acquisition of a business
   • Automobile
   • Heavy truck
   • Machinery
   • Building used in manufacturing activities

   a. Which of the assets above are eligible for depreciation under the MACRS rules or amortization under Sec. 197?
   b. What recovery period should be used for each of the assets listed above that come under the MACRS rules or under Sec. 197?

I:10-5 Robert is a sole proprietor who uses the calendar year as his tax year. On July 20, 2009 he acquired and placed in service a business machine, a 7-year asset, for $50,000. No other property was acquired in 2009.
   a. What is the amount of depreciation allowed in 2009 and 2010 if neither bonus depreciation nor Sec. 179 depreciation (first-year expense election) was elected?
   b. What is the amount of depreciation allowed in 2009 and 2010 if bonus depreciation was taken but not Sec. 179?
   c. What is the amount of depreciation allowed in 2009 and 2010 if Sec. 179 was elected?

I:10-6 Roberta, a sole proprietor who uses the calendar year as her tax year, acquires and places in service two business machines during 2010. Machine C, a 7-year asset, was acquired on January 20, 2010, for $270,000 and Machine D, a 5-year asset, was acquired on August 1, 2010, for $50,000. No other property was acquired in 2010.
   a. What is the amount of depreciation allowed in 2010 if Sec. 179 is not elected?
   b. What is the amount of depreciation allowed in 2010 if Sec. 179 is elected?

I:10-7 Is a deduction allowed under the MACRS rules for depreciable real estate (used in a business or held for investment) in the year the property is sold? If so, explain how it is calculated.

I:10-8 Jose is considering acquiring a new luxury automobile costing $45,000 that will be used 100% in his business. The salesperson at the automobile dealership states that Jose will be entitled to substantial tax benefits in the initial year (2010) including:

If Sec. 179 is elected:

• A deduction for $45,000 of the acquisition cost under Sec. 179.

If Sec. 179 is not elected:

• A $9,000 ($45,000 × 0.2) depreciation deduction.

   a. Are the salesperson's assertions relative to the tax benefits accurate? Explain.
   b. Would your answer to Part a differ if the automobile were used only 60% for business purposes?

c. Would your answer to Part a differ if Jose instead were to lease the automobile?

d. Would your answers to Part a differ if the vehicle were a large SUV (gross vehicle weight rating (GVWR) greater than 6,000 pounds) rather than an automobile?

I:10-9 Would the straight-line MACRS method (using the ADS) be preferable to the regular MACRS method in the following cases? Explain.

a. Ray incurs NOLs in his business for a number of years and has NOL carryovers he would like to use.

b. Rhonda's marginal tax rate is 15% but is expected to increase to 35% in three years.

I:10-10 Rudy is considering whether to make the election under Sec. 179 to expense the maximum amount of the acquisition cost related to certain fixed asset additions. What advantages are associated with the Sec. 179 election?

I:10-11 Luby Corporation has maintained an office in a leased building for several years. The corporation has decided to make some significant leasehold improvements to enhance the property. How should Luby Corporation depreciate the leasehold improvements?

I:10-12 Your client is a self-employed attorney who is considering the purchase of a $32,000 automobile that will be used 80% of the time for business and a $4,000 personal computer that will be used 100% of the time for business, but is located in his home.

a. What depreciation methods and recovery periods may be used under MACRS for the automobile and the personal computer?

b. How would your answer to Part a change if your client were an employee and the computer and automobile were not required as a condition of employment?

c. What tax consequences occur in Part a if the business use of the personal computer or the automobile decreases to 50% or less in a succeeding year? Explain.

I:10-13 Congress enacted provisions in the tax law that permitted 50% bonus depreciation in 2008 and 2009 for certain assets.

a. What types of assets qualified for 50% bonus depreciation?

b. How did bonus depreciation interface with Sec. 179 first-year expensing?

I:10-14 On March 1, 2009, Sarah entered into a three-year lease of an automobile used exclusively in her business. The automobile's FMV was $58,500 at the inception of the lease. Sarah made ten monthly lease payments of $600 each during 2009. Is Sarah able to avoid the luxury automobile restrictions on depreciation by leasing instead of purchasing the automobile? Explain. (The 2009 inclusion amount for Sarah's automobile is found in Table 13 of Appendix C.)

I:10-15 What difference does it make for income tax purposes whether an intangible asset is (1) acquired in connection with a business acquisition, (2) acquired by the purchase of an individual asset (e.g., a patent), or (3) created internally? Explain.

I:10-16 In January of the current year, Park Corporation incurs $34,000 of legal costs associated with a patent that was developed internally and has a legal life of 17 years. Park also acquired for cash the net assets of Central Corporation for $1,000,000. The following assets are specified in the purchase agreement:

Land	$ 200,000
Goodwill and going concern value	100,000
Covenant not to compete	50,000
Licenses	125,000
Customer lists	25,000
Inventory	100,000
Equipment and other tangible depreciable business assets	400,000
Total	$1,000,000

a. What tax treatment should be accorded the intangible assets?

b. Assuming that you were advising Park Corporation during the negotiations before drafting the purchase agreement, what suggestions would you make regarding the allocation of the total purchase price to the individual assets? How could the purchase price of individual assets be substantiated?

I:10-17 Why do most taxpayers prefer to currently expense research and experimental expenditures?

I:10-18 In a business combination, why does the buyer generally prefer to allocate as much of the purchase price to short-lived depreciable assets, ordinary assets such as inventory, and Sec. 197 intangible assets?

I:10-19 Explain the difference between cost depletion and percentage depletion. Which of these two methods generally provides the largest deduction?

I:10-20 Simon acquires an interest in an oil property for $50,000. Intangible drilling costs (IDCs) in the initial year are $10,000. Cost depletion is $5,000 if the IDCs are expensed and $6,000 if the costs are capitalized. Percentage depletion is $15,000 if the IDCs are expensed and $20,000 if the costs are capitalized. The difference in the percentage depletion amounts is due to the 100% taxable income limitation.

a. What method (i.e., expensing or capitalization and amortization) should be elected for the treatment of the IDCs in the initial year if Simon wants to maximize his deductions?

b. Why are intangible drilling costs expensed by most taxpayers?

ISSUE IDENTIFICATION QUESTIONS

I:10-21 Georgia Corporation acquires a business automobile for $30,000 on December 31 of the current year but does not actually place the automobile into service until January 1 of the following year. What tax issues should Georgia Corporation consider?

I:10-22 Paula is planning to either purchase or lease a $50,000 automobile. She anticipates that business use of the auto will be 60% for the first two years but will decline to 40% in years three through five. Currently, Paula's marginal tax rate is 15% but she anticipates that her marginal tax rate will be 35% after a few years. What tax issues should Paula consider relative to the decision to purchase or lease the automobile?

I:10-23 In the current year, Coastal Corporation acquires all of the net assets of Acorn Corporation for $2,000,000. The purchase agreement allocated the following amounts to the individual assets and liabilities:

Land and building	$1,400,000
Accounts receivable	200,000
Inventory	300,000
Goodwill	400,000
Patents (remaining legal life of ten years)	100,000
Covenant not to compete	200,000
Liabilities	(600,000)
Total	$2,000,000

What tax issues should Coastal Corporation consider relative to the asset acquisitions?

I:10-24 Weiskopf, a sole proprietor and a calendar-year taxpayer, purchased $700,000 of equipment during 2010, as follows:

	Cost	Recovery Period
March 1	$200,000	7 years
September 18	$360,000	7 years
October 2	$140,000	5 years

Weiskopf's CPA, to maximize the depreciation deduction, elects $250,000 of Sec. 179 depreciation as follows: $100,000 on the March 1 property and $150,000 on the September 18 property. What tax issue should be considered with respect to the total depreciation deduction for the current year?

PROBLEMS

I:10-25 *Allowed Versus Allowable Depreciation.* Sandy acquired business machinery (which qualified as 7-year MACRS property) on July 15, 2007, for $10,000. In 2007, Sandy claimed a $1,429 regular MACRS depreciation deduction and she elected not to claim Sec. 179 depreciation. Because of net operating losses in 2008–2010, Sandy did not claim any depreciation deduction on her tax returns in those years. She sells the machine on July 1, 2010, for $6,000.
a. What is the adjusted basis of the machine on the sale date?
b. How much gain or loss is recognized on the sale of the machine?

I:10-26 *Conversion of Personal Asset to Business Use.* Sid purchased an automobile for personal use on January 18, 2006 for $10,000. On January 1, 2010, Sid starts a small business and begins to use the automobile exclusively in the business. The automobile's FMV on this date is $6,000. MACRS depreciation deductions are based on a 5-year recovery period.
a. What is the automobile's basis for depreciation when converted to business use in 2010?
b. What is Sid's depreciation deduction in 2010?

I:10-27 *MACRS 40% Test and Bonus Depreciation.* Small Corporation acquired and placed in service the following 100% business-use assets. Small did not elect Sec. 179 expense on any of these properties but claimed 50% bonus depreciation on all eligible property in 2009.

- Truck (light-duty, modified non-personal use) costing $20,000: Placed in service on February 15, 2009 with a 5-year MACRS recovery period.
- Machinery costing $50,000: Placed in service on May 1, 2009 with a 7-year MACRS recovery period.
- Land costing $60,000: Placed in service on July 1, 2009.
- Building costing $100,000: Placed in service on December 1, 2009 with a 39-year MACRS recovery period.
- Equipment costing $40,000: Acquired on December 24, 2009 and placed in service on January 5, 2010 with a 5-year MACRS recovery period.

a. What are Small's total depreciation deductions in 2009 and 2010?
b. What would Small's total depreciation deductions have been in the two years if the machinery had been placed in service on November 1, 2009 instead of May 1, 2009?

I:10-28 *MACRS 40% Test and Partial Year Depreciation.* Large Corporation acquired and placed in service the following 100% business-use assets. Large did not elect Sec. 179 expensing on any of these properties.

- Truck (light-duty, modified non-personal use) costing $36,000: Placed in service on March 3, 2010 with a 5-year MACRS recovery period.
- Machinery costing $85,000: Placed in service on November 15, 2010 with a 7-year MACRS recovery period.
- Land costing $90,000: Placed in service on October 12, 2010.
- Building costing $280,000: Placed in service on December 4, 2010 with a 39-year MACRS recovery period.

a. What is Large's total depreciation deduction in 2010?
b. Large Corporation sells the machinery on February 2, 2012 and sells the building on September 18, 2012. What are the adjusted bases of these two assets on the dates of sale (compute accumulated depreciation to date of sale)?

I:10-29 *Sec. 179 Expensing and MACRS Depreciation.* Ted is in the rental real estate business. During 2010, Ted purchased and placed in service the following assets:

- Apartment building costing $300,000 (exclusive of $80,000 land): Placed in service on May 12 with a 27.5-year MACRS recovery period.
- Office furniture costing $215,000: Placed in service on April 10 with a 7-year MACRS recovery period.
- Office equipment costing $110,000: Placed in service on November 1 with a 5-year MACRS recovery period.

a. What are Ted's total depreciation deductions in 2010 and 2011 assuming he does not elect Sec. 179 expensing?
b. What are Ted's total depreciation deductions in 2010 and 2011 assuming he elects Sec. 179 expensing in 2010 for $215,000 on the furniture and $35, 000 on the equipment?
c. What are Ted's total depreciation deductions in 2010 and 2011 assuming he elects Sec. 179 expensing in 2010 for $140,000 on the furniture and $110,000 on the equipment?

I:10-30 *Sec. 179 Limitations and Carryovers.* In July 2010, Tish acquires and places in service a business machine costing $180,000 with a 7-year MACRS recovery period. Tish elects the maximum allowable Sec. 179 expense on the machine. In August 2010, she also places in service business equipment costing $720,000, with a 5-year MACRS recovery period. Tish's taxable income (before the Sec. 179 expense and the 50% of SE tax deduction) is $60,000.

a. What is Tish's allowable 2010 Sec. 179 expense on the machine? What amount can she carry over to 2011?
b. What is Tish's total 2010 depreciation deduction?
c. What are the limitations on Tish's ability to use the Sec. 179 carryover in 2011?
d. How would your answer to Part a change if Tish's business taxable income (before the Sec. 179 expense and the 50% of SE tax deduction) were $225,000 in 2010 instead of $60,000?

I:10-31 **MACRS Dispositions.** Tampa Corporation sold the following assets in 2010:

	Date Acquired	Date Sold	Original Cost Basis	Depreciation/ Cost-Recovery Method	Recovery Period (Years)	Sales Price
Automobile	1/1/07	12/1/10[a]	$ 9,000	MACRS	5	$ 1,200
Equipment	1/6/07	9/1/10[a]	20,000	MACRS	7	9,500
Building (nonresidental)	4/1/00	12/10/10	100,000	MACRS	39	240,000

[a] The half-year convention was used in the year of acquisition. Tampa did not elect Sec. 179 expense, and bonus depreciation was not in effect during the acquistion years.

a. What is the depreciation deduction for each asset in 2010?
b. Compute the gain or loss on each asset sold.

I:10-32 **Sec. 179 Expensing Election and MACRS Depreciation.** Thad acquires a machine at a cost of $502,000 for use in his business and places it in service on April 1, 2010. The machine is depreciated under MACRS, with a 7-year recovery period. This machine was his only asset acquistion of the year. Thad elects to expense $250,000 of the acquisition cost under Sec. 179.
a. What is Thad's total depreciation deduction for the machine in 2010?
b. Thad then sells the machine on October 5, 2012 for $80,000. Compute Thad's depreciation deductions for 2010 through 2012, the adjusted basis of the machine on October 5, 2012, and the gain or loss on the sale.

I:10-33 **Sec. 179 Expensing and Mid-Quarter Convention.** During 2010, Rita acquired and placed in service two assets for use in her business, as follows:

- Asset A: Placed in service in February at a cost of $540,000 with a 7-year MACRS recovery period.

- Asset B: Placed in service in November at a cost of $255,000 with a 7-year MACRS recovery period.

Rita elects to expense $250,000 under Sec. 179. Compute Rita's total depreciation deduction for 2010 under each of the following assumptions:
a. Rita allocates the entire $250,000 Sec. 179 expense to Asset A.
b. Rita allocates the entire $250,000 Sec. 179 expense to Asset B.

I:10-34 **Straight-Line Depreciation.** Long Corporation has been unprofitable for several years and has substantial NOL carryovers. Therefore, the company has elected to use straight-line MACRS for property acquisitions. Long acquires, holds, or sells the following assets in 2010:

	Date Acquired	Date Sold	Original Cost Basis	Selling Price	Depreciation Method	Recovery Period (Years)
Equipment	6/1/10	—	$40,000	—	SL ADS	7
Light duty truck (Nonpersonal-use)	5/1/06	12/1/10	30,000	$ 8,000	SL ADS	5
Furniture	3/1/06	—	10,000	—	SL ADS	7
Automobile	7/1/07	12/1/10	12,000	10,000	SL ADS	5

Long did not make the Sec. 179 election in any year.
a. What is the depreciation deduction for each asset in 2010?
b. What amount of gain or loss does Long recognize on the properties sold in 2010?

I:10-35 **Mixed Personal/Business Use.** In 2010, Trish, a self-employed CPA and calendar year taxpayer, acquires and places in service an automobile and a personal computer. Pertinent data include the following:

Asset	Date Acquired	Total Original Cost Basis	Portion of Business Usage	Sec. 179 Election
Automobile	1/2/10	$21,000	60%	No
Personal computer	7/1/10	4,000	40%	No

For each asset, calculate the MACRS current year depreciation deduction assuming Trish does not elect Sec. 179 expensing.

I:10-36 *Employee Listed Property.* Assume the same facts as in Problem I:10-35, except Trish is an employee who uses the automobile and personal computer for employment-related activities. While both assets are helpful to Trish in performing her job duties, her employer does not require employees to purchase a car or a personal computer as a condition of employment. What is the amount of depreciation for each asset?

I:10-37 *Recapture of Depreciation Deductions Due to Personal Use.* Tammy acquired an automobile for $20,000 on July 1, 2007. She used the automobile partially for business purposes during the 2007–2010 period. The percentage of business use is as follows: 2007, 70%, 2008, 70%; 2009, 40%; 2010, 35%. The automobile is 5-year recovery property, and Tammy did not elect Sec. 179 expensing. Bonus depreciation was not in effect in 2007.
a. Compute the MACRS depreciation deductions for 2007–2010.
b. What amount of previously claimed depreciation deductions (if any) must Tammy recapture in 2010?

I:10-38 *Luxury Auto Limitations.* Lutz Corporation acquired a 100% business-use automobile (MACRS 5-year recovery) on July 1, 2008 for $64,000. The company did not elect Sec. 179 expensing, but the company otherwise claimed the maximum depreciation deduction available, including 50% bonus depreciation. What is depreciation for 2008–2010, and any subsequent years?

I:10-39 *Luxury Auto Limitations.* Luby Corporation acquires a 100% business-use automobile (MACRS 5-year recovery) on July 1, 2010 for $36,000. Luby does not elect Sec. 179, but the company otherwise desires to claim the maximum MACRS depreciation. What are depreciation deductions for 2010–2012?

I:10-40 *Luxury Auto Limitations.* Tracy acquires an automobile (MACRS 5-year recovery) on March 1, 2010. He uses the automobile 70% of the time in his business and 30% of the time for personal use. The automobile cost $36,000, and no amounts are expensed under Sec. 179.
a. What is depreciation for 2010–2015 and any subsequent years?
b. How would your answer to Part a change if the vehicle were a SUV with a gross vehicle weight rated (GVWR) of over 6,000 pounds and Tracy elected to expense the SUV under Sec. 179?

I:10-41 *Luxury Auto Limitations—Leasing.* Troy entered into a three-year lease of a luxury automobile on January 1, 2009, for use 80% in business and 20% for personal use. The FMV of the automobile at the inception of the lease was $40,500, and Troy made 12 monthly lease payments of $600 in 2009 and 2010.
a. What amount of lease payments are deductible in 2009 and 2010?
b. What portion, if any, of the "inclusion amount" must reduce Troy's lease deduction in 2009 and 2010?
c. How would your answers to Parts a and b change if the FMV of the auto was $15,000 and the monthly lease payments are $200?

I:10-42 *Amortization of Intangibles.* On January 1 of the current year, Palm Corporation purchases the net assets of Vicki's unincorporated business for $600,000. The tangible net assets have a $300,000 book value and a $400,000 FMV. The purchase agreement states that Vicki will not compete with Palm Corporation by starting a new business in the same area for a period of five years. The stated consideration received by Vicki for the covenant not to compete is $50,000. Other intangible assets included in the purchase agreement are as follows:

- Goodwill: $70,000
- Patents (12-year remaining legal life): $30,000
- Customer list: $50,000

a. How would Vicki's assets be recorded for tax purposes by Palm Corporation?
b. What is the amortization amount for each intangible asset in the current year?

I:10-43 *R&E Expenditures.* Park Corporation incurs the following costs in the initial year of doing business:

Materials and supplies for research laboratory	$ 80,000
Utilities and depreciation on research laboratory and equipment	40,000
Costs of acquiring another entity's patent for a new product	20,000
Market research salaries for surveys relative to proposed new products	60,000
Labor and supplies for quality control tests	50,000
Research costs subcontracted to a local university	35,000
Total	$285,000

Park's controller states that all of these costs are qualifying R&E expenditures and that the company policy is to expense such amounts for tax purposes in the year they are incurred. Which of these expenditures are deductible as R&E costs under Sec. 174?

I:10-44   *R&E Expenditures.* In 2010, Phoenix Corporation acquires a new research facility and hires several scientists to develop new products. No new products are developed until 2009, although the following expenditures were incurred:

Laboratory materials	$ 40,000
Research salaries	80,000
Overhead attributable to the research facility	30,000
R&E equipment placed into service (5-year MACRS recovery period)	100,000
Total	$250,000

a. What are Phoenix Corporation's deductions for R&E expenditures in 2010 and 2011 if the expensing method is elected?

b. How would your answer to Part a change if the deferral and amortization method were elected and the amortization period were 60 months?

I:10-45   *Computer Software.* Phillips Corporation, a construction company that specializes in home construction, uses special computer software to schedule jobs and keep track of job costs. It uses generic software for bookkeeping and spreadsheet analysis. During 2010, Phillips Corporation had the following transactions relating to computer software:

• The corporation purchased a new computer system on May 12, 2010, for $15,000. The system included computer hardware and built-in computer software valued at $3,000. The corporation has never separated computer software from the hardware in prior years when a computer system was purchased.

• The corporation separately purchased new bookkeeping software on September 1, 2010, for $5,760.

• On June 1, 2010, Phillips Corporation acquired another home building company to strengthen its position in higher-priced homes. The total purchase price was $700,000 allocated to specific assets as follows:

Equipment	$500,000
Goodwill	150,000
Computer software	50,000

What amount can Phillips Corporation deduct in 2010 with respect to computer software?

I:10-46   *Cost Depletion.* Tina acquires an oil and gas property interest for $200,000 in the current year. The following information about current year operations is supplied for purposes of computing the amount of Tina's depletion and intangible drilling and development cost (IDC) deductions:

Estimated recoverable units	20,000
Units produced	6,000
Units sold	4,000
IDCs	$20,000
Percentage depletion (after limitations)	$25,000

a. What is the cost depletion amount if the IDCs are expensed?

b. What is the cost depletion amount if the IDCs are capitalized?

c. How much depletion is deducted on the tax return?

d. Should the IDCs be capitalized or expensed? Explain.

I:10-47 *Percentage Depletion.* Tony has owned an oil and gas property for a number of years. The following information is provided about the property's operations in the current year:

Gross income	$500,000
Minus: Expenses (including IDCs of $100,000)	(300,000)
Taxable income (before depletion)	$200,000
Cost depletion (if IDCs are expensed)	$ 20,000
Cost depletion (if IDCs are capitalized)	$ 30,000

a. What is the percentage depletion amount if the IDCs are expensed?
b. What is the percentage depletion amount if the IDCs are capitalized?
c. What is the depletion deduction amount assuming that the IDCs are expensed?
d. Based on the information above, which method should be used for the IDCs? Explain.

COMPREHENSIVE PROBLEM

I:10-48 John and Ellen Brite (SSN 265-32-1497 and 571-07-7345, respectively) are married and file a joint return. They have no dependents. John owns an unincorporated specialty electrical lighting retail store, Brite-On. Brite-On had the following assets on January 1, 2009:

Assets	*Cost*
Old store building purchased April 1, 1999	$100,000
Equipment (7-year recovery) purchased January 10, 2004	30,000
Inventory valued using FIFO method: 4,000 light bulbs	$5/bulb

Brite-On purchased a competitor's store on March 1, 2009, for $107,000. The purchase price included the following:

New store building	$60,000 (FMV)
Land	18,000 (FMV)
Equipment (5-year recovery)	11,000 (FMV)
Inventory: 3,000 light bulbs	$ 6/bulb (cost)

On June 30, 2009, Brite-On sold the 7-year recovery period equipment for $12,000. Brite-On leased a $30,500 car for $500/month beginning on January 1, 2009. The car is used 100% for business and was driven 14,000 miles during the year.

Brite-On sold 8,000 light bulbs at a price of $15/bulb during the year. Also, Brite-On made additional purchases of 4,000 light bulbs in August 2009 at a cost of $7/bulb. Brite-On had the following revenues (in addition to the sales of light bulbs) and additional expenses:

Service revenues	$64,000
Interest expense on business loans	4,000
Auto expenses (gas, oil, etc.)	3,800
Taxes and licenses	3,300
Utilities	2,800
Salaries	24,000

John and Ellen also had some personal expenses:

Medical bills	$4,500
Real property taxes	3,800
Home mortgage interest	9,000
Charitable contributions (cash)	600

The Brites received interest income on a bank savings account of $275. John and Ellen made four $5,000 quarterly estimated tax payments. For self-employment tax purposes, assume John spent 100% of his time at the store while Ellen spends no time at the store.

Additional Facts:

• Equipment acquired in 2004: The Brites elected out of bonus depreciation and did not elect Sec. 179.

- Equipment acquired in 2009: The Brites elected Sec. 179 to expense the cost of the 5-year equipment but elected out of bonus depreciation.
- Lease inclusion rules require that Brite-On reduce its deductible lease expense by $35 (Appendix C, Table 13).

Compute the Brite's taxable income and balance due or refund for 2009.

TAX STRATEGY PROBLEM

I:10-49 Stan Bushart works as a customer representative for a large corporation. Stan's job entails traveling to meet with customers, and he uses his personal car 100% for business use. In 2010, Stan must decide whether to buy or lease a new car. After bargaining with several car dealers, Stan has agreed to a price of $30,000. If he buys the car, he will borrow the entire $30,000 at an annual interest rate of 8%, and his payments will be $608.29 per month over 60 months. Annual principal and interest payments are:

	Total	Principal	Interest
2010	$ 7,299	$ 5,083	$2,216
2011	7,299	5,505	1,794
2012	7,299	5,962	1,337
2013	7,299	6,457	843
2014	7,299	6,993	305
Totals:	$36,495	$30,000	$6,495

If he leases the car, his lease payment will be $450 per month for 60 months. At the end of the lease, he has the option of purchasing the car for $10,000. For simplicity, assume an average lease inclusion amount of $230 per year rather than actual amounts. Stan's marginal tax rate is 28% in each of the five years. Using present value analysis with an 8% discount rate, is Stan better off leasing or buying the car?

If Stan purchases the car, he will not elect Sec. 179 expensing. He will sell the car for $10,000 at the end of five years. If he leases the car, assume he merely turns the car in at the end of the lease.

TAX FORM/RETURN PREPARATION PROBLEMS

I:10-50 Thom Jones (SSN 277-31-7253) is an unincorporated manufacturer of widgets. He uses the LCM method to value his inventory and reports the following for 2009:

Sales (less returns and allowances)	$950,000
Cost of goods sold	500,000
Office expenses	10,000
Depreciation*	?
Legal services	4,000
Salary expenses	36,000
Travel expenses	30,000
Repair expenses	20,000

* Information related to Mr. Jones's depreciation:

Cost of office furniture acquired and placed in service on April 15, 2009 (7-year recovery). Thom elects to expense the maximum amount possible under Sec. 179.	$230,000
Cost of other property acquired and placed in service on August 1, 2009:	
5-year recovery property (computers-not listed property)	6,000
7-year recovery property (equipment)	54,000
Depreciation on assets purchased prior to 2009:	28,000

Complete Thom's 2009 Form 4562 and Schedule C of Form 1040.

I:10-51 Using the facts in Problem I:10-48 for John and Ellen Brite, complete their 2009 Form 1040, Schedules A, C, and SE, and Forms 4562 and 4797.

CASE STUDY PROBLEMS

I:10-52   Able Corporation is a manufacturer of electrical lighting fixtures. Able is currently negotiating with Ralph Johnson, the owner of an unincorporated business, to acquire his retail electrical lighting sales business. Johnson's assets include the following:

Assets	Adjusted Basis	FMV
Inventory of electrical fixtures	$ 30,000	$ 50,000
Store buildings	80,000	100,000
Land	40,000	100,000
Equipment: 7-year recovery period	30,000	50,000
Equipment: 5-year recovery period	60,000	100,000
Total	$240,000	$400,000

Mr. Johnson thinks that a total purchase price of $1 million in cash is warranted for the business because of its high profitability and strategic locations, and Able has agreed. Despite the fact that both parties agree that the $600,000 excess payment is goodwill, Able would prefer that it be designated as a 5-year covenant not to compete so that he can amortize it over a 5-year period.

You are a tax consultant for Able who has been asked to make recommendations as to the structuring of the purchase agreement and the amounts to be assigned to individual assets. Prepare a client memo to reflect your recommendations.

I:10-53   In 2008, the Margate Corporation acquired an automobile with a cost of $30,000 for use in its business. Shortly thereafter, Margate Corporation experienced a decline in sales. Several employees were laid off, and the automobile was not immediately needed for any of the sales personnel. Instead of letting the new automobile sit in the corporate lot, the president decided to permit a corporate officer to use the automobile for personal use. The officer used the automobile in 2008 and 2009 only. In 2010, Margate Corporation hired you as their new CPA (tax consultant). You learn that the officer's personal use of the corporate automobile took place for the two prior years without proper accounting to the IRS. As Margate Corporation's tax consultant, what actions (if any) should you take regarding the proper treatment of the automobile? What are your responsibilities as a CPA regarding this matter under the rules of the AICPA's *SSTS* No. 6? (See the *Statements on Standards for Tax Services (SSTS)* in Appendix E).

TAX RESEARCH PROBLEM

I:10-54   The Morriss Corporation is a very successful and profitable manufacturing corporation. The corporation just completed construction of new corporate offices, primarily for its top executives. The president and founder of the corporation, Mr. Timothy Couch, is an avid collector of artwork and has instructed that the lobby and selected offices be decorated with rare collections of art. These expensive works of art were purchased by the corporation in accordance with Couch's directives. Couch justified the purchase of these artworks on the premise that (1) they are excellent investments and should increase in value in the future, (2) they provide an appropriate and impressive office atmosphere when current and prospective customers visit the corporation's offices, and (3) the artwork is depreciable property and the corporation will be able to take sizable writeoffs against income. The Financial Vice-President of the corporation has requested your advice as to whether the works of art are, in fact, depreciable property. Prepare a research memorandum for the Financial Vice-President on this issue.

A partial list of research sources is provided below.

- *Rev. Rul. 68-232, 1968-1 C.B. 70*
- *Shauna C. Clinger, 60 T.C.M. 598 (1990).*
- *Simon v. Comr., 103 T.C. 247 (1994), aff'd, 95-2 USTC ¶50,552 (2d Cir. 1995) nonacq. 1996-2 C.B.I.*
- *Liddle v. Comr., 103 T.C. 285 (1994), aff'd, 95-2 USTC ¶50,488 (3rd Cir. 1995)*

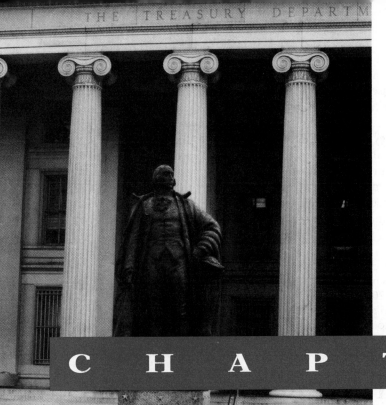

11

CHAPTER

ACCOUNTING PERIODS AND METHODS

LEARNING OBJECTIVES

After studying this chapter, you should be able to

1 ▶ Explain the rules for adopting and changing an accounting period

2 ▶ Explain the differences among cash, accrual, and hybrid accounting

3 ▶ Determine whether specific costs must be included in inventory

4 ▶ Determine the amount of income to be reported from a long-term contract

5 ▶ Compute the gain to be reported from an installment sale

6 ▶ Compute the amount of imputed interest in a transaction

7 ▶ Determine the tax treatment of duplications and omissions that result from changes of accounting methods

An **accounting method** is a system of rules and procedures used to determine the year in which income and expenses are reported for tax purposes. The accounting methods used in computing income for tax purposes generally must be the same as those used in keeping the taxpayer's books and records and determine *when* income and expenses are reported, not whether they are reported. Although the accounting methods used by a taxpayer do not necessarily affect the amount of income reported over the life of a business, they do affect the tax burden in two ways. First, selecting the appropriate accounting method can accelerate deductions or defer income recognition in order to postpone tax payments, and second, because of the progressive tax rate structure, taxpayers can save taxes by spreading income over several accounting periods rather than having income bunched into one period.

EXAMPLE I:11-1 ▶

Jane, a taxpayer using the cash method of accounting, has a 28% marginal tax rate for 2010 and expects to have a 15% marginal tax rate in 2011. Jane plans to make a charitable contribution of $1,000 in January 2011. A contribution in 2011 will reduce Jane's tax by $150 (0.15 × $1,000), whereas a contribution in 2010 will reduce Jane's tax by $280 (0.28 × $1,000). Obviously Jane may wish to accelerate the contribution in order to reduce her tax liability. ◀

ACCOUNTING PERIODS

OBJECTIVE 1

Explain the rules for adopting and changing an accounting period

Taxable income is computed on the basis of the taxpayer's annual **accounting period**, which is ordinarily 12 months (either a calendar year or a fiscal year). A **fiscal year** is a 12-month period that ends on the last day of any month other than December. The tax year must coincide with the year used to keep the taxpayer's books and records. Taxpayers who do not have books (e.g., an individual with wage income) must use the calendar year.[1] A taxpayer with a seasonal business may find a fiscal year to be advantageous. During the slow season, inventories may be lower and employees are available to take inventory and perform other accounting duties associated with the year-end. The tax year is elected on the first tax return that is filed by a taxpayer and cannot be changed without consent from the IRS.[2]

A partnership generally must use the same tax year as the partners who own the majority (greater than 50%) of partnership income and capital. If a majority of partners do not have the same year, the partnership must use the tax year of its principal partners (those with more than a 5% interest in the partnership). If the principal partners do not have the same tax year, the partnership must use the taxable year that results in the least aggregate deferral of income to the partners.[3] An exception is made for partnerships that can establish to the satisfaction of the IRS a business purpose for having a different year.

The purpose of the strict rules for selecting accounting periods is to prevent partners from deferring partnership income by choosing a different tax year for the partnership. For example, calendar-year partners might select a partnership year that ends on January 31. Because partnership income is considered to be earned by the partners on the last day of the partnership's tax year, reporting the profits would thus be deferred 11 months because the partnership year ends after the partner's year. (See the section entitled Required Payments and Fiscal Years in this chapter for further discussion of the calendar-year requirement.)

A similar rule generally requires S corporations and personal service corporations to adopt a calendar year unless the corporation has a business purpose for electing a fiscal year.[4] Taxpayers willing to make required payments or distributions may choose a fiscal year. (See the Required Payments and Fiscal Years section in this chapter.)

 STOP & THINK

Question: The tax rules related to accounting periods essentially require most partnerships, S corporations, and personal service corporations to report on the calendar

---

[1] Sec. 441(g).
[2] Reg. Sec. 1.441-1(b)(4).

[3] Reg. Sec. 1.706-1(a)(3).
[4] Sec. 1378(a).

year basis. Of course, almost all individual taxpayers also report on the calendar year basis. What impact does this have on accountants?

Solution: The principal impact is a compression of tax compliance work into the "accounting busy season." A substantial portion of auditing and other accounting work also takes place at year-end. As a result, these services are also compressed into the accounting busy season. The accounting profession has sought to have these rules changed, but has, at least so far, been unsuccessful.

An improper election to use a fiscal year automatically places the taxpayer on the calendar year.[5] Thus, if the first return is filed late because of oversight, the option to choose a fiscal year is lost.

EXAMPLE I:11-2 ▶ City Corporation receives its charter in 2008 but does not begin operations until 2010. Tax returns are required for 2008 and 2009 as well as for 2010. Timely returns are not filed because the City's officers are unaware that returns must be filed for inactive corporations. Thus, City Corporation must use the calendar year. City Corporation may petition the IRS for approval to use a fiscal year. ◀

While most tax years end on the last day of a month, the tax law allows taxpayers to use a tax year that always ends on the same day of the week, such as the last Friday in October. This means that the tax years will vary in length between 52 and 53 weeks. Taxpayers who regularly keep their books over a period that varies from 52 to 53 weeks may elect the same period for tax purposes. A 52–53-week taxable year must end either the last time a particular day occurs during a calendar month (e.g., the last Friday in October) or the occurrence of the particular day that is closest to the end of a calendar month (e.g., the Saturday closest to the end of November).[6] Under the first alternative, the year may end as many as six days before the end of the month, but must end within the month. Under the second alternative, the year may end as many as three days before or after the end of the month.

The 52–53-week year is especially useful to businesses with inventories. For example, a manufacturer might choose a 52–53-week year that ends on the last Friday in December to permit inventory to be taken over the weekend without interfering with the company's manufacturing activity. Similarly, wage accruals would be eliminated for a company with a weekly payroll if the payroll period always ends on Friday.

Although the 52–53-week year may actually end on a day other than the last day of the month, it is treated as ending on the last day of the calendar month for "effective date" changes in the tax law that would otherwise coincide with the year-end.

EXAMPLE I:11-3 ▶ Eagle Corporation has adopted a 52–53-week year. Eagle's tax year begins on December 29, 2010. Assume that a new tax rate schedule applies to tax years beginning after December 31, 2010. The new tax rate schedule is applicable to Eagle because, in the absence of the 52–53-week year, its tax period would have started on January 1, 2011. ◀

REQUIRED PAYMENTS AND FISCAL YEARS

Virtually all C corporations (other than personal service corporations) have flexibility in choosing an accounting period. Other taxpayers, such as partnerships and S corporations, may use a fiscal year if they have an acceptable business purpose. However, most of these businesses are unable to meet the rather rigid business purpose requirements outlined by the IRS. As a result, these businesses report using the calendar year concentrating most tax work during the early months of the year. Concern over this problem led Congress to enact Sec. 444 which allows partnerships, S corporations, and personal service corporations (such as incorporated medical practices) to elect a taxable year that results in a tax deferral of three months or less (e.g., a partnership with calendar-year partners may elect a September 30 year-end). This is called the **Sec. 444 election**. Furthermore, partnerships,

---

[5] *Q.A. Calhoun v. U.S.*, 33 AFTR 2d 74-305, 74-1 USTC ¶9104 (D.C. Va., 1973).   [6] Sec. 441(f).

S corporations, and personal service corporations may continue using the fiscal year they were using when the current law was passed in 1986 even if that fiscal year results in a deferral beyond three months.

Partnerships and S corporations making the Sec. 444 election, however, must make annual required payments by April 15 of the following year. The purpose of the required payment is to offset the tax deferral advantage obtained when fiscal years are used.

The amount of the required payment is determined by multiplying the maximum tax rate for individuals plus 1% (i.e., 36% in 2010 and 40.6% in 2011) times the previous year's taxable income times a deferral ratio.[7] The deferral ratio is equal to the number of months in the deferral period divided by the number of months in the taxable year. An adjustment is made for deductible amounts distributed to the owners during the year. If the amount due is $500 or less, no payment is required.

ADDITIONAL COMMENT

The American Institute of Certified Public Accountants and accounting firms lobbied extensively for the provision that permits partnerships, S corporations, and personal service corporations to continue to use a fiscal year if annual required payments are made.

EXAMPLE I:11-4 ▶

ABC Partnership begins operations on October 1, 2010, and elects a September 30 year-end under Sec. 444. The partnership's net income for the fiscal year ended September 30, 2011, is $100,000. ABC must make a required payment of $10,150 ($100,000 × 40.6% × 3/12) on or before April 15, 2012. ◀

The owners of businesses making such payments do not claim a credit for the amount paid. Instead, the partnership or S Corporation subtracts the previous year's required payment from the current year's required payment. If the result is negative, then the entity is entitled to a refund.

EXAMPLE I:11-5 ▶

Assume the same facts as in Example I:11-14 except that ABC Partnership's required payment for the year ended September 30, 2012 is $6,000. ABC is entitled to a refund of the difference of $4,150 ($10,150 − $6,000). ◀

Personal service corporations also may elect a fiscal year. However, deductions to shareholder/employees may be limited if distributions to such shareholder/employees during the deferral period do not exceed a minimum amount.[8] Personal service corporations are incorporated medical practices and other businesses owned by individuals who provide their services through the corporation. In general, the rules prevent a distribution pattern that creates a tax deferral. This is achieved by requiring that the deductible payments made to owners during the deferral period be at a rate no lower than during the previous fiscal year.

EXAMPLE I:11-6 ▶

Austin, Inc., is a personal service corporation of attorneys with a fiscal year ending September 30. For the year ended September 30, 2010 the company earned a profit of $480,000 before any salary payments to the owners. The entire profit, however, was paid out as wages to the owners, resulting in a taxable income of zero. To avoid any deduction limitation, Austin must pay salaries to its owners of no less than $120,000 ($480,000 × 3/12) during the period October 1, 2010, to December 31, 2010. If less than $120,000 is paid during this deferral period, deductions are limited for the year ended September 30, 2011. ◀

An option allows personal service corporations to compute the amount of the minimum distribution by using a three-year average of income and distributions.

CHANGES IN THE ACCOUNTING PERIOD

KEY POINT

The use of a natural business year helps in the matching of revenue and expense because the business is normally in a maximum state of liquidity and the problems associated with making estimates involving uncompleted transactions are reduced to a minimum.

Once adopted, an accounting period cannot normally be changed without IRS approval.[9] The IRS will usually approve a change only if the taxpayer can establish a substantial business purpose for the change (e.g., changing to a natural business year).[10] A natural business year ends at or soon after the peak income earning period (e.g., the natural business year for a department store that has a seasonal holiday business may be on January 31). A business without a peak income period may not be able to establish a natural business year and may, therefore, be precluded from changing its tax year. In general, at least

---

[7] Sec. 7519(b).
[8] Sec. 280H(a).

[9] Sec. 442.
[10] Rev. Proc. 74-33, 1974-2 C.B. 489 and Rev. Proc. 87-32, 1989-2 C.B. 32.

25% of revenues must occur during the last two months of the year in order to qualify as a natural business year.

EXAMPLE I:11-7 ▶ USA Department Store's sales peak during the holiday season in December. During January the department store further reduces its inventory through storewide clearance sales. USA elects a "natural" business year-end of January 31 because its inventory levels are lowest at the end of January. Also, USA meets the prescribed test because at least 25% of its revenues for the year occur in December and January. ◀

In a few instances IRS approval is not required to change to another accounting period.

REAL-WORLD EXAMPLE

J.C. Penney, Kmart, and Walmart all use an accounting period ending January 31.

▶ A newly married person may change tax years to conform to that of his or her spouse so that a joint return may be filed. The election must be made in either the first or second year after the marriage date.[11]

▶ A change to a 52–53-week year that ends with reference to the same calendar month in which the former tax year ended.[12]

▶ A taxpayer who erroneously files tax returns using an accounting period other than that on which his or her books are kept is not required to obtain permission to file returns for later years based on the way the books are kept.[13]

▶ A corporation meeting the following specified conditions may change without IRS approval: (1) There has been no change in its accounting period within the past ten calendar years, (2) the resulting year does not have a net operating loss (NOL), (3) the taxable income for the resulting short tax year when annualized is at least 90% of the taxable income for the preceding full tax year, and (4) there is no change in status of the corporation (such as an S corporation election).[14]

▶ An existing partnership can change its tax year without prior approval if the partners with a majority interest have the same tax year to which the partnership changes or if all principal partners who do not have such a tax year concurrently change to such a tax year.[15]

There is one instance, however, when a change in tax years is required: A subsidiary corporation filing a consolidated return with its parent corporation must change its accounting period to conform with its parent's tax year.

Application for permission to change accounting periods is made on Form 1128, Application for Change in Accounting Period, on or before the due date of the return including extensions. The application must be sent to the Commissioner of the IRS, Washington, D.C.

The IRS may establish certain conditions for the taxpayer to meet before it approves the change to a new tax year. For example, the IRS has ruled that if the short period that results from a change involves a NOL greater than $50,000, the taxpayer may have to forgo a carryback of the loss.[16]

RETURNS FOR PERIODS OF LESS THAN 12 MONTHS

Most income tax returns cover an accounting period of 12 months. On two occasions, however, a taxpayer's accounting period may be less than 12 months: when the taxpayer's first or final return is filed and when the taxpayer changes accounting periods.

Taxpayers filing an initial tax return and executors filing a taxpayer's final return or corporations filing their last return are not required to annualize the year's income, nor are personal exemptions or tax credits prorated. These returns are prepared and filed, and taxes are paid as though they are returns for a 12-month period ending on the last day of

---

[11] Reg. Sec. 1.442-1(e). A statement should be attached to the resulting short period return indicating that the change is being made.
[12] Reg. Sec. 1.441-2(c)(2). A statement should be attached to the first return filed under the election indicating that the change is being made.
[13] Rev. Rul. 58-256, 1959-1 C.B. 215.

[14] Reg. Sec. 1.442-1(c). A statement should be attached to the return indicating that each condition is met.
[15] Reg. Sec. 1.442-1(b)(2).
[16] Rev. Proc. 2002-37, 2002-1 C.B. 1030.

the short period. An exception permits the final return of a decedent to be filed as though the decedent lived throughout the entire tax year.[17]

EXAMPLE I:11-8 ► ABC Partnership, which has filed its returns on a calendar-year basis, terminates on June 30, 2010. ABC's final return is due on October 15, 2010. ◄

EXAMPLE I:11-9 ► Joy, a single individual who has filed her returns on a calendar-year basis, dies on June 30, 2010. Joy's final return is due on April 15, 2011. ◄

Taxpayers who change from one accounting period to another must annualize their income for the resulting short period. This prevents income earned during the resulting short period from being taxed at lower rates. Income is annualized as follows:

1. Determine modified taxable income. Individuals must compute their taxable income for the short period by itemizing their deductions (i.e., the standard deduction is not allowed) and personal and dependency exemptions must be prorated.[18]
2. Multiply modified taxable income by the following fraction:

$$\frac{12}{\text{Number of months in short period}}$$

3. Compute the tax on the resulting taxable income using the appropriate tax rate schedule.
4. Multiply the resulting tax by the following fraction:

$$\frac{\text{Number of months in short period}}{12}$$

EXAMPLE I:11-10 ► Pat, a single taxpayer, obtains permission to change from a calendar year to a fiscal year ending on June 30, 2010. During the six months ending June 30, 2010, Pat earns $25,000 and has $5,000 in itemized deductions.[19]

Gross Income	$25,000
Minus: Itemized deductions	(5,000)
Personal exemption [(6 ÷ 12) × $3,650]	(1,825)
Modified taxable income	$18,175
Annualized income [(12 ÷ 6) × $18,175]	$36,350
Tax on annualized income	$ 5,269
Gross tax [(6 ÷ 12) × $5,269]	$ 2,635 ◄

Topic Review I:11-1 summarizes the available accounting periods and the rules for changing accounting periods.

STOP & THINK

Question: Why are taxpayers required to annualize when they change tax years? What provision of the tax law creates this need?

Solution: A change of tax years results in a shortened filing period during the period the change takes place. For example, a taxpayer who changes from a calendar year to a June 30 year-end reports income for only a 6-month period on the first return following the change. Less income is reported, and that income would be taxed at lower rates without annualization. Annualization is necessary because of the progressive tax rate structure.

---

[17] Reg. Sec. 1.443-1(a)(2).
[18] The exemptions are prorated as follows: exemptions × (number of months in the short period ÷ 12).
[19] An alternative method to compute the tax is provided in Sec. 443(b)(2) and Reg. Sec. 1.443-1(b)(2) whereby the taxpayer can elect to compute the tax for a 12-month period beginning on the first day of the short period and then convert the tax to a short-period tax.

Topic Review I:11-1

Accounting Periods and Changes

AVAILABLE YEARS

▶ Available tax years include the calendar year, a fiscal year (a year that ends on the last day of any month other than December), and a 52–53-week year (a year that always ends on the same day of the week).

▶ A partnership must use the tax year of its partners unless the partnership can establish a satisfactory business purpose for having a different year or if the partnership makes required payments.

▶ Similar rules generally require S corporations and personal service corporations to adopt a calendar year unless the corporation has a business purpose for electing a fiscal year. Taxpayers willing to make required payments or distributions may choose a fiscal year ending on September 30, October 31, or November 30.

CHANGE IN ACCOUNTING PERIODS

▶ Once adopted, an accounting period normally cannot be changed without approval by the IRS. The IRS is more likely to approve a change to a natural business year. In general, at least 25% of revenues must occur during the last two months of the year in order to qualify as a natural business year.

▶ Taxpayers who change from one accounting period to another must annualize their income for the resulting short period. This prevents income earned during the resulting short period from being taxed at lower rates.

OVERALL ACCOUNTING METHODS

OBJECTIVE 2

Explain the differences among cash, accrual, and hybrid accounting

A taxpayer's method of accounting determines the year in which income is reported and expenses are deducted. Taxable income must be computed using the method of accounting regularly used by the taxpayer in keeping his or her books if that method clearly reflects income.[20] Permissible overall accounting methods are:

▶ Cash receipts and disbursements method (often called the cash method of accounting)

▶ Accrual method

▶ A combination of the first two methods, often called the hybrid method

KEY POINT

The Code provides the IRS with broad powers in ascertaining whether the taxpayer's accounting method clearly reflects income. It entitles the IRS to more than the usual presumption of correctness.

New taxpayers may generally choose any of the accounting methods listed above. However, the accrual method must be used for sales and cost of goods sold if inventories are an income-producing factor to the business. Exceptions permit businesses with inventories to use the cash method if their average annual gross receipts for the three preceding years do not exceed $1 million ($10 million if the taxpayer's principal business is not the sale of inventory).[21] The fact that an overall accounting method is used in one trade or business does not mean that the same method must be used in a second trade or business or for nonbusiness income and deductions.

EXAMPLE I:11-11 ▶

Troy, a practicing CPA, also owns an appliance store. The fact that Troy uses the accrual method of reporting income from the appliance store, where inventories are an income-producing factor, does not preclude Troy from using the cash method to report income from his service-based accounting practice. Troy could also use the cash method for reporting nonbusiness income (such as dividends) and nonbusiness expenses (such as itemized deductions). ◀

REAL-WORLD EXAMPLE

It has been held that the cash method of accounting can be used where inventories are inconsequential. *Michael Drazen,* 34 T.C. 1070 (1960).

The term *method of accounting* is used to include not only overall methods of accounting listed above but also the accounting treatment of any item.[22]

CASH RECEIPTS AND DISBURSEMENTS METHOD

Most individuals and service businesses use the cash receipts and disbursements method of accounting. Taxpayers cannot use the cash method in a business for sales and cost of goods

---

[20] Sec. 446.
[21] Rev. Proc. 2000-22, 2000-1 C.B. 1008. This Revenue Procedure has been modified and superseded by Rev. Proc. 2001-10, 2001-1 C.B. 272 and Rev. Proc. 2002-28, 2002-1 C.B. 815.

[22] Reg. Sec. 1.446-1(a)(1). Examples of accounting methods for specific items include Sec. 174, relating to research and experimentation expenses; Sec. 451, relating to reporting income from long-term contracts; and Sec. 453, relating to reporting income from installment sales.

sold if inventories are an income-producing factor.[23] However, as noted above, businesses with inventories are permitted to use the cash method if their average annual gross receipts for the three preceding tax years do not exceed $1 million ($10 million if the taxpayer's principal business is not the sale of inventory). However, C corporations and partnerships with a corporate partner may use the cash method only if their average annual gross receipts for the three preceding tax years do not exceed $5 million or if the business meets the requirements associated with providing personal services (i.e., if it is owned by professionals who are using the business to provide professional services).[24] Thus, a law or accounting firm can use the cash method even if its average receipts exceed $5 million. However, other C corporations with greater than $5 million average gross receipts must use the accrual method even if they have no inventory.

Under the cash receipts and disbursements method of accounting, a taxpayer is required to report income for the tax year in which payments are actually or constructively received. While it might seem that receipts under the cash method of accounting should only be recognized if the taxpayer receives cash, this is not the case. The Regulations clearly provide that gross income under the cash method includes cash, property, or services.[25] Thus, if a CPA accepts a set of golf clubs as payment from a client for services rendered, the CPA must include the fair market value of the golf clubs in his gross income. However, an accounts receivable or other unsupported promise to pay is considered to have no value and, as a result, no income is recognized until the receivable is collected. Expenses are deducted in the year paid. Because the recognition of expense is measured by the flow of cash, a taxpayer can control the year in which an expense is deductible by choosing when to make the payment. Individual taxpayers do not have the same opportunity to determine the year in which income is recognized, because the constructive receipt rule requires taxpayers to recognize income if a payment is available, even if actual payment has not been received. (See Chapter I:3 for a discussion of constructive receipt.)

KEY POINT

A taxpayer using the cash method is entitled to certain deductions that do not involve current year cash disbursements, such as depreciation, depletion, and losses.

CAPITALIZATION REQUIREMENTS FOR CASH-METHOD TAXPAYERS. Taxpayers who use the cash receipts and disbursements method are required to capitalize fixed assets and to recover the cost through depreciation or amortization. The Regulations state that prepaid expenses must be capitalized and deducted over the life of the asset if the life of the asset extends substantially beyond the end of the tax year.[26] Typically, capitalization is required only if the life of the asset extends beyond the close of the tax year following the year of payment.[27]

EXAMPLE I:11-12 ▶

On July 1, 2010, Acme Corporation, a cash basis, calendar-year taxpayer, pays an insurance premium of $3,000 for a policy that is effective July 1, 2010, to June 30, 2011. The full $3,000 is deductible in 2010. ◀

EXAMPLE I:11-13 ▶

Assume the same facts as in Example I:11-12, except that the premium covers a three-year period beginning July 1, 2010, and ending June 30, 2013. Acme Corporation may deduct $500 in 2010, $1,000 in 2011 and 2012, and $500 in 2013. ◀

One notable exception to the one-year rule denies a deduction for prepaid interest. Cash-method taxpayers must capitalize such amounts and allocate interest over the prepayment period. A special rule allows homeowners to deduct points paid on a mortgage used to buy or improve a personal residence. The payment must be an established business practice in the area and not exceed amounts generally charged for such home loans. (See Chapter I:7 for a discussion of the deductibility of points.)

To be deductible, a payment must be more than just a refundable deposit. A taxpayer who has an option of cancelling delivery and receiving a refund of amounts prepaid is not normally entitled to deduct the amount of the deposit.

---

[23] Reg. Sec. 1.471-1. However, Sec. 448(b) permits farmers to use the cash method even though they have inventories. Sec. 448(a) denies tax shelters the right to use the cash method even if they do not have inventories.
[24] Secs. 448(b) and (c).

[25] Reg. Sec. 1.446-1(c)(1)(i).
[26] Reg. Sec. 1.461-1(a)(1).
[27] *Bonaire Development Co.*, 76 T.C. 789 (1981), and *Martin J. Zaninovich v. CIR*, 45 AFTR 2d 80-1442, 80-1 USTC ¶9342 (9th Cir., 1980).

Payments can be made either by a check that is honored in due course or by the use of a credit card.[28] Payment by credit card is considered to be the equivalent of borrowing funds to pay the expense. However, a taxpayer's note is not the equivalent of cash, so if a cash method taxpayer gives a note in payment, he or she cannot take the deduction until the note is paid, even if the note is secured by collateral.[29]

ACCRUAL METHOD

There are two tests used to determine when an item of income must be reported or an expense deducted: the **all-events test** and the **economic performance test**.

ADDITIONAL COMMENT

The phrase *reasonable accuracy* means that approximate amounts are ascertainable. Although the word *accuracy* means exactness or precision, when it is used with the word *reasonable* it implies something less than an exact amount.

ALL-EVENTS TEST. An accrual-method taxpayer reports an item of income when "all events" have occurred that fix the taxpayer's right to receive the item of income and the amount can be determined with reasonable accuracy.[30] Similarly, an expense is deductible when all events have occurred that establish the fact of the liability and the amount of the expense can be determined with reasonable accuracy. For deductions, the all-events test is not satisfied until economic performance has taken place.

ECONOMIC PERFORMANCE TEST. Economic performance (of services or property to be provided to a taxpayer) occurs when the property or services are actually provided by the other party.

EXAMPLE I:11-14 ▶ The owner of a professional football team provides medical benefits for injured players through insurance coverage. Economic performance occurs over the term of the policy rather than when the team enters into a binding contract with the insurance company or during the season when the player earns the right to medical benefits. Thus, a one-year premium is deductible over the year of the insurance coverage rather than over the term of the player's contract under which the benefit is earned. But see below for a possible waiver. ◀

Similarly, if a taxpayer is obligated to provide property or services, economic performance occurs in the year the taxpayer provides the property or service.

EXAMPLE I:11-15 ▶ Assume the same facts as in Example I:11-14 except that medical benefits are required under the terms of a player's contract. Also, the team decides to pay medical costs directly. Economic performance occurs as the team actually provides the benefits. Thus, the deduction is permitted only as medical care is provided. ◀

REAL-WORLD EXAMPLE

Before the economic performance test was added to the tax law, a company engaged in strip mining coal was able to deduct the future land reclamation costs as the coal was mined because the liability was certain and the cost could be estimated. *Ohio River Collieries*, 77 T.C. 1369 (1981).

The requirement that economic performance take place before a deduction is allowed is waived if all of the following five conditions are met:

▶ The all-events test, without regard to economic performance, is satisfied.

▶ Economic performance occurs within a reasonable period (but in no event more than 8½ months) after the close of the tax year.

▶ The item is recurring in nature, and the taxpayer consistently treats items of the same type as incurred in the tax year in which the all-events test is met.

▶ The taxpayer is not a tax shelter.

▶ Either the amount is not material or the earlier accrual of the item results in a better matching of income and expense.[31]

EXAMPLE I:11-16 ▶ Bass Corporation, a calendar year taxpayer, pays its annual insurance premium each year on April 30, the anniversary of the policy. The premium paid this year is $6,000 while last year's premium was $5,400. Accrual accounting indicates that Bass deduct $4,000 ($^{8}/_{12}$ × $6,000) of the premium paid this year along with $1,800 ($^{4}/_{12}$ × $5,400) of the premium paid last year, or a total of $5,800. As all of the conditions for the exception to the economic performance requirements are met, Bass Corporation can deduct $6,000 this year. This assumes that Bass has been consistently following the practice and deducted $5,400 last year. ◀

---

[28] Rev. Rul. 78-39, 1978-1 C.B. 73.
[29] *Frank D. Quinn Exec. v. CIR*, 24 AFTR 927, 40-1 USTC ¶9403 (5th Cir., 1940).

[30] Reg. Sec. 1.451-1(a). (See Chapter I:3 for a discussion of the all-events test as it applies to gross income.)
[31] Sec. 461(h).

TYPICAL MISCONCEPTION

It is sometimes mistakenly believed that taxpayers can deduct warranty expenses and bad debts using the allowance method instead of the direct write-off method.

Reserves for items such as product warranty expense and uncollectible accounts are commonly encountered in financial accounting. The all-events and economic performance tests prevent the use of such reserves for tax purposes. This is because the amount of such expense is not usually determinable with sufficient accuracy.

HYBRID METHOD

Taxpayers may use a combination of accounting methods as long as income is clearly reflected. Taxpayers with inventories are required to use the accrual method to report sales and purchases if their average gross receipts for the three preceding years exceeds $1 million ($10 million if the taxpayer's principal business is not the sale of inventory). These taxpayers may use the cash method to report other items of income and expense. To ensure that income is clearly reflected, certain restrictions have been placed on combining accounting methods.

KEY POINT

A taxpayer who uses the cash method in computing gross income from his or her business must use the cash method in computing expenses of such business.

Taxpayers who use the cash method of accounting in determining gross income from a trade or business must use the cash method for determining expenses of the same trade or business. Similarly, taxpayers who use the accrual method of accounting for expenses must use the accrual method in computing gross income from the trade or business.

The basic rules relating to accounting methods, the all-events test, and economic performance are summarized in Topic Review I:11-2.

 STOP & THINK

Question: If an accountant does tax work for an automobile dealer, in exchange for free use of an automobile, does the accountant have to report any income? Does it make a difference whether the accountant uses the automobile in her business? When is any taxable income reported?

Solution: The rental value of the automobile must be included in gross income. If the automobile is used in the accountant's business, a portion of the rental value is deductible as a business expense. Although it is not entirely clear, it seems that an accrual basis accountant would report income as tax services are provided to the dealer. A cash basis taxpayer would report income over the time the automobile is used.

Topic Review I:11-2

Accounting Methods

AVAILABLE METHODS

▶ Permissible overall accounting methods are the cash receipts and disbursements method, the accrual method, and the hybrid method.

▶ The cash method is available to taxpayers without inventories and to taxpayers with inventories whose average gross receipts during the three preceding years was $1 million or less ($10 million if the taxpayer's principal business is not the sale of inventory). C corporations whose average gross receipts fall between $1 and $5 million thresholds may use the cash method if they do not have inventories. C corporations (other than personal service corporations) may not use the cash method if their average gross receipts in the three preceding tax years exceed $5 million.

ALL-EVENTS TEST AND ECONOMIC PERFORMANCE TEST

▶ An accrual-method taxpayer reports an item of income when all events have occurred that fix the taxpayer's right to receive the item of income and when the amount of the item can be determined with reasonable accuracy.

▶ An expense is deductible when all events have occurred that establish that there is a liability and when the amount of the expense can be determined with reasonable accuracy. The all-events test is not satisfied until economic performance has taken place.

▶ Economic performance takes place when property or services are actually provided.

INVENTORIES

KEY POINT

Taxpayers cannot always use inventory methods for tax purposes that conform with generally accepted accounting principles.

In general, manufacturing and merchandising companies are required to use the accrual method of accounting for purchases and sales of merchandise. The inventory method used by a taxpayer must conform to the best accounting practice in the trade or business, and it must clearly reflect income. However, best accounting practices (synonymous with generally accepted accounting principles) and clear reflection of income (which is determined by the IRS) occasionally conflict. The Supreme Court has held that the standard of clear reflection of income prevails in a case where the two standards conflict. In the *Thor Power Tool Co.* case, the company wrote off the cost of obsolete parts for both tax and financial accounting purposes even though the parts were kept on hand and their selling price was not reduced.[32] Regulation Sec. 1.471-4(b) states that obsolete or other slow-moving inventory cannot be written down unless the selling price is also reduced.

Although the company's practice conformed with generally accepted accounting principles, it did not, according to the Supreme Court, clearly reflect income. Hence, generally accepted accounting principles are used only when the Regulations do not specify the treatment of an item or, alternatively, when the Regulations provide more than one alternative accounting method.

Taxpayers who value inventory at cost may write down goods that are not salable at their normal price (e.g., damaged, obsolete, or shopworn goods) only after the selling price has been reduced. Items may be valued at a bona fide selling price reduced by the direct cost of disposal.[33] The option to write down this type of merchandise is available even if the taxpayers use the LIFO inventory method.

EXAMPLE I:11-17 ▶

KEY POINT

The uniform capitalization rules, included in the Tax Reform Act of 1986, require the capitalization of significant overhead costs that previously were expensed.

Stone Corporation publishes books for small academic audiences in Sanskrit and other ancient languages. There is typically one printing of a few hundred or perhaps a thousand copies of each book. Stone may sell a few copies a year of each book. Only after several years can the Corporation determine whether they will ever sell all copies of a given work. Based upon the *Thor Power Tool Co.* case, Stone Corporation cannot write off unsold copies unless they are destroyed or otherwise disposed of, and they cannot write down unsold copies unless the selling price is reduced below cost. ◀

DETERMINATION OF INVENTORY COST

Inventories may be valued at either cost or at the lower of cost or market value. Taxpayers who use the LIFO inventory valuation method (discussed later in this chapter) may not use the lower of cost or market method. In the case of merchandise purchased, cost is the invoice price less trade discounts, plus freight and other handling charges.

Unlike financial accounting, purchasing costs (e.g., salaries of purchasing agents), warehousing costs, packaging, and administrative costs related to these functions must be allocated between cost of goods sold and inventory. The costs that must be included in inventory are found in Sec. 263A and are referred to as the Uniform Capitalization rules (UNICAP). This requirement is applicable only to taxpayers whose average gross receipts for the three preceding years exceed $10 million.[34]

In the case of goods manufactured by the taxpayer, cost is determined by using the UNICAP rules, which may be thought of as an expanded version of the full absorption costing method. Thus, direct costing and prime costing are not acceptable inventory methods. Direct labor and materials along with manufacturing overhead must be included in inventory. Under UNICAP, the following overhead items are included in inventory:

ETHICAL POINT

The UNICAP rules must be followed by taxpayers. To bring a business into compliance with these rules, the taxpayer may need to make certain estimates. SRTP No. 4 provides that a CPA may use a client's estimates if such use is generally acceptable or if it is impractical to obtain exact data. If a change in the overhead application rate is contemplated, it may be desirable to request IRS approval.

▶ Factory repairs and maintenance, utilities, rent, insurance, small tools, and depreciation (including the excess of tax depreciation over accounting depreciation)

▶ Factory administration and officers' salaries related to production

▶ Taxes (other than the income tax)

---

[32] *Thor Power Tool Co. v. CIR*, 43 AFTR 2d 79-362, 79-1 USTC ¶9139 (USSC, 1979).

[33] Reg. Sec. 1.471-2(c).
[34] Sec. 263A(b)(2)(B).

▶ Quality control and inspection

▶ Rework, scrap, and spoilage

▶ Current and past service costs of pension and profit-sharing plans

▶ Service support such as purchasing, payroll, and warehousing costs

Nonmanufacturing costs (e.g., advertising, selling, and research and experimentation costs) are not required to be included in inventory. Interest must be inventoried if the property is real property, long-lived property, or property requiring more than two years (one year in the case of property costing more than $1 million) to produce.

KEY POINT

Identifying the appropriate additional overhead costs to capitalize can be confusing and extremely time consuming.

The main difference between full absorption costing traditionally used for financial reporting purposes and UNICAP costing required for tax purposes is that UNICAP expands the list of overhead costs to include certain indirect costs that have not always been included in overhead for financial reporting purposes. For example, for financial reporting purposes, the costs of operating payroll and personnel departments have sometimes been considered sufficiently indirect or remote to justify omitting them from manufacturing overhead. This is true even though much of the effort of the payroll and personnel departments may be directed toward manufacturing operations. For simplicity and other reasons, overhead costs included in inventory for financial purposes are often limited to those incurred in the factory. UNICAP requires that costs associated with these departments be allocated between manufacturing and nonmanufacturing functions (e.g., sales, advertising, research and experimentation).

EXAMPLE I:11-18 ▶

Best Corporation manufactures traditional style rocking chairs in a small factory with 34 employees. The office staff consists of four employees who handle payroll, receivables, hiring, and other office responsibilities. The sales staff includes three employees who travel the region selling to furniture and craft stores. The remaining 27 employees all work in the factory. Under UNICAP, factory costs including the wages of the 27 factory workers are generally all manufacturing costs. The costs associated with the sales staff are not manufacturing costs. This would include their compensation along with related costs such as travel. Office expenses including the wages paid to the four office workers can be allocated between manufacturing overhead and sales. Reasonable allocation methods are acceptable. One possibility might be to allocate office overhead between sales and manufacturing on a basis as simple as the number of employees in sales (3) and the number in manufacturing (27). Thus, 90% of the cost of the office operation could be treated as manufacturing-related and 10% sales-related. In such case, 90% of the office expenses would be allocated to manufacturing and 10% deducted as a period cost (i.e., selling expenses). The office expenses allocated to manufacturing would in turn be allocated between cost of sales and ending inventory. This allocation could be done on a basis as simple as multiplying the allocated office expenses by the number of chairs in ending inventory and dividing by the number of chairs in the ending inventory plus the total number of chairs made during the year. ◀

A manufacturer may use standard costs to value inventory if any significant variance is reallocated pro rata to ending inventory and cost of goods sold.[35] Taxpayers may determine inventory costs by the following methods: specific identification method; first-in, first-out method (FIFO); last-in, first-out method (LIFO); or average cost method. A few taxpayers, such as an automobile or large appliance dealer, may find it practical to determine the specific cost of items in inventory. Most taxpayers, however, must rely on a flow of goods assumption (e.g., FIFO or LIFO). A discussion of the LIFO method is presented below.

LIFO METHOD. Many taxpayers use the LIFO cost flow assumption because, during inflationary periods, LIFO normally results in the lowest inventory value and hence the lowest taxable income. Once LIFO has been elected for tax purposes, the taxpayer's financial reports must also be prepared using LIFO.[36] This requirement to conform financial reporting often discourages companies from electing LIFO because lower earnings must be reported to shareholders. However, taxpayers may make footnote disclosure of the amount

---

[35] Reg. Sec. 1.471-11(d)(3).   [36] Sec. 472(c).

of net income that would have been reported under FIFO or other inventory methods.[37] Taxpayers may adopt LIFO by attaching a completed Form 970 (or by a statement acceptable to the IRS) to the return for the tax year in which the method is first used.

STOP & THINK

Question: As noted, many publicly held companies do not use LIFO inventory valuation. This is, in part, attributed to the fact that LIFO ordinarily results in lower reported income for accounting purposes than FIFO, and management prefers to report higher profits. Many small, closely-held companies also use FIFO even though their earnings are not reported to the public. Why wouldn't closely-held companies use LIFO?

Solution: There are a variety of reasons. Some businesses are very interested in how their financial statements look to banks and other lenders and to potential investors. In some industries, such as electronics, FIFO may actually provide lower inventory values. Also, LIFO cannot be used with lower of cost or market. As a result, some businesses may elect FIFO to be eligible to use lower of cost or market.

Perhaps, however, the main reason is that LIFO is more complex, and small businesses prefer to simplify their accounting. The advent of computers, accounting software, and bar codes may be having some impact on inventory valuation choices. Nevertheless, many accounting packages only track units on hand and sales revenue. They do not track inventory value (cost). Thus, the company must assign a value to inventory at year-end, and the complexity of LIFO remains a deterrent.

REAL-WORLD EXAMPLE

An automobile dealer, using the dollar-value LIFO method in maintaining its inventory, was required to use one pool for new automobiles and a separate pool for new trucks. *Fox Chevrolet, Inc.,* 76 T.C. 708 (1981).

Recordkeeping under LIFO can be cumbersome. For this reason, taxpayers are permitted to determine inventories using "dollar-value" pools and government price indexes rather than by maintaining a record of actual costs.[38] Retailers use appropriate categories in the Consumer Price Index; other taxpayers use categories in the Producer Price Index. Taxpayers using the index method must divide their inventories into one or more pools (groups of similar items). Thus, a department store might create separate pools for tools, appliances, clothing, furniture, and other products. Dividing inventory into pools can be critical because of the different inflation rates associated with various goods and because, if a particular pool is depleted, the taxpayer loses the right to use the lower prices associated with past layers. An important exception permits taxpayers with average annual gross receipts of $5 million or less for the current and two preceding tax years to use the **simplified LIFO method.**[39] The simplified LIFO method uses a single LIFO pool, thereby avoiding problems with multiple pools.

EXAMPLE I:11-19 ▶

In 2010, King Department Store changes its inventory method from FIFO to LIFO. Because King's gross receipts have never exceeded $5 million, the simplified LIFO method is available. King's year-end inventories under FIFO are as follows:

2009	$100,000
2010	$130,000

Assume the 2009 price index is 120% and the 2010 index is 125%. King must convert its 2010 inventory to 2009 prices.

$$\frac{120\%}{125\%} \times \$130{,}000 = \$124{,}800$$

A base period inventory of $100,000 is established. The increase in inventory (the 2009 layer) is valued at 2010 prices.

Base inventory (2009)	$100,000
Plus: 2010 layer [(125% ÷ 120%) × ($124,800 − $100,000)]	25,833
2010 ending inventory	$125,833

Assume the 2011 inventory valued under FIFO is $136,000 and the 2010 price index is 130%. The 2011 inventory is converted to 2009 prices.

---

[37] Reg. Sec. 1.472-2(e).
[38] Sec. 472(f).

[39] Sec. 474(c).

$$\frac{120\%}{130\%} \times \$136,000 = \$125,538$$

The 2011 increase in inventory (the 2011 layer) is valued at 2011 prices.

Base inventory (2009)	$100,000
2010 layer	25,833
2011 layer	800[a]
2011 ending inventory	$126,633

[a] [(130% ÷ 120%) × ($125,538 − $124,800)].

◀

ADDITIONAL COMMENT

For tax purposes the lower of cost or market method must ordinarily be applied to each separate inventory item, but for financial accounting purposes it can be applied using an aggregate approach.

LOWER OF COST OR MARKET METHOD.   Inventory may be valued at the **lower of cost or market.** This option is available to all taxpayers other than those who determine cost using the LIFO method.[40] The term *market* refers to replacement cost. On the date an inventory is valued, the replacement cost of each item in the inventory is compared with its cost. The lower figure is used as the inventory value. The lower of cost or market method must ordinarily be applied to each separate item in the inventory.

Recall the *Thor Power Tool* case (discussed earlier in this chapter) in which the Supreme Court distinguished market value from expected selling price. **Market value** is the price at which the taxpayer can replace the goods in question. Replacement cost is used in the lower of cost or market determination. Obsolete or other slow-moving inventory can be written down below replacement cost only if the selling price has been reduced.

CYCLE INVENTORY VALUATION.   Computer technology, including bar codes and software, enables businesses to maintain real-time perpetual inventory records. Many businesses, especially those with multiple locations, do not attempt to count all inventory items on the last day of the taxable period. Instead they count inventory following a scheduled cycle. At year-end, businesses adjust quantities shown in perpetual records for shrinkage since the most recent physical count utilizing estimates based on past experiences. The IRS challenged this practice unsuccessfully arguing that the adjustments failed the "all events" test which requires that amounts must be determined with reasonable accuracy.[41] In midst of the litigation, Congress specifically permitted the method in instances where "the taxpayer makes proper adjustment to such inventories and its estimation method [for] actual shrinkage."[42]

WHAT WOULD YOU DO IN THIS SITUATION?

INVENTORY VALUATION

Jack is a new tax client. He says he and his previous accountant did not get along very well. Jack owns an automobile dealership with sales of $12 million. He has provided you with most of the information you need to prepare his tax return, but he has not yet given you the year-end inventory value. You have completed much of the work on his return, but cannot complete it without the inventory figure. You have called Jack three times about the inventory. Each time he has interrupted, and asked you what his tax liability will be at alternative inventory levels. What problem do you see?

---

[40] Reg. Secs. 1.471-2(b) and (c).
[41] *Wal-Mart Stores Inc. v. CIR*, 82 AFTR 2d 5601, 98-2 USTC ¶50,645 (8th Cir., 1998), *Dayton Hudson Corp. v. CIR*, 82 AFTR 2d 5610, 98-2 USTC

¶50,644 (8th Cir., 1998), and *Kroger Co.*, 1997 RIA T.C. Memo ¶97,002, 73 TCM 1637.
[42] Sec. 471(b).

SPECIAL ACCOUNTING METHODS

The term *method of accounting* is used to include not only overall methods of accounting (i.e., cash, accrual, and hybrid) but also the accounting treatment of specific items. Special rules have been established for two types of transactions that cover long periods of time. One rule applies to installment sales (a sale in which final payment is not received until a subsequent tax year) and a separate set of rules applies to long-term contracts (construction and similar contracts that are not completed in the same year they are started). These special rules permit taxpayers to report income from this type of transaction when they have the wherewithal to pay the tax (i.e., the year in which payment is received).

OBJECTIVE 4

Determine the amount of income to be reported from a long-term contract

LONG-TERM CONTRACTS

Long-term contracts include building, installation, construction, or manufacturing contracts that are not completed in the same tax year in which they began.[43] A manufacturing contract is long-term only if the contract involves the manufacture of either a unique item not normally carried in finished goods inventory or items that normally require more than 12 calendar months to complete. Contracts for services (architectural, accounting, legal, and so on) do not qualify for long-term contract treatment.[44]

EXAMPLE I:11-20 ▶

Diamond Corporation manufactures two types of airplanes: small, general aviation planes that require approximately six months to complete and large jet aircrafts sold to airlines that require two years to complete. Diamond maintains an inventory of the small planes but manufactures the large planes to contract specification. Diamond can use long-term contract accounting only for the large planes. Assume Diamond also offers aircraft design assistance to the government and others who seek such services. The long-term contract method of accounting is not available for such services. ◀

HISTORICAL NOTE

The use of the completed contract method was severely restricted in the Tax Reform Act of 1986 because Congress found that several large corporations, particularly those with large defense contracts, had significant deferred taxes attributable to this method. Many of these companies had extremely low or negative tax rates for several years.

The accounting method selected by a taxpayer must be used for all long-term contracts in the same trade or business.[45] In general, the income and expenses associated with long-term contracts may be accounted for by using either the **percentage of completion method** or the **modified percentage of completion method**. In limited instances (explained below), taxpayers may use the **completed contract method**. Under the percentage of completion method, income from a project is reported in installments as the work progresses. Under the completed contract method, income from a project is recognized upon completion of the contract. The modified percentage of completion method is a hybrid that combines two methods (discussed below). Alternatively, taxpayers may use any other accounting method (e.g., the accrual method) that clearly reflects income.

ADDITIONAL COMMENT

In general, a construction contract must involve what has historically been thought of as construction which includes erecting buildings, building dams, roads, and power plants.

COSTS SUBJECT TO LONG-TERM CONTRACT RULES. Direct contract costs are subject to the long-term contract rules. Labor, materials, and overhead costs must be allocated to the contract and accounted for accordingly. Thus, under the completed contract method, such costs are capitalized and deducted from revenue in the year the contract is completed. Selling, marketing and advertising expenses, expenses for unsuccessful bids and proposals, and research and development costs not associated with a specific contract may be deducted currently.

In general, administrative overhead must be allocated to long-term contracts. (See the earlier list of overhead items that must be included in inventory.) This is not required of taxpayers (other than homebuilders) using the completed contract method, but as noted below, the use of the completed contract method is limited.

As previously mentioned, interest must be capitalized if the property being produced is real property, long-lived property, or property requiring more than two years (one year in

---

[43] Reg. Sec. 1.451-3(b).
[44] Rev. Proc. 2004-34, 2004-1 C.B. 991, modifying and superseding Rev. Proc. 71-21, 1971-2 C.B. 549, does establish rules for service contracts that

extend into the year following the receipt of payment. These rules are discussed in Chapter I:3.
[45] Reg. Sec. 1.451-3(a)(1).

the case of property costing more than $1 million) to produce. Interest costs directly attributable to a contract and those that could have been avoided if contract costs had not been incurred must be allocated to long-term contracts.

COMPLETED CONTRACT METHOD. Under the completed contract method of accounting, income from a contract is reported in the taxable year in which the contract is completed. This is true without regard to whether the contract price is collected in advance, upon completion of the contract, or in installments. Costs associated with the contract are accumulated in a work-in-progress account and deducted upon completion. Several courts are in conflict with regard to determining when a contract is completed. Some courts have required total completion and acceptance of the contract.[46] Other courts have held the contract to have been completed when the only work remaining consists of correcting minor defects or furnishing incidental parts.[47]

The use of the completed contract method may only be used in two limited circumstances. The method can be used by smaller companies (those whose average gross receipts for the three preceding tax years is $10 million or less) for construction contracts that are expected to take two years or less to complete and for home construction contracts.[48] It cannot be used by larger companies for manufacturing, or for other long-term contracts other than construction or for construction contracts expected to last longer than two years.

KEY POINT

In general, taxpayers with long-term contracts must compute income under the percentage of completion method for contracts entered into after July 10, 1989.

PERCENTAGE OF COMPLETION METHOD. Under the percentage of completion method of reporting income, the taxpayer reports a percentage of the gross income from a long-term contract based on the portion of work that has been completed. The portion of the total contract price reported in a given year is determined by multiplying the total contract price by the percentage of work completed in the year. The percentage is determined by dividing current year costs by the expected total costs.

KEY POINT

After a taxpayer has adopted an accounting method for long-term contracts, he or she must continue to use that method unless permission to change methods is granted.

MODIFIED PERCENTAGE OF COMPLETION METHOD. At the beginning of a contract, it is difficult to estimate total costs. For this reason, taxpayers may elect to defer reporting any income from a contract until they have incurred at least 10% of the estimated total cost.[49] This is called the modified percentage of completion method. Under this method, if a contract has just been started as of the end of the year, the taxpayer does not have to estimate the profit on the contract during that year. The next year the taxpayer will report profit on all work that has been completed, including work done during the first year. Of course, this assumes that at least 10% of the work has been completed as of the end of the taxable year. If more than 10% of the costs are incurred during the first year, the modified percentage of completion method is identical to the regular percentage of completion method.

The completed contract method, the percentage of completion method, and the modified percentage of completion method are compared in Example I:11-21.

EXAMPLE I:11-21 ▶

In 2010, a contractor enters into a contract to construct a bridge for $1,400,000. At the outset, the contractor estimates that it will cost $1,200,000 to build the bridge. Actual costs in 2010 are $540,000 (45% of the $1,200,000 total estimated costs). Actual costs in 2011 are less than expected and amount to $600,000. The profits reported in both years of the contract are illustrated below.

	2010	2011
Completed contract		
Revenue	0	$1,400,000
Costs incurred	0	(1,140,000)
Gross profit	0	$ 260,000

---

[46] *E. E. Black Limited v. Alsup*, 45 AFTR 1345, 54-1 USTC ¶9340 (9th Cir., 1954), and *Thompson-King-Tate, Inc. v. U.S.*, 8 AFTR 2d 5920, 62-1 USTC ¶9116 (6th Cir., 1961).
[47] *Ehret-Day Co.*, 2 T.C. 25 (1943), and *Nathan Wohlfeld*, 1958 PH T.C. Memo ¶58,128, 17 TCM 677.

[48] Sec. 460(e).
[49] Sec. 460(a).

Percentage of completion

Revenue	$630,000[a]	$770,000[b]
Costs incurred	(540,000)	(600,000)
Gross profit	$ 90,000	$170,000

[a] 540,000/1,200,000 × $1,400,000 = $630,000.
[b] $1,400,000 − $630,000 = $770,000.

◄

In Example I:11-21, the modified percentage of completion method results in the same income being reported each year as the percentage of completion method because more than 10% of the estimated costs were incurred during the first year. Note that the completed contract method defers reporting income until the contract is completed, causing all income from the project to be reported in a single year. Thus, the tax is deferred but the taxpayer may end up being taxed at higher rates. As noted, the completed contract is available only for home construction contracts and to certain smaller contractors for projects of two years or less.

LOOK-BACK INTEREST. Certain contracts (or portions of a contract) accounted for under either the regular or modified percentage of completion method are subject to a **look-back interest** adjustment. When a contract is completed, a computation is made to determine whether the tax paid each year during the contract is more or less than the tax that would have been paid if the actual total cost of the contract had been used rather than the estimated cost.[50] Interest is paid on any additional tax that would have been paid. The taxpayer receives interest on any additional tax that was paid.

 Look-back interest is applicable only to contracts completed more than two years after the commencement date. Furthermore, look-back interest is applicable only if the contract price equals or exceeds either 1% of the taxpayer's average gross receipts for the three taxable years preceding the taxable year the contract was entered into or $1 million.[51]

 Taxpayers may elect a "de minimis" exception to the "look-back" interest computation. If elected, the exception is applicable to all contracts completed within a year, and the election to use the exception can be revoked only with IRS approval. Under the exception, if income reported each year on a contract is within 10% of the recomputed "look-back income," no interest computation is made for the contract. Whether reported income is within 10% of recomputed income is determined separately for each completed contract.

EXAMPLE I:11-22 ► The contractor in Example I:11-21 is exempt from the look-back rule because the contract is completed within two years after the commencement date. On the other hand, if the contract took more than two years to complete, interest would be owed on the underpaid taxes for the first and subsequent contract years. The underreported income for the first year would be $33,158 [($260,000 profit × $540,000 first year's costs ÷ $1,140,000 total costs) − $90,000 first year reported income]. Assuming a 35% tax bracket, the underpaid tax for the first year is $11,605. Upon completion of the contract, interest would be paid on this amount and underpaid taxes for other years. Even if elected, the "de-minimis" exception would be inapplicable as the reported income in the first year of the contract ($90,000) is not within 10% of the income that would have been reported if actual costs had been used in the computation ($123,158 = $33,158 + $90,000). ◄

OBJECTIVE 5

Compute the gain to be reported from an installment sale

INSTALLMENT SALES METHOD

In general, the gain or loss from the sale of property is reported in the year the property is sold. If the sales proceeds are collected in years after the sale, the taxpayer may find it difficult to pay the tax on the entire amount of the gain in the year of sale. To reduce the burden, the tax law permits taxpayers to spread the gain from installment sales over the collection period. The installment method is applicable only to gains and is used to report income from an installment transaction unless the taxpayer elects not to use the

---

[50] Sec. 460(b)(3).

[51] Sec. 460(b)(3).

installment method. An **installment sale** is any disposition of property where at least one payment is received after the close of the taxable year in which the disposition occurs. The installment method is *not* applicable to sales of:

▶ inventory, or

▶ marketable securities[52]

COMPUTATIONS UNDER SEC. 453. Income under the installment sales method is computed as follows:

STEP 1: Compute the gross profit from the sale.

Selling price	$xx,xxx
Minus: Adjusted basis	(x,xxx)
Selling expenses	(x,xxx)
Depreciation recapture[53]	(x,xxx)
Gross profit	$ x,xxx

STEP 2: Determine the contract price.

Contract price (greater of the gross profit from above or the selling price reduced by any existing mortgage assumed or acquired by the purchaser)	$xx,xxx

STEP 3: Compute the gross profit percentage.

$$\frac{\text{Gross profit}}{\text{percentage}} = \frac{\text{Gross profit}}{\text{Contract price}} = \text{xx}\%$$

STEP 4: Compute the gain to be reported in the year of sale.

Collections of principal received during year (exclusive of interest)	$xx,xxx
Plus: Excess mortgage (if any)[a]	x,xxx
Total	$xx,xxx
Times: Gross profit percentage	× xx%
Net gain recognized in year of sale	$ x,xxx
Plus: Depreciation recapture	x,xxx
Gain reported in year of sale	$ x,xxx

STEP 5: Compute the gain to be reported in subsequent years.

Collections of principal received	$ x,xxx
Times: Gross profit percent	× xx%
Gain reported in each of the subsequent years	$ x,xxx

[a] Mortgage − Basis − Selling expense − Depreciation recapture = Excess mortgage

Note that depreciation recapture (see Chapter I:13) must be reported in the year of the sale even if no payment is received.

EXAMPLE I:11-23 ▶ Gina, a cash basis taxpayer, sells equipment for $200,000. The equipment originally cost $70,000, and $10,000 of MACRS depreciation has been deducted before the sale. The $10,000 of depreciation must be recaptured as ordinary income under Sec. 1245. The buyer assumes the existing mortgage of $50,000, pays $10,000 down, and agrees to pay $10,000 per year for 14 years plus interest at a rate acceptable to the IRS. Selling expenses are $13,000. The selling price is $200,000 [($50,000 + $10,000) + (14 × $10,000)]. The gain to be reported is $127,000 [$200,000 − $13,000 − ($70,000 − $10,000)]. Using the steps listed above, calculations are made as follows:

[52] Sec. 453(b)(2) and (k).   [53] For a discussion of depreciation recapture, (see Chapter I:13.)

STEP 1: Compute the gross profit from the sale.

Selling price	$200,000
Minus: Adjusted basis	(60,000)
Selling expenses	(13,000)
Depreciation recapture	(10,000)
Gross profit	$117,000

STEP 2: Determine the contract price.

Greater of gross profit of $117,000 or selling price minus mortgage assumed by purchaser ($150,000 = $200,000 − $50,000)	$150,000

STEP 3: Compute the gross profit percentage.

$$\text{Gross profit percentage} = \frac{\text{Gross profit (\$117,000)}}{\text{Contract price (\$150,000)}} = 78\%$$

STEP 4: Compute the gain to be reported in the year of sale.

Principal received during year	$ 10,000
Plus: Excess mortgage	0
Total amount realized	$ 10,000
Times: Gross profit percentage	× 0.78
Gross profit	$ 7,800
Plus: Depreciation recapture	10,000
Gain reported in year of sale	$ 17,800

STEP 5: Compute the gain to be reported in subsequent years.

Principal received	$ 10,000
Times: Gross profit percentage	× 78%
Gain reported in each subsequent year	$ 7,800

Thus, the total gain reported is $127,000 [$17,800 + ($7,800 × 14)]. This is equal to the gross profit of $117,000 (which is the amount of Sec. 1231 gain reported on the sale) plus the $10,000 of depreciation recapture. As a cash basis taxpayer Gina will report the interest income as it is collected. (See Figure I:11-1 at the end of this chapter which illustrates this computation on Form 6252, Installment Sale Income.) ◄

REAL-WORLD EXAMPLE

When an installment obligation is assigned as collateral for a loan, the transaction is treated as a disposition of the obligation. Rev. Rul. 65-185, 1965-2 C.B. 153.

DISPOSITION OF INSTALLMENT OBLIGATIONS. A taxpayer who sells property on the installment basis may decide not to hold the obligation until maturity. For example, the holder may sell the obligation to a financial institution for the purpose of raising cash. Alternatively, the holder may not be able to collect the full amount of the installments because of the inability of the buyer to make payments. Thus, the holder must determine the adjusted basis of the obligation in order to compute the gain or loss realized on the disposition. The adjusted basis of an installment obligation is equal to the face amount of the obligation reduced by the gross profit that would be realized if the holder collects the face amount of the obligation. In general, this means the adjusted basis of an obligation is equal to

$$\text{Face amount} \times (100\% - \text{Gross profit percentage})$$

EXAMPLE I:11-24 ► Assume the same facts as in Example I:11-23 except that Gina immediately sells a single $10,000 installment to a bank for $9,700. Gina reports a gain of $7,500 computed as follows:

Selling price	$9,700
Minus: Adjusted basis of installment	(2,200)[a]
Recognized gain	$7,500

[a] $10,000 face amount × (100% − 78% gross profit percentage) = $2,200

Gina would have reported a gain of $7,800 had she decided not to sell the installment but to collect the face amount. Because the obligation is discounted by $300 ($10,000 − $9,700),

the reported gain is reduced by $300. If the installment had not been sold immediately, the bank would probably also pay to Gina an amount for the accrued interest. In such a situation Gina would report the gain from the sale and the accrued interest as income. ◄

EXAMPLE I:11-25 ► Assume that Gina in Example I:11-24 is unable to collect the final $10,000 installment because the individual who purchases the property declares bankruptcy. Gina would be entitled to a bad debt deduction of $2,200, the basis of the installment. Gina does not receive a bad debt deduction for the accrued interest because the interest has not been included in her gross income. ◄

KEY POINT

A donor of property does not normally recognize gain, but a gift of certain installment obligations causes the recognition of gain.

Certain dispositions of installment obligations, such as gifts, are taxable events.[54] The main objective of this rule is to prevent income from being shifted from one taxpayer to another. Thus, if a corporation distributes an installment obligation as a dividend or if a father gives his daughter an installment obligation, gain or loss is recognized. In general, the gain or loss recognized is equal to the difference between the FMV of the obligation and its adjusted basis. In the case of a gift, the gain recognized is equal to the difference between the face of the obligation and its adjusted basis. However, certain exceptions to this rule exist. Transfers to controlled corporations under Sec. 351, certain corporate reorganizations and liquidations, transfers on the taxpayer's death, transfers incident to divorce, distributions by partnerships, and contributions of capital to a partnership are exceptions to this rule. In these cases, the recipients of the obligations report income when the installments are collected.

REPOSSESSIONS OF PROPERTY SOLD ON THE INSTALLMENT BASIS. In general, the repossession of property sold on the installment basis is a taxable event. The gain or loss recognized is generally equal to the difference between the value of the repossessed property (reduced by any costs incurred as a result of the repossession) and the adjusted basis of any remaining installment obligations.

EXAMPLE I:11-26 ► Yuji sells stock of a non–publicly traded corporation with a $7,000 adjusted basis for $10,000. Yuji receives a $1,000 down payment, and the balance of $9,000 is due the following year. In the year of the sale Yuji reports a capital gain of $300 (0.30 × $1,000) under the installment method of accounting. Yuji is unable to collect the $9,000 note, and after incurring legal fees of $500, he repossesses the stock. When Yuji repossesses the stock it is worth $8,700. The adjusted basis of the note is $6,300 (0.70 × $9,000). Yuji must report a capital gain of $1,900 ($8,700 − $500 − $6,300). The basis of the stock to Yuji is its FMV at the time it is repossessed ($8,700). ◄

The amount of gain recognized from the repossession of real property is limited to the lesser of (1) the gross profit in the remaining installments reduced by the costs incurred as a result of the repossession or (2) the cash and FMV of other property received from the buyer in excess of the gain previously recognized.[55] In the case of the repossession of either real or personal property, the gain or loss retains the same character as the gain or loss on the original sale.

EXAMPLE I:11-27 ► Assume the same facts as in Example I:11-26, except that the property sold is land. Yuji reports a capital gain of $700, which is the lesser of $2,200 [(0.30 × $9,000) − $500] or $700 ($1,000 − $300). The basis of the land is $7,500 [$9,000 − (0.30 × $9,000) unrealized profit + $700 gain previously recognized + $500 legal fees]. ◄

INSTALLMENT SALES FOR MORE THAN $150,000. Special rules apply to nondealers who sell property for more than $150,000. The special rules do not apply to sales of personal use property, to sales of property used or produced in the trade or business of farming, or to sales of timeshares or residential lots.

First, if the taxpayer borrows funds using the installment obligations as security, the amount borrowed is treated as a payment received on the installment obligation.[56] This

---

[54] Sec. 453B(a).
[55] Sec. 1038.
[56] Sec. 453A(d).

prevents the taxpayer from using the installment method to defer tax and yet obtain cash by borrowing against the installment obligation. Second, if the installment method is used, interest must be paid to the government on the deferred tax.[57] This rule, however, applies only to deferred principal payments over $5 million.[58]

KEY POINT

Installment sales between related parties cannot be used to defer the recognition of gain by the original owner when the related purchaser receives cash as result of a resale of the property.

INSTALLMENT SALES BETWEEN RELATED PERSONS. Installment sales between related persons are subject to the same rules as other installment sales except when the property is resold by the related purchaser. The primary purpose of the resale rule is to prevent the original owner from deferring gain recognition by selling the property to a related person who, in turn, resells the property.

Sec. 453(e) requires the first seller to treat amounts received by the related person (second seller) as having been personally received. Thus, the first seller would be required to report the gain in the year (or years) in which proceeds are received by the second seller. This acceleration provision is applicable only if the resale takes place within two years of the initial sale. For purposes of Sec. 453(e), the term *related person* includes a spouse, children, grandchildren, and parents. Controlled corporations, partnerships, estates, and trusts are also covered.

DEFERRED PAYMENT SALES

The installment sale rules are not applicable to all sales involving future payments. The installment method cannot be used when the sale of property produces a loss. Also, a taxpayer can elect out of the installment method when a sale results in a gain. The manner in which these transactions are reported depends on the taxpayer's accounting method. For accrual method taxpayers, the total *amount receivable* from the buyer (exclusive of interest) is treated as part of the amount realized. Thus, the entire gain or loss is reported in the year of sale. For cash method taxpayers, the FMV of the installment obligation is treated as part of the amount realized in the year of sale. The amount realized, however, cannot be considered to be less than the FMV of the property sold minus any other consideration received (e.g., cash).[59]

EXAMPLE I:11-28 ▶

USA Corporation, an accrual method taxpayer, sells land for $100,000. USA receives $50,000 down and a $50,000 note payable in 12 months plus 14% interest. Assume the basis of the land is $80,000 and that it is a capital asset. Because of the buyer's poor credit, the value of the note is only $45,000. USA affirmatively elects not to report the installment sale on the installment method. USA reports a capital gain of $20,000 ($100,000 − $80,000). If USA collects the face of the note at maturity, no additional gain or loss is recognized. If USA sells the note for $45,000, a $5,000 capital loss is recognized. ◀

EXAMPLE I:11-29 ▶

Assume the same facts as in Example I:11-28, except that USA is a cash method taxpayer. If the FMV of the land is $100,000 (the stated selling price), the treatment of the transaction is exactly the same as it is using the accrual method. If the FMV of the land is assumed to be $95,000 (cash received plus FMV of the note received), USA recognizes a $15,000 ($95,000 − $80,000) capital gain in the year of the sale. If USA collects the face of the note at maturity, $5,000 of ordinary income is recognized. If USA sells the note for $45,000, no gain or loss is recognized. ◀

ADDITIONAL COMMENT

A contingent payment sale is a sale or other disposition of property in which the aggregate selling price cannot be determined by the close of the tax year in which the sale took place.

INDETERMINATE MARKET VALUE. In certain transactions, the value of obligations received cannot be determined (e.g., a mineral interest is sold for an amount equal to 10% of the value of future production). Under the Regulations, the value of obligations with an **indeterminate market value** is assumed to be no lower than the value of the property sold less the value of other property received.[60] Hence, if the value of property sold is determinable, the recognized gain equals the excess of the value of the property sold over its basis. On occasion, however, neither the value of the obligation received nor the value of property sold can be determined.

Temporary regulations specify how these types of transactions are to be treated.[61] The basic rules relating to special accounting methods are summarized in Topic Review I:11-3.

---

[57] The interest computation is described in Sec. 453A(c).
[58] Sec. 453A(b)(2)(B).
[59] Temp. Reg. Sec. 15A.453-1(d)(2)(ii)(A).

[60] Reg. Sec. 1.453-1(d)(3)(iii).
[61] Temp. Reg. Sec. 15A.453-1(c).

Topic Review I:11-3

Special Accounting Methods

LONG-TERM CONTRACTS

▶ Long-term contracts include building, installation, construction, or manufacturing contracts that are not completed in the same tax year in which they are entered into. A manufacturing contract is long-term only if the contract involves the manufacture of either a unique item not normally carried in inventory or an item that normally requires more than 12 calendar months to complete.

▶ Long-term contracts may be reported under the regular or the modified percentage of completion method. Under both methods income is reported as work is completed, except that under the modified percentage of completion method no income is reported until at least 10% of the work is completed.

▶ The completed contract method is available only for home construction contracts, for construction contracts expected to take two years or less to complete, and for use by smaller companies (those whose average gross receipts for the three preceding tax years are $10 million or less).

INSTALLMENT METHOD

▶ Under the installment method gain is reported as the sales proceeds are collected. The installment method is generally not available for sales of inventory or publicly traded property. Furthermore, the method is available only for gains.

▶ Gain is reported as sales proceeds are collected. However, both depreciation recapture and any mortgage in excess of basis must be reported in the year of sale. Gain recognition is also accelerated in certain situations if the seller borrows against the installment obligation or if a related buyer resells the property within two years.

IMPUTED INTEREST

OBJECTIVE 6

Compute the amount of imputed interest in a transaction

KEY POINT

Imputed interest is important because it alters the amount of gain on the sale and causes an interest expense deduction for the buyer and interest income for the seller.

TYPICAL MISCONCEPTION

Some people mistakenly assumed that the imputed interest rules do not apply if the property is sold for a loss.

Before the enactment of Sec. 1274 and the amendment of Sec. 483, property could be sold on an installment basis in a contract providing for little or no interest. Instead of charging interest, the seller charged a higher price for the property. If the property sold was a capital asset, the result of the arrangement was to reduce the interest income reported by the seller and to increase the amount of favorably taxed capital gain. Sections 483 and 1274 now *impute* interest in a deferred payment contract where no interest or a low rate of interest is provided. Another impact of the **imputed interest rules** on sellers is to reallocate payments received between interest (which is fully taxable) and principal (only the gain portion of which is taxable). The result is often an increase in the income reported in early years and a decrease in later years. The rules are generally applicable to both buyers and sellers. In certain instances, the buyer may want interest to be imputed in order to increase his interest deduction in early years.

The following transactions are exempt from the imputed interest rules:

▶ Debt subject to original issue discount provisions (basically bonds issued for less than face where amortization of the discount is required under Sec. 1274; see Chapter I:5)

▶ Sales of property for $3,000 or less

▶ Any sales where all of the payments are due within six months

▶ Sales of patents to the extent the payment is contingent on the use or disposition of the patent

▶ Certain carrying charges for personal property or educational services covered by Sec. 163(b) when the interest charge cannot be ascertained

▶ Charges for the purchase of personal-use property (purchaser only)[62]

---

[62] Sec. 483(d). The rule lowers the basis of a personal-use asset in order to increase any gain on the future sale of the property.

EXAMPLE I:11-30 ▶ Joan is involved in several transactions during the current year. No interest is stated on any of the transactions. The terms of the transactions and the applicability of the imputed interest rules are summarized below:

Transaction	*Imputation of Interest*
Purchases furniture costing $8,000 for her residence. Full price is payable within four months.	Not applicable because property is for personal use. Also, all payments are due within six months.
Sells a boat for $2,000. Payment is due in a year.	Not applicable because sales price is not more than $3,000.
Sells land for $100,000. Payment is due in five years.	Interest must be imputed because no exception is applicable.
Purchases a newly issued bond for $650 (face of $1,000).	Not applicable because transaction is subject to the original issue discount rules in Sec. 1274. Also, the price is not more than $3,000. ◀

IMPUTED INTEREST COMPUTATION

In order to avoid the imputation of interest, the stated interest rate must be at least equal to 100% of the applicable federal rate (110% of the applicable federal rate in the case of sale–lease back arrangements). Lower rates are specified for two types of transactions: (1) If the stated principal amount for qualified debt obligations that are issued in exchange for property under Sec. 1274A does not exceed $2,800,000, the interest rate is limited to 9% compounded semiannually; and (2) the interest rate is limited to 6% compounded semiannually in the case of sales of land between related individuals (unless the sales price exceeds $500,000).

The **applicable federal rate** is determined monthly and is based on the rate paid by the federal government on borrowed funds. The rate varies with the terms of the loan. Loans are divided into short-term (not over three years), mid-term (over three years but not over nine years), and long-term (over nine years).

EXAMPLE I:11-31 ▶ Kasi sells land for $100,000 to Bill, an unrelated person. The sales price is to be paid to Kasi at the end of five years in a single installment with no stated interest. Kasi paid $60,000 for the land. Assume the current federal rate is 10%. Because the amount of the stated principal is less than $2,800,000, interest is imputed at a rate not to exceed 9% compounded semiannually. As a result, the effective rate is 9.2025% (9% compounded semiannually), and the present value factor is .64393 $(1 \div 1.092025^5)$. Thus, the present value of the final payment is $64,393 (0.64393 × $100,000). Kasi reports a $4,393 ($64,393 − $60,000) gain on the sale of the land and $35,607 ($100,000 − $64,393) interest income instead of a $40,000 gain and no interest income. The buyer is treated as incurring $35,607 in interest and has a $64,393 basis in the land. Whether the interest is deductible depends on a variety of other factors (see Chapter I:7). ◀

ACCRUAL OF INTEREST

Is imputed interest reported under the cash or the accrual method? In other words, is imputed interest reported when it accrues or when it is paid? In general, imputed interest is reported as it accrues. However, there are some major exceptions, as follows:

ADDITIONAL COMMENT

The $2,000,000 limit on the stated principal is subject to inflation adjustments for calendar years beginning after 1989.

▶ Sales of personal residences

▶ Most sales of farms for $1 million or less

▶ Sales involving aggregate payments of $250,000 or less

▶ Sales of land between related persons unless the sales price exceeds $500,000[63]

In addition, if the borrower and lender jointly elect, and if the stated principal does not exceed $2,000,000, accrual of interest is not required. This election is not available if the lender is an accrual method taxpayer or a dealer with respect to the property sold or exchanged.[64]

---

[63] Sec. 1274(c)(4).

[64] Sec. 1274A(c).

EXAMPLE I:11-32 ▶ Assume the same facts as in Example I:11-31. Because the aggregate payments do not exceed $250,000, the transaction is exempt from the requirement that interest be accrued. As a result, Kasi reports interest income and Bill reports interest expense in the fifth year when the final payment is made on the transaction. Under the installment method, $4,393 gain on the sale is recognized in the fifth year. ◀

GIFT, SHAREHOLDER, AND OTHER LOANS

Imputed interest rules are not limited to installment transactions. Sec. 7872 applies to transactions involving related parties whose taxes are lowered as a result of low interest or interest-free loans. These situations include

▶ *Gift loans.* For example, parents in higher tax brackets loan money to their adult children without charging interest. If the children invest the borrowed money and are taxed on the income at a lower rate, the family has reduced its total tax liability in the absence of imputed interest rules.

▶ *Corporation shareholder loans.* In the absence of imputed interest rules, taxes may be saved by a corporation that makes an interest-free loan to a shareholder. If the corporation had invested the money and paid out the resulting income as a dividend, it would have first been taxed on the profit. By making the interest-free loan, the corporation could, in the absence of imputed interest rules, reduce its taxes by avoiding the otherwise taxable income.

▶ *Compensation-related loans.* Employers may loan money to employees without charging interest. Without the requirement to impute interest, this could produce tax savings if the employer was unable to deduct additional compensation because of the reasonable compensation limitation or if the employee was unable to deduct the interest, say, because the borrowed funds were used to purchase personal use property.

▶ *Other tax avoidance loans.* Any other low-interest or interest-free loan that produces tax savings may be subject to the imputed interest rules. For example, a club may offer its members a choice of either paying dues or making a large refundable deposit. The club can invest the money and earn interest perhaps equal to the dues. In the absence of imputed interest rules, the member avoids taxes by not having to report the income that would have been earned if the member personally invested the funds. The club is indifferent between the alternatives because both the dues and the interest income are taxable.

In general, interest is imputed on the above loans by applying the applicable federal rates discussed earlier. The resulting interest income is taxable to the lender. Whether the interest expense is deductible by the borrower is determined by applying the usual interest deduction rules (see Chapter I:7).

The imputation process involves a second step. The lender is treated as returning the imputed interest to the borrower. This is necessary because the interest was not actually paid. For example, in the case of a gift loan, the lender is treated as giving the imputed interest back to the borrower. This would not normally have income tax implications, but if the imputed interest were large enough, it could result in a gift tax. In the case of the corporation-shareholder loan, the corporation is treated as paying the imputed interest back to the shareholder as a dividend. Typically, this does not increase the corporation's tax, but it results in the recognition of dividend income to the shareholder. For compensation-related loans, the second step is to impute compensation paid by the employer and received by the employee. The compensation is taxable to the employee and, if reasonable in amount, is deductible by the employer.

There are several important exceptions intended to limit the application of imputed interest in situations where tax avoidance may be immaterial:

▶ Interest is not imputed on gift loans between two individuals totaling $10,000 or less, except when the borrowed funds are used to purchase income-producing property.

▶ If the gift loans between two individuals total $100,000 or less, the imputed interest is limited to the borrower's "net investment income" as defined by Sec. 163(d)(4). (See Chapter I:7 for a discussion of net investment income.) If the net investment income is $1,000 or less, it is not necessary to impute interest.

▶ Interest is not imputed on compensation-related and corporate shareholder loans totaling $10,000 or less.

These exceptions do not apply when tax avoidance is one of the principal purposes of the loans.

EXAMPLE I:11-33 ▶ Linda made interest-free gift loans to each of her four children: Andy, Bob, Cathy, and Donna. Andy borrowed $9,000 to purchase an automobile. Bob borrowed $25,000 to buy stock. Bob's net investment income is $800. Cathy also borrowed $25,000 to buy stock, but her net investment income is $1,100. Donna borrowed $120,000 to purchase a residence, and her net investment income is $500. Tax avoidance is not a motive for any of the loans. Imputation of interest is not required for the loans to Andy or Bob. The loan to Andy is exempt because the amount is less than $10,000, and the loan to Bob is exempt because his net investment income is under $1,000. Imputation of interest is required for the loans to Cathy and Donna. In the case of Cathy, the amount of imputed interest is limited to her net investment income of $1,100. The imputed interest for Donna, however, is not limited to her net investment income because the amount of the loan is over $100,000. ◀

The imputed interest rules are summarized in Topic Review I:11-4.

CHANGE IN ACCOUNTING METHODS

In general, a new taxpayer elects an accounting method by simply applying the selected method when computing income for the initial tax return.[65] If a particular item does not occur in the first year, the accounting method is elected the first year in which the item occurs.

EXAMPLE I:11-34 ▶ Gordon opened a beauty shop several years ago. Because he had no inventory, no inventory method was selected. In the current year, Gordon expanded his business to offer beauty supplies to his customers. Gordon can delay electing an inventory method until the year in which he first has an inventory. ◀

Topic Review I:11-4

Imputed Interest

PURPOSE

The imputed interest rules are intended to prevent taxpayers from reducing their taxes by charging little or no interest on installment payment transactions and loans.

APPLIES TO

In most cases applies to both parties, the debtor and the creditor. The result is to impute interest income to the lender and interest expense to the borrower. Several exceptions exempt small transactions from imputed interest. For example, sales involving payments of $3,000 or less are generally exempt as are loans of less than $10,000.

RATE

Interest is imputed at the applicable federal rate if the stated interest rate is lower. The applicable federal rate is the rate the federal government pays on borrowed funds and is determined monthly. In general, the current rate at the time of the transaction is used throughout the term of the loan. The rate varies with the term of the loan. Loans are divided into short-term (not over three years), mid-term (over three years but not over nine years), and long-term (over nine years).

---

[65] Reg. Sec. 1.446-1(e)(1).

OBJECTIVE 7

Determine the tax treatment of duplications and omissions that result from changes of accounting methods

In general, once an accounting method is chosen, it cannot be changed without IRS approval. There are a few exceptions. For example, taxpayers may adopt the LIFO inventory method without prior IRS approval.[66] Once such methods are adopted, however, they cannot be changed without IRS approval.

As previously noted, the term *accounting method* indicates not only the overall accounting method used by the taxpayer, but also the treatment of any item of income or deduction.[67] A change of accounting methods should not be confused with the correction of an error. Errors include mathematical mistakes, posting errors, deductions of the wrong amount for an expense, omission of an item of taxable income, or incorrect computation of a credit. An error is normally corrected by filing an amended return for the tax year or years in which the error occurs. In general, there is a three-year statute of limitations on the correction of errors. After three years, the tax year is closed and changes cannot be made.[68]

Taxpayers wishing to change accounting methods must file Form 3115 with the IRS in Washington, D.C., on or before the due date of the tax return including extensions. A duplicate copy of Form 3115 must be filed with the tax return for the year. A taxpayer who amends the original income tax return within six months of its due date may request a change of accounting methods with the amended return.[69]

In general, taxpayers initiate a change in accounting methods from an incorrect to a correct method are exempt from penalty and from retroactive application of the new reporting method. Although changes in accounting methods require IRS approval, the IRS states that approval will automatically be granted for a wide variety of changes if the taxpayer meets specific requirements that include proper filing of both Form 3115 and the current year's tax return, agreeing to take into account the Sec. 481(a) adjustment (as described below), not being under examination, and not having changed the same method of accounting within the last four years.[70] Although the IRS retains the right to again change any method of accounting adopted under these procedures it states that such changes will not be retroactive except in rare or unusual circumstances. Examples of situations where retroactive application may occur include misstatement or omission of material facts, change in material facts, and changes in applicable authority.

AMOUNT OF CHANGE

A change in accounting methods usually results in duplications or omissions of items of income or expense.

REAL-WORLD EXAMPLE

The write-down of soil aggregate to its market value by a paving company was a change in accounting method rather than the mere correction of an accounting error. The soil aggregate was included in its election to adopt the LIFO inventory method, and the use of this method required that the soil aggregate be included at cost regardless of market value. *First National Bank of Gainesville, Trustee,* 88 T.C. 1069 (1987).

REAL-WORLD EXAMPLE

An extension of time to file the application for change of accounting method was granted because of the death of the accountant in charge of filing the application. Rev. Rul. 79-417, 1979-2 C.B. 202.

EXAMPLE I:11-35 ▶ Bonnie, a practicing CPA, has been reporting income using the cash method. In the current year, Bonnie obtains permission to change to the accrual method. At the beginning of the current year, Bonnie has $80,000 of receivables that have not been reported in prior years. The receivables were not reported in prior years because they were not collected. Although the receivables are collected in the current year, they are not taxable because, under the accrual method, Bonnie now reports income as it is earned and the income is not earned in the current year. In this case, the income was earned in prior years.

Also, assume Bonnie has accounts payable of $15,000 at the beginning of the current year. The accounts payable were not deducted in prior years because the expenses had not been paid. Furthermore, the accounts payable are not deductible in the current year even if they are paid. This is because the expenses were incurred in prior years. Obviously, the IRS expects to collect the tax on the $80,000 of receivables, and Bonnie is entitled to deduct the $15,000 of payables. In the absence of any special provision, both amounts would be omitted from the computation of taxable income. On the other hand, if the change were from the accrual

---

[66] A taxpayer may adopt LIFO by merely determining year-end inventory by that method and attaching Form 970 to the tax return for the year (Reg. Sec. 1.472-3(a)).

[67] Reg. Sec. 1.446-1(e)(2)(ii)(b).

[68] Exceptions are applicable when the taxpayer omits from the return an amount of income that is over 25% of the gross income stated on the return (6 years) or where fraud occurs (no limitation).

[69] The extension will be granted if the taxpayer (a) files the original income

tax return on time, (b) uses the new method of accounting on the amended return, (c) attaches the application to change methods to the amended return, (d) files a copy of the application with the national office no later than when the original is filed with the amended return, and (e) writes at the top of the application "FILED PURSUANT TO §301.9100-2." Rev. Proc. 99-49, 1999-2, C.B. 725.

[70] Rev. Proc. 97-37, 1997-2 C.B. 455.

method to the cash method, both amounts would be reported twice (in the year prior to the change because they had accrued and in the year of the change because they are collected or paid). Thus, a special provision is also needed for duplications. ◄

REPORTING THE AMOUNT OF THE CHANGE

The net amount of the change must be taken into account.[71] A positive adjustment is added to income, whereas a negative adjustment is subtracted from income. This adjustment can, of course, be made in the year of the change. If the amount is small, recognizing the full amount of the net adjustment in the year of the change is both simple and equitable. Reporting a large positive adjustment in one year could push the taxpayer into a higher marginal tax bracket and result in a significant tax increase. Because the extra income is due to changing accounting methods, not increasing cash flows, the taxpayer may not have the wherewithal to pay the additional tax.

As a result, there are alternative methods that may be used to report the amount of the change. The methods that are available depend on whether the change is voluntary (a change that is initiated by the taxpayer) or involuntary (a change from an unacceptable to an acceptable method that is required by the IRS).

In the case of an involuntary change, several alternative methods are available to the IRS.[72]

In the case of voluntary changes, taxpayers must agree to report the adjustment over a period not to exceed four years. When the amount of the adjustment is $25,000 or less, taxpayers may elect to include the full amount in the current year.[73] In the case of a change spread over four years, equal portions of the change are reported in each of the four years beginning with the year of the change.

EXAMPLE I:11-36 ▶ In 2010, Diana obtains permission to change from the accrual to the cash method of reporting income. The change results in a $30,000 negative adjustment to income. The IRS requires Diana to spread the adjustment over four years. As a result, she may deduct $7,500 in 2010 and $7,500 per year through year 2013. Note that because the amount of the adjustment is spread over the current and future years, the tax savings associated with the deduction are deferred. ◄

In general, the amount of the adjustment cannot be spread over a period longer than the method being changed has been used.

OBTAINING IRS CONSENT

Most changes in accounting method require IRS approval. Sec. 446(e) states that a taxpayer changing the method of accounting "on the basis of which he regularly computes his income in keeping his books" must obtain consent before computing taxable income under the new method. This implies that a taxpayer who has been computing taxable income on a method other than that used in computing book income does not need approval to conform the computation of taxable income to the method regularly used on the taxpayer's books. This conclusion is supported by Sec. 441(a), which requires that the same method of accounting be used in computing taxable income as is used in keeping the books. The alternative might be to require the taxpayer to conform his or her book accounting method with the tax accounting method. The answer may well be in how one defines "books." The IRS has ruled that a reconciliation of taxable income with accounting income was a part of the taxpayer's auxiliary records.[74] Hence, the taxpayer was using the same accounting method for book and tax reporting. As a result, a taxpayer who changes the method of accounting used for financial reporting may not be required to change the method of accounting used for tax reporting as long as financial income and book income are reconciled.

[71] Sec. 481.
[72] Secs. 481(a), (b)(1), (b)(2), and (c).
[73] Rev. Procs. 2008-52, 2008-1 C.B. 587 and 2009-39 I.R.B. 38.
[74] Rev. Rul. 58-601, 1958-2 C.B. 81.

TAX PLANNING CONSIDERATIONS

ACCOUNTING PERIODS

New corporations often routinely adopt a calendar year. Consideration should be given, however, to adopting a tax year for the initial reporting period that ends before the amount of taxable income exceeds the amount that is taxed at the lowest tax rates (e.g., when taxable income is $50,000 or less). This is less critical for a corporation suffering losses because the NOLs may be carried forward for a 20-year period.

In the past, taxpayers were able to defer income by selecting different tax years for partners and partnerships or S corporations and shareholders. Current law limits this opportunity. Nevertheless, partnerships and S corporations may adopt a tax year that differs from that of their owners if that year qualifies as a natural business year (i.e., at least 25% of revenues occur during the last two months of the year). Furthermore, deferral is possible in the case of estates, because they are not subject to similar restrictions on the choice of tax years.

ACCOUNTING METHODS

New businesses should consider the tax implications of electing an accounting method. For example, taxpayers may benefit from the LIFO inventory method because LIFO typically reduces gross profit and defers the payment of taxes during inflationary periods. Similarly, service companies usually choose the cash method of reporting income because it permits receivables to be reported when collected rather than when the income is earned. Choosing an accounting method requires an understanding not only of the available accounting methods, but also the nature of the taxpayer's business. Will a specific election be to the tax advantage of the taxpayer? LIFO inventory is often recommended because, during inflationary periods, it tends to reduce inventory values and increase the cost of goods sold. In certain industries, such as the computer industry, however, costs are declining, and LIFO actually may result in a higher inventory value.

In other industries, inventories may fluctuate widely from one year to the next because of changing demand, shortages of materials, strikes, or other causes. LIFO layers may have to be depleted simply to continue business operations. This can cause one of two things to happen: (1) incurring extra recordkeeping costs of LIFO for little or no benefit because the inventories are depleted before they produce significant tax deferrals or (2) depleting low-cost layers from years past, resulting in a substantial increase in taxable income in the year of occurrence.

INSTALLMENT SALES

Taxpayers normally choose the installment method of reporting income from casual sales of property. By spreading the gain from a sale over more than one tax year, the taxpayer normally remains in lower tax brackets and defers the tax. A taxpayer with low current taxable income may elect not to use the installment sale method in order to take advantage of the lower current tax rates.

COMPLIANCE AND PROCEDURAL CONSIDERATIONS

REPORTING INSTALLMENT SALES ON FORM 6252

Form 6252 (Installment Sale Income) is used to report income under the installment method from sales of real property and casual sales of personal property other than inventory. Figure I:11-1 illustrates how an installment sale transaction is reported. The illustration is based on Example I:11-23. A separate Form 6252 is normally used for each installment sale. Form 6252 is used in the year of the sale and any year in which the taxpayer receives a payment from the sale. Taxpayers who do not wish to use the installment method may report the transaction on either Schedule D or on Form 4797.

Form **6252**

Department of the Treasury
Internal Revenue Service

Installment Sale Income

▶ Attach to your tax return.

▶ Use a separate form for each sale or other disposition of property on the installment method.

OMB No. 1545-0228

2009

Attachment Sequence No. **79**

Name(s) shown on return

Gina Green

Identifying number

1	Description of property ▶ Equipment			
2a	Date acquired (mm/dd/yyyy) ▶ 7 01 2006	**b** Date sold (mm/dd/yyyy) ▶ 8 31 2009		
3	Was the property sold to a related party (see instructions) after May 14, 1980? If "No," skip line 4		☐ Yes ☒ No	
4	Was the property you sold to a related party a marketable security? If "Yes," complete Part III. If "No," complete Part III for the year of sale and the 2 years after the year of sale		☐ Yes ☒ No	

Part I — Gross Profit and Contract Price. Complete this part for the year of sale only.

5	Selling price including mortgages and other debts. **Do not** include interest whether stated or unstated		**5**	200,000
6	Mortgages, debts, and other liabilities the buyer assumed or took the property subject to (see instructions)	**6** 50,000		
7	Subtract line 6 from line 5.	**7** 150,000		
8	Cost or other basis of property sold	**8** 70,000		
9	Depreciation allowed or allowable	**9** 10,000		
10	Adjusted basis. Subtract line 9 from line 8	**10** 60,000		
11	Commissions and other expenses of sale	**11** 13,000		
12	Income recapture from Form 4797, Part III (see instructions) . . .	**12** 10,000		
13	Add lines 10, 11, and 12		**13**	83,000
14	Subtract line 13 from line 5. If zero or less, **do not** complete the rest of this form (see instructions)		**14**	117,000
15	If the property described on line 1 above was your main home, enter the amount of your excluded gain (see instructions). Otherwise, enter -0-		**15**	
16	**Gross profit.** Subtract line 15 from line 14		**16**	117,000
17	Subtract line 13 from line 6. If zero or less, enter -0-		**17**	
18	**Contract price.** Add line 7 and line 17		**18**	150,000

Part II — Installment Sale Income. Complete this part for the year of sale **and** any year you receive a payment or have certain debts you must treat as a payment on installment obligations.

19	Gross profit percentage (expressed as a decimal amount). Divide line 16 by line 18. For years after the year of sale, see instructions		**19**	78%
20	If this is the year of sale, enter the amount from line 17. Otherwise, enter -0-		**20**	
21	Payments received during year (see instructions). **Do not** include interest, whether stated or unstated		**21**	10,000
22	Add lines 20 and 21		**22**	10,000
23	Payments received in prior years (see instructions). **Do not** include interest, whether stated or unstated	**23**		
24	**Installment sale income.** Multiply line 22 by line 19		**24**	7,800
25	Enter the part of line 24 that is ordinary income under the recapture rules (see instructions) . . .		**25**	
26	Subtract line 25 from line 24. Enter here and on Schedule D or Form 4797 (see instructions). . .		**26**	7,800

Part III — Related Party Installment Sale Income. **Do not** complete if you received the final payment this tax year.

27	Name, address, and taxpayer identifying number of related party

28	Did the related party resell or dispose of the property ("second disposition") during this tax year?	☐ Yes ☐ No
29	**If the answer to question 28 is "Yes," complete lines 30 through 37 below unless one of the following conditions is met. Check the box that applies.**	
a	☐ The second disposition was more than 2 years after the first disposition (other than dispositions of marketable securities). If this box is checked, enter the date of disposition (mm/dd/yyyy) . . . . . ▶	
b	☐ The first disposition was a sale or exchange of stock to the issuing corporation.	
c	☐ The second disposition was an involuntary conversion and the threat of conversion occurred after the first disposition.	
d	☐ The second disposition occurred after the death of the original seller or buyer.	
e	☐ It can be established to the satisfaction of the Internal Revenue Service that tax avoidance was not a principal purpose for either of the dispositions. If this box is checked, attach an explanation (see instructions).	

30	Selling price of property sold by related party (see instructions)	**30**	
31	Enter contract price from line 18 for year of first sale	**31**	
32	Enter the **smaller** of line 30 or line 31	**32**	
33	Total payments received by the end of your 2009 tax year (see instructions)	**33**	
34	Subtract line 33 from line 32. If zero or less, enter -0-	**34**	
35	Multiply line 34 by the gross profit percentage on line 19 for year of first sale	**35**	
36	Enter the part of line 35 that is ordinary income under the recapture rules (see instructions) . .	**36**	
37	Subtract line 36 from line 35. Enter here and on Schedule D or Form 4797 (see instructions) . .	**37**	

For Paperwork Reduction Act Notice, see page 4.   Cat. No. 13601R   Form **6252** (2009)

FIGURE I:11-1 ▶ REPORTING INSTALLMENT SALE INCOME ON FORM 6252 (BASED ON EXAMPLE I:11-23)

11-29

PROCEDURES FOR CHANGING TO LIFO

The LIFO method may be adopted in the initial year that inventories are maintained by merely using the method in that year. In addition, advance approval (e.g., within 180 days following the start of the year) from the IRS is not required for an adoption of the LIFO method in the initial year that inventories are maintained on the LIFO method. However, Form 970 should be filed along with the taxpayer's tax return for the year of the change.[75] The application must include an analysis of the beginning and ending inventories. Further, if a taxpayer is changing to the LIFO method from another method (e.g., FIFO), advance approval from the IRS is also not required. Form 970 must be filed with the return and the beginning inventory for LIFO purposes is the same as under the former inventory method.[76]

If the former inventory is valued based on the lower of cost or market (LCM) method, an adjustment is required to restate the beginning inventory to cost because the LCM method cannot be used under LIFO. Generally, the beginning LIFO inventory is the same as the closing inventory for the prior year, except for the required restatement of previous writedowns to market. This adjustment to the beginning inventory can be spread ratably over the year of the change and the next two years.[77]

EXAMPLE I:11-37 ▶ Delaware Corporation elects to change to the LIFO inventory method for 2010. In 2009 Delaware's inventories are valued using the LCM method based on the FIFO cost-flow assumption. The FIFO cost for the ending inventory in 2009 is $50,000, and its LCM amount is $35,000. The initial inventory for 2010 under LIFO must be restated to its cost, or $50,000. The $15,000 ($50,000 cost − $35,000 LCM value) difference can be included in taxable income over the current year and next two years. $5,000 is added to taxable income in 2010, 2011, and 2012. ◀

PROBLEM MATERIALS

DISCUSSION QUESTIONS

I:11-1 Do accounting rules determine the amount of income to be reported by a taxpayer?

I:11-2 How does a taxpayer's tax accounting method affect the amount of tax paid?

I:11-3 Most individuals use the calendar year as their tax year. What requirement, if any, in the tax law causes this?

I:11-4 Why is it desirable for a new taxpayer to select an appropriate tax year?

I:11-5 What restrictions apply to partnerships selecting a tax year?

I:11-6 Does a similar restriction apply to S corporations? Explain.

I:11-7 How could the 52–53-week year prove to be beneficial to taxpayers? Explain.

I:11-8 Under what circumstances can an individual taxpayer change tax years without IRS approval?

I:11-9 Is there any instance in which a change in tax years is required? Explain.

I:11-10 a. In what situations will a tax year cover a period of less than 12 months?
b. Under what conditions is a taxpayer required to annualize income?
c. Does annualizing income increase or decrease the taxpayer's tax liability? Explain.

I:11-11 When is a final tax return due for an individual who uses a calendar year and who dies during the year?

I:11-12 a. Is it correct to say that businesses with inventories must use the accrual method?
b. What other restrictions apply to taxpayers who are choosing an overall tax accounting method?
c. Why is the cash method usually preferred to the accrual method?

I:11-13 a. Does the term *method of accounting* refer only to overall methods of accounting? Explain.

---

[75] An acceptable election is considered to have been made even if Form 970 is not filed as long as all of the information required by Reg. Sec. 1.472-3(a) is provided by the taxpayer.

[76] Reg. Sec. 1.472-2(c).
[77] Sec. 472(d).

b. Does a taxpayer's accounting method affect the total amount of income reported over an extended time period?

c. How can the use of an accounting method affect the total amount of tax paid over time?

I:11-14 a. When are expenses deductible by a cash method taxpayer?

b. Are the rules that determine when interest is deductible by a cash method taxpayer the same as for other expenses?

c. Is a cash method taxpayer subject to the same rules for depreciable assets as accrual method taxpayers?

I:11-15 Who may use the completed contract method of reporting income from long-term contracts?

I:11-16 When is a cash method taxpayer allowed to deduct deposits?

I:11-17 What constitutes a payment in determining when a cash-basis taxpayer is entitled to deduct an expense?

I:11-18 What is meant by economic performance?

I:11-19 What conditions must be met if the economic performance test is to be waived for an accrual-method taxpayer?

I:11-20 Is an accrual method taxpayer permitted to deduct estimated expenses? What about prepaid expenses? Explain.

I:11-21 What is the significance of the *Thor Power Tool Co.* decision?

I:11-22 a. How are overhead costs treated in determining a manufacturing company's inventory?

b. Do retailers have a similar rule?

c. Are these rules the same as for financial accounting? If not, explain.

I:11-23 What transactions are subject to the long-term contract method of reporting?

I:11-24 a. What conditions must be met in order to use the installment method?

b. Why would a taxpayer elect not to use the installment method?

I:11-25 What is the impact of having the entire gain on an installment sale consist of ordinary income from depreciation recapture?

I:11-26 What impact does the gifting of an installment obligation have on the donor?

I:11-27 What treatment is given to an installment sale involving related people?

I:11-28 What is the primary impact of the imputed interest rules on installment sales?

I:11-29 What changes in accounting method can be made without IRS approval?

I:11-30 Can the IRS require a taxpayer to change accounting methods?

I:11-31 Explain the purpose of the four-year method used in computing the tax resulting from a net adjustment due to a change in accounting methods.

I:11-32 If a taxpayer changes the method of accounting used for financial reporting purposes, must the taxpayer also change his or her method of accounting for tax purposes?

ISSUE IDENTIFICATION QUESTIONS

I:11-33 Judy's Cars, Inc., sells collectible automobiles to consumers. She employs the specific identification inventory valuation method. Prices are negotiated by Judy and individual customers. Judy accepts trade-ins when she sells an automobile. Judy negotiates the allowance for trade with the customer. Occasionally, Judy finds that it can take two or three years to sell a given automobile. Judy now has four automobiles that she has held for over two years. She expects to eventually sell those automobiles, but expects that they will sell for less than their original cost. What tax issues should Judy consider?

I:11-34 Lana operates a real estate appraisal service business in a small town serving local lenders. After noting that lenders must pay to bring in a surveyor from out of town, she completes a course and obtains a surveyor's license that enables her to provide this service also. She now provides both services as a proprietor. What tax issues should Lana consider?

I:11-35 John owns a small farm on a lake. A local developer offers John $400,000 cash for his farm. The developer believes John's farm will be very attractive to home buyers because it is on a lake. After John turns down the initial offer, the developer offers to pay John $250,000 plus an amount equal to 10% of the selling price for the homes that are developed and sold. Identify the tax issues John should consider if he accepts the offer.

I:11-36 Lee is starting a small lawn service. On the advice of his accountant, Lee has formed a corporation and made an S corporation election. The accountant has asked Lee to consider electing a fiscal year ending on the last day in February. The accountant pointed out that Lee's business is likely to slow down in the winter. Also, the accountant indicated that the February year end would permit the accountant to do Lee's accounting work after the busy season in accounting is over. What tax issues should Lee consider?

PROBLEMS

I:11-37 *Allowable Taxable Year.* For each of the following cases, indicate whether the taxpayer has selected an allowable tax year in an initial year. If the year selected is not acceptable, indicate what an acceptable year would be.

a. A corporation selects a January 15 year-end.

b. A corporation selects a March 31 year-end.

c. A corporation selects a year that ends on the last Friday in March.

d. A partnership selects a year that ends on December 31 and has three equal partners whose years end on March 31, April 30, and June 30.

e. An S corporation selects a December 31 year-end.

I:11-38 *Change in Accounting Period.* In which of the following instances is a taxpayer permitted to change accounting periods without IRS approval?

a. A calendar-year taxpayer who wishes to change to a year that ends on the last Friday in December.

b. ABC Partnership has filed its tax return using a fiscal-year ending on March 31 for over 40 years. The partnership wishes to change to a calendar year-end that coincides with its partners' year-end.

c. Iowa Corporation, a newly acquired subsidiary, wishes to change its year-end to coincide with its parent.

I:11-39 *Annualization.* Each of the following cases involves a taxable year of less than 12 months. In which situations is annualization required?

a. A new corporation formed in September elects a calendar year.

b. A calendar-year individual dies on June 15.

c. Jean, who has been using a calendar year, marries Hank, a fiscal-year taxpayer. Soon after the marriage, Jean changes her tax year to coincide with her husband's tax year.

d. A calendar-year corporation liquidates on April 20.

I:11-40 *Short Period Return.* Lavanya, a single taxpayer, is a practicing accountant. She obtains permission to change her tax year from the calendar year to a year ending July 31. Her practice income for the seven months ending July 31 is $40,000. In addition, Lavanya has $3,000 of interest income and $6,250 of itemized deductions. She is entitled to one exemption. What is her tax for the short period?

I:11-41 *Cash Basis Expenses.* How much of the following expenses are currently deductible by a cash basis taxpayer?

a. Medical prescriptions costing $20 paid by credit card (medical expenses already exceed the 7.5% of AGI floor).

b. Prepaid interest (not related to points) of $200 on a residential loan.

c. Taxpayer borrows $300 from the bank to make a charitable contribution. The $300 is paid to the charitable organization before the end of the tax year.

d. Taxpayer gives a note to his church indicating an intent to contribute $300.

e. A calendar-year individual mails a check for $200 to his church on December 31. The check is postmarked December 31 and clears the bank on January 4.

I:11-42 *Economic Performance.* In light of the economic performance requirement, how much is deductible by the following accrual-basis corporate taxpayers this year?

a. Camp Corporation sells products with a one-year warranty. Camp estimates that the warranty costs on products sold during this year will amount to $80,000. Camp performs $38,000 of warranty work on products sold last year and $36,000 of warranty work on products sold this year.

b. Data Corporation agrees to pay $10,000 this year and $10,000 next year to a software developer. The developer completes all work on the software and delivers the product to Data this year.

c. Palm Corporation pays $5,000 to a supplier to guarantee delivery of raw materials. The $5,000 is refundable if Palm decides not to acquire the materials.

d. This year North Corporation pays a $1,000 security deposit on space it rents for a new office. In addition, North pays rent of $18,000. The security deposit is refundable if the property is returned in good condition.

I:11-43 *Manufacturing Inventory.* Which of the following costs must be included in inventory by a manufacturing company?

a. Raw materials
b. Advertising
c. Payroll taxes for factory employees
d. Research and experimental costs
e. Factory insurance
f. Repairs to factory equipment
g. Factory utility costs
h. Factory rent

I:11-44 *Single Pool LIFO.* Prime Corporation begins operations in late 2010. Prime decides to use the single pool LIFO method. Year-end inventories under FIFO are as follows:

2010	$110,000
2011	134,000
2012	125,000

The price index for 2010 is 130%; for 2011, 134%; and 2012, 140%. What are 2011 and 2012 inventories?

I:11-45 *Installment Sale.* In 2010, Ace Construction Company sells a used crane to Go Construction Company. The crane, which cost $87,000 in 2002, sells for $80,000. Ace has deducted the entire cost of the crane under MACRS depreciation. Ace receives $20,000 down and is to receive $20,000 per year plus 10% interest for four years. Under the Sec. 1245 depreciation recapture rules, the entire gain is taxable as ordinary income. There is no applicable installment obligation. How much of the gain is taxable in 2010? 2011?

I:11-46 *Inventory Method.* Zap Company manufactures computer hard drives. The cost of hard drives has been declining for years. Sales totaled $4,000,000 last year. Zap's ending inventory was valued at $300,000 under FIFO. The company's new president is trying to cut taxes and asks you whether the company should switch to LIFO. What do you recommend?

I:11-47 *Installment Sales.* First Company sold the following assets during the year. Indicate whether First Company can use the installment method to report each transaction. If not, how is the transaction reported? Assume First Company is an accrual basis taxpayer.
   a. First Company sold stock in a publicly held company costing $35,000. First Company received a $20,000 down payment and is to receive $20,000 per year for two years plus interest.
   b. First Company sold land costing $150,000. First Company received a $20,000 down payment and is to receive $20,000 per year for five years plus interest.
   c. First Company initiated credit sales of merchandise. The company previously sold merchandise only to cash customers. Cash sales this year totaled $4,000,000. Credit sales totaled $500,000. At year end, First Company has receivables of $100,000. The company expects to collect only $85,000 of the current receivables.

I:11-48 *Installment Sale.* On December 31, 2010, Dan sells unlisted stock with a cost of $14,000 for $20,000. Dan collects $5,000 down and is scheduled to receive $5,000 per year for three years plus interest at a rate acceptable to the IRS.
   a. How much gain must Dan recognize in 2010? Assume Dan uses the installment method to report the gain.
   b. In early January 2011, Dan sells the three installments for a total of $13,800. How much gain or loss must Dan recognize from the sale?

I:11-49 *Repossession.* Lina, an attorney, sold an antique rug for $45,000 that had been in her home. The rug cost Lina $12,000 several years ago. Lina collected $15,000 down and received a one-year interest bearing note for the balance. She is unable to collect the balance, and after incurring court costs of $500, she repossesses the rug. The rug is damaged when she recovers it and is now worth only $30,000.
   a. How much gain must Lina report in the year of the sale?
   b. How much gain, if any, must Lina report in the year she repossesses the rug?
   c. What is the basis of the rug after the repossession?

I:11-50 *Deferred Payment Sale.* Joe sells land with a $60,000 adjusted basis for $42,000. He incurs selling expenses of $2,000. The land is subject to a $10,000 mortgage. The buyer, who assumes the mortgage, pays $8,000 down and agrees to pay Joe $8,000 per year for three years plus interest. The installment obligations are worth $24,000.

a. How much gain or loss does Joe report in the year of the sale?

b. When does Joe report the interest income from the sale?

c. Does Joe report gain or loss when he collects the installment payments?

I:11-51 *Imputed Interest.* On January 30, 2010, Amy sells land to Bob for a stated price of $200,000. The full $200,000 is payable on January 30, 2012. No interest is stated. Amy, a cash-method taxpayer, purchased the land in 2005 for $130,000.

a. How much interest income must be reported by Amy on the sale? Assume a 9% rate compounded semiannually. The present value factor is 0.83856.

b. In what year is the interest reported?

c. How much gain is reported by Amy on the sale?

d. In what year is the gain reported?

e. What is Bob's basis in the land?

I:11-52 *Change of Accounting Method.* Dana manages real estate and is a cash method taxpayer. She changes to the accrual method in 2011. Dana's business income for 2011 is $30,000 computed on the accrual method. Her books show the following:

	December 31, 2010	December 31, 2011
Accounts receivable	$16,000	$25,300
Accounts payable	15,200	11,800

a. What adjustment is necessary to Dana's income?

b. How should Dana report the adjustment?

I:11-53 *Required Payment.* BCD Partnership has, for many years, had a March 31 year-end. The partnership's net income for the fiscal year ended March 31, 2011 is $400,000. Because of its fiscal year, BCD has $100,000 on deposit with the IRS from 2010.

a. How much must BCD add to the deposit?

b. When must BCD make the addition?

c. Will the partners receive any credit for the deposit? That is, are they permitted to treat the amount as estimated payments?

I:11-54 *Change to LIFO.* Lance Corporation's management has asked whether they may change their inventory valuation method to LIFO. They now report their inventory using FIFO. If they can change, how would they go about it? How is the related adjustment handled?

I:11-55 *Imputed Interest.* Jane loans $80,000 to John, her son, to permit him to purchase a principal residence. The loan principal is secured by John's residence, but the agreement does not specify any interest. The applicable federal rate for the year is 8%. John's net investment income is $800.

a. How much interest is imputed on the loan each year?

b. Assume that the amount of the loan is $125,000. How much interest is imputed on the loan?

c. Is John allowed to deduct the imputed interest?

d. What other tax implications are there for the loan?

I:11-56 *Long-Term Contract.* King Construction Company is engaged in a road construction contract to build a highway over a three-year period. King will receive $11,200,000 for building five miles of highway. King estimates that it will incur $10,000,000 of costs before the contract is completed. As of the end of the first year King incurred $3,000,000 of costs allocated to the contract.

a. How much income from the contract must King report during the first year?

b. Assume King incurs an additional $5,000,000 of costs during the second year. How much income is reported during that year?

c. Assume that King incurs an additional $2,500,000 of costs in the third and final year of the contract. How much does King report during the third year?

d. Will King receive or pay look-back interest? Explain.

COMPREHENSIVE PROBLEM

I:11-57 Dan turned age 65 and retired this year. He owned and operated a tugboat in the local harbor before his retirement. The boat cost $100,000 when he purchased it two years ago. A tugboat is 10-year property. Dan deducted $10,000 of depreciation on the boat the

year he purchased it and he deducted $18,000 of depreciation last year. He sold the tugboat in November of this year for $90,000 collecting an $18,000 down payment. The buyer agreed to pay 8% interest annually on the unpaid balance and to pay $18,000 annually for four years toward the principal. The four $18,000 principal payments and related interest payments begin next year. Dan received $72,000 of business income and incurred other business expenses of $30,000 this year before he retired. He received Social Security benefits of $2,000 and withdrew $10,000 from a regular IRA account. He contributed $4,000 to his church, paid real property taxes of $2,000, and home mortgage interest of $6,500. Dan paid $200 of state income taxes when he filed last year's return earlier this year and he made estimated state income tax payments of $800 during the this year and $220 after year end. In addition, Dan made federal estimated payments of $8,000. Dan is a single, cash basis taxpayer. Ignore self-employment taxes.

a. Compute the depreciation for the current year on the tugboat.
b. Compute the amount of gain to be reported currently on the sale of the tugboat. Assume that Dan wants to use the installment method if it can be used. The accumulated depreciation on the tugboat is subject to Sec. 1245 depreciation recapture and must be reported currently.
c. How much interest, if any, must Dan report this year?
d. What is the income from the business, excluding the gain on the sale of the tugboat?
e. What is Dan's AGI?
f. What is the amount of Dan's itemized deductions?
g. What is Dan's taxable income?

TAX STRATEGY PROBLEMS

I:11-58 Leon has a substantial portfolio of stocks and bonds as well as cash from some bonds that have recently matured. He has been looking at investing $200,000 in corporate bonds that pay 7% interest. The $14,000 of annual interest would be used to pay his 24-year-old son's tuition at State University. A friend suggested that Leon loan the money "interest free" to his son, a student who has no other income. The son would then invest the $200,000 in the corporate bonds and use the $14,000 interest to pay his tuition. Leon is in the 28% tax bracket. Would such a strategy reduce his family's tax? Assume the applicable federal rate is 6.5%.

I:11-59 Linda is selling land she has owned for many years. The land cost $80,000 and will sell for $200,000. The buyer has offered to pay $100,000 down and pay the balance next year plus interest at 8%. Assume that Linda's after tax rate of return on investments is 10%. Would she be better off receiving the installment payments or receiving cash? Assume her ordinary income is taxed at 28% and that long-term capital gains are taxed at 15%.

TAX FORM/RETURN PREPARATION PROBLEM

I:11-60 Barbara B. Kuhn (SSN 987-65-4321) purchases a fourplex on January 8, 2006, for $175,000. She allocates $25,000 of the cost to the land, and she deducts MACRS depreciation totaling $16,364. Barbara sells the fourplex on January 6, 2009, for $225,000. The buyer assumes the existing mortgage of $180,000, pays $15,000 down, and agrees to pay $15,000 per year for two years plus 12% interest. Barbara incurs selling expenses of $18,000. Complete Form 6252.

CASE STUDY PROBLEMS

I:11-61 Lavonne just completed medical school and residency. She plans to open her medical practice soon. She is not familiar with the intricacies of accounting methods and periods. On advice of her attorney, she plans to form a professional corporation (a form of organization permitted under the laws of most states that does not have the usual limited liability found with business corporations, but is taxed as a corporation). She has asked you whether she should elect a fiscal year and whether she should use the cash or accrual method of reporting income. Discuss whether the options are available to her and the implications of available choices.

I:11-62 Don owns equipment that he purchased several years ago for $400,000. Over the years he properly deducted $110,000 of depreciation. The depreciation will have to be recaptured as ordinary income on the sale. There is a $90,000 mortgage on the property. Don has an offer for the equipment from an individual who says he will pay $100,000 down and $100,000 per year for five years. There is no mention of interest. As the mortgage is nonassumable, Don will pay off the mortgage using most of the down payment. Don is age 61, and proceeds from the sale along with a pension from his employer will provide for his retirement. Don plans to retire next year. He currently has a 25% marginal tax rate. Discuss the tax implications of the sale. Is there anything Don can do to improve his situation?

I:11-63 Troy Tools manufactures over one hundred different hand tools used by mechanics, carpenters, and plumbers. Troy's cost accounting system has always been very simple. The costs allocated to inventory have included only materials, direct labor, and factory overhead. Other overhead costs such as costs of the personnel department, purchasing, payroll, and computer services have never been treated as manufacturing overhead even though many of the activities of the departments relate to the manufacturing operations. You are preparing Troy's tax return for the first time and determine that the company is not following the uniform capitalization rules prescribed in the tax law. You have explained to the company's president that there is a problem, and she is reluctant to change accounting methods. She says allocating these costs to the many products the company makes will be a time-consuming and expensive process. She feels that the cost of determining the additional amounts to include in inventory under the uniform capitalization rules will probably be more than the additional tax that the company will pay. What is the appropriate way to handle this situation? (See the *Statements on Standards for Tax Services* section in Chapter I:15 for a discussion of these issues.)

TAX RESEARCH PROBLEMS

I:11-64 Eagle and Hill Corporations discuss the terms of a land sale, and they agree to a price of $230,000. Eagle wants to use the installment sale method, but is not sure Hill is a reliable borrower. As a result, Eagle requires Hill to place the entire purchase price in escrow to be released in five yearly installments by the escrow agent. Is the installment method available to Eagle?

A partial list of research sources is:

- Rev. Rul. 77-294, 1977-2 C.B. 173
- Rev. Rul. 79-91, 1979-1 C.B. 179
- *H. O. Williams v. U.S.*, 46 AFTR 1725, 55-1 USTC ¶9220 (5th Cir., 1955)

I:11-65 Texas Corporation disassembles old automobiles for the purpose of reselling their components (i.e., different types of metals, plastics, rubber, and other materials). Texas sells some of the items for scrap, but must pay to dispose of environmentally hazardous plastics and rubber. At year-end, Texas Corporation has a difficult time determining the cost of the individual parts that are stacked in piles. In fact, it would be very expensive to even weigh some of the materials on hand. Texas has followed the practice of having two experienced employees estimate the weight of different stacks and then price them based on quotes found in trade journals. If Texas must pay to dispose of an item, it is assigned a value of zero. In other words, Texas does not value its inventory using standard FIFO or LIFO methods. Is such a practice acceptable?

A partial list of research sources is:

- Reg. Secs. 1.471-2(a) and 1.471-3(d)
- *Morrie Chaitlen*, 1978 PH T.C. Memo ¶78,006, 37 TCM 17
- *Justus & Parker Co.*, 13 BTA 127 (1928)

I:11-66 Apple Corporation has never been audited before the current year. An audit is now needed from a CPA because the company is expanding rapidly and plans to issue stock to the public in a secondary offering. A CPA firm has been doing preliminary evaluations of the Apple Corporation's accounts and records. One major problem involves the valuation of inventory under GAAP. Apple Corporation has been valuing its inventory under the cost method and no write-downs have been made for obsolescence. A review of the inventory indicates that obsolescence and excess spare parts in the inventory are two major

problems. The CPA states that for GAAP the company will be required to write down its inventory by 25% of its stated amount, or $100,000, and charge this amount against net income from operations for the current period. Otherwise, a "clean opinion" will not be rendered. The company controller asks your advice regarding the tax consequences from the obsolescence and spare parts inventory write-downs for the current year and the procedures for changing to the LCM method for tax purposes. Apple Corporation is on a calendar year, and the date of your contact with the company is December 1 of the current year.

A partial list of research sources is:

- Secs. 446 and 471
- Reg. Secs. 1.446-1(e)(3), 1.471-2 and 1.471-4
- *American Liberty Pipe Line Co. v. CIR*, 32 AFTR 1099, 44-2 USTC ¶9408 (5th Cir., 1944)
- *Thor Power Tool Co. v. CIR*, 43 AFTR 2d 79-362, 79-1 USTC ¶9139 (USSC, 1979)

problems: The CPA states that if the IRS of the company will be required to write down its inventory by 25% of this stock amount, or $100,000, and charge this amount against not receive into operations for the current period. Otherwise, a clean opinion will not be rendered. The company's controller takes your advice regarding the tax consequences from the objectionable balance sheet items for you to determine for the client whether to file reductions of claims to the LIFO method from expenses. Apply Corporation with a calendar year and the date of announcement with the company, and notified of the client's year.

A partial list of research sources is:

• Sections 446 and 471

• Treas. Reg. §446-1(e)(2)(i)(a); §471-1 and 1.471-2

• American Lighting Operating Co., Inc., B-A-FTC 100, 73-2 USTC ¶9606 (4th Cir. 1991).

• Thor Power Tool Corp. CIR 439 U.S. 522, 99 S. Ct. 773, 79-1 USTC ¶9139 (USSC 1979).

12

CHAPTER

PROPERTY TRANSACTIONS: NONTAXABLE EXCHANGES

LEARNING OBJECTIVES

After studying this chapter, you should be able to

▶1 Understand the tax consequences arising from a like-kind exchange

▶2 Determine the basis of property received in a like-kind exchange

▶3 Determine whether gain from an involuntary conversion may be deferred

▶4 Determine the basis of replacement property in an involuntary conversion

▶5 Determine when a gain resulting from the sale of a principal residence is excluded

Taxpayers who sell or exchange property for an amount greater or less than their basis in that property have a realized gain or loss on the sale or exchange. Almost any transfer of property is treated as a sale or other disposition (see Chapter I:5). The realized gain or loss must be recognized unless a specific Code section provides for nonrecognition treatment. If the realized gain or loss is not recognized at the time of the transaction, the nonrecognized gain or loss may be deferred in some cases and excluded in others.

The general rules related to the computation of realized and recognized gains or losses are covered in Chapter I:5. This chapter discusses three of the most common transactions that may result in *nonrecognition* of a realized gain or loss:

▶ Like-kind exchanges under Sec. 1031 (deferred gain or loss)

▶ Involuntary conversions under Sec. 1033 (deferred gain)

▶ Sales of a personal residence under Sec. 121 (excluded gain)

KEY POINT

The transactions examined in this chapter override the normal rule that provides for the recognition of realized gains and realized losses on property used in a business or held for investment.

Nonrecognition of gain treatment for like-kind exchanges, involuntary conversions, and the sale of a residence may be partially justified by the fact that taxpayers may lack the wherewithal to pay the tax despite the existence of a realized gain. For example, a taxpayer who realizes a gain due to an involuntary conversion of property (damage from fire, storm, etc.) may have to use the amount received to replace the converted property.

A typical requirement in a nontaxable exchange is that the taxpayer is required to maintain a continuing investment in comparable property (e.g., a building is exchanged for another building). In essence, a change in form rather than a change in substance occurs.

A transaction generally considered to be nontaxable may be taxable in part. In a like-kind exchange, for example, the taxpayer may also receive money or property that is not like-kind property. If non–like-kind property or money is received, the realized gain is taxable to the extent of the sum of the money and the fair market value (FMV) of the non–like-kind property received.[1]

LIKE-KIND EXCHANGES

OBJECTIVE 1

Understand the tax consequences arising from a like-kind exchange

Section 1031(a) provides that "No gain or loss shall be recognized on the exchange of property held for productive use in a trade or business or for investment if such property is exchanged solely for property of like-kind which is to be held either for productive use in a trade or business or for investment."[2]

In a **like-kind exchange**, both the property transferred and the property received must be held either for productive use in the trade or business or for investment.

EXAMPLE I:12-1 ▶

Tom owns land used in his trade or business. He exchanges the land for other land, which is to be held for investment. No gain or loss is recognized by Tom because he has exchanged property used in a trade or business for like-kind property to be held for investment. ◀

EXAMPLE I:12-2 ▶

REAL-WORLD EXAMPLE

An exchange or trade of professional football player contracts qualifies as a like-kind exchange. Rev. Rul. 71-137, 1971-1 C.B. 104.

Dawn's automobile is held for personal use. She exchanges the automobile, with a $10,000 basis, for stock of AT&T with a $12,000 FMV. The stock is held for investment. A $2,000 gain is recognized because the automobile is not used in Dawn's trade or business or held for investment. The exchange is not a like-kind exchange because neither personal-use assets nor stock qualify as like-kind property. ◀

ADDITIONAL COMMENT

The mandatory nonrecognition of loss under Sec. 1031 can be avoided by selling the old property in one transaction and buying the new property in a separate, unrelated transaction.

Section 1031 is not an elective provision. If the exchange qualifies as a like-kind exchange, nonrecognition of gain or loss is mandatory. To qualify for like-kind exchange treatment, a direct exchange must occur and the property exchanged must be like-kind. A taxpayer who prefers to recognize a loss on an exchange must structure the transaction to avoid having the exchange qualify as a like-kind exchange.

LIKE-KIND PROPERTY DEFINED

CHARACTER OF THE PROPERTY. To be a nontaxable exchange under Sec. 1031, the property exchanged must be like-kind. The Treasury Regulations specify that "the words

---

[1] Sec. 1031(b).

[2] Sec. 1031(a).

'like-kind' have reference to the nature or character of the property and not to its grade or quality."[3] Thus, exchanges of real property qualify even if the properties are dissimiliar.

EXAMPLE I:12-3 ▶ Eric owns an apartment building held for investment. Eric exchanges the building for farmland to be used in his trade or business. The exchange is a like-kind exchange because both the building and the farmland are classified as real property and both properties are used either in business or held for investment. ◀

EXAMPLE I:12-4 ▶ Trail Corporation exchanges improved real estate for unimproved real estate, both of which are held for investment. The exchange is a like-kind exchange.[4] ◀

ADDITIONAL COMMENT

Real property is often referred to as real estate.

LOCATION OF THE PROPERTY. Transfers of real property located in the U.S. and real property located outside the U.S. after July 9, 1989, are not like-kind exchanges. Exchanges of personal property predominantly used in the United States and personal property used outside of the United States that occur after June 8, 1997, are not like-kind exchanges. To determine where the property is predominantly used, the two-year period ending on the date the property is exchanged is analyzed. For property received, the location of predominant use is determined by analyzing the use during the two-year period after the property is received.

PROPERTY MUST BE THE SAME CLASS. An exchange is not a like-kind exchange when property of one class is exchanged for property of a different kind or class.[5] For example, if real property is exchanged for personal property (or vice versa), no like-kind exchange occurs.[6]

EXAMPLE I:12-5 ▶ Gail exchanges an office building with a $400,000 adjusted basis for an airplane with a $580,000 FMV to be used in business. This is not a like-kind exchange because the office building is real property and the airplane is personal property. Gail must recognize a $180,000 ($580,000 − $400,000) gain. ◀

EXAMPLE I:12-6 ▶ Gary exchanges a business truck for another truck to use in his business. This is an exchange of like-kind property. ◀

ADDITIONAL COMMENT

The rules in the Regulations dealing with exchanges of personal property are not interpreted as liberally as the rules relating to real property.

PROPERTY OF A LIKE CLASS. The Treasury Regulations provide that personal property of a **like class** meets the definition of *like-kind*.[7] Like class property is defined as depreciable tangible personal properties within the same General Asset Class or within the same Product Class.[8] Property within a General Asset Class consists of depreciable tangible personal property described in one of the asset classes provided in Rev. Proc. 87-56 for depreciation.[9] Some of the General Asset Classes are as follows:

▶ Office furniture, fixtures, and equipment (Asset Class 00.11)

▶ Information systems such as computers and peripheral equipment (Asset Class 00.12)

▶ Automobiles and taxis (Asset Class 00.22)

▶ Buses (Asset Class 00.23)

▶ Light general purpose trucks (Asset Class 00.241)

▶ Heavy general purpose trucks (Asset Class 00.242)

▶ Vessels, barges, tugs, and similar water-transportation equipment except those used in marine construction (Asset Class 00.28)

For purposes of the like-kind exchange provisions, a single property may not be classified in more than one General Asset Class or more than one Product Class. Furthermore, property in any General Asset Class may not be classified in a Product Class. A property's General Asset Class or Product Class is determined as of the exchange date.

---

[3] Reg. Sec. 1.1031(a)-1(b).
[4] *Ibid.*
[5] *Ibid.*
[6] Real property includes land and property attached to land in a relatively permanent manner. Personal property that is affixed to real property in a rel-

atively permanent manner is a fixture and is considered part of the real property. Personal property is all property that is not real property or a fixture.
[7] Reg. Sec. 1.1031(a)-2.
[8] Reg. Sec. 1.1031(a)-2(b).
[9] 1987-2 C.B. 674.

EXAMPLE I:12-7 ▶ Wint transfers a personal computer used in his trade or business for a printer to be used in his trade or business. The exchange is a like-kind exchange because both properties are in the same General Asset Class (00.12). ◀

EXAMPLE I:12-8 ▶ Renee transfers an airplane (Asset Class 00.21) used in her trade or business for a heavy general purpose truck to use in her trade or business. The properties are not of a like class because they are in different General Asset Classes. The heavy general purpose truck is in Asset Class 00.242. ◀

Example I:12-8 is taken from the Treasury Regulations, which further state: "Because each of the properties is within a General Asset Class, the properties may not be classified within a Product Class. The airplane and heavy general purpose truck are also not of a like kind. Therefore, the exchange does not qualify for nonrecognition of gain or loss under Sec. 1031."[10]

If two properties are not within a General Asset Class, it still may be possible to be considered like-kind if the properties are within the same Product Class. Property in a Product Class consists of depreciable tangible personal property listed in the North American Classification System prepared by the Office of Management and Budget.[11] The Regulations state that an exchange of a grader for a scraper is an exchange of properties of like class because neither property is in a General Asset Class and both properties are listed in the same Product Class.[12]

There are no like classes for intangible personal property, nondepreciable personal property, or personal property held for investment. To have a like-kind exchange of property held for investment, the property must be exchanged for like-kind property. To determine whether an exchange of intangible personal property is a like-kind exchange, one must consider the type of right involved as well as the underlying property to which the intangible property relates. An exchange of a copyright for a novel for a copyright on a different novel is a like-kind exchange, but the exchange of a copyright on a novel for a copyright on a song is not a like-kind exchange.[13]

NON–LIKE-KIND PROPERTY EXCHANGES. An exchange of inventory or securities does not qualify as a like-kind exchange.[14]

EXAMPLE I:12-9 ▶ Antonio, a dealer in farm equipment, exchanges a new combine for other property in the same General Asset Class to be used in Antonio's trade or business. Because Antonio is a dealer, the new combine is inventory and the exchange does not qualify as a like-kind exchange. ◀

EXAMPLE I:12-10 ▶ Nancy owns Able Corporation stock as an investment. Nancy exchanges the stock for antiques to be held as investments. This exchange is taxable because stock does not qualify as like-kind property. ◀

In most cases, to qualify as a like-kind exchange of personal property, the property must be nearly identical. For example, livestock of different sexes are not like-kind property.[15] An exchange of gold bullion held for investment for silver bullion held for investment is not a like-kind exchange. Silver and gold are intrinsically different metals and primarily are used in different ways.[16] Currency exchanges are not like-kind exchanges,[17] and the exchange of a partnership interest for an interest in another partnership is not a like-kind exchange.[18]

---

[10] Reg. Sec. 1.1031(a)-2(b)(7) Ex. 2.
[11] Reg. Sec. 1.1031(a)-2(b)(3).
[12] Reg. Sec. 1.1031(a)-2(b)(7) Ex. 3.
[13] Reg. Sec. 1.1031(a)-2(c)(1).
[14] Sec. 1031(a)(2). An exchange of stock is not a like-kind exchange. However, an exchange of stock is a nontaxable exchange if the exchange is related to a tax-free reorganization.

[15] Sec. 1031(e).
[16] Rev. Rul. 82-166, 1982-2 C.B. 190.
[17] Rev. Rul. 74-7, 1974-1 C.B. 198.
[18] Sec. 1031(a)(2).

EXCHANGE OF SECURITIES. The like-kind exchange rules do not apply to stocks, bonds, or notes.[19] However, Sec. 1036 provides that no gain or loss is recognized on the exchange of common stock for common stock or preferred stock for preferred stock in the same corporation. Sec. 1036 applies even if voting common stock is exchanged for nonvoting common stock of the same corporation. The nontaxable exchange of stock of the same corporation may be between two stockholders or a stockholder and the corporation.[20]

Section 1036 does not apply to exchanges of common stock for preferred stock; stock for bonds of same corporation, or any kind of stock in different corporations.

EXAMPLE I:12-11 ▶ Kelly owns common stock of Best Corporation. Best issues class B common stock to Kelly in exchange for her common stock. No gain or loss is recognized because this is an exchange of common stock for common stock in the same corporation. If Best issues its preferred stock for Kelly's common stock, Kelly will have a recognized gain or loss unless the exchange is part of a tax-free reorganization. ◀

EXAMPLE I:12-12 ▶ Shirley owns 100 shares of Top Corporation common stock. The stock has a $40,000 adjusted basis and a $50,000 FMV. Bob owns 100 shares of Star Corporation common stock with a $50,000 FMV. If Shirley and Bob exchange their stock, the exchange is taxable, and Shirley has a $10,000 ($50,000 − $40,000) recognized gain. The exchange is neither a like-kind exchange nor an exchange of stock for stock of the same corporation. ◀

A DIRECT EXCHANGE MUST OCCUR

To qualify as a like-kind exchange, a direct exchange of property must occur.[21] Thus, the sale of property and the subsequent purchase of like-kind property does not qualify as a like-kind exchange unless the two transactions are interdependent.

EXAMPLE I:12-13 ▶ Karen sells a lathe used in her business to Rashad for an amount greater than the lathe's adjusted basis. After the sale, Karen purchases another lathe from David. The gain is recognized because these two transactions do not qualify as an exchange of like-kind property. ◀

A sale and a subsequent purchase may be treated as an exchange if the two transactions are interdependent. The IRS indicates that a nontaxable exchange may exist when the taxpayer sells property to a dealer and then purchases like-kind property from the same dealer.[22]

THREE-PARTY EXCHANGES

The typical two-party exchange is not always practical. If both parties do not own like-kind property that meets each other's needs, a three-party exchange might be necessary. A three-party exchange is also useful when the taxpayer is willing to exchange property for like-kind property but is not willing to sell the property to a prospective buyer. The taxpayer's unwillingness to sell the property may be motivated by the desire to avoid an immediate tax on a gain resulting from the sale of the property. Therefore, the taxpayer may arrange to have the prospective buyer purchase property from a third party that fulfills the taxpayer's needs. The three-party exchange can be an effective way of allowing the taxpayer to consummate a like-kind exchange.

EXAMPLE I:12-14 ▶ Kathy owns a farm in Nebraska, which Dick offers to purchase. Kathy is not willing to sell the farm but is willing to exchange the farm for an apartment complex in Arizona. The complex is available for sale. Dick purchases the apartment complex in Arizona from Allyson and transfers it to Kathy in exchange for Kathy's farm. The farm and the apartment complex each have a $900,000 FMV. For Kathy, the transaction qualifies as a like-kind exchange because it is a direct exchange of business real property (the farm) for investment real estate (the apartment complex). For Dick, the exchange is not a like-kind exchange. ◀

KEY POINT
Transfers of property in a three-party exchange must be part of a single, integrated plan. It is important that the taxpayers can show their intent to enter into a like-kind exchange even though contractual interdependence is not necessary to the finding of an exchange.

In the example above, the exchange is convenient for all the parties. However, it is not always this convenient to execute a three-party exchange. For example, Kathy may want

---

[19] Reg. Sec. 1.1031(a)-1(a)(1)(ii).
[20] Reg. Sec. 1.1036-1(a).

[21] Sec. 1031(a).
[22] Rev. Rul. 61-119, 1961-1 C.B. 395.

to own an apartment complex in Arizona, but the property she prefers may not be currently available. In this case, a nonsimultaneous exchange may occur.

NONSIMULTANEOUS EXCHANGE. A nonsimultaneous exchange is treated as a like-kind exchange if the exchange is completed within a specified time period. The property to be received in the exchange must be identified within 45 days after the date of the transfer of the property relinquished in the exchange. The replacement property must be received within the earlier of 180 days after the date the taxpayer transfers the property relinquished in the exchange or the due date for filing a return (including extensions) for the year in which the transfer of the relinquished property occurs.[23]

EXAMPLE I:12-15 ▶ On May 5, 2010, Joal transfers property to Lauren, who transfers cash to an escrow agent. The escrow agent is to purchase suitable like-kind property for Joal. Joal does not have actual or constructive receipt of the cash during the delayed period. To be a like-kind exchange for Joal, the suitable like-kind property must be identified by June 19, 2010 (45 days after the transfer), and Joal must receive the property by November 1, 2010 (180 days after the transfer). ◀

EXAMPLE I:12-16 ▶ Assume the same facts as in the above example except that the transfer by Joal occurs on November 10, 2010. To be a like-kind exchange for Joal, the suitable like-kind property must be identified by December 25, 2010, and Joal must receive the property by April 15, 2011, unless Joal files an automatic four-month extension for the filing of his return (i.e., the due date is extended until August 15, 2011). In such a case, the property must be received no later than 180 days following the transfer of the property relinquished in the exchange, or by May 9, 2011 (i.e., 180 days after November 10, 2010). ◀

RECEIPT OF BOOT

Taxpayers who want to exchange property do not always own property of equal value. To complete the exchange, non–like-kind property or money may be given or received. Cash and non–like-kind property constitute **boot**.

Gain is recognized to the extent of the boot received. However, the amount of recognized gain is limited to the amount of the taxpayer's realized gain.[24] In effect, the realized gain serves as a ceiling for the amount of the recognized gain. The receipt of boot as part of a nontaxable exchange does not cause a realized loss to be recognized.[25]

EXAMPLE I:12-17 ▶ Mario exchanges business equipment with a $50,000 adjusted basis for $10,000 cash and business equipment with a $65,000 FMV. The realized gain is $25,000 ($75,000 − $50,000). Because the $10,000 of boot received is less than the $25,000 realized gain, the recognized gain is $10,000. ◀

EXAMPLE I:12-18 ▶ Mary exchanges business equipment with a $70,000 adjusted basis for $20,000 cash and business equipment with a $65,000 FMV. Her realized gain is $15,000 ($85,000 − $70,000). Because the $20,000 of boot received is more than the $15,000 realized gain, $15,000 of gain is recognized. ◀

Taxing part or all of the gain when cash is received in like-kind exchanges is consistent with the wherewithal-to-pay concept. However, boot may not always be in the form of a liquid asset. If non–like-kind property other than cash is received as boot, the amount of the boot is the property's FMV.

EXAMPLE I:12-19 ▶ Jane exchanges land held as an investment with a $70,000 basis for other land with a $100,000 FMV and a motorcycle with a $2,000 FMV. The acquired land is to be held for investment, and the motorcycle is for personal use. Personal-use property is non–like-kind property and constitutes boot. The realized gain is $32,000 [($100,000 + $2,000) − $70,000]. The amount of boot received is equal to the FMV of the motorcycle. The recognized gain is $2,000, the lesser of the amount of boot received ($2,000) or the realized gain ($32,000). ◀

---

[23] Secs. 1031(a)(3)(A) and (B).
[24] Sec. 1031(b).
[25] Sec. 1031(c).

EXAMPLE I:12-20 ▶
SELF-STUDY
QUESTION

Why is the relief of a liability treated as if one has received cash?

ANSWER

If it were not treated as such, a taxpayer could receive cash shortly before the exchange by borrowing from a bank, using the property as collateral. Then, if the taxpayer is relieved of the debt in the like-kind exchange, he or she would still have cash without having paid a tax on the gain.

Assume the same facts in Example I:12-19 except that Jane uses the motorcycle in a business. The motorcycle is boot, and a $2,000 gain is still recognized because the exchange of real property for personal property is not a like-kind exchange. ◀

PROPERTY TRANSFERS INVOLVING LIABILITIES. If a liability is assumed (or the property is taken subject to a liability), the amount of the liability is considered money received by the taxpayer on the exchange.[26] One who assumes the debt or takes the property subject to a liability is treated as having paid cash, while the party that is relieved of the debt is treated as having received cash. If each party assumes a liability of the other party, only the net liability given or received is treated as boot.[27]

EXAMPLE I:12-21 ▶

Mary exchanges land with a $550,000 FMV that is used in her business for Doug's building, which has a $450,000 FMV. Mary's basis in the land is $400,000, and the land is subject to a liability of $100,000, which Doug assumes. Mary's realized gain is $150,000 [($450,000 + $100,000) − $400,000]. Because assumption of the $100,000 liability is treated as boot, Mary recognizes a $100,000 gain. ◀

EXAMPLE I:12-22 ▶

Matt owns an office building with a $700,000 basis, which is subject to a liability of $200,000. Susan owns an apartment complex with a $900,000 FMV, which is subject to a $150,000 liability. Matt and Susan exchange buildings and assume the related liabilities. Matt's realized gain is $250,000 [($900,000 + $200,000) − ($700,000 + $150,000)]. Matt receives boot of $50,000 ($200,000 − $150,000) and recognizes a $50,000 gain. ◀

BASIS OF PROPERTY RECEIVED

OBJECTIVE 2

Determine the basis of property received in a like-kind exchange

LIKE-KIND PROPERTY RECEIVED. The basis of property received in a nontaxable exchange is equal to the adjusted basis of the property exchanged increased by gain recognized and reduced by any boot received or loss recognized on the exchange.[28]

Basis of property received in a nontaxable exchange	=	Basis of property exchanged	−	Boot received	+	Gain recognized	−	Loss recognized[29]

EXAMPLE I:12-23 ▶

ADDITIONAL COMMENT

In effect the formula used to calculate the basis of the new property involves nothing more than journalizing the transaction and adjusting the basis of the new property by an amount needed to make the entry balance.

Chuck, who is in the business of racing horses, exchanges a racehorse with a $30,000 basis for $10,000 cash and a trotter with an $80,000 FMV. Chuck's realized gain is $60,000 [($80,000 + $10,000) − $30,000], and $10,000 of the gain is recognized because the boot received is less than the realized gain. Chuck's basis for the replacement property (i.e., the trotter) is $30,000 ($30,000 basis of property exchanged − $10,000 of boot received + $10,000 of gain recognized). ◀

The basis of the like-kind property received can also be computed by subtracting the unrecognized gain from its FMV or by adding the unrecognized loss to its FMV. Chuck's $30,000 basis for the trotter in Example I:12-23 may be computed by subtracting the $50,000 of unrecognized gain from the $80,000 FMV.

EXAMPLE I:12-24 ▶

KEY POINT

The basis adjustment is the mechanism that ensures that gain or loss is temporarily postponed rather than permanently excluded.

Pam, who operates a circus, exchanges an elephant with a $15,000 basis for $3,000 cash and a tiger with a $10,000 FMV. The $2,000 realized loss [($10,000 + $3,000) − $15,000] is not recognized. The receipt of boot does not cause a realized loss to be recognized. Pam's basis for the replacement property (i.e., the tiger) is $12,000 ($15,000 basis of property exchanged − $3,000 boot received). ◀

As indicated earlier, realized gains and losses resulting from nontaxable exchanges are deferred. This deferral is reflected in the basis of property received and is illustrated in the

---

[26] Sec. 1031(d). If a liability is assumed, the taxpayer agrees to pay the debt. If property is taken subject to the liability, the taxpayer is responsible for the debt only to the extent that the property could be used to pay the debt.
[27] Reg. Sec. 1.1031(b)-1(c).

[28] Sec. 1031(d).
[29] A loss is recognized only when the taxpayer transfers boot with a basis greater than its FMV. Transfers of non–like-kind property (i.e., boot) are discussed in a separate section of this chapter.

two preceding examples. In Example I:12-23, the $50,000 ($60,000 − $10,000) unrecognized gain may be recognized when the trotter is sold or exchanged in a taxable transaction, because the basis of the replacement property is less than its FMV by the amount of the deferred gain. For example, if the trotter is sold in a taxable transaction for its $80,000 FMV, the $50,000 ($80,000 − $30,000 basis) of previously unrecognized gain would be recognized. In Example I:12-24, the $2,000 unrecognized loss is reflected in the basis of the tiger. If Pam sells the tiger for its $10,000 FMV, a $2,000 loss ($10,000 − $12,000 basis) is recognized.

If more than one item of like-kind property is received, the basis is allocated among the properties in proportion to their relative FMVs on the date of the exchange.

EXAMPLE I:12-25 ▶

Saul, who operates a zoo, exchanges a boa constrictor with a $300 basis for a python with a $400 FMV and an anaconda with a $600 FMV. The $700 realized gain [($400 + $600) − $300] is not recognized. The total bases of the properties received is $300. This amount is allocated to the properties (i.e., the python and the anaconda) based on their relative FMVs. Saul's basis for the python is $120 [($400 ÷ $1,000) × $300], and the basis for the anaconda is $180 [($600 ÷ $1,000) × $300]. ◀

NON–LIKE-KIND PROPERTY RECEIVED. The basis of non–like-kind property received is "an amount equivalent to its FMV at the date of the exchange."[30]

EXAMPLE I:12-26
KEY POINT

Steve had basis of $20,000 before the exchange. Since he recognized gain of $5,000, the total basis of the two assets should be $25,000.

Steve exchanges a punch press with a $20,000 adjusted basis for a press brake with a $50,000 FMV and $5,000 of marketable securities. Steve's realized gain is $35,000 [($50,000 + $5,000) − $20,000], and $5,000 of the realized gain is recognized due to the receipt of boot. Steve's basis for the marketable securities is $5,000, and the basis for the press brake is $20,000 ($20,000 basis of property exchanged − $5,000 boot received + $5,000 gain recognized). ◀

STOP & THINK

Question: Chris Reedy owns 40 houses that he uses as rental property. All houses have a FMV greater than their adjusted basis. Chris wishes to diversify his investments and is considering selling ten of his houses and using the proceeds to purchase other types of investment assets such as stocks, bonds, commercial parking lots and land near town that he expects to increase in value. He asks you for advice.

Solution: If he sells the ten houses, he will have a gain and must pay taxes on the gain. He could defer the gain by exchanging the houses for like-kind property. Stocks and bonds are not like-kind property, but the commercial parking lots and the land should qualify as like-kind property, therefore the tax law encourages him to exchange the houses for the commercial parking lot and/or the land.

ADDITIONAL COMMENT

The running of the two-year holding period is suspended during any period in which the property holder's risk of loss is substantially diminished.

EXCHANGES BETWEEN RELATED PARTIES

Prior to 1990, related taxpayers could often use the like-kind exchange provisions to lower taxes because the tax basis for the property received is determined by the basis of the property exchanged. Related taxpayers could take advantage of the shift in tax basis to transfer a gain on a subsequent sale to a related party.[31] However, exchanges of property between related parties are not like-kind exchanges under current law if either party disposes of the property within two years of the exchange. Any gain resulting from the original exchange is recognized in the year of the subsequent disposition.[32] Dispositions due to death or involuntary conversion, or for non–tax avoidance purposes are disregarded.[33]

EXAMPLE I:12-27 ▶

Melon Corporation, which is 100% owned by Linda, owned land with a basis of $200,000 that was held for investment. Rick wanted to purchase the land for $900,000. Linda owned an office building with a basis of $750,000 and a FMV of $900,000. Instead of selling the land to Rick, Melon Corporation exchanged the land for Linda's office building in December 2009.

---

[30] Reg. Sec. 1.1031(d)-1(c).
[31] The definition of *related parties* is the same as those for Sec. 267(a) which is discussed in Chapter I:6, and includes brothers, sisters, parents, children, and corporations where the taxpayer owns at least 50% in value. (See Sec. 1031(f)(3).)

[32] Sec. 1031(f)(1)(C).
[33] Sec. 1031(f)(2).

ADDITIONAL
COMMENT

If Linda in Example I:12-27 sells the land to Rick for $910,000, she has a $150,000 recognized gain on the exchange and a $10,000 recognized gain on the sale.

Two months later, Linda sells the land to Rick for $900,000. The exchange of the land for the office building is not a like-kind exchange because one of the related parties disposes of the property within two years of the exchange. In 2010, Melon's recognized gain on the exchange of the land is $700,000 ($900,000 − $200,000) and Linda's recognized gain on the exchange of the office building is $150,000 ($900,000 − $750,000). Because Linda's basis for the land is now $900,000, no gain is recognized on the sale of the land to Rick. ◄

If the parties in Example I:12-27 were not related, a like-kind exchange occurred in 2009 and Linda's gain on the sale of the land to Rick is $150,000 ($900,000 − $750,000). Importantly, the exchange is not a like-kind exchange if Linda does not hold the land for investment or for use in her trade or business after receiving it from Melon.

TRANSFER OF NON–LIKE-KIND PROPERTY

In all of the preceding examples that include a transfer of boot, the transferor (i.e., the taxpayer) received boot. If the taxpayer transfers non–like-kind property, gain or loss equal to the difference between the FMV and the adjusted basis of the non–like-kind property surrendered must be recognized. However, if the non–like-kind property is a personal use asset, the loss is not recognized.

EXAMPLE I:12-28 ▶ Shirley exchanges land with a $30,000 basis ($46,000 FMV) and marketable securities with a $10,000 basis ($14,000 FMV) to David for land with a $60,000 FMV in a transaction that otherwise qualifies as a like-kind exchange. Because the non–like-kind property that Shirley transfers has a FMV greater than its basis, she recognizes $4,000 ($14,000 − $10,000) of gain. Shirley's basis for the land received is $44,000 ($30,000 + $10,000 + $4,000), which is the basis of both assets exchanged plus the gain recognized on the exchange. ◄

EXAMPLE I:12-29 ▶ Paul exchanges timberland held as an investment for undeveloped land with a $200,000 FMV to use in his business. Paul's basis for the timberland is $125,000. His tractor with a $6,000 basis and a $4,000 FMV is also transferred. Because the non–like-kind property (i.e., the tractor) that Paul transfers has a FMV less than its basis, he recognizes a $2,000 ($4,000 − $6,000) loss. Paul's basis for the undeveloped land is $129,000 ($125,000 + $6,000 − $2,000). ◄

In Example I:12-29, Paul recognizes a loss on the non–like-kind property he surrenders, despite receiving property in the aggregate with a FMV greater than the total adjusted basis of the transferred assets. Paul is actually making two exchanges. His exchange of timberland with a basis of $125,000 for undeveloped land with a $196,000 FMV is a like-kind exchange, but his exchange of the tractor with a basis of $6,000 for undeveloped land with a $4,000 FMV is a taxable exchange. In Example I:12-30 below, Ed also makes two exchanges. He has a realized and recognized gain as well as a realized but unrecognized loss.

EXAMPLE I:12-30 ▶

KEY POINT

A taxpayer who exchanges like-kind property and non–like-kind property is actually making two exchanges.

Ed owns equipment used in business with a $20,000 adjusted basis and a $15,000 FMV and marketable securities with a $10,000 basis and an $18,000 FMV. Ed exchanges the marketable securities and the equipment for business equipment in the same General Asset Class with a $33,000 FMV. Although the net realized gain is $3,000 [$33,000 − ($20,000 + $10,000)], Ed recognizes an $8,000 gain because he has transferred non–like-kind property with a $10,000 basis and an $18,000 FMV. The $5,000 realized loss on the transfer of equipment is not recognized due to the nonrecognition of gain or loss rules of Sec. 1031. Ed's basis for the equipment received is $38,000 ($20,000 + $10,000 + $8,000). ◄

HOLDING PERIOD FOR PROPERTY RECEIVED

ADDITIONAL
COMMENT

The holding period is relevant only when the asset is a capital asset or a Sec. 1231 asset.

LIKE-KIND PROPERTY. The holding period of like-kind property received in a nontaxable exchange includes the holding period of the property exchanged if the like-kind property surrendered is a capital asset or an asset that is Sec. 1231 property. In essence, the holding period of the property exchanged carries over to the holding period of the like-kind property received.[34] The rule regarding the holding period carryover is consistent with the notion of a continuing investment in the underlying property that has been transferred.

---

[34] Sec. 1223(1) and Reg. Sec. 1.1223-1(a).

BOOT. The holding period for the boot property received begins the day after the date of the exchange.[35]

EXAMPLE I:12-31 ▶ Mario owns a Van Gogh painting acquired on May 1, 1995, as an investment. He exchanges the painting on April 10, 2010, for a Picasso sculpture and marketable securities to be held as investments. The holding period for the sculpture begins on May 1, 1995, and the holding period for the marketable securities starts on April 11, 2010. ◀

The like-kind exchange provisions are summarized in Topic Review I:12-1.

Topic Review I:12-1

Section 1031—Like-Kind Exchanges

▶ Gains and losses are not recognized for like-kind exchanges.

▶ Nonrecognition of gains and losses is mandatory if the exchange is a like-kind exchange.

▶ Section 1031 applies to exchanges of property used in a trade or business or held for investment.

▶ Property exchanged and received must be like-kind.

▶ Subject to certain time constraints, a nonsimultaneous exchange may qualify as a like-kind exchange.

▶ Some gain may be recognized if the taxpayer receives or gives non–like-kind property (boot) in an otherwise like-kind exchange.

▶ A loss may be recognized if the taxpayer transfers non–like-kind property (boot) in an otherwise like-kind exchange.

▶ The basis of property received in an exchange is the basis of the property exchanged less the boot received plus the gain recognized and less any loss recognized.

▶ The nonrecognized gain or loss is deferred.

▶ The holding period of like-kind property received includes the holding period of the property exchanged.

▶ Like-kind exchange treatment does not apply between related parties if property is disposed of within two years of exchange.

INVOLUNTARY CONVERSIONS

OBJECTIVE 3

Determine whether gain from an involuntary conversion may be deferred

Taxpayers who realize a gain due to the involuntary conversion of property may elect to defer recognition of the entire gain if qualifying replacement property is acquired within a specified time period at a cost equal to or greater than the amount realized from the involuntary conversion. No gain is recognized if the property is converted "into property similar or related in service or use to the property so converted."[36]

The opportunity provided in Sec. 1033 to defer recognition of the gain reflects the fact that the taxpayer maintains a continuing investment and may lack the wherewithal to pay tax on the gain that would otherwise be recognized. Furthermore, the involuntary conversion is beyond the taxpayer's control.

KEY POINT

Unlike the like-kind exchange provisions which are mandatory, the involuntary conversion provisions are elective. Further, the involuntary conversion rules apply only to gains, not losses.

Note that the gain is deferred, not excluded. The basis of the replacement property is the property's cost reduced by the amount of gain deferred. The tax treatment for an involuntary conversion is similar to the tax treatment of a like-kind exchange.

EXAMPLE I:12-32 ▶
ADDITIONAL COMMENT

Property involved in an involuntary conversion need not be used in a trade or business or held for investment to qualify for the deferral of gain.

Lenea's warehouse with a $500,000 basis is destroyed by a hurricane. She collects $650,000 from the insurance company and purchases a new warehouse for $720,000. Lenea may elect to defer recognition of the $150,000 gain ($650,000 − $500,000). If the election is made, the basis of the new warehouse is $570,000 ($720,000 − $150,000). The $150,000 gain is merely deferred rather than excluded, because an immediate sale of the replacement property at its $720,000 FMV results in a recognized gain equal to the deferred gain on the involuntarily converted property. For example, if the new warehouse is sold for $720,000, the recognized gain is $150,000 ($720,000 − $570,000). ◀

---

[35] Sec. 1223 and Reg. Sec. 1.1223-1(a).   [36] Sec. 1033(a)(1).

**TYPICAL
MISCONCEPTION**

Occasionally, taxpayers fail to
realize that Sec. 1033 applies only
to gains, not losses.

Section 1033 does not apply to losses realized from an involuntary conversion. A taxpayer may not elect to defer recognition of a loss resulting from an involuntary conversion.

EXAMPLE I:12-33 ▶

Barry's offshore drilling rig with an $800,000 adjusted basis is destroyed by a tsunami. He collects $700,000 from the insurance company and purchases a new drilling rig for $760,000. The $100,000 loss ($700,000 − $800,000) is recognized as a casualty loss, and the basis of the new drilling rig is its $760,000 purchase price. ◀

INVOLUNTARY CONVERSION DEFINED

**ADDITIONAL
COMMENT**

Typically, an involuntary conversion consists of either a casualty or a condemnation.

For Sec. 1033 to apply, property must be compulsorily or involuntarily converted into money or other property. An **involuntary conversion** may be due to theft, seizure, requisition, condemnation, or destruction of the property. Destruction of the property may be complete or partial.[37] For purposes of Sec. 1033, destruction of property does not have to meet the "suddenness" test if the cause of destruction otherwise falls within the general concept of a casualty.[38]

An involuntary conversion occurs when a governmental unit exercises its power of eminent domain to acquire the taxpayer's property without the taxpayer's consent. Furthermore, the threat or imminence of requisition or condemnation of property may permit a taxpayer to defer recognition of gain from the sale or exchange of property under the involuntary conversion rules. Taxpayers who transfer property due to such a threat must be careful to confirm that a decision to acquire their property for public use has been made.[39] Written confirmation of potential condemnation is particularly helpful.[40]

EXAMPLE I:12-34 ▶

Bruce owns an automobile dealership near a state university campus. On a number of occasions, the president of the university expressed an interest in acquiring Bruce's property for additional parking space. The president is not certain about the availability of funds for the purchase, and the university is reluctant to have the property condemned for its use. Based on the university's interest in the property, Bruce sells the property to the Jet Corporation. The threat or imminence of conversion does not exist merely because the property is being considered for acquisition. The sale does not constitute an involuntary conversion.[41] ◀

THREAT OF CONDEMNATION. If a threat of condemnation exists and the taxpayer has reasonable grounds to believe that the property will be condemned, Sec. 1033 applies even if the taxpayer sells the property to an entity other than the governmental unit that is threatening to condemn the property.[42]

EXAMPLE I:12-35 ▶

**ADDITIONAL
COMMENT**

If the property in Example I:12-35 is later condemned, Marty may be able to defer part or all of the gain.

At its regular meeting on Tuesday night, the city commission authorized the city attorney to start the process of condemning two lots owned by Beth for use as a public park. On Wednesday afternoon, Beth sells the two lots to Marty at a gain. The sale of property to Marty is an involuntary conversion, and Beth may elect to defer recognition of the gain if she satisfies the Sec. 1033 requirements. ◀

CONVERSION MUST BE INVOLUNTARY. The conversion must be involuntary. For example, an involuntary conversion does not occur when a taxpayer pays someone to set fire to his or her building.[43] An involuntary conversion also does not occur when a taxpayer who is developing a subdivision reserves certain property for a school site and later sells the property to the school district under condemnation proceedings. In this situation, the taxpayer was required to reserve property for a school site in order to receive zoning approval for development of the subdivision.[44]

---

[37] Reg. Sec. 1.1033(a)-1.
[38] Rev. Rul. 59-102, 1959-1 C.B. 200.
[39] Rev. Rul. 63-221, 1963-2 C.B. 332, and *Joseph P. Balistrieri*, 1979 PH T.C. Memo ¶79,115, 38 TCM 526.
[40] Rev. Rul. 63-221, 1963-2 C.B. 332.

[41] *Forest City Chevrolet*, 1977 PH T.C. Memo ¶77,187, 36 TCM 768.
[42] Rev. Rul. 81-180, 1981-2 C.B. 161, and *Creative Solutions, Inc. v. U.S.*, 12 AFTR 2d 5229, 1963-2 USTC ¶9615 (5th Cir., 1963).
[43] Rev. Rul. 82-74, 1982-1 C.B. 110.
[44] Rev. Rul. 69-654, 1969-2 C.B. 162.

REAL-WORLD EXAMPLE

Because of mounting losses and declining property values, a taxpayer decided to burn down his building to collect the fire insurance proceeds. Although the building was converted into money (insurance proceeds) as a result of its destruction, this conversion was not involuntary within the meaning of Sec. 1033. Rev. Rul. 82-74, 1982-1 C.B. 110.

Although the typical involuntary conversion generally results from a casualty or condemnation, Sec. 1033 provides that certain transactions involving livestock are to be treated as involuntary conversions.[45] For example, the destruction or sale of livestock because of disease is an involuntary conversion.

TAX TREATMENT OF GAIN DUE TO INVOLUNTARY CONVERSION INTO BOOT

Gain may be deferred if the property is involuntarily converted into money or property that is not similar or related in service or use to the converted property.[46] The taxpayer must make a proper replacement of the converted property within a specific time period and elect to defer the gain.

REALIZED GAIN. The taxpayer's realized gain is the excess of the amount received due to the involuntary conversion over the adjusted basis of the property converted. The total award or proceeds received are reduced by expenses incurred to determine the amount realized (e.g., attorney's fees incurred in connection with determining the settlement to be received from a condemnation). If the payment of the award or proceeds is delayed, any amounts paid as interest are not included in determining the amount realized.[47] Amounts received as interest on an award for property condemned are taxed as ordinary income even if the interest is paid by a state or political subdivision.[48]

EXAMPLE I:12-36 ▶ Richard's property with a $100,000 basis is condemned by the city of Phoenix. Richard receives a $190,000 award and pays $1,000 in legal expenses for representation at the condemnation proceedings and $800 for an appraisal of the property. The amount realized is $188,200 [$190,000 − ($1,000 + $800)], and the realized gain is $88,200 ($188,200 − $100,000). Richard may elect to defer part or all of the realized gain if the requirements of Sec. 1033 are satisfied. ◀

ADDITIONAL COMMENT

Some or all of the realized gain is recognized if the cost of the replacement property is less than the amount realized.

GAIN RECOGNIZED. To defer the entire gain, one must purchase replacement property with a cost equal to or greater than the amount realized from the involuntary conversion. If the replacement property is purchased for an amount less than the amount realized, that portion of the realized gain equal to the excess of the amount realized from the conversion over the cost of the replacement property must be recognized.[49] Stated differently, the recognized gain is the lesser of the realized gain or the excess of the amount realized over the cost of the replacement property.

EXAMPLE I:12-37 ▶ Bob owns a restaurant with a $200,000 basis. The restaurant is destroyed by fire, and he receives insurance proceeds of $300,000. Bob's realized gain is $100,000 ($300,000 − $200,000). He purchases another restaurant for $275,000. Bob may elect to defer $75,000 of the gain under Sec. 1033, and $25,000 ($300,000 − $275,000) of Bob's gain must be recognized because he failed to reinvest all of the $300,000 insurance proceeds in a suitable replacement property. ◀

EXAMPLE I:12-38 ▶ Stacey owns a racehorse with a $450,000 basis used for breeding purposes. The racehorse is killed by lightning, and she collects $800,000 from the insurance company. Stacey's realized gain is $350,000 ($800,000 − $450,000). She purchases another racehorse for $430,000. The entire $350,000 of gain is recognized, because the amount realized from the involuntary conversion exceeds the cost of the replacement property by $370,000 ($800,000 − $430,000) which is more than the realized gain. ◀

OBJECTIVE 4

Determine the basis of replacement property in an involuntary conversion

BASIS OF REPLACEMENT PROPERTY. If replacement property is purchased, the basis of the replacement property is its cost less any deferred gain. If the taxpayer elects to defer the gain, the holding period of the replacement property includes the holding period of the converted property.[50]

[45] Secs. 1033(d) and (e). If a taxpayer sells or exchanges more livestock than normal because of a drought, the sale or exchange of the excess amount is treated as an involuntary conversion. The livestock must be other than poultry and be held by the taxpayer for draft, breeding, or dairy purposes.
[46] Sec. 1033(a)(2).
[47] *Flushingside Realty & Construction Co.*, 1943 PH T.C. Memo ¶43,286, 2 TCM 259.
[48] *Spencer D. Stewart v. CIR*, 52 AFTR 2d 83-5885, 83-2 USTC ¶9573 (9th Cir., 1983).
[49] Sec. 1033(a)(2)(A).
[50] Sec. 1223(1)(A).

EXAMPLE I:12-39 ▶ Tracy owns a yacht that is held for personal use and has a $20,000 basis. The yacht is destroyed by a storm, and Tracy collects $24,000 from the insurance company. She purchases a new $35,000 yacht for personal use and elects to defer the $4,000 ($24,000 − $20,000) gain. The basis of the new yacht is $31,000 ($35,000 − $4,000). The holding period for the new yacht includes the holding period of the destroyed yacht. ◀

SEVERANCE DAMAGES. If a portion of the taxpayer's property is condemned, the taxpayer may receive **severance damages** as compensation for a decline in the value of the retained property. For example, if access to the retained property becomes difficult or if the property is exposed to greater damage from flooding or erosion, its value may decline.

The IRS considers severance damages to be "analogous to the proceeds of property insurance; they represent compensation for damages to the property."[51] Amounts received as severance damages reduce the basis of the retained property, and any amount received in excess of the property's basis is treated as gain.[52]

EXAMPLE I:12-40 ▶ Cindy owns a 500-acre farm with a $200 basis per acre ($100,000 basis). The state condemns ten acres across the northwest corner of her farm to build a major highway. Cindy receives a condemnation award of $500 per acre for the ten acres. The highway separates the farm into a 25-acre tract and a 465-acre tract. Because her ability to efficiently use the 25-acre tract for farming is reduced, the state pays additional severance damages of $90 per acre for the 25 acres. Cindy's gain realized from condemnation of the ten acres is $3,000 [$5,000 − ($200 × 10 acres)]. The $2,250 ($90 × 25 acres) of severance damages reduce the basis of the 25-acre tract from $5,000 to $2,750 [($200 × 25 acres) − $2,250]. The reduction in basis is applied solely to the 25 acres because of its decline in value as farmland. ◀

The Sec. 1033 provisions concerning nonrecognition of gain may apply to severance damages. For instance, if severance damages are used to restore the retained property, only that portion of severance damages not spent for restoration reduces the basis of the retained property. A taxpayer who uses severance damages to purchase adjacent farmland to replace the portion of the farm condemned may use Sec. 1033 to defer a gain due to the receipt of the severance damages.[53]

REPLACEMENT PROPERTY

To qualify for nonrecognition of gain due to an involuntary conversion, the taxpayer must acquire qualified replacement property. With some exceptions, the **replacement property** must be "similar or related in service or use to the property so converted."[54] Taxpayers who own and use the property must use the functional-use test although replacement may be made with like-kind property in certain cases. A taxpayer who owns and leases the property that is involuntarily converted may use the taxpayer-use test.

FUNCTIONAL-USE TEST. The **functional-use test** is more restrictive than the like-kind test. To be considered similar or related in service or use, the replacement property must be functionally the same as the converted property. For example, the exchange of a business building for land used in business qualifies as a like-kind exchange. Replacing a building with land does not qualify as replacement property under the involuntary conversion rules. The building must be replaced with a building that is functionally the same as the converted building.

EXAMPLE I:12-41 ▶ Julie's movie theater is destroyed by fire, and she uses the insurance proceeds to purchase a skating rink. The converted property has not been replaced with property that is similar or related in service or use under the functional-use test. The election to defer gain under Sec. 1033 is not available. ◀

---

[51] Rev. Rul. 53-271, 1953-2 C.B. 36.
[52] Rev. Rul. 68-37, 1968-1 C.B. 359.
[53] Rev. Ruls. 69-240, 1969-1 C.B. 199, 73-35, 1973-1 C.B. 367, and 83-49, 1983-1 C.B. 191.
[54] Secs. 1033(a)(2)(A) and 1033(f). The replacement of property requirement

is modified when proceeds from the involuntary conversion of livestock may not be reinvested in property similar or related in use to the converted livestock because of soil contamination or other environmental contamination. Sec. 1033(f) permits the livestock to be replaced with other property, including real property, used for farming purposes.

REPLACEMENT WITH LIKE-KIND PROPERTY. If real property held for productive use in a trade or business or for investment is **condemned**, a proper replacement may be made by acquiring like-kind property.[55] This exception to the functional-use test applies only to real property used in a trade or business or held for investment.

EXAMPLE I:12-42 ▶ Ken owns a building used in his business that is condemned by the state to widen a highway. He uses the proceeds to purchase land to be held for investment. The land is a qualified replacement property because the condemned building is real property used in a trade or business, and the like-kind exchange rule may be applied to the condemnation. ◀

EXAMPLE I:12-43 ▶ Assume the same facts as in Example I:12-42 except that the building is destroyed by a violent windstorm. Ken's purchase of the investment land is not qualified replacement property because the more flexible like-kind exchange rules apply only to condemnations. He must purchase property with the same functional use as the business building. ◀

REAL-WORLD EXAMPLE

A nursery with its trees and shrubs was condemned, and the taxpayer replaced the condemned property with land and greenhouses. The replacement was considered to have been made with like-kind property. *Evert Asjes, Jr.,* 74 T.C. 1005 (1980).

If business or investment property is involuntarily converted as a result of a Presidentially declared disaster after 1994, the taxpayer may replace the property with any tangible property that is held for productive use in a trade or business.

TAXPAYER-USE TEST. The **taxpayer-use test** applies to the involuntary conversion of rental property owned by an investor. This test permits greater flexibility than the functional-use test. The principal requirement is that the owner-investor must lease out the replacement property that is acquired. However, the lessee is not required to use the leased property for the same functional use.[56]

EXAMPLE I:12-44 ▶ Sally owns an apartment complex that is rented to college students. The apartment complex is destroyed by fire. She uses the insurance proceeds to purchase a medical building that is leased to physicians. Sally has acquired a qualified replacement property under the taxpayer-use test, and the gain, if any, may be deferred if an election is made under Sec. 1033. ◀

 STOP & THINK

Question: Greg Stacey's motel is destroyed by fire on March 10 of the current year. The basis of the property is $400,000 and he receives $2,000,000 from the insurance company. Greg is concerned about the possibility of having to pay income tax on the $1,600,000 gain and is aware of the tax rules relating to involuntary conversions. Greg is considering replacing the destroyed motel by building either a new motel or an ice skating rink on the vacant lot. The cost of a new motel or an ice skating rink is expected to be $2,500,000, and he expects to borrow 60% of the cost. What tax advice would you give him?

Solution: Greg may defer the $1,600,000 gain if the involuntary conversion requirements are met and he makes a proper election. The principal issue is whether the replacement property is considered to be "similar in service or use" to the converted property. Because the functional-use test is applicable in this case, an ice skating rink is not similar property and the gain of $1,600,000 must be recognized. Conversely, the new motel is similar property and, since Greg is reinvesting an amount greater than $2,000,000, none of the gain is recognized. His basis in the new motel is $900,000 ($2,500,000 − deferred gain of $1,600,000). The fact that he borrows money and does not spend the $2,000,000 insurance proceeds does not prevent him from electing to defer the gain. The tax requirement is only that he must reinvest an amount equal to or greater than the $2,000,000 insurance proceeds. In this case, the tax law clearly encourages the taxpayer to build a new motel rather than an ice skating rink.

REAL-WORLD EXAMPLE

Taxpayer owned land and a warehouse held for rental purposes. Upon condemnation of this property, taxpayer invested the proceeds in a gas station on land already owned by the taxpayer which was also held for rental purposes. The taxpayer-use test applied, and taxpayer was able to defer the gain. Rev. Rul. 71-41, 1971-1 C.B. 223.

OBTAINING REPLACEMENT PROPERTY

The general rule is that the taxpayer must purchase the replacement property.[57] Taxpayers may purchase replacement property indirectly by purchasing control (i.e., 80% or more of the stock) of a corporation that owns the replacement property.[58] However,

---

[55] Sec. 1033(g)(1).
[56] Rev. Rul. 64-237, 1964-2 C.B. 319.
[57] To qualify as a purchase of property or stock under Sec. 1033(a)(2)(A)(ii), the unadjusted basis of the property or stock must be its cost within the mean-

ing of Sec. 1012 without considering the basis adjustment for the deferred gain. Property acquired by inheritance, gift, or a nontaxable exchange does not qualify as replacement property (see Reg. Sec. 1.1033(a)-2(c)(4)).
[58] Sec. 1033(a)(2)(A) and Reg. Sec. 1.1033(a)-2(c).

this exception is not applicable to the purchase of like-kind property to replace condemned real property used in a trade or business or held for investment.[59]

EXAMPLE I:12-45 ▶ Hank's airplane, used in business, is hijacked and taken to a foreign country. He uses the insurance proceeds to purchase 80% of Fast Corporation stock. Fast Corporation owns an airplane which is qualified replacement property. The involuntary conversion requirements are satisfied if Hank elects to defer any gain realized. ◀

EXAMPLE I:12-46 ▶ Lynn's farm is condemned by the state for public use. She uses the proceeds to purchase 80% of Vermont Corporation stock. Vermont Corporation owns eight parking lots. A qualified replacement property has not been obtained through the stock purchase because the parking lots are not functionally the same as the farm. A qualified replacement does occur if she buys the parking lots from the Vermont Corporation. ◀

TIME REQUIREMENTS FOR REPLACEMENT

TYPICAL MISCONCEPTION

The first taxable year in which any part of the gain on the conversion is realized is the year in which the insurance proceeds are received, not the year in which the involuntary conversion took place.

To qualify for nonrecognition of gain treatment, the converted property must be replaced within a specified time period. The general rule is that the period begins with the date of disposition of the converted property and ends "two years after the close of the first taxable year in which any part of the gain upon the conversion is realized."[60] If the involuntary conversion is due to condemnation or requisition, or the threat of such, the replacement period begins on the date of the threat or imminence of the requisition or condemnation. The replacement period may be extended by obtaining permission from the IRS.[61]

EXAMPLE I:12-47 ▶ On December 8, 2010, Craig's business property was destroyed by fire. Craig receives insurance proceeds in 2011 and elects to defer recognition of the gain. He must replace the property between December 8, 2010, and December 31, 2013. The two-year time period includes 2013 because the gain is realized when the insurance proceeds are received in 2011. ◀

KEY POINT

The replacement period is three years instead of two years on the condemnation of real property used in a business or held for investment.

The replacement period is longer if the involuntary conversion is due to the condemnation of real property (excluding inventory) held for productive use in a trade or business or for investment. The replacement period ends three years after the close of the first tax year in which any part of the gain is realized.[62] This provision for a longer replacement period applies to the same type of real property that may be replaced with like-kind property.

EXAMPLE I:12-48 ▶ Beth owns a building used in her dry cleaning business. In 2010, the state condemns the building and awards Beth an amount greater than the adjusted basis of the building. Beth may replace the property with like-kind property, and the replacement period ends on December 31, 2013. ◀

The involuntary conversion rules are summarized in Topic Review I:12-2.

Topic Review I:12-2

Section 1033: Involuntary Conversions

1. Section 1033 applies only to gains, not losses.
2. Nonrecognition of gain under Section 1033 is elective. (Nonrecognition of gain is mandatory in a direct conversion, but direct conversions seldom occur.)
3. Section 1033 applies to involuntary conversions of all types of properties.
4. Some gain may be recognized if the taxpayer replaces the involuntarily converted property with property that costs less than the amount realized in the involuntary conversion.
5. The nonrecognized gain is deferred.
6. The basis of property acquired to replace the involuntarily converted property is the cost of the property less the deferred gain.
7. Property acquired to replace the involuntarily converted property generally must be functionally related property.
8. The required replacement period generally begins with the date of disposition of the converted property and ends two years after the close of the first taxable year in which any part of the gain on the conversion is realized. (A three-year period applies to condemnations of real property used in a trade or business or held for the production of income.)

---

[59] Sec. 1033(g)(2).
[60] Sec. 1033(a)(2)(B).
[61] Sec. 1033(a)(2)(B)(ii).
[62] Sec. 1033(g)(4).

SALE OF PRINCIPAL RESIDENCE

OBJECTIVE 5

Determine when a gain resulting from the sale of a principal residence is excluded

Congress uses the tax law to encourage home ownership in many ways: (1) Real estate taxes and interest on a mortgage used to acquire a principal or second residence are deductible (see Chapter I:7), (2) part or all of the interest on home equity debt may be deductible, and (3) taxpayers may elect to exclude up to $250,000 ($500,000 on a joint return) of gain from the sale of a principal residence.

Individuals who sell or exchange their personal residence after May 6, 1997, may exclude up to $250,000 of gain if it was owned and occupied as a principal residence for at least two years of the five-year period before the sale or exchange. A married couple may exclude up to $500,000 when filing jointly if both meet the use test, at least one meets the ownership test and neither spouse is ineligible for the exclusion because he or she sold or exchanged a residence within the last two years.[63]

The Sec. 121 exclusion is available regardless of age, and taxpayers do not have to purchase a replacement residence. Any gain not excluded is capital gain because a personal residence is a capital asset. A loss on the sale or exchange of a personal residence is not deductible because the residence is personal-use property.[64]

EXAMPLE I:12-49 ▶ Maki, who is single and 35 years old, sells her principal residence that she purchased four years ago and realizes a $230,000 gain. Maki may exclude the entire gain regardless of her age or whether she purchases a new principal residence. ◀

EXAMPLE I:12-50 ▶ Assume the same facts as in the above example except the realized gain is $320,000. Maki may exclude $250,000 and recognize a $70,000 LTCG. ◀

EXAMPLE I:12-51 ▶ Assume the same facts as in Example I:12-50 except Maki is married to Yixin, and they have owned and occupied the residence for the last four years. They may exclude the entire $320,000 gain. ◀

ADDITIONAL COMMENT

The elimination of taxes on up to $500,000 of gain from the sale of a personal residence has been a great benefit for many taxpayers who had large built-in gains.

Prior to the Taxpayer Relief Act of 1997, taxpayers could defer gain resulting from sale of a personal residence if they purchased another principal residence within two years at a cost greater than the adjusted sales price. Taxpayers who were at least 55 years old could exclude up to $125,000 of gain resulting from the sale of a personal residence. The deferral provision of Sec. 1034 has been repealed; the exclusion has been increased to $250,000 or $500,000; and taxpayers may exclude gain regardless of age and use the exclusion more than once.

Today, the rules for excluding gain resulting from the sale of a personal residence are more favorable for most taxpayers than the old rules because Congress wanted to eliminate the need for homeowners to maintain records for long periods of time. However, taxpayers who expect to sell their homes and have a realized gain of more than $250,000 ($500,000 if a joint return is filed) still need to maintain records. Also, taxpayers who convert their personal residence to business property or rental property will need to know the property's correct adjusted basis to compute depreciation.

DETERMINING THE REALIZED GAIN. Gain realized is the excess of the amount realized over the property's adjusted basis.[65] The amount realized on the sale of the property is equal to the selling price less selling expenses.[66] Selling expenses include commissions, advertising, deed preparation costs, and legal expenses incurred in connection with the sale.[67]

EXAMPLE I:12-52 ▶ Kirby sells his personal residence, which has a $100,000 basis, to Maxine. To make the sale, Kirby pays a $7,000 sales commission and incurs $800 of legal costs. Maxine pays $30,000 cash and assumes Kirby's $90,000 mortgage. The amount realized is $112,200 [($30,000 + $90,000) − ($7,000 + $800)]. The realized gain is $12,200 ($112,200 − $100,000). ◀

---

[63] Sec. 121(a) and (b).
[64] Reg. Secs. 1.165-9(a) and 1.262-1b(4).
[65] Reg. Sec. 1.1034-1(b)(5).

[66] Reg. Sec. 1.1034-1(b)(4).
[67] Reg. Sec. 1.1034-1(b)(4)(i).

ADJUSTED BASIS OF RESIDENCE. The original basis of a principal residence is a function of how the residence is obtained. It could be purchased, received as a gift, or inherited. The cost of a residence includes all amounts attributable to the acquisition including commissions and other purchasing expenses paid to acquire the residence.[68] Capital improvements, but not repairs, increase the adjusted basis of the residence. The costs of adding a room, installing an air conditioning system, finishing a basement, and landscaping are capital improvements. Expenses incurred to protect the taxpayer's title in the residence are also capitalized. Under Sec. 1034, which was repealed in 1997, a taxpayer who deferred gain on the sale of a principal residence was required to reduce the basis of the replacement residence by the amount of the deferred gain.[69]

EXAMPLE I:12-53 ▶

REAL-WORLD EXAMPLE

An unmarried taxpayer plans to make good use of the multiple exclusion allowance. He has purchased two houses; one to live in and one to use as rental property. After a certain number of years he will sell his personal residence and move into the rental house. After at least two more years he will then sell the second house. Except for the gain due to depreciation on the rental house, the gain from both houses will be tax-free up to $250,000 each.

In 1996, Susan paid $200,000 to purchase a new residence. She paid a realtor $4,000 to help locate the house and paid legal fees of $1,200 to make certain that the seller had legal title to the property. As a result of the purchase, she deferred a gain of $50,000 from the sale a former residence in 1995. In 1997, she added a new porch to the house at a cost of $6,000 and installed central air conditioning at a cost of $5,200. Since purchasing the house, she has paid $1,500 for repairs. The adjusted basis of her house is $166,400 [$200,000 + $4,000 + $1,200 − $50,000 + $6,000 + $5,200]. ◀

MULTIPLE USE OF THE EXCLUSION. Previously under Sec. 121, a taxpayer was limited to the exclusion once in their lifetime, and a married taxpayer whose spouse had taken the exclusion could not use the exclusion even if the taxpayer filed as married filing separately. The exclusion is now determined on an individual basis. An individual may claim the exclusion even if the individual's spouse used the exclusion within the past two years. Also, for a married couple filing a joint return when each spouse maintains a separate principal residence, the $250,000 exclusion is available for the sale or exchange of each spouse's principal residence.

EXAMPLE I:12-54 ▶

Krista, who has owned and used a house as her principal residence for the last seven years, marries Josh in January 2010. Josh sold his residence in October 2009 and excluded a $145,000 gain. Krista sells her residence in December 2010 and realizes a gain of $378,000. She may exclude $250,000 of the gain.

Assuming that Krista and Josh use her residence in the above example for a two-year period starting in January 2010, they could exclude up to $500,000 if she waits to sell the house until January 2012. ◀

PRINCIPAL RESIDENCE DEFINED

For Sec. 121 to apply, taxpayers must sell property that qualifies as their principal residence. Whether property is used as the taxpayer's principal residence depends upon all the facts and circumstances. If a taxpayer uses more than one property as a residence during the year, the property used a majority of the time will normally be the principal residence.[70]

EXAMPLE I:12-55 ▶

KEY POINT

A taxpayer may own two or more residences, but only one of them qualifies as the principal residence.

Lanny, a 40-year-old college professor, owns and occupies a house in Oklahoma. During the summer, he lives in a cabin in Idaho. After owning the cabin for eight years, Lanny sells it for $50,000 and realizes a gain. Gain on the sale of the cabin in Idaho must be recognized because Lanny's principal residence is in Oklahoma. ◀

Factors other than use of the property that are relevant when determining a taxpayer's principal residence include place of employment, mailing address for bills and correspondence, address for tax returns and voter registration, and location of religious organizations and recreational clubs with which the taxpayer is affiliated. The principal place of abode for the taxpayer's family members is also relevant.[71]

The property does not have to be one's principal residence at time of the sale to qualify for the exclusion. The exclusion applies if the property has been used as a principal residence for at least two of the five years before the sale or exchange and the exclusion has not been used within the past two years.

---

[68] Reg. Sec. 1.1034-1(c)(4).
[69] Sec. 1034(e).

[70] Reg. Sec. 1.121-1(b)(2).
[71] Reg. Sec. 1.121-1(b)(2).

EXAMPLE I:12-56 ▶ Canan owns and uses a house in Buffalo as her principal residence from March 10, 2006, until November 21, 2008, when she purchases a new house in Kansas on December 1, 2008. Her brother lives in the house in Buffalo until Canan sells it on July 10, 2010, and realizes a gain of $288,000. She may exclude $250,000 and recognize a $38,000 LTCG. ◀

Condominium apartments, houseboats, and housetrailers may qualify as principal residences.[72] Stock held by a tenant-stockholder in a cooperative housing corporation is a principal residence if the dwelling that the taxpayer is entitled to occupy as a stockholder is used as his or her principal residence.[73]

ADDITIONAL COMMENT

The taxpayer does not have to be occupying the old residence at the date of sale. The taxpayer may have already moved to a new residence and be renting the old residence temporarily before its sale.

SALE OF MORE THAN ONE PRINCIPAL RESIDENCE WITHIN A TWO-YEAR PERIOD

The new exclusion provided by Sec. 121 applies to only one sale or exchange every two years. However, a portion of the gain may be excluded in certain circumstances even if the two-year requirement is not satisfied.

If a principal residence is sold within two years of a previous sale or exchange of a residence, part of the gain may be excluded if the sale or exchange is due to a change in employment, health or unforeseen circumstances. The portion of the gain excluded is based on a ratio with a numerator in days or months and a denominator of 730 days or 24 months.[74] The numerator is the shorter of:

(1) the period during which the ownership and use tests were met during the five-year period ending on the date of sale, or

(2) the period of time after the date of the most recent prior sale or exchange for which the exclusion applied until the date of the current sale or exchange.[75]

The amount excluded is $250,000 or $500,000 times the above ratio.

EXAMPLE I:12-57 ▶ Winnie, who is single, sold her principal residence in Detroit on November 1, 2010, and excluded the $127,000 gain because she owned and used the residence for two of the last five years. Winnie had purchased another residence in Cleveland on October 1, 2010. She occupies the residence in Cleveland until June 12, 2011, when she moves to Dallas to accept a new job. She sells the residence in Cleveland on November 15, 2011, and realizes a gain of $40,000. Winnie may exclude all of the gain because the sale of her Cleveland residence was due to a change in employment and 254/730 of $250,000 is more than the $40,000 realized gain. She owns and uses the residence in Cleveland for 254 days, and the period between the sale of the residence in Detroit and the sale in Cleveland is 378 days. ◀

ADDITIONAL COMMENT

If Winnie's gain in Example I:12-57 is $100,000, she may exclude $86,986 (254/730 × $250,000).

OWNERSHIP AND USE TESTS If a principal residence is sold before satisfying the ownership and use tests, part of the gain may be excluded if the sale is due to a change in employment, health, or unforeseen circumstances. The portion of the gain excluded is determined by multiplying the amount of the exclusion (i.e., $250,000 or $500,000) by a fraction whose numerator is the number of days the use and ownership tests were met and whose denominator is 730 days (or 24 months).

EXAMPLE I:12-58 ▶ Tim, a single taxpayer who purchased his home on January 1, 2010, for $500,000, recently became ill and sells his home in order to move closer to a relative who can care for him. Tim sells his principal residence on June 14, 2010, for $620,000, realizing a gain of $120,000. Because he owned and occupied the residence for 165 days and the sale was due to a change in his health, he may exclude $56,164 ($250,000 × 164/730). ◀

For purposes of the two-year ownership rule, a taxpayer's period of ownership includes the period during which the taxpayer's deceased spouse owned the residence. When a taxpayer receives a residence from a spouse or an ex-spouse incident to a divorce, the taxpayer's period of owning the property includes the time the residence was owned by the spouse or ex-spouse.[76] When attempting to determine if the taxpayer has occupied the residence for two years, short temporary absences such as for vacation or other seasonal absence are counted as use by the taxpayer.[77]

---

[72] Rev. Rul. 64-31, 1964-1 C.B. 300.
[73] Reg. Sec. 1.1034-1(c)(3).
[74] Reg. Sec. 1.121-3(g).

[75] Sec. 121(c).
[76] Sec. 121(d)(2) and (3).
[77] Reg. Sec. 1.121-1(c)(2)(i).

EXAMPLE I:12-59 ▶

Sachie receives an $800,000 residence owned for six years by Richard, her former spouse, as part of a divorce settlement. Richard's basis for the residence is $430,000. They lived in the house for five years prior to the divorce. Three months after transfer of the residence to Sachie, she sells it for $825,000, and $250,000 of her $395,000 realized gain is excluded. Sachie must recognize a $145,000 LTCG. Sachie's period of ownership includes the six years Richard owned the residence. ◀

ADDITIONAL COMMENT

The five-year period does not include any period up to ten years during which the taxpayer or the taxpayer's spouse is on qualified official extended duty as a member of the uniformed services.

CHANGE DUE TO EMPLOYMENT, HEALTH, OR UNFORESEEN CIRCUMSTANCES. The Treasury has issued Regulations to provide guidance as to how a homeowner may qualify for partial exclusion if the sale was before the two-year use and ownership test is satisfied or if the sale occurs within two years of a previous sale where the exclusion was used. The exceptions may apply even if a person other than the taxpayer has a change in employment or health.

A taxpayer is viewed as being eligible for partial exclusion if she sells her residence because a qualified individual has a change in employment that satisfies the test under Sec. 217 for the moving expense deduction. A qualified individual includes the taxpayer, the taxpayer's spouse, co-owner of the residence, or a person who uses the residence as a principal place of abode. Taxpayers may qualify for the exclusion and the moving expense deduction if moving to take a new job, continue with present employer or accept a job if the 50-mile distance test is satisfied. The change in employment must occur when the taxpayer is satisfying the ownership and use test for the residence except for the two-year requirement.[78]

EXAMPLE I:12-60 ▶

Mark has lived in his first house for one year in Omaha when he marries Karen. Six months later, Karen receives a job offer and they move to Florida. Mark may exclude a realized gain equal to $18/24$ of $250,000, because the move is due to a change in employment of a qualified individual. ◀

When determining if the sale or exchange of the residence is due to a change in health, the definition of a "qualified individual" is expanded to include relatives who satisfy the relationship test used to determine if one is a dependent of the taxpayer. The relative must satisfy the relationship test but does not have to be a dependent to be a qualified individual. A sale or exchange is because of health if the primary reason is "to obtain, provide, or facilitate the diagnosis, cure, mitigation, or treatment of a disease, illness, or injury of a qualified individual."[79]

EXAMPLE I:12-61 ▶

Daniel has lived in his first house in Virginia for eight months when he sells the house and moves to Texas to take care of his 60-year-old father who recently suffered a stroke. Daniel may exclude a realized gain equal to $8/24$ of $250,000 because the primary reason for the sale is due to the health of a qualified individual. ◀

REAL-WORLD EXAMPLE

In LTR 200601009, taxpayers who sold their home within two years of the purchase because they became aware of various criminal activities occurring in their neighborhood were allowed to utilize Sec. 121. In addition to their son being assaulted and threatened, one of the taxpayers was assaulted by the neighbors.

A sale or exchange is due to unforeseen circumstances if the primary reason for the sale or exchange is an event that the taxpayer could not reasonably have anticipated before purchasing and occupying the residence. For the unforeseen circumstances exception, a qualified individual is the same as a qualified individual for the change in employment test.

The following are specific events considered to qualify as unforeseen circumstances:

1. Involuntary conversion of residence;
2. Natural or man-made disasters or acts of war or terrorism resulting in a casualty to the residence;
3. Death of a qualified individual;
4. Loss of employment by a qualified individual if the individual is eligible for unemployment compensation;
5. Change of employment that results in the taxpayer's inability to pay housing costs and reasonable basic living expenses;
6. Divorce or legal separation;
7. Multiple births from the same pregnancy.[80]

Note that marriage and adoption are not included in the above safe-harbor list of unforeseen circumstances. One who sells her residence before meeting the two-year test because she has adopted a child will not be assured of qualifying for possible exclusion

---

[78] Reg. Sec. 1.121-3(c).
[79] Reg. Sec. 1.121-3(d).
[80] Reg. Sec. 1.121-3T(e).

under the unforeseen circumstances exception. She will have to argue that the facts and circumstances justify her use of the partial exclusion.

The IRS has issued a number of letter rulings that suggest that it is willing to consider many different reasons for selling due to unforseen circumstances. In LTR 200601022, a taxpayer purchased a house, but then married someone with a child who attended a school in a different school district. They decided to temporarily use their house as rental property and rent another house for their use located in the child's school district. While living in the rented house, they had a child and decided to sell the first house because it was too small for their expanding family. Despite the fact that the taxpayer did not use the house as a principal residence, they were allowed to utilize Sec. 121.

EXAMPLE I:12-62 ▶ Benjamin purchases a house near the airport and sells it four months later because of noise caused by planes. He may not exclude any of the gain, because the airport noise is not an unforeseen circumstance. ◀

STOP & THINK

Question: Rebecca's uncle told her that she could purchase his house for $150,000 in five years provided that she could pay at least $30,000 of the purchase price in cash. Rebecca has $15,000 and is considering two alternative methods to obtain the remaining $15,000 in five years. The first alternative is to purchase $15,000 of non-dividend paying stock that she expects to increase in value to $30,000 within five years. The second alternative is to purchase an $80,000 residence by paying $15,000 and borrowing $65,000. Payments on the mortgage will be interest only for five years and amount to $450 per month. Insurance, property taxes, and other home ownership expenses average $90 per month. She expects the house to be worth $95,000 at the end of five years. She will rent an apartment for $540 per month, including utilities, if she buys the stock. Ignoring transaction costs and assuming that she does not itemize deductions, should Rebecca purchase the stock or the house?

Solution: The $15,000 gain resulting from sale of the stock is LTCG and probably taxed at 15%. If the rate is 15%, she must pay taxes of $2,250 and has only $27,750 available to purchase her uncle's house. She will have a gain of $15,000 if she sells the house but the gain is excluded. She has $30,000 of cash and is able to buy her uncle's house. The tax law encourages Rebecca to buy a principal residence.

NONQUALIFIED USE AFTER 2008

A taxpayer who owns a principal residence and a second home (rental property, vacation home, etc.) that has appreciated in value has an incentive to convert the second home to a principal residence if planning to sell the second home. The Housing Assistance Tax Act of 2008 reduced the advantage of converting residences that have not been the principal residence to one's principal residence.

Gain from the sale of a principal residence that is allocable to periods of nonqualified use is not excluded from income. Gain allocated to periods of nonqualified use after 2008 is based on the ratio which the aggregate periods of nonqualified use bears to the total time the property was owned. A period of nonqualified use is any period that the property is not used as a principal residence after 2008. As under prior law, any depreciation attributable to periods of business use is subject to taxation.

Any portion of the five-year period ending on the date of sale that is after the property ceases to be used as a principal residence is not considered nonqualified use, thus the taxpayer may vacate the residence before selling it without recognizing that time after moving out as nonqualified use. Absences due to change in employment, health condition, or other unforeseen circumstances are not considered nonqualified use. Also, nonqualified use does not include any period in which the taxpayer or taxpayer's spouse is serving on qualified official extended duty.

EXAMPLE I:12-63 ▶ The Eberts have owned and lived in a house on Mill Street as their personal residence for 20 years. They also own a house on Elm Street that has been used as rental property for 18 years. Starting May 1, 2008, they moved into the Elm Street house as their principal residence until December 22, 2010 when they sell the Elm Street property and realize a $700,000 gain. Any of the gain due to depreciation must be recognized, but they are eligible to exclude up to $500,000 of the remaining gain. The use of the property as rental property is not nonqualified use because it occurred before 2009. ◀

EXAMPLE I:12-64 ▶ Assume the same facts as in Example I:12-63 except the Eberts do not move into the Elm Street property until May 1, 2011 and will sell the property on December 22, 2013. In this case, the period from January 1, 2009 through April 30, 2011 is nonqualified use and a prorata share of the gain after considering the gain due to depreciation is not eligible for the $500,000 exclusion. ◀

EXAMPLE I:12-65 ▶ Dale owned a house and used it as rental property for six years until January 1, 2010, when he moved into the house and used it as a principal residence. Depreciation for the six years that it was used as rental property is $30,000. If he sells the house on January 1, 2013, and realizes a gain of $210,000, the first $30,000 of gain is recognized. He may exclude 8/9 of the remaining gain of $180,000, and must recognize another $20,000 (1/9 of $180,000) due to the nonqualified use in 2009. The years before 2009 are not considered nonqualified use (5 years) as he used the property as a principal residence for 3 years. So, eight of the nine year period are eligible for the Sec. 121 exclusion. He must recognize $50,000 of the $210,000 gain and may exclude $160,000. ◀

INVOLUNTARY CONVERSION OF A PRINCIPAL RESIDENCE

Ordinarily, the involuntary conversion of a principal residence is governed by Sec. 1033, discussed earlier in this chapter. A gain due to an involuntary conversion of a personal residence may be deferred if the requirements of Sec. 1033 are satisfied. The functional-use test must be satisfied regardless of the type of involuntary conversion.

For purposes of Sec. 121, the destruction, theft, seizure, requisition, or condemnation of property is treated as a sale.[81] Thus, taxpayers may exclude a gain of up to $250,000 or $500,000 due to the involuntary conversion of a principal residence if the use and ownership tests are satisfied. Taxpayers normally prefer to exclude gain if the use and ownership tests are satisfied rather than defer gain under the involuntary conversion provisions.

If taxpayers make a proper and timely replacement of the residence subject to the involuntary conversion, gain may be excluded up to $250,000, or $500,000, and the remaining gain may be deferred. For purposes of applying the involuntary conversion provisions, the amount realized due to the involuntary conversion is reduced by any gain excluded under Sec. 121.[82]

EXAMPLE I:12-66 ▶ The Kochs' principal residence, with an adjusted basis of $200,000, has been used and owned by them for nine years. The house is destroyed by a hurricane, and the Kochs receive insurance proceeds of $820,000. Four months later, they purchase another residence for $900,000. The Kochs have a realized gain of $620,000 and may exclude $500,000 under Sec. 121. The remaining $120,000 gain may be deferred and the basis of their replacement residence is $780,000 ($900,000 − $120,000). ◀

Because the amount realized is reduced by the gain excluded, the Kochs could have deferred the $120,000 gain in the above example by investing only $320,000 in a replacement residence.

If gain due to the involuntary conversion of a principal residence is deferred under Sec. 1033, the holding period of the replacement residence includes the holding period of the converted property for purposes of satisfying the use and ownership tests of Sec. 121.[83] The Kochs satisfy the use and ownership requirements for Sec. 121 with respect to their new residence in Example I:12-65 because gain is deferred under Sec. 1033.

A loss due to a condemnation of a personal residence is not recognized. If the loss is due to a casualty, the loss is deductible and is treated like other casualty losses of nonbusiness property (see Chapter I:8).

TAX PLANNING CONSIDERATIONS

AVOIDING THE LIKE-KIND EXCHANGE PROVISIONS

In some cases, a taxpayer may prefer a taxable exchange to a nontaxable like-kind exchange. For instance, if the gain is taxed as a capital gain and the taxpayer has capital losses to offset the gain, the taxpayer may prefer to recognize the gain during the current year. If gain on the exchange is recognized instead of deferred, the basis of the property received in the exchange is higher.

---

[81] Sec. 121(d)(5)(A).
[82] Sec. 121(d)(5)(B).

[83] Sec. 121(d)(8).

EXAMPLE I:12-67 ▶ Connie owns land with a $20,000 basis. The land is held as an investment. Connie exchanges the land for a duplex with a $100,000 FMV. Because the exchange qualifies as a like-kind exchange, no gain is recognized and Connie's basis for the duplex is $20,000. If the exchange does not qualify as a like-kind exchange (e.g., the land is a personal-use asset), Connie recognizes an $80,000 capital gain. Connie's basis for the duplex is $100,000. The basis of the duplex, except for the portion allocable to land, is eligible for depreciation. ◀

If an exchange qualifies as a like-kind exchange, no loss on the exchange is recognized. A taxpayer who prefers to recognize a loss should avoid making a like-kind exchange. It may be advantageous to sell the property to recognize the loss and then purchase the replacement asset in two independent transactions. If the sale and purchase transactions are with the same party, the IRS may maintain that the like-kind exchange rules apply because the two transactions are in substance a like-kind exchange (i.e., the judicial doctrine of substance over form might be applied).

SALE OF A PRINCIPAL RESIDENCE

ELECTION PROVISION. When the requirements of Sec. 121 are satisfied, gain is excluded unless the taxpayer elects not to have Sec. 121 apply.[84]

EXAMPLE I:12-68 ▶ Paula has owned a house in Wyoming for eight years and occupied it until 18 months ago when she moved to Idaho and purchased a new house. She sells the house in Wyoming on May 23, 2010, and the realized gain is $25,000. Paula anticipates that she will move next year and have to sell the house in Idaho which has appreciated more than $100,000 since purchased. Paula may want to elect not to have Sec. 121 apply and recognize the $25,000 gain and then use the exclusion when she sells the house in Idaho next year. ◀

PROPERTY USED AS RESIDENCE AND FOR BUSINESS. If a house is used for both residential use and business use, the tax treatment depends on whether or not the business portion of the house is conducted in a separate structure. If the business portion of the house is conducted in a separate structure, the sale should be treated as a sale of two assets, the residence and the portion of the property used as a business. The Sec. 121 exclusion only applies to the residence portion of the property.

EXAMPLE I:12-69 ▶

ADDITIONAL COMMENT

As explained in Chapter I:13, Mormor's $24,000 gain in Example 69 is a Sec. 1231 gain and $6,000 is taxed at a maximum rate of 25% because it is unrecaptured Sec. 1250 gain.

Mormor owns a one-acre lot with a house she uses as her residence and a barn that she uses to display and sell antiques. She purchased the property in 1990 for $100,000 and $10,000 of the purchase price was allocated to the barn. Depreciation of $4,000 has been allowed for the barn. She sells the property during the current year for $300,000 and estimates that 10% of the price received is for the barn. She may exclude the $180,000 ($270,000 − $90,000) gain on the sale of the residence. Her $24,000 ($30,000 − $6,000) gain on the sale of the barn is recognized.[85] ◀

If the business activity is conducted within the house and not in a separate structure, the sale does not have to be treated as a sale of two different assets. However, gain attributable to depreciation after May 6, 1997, is not eligible for the exclusion. The remaining gain is eligible for the exclusion.

EXAMPLE I:12-70 ▶ Kate purchased a house in 2001 for $200,000 and uses 15% of the house as an office. The office is used on a regular and exclusive basis and is her principal place of business. Depreciation of $3,400 has been deducted when she sells the house for $430,000. Her gain is $233,400 ($430,000 − $196,600), and she may exclude $230,000 but must recognize $3,400 of the gain. ◀

The government's decision to allow Kate to treat the property in the above example as one property instead of two is beneficial for her. If the property was viewed as two properties or if the office was in a separate structure, only $195,500 ($365,500 − $170,000) of the gain would qualify for the exclusion.

---

[84] Sec. 121(f).
[85] As explained in Chapter I:13, the gain is Sec. 1231 gain and $4,000 is unrecaptured Sec. 1250 gain.

EXAMPLE I:12-71 ▶ Bobbi purchased a house on March 1, 2000 and used it as her principal residence until March 1, 2003, when she rented the house to the Allens while she lived with her mother. On November 1, 2009, the Allens' lease expired and she moved back into the house. She sells the house on July 12, 2010, and realizes a gain of $210,000. She may not exclude any of the gain because she has not used the property as her principal residence for two of the last five years. ◀

If Bobbi in the above example did satisfy the two-out-of-five-year requirement, gain equal to depreciation would first be recognized. A portion of the remaining gain could not be excluded because of the nonqualified use.

EXAMPLE I:12-72 ▶ Assume the same facts as in the above example except that Bobbi sells the house on December 1, 2011. Because she has used the property as her principal residence for two of the last five years, she may exclude part of the excess of the $210,000 gain over depreciation allowed after May 6, 1997. Ten months of the use is nonqualified use because of its use as rental property for ten months after 2008. Because she owned the property for 141 months and nonqualified use amounted to ten months, 10/141 of the gain remaining after gain recognized due to depreciation. ◀

COMPLIANCE AND PROCEDURAL CONSIDERATIONS

REPORTING OF INVOLUNTARY CONVERSIONS

ADDITIONAL COMMENT

The failure to include gain from an involuntary conversion in gross income is deemed to be an election even though the details are not reported.

The election to defer recognition of the gain from an involuntary conversion is made by not reporting the gain as income for the first year in which gain is realized. All details pertaining to the involuntary conversion (including those relating to the replacement of the converted property) should be reported for the taxable year or years in which any of the gain is realized.[86]

A taxpayer who elects to defer recognition of the gain but does not make a proper replacement of the property within the required period of time must file an amended return for the year or years for which the election was made. An amended return may be needed if the cost of the replacement property is less than expected at the time of the election. All details pertaining to the replacement of converted property must be reported in the year in which replacement occurs.[87]

EXAMPLE I:12-73 ▶ Bob's property, with a $40,000 adjusted basis, was destroyed by a storm in 2009. Bob received $45,000 insurance proceeds in 2009 and planned to purchase property similar to the converted property in 2010 at a cost of $47,000. Bob elected to defer recognition of the gain in 2009. In 2010 the replacement property is purchased for $44,500. Bob must file an amended return for 2009 and recognize a $500 ($45,000 − $44,500) gain. ◀

ADDITIONAL COMMENT

The replacement period may be extended if special permission is obtained from the IRS.

A taxpayer who either is ineligible or does not want to defer the gain must report the gain in the usual manner. If a taxpayer does not elect to defer the gain in the year the gain is realized and the replacement period has not expired, a subsequent election may be made. In such an event, a refund claim should be filed for the tax year in which the gain was realized and previously recognized.[88]

Taxpayers who do not initially elect to defer the gain from an involuntary conversion may later make the election, but the election may not subsequently be revoked. The Tax Court has ruled that the Treasury Regulations allow the filing of an amended return for a year in which the election is made only if proper replacement is not made within the specified time period or the replacement is made at a cost lower than anticipated at the time of the election.[89] The IRS takes the position that taxpayers who designate qualifying property as replacement property may not later designate other qualifying property as the replacement property.[90]

EXAMPLE I:12-74 ▶ In 2008 Troy collected $200,000 from an insurance company as the result of the destruction of rental property with a $140,000 basis. He made the election to defer the gain realized in 2008 and attached a supporting schedule of details regarding the involuntary conversion including

---

[86] Reg. Sec. 1.1033(a)-2(c)(2).
[87] *Ibid.*
[88] *Ibid.*

[89] *John McShain*, 65 T.C. 686 (1976).
[90] Rev. Rul. 83-39, 1983-1 C.B. 190.

a designation of replacement property to be acquired in 2009. In 2009 Troy purchased the designated replacement rental property for $225,000. In 2010 Troy purchases other rental property for $400,000 and now wants to designate that property as the replacement property for the property destroyed in 2008. Troy may not designate the property acquired in 2010 as the replacement property because the rental property purchased in 2009 was already designated as such. ◄

REPORTING OF SALE OR EXCHANGE OF A PRINCIPAL RESIDENCE

Taxpayers only have to report the sale if any of the gain is not excluded. If the taxpayer does not qualify to exclude all of the gain or elects not to exclude the gain, the entire gain realized is reported on Schedule D either on line 1, if residence is held for one year or less, or on line 8. On the line below where the entire gain is shown, the taxpayer should indicate on the following line the amount of the gain that is being excluded as a loss (i.e., show in parentheses).

Publication 523, Selling Your Home, provides the following worksheet that may be used to determine if any gain is recognized. If the taxpayer has to utilize the exceptions to the two-year ownership and use tests, a different worksheet is provided.

Worksheet 2. Gain (or Loss), Exclusion, and Taxable Gain

Part 1–Gain (or Loss) on Sale

1. Selling price of home . . . . _____
2. Selling expenses. . . . . _____
3. Subtract line 2 from line 1 . . . . _____
4. Adjusted basis of home sold. (From Worksheet 1, line 15.) . . . . _____
5. Subtract line 4 from line 3. This is the **gain (or loss)** on the sale. If this is a loss, stop here . . _____

Part 2–Exclusion and Taxable Gain

6. Maximum exclusion. (See *Amount of Exclusion* in this chapter.) . . . . _____
7. Enter any depreciation claimed on the property for periods after May 6, 1997. If none, enter zero _____
8. Subtract line 7 from line 5. (If the result is less than zero, enter zero.) . . . . _____
9. Subtract line 7 from line 6. . . . . _____
10. Enter the smaller of line 8 or 9. This is your exclusion. If you are reporting the sale on the installment method, enter this amount on line 15 of Form 6252 . . . . _____
11. Subtract line 10 from line 5. This is your taxable gain. Report it on Schedule D (Form 1040) as described under *Reporting the Gain* in this chapter. If the amount on this line is zero, do not report the sale or exclusion on your tax return . . . . _____

PROBLEM MATERIALS

DISCUSSION QUESTIONS

I:12-1 Evaluate the following statement: The underlying rationale for the nonrecognition of a gain or loss resulting from a like-kind exchange is that the exchange constitutes a liquidation of the taxpayer's investment.

I:12-2 Why might a taxpayer want to avoid having an exchange qualify as a like-kind exchange?

I:12-3 Debbie owns office equipment with a basis of $300,000 and a holding period starting on May 10, 2000. Debbie exchanges the equipment for other office equipment owned by Doug on July 23, 2010. Doug's equipment has an FMV of $500,000. Both Debbie and Doug use the equipment in their businesses.

a. What is Debbie's basis for the office equipment received in the exchange and when does the holding period start for that equipment?

b. If Debbie and Doug are related taxpayers, explain what action could occur that would cause the exchange not to qualify as a like-kind exchange.

I:12-4 Kay owns equipment used in her business and exchanges the equipment for other like-kind equipment and marketable securities.

a. Will Kay's recognized gain ever exceed the realized gain?

b. Will Kay's recognized gain ever exceed the FMV of the marketable securities?

c. What is the basis of the marketable securities received?

d. When does the holding period of the marketable securities begin?

I:12-5 Demetrius sells word processing equipment used in his business to Edith. He then purchases new word processing equipment from Zip Corporation.

a. Do the sale and purchase qualify as a like-kind exchange?

b. When may a sale and a subsequent purchase be treated as a like-kind exchange?

I:12-6 When determining whether property qualifies as like-kind property, is the quality or grade of the property considered?

I:12-7 What is personal property of a like class that meets the definition of like-kind?

I:12-8 When does a nonsimultaneous exchange qualify as a like-kind exchange?

I:12-9 Burke is anxious to purchase land owned by Kim for use in his trade or business. Kim's basis for the land is $150,000, and Burke has offered to pay $800,000 if she will sell within the next 10 days. Kim is interested in selling but wants to avoid recognizing gain. What advice would you give?

I:12-10 Lanny wants to purchase a farm owned by Jane, but Jane does not want to recognize a gain on the transfer of the appreciated property. Explain how a three-party exchange might be used to allow Lanny to obtain the farm without Jane having to recognize a gain.

I:12-11 Does the receipt of boot in a transaction that otherwise qualifies as a like-kind exchange always cause the exchange to be at least partially taxable?

I:12-12 When must a taxpayer who gives boot recognize a gain or loss?

I:12-13 What is the justification for Sec. 1033, which allows a taxpayer to elect to defer a gain resulting from an involuntary conversion? May a taxpayer elect under Sec. 1033 to defer recognition of a loss resulting from an involuntary conversion?

I:12-14 Must property be actually condemned for the conversion of property to be classified as an involuntary conversion? Explain.

I:12-15 What are severance damages? What is the tax treatment for severance damages received if the taxpayer does not use the severance damages to restore the retained property?

I:12-16 The functional use test is often used to determine whether the replacement property is similar or related in service or use to the property converted. Explain the functional use test.

I:12-17 In what situations may a gain due to an involuntary conversion of real property be deferred if like-kind property is purchased to replace the converted property?

I:12-18 Prior to the Taxpayer Relief Act of 1997, taxpayers could defer a gain on the sale of a principal residence sold before May 7, 1997, if they purchased and occupied a new principal residence within two years before or after the sale and the cost of the new residence was at least equal to the adjusted sales price of the old residence. Some taxpayers who were at least 55 years old had a once-in-a-lifetime exclusion up to $125,000 if they owned and used the property as a principal residence for at least three years of the five-year-period ending on the date of sale. Discuss why current law with respect to the sale of a personal residence is more favorable than the law prior to the Taxpayer Relief Act of 1997.

I:12-19 One reason Congress expanded the exclusion of gain on the sale of a principal residence and eliminated the deferral provision was to eliminate the need for many taxpayers to keep records of capital improvements that increase the basis of their residence. Why might taxpayers still need to maintain such records to substantiate the adjusted basis of their principal residence?

I:12-20 Steve maintains that the cost of wallpapering his three-bedroom house is a capital expenditure while Martha maintains that the cost of wallpapering her three-bedroom house is an expense. Steve uses his house as his personal residence while Martha's house is rental property. Explain why Steve and Martha view the cost of wallpapering differently.

I:12-21 The Nelsons purchased a new residence in 1992 for $300,000 from David who owned and used the residence as rental property. When the Nelsons wanted to purchase the property, it was being rented to tenants who had four months remaining on their lease. The Nelsons paid the tenants $1,000 to relinquish the lease and vacate the property. In 1996, they added a family room to the house at a cost of $79,200. In 1998, they suffered hail damage to the roof and received $7,000 from the insurance company. They did not repair the damaged roof, and no casualty loss deduction was allowed. What is their adjusted basis for the house today?

I:12-22 What requirements must be satisfied by an unmarried taxpayer under Sec. 121 to be eligible for the election to exclude a gain up to $250,000 on the sale or exchange of a principal residence?

ISSUE IDENTIFICATION QUESTIONS

I:12-23 John owns 25% of the ABC Partnership and Jane owns 25% of the XYZ Partnership. The ABC Partnership owns a farm and produces corn and the XYZ Partnership owns a farm and produces soybeans. John and Jane agree to exchange their partnership interests. What tax issues should John and Jane consider?

I:12-24 Chauvin Oil Corporation operates primarily in the United States and owns an offshore drilling rig with an adjusted basis of $400,000 that it uses near Louisiana. Chauvin exchanges the rig for a new rig with a FMV of $1,000,000, and Chauvin also pays $250,000. Chauvin plans to expand its drilling operations to offshore sites near Finland. What tax issues should the Chauvin Oil Corporation consider?

I:12-25 Jaharta, Inc., owns land used for truck farming and cattle raising. The California Division of Highways condemned 36 acres of Jaharta's land to build a new highway. Jaharta owned a 50% interest in property being used for apricot, prune, and walnut orchards. Jaharta used the proceeds received as a result of the condemnation to purchase the remaining interest in the property being used for orchards. What tax issues should Jaharta consider?

PROBLEMS

I:12-26 *Like-Kind Property.* Which of the following exchanges qualify as like-kind exchanges under Sec. 1031?
  a. Acme Corporation stock held for investment purposes for Mesa Corporation stock also held for investment purposes
  b. A motel used in a trade or business for an apartment complex held for investment
  c. A pecan orchard in Texas used in a trade or business for an orange grove in Florida used in a trade or business
  d. A one-third interest in a general partnership for a one-fourth interest in a limited partnership
  e. Inventory for equipment used in a trade or business
  f. Unimproved land held as an investment for a warehouse used in a trade or business
  g. An automobile used as a personal-use asset for marketable securities held for investment

I:12-27 *Like-Kind Property.* Which of the following exchanges qualify as like-kind exchanges under Sec. 1031?
  a. A motel in Texas for a motel in Italy
  b. An office building held for investment for an airplane to be used in the taxpayer's business
  c. Land held for investment for marketable securities held for investment
  d. Land held for investment for a farm to be used in the taxpayer's business

I:12-28 *Like-Kind Exchange: Boot.* Determine the realized gain or loss, the recognized gain or loss, and the basis of the equipment received for the following like-kind exchanges:

Basis of Equipment Exchanged	FMV of Boot Received	FMV of Equipment Received
$20,000	$ –0–	$85,000
45,000	14,000	70,000
60,000	25,000	65,000
70,000	38,000	60,000
90,000	22,000	55,000

I:12-29 *Like-Kind Exchange: Personal Property.* Beach Corporation owns a computer with a $34,000 adjusted basis. The computer is used in the company's trade or business. What is the realized and recognized gain or loss for each of the following independent transactions where the computer is exchanged for?
  a. A used computer with a $70,000 FMV plus $16,000 cash.
  b. A used computer with a $18,000 FMV plus $7,000 cash.
  c. Marketable securities with a $61,000 FMV.

I:12-30 *Like-Kind Exchange: Personal Property.* Boise Corporation exchanges a machine with a $14,000 basis for a new machine with an $18,000 FMV and $3,000 cash. The machines are used in Boise's business and are in the same General Asset Class.
  a. Determine Boise Corporation's recognized gain and the basis for the new machine.
  b. How would your answer to Part a change if the corporation's machine is also subject to a $6,000 liability, and the liability is assumed by the other party?

I:12-31   *Exchange of Personal Property.* Lithuania Corporation operates a ferry service and owns four barges. Lithuania exchanges one of the barges with an adjusted basis of $350,000 for a used smaller barge with a FMV of $444,000 and a $26,000 computer. Without considering the exchange, Lithuania Corporation's taxable income is $700,000. Determine Lithuania's
   a. realized gain on the exchange.
   b. recognized gain.
   c. basis of the new barge.
   d. basis of the computer.
   e. Assume that the recognized gain is $26,000 and the gain is not capital gain. What is the increase in Lithuania's tax liability as a result of the exchange?

I:12-32   *Like-Kind Exchange: Liabilities.* Paul owns a building used in his business with an adjusted basis of $340,000 and a $750,000 FMV. He exchanges the building for a building owned by David. David's building has a $950,000 FMV but is subject to a $200,000 liability. Paul assumes David's liability and uses the building in his business. What is Paul's
   a. realized gain?
   b. recognized gain?
   c. basis for the building received?

I:12-33   *Like-Kind Exchange: Liabilities.* Helmut exchanges his apartment complex for Heidi's farm, and the exchange qualifies as a like-kind exchange. Helmut's adjusted basis for the apartment complex is $600,000 and the complex is subject to a $180,000 liability. The FMV of Heidi's farm is $770,000 and the farm is subject to a $100,000 liability. Each asset is transferred subject to the liability. What is Helmut's recognized gain and the basis of the new farm?

I:12-34   *Like-Kind Exchange: Liabilities.* Sheila owns land with a basis of $100,000 and FMV of $230,000. The land is subject to an $80,000 liability. Sheila plans to exchange the land for land owned by Tony that has a $250,000 FMV but is subject to a liability of $150,000. Sheila plans to assume Tony's debt and Tony will assume her $80,000 debt. Because the exchange is not of equal value, how much cash must Tony transfer to equalize the exchange?

I:12-35   *Like-Kind Exchange: Transfer of Boot.* Wayne exchanges unimproved land with a $50,000 basis and marketable securities with a $10,000 basis for an eight-unit apartment building having a $150,000 FMV. The land and marketable securities are held by Wayne as investments, and the apartment building is held as an investment. The marketable securities have a $25,000 FMV. What is his realized gain, recognized gain, and the basis for the apartment building?

I:12-36   *Like-Kind Exchange: Related Parties.* Bob owns a duplex used as rental property. The duplex has a basis of $86,000 and $300,000 FMV. He transfers the duplex to Cindy, his sister, in exchange for a triplex that she owns. The triplex has a basis of $279,000 and a $300,000 FMV. Two months after the exchange, Cindy sells the duplex to a business associate for $312,000. Determine:
   a. Bob's realized and recognized gain on the exchange.
   b. Cindy's realized and recognized gain on the exchange.

I:12-37   *Like-Kind Exchange: Related Parties.* Assume the same facts as in I:12-36 except Cindy sells the duplex to a nonrelated individual more than two years after the exchange with Bob. Ignore any changes in adjusted basis due to depreciation that would have occurred after the exchange. Determine:
   a. Bob's realized and recognized gain on the exchange.
   b. Cindy's realized and recognized gain on the exchange.
   c. Cindy's realized and recognized gain on the sale.

I:12-38   *Involuntary Conversion.* Duke Corporation owns an office building with a $400,000 adjusted basis. The building is destroyed by a tornado. The insurance company paid $750,000 as compensation for the loss. Eight months after the loss, Duke uses the insurance proceeds and other funds to acquire a new office building for $682,000 and machinery for one of the company's plants at a $90,000 cost. Assuming that Duke elects to defer as much of the gain as possible, what is the recognized gain, the basis for the new office building, and the basis for the machinery acquired?

I:12-39   *Involuntary Conversion: Replacement Period.* The Madison Corporation paid $3,000 for several acres of land in 1993 to use in its business. The land is condemned and taken by the state in March 2010. The company receives $25,000 from the state. Whenever possible, the corporation elects to minimize taxable income. For each of the following

independent cases, what is the recognized gain or loss in 2010 on the conversion and the tax basis of the replacement property (replacement land will be purchased in July)?
   a. 2011 for $22,500.
   b. 2012 for $28,500.
   c. 2013 for $23,600.

I:12-40 *Involuntary Conversion of Real Property.* On April 27, 2010, an office building owned by Newark Corporation, an offshore drilling company that is a calendar-year taxpayer, is destroyed by a hurricane. The basis of the office building is $600,000, and the corporation receives $840,000 from the insurance company.
   a. To defer the entire gain due to the involuntary conversion, what amount must the corporation pay for replacement property?
   b. To defer the gain due to the involuntary conversion, by what date must the corporation replace the converted property?
   c. If Newark replaces the office building by purchasing a 900,000 gallon storage tank for $810,000, may it defer any of the gain due to the involuntary conversion?
   d. Will answers to Parts b and c change if the office building had been condemned by the state? Explain.

I:12-41 *Involuntary Conversion: Different Methods of Replacement.* On September 3, 2010, Federal Corporation's warehouse is totally destroyed by fire. $800,000 of insurance proceeds are received, and the realized gain is $300,000. Whenever possible, Federal elects to defer gains. For each of the following independent situations, what is the amount of gain recognized? Explain why the gain is not deferred, if applicable.
   a. On October 23, 2010, Federal purchases a warehouse for $770,000.
   b. On February 4, 2011, Federal purchases 100% of the Park Corporation, which owns a warehouse. Federal pays $895,000 for the stock.
   c. On March 10, 2011, Federal receives a capital contribution from its majority shareholder. The shareholder transfers a warehouse to the corporation. The warehouse's FMV is $975,000. The shareholder's basis in the warehouse is $635,000.
   d. On November 20, 2012, Federal purchases an apartment complex for $900,000.
   e. On March 26, 2013, Federal purchases a warehouse for $888,000.

I:12-42 *Severance Damages.* Twelve years ago, Marilyn purchased two lots in an undeveloped subdivision as an investment. Each lot has a $10,000 basis and a $40,000 FMV when the city condemns one lot for use as a municipal sewage treatment plant. As a result of the condemnation, Marilyn receives $40,000 from the city. Because the value of the other lot is reduced, the city pays $7,500 severance damages. She does not plan to replace the condemned lot. What is her:
   a. recognized gain due to the condemnation?
   b. recognized gain from the receipt of the severance damages?
   c. basis for the lot she continues to own?

I:12-43 *Sale of a Principal Residence.* Marc, age 45, sells his personal residence on May 15, 2010, for $180,000. He pays $8,000 in selling expenses and $900 in repair expenses to help sell the residence. He has lived in the residence since 1980, when he purchased it for $55,000. In 1995, he paid $6,000 to install central air conditioning. If Marc purchases a new principal residence in December of the current year for $162,000, what is the realized gain, recognized gain, and the basis for the new residence?

I:12-44 *Sale of a Principal Residence.* Mr. and Mrs. Rusbarsky purchased a residence on June 12, 2007, for $200,000. On March 12, 2010, they sell the residence for $300,000, and selling expenses amount to $11,000. They purchase another house in a new subdivision for $275,000. Determine the gain realized and recognized.

I:12-45 *Sale of a Principal Residence.* On January 10, 2010, Kirsten married Joe. Joe sold his personal residence on October 25, 2009, and excluded the entire gain of $175,000. Although they had originally planned to live in the house that Kirsten had received as a gift from her parents in 2001, they decided to purchase a larger house, and Kirsten sold her house and realized a $370,000 gain.
   a. If they file a joint return, how much of the $370,000 gain may be excluded?
   b. If Kirsten files as married filing separately, how much of the $370,000 gain may be excluded?

I:12-46 *Involuntary Conversion of Principal Residence.* Mr. and Mrs. Snell own and live in a house, with an adjusted basis of $300,000, that was purchased in 1994. The house is destroyed by a tornado on March 10 of the current year, and the Snells receive insurance proceeds of $410,000. They purchase another residence for $480,000 four months later.

a. May they exclude the $110,000 gain, and if so, what is the basis of the residence purchased in July?

b. May they defer the $110,000 gain, and if so, what is the basis of the residence purchased in July?

I:12-47 *Sale of a Principal Residence.* Mr. and Mrs. Kitchens purchased their first home in Ohio for $135,000 on October 1, 2009. Because Mr. Kitchens' employer transferred him to Utah, they sold the house for $160,000 on January 10, 2010. How much of the gain is recognized?

I:12-48 *Sale of a Principal Residence.* Prior to the Taxpayer Relief Act of 1997, taxpayers could defer a gain on the sale of a principal residence sold before May 7, 1997. To defer all of the gain, the taxpayer had to make a timely purchase of a replacement residence that cost more than the adjusted sales price of the residence sold. The basis of the replacement residence was reduced by the gain deferred.

Answer the following questions to demonstrate why Beverley and George might prefer the law prior to the Taxpayer Relief Act if they sell their principal residence for $900,000, with an adjusted basis of $200,000. Selling expenses of $20,000 were paid. They owned and occupied the home for 20 years and file a joint return. The amount realized is equal to the adjusted sales price, and they purchase a new residence for $1,000,000 two weeks after the sale.

a. Under current law, what is the gain recognized and the basis of their new residence?

b. If the sale had occurred prior to May 7, 1997, what is the gain recognized and the basis of their new residence?

c. Which law might they prefer?

I:12-49 *Unqualified Use.* Sherron, who is single, purchased a house to use as rental property on April 1, 2007, for $300,000. He moved into the house on June 1, 2009, and used it as a personal residence until August 1, 2010, when he sells the house for $500,000. Depreciation allowed while property was used as rental property amounts to $25,000. Determine his:

a. realized gain on the sale

b. recognized gain on the sale

c. recognized gain on the sale if the house is sold on August 1, 2011, for $500,000

I:12-50 *Sale of a Principal Residence: Rental Property.* For the last five years, Mr. and Mrs. Cockrell rented their furnished basement to local college students. When determining their taxable income each year, they deducted a portion of the utilities, property taxes, interest, and depreciation based on the fact that 15% of the house is used for rental purposes. The original basis of the property is $100,000, and depreciation of $4,000 has been allowed on the rental portion of the property. During the current year, Mr. and Mrs. Cockrell sell the house for $300,000. No selling expenses or fixing-up expenses are incurred. Determine:

a. realized gain on the sale.

b. recognized gain on the sale.

I:12-51 *Multiple Sales of a Principal Residence.* Consider the following information for Mr. and Mrs. Di Palma:

- On June 10, 2009, they sold their principal residence for $80,000 and incur $6,000 of selling expenses. The basis of the residence, acquired in 2002, is $50,000.

- On June 25, 2009, they purchased a new principal residence for $90,000 and occupied it immediately.

- On May 10, 2010, they purchase their neighbor's residence for $115,000 and occupy the residence immediately.

- On August 29, 2010, they sell the residence purchased on June 25, 2009, for $148,000. They pay $7,000 of selling expenses. Determine:

a. realized gain on the sale of the residence in 2009.

b. recognized gain on the sale of the residence in 2009.

c. realized gain on the sale of the residence in 2010.

d. recognized gain on the sale of the residence in 2010.

I:12-52 *Multiple Sales of a Principal Residence.* Consider the following information for Mr. and Mrs. Gomez:

- On May 26, 2009, they sold their principal residence, acquired in 1999, for $200,000. They paid $8,000 of selling expenses. Their basis in the residence was $70,000.

- On July 25, 2009, they purchased a new principal residence for $250,000.

- On June 2, 2010, Mr. Gomez, a bank officer, is transferred to another bank in the northern part of the state and they vacate their house.

- On July 1, 2010, they purchase a new principal residence for $420,000.
- On October 6, 2010, they sell the residence that was purchased on July 25, 2009, for $520,000. They pay $30,000 of selling expenses. Determine:
a. realized gain on the sale of the residence in 2009.
b. recognized gain on the sale of the residence in 2009.
c. realized gain on the sale of the residence in 2010.
d. recognized gain on the sale of the residence in 2010.

COMPREHENSIVE PROBLEM

I:12-53   Paden, who is single and has been employed as an accountant for 27 years with Harper, Inc., lost his job due to company downsizing. His last day of employment is July 31, 2010, and Harper provides a $9,000 severance payment. The severance payments are based on an employee's time of employment. During the year, Paden received a salary from Harper of $36,000. Harper also paid $1,500 of Paden's medical insurance premiums.

In May 2010, Paden, who had always wanted to be associated with a football team, applied for the head coaching job at Hawk University in Iowa and, much to his surprise, received the job beginning on August 1. In June and July, Paden paid $4,500 to take courses in sports management at the local university. Hawk University is substantially short of funding and Paden paid $2,000 for entertainment expenses related to his job and $500 for supplies. No reimbursement was received.

His salary from Hawk is $4,000 per month payable at the end of each month. His salary for December was not received until January 6, 2011.

On August 1, he sold his house for $329,000 and paid a sales commission of $14,000. He inherited the house 20 years ago when his mother died. Her basis for the house was $37,000 and the FMV when she died was $50,000. Property taxes for the 2010 calendar year amount to $3,600, and property taxes were apportioned at the closing. Property taxes are payable on October 1. He paid $12,000 of interest on home equity debt of $150,000.

To move to Iowa, he drove 700 miles and spent $45 for meals during the trip. Movers charged $4,150 to move his household items. The standard mileage rate for moving expenses for 2009 is 24 cents per mile. He purchased a new house in Iowa for $150,000 on August 15 and borrowed $110,000. He also agreed to pay all property taxes for 2010. Real property taxes for the home in Iowa will be paid on January 30, 2011, and amount to $1,500. Interest on the $110,000 debt during the current year is $1,475. To obtain the loan, Paden paid points of $1,000.

He contributed common stock (basis of $1,000 and FMV of $6,000) held as an investment for three years to Hawk University and cash of $1,765 to the First United Methodist Church. He paid personal property taxes of $435 for his car.

Paden sold 200 shares of Dell Corporation stock on April 10 for $100 per share. His basis was $145 per share. On May 1, he purchased 300 shares of Dell at $89 per share.
Determine:
1. gross income without considering the sale of his house or the Dell Corporation stock.
2. recognized gain due to the sale of his house.
3. net capital gain.
4. adjusted gross income.
5. total amount of itemized deductions.
6. taxable income.
7. basis of his house in Iowa.
8. if the sales price for his home was $470,000 instead of $370,000, would his taxable income increase by more than $100,000. If yes, explain.

TAX STRATEGY PROBLEM

I:12-54   *Sale of a Principal Residence.* Ray and Ellie have each owned a principal residence used for more than five years. Ray's residence has an adjusted basis of $100,000 and a FMV of $325,000, while Ellie's residence has an adjusted basis of $300,000 and a FMV of $490,000. They plan to marry and will purchase another house.
a. Should they sell their houses before the marriage in order to minimize their taxes?
b. Will your answer to Part a change if the FMV of Ellie's house is $690,000?
c. In Part b, what tax strategy should Ray and Ellie consider?

TAX FORM/RETURN PREPARATION PROBLEMS

I:12-55 On October 29, 2010, Miss Joan Seely (SSN 123-45-6789) sells her principal residence for $150,000 cash. She purchased the residence on May 12, 2001, for $85,000. She spent $12,000 for capital improvements in 2001. To help sell the house, she pays $300 for minor repairs. The realtor's commission amounts to $7,500. Her old residence is never rented out or used for business. Complete the worksheet on page 12-23 for Miss Seely for 2010.

I:12-56 At the beginning of the current year, Donna Harp was employed as a cinematographer by Farah Movie, Inc., a motion picture company in Los Angeles, California. In June, she accepted a new job with Ocala Production in Orlando, Florida. Donna is single and her Social Security number is 223-77-6793. She sold her house in California on August 10 for $500,000. She paid a $14,000 sales commission. The house was acquired on March 23, 1987, for $140,000.

The cost of transporting her household goods and personal effects from California to Orlando amounted to $2,350. To travel from California to Florida, she paid travel and lodging costs of $370 and $100 for meals.

On July 15, she purchased a house for $270,000 on 1225 Minnie Lane in Orlando. To purchase the house, she incurred a 20-year mortgage for $170,000. To obtain the loan, she paid points of $3,400. The $3,600 of property taxes for the house in Orlando were prorated with $1,950 being apportioned to the seller and $1,650 being apportioned to the buyer. In December of the current year she paid $3,600 for property taxes.

Other information related to her return:

Salary from Farah Movie, Inc.	$30,000
Salary from Ocala Production, Inc.	70,000
Federal income taxes withheld by Farah	6,000
Federal income taxes withheld by Ocala	22,000
FICA taxes withheld by Farah	2,295
FICA taxes withheld by Ocala	5,355
Dividend income	10,000
Interest paid for mortgage:	
Home in California	6,780
Home in Orlando	3,800
Property taxes paid in California	4,100
Sales taxes paid in California and Florida	3,125
State income taxes paid in California	2,900
Interest income from Sun National Bank	1,800

Prepare Form 1040 including Schedules A, B, and D and Form 3903. Use the worksheet on page 12-23 to determine the amount of recognized gain on the sale of the residence.

I:12-57 Jim Sarowski (SSN 344-77-9255) is 70 years old and single. He received Social Security benefits of $16,000. He works part-time as a greeter at a local discount store and received wages of $7,300. Federal income taxes of $250 were withheld from his salary. Jim lives at Rt. 7 in Daingerfield, Texas.

In March of the current year, he purchased a duplex at 2006 Tennessee Street to use as rental property for $100,000, with 20% of the price allocated to land. During the current year, he had the following receipts and expenditures with respect to the duplex:

Rent receipts	$8,800
Interest paid	5,900
Property taxes	1,400
Insurance	800
Maintenance	300

Other expenditures during the current year:

Contributions to the church	$2,600
Personal property taxes	225
Sales tax	345

On July 24 of the current year, he exchanged ten acres of land for a car with a $16,500 FMV to be held for personal use. The land was purchased on November 22, 1991, for $18,000 as an investment. Because of pollution problems in the area, the value of the land declined.

On December 1 of the current year, he sold his residence, which had been his home for 30 years, for $475,000. Sales commissions of $16,000 were paid, and the adjusted basis for his home is $110,000. He plans to rent an apartment and does not plan to purchase another home. His only other sale of a principal residence occurred 32 years ago.

Prepare Forms 1040 and 4562 and Schedules D and E. Use the worksheet on page 12-23 to determine the amount of recognized gain on the sale of the residence.

CASE STUDY PROBLEMS

I:12-58 The Electric Corporation, a publicly held corporation, owns land with a $1,600,000 basis that is being held for investment. The company is considering exchanging the land for two assets owned by the Quail Corporation: land with a FMV of $4,000,000 and marketable securities with a $1,000,000 FMV. Both assets will be held by the Electric Corporation for investment, although the corporation is considering the possibility of developing the land and building residential houses. The president of the corporation has hired you to prepare a report explaining how the exchange will affect the corporation's reported net income and its tax liability. The corporation has a tax rate of 34%.

TAX RESEARCH PROBLEMS

I:12-59 For the last nine years, Mr. and Mrs. Orchard live in a residence located on eight acres. In January of the current year they sell the home and two acres of land. The purchaser of the residence does not wish to own the entire eight acres of land. In December they sell the remaining six acres of land to another individual for $60,000. The house and the land have never been used by the Orchards in a trade or business or held for investment. The realized gains resulting from the two sales are computed as follows:

	House and Two Acres January Sales	Eight Acres December Sale
Selling price	$140,000	$60,000
Minus: Selling expenses	(8,000)	(3,000)
Amount realized	$132,000	$57,000
Minus: Basis	(80,000)	(18,000)
Realized gain	$ 52,000	$39,000

As a result of the sales described above, what is the amount of realized gain that must be recognized during the current year?

A partial list of research sources is:

- Reg. Sec. 1.121-1(b)

I:12-60 George, age 68, decides to retire from farming and is considering selling his farm. The farm has a $100,000 basis and a $400,000 FMV. George's two sons are not interested in farming. Both sons have large families and would like to own houses suitable for their needs. The Iowa Corporation is willing to purchase George's farm. George's tax advisor suggests that Iowa Corporation should buy the two houses the sons want to own for $400,000 and then exchange the houses for George's farm. After the exchange, George could make a gift of the houses to the sons.

a. If the transactions are executed as suggested by the tax advisor, George's recognized gain will be $300,000. Explain why the transaction does not qualify as a like-kind exchange.

b. George wants the exchange to qualify as a like-kind exchange and still help his sons obtain the houses. What advice do you have for him?

A partial list of research sources is:

- *Dollie H. Click,* 78 T.C. 225 (1982)

- *Fred S. Wagensen,* 74 T.C. 653 (1980)

I:12-61 On March 10, 2007, Elizabeth, a college professor, purchased a house for $300,000. She did not move into the house until August 8, 2007. On August 1, 2008, she accepted a position as a visiting professor at Hogwatts University for one year and moved to Liverpool where she rented an apartment. While away at Hogwatts, two of her former students lived in the house but did not pay rent. She returned to the house on August 1,

2009, and lived in the house until July 15, 2010, when she sold the house for $500,000. The realtor's commission was $35,000. Determine her recognized gain.

A partial list of research sources is:

- Reg. Sec. 1.121-1(c)

I:12-62 Mr. and Mrs. Hattan have lived in their residence for 20 years and purchased the house for $100,000 as joint tenants with right of survivorship. Mr. Hattan died in May of the current year when the house's FMV was $800,000. Mrs. Hattan wants to sell the house. What is the tax effect of selling the house this year for $825,000 or next year for $830,000?

A partial list of research sources is:

- Sections 121 and 1014

I:12-63 Joseph Allen, who is single, purchased his first house in Orono, ME. one year ago for $200,000. Katahdin wants to purchase the house for $360,000. Refer to the regulations to determine if he may exclude part of the gain in the following independent cases:

a. He has been unemployed for 16 months and has a chance to start work for Penobscot Manufacturing whose plant is located 62 miles from Joseph's home in Orono.

b. His dependent son, Ryan, has chronic asthma, and the son's doctor has advised Joseph that Ryan should live in a warm, dry climate to mitigate the chronic asthma. Joseph and Ryan move to Nevada.

c. Joseph has become increasingly annoyed at the amount of traffic in his neighborhood although the amount of traffic has not increased much compared to the traffic when he purchased the house.

A partial list of research sources is:

- Reg. Sec. 1.121-3(c), (d) and (e)

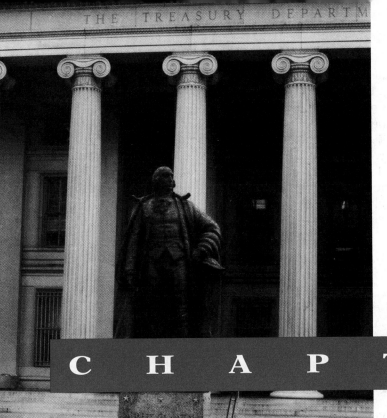

13

C H A P T E R

PROPERTY TRANSACTIONS: SECTION 1231 AND RECAPTURE

LEARNING OBJECTIVES

After studying this chapter, you should be able to

1 ▶ Identify Sec. 1231 property

2 ▶ Understand the tax treatment for Sec. 1231 transactions

3 ▶ Apply the recapture provisions of Sec. 1245

4 ▶ Apply the recapture provisions of Sec. 1250

5 ▶ Describe other recapture applications

Chapter I:5 states that all recognized gains and losses must eventually be designated as either capital or ordinary. However, gains or losses on certain types of property are designated as Sec. 1231 gains or losses, which are given preferential treatment under the tax law. Sec. 1231 property primarily is business property, either real or depreciable property used in a trade or business.[1] A net Sec. 1231 loss, defined as the excess of Sec. 1231 losses over Sec. 1231 gains, is treated as an ordinary loss.[2] Net Sec. 1231 gain, the excess of Sec. 1231 gains over Sec. 1231 losses, is generally treated as long-term capital gain.[3] However, the preferential treatment of Sec. 1231 gains is diminished, principally by the so-called depreciation recapture rules and the five-year lookback rule. This chapter discusses the important rules dealing with Sec. 1231 gains and losses and depreciation recapture.

HISTORY OF SEC. 1231

KEY POINT

Taxpayers normally prefer to have gains treated as capital gains, and losses treated as ordinary losses. Because Sec. 1231 property receives the preferable treatment for both net gains and losses, it has been said that this property enjoys the best of both worlds.

During the depressed economy of the early and mid-1930s, business property was classified as a capital asset. Many business properties were worth less than their adjusted basis. Instead of selling business properties, taxpayers found it advantageous to retain assets that had declined in value because they could recover the full cost as depreciation. Capital losses had only limited deductibility during this period. To encourage the mobility of capital (i.e., the replacement of business fixed assets), the Revenue Act of 1938 added business property to the list of properties not considered to be capital assets.

From 1938 to 1942, gains and losses on the sale or exchange of business property were treated as ordinary gains and losses. Favorable capital gain treatment was eliminated and taxpayers with appreciated business properties were reluctant to sell the assets because of the high tax cost. This restriction on the mobility of capital was more significant than usual because business assets had to be shifted into industries that were more heavily involved in the production of military goods. Furthermore, taxpayers were often forced to recognize ordinary gains because the government used the condemnation process to obtain business property for the war effort. In 1942, Congress created the predecessor of Sec. 1231, which allowed taxpayers to treat net gains from the sale of business property as capital gains and net losses as ordinary losses. Before 1987, only 40% of an individual's net capital gain might be subject to tax because of the 60% long-term capital gain deduction.

The Tax Reform Act of 1986 eliminated the 60% long-term capital gain deduction for net capital gains. Favorable long-term capital gain treatment was reinstated into the tax law in 1991 in the form of a 28% maximum tax rate applying to net capital gains for noncorporate taxpayers. The Taxpayer Relief Act of 1997 significantly increased the preferential tax treatment by reducing the maximum rate to 20% for net capital gain that is adjusted net capital gain. The maximum rate was reduced by the Jobs and Growth Tax Relief Reconciliation Act of 2003 (2003 Tax Act) to 15%, for sales after May 5, 2003.

It may also be advantageous to have gains classified as capital or Sec. 1231 if taxpayers have capital losses or capital loss carryovers because of the limitations imposed on the deductibility of capital losses. Furthermore, there are other situations where it may be important for the property to be Sec. 1231 property (e.g., a contribution of appreciated property to a charitable organization).

---

[1] (See page I:13-5 for a more complete definition of Sec. 1231 property.)
[2] Secs. 1231(c)(4) and (a)(2).

[3] Secs. 1231(c)(3) and (a)(1). There are several exceptions to this rule that are covered later in this chapter.

OVERVIEW OF BASIC TAX TREATMENT FOR SEC. 1231

NET GAINS

At the end of the tax year, Sec. 1231 gains are netted against Sec. 1231 losses. If the over-all result is a net Sec. 1231 gain, the gains and losses are treated as long-term capital gains (LTCGs) and long-term capital losses (LTCLs), respectively.[4] For the sake of expediency, it is often stated that a net Sec. 1231 gain is treated as a LTCG. For tax years beginning after 1984, however, a portion or all of the net Sec. 1231 gain may be treated as ordinary income because of a special five-year lookback rule (see discussion below).

EXAMPLE I:13-1 ▶ Dawn owns a business that has $20,000 of Sec. 1231 gains and $12,000 of Sec. 1231 losses dur-ing the current year. Because the Sec. 1231 gains exceed the Sec. 1231 losses, the gains and losses are treated as LTCGs and LTCLs. After the gains and losses are offset, there is an $8,000 net long-term capital gain (NLTCG). ◀

EXAMPLE I:13-2 ▶ Assume the same facts as in Example I:13-1 except that Dawn also recognizes a $7,000 LTCG from the sale of a capital asset. After considering the $8,000 net Sec. 1231 gain, which is treated as a LTCG, Dawn has a $15,000 NLTCG ($8,000 + $7,000). ◀

NET LOSSES

If the netting of Sec. 1231 gains and losses at the end of the year results in a net Sec. 1231 loss, the Sec. 1231 gains and losses are treated as ordinary gains and losses.[5] For expedi-ency, it is often stated that the net Sec. 1231 loss is treated as an ordinary loss.

EXAMPLE I:13-3 ▶ David owns an unincorporated business and has $30,000 of Sec. 1231 gains and $40,000 of Sec. 1231 losses in the current year. Because the losses exceed the gains, they are treated as ordinary losses and gains. ◀

EXAMPLE I:13-4 ▶ Assume the same facts as in Example I:13-3 except that David receives a $37,000 salary as a cor-porate employee. David has no other income, losses, or deductions affecting his adjusted gross income (AGI). The Sec. 1231 gains and losses are treated as ordinary gains and losses, and David's AGI is $27,000 ($37,000 salary − $10,000 of ordinary loss). The $40,000 of ordinary losses offsets the $30,000 of ordinary gains and $10,000 of David's salary. ◀

TYPICAL MISCONCEPTION

It is sometimes erroneously thought that each Sec. 1231 gain should be treated as a LTCG and each Sec. 1231 loss as an ordinary loss. However all Sec. 1231 gains and losses must be combined to determine whether the Sec. 1231 gains and losses are LTCGs and LTCLs or ordinary gains and losses.

One important advantage of Sec. 1231 is illustrated in Example I:13-4. Because the Sec. 1231 gains and losses are treated as ordinary, the $10,000 net Sec. 1231 loss is fully deductible in the current year. If the gains and losses were classified as long-term capital gains and losses, David would have a $10,000 net long-term capital loss (NLTCL). Only $3,000 of the $10,000 NLTCL would have been deductible against David's other income. As explained in Chapter I:5, only $3,000 of net capital losses may be deducted from non-capital gain income per year.

ADDITIONAL COMMENT

A taxpayer's share of a Sec. 1231 loss from a partnership or S Corporation may be subject to the passive activity loss rules.

FIVE-YEAR LOOKBACK RULE Beginning in 1985, the benefits of Sec. 1231 were reduced. For tax years beginning after 1984, any net Sec. 1231 gain is ordinary gain to the extent of any nonrecaptured net Sec. 1231 losses from the previous five years.[6] This pro-vision is referred to as the *five-year lookback rule*. In essence, net Sec. 1231 losses previ-ously deducted as ordinary losses are recaptured by changing what would otherwise be a LTCG into ordinary income.

EXAMPLE I:13-5 ▶ In 2010, Craig recognizes $25,000 of Sec. 1231 gains and $15,000 of Sec. 1231 losses. In 2006, Craig reported $14,000 of Sec. 1231 losses and no Sec. 1231 gains. No other Sec. 1231 gains or losses were recognized by Craig during the prior five-year period, 2005–2009. The $10,000

---

[4] Sec. 1231(a)(1).
[5] Sec. 1231(a)(2).

[6] Sec. 1231(c)(1).

HISTORICAL NOTE

Congress reduced the benefits of Sec. 1231 by requiring the recapture of any nonrecaptured net Sec. 1231 loss. This recapture is required because taxpayers have a certain amount of control over the timing of the recognition of Sec. 1231 gains or losses. Taxpayers had attempted to recognize Sec. 1231 losses in one year and Sec. 1231 gains in another year to avoid the netting process.

($25,000 − $15,000) of net Sec. 1231 gain in 2010 is treated as ordinary income due to the $14,000 of nonrecaptured net Sec. 1231 losses. ◄

To determine the amount of nonrecaptured net Sec. 1231 losses, compare the aggregate amount of net Sec. 1231 losses for the most recent preceding five tax years with the amount of such losses recaptured as ordinary income for those preceding tax years. The excess of the aggregate amount of net Sec. 1231 losses over the previously recaptured loss is the nonrecaptured net Sec. 1231 loss. In Example I:13-5, $4,000 of nonrecaptured net Sec. 1231 losses remain that can be recaptured in 2011. In 2011, the preceding five-year period includes 2006 through 2010.

TAX RATE FOR NET SEC. 1231 GAIN

In general, net Sec. 1231 gains are taxed similarly to the taxation of net long-term capital gains. Thus, a Sec. 1231 gain may be taxed at a rate of 15% (or zero if the taxpayer's regular tax rate is 15% or less). Sec. 1231 property must have a holding period of more than one year. Recall from Chapter I:5 that adjusted net capital gain (ANCG) is net capital gain (NCG) determined *without* regard to:

(1) the 28% rate gain, and
(2) unrecaptured Sec. 1250 gain, which is taxed at no more than 25% as explained later.

ANCG might be taxed at 15% or zero beginning in 2008. For years before 2008, the rate of tax on ANCG for taxpayers in the 10% or 15% tax brackets was 5%. If Sec. 1231 property is sold at a gain, the Sec. 1231 gain is LTCG if there are no Sec. 1231 losses or nonrecaptured net Sec. 1231 losses. However, all or part of this gain is unrecaptured Section 1250 gain if the asset is a building. Thus, net Sec. 1231 gain might be taxed today at 15%, or 25% depending on the taxpayer's tax rate and whether or not the gain is unrecaptured section 1250 gain. Part or all of Sec. 1231 gain due to the sale of real property subject to depreciation that is unrecaptured Sec. 1250 gain is taxed at a maximum of 25%.

EXAMPLE I:13-6 ▶   Savannah, whose tax rate is 28%, sells land at a gain of $10,000 and other land at a gain of $15,000. Both tracts of land qualify as Sec. 1231 property. She has no other transactions involving capital assets or 1231 property and no nonrecaptured net Sec. 1231 losses. Savannah has net Sec. 1231 gain of $25,000 that is NLTCG and her NCG is $25,000. Her ANCG is $25,000 taxed at a rate of 15%. ◄

EXAMPLE I:13-7 ▶   Assume the same facts as in Example I:13-6 except Savannah also has a $7,000 loss from the sale of a third tract of land that is Sec. 1231 property. Her net Sec. 1231 gain is $18,000. Her NCG is $18,000 and her ANCG is $18,000 taxed at a rate of 15%. ◄

EXAMPLE I:13-8 ▶   Grace, whose tax rate is 15% or less, sells land that is Sec. 1231 property at a gain of $2,000. She has no other transactions involving capital assets or 1231 property and no nonrecaptured net Sec. 1231 losses. The $2,000 gain is not taxed since her tax rate is 15% or less. In 2007 and earlier years, the $2,000 gain would be taxed at 5%. ◄

ADDITIONAL COMMENT

Because Sec. 1231 property in Examples I:13-6, I:13-7, and I:13-8 is land, none of the gain is unrecaptured Section 1250 gain.

APPLYING THE FIVE-YEAR LOOKBACK RULE.   As explained earlier, net Sec. 1231 gain is ordinary income to the extent of nonrecaptured net Sec. 1231 losses. Net Sec. 1231 gain is recharacterized as ordinary income under the five-year lookback rule in the following order:

(1) Net Sec. 1231 gain in the 25% group (unrecaptured Sec. 1250 gain)
(2) Net Sec. 1231 gain in the 15% group

EXAMPLE I:13-9 ▶   Chris, whose tax rate is 33%, has nonrecaptured net Sec. 1231 losses of $20,000 at the beginning of the current year when he recognizes gains from the sale of two assets used in his trade or business and held more than one year. Asset #1 is a building and the entire $14,000 Sec. 1231 gain is unrecaptured Sec. 1250 gain. Asset #2 is land and the Sec. 1231 gain is $15,000. All gain resulting from the sale of asset #1 is ordinary income and $6,000 of the gain from the sale of asset #2 is ordinary income because of the five-year lookback rule. The remaining $9,000 gain from the sale of asset #2 (land) is taxed at 15%. ◄

SECTION 1231 PROPERTY

OBJECTIVE 1

Identify Sec. 1231 property

SECTION 1231 PROPERTY DEFINED

Section 1231 property includes the following types of property:

▶ Real property or depreciable property used in a trade or business with a holding period of more than one year

▶ Timber, coal, or domestic iron ore

▶ Livestock

▶ Unharvested crops

Each of these types of Sec. 1231 assets are discussed below.

REAL OR DEPRECIABLE PROPERTY USED IN TRADE OR BUSINESS

KEY POINT

Inventory, free publications of the U.S. government, copyrights, as well as literary, musical, or artistic compositions are not capital assets.

As noted in Chapter I:5, the Code does not provide a definition of a capital asset. Instead, Sec. 1221 provides a list of noncapital assets. This list includes both depreciable property and real property used in a trade or business.[7] These properties are treated as Sec. 1231 properties if held for more than one year. Depreciable property and real property used in a trade or business and held for **one year or less** are neither capital assets nor Sec. 1231 property. Any gain or loss resulting from the disposition of such assets is ordinary.

EXAMPLE I:13-10 ▶

The Prime Corporation owns land held as an investment and land used as an employee parking lot. The land held as an investment is a capital asset. The land used as a parking lot is real property used in a trade or business and is not a capital asset. The land used as a parking lot is a Sec. 1231 asset if held for more than one year. ◀

EXAMPLE I:13-11 ▶

KEY POINT

Only property used in a trade or business is included in the definition of Sec. 1231 property. Gains and losses on property held for investment may be included only if the result of a condemnation or casualty.

Dale, a self-employed plumber, owns an automobile held for personal use and a truck used in his trade. The automobile is a capital asset because it is held for personal use, but the truck is a Sec. 1231 asset if held for more than one year. As described later, a portion or all of any gain realized on the sale of the truck may be taxed as ordinary income due to the Sec. 1245 depreciation recapture provisions which are explained on page 8. ◀

Certain types of property do not qualify as Sec. 1231 property, even if used in a trade or business. For example, inventory is not Sec. 1231 property. Thus, a sale of inventory results in ordinary gain or loss. Publications of the U.S. Government received other than by purchase at its regular sale price; a copyright; literary, musical, or artistic compositions; letters or memorandums; or similar properties held by certain taxpayers are not classified as Sec. 1231 property.[8]

EXAMPLE I:13-12 ▶

KEY POINT

The record company in example I:13-12 may amortize the cost of the copyright. The copyright is Sec. 1231 property if held more than one year.

Carl, who owns a recording studio, writes a musical composition and obtains a copyright that is sold to a record company. Because the musical composition is created by the personal efforts of the taxpayer, the musical composition is not Sec. 1231 property, and the sale results in ordinary gain from the sale of an ordinary asset. ◀

REAL-WORLD EXAMPLE

Christmas trees can be included in the definition of Sec. 1231 property.

TIMBER.   Section 631 allows taxpayers to elect to treat the cutting of timber as a sale or exchange of such timber. To be eligible to make this election, the taxpayer must own the timber or hold the contract right on the first day of the year and for more than one year. Furthermore, the timber must be cut for sale or for use in the taxpayer's trade or business.[9]

The gain or loss is determined by comparing the timber's adjusted basis for depletion with its fair market value (FMV) on the first day of the tax year in which it is cut. If the timber is eventually sold for more or less than its FMV (determined on the first day of the year the timber is cut), the difference is ordinary gain or loss.

---

[7] Sec. 1221(2).
[8] Sec. 1231(b)(1).

[9] Sec. 631(a) and Reg. Sec. 1.631-1.

EXAMPLE I:13-13 ▶ Vermont Corporation owns timber with a $60,000 basis for depletion. The timber, acquired four years ago, is cut during the current year for use in the corporation's business. The FMV of the timber on the first day of the current year is $200,000. Vermont Corporation may elect to treat the cutting of the timber as a sale or exchange and recognize a $140,000 ($200,000 − $60,000) gain. ◀

If the election is made to treat the cutting of timber as a sale or exchange, the timber is considered Sec. 1231 property.[10] Thus, the $140,000 gain in Example I:13-13 is Sec. 1231 gain. If the taxpayer does not make the election, the character of any gain or loss depends on whether the timber is held for sale in the ordinary course of the taxpayer's trade or business, held for investment, or held for use in a trade or business.

COAL OR DOMESTIC IRON ORE.   An owner who disposes of coal (including lignite) or domestic iron ore while retaining an economic interest in it must treat the disposal as a sale.[11] The coal or iron ore is considered Sec. 1231 property.[12] The owner must own and retain an economic interest in the coal or iron ore in place.[13] An economic interest is owned when one acquires by investment any interest in mineral in place and seeks a return of capital from income derived from the extraction of the mineral.

LIVESTOCK.   Livestock held by the taxpayer for draft, breeding, dairy, or sporting purposes is considered Sec. 1231 property if held for 12 months or more from the date of acquisition. However, cattle and horses must be held for 24 months or more from the date of acquisition to qualify as Sec. 1231 property.[14]

UNHARVESTED CROPS AND LAND.   An unharvested crop growing on land used in a trade or business is considered Sec. 1231 property if the crop and the land are both sold at the same time to the same person and the land is held more than one year.[15] Section 1231 does not apply to the sale or exchange of an unharvested crop if the taxpayer retains any right or option to reacquire the land.[16]

If Sec. 1231 applies to the sale or exchange of an unharvested crop sold with the land, no deductions are allowed for expenses attributable to the production of the unharvested crop.[17] Instead, costs of producing the crop must be capitalized.

INVOLUNTARY CONVERSIONS

Gains and losses from involuntary conversions of property used in a trade or business generally are classified as Sec. 1231 gains and losses. Involuntary conversions of capital assets that are held in connection with a trade or business or in a transaction entered into for profit also generally qualify for Sec. 1231 treatment. The property that is involuntarily converted must be held more than one year. Certain involuntary conversions are treated differently for income tax purposes. For example, the tax rules are different for condemnations and casualties, even though both are involuntary conversions of property.

CONDEMNATIONS

Gains and losses resulting from condemnations of Sec. 1231 property and capital assets held more than one year are classified as Sec. 1231 gains and losses. As indicated above, the capital assets must be held in connection with a trade or business or with a transaction entered into for profit.[18]

EXAMPLE I:13-14 ▶ Kathryn owns land with a $20,000 basis and a $30,000 FMV as well as a building with a $40,000 adjusted basis and a $26,000 FMV. Both assets are used in her trade or business and have been held for more than one year. As a result of the state exercising its powers of requisition or con-

---

[10] Sec. 1231(b)(2) and Reg. Sec. 1.631-1(d)(4).
[11] Sec. 631(c) and Reg. Sec. 1.631-3(a)(1).
[12] Sec. 1231(b)(2) and Reg. Sec. 1.631-3(a)(2).
[13] Reg. Sec. 1.631-3(b)(4).
[14] Sec. 1231(b)(3).

[15] Sec. 1231(b)(4) and Reg. Secs. 1.1231-1(c)(5) and 1(f).
[16] Reg. Sec. 1.1231-1(f).
[17] Sec. 268 and Reg. Sec. 1.268-1.
[18] Secs. 1231(a)(3)(A) and (4)(B).

demnation, Kathryn is required to transfer both properties to the state for cash equal to their FMVs. No other transfers of assets occur during the current year. The $10,000 gain due to condemnation of the land is a Sec. 1231 gain and the $14,000 loss due to condemnation of the building is a Sec. 1231 loss. ◄

OTHER INVOLUNTARY CONVERSIONS

TYPICAL MISCONCEPTION

The inclusion of gains and losses from condemnations in the netting of the other involuntary conversions is a common error.

Gains or losses resulting from an involuntary conversion arising from fire, storm, shipwreck, other casualty, or theft are not classified as Sec. 1231 gains or losses if the recognized losses from such conversions exceed the recognized gains.[19] In such a case, the involuntary conversions are treated as ordinary gains and losses. However, if the gains from such involuntary conversions exceed the losses, both are classified as Sec. 1231 gains and losses.

EXAMPLE I:13-15 ▶ Jose owns equipment having a $50,000 adjusted basis and a $42,000 FMV and a building having a $30,000 adjusted basis and a $35,000 FMV which are used in Jose's trade or business. The straight-line method of depreciation is used for the building. Both assets are held for more than a year. As a result of a fire, both assets are destroyed, and Jose collects insurance proceeds equal to the assets' FMV. No other transfers of assets occur during the current year. Because the $8,000 ($42,000 − $50,000) recognized loss exceeds the $5,000 ($35,000 − $30,000) recognized gain, the recognized loss and gain are both treated as ordinary. ◄

PROCEDURE FOR SEC. 1231 TREATMENT

OBJECTIVE 2

Understand the tax treatment for Sec. 1231 transactions

After determining the recognized gains and losses from transfers of property qualifying for Sec. 1231 treatment, it is necessary to determine whether any gain must be recaptured as ordinary income under Secs. 1245 and 1250. The recaptured gain, discussed later in this chapter, is not eligible for Sec. 1231 treatment. After eliminating the gain recaptured as ordinary income due to the recapture of depreciation, the procedure for analyzing Sec. 1231 transactions is as follows:

STEP 1. Determine all gains and losses resulting from casualties or thefts of Sec. 1231 property and non–personal-use capital assets held for more than one year. Gains and losses are netted and the net gain is treated as Sec. 1231 gain if the gains exceed the losses.

If the losses exceed the gains, both are treated as ordinary losses and gains and do not, therefore, enter into the Sec. 1231 netting procedure. Recall from Chapter I:7 that business casualty losses are deductible *for* AGI and other casualty losses are deductible *from* AGI.

KEY POINT

Gains that are recaptured under Secs. 1245 and 1250 are not eligible for Sec. 1231 treatment.

STEP 2. Combine the following gains and losses to determine whether Sec. 1231 gains exceed Sec. 1231 losses or vice versa:

▶ Net casualty and theft *gains* resulting from Step 1, if any

▶ Gains and losses resulting from the sale or exchange of Sec. 1231 property

▶ Gains and losses resulting from the condemnation of Sec. 1231 property and non–personal-use capital assets held more than one year.

If a net Sec. 1231 loss is the result, the losses and gains are treated as ordinary losses and gains. If a net Sec. 1231 gain is the result, the gains and losses are treated as LTCGs and LTCLs, although a portion or all of the capital gain may be recaptured as ordinary income as outlined in Step 3 (five-year lookback rule) below.

STEP 3. If a net Sec. 1231 gain is the result of Step 2, determine if the taxpayer has any nonrecaptured net Sec. 1231 losses. Nonrecaptured net Sec. 1231 losses are the excess of aggregate net Sec. 1231 losses for the preceding five years over losses previously recaptured as ordinary income due to the recapture provision of Sec. 1231. Net Sec. 1231 gains to the extent of any nonrecaptured net Sec. 1231 losses are treated as ordinary income. Sec. 1231 gain that is unrecaptured Sec. 1250 gain is first treated as ordinary income to the extent of nonrecaptured net Sec. 1231 losses. Any net Sec. 1231 gain in excess of nonrecaptured net Sec. 1231 loss is treated as a LTCG.

---

[19] Sec. 1231(a)(4)(C).

EXAMPLE I:13-16 ▶ The following gains and losses pertain to Danielle's business assets that qualify as Sec. 1231 property. Danielle does not have any nonrecaptured net Sec. 1231 losses from previous years, and the portion of gain recaptured as ordinary income due to the depreciation recapture provisions has been considered.

Gain due to an insurance reimbursement for fire damage	$10,000
Loss due to condemnation	(19,000)
Gain due to the sale of Sec. 1231 property	22,000

The $10,000 casualty gain is classified as a Sec. 1231 gain because gains resulting from casualties or thefts of Sec. 1231 property exceed losses. Danielle has $32,000 ($10,000 + $22,000) of Sec. 1231 gains and a $19,000 Sec. 1231 loss. Danielle's $13,000 net Sec. 1231 gain is treated as a LTCG. No portion of the $13,000 LTCG is recaptured as ordinary income because Danielle does not have any nonrecaptured net Sec. 1231 losses during the preceding five-year period. ◀

EXAMPLE I:13-17 ▶ Assume the same facts as in Example I:13-16 except that Danielle has a $10,000 loss because of the fire instead of a $10,000 gain. The $10,000 casualty loss is an ordinary loss, not a Sec. 1231 loss because losses resulting from casualties or thefts of Sec. 1231 property exceed gains. Because the loss is a business loss, it is deductible *for* AGI. Due to the $19,000 condemnation loss and the $22,000 of Sec. 1231 gain, she has a $3,000 net Sec. 1231 gain that is treated as a LTCG. ◀

EXAMPLE I:13-18 ▶ The following gains and losses recognized in 2010 pertain to Fred's business assets that were held for more than one year. The assets qualify as Sec. 1231 property.

Gain due to an insurance reimbursement for a casualty	$15,000
Gain due to a condemnation	25,000
Loss due to the sale of Sec. 1231 property	(12,000)

A summary of Fred's net Sec. 1231 gains and losses for the previous five-year period is as follows:

Year	Sec. 1231 Gain	Sec. 1231 Loss	Cumulative Nonrecaptured Net Sec. 1231 Losses (from five prior years)
2005	$ 5,000		–0–
2006		$2,000	$2,000
2007		6,000	8,000
2008	13,000		–0–
2009		9,000	9,000

The $15,000 gain due to the insurance reimbursement for a casualty is treated as a Sec. 1231 gain. The $25,000 gain from the condemnation is also a Sec. 1231 gain. Fred's net Sec. 1231 gain in 2010 is $28,000 [($15,000 + $25,000) − $12,000]. However, $9,000 of the Sec. 1231 gain is recaptured as ordinary income due to the $9,000 of nonrecaptured net Sec. 1231 loss from 2009. The remaining $19,000 of net Sec. 1231 gain is a LTCG. ◀

RECAPTURE PROVISIONS OF SEC. 1245

OBJECTIVE 3

Apply the recapture provisions of Sec. 1245

In 1962, Congress enacted Sec. 1245, which substantially reduced the advantages of Sec. 1231. A gain from the disposition of Sec. 1245 property is treated as ordinary income to the extent of the total amount of depreciation (or cost-recovery) deductions allowed since January 1, 1962. The gain recaptured as ordinary income cannot exceed the amount of the realized gain.

EXAMPLE I:13-19 ▶ Adobe Corporation sells equipment used in its trade or business for $95,000. The equipment was acquired several years ago for $110,000 and is Sec. 1245 property.[20] The equipment's adjusted basis is $60,000 because $50,000 of depreciation was deducted. The entire $35,000 ($95,000 − $60,000) gain is treated as ordinary income because the total amount of depreciation taken ($50,000) is greater than the $35,000 realized gain. ◀

---

[20] Throughout this chapter, property is considered to be placed in service when it is purchased or acquired. The term *Sec. 1245 property* is used here to refer to either recovery property under the ACRS or MACRS rules or nonrecovery property that falls outside of the ACRS or MACRS rules.

The recapture provisions of Sec. 1245 apply to the total amount of depreciation (or cost recovery) allowed or allowable for Sec. 1245 property. It makes no difference which method of depreciation is used.[21]

Generally, the entire gain from the disposition of Sec. 1245 property is recaptured as ordinary income because the total amount of depreciation (or cost recovery) is greater than the gain realized. A portion of the gain will receive Sec. 1231 treatment if the realized gain exceeds total depreciation or cost recovery.

EXAMPLE I:13-20 ▶   Assume the same facts as in Example I:13-19 except that the asset is sold for $117,000. Because the $57,000 ($117,000 − $60,000) realized gain is greater than the $50,000 of total depreciation, $50,000 of the gain is ordinary income and the remaining $7,000 is a Sec. 1231 gain. ◀

PURPOSE OF SEC. 1245

The purpose of Sec. 1245 is to eliminate any advantage taxpayers would have if they were able to reduce ordinary income by deducting depreciation and subsequently receive Sec. 1231 treatment when the asset was sold. For individuals, Sec. 1245 recapture prevents net Sec. 1231 gain from being treated as LTCG. The conversion of Sec. 1231 gain to Sec. 1245 ordinary income also prevents taxpayers from possibly using capital losses.

EXAMPLE I:13-21 ▶   During the current year, Coastal Corporation has capital losses of $50,000 and no capital gains for the current year or the preceding three years. The corporation owns equipment purchased several years ago for $90,000, and depreciation deductions of $48,000 have been allowed. If Coastal sells the equipment for $72,000, the entire $30,000 ($72,000 − $42,000) gain, which is due to the depreciation deductions, is Sec. 1245 ordinary income. Without Sec. 1245, the $30,000 gain is a Sec. 1231 gain that could be offset by $30,000 of the corporation's capital loss. ◀

Note that Sec. 1245 does not apply to losses. If Coastal Corporation sells the equipment in Example I:13-21 for $40,000, a $2,000 ($40,000 − $42,000 basis) Sec. 1231 loss is recognized.

SECTION 1245 PROPERTY. **Section 1245 property** is certain property subject to depreciation and, in some cases, amortization. The most common example of Sec. 1245 property is depreciable personal property such as equipment. Automobiles, livestock, railroad grading, and single-purpose agricultural or horticultural structures are Sec. 1245 properties as well as intangible assets subject to amortization under Sec. 197 (see Chapter I:10).[22] Except for certain buildings placed in service after 1980 and before 1987, buildings and structural components generally are not Sec. 1245 property.[23]

EXAMPLE I:13-22 ▶   Buckeye Corporation owns the following assets acquired in 1999: equipment, a patent, an office building (including structural components), and land. The equipment and patent are Sec. 1245 property. The office building and the land are not Sec. 1245 property. ◀

In many cases, taxpayers are allowed preferential treatment with respect to amortizing certain costs. For example, taxpayers may elect to expense up to $15,000 of the cost of making any business facility more accessible to handicapped and elderly people,[24] or to amortize pollution control facilities over 60 months[25] and reforestation expenditures over 84 months.[26] If taxpayers have amortized the costs of any real property under the special provisions, Sec. 1245 applies to the gain resulting from the disposition of such property.[27]

If taxpayers elect to expense certain depreciable property under Sec. 179, the amount deducted is treated as a depreciation deduction for purposes of the Sec. 1245 recapture provisions.[28]

---

[21] As explained later in this chapter, the method of cost recovery used determines whether certain real property is treated as Sec. 1245 recovery property.
[22] Sec. 1245(a)(3).
[23] Sec. 1245(a)(3)(B)(i). Tangible real property "used as an integral part of the manufacturing, production, extraction, or furnishing of transportation, communication, electrical energy, gas, water, or sewage disposal services" is Sec. 1245 property.
[24] Sec. 190.

[25] Sec. 169(a).
[26] Sec. 194(a).
[27] Sec. 1245(a)(3)(C). The Sec. 1245 rules recapture amortization deductions claimed on real property under Secs. 169, 179, 185, 188, 190, 193, and 194.
[28] Sec. 1245(a)(2)(C). The maximum amount deductible under Sec. 179 is $250,000 in 2008–2010, $125,000 in 2007, $108,000 in 2006 and $105,000 in 2005.

EXAMPLE I:13-23 ▶ Compact Corporation purchased $90,000 of five-year equipment on March 10, 2009, and elected to expense $20,000 of the cost under Sec. 179. Compact sells the equipment on July 30, 2010, for $95,000. Regular depreciation allowed under MACRS for 2009 and 2010 is $14,000 and $11,200 (½ year), respectively. The adjusted basis of the equipment on the date of sale is $44,800 ($90,000 − $20,000 − $25,200 depreciation). The realized gain is $50,200 ($95,000 − $44,800), and $45,200 ($20,000 + $25,200) of the gain is Sec. 1245 ordinary income. The remaining $5,000 is Sec. 1231 gain. ◀

TYPICAL MISCONCEPTION

The categorization of nonresidential real estate acquired between 1981 and 1986 on which an accelerated depreciation method was used as Sec. 1250 property rather than as Sec. 1245 property is a common error.

APPLICATION OF SEC. 1245 TO NONRESIDENTIAL REAL ESTATE. Most real property is not affected by Sec. 1245. However, Sec. 1245 does apply to nonresidential real estate that qualified as recovery property under the ACRS rules (i.e., placed in service after 1980 and before 1987) unless the taxpayer elected to use the straight-line method of cost recovery.[29] Section 1245 does not apply to nonresidential real estate acquired after 1986, because only straight-line depreciation may be used for nonresidential real estate acquired after 1986 (see Chapter I:10).

EXAMPLE I:13-24 ▶ Brad sells two warehouses during the current year that are totally depreciated because their recovery period is 19 years.

KEY POINT

Taxpayers acquiring nonresidential real property between 1981 and 1986 were confronted with choosing between straight-line ACRS and ACRS using the statutory rates. In making the decision, these taxpayers should have considered the number of years the property would be held, the estimated selling price, the present value of the additional depreciation deductions, and any preferential treatment for net capital gains.

	Warehouse 1	Warehouse 2
Year of purchase	1985	1985
Cost*	$720,000	$900,000
Cost recovery—straight line ACRS	720,000	
Cost recovery—ACRS statutory rates (accelerated)		900,000
Adjusted basis	0	0
Selling price	700,000	800,000

*does not consider the cost of land

Both warehouses were placed in service after 1980 and before 1987 and qualify as recovery property under ACRS. The $700,000 ($700,000 − $0) gain on the sale of Warehouse 1 is a Sec. 1231 gain. Section 1245 does not apply because the straight-line method of cost recovery was used. Section 1245 applies to the sale of Warehouse 2 because ACRS was used and the property is nonresidential real estate placed in service after 1980 and before 1987. Therefore, the $800,000 ($800,000 − $0) gain is Sec. 1245 ordinary income because the $800,000 gain is less than the $900,000 total ACRS cost-recovery allowance. ◀

As illustrated in the example above, nonresidential buildings placed in service after 1980 and before 1987 are Sec. 1245 property if an accelerated method of cost recovery was used.

If the properties in Example I:13-24 were acquired before 1981 or after 1986, they would not be subject to the Sec. 1245 recapture rules regardless of the method of depreciation used. However, nonresidential real estate (e.g., a warehouse) acquired after 1970 and before 1981 is subject to the Sec. 1250 recapture rules, and a portion of the gain from its disposition may be treated as ordinary income if accelerated depreciation was used.[30]

The Sec. 1245 recapture rules are summarized in Topic Review I:13-1.

RECAPTURE PROVISIONS OF SEC. 1250

OBJECTIVE 4

Apply the recapture provisions of Sec. 1250

In 1964, Sec. 1250 was enacted to extend the recapture concept to include most depreciable real property. Unlike Sec. 1245, where the recapture is based upon the total amount of depreciation (or cost recovery) allowed, Sec. 1250 applies solely to additional depreciation. **Additional depreciation,** also referred to as **excess depreciation,** is the excess of the actual amount of accelerated depreciation (or cost-recovery deductions under ACRS) over

---

[29] Sec. 1245(a)(5).

[30] Gain due to the sale or exchange of Sec. 1250 property placed in service before 1981 is ordinary income to the extent of additional depreciation.

Topic Review I:13-1

Section 1245 Recapture

- ▶ Section 1245 affects the character of the gain, not the amount of gain.
- ▶ Section 1245 does not apply to assets sold or exchanged at a loss.
- ▶ Section 1245 ordinary income is never more than the realized gain.
- ▶ Section 1245 recapture applies to the total depreciation or amortization allowed or allowable but not more than the realized gain.
- ▶ Section 1245 property includes depreciable personal property and amortizable intangible assets (e.g., a patent).
- ▶ Section 1245 property includes nonresidential real estate placed in service after 1980 and before 1987 under the ACRS rules *unless* the taxpayer elected to use the straight-line method of cost recovery.
- ▶ Section 1245 does not apply to any buildings placed in service after 1986.

the amount of depreciation that would be deductible under the straight-line method. Any gain due to excess depreciation is Sec. 1250 ordinary income.

EXAMPLE I:13-25 ▶ Wyatt sells a building that was placed in service before 1981 and the gain is $50,000. Accelerated depreciation was used and excess depreciation amounts to $74,000. All $50,000 of the gain is Sec. 1250 ordinary income. If the gain is $90,000, $74,000 is Sec. 1250 ordinary income and $16,000 is Sec. 1231 gain. ◀

PURPOSE OF SEC. 1250

Section 1250 has the effect of converting a portion of the Sec. 1231 gain into ordinary income when real property is sold or exchanged. The incremental benefits from using accelerated depreciation or ACRS cost recovery may be recaptured when the property is sold. Noncorporate taxpayers can avoid Sec. 1250 recapture by either using the straight-line method of depreciation or cost recovery or holding the Sec. 1250 property for its entire useful life or recovery period.

The Sec. 1250 recapture rules are applied solely to the additional depreciation amount instead of total depreciation claimed as is the case for Sec. 1245 property. Sec. 1250 provides for less depreciation recapture than Sec. 1245.

ADDITIONAL COMMENT

Elevators and escalators are Sec. 1245 property if placed in service before 1987, but Sec. 1250 property if placed in service after 1986.

KEY POINT

An apartment building is the most common type of property classified as residential real estate.

SECTION 1250 PROPERTY DEFINED

Section 1250 property is any depreciable real property other than Sec. 1245 property.[31] As stated on page 10, nonresidential real estate placed in service after 1980 and before 1987 is Sec. 1245 property unless the straight-line method of cost recovery is elected. The property is Sec. 1250 property if straight-line cost recovery is elected.

Depreciation recapture is not required on real property placed in service after 1986 because such property must be depreciated under the straight-line MACRS rules.[32]

EXAMPLE I:13-26 ▶ Frances sells an office building during the current year for $800,000. The office building was purchased in 1980 for $700,000* and depreciation of $500,000 has been allowed using an accelerated method of depreciation. If the straight-line method was used, depreciation would be $420,000. The office building is Sec. 1250 property. Her recognized gain is $600,000 and $80,000 is Sec. 1250 ordinary income due to excess depreciation ($500,000 – $420,000). The remaining $520,000 gain is Sec. 1231 gain.

ADDITIONAL COMMENT

If the building in Example I:13-26 was placed in service after 1980 and before 1987, the building is Sec. 1245 property if Frances uses accelerated cost recovery and not the straight-line method.

If Frances purchased the building after 1986, she was required to use the straight-line method. Thus her recognized gain is $520,000 ($800,000 – $280,000) with straight-line depreciation being $420,000. None of the gain is Sec. 1250 ordinary income. The gain is Sec. 1231 gain. ◀

*does not consider the cost of land

---

[31] Sec. 1250(c).
[32] As explained in the Additional Recapture for Corporations section in this chapter, corporations may have depreciation recapture under Sec. 291(a) despite the use of straight-line depreciation.

SELF-STUDY QUESTION

In Example I:13-24, how much of the $700,000 Sec. 1231 gain resulting from the sale of warehouse #1 is unrecaptured Sec. 1250 gain?

ANSWER

All $700,000

HISTORICAL NOTE

Prior to the Taxpayer Relief Act of 1997, all LTCGs were taxed at a maximum rate of 28%. When the maximum rate was reduced to 20% (now 15%), Congress did not extend this favorable treatment to depreciable real estate. The maximum rate on this type of property was reduced from 28% to 25%. Even though Congress recently reduced the maximum LTCG rate to 15%, this lower rate still does not apply to depreciable real estate for unrecaptured Sec. 1250 gain.

As explained below, $420,000 of the Sec. 1231 gain in Example 13-26 is taxed at a maximum rate of 25% and $100,000 is taxed at 15% if there are no Sec. 1231 losses, nonrecaptured net Sec. 1231 losses, and no capital gains and losses from other transactions. Recall from Chapter I:5 that the tax rate on adjusted net capital gain may be 15% or zero.

UNRECAPTURED SECTION 1250 GAIN

For sales of real property, some or all of the Sec. 1231 gain may be LTCG that is unrecaptured Sec. 1250 gain taxed at a maximum rate of 25%. Unrecaptured Sec. 1250 gain is the amount of LTCG which would be taxed as ordinary if Sec. 1250 provided for the recapture of all depreciation and not just additional depreciation. When a taxpayer sells Sec. 1250 property (e.g., an office building) at a gain, any gain due to excess depreciation is ordinary income. Any remaining gain is Sec. 1231 gain and may be LTCG; however, any of the LTCG due to depreciation other than excess depreciation is unrecaptured Sec. 1250 gain taxed at a maximum rate of 25%.

An individual taxpayer who uses straight-line depreciation for Sec. 1250 property does not have any additional depreciation that would be recaptured as ordinary gain under Sec. 1250. Therefore, for buildings placed in service after 1986, all of the Sec. 1231 gain to the extent of the depreciation is unrecaptured Sec. 1250 gain subject to a maximum tax rate of 25% because only straight-line depreciation may be used. In Example I:13-26, $420,000 of the Sec. 1231 gain is unrecaptured Sec. 1250 gain because $420,000 of the gain would be taxed as ordinary income if all depreciation had been recaptured.

EXAMPLE I:13-27 ▶

Linnie owns a building used in her trade or business that was placed in service in 1994. She has no Sec. 1231 losses, nonrecaptured net Sec. 1231, losses or capital gains and losses. The building cost $400,000* and depreciation-to-date amounts to $172,000. If she sells the building for $350,000, her $122,000 gain ($350,000−$228,000) is Sec. 1231 gain and there is no depreciation recapture under Sec. 1250 because straight-line depreciation was allowed. The $122,000 Sec. 1231 gain is LTCG taxed at a maximum rate of 25% because it is unrecaptured Sec. 1250 gain. ◀

*does not consider the cost of land

STOP & THINK

Question: What is the difference between *Sec. 1250 depreciation recapture* and *unrecaptured Sec. 1250 gain*?

Solution: Section 1250 depreciation recapture is the recharacterization of some or all of the Sec. 1231 gain on a building to ordinary income. Section 1250 depreciation recapture only applies to a noncorporate taxpayer if accelerated depreciation was used. Because accelerated depreciation is not allowed after 1986, this provision does not apply to noncorporate taxpayers for buildings placed in service after 1986. Unrecaptured Sec. 1250 gain is taxed at a maximum rate of 25% and occurs when there is a sale or an exchange of a building that is not Sec. 1245 property. If straight-line depreciation is used for a building, the gain is Sec. 1231 gain and the portion of the gain due to depreciation is unrecaptured Sec. 1250 gain. Part or all of the Sec. 1231 gain is taxed at a maximum rate of 25% with any excess taxed at 15%.

EXAMPLE I:13-28 ▶

Assume the same facts as in Example I:13-27 except Linnie sells the building for $500,000. Her Sec. 1231 gain is $272,000 ($500,000−$228,000), and $172,000 of the gain is taxed at 25% because it is unrecaptured Sec. 1250 gain. The remaining $100,000 of gain is taxed at 15%. ◀

ADDITIONAL COMMENT

When a building is sold at a gain, different tax rates might apply to portions of the gain: rate for ordinary income, 25% for unrecaptured Sec. 1250 gain, and 15% for ANCG.

TAXATION OF GAINS ON SALE OR EXCHANGE OF DEPRECIABLE REAL PROPERTY

Noncorporate taxpayers who placed real property in service after 1963 and before 1981 may have to recognize Sec. 1250 ordinary income if they used a depreciation method greater than straight-line. Only noncorporate taxpayers may have gain treated as unrecaptured Sec. 1250 gain and the amount of unrecaptured Sec. 1250 gain is not greater than the amount of depreciation allowed.

There is a difference between Sec. 1250 ordinary income and unrecaptured Sec. 1250 gain. Sec. 1250 ordinary income could be taxed at 35% for noncorporate taxpayers while

unrecaptured Sec. 1250 gain is taxed at a maximum rate of 25%. To have unrecaptured Sec. 1250 gain, the property must have a holding period greater than one year.

EXAMPLE I:13-29 ▶ Erin, whose tax rate is 35%, owns an office building purchased for $1,000,000* on April 10 of last year. The building is sold on March 28 of the current year for $990,000 when its adjusted basis is $966,850. The $23,150 gain is not Sec. 1231 gain and none of the gain is unrecaptured Sec. 1250 gain because the holding period is not more than one year. The $23,150 gain is ordinary taxed at 35%. If the holding period was more than one year, the Sec. 1231 gain of $23,150 is LTCG that is unrecaptured Sec. 1250 gain taxed at 25%. ◀

*does not consider the cost of land

The proper tax treatment for depreciable real estate depends on the method of depreciation, when the property was placed in service, and how the property is used. Section 1245 applies to a building placed in service after 1980 and before 1987 if accelerated cost recovery is allowed and the building is not used as residential rental property.

Real property used as residential rental property placed in service before 1987 may be taxed more favorably than other types of real property because the Sec. 1250 recapture of excess depreciation rules apply only to additional depreciation allowed after 1975 for residential rental property. Also, buildings used as residential rental property are never subject to the Sec. 1245 recapture rules.

For a building or structure to qualify as residential rental property, 80% or more of the gross rental income from the building or structure must be rental income from dwelling units. Residential rental property does not include any unit in a hotel, motel, inn, or other establishment if more than one-half of the units are used on a transient basis.[33]

When a building is sold at a gain, different tax rates may apply to portions of the gain:

Rate for ordinary income − Sec. 1250 due to recapture of excess depreciation or 1245 due to recapture of depreciation

25% − unrecaptured Sec. 1250 gain

15% (or zero) − portion of Sec. 1231 gain that becomes adjusted net capital gain

DEPRECIABLE REAL PROPERTY PLACED IN SERVICE BEFORE 1981. Taxpayers who elected to use accelerated depreciation on real property placed in service before 1981 may have some or all of their gain treated as Sec. 1250 ordinary income. Gain due to excess depreciation allowed after 1963 is Sec. 1250 ordinary income unless the building is used as residential rental property where gain due to excess depreciation after 1975 is ordinary income. The Sec. 1250 recapture rules are the same for residential rental property and other real property placed in service after 1975.

EXAMPLE I:13-30 ▶
ADDITIONAL COMMENT

If the selling price in Example I:13-30 is $172,000, all of the gain is Sec. 1250 ordinary income.

Selling Price	$172,000
Adjusted Basis	100,000
Realized Gain	$ 72,000
Ordinary Gain	$ 72,000

ADDITIONAL COMMENT

If Buddy's apartment complex (residential rental property) in Example 13-30 was placed in service before 1976, only excess depreciation after 1975 is subject to recapture as Sec. 1250 ordinary income.

Buddy sells an apartment complex used as residential rental property and placed in service on January 1, 1977. The cost of the apartment complex is $900,000,* and the complex is sold on January 1, 2010, for $700,000. Depreciation claimed by Buddy on the property is as follows:

Time Period	Depreciation Allowed	Straight-Line Depreciation	Additional Depreciation
Jan. 1, 1977–Jan. 1, 2010	$800,000	$710,000	$90,000

On the date of sale, the adjusted basis of the apartment is $100,000 ($900,000 − $800,000) and the realized gain is $600,000 ($700,000 − $100,000). All $90,000 of additional depreciation allowed is recaptured as ordinary income because the additional depreciation is less than the realized gain. The remaining $510,000 ($600,000 − $90,000) of gain is a Sec. 1231 gain. The Sec. 1231 gain is LTCG if 1231 gains exceed 1231 losses and is taxed at 25% because it is unrecaptured Sec. 1250 gain. ◀

*does not consider the cost of land

[33] Reg. Sec. 1.167(j)-3(b)(1)(i).

EXAMPLE I:13-31 ▶ Assume the same facts as in Example I:13-30 except the building is nonresidential real estate such as a warehouse, manufacturing plant or an office building. The tax treatment is the same for both examples. Buddy has $90,000 of ordinary income and Sec. 1231 gain of $510,000. The Sec. 1231 gain is LTCG if 1231 gains exceed 1231 losses and is taxed at 25% because it is unrecaptured Sec. 1250 gain. ◀

There is no additional depreciation, and thus no Sec. 1250 ordinary income if the building is fully depreciated when sold or exchanged. As each year passes, noncorporate shareholders are increasingly less likely to have Sec. 1250 ordinary income.

EXAMPLE I:13-32 ▶ Assume the same facts as in Examples 30 and 31 except the buildings are fully depreciated and the selling price is $720,000. For both buildings, the realized gain of $720,000 is Sec. 1231 gain and is unrecaptured Sec. 1250 gain taxed at a maximum rate of 25%. ◀

DEPRECIABLE REAL PROPERTY PLACED IN SERVICE AFTER 1980 AND BEFORE 1987. Gain due to additional depreciation for buildings used as residential rental property placed in service after 1980 and before 1987 is Sec. 1250 ordinary income. Because the recovery period for buildings placed in service during this period is 15, 18 or 19 years, all such buildings will be fully depreciated if sold in 2010, thus there is no additional depreciation and no Sec. 1250 ordinary income.

The method of depreciation used for other buildings placed in service during this period is a critical factor in determining the tax treatment when sold. If accelerated cost recovery was used, the nonresidential real estate is Sec. 1245 property where all gain due to depreciation is ordinary income. If the straight-line method is used, the property is Sec. 1250 property and none of the gain is ordinary income for noncorporate taxpayers.

EXAMPLE I:13-33 ▶ Ford purchased three buildings (A, B and C) in 1982 for $500,000 each*. The recovery period for each building is 15 years, so each building is fully depreciated when he sells the buildings during the current year for $400,000 each.

*does not consider the cost of land

Building	Use of Property	Method of Cost Recovery (Depreciation)
A	residential rental property	accelerated or straight-line
B	office building	accelerated
C	warehouse	straight-line

Building B is Sec. 1245 property, and the $400,000 gain is Sec. 1245 ordinary income. For buildings A and C, the $400,000 gain is Sec. 1231 gain and is unrecaptured Sec. 1250 gain because the gain is due to depreciation. ◀

EXAMPLE I:13-34 ▶ Assume the same facts as in Example I:13-33 except the selling price is $570,000. For building B, Ford must recognize $500,000 of Sec. 1245 ordinary income and $70,000 of Sec. 1231 gain taxed at 15%. For buildings A and C, the $570,000 gain is Sec. 1231 gain with $500,000 taxed at 25% and $70,000 taxed at 15%. ◀

DEPRECIABLE REAL PROPERTY PLACED IN SERVICE AFTER 1986. The straight-line method of depreciation is the only method of depreciation allowed for buildings placed in service after 1986, and thus noncorporate taxpayers will not have any Sec. 1250 ordinary income when they sell or exchange buildings placed in service after 1986. Gain due to depreciation is unrecaptured Sec. 1250 gain subject to a maximum tax rate of 25%.

The tax treatment for residential rental property and other real property placed in service after 1986 is the same, but taxpayers may depreciate residential rental property over 27.5 years and other real property placed in service after May 12, 1993, over 39 years.

EXAMPLE I:13-35 ▶ Stella purchased an apartment complex on October 10, 2003, for $275,000 (exclusive of land) while Mack purchased an office building for $275,000 on the same day. Stella and Mack sell the

▼ **TABLE I:13-1**

CHARACTER OF GAIN ON SALE OR EXCHANGE OF DEPRECIABLE REAL PROPERTY FOR NONCORPORATE TAXPAYERS

	Sec. 1245 Ordinary	Sec. 1250 Ordinary	Sec. 1231	Unrecaptured Sec. 1250 (Maximum rate of 25%)
RESIDENTIAL RENTAL				
Placed in Service Before 1981				
Use straight-line depreciation	No	No	Yes	Yes
Use accelerated depreciation	No	Yes*	Yes**	Yes
Placed in Service After 1980 & Before 1987				
Use straight-line depreciation	No	No	Yes	Yes
Use accelerated depreciation	No	Yes*	Yes**	Yes
Placed in Service After 1986				
Use straight-line depreciation	No	No	Yes	Yes
NONRESIDENTIAL				
Placed in Service Before 1981				
Use straight-line depreciation	No	No	Yes	Yes
Use accelerated depreciation	No	Yes*	Yes**	Yes
Placed in Service After 1980 & Before 1987				
Use straight-line depreciation	No	No	Yes	Yes
Use accelerated depreciation	Yes	No	Yes***	No
Placed in Service After 1986				
Use straight-line depreciation	No	No	Yes	Yes

* Portion of gain due to excess depreciation
** To extent gain is greater than excess depreciation
*** To extent gain is greater than total depreciation

buildings on April 22, 2010, for $250,000. At the date of sale, Stella's adjusted basis in the apartment complex is $210,005 based on a 27.5 year recovery period and Mack's adjusted basis in the office building is $229,166 based on a 39 year recovery period. Stella has a Sec. 1231 gain of $39,995 [$250,000 − $210,005 adjusted basis], and all of the gain is unrecaptured Sec. 1250 gain. Mack has a Sec. 1231 gain of $20,834 [$250,000 − $229,166 adjusted basis], and all of the gain is unrecaptured Sec. 1250 gain. ◄

LOW-INCOME HOUSING

Congress has provided incentives for the construction and rehabilitation of low-income housing. For tax years after 1986, a low-income housing credit is available to owners of qualified low-income housing projects.[34]

If the low-income housing unit is held for 16 years and 8 months, none of the additional depreciation is subject to recapture as ordinary income.[35] Thus noncorporate taxpayers will not have any Sec. 1250 ordinary income if the low-income housing is sold after 2002.

The Sec. 1250 recapture rules for noncorporate taxpayers are summarized in Topic Review I:13-2.

---

[34] Sec. 42.   [35] Secs. 1250(a)(1)(B)(i), (ii), (iii), and (iv).

Topic Review I:13-2

Section 1250 Recapture for Noncorporate Taxpayers

► Section 1250 affects the character of the gain, not the amount of gain.

► Section 1250 does not apply to assets sold or exchanged at a loss.

► Section 1250 ordinary income is never more than the realized gain.

► Section 1250 ordinary income is never more than the *additional* depreciation allowed. (Note, that this statement is not true for corporate taxpayers.)

► Section 1250 property includes depreciable real property unless the real property is nonresidential real estate placed in service in 1980 and before 1987 under the ACRS rules and the straight-line method is not elected.

► Section 1250 ordinary income does not exist if the straight-line method of depreciation is used. (This statement is not true for corporate taxpayers because of the additional recapture requirements under Sec. 291.)

ADDITIONAL RECAPTURE FOR CORPORATIONS

KEY POINT

Section 291 has no effect on Sec. 1245 property because gain is already recaptured to the extent of all depreciation.

ADDITIONAL COMMENT

Corporations are subject to an additional 20% depreciation recapture rule under Sec. 291 on sales of Sec. 1250 property.

Corporations are subject to additional recapture rules under Sec. 291 if depreciable real estate is sold or otherwise disposed of. This recapture is in addition to the normal recapture rules under Sec. 1250. The additional ordinary income that is recaptured effectively reduces the amount of the Sec. 1231 gain.

The additional recapture amount under Sec. 291 is equal to 20% of the difference between the amount that would be recaptured if the property was Sec. 1245 property and actual recapture amount under Sec. 1250.[36]

EXAMPLE I:13-36 ►

SELF-STUDY QUESTION

If the taxpayer in Example I:13-36 is a noncorporate taxpayer, how much of the gain is Sec. 1250 ordinary income?

ANSWER

$60,000

In 1980, Orlando Corporation purchased an office building for $500,000* for use in its business. The building is sold during the current year for $480,000. Pertinent details relating to depreciation of the building and realized gain on the sale are below:

► Total depreciation allowed for the building is $420,000.

► If straight-line depreciation had been used, depreciation allowed would have been $360,000.

► Building's adjusted basis is $80,000 ($500,000 − $420,000).

► Realized and recognized gain is $400,000 ($480,000 − $80,000).

To determine the character of the $400,000 gain, the following analysis must be made:

► Additional depreciation is $60,000 ($420,000 − $360,000). Gain to the extent of additional depreciation is recaptured as Sec. 1250 ordinary income.

► Section 291 depreciation recapture applies because the taxpayer is a corporation. If the property was Sec. 1245 property, $400,000 of the gain would be ordinary income.

► Because of Sec. 291, Orlando has more Sec. 1250 ordinary income: $68,000 [0.20 × ($400,000 − $60,000)].

In summary, of the total recognized gain of $400,000, $128,000 is recaptured as ordinary income ($60,000 + $68,000) and the remaining $272,000 ($400,000 − $128,000) is Sec. 1231 gain. ◄

*does not consider the cost of land

EXAMPLE I:13-37 ►

Pacific Corporation purchased an office building in 1981 for $800,000* for use in its trade or business. The building is sold during the current year for $850,000. Pacific elected to use the straight-line method of cost recovery and $800,000 cost-recovery deductions have been allowed. The realized gain is $850,000 ($850,000 − 0). There is no excess depreciation, so none of the gain is ordinary income under Sec. 1250 if Sec. 291 is not considered. If the building were instead Sec. 1245 recovery property, $800,000 of the gain would be treated as ordinary income.

---

[36] Sec. 291(a)(1).

The amount of Sec. 1250 ordinary income under Sec. 291 is $160,000 [0.20 × ($800,000 − $0)]. The remaining $690,000 ($850,000 − $160,000) gain is Sec. 1231 gain. ◀

*does not consider the cost of land

For corporations, none of the Sec. 1231 gain is unrecaptured Sec. 1250 gain.

SUMMARY OF SECS. 1231, 1245, AND 1250 GAINS

Section 1231 property is depreciable property and nondepreciable real property used in one's trade or business and held for more than one year. Net Sec. 1231 gain, the excess of Sec. 1231 gain over Sec. 1231 loss, is LTCG unless the five-year lookback rule applies in which case the gain is ordinary to the extent of the nonrecaptured net Sec. 1231 loss. Net Sec. 1231 loss, the excess of Sec. 1231 loss over Sec. 1231 gain, is ordinary.

Section 1245 applies to depreciable personal property and amortizable intangible assets. It also applies to certain nonresidential real property placed in service during ACRS (after 1980 and before 1987) if accelerated cost recovery is used. Gain to the extent of depreciation is ordinary income. All of the gain resulting from the sale of Sec. 1245 property is ordinary income unless the asset is sold for more than its original basis.

Section 1250 property is depreciable real property, and gain is ordinary income to the extent of additional depreciation, the excess of accelerated depreciation over straight-line. After 1986, the straight-line method must be used for real property and thus noncorporate taxpayers will not have any Sec. 1250 ordinary income on the sale of depreciable real property placed in service after 1986. Unfortunately, Congress made the sale and exchange of buildings more complicated in 1997 when it created the concept of unrecaptured Sec. 1250 gain that is taxed at 25%. When a noncorporate taxpayer sells depreciated buildings at a gain, any gain to the extent of straight-line depreciation is Sec. 1231 gain but is taxed at a rate no higher than 25% because it is unrecaptured Sec. 1250 gain.

To further illustrate Sec. 1231, 1245, and 1250, refer to Topic Review I:13-3 where a noncorporate taxpayer with a 35% tax rate sells various assets during the current year. Each asset was purchased in 1997 and the selling price is $450,000 for each of the first three assets. All assets are used in a trade or business. There are no other gains and losses and no nonrecaptured net Sec. 1231 losses.

Topic Review I:13-3

Sections 1231, 1245, and 1250—Comparison of Various Assets

The taxpayer is a noncorporate taxpayer with a 35% tax rate who sells each of the first three assets for $450,000. Each asset was purchased in 1997 and is used in a trade or business. The difference between the original basis and the adjusted basis of the equipment and building is attributable to depreciation. There are no other gains and losses and no nonrecaptured net Sec. 1231 losses.

	ORIGINAL BASIS	ADJUSTED BASIS	TAX TREATMENT
1. Land	$400,000	$400,000	$50,000 Sec. 1231 gain taxed at 15%.
2. Equipment	600,000	400,000	$50,000 Sec. 1245 ordinary income taxed at 35%. All gain is due to depreciation.
3. Building	500,000	400,000	$50,000 Sec. 1231 gain which is unrecaptured Sec. 1250 gain taxed at 25%.

For assets 4, 5, & 6, assume the selling price is $700,000.

	ORIGINAL BASIS	ADJUSTED BASIS	TAX TREATMENT
4. Land	$400,000	$400,000	$300,000 Sec. 1231 gain taxed at 15%.
5. Equipment	600,000	400,000	$200,000 Sec. 1245 ordinary income taxed at 35% and $100,000 Sec. 1231 gain taxed at 15%.
6. Building	500,000	400,000	$300,000 Sec. 1231 gain with $100,000 of unrecaptured Sec. 1250 gain taxed at 25% and $200,000 taxed at 15%.

RECAPTURE PROVISIONS— OTHER APPLICATIONS

OBJECTIVE 5

Describe other recapture applications

Secs. 1245 and 1250 recapture provisions take precedence over other provisions of the tax law.[37] Unless an exception or limitation is specifically stated in Secs. 1245 or 1250, gain is recognized under Secs. 1245 or 1250 despite the existence of provisions elsewhere in the Code that allow nonrecognition of gain.[38]

GIFTS OF PROPERTY SUBJECT TO RECAPTURE

A gift of appreciated depreciable property does not result in the recapture of depreciation or cost-recovery deductions under Secs. 1245 or 1250.[39] The donee must consider the recapture potential when disposing of the property. The recapture amount for the donee is computed by including the recaptured amount attributable to the donor.[40]

EXAMPLE I:13-38 ▶ Ashley makes a gift of equipment with an $8,200 FMV to Helmut. Ashley paid $10,000 for the equipment and deducted $4,000 of depreciation before making the gift. Ashley does not have to recapture any depreciation when making the gift. Helmut's basis for the equipment is $6,000 and the potential depreciation recapture carries over to Helmut. ◀

EXAMPLE I:13-39 ▶

ADDITIONAL COMMENT

If the taxpayer in Topic Review I:13-3 is a corporation, the character of the gain is the same for assets 1, 2, 4, and 5. For asset 3, $10,000 of the gain is Sec. 1250 ordinary income because of Sec. 291 and $40,000 is Sec. 1231 gain. For asset 6, $20,000 is Sec. 1250 ordinary income because of Sec. 291 and $280,000 is Sec. 1231 gain.

Assume the same facts as in Example I:13-38 except that Helmut uses the equipment in a trade or business, deducts $1,500 of depreciation, and sells the equipment for $7,100. When determining the amount of depreciation subject to recapture, Helmut must also consider the depreciation allowed to Ashley. The entire $2,600 [$7,100 − ($6,000 − $1,500)] gain is recaptured as ordinary income because it is less than the $5,500 ($4,000 + $1,500) of depreciation claimed. ◀

TRANSFER OF PROPERTY SUBJECT TO RECAPTURE AT DEATH

The transfer of appreciated property at death does not cause a recapture of depreciation deductions to the decedent's estate under Secs. 1245 and 1250.[41] In addition, recapture potential does not carry over to the person who receives the property from the decedent.

EXAMPLE I:13-40 ▶

KEY POINT

Death is one of the few ways to avoid the recapture provisions.

Jackie dies while owning a building with a $900,000 FMV. The building is Sec. 1245 property acquired in 1985 for $800,000* on which cost-recovery deductions of $800,000 have been claimed. Pam inherits the building from Jackie. Pam's basis for the building is $900,000, and the $800,000 of cost-recovery deductions are not recaptured. If Pam immediately sells the building, there is no depreciation recapture attributable to the $800,000 of cost-recovery deductions taken by the decedent. ◀

*does not include cost of land

CHARITABLE CONTRIBUTIONS

As discussed in Chapter I:7, the deduction for a charitable contribution of appreciated ordinary income property is generally limited to its adjusted basis (i.e., the amount of the contribution deduction is equal to the FMV of the property less the amount of gain that would not have been LTCG [or Sec. 1231 gain] if the contributed property had been sold by the taxpayer at its FMV).[42] Thus, the contribution deduction for recapture property is reduced to reflect the ordinary income that would be recognized if the property were sold rather than contributed to the charity.

EXAMPLE I:13-41 ▶ Ralph makes a gift of an organ to a church. The organ is used in Ralph's trade or business and has a $6,300 FMV. Ralph paid $10,000 for the organ, and $8,000 depreciation has been claimed. If the organ were sold for its $6,300 FMV, the realized and recognized gain would be $4,300 ($6,300 − $2,000) and all of the gain would be ordinary income due to the recapture of depreciation under Sec. 1245. The charitable contribution deduction is limited to $2,000 ($6,300 − $4,300), because none of the $4,300 gain would be taxed as a LTCG if the organ were sold. ◀

---

[37] Secs. 1245(d) and 1250(i).
[38] Reg. Secs. 1.1245-6(a) and 1.1250-1(c)(1).
[39] Secs. 1245(b)(1) and 1250(d)(1).
[40] Reg. Secs. 1.1245-2(a)(4) and 1.1250-2(d).
[41] Secs. 1245(b)(2) and 1250(d)(2).
[42] Sec. 170(e)(1)(A).

LIKE-KIND EXCHANGES

A taxpayer who receives boot (i.e., non–like-kind property) in a transaction that otherwise qualifies as a like-kind exchange recognizes gain equal to the lesser of the realized gain or the amount of boot received. If the property is Sec. 1245 or 1250 property, the gain is first considered to be ordinary income up to the maximum amount of the gain that is subject to the recapture provisions.

EXAMPLE I:13-42 ▶

Virginia owns a duplex that is residential rental property. The duplex cost $300,000* in 1979 and has a $60,000 adjusted basis. Additional depreciation (i.e., excess of accelerated depreciation over straight-line) of $22,000 has been deducted. Virginia exchanges the duplex for a four-unit apartment building with a $250,000 FMV and $25,000 in cash. Gain realized on the exchange is $215,000 [($250,000 + $25,000) − $60,000)], and the recognized gain is $25,000. Gain recognized is the lesser of the $25,000 boot received or the $215,000 gain realized. Because additional depreciation is recaptured as ordinary income under Sec. 1250, $22,000 of the gain is ordinary income and $3,000 of the gain is Sec. 1231 gain which may be taxed at 25% because it is unrecaptured Sec. 1250 gain. ◀

*does not include cost of land

If gain is not recognized in a like-kind exchange, the recapture potential carries over to the replacement property (i.e., any recapture potential associated with the property exchanged attaches to the property received in the exchange).[43]

EXAMPLE I:13-43 ▶

Melissa owns a Chevrolet pickup truck used in her trade or business that cost $10,000 and has a $6,000 adjusted basis due to $4,000 in depreciation deductions she has claimed. The truck is exchanged for a Ford pickup truck with a $9,000 FMV. The Ford truck is used in Melissa's business. Melissa does not recognize any portion of the $3,000 realized gain because the exchange qualifies as a like-kind exchange and no boot is received. Her basis for the Ford truck is $6,000 (i.e., a substituted basis).

After deducting $2,000 of depreciation, Melissa sells the Ford truck for $7,300. All of the recognized gain of $3,300 ($7,300 − $4,000) is ordinary income. The depreciation recapture amount under Sec. 1245 is equal to the total $6,000 in depreciation (including $4,000 on the Chevrolet pickup truck) but the recognized gain is only $3,300.[44] ◀

INVOLUNTARY CONVERSIONS

If an involuntary conversion of Sec. 1245 property occurs and all or a portion of the gain is not recognized,[45] the amount of gain that is considered to be Sec. 1245 ordinary income is limited and cannot be more than the recognized gain.[46] A similar provision exists for the involuntary conversion of Sec. 1250 property.[47]

EXAMPLE I:13-44 ▶

The Ryan Corporation's printing equipment with original cost of $600,000 and adjusted basis of $200,000 is destroyed by fire. Ryan, Inc. receives $550,000 of insurance proceeds and purchases $510,000 of printing equipment. If the corporation elects to defer gain, it must recognize a $40,000 gain which is Sec. 1245 ordinary income. The basis of the printing equipment acquired is $200,000. ◀

INSTALLMENT SALES

As discussed in Chapter I:11, gain resulting from an installment sale is generally recognized as payments are received. Thus, the gain may be spread over more than one accounting period. An installment sale of depreciable property may result in all of the recaptured gain being taxed in the year of the sale.[48] Recapture income is "the aggregate amount which would be treated as ordinary income under Sec. 1245 or 1250 for the taxable year of the disposition if all payments to be received were received in the taxable year of disposition."[49] Recapture income must be recognized in the year of sale, even if no payments are received.

---

[43] Reg. Sec. 1.1245-2(c)(4).
[44] Reg. Sec. 1.1245-2(a)(4).
[45] As discussed in Chapter I:12, one may elect to defer recognition of the gain if the Sec. 1033 requirements are satisfied.

[46] Sec. 1245(b)(4) and Reg. Sec. 1.1245-4(d)(1).
[47] Sec. 1250(d)(4) and Reg. Sec. 1.1250-3(d).
[48] Sec. 453(i)(1).
[49] Sec. 453(i)(2).

EXAMPLE I:13-45 ▶

KEY POINT

In the case of an installment sale of Sec. 1245 or 1250 property, it is possible to report a large taxable gain even though the taxpayer has not yet received the cash to pay the tax on such gain.

Pat owns equipment with a $100,000 acquisition cost and a $42,000 adjusted basis. During the current year, Pat sells the property for $30,000 cash and a $60,000 interest-bearing note to be paid over a ten-year period. The realized gain is $48,000 ($90,000 − $42,000), and the recapture income amount is $48,000 (the lesser of total depreciation deductions of $58,000 or the $48,000 realized gain). The $48,000 gain is all recognized as ordinary income in the current year, despite the fact that the transaction qualifies as an installment sale and only $30,000 of cash is received in the year of sale. ◀

If gain realized from the installment sale exceeds the recapture income, the excess gain is reported under the installment method.[50] The amount of recapture income recognized is added to the adjusted basis to determine the gross profit ratio.

EXAMPLE I:13-46 ▶

SELF-STUDY QUESTION

What method of cost recovery did Bob use in Example I:13-46?

ANSWER

Accelerated cost recovery. The office building is subject to Sec. 1245 recapture.

Bob owns an office building acquired for $700,000* in 1986 and subject to the Sec. 1245 recapture rules. After claiming $700,000 of cost recovery deductions, Bob sells the building to Janet in 2010 for $1,000,000. Bob receives $200,000 in cash and an $800,000 interest-bearing note. The note is to be paid with annual principal payments of $100,000 and interest on the unpaid balance beginning in 2011. The total amount of realized gain is $1,000,000 ($1,000,000 − 0). In 2010, Bob recognizes $700,000 of Sec. 1245 ordinary income. The gross profit ratio is determined by adding $700,000 recapture income to the $0 basis. The gross profit ratio is 30% [($1,000,000 − $700,000) ÷ $1,000,000]. In addition to recognizing $700,000 of ordinary income, Bob recognizes $60,000 (0.30 × $200,000) Sec. 1231 gain in 2010 because a $200,000 cash down payment was received in the year of the sale. In 2011 and in each subsequent year, $30,000 (0.30 × $100,000) of Sec. 1231 gain is recognized as the cash payments on the principal are received. ◀

*does not include cost of land

SECTION 179 EXPENSING ELECTION

In lieu of capitalizing the cost of new or used tangible personal business property, taxpayers may elect to expense up to $250,000 of the acquisition cost in 2010[51] (see Chapter I:10). If the property is subsequently converted to nonbusiness use, previous tax benefits derived from the immediate expensing election must be recaptured and added to the taxpayer's gross income in the year of the conversion.[52] The recaptured amount equals the difference between the amount expensed under Sec. 179 and the total depreciation that would otherwise have been claimed for the period of business use.

EXAMPLE I:13-47 ▶

SELF-STUDY QUESTION

If Behren in Example I:13-47 sells the equipment for $15,000 instead of converting it to a non-business use, what is the character of the gain?

ANSWER

$15,000 of Sec. 1245 ordinary income

Behren purchased business equipment (a five-year recovery period) in 2009 for $18,100 and elected to expense the entire amount under Sec. 179. In 2010, he converts the equipment to nonbusiness use. Depreciation of $3,620 (0.20 × $18,100) under the MACRS rules would have been allowed during the period the equipment was held for business use if Behren had not elected to expense the $18,100 cost. Behren must recognize $14,480 ($18,100 − $3,620) of Sec. 1245 ordinary income the current year. ◀

CONSERVATION AND LAND CLEARING EXPENDITURES

Taxpayers engaged in the business of farming may deduct expenditures paid or incurred during the taxable year for soil and water conservation or the prevention of erosion. The expenditures must be made with respect to land used in farming and would be capital expenditures except for this provision.[53]

The deductions for conservation expenditures may be partially or fully recaptured as ordinary income if the farmland is disposed of before the land is held for more than nine years.[54] The amount of deductions recaptured as ordinary income under Sec. 1252 is a percentage of the aggregate deductions allowed for conservation expenditures. The amount of ordinary income recognized under Sec. 1252 is limited to the lesser of the taxpayer's realized gain or the applicable recapture percentage times the total conservation expenditures.

---

[50] Sec. 453(i)(1)(B).0.
[51] Secs. 179(a) and (b)(1). At the date of publication of this textbook, Congress had not officially extended the maximum Sec. 179 deduction for 2010 to $250,000. The Sec. 179 deduction will be $134,000 if Congress does not extend this amount.

[52] Sec. 179(d)(10) and Reg. Sec. 1.179-1(e).
[53] Sec. 175(a).
[54] Sec. 1252(a)(1).

WHAT WOULD YOU DO IN THIS SITUATION?

You recently graduated with an advanced degree in taxation and have accepted a job with a CPA firm in the tax department. One of the firm's clients, a wealthy individual, was in need of cash and decided to sell some assets to raise the cash. The client asked the firm to advise him, from a tax standpoint, which assets he should sell. The client is in the 35% tax bracket. You suggested in a written memo that the client sell one of the client's jet airplanes. The plane you recommended to be sold had originally cost $16 million and now had an adjusted basis of $5 million. A buyer had offered to buy the plane for $12 million on the installment basis, paying $4 million per year for three years plus interest at 9%. The principal reason for selling that particular plane is that it would raise $12 million over three years, but the tax could be spread over three years by using the installment sale method. The client took your advice and sold the plane in the current year.

Later, when preparing the client's tax return, you realize that gain due to depreciation of the airplane must be recognized in the year of sale, even if the property is sold under the installment sale method. Thus, *all* of the gain on the sale of the plane must be recognized in the year of sale, not spread over three years. You go to your manager and tell him about your major mistake. Your manager, who reviewed your original memo, indicates that he thinks that the two of you should not tell anyone about the mistake as it will negatively impact both of your careers. The manager thinks that because the client has such a large amount of income, reporting the entire gain on the sale of the plane on the client's return might not be detected by the client. Thus, the manager instructs you to prepare the current year return with the entire $7 million of gain and not tell anyone about the mistake. What should you do in this situation?

KEY POINT

There is no recapture of conservation costs if the farmland is held for at least 10 years.

The recapture percentage is 100% if the farmland is disposed of within five years after the date it is acquired. The percentage declines by 20 percentage points for each additional year the property is held. If the land is disposed of after being held for more than nine years, none of the expenses are recaptured.[55]

EXAMPLE I:13-48 ▶

Paula owns farmland with a $400,000 basis. She has deducted $50,000 for soil and water conservation expenditures. After farming the land for six years and five months, Paula sells the land for $520,000. The realized gain is $120,000 ($520,000 − $400,000) and the recapture percentage is 60%, because the farmland is disposed of within the seventh year after it was acquired. The amount of ordinary income due to recapture under Sec. 1252 is $30,000, the lesser of the $120,000 realized gain or the $30,000 (0.60 × $50,000) recapture amount. ◀

ADDITIONAL COMMENT

Intangible drilling and development costs represent the major cost of operations and can provide investors with working interests in oil and gas properties with a first-year write-off of substantially all of their investment.

INTANGIBLE DRILLING COSTS AND DEPLETION

Taxpayers may elect to either expense or capitalize intangible drilling and development costs (IDC).[56] If the election to expense is not made, the costs are capitalized and recovered through additional depletion deductions. Intangible drilling and development costs include "all expenditures made by an operator for wages, fuel, repairs, hauling, supplies, etc., incident to and necessary for the drilling of wells and the preparation of wells for the production of oil or gas."[57]

Part or all of the gain from the sale of oil and gas properties may be recaptured as ordinary income due to the recapture of the IDC deduction and the deduction for depletion. However, the amount of ordinary income recognized from the recapture of IDC and depletion is limited to the gain realized from disposition of the property.[58]

EXAMPLE I:13-49 ▶

In 2003, Marty purchased undeveloped property to drill for oil and gas. Intangible drilling and development costs of $400,000 were paid in 2003, and Marty elected to expense the IDC. During the current year, Marty sells the property and realizes a $900,000 gain. $300,000 of cost depletion was allowed. Marty must recognize $700,000 of ordinary income because of the recapture of IDC ($400,000) and the recapture of depletion ($300,000). The remaining $200,000 ($900,000 − $700,000) gain is Sec. 1231 gain. ◀

---

[55] Sec. 1252(a)(3).
[56] Sec. 263(c).

[57] Reg. Sec. 1.612-4(a).
[58] Sec. 1254(a)(1).

EXAMPLE I:13-50 ▶

SELF-STUDY QUESTION

If Tina in Example I:13-50 sells the properties for $990,000, what is her gain?

ANSWER

$280,000 of ordinary income and $90,000 of Sec. 1231 gain

In 2000, Tina acquired oil and gas properties for $700,000 and paid $200,000 for intangible drilling costs. During 2000, she elected to expense the $200,000 of IDC. Total depletion allowed was $80,000. During the current year, Tina sells the property for $840,000 and realizes a $220,000 [($840,000 − ($700,000 − $80,000)] gain. The amount of ordinary income due to recapture is $220,000, because both IDC and depletion must be recaptured only to the extent of the gain. ◀

GAIN ON SALE OF DEPRECIABLE PROPERTY BETWEEN RELATED PARTIES

All gain recognized on the sale or exchange of property between related parties is ordinary income if the property is subject to depreciation in the hands of the transferee (i.e., the person who purchases the property). The sale or exchange may be direct or indirect.[59]

EXAMPLE I:13-51 ▶

SELF-STUDY QUESTION

If Phil sells the building in Example I:13-51 to an unrelated party, what is the character of the gain?

ANSWER

$300,000 of Sec. 1231 gain. If the Sec. 1231 gain becomes LTCG, $200,000 of the gain is unrecaptured Sec. 1250 gain taxed at a maximum rate of 25%

Phil owns a building with a $500,000 adjusted basis and $800,000 FMV. The building, which cost $700,000, is used in his business, and the straight-line method of depreciation is used. $200,000 of depreciation deductions were allowed. If the building is sold to Phil's 100%-owned corporation for $800,000, the $300,000 realized gain ($800,000 − $500,000) is treated as ordinary income under Sec. 1239, because the property is subject to depreciation in the hands of the transferee and the corporation and Phil are related parties. ◀

A sale or exchange of property could be subject to depreciation recapture under Sec. 1245 or 1250 as well as the Sec. 1239 related party rules. If so, recapture under Sec. 1245 or 1250 is considered before recapture under Sec. 1239.[60]

EXAMPLE I:13-52 ▶

Assume the same facts as in Example I:13-51 except that Phil sells equipment to the corporation instead of a building. All of the $300,000 realized gain is treated as ordinary income. The recapture amount under Sec. 1245 is $200,000, and Sec. 1239 applies to the remaining $100,000 gain. ◀

REAL-WORLD EXAMPLE

A taxpayer sold a secret formula for typing correction fluid to a corporation that was a related party. The gain on the sale was treated as a capital gain, not as ordinary income under Sec. 1239, because the secret formula was not depreciable. *Bette C. Graham v. U.S.*, 43 AFTR 2d 79-1013, 79-1 USTC ¶9274 (D.C. Tx., 1979).

PURPOSE OF SEC. 1239. Without Sec. 1239, a taxpayer could transfer appreciated depreciable property to a related party and recognize a Sec. 1231 gain on the sale. Net Sec. 1231 gain is treated as LTCG. The related purchaser of the property would receive a step up in the depreciable basis of the property to its FMV and be able to claim a larger amount of depreciation. In Example I:13-51, Phil might prefer to recognize a $300,000 Sec. 1231 gain if the 100%-owned corporation was able to obtain a step-up in the property's basis to $800,000. Because Sec. 1239 applies, Phil must recognize $300,000 of ordinary income rather than Sec. 1231 gain. This rule prevents an individual taxpayer from receiving favorable Sec. 1231 gain treatment and prevents all taxpayers having large capital loss carryovers from using a related party to recognize a Sec. 1231 or capital gain which can be offset against their capital losses.

RELATED PARTIES. A person is related (1) to any corporation if the individual owns (directly or indirectly) more than 50% of the value of the outstanding stock and (2) to any partnership in which the person has a capital or profits interest of more than 50%.[61] Constructive ownership rules apply when determining whether the person owns more than 50% of the corporation or has more than a 50% interest in the partnership. Thus, an individual is considered to own stock that is owned by other family members and related entities (e.g., corporations, partnerships, estates, and trusts).

EXAMPLE I:13-53 ▶

Tony sells a truck used for nonbusiness purposes to the Able Corporation for $15,000 when its adjusted basis is $12,000. Tony owns 30% of Able and his spouse owns 40% of Able. Tony and Able are related parties because Tony is deemed to own 70% of Able under the constructive ownership rules and $3,000 of ordinary income must be recognized under Sec. 1239. ◀

A person is related to any trust in which such a person or the person's spouse is a beneficiary.[62] Section 1239 also applies to a sale or exchange of depreciable property between two corporations if the same individual owns more than 50% of each corporation.[63]

---

[59] Sec. 1239(a).
[60] Reg. Sec. 1.1245-6(f).
[61] Sec. 1239(c).
[62] Sec. 1239(b)(2).
[63] Rev. Rul. 79-157, 1979-1 C.B. 281.

TAX PLANNING CONSIDERATIONS

For noncorporate taxpayers, net Sec. 1231 gains are generally preferable to ordinary gains because of the possible lower tax rate applicable to net capital gains. The tax rate could be zero, 15%, or 25%. For corporate taxpayers, however, after 1986 it usually does not make any difference whether a gain is classified as Sec. 1231 or ordinary unless the corporation has capital losses. Corporations do not have preferential tax rates on net capital gains.

EXAMPLE I:13-54 ▶ Western Corporation has taxable income of $550,000 without considering the sale of equipment for $400,000 during the current year. The equipment originally cost $500,000 and has a $350,000 adjusted basis after deducting depreciation. The corporation has no other gains and losses during the year or any capital loss carryovers from previous years. For Western Corporation, it does not make any difference whether the gain is Sec. 1245 ordinary income or Sec. 1231 gain. The effect on the corporation's taxable income and tax liability is the same regardless of how the gain is classified. ◀

The avoidance of the recapture provisions is important to both corporate and noncorporate taxpayers if capital loss carryovers exist. For example, if Western Corporation has a capital loss carryforward of $40,000 in Example I:13-54, the corporation's taxable income is increased by $10,000 ($50,000 − $40,000) if the $50,000 gain is Sec. 1231 gain. However, because the gain is Sec. 1245 ordinary income, the corporation's taxable income is increased by $50,000. The $40,000 capital loss carryforward is deductible only if Western has capital gain or net Sec. 1231 gain which becomes capital gain.

AVOIDING THE RECAPTURE PROVISIONS

In view of the pervasiveness of the recapture provisions discussed in this chapter, recapture is difficult to avoid. In some cases, recapture can be avoided by holding the property a specific length of time before disposing of it (e.g., the recapture of conservation and land clearing expenses can be avoided by holding the farmland for more than nine years).[64] Contributing appreciated property to a qualified charitable organization cannot be used to circumvent the recapture provisions because in such case the amount of the charitable contribution is reduced by the amount of the gain that would not be a LTCG if the property were sold by the taxpayer.[65]

Although it is often difficult to avoid the recapture provisions, taxpayers may dispose of the property and defer recapture if the disposition is a nontaxable exchange. In a like-kind exchange where no boot is received, the recapture potential is carried over to the property received in the exchange.

Proper timing of the asset's disposition may be advantageous. Disposition may be delayed until the taxpayer's tax rate is low or the property can be sold in the same year that the taxpayer has an NOL that is about to expire.

Taxpayers can shift the recapture potential to other taxpayers by making a gift of property subject to recapture. The recapture potential remains with the property and must be considered when the donee disposes of the property.

TRANSFER PROPERTY AT DEATH. One way to avoid the recapture provisions is to transfer the property at death. No recapture occurs at the time of the transfer, and the basis of property received from a decedent is generally the FMV of the property at the date of the decedent's death.[66] The property's recapture potential does not carry over to the beneficiary as in the case of a gift made to a donee.

---

[64] Sec. 1252(a)(1).
[65] Sec. 170(e)(1)(A).

[66] Sec. 1014(a).

ADDITIONAL COMMENT

Form 4797 has four major parts. In completing this form one should normally begin with Part III on page 2, where the recapture of depreciation is calculated. Note that the total amount recaptured from line 31 is carried forward to Part II, where it is combined with other ordinary gains and losses. Any unrecaptured gain from line 32 is carried forward to Part I, where it is netted with other Sec. 1231 gains and losses.

COMPLIANCE AND PROCEDURAL CONSIDERATIONS

Form 4797, Supplemental Schedule of Gains and Losses, is used to report gains and losses from sales or exchanges of assets used in a trade or business (see Figures I:13-1 through I:13-3). The form is also used to report gains or losses resulting from involuntary conversions, other than casualties or thefts, of property used in the trade or business and capital assets held more than a year. If gains or losses due to casualties or thefts of property used in a trade or business or property held to produce income are recognized, they are reported on Form 4684, Casualties and Thefts (see Figure I:13-3). If such casualties or thefts occur, Form 4684 is prepared either before or at the same time as Form 4797.

REPORTING SEC. 1231 GAINS AND LOSSES ON FORM 4797

Part I of Form 4797, which is reproduced in Figure I:13-1, is used to report gains and losses resulting from

▶ The sale or exchange of Sec. 1231 property

▶ An involuntary conversion, other than a casualty or theft, of Sec. 1231 property

▶ An involuntary conversion, other than a casualty or theft, of capital assets held more than one year and used to produce income.

As indicated on lines 3 through 6 in Part I of Form 4797, gains and losses recorded on other forms and in Part III of Form 4797 are reported in Part I. The netting of Sec. 1231 gains and losses occurs in Part I of Form 4797. All gains and losses are recorded in column (g). If line 7(g) has a loss, Sec. 1231 losses exceed Sec. 1231 gains and the net loss is reported on line 11 as ordinary loss. If there is no nonrecaptured net section 1231 losses, all gain reported on line 7(g) is transferred to Schedule D. If the taxpayer does have nonrecaptured net Sec. 1231 losses, that amount is reported on line 8. Gains reported on line 7(g) will be recharacterized as ordinary income to the extent of the nonrecaptured net Sec. 1231 losses and reported as ordinary income on line 12.

Ordinary gains and losses recognized including those recorded on other forms and in Parts I and III of Form 4797 are reported on lines 11 through 17 in Part II of Form 4797.

REPORTING GAINS RECAPTURED AS ORDINARY INCOME ON FORM 4797

Part III of Form 4797 for 2009, reproduced in Figure I:13-2, is completed before Parts I and II to determine and report ordinary income due to the recapture provisions of Secs. 1245, 1250, 1252, 1254, and 1255. To illustrate the use of Part III, assume an individual sells equipment (7-year recovery) used in a trade or business for $60,000 on April 30, 2009. The equipment cost $58,000 on March 10, 2007, and depreciation deductions through the date of sale of $27,565 were allowed. The $29,565 ($60,000 − $30,435) total gain is reported on line 24. On line 30, total gains resulting from the sale of all properties ($29,565 in this illustration) reported in Part III are combined. The total amount of ordinary income due to the recapture provisions ($27,565 in this illustration) is reported on line 31 and then reported as ordinary income on line 13 in Part II. The excess of the gain over the amount of ordinary income is reported on line 32. The portion of this gain not due to casualty or theft ($2,000 in this illustration) is a Sec. 1231 gain and is reported on line 6 of Part I of Form 4797. If any of the gain is due to casualty or theft, that portion of the gain is reported on Section B of Form 4684.

REPORTING CASUALTY OR THEFT GAIN OR LOSS ON FORM 4684

Section A of Form 4684 is used to report gains and losses resulting from a casualty or theft of personal-use property. These gains and losses are not Sec. 1231 transactions, and Sec. A of Form 4684 is not discussed in this chapter.

Section B of Form 4684, reproduced in Figure I:13-3, is used to report gains and losses resulting from a casualty or theft of property used in a trade or business or held for the

Form **4797**	**Sales of Business Property**	OMB No. 1545-0184
Department of the Treasury Internal Revenue Service (99)	(Also Involuntary Conversions and Recapture Amounts Under Sections 179 and 280F(b)(2)) ▶ Attach to your tax return. ▶ See separate instructions.	**2009** Attachment Sequence No. **27**

Name(s) shown on return	Identifying number

Part I **Sales or Exchanges of Property Used in a Trade or Business and Involuntary Conversions From Other Than Casualty or Theft—Most Property Held More Than 1 Year** (see instructions)

1 Enter the gross proceeds from sales or exchanges reported to you for 2009 on Form(s) 1099-B or 1099-S (or substitute statement) that you are including on line 2, 10, or 20 (see instructions) **1**

2	(a) Description of property	(b) Date acquired (mo., day, yr.)	(c) Date sold (mo., day, yr.)	(d) Gross sales price	(e) Depreciation allowed or allowable since acquisition	(f) Cost or other basis, plus improvements and expense of sale	(g) Gain or (loss) Subtract (f) from the sum of (d) and (e)

3	Gain, if any, from Form 4684, line 43	**3**	
4	Section 1231 gain from installment sales from Form 6252, line 26 or 37	**4**	
5	Section 1231 gain or (loss) from like-kind exchanges from Form 8824	**5**	
6	Gain, if any, from line 32, from other than casualty or theft.	**6**	*2,000*
7	Combine lines 2 through 6. Enter the gain or (loss) here and on the appropriate line as follows:	**7**	*2,000*

Partnerships (except electing large partnerships) and S corporations. Report the gain or (loss) following the instructions for Form 1065, Schedule K, line 10, or Form 1120S, Schedule K, line 9. Skip lines 8, 9, 11, and 12 below.

Individuals, partners, S corporation shareholders, and all others. If line 7 is zero or a loss, enter the amount from line 7 on line 11 below and skip lines 8 and 9. If line 7 is a gain and you did not have any prior year section 1231 losses, or they were recaptured in an earlier year, enter the gain from line 7 as a long-term capital gain on the Schedule D filed with your return and skip lines 8, 9, 11, and 12 below.

8	Nonrecaptured net section 1231 losses from prior years (see instructions)	**8**	
9	Subtract line 8 from line 7. If zero or less, enter -0-. If line 9 is zero, enter the gain from line 7 on line 12 below. If line 9 is more than zero, enter the amount from line 8 on line 12 below and enter the gain from line 9 as a long-term capital gain on the Schedule D filed with your return (see instructions)	**9**	

Part II **Ordinary Gains and Losses** (see instructions)

10 Ordinary gains and losses not included on lines 11 through 16 (include property held 1 year or less):

11	Loss, if any, from line 7	**11**	( )
12	Gain, if any, from line 7 or amount from line 8, if applicable	**12**	
13	Gain, if any, from line 31	**13**	*27,565*
14	Net gain or (loss) from Form 4684, lines 35 and 42a	**14**	
15	Ordinary gain from installment sales from Form 6252, line 25 or 36	**15**	
16	Ordinary gain or (loss) from like-kind exchanges from Form 8824.	**16**	
17	Combine lines 10 through 16	**17**	*27,565*

18 For all except individual returns, enter the amount from line 17 on the appropriate line of your return and skip lines a and b below. For individual returns, complete lines a and b below:

  a If the loss on line 11 includes a loss from Form 4684, line 39, column (b)(ii), enter that part of the loss here. Enter the part of the loss from income-producing property on Schedule A (Form 1040), line 28, and the part of the loss from property used as an employee on Schedule A (Form 1040), line 23. Identify as from "Form 4797, line 18a." See instructions . . | **18a** |

  b Redetermine the gain or (loss) on line 17 excluding the loss, if any, on line 18a. Enter here and on Form 1040, line 14 | **18b** | *27,565* |

For Paperwork Reduction Act Notice, see separate instructions.   Cat. No. 13086I   Form **4797** (2009)

FIGURE I:13-1   ▶   PART I AND PART II OF FORM 4797

Part III	Gain From Disposition of Property Under Sections 1245, 1250, 1252, 1254, and 1255

(see instructions)

19	(a) Description of section 1245, 1250, 1252, 1254, or 1255 property:	(b) Date acquired (mo., day, yr.)	(c) Date sold (mo., day, yr.)
A	Equipment	3-10-07	4-30-09
B			
C			
D			

These columns relate to the properties on lines 19A through 19D. ▶		Property A	Property B	Property C	Property D
20	Gross sales price (**Note:** *See line 1 before completing.*)	20	60,000			
21	Cost or other basis plus expense of sale	21	58,000			
22	Depreciation (or depletion) allowed or allowable	22	27,565			
23	Adjusted basis. Subtract line 22 from line 21	23	30,435			
24	Total gain. Subtract line 23 from line 20	24	29,565			
25	**If section 1245 property:**					
a	Depreciation allowed or allowable from line 22	25a	27,565			
b	Enter the **smaller** of line 24 or 25a	25b	27,565			
26	**If section 1250 property:** If straight line depreciation was used, enter -0- on line 26g, except for a corporation subject to section 291.					
a	Additional depreciation after 1975 (see instructions)	26a				
b	Applicable percentage multiplied by the **smaller** of line 24 or line 26a (see instructions)	26b				
c	Subtract line 26a from line 24. If residential rental property **or** line 24 is not more than line 26a, skip lines 26d and 26e	26c				
d	Additional depreciation after 1969 and before 1976	26d				
e	Enter the **smaller** of line 26c or 26d	26e				
f	Section 291 amount (corporations only)	26f				
g	Add lines 26b, 26e, and 26f	26g				
27	**If section 1252 property:** Skip this section if you did not dispose of farmland or if this form is being completed for a partnership (other than an electing large partnership).					
a	Soil, water, and land clearing expenses	27a				
b	Line 27a multiplied by applicable percentage (see instructions)	27b				
c	Enter the **smaller** of line 24 or 27b	27c				
28	**If section 1254 property:**					
a	Intangible drilling and development costs, expenditures for development of mines and other natural deposits, and mining exploration costs (see instructions)	28a				
b	Enter the **smaller** of line 24 or 28a	28b				
29	**If section 1255 property:**					
a	Applicable percentage of payments excluded from income under section 126 (see instructions)	29a				
b	Enter the **smaller** of line 24 or 29a (see instructions)	29b				

Summary of Part III Gains. Complete property columns A through D through line 29b before going to line 30.

30	Total gains for all properties. Add property columns A through D, line 24	30	29,565
31	Add property columns A through D, lines 25b, 26g, 27c, 28b, and 29b. Enter here and on line 13	31	27,565
32	Subtract line 31 from line 30. Enter the portion from casualty or theft on Form 4684, line 39. Enter the portion from other than casualty or theft on Form 4797, line 6	32	2,000

Part IV	Recapture Amounts Under Sections 179 and 280F(b)(2) When Business Use Drops to 50% or Less

(see instructions)

			(a) Section 179	(b) Section 280F(b)(2)
33	Section 179 expense deduction or depreciation allowable in prior years	33		
34	Recomputed depreciation (see instructions)	34		
35	Recapture amount. Subtract line 34 from line 33. See the instructions for where to report	35		

Form **4797** (2009)

FIGURE I:13-2   ▶   PART III OF FORM 4797

Name(s) shown on tax return. Do not enter name and identifying number if shown on other side.   **Identifying number**

SECTION B—Business and Income-Producing Property

Part I   **Casualty or Theft Gain or Loss** (Use a separate Part I for each casualty or theft.)

23   Description of properties (show type, location, and date acquired for each property). Use a separate line for each property lost or damaged from the same casualty or theft.

Property **A** _____

Property **B** _____

Property **C** _____

Property **D** _____

		Properties			
		A	**B**	**C**	**D**
24 Cost or adjusted basis of each property	**24**				
25 Insurance or other reimbursement (whether or not you filed a claim). See the instructions for line 3	**25**				
Note: *If line 24 is **more** than line 25, skip line 26.*					
26 Gain from casualty or theft. If line 25 is **more** than line 24, enter the difference here and on line 33 or line 38, column (c), except as provided in the instructions for line 37. Also, skip lines 27 through 31 for that column. See the instructions for line 4 if line 25 includes insurance or other reimbursement you did not claim, or you received payment for your loss in a later tax year.	**26**				
27 Fair market value **before** casualty or theft	**27**				
28 Fair market value **after** casualty or theft	**28**				
29 Subtract line 28 from line 27	**29**				
30 Enter the **smaller** of line 24 or line 29	**30**				
Note: *If the property was totally destroyed by casualty or lost from theft, enter on line 30 the amount from line 24.*					
31 Subtract line 25 from line 30. If zero or less, enter -0-	**31**				

32   Casualty or theft loss. Add the amounts on line 31. Enter the total here and on line 33 **or** line 38 (see instructions)   **32**

Part II   **Summary of Gains and Losses** (from separate Parts I)

(a) Identify casualty or theft	(b) Losses from casualties or thefts		(c) Gains from casualties or thefts includible in income
	(i) Trade, business, rental or royalty property	(ii) Income-producing and employee property	

Casualty or Theft of Property Held One Year or Less

		(i)	(ii)	(c)
33 _____		( )	( )	
_____		( )	( )	
34 Totals. Add the amounts on line 33	**34**	( )	( )	

35   Combine line 34, columns (b)(i) and (c). Enter the net gain or (loss) here and on Form 4797, line 14. If Form 4797 is not otherwise required, see instructions   **35**

36   Enter the amount from line 34, column (b)(ii) here. Individuals, enter the amount from income-producing property on Schedule A (Form 1040), line 28, or Form 1040NR, Schedule A, line 16, and enter the amount from property used as an employee on Schedule A (Form 1040), line 23, or Form 1040NR, Schedule A, line 11. Estates and trusts, partnerships, and S corporations, see instructions   **36**

Casualty or Theft of Property Held More Than One Year

		(i)	(ii)	(c)
37 Casualty or theft gains from Form 4797, line 32	**37**			
38 _____		( )	( )	
_____		( )	( )	
39 Total losses. Add amounts on line 38, columns (b)(i) and (b)(ii)	**39**	( )	( )	

40   Total gains. Add lines 37 and 38, column (c)   **40**

41   Add amounts on line 39, columns (b)(i) and (b)(ii)   **41**

42   If the loss on line 41 is **more** than the gain on line 40:

   a Combine line 39, column (b)(i) and line 40, and enter the net gain or (loss) here. Partnerships (except electing large partnerships) and S corporations, see the note below. All others, enter this amount on Form 4797, line 14. If Form 4797 is not otherwise required, see instructions   **42a**

   b Enter the amount from line 39, column (b)(ii) here. Individuals, enter the amount from income-producing property on Schedule A (Form 1040), line 28, or Form 1040NR, Schedule A, line 16, and enter the amount from property used as an employee on Schedule A (Form 1040), line 23, or Form 1040NR, Schedule A, line 11. Estates and trusts, enter on the "Other deductions" line of your tax return. Partnerships (except electing large partnerships) and S corporations, see the note below. Electing large partnerships, enter on Form 1065-B, Part II, line 11   **42b**

43   If the loss on line 41 is **less** than or **equal** to the gain on line 40, combine lines 40 and 41 and enter here. Partnerships (except electing large partnerships), see the note below. All others, enter this amount on Form 4797, line 3   **43**

Note: *Partnerships, enter the amount from line 42a, 42b, or line 43 on Form 1065, Schedule K, line 11. S corporations, enter the amount from line 42a or 42b on Form 1120S, Schedule K, line 10.*

Form **4684** (2009)

FIGURE I:13-3 ▶   SECTION B OF FORM 4684

production of income. Note that a separate Part I is used for each different casualty or theft. Gains are reported on line 26, and losses are reported on line 32. For properties held a year or less, the gains and losses are reported on lines 33 through 36 of Part II. These gains and losses are either recorded as ordinary gains and losses on line 14 of Part II of Form 4797 or as itemized deductions on Schedule A of Form 1040.

For properties held more than a year, the gains and losses are reported on lines 40 and 41. If gains exceed losses, the net gain is reported on line 43 and then on line 3 of Part I of Form 4797 (i.e., the gains and losses are treated as Sec. 1231 gains and losses). If the losses exceed the gains, all or part of the gains and losses are reported as ordinary in Part II of Form 4797 and/or on Schedule A of Form 1040.

PROBLEM MATERIALS

DISCUSSION QUESTIONS

I:13-1 Explain how the gain on the sale or exchange of land could be classified as either ordinary income, a Sec. 1231 gain, or a LTCG, depending on the facts and circumstances.

I:13-2 Why were taxpayers reluctant to sell appreciated business property between 1938 and 1942? What effect did this reluctance have on the tax law?

I:13-3 Alice owns timber, purchased six years ago, with an adjusted basis of $50,000. The timber is cut for use in her furniture business on October 1, when the FMV of the timber is $200,000. The FMV of the timber on January 1 is $190,000. May Alice treat any of the gain as Sec. 1231 gain? If so, how much?

I:13-4 Explain how the gain from an involuntary conversion of business property held more than one year is taxed if the involuntary conversion is the result of a condemnation. Explain the tax treatment if the involuntary conversion is due to a casualty.

I:13-5 When is livestock considered Sec. 1231 property?

I:13-6 When is a net Sec. 1231 gain treated as ordinary income?

I:13-7 Carlie has a Sec. 1231 gain of $10,000 and no Sec. 1231 losses during the current year. Explain why the gain might be taxed at (a) 15%, (b) 35%, (c) 25%, or (d) zero.

I:13-8 Why is it unlikely that gains due to the sale of equipment will be treated as Sec. 1231 gains?

I:13-9 Hank sells equipment used in a trade or business for $25,000. The equipment costs $30,000 and has an adjusted basis of $25,500. Why is it important to know the holding period?

I:13-10 Jackie purchases equipment during the current year for $800,000 that has a seven-year MACRS recovery period. She expects to sell the property after three years. Jackie anticipates that her marginal tax rate in the year of sale will be significantly higher than her current marginal tax rate.

Why might it be advantageous for her to use the straight-line method of depreciation?

I:13-11 Karen purchased a computer three years ago for $15,300 to use exclusively in her business. She expensed the entire cost of the computer under Sec. 179. If she sells the computer during the current year for $3,721, what is the amount and character of her recognized gain?

I:13-12 Sheila owns a motel that is used in a trade or business. If she sells the motel, the gain will be Sec. 1245 ordinary income. During what period of time was the motel placed into service?

I:13-13 How may a taxpayer avoid having additional depreciation for purposes of Sec. 1250?

I:13-14 Marty sells his fully depreciated building at a gain to an unrelated party. The building is purchased before 1981. Is any of the gain taxed as ordinary income?

I:13-15 Which of the following assets (assume all assets have a holding period of more than one year) do not qualify as Sec. 1231 property: inventory, a pig held for breeding, land used as a parking lot for customers, and marketable securities?

I:13-16 When is an office building subject to the depreciation recapture rules of Sec. 1245?

I:13-17 Does a building that is 60% rented for residential use and 40% for commercial use qualify as residential rental property?

I:13-18 Roger owns an apartment complex with a FMV of $2 million. If he sells the apartment complex, $700,000 of the gain is Sec. 1231 gain with $600,000 taxed at 25% because it is unrecaptured Sec. 1250 gain. If he dies before selling the apartment complex and his estate sells the property for $2 million, how much ordinary income must the estate recognize?

I:13-19 Rashad owns a duplex used 100% as residential rental property. Under what conditions, if any,

will any gain that he recognizes be Sec. 1245 ordinary income?

I:13-20 John and Karen are unrelated individuals. John sold land that is Sec. 1231 property held for three years and recognized a $50,000 gain. Karen sold a building that is Sec. 1231 property held for three years and recognized a $50,000 gain. Straight-line depreciation was used. John and Karen both have a 30% tax rate, no other transactions involving capital assets or 1231 assets, and no nonrecaptured Sec. 1231 losses. Except for the sales of different assets, their tax situation is exactly the same. As a result of selling his Sec. 1231 property, will John pay more, less or the same amount of taxes than Karen as a result of selling her Sec. 1231 property? Explain.

I:13-21 Why may a corporation recognize a greater amount of ordinary income due to the sale of Sec. 1250 property than a noncorporate taxpayer?

I:13-22 Assume a taxpayer sells equipment used in a trade or business for a gain that is less than the depreciation allowed. If the taxpayer is a corporation, will a greater amount of Sec. 1245 income be recognized than if the taxpayer is an individual? Explain.

I:13-23 Dale owns business equipment with a $100,000 FMV and an adjusted basis of $60,000. The property was originally acquired for $150,000. Which one of the following transactions would result in recognition of $40,000 ordinary income by Dale due to the depreciation recapture rules of Sec. 1245?

a. He makes a gift of the property to a daughter.

b. He contributes the property to a qualified charitable organization.

c. He disposes of the equipment in an installment sale and receives $10,000 cash in the year of sale.

I:13-24 Carlos owns an office building with an $800,000 acquisition cost, a $270,000 adjusted basis, and a $500,000 FMV. The office building was acquired before 1981, and additional depreciation amounts to $175,000. Carlos makes a gift of the building to a charitable organization. What is the amount of his charitable contribution deduction?

I:13-25 Ted owns a warehouse that cost $850,000 in 1984 and is subject to depreciation recapture under Sec. 1245. The warehouse, which has an adjusted basis of zero, is destroyed by a tornado and Ted receives $580,000 from the insurance company. Within nine months, he pays $500,000 for a new warehouse and an election is made to defer the gain under Sec. 1033. What is the amount and character of Ted's recognized gain?

I:13-26 When a taxpayer disposes of oil, gas, or geothermal property, part or all of the gain may be recaptured as ordinary income. Explain how the recapture amount is determined for oil and gas and geothermal properties.

I:13-27 William owns two appreciated assets, land and a building, which have been used in his trade or business since purchased in 1990. If he sells the two assets to his 100%-owned corporation, will William have to recognize any ordinary income? Explain.

ISSUE IDENTIFICATION QUESTIONS

I:13-28 Six years ago Joelle started raising chinchillas. She separates her chinchillas into two groups, a breeding group and a market group. During the year, she had the following sales of chinchillas from her market group: 400 to producers of fur products; 100 to pet stores; and 25 to individuals to use as pets. From her breeding stock, she sold six chinchillas to Rebecca, an individual who is starting a chinchilla ranch, and five to Fur Pelts, a producer of fur products. All 11 chinchillas from the breeding group have been held for at least 22 months, and the five sold to Fur Pelts were poor performers.

I:13-29 Green Acres, Inc., owns 1,400 acres adjacent to land owned by the U.S. government. The government, wanting to sell timber from its land, had to assure prospective bidders of access to the timber. The government entered into an agreement with Green Acres for a logging road easement across land owned by Green Acres. The government agreed to pay $2 per thousand board feet of timber removed up to a maximum of $130,000. Bidders for the rights to obtain the government's timber had to agree to pay the fee to Green Acres as part of their bids for the timber. Stanley Lumberyard, Inc. provided the highest bid and paid $80,000 to Green Acres during the first year of cutting and removing the timber and $50,000 during the second year. What tax issues should Green Acres and Stanley Lumberyard consider?

I:13-30 Sarah, who has been in the business of erecting, maintaining, and renting outdoor advertising displays for 18 years, has an offer to purchase her business. Two basic types of advertising displays are used in her business: structure X and structure Y. Structure X consists of a single sign face nailed to a wooden support frame and attached to wooden poles 30 feet long. Its structure is rather easy to dismantle and move from one location to another. In contrast, structure Y is a permanent sign that is designed to withstand winds

of up to 100 miles per hour. None of the Structure Y signs have ever been moved. What tax issues should Sarah consider?

I:13-31 Sylvester owns and operates an unincorporated pizza business that delivers pizza to customers. Three years ago, he acquired an automobile for $10,000 to provide delivery service. Recently, Sylvester hired an employee who prefers to use his personal automobile to make the deliveries. Thus, Sylvester decided to permit his 18-year old daughter to use the automobile for her personal use. The automobile's adjusted basis is $3,080 and its FMV is $4,700. What tax issues should Sylvester consider?

PROBLEMS

I:13-32 *Secs. 1231, 1245, and 1250 Transactions.* All assets listed below have been held for more than one year. Which assets might be classified as Sec. 1231, Sec. 1245, or Sec. 1250 property? An asset may be classified as more than one type of property.
a. Land on which a factory is located
b. Equipment used in the factory
c. Raw materials inventory
d. Patent purchased to allow use of a manufacturing process
e. Land held primarily for sale
f. Factory building acquired in 1986 (the straight-line ACRS recovery method is used)

I:13-33 *Sec. 1231 Gains and Losses.* Vivian's AGI is $40,000 without considering the gains and losses below. Determine her revised AGI after the inclusion of any applicable gains or losses for the following independent cases. Assume she has no nonrecaptured net Sec. 1231 losses at the beginning of the year.

	Case A	Case B	Case C	Case D
Sec. 1231 gain	$19,000	$10,000	$30,000	$ 5,000
Sec. 1231 loss	5,000	22,000	39,000	12,000
LTCG	–0–	–0–	6,300	–0–
LTCL	–0–	–0–	–0–	4,200

I:13-34 *Sec. 1231 Gains and Losses.* Edith, who has no other sales or exchanges and no nonrecaptured Sec. 1231 losses, sells three tracts of land that are used in her trade or business. Her regular income tax rate is 35%.
Asset #1—$15,000 gain and holding period of 20 months
Asset #2—$17,000 loss and holding period of 25 months
Asset #3—$ 5,000 gain and holding period of 13 months
a. What is the increase in her taxes as a result of the three sales?
b. If the holding period for Asset #2 is nine months, what is the decrease in her taxes as a result of the three sales?

I:13-35 *Sec. 1231 Transactions.* Which of the following transactions or events is treated as a Sec. 1231 gain or loss? All assets are held for more than one year.
a. Theft of uninsured diamond ring, with an $800 basis and a $1,000 FMV.
b. Gain due to condemnation of land used in business.
c. Loss on the sale of a warehouse.
d. Gain of $4,000 on the sale of equipment. Depreciation deductions allowed amount to $10,000.

I:13-36 *Capital Loss Versus Sec. 1231 Loss.* Vicki has an AGI of $70,000 without considering the sale of a nondepreciable asset for $23,000. The asset was acquired six years ago and has an adjusted basis of $35,000. She has no other sales or exchanges. Determine her AGI for the following independent situations when the asset is:
a. A capital asset.
b. Sec. 1231 property.

I:13-37 *Ordinary Income Versus Sec. 1231 Gain.* At the beginning of 2010, Silver Corporation has a $95,000 capital loss carryforward from 2009. During 2010, the corporation sells land, held for four years, and realizes an $80,000 gain. Silver has no unrecaptured net Sec. 1231 losses, and it made no other sales during the current year. Determine the amount of capital loss carryforward that Silver can use in 2010 if the land is:
a. Sec. 1231 property.
b. Not a capital asset or Sec. 1231 property.

I:13-38 *Sec. 1231 Transactions.* During the current year, Sean's office building is destroyed by fire. After collecting the insurance proceeds, Sean has a $50,000 recognized gain. The building was acquired in 1998, and the straight-line method of depreciation has been used. He does not plan to acquire a replacement building. In addition to the gain on the building, consider the following independent cases and determine his total net capital gain. For each case, include the $50,000 casualty gain described above.

a. Land used in his trade or business and held more than a year is condemned by the state. The recognized gain is $60,000.

b. Assume the same facts as in Part a, except the condemnation results in a $60,000 loss.

c. An apartment building used as residential rental property and held more than one year is destroyed by a sudden, unexpected mudslide. The building is not insured, and the loss amounts to $200,000.

I:13-39 *Nonrecaptured Net Sec. 1231 Losses.* Consider the following summary of Sec. 1231 gains and losses recognized by Janet during the period 2005–2010. If Janet has no capital gains and losses during the six-year period, determine her net capital gain for each year.

	Sec. 1231 Gains	Sec. 1231 Losses
2005	$ 9,000	$ 7,000
2006	20,000	24,000
2007	12,000	19,000
2008	9,000	4,000
2009	25,000	13,200
2010	10,000	17,000

I:13-40 *Nonrecaptured Net Sec. 1231 Losses.* Dillion has a tax rate of 33% on his ordinary income and $40,000 of net nonrecaptured Sec. 1231 losses at the start of the year. During the year, he recognizes a Sec. 1231 gain of $53,000 from the sale of land. As a result of the sale, how much does Dillion's tax liability increase?

I:13-41 *Sec. 1245.* The Pear Corporation owns equipment with a $300,000 adjusted basis. The equipment was purchased six years ago for $650,000. If Pear sells the equipment for the selling prices given in the three independent cases below, what are the amount and character of Pear's recognized gain or loss?

Case	Selling Price
A	$407,000
B	752,000
C	245,000

I:13-42 *Sec. 1245.* Elizabeth owns equipment that cost $500,000 and has an adjusted basis of $230,000. If the straight-line method of depreciation had been used, the adjusted basis would be $300,000.

a. What is the maximum selling price that she could sell the equipment for without having to recognize Sec. 1245 ordinary income?

b. If she sold the equipment and had to recognize $61,000 of Sec. 1245 ordinary income, what was the selling price?

I:13-43 *Sale of Business and Personal-Use Property.* Arnie, a college student, purchased a truck in 2008 for $6,000. He used the truck 70% of the time as a distributor for the local newspaper and 30% of the time for personal use. The truck has a five-year recovery period, and he claimed depreciation deductions of $840 in 2008 and $1,344 in 2009. Arnie sells the truck on June 20, 2010, for $3,000.

a. What is the amount of allowable depreciation in 2010?

b. Determine Arnie's realized and recognized gain or loss and its character.

I:13-44 *Like-Kind Exchange of Sec. 1245 Property.* General Corporation owns equipment which cost $70,000 and has a $44,000 adjusted basis. General exchanges the equipment for other equipment ($42,000 FMV) and marketable securities ($30,000 FMV). Determine the following:

a. Realized gain

b. Recognized gain

c. Gain treated as ordinary income

d. Gain treated as Sec. 1231 gain

e. Basis of marketable securities received

f. Basis of equipment received

I:13-45 *Like-Kind Exchange of Sec. 1245 Property.* Leroy owns a truck used in his trade or business that cost $50,000 and has an adjusted basis of $34,000. The truck is exchanged for a new truck that is like-kind property with a FMV of $40,000. Prior to selling the new truck two years later, Leroy is allowed depreciation of $13,000 for the new truck. Determine:
a. Realized gain on the exchange
b. Recognized gain on the exchange
c. Basis of truck received
d. Recognized gain, and the character of the gain, if the sales price of the truck is $41,000
e. Recognized gain, and the character of the gain, if the sale price of the truck is $52,000

I:13-46 *Purpose of Sec. 1245.* Martin owns equipment used in his trade or business purchased four years ago for $200,000. Martin sells the equipment in the current year for $110,000 when its adjusted basis is $52,000. No other sales or exchanges are made this year or the preceding five years. His tax rate is 35% for all years since the year of purchase.
a. Determine the increase in Martin's AGI for the current year as a result of the sale if Sec. 1245 did not exist.
b. Determine the increase in Martin's AGI for the current year as a result of the sale if Sec. 1245 does exist.
c. Given that Sec. 1245 does exist, how much higher is his tax in (b) than in (a)?

I:13-47 *Secs. 1231 and 1250-Real Property Placed in Service Before 1981.* Charles owns an office building and land that are used in his trade or business. The office building and land were acquired in 1978 for $800,000 and $100,000, respectively. During the current year, the properties are sold for $900,000 with 20% of the selling price being allocated to the land. The assets as shown on the taxpayer's books before their sale are as follows:

Building	$800,000	
Accumulated depreciation	690,000[a]	$110,000
Land		100,000

[a]If the straight-line method of depreciation had been used, the accumulated depreciation would be $560,000.

a. What is the recognized gain due to the sale of the building?
b. What is the character of the recognized gain due to the sale of the building?
c. What is the recognized gain and character of the gain due to the sale of the land?

I:13-48 Assume the same facts as in Problem I:13-47 except the taxpayer is a corporation. Answer the same questions.

I:13-49 *Secs. 1231, 1245, and Unrecaptured Sec. 1250.* Brigham is single, in the 33% marginal income tax bracket, and has the sales or exchanges below. At the beginning of the year, he has nonrecaptured net Sec. 1231 losses of $10,000. Determine the increase or decrease in Brigham's tax liability as a result of the following independent sales or exchanges.
a. Sells equipment used in his trade or business for $40,000. The equipment was purchased for $100,000 and depreciation allowed amounts to $72,000.
b. Sells land used in his trade or business for $80,000. The land was purchased four years ago for $61,000.
c. He sells a building used in his trade or business for $163,000. The building was purchased in 1988 for $250,000 and depreciation allowed amounts to $110,000.
d. Same as Part c except he sells the building for $127,000.

I:13-50 *Secs. 1245 and 1231.* The LaPoint Corporation placed in service $350,000 of equipment (7-year recovery property) on June 3, 2009 and elected to expense $250,000 as Sec. 179 expense. The maximum amount deductible due to Sec. 179 was $250,000. LaPont sold the equipment for $150,000 on November 22, 2010. Determine the following:
a. Depreciation allowed in 2009 if the corporation wants to maximize total deductions. 50% bonus depreciation (determined after the Sec. 179 expense deduction) was allowed in 2009
b. Depreciation allowed during 2010, assume no bonus depreciation
c. Amount of gain or loss and character

I:13-51 *Unrecaptured Sec. 1250 Gain and 1231.* Mr. Briggs purchased an apartment complex on January 10, 2008, for $2,000,000 with 10% of the price allocated to land. He sells the complex on October 22, 2010, for $2,500,000.
a. How much depreciation was allowed for 2008?
b. How much depreciation is allowed for 2010?
c. Will any of the gain be ordinary income?
d. What is the amount of gain and the character of the gain on the sale of the building?

e. What is the amount of gain and the character of the gain on the sale of the land?

f. Will any of the gain be taxed at 25%?

I:13-52 *Sec. 1250 Residential Rental Property-Placed in Service After 1981 and Before 1987.* Jesse owns a duplex used as residential rental property. The duplex cost $100,000 in 1986, and 10% of the cost was allocated to the land. Total cost-recovery deductions allowed amount to $90,000. The statutory percentages were used to compute cost-recovery deductions. If the straight-line method of cost recovery were used instead, $90,000 of cost-recovery deductions would have been allowed.

a. What is the amount of recognized gain and the character of the gain if Jesse sells the duplex for $125,000 with 10% of the price allocated to land?

b. Same as (a) except the building is an office building.

I:13-53 *Sec. 1250-Real Property Placed in Service Before 1981.* Rosemary owns an office building placed in service in 1980 that cost $625,000 and has an adjusted basis of $227,000. If the straight-line method of depreciation were used, the adjusted basis would be $300,000.

a. What is the maximum selling price that she could sell the building for without having to recognize Sec. 1250 ordinary income?

b. If she sold the building and had to recognize $51,000 of Sec. 1250 ordinary income, what was the selling price?

I:13-54 *Nonresidential Real Property-Noncorporate Taxpayer.* Consider three office buildings placed in service as shown below and answer the following true-false questions. Assume all assets are sold by a noncorporate taxpayer at a gain and there are no other sales or exchanges or nonrecaptured Sec. 1231 loss unless told otherwise. None of the buildings are fully depreciated when sold and the taxpayer's tax rate is more than 25%.

	Placed in Service
Building #1	Before 1981
Building #2	After 1980 and before 1987
Building #3	After 1986

1. Some or all of the gain on sale of #1 is ordinary if accelerated depreciation was used.
2. If the straight-line method of depreciation was used for #1, some or all of the gain may be taxed at 25%.
3. Gain on the sale of #2 could be Sec. 1245 ordinary income.
4. Gain on the sale of #2 could be Sec. 1231 gain.
5. Part of the gain on the sale of #2 could be Sec. 1245 ordinary income and part could be Sec. 1231 gain.
6. If the straight-line method of depreciation was used for #2, some or all of the gain may be taxed at 25%.
7. Some or all of the gain on the sale of #3 could be Sec. 1245 ordinary income.
8. Some or all of the gain on the sale of #3 could be taxed at 25%.
9. Some of the gain on the sale of #3 could be Sec. 1250 ordinary income.
10. If the taxpayer has a nonrecaptured Sec. 1231 loss of $30,000 and the gain on the sale of #3 is $40,000, all $40,000 of the gain is taxed as ordinary income.

I:13-55 *Nonresidential Real Property-Corporate Taxpayer.* Assume the same facts as in Problem I:13-54 except the taxpayer is a corporate taxpayer with a 34% tax rate and answer the ten true-false questions.

I:13-56 *Secs. 1231 and 1250-Placed in Service After 1986.* Molly, whose tax rate is 35%, sells an apartment complex for $4,500,000 with 10% of the price allocated to land. The apartment complex was purchased in 1991. She has no other sales or exchanges during the year and no nonrecaptured net Sec. 1231 losses. Information about the assets at the time of sale is:

	Building	Land
Original Cost	$2,700,000	$300,000
Accumulated Depreciation	1,000,000	0

a. What is the recognized gain on the sale of the building and the character of the gain?

b. What is the recognized gain on the sale of the land and the character of the gain?

c. How much of the Sec. 1231 gain is taxed at 25%?

d. If Molly has NSTCL of $50,000, will the capital loss reduce the Sec. 1231 gain taxed at 25% or 15%?

I:13-57 *Secs. 1231 and 1250 for Corporate Taxpayer.* Assume the same facts as in Problem I:13-56 except the taxpayer is a corporation instead of an individual.
  a. What is the recognized gain on the sale of the building and the character of the gain?
  b. What is the recognized gain on the sale of the land and the character of the gain?
  c. How much of the Sec. 1231 gain is taxed at 25%?

I:13-58 *Charitable Contribution of Sec. 1231 Property.* Raquel owns land used in her trade or business for more than one year. The basis is $10,000 and its FMV is $40,000. Her tax rate is 33% and her AGI is $150,000. She makes no other charitable contributions except for the ones considered below.
  a. If she gives the land to a university, determine her tax savings.
  b. If she sells the land for $40,000, pays the tax and then contributes the remainder of the cash to the charity, determine her tax savings because of the contribution and the amount that the university receives. Assume that she has no other sales or exchanges during the year.

I:13-59 *Secs. 1231, 1245 and 1250.* Glen, whose tax rate is 33%, sells each of the following assets for $200,000. Each case is an independent case.

	Sec. 1231 Gain (Loss)	Ordinary Income	Taxed at 33%	Taxed at 25%	Taxed at 15%
Building purchased in 1995 for $220,000 with adjusted basis of $165,000.					
Equipment purchased in 2006 for $300,000 with adjusted basis of $144,000					
Land purchased in 1990 for $30,000 to use as a building site					
Building purchased in 1994 for $150,000 with adjusted basis of $112,000					
Equipment purchased in 2007 for $180,000 with adjusted basis of $140,000					

I:13-60 *Recapture of Soil and Water Conservation Expenditures.* Bob owns farmland with a $600,000 basis, and he elects to expense $100,000 of expenditures incurred for soil and water conservation purposes. Bob sells the farmland after farming for seven years and four months. What is the amount of the recognized gain and the character of the gain if the selling price is
  a. $825,000
  b. $615,000

I:13-61 *Recapture of Intangible Drilling Costs.* Jeremy purchased undeveloped oil and gas property five years ago. He paid $300,000 for intangible drilling and development costs and elected to expense the $300,000. During the current year, Jeremy sells the property, which has an $800,000 adjusted basis, for $900,000. What is the amount of gain treated as ordinary income under Sec. 1254 because of the election to expense intangible drilling and development costs?

I:13-62 *Recapture of Intangible Drilling Costs and Depletion.* In 1999, Jack purchased undeveloped oil and gas property for $900,000 and paid $170,000 for intangible drilling and development costs. He elected to expense the intangible drilling and development costs. During the current year he sells the property for $950,000 when the property's adjusted basis is $700,000. Depletion of $200,000 was allowed on the property.
  a. What is the realized gain and how much of the gain is ordinary income?
  b. For Jack to have a Sec. 1231 gain, the selling price must exceed what amount?

I:13-63 *Related Party Transactions.* Ed operates a storage business as a sole proprietorship and owns the following assets acquired in 1987:

Warehouse	$400,000
Minus: Accumulated depreciation	(230,000)

| Adjusted basis | $170,000 |
| Land | 65,000 |

The FMV of the warehouse and the land are $500,000 and $200,000, respectively. Ed owns 75% of the stock of the Crane Corporation. If he sells the two assets to Crane at a price equal to the FMV of the assets, determine the recognized gain and its character due to the sale of the:
a. Building
b. Land

COMPREHENSIVE PROBLEM

I:13-64 Betty, whose tax rate is 33%, is in the business of breeding and racing horses. Except for the transactions below, she has no other sales or exchanges and she has no unrecaptured net Sec. 1231 losses. Consider the following transactions that occur during the year:

- A building with an adjusted basis of $300,000 is destroyed by fire. Insurance proceeds of $500,000 are received, but Betty does not plan to replace the building. The building was built 12 years ago at a cost of $430,000 and used to provide lodging for her employees. Straight-line depreciation has been used.
- Four acres of the farm are condemned by the state to widen the highway and Betty receives $50,000. The land was inherited from her mother 15 years ago when its FMV was $15,000. Her mother purchased the land for $10,300. Betty does not plan to purchase additional land.
- A racehorse purchased four years ago for $200,000 was sold for $550,000. Total depreciation allowed using the straight-line method amounts to $160,000.
- Equipment purchased three years ago for $200,000 is exchanged for $100,000 of IBM common stock. The adjusted basis of the equipment is $120,000. If straight-line depreciation had been used, the adjusted basis would be $152,000.
- An uninsured pony, with an adjusted basis of $20,000 and FMV of $35,000, that her daughter uses only for personal use is injured while attempting a jump. Because of the injury, the uninsured pony has to be destroyed by a veterinarian.

a. What amount of Sec. 1245 ordinary income must be recognized?
b. What amount of Sec. 1250 ordinary income must be recognized?
c. Will the loss resulting from the destruction of her daughter's pony be used to determine net Sec. 1231 gains or losses?
d. What is the amount of the net Sec. 1231 gain or loss?
e. After all of the netting of gains or losses is completed, will the gain resulting from the involuntary conversion of the building be treated as LTCG?
f. What is the amount of her unrecaptured Sec. 1250 gain?

TAX STRATEGY PROBLEMS

I:13-65 Russ has never recognized any Sec. 1231 gains or losses. In December 2010, Russ is considering the sale of two Sec. 1231 assets. The sale of one asset will result in a $20,000 Sec. 1231 gain while the sale of the other asset will result in a $20,000 Sec. 1231 loss. Russ has no other capital or Sec. 1231 gains and losses in 2010 and does not expect to have any other capital or Sec. 1231 gains and losses in 2010. He is aware that it might be advantageous to recognize the Sec. 1231 gain and the Sec. 1231 loss in different tax years. However, he does not know whether he should recognize the Sec. 1231 gain in 2010 and the Sec. 1231 loss in 2011 or vice versa. His marginal tax rate for each year is expected to be 33%. Advise the taxpayer with respect to these two alternatives:
a. Recognize the $20,000 Sec. 1231 loss in 2010 and the $20,000 Sec. 1231 gain in 2011.
b. Recognize the $20,000 Sec. 1231 gain in 2010 and the $20,000 Sec. 1231 loss in 2011.

I:13-66 Holly has recognized a $9,000 STCL. She has no other recognized capital gains and losses in 2010. She is considering the sale of a Sec. 1231 asset held for four years at a $5,000 gain in 2010. She had not recognized any Sec. 1231 losses during the previous five years and does not expect to have any other Sec. 1231 transactions in 2010. Her marginal tax rate for 2010 is 31%. What is the amount of increase in her 2010 taxes if Holly recognizes the $5,000 Sec. 1231 gain in 2010?

TAX FORM/RETURN PREPARATION PROBLEMS

I:13-67 George Buckner sells an apartment building on October 10th of the current year for $1,750,000. The building was purchased on January 1, 1995, for $2,000,000. Depreciation of $420,000 has been taken. The figures given above do not include the purchase price or the selling price of the land. Mr. Buckner's adjusted basis for the land is $200,000, and the sales price is $350,000. Mr. Buckner, who owns and operates a taxi business, sells one of the automobiles for $1,800 on November 14th. The automobile's adjusted basis is zero, and the original cost is $15,000. The automobile was purchased on April 25, 2004. Mr. Buckner has no other gains and losses during the year, and nonrecaptured net Sec. 1231 losses amount to $32,000. Prepare Form 4797 for the current year.

I:13-68 Julie Hernandez is single and has no dependents. She operates a dairy farm and her Social Security number is 510-88-6387. She lives at 1325 Vermont Street in Costa, Florida. Consider the following information for the current year:

- Schedule C was prepared by her accountant and the net profit from the dairy operations is $48,000.

- Itemized deductions amount to $4,185.

- Dividend income (qualified dividend) amounts to $280.

- State income tax refund received during the year is $125. She did not itemize last year.

- In June, a burglar broke into her house and stole the following two assets, which were acquired in 1988:

	Basis	FMV	Insurance Proceeds Received
Painting	$2,000	$10,000	$9,000
Sculpture	1,700	1,500	0

The following assets used in her business were sold during the year:

	Acquisition Date	Original Cost	Depreciation to Date of Sale	Date of Sale	Selling Price
Tractor	June 10, 1999	$25,000	$25,000	Oct. 20	$ 8,300
Barn	May 23, 1989	90,000	61,000	May 13	87,000
Land	May 23, 1989	15,000	–0–	May 13	27,000
Cows	Sept. 7, 2007	20,000	13,000	Nov. 8	21,000

In August, three acres of the farm were taken by the state under the right of eminent domain for the purpose of building a highway. The basis of the three acres is $1,500, and the state paid the FMV, $22,000, on February 10. The farm was purchased on August 12, 1971.

Nonrecaptured net Section 1231 losses from the five most recent tax years preceding the current year amount to $7,000. Estimated taxes paid during the year amount to $32,000.

Prepare Forms 1040, 4684 Section A, 4797, and Schedule D for the current year. (Do not consider self-employment taxes discussed in Chapter I:14.)

CASE STUDY PROBLEMS

I:13-69 Your client, Kent Earl, whose tax rate is 35%, owns a bowling alley and has indicated that he wants to sell the business for $1,000,000 and purchase a minor league baseball franchise. His business consists of the following tangible assets:

	Acquisition Date	Original Cost	Adjusted Basis
Equipment	1998	$600,000	$150,000
Building	1988	900,000	494,000
Land	1978	100,000	100,000
Inventory	Current year	50,000	50,000

Because you have another client, Tom Quick, who is interested in purchasing a business, you informed Tom of Kent's interest in selling. Tom wants to purchase the bowling alley, and the price sounds right to him. The bowling alley business has been very profitable in the last few years because Kent has developed a loyal group of customers by promoting bowling leagues during the week days and a special Saturday afternoon session for chil-

dren in the elementary school grades. Kent and Tom have come to you and want to know how the transaction should be handled for the best tax results. You know that the $1,000,000 purchase price will have to be allocated among the assets and it will be necessary to estimate the FMV of all assets. Because FMV is often subjective, Kent and Tom recognize that some flexibility might exist in allocating the purchase price. For example, it might be just as easy to justify a FMV of $300,000 or $325,000 for the equipment.

a. What advice do you have for Kent with respect to the allocation (i.e., should he be interested in allocating more to some assets than others)? Explain the reasoning for your advice.

b. Would your advice to Kent be different if he had a large amount of capital losses and no nonrecaptured net Sec. 1231 losses?

c. What advice do you have for Tom with respect to the allocation (i.e., should he be interested in allocating more of the purchase price to some assets than to others)? Explain the reasoning for your advice.

d. What advantages might result from having Kent sign an agreement not to compete (i.e., operate a bowling alley)?

e. Should you have a concern about the ethical implications of advising both Kent and Tom?

I:13-70 Assume the same facts as in Case Study Problem I:13-69 except you have the following market values as a result of an appraisal:

Equipment	$ 250,000
Building	500,000
Land	140,000
Inventory	110,000
Total	$1,000,000

Tom insists that $150,000 of the purchase price should be allocated to inventory and $100,000 should be allocated to land. He refuses to complete the purchase unless the allocation is made as he requests. What action should you take with respect to Tom's request? (See Chapter I:10 for a discussion of valuation issues in the purchase and sale of a business.)

TAX RESEARCH PROBLEM

I:13-71 Berkeley Corporation has a policy of furnishing new automobiles to the athletic department of the local university. The automobiles are used for short periods of time by the extremely popular head basketball coach. When the automobiles are returned to Berkeley Corporation, they are sold to regular customers. The owner of Berkeley Corporation maintains that any such cars held for more than one year should qualify as Sec. 1231 property. Do you agree?

Research sources include:

• Rev. Rul. 75-538, 1975-2 C.B. 34

14

CHAPTER

SPECIAL TAX COMPUTATION METHODS, TAX CREDITS, AND PAYMENT OF TAX

LEARNING OBJECTIVES

After studying this chapter, you should be able to

1. ► Calculate the alternative minimum tax

2. ► Describe what constitutes self-employment income and compute the self-employment tax

3. ► Describe the various business and personal tax credits

4. ► Understand the mechanics of the federal withholding tax system and the requirements for making estimated tax payments

Chapter I:2 discussed the basic tax computation for individuals using the tax table and tax rate schedules. This chapter completes the discussion of the tax computation by examining three principal topics:

1. Two special methods of tax computation: the alternative minimum tax and self-employment tax;
2. Various tax credits that are available to reduce tax liability; and
3. Methods for payment of an individual's tax liability, including the pay-as-you-go withholding rules and estimated tax payment requirements.

ALTERNATIVE MINIMUM TAX

OBJECTIVE 1

Calculate the alternative minimum tax

Over the years, Congress has used the income tax law for a variety of purposes other than just raising revenue to fund government operations, such as enacting provisions to promote economic and social goals. As the number of special tax provisions increased, many taxpayers were able to carefully plan their financial affairs to substantially reduce or eliminate their entire income tax liability. As a result, in 1969, Congress passed a new set of rules to ensure that all taxpayers would pay at least a minimum amount of income tax. Thus was born what is known today as the **alternative minimum tax** (**AMT**).

The original minimum tax was called an add-on minimum tax because it was added to the taxpayer's regular income tax liability. The present AMT system was created in 1978 and is no longer an add-on tax, but is a separate and parallel tax system. Taxpayers are first required to compute their regular income tax liability and then recompute their tax under the AMT system. The AMT system requires taxpayers to adjust their regular taxable income by a number of adjustments and preferences and then subtract an exemption amount to arrive at the AMT base. The AMT base is then multiplied by special rates to compute the tax, which is called the Tentative Minimum Tax (TMT). Taxpayers are required to pay the *greater* of (1) the regular income tax, or (2) the TMT.

HISTORICAL NOTE

The original add-on minimum tax, enacted in 1969, was 10% of the taxpayer's tax preferences in excess of a $30,000 statutory exemption.

LEGISLATIVE NOTE

The American Recovery and Reinvestment Act of 2009 enacted an AMT patch setting the 2009 exemption amounts at $70,950 for married taxpayers filing jointly and $46,700 for unmarried taxpayers. At the time this textbook went to press, Congress had not enacted a similar patch for 2010. The authors, however, believe that Congress eventually will enact such a patch rather than let the exemption amounts revert to their previous low levels ($45,000 married filing jointly; $33,750 unmarried). Accordingly, we will use the 2009 exemption amounts for both 2009 and 2010 in this chapter.

The present AMT system applies to individuals, corporations, estates, and trusts.[1] Most individual taxpayers are not subject to the AMT because their regular income tax is greater than the TMT. This is primarily because many taxpayers do not have substantial adjustments and preferences, and the AMT exemption is fairly liberal in amount. For tax years beginning in 2009 the exemption was $70,950 for married individuals filing a joint return and $46,700 for unmarried individuals, and for this chapter we are using the same amounts for 2010 (see Legislative Update in the margin). However, in recent years more and more individuals have been subjected to the AMT. Many of these are not the high-income individuals for which the AMT was intended. The primary reason for this unusual phenomenon is the structure of the AMT system and the fact that the AMT is not indexed for inflation. To date, Congress has not found a cure for the unintended consequences of the AMT, but it has applied an annual patch to alleviate it.

EXAMPLE I:14-1 ▶

Ricardo and Sue are married and file a joint return with regular taxable income of $30,000 and tax preferences and adjustments of $12,000. Their alternative minimum taxable income (AMTI) is $42,000 ($30,000 + $12,000), but the alternative minimum tax base is zero because of the $70,950 exemption. Thus, their tax liability is based on the regular tax computation, and they owe no AMT liability. ◀

---

[1] The AMT applicable to corporations is discussed in Chapter C:5 of *Prentice Hall's Federal Taxation: Corporations, Partnerships, Estates, and Trusts* text and in the *Comprehensive* volume.

EXAMPLE I:14-2 ▶ Assume the same facts for Ricardo and Sue as in Example I:14-1 for 2010, except they have tax preferences and adjustments of $61,000. Their alternative minimum taxable income (AMTI) is $91,000. Their tentative minimum tax (TMT) is $5,213 [$91,000 − $70,950 exemption = $20,050 × 0.26 = $5,213.] Regular tax on taxable income of $30,000 is $3,663. Ricardo and Sue must pay the TMT of $5,213 because it exceeds the regular tax of $3,663. ◀

AMT COMPUTATION

The alternative minimum tax for individuals uses a two-tiered graduated rate schedule. The AMT tax base consists of the following items:[2]

ADDITIONAL COMMENT

Some tax advisors recommend accelerating income into a year in which the taxpayer is subject to the AMT because the income will be taxed at a 26% or a 28% rate rather than a possibly higher rate in a later year.

TAXABLE INCOME   (computed under the regular income tax system)
Plus: AMT tax preference items[3]
Plus: Personal and dependency exemptions
         The standard deduction if the taxpayer does not itemize
Plus or   AMT adjustments
minus:

ALTERNATIVE MINIMUM TAXABLE INCOME (AMTI)
Minus: Exemption amount[a][4]

ALTERNATIVE MINIMUM TAX BASE
Times: Tax rate (26% of first $175,000; 28% of amounts in excess of $175,000)[5]
Minus: Nonrefundable personal credits

TENTATIVE MINIMUM TAX
Minus: Regular tax after nonrefundable personal credits

ALTERNATIVE MINIMUM TAX

[a]*Exemption Amount:*	*Basic AMT Exemption:*	*Phaseout: Basic Minus 25% of AMTI in Excess of:*
(See Legislative Update, Page I:14-2)		
Married filing jointly and surviving spouse	$70,950	$150,000
Unmarried	$46,700	$112,500
Married filing separately	$35,475	$ 75,000

EXAMPLE I:14-3 ▶ Rita, an unmarried taxpayer filing single, has regular taxable income of $185,000 in 2010, a regular tax liability after credits of $46,167, a positive AMT adjustment (due to limitations on itemized deductions) of $25,300, and tax preferences of $10,000. Rita's nonrefundable tax cedits were an adoption credit of $1,000 and a child and dependent care credit of $600. Rita's alternative minimum tax is calculated as follows:

KEY POINT

For purposes of the alternative minimum tax, no deduction is allowed for personal exemptions or the standard deduction.

Taxable income		$185,000
Plus:	Tax preferences	10,000
Plus:	Adjustments related to itemized deductions	25,300
Plus:	Personal exemption	3,650
Alternative minimum taxable income (AMTI)		$223,950
Minus:	Exemption amount ($46,700 − $27,863[b])	(18,837)
Alternative minimum tax base		$205,113

HISTORICAL NOTE

In the Revenue Reconciliation Act of 1993, Congress created a two-tier alternative minimum tax schedule in order to make the individual income tax system more progressive.

---

[2] Sec. 55(b)(1).
[3] Sec. 57 (See page I:14-4).
[4] Sec. 55(d)(3). The 2009 AMT patch for exemption amounts was passed in the American Recovery and Reinvestment Act of 2009. It is only a one-year patch. As of publication date, Congress had not enacted a patch for 2010.

[5] The AMT rate on net capital gains has been reduced from the 26%/28% rates to 15%/5% to correspond with the reduction in rates on net capital gains for regular tax purposes.

Tax on first $175,000: ($175,000 × 0.26)	$ 45,500
Tax on excess over $175,000: ($30,113 × 0.28)	8,432
Tentative minimum tax	$ 53,932
Minus: Nonrefundable tax credits	$ (1,600)
Regular tax	(46,167)
Alternative minimum tax (AMT)	$ 6,165

Rita has a total federal income tax liability of $52,332 ($46,167 regular tax + $6,165 AMT).

[b]Exemption phaseout: [0.25 × ($223,950 − $112,500)] = $27,863 ◄

AMT PREFERENCE ITEMS

Certain provisions in the Internal Revenue Code grant favorable treatment to taxpayers. However, Congress is concerned that some taxpayers may take over-advantage of these favorable provisions and has therefore classified them as tax preferences (IRC Sec. 57). For example, accelerated depreciation allowed for real property placed in service before 1987 is a tax preference item. (See Chapter I:10 for a discussion of ACRS depreciation.) However, not all items receiving preferential treatment are tax preference items. For example, most municipal bond interest income is exempt from the federal income tax but is not a tax preference item.

To compute the AMT tax base, the tax preferences designated in Sec. 57 must be added to regular taxable income. Some of the most common tax preference items are:

▶ Excess of accelerated depreciation (or ACRS cost recovery) claimed over a hypothetical straight-line depreciation amount for real property placed in service before 1987 (computed on an item-by-item basis).

▶ Tax-exempt interest on certain private activity bonds issued before 2009 or after 2010. In general, private activity bonds are state or local bonds that are issued to help finance a private business.

▶ Excess of percentage depletion over the adjusted basis of the property. This item of tax preference does not apply to the percentage depletion deduction claimed by independent oil and gas producers and royalty owners.

▶ Exclusion of gain on the sale of certain small business stock. The exclusion is 7% of the gain on the disposition of qualified small business stock under Sec. 1202[6] (see Chapter I:5).

EXAMPLE I:14-4 ▶ Richard, an unmarried taxpayer filing single, has the following tax preference items for the current year:

▶ $15,000 ACRS cost-recovery deduction on real property placed in service before 1987 and held for investment. The straight-line ACRS deduction would have been $10,000.

▶ $10,000 of tax-exempt interest on private activity bonds.

Richard's total tax preferences are $15,000, consisting of $5,000 excess cost recovery deductions and $10,000 tax-exempt interest on the private activity bonds. ◄

As one can see from the discussion above, most taxpayers will have few, if any, tax preferences.

AMT ADJUSTMENTS

As previously discussed, AMTI equals taxable income increased or decreased by adjustments and increased by tax preference items. For most individual taxpayers, adjustments are either itemized deductions that are not allowed in computing AMTI or timing differences relating to the deferral of income or the acceleration of deductions under the regular tax rules. These adjustments generally increase the AMT tax base, although the AMT tax base may be reduced when the timing differences reverse. Some of the more important adjustments are:

ADDITIONAL COMMENT

Most taxpayers will not have tax preference items. Over the years, tax preference items have diminished in importance while adjustments have increased in impacting AMT liabilities.

ADDITIONAL COMMENT

Under the American Recovery and Reinvestment Act of 2009, interest on private activity bonds issued in 2009 or 2010 is not treated as a tax preference item.

ADDITIONAL COMMENT

Some tax advisors recommend that cash basis taxpayers prepay their local property taxes or state income taxes before the end of the year to reduce the current year's tax liability. However, if the taxpayer is subject to the AMT, this may not be a valid tax planning strategy.

---

[6] Sec. 57(a)(7). The 7% rate was formerly 28%. Before 2001, the 28% rate was 42%.

LIMITATION ON ITEMIZED DEDUCTIONS. Only certain itemized deductions are allowed in computing AMTI. Additionally, the standard deduction is not allowed if an individual does not itemize deductions. The following items *are deductible* for AMT purposes:

▶ Casualty and theft losses in excess of 10% of AGI

▶ Charitable contributions (but not in excess of the 20%, 30%, and 50% of AGI limitation amounts)

▶ Medical expenses in excess of 10% of AGI (a 7.5% ceiling applies to the regular tax computation)

▶ Qualified housing interest and certain other interest (up to the amount of qualified net investment income included in the AMT base).

▶ Estate tax deduction on income in respect of a decedent

▶ Gambling losses

Some of the more significant itemized deductions that *are not deductible* for the AMT include miscellaneous itemized deductions (e.g., unreimbursed employee business expenses), state, local, and foreign income taxes, and real and personal property taxes. The overall phaseout of itemized deductions does not apply to the AMT.

EXAMPLE I:14-5 ▶ Robin, an unmarried taxpayer filing single, has AGI of $100,000 and the following itemized deductions:

Charitable contributions	4,000
Medical expenses not reimbursed by insurance	10,500
Mortgage interest on Robin's personal residence	18,500
Real estate taxes	4,000
State income taxes	6,000
Personal casualty loss, net of insurance, before any limitations	$15,000

From the information above, Robin's regular taxable income would be:

AGI			$100,000
Itemized deductions:			
Charitable contributions		$ 4,000	
Medical expenses	$10,500		
Less 7.5% of AGI	(7,500)	3,000	
Mortgage interest		18,400	
Real estate taxes		4,000	
State income taxes		6,000	
Personal casualty loss	$15,000		
Less $100 floor	(100)		
Less 10% of AGI	(10,000)	4,900	(40,300)
Personal exemption			(3,650)
Taxable income			$56,050

To compute her AMTI, Robin must make adjustments to her regular taxable income. Assume that Robin also has $20,000 of tax preferences. Her AMTI would be computed as follows:

Taxable income	$56,050
Tax preferences	20,000
AMT adjustments:	
Medical expenses: (only $500 allowed for AMTI [$10,500 − .10($100,000)]	2,500
Real estate and state income taxes (not allowed for AMTI)	10,000
Personal exemption (not allowed for AMTI)	3,650
AMTI	$92,200 ◀

TIMING DIFFERENCES. Other adjustments are required when the rules for calculating regular taxable income permit the taxpayer to temporarily defer the recognition of income or to accelerate deductions (timing differences). The most common AMT adjustments for timing differences are:

▶ For personal property placed in service after 1998, the difference between the MACRS deduction and the amount determined by using the 150% declining balance method

(switching to the straight-line method) over the recovery period used for regular tax purposes.[7] Bonus depreciation (50% or 30%), where applicable, is allowed in full for purposes of the AMT.

▶ For real property placed in service after 1986 and before January 1, 1999, the difference between the MACRS depreciation claimed using the property's actual recovery period and a hypothetical straight-line depreciation amount calculated using a 40-year life (see Chapter I:10 for a discussion of the alternative depreciation system).[8]

▶ For incentive stock options, the excess of the option's fair market value over the price paid by the individual for the option. This adjustment is measured on the date the rights to the underlying stock are freely transferable or are not subject to a substantial risk of forfeiture.

▶ For research and experimental (R&E) expenditures, the difference between the amount expensed and the deduction that would have been allowed if the expenditures were capitalized and amortized over a ten-year period.[9]

EXAMPLE I:14-6 ▶

Rob has the following AMT adjustments caused by timing differences in 2009:

▶ Depreciation in 2010 on residential rental property costing $100,000 and placed in service in January 1998 is $3,636 using the straight-line method and a 27½-year recovery period under MACRS rules. Depreciation for AMT purposes is $2,500 using the straight-line method and a 40-year recovery period under the alternative depreciation system. Thus, the positive AMT adjustment is $1,136 ($3,636 − $2,500).

▶ Depreciation on a computer used in business costing $10,000 and placed in service in January 2010 is $2,000 based on MACRS rules (i.e., 200% DB method, a half-year convention, and a five-year recovery period). Depreciation for AMT purposes is $1,500 based on the alternative depreciation system (i.e., 150% DB method, half-year convention, and a five-year recovery period). Thus, the positive AMT adjustment is $500 ($2,000 − $1,500).

ADDITIONAL COMMENT

For corporate taxpayers only, there is a 0.12% environmental tax imposed on the excess of the corporation's modified alternative minimum taxable income over $2 million. This additional tax levy is primarily imposed on corporations larger than "mom and pop" entities.

▶ R&E expenditures amounting to $50,000 are expensed in the current year. For AMT purposes, the R&E deduction would be $5,000 ($50,000 ÷ 10 years) since the expenditures are capitalized and amortized over a 10-year period. Thus, the positive AMT adjustment is $45,000 ($50,000 − $5,000).

Rob's total positive AMT adjustment to taxable income to arrive at AMTI is $46,636 ($1,136 + $500 + $45,000). ◀

AMT CREDITS

CREDITS THAT REDUCE THE AMT. As we will discuss later in this chapter, a number of credits are allowed to reduce a taxpayer's regular tax liability. However, for purposes of the AMT, only the foreign tax credit and nonrefundable personal credits are allowed. The foreign tax credit that applies to the AMT is a specially computed credit, called the "alternative minimum tax foreign tax credit" and is beyond the scope of this text. For tax years beginning in 2000–2010, taxpayers can apply allowable nonrefundable personal tax credits against both regular tax and the AMT. They are discussed on pp. I:14-10–19 and are summarized in Topic Review I:14-2.

 STOP & THINK

Question: What are the most common characteristics of taxpayers who are subject to the AMT?

Solution: While each situation is unique, certain taxpayers are more likely to be subject to the AMT. First, taxpayers who have materially invested in real estate before January 1, 1999 are likely candidates for the AMT because they will have a large positive adjustment caused from differences in depreciation. Second, as discussed above, taxpayers who use credits to reduce their regular tax liability may be subject to the AMT because only certain credits reduce the AMT. Third, taxpayers who have very large itemized deductions, primarily from large state and local tax liabilities, may be subject to the AMT because state and

---

[7] For personal property placed in service after 1986 and prior to 1999, the 150% declining balance method (switching to the straight-line method) was used for AMT purposes, but the ADS recovery period was required rather than the recovery period for regular tax purposes.

[8] For real property being depreciated under the straight-line method and

placed in service after 1998, the Taxpayer Relief Act of 1997 eliminates this adjustment.

[9] Sec. 56(b)(2). However, this adjustment does not apply if the taxpayer materially participates in the activity, Sec. 56(b)(2)(D).

ADDITIONAL COMMENT

The American Recovery and Reinvestment Act of 2009 allows taxpayers with deferred credits from tax years beginning before 2006 (deferred research credits or deferred AMT credits) to turn these into refundable credits in lieu of taking bonus and accelerated depreciation on qualified eligible property (see Chapter I:10.)

local taxes are not deductible for AMT purposes. Fourth, taxpayers who have very large personal exemptions; large families in high-tax states may be subject to the AMT.

FUTURE AMT CREDIT. Under Sec. 53, individual taxpayers are allowed a credit for AMT paid in the past against future *regular tax liability*. While this may seem unusual, the logic is as follows: The AMT may be caused by adjustments that will reverse in the future, and the taxpayer will actually pay a higher regular tax in those future years. Thus, the combination of a prior year AMT and current year regular tax essentially constitutes double taxation. A taxpayer who paid AMT in prior years but is not subject to AMT in the current year may be entitled to an AMT credit against his regular tax liability in the current year.[10]

SUMMARY ILLUSTRATION OF THE AMT COMPUTATION

EXAMPLE I:14-7 ▶

Roger and Kate are married, file a joint return, and have four dependent children. All the children are under age 17. The following items were used to compute regular taxable income in 2010:

ADDITIONAL COMMENT

In some circumstances, the AMT applies to unsuspecting taxpayers. In a classic case, *D.R. Klaassen*, T.C. Memo 1998-241 (affd, CA-10), the taxpayers had 12 personal exemptions and were subject to the AMT even though they had no tax preferences or adjustments.

Gross income:		
Salary		$ 70,000
Interest income		10,000
Business income		30,000[a]
AGI		$110,000
Itemized deductions:		
State and local taxes	$9,400	
Mortgage interest on their personal residence	12,000	
Charitable contributions	3,000	(24,400)
Personal and dependency exemptions ($3,650 × 6)		(21,900)
Taxable income		$ 63,700
Regular tax		$8,718
Child tax credit (nonrefundable personal tax credit)		(4,000)
Net regular tax		$ 4,718

[a]MACRS depreciation deductions of $70,000 on personal property placed in service after 1986 were claimed in arriving at business income. Only $50,000 of depreciation would be claimed under the alternative depreciation system using the 150% declining balance method.

Their AMT is computed as follows:		
Taxable income		$ 63,700
Personal and dependency exemptions		21,900
AMT adjustments:		
Excess depreciation ($70,000 − $50,000)	$20,000	
State and local taxes	9,400	29,400
AMTI		$115,000
AMT exemption (see Legislative Update on page I:14-2)		(70,950)
Tax base		$ 44,050
Tax rate		× 0.26
Tentative minimum tax before credit		$ 11,453
Child tax credit (nonrefundable personal tax credit)		(4,000)
Tentative minimum tax		$ 7,453
Net regular tax after child tax credit		(4,718)
Alternative minimum tax		$ 2,735[b]

[b]An AMT credit may be available in future years to offset regular tax. However, the AMT credit applies only to the AMT that results from timing differences such as depreciation adjustments and not from exclusions (e.g., personal exemptions and taxes).

The total tax liability for Roger and Kate for 2010 is $7,453 ($4,718 + $2,735). ◀

---

[10] The AMT credit essentially is applicable to timing adjustments rather than permanent adjustments. A detailed discussion of the rules for computing the AMT credit is beyond the scope of this book. (See Sec. 53 for additional information.)

SELF-EMPLOYMENT TAX

Most individuals are classified as employees and are not subject to the self-employment tax. Employees pay their employment taxes under the Federal Insurance Contributions Act (FICA) through payroll withholding. Employers must withhold the employee's share of the FICA tax and also pay a matching amount. Employees are not subject to an additional employment tax when they file their federal income tax returns.

The self-employment tax is imposed to finance Social Security coverage for self-employed individuals. Thus, the distinction between a self-employed individual (often referred to as an independent contractor) and an employee is important because no matching employer FICA contribution is required if the payee is deemed to have independent contractor status. Independent contractors are subject to self-employment tax on the amount of net earnings from the self-employment activity. Employees who have a small business in addition to their regular employment (e.g., an accountant who is an employee for a large corporation and also prepares tax returns in a sideline consulting practice) may be subject to self-employment tax on the outside income in addition to the FICA tax on wages.

ETHICAL POINT

An employer must have a reasonable basis for treating a worker as an independent contractor or meet the general common law rules for determining whether an employer-employee relationship exists. Otherwise, the employer is liable for federal and state income tax withholding, FICA and FUTA taxes, interest, and penalties associated with the misclassification.

HISTORICAL NOTE

The ceiling amount on income from self-employment was $7,800 in 1971.

COMPUTING THE TAX

Self-employed individuals are subject to the self-employment (SE) tax if their net earnings are $400 or more.[11] The SE tax rate is a total of 15.3%, comprised of 12.4% for old-age, survivors, and disability insurance (OASDI) up to a ceiling amount of $106,800 in 2010 ($106,800 in 2009), commonly referred to as Social Security, and 2.9% for hospital insurance (HI), commonly referred to as Medicare taxes. No ceiling applies to the HI portion. The SE tax rates are exactly twice the rates for employees under FICA (6.2% for OASDI up to a ceiling amount of $106,800 in 2010, and 1.45% for HI). For employee wages, the 6.2% and 1.45% (total of 7.65%) must be matched by the employer. This matching requirement for employers effectively equalizes Social Security taxes for employees and self-employed individuals.

One-half of the self-employment tax is allowed as a *for*-AGI deduction.[12] Net earnings from self-employment are determined by multiplying self-employment income by 0.9235 (equivalent to 100% of self-employment income minus one-half of self-employment taxes, or 7.65%).

EXAMPLE I:14-8 ▶

HISTORICAL NOTE

The Revenue Reconciliation Act of 1993 eliminated the wage cap on the hospital insurance component of wages. Though presented as a tax increase for high-income individuals, it also increases the tax burden for employers of high-income individuals.

Rose is a CPA who operates her practice as a sole proprietorship. She has $120,000 of earnings from self-employment in 2010. Her net earnings from self-employment is $110,820 ($120,000 × 0.9235). The OASDI portion of the tax is $13,243 ($106,800 × 0.124). The amount of self-employment income subject to the hospital insurance portion of the tax is $110,820 and the HI tax is $3,214 ($110,820 × 0.029). Thus, the total self-employment tax reported on Schedule SE is $16,457. Rose also receives a *for*-AGI tax deduction of $8,229 ($16,457 × 0.50). ◀

If an individual is an employee and also has income from self-employment, the tax base for computing the SE tax is reduced by the wages that are subject to the FICA tax. The SE tax base for the OASDI component is equal to the lesser of (a) the primary ceiling ($106,800 in 2010) reduced by the FICA wages, or (b) the SE income multiplied by 0.9235.

EXAMPLE I:14-9 ▶

Sandy receives $75,000 wages as an employee in 2010 that are subject to FICA tax. In addition, Sandy has a small consulting practice that generates $10,000 of income from self-employment. The tentative tax base for computing the SE tax is $9,235 ($10,000 × 0.9235) net earnings from self-employment. The tax base for computing the OASDI portion of the SE tax is the lesser of $9,235 net earnings from self-employment or $31,800 ($106,800 ceiling − $75,000 FICA wages). Sandy's self-employment tax for the OASDI component is $1,145 ($9,235 × 0.124) and the HI component is $268 ($9,235 × 0.029) The total amount of SE tax is therefore $1,413 ($1,145 + $268) and Sandy also receives a *for*-AGI deduction of $707 ($1,413 × 0.50). ◀

---

[11] Sec. 6017. [12] Sec. 164(f).

EXAMPLE I:14-10 ▶

LEGISLATIVE UPDATE

The Hiring Incentives to Restore Employment (HIRE) Act of 2010 created a limited payroll tax holiday. Qualified employers would be exempt from the employer portion of OASDI on wages paid from March 18, 2010 through December 31, 2010 to qualified employees (new hires from the ranks of the unemployed). Employers who take advantage of the payroll tax holiday would not be eligible for the Work Opportunity Credit with respect to those employees.

Assume the same facts as Example I:14-9 except that Sandy's wages are $125,000. Sandy's taxable self-employment income for the OASDI portion of the SE tax is zero because her FICA wages exceed the $106,800 primary ceiling amount. However, she is subject to SE tax with respect to the HI portion. The tax base for the HI portion is her $9,235 net earnings from self-employment because no ceiling amount is applicable. The HI portion of the SE tax is $268 ($9,235 × 0.029) and Sandy also receives a *for*-AGI deduction for $134 ($268 × 0.50). ◀

CREDIT FOR EXCESS SOCIAL SECURITY TAX PAID

If an employee works for more than one employer during the year and earns, in total, more than the social security ceiling ($106,800 in 2010), the several employers may have withheld more than the total required OASDI portion of social security tax. The taxpayer is entitled to a credit or a refund for this overpayment of tax on his or her regular income tax return, Form 1040.

WHAT CONSTITUTES SELF-EMPLOYMENT INCOME

Individuals who carry on a trade or business as a proprietor or partnership are subject to the SE tax. If an individual has two separate self-employment activities, the *net* earnings from each activity are aggregated. However, where a husband and wife file a joint return and both have self-employment income, the SE tax must be computed for each individual separately.

EXAMPLE I:14-11 ▶

KEY POINT

In the case of married taxpayers filing joint returns, it is important on Schedule SE of Form 1040 to fill in the name and Social Security number of the spouse with the self-employment income. This information is used to establish specific benefit eligibility.

ADDITIONAL COMMENT

For some self-employed taxpayers, the amount of SE tax exceeds the amount of income tax for the year. For example, a married couple with two children and $17,000 of self-employment income would not owe any income tax, but would have a $2,402 (17,000 × .9235 × 15.3%) SE tax liability.

Bob and Ruth are married and file a joint return. Bob has $13,000 net earnings from a consulting business and a $4,000 net loss from a retail store that he operates as a sole proprietorship. Ruth has wages of $50,000 from her employer that are subject to FICA taxes. Bob's net earnings from self-employment are $8,312 ($9,000 × 0.9235). No reduction in Bob's SE tax base is allowed for Ruth's wages because Ruth is not self-employed. The SE tax is computed separately for Bob and Ruth. ◀

Among the items that constitute earnings subject to the SE tax are:

▶ Net earnings from a sole proprietorship
▶ Director's fees[13]
▶ Taxable research grants
▶ Distributive share of partnership income plus guaranteed payments from the partnership

The self-employment tax is computed on Schedule SE of Form 1040 (see Appendix B). The rules for computing the SE tax are summarized in Topic Review I:14-1.

Topic Review I:14-1

Self-Employment Tax Summary

▶ SE tax is imposed on net earnings from self-employment over $400.
▶ The tax base is generally the amount of self-employment income multiplied by 0.9235.
▶ A $106,800 (2010) ceiling applies to the old age, survivors, and disability (OASDI) portion. No ceiling applies to the hospital insurance (HI) portion of the tax.
▶ SE tax is computed separately for married individuals filing joint returns.
▶ One-half of the SE tax imposed is allowed as a business deduction *for* AGI.
▶ The SE tax rate is 15.3%, which includes 12.4% for the OASDI portion and 2.9% for the hospital insurance (HI) portion.

---

[13] Rev. Rul. 57-246, 1957-1 C.B. 338. It is a factual question whether an officer who also serves as a director is performing services as an employee or as an independent contractor. The courts have recognized that an individual can perform services as a director and also perform employment-related services, but the director fees may be recharacterized by the courts if the fees are in reality compensation for services rendered as an employee. (See *Peter H. Jacobs*, 1993 RIA T.C. Memo ¶ 93, 570, 66 TCM 1470.)

OVERVIEW OF TAX CREDITS

Describe the various business and personal tax credits

USE AND IMPORTANCE OF TAX CREDITS

Tax credits are often used by the federal government to implement tax policy objectives. For example, tax credits may help to increase employment, encourage energy conservation and research and experimental activities, encourage certain socially desired activities, and provide tax relief for low-income taxpayers. Tax credits are also used to mitigate the effects of double taxation on income from foreign countries. Thus, tax credits are an important part of the income tax law.

Credits are classified into two broad categories, **nonrefundable** and **refundable.** Nonrefundable credits only offset tax liability. Refundable credits, on the other hand, not only offset tax liability but if the credits exceed the tax liability, the excess will be paid (refunded) directly to the taxpayer. Topic Review I:14-2 provides a summary of selected tax credits and the rationale for their inclusion in the tax law. Note that most tax credits are nonrefundable. The principal refundable credit is the earned income credit. Taxes withheld from employee wages are prepayments of tax, but are also frequently called refundable credits.

ADDITIONAL COMMENT

The American Recovery and Reinvestment Act of 2009 has expanded and increased both nonrefundable and refundable credits.

VALUE OF A CREDIT VERSUS A DEDUCTION

As discussed previously in Chapter I:2, tax credits reduce tax liability on a dollar-for-dollar basis. This is in contrast to a tax deduction, which reduces taxable income; so the value of a tax deduction is limited by the taxpayer's marginal tax rate. Thus, tax deductions are more valuable to high-income taxpayers than to lower-income taxpayers because their marginal tax rate is higher. Tax credits, however, benefit all taxpayers in the same amount regardless of their marginal tax rate.

EXAMPLE I:14-12 ▶

Tasha and Sean are both single taxpayers and each has an $800 expenditure that qualifies as either a tax deduction or a 20% credit. Tasha is in the 15% marginal tax bracket while Sean is in the 33% marginal tax bracket. If the $800 is claimed as a deduction, Tasha would receive a tax benefit of $120 ($800 × 15%) whereas Sean would receive a tax benefit of $264 ($800 × 33%). Thus, higher income taxpayers realize greater benefits from the same amount of deduction because of the progressive nature of the federal income tax system. Conversely, if the credit is claimed, both Tasha and Sean would benefit equally as the $160 credit ($800 × 20%) would reduce each taxpayer's tax liability on a dollar-for-dollar basis. Thus, tax credits provide the same benefit to taxpayers regardless of the applicable marginal tax bracket. In this case, Tasha would prefer the credit while Sean would prefer the tax deduction. ◀

NONREFUNDABLE PERSONAL TAX CREDITS

As a result of tax legislation in the last few years, the number of personal tax credits for individual taxpayers has increased significantly. Most personal tax credits have been enacted for social welfare rather than economic reasons. Nonrefundable personal credits offset both an individual's regular tax and AMT, to the extent the aggregate credits do not exceed the sum of (1) regular tax liability minus foreign tax credit, plus (2) excess of tentative minimum tax over regular tax (the AMT).[14] The more important nonrefundable personal tax credits are discussed below.

CHILD TAX CREDIT

Taxpayers are allowed a credit of $1,000 for each qualifying child[15] under the age of 17. The definition of qualifying child is found in Chapter I:2, but the child tax credit also

---

[14] Sec. 26. The 2008 Extenders Act continues to offset the AMT with nonrefundable personal two credits to tax years beginning in 2008.

[15] Sec. 24(c).

requires that each qualifying child be younger than the person claiming the credit for the child, be unmarried, and be the taxpayer's dependent.[16] Congress intends that only a child's parents be eligible to take the child tax credit.

The credit phases out in both 2010 and 2009 when modified AGI[17] reaches $110,000 (MFJ), $75,000 (Single), or $55,000 (MFS). The phaseout equals modified AGI less the applicable floor, times $50 for each $1,000 or fraction of the excess. Thus, a married couple filing jointly with one qualifying child and modified AGI of $124,000 will have a tentative child tax credit of $1,000. The credit will be subject to a phaseout of $700 [($124,000 − $110,000) ÷ $1,000 × $50 = $700]. Their allowable credit will be $300.

The child tax credit is generally *nonrefundable*. However, if taxpayer's tentative child tax credit is greater than the total tax liability, part of the credit (the "additional" child tax credit) is *refundable*. The refundable portion is the greater of (1) 15% of taxpayer's earned income in excess of $3,000 in both 2009 and 2010; or (if taxpayer has three or more qualifying children) the excess of taxpayer's social security and medicare taxes over taxpayer's allowable earned income credit (EIC). Form 8812 is used to compute the refundable portion of the child tax credit.

CHILD AND DEPENDENT CARE CREDIT

The child and dependent care credit provides relief for taxpayers who incur child and dependent care expenses because of employment activities.[18] To qualify for the credit, which ranges from 20% to 35% of eligible expenses, an individual must meet two requirements: (1) expenses for the care of a qualifying individual must be incurred to enable the taxpayer to be gainfully employed, and (2) the qualifying individual must be either a qualifying child under age 13 or an incapacitated dependent or spouse who lived with the taxpayer for more than one-half of the year.[19]

EXAMPLE I:14-13 ▶ Tim and Tina are married and have two children under age 13. They incur child care expenses (e.g., a housekeeper and nurse) to enable both Tim and Tina to work on a full-time basis. These expenditures are eligible for the child and dependent care credit because Tim and Tina incurred them to be gainfully employed. Alternatively, if Tina were not employed, but incurred the child care expenses to play tennis and other social activities, the expenditures would not be eligible for the child and dependent care credit. ◀

QUALIFYING EMPLOYMENT-RELATED EXPENSES. Eligible expenses include amounts spent for housekeeping, nursing, cooking, baby-sitting, etc. in the taxpayer's home, but do not include expenses for a chauffeur or gardener. If the child or dependent care is provided outside the home by a dependent care facility (e.g., a day care facility), the amounts generally will qualify only if the dependent care facility provides care for more than six individuals. Employment-related expenses do not include amounts paid for services outside of the taxpayer's household at a camp where the qualifying individual stays overnight. In addition, amounts paid for services outside of the taxpayer's household (e.g., adult day care) that are spent for the care of an incapacitated dependent or spouse qualify only if the individual lives in the taxpayer's home for at least eight hours a day.

EXAMPLE I:14-14 ▶ Tony is divorced and has two children under age 13. He is employed and incurs child care expenses at a preschool nursery for one of the children. He also has a live-in nanny who provides housekeeping services and a gardener to care for his yard. The expenditures for the preschool nursery and the live-in nanny qualify because these services constitute eligible household services and care of a qualifying individual. However, the payments to the gardener do not constitute qualifying household services. ◀

---

[16] Sec. 24(a), as amended by the 2008 Adoption Act.
[17] Modified AGI means AGI increased by any amount excluded from gross income under Secs. 911, 931, or 933. Sec. 911, 931, and 933 are special exclusions in the international tax area.

[18] Sec. 21. The complete title of this credit is *Expenses for Household and Dependent Care Services Necessary for Gainful Employment.*
[19] Secs. 21(b)(1) and (e)(1). Married individuals must generally file a joint return to obtain the credit.

The following special rules apply:

▶ The maximum amount of child and dependent care expenses that qualify for the credit is $3,000 for one qualifying individual and $6,000 for two or more qualifying individuals.[20] These qualifying expense ceilings are reduced by the amount excludable from gross income relating to employer-provided dependent care assistance programs (see below). No carryover is permitted for excess expenses.

▶ Payments to a relative are qualifying expenses unless the relative is a dependent or a child (under age 19) of the taxpayer.[21]

▶ Gratuitous services performed by the taxpayer for charitable organizations are not considered gainful employment.[22]

▶ The maximum qualifying expenses cannot exceed the individual's earned income. For married individuals, the limitation is applied to the earned income of the spouse with the smaller earned income.

▶ A spouse who either is a full-time student or is incapacitated is deemed to have an earned income of $250 per month.[23] The amount is increased to $500 per month if there are two or more qualifying individuals in the household.

▶ The credit will not be allowed unless the qualifying individual's Social Security number is reported on the return on which the credit is claimed.

EXAMPLE I:14-15 ▶

KEY POINT

The percentage used to calculate the credit varies from 20% to 35% depending on the taxpayer's AGI.

Troy and Tracy are married and in 2010 incur qualifying child care expenses of $4,000 to take care of their two children, ages 1 and 3. Tracy's earned income is $20,000, and Troy's earned income from a part-time job is $3,500. Although the overall qualifying expense limitation of $6,000 is not exceeded, the earned income limitation applies because Troy's earned income ($3,500) is less than the child care expenses ($4,000). Therefore, the amount of child care expenses eligible for the credit is limited to $3,500. ◀

COMPUTATION OF THE CREDIT RATE AND AMOUNT. The credit is 35% of qualifying expenses (not to exceed the ceiling limitations of $3,000 or $6,000). The credit rate is reduced by one percentage point for each $2,000 (or fraction thereof) of adjusted gross income in excess of $15,000. However, the rate goes no lower than 20%. The minimum credit (20%) is applied once a taxpayer's AGI exceeds $43,000.

EXAMPLE I:14-16 ▶

Mark and Vicki are married, file a joint return in 2010, and have three children under age 13. Mark and Vicki's employment-related earnings are $25,000 and $10,000, respectively. Including all sources of income, their AGI is $36,000. They incur $8,000 of child care expenses during the year. The eligible child care expenses are limited to $6,000 because Mark and Vicki have more than one qualifying child and the ceiling limitation is less than either Vicki's earned income or the actual expenses incurred. Because their AGI is greater than $15,000, the credit rate is reduced from 35% to 24%, computed as follows:

Adjusted gross income (AGI)	$36,000
Base amount	(15,000)
Excess	21,000
Divided by $2,000	10.5
Rounded up to	11
Applicable credit (35% − 11%)	24%

Therefore, Mark and Vicki's child and dependent care credit for the year is $1,440 ($6,000 × 0.24). ◀

DEPENDENT CARE ASSISTANCE. An employee may exclude up to $5,000 from gross income for dependent care assistance payments made by the individual's employer.[24] The exclusion amount is limited to the earned income of the employee (or in the case of a

---

[20] Qualifying expenses may be incurred at any time during the year.
[21] Sec. 21(e)(6).
[22] Rev. Rul. 73-597, 1973-2 CB 69.
[23] Sec. 21(d)(2). To qualify as a full-time student, the individual must enroll in

an educational institution on a full-time basis for at least five calendar months of the year (Reg. Sec. 1.44A-2(b)(3)(B)(ii)).
[24] Sec. 129. (See Chapter I:4 for a discussion of the requirements for exclusion.)

married taxpayer, the lesser of the employee's earned income or the earned income of the spouse). To avoid a double benefit, the otherwise eligible expenses for purposes of computing the child and dependent care credit are reduced by the amount of assistance that is excluded from gross income.[25]

EXAMPLE I:14-17 ▶

Assume the same facts as in Example I:14-16 except that Mark was reimbursed $4,000 by his employer under a qualified dependent care assistance program and this amount was excluded from his gross income. Thus, expenses eligible for the child and dependent care credit are reduced to $2,000 ($6,000 − $4,000) and the child care credit is $480 ($2,000 × 0.24). ◀

ADDITIONAL COMMENT

The tax credit for the elderly or disabled has been declining in recent years and amounted to only $12.5 million in 2007.

TAX CREDIT FOR THE ELDERLY AND DISABLED

A limited credit is provided for certain low-income individuals who have attained age 65 before the end of the tax year or who retired because of a permanent and total disability. Most elderly or disabled taxpayers are ineligible for the credit because they either receive Social Security benefits in excess of ceiling limitations or they have AGI amounts in excess of the limitations, which effectively reduces or eliminates the allowable credit.

The maximum credit is 15% of an initial amount of $5,000 ($7,500 for married individuals filing jointly if both spouses qualify).[26] This initial amount is reduced by:

▶ Nontaxable Social Security, railroad retirement, or Veterans Administration pension or annuity benefits, and

▶ One-half of AGI in excess of $7,500 for a single individual ($10,000 for married taxpayers filing a joint return).[27]

EXAMPLE I:14-18 ▶

Wayne and Tammy are both 67 years old and file a joint return. They have AGI of $11,000 and receive nontaxable Social Security benefits of $3,000 during the current year. Their tax credit for the elderly is computed as follows:

Initial ceiling amount		$7,500
Minus: Nontaxable social security benefits	$3,000	
One-half of AGI in excess of $10,000		
(0.50 × [$11,000 − $10,000])	500	(3,500)
Total credit base		$4,000
		× 0.15
Tax credit		$ 600

The $600 credit is nonrefundable, i.e., is allowed only to the extent that Wayne and Tammy's total personal tax credits do not exceed the actual tax due before credits. ◀

ADOPTION CREDIT

LEGISLATIVE UPDATE

The Health Reform Act increases maximum allowable qualified adoption expenses to $13,170 for 2010 and 2011. The Act also makes this credit refundable rather than nonrefundable.

A nonrefundable credit is allowed for qualified adoption expenses of up to $12,170 ($12,150 in 2009) and generally is allowable in the year the adoption is finalized.[28] If adoption expenses are paid *prior* to the year the adoption is finalized, such expenses are not eligible for the credit until the year the adoption is finalized. If the adoption expenses are paid during or after the year the adoption is finalized, the credit is allowable in the year the expenses are paid or incurred. For taxpayers with AGI above $182,520 ($182,180 in 2009), the credit is ratably phased out over a range of $40,000.[29] In the case of the adoption of a child with special needs, $12,170 is allowed as an adoption credit regardless of whether the taxpayer has qualified adoption expenses.

Qualified adoption expenses include reasonable and necessary adoption fees, court costs, attorney fees, and other expenses that are directly related to the legal adoption of an eligible child. Qualified adoption expenses are reduced by any reimbursements from an

---

[25] Sec. 21(c).
[26] Sec. 22(c)(2). The initial amount is $5,000 if one spouse filing a joint return is less than age 65 and is $3,750 for a married individual filing a separate return. Unless married individuals live apart for the entire year, they must file a joint return to obtain the credit.
[27] The AGI ceiling is $5,000 for married individuals filing a separate return.

[28] The credit as well as the AGI phaseout amounts are adjusted for inflation each year.
[29] For purposes of the phase-out, AGI must be modified. AGI is determined without regard to the exclusions from gross income for foreign earned income and after the application of the rules relating to the taxation of Social Security, as well as selected other items. (See Sec. 23.)

employer plan. An eligible child is defined as a child who has not reached 18 years old when the adoption takes place or is physically or mentally incapable of self-care.

EXAMPLE I:14-19 ▶ Oscar and Betty began proceedings in June 2009 to adopt an infant child. They incurred $5,000 of attorney fees and adoption agency fees in 2009. In 2010, they incurred an additional $8,000 of qualified adoption expenses when the adoption became final. Oscar and Betty's AGI in 2010 is $190,000. The adoption credit is allowable in 2010 in the amount of $9,775, computed as follows:

Total qualified adoption expenses in 2009 and 2010	$13,000
Maximum credit	12,170
Phase-out percentage ($7,480*/$40,000)	18.7%
Amount of credit disallowed ($12,170 × 0.187)	2,276
Amount of credit allowed ($12,170 − $2,276)	9,894

Oscar and Betty can use only $9,894 of expenses (maximum) and must claim the credit in 2010, the year the adoption becomes final. Finally, the adoption credit is limited based on their AGI.

*(AGI $190,000 − $182,520) ◀

AMERICAN OPPORTUNITY TAX CREDIT

Two credits are available to assist taxpayers who incur higher education expenses for themselves, their spouses, and dependents. The two credits are the "American Opportunity Tax Credit (AOTC)" and the "Lifetime Learning credit."[30]

Under the AOTC, taxpayers are allowed a credit for qualified tuition and related expenses paid during the taxable year for each qualified student (up to $2,500 in 2010). Qualified tuition and related expenses include tuition and fees required for enrollment and course materials including textbooks. They do not include room and board, student activity fees, and other expenses unrelated to an individual's academic course of instruction. Below are a number of requirements and limitations for the AOTC:

▶ The $2,500 credit is allowed for a maximum of four years per student and is computed as 100% of the first $2,000 of qualified expenses *plus* 25% of the second $2,000 of qualified expenses ($2,000 + $500 = $2,500).

▶ Qualified tuition and related expenses eligible for the AOTC are limited to the first four years of postsecondary education. The first four years of postsecondary education are measured at the *beginning* of the taxable year. If a student has not completed the first four years of postsecondary education by the beginning of the taxable year, qualified tuition and related fees are eligible for the AOTC. The first four years are determined based on whether the educational institution awards the student four years of academic credit at that institution.

▶ If a taxpayer pays qualified education expenses in one year but the expenses relate to an academic period that begins during January, February, or March of the next taxable year, the academic period is treated as beginning during the taxable year in which the payment is made. Thus, a payment of tuition in December 2010 for the Spring Semester, 2011 (which begins in January 2011) would be eligible for the AOTC in 2010.

▶ An eligible student must carry at least one-half of the normal full-time load for the course of study the student is pursuing.

▶ The AOTC is not available to any student who has been convicted of a federal or state felony offense for possession or distribution of a controlled substance as of the end of the taxable year for which the credit is claimed.

▶ Qualified tuition and related expenses eligible for the AOTC must be reduced by amounts received under other sections of the tax law, such as scholarships (Sec. 117), employer-sponsored educational reimbursement plans (Sec. 127), Education IRAs (Sec. 530), or other provisions of the tax law.

ADDITIONAL COMMENT

The American Recovery and Reinvestment Act of 2009 expanded the Hope Scholarship Credit for tax years beginning in 2009 and 2010 and renamed it the American Opportunity Tax Credit (AOTC.) The AOTC interacts with the Lifetime Learning Credit in a manner similar to the old Hope Scholarship Credit.

ADDITIONAL COMMENT

In addition to the AOTC and Lifetime Learning credits, there have been a plethora of new tax laws that encourage education, including:
(1) a *for* AGI deduction of up to $4,000 annually through 2009;
(2) Sec. 529 plans;
(3) Improved student loan interest deduction rules;
(4) Increased limits for Coverdell Education IRAs.

---

[30] Sec. 25A. Both credits are contained in Sec. 25A. The AOTC is specifically described in Sec. 25A(b) while the lifetime learning credit is described in Sec. 25A(c). The various definitions contained in Sec. 25A apply to both credits.

▶ The allowable credit (AOTC) is reduced for taxpayers who have modified AGI above certain amounts. The phase-out for taxpayers filing joint returns occurs over a $20,000 range and begins when modified AGI is $160,000 in 2010 as follows:

$$\text{Tentative AOTC} \times \frac{\text{Modified AGI} - \$160,000}{\$20,000} = \text{Phaseout for MFJ taxpayers}$$

For taxpayers other than joint filers, the $160,000 is replaced with $80,000 and the $20,000 is replaced with $10,000.

It is important to understand that the AOTC applies to each student. Thus, parents who have two children in their first four years of college may claim up to $2,500 for each child. For tax years beginning in 2009 and 2010, up to 40% of the allowable AOTC is refundable.

LIFETIME LEARNING CREDIT

ADDITIONAL COMMENT

The education expenses for the AOTC and lifetime learning credits must be incurred at an educational institution that is eligible to participate in Department of Education student aid programs.

The Lifetime Learning (LL) credit is computed differently than the AOTC and is less restrictive; however, most of the definitions regarding eligible students and qualified expenses are identical. The LL credit is 20% of a maximum $10,000 per year of qualified tuition and fees paid by the taxpayer for one or more eligible students. However, unlike the AOTC, the $10,000 LL limitation is imposed at the taxpayer level, not on a per student basis. Below are some important requirements for the Lifetime Learning credit:

▶ The definition of qualified tuition and related expenses is the same as for the AOTC.

▶ The LL credit is available for an *unlimited* number of years and may be used for undergraduate, graduate, and professional degree expenses. Thus, the LL credit is available to eligible students when the AOTC is not.

▶ The LL credit and AOTC may not be taken in the same tax year with respect to the same student's tuition and related expenses, i.e., no doubling-up is permitted. For example, if Son A's tuition for the academic year is $10,000 and is used to claim the $2,500 AOTC, none of the $10,000 may be used for the LL credit with respect to Son A. However, if Daughter B also has tuition expenses in the same tax year, either the LL credit or the AOTC is allowed for Daughter B.

▶ The LL credit may be claimed for any course (degree or nondegree)at a college or university that helps an individual acquire or improve job skills, such as credit or noncredit courses that qualify as continuing professional education (CPE). Also, the requirement that a student take at least one-half of a full load does not apply to the lifetime learning credit.

▶ The LL credit phases out over a $20,000 range for taxpayers filing joint returns with modified AGI beginning at $100,000. The phaseout for all other taxpayers is a $10,000 range with modified AGI beginning at 50,000.

EXAMPLE I:14-20 ▶ Mark and Jane Green are married, file a joint return, and have three dependent children in college, Ron, Susan, and Bill. Ron and Susan attend State University and Bill attends Private University. The Green's modified AGI in 2010 is $164,000. The children's classifications and expenses are as follows:

	Spring Semester 2010 (Paid in January 2010)	Fall Semester 2010 (Paid in August 2010)
Ron:	Senior	5th year Senior
Tuition and fees	$1,500	$1,550
Course materials (books)	300	300
Room and board	3,500	3,700
Susan:	Junior	Senior
Tuition and fees	$1,500	$1,550
Course materials (books)	300	300
Room and board	3,500	3,700
Bill:		Freshman
Tuition and fees	—	$3,700
Course materials (books)	—	300
Room and board	—	3,700

The Greens claimed for Ron and Susan the HOPE credit in 2008 and the AOTC and LL in 2009. In 2010, they are allowed to claim the American Opportunity tax credit (AOTC) and the Lifetime Learning credit (LL) as follows:

AOTC: Ron qualifies for the AOTC only in Spring 2010 because the credit is limited to the first four years of post-secondary education. His tentative credit is $1,800 ($1,800 × 100%.) Susan qualifies for the AOTC in both semesters. Her tentative credit is $2,413 (the first $2,000 × 100%, plus $1,650 × 25%.) Bill qualifies for the AOTC only in Fall 2010 because he began post-secondary education in that semester. His tentative credit is $2,500 (the first $2,000 × 100%, plus the next $2,000 × 25%.) The Green's total tentative AOTC is $6,713. The phaseout is $1,343 [$6,713 × ($164,000 − $160,000) / $20,000.] Thus, the Green's total allowable AOTC is $5,370 ($6,713 − $1,343.)

Lifetime Learning credit: Ron qualifies for the LL credit in Fall 2010 because the LL credit is not limited to four years of post-secondary education. His qualified education expenses total $1,850, so the Green's tentative LL credit is $370 ($1,850 × 20%.) The phaseout is $370 ($370 × ($164,000 − $100,000) / $20,000.] Thus, the Green's total allowable LL credit is zero. ◄

RESIDENTIAL ENERGY CREDITS

Congress has enacted a wide range of incentives for both individuals and businesses to promote domestic energy production and conservation. Most of these incentives are in the form of tax credits. Two major credits for individual taxpayers are (1) the nonbusiness energy property credit, and (2) the residential energy efficient property credit.

NONBUSINESS ENERGY PROPERTY CREDIT. Individuals are allowed a nonrefundable tax credit for nonbusiness energy property, such as residential windows and exterior doors, insulation, heat pumps, furnaces, central air conditioners, and water heaters. The credit is limited to $1,500 per taxpayer. It applies to property placed into service after December 31, 2008, and before January 1, 2011.[31]

The credit is the sum of (1) 30% of the cost of *qualified energy efficiency improvements* plus (2) 30% of the cost of the *residential energy property expenditures* installed during the year at the taxpayer's principal residence. Qualified energy efficiency improvements include insulation materials, exterior windows (including skylights), exterior doors, and metal or asphalt roofs with special coatings. These improvements must meet specific energy efficiency requirements, original use must begin with the taxpayer, and the improvement must be reasonably expected to remain in use for at least five years. Residential energy property includes electric heat pumps, central air conditioners, water heaters, and advanced main air circulating fans. This property must also meet minimum energy standards to qualify. These energy standards are stringent, which means only expensive equipment generally will qualify.

Below are other selected features of the credit:

▶ The taxpayer's basis in the property is reduced by the amount of the credit.

▶ If a dwelling unit is owned and occupied by more than one owner, the $1,500 maximum credit must be allocated among the owners.

▶ The cost of labor for installation of residential energy property expenditures is specifically eligible for the credit. However, the new law is silent with respect to labor for qualified energy efficiency improvements. While it seems reasonable to assume that labor costs would qualify, the fact that the law is specific as to energy property and silent as to energy improvements would lead one to assume that labor is not includible for energy improvements. Additional guidance in this area should be forthcoming.

▶ Rental property and vacation homes do not qualify for the credit, as they are not the principal residence of the owner.

▶ If less than 80% of the use of the dwelling is nonbusiness, then only the percentage of nonbusiness use can be taken into account.

---

[31] Sec. 25C, as amended by the American Recovery and Reinvestment Act of 2009.

EXAMPLE I:14-21 ▶ Tom and Sandra Mireaut are married, file a joint return, and own and live in a home that is their principal residence. In 2010, they install new energy efficient windows in their home at a cost of $3,500 and purchase and install a new replacement energy efficient heat pump at a cost of $2,500. Their nonbusiness energy property credit for 2010 is $1,500 ($6,000 × 0.30 = $1,800 tentative credit, limited to $1,500). ◀

RESIDENTIAL ENERGY EFFICIENT PROPERTY (REEP) CREDIT. For tax years beginning after December 31, 2005 and before January 1, 2017, a tax credit is allowed for several types of energy efficient property installed on a taxpayer's principal residence:[32]

- ▶ Solar hot water heaters
- ▶ Qualified solar electric property
- ▶ Fuel cell property
- ▶ Residential wind property
- ▶ Geothermal heat pumps

The credit is 30% of the cost of eligible property. Other features of the REEP credit are:

- ▶ Labor costs to install the property are included in the qualified cost of the property.
- ▶ Second homes or vacation homes do not qualify for some parts of the credit.
- ▶ If less than 80% of the use of the dwelling is for nonbusiness use, then only the percentage of nonbusiness use can be taken into account.
- ▶ The taxpayer's basis in the property is reduced by the amount of the credit.
- ▶ The credit is not available for use with swimming pools or hot tubs.
- ▶ Credits earned but not used in the current year can be carried forward to the next year.

ALTERNATIVE MOTOR VEHICLE CREDIT

NEW TAX ACT

The American Recovery and Reinvestment Act of 2009 significantly expanded tax credits for alternative motor vehicles.

Congress has enacted several nonrefundable personal credits to encourage taxpayers to invest in alternative vehicles. The comprehensive alternative motor vehicle credit (AMVC) contains the:

- ▶ Qualified fuel cell credit
- ▶ Advanced lean-burn technology credit
- ▶ Qualified hybrid credit
- ▶ Qualified alternative fuel refueling property credit
- ▶ Plug-in conversion credit
- ▶ Plug-in electric vehicle credit

Details on these credits are beyond the scope of this text.

QUALIFIED RETIREMENT SAVINGS CONTRIBUTIONS CREDIT ("SAVER'S CREDIT")

To encourage low and middle income taxpayers to save for retirement, a *permanent*, nonrefundable credit for contributions or deferrals to qualified retirement plans has been established for tax years beginning after December 31, 2001.[33] The saver's credit is allowed *in addition* to otherwise allowable exclusions or deductions from gross income for retirement plan contributions or deferrals.

To be eligible for the saver's credit, a taxpayer must be at least 18 years of age as of the close of the tax year, must not be claimed as a dependent on someone else's tax return, and must not be a full-time student as defined in Sec. 152(f)(2) for purposes of the dependency exemption (full-time student for at least 5 calendar months).

The saver's credit is computed by multiplying the amount contributed (maximum $2,000 per eligible individual per year) by an applicable percentage. The percentage for 2010 depends on the taxpayer's adjusted gross income, as shown in the following table:

---

[32] Sec. 25D, as amended by the American Recovery and Reinvestment Act of 2009.

[33] Sec. 25B. The Pension Protection Act of 2006 made the credit permanent.

Applicable Percentage	MFJ		Head of Household		All Other Statuses	
	AGI Over	Not Over	AGI Over	Not Over	AGI Over	Not Over
50%	$ 0	$33,500	$ 0	$25,125	$ 0	$16,750
20%	33,500	36,000	25,125	27,000	16,750	18,000
10%	36,000	55,500	27,000	41,625	18,000	27,750
0%	55,500		41,625		27,750	

Annual qualified retirement savings contribution equals the sum of contributions or deferrals by the taxpayer to specified retirement plans, including IRAs (Roth and Traditional), 401(k) plans, 403(b) plans, and certain other plans, reduced by any distributions from such plans. The maximum contribution eligible for the credit for each individual is $2,000 per year.

EXAMPLE I:14-22 ▶ Steve is unmarried filing single and has AGI of $17,000 in 2010. During the year, he contributes $2,000 to his Roth IRA. Steve is eligible for a Qualified Retirement Savings Contributions Credit in the amount of $400 ($2,000 × 20%). The credit would be the same if he contributed $2,000 to a traditional IRA. In addition to the $400 credit, Steve also would be permitted to deduct the $2,000 contribution to the traditional IRA on his individual return. ◀

LIMITATION ON NONREFUNDABLE PERSONAL CREDITS

As mentioned on pg. I:14-10, nonrefundable personal credits may not exceed the sum of (1) the regular tax liability minus foreign tax credit, and (2) the excess of tentative minimum tax over regular tax.[34] Thus, individual taxpayers may offset both their regular tax liability and AMT liability with nonrefundable personal credits.

MISCELLANEOUS CREDITS

With the exception of the foreign tax credit, miscellaneous credits are highly-specialized, such as the nonconventional source fuel credit. For this reason, only the foreign tax credit is discussed in this text.

FOREIGN TAX CREDIT

U.S. citizens, resident aliens, and U.S. corporations are subject to U.S. taxation on their worldwide income.[35] The foreign-source portion of worldwide income is also subject to taxation by the foreign country. To reduce possible double taxation, Federal tax law provides a foreign tax credit (FTC) for income taxes paid or accrued to a foreign country or a U.S. possession.[36]

In lieu of the FTC, taxpayers may elect to take a deduction for foreign taxes paid or accrued.[37] In general, the FTC results in a greater tax benefit because (as previously discussed) a credit is fully offset against the tax liability, while a deduction merely reduces taxable income.

Computation of Allowable Credit. The **foreign tax credit** equals the lesser of (1) foreign tax paid or accrued, or (2) the portion of U.S. income tax liability attributable to income earned in all foreign countries (FTC limitation).[38] This limitation restricts claiming foreign tax credit if the effective foreign tax rate on foreign earnings exceeds the effective U.S. tax rate on these earnings. It also may result in double taxation if the unused credit cannot be used as a carryback or carryover (see discussion under the next heading). The FTC limitation is computed using the following formula:

---

[34] Sec. 26. Allowing taxpayers to reduce AMT with nonrefundable personal credits was extended to tax years beginning in 2009 and 2010 by the American Recovery and Reinvestment Tax Act of 2009.

[35] Certain exceptions are provided by treaty agreements between the United States and foreign countries whereby certain types of foreign-source income may be exempt from taxation or taxed at a reduced tax rate in the foreign country.

[36] Under Sec. 911, in 2010, U.S. citizens and resident aliens may elect to exclude from gross income up to $91,500 of foreign-earned income and certain housing cost amounts. Foreign taxes attributable to excluded income cannot be taken as a credit. (See Chapter I:4 for a discussion of these exclusions.)

[37] Sec. 164(a)(3).

[38] Sec. 904.

$$\frac{\text{Foreign source taxable income}}{\text{Worldwide taxable income}} \times \frac{\text{U.S. income tax}}{\text{before credits}} = \text{FTC limitation}$$

EXAMPLE I:14-23 ▶ Edison Corporation has $200,000 of U.S. source taxable income and $100,000 of foreign source taxable income from country A. Total worldwide taxable income is $300,000 ($200,000 + $100,000). Country A levies $40,000 in foreign income taxes on the foreign source taxable income (i.e., a 40% effective tax rate). The U.S. tax before credits is $100,250 on the $300,000 of worldwide taxable income. Using the formula given above, the overall FTC limitation is computed as follows:[39]

$$\frac{\$100,000}{\$300,000} \times \$100,250 = \$33,417$$

Because the foreign tax payments ($40,000) exceed the U.S. tax attributable to the foreign source income ($33,417), the limitation applies. Thus, $6,583 ($40,000 − $33,417) of FTC cannot be used in the current year. ◀

STOP & THINK *Question:* Since a credit is generally more valuable than a deduction, under what circumstances would it be beneficial for a taxpayer to take a deduction for foreign taxes in lieu of the foreign tax credit?

Solution: If a taxpayer has foreign source taxable income from one country and an equal loss from another foreign country, the foreign tax credit limitation is zero because the net foreign-source taxable income is zero. Because none of the taxes paid in the foreign country in which taxable income was produced can be claimed as a credit, the taxpayer may choose to deduct them (unless the unused credits can be carried back or forward.)

Treatment of Unused Credits. Unused foreign tax credits are carried back one year and then forward for ten years to tax years where the limitation is not exceeded (i.e., the foreign tax payment is lower than the U.S. taxes attributable to the foreign-source income in the carryback or carryover years). Unused credits are lost if they are not used by the end of the ten-year carryover period.

GENERAL BUSINESS CREDITS

The tax credits commonly available to businesses are grouped into a special category called **general business credits**. These credits are combined for the purpose of computing an overall dollar limitation based on the taxpayer's tax liability, discussed in more detail on page I:14-24. If the general business credits earned in the current year exceed the limitation, the excess may be carried back one year and carried forward 20 years.[40]

Earned credits are used as follows:

▶ Carryforwards from prior years (used in FIFO order)

▶ Current year's earned credit

▶ Carrybacks

EXAMPLE I:14-24 ▶ Eastern Corporation had unused general business tax credits of $10,000 in 2009 that are carried forward to 2010. Eastern earns $5,000 of additional credits in 2010 and computes an overall credit limitation of $12,000 for the year. The allowable $12,000 credit consists of the $10,000 carryover from 2009 and $2,000 from 2010. The $3,000 of unused 2010 credit ($5,000 − $2,000) is carried forward to 2011. ◀

The more important general business credits are discussed below. They are all nonrefundable.

---

[39] Two types of income have a separate foreign tax credit limitation: passive income and all other income. (See Chapter C:16 of *Prentice Hall's Federal Taxation: Corporations, Partnerships, Estates, and Trusts* for a more detailed discussion of these separate limitations.)

[40] For tax years prior to 1998, the carryback period was three years and the carryforward period was 15 years.

TAX CREDIT FOR REHABILITATION EXPENDITURES

Congress provides incentives for the rehabilitation of older industrial and commercial buildings and certified historic structures.[41] A credit for rehabilitation expenditures is available subject to the following special rules and qualification requirements:

► The credit is 10% for structures that were originally placed in service before 1936 and 20% for certified historic structures. In the aftermath of Hurricane Katrina, expenditures paid or incurred after August 28, 2005 and before January 1, 2010 on qualified structures in the Gulf Opportunity (GO) Zone are eligible for a credit of 13% for any qualified building other than a certified historic structure, and 26% for any certified historic structure.[42]

► The credit applies only to depreciable trade or business property and depreciable property held for investment. Residential rental property does not qualify unless the building is a certified historic structure.

► Rehabilitation includes renovation, restoration, or construction of a building, but not an enlargement or new construction. For buildings other than certified historic structures, a rehabilitation project must meet certain structural tests.[43]

► For certified historic structures, the total rehabilitation must be certified by the Department of the Interior as being consistent with the historic character of the building.

► Straight-line depreciation generally must be used with the applicable Sec. 168 recovery periods with respect to rehabilitation expenditures. The regular MACRS depreciation rules apply to the portion of the property's basis that is not eligible for the credit.

► The basis of the property for depreciation is reduced by the full amount of the credit taken.[44]

► Rehabilitation expenditures must exceed the greater of the property's adjusted basis or $5,000.

► The rehabilitation credit is recaptured at a rate of 20% per year if there is an early disposition of the property.

EXAMPLE I:14-25 ►

During the current year, Ted incurs $40,000 of rehabilitation expenditures in connection with a certified historic structure used in his business. The adjusted basis of the certified historic structure was $38,000 at the time the rehabilitation began. The property qualifies for the rehabilitation credit because:

► It is used in Ted's trade or business and is depreciable.

► The property is a certified historic structure.

► The amount of the expenditure exceeds the greater of the property's $38,000 adjusted basis or the $5,000 statutory minimum.

Thus, the credit is $8,000 (0.20 × $40,000). The basis of the rehabilitation expenditures for depreciation purposes is reduced by the full amount of the credit to $32,000 ($40,000 − $8,000). If the property is disposed of after one year, $1,600 of the credit (0.20 × $8,000) is earned and $6,400 ($8,000 − $1,600) is recaptured. ◄

BUSINESS ENERGY TAX CREDITS

To encourage energy conservation measures, credits are available to businesses that invest in energy-conserving properties (e.g., solar and geothermal property).[45] The credit for geothermal energy property is 10% of the property's basis. The credit for solar energy property and qualified fuel cell property purchased in tax years ending after December 31, 2005 and before January 1, 2016 is 30% of the property's basis. Construction, reconstruction, or erection of the property must be completed by the taxpayer, and its original use must begin with the taxpayer. This credit is part of, and is subject to, the limitations of the general business credit.

---

[41] Secs. 47(a)(1) and (2). A certified historic structure must be certified by the Department of the Interior and must be located in a registered historic district or listed in the *National Register*.
[42] Sec. 47 and Sec. 1400N.

[43] Sec. 47(c)(1)(A).
[44] Sec. 50(c)(1).
[45] Sec. 48(a)(2).

Recent tax law changes have set up a complex interaction among the energy credit, renewable energy grants, and an electricity production credit. Details are beyond the scope of this text, but essentially, taxpayers must choose to receive grants or take credits, but not both.

WORK OPPORTUNITY TAX CREDIT

ADDITIONAL COMMENT

The employer must receive or request the certification in writing no later than the employee's first day of work.

Employers who hire members of one or more targeted groups may elect the Work Opportunity Tax Credit (WOTC).[46] This credit is intended to reduce unemployment for individuals who are considered economically disadvantaged. To qualify for the credit the employer must obtain a certification from a local jobs service office of a state employment security agency stating that the unemployed individual is a qualified member of a targeted group. Rehired employees do not qualify their employers for the credit.

The credit is computed based on qualified first-year wages paid or incurred for employees in groups 1-10, and on qualified first-year and second-year wages paid or incurred for employees in group 11. The targeted groups are:[47]

ADDITIONAL COMMENT

The American Recovery and Reinvestment Act of 2009 added two new groups to the Work Opportunity Credit, qualified unemployed veterans and qualified disconnected youth.

(1) Qualified TANF (temporary assistance to needy families) recipients
(2) Qualified veterans (eligible for food stamps and service-connected disability compensation)
(3) Qualified unemployed veterans and
(4) Qualified ex-felons
(5) Designated community residents (empowerment zone and enterprise communities)
(6) Qualified disconnected youth
(7) Vocational rehabilitation referrals
(8) Qualified summer youth employee
(9) Qualified food stamp recipient
(10) Qualified SSI (supplemental security income) recipients
(11) Qualified LTFA (long-term family assistance) recipients

LEGISLATIVE UPDATE

The Hiring Incentives to Restore Employment (HIRE) Act of 2010 created a limited payroll tax holiday. Qualified employers would be exempt from the employer portion of OASDI on wages paid from March 18, 2010 through December 31, 2010 to qualified employees (new hires from the ranks of the unemployed). Employers who take advantage of the payroll tax holiday would not be eligible for the Work Opportunity Credit with respect to those employees.

Qualified wages: For members of the first ten targeted groups, qualified first-year wages are a maximum of $6,000 ($3,000 for qualified summer youth employees) per employee. No credit is allowed for second-year wages. For members of the eleventh targeted group, qualified wages are $10,000 per employee in both the first and second years of employment.

A disadvantage associated with electing the WOTC is that the employer's deduction for wages is reduced by the amount of the credit. This provision applies to hires from all eleven groups.

CALCULATION OF THE CREDIT   First-year wages: If an employer hires a member of the first nine targeted groups, the credit equals 40% of qualified first-year wages (25% if employment is at least 120 hours but less than 400 hours). Thus, the maximum credit per employee is $2,400 (the first $6,000 of qualified first-year wages × 0.40). If an employer hires a qualified summer youth employee, the maximum credit is $1,200 (the first $3,000 of qualified first-year wages × 0.40). If an employer hires a member of the tenth targeted group, the maximum credit is $4,000 (the first $10,000 of qualified wages × 0.40). No credit is allowed for qualified wages paid to employees who work less than 120 hours in the first year of employment.

Second year wages: If an employer hires a member of the tenth targeted group, the maximum credit in the second year of employment is $5,000 (the first $10,000 of qualified wages × 0.50), for a maximum total credit of $9,000.

EXAMPLE I:14-26 ▶ Jet Corporation hires two individuals in the current year, one a qualified ex-felon and the other a qualified food stamp recipient. Both individuals are properly certified by the state agency. One of the individuals is paid $8,000 of wages during the year, and the second individual is paid $4,000. The amount of wages eligible for the work opportunity credit is $10,000 ($6,000 ceiling limit for the first employee plus $4,000 actual wages paid to the second employee). The credit

[46] The Tax Relief and Health Care Act of 2006 combined two credits, the former WOTC and the Welfare-to-Work credit, into the new WOTC, which is effective for qualified individuals hired after December 31, 2006 and before January 1, 2008. The Small Business and Work Opportunity Tax Act of 2007 extended the expiration date to August 31, 2011.
[47] Sec. 51.

is $4,000 (40% × $10,000). Jet must reduce its $12,000 deduction for wages paid to the two individuals by the $4,000 amount of the credit in the current year. ◀

This credit is part of, and is subject to, the limitations of the general business credit.

EMPLOYER-PROVIDED CHILD CARE CREDIT

Adequate and affordable child care for working parents is a major problem in the United States. To create an incentive for small and medium-sized businesses to provide child care for their employees, the employer-provided child care credit was enacted effective for taxable years beginning after December 31, 2001.[48] The credit is the *sum* of the following two amounts:

▶ 25% of qualified child care expenses. These expenses are amounts paid to acquire, construct, rehabilitate, expand, and operate a qualified child care facility; plus

▶ 10% of qualified child care resources and referral expenditures. These are expenses paid or incurred by a taxpayer under a contract to provide child care resource and referral services to employees.

These are several special rules with regard to the credit, including:

▶ The total credit amount allowed for any given year cannot exceed $150,000.

▶ Employers claiming this credit are not permitted a double benefit, that is, they cannot claim a deduction for child care expenses and also claim the credit. Expenses that would be otherwise deductible must be reduced by the amount of the credit claimed.

▶ If an employer ceases child care operations or otherwise terminates the child care services, all or part of the credits claimed must be recaptured as an increase in tax. The recapture amount depends on how long the child care services have been provided. For example, if the recapture event occurs within the first three years, 100% of the credits are recaptured. No recapture results if the child care services are provided for more than ten years.

This credit is part of, and is subject to, the limitations of the general business credit.

EXAMPLE I:14-27 ▶

Gamechicken, Inc., began a child care facility for its employees during the year. The corporation incurred the following expenses:

Rent on facility	$ 25,000
Leasehold improvements	60,000
Equipment, toys, etc.	18,000
Salaries of child care employees	30,000
Other operating expenses of facility	12,000
Qualified child care referral fees*	8,000
Total expenses	$153,000

*Fees paid to a firm to place children in other facilities.

Gamechicken's credit for the year would be $37,050 [($145,000 × 25%) + ($8,000 × 10%)]. All of the above amounts are also deductible, but would need to be reduced by the amount of the credit. So, the rent, salaries, and operating expenses of $67,000 ($25,000 + $30,000 + $12,000) must be reduced by a total of $16,750 ($67,000 × 25%), the referral fees must be reduced by $800 ($8,000 × 10%), and the basis of the leasehold improvements and equipment must be reduced by $19,500 ($78,000 × 25%). ◀

DISABLED ACCESS CREDIT

A nonrefundable tax credit is available to eligible small businesses for expenditures incurred to make existing business facilities accessible to disabled individuals. Eligible expenditures include payments for removing architectural, communication, physical, or transportation barriers that prevent a business from being accessible. Expenditures made in connection with *new* construction are not eligible for the credit.

[48] Sec. 45F.

The disabled access credit is equal to 50% of eligible expenditures that exceed $250 but do not exceed $10,250.[49] Thus, the annual credit limitation is $5,000 [0.50($10,250 − $250)]. The basis of the property is reduced by the allowable credit. An eligible small business is any business that either (1) had gross receipts of $1 million or less in the preceding year or, (2) in the case of a business failing the first test, had no more than 30 full-time employees in the preceding year and makes a timely election to claim the credit.

EXAMPLE I:14-28 ▶

Crane Corporation had 14 employees during the preceding tax year and $2 million of gross receipts. During the current year, Crane installed concrete access ramps at a total cost of $14,000. Crane is an eligible small business because the company had 30 or fewer full-time employees during the preceding year even though its gross receipts exceed the threshold amount (i.e., $1 million). Only $10,000 of eligible expenditures qualify for the credit, thereby limiting the credit to $5,000 ($10,000 × 0.50). The depreciable basis of the property is reduced by the credit amount to $9,000 ($14,000 − $5,000). ◀

This credit is part of, and is subject to, the limitations of the general business credit.

LEGISLATIVE UPDATE

At the time this textbook went to press, Congress was considering extending the tax credit for qualified rehabilitation expenditures through December 31, 2010.

CREDIT FOR RESEARCH ACTIVITIES

To encourage businesses to conduct research and experimentation, a credit is allowed under Sec. 41. The research credit is equal to the sum of:

(1) Regular Research Credit: 20% of the excess of qualified research expenses over a base amount for taxable years after December 31, 2005 and before January 1, 2010.

(2) University Basic Research Credit: 20% of basic research payments made to qualified organizations, such as universities and scientific research organizations, over a qualified organization base period amount. Discussion of this credit is beyond the scope of this book.

(3) Energy Research Consortium Credit: 20% of all qualified energy research expenses. Discussion of this credit is beyond the scope of this book.

REGULAR RESEARCH CREDIT. Qualified research expenses are defined in the Treasury Regulations[50] and essentially are internal and external research expenses that are incident to the development or improvement of a product or component. Only incremental expenditures (the excess over a base amount) are eligible for the credit. Research conducted after the start of commercial production does not qualify for the credit, nor do marketing, advertising, or production expenses.

The base amount is computed by multiplying (1) the taxpayer's fixed-base percentage (see below) times (2) the average annual gross receipts for the four tax years preceding the credit year. The base amount may not be less than 50% of the qualified research expenses for the year of the credit. The fixed-base percentage for start-up companies generally begins and remains at 3% for five years and then is adjusted annually through a complicated formula that is beyond the scope of this textbook.

EXAMPLE I:14-29 ▶

Northern Inc. began operations in 2006 and had the following gross receipts for the period 2006–2009:

2006	$4,500,000
2007	7,000,000
2008	8,000,000
2009	8,500,000

Northern's average annual gross receipts for the four-year period is $7,000,000. Assuming Northern Inc. uses a fixed-base percentage of 3%, the corporation's base amount for 2010 would be $210,000 ($7,000,000 × 3%) if Congress extends the credit into 2010. ◀

---

[49] Sec. 44.

[50] Reg. Sec. 1.41-2.

EXAMPLE I:14-30 ▶ Using the information in the previous example, if Northern Inc. incurred qualified research expenses of $500,000 in 2010 and if Congress extends the credit into 2010, the corporation's regular research credit would be $58,000 [($500,000 − $210,000) × 20%]. ◀

ALTERNATIVE SIMPLIFIED RESEARCH CREDIT. Taxpayers may elect a new simplified credit in lieu of the Regular or Incremental Research Credit, effective for tax years ending after December 31, 2006. This new credit is not based on historical gross receipts, thus opening the research credit to new businesses. The base and credit percentage is computed as follows:

▶ For tax years ending before January 1, 2009, 12% of the excess of qualified research expenses of the current year over 50 percent of the average qualified research expenses for the three preceding taxable years (14% for tax years ending after December 31, 2008); or

▶ 6% of qualified research expenses of the current year if the taxpayer has no qualified research expenses in any one of the three preceding taxable years.

EXAMPLE I:14-31 ▶ Howell Company is a calendar year taxpayer. In 2010, it incurs $175,000 of qualified research expenses. In the three preceding tax years, Howell's qualified research expenses averaged $40,000 per year. Howell can elect a simplified research credit of $18,600 [($175,000 − $20,000) × 0.12)]. If Howell had no qualified research expenses in the three preceding years, its credit would be $10,500 ($175,000 × .06). ◀

An election to use the alternative simplified credit applies to all succeeding taxable years unless revoked with IRS consent. It cannot be used in any taxable year for which an election to use the alternative incremental credit is in effect.

INTERACTION WITH THE RESEARCH DEDUCTION. A business deduction is allowed for research and experimentation expenditures under Sec. 174. This deduction must be reduced by the amount of the research credit.[51]

The research credit is part of, and is subject to the limitations of, the general business credit.

LEGISLATIVE UPDATE

The Hiring Incentives to Restore Employment (HIRE) Act of 2010 created a Retained Worker Credit for employers that retain newly hired individuals for a period of not less than 52 consecutive weeks in any tax year ending after March 18, 2010. It is part of the general business credit. The credit with respect to each qualified worker is the lesser of $1,000 or 6.2% of wages during that period.

GENERAL BUSINESS CREDIT OVERALL LIMITATION

As mentioned on page I:14-19, there is an overall dollar limitation of the general business credit based on tax liability. The general business credit may not exceed *net income tax* minus the greater of (1) the tentative minimum tax (even if no AMT is owed) or 25% of the *net regular tax liability* above $25,000.[52] *Net income tax* means the sum of the regular tax liability and the AMT, reduced by the nonrefundable personal credits and the foreign tax credit. *Net regular tax liability* means the regular tax liability reduced by nonrefundable personal credits and the foreign tax credit. The limitation also prevents a taxpayer from claiming a general business credit in the same tax year that the taxpayer has alternative minimum tax. An exception exists with respect to the empowerment zone employment credit but a discussion of this exception is outside the scope of this textbook. The overall credit limitation is demonstrated in the example below.

EXAMPLE I:14-32 ▶ Steve's general business tax credit before limitation is $50,000 (a $40,000 research credit and a $10,000 work opportunity credit). Steve's regular tax liability (before credits) is $45,000, and his tentative minimum tax is $10,000 (thus, Steve is not subject to the AMT). His nonrefundable tax credits also include a $1,200 child and dependent care credit and an $1,800 foreign tax credit. Steve's general business tax credit is initially limited to net income tax of $42,000 ($45,000 − $1,200 − $1,800). This amount is reduced by the $10,000 tentative minimum tax because it is

---

[51] Sec. 280(c)(2)
[52] The limitation discussed above actually must be separated into two parts: (1) all general business credits other than the empowerment zone and New York Liberty Zone employment credits and (2) the empowerment zone and

New York Liberty Zone employment credits. Only the first part is covered here. The second part allows these credits to reduce, in whole or part, the AMT. (See Sec. 38(c) for details.)

greater than the net regular tax ceiling of $4,250 [0.25 × ($42,000 − $25,000)]. Thus, the limitation on the $50,000 of general business tax credit is $32,000 ($42,000 − $10,000), and Steve's credit is $32,000. ◄

REFUNDABLE CREDITS

As mentioned earlier, refundable credits not only offset a taxpayer's income tax liability but can create a refund. If the refundable credits exceed the tax liability, such excess will be refunded to the taxpayer.

EARNED INCOME CREDIT

The earned income credit (EIC) is refundable and, as such, it is a special type of "negative income tax" or welfare benefit for certain low-income families. It is designed to encourage low-income individuals to become gainfully employed.[53] The credit is based on earned income, which includes wages, salaries, tips, and other employee compensation plus net earnings from self-employment. Earned income does not include any form of employee compensation that is not includible in the taxpayer's income for the year.

DISQUALIFIED INCOME. The EIC is denied to taxpayers whose "disqualified income" exceeds $3,100 in both 2010 and 2009. Disqualified income includes taxable interest and dividends, tax-exempt interest, net income from nonbusiness rents or royalties, net capital gains, and net passive activity income.

ELIGIBILITY RULES. The credit is available to individuals with qualifying children (see Chapter I:2 for the uniform definition of a qualifying child) and also to certain individuals without children if earned income and AGI thresholds are met.[54] The EIC applies to married individuals only if a joint return is filed. The qualifying child's name, age, and taxpayer identification number must be included on the return. Individuals without children are eligible only if the following requirements are met:

▶ The individual's principal place of abode is in the United States for more than one-half of the tax year.

▶ The individual (or spouse if married) is at least age 25 and not more than age 64 at the end of the tax year.

▶ The individual is not a dependent or the qualifying child of another taxpayer for the tax year.[55]

COMPUTATION OF THE CREDIT AMOUNT. Earned income credit percentages and the maximum amount of earned income allowed for the credit in 2010 are summarized in Table I:14-1. These vary based on the number of qualifying children (from none to three or more) and the taxpayer's filing status. The maximum allowable credit phases out when the taxpayer's AGI or earned income (whichever is greater) exceeds a specified amount (see Table I:14-2).[56]

EXAMPLE I:14-33 ▶ Vivian is not married, has one qualifying child, and is eligible for the earned income credit in 2010. Vivian's AGI is $19,500 ($15,900 of wages and $3,600 of alimony). The wages are considered earned income; the alimony is not earned income. Using Table I:14-1, the tentative credit is $3,050. Using Table I:14-2, the phaseout is $487 [0.1598 × ($19,500 AGI − $16,450 phaseout floor)].[57] The allowable credit is therefore $2,563 ($3,050 − $487), and this amount is refundable to Vivian. ◄

HISTORICAL NOTE

The earned income credit was claimed on 28.1 million tax returns in 2006 and amounted to $44.4 billion. This compares with 19.4 million returns and $32.5 billion in 2000.

ADDITIONAL COMMENT

Under tax law enacted in 2002, kidnapped children will now meet the principal place of abode test. Such children must be presumed by law enforcement authorities to have been kidnapped by someone other than a family member.

---

[53] (See Chapter I:2 for a discussion of the relationship between the child tax credit and the earned income credit.)
[54] Sec. 32(c).
[55] Sec. 32(c)(1)(A), as amended by the 2008 Adoption Act.

[56] The percentages are adjusted annually for inflation.
[57] Sec. 32(b)(1). $19,500 is used in the formula because AGI of $19,500 is greater than $15,900 of earned income.

▼ TABLE I:14-1

2010 Earned Income Credit Table

Number of Qualifying Children	Basic Percentage	Maximum Amount of Earned Income allowed for Credit	Tentative Credit
All taxpayers:			
No children	7.65%	$ 5,980	$ 457
One child	34.0%	8,970	3,050
Two children	40.0%	12,590	5,036
Three or more children	45.0%	12,590	5,666

▼ TABLE I:14-2

2010 Earned Income Credit Phaseout Table

Number of Qualifying Children	Phaseout Begins at[a]	Phaseout Percentage	Phaseout Ends at
Married filing joint return:			
No children	$12,490	7.65%	$18,470
One child	21,460	15.98%	40,545
Two children	21,460	21.06%	45,372
Three or more children	21,460	21.06%	48,362
Other taxpayers:			
No children	$ 7,480	7.65%	$13,460
One child	16,450	15.98%	35,535
Two children	16,450	21.06%	40,363
Three or more children	16,450	21.06%	43,352

[a]Greater of AGI or earned income.
[b]EIC will be zero at AGI or earned income above these figures.

ADDITIONAL COMMENT

The American Recovery and Reinvestment Act of 2009 provides additional temporary relief from the marriage tax penalty by expanding the earned income credit for large families.

Taxpayers who have at least one qualifying child can receive advance payments on their refundable EIC by applying for employer withholding reduction.

HOMEBUYER TAX CREDIT (HTC)

ADDITIONAL COMMENT

The American Recovery and Reinvestment Act of 2009 and the Worker, Homeownership, and Business Assistance Act of 2009 expanded the first-time homebuyers' credit to encourage home ownership.

The 2008 Housing Assistance Tax Act introduced a refundable tax credit equal to the lesser of 10% of the purchase price of a principal residence or $7,500. The Homebuyer Tax Credit (HTC) applied to *first-time homebuyers* who purchased a principal residence after April 8, 2008 and before July 1, 2009. It was in fact an interest-free loan that involved recapture over 15 years, beginning in the second year after the tax year in which the home was purchased. Taxpayers who claimed the HTC in 2008 will begin recapture in 2010. Recapture of the refundable HTC increases tax liability, generally by $500 per year ($7,500/15 years).

The American Recovery and Reinvestment Act of 2009 increased the maximum HTC to $8,000 and extended the purchase deadline to December 1, 2009.

The Worker, Homeownership and Business Assistance Act of 2009 further extended the HTC as follows:

▶ The definition of eligible taxpayers now includes *existing homebuyers* who purchased a principal residence between November 7, 2009 and April 30, 2010.

▶ The purchase deadline for both *first-time homebuyers* and *existing homebuyers* is now May 1, 2010 (closing must occur before July 1, 2010).

▶ The recapture requirement is eliminated, unless the taxpayer sells the home within three years.

> ▶ Phaseout thresholds based on modified AGI are increased.

> ▶ No HTC is allowed for residences costing more than $800,000.

ELIGIBLITY RULES.   A *first-time homebuyer* is any individual who did not own a principal residence during the three-year period preceding the new residence purchase. An *existing homebuyer* is any individual who owned and used a principal residence in five consecutive years out of the eight years preceding the new residence purchase. If a married filing jointly couple, only one individual needs to meet the own-and-use requirement.

COMPUTATION OF THE HTC.   For *first-time homebuyers*, the HTC in 2010 is the lesser of 10% of the home's purchase price or $8,000. For purchases after November 7, 2009, the HTC phases out ratably over a $20,000 range for taxpayers with modified AGI beginning at $225,000 (MFJ) or $125,000 (other filing statuses.) For purchases before that date, the phaseout thresholds were $150,000 and $75,000, respectively.

For *existing homebuyers*, the HTC in 2010 is the lesser of 10% of the home's purchase price or $6,500. Phaseout thresholds are the same as above.

Taxpayers eligible for the HTC based on a purchase before December 1, 2009 were allowed to claim the credit on either their 2008 or 2009 return. Taxpayers eligible for the HTC based on a subsequent purchase may claim the credit on either their 2009 or 2010 return.

EXAMPLE I:14-34 ▶ In 2008, Joanne was unmarried filing single. She was a qualified *first-time homebuyer*. On April 10, 2008, she purchased a home for $100,000. Her modified AGI for the year was $70,000. Her tentative HTC was $7,500, computed as follows: ($100,000 × .10 = $10,000) which was then limited to the maximum of $7,500. No phaseout applied because Joanne's modified AGI was less than $75,000. Thus, her refundable 2008 HTC was $7,500. Recapture of the HTC begins with Joanne's 2010 tax return. She will pay an additional $500 tax ($7,500 ÷ 15) in each of the years 2010–2025, unless she sells the home during that period. In that case, she will recapture all remaining credit in the year of sale. ◀

EXAMPLE I:14-35 ▶ In 2010, Steve and Julie are married filing jointly. They are qualified *existing homebuyers*. On February 15, 2010, they purchased a principal residence for $685,000. Their modified AGI for the year is $235,000. Their tentative HTC is $6,500, computed as follows: ($685,000 × .10 = $6,850) which is then limited to the maximum of $6,500. Phaseout based on modified AGI is $1,788 ($230,500 − $225,000 = $5,500 ÷ $20,000 = 0.275 × $6,500 = $1,788). Thus, their refundable HTC is $4,712. No recapture applies. ◀

As of publication date, Congress has not passed any further extension of the Homebuyer Tax Credit.

MAKING WORK PAY CREDIT AND ECONOMIC RECOVERY PAYMENTS

ADDITIONAL COMMENT

The Making Work Pay credit is intended to offset social security taxes paid.

The American Recovery and Reinvestment Act of 2009 included a new refundable credit, the Making Work Pay (MWP) credit. It applies to tax years beginning in 2009 and 2010, and can be claimed as a refund on the individual's tax return or through reductions in either withholding taxes (employed individuals) or estimated tax payments (self-employed individuals.)

ELIGIBILITY RULES.   The MWP credit is available to individuals other than nonresident aliens and those who can be claimed as a dependent on another taxpayer's return. Earned income is defined as it is in the earned income credit.

COMPUTATION OF THE CREDIT.   The MWP credit is the lesser of 6.2% of the individual's earned income or $400 ($800 for individuals filing a joint return.) Thus, individuals who file jointly will receive the maximum $800 credit at earned income of $12,903 ($12,903 × 0.062 = $800) and other filing statuses will receive the maximum $400 credit at earned income of $6,452 ($6,452 × 0.062 = $400.)

PHASEOUT.   The MWP credit is reduced by 2% of modified adjusted gross income (MAGI) above $150,000 for joint filers, or $75,000 for all other filing statuses. MAGI is defined as AGI plus amounts excluded under the foreign earned income exclusion and

other less common exclusions. Thus, taxpayers filing jointly with MAGI of $190,000 will lose the entire $800 MWP credit [($190,000 − $150,000) × .02 = $800]. Taxpayers of other filing statuses will lose the entire $400 MWP credit when MAGI reaches $95,000 [($95,000 − $75,000) × .02 = $400].

INTERACTION WITH ECONOMIC RECOVERY PAYMENTS. Because earned income does not include benefits received from social security, railroad retirement, supplemental security income, or veterans' benefits, some individuals will not be eligible for the MWP credit. Thus, the American Recovery and Reinvestment Act of 2009 provides for a one-time *economic recovery payment (ERP)* of $250 in 2009 to these individuals ($500 on a joint return where both individuals are eligible) if they are certified under any of these benefit programs in any of the three months November 2008 through January 2009, have a valid social security number, and live in the U.S. or its territories.

Individuals who qualify for the MWP credit and also qualify for the ERP must reduce their MWP credit by $250.

Topic Review I:14-2

Summary of Selected Tax Credits Discussed in Chapter 14

TAX CREDIT ITEM	RATIONALE FOR INCLUSION IN TAX LAW
NONREFUNDABLE PERSONAL CREDITS:	
Adoption credit (Sec. 23)	Provides relief for taxpayers who incur expenses in the adoption of children
Child tax credit (Sec. 24)	Reduces the tax burden on families with dependent children
Child and Dependent care credit (Sec. 21)	Provides relief for employed parents and other individuals who incur expenses for dependent care
Elderly and Disabled credit (Sec. 22)	Provides relief for elderly taxpayers who are not substantially covered by Social Security
HOPE scholarship and Lifetime Learning credit (Sec. 25A)	Assists students and families with the cost of post-secondary education
Qualified retirement savings contributions credit (Sec. 25B)	Encourages low- and middle-income taxpayers to save for retirement
Residential energy credits (Sec. 25C & D)	Encourages energy conservation measures on principal residences
MISCELLANEOUS CREDITS:	
Foreign tax credit (Sec. 27)	Mitigates the effects of double taxation on foreign-source income
GENERAL BUSINESS CREDITS:	
Business energy credits (Sec. 48)	Encourages energy conservation measures
Disabled access credit (Sec. 44)	Encourages small businesses to provide access for disabled persons
Employer-provided child care credit (Sec. 45F)	Provides incentive for businesses to provide child care for employees
Rehabilitation expenditures credit (Sec. 21)	Encourages the rehabilitation of older buildings
Research credit (Sec. 41)	Encourages research and experimental activities
Work opportunity credit (Sec. 51)	Provides incentive for employers to hire people from disadvantaged groups
REFUNDABLE PERSONAL CREDITS:	
Earned income credit (Sec. 32)	Provides incentive for low-income individuals to work
First-time homebuyers' credit (Sec. 36)	Encourages first-time home ownership.
Making Work Pay credit	Mitigates the effect of social security taxes for low-income individuals
Overpayment of social security taxes (Sec. 31)	Provides a credit or refund for social security taxes overpaid when a taxpayer has multiple employers
Taxes withheld from wages and other income (Sec. 31)	Recognizes taxpayer's prepayment of tax

PAYMENT OF TAXES

OBJECTIVE 4

Understand the mechanics of the federal withholding tax system and the requirements for making estimated tax payments

The IRS collects federal income taxes during the year either through withholding on wages or quarterly estimated tax payments. If the total of withholdings and estimated taxes is less than the amount of tax liability, the taxpayer must pay the balance of the tax due when the tax return is filed. If there has been an overpayment of tax, the taxpayer may either request a refund or choose to apply the overpayment to the following year's quarterly estimated taxes.

Substantial penalties are imposed if an employer fails to withhold federal income tax and pay such amounts to the IRS.[58] In addition, a taxpayer may be subject to a nondeductible penalty upon an underpayment of estimated tax.[59]

WITHHOLDING OF TAXES

Employers must withhold federal income taxes and FICA taxes from an employee's wages. No withholdings are required if an employer-employee relationship does not exist (e.g., an individual who performs services as an independent contractor). Generally, unless a specific exemption is provided, withholding is required on all forms of remuneration paid to an employee. Thus, salaries, fees, bonuses, dismissal payments, commissions, vacation pay, and taxable fringe benefits are all subject to withholding.[60] Below are some special rules relating to withholding of federal taxes:

▶ *More than one employer during the same year.* Each employer must withhold FICA and federal income taxes without regard to the fact that the employee has more than one employer. As discussed on page I:14-9, this may cause an overwithholding of FICA taxes if the employee's wages exceed the ceiling amount on the OASDI portion of the tax. In the event of overwithholding of FICA taxes, the employee may credit the excess amount as an additional payment of tax. However, the matching employer excess FICA contributions are not refundable or creditable against the tax liabilities of either employer or employee.

▶ *Overall exemption.* Taxpayers are exempt from withholding in the current year if they (1) had no tax liability in the prior year; (2) expect no tax liability in the current year; and (3) can be claimed as dependent by another taxpayer and report no more than $900 total income, no more than $300 of which is unearned. The earnings of such individuals are still fully taxable, and an employer may be liable for matching FICA tax payments on these earnings.

▶ *Exemption for certain employment activities.* Certain employees, such as agricultural laborers, ministers, household employees, newspaper carriers under age 18, and those earning tips of less than $20 per month from an employer, are exempt from withholding. The earnings of such individuals are still fully taxable, and an employer may be liable for matching FICA tax payments on these earnings.[61]

▶ *Special rules for supplemental wage payments.* Supplemental wages payments include items such as bonuses, commissions, overtime, accumulated sick pay, severance pay, awards, prizes, back pay, and retroactive pay increases. If an employee receives supplemental wage payments, the federal income tax withholding amount is determined under either of two methods:[62]

---

[58] Sec. 3403. Employers are liable for payment of the full amount that must be withheld and paid to the IRS. In addition, responsible individuals (e.g., corporate officers, directors, and consultants) may be held personally liable for payment of the tax. (See *Renate Schiff v. U.S.,* 69 AFTR 2d 92-804, 92-1 USTC ¶50,248 (D.C. NV, 1992), *Ted E. Tsouprake v. U.S.,* 69 AFTR 2d 92-821, 92-1 USTC ¶50,249 (D.C. FL, 1992), and *Ralph M. Guito, Jr. v. U.S.,* 67 AFTR 2d 91-1066, 92-1 USTC ¶ 50,231 (D.C. FL, 1991).)

[59] Sec. 6654.
[60] Reg. Sec. 31.3401(a)-1(a)(2).
[61] Reg. Sec. 31.3401(a)(10)-1(a). An employer is liable for FICA tax payments for domestic servants if $1,400 or more is paid to an individual in any calendar year.
[62] Reg. Sec. 31.3402(g)-1(a).

- Concurrent payments—if the supplemental wages are included in the payment of regular wages, the tax is withheld as if the total was a single wage payment for the payroll period.
- Separate payments—if the supplemental wages are paid separately, the tax withheld is either a flat 25%, or the percentage that applies to the aggregate of the supplemental wage payment with wages paid within the same calendar year for the last preceding payroll period or the current payroll period.

▶ *Backup withholding.* Backup withholding rules were enacted to prevent abusive noncompliance situations, such as not providing the payor of a dividend with the payee's Social Security number. A 28% withholding rate is required on most types of payments that are reported on Form 1099 (e.g., interest, dividends, royalties, etc.) where a proper taxpayer identification number is not provided.

▶ *Other special rules.* There are many other special rules on withholding in certain circumstances, such as for fringe benefits, pension and annuity payments, etc. that are beyond the scope of this text.

WITHHOLDING ALLOWANCES AND METHODS. On commencement of employment, every employee must file with his/her employer an employee's withholding allowance certificate (Form W-4), which lists the employee's marital status and number of withholding allowances. The W-4 becomes the input to the employer for computation of the amount of federal income tax to be withheld. If an employee's circumstances change (e.g., a married taxpayer is divorced during the year), an amended Form W-4 must be filed within 10 days. In general, the employee's Form W-4 is sent by the employer to the IRS when the number of withholding allowances exceeds 10, or an employee with earnings of more than $200 per week claims exemption from withholding.[63] This procedure is intended to prevent employees from avoiding income tax withholding.

The number of withholding allowances claimed on Form W-4 is typically the same as the number of personal and dependency exemptions that will be taken on the employee's tax return for the year. An additional withholding allowance (reflecting the standard deduction) may be claimed by a taxpayer who has one job or, if married, has a spouse who is unemployed.[64] Further additional withholding allowances may be claimed if an individual has deductions, losses, or credits from a wide variety of sources, including itemized deductions, alimony payments, moving expenses, and losses from a trade or business, rental property, or a farm. Form W-4 contains tables and a worksheet to help employees compute the number of additional withholding allowances.[65]

EXAMPLE I:14-36 ▶

Sam and Sally are married and have three dependent children. They file a joint return. Sally is not employed, and Sam does not claim additional withholding allowances for unusually large deductions or tax credits. Sam may claim six allowances (two personal exemptions [for Sam and Sally] plus three dependency exemptions, plus one special allowance to reflect the standard deduction). The special allowance is available because Sally is not employed and Sam has only one job. ◀

 STOP & THINK

Question: Many taxpayers believe that they must claim the same number of withholding allowances for withholding purposes as the number of personal exemptions on their income tax return. Why is this not correct?

Solution: While the starting point for determining withholding allowances is the taxpayer's marital status and number of personal exemptions, taxpayers are allowed to claim more or fewer withholding allowances based on their individual situation. Taxpayers may claim additional withholding allowances for two principal reasons: (1) a taxpayer has high deductions, losses, or credits; or (2) an unmarried taxpayer qualifies for head of

---

[63] Reg. Sec. 31.3402(f)(2)-1.
[64] Sec. 3402(f)(1)(E).

[65] Married taxpayers who are both employed may allocate withholding allowances as they see fit as long as the same allowance is not claimed more than once.

household filing status. The withholding tables are constructed assuming that the taxpayer will use the standard deduction. Therefore, if a taxpayer has much higher itemized deductions than the standard deduction, the withholding tables may prescribe too much withholding, and the taxpayer would have a large refund at the end of the year. To alleviate this situation, taxpayers are allowed to claim additional withholding allowances. Similarly, the withholding tables only have two categories for marital status, single or married. Thus, if an unmarried taxpayer qualifies for head of household status, the "single" withholding tables may cause over-withholding of tax.

COMPUTATION OF FEDERAL INCOME TAX WITHHELD. Employers use either wage bracket tables or an optional percentage method to compute the actual amount of withholding. Both methods produce approximately the same results. Wage bracket tables are available for daily, weekly, biweekly, and monthly payroll periods. Separate tables are used for single (including heads-of-household) and married individuals. Partial wage bracket tables for married and single persons using a monthly payroll period for wages are located in the 2009 Tax Tables and Rate Schedules on page T-16.

EXAMPLE I:14-37 ▶ Henry is married and claims four withholding allowances. His monthly salary is $3,000. The federal income tax withheld per month for 2009 using the wage bracket table on page T-16 is $66. ◀

ESTIMATED TAX PAYMENTS

ADDITIONAL COMMENT

The IRS does not mail reminder statements for the required quarterly estimated payments.

Certain types of income are not subject to withholding (e.g., investment income, rents, income from self-employment, and capital gains). Taxpayers who earn this type of income must make quarterly estimated tax payments.

The purpose of the estimated tax payment system is to ensure that all taxpayers have paid enough tax by the end of the tax year to cover most of their tax liability. Thus, estimated tax payments may also be required if insufficient tax is being withheld from an individual's salary, pension, or other income (although many taxpayers prefer to file an amended Form W-4 to reduce the number of withholding allowances). The amount of estimated tax is the taxpayer's estimated tax liability (including self-employment tax and alternative minimum tax) reduced by withholdings, tax credits, and any excess FICA amounts.[66]

ADDITIONAL COMMENT

The comedian, Red Skelton, on the IRS: "I get even with them. I send in an estimated tax form, but I don't sign it. If I've got to guess what I'm making, let them guess who's making it."

REQUIRED ESTIMATED TAX PAYMENTS. For calendar-year individuals, required quarterly payments are due by April 15, June 15, September 15 of the current year, and January 15 of the following year. To avoid an underpayment penalty,[67] total estimated tax payments must equal or exceed any of the following three "safe harbor" amounts:

▶ 90% of the tax liability shown on the return for the current year;

▶ 100% of the tax liability shown on the return for the prior year if the taxpayer's AGI for such prior year was $150,000 or less. If the taxpayer's AGI was greater than $150,000, no penalty will be imposed if the taxpayer pays estimated tax payments in the current year equal to 110% of the preceding year's income tax liability.

▶ 90% of the tax liability shown on the return for the current year computed on an annualized basis.

Further, no penalty is imposed if (1) the estimated tax for the current year is less than $1,000 or (2) the individual had no tax liability for the prior year.

No penalty is imposed for failure to *file* quarterly estimated tax payments, even though the IRC includes specific filing requirements. A penalty is imposed only if the taxpayer fails to meet the minimum payment requirements or one of the previously mentioned exceptions does not apply.

[66] Excess FICA payments will likely occur if an employee has more than one employer during the year and the total FICA withholding from all employers exceed in the aggregate the ceiling on FICA taxes.

[67] Sec. 6654.

WHAT WOULD YOU DO IN THIS SITUATION?

THE NANNY TAX: DON'T PAY NOW, WORRY LATER

You are a CPA engaged in tax practice, and one of your clients is Mr. Throckmorton D. Princeton, J.D. He is a senior partner in the prestigious employment litigation firm of Huey, Dewey and Fooey. Mr. Princeton is known for his ruthless litigation style.

Things were rosy for Mr. Princeton until last week, when there was some speculation in the press about his being appointed to a cabinet-level position by the President. A TV news magazine show looked into Mr. Princeton's domestic worker situation. It appears that Mr. Princeton has long engaged in the practice of hiring part-time workers in his household to clean his house, tend to his gardens, walk his dogs, cook his meals, service his car, and nurse him when he is ill. All told, he used over twenty-five people at one time or another in the past year. These workers were paid as little as possible, and all were asked to sign a contract with Mr. Princeton stating that they were to be classified as independent contractors. The total amount paid to these workers was $50,000. Mr. Princeton paid no payroll taxes, although he did file Forms 1099 with the IRS. What tax and ethical issues should be considered?

EXAMPLE I:14-38 ▶ Sarah does not make quarterly estimated tax payments for 2010, even though she has a substantial amount of income not subject to withholding. Her taxable income in 2010 is $140,000. Her actual tax liability (including self-employment taxes and the alternative minimum tax) for 2010 is $40,000. Withholdings from her salary are $30,000. She pays the $10,000 balance due to the IRS when she files her 2010 return on April 3, 2011. Sarah's tax liability for 2009 was $28,000. There is no penalty for failure to make the quarterly estimated tax payments because she meets the second exception: the $30,000 of withholdings is more than 100% of her $28,000 tax liability for 2009. ◀

EXAMPLE I:14-39 ▶ Assume the same facts in Example I:14-38 except Sarah's AGI in 2009 was $180,000. Since her AGI exceeded $150,000 in 2009, the second safe harbor amount would be $110% (instead of 100%) of the prior year's tax or $30,800 ($28,000 × 1.10). Because the $30,000 of withholding is less than 110% of her $28,000 tax liability, Sarah would not meet either exception and would be subject to the underpayment penalty. ◀

Form 2210 (see Appendix B) should be completed and submitted with the tax return if a possible underpayment of tax is indicated. This form is used to determine whether one of the exceptions applies and, if not, to compute the amount of the underpayment penalty. The actual computation of the underpayment penalty is not shown here because of the length and complexity of the rules. Topic Review I:14-3 summarizes the withholding tax and estimated payment requirements.

TAX PLANNING CONSIDERATIONS

AVOIDING THE ALTERNATIVE MINIMUM TAX

KEY POINT

The alternative minimum tax can be avoided or its impact lessened by various tax strategies.

Taxpayers with substantial amounts of tax preference items and/or positive AMT adjustments and a correspondingly low regular tax liability may be subject to the AMT. These taxpayers need to engage in tax planning to minimize or avoid the AMT.

A liberal AMT exemption is provided for most individuals, so taxpayers can plan for full use of the exemption by timing certain income and deduction items each year. For example, the AMT may be avoided by delaying payment of certain itemized deductions (e.g., state and local taxes) that reduce the regular income tax but do not reduce the AMT. A cash method taxpayer who defers payment of state income taxes into the following year triggers an increase in the regular tax for the current year. This increase can eliminate the

Topic Review I:14-3

Withholding Taxes and Estimated Payments

EMPLOYER WITHHOLDING OF TAXES:

	FICA	INCOME TAX
Subject to withholding:	For OASDI, all employee earnings up to $106,800 (in 2010) per employer. No ceiling applies to HI earnings.	All employee wages, salaries, fees, bonuses, commissions, taxable fringe benefits, and so on.[a]
Withholding amounts:	7.65% of FICA wages including 6.2% on OASDI earnings and 1.45% on HI earnings.	Determined by using withholding tables or the percentage method based on an individual's filing status and number of withholding allowances.

[a]Exceptions are provided for certain nontaxable fringe benefits.

ESTIMATED TAX PAYMENTS:

▶ To avoid an underpayment penalty, estimated tax payments and withholdings for the year must equal or exceed any one of the following: 90% of the tax liability shown on the return for the current year; or 100% of the tax liability shown on the return for the prior year (110% if AGI for the prior year exceeds $150,000); or 90% of the tax liability shown on the return for the current year computed on an annualized basis.

▶ The underpayment penalty is not deductible for income tax purposes.

▶ Form 2210 should be completed and submitted with the tax return if an underpayment is indicated.

AMT liability. However, it is necessary to consider tax effects for both the current and following years, because state income taxes are deductible for purposes of the regular tax calculation when payment is made in the following year. This reduction may affect the AMT calculation in such a year and increase the amount of tax owed.

Certain tax-exempt investments, such as interest on private activity bonds, generate additional tax preferences for the investor. Before such investments are acquired, an investor should determine the potential AMT impact.

AVOIDING THE UNDERPAYMENT PENALTY FOR ESTIMATED TAX

Many taxpayers find it difficult to estimate their taxes for the purposes of making quarterly estimated payments and are uncertain whether their withholdings and estimated tax will equal or exceed 90% or more of their actual tax liability for the year. A common planning technique to avoid a possible underpayment tax penalty is to make estimated tax payments and withholdings in an amount that is at least 100% (or 110%[68] if AGI was in excess of $150,000 for the prior year) of the actual tax liability for the prior year, thereby meeting one of the exceptions that prevents the underpayment penalty from being imposed. This technique is commonly referred to as a "safe harbor estimate."

EXAMPLE I:14-40 ▶ Yong expects his 2010 federal income tax withholdings to be $14,000 and estimates that his income tax liability will be $24,000. Yong's actual federal income taxes in 2009 were $20,000. If estimated taxes of at least $6,000 are paid during the year, Yong's estimated taxes plus withholding will be at least 100% of his prior year's tax liability ($14,000 + $6,000 = $20,000) and no underpayment penalty will be imposed, despite the fact that there is a $4,000 ($24,000 − $20,000) balance due of the actual tax liability. If Yong's 2009 AGI was in excess of $150,000, his estimated taxes plus withholding must be at least 110% of his 2009 tax liability or $22,000 (1.10 × $20,000) to avoid the underpayment penalty. Thus, his estimated tax payments must be at least $8,000. ◀

---

[68] The 110% is applicable for tax years 2003 and thereafter.

CASH-FLOW CONSIDERATIONS

Assuming that the underpayment penalty can be avoided, it is generally preferable to have an underpayment of tax to the government at the time for filing the return rather than to receive a refund resulting from an overpayment of tax. No interest is paid on a refund if the IRS pays the refund within 45 days from the later of the due date of the return or its filing date.[69] In addition, the IRS has, in effect, received an interest-free loan from the taxpayer during the period such overpayment is made. To avoid an overpayment, a taxpayer may file an amended W-4 form and claim additional withholding allowances if the requirements are met (e.g., the taxpayer has unusually large itemized deductions, tax credits, alimony payments, etc.).

If an individual anticipates that her combined estimated tax payments and withholdings will be insufficient to avoid the underpayment penalty, it may be preferable to increase amounts withheld before the end of the tax year (e.g., amounts withheld in the fourth quarter) rather than increase the estimated tax payments.[70] This technique may be advantageous because the penalty is calculated on a quarterly basis, while withholdings are considered to be spread evenly over the year, even when withholding amounts are increased near the end of the year. The end result is a cash-flow savings to the taxpayer. Another way to avoid the underpayment penalty is to accelerate certain deductions (e.g., real estate taxes on a personal residence) by paying such amounts before the end of the current tax year. Additionally, otherwise deductible contributions to an IRA made between the end of the tax year and the due date for the tax return may be treated as a deduction for the prior year, thereby avoiding the underpayment penalty (see Chapter I:9).

USE OF GENERAL BUSINESS TAX CREDITS

Taxpayers must consider the priority and interrelated aspects of credits to ensure that a particular credit is fully used. For example, an individual's nonrefundable personal tax credits reduce tax liability before the foreign tax credit limitation is applied. Then, the nonrefundable personal tax credits and foreign tax credit are deducted from the individual's tax liability before limitations are applied to the general business tax credit.

FOREIGN TAX CREDITS AND THE FOREIGN EARNED INCOME EXCLUSION

Individuals who accept foreign job assignments should consider federal income tax implications, because U.S. citizens are subject to U.S. tax on their worldwide income. Assuming that certain requirements and limitations are met, an individual may elect to take either a foreign tax credit or a foreign-earned income exclusion of $91,500 in 2010 ($91,400 in 2009) with respect to salaries, allowances, and other forms of earned income that are earned while on extended non-U.S. assignments.[71] Any taxes paid or accrued with respect to the excluded income are not available as a foreign tax credit. In general, when the effective foreign tax rate is less than the effective U.S. tax rate, the exclusion is preferable because the foreign tax credit that can be claimed does not equal the gross U.S. tax owed on the income. When the effective foreign tax rate exceeds the effective U.S. tax rate, U.S. taxpayers ordinarily elect not to use the exclusion. Instead, the excess tax credits on earned income are used to offset the U.S. taxes owed on other types of foreign income. Detailed coverage of the interaction between foreign tax credits and the exclusion is contained in Chapter C:16 of the *Prentice Hall's Federal Taxation: Corporations, Partnerships, Estates, and Trusts* text.

---

[69] Sec. 6611(e).

[70] To completely avoid the underpayment penalty, the tax law generally requires the estimated payments to be made equally on the four installment dates.

[71] Sec. 911(a). The foreign income exclusion requirements are discussed in Chapter I:4.

COMPLIANCE AND PROCEDURAL CONSIDERATIONS

ALTERNATIVE MINIMUM TAX (AMT) FILING PROCEDURES

Individual taxpayers use Form 6251 to compute the AMT, and corporations use Form 4626 (see Appendix B for both forms). Form 6251 must be completed and attached to an individual's income tax return in any of the following situations:

▶ An AMT tax liability actually exists.

▶ The taxpayer has tax credits that are limited by the tentative minimum tax.

▶ The AMT base exceeds the exemption amounts, and the individual has AMT adjustment or tax preference items.

WITHHOLDINGS AND ESTIMATED TAX PAYMENTS

Taxpayers who have income taxes withheld from wages, pensions, and other income should receive a Form W-2 (or Form 1099-R for pensions) from the employer by January 31. These forms should be attached to the individual's tax return to substantiate the amount of withholdings. If the form is incorrect, the taxpayer should request a corrected form from the employer.

Taxpayers who make quarterly estimated tax payments may not file Form 1040A or Form 1040EZ. Married individuals may make either joint or separate estimated tax payments. If joint estimated tax payments are made and the married individuals subsequently file separate returns (e.g., in the case of a divorce that is pending or a divorce completed before the end of the year), the joint estimated tax payments are divided in proportion to each spouse's individual tax if no agreement is reached concerning an appropriate division.

EXAMPLE I:14-41 ▶ George and Alice are married and make joint estimated tax payments of $10,000 during 2010. George and Alice are separated in February 2011 and Alice refuses to file a joint return with George for tax year 2010. George 's tax liability for 2010 on his separate return is $20,000 and Alice's tax liability on her separate return is $5,000. If no agreement is reached concerning the allocation of the joint estimated payments of $10,000, Alice is entitled to claim $2,000 of the estimated tax payments on her return [($5,000 ÷ $25,000) × $10,000]. The remaining $8,000 is apportioned to George. ◀

GENERAL BUSINESS TAX CREDITS

The computation of the business energy credit is made on Form 3468. Individuals then transfer the totals to page 2 of Form 1040. Form 3800 must be filed if any other general business credits are claimed.

NONREFUNDABLE PERSONAL TAX CREDITS

KEY POINT

The earned income credit is available even in cases where the taxpayer has no tax liability. The refund of taxes not paid or incurred is often called a negative income tax.

Nonrefundable personal tax credits are reported on page 2 of Form 1040. These credits are deducted from the taxpayer's tax liability before other credits. The credits section on page 2 of Form 1040 limits the deduction for nonrefundable personal tax credits to the amount of tax due. Form 2441 (see Appendix B) must be filed to claim the child and dependent care credit. Taxpayers who claim the child and dependent care credit must also include the care provider's name, address, and taxpayer identification number on their tax return. If the caregiver will not provide the required information, the taxpayer has the option to supply the name and address of the caregiver on Form 2441 and attach a statement explaining that the caregiver has refused to provide his or her taxpayer identification number (TIN). Schedule R of Form 1040 (see Appendix B) is filed to claim the credit for the elderly and disabled. An eligible individual may elect to have the IRS compute the tax and the amount of the tax credit.[72]

---

[72] Sec. 6014. (See Form 1040 instructions for more reporting details.)

The earned income tax credit is refundable to an individual even if no tax is owed. The IRS will automatically compute the credit amount.[73] However, tax tables to assist in the process are included in the IRS instructions to Forms 1040 and 1040A. Schedule EIC of Form 1040 (see Appendix B) is used to compute the credit if Form 1040 is used. If an individual expects to be eligible for the earned income credit, he or she can obtain advance payments of the credit amount by filing Form W-5 (Earned Income Credit Advance Payment Certificate) with his or her employer, who will increase the employee's pay by the amount of the credit. Individuals who receive advance payments must file Form 1040 or Form 1040A to obtain the credit even if they are not required to file a tax return. Taxpayers who are eligible for the earned income credit cannot use Form 1040EZ.

The foreign tax credit for individuals is computed on Form 1116 (see Appendix B). The foreign tax credit amount so determined is entered on page 2 of Form 1040.

PROBLEM MATERIALS

Note: For problems related to the AMT, we assume the same exemption amounts for 2009 and 2010 (See Legislative Update on page I:14-2).

DISCUSSION QUESTIONS

I:14-1 Why are most taxpayers not subject to the alternative minimum tax (AMT)?

I:14-2 Does the AMT apply if an individual's tax liability as computed under the AMT rules is less than his or her regular tax amount?

I:14-3 Which of the following are tax preference items for purposes of computing the individual AMT?
a. Net long-term capital gain
b. Excess depreciation for real property placed in service before 1987
c. Straight-line depreciation on residential real estate acquired in 1992
d. Appreciated element for charitable contributions of capital gain real property

I:14-4 Which of the following are individual AMT adjustments (more than one answer may be correct)?
a. Itemized deductions that are allowed for regular tax purposes but not allowed in computing AMTI.
b. Excess of MACRS depreciation over depreciation computed under the alternative depreciation system for real property placed in service after 1986 and before 1999.
c. Excess of MACRS depreciation over depreciation computed under the alternative depreciation system for personal property placed in service after 1986.
d. Tax-exempt interest earned on State of Michigan general revenue bonds.

I:14-5 Which of the following itemized deductions are deductible when computing the alternative minimum tax for individuals (more than one answer may be correct)?
a. Charitable contributions

b. Mortgage interest on a personal residence
c. State and local income taxes
d. Interest related to an investment in undeveloped land where the individual has no investment income
e. Medical expenses amounting to 9% of AGI

I:14-6 Why are most individuals not subject to the self-employment tax?

I:14-7 Tony, who is single and 58 years old, is considering early retirement from his salaried job. He currently has $70,000 salary and also earns $50,000 profit from a consulting business. What advice would you give Tony relative to the need to make Social Security tax payments if he retires and continues to be actively engaged as a consultant during his retirement?

I:14-8 Theresa is a college professor who wants to work for a consulting firm during the summer. She will be working on special projects relating to professional development programs. What advantages might accrue to the consulting firm if the engagement is set up as a consulting arrangement rather than an employment contract?

I:14-9 Ted and Tina, a married couple, both have self-employment income and file a joint return in 2010. Ted has self-employment income of $20,000 and receives a $34,800 salary from his employer. Tina has no salary and self-employment income from a sole proprietorship of $10,000.
a. How much self-employment tax is due for Ted and Tina on a joint return?
b. How much, if any, of the self-employment tax payments may be deducted on Ted and Tina's income tax return?

---

[73] Sec. 6695(g) requires preparers to meet due diligence requirements with respect to the earned income tax credit (EIC). If the EIC is incorrectly computed or overlooked, the *preparer* could be subject to a $100 penalty.

I:14-10 Discuss the underlying rationale for the following tax credit items:
a. Foreign tax credit
b. Research credit
c. Business energy credit
d. Work opportunity credit
e. Child and dependent care credit
f. Earned income credit
g. American Opportunity credit
h. Adoption credit

I:14-11 If Congress is considering a tax credit or deduction as an incentive to encourage certain activities, is a $40 tax credit more valuable than a $200 tax deduction for a taxpayer with a 15% marginal rate? a 25% marginal rate?

I:14-12 What are the more significant tax credit items included in the computation of the general business tax credit?

I:14-13 Discuss the limitations that have been imposed on the general business tax credit, including the following:
a. Overall ceiling limitation based on the tax liability
b. Priority of general business and personal credits
c. Carryback and carryover of unused credits (including the application of the FIFO method)

I:14-14 Sarah, a married taxpayer who files a joint return, is considering a foreign assignment for two years. In 2010, she will earn $120,000 in the foreign country. Sarah has no other income. She will be eligible for either the foreign tax credit or the foreign-earned income exclusion. The average tax rate on Sarah's earnings if fully taxable under U.S. law would be 30%. The average tax rate for the foreign salary is 20% under the foreign country's laws.
a. Discuss in general terms the computation of the foreign tax credit and its limitation.
b. Would Sarah be better off electing the foreign tax credit or the foreign earned income exclusion? Explain.

I:14-15 King Corporation is expanding its business and is planning to hire four additional employees at an annual labor cost of $12,000 each. What will the tax consequences in the first year be if King hires employees who are eligible in one of targeted groups 1-10 for the work opportunity tax credit?

I:14-16 Queen Corporation has been in business since 1989. During the preceding year, the company had 25 full-time employees and gross receipts of $8,000,000. During the current year, Queen spent $20,000 to install access ramps for disabled individuals. Is Queen Corporation eligible for the disabled access credit? If so, what is the credit amount and the basis reduction (if any) for the depreciable property?

I:14-17 Discuss the special tax rules that apply to the tax credit for rehabilitation expenditures including the following:

a. Types of eligible expenditures
b. Applicable tax credit rates
c. Restrictions on depreciation methods
d. Calculation of basis for expenditures
e. Potential recapture of the credit

I:14-18 What types of business property qualify for the business energy credit?

I:14-19 What is the underlying reason for enactment of most of the personal tax credits?

I:14-20 Discuss the difference between a refundable tax credit and a nonrefundable tax credit. Give at least one example of each type of credit.

I:14-21 If an individual is not employed and has no earned income, is it possible to take a child and dependent care credit for otherwise qualifying child and dependent care expenses? Explain.

I:14-22 Discuss the major differences between the American Opportunity credit and the Lifetime Learning credit. Include in your discussion the type of taxpayers who would likely qualify for each of the credits.

I:14-23 What is the maximum child and dependent care credit available to an employed individual who has $8,000 of qualifying child care expenses and two or more qualifying children or incapacitated dependents?

I:14-24 Vivian is a single taxpayer with two children who qualify for the child and dependent care credit. She incurred $7,000 of qualifying child care expenses during the current year. She also received $4,000 in reimbursements from her employer from a qualified employee dependent care assistance program. What is the maximum child and dependent care credit available to Vivian if her AGI is $24,500?

I:14-25 The adoption credit is intended to assist taxpayers with the financial burden of adopting children.
a. Discuss how the credit is computed.
b. Why did Congress impose a phase out of the credit for taxpayers based on AGI?

I:14-26 Alice is a single mother, 37 years old, and has two qualifying children, ages 3 and 6. She receives $3,600 alimony and earns $18,000 in wages resulting in $21,600 of AGI in 2010. Is Alice eligible for the earned income credit? If so, is it possible for her to receive advance payments of the credit rather than receiving a tax refund when her tax return is filed?

I:14-27 Why are most elderly people unable to qualify for the tax credit for the elderly?

I:14-28 If an employer fails to withhold federal income taxes and FICA taxes on wages or fails to make payment to the IRS, what adverse tax consequences may result? May corporate officers or other corporate officials be held responsible for the underpayment?

I:14-29 Taxpayers are permitted to contribute money to qualified retirement plans and receive very

favorable tax benefits. Congress has provided further incentives to contribute money to such plans by enacting the Qualified Retirement Savings Contributions Credit.
a. Why did Congress enact this credit when such contributions already receive favorable tax treatment?
b. Briefly describe how the credit is computed.

I:14-30 The credit for employer-provided child care has two major components, a credit for qualified child care expenses and a credit for qualified child care resources and referral expenditures.
a. Discuss each of the two components. What type of expenses are included in each component?
b. The two components are added together to compute the credit for employer-provided child care. Discuss the rates for each component, the limitation for the credit, and the tax result if the employer ceases to offer child care operations within the first three years after claiming the credit.

I:14-31 A credit is allowed to encourage businesses to conduct research and experimentation. One feature of the research credit is that only incremental expenditures are eligible. Explain the concept that the credit is allowed for *increasing* research activities.

I:14-32 Although Virginia is entitled to five personal and dependency exemptions on her income tax return, she claims only one withholding allowance on Form W-4.
a. Is it permissible to claim fewer allowances than an individual is entitled to?
b. Why would an individual claim fewer allowances?
c. Is it possible for Virginia to claim more than five withholding allowances?

I:14-33 Mario is a college student who had no income tax liability in the prior year and expects to have no tax liability for the current year.
a. What steps should Mario take to avoid having amounts withheld from his summer employment wages?
b. What are the cash-flow implications to Mario if the employer withholds federal income taxes?

I:14-34 What is backup withholding? What is its purpose?

I:14-35 In March 2010, Vincent anticipates that his actual tax liability for the 2010 tax year will be $12,000 and that federal income taxes withheld from his salary will be $9,000. Thus, when he files his 2010 income tax return in 2011, he will have a $3,000 balance due. His actual federal income tax liability for 2009 was $8,000 and his AGI in 2009 was less than $150,000.
a. Is Vincent required to make estimated tax payments in 2010?
b. If no estimated tax payments are made, will Vincent be subject to an underpayment penalty if the actual tax liability for the 2010 tax year is $12,000? Why or why not?
c. Will Vincent be subject to an underpayment penalty if his actual tax liability for 2010 is instead $25,000? Why?

I:14-36 An individual has increasing levels of income each year and is uncertain regarding the amount of his estimated taxable income for any given year. What tax planning strategy can you suggest to avoid the penalty for underpayment of estimated tax?

I:14-37 From a cash-flow perspective, why is it generally preferable to have an underpayment of tax (assuming no underpayment penalty is imposed) rather than an overpayment of tax?

I:14-38 Why do many taxpayers intentionally overpay their tax through withholdings to obtain a tax refund?

ISSUE IDENTIFICATION QUESTIONS

I:14-39 Daryl is an executive who has an annual salary of $120,000. He is considering early retirement so he can pursue a career as a management consultant. Daryl estimates that he could earn approximately $80,000 annually from his consulting business. What tax issues should Daryl consider?

I:14-40 Jennifer recently received a check for $30,000 and securities with an FMV of $200,000 from her former husband pursuant to a divorce. The $30,000 represents alimony and the securities were transferred pursuant to the property settlement. The property settlement is nontaxable to Jennifer. Assuming the alimony is taxable and no income taxes are withheld, what tax issues should Jennifer consider?

I:14-41 Coastal Corporation is planning an expansion of its production facilities and is considering whether to hire additional employees from economically disadvantaged groups to avail itself of the Work Opportunity credit. The company plant is not located in an empowerment zone. New employees are paid approximately $18,000 per year. If economically disadvantaged employees are hired, additional job training expenses of $5,000 per employee will be required. What tax issues should Coastal consider with regard to the hiring and training of its new employees?

PROBLEMS

Note: For problems related to the AMT, we assume the same exemption amounts for 2009 and 2010 (See Legislative Update on page I:14-2).

I:14-42   *AMT Computation.* William and Maria Smith are a married couple filing jointly. They have no children and report the following items in 2010:

Taxable income	$70,000
Tax preferences	20,000
AMT adjustments related to itemized deductions	15,000
Regular tax liability	9,863

    a. What is the Smith's AMT liability?
    b. What would be William's AMT liability if he were an unmarried taxpayer filing single with a regular tax liability of $13,681?

I:14-43   *AMT Computation.* Jose, an unmarried taxpayer filing single with no dependents, has AGI of $200,000 and reports the following items in 2010:

Taxable income	$160,000
Tax preferences	10,000
AMT adjustments related to itemized deductions	30,000
Regular tax liability	38,509

    What is Jose's AMT liability?

I:14-44   *AMT Computation.* Harry and Mary Prodigious are married filing jointly and have 12 children. Six of the children are under age 17 in 2010. With the large number of children, they live in a very austere manner. Harry, in his spare time, works a large garden that provides most of their food. Mary makes all the children's clothes. Harry works for a local engineering firm and earns a salary of $100,000 in 2010. Mary does not work outside the home. The only other income is taxable interest in the amount of $8,000. They claim the standard deduction in filing their 2010 return and have no tax preferences or adjustments for purposes of the AMT.
    a. Compute Harry and Mary's regular tax and AMT under the facts above.
    b. Comment on the tax policy implications of your answer in Part a above.

I:14-45   *AMT Adjustments and Computation of Tax.* Allen, an unmarried taxpayer filing single, has no dependents and reports the following items on his 2010 federal income tax return:

Adjusted gross income	$75,000
Taxable income	48,000
Regular tax liability	8,181
Tax preferences	20,000
Itemized deductions including:	
Charitable contributions	7,500
Medical expenses (before AGI floor)	10,000
Mortgage interest on personal residence	10,000
State income taxes	5,000
Real estate taxes	8,000

    a. What is the amount of Allen's AMT adjustments related to itemized deductions?
    b. What is Allen's AMT liability?

I:14-46   *Self-Employment Tax.* In the current year, Amelia has wages of $45,000 and net income from a small unincorporated business of $70,000.
    a. What is the amount of Amelia's self-employment tax and *for* AGI deduction relative to her self-employment tax?
    b. How would your answer to Part a change if Amelia's wages were $110,000 rather than $45,000?

I:14-47   *Self-Employment Tax.* Arnie and Angela are married and file a joint return in the current year. Arnie is a partner in a public accounting firm. His share of the partnership's income in the current year is $40,000, and he receives guaranteed payments of $35,000. Angela receives wages of $50,000 from a large corporation. What is each taxpayer's self-employment tax amount? (Hint: Guaranteed payments received from a partnership are considered self-employment income.)

I:14-48   *Self-Employment Tax.* Anita, a single taxpayer, reports the following items for the current year:

Salary (subject to withholding)	$20,000
Income for serving on the Board of Directors for XYZ Corporation	11,000
Consulting gross income	9,000
Expenses related to consulting practice	(15,000)

a. What is the amount of Anita's self-employment tax?
b. How would your answer to Part a change if Anita's salary were $110,000?

I:14-49 *Computation of Tax Credits.* During the current year, Becky has personal credits as well as business credits related to her sole proprietorship. Her tentative tax credits for the current year include the following:

Work opportunity credit	$ 1,000
Child and dependent care credit	1,200
Research credit	14,000
Business energy credit	600
Total	$16,800

Becky's regular tax liability before credits is $13,800. Assume that she has no alternative minimum tax liability.
a. What is the amount of allowable personal tax credits?
b. What is the amount of allowable business tax credits?
c. What treatment is accorded to the unused tax credits for the current year?

I:14-50 *Child and Dependent Care Credit.* In each of the following independent situations, determine the amount of the child and dependent care tax credit. (Assume that both taxpayers are employed.)
a. Brad and Bonnie are married and file a joint return, with earned income of $40,000 and $14,000, respectively. Their combined AGI is $52,000. They have two children, ages 10 and 12, and employ a live-in nanny at an annual cost of $9,000.
b. Assume the same facts as in Part a, except that Brad and Bonnie employ Bonnie's mother, who is not their dependent, as the live-in nanny.
c. Bruce is divorced and has two children, ages 10 and 16. He has AGI and earned income of $27,000. Bruce incurs qualifying child care expenses of $8,000 during the year, incurred equally for both children. Bruce's employer maintains an employee dependent care assistance program. $1,000 was paid to Bruce from this program and excluded from Bruce's gross income.
d. Buddy and Candice are married and file a joint return. Their combined AGI is $50,000. Buddy earns $46,000, and Candice's salary from a part-time job is $4,000. They incur $5,000 of qualifying child care expenses for a day-care facility for their two children, ages 2 and 4.
e. Ben and Bunny are married and file a joint return. Their AGI is $75,000, all earned by Bunny. Ben was a full-time student for two semesters (10 months) at State University during the year. They incur $7,000 of qualifying child care expenses for their two children, ages 6 and 4.

I:14-51 *Adoption Credit.* Brad and Valerie decided to adopt a child and contacted an adoption agency in August 2009. After extensive interviews and other requirements (such as financial status, etc.), Brad and Valerie were approved as eligible parents to adopt a child. The agency indicated that it might take up to two years to find a proper match. In November 2010, the adoption became final, and Brad and Valerie adopted an infant daughter (not a special needs child). Below is a list of expenses that they incurred:

2009:	Agency fees (first installment)	$5,000
	Travel expenses for interviews, etc.	1,500
	Publications for prospective adoptive parents	300
	Legal fees connected with the adoption	1,000
	Kennel fees for dog while on adoption trips	250
2010:	Agency fees (final installment)	$4,000
	Travel expenses	400
	Court costs for adoption	200
	Kennel fees	100
	Nursery furniture (baby's room) and supplies	2,000

Brad and Valerie's AGI in 2009 was $70,000 and in 2010 was $90,000.
a. Compute Brad and Valerie's qualified adoption expenses for 2009 and 2010.
b. Compute Brad and Valerie's adoption credit. What year(s) may the credit be taken?
c. Would your answer to Part b change if the adopted child was a special needs child?

I:14-52 *American Opportunity Tax Credit and Lifetime Learning Credit.* Lou and Stella North are married, file a joint return, and have two dependent children in college, Phil and Jaci. Both attend State University, and neither receives any type of financial assistance. The North's modified AGI in 2009 is $112,000. The children's classifications and expenses are as follows:

	Spring Semester 2010 (paid in January 2010)	Fall Semester 2010 (paid in July 2010)
Phil:	Senior	Master's candidate
Tuition	$7,500	$8,000
Laboratory fees	500	500
Student activity fees	100	100
Course materials (books)	400	450
Room and board	3,200	3,200
Jaci:	Sophomore	Junior
Tuition	$1,600	$1,750
Student activity fees	100	100
Course materials (books)	250	300
Room and board	3,500	3,700

The Norths claimed the HOPE scholarship credit for both Phil and Jaci in 2008 and the AOTC 2009.
a. Compute any education credits that the Norths may claim in 2010.
b. How would your answer in Part a change if Phil received an academic scholarship of $3,000 (excluded from gross income) for each semester in 2010?
c. How would your answer in Part a change if Lou and Stella's modified AGI for 2010 was $175,000?
d. How would your answer in Part a change if Phil had been a junior during Spring semester 2010 and a senior during Fall semester 2010?

I:14-53 *Tax Credit for the Elderly.* Caroline, age 66 and unmarried filing single, received the following income items for the current year:

Social Security benefits (nontaxable)	$ 3,000
Pension benefits (taxable)	6,450
Interest income (taxable)	2,050
Total	$11,500

Caroline's tax liability (before credits) is $300.
a. What is Caroline's tentative tax credit for the elderly (before the tax liability limitation is applied)?
b. What is Caroline's allowable tax credit?

I:14-54 *General Business Tax Credit Limitation.* During 2010, Joule Company, a sole proprietorship, earned general business tax credits of $30,000 for energy conservation and rehabilitation expenditures. The owner, Mark Joule, knows that the overall credit will be limited. He provides you with the following information for 2010: regular tax (before credits) = $37,500; tentative minimum tax = $20,200; alternative minimum tax = $0; foreign tax credit = $4,500; other nonrefundable credits = $6,100. Mark also has a $3,000 carryforward of general business credit from 2009.
a. What is the 2010 limitation on Mark's general business credit?
b. What is Mark's allowable general business credit in 2010 and where does it come from?
c. What is Mark's general business credit carryover to 2011?

I:14-55 *Foreign Tax Credit.* Laser Corporation, a U.S. corporation, has a foreign office that conducts business in France. Laser pays foreign taxes of $74,000 on foreign-source taxable income of $185,000. Its U.S.-source taxable income is $320,000, total U.S. taxable income (worldwide) of $505,000, and U.S. tax liability (before reductions for the foreign tax credit) is $171,700. What is Laser's foreign tax credit? What is Laser's foreign tax credit carryback or carryover?

I:14-56 *Work Opportunity Credit.* Lang Corporation hires two economically disadvantaged youths (qualified for the work opportunity credit in groups 1-10) in August of the current year. Each employee earns $8,000 of wages in the current year. Salaries and wages paid to other employees in the current year totaled $50,000. Lang has a regular income tax liability of $40,000 in the current year before deducting tax credits (assuming the appropriate deduction is claimed for the youths' salaries). Its tentative minimum tax is $10,000. Business tax credits other than the work opportunity credit amount to $35,000.

    a. What is Lang's tentative work opportunity credit (before limitations) in the current year?

    b. What total general business credit can Lang use in the current year? What amount is available for carryover or carryback?

    c. What is Lang's deduction for salaries and wages paid to the two youths and its total deduction for salaries and wages in the current year?

I:14-57 *Rehabilitation Tax Credit.* In the current year, Bob acquired a certified historic structure on and placed it in service August 4 of the current year to be used as an office for his business. He paid $20,000 for the building (exclusive of the land) and spent $40,000 for renovation costs.

    a. Assuming Congress extends the credit into 2010, what is the rehabilitation tax credit (before limitations)?

    b. Compute the depreciation that Bob can take on the building for the current year.

    c. What is the basis of the building for MACRS depreciation purposes?

I:14-58 *Research Credit.* Pharm Inc. is a small pharmaceutical company that is heavily involved in drug research. During 2010, Pharm Inc. incurred the following expenditures related to the company's research efforts:

Salaries of research scientists and technicians	$180,000
Supplies and materials	42,000
Depreciation on research equipment	30,000

For the years 2006–2009, Pharm Inc. had average gross receipts of $5,000,000 and the company's fixed-base percentage is 3%. Also, during 2010 the company paid $200,000 to State University for the express purpose of doing basic research in the scientific field. Pharm Inc.'s qualified organization base period amount is $120,000. Assuming Congress extends the credit into 2010, compute Pharm Inc.'s credit for research activities. Is Pharm Inc. entitled to claim any deduction for research and experimentation expenses for the year?

I:14-59 *Earned Income Credit.* Carolyn is unmarried and has one dependent child, age 6, who lived with her for the entire year. She has earned income of $12,000 of wages and $6,000 of alimony in 2010. Her AGI is $18,000.

    a. What is Carolyn's tentative earned income credit (before phaseout)?

    b. What is Carolyn's allowable earned income credit?

    c. If Carolyn has no income tax liability (before the earned income credit is subtracted), is she entitled to a refund in the current year?

    d. How will your answers to Parts a and b change if Carolyn is married filing a joint return with three qualifying children?

I:14-60 *Earned Income Credit.* Jose is unmarried with no qualifying children. He has $8,300 of wages during the current year and is otherwise eligible for the earned income credit. Jose has $200 of interest income and no *for* AGI deductions. His AGI is $8,500.

    a. What is Jose's tentative earned income credit before phaseout?

    b. What is Jose's allowable earned income credit?

    c. If Jose has no income tax liability (before the earned income credit is subtracted), is he entitled to a refund for the current year?

    d. Would your answer to Part b change if Jose had dividend and interest income of $3,200 during the taxable year?

I:14-61 *Homebuyer Credit.* Loren and Sally Wilson are married taxpayers filing jointly. On April 1, 2010, they purchased a home for the first time at a cost of $225,000 (their principal residence.) Their 2010 modified AGI is $93,000, and their tax liability before credits is $6,000.

    a. What is the Wilsons' allowable homebuyer credit?

    b. How will the credit impact the Wilsons' tax liability?

    c. Will the recapture rules apply?

    d. How would you answer to a. above change if the Wilsons' modified AGI were $165,000 rather than $93,000?

I:14-62 *Refundable Credits.* The following are independent cases.
   a. Latisha is an unmarried taxpayer, filing head of household. She has two dependent children who lived with her all year. Her 2010 earned income was $18,600 and her AGI was $22,400. She uses the standard deduction. Compute:
      1. Taxable income and regular tax before credits
      2. Latisha's earned income credit (EIC) and Making Work Pay (MWP) credit.
      3. Balance due or refund.
   b. Marcus is an unmarried taxpayer, filing single. On July 15, 2010, he purchased a home for the first time at a cost of $124,000. His 2010 AGI was $85,000.
      1. Compute his Homebuyer Credit.
      2. Under what circumstances would Marcus be subject to recapture of the credit?
   c. Jillian is an unmarried taxpayer, filing single. She is 78 years old and received $9,520 of Social Security benefits in 2010. She also worked part-time and earned $4,900. Compute her 2010 Making Work Pay credit.

I:14-63 *Penalties for Nonpayment of Withholding and FICA Taxes.* Lake Corporation has some severe cash-flow problems. You are the company's financial and tax consultant. The treasurer of the company has informed you that the company has failed to make FICA and federal income tax withholding payments to the IRS (both the employer and employee contributions) for a period of approximately six months.
   a. What advice can you give to the company treasurer regarding the nonpayment of taxes?
   b. Can the liability for payment of the taxes extend to parties other than the corporation? Explain.

I:14-64 *Exemptions from Withholding.* Which of the following categories of individuals or income are exempt from the federal income tax withholding requirements?
   a. Domestic servants
   b. Independent contractors
   c. Newspaper carriers over age 18
   d. Bonuses
   e. Commissions
   f. Vacation pay
   g. Tips under $20 per month from a single employer

I:14-65 *Withholding Exemptions.* Barry is a college student who is employed as a waiter during the summer. He earns approximately $1,500 during the summer and estimates that he will not be required to file a tax return and will have no federal income tax liability. Last year, however, he made $6,000 and was required to file a return and pay $400 in taxes. Barry is unmarried filing single and is supported by his parents. He has no dependents and does not have any other sources of income or deductions.
   a. Can Barry claim exempt status on Form W-4 for withholding purposes?
   b. Can Barry claim more than one exemption on Form W-4 (e.g., additional withholding allowances or the standard deduction allowance) to minimize the amount withheld? Explain.

I:14-66 *Withholding Allowances.* Bart and Jane Lee are married, file a joint return and have two dependent children. Bart begins a new job and is asked to fill out a Form W-4. His monthly gross earnings will be $3,000. Jane is unemployed. Bart can claim three additional withholding allowances because he will have a large for-AGI deduction for substantial alimony paid to his ex-wife, Sue.
   a. What is the correct number of withholding allowances on Form W-4?
   b. What is the federal income tax to be withheld using the wage bracket tables (see withholding table on page T-15)?
   c. What disclosure procedures must Bart's employer follow if Bart claims more than ten allowances?

I:14-67 *Estimated Tax Requirements.* Anna does not make quarterly estimated tax payments even though she has substantial amounts of income that are not subject to withholding. In 2009, Anna's tax liability was $18,000. In 2010, Anna's actual tax liability is $30,000, and $18,200 was withheld from her salary. Anna's AGI for 2009 was $135,000.
   a. Is Anna subject to the underpayment penalty? Why?
   b. If Anna's withholdings were only $15,000, would she be subject to the underpayment penalty? Why?
   c. If Anna is subject to an underpayment penalty, can she deduct this amount as interest? Explain.

I:14-68 *Estimated Tax Underpayment Penalty.* Jane's estimated tax payments for 2010 are $14,000 and federal income taxes withheld from her salary amount to $12,000. Jane's actual tax liability for 2010 is $30,000. Her income was earned evenly throughout the current year. Jane's AGI for 2009 was $160,000 and her tax liability in 2009 was $25,000. Is Jane subject to the underpayment penalty? Explain.

COMPREHENSIVE PROBLEM

I:14-69 Mike Webb, married to Nancy Webb, is employed by a large pharmaceutical company and earns a salary. In addition, Mike is an entrepreneur and has two small businesses on the side, both operated as sole proprietorships. One is a consulting business where Mike provides financial and retirement assistance to pharmacists. The consulting business is doing very well. The other involves the manufacture of Christmas novelties in China, selling the products in gift shops in the U.S. This business is struggling. However, Mike feels the Christmas novelty business has great potential. In 2010, Mike reports the following:

Salary			$150,000
Consulting practice:	Revenues	$65,000	
	Ordinary expenses	12,000	53,000
Sole proprietorship:	Revenues	$22,000	
	Ordinary Expenses	40,000	(18,000)
Interest (none tax-exempt)			3,000
Dividends, qualified			9,000
LTCG		$24,000	
STCL		(4,000)	20,000
Itemized deductions:			
State and local taxes		$14,000	
Real estate taxes		5,000	
Mortgage interest on personal residence		10,000	
Charitable contributions		8,000	37,000

Child care expenses:
The Webb's have two dependent children, ages 13 and 11, and pay child care expenses of $4,000 per year for each child, for a total of $8,000. Nancy is not employed, but is a full-time student at State University, majoring in Accounting.

Federal income tax withheld from salary	$21,000
Estimated taxes paid for 2010	14,000

Mike and Nancy's AGI in 2009 was $175,000 and actual federal income tax liability for 2009 was $29,000.

Compute Mike and Nancy's federal income tax liability for 2010, including self-employment taxes and AMT, if applicable. Also, are Mike and Nancy subject to any underpayment penalties for 2010?

TAX STRATEGY PROBLEM

I:14-70 Jeff and Linda Foley are married and file a joint income tax return. Jeff is a lawyer and a partner in the firm of Foley & Looby, Attorneys at Law. Jeff is a 50% partner in the firm along with his partner, John Looby who is the other 50% partner. Foley & Looby (F&L) currently rent office space in a prestigious building and pay rent of $6,000 per month or $72,000 per year for their 4,000 square foot office. Thus, the firm pays $18 per square foot per year. As no equity is being generated by paying rent, Jeff and John are considering buying an office building. They have two buildings under consideration, as follows:

Building #1

Building #1 is a relatively new building and has 10,000 square feet of space. The new building can be purchased for a total price of $1,000,000. F&L would only use 4,000 square feet of the space and have other businesses that would rent the other 6,000 square feet from F&L for $15 per square foot per year, a total of $90,000 per year. Maintenance costs would amount to approximately $10 per square foot per year. The building is in

excellent condition and is ready to be moved into immediately and would require very few other outlays by F&L.

Building #2

Building #2 is located in the downtown area in a certified historic district and would qualify as a certified historic structure. This building, nearly 80 years old, also has 10,000 square feet and, like Building #1, the other 6,000 square feet can be rented to other tenants at $15 per square foot per year, a total of $90,000 per year. However, Building #2 is not in as good condition as Building #1. The purchase price of the building would be $400,000, and Jeff and John estimate that approximately $600,000 would have to be invested in capital expenditures to make the building suitable for their business. After the significant capital expenditures, F&L estimates the maintenance costs to be similar to Building #1, or $10 per square foot per year.

Both buildings can be 100% financed at 8% annual interest rate for 15 years. The annual cash payment on the $1,000,000 mortgage would be $117,000. Assume both buildings will appreciate at a rate of 8% per year.

Jeff and John have come to you as their financial and tax advisor to help them make the decision as to which building to purchase. If the buildings are equally desirable from a non-financial and non-tax standpoint, what is the best decision for them? That is, should they stay where they are and rent, or purchase one of the two buildings? Assume both Jeff and John are in the top 35% marginal tax bracket and that Congress extends the rehabilitation credit into 2010.

TAX FORM/RETURN PREPARATION PROBLEMS

I:14-71 Len and Christy Vole, ages 42 and 39 respectively, are married and file jointly in 2009. Len is a contractor operating as a sole proprietorship (EIN 36-278114). Christy is employed part-time as a paralegal. They have two dependent children, Jill, age 8 and Lee, age 5. In 2009, Len's earned income was $95,000, Christy's was $28,000, and they received $4,550 of taxable interest income. Thus, their AGI was $127,550. Their allowable itemized deductions were $13,700 and taxable income was $99,250. Regular tax before credits was $17,188, and Len's self-employment tax was $13,423. Federal income tax withholding was $7,500 and estimated tax payments were $13,000. The Voles also incurred $7,000 of qualifying child care expenses to enable them to work ($3,500 for each child). It was paid to HiTop Daycare, 327 Fowler St., Indianapolis, IN 46802 (EIN 36-415679).

Len also incurred the following expenses that qualify for the general business credit: $6,000 for disabled access and $8,500 of first-year wages paid to an employee who qualifies Len's business for the work opportunity credit and worked 500 hours during the year. No adjustments are required to either credit and there are no carrybacks or carryforwards.

Social security numbers are: Len, 342-54-6859; Christy, 490-67-5321; Jill, 311-68-3905; Lee, 311-30-6785.

Complete page 2 of the Vole's 2009 Form 1040, along with supporting Forms 2441 (child and dependent care credit), Form 3800 (general business credit), Form 8826 (disabled access credit), and Form 5884 (work opportunity credit). Show detail of the child tax credit computation (with any phaseout) at the bottom of Form 1040, page 2.

I:14-72 Harold J. Milton (SSN 574-45-5477) is unmarried filing single with no dependents. He had the following income and deductions for 2009:

Salary	$177,000	State income taxes	$18,000
Interest income from bank	12,000	Mortgage interest expense	
Dividend income (qualified)	18,000	on residence	19,000
Deductible IRA contribution	5,000	Interest expense on car loan	3,000
Tax-exempt interest		Real estate taxes	
from municipal bonds	24,000	on residence	2,000
Charitable contributions	27,000	Miscellaneous deductions—other	
		(before the 2% AGI floor)	7,000
		Income taxes withheld	20,000
		Estimated tax payments	
		($2,500 per quarter)	10,000

Complete Milton's 2009 Form 1040, Schedule A, B, D, Form 6251, and Form 2210. Milton had AGI in 2008 of $200,000 and his 2008 income tax liability was $46,000. (Note: Milton is eligible to use the Short Method on Form 2210.)

CASE STUDY PROBLEMS

I:14-73 Barbara was divorced in 2007. However, the final property settlement and determination of alimony payments was not made until February 2010 because of extended litigation. Barbara received a $20,000 payment of back alimony in March 2010 and will receive monthly alimony payments of $2,000 for the period April through December 2010. Last year, in 2009, Barbara's income consisted of $15,000 salary and $2,000 of taxable interest income. She used the standard deduction and had no dependents. In 2009, Barbara's tax liability was $1,900. In 2010, she expects to continue working at an annual salary of $15,000 and will have $2,000 of interest income. Federal income taxes withheld from her salary in 2010 will be $1,500. Her monthly alimony payments of $2,000 are also expected to continue for an indefinite period.

In early April 2010 Barbara requests your advice regarding the payment of quarterly estimated taxes for 2010. Prepare a memo to your client that discusses these requirements, including any possible penalties for not making quarterly payments and nontax issues such as cash-flow and investment income decisions.

I:14-74 Chips-R-Us is a computer technology corporation that designs hardware and software for use in large businesses. The corporation regularly pays individuals to install programs and give advice to companies that buy their software. In the current year, Simone, a computer expert, was sent to a customer of Chips-R-Us to perform computer services. Simone is not a regular employee of the corporation and the corporation did not train Simone for the task. Simone keeps track of the time spent on the job at the customer and reports to the corporation, which pays Simone for her services. The corporation specifies the work to be done for their client. The corporation can also replace Simone with another individual if her work is not satisfactory. Chips-R-Us treats Simone as an independent contractor for employment tax purposes.

In the current year the IRS challenges the corporation that it has failed to remit FICA taxes and income taxes that should have been withheld with respect to Simone's employment. Chips-R-Us refuses to pay the amount, stating that it is not required to do so because Simone is not an employee of the corporation. What will be the likely outcome of the IRS's challenge concerning Simone's status as an employee or independent contractor? Who may be liable for payment of the employment taxes, interest, and penalties to the government? What ethical responsibilities should be followed in the remittance of withheld employee taxes?

TAX RESEARCH PROBLEM

I:14-75 Lean Corporation was incorporated in 1981 by Bruce Smith, who has served as an officer and member of the Board of Directors. Carl Jones has served as the secretary-treasurer of the company as a convenience to his friend Bruce. Carl acted as a part-time bookkeeper but did not run the everyday business affairs and paid only the bills he was instructed to pay. Carl was an authorized signatory for the corporate bank accounts but had no final control over expenditures.

Beginning in the last quarter of 2009, the company failed to pay all of the taxes withheld from employees and the employer's share of FICA taxes to the IRS. Despite this delinquency, the corporation continued to pay other creditors, including its employees, in preference to the IRS.

In January, 2010 Lean Corporation entered into an installment agreement with the IRS to keep current on its withholding taxes and to make payments on the past due balance until paid in full. The company subsequently defaulted on the agreement in April 2010. During this period, Bruce Smith was serving as chief financial officer and was a member of the board of directors. He had the authority to make policy decisions. He was responsible for negotiating the installment agreement with the IRS and the decision to default on the agreement.

Who is liable for the penalty for the nonpayment of the payroll tax withholdings?

A partial list of research sources is:

- Sec. 6672

- *Ernest W. Carlson v. U.S.*, 67 AFTR 2d 91-1104, 91-1 USTC ¶50,262 (D.C. UT, 1991)

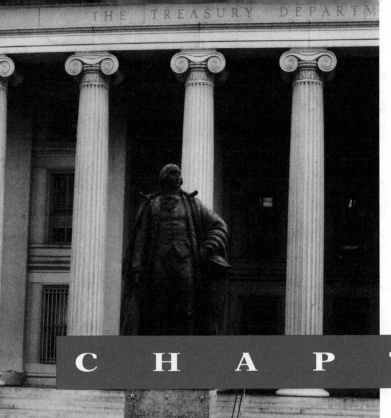

15

CHAPTER

TAX RESEARCH

LEARNING OBJECTIVES

After studying this chapter, you should be able to

▶ 1 Describe the steps in the tax research process

▶ 2 Explain how the facts influence the tax consequences

▶ 3 Identify the sources of tax law and understand the authoritative value of each

▶ 4 Consult tax services to research an issue

▶ 5 Grasp the basics of Internet-based tax research

▶ 6 Use a citator to assess tax authorities

▶ 7 Understand professional guidelines that CPAs in tax practice should follow

▶ 8 Prepare work papers and communicate to clients

This chapter introduces the reader to the tax research process. Its major focus is the sources of the tax law (i.e., the Internal Revenue Code and other tax authorities) and the relative weight given to each source. The chapter describes the steps in the tax research process and places particular emphasis on the importance of the facts to the tax consequences. It also describes the features of frequently used tax services and computer-based tax research resources. Finally, it explains how to use a citator.

The end product of the tax research process—the communication of results to the client—also is discussed. This text uses a hypothetical set of facts to provide a comprehensive illustration of the process. Sample work papers demonstrating how to document the results of research are included in Appendix A. The text also discusses two types of professional guidelines for CPAs in tax practice: the American Institute of Certified Public Accountants' (AICPA's) *Statements on Standards for Tax Services* (reproduced in Appendix E) and Treasury Department *Circular 230*.

OVERVIEW OF TAX RESEARCH

Tax research is the process of solving tax-related problems by applying tax law to specific sets of facts. Sometimes it involves researching several issues and often is conducted to formulate tax policy. For example, policy-oriented research would determine how far the level of charitable contributions might decline if such contributions were no longer deductible. Economists usually conduct this type of tax research to assess the effects of government policy.

Tax research also is conducted to determine the tax consequences of transactions to specific taxpayers. For example, client-oriented research would determine whether Smith Corporation could deduct a particular expenditure as a trade or business expense. Accounting and law firms generally engage in this type of research on behalf of their clients.

This chapter deals only with client-oriented tax research, which occurs in two contexts:

ADDITIONAL COMMENT

Closed-fact situations afford the tax advisor the least amount of flexibility. Because the facts are already established, the tax advisor must develop the best solution possible within certain predetermined constraints.

1. **Closed-fact or tax compliance situations:** The client contacts the tax advisor after completing a transaction or while preparing a tax return. In such situations, the tax consequences are fairly straightforward because the facts cannot be modified to obtain different results. Consequently, tax saving opportunities may be lost.

EXAMPLE I:15-1 ▶

Tom informs Carol, his tax advisor, that on November 4 of the current year, he sold land held as an investment for $500,000 cash. His basis in the land was $50,000. On November 9, Tom reinvested the sales proceeds in another plot of investment property costing $500,000. This is a closed fact situation. Tom wants to know the amount and the character of the gain (if any) he must recognize. Because Tom solicits the tax advisor's advice after the sale and reinvestment, the opportunity for tax planning is limited. For example, the possibility of deferring taxes by using a like-kind exchange or an installment sale is lost. ◀

ADDITIONAL COMMENT

Open-fact or tax-planning situations give a tax advisor flexibility to structure transactions to accomplish the client's objectives. In this type of situation, a creative tax advisor can save taxpayers dollars through effective tax planning.

2. **Open-fact or tax-planning situations:** Before structuring or concluding a transaction, the client contacts the tax advisor to discuss tax planning opportunities. Tax-planning situations generally are more difficult and challenging because the tax advisor must consider the client's tax and nontax objectives. Most clients will not engage in a transaction if it is inconsistent with their nontax objectives, even though it produces tax savings.

EXAMPLE I:15-2 ▶

Diane is a widow with three children and five grandchildren and at present owns property valued at $10 million. She seeks advice from Carol, her tax advisor, about how to minimize her estate taxes while conveying the greatest value of property to her descendants. This is an open-fact situation. Carol could advise Diane to leave all but a few hundred thousand dollars of her property to a charitable organization so that her estate would owe no estate taxes. Although this recommendation would eliminate Diane's estate taxes, Diane is likely to reject it because she wants her children or grandchildren to be her primary beneficiaries. Thus, reducing estate

taxes to zero is inconsistent with her objective of allowing her descendants to receive as much after-tax wealth as possible. ◀

When conducting research in a tax-planning context, the tax professional should keep a number of points in mind. First, the objective is not to minimize taxes per se but rather to maximize a taxpayer's after-tax return. For example, if the federal income tax rate is a constant 30%, an investor should not buy a tax-exempt bond yielding 5% when he or she could buy a corporate bond of equal risk that yields 9% before tax and 6.3% after tax. This is the case even though his or her explicit taxes (actual tax liability) would be minimized by investing in the tax-exempt bond.[1] Second, taxpayers typically do not engage in unilateral or self-dealing transactions; thus, the tax ramifications for all parties to the transaction should be considered. For example, in the executive compensation context, employees may prefer to receive incentive stock options (because they will not recognize income until they sell the stock), but the employer may prefer to grant a different type of option (because the employer cannot deduct the value of incentive stock options upon issuance). Thus, the employer might grant a different number of options if it uses one type of stock option versus another type as compensation. Third, taxes are but one cost of doing business. In deciding where to locate a manufacturing plant, for example, factors more important to some businesses than the amount of state and local taxes paid might be the proximity to raw materials, good transportation systems, the cost of labor, the quantity of available skilled labor, and the quality of life in the area. Fourth, the time for tax planning is not restricted to the beginning date of an investment, contract, or other arrangement. Instead, the time extends throughout the duration of the activity. As tax rules change or as business and economic environments change, the tax advisor must reevaluate whether the taxpayer should hold onto an investment and must consider the transaction costs of any alternatives.

One final note: the tax advisor should always bear in mind the financial accounting implications of proposed transactions. An answer that may be desirable from a tax perspective may not always be desirable from a financial accounting perspective. Though interrelated, the two fields of accounting have different orientations and different objectives. Tax accounting is oriented primarily to the Internal Revenue Service (IRS). Its objectives include calculating, reporting, and predicting one's tax liability according to legal principles. Financial accounting is oriented primarily to shareholders, creditors, managers, and employees. Its objectives include determining, reporting, and predicting a business's financial position and operating results according to Generally Accepted Accounting Principles. Because tax and financial accounting objectives may differ, planning conflicts could arise. For example, management might be reluctant to engage in tax reduction strategies that also reduce book income and reported earnings per share. Success in any tax practice, especially at the managerial level, requires consideration of both sets of objectives and orientations.

STEPS IN THE TAX RESEARCH PROCESS

In both open- and closed-fact situations, the tax research process involves six basic steps:

1. Determine the facts.
2. Identify the issues (questions).
3. Locate the applicable authorities.
4. Evaluate the authorities and choose those to follow where the authorities conflict.
5. Analyze the facts in terms of the applicable authorities.
6. Communicate conclusions and recommendations to the client.

---

[1] For an excellent discussion of explicit and implicit taxes and tax planning see M. S. Scholes, M. A. Wolfson, M. Erickson, L. Maydew, and T. Shevlin, *Taxes and Business Strategy: A Planning Approach,* fourth edition (Upper Saddle River, NJ: Pearson Prentice Hall, 2008). Also see Chapter I:18 of the *Individuals* volume. An example of an implicit tax is the excess of the before-tax earnings on a taxable bond over the risk-adjusted before-tax earnings on a tax-favored investment (e.g., a municipal bond).

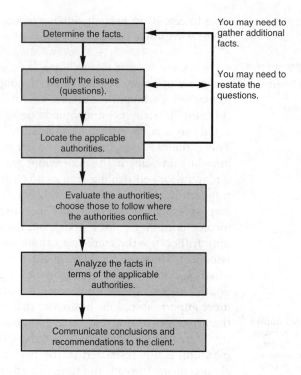

FIGURE I:15-1 ▶ STEPS IN THE TAX RESEARCH PROCESS

ADDITIONAL COMMENT

The steps of tax research provide an excellent format for a written tax communication. For example, a good format for a client memo includes (1) statement of facts, (2) list of issues, (3) discussion of relevant authority, (4) analysis, and (5) recommendations to the client of appropriate actions based on the research results.

Although the above outline suggests a linear approach, the tax research process often is circular. That is, it does not always proceed step-by-step. Figure I:15-1 illustrates a more accurate process, and Appendix A provides a comprehensive example of this process.

In a closed-fact situation, the facts have already occurred, and the tax advisor's task is to analyze them to determine the appropriate tax treatment. In an open-fact situation, by contrast, the facts have not yet occurred, and the tax advisor's task is to plan for them or shape them so as to produce a favorable tax result. The tax advisor performs the latter task by reviewing the relevant legal authorities, particularly court cases and IRS rulings, all the while bearing in mind the facts of those cases or rulings that produced favorable results compared with those that produced unfavorable results. For example, if a client wants to realize an ordinary loss (as opposed to a capital loss) on the sale of several plots of land, the tax advisor might consult cases involving similar land sales. The advisor might attempt to distinguish the facts of those cases in which the taxpayer realized an ordinary loss from the facts of those cases in which the taxpayer realized a capital loss. The advisor then might recommend that the client structure the transaction based on the fact pattern in the ordinary loss cases.

TYPICAL MISCONCEPTION

Many taxpayers think the tax law is all black and white. However, most tax research deals with gray areas. Ultimately, when confronted with tough issues, the ability to develop strategies that favor the taxpayer and then to find relevant authority to support those strategies will make a successful tax advisor. Thus, recognizing planning opportunities and avoiding potential traps is often the real value added by a tax advisor.

Often, tax research involves a question to which no clearcut, unequivocally correct answer exists. In such situations, probing a related issue might lead to a solution pertinent to the central question. For example, in researching the issue described in the previous paragraph, i.e., whether the taxpayer may deduct a loss as ordinary instead of capital, the tax advisor might research the related issue of whether the presence of an investment motive precludes classifying a loss as ordinary. The solution to the latter issue might be relevant to the central question of whether the taxpayer may deduct the loss as ordinary.

Identifying the issue(s) to be researched often is the most difficult step in the tax research process. In some instances, the client defines the issue(s) for the tax advisor, such as where the client asks, "May I deduct the costs of a winter trip to Florida recommended by my physician?" In other instances, the tax advisor, after reviewing the documents submitted to him or her by the client, identifies and defines the issue(s) himself or herself. Doing so presupposes a firm grounding in tax law.[2]

---

[2] Often, in an employment context, supervisors define the questions to be researched and the authorities that might be relevant to the tax consequences.

Once the tax advisor locates the applicable legal authorities, he or she might have to obtain additional information from the client. Example I:15-3 illustrates the point. The example assumes that all relevant tax authorities are in agreement.

EXAMPLE I:15-3 ▶ Mark calls his tax advisor, Al, and states that he (1) incurred a loss on renting his beach cottage during the current year and (2) wonders whether he may deduct the loss. He also states that he, his wife, and their minor child occupied the cottage only eight days during the current year.

This is the first time Al has dealt with the Sec. 280A vacation home rules. On reading Sec. 280A, Al learns that a loss is *not* deductible if the taxpayer used the residence for personal purposes for longer than the greater of (1) 14 days or (2) 10% of the number of days the unit was rented at a fair rental value. He also learns that the property is *deemed* to be used by the taxpayer for personal purposes on any days on which it is used by any member of his or her family (as defined in Sec. 267(c)(4)). The Sec. 267(c)(4) definition of family members includes brothers, sisters, spouse, ancestors, or lineal descendants (i.e., children and grandchildren).

Mark's eight-day use is not long enough to make the rental loss nondeductible. However, Al must inquire about the number of days, if any, Mark's brothers, sisters, or parents used the property. (He already knows about use by Mark, his spouse, and his lineal descendants.) In addition, Al must find out how many days the cottage was rented to other persons at a fair rental value. Upon obtaining the additional information, Al proceeds to determine how to calculate the deductible expenses. Al then derives his conclusion concerning the deductible loss, if any, and communicates it to Mark. (This example assumes the passive activity and at-risk rules restricting a taxpayer's ability to deduct losses from real estate activities will not pose a problem for Mark. See Chapter I:8 of *Prentice Hall's Federal Taxation: Individuals* for a comprehensive discussion of these topics.) ◀

Many firms require that a researcher's conclusions be communicated to the client in writing. Members or employees of such firms may answer questions orally, but their oral conclusions should be followed by a written communication. According to the AICPA's *Statements on Standards for Tax Services* (reproduced in Appendix E),

> Although oral advice may serve a client's needs appropriately in routine matters or in well-defined areas, written communications are recommended in important, unusual, or complicated transactions. The member may use professional judgment about whether, subsequently, to document oral advice in writing.[3]

In addition, Treasury Department *Circular 230* covers all written advice communicated to clients. These requirements are more fully discussed at the end of this chapter and in Chapter C:15 (*Corporations, Partnerships, Estates, and Trusts* volume).

IMPORTANCE OF THE FACTS TO THE TAX CONSEQUENCES

OBJECTIVE 2

Explain how the facts influence the tax consequences

Many terms and phrases used in the Internal Revenue Code (IRC) and other tax authorities are vague or ambiguous. Some provisions conflict with others or are difficult to reconcile, creating for the researcher the dilemma of deciding which rules are applicable and which tax results are proper. For example, as a condition to claiming another person as a dependent, the taxpayer must provide a certain level of support for such person.[4] Neither the IRC nor the Treasury Regulations define "support." This lack of definition could be problematic. For example, if the taxpayer purchased a used automobile costing $8,000 for an elderly parent whose only source of income is $7,800 in Social Security benefits, the question of whether the expenditure constitutes support would arise. The tax advisor would have to consult court opinions, revenue rulings, and other IRS pronouncements to ascertain the legal meaning of the term "support." Only after thorough research would the meaning of the term become clear.

---

[3] AICPA, *Statement on Standards for Tax Services*, No. 7, "Form and Content of Advice to Taxpayers," 2010, Para. 6.

[4] Sec. 152(e)(1)(A) and Sec. 152(d)(1)(C).

In other instances, the legal language is quite clear, but a question arises as to whether the taxpayer's transaction conforms to a specific pattern of facts that gives rise to a particular tax result. Ultimately, the peculiar facts of a transaction or event determine its tax consequences. A change in the facts can significantly change the consequences. Consider the following illustrations:

Illustration One

Facts: A holds stock, a capital asset, that he purchased two years ago at a cost of $1,000. He sells the stock to B for $920. What are the tax consequences to A?

Result: Under Sec. 1001, A realizes an $80 capital loss. He recognizes this loss in the current year. A must offset the loss against any capital gains recognized during the year. Any excess loss is deductible from ordinary income up to a $3,000 annual limit.

Change of Facts: A is B's son.

New Result: Under Sec. 267, A and B are related parties. Therefore, A may not recognize the realized loss. However, B may use the loss if she subsequently sells the stock at a gain.

Illustration Two

Facts: C donates to State University ten acres of land that she purchased two years ago for $10,000. The fair market value (FMV) of the land on the date of the donation is $25,000. C's adjusted gross income is $100,000. What is C's charitable contribution deduction?

Result: Under Sec. 170, C is entitled to a $25,000 charitable contribution deduction (i.e., the FMV of the property unreduced by the unrealized long-term gain).

Change of Facts: C purchased the land 11 months ago.

New Result: Under the same IRC provision, C is entitled to only a $10,000 charitable contribution deduction (i.e., the FMV of the property reduced by the unrealized short-term gain).

Illustration Three

Facts: Acquiring Corporation pays Target Corporation's shareholders one million shares of Acquiring voting stock. In return, Target's shareholders tender 98% of their Target voting stock. The acquisition is for a bona fide business purpose. Acquiring continues Target's business. What are the tax consequences of the exchange to Target's shareholders?

Result: Because the transaction qualifies as a reorganization under Sec. 368(a)(1)(B), Target's shareholders are not taxed on the exchange, which is solely for Acquiring voting stock.

Change of Facts: In the transaction, Acquiring purchases the remaining 2% of Target's shares with cash.

New Result: Under the same IRC provision, Target's shareholders are now taxed on the exchange, which is not solely for Acquiring voting stock.

CREATING A FACTUAL SITUATION FAVORABLE TO THE TAXPAYER

TYPICAL MISCONCEPTION

Many taxpayers believe tax practitioners spend most of their time preparing tax returns. In reality, providing tax advice that accomplishes the taxpayer's objectives is one of the most important responsibilities of a tax advisor. This latter activity is tax consulting as compared to tax compliance.

Based on his or her research, a tax advisor might recommend to a taxpayer how to structure a transaction or plan an event so as to increase the likelihood that related expenses will be deductible. For example, suppose a taxpayer is assigned a temporary task in a location (City Y) different from the location (City X) of his or her permanent employment. Suppose also that the taxpayer wants to deduct the meal and lodging expenses incurred in City Y as well as the cost of transportation thereto. To do so, the taxpayer must establish that City X is his or her tax home and that he or she temporarily works in City Y. (Section 162 provides that a taxpayer may deduct travel expenses while "away from home" on business. A taxpayer is deemed to be "away from home" if his or her employment at the new location does not exceed one year, i.e., it is "temporary.") Suppose the taxpayer wants to know the tax consequences of his or her working in City Y for ten months and then, within that ten-month period, finding permanent employment in City Y. What is tax research likely to reveal?

Tax research will lead to an IRS ruling stating that, in such circumstances, the employment will be deemed to be temporary until the date on which the realistic expectation about the temporary nature of the assignment changes.[5] After this date, the employment

---

[5] Rev. Rul. 93-86, 1993-2 C.B. 71.

will be deemed to be permanent, and travel expenses relating to it will be nondeductible. Based on this finding, the tax advisor might advise the taxpayer to postpone his or her permanent job search in City Y until the end of the ten-month period and simply treat his or her assignment as temporary. So doing would lengthen the time he or she is deemed to be "away from home" on business and thus increase the amount of meal, lodging, and transportation costs deductible as travel expenses. The taxpayer should compare the tax savings to any additional personal costs of maintaining two residences.

THE SOURCES OF TAX LAW

OBJECTIVE 3

Identify the sources of tax law and understand the authoritative value of each

The language of the IRC is general; that is, it prescribes the tax treatment of broad categories of transactions and events. The reason for the generality is that Congress can neither foresee nor provide for every detailed transaction or event. Even if it could, doing so would render the statute narrow in scope and inflexible in application. Accordingly, interpretations of the IRC—both administrative and judicial—are necessary. Administrative interpretations are provided in Treasury Regulations, revenue rulings, and revenue procedures. Judicial interpretations are presented in court opinions. The term *tax law* as used by most tax advisors encompasses administrative and judicial interpretations in addition to the IRC. It also includes the meaning conveyed in reports issued by Congressional committees involved in the legislative process.

THE LEGISLATIVE PROCESS

Tax legislation begins in the House of Representatives. Initially, a tax proposal is incorporated in a bill. The bill is referred to the House Ways and Means Committee, which is charged with reviewing all tax legislation. The Ways and Means Committee holds hearings in which interested parties, such as the Treasury Secretary and IRS Commissioner, testify. At the conclusion of the hearings, the Ways and Means Committee votes to approve or reject the measure. If approved, the bill goes to the House floor where it is debated by the full membership. If the House approves the measure, the bill moves to the Senate where it is taken up by the Senate Finance Committee. Like Ways and Means, the Finance Committee holds hearings in which Treasury officials, tax experts, and other interested parties testify. If the committee approves the measure, the bill goes to the Senate floor where it is debated by the full membership. Upon approval by the Senate, it is submitted to the President for his or her signature. If the President signs the measure, the bill becomes public law. If the President vetoes it, Congress can override the veto by at least a two-thirds majority vote in each chamber.

Generally, at each stage of the legislative process, the bill is subject to amendment. If amended, and if the House version differs from the Senate version, the bill is referred to a House-Senate conference committee.[6] This committee attempts to resolve the differences between the House and Senate versions. Ultimately, it submits a compromise version of the measure to each chamber for its approval. Such referrals are common. For example, in 1998 the House and Senate disagreed over what the taxpayer must do to shift the burden of proof to the IRS. The House proposed that the taxpayer assert a "reasonable dispute" regarding a taxable item. The Senate proposed that the taxpayer introduce "credible evidence" regarding the item. A conference committee was appointed to resolve the differences. This committee ultimately adopted the Senate proposal, which was later approved by both chambers.

ADDITIONAL COMMENT

Committee reports can be helpful in interpreting new legislation because they indicate the intent of Congress. With the proliferation of tax legislation, committee reports have become especially important because the Treasury Department often is unable to draft the needed regulations in a timely manner.

After approving major legislation, the Ways and Means Committee and Senate Finance Committee usually issue official reports. These reports, published by the U.S. Government Printing Office (GPO) as part of the *Cumulative Bulletin* and as separate documents, explain the committees' reasoning for approving (and/or amending) the legislation.[7] In addition, the GPO publishes both records of the committee hearings and transcripts of the floor debates. The records are published as separate House or Senate documents. The transcripts are incorporated in the *Congressional Record* for the day of the

---

[6] The size of a conference committee can vary. It is made up of an equal number of members from the House and the Senate.

[7] The *Cumulative Bulletin* is described in the discussion of revenue rulings on page I:15-12.

debate. In tax research, these records, reports, and transcripts are useful in deciphering the meaning of the statutory language. Where this language is ambiguous or vague, and the courts have not interpreted it, the documents can shed light on **Congressional intent,** i.e., what Congress *intended* by a particular term, phrase, or provision.

EXAMPLE I:15-4 ▶ As mentioned earlier, in 1998 Congress passed legislation concerning shifting the burden of proof to the IRS. This legislation was codified in Sec. 7491. The question arises as to what constitutes "credible evidence." (Remember, the taxpayer must introduce "credible evidence" to shift the burden of proof to the IRS). Section 7491 does not define the term. Because the provision was relatively new, few courts had an opportunity to interpret what "credible evidence" means. In the absence of relevant statutory or judicial authority, the researcher might have looked to the committee reports to ascertain what Congress intended by the term. Senate Report No. 105-174 states that "credible evidence" means evidence of a quality, which, "after critical analysis, the court would find sufficient upon which to base a decision on the issue if no contrary evidence were submitted."[8] This language suggests that Congress intended the term to mean evidence of a kind sufficient to withstand judicial scrutiny. Such a meaning should be regarded as conclusive in the absence of other authority. ◀

THE INTERNAL REVENUE CODE

The IRC, which comprises Title 26 of the United States Code, is the foundation of all tax law. First codified (i.e., organized into a single compilation of revenue statutes) in 1939, the tax law was recodified in 1954. The IRC was known as the Internal Revenue Code of 1954 until 1986, when its name was changed to the Internal Revenue Code of 1986. Whenever changes to the IRC are approved, the old language is deleted and new language added. Thus, the IRC is organized as an integrated document, and a researcher need not read through the relevant parts of all previous tax bills to find the current version of the law. Nevertheless, a researcher must be sure that he or she is working with the law in effect when a particular transaction occurred.

ADDITIONAL COMMENT

The various tax services, discussed later in this chapter, provide IRC histories for researchers who need to work with prior years' tax law.

The IRC contains provisions dealing with income taxes, estate and gift taxes, employment taxes, alcohol and tobacco taxes, and other excise taxes. Organizationally, the IRC is divided into subtitles, chapters, subchapters, parts, subparts, sections, subsections, paragraphs, subparagraphs, and clauses. Subtitle A contains rules relating to income taxes, and Subtitle B deals with estate and gift taxes. A set of provisions concerned with one general area constitutes a subchapter. For example, the topics of corporate distributions and adjustments appear in Subchapter C, and topics relating to partners and partnerships appear in Subchapter K. Figure I:15-2 presents the organizational scheme of the IRC.

An IRC section contains the operative provisions to which tax advisors most often refer. For example, they speak of "Sec. 351 transactions," "Sec. 306 stock," and "Sec. 1231 gains and losses." Although a tax advisor need not know all the IRC sections, paragraphs, and parts, he or she must be familiar with the IRC's organizational scheme to read and interpret it correctly. The language of the IRC is replete with cross-references to titles, paragraphs, subparagraphs, and so on.

EXAMPLE I:15-5 ▶ Section 7701, a definitional section, begins, "When used in this title . . ." and then provides a series of definitions. Because of this broad reference, a Sec. 7701 definition applies for all of Title 26; that is, it applies for purposes of the income tax, estate and gift tax, excise tax, and other taxes governed by Title 26. ◀

EXAMPLE I:15-6 ▶ Section 302(b)(3) allows taxpayers whose stock holdings are completely terminated in a redemption (a corporation's purchase of its stock from one or more of its shareholders) to receive capital gain treatment on the excess of the redemption proceeds over the stock's basis instead of ordinary income treatment on the entire proceeds. Section 302(c)(2)(A) states, "In the case of a distribution described in subsection (b)(3), section 318(a)(1) shall not apply if. . . ." Further, Sec. 302(c)(2)(C)(i) indicates "Subparagraph (A) shall not apply to a distribution to any entity unless. . . ." Thus, in determining whether a taxpayer will receive capital gain treatment in a stock redemption, a tax advisor must be able to locate and interpret various cross-referenced IRC sections, subsections, paragraphs, subparagraphs, and clauses. ◀

---

[8] S. Rept. No. 105-174, 105th Cong., 1st Sess. (unpaginated) (1998).

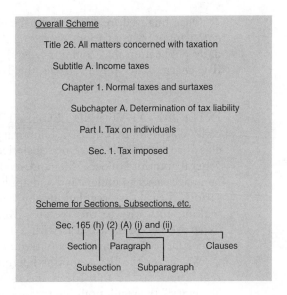

FIGURE I:15-2 ▶ ORGANIZATIONAL SCHEME OF THE INTERNAL REVENUE CODE

TREASURY REGULATIONS

The Treasury Department issues regulations that expound upon the IRC. Treasury Regulations often provide examples with computations that assist the reader in understanding how IRC provisions apply.[9]

Because of frequent IRC changes, the Treasury Department does not always update the regulations in a timely manner. Consequently, when consulting a regulation, a tax advisor should check its introductory or end note to determine when the regulation was adopted. If the regulation was adopted before the most recent revision of the applicable IRC section, the regulation should be treated as authoritative to the extent consistent with the revision. Thus, for example, if a regulation issued before the passage of an IRC amendment specifies a dollar amount, and the amendment changed the dollar amount, the regulation should be regarded as authoritative in all respects except for the dollar amount.

PROPOSED, TEMPORARY, AND FINAL REGULATIONS. A Treasury Regulation is first issued in proposed form to the public, which is given an opportunity to comment on it. Parties most likely to comment are individual tax practitioners and representatives of organizations such as the American Bar Association, the Tax Division of the AICPA, and the American Taxation Association. The comments may suggest that the proposed rules could affect taxpayers more adversely than Congress had anticipated. In drafting a final regulation, the Treasury Department generally considers the comments and may modify the rules accordingly. If the comments are favorable, the Treasury Department usually finalizes the regulation with minor revisions. If the comments are unfavorable, it finalizes the regulation with major revisions or allows the proposed regulation to expire.

Proposed regulations are just that—proposed. Consequently, they carry no more authoritative weight than do the arguments of the IRS in a court brief. Nevertheless, they represent the Treasury Department's official interpretation of the IRC. By contrast, **temporary regulations** are binding on the taxpayer. Effective as of the date of their publication, they often are issued immediately after passage of a major tax act to guide taxpayers and their advisors on procedural or computational matters. Regulations issued as temporary are concurrently issued as proposed. Because their issuance is not preceded by a public comment period, they are regarded as somewhat less authoritative than final regulations.

---

[9] Treasury Regulations are formulated on the basis of Treasury Decisions (T.D.s). The numbers of the Treasury Decisions that form the basis of a Treasury Regulation usually are found in the notes at the end of the regulation.

Once finalized, regulations can be effective as of the date they were proposed or the date temporary regulations preceding them were first published in the *Federal Register*, a daily publication that contains federal government pronouncements. For changes to the IRC enacted after July 29, 1996, the Treasury Department generally cannot issue regulations with retroactive effect.

INTERPRETATIVE AND LEGISLATIVE REGULATIONS. In addition to being officially classified as proposed, temporary, or final, Treasury Regulations are unofficially classified as interpretative or legislative. **Interpretative regulations** are issued under the general authority of Sec. 7805 and, as the name implies, merely make the IRC's statutory language easier to understand and apply. In addition, they often illustrate various computations. **Legislative regulations**, by contrast, arise where Congress delegates its rule-making authority to the Treasury Department. When Congress believes it lacks the expertise necessary to deal with a highly technical matter, it instructs the Treasury Department to set forth substantive tax rules relating to the matter.

Whenever the IRC contains language such as "The Secretary shall prescribe such regulations as he may deem necessary" or "under regulations prescribed by the Secretary," the regulations interpreting the IRC provision are legislative. The consolidated tax return regulations are an example of legislative regulations. In Sec. 1502, Congress delegated to the Treasury Department authority to issue regulations that determine the tax liability of a group of affiliated corporations filing a consolidated tax return. As a precondition to filing such a return, the corporations must consent to follow the consolidated return regulations.[10] Such consent generally precludes the corporations from later arguing in court that the regulatory provisions are invalid.

AUTHORITATIVE WEIGHT. Final regulations are presumed to be valid and have almost the same authoritative weight as the IRC. Despite this presumption, taxpayers occasionally argue that a regulation is invalid and, consequently, should not be followed. A court will not strike down an interpretative regulation unless, in its opinion, the regulation is "unreasonable and plainly inconsistent with the revenue statutes."[11] In other words, a court is unlikely to invalidate a legislative regulation because it recognizes that Congress has delegated to the Treasury Department authority to issue a specific set of rules. Nevertheless, courts have invalidated legislative regulations where, in their opinion, the regulations exceeded the scope of power delegated to the Treasury Department,[12] were contrary to the IRC,[13] or were unreasonable.[14]

In assessing the validity of Treasury Regulations, some courts apply the **legislative reenactment doctrine**. Under this doctrine, a regulation is deemed to receive Congressional approval whenever the IRC provision under which the regulation was issued is reenacted without amendment.[15] Underlying this doctrine is the rationale that, if Congress believed that the regulation offered an erroneous interpretation of the IRC, it would have amended the IRC to conform to its belief. Congress's failure to amend the IRC signifies approval of the regulation.[16] This doctrine is predicated on Congress's constitutional authority to levy taxes. This authority implies that, if Congress is dissatisfied with the manner in which either the executive or the judiciary have interpreted the IRC, it can invalidate these interpretations through new legislation.

KEY POINT

The older a Treasury Regulation becomes, the less likely a court is to invalidate the regulation. The legislative reenactment doctrine holds that if a regulation did not reflect the intent of Congress, lawmakers would have changed the statute in subsequent legislation to obtain their desired objectives.

 STOP & THINK

Question: You are researching the manner in which a deduction is calculated. You consult Treasury Regulations for guidance because the IRC states that the calculation is to be done "in a manner prescribed by the Secretary." After reviewing these authorities, you

---

[10] Sec. 1501.

[11] *CIR v. South Texas Lumber Co.*, 36 AFTR 604, 48-1 USTC ¶5922 (USSC, 1948). In *U.S. v. Douglas B. Cartwright, Executor*, 31 AFTR 2d 73-1461, 73-1 USTC ¶12,926 (USSC, 1973), the Supreme Court concluded that a regulation dealing with the valuation of mutual fund shares for estate and gift tax purposes was invalid.

[12] *McDonald v. CIR*, 56 AFTR 2d 5318, 85-2 USTC ¶9494 (5th Cir., 1985).

[13] *Jeanese, Inc. v. U.S.*, 15 AFTR 2d 429, 65-1 USTC ¶9259 (9th Cir., 1965).

[14] *United States v. Vogel Fertilizer Co.*, 49 AFTR 2d 82-491, 82-1 USTC ¶9134 (USSC, 1982).

[15] *United States v. Homer O. Correll*, 20 AFTR 2d 5845, 68-1 USTC ¶9101 (USSC, 1967).

[16] One can rebut the presumption that Congress approved of the regulation by showing that Congress was unaware of the regulation when it reenacted the statute.

conclude that another way of doing the calculation arguably is correct under an intuitive approach. This approach would result in a lower tax liability for the client. Should you follow the Treasury Regulations or use the intuitive approach and argue that the regulations are invalid?

Solution: Because of the language "in a manner prescribed by the Secretary," the Treasury Regulations dealing with the calculation are legislative. Whenever Congress calls for legislative regulations, it explicitly authorizes the Treasury Department to write the "rules." As a consequence, such regulations are more difficult than interpretative regulations to be overturned by the courts. Thus, unless you intend to challenge the Treasury Regulations and believe you will prevail in court, you should follow them.

ADDITIONAL COMMENT

Citations serve two purposes in tax research: first, they substantiate propositions; second, they enable the reader to locate underlying authority.

CITATIONS. Citations to Treasury Regulations are relatively easy to understand. One or more numbers appear before a decimal place, and several numbers follow the decimal place. The numbers immediately following the decimal place indicate the IRC section being interpreted. The numbers preceding the decimal place indicate the general subject of the regulation. Numbers that often appear before the decimal place and their general subjects are as follows:

Number	General Subject Matter
1	Income tax
20	Estate tax
25	Gift tax
301	Administrative and procedural matters
601	Procedural rules

The number following the IRC section number indicates the numerical sequence of the regulation, such as the fifth regulation. No relationship exists between this number and the subsection of the IRC being interpreted. An example of a citation to a final regulation is as follows:

Reg. Sec. 1.165 – 5

Income tax   IRC section   Fifth regulation

Citations to proposed or temporary regulations follow the same format. They are referenced as Prop. Reg. Sec. or Temp. Reg. Sec. For temporary regulations the numbering system following the IRC section number always begins with the number of the regulation and an upper case T (e.g., -1T).

Section 165 addresses the broad topic of losses and is interpreted by several regulations. According to its caption, the topic of Reg. Sec. 1.165-5 is worthless securities, which also is addressed in subsection (g) of IRC Sec. 165. Parenthetical information following the text of the Treasury Regulation indicates that the regulation was last revised on March 11, 2008, by Treasury Decision (T.D.) 9386. Section 165(g) was last amended in 2000. A researcher must always check when the regulations were last amended and be aware that an IRC change may have occurred after the most recent regulation amendment, potentially making the regulation inapplicable.

When referencing a regulation, the researcher should fine-tune the citation to indicate the precise passage that supports his or her conclusion. An example of such a detailed citation is Reg. Sec. 1.165-5(i), Ex. 2(i), which refers to paragraph (i) of Example 2, found in paragraph (i) of the fifth regulation interpreting Sec. 165.

TYPICAL MISCONCEPTION

Even though revenue rulings do not have the same weight as Treasury Regulations or court cases, one should not underestimate their importance. Because a revenue ruling is the official published position of the IRS, in audits the examining agent will place considerable weight on any applicable revenue rulings.

ADMINISTRATIVE PRONOUNCEMENTS

The IRS interprets the IRC through **administrative pronouncements,** the most important of which are discussed below. After consulting the IRC and Treasury Regulations, tax advisors are likely next to consult these pronouncements.

REVENUE RULINGS.   In **revenue rulings**, the IRS indicates the tax consequences of specific transactions encountered in practice. For example, in a revenue ruling, the IRS might indicate whether the exchange of stock for stock derivatives in a corporate acquisition is tax-free.

The IRS issues more than 50 revenue rulings a year. These rulings do not rank as high in the hierarchy of authorities as do Treasury Regulations or federal court cases. They simply represent the IRS's view of the tax law. Taxpayers who do not follow a revenue ruling will not incur a substantial understatement penalty if they have substantial authority for different treatment.[17] Nonetheless, the IRS presumes that the tax treatment specified in a revenue ruling is correct. Consequently, if an examining agent discovers in an audit that a taxpayer did not adopt the position prescribed in a revenue ruling, the agent will contend that the taxpayer's tax liability should be adjusted to reflect that position.

Soon after it is issued, a revenue ruling appears in the weekly *Internal Revenue Bulletin* (cited as I.R.B.), published by the U.S. Government Printing Office (GPO). Revenue rulings later appear in the *Cumulative Bulletin* (cited as C.B.), a bound volume issued semiannually by the GPO. An example of a citation to a revenue ruling appearing in the *Cumulative Bulletin* is as follows:

> Rev. Rul. 97-4, 1997-1 C.B. 5.

This is the fourth ruling issued in 1997, and it appears on page 5 of Volume 1 of the 1997 *Cumulative Bulletin.* Before the GPO publishes the pertinent volume of the *Cumulative Bulletin,* researchers should use citations to the *Internal Revenue Bulletin.* An example of such a citation follows:

> Rev. Rul. 2009-3, 2009-5 I.R.B. 382.

For revenue rulings (and other IRS pronouncements) issued after 1999, the full four digits of the year of issuance are set forth in the title. For revenue rulings (and other IRS pronouncements) issued before 2000, only the last two digits of the year of issuance are set forth in the title. The above citation represents the third ruling for 2009. This ruling is located on page 382 of the *Internal Revenue Bulletin* for the fifth week of 2009. Once a revenue ruling is published in the *Cumulative Bulletin,* only the citation to the *Cumulative Bulletin* should be used. Thus, a citation to the I.R.B. is temporary.

REVENUE PROCEDURES.   As the name suggests, **revenue procedures** are IRS pronouncements that usually deal with the procedural aspects of tax practice. For example, one revenue procedure deals with the manner in which tip income should be reported. Another revenue procedure describes the requirements for reproducing paper substitutes for informational returns such as Form 1099.

As with revenue rulings, revenue procedures are published first in the *Internal Revenue Bulletin,* then in the *Cumulative Bulletin.* An example of a citation to a revenue procedure appearing in the *Cumulative Bulletin* is as follows:

> Rev. Proc. 97-19, 1997-1 C.B. 644.

This pronouncement is found in Volume 1 of the 1997 *Cumulative Bulletin* on page 644. It is the nineteenth revenue procedure issued in 1997.

In addition to revenue rulings and revenue procedures, the *Cumulative Bulletin* contains IRS notices, as well as the texts of proposed regulations, tax treaties, committee reports, and U.S. Supreme Court decisions.

LETTER RULINGS.   **Letter rulings** are initiated by taxpayers who ask the IRS to explain the tax consequences of a particular transaction.[18] The IRS provides its explanation in the form of a letter ruling, that is, a response personal to the taxpayer requesting an answer.

---

[17] Chapter C:15 discusses the authoritative support taxpayers and tax advisors should have for positions they adopt on a tax return.

[18] Chapter C:15 further discusses letter rulings.

Only the taxpayer to whom the ruling is addressed may rely on it as authority. Nevertheless, letter rulings are relevant for other taxpayers and tax advisors because they offer insight into the IRS's position on the tax treatment of particular transactions.

Originally the public did not have access to letter rulings issued to other taxpayers. As a result of Sec. 6110, enacted in 1976, letter rulings (with confidential information deleted) are accessible to the general public and have been reproduced by major tax services. An example of a citation to a letter ruling appears below:

Ltr. Rul. 200130006 (July 30, 2001).

The first four digits (two if issued before 2000) indicate the year in which the ruling was made public, in this case, 2001.[19] The next two digits denote the week in which the ruling was made public, here the thirtieth. The last three numbers indicate the numerical sequence of the ruling for the week, here the sixth. The date in parentheses denotes the date of the ruling.

OTHER INTERPRETATIONS

<table>
<tr><td>

ADDITIONAL COMMENT

A technical advice memorandum is published as a letter ruling. Whereas a taxpayer-requested letter ruling deals with prospective transactions, a technical advice memorandum deals with past or consummated transactions.

</td><td>

Technical Advice Memoranda. When the IRS audits a taxpayer's return, the IRS agent might ask the IRS national office for advice on a complicated, technical matter. The national office will provide its advice in a **technical advice memorandum**, released to the public in the form of a letter ruling.[20] Researchers can identify which letter rulings are technical advice memoranda by introductory language such as, "In response to a request for technical advice. . . ." An example of a citation to a technical advice memorandum is as follows:

</td></tr>
</table>

T.A.M. 9801001 (January 2, 1998).

This citation refers to the first technical advice memorandum issued in the first week of 1998. The memorandum is dated January 2, 1998.

Information Releases. If the IRS wants to disseminate information to the general public, it will issue an **information release**. Information releases are written in lay terms and are dispatched to thousands of newspapers throughout the country. The IRS, for example, may issue an information release to announce the standard mileage rate for business travel. An example of a citation to an information release is as follows:

I.R. 86-70 (June 12, 1986).

This citation is to the seventieth information release issued in 1986. The release is dated June 12, 1986.

<table>
<tr><td>

ADDITIONAL COMMENT

Announcements are used to summarize new tax legislation or publicize procedural matters. Announcements generally are aimed at tax practitioners and are considered to be "substantial authority" [Rev. Rul. 90-91, 1990-2 C.B. 262].

</td><td>

Announcements and Notices. The IRS also disseminates information to tax practitioners in the form of **announcements** and **notices**. These pronouncements generally are more technical than information releases and frequently address current tax developments. After passage of a major tax act, and before the Treasury Department has had an opportunity to issue proposed or temporary regulations, the IRS may issue an announcement or notice to clarify the legislation. The IRS is bound to follow the announcement or notice just as it is bound to follow a revenue procedure or revenue ruling. Examples of citations to announcements and notices are as follows:

</td></tr>
</table>

Announcement 2007-3, 2007-4 I.R.B. 376.
Notice 2007-9, 2007-5 I.R.B. 401.

The first citation is to the third announcement issued in 2007. It can be found on page 376 of the fourth *Internal Revenue Bulletin* for 2007. The second citation is to the ninth

---

[19] Sometimes a letter ruling is cited as PLR (private letter ruling) instead of Ltr. Rul.

[20] Technical advice memoranda are discussed further in Chapter C:15.

notice issued in 2007. It can be found on page 401 of the fifth *Internal Revenue Bulletin* for 2007. Notices and announcements appear in both the *Internal Revenue Bulletin* and the *Cumulative Bulletin*.

JUDICIAL DECISIONS

Judicial decisions are an important source of tax law. Judges are reputed to be unbiased individuals who decide questions of fact (the existence of a fact or the occurrence of an event) or questions of law (the applicability of a legal principle or the proper interpretation of a legal term or provision). Judges do not always agree on the tax consequences of a particular transaction or event. Therefore, tax advisors often must derive conclusions against a background of conflicting judicial authorities. For example, a U.S. district court might disagree with the Tax Court on the deductibility of an expense. Likewise, one circuit court might disagree with another circuit court on the same issue.

OVERVIEW OF THE COURT SYSTEM.   A taxpayer may begin tax litigation in any of three courts: the U.S. Tax Court, the U.S. Court of Federal Claims (formerly the U.S. Claims Court), or U.S. district courts. Court precedents are important in deciding where to begin such litigation (see page I:15-21 for a discussion of precedent). Also important is when the taxpayer must pay the deficiency the IRS contends is due. A taxpayer who wants to litigate either in a U.S. district court or in the U.S. Court of Federal Claims must first pay the deficiency. The taxpayer then files a claim for refund, which the IRS is likely to deny. Following this denial, the taxpayer must petition the court for a refund. If the court grants the taxpayer's petition, he or she receives a refund of the taxes in question plus accrued interest. If the taxpayer begins litigation in the Tax Court, on the other hand, he or she need not pay the deficiency unless and until the court decides the case against him or her. In that event, the taxpayer also must pay interest and penalties.[21] A taxpayer who believes that a jury would be sympathetic to his or her case should litigate in a U.S. district court, the only forum where a jury trial is possible.

If a party loses at the trial court level, it can appeal the decision to a higher court. Appeals of Tax Court and U.S. district court decisions are made to the court of appeals for the taxpayer's circuit. The appeals court system is comprised of 11 geographical circuits designated by numbers, the District of Columbia Circuit, and the Federal Circuit.[22] Table I:15-1 shows the states that lie in the various circuits. California, for example, lies in the Ninth Circuit. When referring to these appellate courts, instead of saying, for example, "the Court of Appeals for the Ninth Circuit," one generally says "the Ninth Circuit." All decisions of the U.S. Court of Federal Claims are appealable to one court—the Court of Appeals for the Federal Circuit—irrespective of where the taxpayer resides or does business.[23] The only cases the Federal Circuit hears are those that originate in the U.S. Court of Federal Claims.

The party losing at the appellate level can petition the U.S. Supreme Court to review the case under a **writ of certiorari**. If the Supreme Court agrees to hear the case, it grants certiorari.[24] If it refuses to hear the case, it denies certiorari. In recent years, the Court has granted certiorari in only about six to ten tax cases per year. Figure I:15-3 and Table I:15-2 provide an overview and summary of the court system with respect to tax matters.

THE U.S. TAX COURT.   The U.S. Tax Court was created in 1942 as a successor to the Board of Tax Appeals. It is a court of national jurisdiction that hears only tax-related cases. All taxpayers, regardless of their state of residence or place of business, may litigate in the Tax Court. It has 19 judges, including one chief judge.[25] The President, with the consent of the Senate, appoints the judges for a 15-year term and may reappoint them for an additional

---

[21] Revenue Procedure 2005-18, 2005-1 C.B. 638, provides procedures for taxpayers to make remittances or apply overpayments to stop the accrual of interest on deficiencies.

[22] The Federal Circuit has nationwide jurisdiction to hear appeals in specialized cases, such as those involving patent laws.

[23] The Court of Claims was reconstituted as the United States Court of Claims in 1982. In 1992, this court was renamed the U.S. Court of Federal Claims.

[24] The granting of certiorari signifies that the Supreme Court is granting an appellate review. The denial of certiorari does not necessarily mean that the Supreme Court endorses the lower court's decision. It simply means the court has decided not to hear the case.

[25] The Tax Court also periodically appoints, depending on budgetary constraints, a number of trial judges and senior judges who hear cases and render decisions with the same authority as the regular Tax Court judges.

▼ **TABLE I:15-1**
Federal Judicial Circuits

Circuit	States Included in Circuit
First	Maine, Massachusetts, New Hampshire, Rhode Island, Puerto Rico
Second	Connecticut, New York, Vermont
Third	Delaware, New Jersey, Pennsylvania, Virgin Islands
Fourth	Maryland, North Carolina, South Carolina, Virginia, West Virginia
Fifth	Louisiana, Mississippi, Texas
Sixth	Kentucky, Michigan, Ohio, Tennessee
Seventh	Illinois, Indiana, Wisconsin
Eighth	Arkansas, Iowa, Minnesota, Missouri, Nebraska, North Dakota, South Dakota
Ninth	Alaska, Arizona, California, Hawaii, Idaho, Montana, Nevada, Oregon, Washington, Guam, Northern Marina Islands
Tenth	Colorado, Kansas, New Mexico, Oklahoma, Utah, Wyoming
Eleventh	Alabama, Florida, Georgia
D.C.	District of Columbia
Federal	All jurisdictions (for taxpayers appealing from the U.S. Court of Federal Claims)

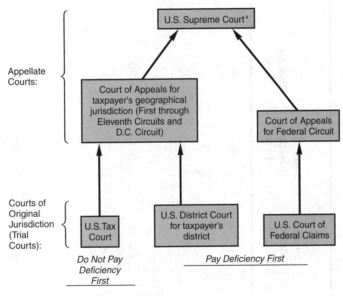

ᵃ Cases are heard only if the Supreme Court grants certiorari.

FIGURE I:15-3 ▶ OVERVIEW OF COURT SYSTEM—TAX MATTERS

term. The judges, specialists in tax-related matters, periodically travel to roughly 100 cities throughout the country to hear cases. In most instances, only one judge hears a case.

The Tax Court issues both regular and memorandum (memo) decisions. Generally, the first time the Tax Court decides a legal issue, its decision appears as a **regular decision. Memo decisions,** on the other hand, usually deal with factual variations of previously decided cases. Nevertheless, regular and memo decisions carry the same authoritative weight.

At times, the chief judge determines that a particular case concerns an important issue that the entire Tax Court should consider. In such a situation, the words *reviewed by the court* appear at the end of the majority opinion. Any concurring or dissenting opinions follow the majority opinion. A judge who issues a concurring opinion agrees with the basic outcome of the majority's decision but not with its rationale. A judge who issues a dissenting opinion believes the majority reached an erroneous conclusion.

▼ TABLE I:15-2
Summary of Court System—Tax Matters

Court(s) (Number of)	Number of Judges on Each	Personal Jurisdiction	Subject Matter Jurisdiction	Determines Questions of Fact	Trial by Jury	Precedents Followed	Where Opinions Published
U.S. district courts (over 95)	1–28*	Local	General	Yes	Yes	Same court Court for circuit where situated U.S. Supreme Court	Federal Supplement American Federal Tax Reports United States Tax Cases
U.S. Tax Court (1)	19	National	Tax	Yes	No	Same court Court for taxpayer's circuit U.S. Supreme Court	Tax Court of the U.S. Reports CCH Tax Court Memorandum Decisions RIA Tax Court Memorandum Decisions
U.S. Court of Federal Claims (1)	16	National	Claims against U.S. Government	Yes	No	Same court Federal Circuit Court U.S. Supreme Court	Federal Reporter (pre-1982) U.S. Court of Federal Claims American Federal Tax Reports United States Tax Cases
U.S. Courts of Appeals (13)	About 20	Regional	General	No	No	Same court U.S. Supreme Court	Federal Reporter American Federal Tax Reports United States Tax Cases
U.S. Supreme Court (1)	9	National	General	No	No	Same court	U.S. Supreme Court Reports Supreme Court Reporter United States Reports, Lawyers' Edition American Federal Tax Reports United States Tax Cases

*Although the number of judges assigned to each court varies, only one judge hears a case.

Another phrase sometimes appearing at the end of a Tax Court opinion is *Entered under Rule 155.* This phrase signifies that the court has reached a decision concerning the tax treatment of an item but has left computation of the deficiency to the two litigating parties.

Small Cases Procedure. Taxpayers have the option of having their cases heard under the **small cases procedure** of the Tax Court if the amount in controversy on an annual basis does not exceed $50,000.[26] This procedure is less formal than the regular Tax Court procedure, and taxpayers can represent themselves without an attorney.[27] The cases are heard by special commissioners instead of by one of the 19 Tax Court judges. A disadvantage of the small cases procedure for the losing party is that the decision cannot be appealed. The opinions of the commissioners generally are not published and have no precedential value.

Acquiescence Policy. The IRS has adopted a policy of announcing whether, in future cases involving similar facts and similar issues, it will follow federal court decisions that are adverse to it. This policy is known as the IRS **acquiescence policy.** If the IRS wants taxpayers to know that it will follow an adverse decision in future cases involving similar facts and issues, it will announce its "acquiescence" in the decision. Conversely, if it wants taxpayers to know that it will not follow the decision in such future cases, it will announce its "nonacquiescence." The IRS does not announce its acquiescence or nonacquiescence in every decision it loses.

The IRS publishes its acquiescences and nonacquiescences as "Actions on Decision" first in the *Internal Revenue Bulletin,* then in the *Cumulative Bulletin.* Before 1991, the IRS acquiesced or nonacquiesced in regular Tax Court decisions only. In 1991, it broadened the scope of its policy to include adverse U.S. Claims Court, U.S. district court, and U.S. circuit court decisions.

In cases involving multiple issues, the IRS may acquiesce in some issues but not others. In decisions supported by extensive reasoning, it may acquiesce in the result but not the rationale (*acq. in result*). Furthermore, it may retroactively revoke an acquiescence or nonacquiescence. The footnotes to the relevant announcement in the *Internal Revenue Bulletin* and *Cumulative Bulletin* indicate the nature and extent of IRS acquiescences and nonacquiescences.

These acquiescences and nonacquiescences have important implications for taxpayers. If a taxpayer bases his or her position on a decision in which the IRS has nonacquiesced, he or she can expect an IRS challenge in the event of an audit. In such circumstances, the taxpayer's only recourse may be litigation. On the other hand, if the taxpayer bases his or her position on a decision in which the IRS has acquiesced, he or she can expect little or no challenge. In either case, the examining agent will be bound by the IRS position.

Published Opinions and Citations. Regular Tax Court decisions are published by the U.S. Government Printing Office in a bound volume known as the *Tax Court of the United States Reports.* Soon after a decision is made public, Research Institute of America (RIA) and CCH Incorporated (CCH) each publish the decision in its respective reporter of Tax Court decisions. An official citation to a Tax Court decision is as follows:[28]

MedChem Products, Inc., 116 T.C. 308 (2001).

The citation indicates that this case appears on page 308 in Volume 116 of *Tax Court of the United States Reports* and that the case was decided in 2001.

---

[26] Sec. 7463. The $50,000 amount includes penalties and additional taxes but excludes interest.

[27] Taxpayers can represent themselves in regular Tax Court proceedings also, even though they are not attorneys. Where taxpayers represent themselves, the words *pro se* appear in the opinion after the taxpayer's name. The Tax Court is the only federal court before which non-attorneys, including CPAs, may practice.

[28] In a citation to a case decided by the Tax Court, only the name of the plaintiff (taxpayer) is listed. The defendant is understood to be the Commissioner of Internal Revenue whose name usually is not shown in the citation. In cases decided by other courts, the name of the plaintiff is listed first and the name of the defendant second. For non-Tax Court cases, the Commissioner of Internal Revenue is referred to as *CIR* in our footnotes and text.

From 1924 to 1942, regular decisions of the Board of Tax Appeals (predecessor of the Tax Court) were published by the U.S. Government Printing Office in the *United States Board of Tax Appeals Reports*. An example of a citation to a Board of Tax Appeals case is as follows:

J.W. Wells Lumber Co. Trust A., 44 B.T.A. 551 (1941).

This case is found in Volume 44 of the *United States Board of Tax Appeals Reports* on page 551. It is a 1941 decision.

ADDITIONAL COMMENT

Once the IRS has acquiesced in a federal court decision, other taxpayers generally will not need to litigate the same issue. However, the IRS can change its mind and revoke a previous acquiescence or nonacquiescence. References to acquiescences or nonacquiescences in federal court decisions can be found in the citators.

If the IRS has acquiesced or nonacquiesced in a federal court decision, the IRS's action should be denoted in the citation. At times, the IRS will not announce its acquiescence or nonacquiescence until several years after the date of the decision. An example of a citation to a decision in which the IRS has acquiesced is as follows:

Security State Bank, 111 T.C. 210 (1998), *acq.* 2001-1 C.B. xix.

The case appears on page 210 of Volume 111 of the *Tax Court of the United States Reports* and the acquiescence is reported on page xix of Volume 1 of the 2001 *Cumulative Bulletin.* In 2001, the IRS acquiesced in this 1998 decision. A citation to a decision in which the IRS has nonacquiesced is as follows:

Estate of Algerine Allen Smith, 108 T.C. 412 (1997), *nonacq.* 2000-1 C.B. xvi.

The case appears on page 412 of Volume 108 of the *Tax Court of the United States Reports.* The nonacquiescence is reported on page xvi of Volume 1 of the 2000 *Cumulative Bulletin.* In 2000, the IRS nonacquiesced in this 1997 decision.

Tax Court memo decisions are not published by the U.S. Government Printing Office. They are, however, published by RIA in *RIA T.C. Memorandum Decisions* and by CCH in *CCH Tax Court Memorandum Decisions.* In addition, shortly after its issuance, an opinion is made available electronically and in loose-leaf form by RIA and CCH in their respective tax services. The following citation is to a Tax Court memo decision:

KEY POINT

To access all Tax Court cases, a tax advisor must refer to two different publications. The regular opinions appear in the *Tax Court of the United States Reports,* published by the U.S. Government Printing Office, and the memo decisions are published by both RIA (formerly PH) and CCH in their own court reporters.

Edith G. McKinney, 1981 PH T.C. Memo ¶81,181, 41 TCM 1272.

McKinney is found at Paragraph 81,181 of Prentice Hall's (now RIA's)[29] 1981 *PH T.C. Memorandum Decisions* reporter, and in Volume 41, page 1272, of CCH's *Tax Court Memorandum Decisions.* The 181 in the PH citation indicates that the case is the Tax Court's 181st memo decision of the year. A more recent citation is formatted in the same way but refers to RIA memo decisions.

Paul F. Belloff, 1992 RIA T.C. Memo ¶92,346, 63 TCM 3150.

U.S. DISTRICT COURTS. Each state has at least one U.S. district court, and more populous states have more than one. Each district court is independent of the others and is thus free to issue its own decisions, subject to the precedential constraints discussed later in this chapter. Different types of cases—not just tax-related—are adjudicated in this forum. A district court is the only forum in which the taxpayer may have a jury decide questions of fact. Depending on the circumstances, a jury trial might be advantageous for the taxpayer.[30]

District court decisions are officially reported in the *Federal Supplement* (cited as F. Supp.) published by West Publishing Co. (West). Some decisions are not officially

---

[29] For several years the Prentice Hall Information Services division published its *Federal Taxes 2nd* tax service and a number of related publications, such as the *PH T.C. Memorandum Decisions.* Changes in ownership occurred, and in late 1991 Thomson Professional Publishing added the former Prentice Hall tax materials to the product line of its RIA tax publishing division. Some

print products such as the *PH T.C. Memorandum Decisions* still have the Prentice Hall name on the spine of older editions.

[30] Taxpayers might prefer to have a jury trial if they believe a jury will be sympathetic to their case.

reported and are referred to as **unreported decisions**. Decisions by U.S. district courts on the topic of taxation also are published by RIA and CCH in secondary reporters that contain only tax-related opinions. RIA's reporter is *American Federal Tax Reports* (cited as AFTR).[31] CCH's reporter is *U.S. Tax Cases* (cited as USTC). A case not offically reported nevertheless might be published in the AFTR and USTC. An example of a complete citation to a U.S. district court decision is as follows:

> *Alfred Abdo, Jr. v. IRS*, 234 F. Supp. 2d 553, 90 AFTR 2d 2002-7484, 2003-1 USTC ¶50,107 (DC North Carolina, 2002).

ADDITIONAL COMMENT

A citation, at a minimum, should contain the following information: (1) the name of the case, (2) the reporter that publishes the case along with both a volume and page (or paragraph) number, (3) the year the case was decided, and (4) the court that decided the case.

In the example above, the **primary citation** is to the *Federal Supplement*. The case appears on page 553 of Volume 234 of the second series of this reporter. **Secondary citations** are to *American Federal Tax Reports* and *U.S. Tax Cases*. The same case is found in Volume 90 of the second series of the AFTR, page 2002-7484 (meaning page 7484 in the volume containing 2002 cases) and in Volume 1 of the 2003 USTC at Paragraph 50,107. The parenthetical information indicates that the case was decided in 2002 by the U.S. District Court for North Carolina. Because some judicial decisions have greater precedential weight than others (e.g., a Supreme Court decision versus a district court decision), information relating to the identity of the adjudicating court is useful in evaluating the authoritative value of the decision.

ADDITIONAL COMMENT

The U.S. Court of Federal Claims adjudicates claims (including suits to recover federal income taxes) against the U.S. Government. This court usually hears cases in Washington, D.C., but will hold sessions in other locations as the court deems necessary.

U.S. COURT OF FEDERAL CLAIMS. The U.S. Court of Federal Claims, another court of first instance that addresses tax matters, has nationwide jurisdiction. Originally, this court was called the U.S. Court of Claims (cited as Ct. Cl.), and its decisions were appealable to the U.S. Supreme Court only. In a reorganization, effective October 1, 1982, the reconstituted court was named the U.S. Claims Court (cited as Cl. Ct.), and its decisions became appealable to the Circuit Court of Appeals for the Federal Circuit. In October 1992, the court's name was again changed to the U.S. Court of Federal Claims (cited as Fed. Cl.).

Beginning in 1982, U.S. Claims Court decisions were reported officially in the *Claims Court Reporter*, published by West from 1982 to 1992.[32] An example of a citation to a U.S. Claims Court decision appears below:

> *Benjamin Raphan v. U.S.*, 3 Cl. Ct. 457, 52 AFTR 2d 83-5987, 83-2 USTC ¶9613 (1983).

The *Raphan* case appears on page 457 of Volume 3 of the *Claims Court Reporter*. Secondary citations are to Volume 52, page 83-5987 of the AFTR, Second Series, and to Volume 2 of the 1983 USTC at Paragraph 9613.

Effective with the 1992 reorganization, decisions of the U.S. Court of Federal Claims are now reported in the *Federal Claims Reporter*. An example of a citation to an opinion published in this reporter is presented below:

> *Jeffrey G. Sharp v. U.S.*, 27 Fed. Cl. 52, 70 AFTR 2d 92-6040, 92-2 USTC ¶50,561 (1992).

The *Sharp* case appears on page 52 of Volume 27 of the *Federal Claims Reporter*, on page 6040 of the 70th volume of the AFTR, Second Series, and at Paragraph 50,561 of Volume 2 of the 1992 USTC reporter. Note that, even though the name of the reporter published by West has changed, the volume numbers continue in sequence as if no name change had occurred.

---

[31] The *American Federal Tax Reports* (AFTR) is published in two series. The first series, which includes opinions issued up to 1957, is cited as AFTR. The second series, which includes opinions issued after 1957, is cited as AFTR 2d. The *Alfred Abdo, Jr.* decision cited as an illustration of a U.S. district court decision appears in the second *American Federal Tax Reports* series.

[32] Before the creation in 1982 of the U.S. Claims Court (and the *Claims Court Reporter*), the opinions of the U.S. Court of Claims were reported in either the *Federal Supplement* (F. Supp.) or the *Federal Reporter, Second Series* (F.2d). The *Federal Supplement* is the primary source of U.S. Court of Claims opinions from 1932 through January 19, 1960. Opinions issued from January 20, 1960, to October 1982 are reported in the *Federal Reporter, Second Series*.

CIRCUIT COURTS OF APPEALS. Lower court decisions are appealable by the losing party to the court of appeals for the circuit in which the litigation originated. Generally, if the case began in the Tax Court or a U.S. district court, the case is appealable to the circuit for the individual's residence as of the appeal date. For a corporation, the case is appealable to the circuit for the corporation's principal place of business. The Federal Circuit hears all appeals of cases originating in the U.S. Court of Federal Claims.

As mentioned earlier, there are 11 geographical circuits designated by numbers, the District of Columbia Circuit, and the Federal Circuit. In October 1981, the Eleventh Circuit was created by moving Alabama, Georgia, and Florida from the Fifth to a new geographical circuit. The Eleventh Circuit has adopted the policy of following as precedent all decisions of the Fifth Circuit during the time the states currently constituting the Eleventh Circuit were part of the Fifth Circuit.[33]

EXAMPLE I:15-7 ▶ In the current year, the Eleventh Circuit first considered an issue in a case involving a Florida taxpayer. In 1980, the Fifth Circuit had ruled on the same issue in a case involving a Louisiana taxpayer. Because Florida was part of the Fifth Circuit in 1980, under the policy adopted by the Eleventh Circuit, it will follow the Fifth Circuit's earlier decision. Had the Fifth Circuit's decision been rendered in 1982—after the creation of the Eleventh Circuit—the Eleventh Circuit would not have been bound by the Fifth Circuit's decision. ◀

As the later discussion of precedent points out, different circuits may reach different conclusions concerning similar facts and issues.

Circuit court decisions—regardless of topic (e.g., civil rights, securities law, and taxation)—are now reported officially in the *Federal Reporter, Third Series* (cited as F.3d), published by West. The third series was created in October 1993 after the volume number for the second series reached 999. The primary citation to a circuit court opinion should be to the *Federal Reporter*. Tax decisions of the circuit courts also appear in the *American Federal Tax Reports* and *U.S. Tax Cases*. Below is an example of a citation to a 1994 circuit court decision:

> *Leonard Greene v. U.S.*, 13 F.3d 577, 73 AFTR 2d 94-746, 94-1 USTC ¶50,022 (2nd Cir., 1994).

The *Greene* case appears on page 577 of Volume 13 of the *Federal Reporter, Third Series*. It also is published in Volume 73, page 94-746 of the AFTR, Second Series, and in Volume 1, Paragraph 50,022, of the 1994 USTC. The parenthetical information indicates that the Second Circuit decided the case in 1994. (A *Federal Reporter, Second Series* reference is found in footnote 33 of this chapter.)

ADDITIONAL COMMENT

A judge is not required to follow judicial precedent beyond his or her jurisdiction. Thus, the Tax Court, the U.S. district courts, and the U.S. Court of Federal Claims are not required to follow the others' decisions, nor is a circuit court required to follow the decision of a different circuit court.

U.S. SUPREME COURT. Whichever party loses at the appellate level can request that the U.S. Supreme Court hear the case. The Supreme Court, however, hears very few tax cases. Unless the circuits are divided on the tax treatment of an item, or the issue is deemed to be of great significance, the Supreme Court probably will not hear the case.[34] Supreme Court decisions are the law of the land and take precedence over all other court decisions, including the Supreme Court's earlier decisions. As a practical matter, a Supreme Court interpretation of the IRC is almost as authoritative as an act of Congress. If Congress does not agree with the Court's interpretation, it can amend the IRC to achieve a different result and has in fact done so on a number of occasions. If the Supreme Court declares a tax statute to be unconstitutional, the statute is invalid.

All Supreme Court decisions, regardless of subject, are published in the *United States Supreme Court Reports* (cited as U.S.) by the U.S. Government Printing Office, the *Supreme Court Reporter* (cited as S. Ct.) by West, and the *United States Reports, Lawyers' Edition* (cited as L. Ed.) by Lawyer's Co-operative Publishing Co. In addition,

---

[33] *Bonner v. City of Prichard*, 661 F.2d 1206 (11th Cir., 1981).
[34] *Vogel Fertilizer Co. v. U.S.*, 49 AFTR 2d 82-491, 82-1 USTC ¶9134 (USSC, 1982), is an example of a case the Supreme Court heard to settle a split in judicial authority. The Fifth Circuit, the Tax Court, and the Court of Claims had reached one conclusion on an issue, while the Second, Fourth, and Eighth Circuits had reached another.

the AFTR and USTC reporters published by RIA and CCH, respectively, contain Supreme Court decisions concerned with taxation. An example of a citation to a Supreme Court opinion appears below:

> *Boeing Company v. U.S.*, 537 U.S. 437, 91 AFTR 2d 2003-1088, 2003-1 USTC ¶50,273 (USSC, 2003).

According to the primary citation, this case appears in Volume 537, page 437, of the *United States Supreme Court Reports*. According to the secondary citation, it also appears in Volume 91, page 2003-1088, of the AFTR, Second Series, and in Volume 1, Paragraph 50,273, of the 2003 USTC.

Table I:15-3 provides a summary of how the IRC, court decisions, revenue rulings, revenue procedures, and other administrative pronouncements should be cited. Primary citations are to the reporters published by West or the U.S. Government Printing Office, and secondary citations are to the AFTR and USTC.

PRECEDENTIAL VALUE OF VARIOUS DECISIONS.

Tax Court. The Tax Court is a court of national jurisdiction. Consequently, it generally rules uniformly for all taxpayers, regardless of their residence or place of business. It follows U.S. Supreme Court decisions and its own earlier decisions. It is not bound by cases decided by the U.S. Court of Federal Claims or a U.S. district court, even if the district court has jurisdiction over the taxpayer.

In 1970, the Tax Court adopted what is known as the *Golsen* Rule.[35] Under this rule, the Tax Court departs from its general policy of adjudicating uniformly for all taxpayers and instead follows the decisions of the court of appeals to which the case in question is appealable. Stated differently, the *Golsen* Rule mandates that the Tax Court rule consistently with decisions of the court for the circuit where the taxpayer resides or does business.

EXAMPLE I:15-8 ▶ In the year in which an issue was first litigated, the Tax Court decided that an expenditure was deductible. The government appealed the decision to the Tenth Circuit Court of Appeals and won a reversal. This is the only appellate decision regarding the issue. If and when the Tax Court addresses this issue again, it will hold, with one exception, that the expenditure is deductible. The exception applies to taxpayers in the Tenth Circuit. Under the *Golsen* Rule, these taxpayers will be denied the deduction. ◀

U.S. District Court. Because each U.S. district court is independent of the other district courts, the decisions of each have precedential value only within its own jurisdiction (i.e., only with respect to subsequent cases brought before that court). District courts must follow decisions of the U.S. Supreme Court, the circuit court to which the case is appealable, and the district court's own earlier decisions regarding similar facts and issues.

EXAMPLE I:15-9 ▶ The U.S. District Court for Rhode Island, the Tax Court, and the Eleventh Circuit have decided cases involving similar facts and issues. Any U.S. district court within the Eleventh Circuit must follow that circuit's decision in future cases involving similar facts and issues. Likewise, the U.S. District Court for Rhode Island must decide such cases consistently with its previous decision. Tax Court decisions are not binding on the district courts. Thus, all district courts other than the one for Rhode Island and those within the Eleventh Circuit are free to decide such cases independently. ◀

U.S. Court of Federal Claims. In adjudicating a case, the U.S. Court of Federal Claims must rule consistently with U.S. Supreme Court decisions, decisions of the Circuit Court of Appeals for the Federal Circuit, and its own earlier decisions, including those rendered when the court had a different name. It need not follow decisions of other circuit courts, the Tax Court, or U.S. district courts.

---

[35] The *Golsen* Rule is based on the decision in *Jack E. Golsen*, 54 T.C. 742 (1970).

▼ TABLE I:15-3
Summary of Tax-related Primary Sources—Statutory and Administrative

Source Name	Publisher	Materials Provided	Citation Example
U.S. Code, Title 26	Government Printing Office	Internal Revenue Code	Sec. 441(b)
Code of Federal Regulations, Title 26	Government Printing Office	Treasury Regulations (final)	Reg. Sec. 1.461-1(c)
		Treasury Regulations (temporary)	Temp. Reg. Sec. 1.62-1T(e)
Internal Revenue Bulletin	Government Printing Office	Treasury Regulations (proposed)	Prop. Reg. Sec. 1.671-1(h)
		Treasury decisions	T.D. 8756 (January 12, 1998)
		Revenue rulings	Rev. Rul. 2009-33, 2009-40 I.R.B. 447
		Revenue procedures	Rev. Proc. 2009-52, 2009-49 I.R.B. 744
		Committee reports	S.Rept. No. 105-33, 105th Cong., 1st Sess., p. 308 (1997)
		Public laws	P.L. 105-34, Sec. 224(a), enacted August 6, 1997
		Announcements	Announcement 2007-3, 2007-4 I.R.B. 376
		Notices	Notice 2009-21, 2009-13 I.R.B. 724
Cumulative Bulletin	Government Printing Office	Treasury Regulations (proposed)	Prop. Reg. Sec. 1.671-1(h)
		Treasury decisions	T.D. 8756 (January 12, 1998)
		Revenue rulings	Rev. Rul. 84-111, 1984-2 C.B. 88
		Revenue procedures	Rev. Proc. 77-28, 1977-2 C.B. 537
		Committee reports	S.Rept. No. 105-33, 105th Cong., 1st Sess., p. 308 (1997)
		Public laws	P.L. 105-34, Sec. 224(a), enacted August 6, 1997
		Announcements	Announcement 2009-8, 2009-8 I.R.B. 598
		Notices	Notice 88-74, 1988-2 C.B. 385

Summary of Tax-related Primary and Secondary Sources—Judicial

Reporter Name	Publisher	Decisions Published	Citation Example
U.S. Supreme Court Reports	Government Printing Office	U.S. Supreme Court	Boeing Company v. U.S., 537 U.S. 437 (2003)
Supreme Court Reports	West Publishing Company	U.S. Supreme Court	Boeing Company v. U.S., 123 S. Ct. 1099 (2003)
Federal Reporter (1st–3rd Series)	West Publishing Company	U.S. Court of Appeal Pre-1982 Court of Claims	Leonard Greene v. U.S., 13 F.3d 577 (2nd Cir., 1994)
Federal Supplement Series	West Publishing Company	U.S. District Court	Alfred Abdo, Jr. v. IRS, 234 F. Supp. 2d 553 (DC North Carolina, 2002)
U.S. Court of Federal Claims	West Publishing Company	Court of Federal Claims	Jeffery G. Sharp v. U.S., 27 Fed. Cl. 52 (1992)
Tax Court of the U.S. Reports	Government Printing Office	U.S. Tax Court regular	Security State Bank, 111 T.C. 210 (1998), acq. 2001-1 C.B. xix
Tax Court Memorandum Decisions	CCH Incorporated	U.S. Tax Court memo	Paul F. Belloff, 63 TCM 3150 (1992)
RIA Tax Court Memorandum Decisions	Research Institute of America	U.S. Tax Court memo	Paul F. Belloff, 1992 RIA T.C. Memo ¶92,346
American Federal Tax Reports	Research Institute of America	Tax: all federal courts except Tax Court	Boeing Company v. U.S., 91 AFTR 2d 2003-1 (USSC, 2003)
U.S. Tax Cases	CCH Incorporated	Tax: all federal courts except Tax Court	Ruddick Corp. v. U.S., 81-1 USTC ¶9343 (Ct. Cls., 1981)

EXAMPLE I:15-10 ▶ Assume the same facts as in Example I:15-9. In a later year, a case involving similar facts and issues is heard by the U.S. Court of Federal Claims. This court is not bound by precedents set by any of the other courts. Thus, it may reach a conclusion independently of the other courts. ◀

Circuit Courts of Appeals. A circuit court is bound by U.S. Supreme Court decisions and its own earlier decisions. If neither the Supreme Court nor the circuit in question has already decided an issue, the circuit court has no precedent that it must follow, regardless of whether other circuits have ruled on the issue. In such circumstances, the circuit court is said to be writing on a clean slate. In rendering a decision, the judges of that court may adopt another circuit's view, which they are likely to regard as relevant.

EXAMPLE I:15-11 ▶ Assume the same facts as in Example I:15-9. Any circuit other than the Eleventh would be writing on a clean slate if it adjudicated a case involving similar facts and issues. After reviewing the Eleventh Circuit's decision, another circuit might find it relevant and rule in the same way. ◀

In such a case of "first impression," when the court has had no precedent on which to base a decision, a tax practitioner might look at past opinions of the court to see which other judicial authority the court has found to be "persuasive."

Forum Shopping. Not surprisingly, courts often disagree on the tax treatment of the same item. This disagreement gives rise to differing precedents within the various jurisdictions (what is called a "split in judicial authority"). Because taxpayers have the flexibility of choosing where to file a lawsuit, these circumstances afford them the opportunity to **forum shop.** Forum shopping involves choosing where among the courts to file a lawsuit based on differing precedents.

An example of a split in judicial authority concerned the issue of when it became too late for the IRS to question the tax treatment of items that "flowed through" an S corporation's return to a shareholder's return. The key question was this: if the time for assessing a deficiency (limitations period) with respect to the corporation's, but not the shareholder's, return had expired, was the IRS precluded from collecting additional taxes from the shareholder? In *Kelley*,[36] the Ninth Circuit Court of Appeals ruled that the IRS would be barred from collecting additional taxes from the shareholder if the limitations period for the *S corporation's* return had expired. In *Bufferd*,[37] *Fehlhaber*,[38] and *Green*,[39] three other circuit courts ruled that the IRS would be barred from collecting additional taxes from the shareholder if the limitations period for the *shareholder's* return had expired. The Supreme Court affirmed the *Bufferd* decision,[40] establishing that the statute of limitations for the shareholder's return governed. This action brought about certainty and uniformity within the judicial system.

Dictum. At times, a court may comment on an issue or a set of facts not central to the case under review. A court's remark not essential to the determination of a disputed issue, and therefore not binding authority, is called *dictum.* An example of dictum is found in *Central Illinois Public Service Co.*[41] In this case, the U.S. Supreme Court addressed whether lunch reimbursements received by employees constitute wages subject to withholding. Justice Blackman remarked in passing that earnings in the form of interest, rents, and dividends are not wages. This remark is dictum because it is not essential to the determination of whether lunch reimbursements are wages subject to withholding. Although not authoritative, dictum may be cited by taxpayers to bolster an argument in favor of a particular tax result.

---

[36] *Daniel M. Kelley v. CIR,* 64 AFTR 2d 89-5025, 89-1 USTC ¶9360 (9th Cir., 1989).

[37] *Sheldon B. Bufferd v. CIR,* 69 AFTR 2d 92-465, 92-1 USTC ¶50,031 (2nd Cir., 1992).

[38] *Robert Fehlhaber v. CIR,* 69 AFTR 2d 92-850, 92-1 USTC ¶50,131 (11th Cir., 1992).

[39] *Charles T. Green v. CIR,* 70 AFTR 2d 92-5077, 92-2 USTC ¶50,340 (5th Cir., 1992).

[40] *Sheldon B. Bufferd v. CIR,* 71 AFTR 2d 93-573, 93-1 USTC ¶50,038 (USSC, 1993).

[41] *Central Illinois Public Service Co. v. CIR,* 41 AFTR 2d 78-718, 78-1 USTC ¶9254 (USSC, 1978).

STOP & THINK

Question: You have been researching whether an amount received by your new client can be excluded from her gross income. The IRS is auditing the client's prior year tax return, which another firm prepared. In a similar case decided a few years ago, the Tax Court allowed an exclusion, but the IRS nonacquiesced in the decision. The case involved a taxpayer in the Fourth Circuit. Your client is a resident of Maine, which is in the First Circuit. Twelve years ago, in a case involving another taxpayer, the federal court for the client's district ruled that this type of receipt is not excludable. No other precedent exists. To sustain an exclusion, must your client litigate? Explain. If your client litigates, in which court of first instance should she begin her litigation?

Solution: Because of its nonacquiescence, the IRS is likely to challenge your client's tax treatment. Thus, she may be compelled to litigate. She would not want to litigate in her U.S. district court because it would be bound by its earlier decision, which is unfavorable to taxpayers generally. A good place to begin would be the Tax Court because it is bound by appellate court, but not district court, decisions and because of its earlier pro-taxpayer position. No one can predict how the U.S. Court of Federal Claims would rule because no precedent that it must follow exists.

ADDITIONAL COMMENT

A tax treaty carries the same authoritative weight as a federal statute (IRC). A tax advisor should be aware of provisions in tax treaties that will affect a taxpayer's worldwide tax liability.

TAX TREATIES

The United States has concluded **tax treaties** with numerous foreign countries. These treaties address the alleviation of double taxation and other matters. A tax advisor exploring the U.S. tax consequences of a U.S. corporation's operations in another country should determine whether a treaty between that country and the United States exists. If one does, the tax advisor should ascertain the applicable provisions of the treaty. (See Chapter I:16 of this text for a more extensive discussion of treaties.)

KEY POINT

Tax articles can be used to help *find* answers to tax questions. Where possible, the underlying statutory, administrative, or judicial sources referenced in the tax article should be cited as authority and not the author of the article. The courts and the IRS will place little, if any, reliance on mere editorial opinion.

TAX PERIODICALS

Tax periodicals assist the researcher in tracing the development of, and analyzing tax law. These periodicals are especially useful when they discuss the legislative history of a recently enacted IRC statute that has little or no administrative or judicial authority on point.

Tax experts write articles on landmark court decisions, proposed regulations, new tax legislation, and other matters. Frequently, those who write articles of a highly technical nature are attorneys, accountants, or professors. Among the periodicals that provide in-depth coverage of tax-related matters are the following:

> *The Journal of Taxation*
> *The Tax Adviser*
> *Practical Tax Strategies*
> *Taxes—The Tax Magazine*
> *Tax Law Review*
> *Tax Notes*
> *Corporate Taxation*
> *Business Entities*
> *Real Estate Taxation*
> *Estate Planning*

The first six journals are generalized; that is, they deal with a variety of topics. As their titles suggest, the next four are specialized; they deal with specific subjects. All these publications (other than *Tax Notes,* which is published weekly) are published either monthly or quarterly. Daily newsletters, such as the *Daily Tax Report,* published by the Bureau of National Affairs (BNA) in print and electronic formats, are used by tax professionals when they need updates more timely than can be provided by monthly or quarterly publications.

Tax periodicals and tax services are secondary authorities. The IRC, Treasury Regulations, IRS pronouncements, and court opinions are primary authorities. In presenting research results, the tax advisor should always cite primary authorities.

TAX SERVICES

OBJECTIVE 4

Consult tax services to research an issue

Various publishers provide multivolume commentaries on the tax law in what are familiarly referred to as **tax services**. Researchers often consult tax services at the beginning of the research process because a tax service helps identify the tax authorities pertaining to a particular tax issue. The actual tax authorities (e.g., IRC, Treasury Regulations, IRS pronouncements, and court cases), and not the tax services, are generally cited as support for a particular tax position. The services are available in print form via the publishers and electronic form via the Internet. (See further discussion at "The Internet as a Research Tool" later in this chapter). Although each major tax service is an outstanding resource, significant differences exist in the content and organizational scheme from one publisher to the next. For example, each service has its own special features and editorial approach to tax issues along with a great deal of proprietary content. The best way to acquaint oneself with the various tax services and the advantages and disadvantages of each is to use them in researching hypothetical or actual problems.

Organizationally, tax services fall into two types: annotated and topical (although this distinction has become somewhat blurred in the Internet version of these services). An **annotated tax service** is organized by IRC section. The IRC-arranged subdivisions of this service are likely to encompass several topics. The annotations accompany editorial commentaries and include digests or summaries of IRS pronouncements and court opinions that interpret a particular IRC section. They are classified by subtopic and cite pertinent primary authorities. A **topical tax service,** on the other hand, is organized by broad topic, including income taxes, estate and gift taxes, and excise taxes. The topically arranged subdivisions of this service are likely to encompass several IRC sections.

Annotated tax services include the *United States Tax Reporter* and the *Standard Federal Income Tax Reporter* services, both of which are organized by IRC section. Many tax advisors find these reporters easy to use because of their extensive indexing system. Topical tax services include RIA's *Federal Tax Coordinator 2d* and BNA's *Tax Management Portfolios*. *Tax Management Portfolios* are popular with many tax advisors because they are very readable yet still provide a comprehensive discussion of a broad range of tax issues. Each portfolio (e.g., Passive Loss Rules, Portfolio 549) covers a particular topic in great detail. However, because the published portfolios do not cover all areas of the tax law, another service may be necessary to supplement the gaps in a portfolio's coverage. Table I:15-4 summarizes the organization and key features of the major tax services.

▼ TABLE I:15-4
Summary of Key Features of Tax Services

Name	Publisher	Organization	Key Features
United States Tax Reporter	Thomson Reuters/RIA	IRC section number	• Editorial commentary • Index and findings list • Annotations
Standard Federal Income Tax Reporter	Wolters Kluwer/CCH	IRC section number	• Editorial commentary • Index and findings list • Annotations
Federal Tax Coordinator 2d	Thomson Reuters/RIA	Tax topic (income tax by topic, estate and gift taxes, excise taxes)	• Commentary organized by topic with references to primary authority and tabbed access to IRC and Treasury Regulations.
Tax Management Portfolios	Bureau of National Affairs (BNA)	U.S. income, foreign income, state tax, estate and gift tax	• Over 400 specialized booklets with extensive commentary by topic, heavily footnoted and referenced to primary authority.

THE INTERNET AS A RESEARCH TOOL

OBJECTIVE 5

Grasp the basics of Internet-based tax research

Internet databases are rapidly replacing print-based services as the principal source of tax related information. These databases encompass not only the IRC, Treasury Regulations, court cases, state laws, and other primary authorities, but also citators and secondary sources such as tax service reporters, treatises, journals, and newsletters. The principal advantages of using Internet-based tax services are ease and speed of access. These services eliminate the need for searching through several volumes of text, the need for consulting numerous cumulative supplements, and the time required to regularly update a print-based library. In addition, Internet based research tools put a vast amount of information in the hands of a tax practitioner without the cost and space requirements of a well equipped print-based tax library.

Because of these advantages, the Internet has become the principal medium for conveying tax related information to professionals. The most widely used Internet-based research services are RIA's Checkpoint™ (hereafter CHECKPOINT), accessible at *http://checkpoint.riag.com*, and CCH IntelliConnect™ (hereafter INTELLICONNECT), accessible at *http://intelliconnect.cch.com*.[42] Westlaw® and LexisNexus® are online legal research services that are predominately used by legal professionals.[43] This chapter limits its discussion to CHECKPOINT and INTELLICONNECT. Both services are updated continuously and store information in databases, called libraries, principal among which are the following:[44]

CHECKPOINT	*INTELLICONNECT*
Newsstand	Tax News, Journals, and Newsletters
Federal	Federal Tax
State and Local	State Tax
International	International Tax
Estate Planning	Financial and Estate Planning
Pension and Benefits	Pension
Payroll	Payroll

Newsstand on CHECKPOINT and *Tax News, Journals, and Newsletters* on INTELLICONNECT provide daily updates on recent tax developments. The *Federal* library on both series contains the text of the IRC, Treasury Regulations, IRS pronouncements, court opinions, and other primary sources. In addition to primary sources, the *Federal* library on CHECKPOINT contains the RIA citator, *Federal Tax Coordinator 2d*, and *United States Tax Reporter* annotations and explanations. The *Federal* library on INTELLICONNECT contains the *Standard Federal Income Tax Reporter* and the *Standard Federal Income Tax Reporter Explanations*. Tax reporters for all 50 states as well as multistate tax guides are found in the *State and Local* library on CHECKPOINT and the *State Tax* library on INTELLICONNECT. International tax treaties are found in the *International* library of both services. CHECKPOINT's *Estate Planning* offers the text of estate tax treaties, newsletters, journals, and Warren, Gorham & Lamont tax treatises. INTELLICONNECT's *Financial and Estate Planning* library supplies the *Federal Estate and Gift Tax Reporter*, as well as the text of estate and gift tax statutes, cases, and rulings. Finally, *Pension and Benefits* on CHECKPOINT and *Pension* on INTELLICONNECT contain the text of the Employee Retirement Income Security Act (ERISA), related Treasury Regulations, and Congressional committee reports, while *Payroll* provides the text of state and federal employment regulations and current withholding tables.

---

[42] Commerce Clearing House (CCH) is a member of the Wolters Kluwer Tax, Accounting and Legal Division. During 2009, CCH completed a major revision to its online research service, transitioning from the former Tax Research Network to IntelliConnect™ (hereafter INTELLICONNET).

[43] The research products discussed in this section (e.g., CHECKPOINT, INTELLICONNECT, Westlaw, and LexisNexus) generally are available only to paid subscribers.

[44] INTELLICONNECT has numerous other databases, including Accounting and Audit, Banking, Corporate Government, Energy & Natural Resources, Health Care Compliance and Reimbursement. These specialty areas generally fall outside the tax arena and therefore are not described in this chapter.

CHECKPOINT and INTELLICONNECT libraries and databases can be searched in four basic ways:

▶ By keyword
▶ By index
▶ By citation
▶ By content

EXAMPLE I:15-12 ▶ Rhonda Researcher's client is a real estate developer and wants to exchange an office building for a residential condominium in the same town. The client wants to know if he can structure the transaction in a tax advantaged way. Rhonda immediately recognizes the situation as a potential like-kind exchange of real property. Therefore, she undertakes a keyword search of INTELLICONNECT using the term *like kind exchange* to quickly uncover potentially applicable documents. She also knows that Sec. 1031 is the relevant IRC section and can search the IRC or Treasury Regulations by citation. On the other hand, if she were unfamiliar with the topic, she could employ several other options. For example, INTELLICONNECT's Federal Tax editorial content has a heading for topic indexes. The "Exchange of property" term in the topical index directs Rhonda to "See Like-kind Exchanges; Sales and Exchanges; and Tax-free Exchanges." The index entries under these headings direct Rhonda to a number of entries potentially applicable to the transaction. Rhonda also conducts a similar research procedure on CHECKPOINT to see whether this alternative service provides any additional information. In particular, she searches in the *Federal Tax Coordinator 2d,* which is RIA's topical service. ◀

KEY WORD SEARCHES

Searching CHECKPOINT and INTELLICONNECT by keyword is relatively simple, particularly if the researcher is familiar with the Internet. The first step is to activate a database or multiple databases and refine the results after the initial query. The researcher can choose to search across any combination of the available databases. The CHECKPOINT Federal databases include primary sources such as the Internal Revenue Code, Treasury Regulations, and Federal Tax Cases along with editorial databases such as RIA's *Federal Tax Coordinator 2d*. Similar choices exist for INTELLICONNECT. Deciding which database to include in the search depends partly on the expected complexity of the research question and on the researcher's familiarity with the topic.

The search engines within the services look for the terms selected and many variations of the terms. For example, the search for *auto* will return documents with auto, car, automobile, motor vehicle, passenger vehicle, sedan, and others.[45] Searches will include both singular and plural variations. Any document with the term or terms is returned and ranked by best match according to the search. If two terms are used, the best matches generally are documents where the terms are close together. Picking key words and search terms is critical to success. The search must be broad enough to include relevant documents but not so broad to include hundreds or thousands of documents unlikely to be on point.

For example, if the researcher selects only the INTELLICONNECT Cases database, the term *property exchange* returns thousands of results that have both the words *property* and *exchange* somewhere in the document. Clearly this outcome is too broad for a researcher just beginning his or her research. Fortunately, several methods of narrowing the search exist. For example, the search for *property exchange* can be limited to all terms, any terms, near phrase, or exact phrase. Specifically, the keyword search "property exchange" that uses quotation marks around the search phrase will return documents only with that exact phrase. Using Boolean connectors is helpful as well. These connectors force the search engine to narrow the search based on the parameters set. Table I:15-5 provides a partial list of connectors available in CHECKPOINT and INTELLICONNECT.

Another way to narrow a search is to focus on terms unique to the research question at hand. The goal is to identify tax related terms likely to appear only in relevant tax

---

[45] Both CHECKPOINT and INTELLICONNECT provide a thesaurus tool, which can identify synonyms and suggest alternative terms related to search terms used by the researcher. The search engine automatically searches for synonyms unless the researcher restricts the search to specific terms using Boolean connectors or quotation marks. For example, a search for the specific phrase "automobile depreciation" will not return documents that refer to *auto, car,* or *vehicle*.

▼ TABLE I:15-5

Connectors Used in INTELLICONNECT and CHECKPOINT

INTELLICONNECT	CHECKPOINT	Description	Examples
and	&, and	Retrieves documents with both terms.	INTELLICONNECT: property and exchange CHECKPOINT: property & exchange
or	|, or	Retrieves documents with either term.	INTELLICONNECT: property or exchange CHECKPOINT: property | exchange
not	^	Retrieves documents with one term but not the other.	INTELLICONNECT: property not exchange CHECKPOINT: property ^ exchange
w/n	/n	Retrieves documents in which the first term is separated from the second term by no more than n number of words.	INTELLICONNECT: property w/5 exchange CHECKPOINT: property /5 exchange Locates property within 5 words of exchange
w/sen	/s	Retrieves documents that contain the first term within 20 words of the second term (or within the same sentence for RIA).	INTELLICONNECT: property w/sen exchange CHECKPOINT: property /s exchange
w/par	/p	Retrieves documents that contain the first term within 80 words of the second term (or within the same paragraph for RIA).	INTELLICONNECT: property w/par exchange CHECKPOINT: property /p exchange
" "	" "	Exact phrase.	INTELLICONNECT and CHECKPOINT: "property exchange"
*	*	Keyword variation.	Depracia* returns depreciation, depreciate, depreciated, depreciating

authorities. For example, stamps are a type of collectible, but the term also will appear in documents discussing taxation of distilled spirits, food stamps, and store stamps and coupons. The researcher should begin the search with limiting terms such as *collectible* rather than the broader term *stamps*. Also, researchers with a good working knowledge of the IRC quickly learn that using IRC sections in search terms is a great way to obtain relevant documents.

Searching using key words is a skill that improves with practice. Researchers becoming familiar with using the databases will learn to craft search terms that include the most relevant elements of the question at hand. Once the researcher finds a document on point, the information within that document often can be used to narrow future searches. The search can be repeated by adding terms, or the documents returned originally can be searched using a new set of terms. However, if searches by key word search do not return the desired results, other options exist.

SEARCH BY INDEX

Both CHECKPOINT and INTELLICONNECT offer traditional indexes. With INTELLICONNECT, the user can click on most databases to see an index of the contents. For example, clicking on the *Standard Federal Income Tax Reporter* Topical Index listed in the Federal Tax Editorial content database reveals a list from A to Z, and the researcher can easily click on a hyperlink for any letter and scroll through the alphabetized topics list. As an example, one can find the letter C, then scroll through the screens and find the topic "casualty losses" that directs the researcher to a variety of subheadings. CHECKPOINT has an Index option under the Search area of the Research tab. In CHECKPOINT, the researcher can choose the *Federal Tax Coordinator 2d* Topic Index database. Again, the

researcher will find the letter C and scroll through the topics to find "casualty losses," which leads the researcher to subheadings with hyperlinks to CHECKPOINT's editorial materials.

In addition, both INTELLICONNECT and CHECKPOINT have topical indexes that use hyperlinks to the Internal Revenue Code. In INTELLICONNECT, the researcher selects the index Internal Revenue Code Topic Index and begins his or her research with an A to Z list. In CHECKPOINT, the researcher selects the Current Code Topic Index.

SEARCH BY CITATION

Often the desired document is a specific IRC section, Treasury Regulation, court case, IRS pronouncement, or other document. If so, both services offer searches by specific citation. Researchers must be careful to use exact citations using this tool because close matches will not return the desired document.

Both CHECKPOINT and INTELLICONNECT citation search tools provide dedicated boxes in which to type the specific type of document requested. For example, to search for IRC Sec. 267, the researcher simply types 267 in the box labeled Current Code in CHECK-POINT or IRC Code & Hist. Sec. in INTELLICONNECT. Specific boxes also exist for various court decisions, revenue rulings, revenue procedures, and other IRS pronouncements.

SEARCH BY CONTENT

Each database also can be searched by content. Clicking on the hyperlink for each database will return a table of contents. Clicking through an entry will take the researcher further into the table of contents. For example, in INTELLICONNECT, several documents discussing adoption credits can be located by clicking on the following series of hyperlinks:

> Federal Tax
> > Federal Tax Editorial Content
> > > Standard Federal Income Tax Reporter
> > > > Credits
> > > > > Adoption expenses – Sec. 23
> > > > > > Credit for adoption expenses –
> > > > > > §23 [¶3700] – Explanations

CHECKPOINT also has a Table of Contents, located in the upper right corner of the primary research screen. Documents discussing adoption credits may be found by clicking on the following series of hyperlinks:

> Federal Library
> > Federal Editorial Materials
> > > Federal Tax Coordinator 2d
> > > > Chapter A Individuals and Self-Employment Tax
> > > > > A-4400 Adoption Expense Credit
> > > > > > A-4401 Allowance of the adoption expense credit

NONCOMMERCIAL INTERNET SERVICES

Many noncommercial institutions, such as governments and universities, allow access to their tax-related databases via the Internet. In "tax-surfing" the Internet, the researcher might first visit the IRS site located at *http://www.irs.gov*. Although oriented to the layman, this site contains a wealth of information useful to the tax professional. Such information includes guidelines for electronic filing, IRS forms and instructions, the full text of Treasury Regulations, and recent issues of the *Internal Revenue Bulletin*. Other useful sites include those maintained by the Library of Congress at *http://thomas.loc.gov* and the Government Printing Office at *http://www.gpoaccess.gov*. From these sites, the researcher can retrieve the text of recent court opinions, tax legislation, committee reports, state and federal tax laws, and much more.

An excellent gateway for starting tax related research is the Tax, Accounting, and Payroll Sites Directory at *http://www.taxsites.com*, maintained by AccountantsWorld,

LLC. This site provides hundreds of hyperlinks to federal, state, and international tax law and tax form databases. Instrumental in financial accounting searches is the Electronic Data Gathering, Analysis, and Retrieval (EDGAR) site at *http://www. sec.gov/edgar.shtml*. EDGAR is a document filing and retrieval service sponsored by the U.S. Securities and Exchange Commission (SEC). It provides access to the full text of documents filed with the SEC by publicly traded companies. These documents include annual financial statements on Form 10-K, quarterly financial statements on Form 10-Q, proxy statements, and prospectuses. The EDGAR database extends from January 1994 to the present and is accessible by company name, central index key, document file number, and keyword.

CITATORS

OBJECTIVE 6

Use a citator to assess tax authorities

Citators serve two functions. First, they trace the judicial history of a particular case (e.g., if the case under analysis is an appeals court decision, the citator indicates the lower court that heard the case and whether the Supreme Court reviewed the case). Second, they list other authorities (e.g., cases and IRS pronouncements) that cite the case or authority in question. These listed authorities are called *citing cases* or *citing rulings*. The judicial history also indicates whether the case is affirmed, reversed or remanded.[46]

Because tax law relies heavily on precedent, the citator provides an index of citing cases and rulings that help the researcher determine the strength of the case or ruling he or she is evaluating. The citator gives full citations for the citing case and lists where the citing cases can be found. It is important to note that the same case may have as many as three decisions (i.e., lower court, court of appeals, and Supreme Court) with each listing having its own list of citing cases. Therefore, if a citing case cites only the Supreme Court decision, the citator will list it only under the Supreme Court cite.

Two principal tax related commercial citators are those in INTELLICONNECT and CHECKPOINT. Both citators allow the researcher to enter case names or case citations. The discussion in this section focuses on the electronic version of the citators, although both CCH and RIA offer print versions as well.

The INTELLICONNECT citator analyzes every decision reported in the *Standard Federal Income Tax Reporter*, the *Excise Tax Reporter*, and the *Federal Estate and Gift Tax Reporter* and selectively lists cases that cite the decision under analysis. INTELLICONNECT lists only the citing cases that its editors believe will influence the precedential weight of the decision under analysis.

The CHECKPOINT citator also provides the history of each authority and lists the cases and pronouncements that have cited the authority. This citator, however, differs from the INTELLICONNECT citator in a couple of important ways. First, CHECKPOINT lists all citing cases, and not just those that the editors believe will serve as relevant precedent. Second, the CHECKPOINT citator provides additional information about the citing case, showing whether the citing authorities comment favorably or unfavorably on the cited case or whether they can be distinguished from the cited case.[47]

In addition to tax cases, the CHECKPOINT and INTELLICONNECT citators evaluate revenue rulings and other IRS pronouncements and lists any status changes. Before relying on a revenue ruling or pronouncement, a researcher must confirm that the pronouncement reflects the current position of the IRS. For example, a revoked ruling is

---

[46] If a case is *affirmed*, the decision of the lower court is upheld. *Reversed* means the higher court invalidated the decision of the lower court because it reached a conclusion different from that derived by the lower court. *Remanded* signifies that the higher court sent the case back to the lower court with instructions to address matters consistent with the higher court's ruling.

[47] When a court distinguishes the facts of one case from those of an earlier case, it suggests that its departure from the earlier decision is justified because the facts of the two cases are different.

▼ TABLE I:15-6
Terms to Describe Status Changes to IRS Rulings

Term	Description of Term
Amplified	No change in the prior published position has occurred, but the prior position is extended to cover a variation of the fact situation previously addressed.
Clarified	Language used in a prior published position is being made clear because the previous language has caused or could cause confusion.
Distinguished	The ruling mentions a prior ruling but points out an essential difference between the two rulings.
Modified	The substance of a previously published ruling is being changed, but the prior ruling remains in effect.
Obsoleted	A previously published ruling is no longer determinative with respect to future transactions, e.g., because laws or regulations have changed, or the substance of the ruling has been adopted into regulations.
Revoked	A previously published ruling has been determined to be incorrect, and the correct position is being stated in the new ruling.
Superseded	The new ruling merely restates the substance of a previously published ruling or series of rulings.
Supplemented	The ruling expands a previous ruling, e.g., by adding items to a list.
Suspended	The previously published ruling will not be applied pending some future action, such as the issuance of new or amended regulations.

Source: www.irs.gov.

one in which the ruling is no longer correct and the correct position is being stated in the new ruling. The IRS does not remove the old ruling from the *Internal Revenue Bulletin* or *Cumulative Bulletin*, but the old ruling does not have authority regarding a transaction occurring after the revocation. Thus, failure to confirm its status could result in an incorrect conclusion. Table I:15-6 provides a list of terms the IRS uses to describe changes in the status of a ruling.

USING THE CITATOR

Internet-based versions of the citators are easier to use than print-based citators. For example, assume the researcher is currently reading *Leonarda C. Diaz v. Commissioner of Internal Revenue*, 70 TC 1067 (1978). Using INTELLICONNECT, the researcher can click on the Citator button in the left column at the top left of the page, and the service opens up a new tab with a summary of activity of the case. The information in bold print with bullets to the left denotes that the *Diaz* case was first decided by the Tax Court (i.e., TC), and then by the Second Circuit Court of Appeals (i.e., CA-2). It shows that the Second Circuit affirmed (upheld) the Tax Court's decision. The three cases underneath the Second Circuit decision cite the *Diaz* decision and might be useful for the researcher to better understand the impact of the case. The seven cases listed beneath the Tax Court decision cite the Tax Court's opinion.

The CHECKPOINT citator is similarly easy to use. Once again, if the researcher is reading the *Diaz* case, he or she simply clicks on the Citator button at the top of the case window. The two main decisions (Tax Court and Second Circuit) appear in a list. Clicking on either case brings up the court decisions that have cited the *Diaz* decision. CHECKPOINT sometimes lists more cases than does INTELLICONNECT. In this example, CHECKPOINT lists ten cases that have cited the *Diaz* Second Circuit decision and 25 cases that have cited the Tax Court decision. CHECKPOINT also adds a brief description of the type of citation— cited favorably, cited unfavorable, case distinguished, or reasoning followed.

PROFESSIONAL GUIDELINES FOR TAX SERVICES

Professional guidelines for tax services are contained in both government-imposed and professional-imposed tax standards. The following sections briefly describe two types of guidelines—Treasury Department *Circular 230* (Rev. 4-2008) and the American Institute of Certified Public Accountants (AICPA) *Statements on Standards for Tax Services (SSTSs)*. A fuller discussion of these standards appears in Chapter C:15.

TREASURY DEPARTMENT *CIRCULAR 230*

Circular 230 sets forth rules to practice before the Internal Revenue Service and pertains to certified public accountants, attorneys, enrolled agents, and other persons representing taxpayers before the IRS. It presents the duties and restrictions relating to such practice and prescribes sanctions and disciplinary proceedings for violating these regulations.

Circular 230 rules, however, are not ethical standards. Instead, the document focuses on the right to represent clients before the IRS. These standards differ from the AICPA's SSTSs in the following ways:

▶ They apply only to federal tax issues and not state authorities.

▶ They generally apply only to federal income tax practice.

▶ They do not provide the depth of guidance found in the SSTSs.

▶ They give the government the authority to impose monetary penalties for violations of the rules.

Circular 230 also provides guidelines for written advice to taxpayers. These guidelines fall into two categories: (1) covered opinions[48] and (2) all other written advice.[49] The rules govern written advice in opinion letters, memoranda, presentations, studies, facsimiles, e-mail, and instant messaging, but they exclude oral advice, tax return preparation, certain post-filing advice, and internal written advice.

Tax advisors are often asked to give their opinion on the tax treatment of a transaction or proposed transaction. The advisor's written conclusions are called "reliance opinions" in *Circular 230* and include any written advice that concludes, at a confidence level of more likely than not, that a tax issue would be resolved in a taxpayer's favor. These opinions might include many routine tax issues encountered in a standard practice. Rather than comply with the detailed due diligence burdens imposed by *Circular 230*, many practitioners now include a standard disclaimer for routine written advice. See the sample client letter in Appendix A for the language of such disclaimers.

AICPA'S STATEMENTS ON TAX STANDARDS

Tax advisors confronted with ethical issues frequently turn to a professional organization for guidance. Although the guidelines set forth by such organizations are not *legally* enforceable, they carry significant moral weight, and may be cited in a negligence lawsuit as the proper "standard of care" for tax practitioners. They also may provide grounds for the termination or suspension of one's professional license. One such set of guidelines is the *Statements on Standards for Tax Services* (SSTSs),[50] issued by the American Institute of Certified Public Accountants (AICPA) and reproduced in Appendix E.

The SSTSs provide an ethical framework to govern the normative relationship between a tax advisor and his or her client, where, unlike an auditor, a tax advisor acts as the client's advocate. Thus, his or her primary duty is to the client, not the IRS. In

---

[48] Covered opinions include tax shelters, reportable transactions, marketed opinions as well as reliance opinions.
[49] *Circular 230* Section 10.35 applies to covered opinions and Section 10.37 applies to all other written advice.

[50] AICPA, *Statements on Standards for Tax Services*, 2009, effective January 1, 2010.

fulfilling this duty, the advisor is bound by the highest standards of care. The most recent version of the SSTSs includes seven standards that provide guidance for AICPA members in their professional tax practice.

SSTS No. 1—Tax Return Positions. Tax professionals often provide tax advice in situations where the authority is unclear or evolving. Frequently this advice involves recommending positions that could be reversed upon audit. This statement describes the minimum level of confidence a CPA must achieve to recommend a tax return position to a taxpayer. Members first must determine and comply with all standards imposed by the various taxing authorities. Regardless of those standards, a member should not recommend a position unless he or she has a good faith belief that the position has a "realistic possibility" of being sustained administratively or judicially on its merits if challenged. Members are not permitted to take the probability of audit into account.

If the position does not meet the realistic probability standard, a member still may recommend a tax return position if he or she concludes that the position has a "reasonable basis" and the position is properly disclosed. When recommending a tax return position and when preparing or signing a return on which a tax return position is taken, a member should, when relevant, advise the taxpayer regarding potential penalty consequences of such tax return position and the opportunity, if any, to avoid such penalties through disclosure.

The standard highlights the dual responsibility of the member. The U.S. tax system can function only when taxpayers file "true, correct, and complete" returns, but taxpayers also have no obligation to pay more in tax than they legally owe. The tax professional's duty is to meet his or her responsibilities to both the tax system and the taxpayer client.

SSTS No. 2—Answers to Questions on Returns. Return preparers often must sign a declaration that the return is "true, correct, and complete." A member should make a reasonable effort to obtain from the taxpayer the information necessary to provide appropriate answers to all questions on a tax return before signing as preparer. However, in certain circumstances, questions or information applicable to the taxpayer may be omitted. Reasonable grounds include the following situations:

▶ The omitted information is not readily available or is immaterial and has little effect on taxable income or loss or the tax liability.

▶ The meaning of the question as it relates to the taxpayer is uncertain.

▶ The requested information is voluminous, in which case the taxpayer can attach a statement indicating that the requested information will be supplied upon request.

SSTS No. 3—Certain Procedural Aspects of Preparing Returns. Tax returns are based on information provided by the client. This statement sets forth the applicable standards for members concerning this information. Specifically, in preparing or signing a return, members are not required to examine or verify a client's supporting data. A member may rely on information supplied by the taxpayer unless the information appears to be incorrect, incomplete, inconsistent, or unreasonable under the circumstances. However, if the applicable law or regulations impose a specific record keeping requirement to claim a deduction, the member should inquire and satisfy himself or herself that the required records do exist.

Members are specifically encouraged to make use of a taxpayer's returns for one or more prior years in preparing the current return, whenever feasible. The practice should help avoid the omission or duplication of items and provide a basis for the treatment of similar or related transactions.

SSTS No. 4—Use of Estimates. For various reasons, precise information about an amount required on a tax return might not be available at the time the tax return is prepared. For

example, the taxpayer might not have a record of small transactions or might be missing certain records. In such cases, a member may advise on estimates used in the preparation of the tax return, but the taxpayer has the responsibility to provide the estimated data. Appraisals and valuations are not considered estimates.

If estimates are used, they generally need not be labeled as estimates, but they should not be presented in a manner that provides a misleading impression about the degree of factual accuracy. However, disclosure that estimates were used should be made in some unusual situations, including:

▶ A taxpayer has died or is ill at the time the return is prepared.

▶ A taxpayer has not received a schedule K-1 at the time the tax return is to be filed.

▶ Litigation is pending that affects the return.

▶ Fire, computer failure, or a natural disaster has destroyed the relevant records.

Notwithstanding this statement, the tax practitioner may not use estimates when such use is implicitly prohibited by the IRC. For example, Sec. 274(d) disallows deductions for certain expenses (e.g., meals and entertainment) unless the taxpayer can substantiate the expenses with adequate records or sufficient corroborating information. The documentation requirement effectively precludes the taxpayer from estimating such expenses and the practitioner from using such estimates.

SSTS No. 5—Departure from a Position Previously Concluded in an Administrative Proceeding or Court Decisions.

Members can take positions that differ from a position determined in an administrative proceeding with respect to the taxpayer's prior return (such as an IRS audit, IRS appeals conference, or a court decision.) Departure might be warranted because of a change in the law or regulations, or favorable court decisions. In any event, if the member can otherwise meet the standards of SSTS No. 1, departure from previous positions is permissible.

SSTS No. 6—Knowledge of Error: Return Preparation and Administrative Proceedings.

For purposes of this standard, the definition of an error has the common meaning, including a mathematical error, but the definition also encompasses any position that does not meet the standards of SSTS No. 1. A position also qualifies as an error if it met the standard when a return was originally filed but no longer does because of a retroactive legislative or legal proceeding. An error for this purpose does not include immaterial items.

A member should inform the taxpayer promptly upon becoming aware of (1) an error in a previously filed return, (2) an error in a return that is the subject of an administrative proceeding (e.g., an IRS audit or appeals conference), or (3) a taxpayer's failure to file a required return. A member should advise the taxpayer of the potential consequences of the error and recommend corrective measures to be taken. This advice can be given orally. The member is not obligated to inform the taxing authority of an error and, in fact, may not do so without the taxpayer's permission except when required by law.

However, if the taxpayer requests that a member prepare the current year's return and the taxpayer has not taken appropriate action to correct an error in a prior year's return, the member should consider whether to withdraw from preparing the return and whether to continue a professional or employment relationship with the taxpayer.

The standard recognizes that conflicts can arise between the member's interests and those of the client. For example, withdrawal from an engagement could have an adverse impact on the taxpayer. In some situations, the member should consult his or her own legal counsel before deciding on recommendations to the taxpayer and whether to continue the engagement. In situations involving potential fraud or criminal charges, the member should advise the client to consult with an attorney before taking any action.

SSTS No. 7—Form and Content of Advice to Taxpayers.

A member should use professional judgment to ensure that tax advice provided to a taxpayer reflects competence and

appropriately serves the taxpayer's needs. The advice can be communicated in writing or orally. When communicating tax advice to a taxpayer in writing, a member should comply with relevant taxing authorities' standards applicable to written tax advice. A member should use professional judgment about any need to document oral advice.

In deciding on the form of advice provided to a taxpayer, a member should consider factors such as:

▶ The importance of the transaction and the amounts involved

▶ The technical complexity involved

▶ The existence of authorities and precedents

▶ The tax sophistication of the taxpayer

▶ The need to seek other professional advice

▶ The potential penalty consequences of a tax return position and whether any penalties can be avoided through disclosure

This statement implies that practitioner-taxpayer dealings should not be casual, nonconsensual, or open ended. Rather, they should be professional, contractual, and definite. Oral advice may be appropriate in routine matters, but written communications are recommended in important, complicated, or significant dollar value transactions.

In addition to these obligations, the tax advisor has a strict duty of confidentiality to the client. Although not encompassed under the SSTSs, this duty is implied in the accountant client privilege. (For a discussion of this privilege, see Chapter C:15.)

STOP & THINK

Question: As described in the Stop & Think box on pages I:15-10 and I:15-11, you are researching the manner in which a deduction is calculated. The IRC states that the calculation is to be made "in a manner prescribed by the Secretary." After studying the IRC, Treasury Regulations, and committee reports, you conclude that another way of doing the calculation is arguably correct under an intuitive approach. This approach would result in a lower tax liability for the client. According to the *Statements on Standards for Tax Services,* may you take a position contrary to final Treasury Regulations based on the argument that the regulations are not valid?

Solution: You should not take a position contrary to the Treasury Regulations unless you have a "good-faith belief that the position has a realistic possibility of being sustained administratively or judicially on its merits." However, you can take a position that does not meet the above standard, provided you adequately disclose the position, and the position has a reasonable basis. Whether or not you have met the standard depends on all the facts and circumstances. Chapter C:15 discusses tax return preparer positions contrary to Treasury Regulations.

WHAT WOULD YOU DO IN THIS SITUATION?

Regal Enterprises and Macon Industries, unaffiliated corporations, have hired you to prepare their respective income tax returns. In preparing Regal's return, you notice that Regal has claimed a depreciation deduction for equipment purchased from Macon on February 22 at a cost of $2 million. In preparing Macon's return, you notice that Macon has reported sales proceeds of $1.5 million from the sale of equipment to Regal on February 22. One of the two figures must be incorrect. How do you proceed to correct it? Hint: See SSTS No. 3 in Appendix E.

SAMPLE WORK PAPERS AND CLIENT LETTER

OBJECTIVE 8

Prepare work papers and communicate to clients

Appendix A presents a set of sample work papers, including a draft of a client letter and a memo to the file. The work papers indicate the issues to be researched, the authorities addressing the issues, and the researcher's conclusions concerning the appropriate tax treatment, with rationale therefor.

The format and other details of work papers differ from firm to firm. The sample in this text offers general guidance concerning the content of work papers. In practice, work papers may include less detail.

PROBLEM MATERIALS

DISCUSSION QUESTIONS

I:15-1 Explain the difference between closed-fact and open-fact situations.

I:15-2 According to the AICPA's *Statements on Standards for Tax Services*, what duties does the tax practitioner owe the client?

I:15-3 Explain what is encompassed by the term *tax law* as used by tax advisors.

I:15-4 The U.S. Government Printing Office publishes both hearings on proposed legislation and committee reports. Distinguish between the two.

I:15-5 Explain how committee reports can be used in tax research. What do they indicate?

I:15-6 A friend notices that you are reading the Internal Revenue Code of 1986. Your friend inquires why you are consulting a 1986 publication, especially when tax laws change so frequently. What is your response?

I:15-7 Does Title 26 contain statutory provisions dealing only with income taxation? Explain.

I:15-8 Refer to IRC Sec. 301.
   a. Which subsection discusses the general rule for the tax treatment of a property distribution?
   b. Where should one look for exceptions to the general rule?
   c. What type of Treasury Regulations would relate to subsection (e)?

I:15-9 Why should tax researchers note the date on which a Treasury Regulation was adopted?

I:15-10 a. Distinguish between proposed, temporary, and final Treasury Regulations.
   b. Distinguish between interpretative and legislative Treasury Regulations.

I:15-11 Which type of regulation is more difficult for a taxpayer to successfully challenge, and why?

I:15-12 Explain the legislative reenactment doctrine.

I:15-13 a. Discuss the authoritative weight of revenue rulings.

   b. As a practical matter, what consequences are likely to ensue if a taxpayer does not follow a revenue ruling and the IRS audits his or her return?

I:15-14 a. In which courts may litigation dealing with tax matters begin?
   b. Discuss the factors that might be considered in deciding where to litigate.
   c. Describe the appeals process in tax litigation.

I:15-15 May a taxpayer appeal a case litigated under the Small Cases Procedure of the Tax Court?

I:15-16 Explain whether the following decisions are of the same precedential value: (1) Tax Court regular decisions, (2) Tax Court memo decisions, (3) decisions under the Small Cases Procedures of the Tax Court.

I:15-17 Does the IRS acquiesce in decisions of U.S. district courts?

I:15-18 The decisions of which courts are reported in the AFTR? In the USTC?

I:15-19 Why do some revenue ruling citations refer to the *Internal Revenue Bulletin* (I.R.B.) and others to a *Cumulative Bulletin* (C.B.)?

I:15-20 Explain the *Golsen* Rule. Give an example of its application.

I:15-21 Assume that the only precedents relating to a particular issue are as follows:

Tax Court—decided for the taxpayer
Eighth Circuit Court of Appeals—decided for the taxpayer (affirming the Tax Court)
U.S. District Court for Eastern Louisiana—decided for the taxpayer
Fifth Circuit Court of Appeals—decided for the government (reversing the U.S. District Court of Eastern Louisiana)

   a. Discuss the precedential value of the foregoing decisions for your client, who is a California resident.

b. If your client, a Texas resident, litigates in the Tax Court, how will the court rule? Explain.

I:15-22 Which official publication(s) contain(s) the following:
   a. Transcripts of Senate floor debates
   b. IRS announcements
   c. Tax Court regular opinions
   d. Treasury decisions
   e. U.S. district court opinions
   f. Technical advice memoranda

I:15-23 Under what circumstances might a tax advisor find the provisions of a tax treaty useful?

I:15-24 What two functions does a citator serve?

I:15-25 Describe two ways that the information available from the CHECKPOINT citator differs from that available from the INTELLICONNECT citator.

I:15-26 List four methods of searching the CHECKPOINT and INTELLICONNECT databases.

I:15-27 Access INTELLICONNECT at *http://intelliconnect.cch.com* and RIA CHECKPOINT™ at *http://checkpoint.riag.com*. Then answer the following questions:
   a. What are the principal primary sources found in both Internet tax services?
   b. What are the principal secondary sources found in each Internet tax service?

I:15-28 Compare the features of the computerized tax services with those of Internet sites maintained by noncommercial institutions. What are the relative advantages and disadvantages of each? Could the latter sites serve as a substitute for a commercial tax service?

I:15-29 According to the *Statements on Standards for Tax Services,* what belief should a CPA have before taking a pro-taxpayer position on a tax return?

I:15-30 List an advisor's duties that are excluded under the AICPA's *Statements on Standards for Tax Services.*

I:15-31 List the two classifications of written advice under Treasury Department *Circular 230.*

I:15-32 Explain how Treasury Department *Circular 230* differs from the AICPA's *Statements on Standards for Tax Services.*

PROBLEMS

I:15-33 *Interpreting the IRC.* Under a divorce agreement executed in the current year, an ex-wife receives from her former husband cash of $25,000 per year for eight years. The agreement does not explicitly state that the payments are excludable from gross income.
   a. Does the ex-wife have gross income? If so, how much?
   b. Is the former husband entitled to a deduction? If so, is it for or from AGI?
   Refer only to the IRC in answering this question. Start with Sec. 71.

I:15-34 *Interpreting the IRC.* Refer to Sec. 385 and answer the questions below.
   a. Whenever Treasury Regulations are issued under this section, what type are they likely to be: legislative or interpretative? Explain.
   b. Assume Treasury Regulations under Sec. 385 have been finalized. Will they be relevant to estate tax matters? Explain.

I:15-35 *Using IRS Rulings.* Locate PLR 8733007 and Rev. Rul. 81-219.
   a. Briefly summarize the tax issue and conclusion of each ruling.
   b. Under what circumstances can a researcher rely on the private letter ruling?
   c. Under what circumstances can a researcher rely on the revenue ruling?

I:15-36 *Using Treasury pronouncements.* Which IRC section(s) does Rev. Rul. 2001-29 interpret? (Hint: consult the official pronouncement of the IRS.)

I:15-37 *Using CHECKPOINT for a Keyword Search.* The objective is to locate a general overview of available home office deductions. On the main research tab, select the *United States Tax Reporter—Explanations (RIA)* library. How many results does CHECKPOINT return for each search term?
   a. Search term: home office deduction.
   b. Search term: "home office" deduction.
   c. Search term: "home office" /5 deduction.
   d. Perform the search in Part a above. Select *Sort by Relevance.* How does this sort change the results? Does the sort make it easier to locate relevant documents?

I:15-38 *Using INTELLICONNECT for a Keyword Search.* The search objective is to determine the amount generally excludable on the sale of a married couple's home. Using Browse, locate the *Standard Federal Income Tax Reporter—Explanations* library. How many results does INTELLICONNECT return for each search term?
   a. Search term: home sale gain exclusion.
   b. Search term: "home sale" gain exclusion.

      c. Does limiting the results to only those documents containing the specific term "home sale" improve your results?

      d. How do most tax documents refer to a person's home?

I:15-39 *Determining Acquiescence.*

      a. What official action (acquiescence or nonacquiescence) did the IRS Commissioner take regarding the 1986 Tax Court decision in *John McIntosh*? (Hint: Consult Actions on Decisions.)

      b. Did this action concern *all* issues in the case? If not, explain. (Before answering this question, consult the headnote to the court opinion.)

I:15-40 *Determining Acquiescence.*

      a. What original action (acquiescence or nonacquiescence) did the IRS Commissioner take regarding the 1952 Tax Court decision in *Streckfus Steamers, Inc.*? (Hint: Consult Actions on Decisions.)

      b. Was the action complete or partial?

      c. Did the IRS Commissioner subsequently change his mind? If so, when?

I:15-41 *Determining Acquiescence.*

      a. What original action (acquiescence or nonacquiescence) did the IRS Commissioner take regarding the 1956 Tax Court decision in *Pittsburgh Milk Co.*? (Hint: Consult Actions on Decisions.)

      b. Did the IRS Commissioner subsequently change his mind? If so, when?

I:15-42 *Evaluating a Case.* Look up *James E. Threlkeld,* 87 T.C. 1294 (1988) and answer the questions below.

      a. Was the case reviewed by the court? If so, was the decision unanimous? Explain.

      b. Was the decision entered under Rule 155?

      c. Consult a citator. Was the case reviewed by an appellate court? If so, which one?

I:15-43 *Evaluating a Case.* Look up *Bush Brothers & Co.,* 73 T.C. 424 (1979) and answer the questions below.

      a. Was the case reviewed by the court? If so, was the decision unanimous? Explain.

      b. Was the decision entered under Rule 155?

      c. Consult a citator. Was the case reviewed by an appellate court? If so, which one?

I:15-44 *Writing Citations.* Provide the proper citations (including both primary and secondary citations where applicable) for the authorities listed below. (For secondary citations, reference both the AFTR and USTC.)

      a. *National Cash Register Co.,* a 6th Circuit Court decision

      b. *Thomas M. Dragoun v. CIR,* a Tax Court memo decision

      c. *John M. Grabinski v. U.S.,* a U.S. district court decision

      d. *John M. Grabinski v. U.S.,* an Eighth Circuit Court decision

      e. *Rebekah Harkness,* a 1972 Court of Claims decision

      f. *Hillsboro National Bank v. CIR,* a Supreme Court decision

      g. Rev. Rul. 78-129

I:15-45 *Writing Citations.* Provide the proper citations (including both primary and secondary citations where applicable) for the authorities listed below. (For secondary citations, reference both the AFTR and USTC.)

      a. Rev. Rul. 99-7

      b. *Frank H. Sullivan,* a Board of Tax Appeals decision

      c. *Tate & Lyle, Inc.,* a 1994 Tax Court decision

      d. *Ralph L. Rogers v. U.S.,* a U.S. district court decision

      e. *Norman Rodman v. CIR,* a Second Circuit Court decision

I:15-46 *Interpreting Citations.* Indicate which courts decided the cases cited below. Also indicate on which pages and in which publications the authority is reported.

      a. *Lloyd M. Shumaker v. CIR,* 648 F.2d 1198, 48 AFTR 2d 81-5353 (9th Cir., 1981)

      b. *Xerox Corp. v. U.S.,* 14 Cl. Ct. 455, 88-1 USTC ¶9231 (1988)

      c. *Real Estate Land Title & Trust Co. v. U.S.,* 309 U.S. 13, 23 AFTR 816 (USSC, 1940)

      d. *J. B. Morris v. U.S.,* 441 F. Supp. 76, 41 AFTR 2d 78-335 (DC TX, 1977)

      e. Rev. Rul. 83-3, 1983-1 C.B. 72

      f. *Malone & Hyde, Inc. v. U.S.,* 568 F.2d 474, 78-1 USTC ¶9199 (6th Cir., 1978)

I:15-47 *Using a Tax Service.* Use the topical index of the *United States Tax Reporter* to locate authorities dealing with the deductibility of the cost of a facelift.

      a. In which paragraph(s) does the *United States Tax Reporter* summarize and cite these authorities?

      b. List the authorities.

      c. May a taxpayer deduct the cost of a facelift paid in the current year? Explain.

I:15-48   *Using a Tax Service.* Locate Reg. Sec. 1.302-1 using either CHECKPOINT or INTELLI-CONNECT. Does this Treasury Regulation reflect recent amendments to the IRC? Explain.

I:15-49   *Using a Tax Service.* Using the topical index of the *Standard Federal Income Tax Reporter* in INTELLICONNECT, locate authorities addressing whether termite damage constitutes a casualty loss.
a. In which paragraph(s) does the *Standard Federal Income Tax Reporter* summarize and cite these authorities?
b. List the authorities.

I:15-50   *Using a Tax Service.*
a. Using the *Standard Federal Income Tax Reporter* in INTELLICONNECT, locate where Sec. 303(b)(2)(A) appears. This provision states that Sec. 303(a) applies only if the stock in question meets a certain percentage test. What is the applicable percentage?
b. Locate Reg. Sec. 1.303-2(a) in the same service. Does this Treasury Regulation reflect recent amendments to the IRC with respect to the percentage test addressed in Part a? Explain.

I:15-51   *Using a Tax Service.* Using the BNA tax service, identify the number of the BNA portfolio for the following subjects.
a. Innocent spouse relief.
b. Accounting methods.
c. Involuntary conversions.
d. IRAs.
e. Deductibility of legal and accounting fees, bribes, and illegal payments.

I:15-52   *Using a Tax Service.* This problem deals with CHECKPOINT's *Federal Tax Coordinator 2d*. Use the topical index CHECKPOINT to locate authorities dealing with the deductibility of the cost of work clothing by ministers (clergymen). List the authorities.

I:15-53   *Using a Citator.* Trace *Biltmore Homes, Inc.,* a 1960 Tax Court memo decision, in both the INTELLICONNECT and CHECKPOINT citators.
a. According to the CHECKPOINT citator, how many times has the Tax Court decision been cited by other courts on Headnote Number 5?
b. How many issues did the lower court address in its opinion? (Hint: Refer to the case headnote numbers.)
c. Did an appellate court review the case? If so, which one?
d. According to the INTELLICONNECT citator, how many times has the Tax Court decision been cited by other courts?
e. According to the INTELLICONNECT citator, how many times has the circuit court decision been cited by other courts on Headnote Number 5?

I:15-54   *Using a Citator.* Trace *Stephen Bolaris,* 776 F.2d 1428, in both the INTELLICONNECT and CHECKPOINT citators.
a. According to the CHECKPOINT citator, how many times has the Ninth Circuit's decision been cited?
b. Did the decision address more than one issue? Explain.
c. Was the decision ever cited unfavorably? Explain.
d. According to the INTELLICONNECT citator, how many times has the Ninth Circuit's decision been cited?
e. According to the INTELLICONNECT citator, how many times has the Tax Court's decision been cited on Headnote Number 1?

I:15-55   *Interpreting a Case.* Refer to the *Holden Fuel Oil Company* case (31 TCM 184).
a. In which year was the case decided?
b. What controversy was litigated?
c. Who won the case?
d. Was the decision reviewed at the lower court level?
e. Was the decision appealed?
f. Has the decision been cited in other cases?

I:15-56   *Internet Research.* Access the IRS Internet site at *http://www.irs.gov* and answer the following questions:
a. How does one file a tax return electronically?
b. How can the taxpayer transmit funds electronically?
c. What are the advantages of electronic filing?

I:15-57 *Internet Research.* Access the IRS Internet site at *http://www.irs.gov* and indicate the titles of the following IRS forms:
  a. Form 4506
  b. Form 973
  c. Form 8725

I:15-58 *Internet Research.* Access the Federation of Tax Administrators Internet site at *http://www.taxadmin.org/fta/link/forms.html* and indicate the titles of the following state tax forms and publications:
  a. Minnesota Form M-100
  b. Illinois Individual Schedule CR
  c. New York State Corporate Form CT-3-C

I:15-59 *Internet Research.* Access the Urban Institute and Brookings Institution Tax Policy Center at *http://taxpolicycenter.org*. On the home page, search for *state individual income tax rates* and locate the Tax Policy Center's latest summary of each state's rates. Researchers also can locate the file by looking under the *State* tab, *Main Features of State Tax Systems*.
  a. How many states do not have a state individual income tax?
  b. How many states tax only interest and dividends for individuals?
  c. What is the top marginal individual income tax rate in Oregon?
  d. Of those that do impose an income tax, which state's top marginal rate is lowest?

COMPREHENSIVE PROBLEM

I:15-60 Your client, a physician, recently purchased a yacht on which he flies a pennant with a medical emblem on it. He recently informed you that he purchased the yacht and flies the pennant to advertise his occupation and thus attract new patients. He has asked you if he may deduct as ordinary and necessary business expenses the costs of insuring and maintaining the yacht. In search of an answer, consult either INTELLICONNECT's *Standard Federal Income Tax Reporter* or CHECKPOINT's *United States Tax Reporter*. Explain the steps taken to find your answer.

TAX STRATEGY PROBLEM

I:15-61 Your client, Home Products Universal (HPU), distributes home improvement products to independent retailers throughout the country. Its management wants to explore the possibility of opening its own home improvement centers. Accordingly, it commissions a consulting firm to conduct a feasibility study, which ultimately persuades HPU to expand into retail sales. The consulting firm bills HPU $150,000, which HPU deducts on its current year tax return. The IRS disputes the deduction, contending that, because the cost relates to entering a new business, it should be capitalized. HPU's management, on the other hand, firmly believes that, because the cost relates to expanding HPU's existing business, it should be deducted. In contemplating legal action against the IRS, HPU's management considers the state of judicial precedent: The federal court for HPU's district has ruled that the cost of expanding from distribution into retail sales should be capitalized. The appellate court for HPU's circuit has stated in *dictum* that, although in some circumstances switching from product distribution to product sales entails entering a new trade or business, improving customer access to one's existing products generally does not. The Federal Circuit Court has ruled that wholesale distribution and retail sales, even of the same product, constitute distinct businesses. In a case involving a taxpayer from another circuit, the Tax Court has ruled that such costs invariably should be capitalized. HPU's Chief Financial Officer approaches you with the question, "In which judicial forum should HPU file a lawsuit against the IRS: (1) U.S. district court, (2) the Tax Court, or (3) the U.S. Court of Federal Claims?" What do you tell her?

CASE STUDY PROBLEM

I:15-62 A client, Mal Manley, fills out his client questionnaire for the previous year and on it provides information for the preparation of his individual income tax return. The IRS has never audited Mal's returns. Mal reports that he made over 100 relatively small cash contributions totaling $24,785 to charitable organizations. In the last few years, Mal's charitable contributions have averaged about $15,000 per year. For the previous

year, Mal's adjusted gross income was roughly $350,000, about a 10% increase from the year before.

Required: Applying *Statements on Standards for Tax Services* No. 3, determine whether you can accept at face value Mal's information concerning his charitable contributions. Now assume that the IRS recently audited Mal's tax return for two years ago and denied 75% of that year's charitable contribution deduction because the deduction was not substantiated. Assume also that Mal indicates that, in the previous year, he contributed $25,000 (instead of $24,785). How do these changes of fact affect your earlier decision?

TAX RESEARCH PROBLEMS

I:15-63 The purpose of this problem is to enhance your skills in interpreting the authorities that you locate in your research. In answering the questions that follow, refer only to *Thomas A. Curtis, M.D., Inc.,* 1994 RIA TC Memo ¶94,015.

a. What was the principal controversy litigated in this case?
b. Which party—the taxpayer or the IRS—won?
c. Why is the corporation instead of Dr. and/or Ms. Curtis listed as the plaintiff?
d. What is the relationship between Ellen Barnert Curtis and Dr. Thomas A. Curtis?
e. Approximately how many hours a week did Ms. Curtis work, and what were her credentials?
f. For the fiscal year ending in 1989, what salary did the corporation pay Ms. Curtis? What amount did the court decide was reasonable?
g. What dividends did the corporation pay for its fiscal years ending in 1988 and 1989?
h. To which circuit would this decision be appealable?
i. According to *Curtis,* what five factors did the Ninth Circuit mention in *Elliotts, Inc.* as relevant in determining reasonable compensation?

I:15-64 Josh contributes $5,000 toward the support of his widowed mother, aged 69, a U.S. citizen and resident. She earns gross income of $2,000 and spends it all for her own support. In addition, Medicare pays $3,200 of her medical expenses. She does not receive financial support from sources other than those described above. Must the Medicare payments be included in the support that Josh's mother is deemed to provide for herself?

Prepare work papers and a client letter (to Josh) dealing with the issue.

I:15-65 Amy owns a vacation cottage in Maine. She predicts that the time during which the cottage will be used in the current year is as follows:

By Amy, solely for vacation	12 days
By Amy, making repairs ten hours per day and vacationing the rest of the day	2 days
By her sister, who paid fair rental value	8 days
By her cousin, who paid fair rental value	4 days
By her friend, who paid a token amount of rent	2 days
By three families from the Northeast, who paid fair rental value for 40 days each	120 days
Not used	217 days

Calculate the ratio for allocating the following expenses to the rental income expected to be received from the cottage: interest, taxes, repairs, insurance, and depreciation. The ratio will be used to determine the amount of expenses that are deductible and, thus, Amy's taxable income for the year.

For the tax manager to whom you report, prepare work papers in which you discuss the calculation method. Also, draft a memo to the file dealing with the results of your research.

I:15-66 Look up *Summit Publishing Company,* 1990 PH T.C. Memo ¶90,288, 59 TCM 833, and *J.B.S. Enterprises,* 1991 PH T.C. Memo ¶91,254, 61 TCM 2829, and answer the following questions:

a. What was the principal issue in these cases?
b. What factors did the Tax Court consider in resolving the central issue?
c. How are the facts of these cases similar? How are they dissimilar?

I:15-67 Your supervisor would like to set up a single Sec. 401(k) plan exclusively for the managers of your organization. Concerned that this arrangement might not meet the requirements

for a qualified plan, he has asked you to request a determination letter from the IRS. In a brief memorandum, address the following issues:

a. What IRS pronouncements govern requests for determination letters?
b. What IRS forms must be filed with the request?
c. What information must be provided in the request?
d. What actions must accompany the filing?
e. Where must the request be filed?

16

CHAPTER

CORPORATIONS

LEARNING OBJECTIVES

After studying this chapter, you should be able to

1 ▶ Identify the types of entities that can be classified as a corporation for federal income tax purposes

2 ▶ Calculate the corporate income tax liability

3 ▶ Apply the nonrecognition of gain or loss rules for corporate capitalizations

4 ▶ Understand the significance of earnings and profits

5 ▶ Determine the tax consequences of nonmoney distributions and stock redemptions

6 ▶ Understand the tax implications of a corporate liquidation for the liquidating corporation and its shareholders

ADDITIONAL COMMENT

In 1987, total income tax collections were $568.3 billion. The corporate income tax produced $102.9 billion of federal income tax revenues. Corporate income taxes were 18.1% of federal income tax revenues. Individual income tax revenues were the remaining 81.9% of federal income tax revenues. By 2005, total income tax collections were $1,181.3 billion. Corporate income taxes decreased to 13.5% of federal income tax revenues. Noncorporate (individual, trust, estate, etc.) income taxes increased to 86% of federal income tax revenues.

A business may be organized and operated as a **sole proprietorship, C corporation, S corporation, partnership, limited liability company (LLC),** or **limited liability partnership (LLP)**. These business forms fall into two major categories: taxable entities and flow-through entities. The latter category also is referred to as tax conduits or pass-through entities. Sole proprietorships and C corporations fall into the taxable entity category although sole proprietorships are subject to a single level of tax, while C corporations are subject to two levels of tax. A sole proprietorship is not taxed directly because it is not considered to be a separate legal entity. Rather, the individual owner is taxed directly and reports the sole proprietorship's business income and expenses on Schedule C of Form 1040 (U.S. Individual Income Tax Return). The C corporation also is taxed directly and reports its tax results on Form 1120 (U.S. Corporation Income Tax Return). In addition, the corporation's shareholders are taxed if the C corporation pays dividends to them or if the shareholders sell their stock at a gain.[1] In this way, the C corporation organizational form results in two levels of taxation: once at the corporate level when income is earned and again at the shareholder level when income is distributed.

Despite its double taxation and sometimes complicated legal form, the corporation has the dual advantages of facilitating external financing and limiting the shareholders' legal liability. Some tax analysts question whether the burden of corporate taxation is borne directly by the corporate enterprise. These analysts argue that, depending on market conditions and terms of trade, the corporate enterprise might be able to shift the burden to consumers in the form of higher prices, employees in the form of lower salaries and wages, tenants in the form of higher rents, and shareholders in the form of lower dividends and stock values.

Flow-through entities, such as S corporations, partnerships, and limited liability companies, entail only one level of taxation at the ownership level. Accordingly, the entities themselves are not taxed, and the income and losses pass through to the shareholders of the S corporation, the partners of the partnership, or the members of the limited liability company. The owners then report the pass-through items on their separate tax returns and may offset a pro rata share of entity losses against their separate income. Some of these entities, such as S corporations and limited liability companies, offer federal advantage of limiting all of their owners' legal liability. Such a feature is advantageous, especially where the business incurs extraordinary liability. Nevertheless, flow-through entities involve certain legal complexities and restrictions, which is one disadvantage of this form of organization. A comparison of the number of tax returns filed and taxable income for the four major business forms for tax year 2008 can be found in Table I:16-1.

This chapter explores the tax consequences of forming, operating, and liquidating a C corporation. Chapter I:17 discusses the basic tax rules pertaining to flow-through entities, and Table I:17-2 at the end of that chapter compares the alternative forms of business organizations. Detailed coverage of these two areas of taxation are reserved for this text's companion volume titled *Prentice Hall's Federal Taxation: Corporations, Partnerships, Estates, and Trusts.*

DEFINITION OF A CORPORATION

Identify the types of entities that can be classified as a corporation for federal income tax purposes

Under Treasury Regulations,[2] a business entity with two or more owners may be classified as either a corporation or a partnership. An entity having only one owner may be classified as a corporation or a sole proprietorship. A business entity is a corporation if it is organized under a federal or state statute that refers to the entity as incorporated or as a corporation, body corporate, body politic, joint-stock company, or joint-stock association. Corporations also include insurance companies, state-chartered banks, and business entities wholly owned by a state or political subdivision. In general, with rare exceptions if a business entity incorporates, it is taxed as a corporation.

---

[1] A corporate liquidation is treated as a sale in which a shareholder receives cash and/or other assets from the liquidating corporation in exchange for his or her stock. The shareholder's recognized gain or loss upon a liquidating distribution generally is capital in character (IRC Sec. 331(a)). This topic is explored in greater detail in a later section of this chapter.

[2] Reg. Secs. 301.7701-1, -2, and -3.

▼ Table I:16-1
Comparison—Types of Returns

Taxpayer Class	Number of Returns Filed			
	2008	2007	2006	2005
Individuals	197.409 million	183.091 million	177.404 million	177.494 million
Partnerships	3.307 million	3.097 million	2.773 million	2.665 million
S corporations	4.440 million	4.099 million	3.825 million	3.634 million
C corporations[a, b]	2.538 million	2.508 million	2.454 million	2.494 million
Estates and Trusts	3.075 million	3.718 million	3.697 million	3.684 million

IRS, *Data Book*, 2008.
[a]The number shown includes returns for various types of domestic and foreign corporations and associations.
[b]Tax-exempt organizations filed 815,000 Form 990 series returns in 2005, 833,000 in 2006, 901,000 in 2007, and 901,000 in 2008.

On the other hand, if the business entity has two or more owners and is organized as a partnership, limited liability company, or limited liability partnership, the entity can elect to be *taxed* as either a partnership or corporation. The "check-the-box" regulations replace prior entity classification rules that involved subjective judgment and opened the door to manipulation.

EXAMPLE I:16-1 ▶ Al and Jane incorporate a business in Delaware. Because it is legally incorporated, the business is taxed as a corporation. Bill and Max form a limited liability company in Florida. For federal income tax purposes, the limited liability company can elect to be taxed as a corporation or a partnership. ◀

SIMILARITIES AND DIFFERENCES BETWEEN THE TAXATION OF CORPORATIONS AND INDIVIDUALS

SIMILARITIES

The computation of corporate taxable income is similar to that of sole proprietorship income. For example, under Sec. 162 corporations can deduct ordinary and necessary business expenses. They also may exclude from gross income items such as tax-exempt interest and life insurance proceeds. Corporations also can deduct interest, depreciation, and other business-related expenses in a manner similar to that of unincorporated businesses.

In general, the IRC authorizes all taxpayers to use one of three methods of accounting—the accrual method, the cash method, and the hybrid method.[3] However, with certain exceptions C corporations generally must use the accrual method of accounting unless they meet certain conditions. Sec. 448 permits corporations engaged in a farming business, qualified personal service corporations, and entities having less than $5 million in gross receipts for each of the three prior tax years to use the cash method of accounting.[4] To simplify recordkeeping requirements for small businesses, Rev. Proc. 2002-28 permits qualified small businesses to adopt the cash method of accounting instead of the accrual method.[5]

---

[3] For a more complete discussion of accounting methods, (see Chapter I:11).
[4] Sec. 448(b).
[5] Rev. Proc. 2002-28, 2002-1 C.B. 815. An eligible business has gross receipts of $10 million or less for all prior three-taxable year periods and not prohibited under Sec. 448 from otherwise using the cash method of accounting.

Corporations are entitled to many of the tax benefits available to sole proprietorships. C corporations can elect to claim the Sec. 179 expensing deduction that is available to sole proprietorships and partnerships. In the past, they also were eligible to claim the 50% first-year bonus depreciation. In addition, owners of small corporations are eligible for a special exclusion of part of their gain on the sale of qualifying stock under Sec. 1202. The 2003 Tax Act lowered capital gains rates, thereby reducing the effective cost of selling a stock investment. Most investors will pay a 15% or lower marginal tax rate on a stock gain. Similarly, most dividend income earned by individuals is now taxed at the same low rate.

ADDITIONAL COMMENT

According to a Tax Foundation estimate, Fortune 500 companies spend an average of $2.4 million per year on income-tax compliance. Approximately 70% is attributable to the federal income tax, especially provisions relating to foreign-source income and the alternative minimum tax.

DIFFERENCES

One principal difference in computing corporate taxable income compared to individual taxable income is that personal, consumption-type expenditure write-offs and exemptions apply solely to individuals. A few differences are worth noting:

▶ Computation of *adjusted gross income* (AGI) applies only to individuals.

▶ Corporations are not entitled to the standard deduction or personal and dependency exemptions.

▶ Corporations are entitled to a dividends-received deduction of 70%, 80%, or 100% for qualifying dividends.

▶ For tax years 2003 through 2010, dividends received by an individual from a domestic corporation are taxed at a 15% or 5% tax rate. The 5% tax rate applies only to individuals whose incomes fall in the 10% or 15% tax bracket.

▶ Corporate charitable contribution deductions are limited to 10% of taxable income (with certain adjustments described on page I:16-7 of this chapter), whereas individual charitable contribution deductions generally are limited to 50% of AGI.

▶ Corporations are not allowed preferential tax treatment for net long-term capital gains nor are they allowed to deduct net capital losses against ordinary income. Individuals are allowed preferential tax treatment for net long-term capital gains and may deduct up to $3,000 per year of net capital losses against ordinary income.

SPECIFIC RULES APPLICABLE TO CORPORATIONS

CAPITAL GAINS AND LOSSES

The rules for netting long- and short-term capital gains and losses, netting Sec. 1231 (i.e., business fixed assets) gains and losses, and capital gain and loss holding periods are the same for both corporations and individuals. The netting process can be summarized as follows (see Schedule D of Form 1120–Capital Gains and Losses in Appendix B):

▶ Long-term capital gains (LTCGs) are netted against long-term capital losses (LTCLs).

▶ Short-term capital gains (STCGs) are netted against short-term capital losses (STCLs).

▶ A net long-term capital gain (NLTCG) is then offset against a net short-term capital loss (NSTCL).

▶ A net long-term capital loss (NLTCL) is then offset against a net short-term capital gain (NSTCG).

▶ Following this initial netting process, if a corporation reports both a NLTCG and a NSTCG, both the NSTCG and the NLTCG are taxed at ordinary income rates.

▶ NSTCGs are netted against NLTCLs, and any excess is taxed at ordinary income rates.

▶ NLTCLs and NSTCLs may not be deducted from ordinary income.

EXAMPLE I:16-2 ▶ Gulf Corporation realizes the following capital gains and losses during the current year:

LTCG	$15,000
LTCL	5,000
STCG	3,000
STCL	8,000

Gulf has a $10,000 NLTCG and a $5,000 NSTCL. The NLTCG is offset against the NSTCL, resulting in a $5,000 net capital gain that is taxed at ordinary income rates. ◀

EXAMPLE I:16-3 ▶ High Corporation realizes the following capital gains and losses during the current year:

LTCG	$15,000
LTCL	5,000
STCG	10,000
STCL	8,000

High has a $10,000 NLTCG and a $2,000 NSTCG. Both the $2,000 NSTCG and the $10,000 NLTCG are taxed at ordinary income rates. ◀

EXAMPLE I:16-4 ▶ Huge Corporation realizes the following capital gains and losses during the current year:

LTCG	$ 5,000
LTCL	15,000
STCG	8,000
STCL	10,000

Huge Corporation has a $10,000 NLTCL and a $2,000 NSTCL. In computing its current year taxable income, Huge may not deduct either net loss against its ordinary income. ◀

SELF-STUDY QUESTION

What are the major differences in the taxation of the capital gains and losses of individuals and corporations?

CORPORATE CAPITAL LOSS LIMITATIONS. For corporations, neither a NLTCL nor a NSTCL is deductible against ordinary income in the year it is incurred. Instead, it is eligible for a 3-year carryback and 5-year carryover and may be offset against capital gains in those years.[6] Both the NSTCL and the NLTCL are treated as STCLs for purposes of the carryback and carryover. The corporate capital loss limitations and carryback-carryover rules differ from those applicable to noncorporate taxpayers (see the discussion in Chapter I:5).[7]

EXAMPLE I:16-5 ANSWER

First, an individual can offset $3,000 of capital losses against ordinary income. Second, an individual has an indefinite carryover instead of a 3-year carryback and a 5-year carryover that applies to corporations. Third, all corporate capital loss carrybacks and carryovers are treated as STCLs. Finally, a 15% maximum tax rate applies to most net capital gains (i.e., the excess of net long-term capital gain over net short-term capital loss) for noncorporate taxpayers. A 5% maximum rate applies to individuals in the 10% or 15% tax brackets.

EXAMPLE I:16-5 ▶ Assume the same facts as in Example I:16-4. The $10,000 NLTCL and the $2,000 NSTCL are nondeductible in the current year. The $12,000 ($10,000 + $2,000) is carried back as a STCL to the third previous year. If the net gains in the carryback years are insufficient to absorb the $12,000 STCL, the excess is carried over up to 5 years. ◀

DIVIDENDS-RECEIVED DEDUCTION

Corporations may deduct 80% of dividends received from a domestic corporation if the recipient corporation owns 20% or more of the voting power and value of the dividend-paying corporation's stock.[8] If a corporation owns less than 20% of the dividend-paying corporation's stock, the deduction is 70% of dividends received. The percentage increases to 100% if the dividend is received from an 80%-or-more-owned corporation for which a consolidated tax return election has not been made. This deduction mitigates the onerous effects of triple taxation, where one corporation (a subsidiary) pays dividends to a corporate shareholder (its parent corporation), which in turn distributes an equal amount to its shareholders.

BOOK-TAX ACCOUNTING COMPARISON

The dividends-received deduction is a tax concept. No such expense or adjustment exists for financial reporting purposes.

The following table sets forth the dividends-received deduction percentages.

Percentage of Stock Owned	*Dividends-Received Deduction*
Less than 20%	70%
20% through 79.99%	80%
80% or more	100%

---

[6] Secs. 1211(a) and 1212(a).
[7] Noncorporate taxpayers (e.g., individuals) can deduct up to $3,000 of net capital losses against ordinary income annually. Unused capital losses of a noncorporate taxpayer are carried over (but not carried back) for an indefinite time period and retain their character as long- or short-term.
[8] The dividends-received deduction rules are set forth in Secs. 243 and 246.

The 80% and 70% **dividends-received deductions** are subject to the following limitations:

▶ The dividends-received deduction is limited to 80% (or 70%) of taxable income computed without regard to the net operating loss (NOL) deduction, the dividends-received deduction, or capital loss carrybacks to the limitation year.

▶ The limitation does not apply if the corporation generates an NOL in the current year after taking the dividends-received deduction determined under the general rules.

▶ The dividends-received deduction is not available if the distributing corporation's stock is held by the distributee for 45 or fewer days within the 90-day period that commences 45 days before the ex-dividend date.

EXAMPLE I:16-6 ▶ King Corporation reports the following income and expense items during the current year:

Net income from operations	$ 50,000
Dividends from two 20%-owned corporations	200,000

The dividends-received deduction determined under the general rule is $160,000 (0.80 × $200,000 dividends). The deduction limitation is $200,000 (0.80 × $250,000 of taxable income before the dividends-received deduction). Because the limitation ($200,000) exceeds the dividends-received deduction determined under the general rule ($160,000), the entire $160,000 dividends-received deduction is allowed. ◀

EXAMPLE I:16-7 ▶

Assume the same facts as in Example I:16-6, except that the corporation incurred a $10,000 net loss from operations. The dividends-received deduction determined under the general rule is $160,000 (0.80 × $200,000 dividends). The limitation under the general rule is based on taxable income before the dividends-received deduction of $190,000 ($200,000 − $10,000). The limitation is $152,000 (0.80 × $190,000). As illlustrated below, no NOL results after deducting the entire 80% dividends-received deduction determined under the general rule:

Net loss from operations	$ (10,000)
Plus: Dividends received from 20% (or more) owned corporations	200,000
Minus: Dividends-received deduction (0.80 × $200,000)	(160,000)
Taxable income as determined under the general rule	$ 30,000

Because the dividends-received deduction is limited to $152,000, the recognized taxable income for the year is $38,000 ($190,000 − $152,000). ◀

EXAMPLE I:16-8 ▶ Assume the same facts as in Example I:16-7, except that the loss from operations is $50,000. The dividends-received deduction determined under the general rule is $160,000 (0.80 × $200,000 dividends). The limitation is $120,000 (0.80 × $150,000 of taxable income before the dividends-received deduction). The limitation, however, does not apply because a $10,000 NOL results after taking the entire dividends-received deduction determined under the general rule.

Net loss from operations	$ (50,000)
Plus: Dividends received	200,000
Minus: Dividends-received deduction (0.80 × $200,000)	(160,000)
Taxable income	$ (10,000)

Therefore, the entire $160,000 dividends-received deduction is allowed. ◀

EXAMPLE I:16-9 ▶ On June 1, Lean Corporation acquires 5% of Madison Corporation stock. Madison pays a cash dividend to all shareholders of record on June 15. Lean receives the dividend on June 20. On July 1, Lean sells its Madison stock. A dividends-received deduction is not allowed because Lean does not own the Madison stock for the required 46 days within the 90-day period that commences 45 days before the ex-dividend date (June 15). ◀

NET OPERATING LOSSES

Unlike the computation of individual NOLs, the computation of a corporate **net operating loss (NOL)** does not involve adjusting nonbusiness deductions and capital gains and losses. (See Chapter I:8 for a discussion of these adjustments for individuals.[9]) In the cor-

---

[9] The NOL rules are set forth in Sec. 172.

porate NOL computation, the full dividends-received deduction is allowed. However, no deduction for an NOL carryover or carryback from a preceding or succeeding year is allowed.

EXAMPLE I:16-10 ▶ The computation of Maine Corporation's NOL for 2010 is based on the following taxable items:

Operating income	$ 400,000
Plus: Dividends received from 20% (or more) owned corporations	300,000
Gross income	$ 700,000
Minus: Business operating expenses	(600,000)
Dividends-received deduction (0.80 × $300,000)	(240,000)
Net operating loss	$(140,000)

In general, NOLs are carried back two years (beginning with the earliest NOL tax year). Any excess amounts are carried forward up to 20 years to offset taxable income in those years. Thus, Maine's NOLs can be carried back to 2008 and 2009. Any remaining NOL is carried over to years 2011–2030.[10] ◀

KEY POINT

In deciding whether to forgo the NOL carryback, the corporation should compare the current refund from the potential carryback to the present value of any future benefit from a carryover.

A corporation may elect to forgo the NOL carryback and instead carry the loss forward. For example, if the corporation has taxable income less than $75,000 in the carryback year(s) subject to tax rates less than 34%, the tax benefit of an NOL carryback might be limited because the carryback offsets income taxed at relatively low rates. The tax benefit of the NOL might be greater if the carryback is forgone and the NOL is carried over to a year in which the marginal tax rate is 34% or higher. However, the carryover would defer tax savings, whereas a carryback would produce an immediate tax benefit. The election, if made, applies to all carryback years, and the NOL carries forward for up to 20 years.

ADDITIONAL COMMENT

For purposes of determining the charitable contribution deduction limit, taxable income is calculated without regard to NOL and capital loss carrybacks, but NOL and capital loss carryovers are reflected in calculating taxable income.

CHARITABLE CONTRIBUTIONS

Some of the charitable contribution rules applicable to indiviudals also apply to corporations (e.g., the restriction on contributions of ordinary income property discussed in Chapter I:7).[11] The following rules apply solely to corporations:

▶ Under the general rule, a payment must be made before a contribution deduction is allowed. However, corporations using the accrual method of accounting may accrue a contribution deduction in the year preceding payment if before the end of the tax year the contribution is authorized by the board of directors and is made within 2½ months of the end of the tax year.

▶ Section 170(e) allows an increased charitable deduction for certain corporate property contributions. The increased deduction is available for (1) property used to care for the ill, needy, or infants; (2) scientific research property used by colleges or universities for research and experimentation; and (3) computer technology, software, and peripherals donated to educational institutions for use in grades kindergarten through 12. In each case the amount of the deduction equals the donor's adjusted basis in the property plus one-half of the excess of the property's FMV over its adjusted basis (not to exceed twice the property's adjusted basis).

▶ Corporate charitable contributions are limited to 10% of taxable income (computed without regard to the charitable contribution deduction, NOL and capital loss carry-*backs*, or the dividends-received deduction).

▶ Unused contribution amounts are carried forward 5 years. In the carryover year, the current year's contribution amount first is deducted to the extent of the 10% limitation. Contribution carryovers from the earliest year then are deducted to the extent of any unused limitation amount.

---

[10] NOLs incurred in tax years beginning before August 6, 1997 are carried back three years and forward 15 years. IRC Sec. 172(f) contains special rules that permit three-year or longer carryback periods. Corporate losses eligible for special carrybacks include presidentially declared disaster area losses (one year), product liability losses (10 years), and losses arising in 2001 and 2002 (five years). Losses incurred after 1998 may be carried forward up to 20 years.

[11] Rules pertaining to charitable contributions are set forth in Sec. 170.

EXAMPLE I:16-11 ▶

Mesa Corporation reports the following results for 2010:

Taxable income (before deducting dividends-received and charitable contributions)	$130,000
Dividends-received deduction	10,000
Charitable contributions	20,000

Mesa has never incurred an NOL. The limitation on contributions is $13,000 ($130,000 × 0.10), and taxable income is $107,000 ($130,000 − $13,000 − $10,000). The $7,000 ($20,000 − $13,000) excess contribution amount carries forward 5 years (2011–2015). ◀

EXAMPLE I:16-12 ▶

Assume that the same facts in Example I:16-1 in 2011, except that taxable income (before deducting dividends-received and charitable contributions) is $220,000. The contribution limitation now is $22,000 ($220,000 × 0.10). The $20,000 charitable contribution for 2011 first is deducted to the extent of the $22,000 limitation, leaving a $2,000 unused excess. Thus, $2,000 of the carryover from 2010 is deductible to the extent of this unused limitation, leaving a $5,000 carryover from 2010, which may be used in tax years 2012 through 2015. ◀

COMPENSATION DEDUCTION LIMITATION FOR PUBLICLY HELD CORPORATIONS

A publicly held corporation is denied a deduction for compensation paid to its chief executive officer and its four highest-compensated officers if the compensation for that individual exceeds $1 million per year.[12] Includible compensation includes both cash and noncash benefits. The following types of compensation are not taken into account for purposes of calculating the $1 million limitation:

▶ Remuneration payable on a commission basis

▶ Compensation based on individual performance goals (if approved by certain outside directors and shareholders)[13]

▶ Payments to a qualified retirement plan

▶ Tax-free employee benefits (such as employer-provided health care and Sec. 132 fringe benefits)

EXAMPLE I:16-13 ▶

Pine Corporation is a publicly held company whose securities are listed on the New York Stock Exchange. In the current year, Pine compensates its chief executive officer, Rodney, as follows: salary, $1,200,000; commissions based on sales generated by Rodney, $400,000; payments to a qualified pension plan, $25,000; and tax-free fringe benefits, $10,000. The commissions, payments to the qualified pension plan, and tax-free fringe benefits are not subject to the $1 million annual deduction limitation. Thus, $200,000 ($1,200,000 − $1,000,000) of Rodney's salary is not deductible by Pine even though Rodney is taxed on the entire $1,200,000. ◀

U.S. PRODUCTION ACTIVITIES DEDUCTION

Congress created a special deduction to reduce taxes on U.S. manufacturing activities. Effective as of 2005, the deduction is calculated as a percentage of the lesser of qualified production activities income or taxable income (before considering this deduction). The percentage for the deduction is phased in as follows:

Tax Year	Percentage Deduction
2005 & 2006	3%
2007–2009	6%
2010 and thereafter	9%

---

[12] Sec. 162(m). A publicly held corporation is any corporation issuing any class of securities required to be registered under Section 12 of the Securities Exchange Act of 1934. This corporation generally has securities listed on a national securities exchange, or has at least $5 million or more of assets and 500 or more shareholders.

[13] (See Reg. Sec. 1.162-27 for the requirements relating to the attainment of performance goals.)

The deduction is available for income derived from qualified production property manufactured, produced, grown, or extracted in whole or in significant part in the U.S. The deduction is broad in scope because the definition of qualified production property is quite expansive. Qualified production property includes any tangible personal property, computer software, sound recording, qualified firm, electricity, natural gas, or potable water, erection or renovation of buildings or infrastructure, and architectural or engineering services related to construction.

EXAMPLE I:16-14 ▶ Cedar Corporation manufactures widgets in its factory in Birmingham, Alabama. In 2010, its taxable income (before the production deduction) is $300,000 and its net income from qualified production activities is $237,000. Cedar has a qualified production activities deduction of $21,330 (9% of the lesser of $237,000 or $300,000). After claiming this deduction, its taxable income for 2010 is $278,670 ($300,000 − $21,330). ◀

For a summary of the rules relating to corporate capital gains and losses, dividends-received deduction, net operating losses, charitable contribution deduction, compensation deduction, and U.S. production activities deduction, see Topic Review I:16-1.

Topic Review I:16-1

Summary of Rules for Calculating Corporate Taxable Income

CAPITAL GAINS AND LOSSES

▶ If a net loss results from netting long-term and short-term capital gains and losses, none of this loss can be deducted from ordinary income. Instead, the loss may be carried back 3 years and forward up to 5 years and is treated as short-term in character (i.e., STCL).

▶ Corporate net capital gains do not receive favorable tax treatment. The 15% maximum tax rate for net capital gains applies to individuals but not C corporations.

DIVIDENDS-RECEIVED DEDUCTION

▶ The dividends-received deduction is 80% if the corporate shareholder owns 20% or more of stock in the dividend-paying corporation, and 70% if the corporate shareholder owns less than 20%. A 100% deduction is available for dividends received from an 80%-or-more-owned member of an affiliated group that does not file a consolidated tax return.

▶ The dividends-received deduction is limited to 80% (or 70% as the case may be) of taxable income (after adjustments for the NOL deduction, the dividends-received deduction, and capital loss carrybacks) unless the corporate shareholder generates an NOL after deducting the full amount of dividends-received.

CHARITABLE CONTRIBUTIONS

▶ Accrual-basis corporate donors may accrue a current year deduction if the contribution is authorized by the board of directors and paid within 2½ months after the end of the current tax year.

▶ Corporations are allowed increased deductions for contributions of qualifying property used (1) to care for the ill, needy, or infants, (2) to conduct research or experimentation in colleges or universities, or (3) by educational institutions in grades kindergarten through 12.

▶ Contributions are limited to 10% of taxable income (adjusted for certain taxable items).

▶ Unused charitable contributions are carried forward up to 5 years.

NOLs, COMPENSATION, AND PRODUCTION ACTIVITIES

▶ In general, NOLs may be carried back 2 years (beginning with the earlier year), then forward up to 20 years. The corporation may elect to forgo the 2-year carryback. Longer carryback periods are permitted for special losses (for example, product liability losses and NOLs incurred in 2003 and 2004). NOLs of certain small businesses or a farm business may be carried back five years.

▶ Publicly held corporations are denied a deduction for compensation exceeding $1 million paid to certain key executives.

▶ Businesses engaged in manufacturing activities may deduct 9% of the lesser of qualified production activities income or taxable income (before this deduction) for tax years 2010 and after.

COMPUTATION OF TAX

OBJECTIVE 2

Calculate the corporate income tax liability

COMPUTATION OF TAXABLE INCOME

Table I:16-2 illustrates the computation of *taxable income* for a C corporation.

COMPUTATION OF REGULAR TAX

The corporate tax rate schedule is graduated, as follows:[14]

If Taxable Income Is:			Of the
Over . . .	But Not Over . . .	The Tax Is:	Amount Over . . .
$0	$50,000	15%	$0
50,000	75,000	$7,500 + 25%	50,000
75,000	100,000	13,750 + 34%	75,000
100,000	335,000	22,250 + 39%	100,000
335,000	10,000,000	113,900 + 34%	335,000
10,000,000	15,000,000	3,400,000 + 35%	10,000,000
15,000,000	18,333,333	5,150,000 + 38%	15,000,000
18,333,333		6,416,667 + 35%	18,333,333

▼ TABLE I:16-2

Computation of Corporate Taxable Income

Sales	$600,000
Minus: Cost of goods sold	(300,000)
Gross profit	$300,000
Plus: Other income	
Dividends from 25%-owned corporation	$100,000
Interest	10,000
Long-term capital gain	90,000
Gross income	$500,000
Minus: Deductions:	
Salaries	$ 80,000
Repairs	20,000
Bad debts	27,000
Taxes	10,000
Contributions (subject to the 10% corporate limitation, as discussed on page I:16-7)	5,000
Depreciation	20,000
Pension and profit-sharing contributions	35,000
Total deductions	$197,000
Taxable income before special deductions	$303,000
Minus: Special deductions:	
Net operating loss deduction	(15,000)[a]
Dividends-received deduction	(80,000)[b]
U.S. production activities deduction	(12,600)[c]
Taxable income	$195,400

ADDITIONAL COMMENT

Most states impose an income tax on C corporations. Some states exempt S corporations from the state corporate income tax.

[a]This amount represents a net operating loss carried over from a prior year.
[b]0.80 × $100,000 = $80,000 dividends-received deduction.
[c]Assume qualified production income is $140,000. Taxable income before the U.S. production activities deduction is $208,000. Therefore, the U.S. production activities deduction (in years 2010 and after) is $12,600 ($140,000 × 0.09).

[14] Sec. 11(b)(1).

EXAMPLE I:16-15 ▶ Able Corporation's taxable income for the current year is $100,000. Its regular tax liability is computed as follows:

0.15 × $50,000	=	$ 7,500
0.25 × $25,000	=	6,250
0.34 × $25,000	=	8,500
Total tax		$22,250

The total tax due on the $100,000 of taxable income is $22,250. This tax can be computed directly through the tax rate schedule shown above (or on inside back cover of this textbook). ◀

The 15% and 25% tax rates on the first $75,000 of taxable income, as compared to a flat 34% rate, provide a $11,750 benefit (tax reduction) computed as follows:

Tax on $75,000 at 34%	$25,500
Minus: Tax on $75,000 (from tax rate schedule)	(13,750)
Tax benefit of lower rates	$11,750

Congress wanted only small corporations to obtain this benefit, so it imposed a 5% surtax on taxable income between $100,000 and $335,000. This 5% surtax is reflected in the 39% (34% + 5%) marginal rate in the corporate tax schedule. After taxable income reaches $335,000, the entire benefit of the lower rates is recaptured ($235,000 × 0.05 = $11,750). Thus, corporations with taxable income between $335,000 and $10,000,000 pay a flat tax equal to 34% times taxable income.

EXAMPLE I:16-16 ▶ Ajax Corporation's taxable income for the current year is $335,000. Its tax liability is computed as follows:

0.15 × $ 50,000	=	$ 7,500
0.25 × $ 25,000	=	6,250
0.34 × $260,000	=	88,400
0.05 × $235,000	=	11,750
Total tax		$113,900

The $113,900 tax liability also can be calculated by multiplying 34% times $335,000. Thus, the benefit of the lower rates on the first $75,000 of taxable income is completely phased-out when taxable income reaches $335,000. ◀

KEY POINT

The corporate income tax is essentially flat for corporations with substantial taxable income.

A 35% rate applies to taxable income exceeding $10 million. An additional 3% surtax (reflected in the 38% rate) applies to taxable income between $15 million and $18,333,333. This surtax eliminates the benefit of the 34% rate when taxable income equals or exceeds $18,333,333. Thus, a flat 35% rate applies to taxable income exceeding $18,333,333.

EXAMPLE I:16-17 ▶ Ajax Corporation's taxable income for the current year is $18,333,333. Its tax liability is computed as follows:

0.34 × $10,000,000	=	$3,400,000
0.35 × $5,000,000	=	1,750,000
0.38 × $3,333,333	=	1,266,667
Total tax		$6,416,667

Effectively, at $18,333,333 of taxable income, the average tax rate is 35% (0.35 × $18,333,333 = $6,416,667). ◀

SPECIAL RULE FOR PERSONAL SERVICE CORPORATIONS. Certain personal service corporations are not subject to graduated rates.[15] Rather, a flat 35% rate applies. Applicable personal service corporations are those that perform services in the fields of

---

[15] Sec. 11(b)(2).

health, law, engineering, architecture, accounting, actuarial science, performing arts, or consulting, where substantially all of the corporate stock is held by current or retired employees, or by the estates of deceased employees.

COMPUTATION OF THE CORPORATE ALTERNATIVE MINIMUM TAX (AMT)

The alternative minimum tax (AMT) for corporations is similar to that for individuals (see Chapter I:14 for a discussion of the AMT for individuals).[16] The AMT ensures that taxpayers with substantial economic income pay a minimum amount of federal tax.[17] If a corporation's AMT liability is greater than its regular (income) tax liability, the corporation must pay both the excess amount and the regular tax.

The corporate AMT is 20% of alternative minimum taxable income (AMTI) net of an exemption based on the entity's AMTI. The exemption amount for corporations is $40,000 reduced by 25% of the excess of AMTI over $150,000. This exemption is phased-out when AMTI exceeds $310,000 [$150,000 + (1.0/0.25 × $40,000)].

EXAMPLE I:16-18 ▶

Allied Corporation reports $200,000 of AMTI before the AMT exemption. The $40,000 exemption amount is reduced by $12,500 [0.25 × ($200,000 − $150,000)] to $27,500 ($40,000 − $12,500). Thus, the AMT base is $172,500 ($200,000 − $27,500). ◀

ADDITIONAL COMMENT

For AMTI through $150,000, the exemption amount is $40,000. For AMTI of $310,000 or more, the exemption amount is $0. Thus, the reduction formula need be applied only when AMTI is between $150,000 and $310,000. For all practical purposes, few corporations will benefit from the exemption as their AMTI will exceed $310,000.

COMPUTATION OF AMTI. AMTI equals regular taxable income modified by certain adjustments and increased by tax preference items. Tax preference items are subject to some type of preferential tax treatment in the regular income tax system. As with the individual AMT, these items are *added* to regular taxable income to compute AMTI. Because corporations are more likely to have AMT adjustments than tax preferences,[18] only AMT adjustments are discussed in this chapter.

AMT Adjustments. AMT adjustments reflect timing differences relating to deferred income or accelerated deductions. These adjustments generally increase the AMT tax base, while the reversal of these differences may result in a reduction of the AMT tax base over time. When an AMT is paid, an AMT tax credit is available to the corporation to reduce the regular tax liability in subsequent years if its regular tax exceeds its tentative minimum tax. (See Chapter I:14 for a detailed discussion of this topic.) The most common AMT adjustments include the following:

▶ For real property placed in service after 1986 and before 1999, the difference between the MACRS income tax depreciation claimed and a hypothetical straight-line depreciation amount computed under the alternative depreciation system and a 40-year cost recovery period (see Chapter I:10 for a discussion of the alternative depreciation system).

▶ For personal property placed in service after 1986, the difference between the MACRS income tax depreciation claimed and the amount calculated under the 150% declining balance method and alternative depreciation system.

▶ 75% of the excess of adjusted current earnings (ACE) over AMTI (as calculated before the ACE adjustment and the alternative tax NOL deduction but after all other adjustments and tax preference items).[19]

▶ Regular taxable income (the starting point for calculating AMTI) is net of the U.S. production activities deduction. For regular tax purposes, the deduction is 9% (in 2010 and after) times the lesser of qualified production activities income or taxable income before the deduction. For corporate AMTI purposes, the computation is based on the lesser of qualified production activities income or AMTI before the deduction.

---

[16] The AMT rules are set forth in Secs. 55–58.

[17] The Taxpayer Relief Act of 1997 repealed the corporate AMT for *small corporations* (measured by gross receipts) for tax years beginning after December 31, 1997. For details, see the discussion below.

[18] (See Sec. 57 for a list of tax preference items. Also, see Chapter I:14 for a discussion of these items.)

[19] The term *adjusted current earnings* is based on the earnings and profits definition found in Sec. 312. (See Chapter C:5 of *Prentice Hall's Federal Taxation: Corporations, Partnerships, Estates, and Trusts* for a detailed discussion of this AMT adjustment.)

EXAMPLE I:16-19 ▶ In the current year, Camp Corporation earns taxable income of $100,000, and its regular tax liability is $22,250. Camp's AMT adjustments other than ACE are $80,000, and it has $340,000 of adjusted current earnings. Camp's AMT liability is computed as follows:

Regular taxable income	$100,000
Plus: AMT adjustments other than ACE	80,000
AMTI (before ACE adjustment)	$180,000
Plus: ACE adjustment [0.75 × ($340,000 − $180,000)]	120,000
AMTI	$300,000
Minus: Exemption ($40,000 − [($300,000 − $150,000) × 0.25])	(2,500)
AMT base	$297,500
Times: AMT rate	× .20
Tentative minimum tax	$ 59,500
Minus: Regular tax	(22,250)
AMT liability	$ 37,250

ADDITIONAL COMMENT

Because of the AMT credit, the AMT essentially is a prepaid tax on preference items and adjustments; it affects the timing of the corporation's tax payments.

Camp's total current year tax liability is $59,500 ($22,250 regular tax + $37,250 AMT). In effect, the corporation pays the greater of the regular tax or the tentative minimum tax. Camp also carries over the $37,250 AMT to next year as an AMT credit. For example, if next year's regular tax liability is $30,000 and the tentative minimum tax is $20,000, Camp applies a $10,000 credit against next year's regular tax liability and carries over the remaining $27,250 ($37,250 − $10,000) AMT credit to the following year. The AMT credit has an indefinite life. ◀

 STOP & THINK

Question: Corporations that are subject to the AMT typically must alter their tax planning to minimize their overall tax liability. How might a corporation plan the timing of income recognition and deductions for AMT purposes?

Solution: Under the regular tax regime, a corporation might accelerate deductions to the current year and defer income recognition until a future year. While this technique reduces the regular tax, it increases the AMT and for some corporations may produce no tax benefit. Under the AMT regime, the corporation might consider reversing this strategy by accelerating income recognition and deferring deductions. The interplay of regular tax and AMT planning converges to a point where the income tax is reduced to the lowest possible amount without triggering the AMT.

Exception to AMT for Small Corporations. For tax years beginning after 1997, the AMT does not apply to small business corporations. A small business corporation is a corporation whose average gross receipts for each of the three years preceding the year in which the exemption is claimed is $7.5 million or less.[20]

 STOP & THINK

Question: Why might Alternative Minimum Taxable Income (AMTI) approximate income for financial accounting purposes to a greater extent than would regular taxable income?

Solution: AMTI could approximate financial accounting income to a greater extent than would regular taxable income for three reasons: First, AMTI includes certain items recognized for financial accounting purposes but not regular tax purposes (e.g., interest on private activity bonds). Second, AMTI generally is based on conservative accounting methods (e.g., less accelerated depreciation rates) that often are adopted for financial accounting purposes, but not regular tax purposes. Third, certain deductions allowed in deriving regular taxable income (e.g., U.S. production activities deduction) are not allowed in deriving either AMTI or financial accounting income. As a result, the liability that a company accrues for AMT purposes could approximate the tax expense that it recognizes for financial accounting purposes to a greater extent than would its regular tax liability.

---

[20] The AMT exemption also applies to a noncorporate entity that elects to be taxed as a C corporation under the check-the-box rules. The calculation of gross receipts is based on the entity's tax year. The $7.5 million maximum is reduced to $5 million for the corporation's first three year period that begins after 1993.

PENALTY TAXES

Intended to deter otherwise abusive tax planning practices are two penalty taxes: the accumulated earnings tax and the personal holding company tax. The computation of both taxes is based on complex rules that are discussed in more detail in the companion volume to this text, *Prentice Hall's Federal Taxation: Corporations, Partnerships, Estates, and Trusts*. These rules are summarized below.

ACCUMULATED EARNINGS TAX. The **accumulated earnings tax** aims at discouraging companies from retaining excessive earnings invested in assets unrelated to business needs.[21] A company might avoid liability for this tax if its earnings are reinvested in operating assets or retained for the reasonable needs of the business. If not for this tax, closely held corporations might not pay dividends to their shareholders (thereby avoiding the double taxation of their earnings). The retained earnings then might be used for passive investment purposes.

Reasonable needs of the business are associated with numerous activities, including the following:

▶ Reasonably anticipated business expansion and plant replacement

▶ Acquiring the assets or stock (other than portfolio investments) of another business

▶ Providing working capital for the business

▶ Establishing a sinking fund to retire corporate debt

▶ Investing or lending to suppliers or customers

The accumulated earnings tax generally is imposed on closely held corporations. However, the tax may be imposed on a publicly held corporation if effective control is in the hands of a few related shareholders.[22]

The accumulated earnings tax base is the corporation's accumulated taxable income for a particular year. The accumulated earnings tax rate is 15%. Shareholders in the 10% or 15% marginal tax bracket can reduce the corporation's accumulated earnings tax exposure by having the corporation distribute dividends, taxed to the shareholders at a 5% rate. Accumulated taxable income is computed as follows:

Taxable income
Plus: Dividends-received deduction
       Net operating loss deduction
Minus: Net capital losses
       Net long-term capital gains over net short-term capital
         losses (less federal income tax on such net gains)
       Federal income tax liability
       Charitable contributions exceeding 10% corporate limitation
       Deductions for dividends paid or deemed paid[23]
       Accumulated earnings credit

Accumulated taxable income

The accumulated earnings credit equals the greater of (1) $250,000 minus accumulated earnings and profits (E&P) at the beginning of the year[24] or (2) the amount of E&P for the tax year that is retained for the reasonable needs of the business. The reasonable needs of the business are determined at year-end and are reduced by accumulated E&P at the beginning of the year. Thus, only the amount of E&P that is retained to meet the increase in reasonable business needs may be claimed as a credit. (E&P is defined later in this chapter.)

ADDITIONAL COMMENT

When the highest marginal tax rate on individuals was considerably higher than the corporate tax rate, corporations commonly were used as tax shelters. From 1987 through 1992, corporate tax rates were only slightly higher than individual tax rates, making both the accumulated earnings tax and the personal holding company tax less important. In 1993 and subsequent years, the increase in the highest individual tax rate to 39.6% increased the importance of the two penalty taxes to some degree because the top corporate tax rate is only 35%. The accumulated earnings tax rate was reduced to 15% for tax years beginning after December 31, 2002. The accumulated earnings tax rate was reduced to the tax rate on dividends that would apply to most shareholders if the accumulated earnings of the corporation were distributed to the shareholders. The accumulated earnings tax rate exceeds the tax rate applicable to shareholders having low levels of taxable income who are in either the 5% or 10% marginal tax brackets.

ADDITIONAL COMMENT

The accumulated earnings tax can be avoided by the payment of a large enough dividend or by making an S corporation election. The accumulated earnings tax does not apply during the years the S corporation election is in effect.

---

[21] The basic rules for the accumulated earning tax are set forth in Code Secs. 531–537.
[22] Sec. 532(c) and *Golconda Mining Corp. v. CIR*, 35 AFTR 2d 75-336, 74-2 USTC ¶9845 (9th Cir., 1974).
[23] Sec. 561. The deduction for dividends paid includes dividends actually paid during the tax year and consent dividends (e.g., hypothetical dividends) where the shareholders agree to be taxed on such amounts. Under Sec. 563, dividends paid during the first 2½ months following the end of the tax year are considered paid on the last day of the preceding tax year.
[24] The $250,000 credit amount is reduced to $150,000 for service corporations engaged in the field of health, law, engineering, architecture, accounting, actuarial science, performing arts, or consulting.

EXAMPLE I:16-20 ▶ In the current year, Compact Corporation earns taxable income of $100,000. Compact's federal tax liability is $22,250, and the corporation paid $10,000 in dividends to its shareholders. Compact claims a deduction of $80,000 for $100,000 of dividends received. Accumulated E&P at the beginning of the year for the reasonable needs of the business is $200,000. Compact's reasonable needs of the business at year-end require $220,000 of funding. Accumulated taxable income and the accumulated earnings credit are computed as follows:

Taxable income		$100,000
Plus: Dividends-received deduction		80,000
Minus: Federal income tax liability		(22,250)
Dividends-paid deduction		(10,000)
Accumulated earnings credit—the greater of:		
(1) $250,000 (statutory exemption) − $200,000		
(accumulated E&P at the beginning of the year)	$50,000	
(2) E&P retained for the increased reasonable	or	
needs of the business ($220,000 − $200,000)	$20,000	(50,000)
Accumulated taxable income		$ 97,750

Compact's accumulated earnings tax liability is $14,662 (0.15 × $97,750). It pays this tax in addition to its regular income tax. Compact's total federal tax liability is $36,912 ($22,250 + $14,662). ◀

An IRS auditor will likely examine Schedules L and M-2 of Form 1120 (U.S. Corporation Income Tax Return) to determine if accumulated earnings are excessive. See Appendix C for a completed Form 1120. The auditor will examine Schedule L (the balance sheet) to identify the assets owned by the business. Substantial marketable securities, loans to shareholders, and nonbusiness assets (for example, a boat or resort condominium) might suggest that the corporation is retaining excessive earnings. The corporation could have distributed these earnings to its shareholders in the form of dividends. Loans to shareholders might suggest the corporation's reluctance to distribute its earnings. The IRS auditor will look at Schedule M-2 to see if the corporation has declared and paid any dividends to the shareholders. To avoid the accumulated earnings tax the corporation might argue that it has consistently paid dividends.

WHAT WOULD YOU DO IN THIS SITUATION?

Scott, Steve, and Sean own 100% of the outstanding stock of Sofa Corporation for all of the current year. In its first twelve years of existence, Sofa Corporation, a manufacturer of custom-made sofas, never paid a dividend to its shareholders. It preferred instead to retain its earnings for working capital, additional machinery, and short-term investments. Scott and Steve would like to borrow money from Sofa because Scott is planning to open a florist shop, and Steve needs a loan to pay off personal debts. For these reasons, Sofa will not pay a dividend in the current year. However, the company intends to pay dividends next year when the two loans have been paid off. Sofa has accumulated E&P (before any distributions) exceeding $250,000. As Sofa's tax consultant, you inform the

shareholders of the possibility that the company will be liable for the accumulated earnings tax. The shareholders ask you if they should inform the IRS of potentially excessive earnings, voluntarily pay the tax, or just wait to be audited by the IRS.

a. What advice would you give the shareholders regarding reporting the potentially excessive earnings and the payment of the tax? (See the *Statements on Responsibilities in Tax Practice* section in Chapter I:15 and Appendix E.)

b. What advice would you give the shareholders if the corporation instead reported low operating profits from its sofa-making business and met both personal holding company requirements in the current year?

ADDITIONAL COMMENT

The personal holding company tax is imposed mechanically, whereas the accumulated earnings tax is based on a subjective standard of purpose to avoid the tax.

PERSONAL HOLDING COMPANY TAX. A corporation is considered a personal holding company if both of the following tests are met:[25]

▶ More than 50% of the value of its outstanding stock is owned by five or fewer individuals at some time during the last six months of the tax year.

▶ 60% or more of its adjusted ordinary gross income is personal holding company income. Personal holding company income consists of passive income, including dividends, interest, and in some circumstances, rent.

Many closely held corporations pass the 50% stock ownership test because of family ownership attribution rules. For example, 20 family shareholders (e.g., spouses, children, and grandchildren) may count as a single shareholder for purposes of applying the 50% and five or fewer shareholder tests.

ADDITIONAL COMMENT

The personal holding company tax can be a problem in a corporation's final year as the entity scales down its operations. The corporation may have discontinued its operations, sold its assets, and earned primarily investment income.

The personal holding company tax discourages the conversion of closely held operating companies into nonoperating companies that reinvest substantial earnings in passive investments (e.g., stocks and bonds of other companies). The tax compels a company to distribute its earnings to shareholders if the earnings are not reinvested in operating assets. Liability for the personal holding company tax does not require a tax-avoidance motive. By contrast, liability for the accumulated earnings tax does require an intent to avoid the tax on dividends.

The accumulated earnings tax cannot be imposed in the same year the corporation is deemed to be a personal holding company. Often, a corporation that gradually converts itself into a nonoperating company by reinvesting its earnings in passive investments will incur an accumulated earnings tax liability before incurring a personal holding company tax liability. However, this is not always the case. For example, a newly-formed corporation that temporarily invests surplus funds in nonoperating assets may be deemed to be a personal holding company in its first year of operation, while the $250,000 accumulated earnings credit temporarily shields the same company from the accumulated earnings tax.

Computation of Personal Holding Company Tax. The **personal holding company tax** is the product of the personal holding company tax rate times undistributed personal holding company income. Various adjustments are made to regular taxable income to derive the personal holding company tax base. These adjustments are similar to those made in calculating the accumulated earnings tax, as illustrated in Example I:16-20. The personal holding company tax rate is 15%.

EXAMPLE I:16-21 ▶

Crane Corporation has four shareholders who together own more than 50% of the value of Crane stock at all times during the current year. More than 60% of Crane's adjusted gross income is personal holding company income (dividends, interest, etc.). Crane is a personal holding company for the current year because both the stock ownership and the income tests are met. Crane receives a $25,000 dividend for which it claims a $20,000 dividends-received deduction. It pays $18,750 of dividends to its shareholders. Crane has $200,000 of regular taxable income and a $61,250 regular tax liability.

Crane's personal holding company tax is computed as follows:

ADDITIONAL COMMENT

The personal holding company tax, like the accumulated earnings tax, can be avoided by paying a large enough dividend or by making an S corporation election. A timely S corporation election precludes the corporation from being classified as a personal holding company for the years it is in effect.

Regular taxable income	$200,000
Adjustments:	
Federal income tax liability	(61,250)
Dividends-received deduction	20,000
Dividends-paid deduction[26]	(18,750)
Undistributed personal holding company income	$140,000
Times: Personal holding company tax rate	× 0.15
Personal holding company tax	$ 21,000

---

[25] The basic rules for personal holding companies are set forth in Secs. 541–547.

[26] Secs. 547 and 561. The dividends-paid deduction is available for dividends paid during the tax year, dividends paid within 2½ months following the end of the tax year (subject to certain limitations), consent dividends, and dividends paid within 90 days following an IRS determination that a personal holding company tax is owed (i.e., deficiency dividends). Deficiency dividends are not allowed in computing the accumulated earnings tax.

Topic Review I:16-2

Comparison of the Two Corporate Penalty Taxes

ITEM	ACCUMULATED EARNINGS TAX—SEC. 531	PERSONAL HOLDING COMPANY (PHC) TAX—SEC. 541
Reason for imposing the penalty tax	To discourage companies from retaining excessive earnings if such earnings are invested in nonoperating assets. A primary purpose is to compel the distribution of excessive earnings.	To discourage the conversion of closely held operating companies into passive investment companies. A primary purpose is to compel the distribution of passive income.
Elements of the tax formula	The tax base is regular taxable income plus or minus certain adjustments. The tax computation involves subjective judgment because the accumulated earnings credit (which often reduces the tax base to zero) is a function of retaining earnings for the reasonable needs of the business.	The determination of whether a corporation is a personal holding company and the computation of the tax is mechanical. Once the corporation is deemed to be a PHC, its tax base is regular taxable income plus or minus certain adjustments.
Computation of tax	Adjustments are made to taxable income for items such as the dividends-received deduction, the dividends-paid deduction, the federal income tax liability, and the accumulated earnings credit (see Example I:16-20). The tax rate is 15% of accumulated taxable income.	Adjustments are made to regular taxable income for items such as the dividends-received deduction, dividends-paid deduction, and the federal income tax liability to derive undistributed PHC income (see Example I:16-20). The tax rate is 15% of undistributed PHC income.

Crane's total federal tax liability is $82,250 ($61,250 + $21,000). Payment of the $21,000 personal holding company tax may be avoided if Crane distributes all of the personal holding company income to its shareholders. Special rules allow personal holding companies to distribute this income and avoid the personal holding company tax even after the corporation's year-end. Crane shareholders then pay the regular income tax on the dividend distribution. ◀

Topic Review I:16-2 compares the accumulated earnings tax and personal holding company tax rules.

COMPUTATION OF TAX
FOR CONTROLLED GROUPS

Shareholders in one corporation could realize substantial tax savings by dividing the business into two or more corporations. This tax savings results from the corporations' benefitting from the lower corporate rates for taxable income less than $100,000. To prevent this type of tax avoidance, a **controlled group** must apportion the lower rates among group members as if only one corporation exists.[27] An equal apportionment to each member is required unless all group members consent to a disproportionate allocation. A controlled group, as discussed below, is a group of corporations that are, in general, owned by the same shareholder or group of shareholders.

EXAMPLE I:16-22 ▶ West and East Corporations are members of a controlled group. In the current year West and East each earn taxable income of $100,000. If each corporation were taxed separately, each's tax liability would be $22,250, or a total of $44,500. However, because West and East are members of a controlled group, the lower marginal tax rates must be apportioned to each corporation. The tax liability for each corporation under an equal apportionment is computed as follows:

---

[27] Sec. 1561.

Tax Calculation	Corporation	
	West	East
Tax on initial $50,000 of taxable income apportioned equally between West and East (0.15 × $25,000)	$ 3,750	$ 3,750
Tax on next $25,000 apportioned equally between West and East (0.25 × $12,500)	3,125	3,125
Tax on next $25,000 apportioned equally between West and East (0.34 × $12,500)	4,250	4,250
Tax on remaining $50,000 of taxable income for each corporation (0.39 × $50,000)	19,500	19,500
Tax on $100,000 of taxable income for each corporation	$30,625	$30,625

ADDITIONAL COMMENT

A controlled group of corporations must apportion not only the lower tax rates but also the $250,000 accumulated earnings credit and the $40,000 alternative minimum tax exemption.

The result of being members of a controlled group is that West and East must pay a total tax of $61,250, which is $16,750 ($61,250 − $44,500) more than the amount that each would pay if it were a separate, unrelated corporation. The total tax liability of $61,250 would have resulted if West and East were, in fact, one corporation. ◀

If taxable income of the controlled group exceeds $10 million, a comparable allocation must be made to reflect the lower 34% rate applicable to taxable income up to $10 million. Controlled groups may be classified into three types: brother-sister, parent-subsidiary, and combined. These three types are discussed below.

BROTHER-SISTER CONTROLLED GROUP. The IRC sets forth two definitions of a **brother-sister controlled group.** This textbook will refer to them as the 80%-50% definition and the 50%-only definition. Under the 80%-50% definition, a brother-sister controlled group exists if the following conditions are met:

▶ Five or fewer individuals, estates, or trusts own at least 80% of the voting power or value of all classes of stock of each corporation.[28]

▶ The shareholders commonly own more than 50% of the total voting power or value of all classes of stock. For the purpose of this condition, stock is counted only to the extent that each shareholder owns an identical interest in each corporation.[29] The term *identical interest* means the smallest overlapping percentage of stock owned by the shareholder in any corporation included in the brother-sister group.

ADDITIONAL COMMENT

In practice, brother-sister corporations are associated with one or a small number of taxpayers, owning several small, closely-held corporations.

Thus, under the 80%-50% definition, the five or fewer shareholders not only must have more than 50% common ownership in the corporations, but also must own at least 80% of the stock in each brother-sister corporation. This definition is narrow because the shareholders must meet two tests.

The 50%-only definition is broader because the five or fewer shareholders must satisfy only the 50% common ownership test. Consequently, in situations where the 50%-only definition applies, more corporations may be deemed to be members of a controlled group than under the 80%-50% definition.

The 50%-only definition applies for apportioning the lower marginal tax rates as illustrated in Example I:16-22. It also applies for apportioning the accumulated earnings credit and the AMT exemption. The 80%-50% definition applies for other purposes, such as apportioning the Sec. 179 expense limitation.

EXAMPLE I:16-23 ▶ The single classes of stock in First, Second, and Third Corporations are owned by Amir, Beth, Carol, Dawn, and Edith as follows:

---

[28] The 80% test is met if 80% or more of the total combined voting power of all classes of voting stock *or* at least 80% of the total value of all classes of stock of each corporation is held by five or fewer shareholders on December

31. To be counted for the 80% test, a shareholder must own stock in each corporate member of the brother-sister controlled group.
[29] Sec. 1563(a)(2).

| | Corporation | | | |
Individuals	First	Second	Third	Identical Interest
Amir	40%	20%	20%	20%
Beth	30	30	60	30
Carol	10	40	10	10
Dawn	10	10	—	—
Edith	10	—	10	—
Total	100%	100%	100%	60%

This group meets both the 80%-50% test and the 50%-only test. The 80%-50% test is met because five or fewer individuals own at least 80% of First, Second, and Third stocks and because Amir, Beth, and Carol own 80% of First stock and 90% of Second and Third stocks. For purposes of the 80% test the stock ownership of Dawn and Edith is not counted because they do not own stock in each of the three corporations. The 50% test also is met because common ownership exceeds 50% (60% of identical interests). For purposes of the 50%-only test, the stock ownership of Dawn and Edith is not counted because they do not own stock in each of the three corporations. In this example, the 50%-only test also is met. ◄

PARENT-SUBSIDIARY CONTROLLED GROUPS. A **parent-subsidiary controlled group** exists if the following conditions are met:

▶ A common parent corporation owns at least 80% of the stock in at least one subsidiary.[30]

▶ At least 80% of the stock in each other member of the controlled group is owned by other members of the controlled group.

EXAMPLE I:16-24 ▶ Federal Corporation owns 100% of Apex Corporation stock and 30% of Giant Corporation stock. Apex also owns 50% of Giant stock. Each corporation has only one class of stock outstanding. Because Federal owns at least 80% of Apex stock, it is the common parent of the Federal-Apex-Giant parent-subsidiary controlled group. Giant also is a member of the controlled group because at least 80% of Giant stock is owned by members of the controlled group (Federal and Apex together own 80% [30% + 50%]). The parent-subsidiary controlled group consists of Federal, Apex, and Giant. ◄

COMBINED CONTROLLED GROUPS. A combined controlled group exists if the following two conditions involving three or more corporations are met:

▶ A common parent owns at least 80% of at least one subsidiary (a parent-subsidiary group), and

▶ The common parent is a member of a brother-sister controlled group.[31]

Based on the facts of Example I:16-24, a combined controlled group would have existed if Federal was a member of a brother-sister controlled group that also included National, a situation that would have resulted from Viki's owning 100% of the single classes of stock of Federal and National. Then, Federal, National, Apex, and Giant would have constituted a combined controlled group and would have had to apportion the various tax benefits.

BOOK-TAX ACCOUNTING COMPARISON

Corporations eligible to file a consolidated tax return may differ from those eligible to report on a consolidated financial accounting basis. 80% stock ownership is needed to file a consolidated tax return while only 50% stock ownership is needed to issue a consolidated financial statement.

CONSOLIDATED RETURNS

Corporations that are members of a parent-subsidiary affiliated group are eligible to file a consolidated tax return if they elect to do so under the consolidated return Treasury Regulations. Note, however, that an affiliated group is not the same as a controlled group. (See Chapter C:8 of the *Prentice Hall's Federal Taxation: Corporations, Partnerships, Estates, and Trusts* text for a detailed discussion of the requirements for filing a consolidated tax return.) Brother-sister controlled groups never can file consolidated tax returns. The parent-subsidiary members of a combined controlled group might

---

[30] Sec. 1563(a)(1).

[31] Sec. 1563(a)(3).

constitute an affiliated group and thus could elect to file a consolidated tax return. Although the parent's sister corporation is a member of the same controlled group, the parent's sister may not join in the consolidated tax return election. Once the election is made, IRS permission to discontinue filing on a consolidated basis is required.[32]

The consolidated return regulations treats the affiliated group as a single entity, thereby providing the following advantages: (1) net operating losses of one or more members can be used to offset profits of other members; (2) capital losses of one or more members can be used to offset capital gains of other members; and (3) transactions involving two or more group members are treated as occurring among divisions of a single entity, thus the taxation of profits and gains from such transactions is deferred until a subsequent transaction involving a group member and a party outside the affiliated group.

STOP & THINK

Question: P Corporation owns 100% of S-1 Corporation stock and P and S-1 Corporations each own 50% of S-2 Corporation stock. P and S-1 have owned stock in S-2 since its incorporation. Both P and S-1 are highly profitable and are subject to a flat 34% corporate tax rate. S-2 has generated a net operating loss (NOL) in each year of its existence. Would filing a consolidated tax return benefit P, S-1, and S-2?

Solution: Filing a consolidated return would benefit the corporations because S-2's current year losses can be used to offset P's and S-1's current year profits. Because S-2 has never earned a profit, it would not be able to use the NOL if it filed a separate return. In addition, S-2's prior year losses might be used to offset profits reported by S-1 in current year and future year consolidated tax returns. Filing a consolidated return allows the NOLs of one or more members of an affiliated group to offset the profits of other members and reduce the group's overall tax liability.

TRANSFERS OF PROPERTY TO CONTROLLED CORPORATIONS

OBJECTIVE 3

Apply the nonrecognition of gain or loss rules for corporate formations

Section 351 permits investors to defer recognition of gain or loss on the transfer of property to a corporation. The property may be transferred when a new corporation is formed or when additional capital is contributed to an existing corporation. Without the Sec. 351 nonrecognition rules, a sole proprietorship or a partnership might be discouraged from incorporating because the transfer of appreciated property to the corporation would constitute a taxable event, thereby resulting in a recognized gain.

SECTION 351 NONRECOGNITION REQUIREMENTS

KEY POINT

The nonrecognition provisions of Sec. 351 are mandatory rather than elective if all its conditions are met.

The deferral of gain or loss under Sec. 351 can be justified because the assets merely have been transferred to a corporation that is controlled by the transferors. In addition, the transferors do not have the wherewithal-to-pay the tax on the gains that otherwise would be recognized because they receive only stock in the transferee (controlled) corporation. Section 351 prevents recognition of losses on transfers of property that have declined in value.

Gain or loss is not recognized if all the following conditions are met:

▶ Property (other than services) is transferred to the corporation solely in exchange for stock in the transferee corporation.[33]

▶ Immediately after the exchange, the transferor-shareholders in the aggregate control the transferee corporation through ownership of at least 80% of its stock.[34]

[32] Reg. Sec. 1.1502-75(c).
[33] Section 351(d) provides that services do not qualify as "property". Thus, if an individual transfers services in exchange for stock, the individual is not deemed to be a transferor for purposes of meeting the 80% control requirement, unless the individual also transfers sufficient property. The rendering of

services results in the service provider's recognizing ordinary income equal to the FMV of the services rendered.
[34] Sec. 368(c). "Control" means the ownership of at least 80% of the total combined voting power of all classes of stock and at least 80% of the total number of shares of all other classes of stock.

▶ If a transferor receives money or property (other than stock in the transferee corporation), the transferor recognizes gain (but not loss) equal to the lesser of the "boot" (i.e., money plus the FMV of nonstock property) received or the realized gain.[35] In addition, a corporation that transfers appreciated property (other than its own stock or debt obligations) to the transferor-shareholders also recognizes gain on the exchange.[36]

▶ The character of any gain recognized by the transferor depends on the type of property transferred as follows: capital gain on capital assets, Sec. 1231 gain on Sec. 1231 property, and ordinary income on other property (e.g., inventory).

▶ Depreciation is not recaptured in a Sec. 351 transfer unless the transferor recognizes gain on the depreciable property transferred.[37]

EXAMPLE I:16-25 ▶

Carlos and Fred merge their sole proprietorships by forming the Miami Corporation. Carlos transfers to Miami land and a building with a $50,000 adjusted basis and a $100,000 FMV in exchange for 40% of Miami stock. Fred transfers to Miami equipment with a $60,000 adjusted basis and a $150,000 FMV in exchange for 60% of Miami stock. Miami is controlled by Carlos and Fred because immediately after the exchange together they own at least 80% of Miami's single class of stock. Carlos and Fred recognize no gain because all of the Sec. 351 requirements are met and they received no property other than Miami stock. The depreciation recapture potential on the building and equipment is inherited by Miami. ◀

EXAMPLE I:16-26 ▶

Gail and Gary form Michigan Corporation. Gail transfers inventory with a $50,000 adjusted basis and a $100,000 FMV to Michigan in exchange for $20,000 cash and 50% of Michigan stock worth $80,000. Michigan generated the cash through bank borrowings. Gary transfers equipment with a $150,000 adjusted basis and a $100,000 FMV in exchange for 50% of stock worth $80,000 and a Michigan 10-year note valued at $20,000. The Section 351 requirements are met because property is transferred by the two transferors who together control more than 80% of the Michigan stock immediately after the exchange. The tax consequences to Gail and Gary are as follows:

	Gail	Gary
FMV of stock received	$ 80,000	$ 80,000
Plus: Cash or note received	20,000	20,000
Amount realized	$100,000	$100,000
Minus: Adjusted basis of property transferred	(50,000)	(150,000)
Gain (loss) realized	$ 50,000	$ (50,000)
Gain (loss) recognized	$ 20,000	$ —0—

Gail's recognized gain is the lesser of the $20,000 boot she received or her $50,000 realized gain. This gain is ordinary in character because Gail transferred inventory. Because Gary realized a loss, he recognizes no gain or loss even though he received $20,000 of boot. ◀

BASIS CONSIDERATIONS

STOCK RECEIVED BY THE TRANSFEROR. In Sec. 351 transactions, substituted basis rules apply to stock received by the transferors and carryover basis rules apply to property transferred to the corporation. The transferor's stock basis is computed as follows:

ADDITIONAL COMMENT

When different classes of stock are received in a Sec. 351 exchange, the total substituted basis must be allocated among the different classes in proportion to their relative FMVs.

Basis of property transferred to the corporation
Plus: Any gain recognized by the transferor
         on the exchange (e.g., as a result of boot received)
Minus: Amount of money received (including any transferor
          liabilities assumed by the transferee corporation)
          FMV of any nonmoney boot property received

Basis of stock received[38]

Any boot property received by the tranferor takes a FMV basis.

---

[35] Sec. 351(b). Recognized gain is calculated on an asset-by-asset basis.
[36] Secs. 351(f) and 311(b).
[37] Secs. 1245(b)(3) and 1250(d)(3). The transferee corporation recaptures depreciation if it subsequently sells or disposes of the asset.

[38] Sec. 358(a).

EXAMPLE I:16-27 ▶ George and Gina form New Corporation. George transfers to New land and a building with a $60,000 adjusted basis and a $100,000 FMV in exchange for 50% of New stock. Gina transfers equipment with a $120,000 adjusted basis and a $100,000 FMV for 50% of New stock. George realizes a $40,000 gain, and Gina realizes a $20,000 loss. However, George and Gina recognize no gain or loss because the Sec. 351 requirements have been met. George's basis in his New stock is $60,000, and Gina's basis in her New stock is $120,000. ◀

STOP & THINK

Question: In Example I:16-27, George and Gina recognized no gain or loss. Why does this treatment represent tax deferral rather than permanent nonrecognition?

Solution: George's $40,000 unrecognized gain is reflected in a $60,000 stock basis that is $40,000 *below* its $100,000 FMV. Thus, if George immediately sells his stock for its FMV, he recognizes the $40,000 deferred gain ($100,000 selling price − $60,000 stock adjusted basis). Similarly, Gina's $20,000 unrecognized loss is reflected in a $120,000 stock basis that is $20,000 *above* its $100,000 FMV. Thus, if Gina immediately sells her stock for its FMV, she recognizes the $20,000 deferred loss ($100,000 selling price − $120,000 stock adjusted basis). In this way, the substituted basis rules ensure that realized gains and losses are deferred.

BOOK-TAX ACCOUNTING COMPARISON

Financial accounting requires that the corporation record the transferred assets at their fair market values.

PROPERTY RECEIVED BY TRANSFEREE CORPORATION. Generally, carryover basis rules apply to property received by the transferee corporation. The basis of this property is computed as follows:

Transferor's adjusted basis in property
Plus: Gain recognized by the transferor
_____
Basis of property to the transferee corporation[39]

EXAMPLE I:16-28 ▶ In a tax-free exchange under Sec. 351, North Corporation receives property with a $60,000 adjusted basis and a $100,000 FMV. If no gain is recognized on the transfer, the transferor's $60,000 adjusted basis becomes the transferee corporation's asset basis, as well as the shareholder's stock basis. If the transferor instead had recognized a $10,000 gain because she received boot (e.g., cash) North's asset basis would have been $70,000 ($60,000 adjusted basis in the transferor's hands + $10,000 gain recognized by the transferor), and the transferor's stock basis would have been $70,000. ◀

A special IRC provision is intended to discourage investors from attempting to generate double losses by transferring loss property to a corporation in connection with a Sec. 351 exchange.[40] In general, if the FMV of contributed property is less than the shareholder's adjusted basis in such property, the transferee corporation is required to use the FMV of the loss property as its asset basis.

TREATMENT OF LIABILITIES

TYPICAL MISCONCEPTION

When a corporation assumes a shareholder's liabilities and the shareholder recognizes no gain, one might mistakenly assume that the shareholder's stock basis is not reduced by the liabilities assumed.

NONRECOGNITION OF GAIN. Section 357(a) provides for the nonrecognition of gain upon the transferee corporation's assumption of liabilities or its taking property subject to liabilities. Accordingly, under the general rule, shareholders recognize no gain when they transfer liabilities to a controlled corporation. The shareholders, however, must reduce their stock basis by the amount of liabilities assumed or acquired. This rule is logical because, if a shareholder transfers net assets of $10,000 (i.e., gross assets of $100,000 and liabilities of $90,000), the net contribution to capital is only $10,000 even though the shareholder has transferred $100,000 in gross assets.

EXAMPLE I:16-29 ▶ In a transaction qualifying as tax-free under Sec. 351, Ira transfers land with an $80,000 adjusted basis and a $100,000 FMV to Mega Corporation in exchange for 100% of Mega stock with a $60,000 FMV. The transferred property is subject to a $40,000 liability that the corporation assumes. The tax consequences to Ira are as follows:

---

[39] Sec. 362(a).   [40] Sec. 362(e).

FMV of stock received	$ 60,000
Plus: Liability assumed by Mega	40,000
Amount realized	$100,000
Minus: Adjusted basis of property transferred	(80,000)
Gain realized by Ira	$ 20,000
Gain recognized by Ira	$ –0–
Adjusted basis of property transferred	$ 80,000
Minus: Liability assumed by Mega	(40,000)
Ira's adjusted basis in Mega stock received	$ 40,000

In addition, Mega takes an $80,000 carryover basis in the land. ◄

EXCEPTIONS. Two exceptions to the general rule of Sec. 357 require gain recognition upon the transfer of liabilities to a corporation. The first exception relates to the nature of the exchange. If the principal purpose for the assumption of the liabilities is tax avoidance or if the transaction does not have a bona fide business purpose, all of the transferor's liabilities assumed by the transferee corporation are treated as boot, potentially resulting in gain recognition.[41]

EXAMPLE I:16-30 ▶ In a transaction purportedly meeting the requirements of Sec. 351, Helen transfers to Orlando Corporation land and a building with a $70,000 adjusted basis and a $100,000 FMV in exchange for 100% of Orlando stock. Shortly before the transfer, Helen mortgages the property for $60,000 and uses the mortgage loan to pay off personal debts. The corporation then assumes the $60,000 mortgage and issues to Helen stock worth $40,000. The mortgage assumption lacks a bona fide business purpose because it is intended to place cash in Helen's hands without her recognizing gain under the boot rules. Consequently, for the purpose of determining gain recognized, Helen must treat the entire $60,000 liability assumed as boot. The tax consequences to Helen are as follows:

FMV of stock received	$ 40,000
Plus: Liability assumed by Orlando	60,000
Amount realized	$100,000
Minus: Adjusted basis of property transferred	(70,000)
Gain realized	$ 30,000
Gain recognized	$ 30,000
Adjusted basis of property transferred	$ 70,000
Plus: Gain recognized	30,000
Minus: Liability assumed by Orlando	(60,000)
Adjusted basis of stock received	$ 40,000

Although total boot is $60,000 (the liability assumed), Helen's recognized gain does not exceed her $30,000 realized gain. In addition, the stock basis equals its FMV because Helen recognizes the entire realized gain, with no gain to defer. Finally, Orlando's basis in the land and building is $100,000 ($70,000 adjusted basis in the transferor's hands + $30,000 gain recognized by the transferor). ◄

REAL-WORLD EXAMPLE

Customer deposits representing obligations to perform future services were considered liabilities. Because these liabilities exceeded the basis of the assets transferred to the corporation, gain was recognized. *William P. Orr,* 78 T.C. 1059 (1982).

A second exception applies to excess liabilities. If a transferor's total liabilities assumed by the transferee corporation exceeds the total basis of assets (including cash) transferred by that transferor, the transferor must recognize gain to the extent of the excess.[42] Without this rule, the transferor would take a negative basis in the stock received. Gain is recognized because the transferor has derived a net economic benefit to the extent the liabilities assumed exceed the adjusted basis of the transferred assets.

---

[41] Sec. 357(b).
[42] Sec. 357(c). Accounts receivable and accounts payable with a zero basis for a cash basis transferor are disregarded for purposes of Sec. 357(c). (See Sec. 357(c)(3).)

EXAMPLE I:16-31 ▶ In a transaction otherwise qualifying as tax-free under Sec. 351 Jack transfers to Maple Corporation assets with a $60,000 adjusted basis and a $100,000 FMV. Simultaneously, Maple assumes $75,000 of Jack's liabilities. Jack recognizes a $15,000 gain because the liabilities assumed by Maple exceed the basis of the assets transferred ($75,000 − $60,000). The character of Jack's recognized gain depends on the type(s) of property (capital assets, Sec. 1231 property, inventory, etc.) Jack transferred.[43] Jack's net economic benefit from the exchange is $15,000 ($75,000 liabilities assumed by Maple − $60,000 adjusted basis of assets transferred). Jack's basis in the stock received is zero ($60,000 asset adjusted basis + $15,000 gain recognized − $75,000 liabilities assumed). Because Jack's realized gain is $40,000 of which he recognizes $15,000, only $25,000 of the gain is deferred ($25,000 FMV of stock − $0 basis). Maple's basis in the assets is increased from $60,000 to $75,000 because of Jack's $15,000 recognized gain. ◀

Topic Review I:16-3 summarizes the general rules relating to the transfer of property to a controlled corporation.

CORPORATE CAPITAL STRUCTURE

ADDITIONAL COMMENT

Thin capitalization is primarily a problem for closely-held corporations where the shareholders also hold the debt. It is not normally a problem for large publicly-held corporations.

A corporation may be capitalized with both equity (generally common or preferred stock) and debt. The use of debt in the capital structure offers the following advantages:

▶ Interest on debt is deductible by the corporation, while dividends on stock are not deductible.

▶ Stock redemptions may result in dividend treatment to the shareholders unless certain requirements are met (see pages I:16-28 through I:16-31), while debt repayment represents a tax-free return of capital.

If the corporation is too thinly capitalized (e.g., excessive debt relative to equity), the IRS may attempt to recharacterize part or all of the debt as equity and deny the corporation an interest deduction.

Topic Review I:16-3

Sec. 351 Requirements, Gain Recognition Rules, and Basis Rules

▶ Sec. 351 nonrecognition treatment requires an exchange of property solely for stock. The transferor-shareholders must control (i.e., 80% or more stock ownership) the corporation immediately after the exchange.

▶ Nonqualifying property (e.g., cash, nonmoney property, or debt obligations of the transferee corporation) received by the transferors is treated as boot.

▶ The transferors recognize gain equal to the lesser of the boot received or the realized gain.

▶ Generally, the transferors recognize no gain if they transfer liabilities to a controlled corporation. Exceptions to the nonrecognition rule apply if (1) the principal purpose of the liability transfer is tax avoidance, (2) no bona fide business purpose for the transfer exists, or (3) total liabilities assumed by the corporation exceed the transferor's adjusted basis in the transferred assets.

▶ Substituted basis rules referencing the basis of the asset(s) transferred apply to the stock received by the transferors. Generally, carryover basis rules apply to property contributed to the transferee corporation. However, if the FMV of the property is less than the carryover basis, the corporation must use a FMV basis.

---

[43] Reg. Sec. 1.357-2(a).

EARNINGS AND PROFITS

CALCULATION OF EARNINGS AND PROFITS

Earnings and profits (E&P) measures a C corporation's economic ability to pay dividends out of its current and accumulated earnings without impairing its capital. If the corporation has no E&P, a distribution is treated as a tax-free return of capital, and possibly a capital gain, rather than a taxable dividend.

Current E&P is calculated by making various adjustments to the corporation's regular taxable income.[44] This calculation, as well as the determination of accumulated E&P, is set forth in Table I:16-3.

EXAMPLE I:16-32 ▶

BOOK-TAX ACCOUNTING COMPARISON

E&P is similar to retained earnings in financial accounting although numerous differences exist between the two accounts. For example, issuance of a stock dividend usually reduces retained earnings but does not affect E&P.

Park Corporation, an accrual method taxpayer, reports $100,000 of taxable income in the current year. Its tax accountant made the following adjustments to derive current E&P and the addition to accumulated E&P:

Taxable income	$100,000
Plus:	
Tax-exempt bond interest	2,000
Key officer life insurance proceeds (nontaxable)	10,000
Dividends-received deduction	20,000
MACRS depreciation in excess of ADS depreciation	15,000
Percentage depletion in excess of cost depletion	10,000
U.S. production activities deduction	3,000
	$160,000
Minus:	
Federal income taxes accrued[a]	(22,250)
Net capital losses	(5,000)
Key officer life insurance premiums (not deductible because the corporation is the beneficiary)	(2,000)
Charitable contributions exceeding the 10% limitation	(3,000)
Fine for overweight trucks on city streets	(5,000)
Current E&P	$122,750
Minus: Money distribution	(5,000)
Addition to accumulated E&P	$117,750

[a]An accrual method of accounting corporation reduces its E&P by its accrued federal income taxes for the tax year. A cash method of accounting corporation reduces its E&P by its actual federal income taxes paid during the tax year.

To derive E&P, regular taxable income is increased by nontaxable income—the tax-exempt bond interest and the life insurance proceeds—received by Park. Taxable income also is increased for deductions claimed when calculating regular taxable income but not allowed when calculating E&P. Three of these deductions do not represent economic outlays—the dividends-received deduction, U.S. production activities deduction, and percentage depletion in excess of cost. Another adjustment represents a timing difference that will reverse in later tax years—MACRS depreciation in excess of Alternative Depreciation System (ADS) depreciation. Regular taxable income is reduced by negative adjustments for economic outlays that are not deductible in calculating regular taxable income. These E&P reductions include federal income taxes, capital losses in excess of capital gains, key officer life insurance premiums, excess charitable contributions, and fines. ◀

CURRENT VERSUS ACCUMULATED E&P

Current and accumulated E&P must be distinguished because tracing rules determine whether a distribution is made out of current or accumulated E&P. For example, a distribution to shareholders is deemed to be made first out of current E&P and is therefore taxed as a dividend, even if accumulated E&P is negative. Accumulated E&P represents

---

[44] These adjustments are set forth in Sec. 312 and the related Treasury Regulations.

▼ TABLE I:16-3

Calculation of Earnings and Profits

Regular taxable income

Plus: Exclusions from regular taxable income:
- Tax-exempt interest
- Life insurance proceeds where the corporation is the beneficiary
- Recoveries of bad debts and other prior-year deductions for which the corporation received no tax benefit
- Federal income tax refunds from prior years

Plus: Income deferred to a later year for taxable income purposes:
- Deferred gain on installment sales
- Deferred gain on like-kind exchanges

Plus or minus: Adjustments for items that must be recomputed:
- Income on long-term contracts based on percentage of completion method rather than completed contract method
- Excess of pre-ACRS accelerated depreciation over straight-line depreciation
- Excess of ACRS depreciation over straight-line ACRS depreciation with an extended recovery period
- Excess of regular MACRS depreciation over Alternative Depreciation System (ADS) depreciation
- Excess of percentage depletion over cost depletion

Plus: Deductions not allowed in computing E&P:
- Dividends-received deduction
- NOL carryovers, charitable contribution carryovers, and capital loss carryovers from prior years
- U.S. production activitives deduction

Minus: Expenses and losses not deductible in computing regular taxable income:
- Federal income taxes
- Life insurance premiums where the corporation is the beneficiary
- Excess capital losses not deductible in current year
- Excess charitable contributions not deductible in current year
- Expenses related to production of tax-exempt income
- Nondeductible losses on related party sales
- Nondeductible penalties and fines
- Nondeductible political contributions

Current E&P (or E&P deficit)
Minus: Distributions to shareholders (but not in excess of current E&P)

Addition to accumulated E&P (if any)

the total of all prior years' undistributed current E&P as of the first day of the tax year. Distributions are deemed to be made out of accumulated E&P only after the current E&P balance (if any) is exhausted.[45]

EXAMPLE I:16-33 ▶   Pacific Corporation, a calendar-year taxpayer, reports a $100,000 accumulated E&P deficit and $30,000 of current E&P as of January 1. Pacific makes a $40,000 distribution to its shareholders. In the distribution, $30,000 is treated as a taxable dividend to the extent of current E&P, and the remaining $10,000 is treated as a tax-free return of capital (to the extent that Pacific's shareholders have stock basis) because of the accumulated E&P deficit, which is not increased as a result of the tax-free distribution. ◀

If a shareholder's stock basis is reduced to zero because of a property distribution treated as a tax-free return of capital, the excess of the distribution amount over this basis is treated as a capital gain.

[45] Reg. Sec. 1.316-2.

EXAMPLE I:16-34 ▶ Peach Corporation, a calendar-year taxpayer, has one shareholder, Georgia, who has owned her Peach stock for several years. At the beginning of the current year, Peach has $30,000 of current E&P and $20,000 of accumulated E&P. Georgia's stock basis is $10,000. At the end of the current year, Peach distributes $65,000 to Georgia. The $65,000 distribution is reported as follows:

Taxable dividend paid out of current E&P	$30,000
Taxable dividend paid out of accumulated E&P	20,000
Total taxable dividend	$50,000
Tax-free return of capital	10,000
Long-term capital gain	5,000
Total distribution	$65,000

In addition, Georgia's stock basis is reduced to zero because of the $10,000 portion treated as a return of capital. ◀

If the distributing corporation has a current E&P deficit and a positive accumulated E&P balance, the current deficit and accumulated E&P balance are netted as of the distribution date.[46] The current E&P deficit for the year is prorated on a daily basis unless a nonratable allocation is more appropriate.

EXAMPLE I:16-35 ▶ On January 1 of the current (nonleap) year, Prime Corporation, a calendar-year taxpayer, has a $100,000 positive accumulated E&P balance and a $35,500 current E&P deficit. Prime makes a $30,000 distribution to its shareholders on July 1 (the 182nd day of the year). Because the current deficit is allocated ratably over the year unless the corporation can show that a nonratable allocation is more appropriate, E&P as of July 1 is $82,201 [$100,000 accumulated E&P − (183/365 × $35,500 current E&P deficit)]. The entire $30,000 distribution is taxable as a dividend. ◀

NONMONEY DISTRIBUTIONS

OBJECTIVE 5

Determine the tax consequences of nonmoney distributions and stock redemptions

TAX CONSEQUENCES TO THE SHAREHOLDERS

Occasionally, a corporation distributes nonmoney property (i.e., assets other than its stock or stock rights) to its shareholders. If nonmoney property is distributed, the following tax consequences generally ensue:

▶ The distribution amount equals the FMV of the property (reduced by any associated liabilities).

▶ The distribution amount is treated as a taxable dividend if the corporation has sufficient E&P.

▶ The basis of the distributed property equals its FMV (without reduction for any associated liabilities).

EXAMPLE I:16-36 ▶

REAL-WORLD EXAMPLE

A distribution of $20 Double Eagle gold coins was a nonmoney distribution rather than a money distribution because the gold coins were withdrawn from circulation and had numismatic value. *Warren C. Cordner v. U.S.,* 49 AFTR 2d 82-1353, 82-1 USTC ¶9275 (9th Cir., 1982).

Red Corporation distributes land and a building having a $50,000 adjusted basis and a $100,000 FMV to its sole shareholder, Irene. Red has current and accumulated E&P exceeding $100,000. The property is subject to a $40,000 mortgage, which Irene assumes. The amount distributed to Irene is $60,000 ($100,000 FMV − $40,000 liability). Irene reports a $60,000 taxable dividend because the corporation has E&P exceeding the distribution amount. Irene's basis in the property is its $100,000 FMV. ◀

TAX CONSEQUENCES TO THE DISTRIBUTING CORPORATION

As a general rule, the corporation recognizes no gain or loss upon distributing nonmoney property to its shareholders.[47] However, if a corporation distributes appreciated nonmoney property, the corporation is treated as if it sold the property to the shareholder for its FMV immediately before the distribution and thus recognizes any realized gain.[48] On

---

[46] Reg. Sec. 1.316-2(b).
[47] Sec. 311(a).
[48] Sec. 311(b).

the other hand, a corporation does not recognize loss when it distributes depreciated nonmoney property, even though a sale of such property might otherwise have resulted in a deductible tax loss.

EXAMPLE I:16-37 ▶ Rocket Corporation distributes to its shareholder Peter $75,000 in cash, along with land having a $50,000 adjusted basis and a $60,000 FMV. Rocket recognizes $10,000 ($60,000 − $50,000) of gain on the land distribution. Alternatively, if the land had a $60,000 adjusted basis and a $50,000 FMV, the corporation would not have recognized the $10,000 ($50,000 − $60,000) realized loss. ◀

If the property distributed is subject to a liability that exceeds the property's basis, for the purpose of calculating gain, the FMV of such property is deemed to be the greater of the actual FMV or the amount of the liability.[49]

EXAMPLE I:16-38 ▶ Assume the same facts as in Example I:16-37 except that the land is subject to a $70,000 mortgage. Rocket recognizes a $20,000 ($70,000 − $50,000) gain on the distribution because the mortgage exceeds the land's FMV. ◀

 STOP & THINK

Question: What are the tax consequences of a pro rata stock dividend, that is, a corporation's issuing additional shares of its own single class of stock to existing shareholders?

Solution: The shareholder's economic position does not change as a result of the stock dividend. Although the shareholders receive additional shares of stock, they still own the same proportion of stock in the corporation. Consequently, they realize no economic gain on the stock dividend. Accordingly, they spread the basis of their old shares over their old and new shares, thereby decreasing the per share basis while leaving the total basis unchanged. In addition, the corporation recognizes no gain or loss and does not reduce its E&P balance. Some stock dividends, such as those involving a shareholder election to receive either stock or cash, are taxable.[50] (See Chapter 4 of *Prentice Hall's Corporations, Partnerships, Estates, and Trusts*).

STOCK REDEMPTIONS

Two possible tax consequences ensue when a corporation repurchases (redeems) some of its outstanding stock:

▶ The redemption is treated as a taxable dividend to the shareholder to the extent of the corporation's E&P

▶ The redemption is treated as an exchange of stock, generally resulting in the shareholder's recognizing capital gain or loss

The first prescribed treatment is intended to discourage corporations from paying a disguised dividend in the form of a stock redemption taxable as a capital gain. For example, the corporation might redeem 10% of its sole shareholder's stock rather than pay a cash dividend. After the redemption, the shareholder continues to own all of the outstanding stock, retains the same degree of control over the corporation, and holds the distributed money or other property. Taxing the redemption as an exchange would reduce the tax burden on the shareholder without reducing his/her ownership interest.

The second prescribed tax treatment is significant because individual shareholders are generally subject to a 15% maximum rate on their net capital gains. In addition, exchange treatment is preferable if the shareholders have unused capital losses or capital loss carryovers that otherwise would be of limited tax benefit. Moreover, exchange treatment affords shareholders a tax-free recovery of their stock investment. Such a tax-free recovery does not result if the distribution is treated as a dividend.

---

[49] Secs. 311(b)(2) and 336(b).   [50] Sec. 305(b).

EXAMPLE I:16-39 ▶ Ajax Corporation has two equal shareholders, Rita and Harry. Each shareholder has owned 10 shares of Ajax stock for several years. Each share has a $100 basis and a $150 FMV. Ajax, which has sufficient E&P, redeems 5 shares from each shareholder for the $150 FMV. As a result of the redemption, Rita and Harry each recognize $750 ($150 FMV × 5 shares) of dividend income because each still owns 50% of Ajax stock. Rita's total $1,000 basis in her stock is not decreased as a result of the dividend treatment. On the other hand, her per share basis increases from $100 ($1,000 ÷ 10 shares) to $200 ($1,000 ÷ 5) per share.

If instead, Ajax redeems 5 of Rita's shares but none of Harry's, Rita has substantially reduced her proportionate ownership interest in Ajax. Consequently, she is entitled to exchange treatment and recognizes a $250 capital gain calculated as follows:

Redemption proceeds ($150 × 5)	$750
Minus: Basis of stock redeemed ($100 × 5)	(500)
Capital gain	$250

The capital gain is generally long-term and is taxed at a 15% rate. Moreover, only $250 is taxed in the case of exchange treatment as opposed to $750 in the case of dividend treatment. In the former case, Rita's total $1,000 basis is reduced to $500. The basis of her 5 shares redeemed offsets the $750 redemption amount. Rita's per share basis remains at $100 ($500 ÷ 5 shares) after the redemption. Example I:16-40 on page I:16-30 explains why the first redemption warrants dividend treatment while the second redemption warrants exchange treatment. ◀

DETERMINING WHETHER A REDEMPTION IS A DIVIDEND OR CAPITAL GAIN

A redemption is treated as an exchange taxed as a capital gain or loss if any of the following conditions are met:[51]

▶ The redemption is substantially disproportionate with respect to the shareholder's interest [Sec. 302(b)(2)].

▶ The redemption is not essentially equivalent to a dividend [Sec. 302(b)(1)].[52]

▶ The redemption completely terminates the shareholder's interest [Sec. 302(b)(3)].

SUBSTANTIALLY DISPROPORTIONATE. Constructive stock ownership rules apply to determine whether a redemption is substantially disproportionate.[53] **Constructive stock ownership** means that the redeemed shareholder is considered to own the stock of certain related parties. These related parties include family members, partnerships and corporations in which the shareholder owns an interest, and trusts and estates of which the shareholder is a beneficiary.

For a redemption to be substantially disproportionate, all of the following tests must be met immediately after the redemption:

▶ The shareholder must own less than 80% of his or her former percentage of voting stock (including stock held by related parties).

▶ The shareholder must own less than 80% of his or her former percentage of common (voting and nonvoting) stock (including stock held by related parties).

▶ The shareholder must own less than 50% of all the voting stock (including stock held by related parties).

Under Sec. 302(b)(2) a redemption of solely nonvoting stock will not qualify for capital gains treatment.

NOT ESSENTIALLY EQUIVALENT TO A DIVIDEND. A redemption that is not essentially equivalent to a dividend results in a meaningful reduction in the shareholder's interest.[54] In determining whether a meaningful reduction has occurred, the IRS looks at the shareholder's interest in the following: (1) voting power, (2) participation in earning

[51] Sec. 302.
[52] For example, exchange treatment has been allowed where the redeemed shareholder's voting control, right to share in current earnings, and right to receive corporate assets upon liquidation have been significantly reduced. Ordinarily, this occurs when a shareholder's majority interest is converted to a 50% interest, a majority interest is converted to a minority (less than 50%) interest, or a minority interest is significantly reduced. (See, for example, Rev. Ruls. 75-502 and 76-364 cited in footnotes 55 and 56.)
[53] Sec. 318.
[54] *U.S. v. Maclin P. Davis,* 25 AFTR 2d 70-827, 70-1 USTC ¶9289 (USSC, 1970).

and profits, and (3) share of net assets upon liquidation.[55] This approach usually is adopted if the redemption fails the objective tests for a substantially disproportionate redemption. Specifically, if a shareholder's interest falls below 50% after the redemption, but the redemption does not meet the 80% test, the shareholder might argue that the redemption is not essentially equivalent to a dividend. For example, a reduction in ownership from 27% to 22% fails the 80% test for substantially disproportionate redemptions (80% × 27% = 21.6%) but could be regarded as a meaningful reduction in the shareholder's interest.[56]

EXAMPLE I:16-40 ▶

In Example I:16-39, the redemption of both Rita and Harry's stock failed the substantially disproportionate test. For Rita and Harry to pass the test, each shareholder's current ownership percentage must be less than 80% of his or her former ownership percentage, or 40% (80% × 50% prior ownership) and less than 50% on an absolute basis. After the redemption, Rita and Harry each still own exactly 50% of Ajax's single class of stock, thereby failing both the 80% and 50% tests.

On the other hand, the redemption of only Rita's 5 shares qualifies for exchange treatment because, after the redemption, Rita owns 33⅓% (5 shares Rita still owns ÷ 15 total shares outstanding) of Ajax's single class of stock. Thus, Rita's post-redemption ownership is less than the 40% and 50% thresholds, thereby making the redemption substantially disproportionate. ◀

EXAMPLE I:16-41 ▶

Jane owns 60 shares of Fast Corporation's single class of stock. Her mother owns 20 additional shares of Fast stock. The remaining 20 Fast shares are owned by Peter, who is unrelated to Jane or her mother. Fast redeems 30 shares of Jane's stock for $100,000. Jane's percentage interest before the redemption is 80% [(60 + 20 shares) ÷ 100 shares]. Immediately after the redemption, her percentage interest is 71.4% [(30 + 20 shares) ÷ 70 shares]. To meet the 80% test, Jane's interest must be less than 64% (80% × 80%). Therefore, Jane does not meet the 80% test. Also, Jane does not meet the 50% test because she does not own less than 50% of Fast stock after the redemption. Both tests must be met for the redemption to qualify as substantially disproportionate. Jane likely will not qualify for Sec. 302(b)(1) "not essentially equivalent to a dividend" treatment because she has not reduced her stock interest to 50% or less. Therefore, the $100,000 is treated as a dividend and is taxable to Jane to the extent of Fast's E&P. ◀

COMPLETE TERMINATION.   Under Sec. 302(b)(3), a complete termination of a shareholder's stock interest also qualifies for capital gain or loss treatment. At first glance, this rule appears redundant because the substantially disproportionate rule also applies to a redemption that results in a complete termination of a shareholder's interest. However, the complete termination provision permits a waiver of the family ownership attribution rules. These rules are waived if the former shareholder files an agreement with the IRS that for 10 years he or she will acquire no interest other than that as a creditor of the corporation.[57]

EXAMPLE I:16-42 ▶

REAL-WORLD EXAMPLE

All of a father's stock in a corporation was redeemed, and his children were the remaining shareholders. Then the father entered into a long-term contract with the corporation to perform consulting and advisory services. The contract represented an interest in the corporation and the family attribution rules were not waived. Rev. Rul. 70-104, 1970-1 C.B. 66.

Assume the same facts as in Example I:16-41 except that Fast Corporation redeems all of Jane's 60 shares for $200,000, and Jane's basis in her shares is $90,000. The family ownership attribution rules are waived if Jane agrees not to acquire any interest in Fast for 10 years. Jane's interest is deemed to be completely terminated, and the redemption is treated as a sale of stock, thus eligible for capital gains treatment. Jane recognizes a capital gain of $110,000 ($200,000 − $90,000). If the waiver is not effective because Jane remains an employee of Fast, the substantially disproportionate tests would be applied to determine whether the redemption qualifies as an exchange. Jane would be deemed to own 50% of the stock (20 shares owned ÷ 40 outstanding shares) immediately after the redemption. Thus, the substantially disproportionate test would not be met. Without an effective waiver, the redemption does not qualify as a complete termination because Jane is deemed to own her mother's stock. Consequently, the redemption would be treated as a dividend unless it could qualify for sale treatment under the Sec. 302(b)(1) "not-essentially-equivalent-to-a-dividend" test. ◀

---

[55] Rev. Rul. 75-502, 1975-2 C.B. 111.
[56] Rev. Rul. 76-364, 1976-2 C.B. 91.
[57] Sec. 302(c)(2). The former shareholder cannot serve as an officer, director, or employee for at least 10 years and must notify the IRS if additional stock is acquired (other than by bequest or inheritance). If such stock is subsequently acquired, it usually causes the redemption to be recharacterized as a dividend.

CORPORATE DISTRIBUTIONS IN COMPLETE LIQUIDATION

OBJECTIVE 6

Understand the tax implications of a corporate liquidation for the liquidating corporation and its shareholders

Sometimes shareholders may wish to terminate a corporation's existence. A complete liquidation is similar to a stock redemption except that all (rather than a portion) of the corporation's stock is redeemed. In a complete liquidation, the assets are either distributed in kind to the shareholders in exchange for their stock or sold for cash, which is then distributed to the shareholders in exchange for their stock. The liquidated corporation usually is dissolved under state law.

Surprisingly, the reasons for a complete termination are not always associated with unprofitable operations. For example, a highly-successful closely-held company may have management continuity problems because key officers and shareholders are approaching retirement age. Also, for reasons of organizational management, a parent corporation may wish to liquidate a subsidiary and continue its operations as a separate division of the parent.

TYPICAL MISCONCEPTION

It is sometimes assumed that corporate liquidation always is associated with the discontinuance of business activities. Sometimes, however, the business is operated as a limited liability company, partnership, or sole proprietorship after the liquidation.

TAX CONSEQUENCES TO THE LIQUIDATING CORPORATION

DISTRIBUTION OF ASSETS. In a liquidation, the liquidating corporation is treated as if it had sold its assets for their FMV to its shareholders and thus recognizes gain or loss.[58] If the distributed property is subject to a liability, the FMV of the property is deemed to be the greater of the property's actual FMV or the amount of the liability.

EXAMPLE I:16-43 ▶

In a complete liquidation, Southern Corporation distributes the following assets to its shareholders:

▶ Inventory: $12,000 basis, $20,000 FMV

▶ Investment land: $5,000 basis, $40,000 FMV, subject to a $30,000 liability

▶ Marketable securities: $20,000 basis, $15,000 FMV

Southern recognizes $8,000 ($20,000 − $12,000) of ordinary income on the distribution of the inventory, $35,000 ($40,000 − $5,000) of capital gain on the distribution of the land, and $5,000 ($15,000 − $20,000) of capital loss on the distribution of the marketable securities. ◀

SALE OF ASSETS. The tax consequences of an asset sale closely parallel those of a liquidating distribution. If a corporation sells its assets in a complete liquidation and then distributes the sales proceeds to its shareholders, all gain or loss realized on the sale is recognized by the corporation.

LIMITATION ON LOSS RECOGNITION. Under the general rule, upon liquidating, the corporation recognizes both gains and losses. To prevent abuses, three special rules limit the recognition of losses. First, a liquidating subsidiary recognizes neither gain nor loss when it distributes property to its parent. In addition, a liquidating subsidiary recognizes gain (but not loss) when it distributes property to minority shareholders. (The special rules applying to the liquidation of a subsidiary are set forth below.) Second, a liquidating corporation recognizes no loss when it distributes property to a related person, unless the property is distributed ratably to all shareholders and the property was not contributed in a Sec. 351 transaction or otherwise as capital within the preceding five years. Finally, losses are not recognized upon the sale, exchange, or distribution of property where the property was contributed in a Sec. 351 transaction or otherwise as capital, the principal purpose of which was loss recognition. These special loss limitations are explained further in Chapter C:6 of *Prentice Hall's Federal Taxation: Corporations, Partnerships, Estates, and Trusts.*

---

[58] Sec. 336.

TAX ATTRIBUTES.   Tax attributes, such as NOL carryovers, E&P balances, capital loss carryovers, and tax credits, are extinguished in a corporate liquidation.

TAX CONSEQUENCES TO THE SHAREHOLDERS

KEY POINT

An appraisal may be necessary to determine the FMV of the distributed assets.

Under the general rule for complete liquidations, shareholders are deemed to have sold their stock to the corporation in exchange for money or other property.[59] If the stock is a capital asset, the shareholder recognizes capital gain or loss equal to (1) the money plus the FMV of other property distributed to the shareholder less (2) the adjusted basis of the shareholder's stock.[60] The value of property distributed to a shareholder is its FMV on the distribution date.[61]

EXAMPLE I:16-44 ▶

In a complete liquidation, Sun Corporation distributes land with a $70,000 adjusted basis and a $100,000 FMV to shareholder John, in exchange for his Sun stock. John's adjusted basis in the stock is $40,000. Joan, another shareholder, receives $100,000 cash for her shares. Joan's adjusted basis in her stock is $120,000. John recognizes a $60,000 ($100,000 − $40,000) capital gain. Joan recognizes a $20,000 ($100,000 − $120,000) capital loss. The basis of the land received by John is $100,000 (the land's FMV on the distribution date). ◀

SECTION 332: LIQUIDATION OF A SUBSIDIARY CORPORATION

KEY POINT

Section 351 permits a parent corporation to incorporate a subsidiary corporation tax-free. Section 332 permits a parent corporation to liquidate a controlled subsidiary corporation without adverse tax results where the subsidiary's property has significantly appreciated in value.

GAIN AND LOSS CONSIDERATIONS.   Section 332 carves out an exception to the general rule that gain or loss is recognized in a liquidating distribution. Under this exception, neither a parent nor its 80% or more owned subsidiary recognizes gain or loss when the parent liquidates the subsidiary.[62] In a Sec. 332 liquidation, the subsidiary usually is dissolved, and its assets and liabilities transferred to the parent. The Section 332 nonrecognition rule is mandatory, not elective, if its requirements are met.

For nonrecognition treatment, the subsidiary must:

▶ Distribute all its assets to the parent in complete liquidation within a single tax year.

▶ Make a series of distributions resulting in a complete liquidation over a three-year period that commences at the close of the tax year in which the first liquidating distribution is made.

If a minority interest also is being liquidated, the exception does not apply. The subsidiary recognizes gain (but not loss) on property distributed to a minority shareholder. In addition, the minority shareholder(s), recognize(s) gain or loss.

KEY POINT

A parent corporation whose basis for its subsidiary's stock exceeds the tax basis of its share of the subsidiary's net assets loses the tax benefit of the economic loss if the subsidiary is liquidated under the Sec. 332 rules.

BASIS CONSIDERATIONS.   The basis of the subsidiary's assets carry over to the parent, and the adjusted basis of the parent's stock in the subsidiary disappears.[63] This rule could create inequities because the parent may have paid an amount for the subsidiary stock that is greater (or less) than the parent's basis in the subsidiary's net assets.

EXAMPLE I:16-45 ▶

Several years ago Tampa Corporation acquired 100% of Top Corporation stock for $100,000. In the current year, Top is liquidated, and assets having a $130,000 FMV and a $50,000 basis are transferred to Tampa. Upon receiving the assets, Tampa recognizes no gain or loss. Tampa's $100,000 basis in the Top stock disappears, and Tampa takes only a $50,000 basis in the Top assets. Tampa would recognize an $80,000 ($130,000 − $50,000) gain should it sell the assets for their $130,000 FMV immediately after the liquidation. The character of the gain would depend on the type of assets received by Tampa. ◀

When these carryover basis rules apply, the parent corporation also inherits the tax attributes of the subsidiary.[64] For example, the liquidated subsidiary's NOL and capital

[59] Sec. 331(a)(1).

[60] Certain losses on the sale of small business stock are ordinary in character if the requirements of Sec. 1244 are met (see Chapter I:8).

[61] Sec. 334(a).

[62] Under Sec. 1504(a)(2), the parent corporation must own at least 80% of the total combined voting power of all classes of stock entitled to vote and at least 80% of the total value of all classes of stock.

[63] Sec. 334(b)(1).

[64] Sec. 381.

loss carryovers and E&P balances carry over to the parent. In addition, the subsidiary recognizes no gain under the depreciation recapture rules. Instead, this recapture potential remains with the subsidiary assets distributed to the parent.

Topic Review I:16-4 summarizes the complete liquidation rules.

TAX PLANNING CONSIDERATIONS

CAPITAL STRUCTURE AND SECTION 1244

As mentioned earlier in the chapter, the issuance of long-term debt to capitalize a profitable closely-held C corporation could bolster the corporation's total economic returns and thus increase share values. However, if the corporation is no longer profitable and goes bankrupt, the corporate debt becomes worthless and is treated by noncorporate shareholders as nonbusiness bad debt. As is discussed in Chapter I:8, nonbusiness bad debt is deductible as a short-term capital loss subject to the $3,000 per year limitation.

Topic Review I:16-4

Distributions in Complete Liquidation

SEC. 331 GENERAL LIQUIDATION RULES	LIQUIDATING CORPORATION	SHAREHOLDERS
Gain or loss recognition	Gain or loss equal to the FMV of the property distributed less the property's adjusted basis generally is recognized.	Capital gain or loss equal to the amount of money plus the FMV of other property received less the shareholder's basis of stock in the liquidating corporation is recognized.
Exception to the gain or loss rule	Losses are not recognized on distributions of property to related parties, or property acquired in certain tax-free transactions, where the principal purpose for the transaction is tax avoidance.	Sec. 1244 ordinary loss treatment is available only to individual shareholders.
Basis considerations	Not applicable.	The basis of nonmoney property received is its FMV.
Tax attributes	Tax attributes (e.g., NOL carryovers and E&P) disappear upon liquidation.	Not applicable.

SEC. 332 SUBSIDIARY CORPORATION LIQUIDATION RULES	SUBSIDIARY	PARENT
General requirements	The subsidiary is liquidated, and its assets and liabilities are transferred to its minority shareholders and parent.	Sec. 332 is mandatory. The parent must own at least 80% of subsidiary stock.
Gain or loss recognition	No gain or loss is recognized on the transfer of assets to the parent. Gain but not loss is recognized on distributions to minority shareholders.	The parent recognizes no gain or loss. Minority shareholders recognize gain or loss.
Basis considerations	None.	The basis of subsidiary assets carry over to the parent. Minority shareholders take a FMV basis in the assets they receive.
Tax attributes	Tax attributes are extinguished in the liquidation.	Tax attributes (e.g., NOL carryovers and E&P) are inherited by the parent.

As an alternative to debt, shareholders could capitalize the corporation with stock (equity). If certain conditions are met, this stock would be Sec. 1244 stock (small business corporation stock, see Chapter I:8 for details). If it becomes worthless, the shareholder may deduct up to $50,000 ($100,000 on a joint return) of its value as an ordinary loss. From a tax perspective, ordinary loss treatment is generally better than the capital loss treatment that applies to nonbusiness bad debts.

The two principal components of capital structure clearly yield different results, depending on whether the corporation is profitable or unprofitable. Thus, deciding how to capitalize a corporation ultimately involves an evaluation of its potential profitability. If the owners of a new corporation believe the venture will be profitable, they should prefer debt because of the deductibility of interest payments. Because few entrepreneurs assume that their business will be unsuccessful, advising them to capitalize it with substantially more equity than debt might be difficult.

DIVIDEND POLICY

Dividends paid out of E&P are taxable to shareholders and nondeductible by the corporation. Consequently, in a closely held corporation, where ownership and management are the same, the owner-managers may wish to increase shareholder-employee compensation rather than increase dividends. Likewise, a shareholder may wish to lease property to the corporation instead of contribute it as capital. Even though the increased salary or rental payments are taxable to the shareholders (as are dividends), the corporation may deduct them as long as the amounts are reasonable.

EXAMPLE I:16-46 ▶

Mario and Nancy are equal owners of highly profitable Texas Corporation, which has substantial E&P. Mario and Nancy are the key officers. Each is paid $100,000 compared to $150,000 paid to others in similar positions. To increase earnings distributions to the owners, additional salary of $50,000 might be paid to both Mario and Nancy (rather than increase dividends by the same amount) because the corporation can deduct salary but not dividends. The salary payments result in a single level of taxation, while the dividend payments result in double taxation. The additional $50,000 compensation would subject the employer and the two shareholders to additional payroll taxes (e.g., the 1.45% Medicare portion of the FICA tax. There is no ceiling on the Medicare tax base.) ◀

USE OF LOSSES

A corporation should carefully plan how to use its net operating loss and capital loss carryovers. For example, the sale of appreciated business assets could result in a Sec. 1231 gain that could offset capital loss carryovers. Net Sec. 1231 gains are treated as capital in character. Alternatively, as a result of depreciation recapture, the sale of assets could give rise to ordinary income. Such income could be offset by expiring NOLs.

If a business expects to generate net operating losses or capital losses during its start-up phase, an S corporation election might be desirable because the losses flow thru to the shareholders' separate returns. The S corporation election might be terminated when the corporation becomes profitable so that C corporation treatment is preferred. (See Chapter I:17 for a discussion of S corporations.)

CHARITABLE CONTRIBUTIONS

Many owners of closely held corporations prefer to make charitable contributions through their corporations rather than as individuals because the corporations might be able to take a larger deduction. An accrual method corporation may accelerate a charitable contribution deduction if its board of directors approves the contribution before year-end, and the corporation makes the contribution within 2½ months of the corporation's tax year-end. The alternative to a corporate contribution could be a nondeductible dividend payment to the owner(s) who make(s) (an) individual contribution(s).

DIVIDENDS-RECEIVED DEDUCTION

Corporate shareholders may deduct 80% (in some cases, 70%) of dividends received. However, this deduction is limited to 80% (in some cases, 70%) of taxable income unless the deduction creates or increases an NOL. Thus, a substantial scale-down of the

dividends-received deduction may result if taxable income (before this deduction) is positive, but negligible. If the limitation is likely to diminish the magnitude of the deduction, the corporation might either accelerate business deductions into the current year or postpone the recognition of income to a later year. Either measure could result in the generation of an NOL that renders the limitation inapplicable. (See Examples I:16-7 and I:16-8.)

REDUCED TAXES ON TAXPAYER STOCK SALES

IRC Section 1202(a)(1) permits noncorporate investors to exclude up to 50% of any gain realized on the sale or exchange of small business stock. This exclusion applies only to stock issued by C corporations that meet certain requirements; i.e., a stock holding period of five years or more, the use of at least 80% of the corporation's assets in the active conduct of a business, and a corporate asset value of $50 million or less at the time of stock issuance.

COMPLIANCE AND PROCEDURAL CONSIDERATIONS

FILING REQUIREMENTS

KEY POINT

All corporations must file an income tax return. The filing requirements are not based on minimum amounts of gross income, as in the case of individual taxpayers.

A corporation must file Form 1120 (U.S. Corporation Income Tax Return) even if the corporation exists for only part of the year. Supplementing this form is a separate Schedule D that reports capital gains and losses. In addition, the corporation must file Form 4626 (Alternative Minimum Tax—Corporations) even if no alternative minimum tax is due. Certain small corporations are eligible to file a simplified Form 1120-A (U.S. Corporation Short-Form Income Tax Return) if their gross receipts, total income, and total assets are all less than $500,000. Form 1120-A may not be filed in certain circumstances (e.g., the corporation earns dividend income eligible for an 80% dividends-received deduction, the corporation is in the process of liquidation, or is a member of a controlled group).

Corporations with less than $250,000 of gross receipts and less than $250,000 in assets can avoid reporting on Schedules L, M-1, and M-2 of their Form 1120. Corporations, who file Form 1120-A and are below the $250,000 income threshold, no longer must complete parts III and IV of Form 1120-A.

The regular due date for the corporate return is the fifteenth day of the third month following the end of the tax year (e.g., March 15 for calendar-year corporations). The corporation can obtain an automatic 6-month extension by filing Form 7004 (Application for Automatic Extension of Time to File Corporation Income Tax Return). If an extension is granted, the full amount of the estimated tax must be paid on or before the due date (e.g., March 15 for calendar-year corporations).

Quarterly estimated tax payments must be made on the fifteenth day of the fourth, sixth, ninth, and twelfth months of the tax year. In general, the total required estimated tax payments are the lesser of 100% of the corporation's tax liability for the current year or 100% of the tax shown on the preceding year's return.[65] However, a corporation need not base the quarterly payments on the preceding year's tax liability if that liability was zero.[66] The corporation is subject to a nondeductible penalty to the extent the quarterly payments are less than the actual amounts due.

Through its e-file program, the IRS has developed an electronic procedure for filing Forms 1120 and 1120S. For tax years ending on or after December 31, 2005, corporations with at least $10 million in assets that file at least 250 returns annually are required to file electronically. Corporations not required to file electronically may choose to do so voluntarily. Currently, an amended tax return cannot be filed electronically.

---

[65] Exceptions are provided for large corporations and corporations that earn their income unevenly during the tax year. Large corporations—those with taxable income exceeding $1 million in any of the three preceding tax years—must make quarterly estimated tax payments based on 100% of the tax shown on their current year return. Alternatively, they are permitted to make their first-quarter payment based on 100% of the preceding year's tax liability [Sec. 6655(d)]. Section 6655(e) permits corporations to use an annualized income installment method, or seasonally adjusted installment method if the latter installments are less than the normally-required installment [Sec. 6655(e)].

[66] Rev. Rul. 92-54 1992-2 C.B. 320.

BOOK-TAX ACCOUNTING COMPARISON

The Schedule M-1 adjustments highlight the differences between financial accounting and tax accounting.

SCHEDULE M-1 AND M-2 RECONCILIATIONS

Schedule M-1 is used to reconcile financial accounting net income with taxable income before certain deductions (the NOL and dividends-received deductions). Figure I:16-1 shows a completed Schedule M-1 based on the following adjustments:

Net income per books	$100,000
Plus:	
Federal income tax liability	3,000
Net capital losses	2,000
Nondeductible premiums on life insurance covering key officers	4,000
Minus:	
Tax-exempt interest income	(9,000)
Excess of tax depreciation over financial accounting depreciation	(75,000)
Taxable income (before certain deductions)	$ 25,000

KEY POINT

Many small corporations who file Form 1120 are not required to complete Schedules M-1 and M-2. The exception is applicable to companies with gross receipts and assets below $250,000.

Schedule M-2 reconciles retained earnings (for financial accounting purposes) at the beginning of the year with retained earnings at year-end. This reconciliation accounts for changes in the balance sheet reported on Schedule L, or for items of income, gain, or loss components of retained earnings that have not been reported as part of net income. Figure I:16-2 illustrates a completed Schedule M-2 based on the above facts and the following assumptions: a $140,000 retained earnings balance on January 1, $100,000 of net income for financial accounting purposes, and the payment of a $40,000 cash dividend.

Schedule M-1   **Reconciliation of Income (Loss) per Books With Income per Return**
Note: Schedule M-3 may be required instead of Schedule M-1—see instructions.

1	Net income (loss) per books	100,000	7	Income recorded on books this year not included on this return (itemize):	
2	Federal income tax per books	3,000			
3	Excess of capital losses over capital gains	2,000	a	Tax-exempt interest $ 9,000	
4	Income subject to tax not recorded on books this year (itemize): _____ _____		b	Other (itemize): _____ _____	9,000
5	Expenses recorded on books this year not deducted on this return (itemize):		8	Deductions on this return not charged against book income this year (itemize):	
a	Depreciation . . . . $_____		a	Depreciation . . $ 75,000	
b	Charitable contributions $_____		b	Charitable contributions $	
c	Travel and entertainment $_____		c	Other (itemize): _____ _____	
d	Other (itemize): Premium on Life Insurance 4,000	4,000	9	Add lines 7 and 8	84,000
6	Add lines 1 through 5	109,000	10	Income—line 6 less line 9 . . .	25,000

FIGURE I:16-1   ▶   FORM 1120, SCHEDULE M-1

Schedule M-2   **Analysis of Unappropriated Retained Earnings per Books**

1	Balance at beginning of year	140,000	5	Distributions:	a	Cash	40,000
2	Net income (loss) per books	100,000			b	Stock	
3	Other increases (itemize): _____ _____ _____				c	Property . . .	
			6	Other decreases (itemize): _____			
			7	Add lines 5 and 6			40,000
4	Add lines 1, 2, and 3	240,000	8	Balance at end of year (line 4 less line 7) .			200,000

FIGURE I:16-2   ▶   FORM 1120, SCHEDULE M-2

SCHEDULE M-3 RECONCILIATION

Schedule M-3 (Net Income (Loss) Reconciliation for Corporations with Total Assets of $10 Million or More) reconciles a C corporation's book-tax differences. Reg. Sec. 1.6011-4(b)(6), defines significant book-tax difference in terms of a transaction with respect to which the amount of any item or items of income, gain, expense, or loss for tax purposes differs by more than $10 million in any tax year from the amount of the same item for book purposes. The amount of an item for book purposes is determined under Generally Accepted Accounting Principles.

Each member of an affiliated group must file a separate Schedule M-3. The entire group must file a consolidated Schedule M-3. The IRS is likely to use this schedule as a tool to determine whether or not to audit a corporation. A sample Schedule M-3 is presented on pages I:16-38 to I:16-40.

MAINTENANCE OF E&P RECORDS

Companies are not required to compute E&P on their tax return. They should, however, maintain adequate records of E&P items because the limitations period for contesting these items is indefinite, and the taxpayer has the burden of proof. Thus, if the IRS discovers that a company has current or accumulated E&P and treats a distribution as a taxable dividend rather than a tax-free return of capital, the taxpayer must show that the prescribed IRS treatment is erroneous.

Form 5452 (Corporate Report of Nondividend Distributions) must be filed by any corporation that makes a return-of-capital distribution. This form requires a computation of E&P and a schedule of differences between taxable income and E&P. This form also requires a year-by-year computation of accumulated E&P.

PROBLEM MATERIALS

DISCUSSION QUESTIONS

I:16-1 William Bonney and Pat Garrett incorporate Sales, Inc. on January 1, of the current year, under the laws of the State of Florida.
   a. What federal income tax treatment is required of the new corporation under the check-the-box rules?
   b. Are any elective tax treatments available for Sales, Inc. under the IRC or the check-the-box rules?
   c. How would your answers to Parts a and b change (if at all) should William Bonney be the sole shareholder of Sales, Inc.?

I:16-2 Under the present tax system, C corporation income is taxed twice, once when earned and again when the shareholders receive dividends or sell their stock. Nevertheless, the C corporation form is widely used in the United States, especially for large enterprises. Why would an entrepreneur choose C corporation status instead of one of the flow-through organizational forms?

I:16-3 Some tax analysts contend that many corporations can shift the burden of corporate taxation to consumers in the form of higher prices. In what other ways might a corporation attempt to shift the burden (e.g., to employees, tenants, and/or shareholders)?

I:16-4 For most individual investors, net long-term capital gains and dividends are taxed at the same rate. Yet, in some circumstances, an investor's generating long-term capital gains is more advantageous than earning a dividend. What are these circumstances and why?

I:16-5 Acorn Corporation has a $5,000 NSTCG and a $9,000 NLTCL in the current year. Last year, Acorn had a $3,000 NLTCG. No other capital gains or losses were reported in prior tax years.
   a. Do the NSTCG and NLTCL have to be offset in the current year?
   b. Is any portion of the NLTCL deductible in the current year?
   c. What loss carryback or carryover rules should be applied to any unused capital losses incurred in the current year?

I:16-6 C corporations are allowed a dividends-received deduction (DRD) for dividends received from domestic corporations.
   a. What is the purpose of the DRD?
   b. Does the taxable income limitation on the DRD serve any useful function?
   c. What additional tax liability is incurred by a C corporation when it receives $10,000 of dividend income from a 10%-owned domestic

SCHEDULE M-3
(Form 1120)

Department of the Treasury
Internal Revenue Service

Net Income (Loss) Reconciliation for Corporations With Total Assets of $10 Million or More

▶ Attach to Form 1120 or 1120-C.
▶ See separate instructions.

OMB No. 1545-0123

20**09**

Name of corporation (common parent, if consolidated return)

Employer identification number

Check applicable box(es): (1) ☐ Non-consolidated return   (2) ☐ Consolidated return (Form 1120 only)

(3) ☐ Mixed 1120/L/PC group   (4) ☐ Dormant subsidiaries schedule attached

Part I   **Financial Information and Net Income (Loss) Reconciliation** (see instructions)

1a Did the corporation file SEC Form 10-K for its income statement period ending with or within this tax year?
  ☐ **Yes.** Skip lines 1b and 1c and complete lines 2a through 11 with respect to that SEC Form 10-K.
  ☐ **No.** Go to line 1b. See instructions if multiple non-tax-basis income statements are prepared.
 b Did the corporation prepare a certified audited non-tax-basis income statement for that period?
  ☐ **Yes.** Skip line 1c and complete lines 2a through 11 with respect to that income statement.
  ☐ **No.** Go to line 1c.
 c Did the corporation prepare a non-tax-basis income statement for that period?
  ☐ **Yes.** Complete lines 2a through 11 with respect to that income statement.
  ☐ **No.** Skip lines 2a through 3c and enter the corporation's net income (loss) per its books and records on line 4a.
2a Enter the income statement period: Beginning ___MM/DD/YYYY___   Ending ___MM/DD/YYYY___
 b Has the corporation's income statement been restated for the income statement period on line 2a?
  ☐ **Yes.** (If "Yes," attach an explanation and the amount of each item restated.)
  ☐ **No.**
 c Has the corporation's income statement been restated for any of the five income statement periods preceding the period on line 2a?
  ☐ **Yes.** (If "Yes," attach an explanation and the amount of each item restated.)
  ☐ **No.**
3a Is any of the corporation's voting common stock publicly traded?
  ☐ **Yes.**
  ☐ **No.** If "No," go to line 4a.
 b Enter the symbol of the corporation's primary U.S. publicly traded voting common stock . . . .
 c Enter the nine-digit CUSIP number of the corporation's primary publicly traded voting common stock . . . .

4a Worldwide consolidated net income (loss) from income statement source identified in Part I, line 1 . . .	**4a**	
b Indicate accounting standard used for line 4a (see instructions): (1) ☐ GAAP (2) ☐ IFRS (3) ☐ Statutory (4) ☐ Tax-basis (5) ☐ Other (specify) _____		
5a Net income from nonincludible foreign entities (attach schedule)	**5a** ( )
b Net loss from nonincludible foreign entities (attach schedule and enter as a positive amount)	**5b**	
6a Net income from nonincludible U.S. entities (attach schedule)	**6a** ( )
b Net loss from nonincludible U.S. entities (attach schedule and enter as a positive amount)	**6b**	
7a Net income (loss) of other includible foreign disregarded entities (attach schedule)	**7a**	
b Net income (loss) of other includible U.S. disregarded entities (attach schedule)	**7b**	
c Net income (loss) of other includible entities (attach schedule)	**7c**	
8 Adjustment to eliminations of transactions between includible entities and nonincludible entities (attach schedule)	**8**	
9 Adjustment to reconcile income statement period to tax year (attach schedule)	**9**	
10a Intercompany dividend adjustments to reconcile to line 11 (attach schedule)	**10a**	
b Other statutory accounting adjustments to reconcile to line 11 (attach schedule)	**10b**	
c Other adjustments to reconcile to amount on line 11 (attach schedule)	**10c**	
11 **Net income (loss) per income statement of includible corporations.** Combine lines 4 through 10 . . .	**11**	

Note. Part I, line 11, must equal the amount on Part II, line 30, column (a), and Schedule M-2, line 2.

12 Enter the total amount (not just the corporation's share) of the assets and liabilities of all entities included or removed on the following lines.

	Total Assets	Total Liabilities
a Included on Part I, line 4 . . . . ▶		
b Removed on Part I, line 5 . . . . ▶		
c Removed on Part I, line 6 . . . . ▶		
d Included on Part I, line 7 . . . . ▶		

For Paperwork Reduction Act Notice, see the Instructions for Form 1120.   Cat. No. 37961C   **Schedule M-3 (Form 1120) 2009**

FIGURE I:16-3a   ▶   FORM 1120, SCHEDULE M-3

Schedule M-3 (Form 1120) 2009   Page **2**

Name of corporation (common parent, if consolidated return)	Employer identification number

Check applicable box(es): **(1)** ☐ Consolidated group   **(2)** ☐ Parent corp   **(3)** ☐ Consolidated eliminations   **(4)** ☐ Subsidiary corp   **(5)** ☐ Mixed 1120/L/PC group

Check if a sub-consolidated: **(6)** ☐ 1120 group   **(7)** ☐ 1120 eliminations

Name of subsidiary (if consolidated return)	Employer identification number

Part II   **Reconciliation of Net Income (Loss) per Income Statement of Includible Corporations With Taxable Income per Return** (see instructions)

Income (Loss) Items (Attach schedules for lines 1 through 11)	(a) Income (Loss) per Income Statement	(b) Temporary Difference	(c) Permanent Difference	(d) Income (Loss) per Tax Return
1 Income (loss) from equity method foreign corporations				
2 Gross foreign dividends not previously taxed . .				
3 Subpart F, QEF, and similar income inclusions .				
4 Section 78 gross-up				
5 Gross foreign distributions previously taxed . .				
6 Income (loss) from equity method U.S. corporations .				
7 U.S. dividends not eliminated in tax consolidation				
8 Minority interest for includible corporations . .				
9 Income (loss) from U.S. partnerships				
10 Income (loss) from foreign partnerships				
11 Income (loss) from other pass-through entities .				
12 Items relating to reportable transactions (attach details)				
13 Interest income (attach Form 8916-A)				
14 Total accrual to cash adjustment				
15 Hedging transactions				
16 Mark-to-market income (loss)				
17 Cost of goods sold (attach Form 8916-A) . . .	( )			( )
18 Sale versus lease (for sellers and/or lessors) . .				
19 Section 481(a) adjustments				
20 Unearned/deferred revenue				
21 Income recognition from long-term contracts .				
22 Original issue discount and other imputed interest				
23a Income statement gain/loss on sale, exchange, abandonment, worthlessness, or other disposition of assets other than inventory and pass-through entities				
b Gross capital gains from Schedule D, excluding amounts from pass-through entities				
c Gross capital losses from Schedule D, excluding amounts from pass-through entities, abandonment losses, and worthless stock losses				
d Net gain/loss reported on Form 4797, line 17, excluding amounts from pass-through entities, abandonment losses, and worthless stock losses				
e Abandonment losses				
f Worthless stock losses (attach details)				
g Other gain/loss on disposition of assets other than inventory				
24 Capital loss limitation and carryforward used . .				
25 Other income (loss) items with differences (attach schedule)				
26 **Total income (loss) items.** Combine lines 1 through 25				
27 **Total expense/deduction items** (from Part III, line 36)				
28 Other items with no differences				
29a Mixed groups, see instructions. All others, combine lines 26 through 28				
b PC insurance subgroup reconciliation totals . .				
c Life insurance subgroup reconciliation totals . .				
30 **Reconciliation totals.** Combine lines 29a through 29c				

Note. Line 30, column (a), must equal the amount on Part I, line 11, and column (d) must equal Form 1120, page 1, line 28.

Schedule M-3 (Form 1120) 2009

FIGURE I:16-3b ▶ FORM 1120, SCHEDULE M-3

Name of corporation (common parent, if consolidated return)	Employer identification number

Check applicable box(es): **(1)** ☐ Consolidated group   **(2)** ☐ Parent corp   **(3)** ☐ Consolidated eliminations   **(4)** ☐ Subsidiary corp   **(5)** ☐ Mixed 1120/L/PC group

Check if a sub-consolidated: **(6)** ☐ 1120 group   **(7)** ☐ 1120 eliminations

Name of subsidiary (if consolidated return)	Employer identification number

Part III   **Reconciliation of Net Income (Loss) per Income Statement of Includible Corporations With Taxable Income per Return—Expense/Deduction Items** (see instructions)

Expense/Deduction Items	(a) Expense per Income Statement	(b) Temporary Difference	(c) Permanent Difference	(d) Deduction per Tax Return
1 U.S. current income tax expense				
2 U.S. deferred income tax expense				
3 State and local current income tax expense				
4 State and local deferred income tax expense				
5 Foreign current income tax expense (other than foreign withholding taxes)				
6 Foreign deferred income tax expense				
7 Foreign withholding taxes				
8 Interest expense (attach Form 8916-A)				
9 Stock option expense				
10 Other equity-based compensation				
11 Meals and entertainment				
12 Fines and penalties				
13 Judgments, damages, awards, and similar costs				
14 Parachute payments				
15 Compensation with section 162(m) limitation				
16 Pension and profit-sharing				
17 Other post-retirement benefits				
18 Deferred compensation				
19 Charitable contribution of cash and tangible property				
20 Charitable contribution of intangible property				
21 Charitable contribution limitation/carryforward				
22 Domestic production activities deduction				
23 Current year acquisition or reorganization investment banking fees				
24 Current year acquisition or reorganization legal and accounting fees				
25 Current year acquisition/reorganization other costs				
26 Amortization/impairment of goodwill				
27 Amortization of acquisition, reorganization, and start-up costs				
28 Other amortization or impairment write-offs				
29 Section 198 environmental remediation costs				
30 Depletion				
31 Depreciation				
32 Bad debt expense				
33 Corporate owned life insurance premiums				
34 Purchase versus lease (for purchasers and/or lessees)				
35 Other expense/deduction items with differences (attach schedule)				
36 **Total expense/deduction items.** Combine lines 1 through 35. Enter here and on Part II, line 27, reporting positive amounts as negative and negative amounts as positive				

Schedule M-3 (Form 1120) 2009

FIGURE I:16-3c ▶ FORM 1120, SCHEDULE M-3

corporation? From a 25%-owned domestic corporation? From a more-than-80% owned domestic corporation? Assume that the entity's additional taxable income is taxed at a 34% marginal rate.

d. What is the effective tax rate on the dividend income? Hint: the effective tax rate equals the increase in a C corporation's tax liability divided by the additional gross income that it reports.

I:16-7 Under what circumstances might a corporation elect not to carry back an NOL to its prior tax years?

I:16-8 What requirements must be met for an accrual-basis corporation to deduct a charitable contribution in a year before its payment?

I:16-9 Acorn Corporation is publicly traded on the American Stock Exchange. Its chief executive officer, Carl, currently receives an annual salary of $1 million. The board of directors is considering increasing his compensation by $200,000.

a. What are the income tax consequences to Acorn if Carl's salary is increased to $1,200,000?

b. What alternatives might be considered to increase Carl's annual compensation that would produce more favorable tax consequences for Acorn?

I:16-10 Current tax law imposes a $1 million limitation on the deductibility of executive compensation. Should such limitation be retained or repealed? Give reasons for your opinion.

I:16-11 The current corporate tax structure contains phase-outs (via surtaxes) at various levels of taxable income that eliminate the benefits of lower tax brackets. Identify the two phase-outs in the corporate tax rate structure. How do these phase-outs affect a corporation's marginal and average tax rates? In your opinion, should phase-outs be retained in the tax law or repealed?

I:16-12 Explain the following statement: For a C corporation earning taxable income in excess of $10,000,000, the corporate income tax is in essence a flat tax imposed at a 34% rate.

I:16-13 The new production activities deduction is available based only on income related to U.S. production activities (or taxable income, if a smaller amount). Why did Congress restrict the calculation of the deduction only to income from domestic production?

I:16-14 Spurrier Corporation's taxable income is $50,000, and its tax preference items and positive adjustments for the alternative minimum tax (AMT) are $100,000.

a. Is Spurrier subject to the AMT (assume the corporation is not excluded from the AMT under the small business exception)? If so, what additional taxes (if any) are owed because of the AMT rules?

b. What AMT reporting requirements must Spurrier satisfy in preparing its tax return?

c. Can Spurrier avoid paying the corporate AMT by electing to pay more dividends to its shareholder? What is the tax tradeoff between paying the AMT and paying dividends to a shareholder?

I:16-15 Current tax law provides for a dual system, the regular tax and alternative minimum tax. In effect, a corporation pays the greater of the regular tax or the tentative minimum tax. Why did Congress enact such a dual system? How could Congress replace the dual system with a single tax system?

I:16-16 Collins Corporation pays a $30,000 alternative minimum tax in the current year. What AMT benefit (if any) is available to reduce federal income taxes paid in a prior tax year, in the current tax year, or in a future tax year?

I:16-17 The accumulated earnings tax is efffectively a penalty on corporations.

a. What is the purpose of the accumulated earnings tax?

b. Why does the "reasonable needs of the business" exception either reduce or eliminate the accumulated earnings tax burden for many corporations?

I:16-18 Acme Corporation is a highly profitable closely held corporation that has never paid a dividend. During the past five years, after-tax earnings of $200,000 per year have been retained in the business. All of the earnings ($1 million) have been reinvested in operating assets and to finance an expansion of the business. Is the corporation subject to the accumulated earnings tax because no dividends have been paid?

I:16-19 The personal holding company tax imposes a penalty on corporations.

a. What is the purpose of the personal holding company tax?

b. Two tests are used to classify a corporation as a personal holding company. What are these tests, and how do they serve the purpose of the personal holding company tax?

I:16-20 In terms of a corporation's incurring liability for the tax, what is the difference between the personal holding company tax and the accumulated earnings tax? Do both taxes require a tax avoidance motive?

I:16-21 Why are controlled groups of corporations required to apportion among group members the lower rates applicable to taxable income up to $75,000?

I:16-22 Discuss the underlying rationale for the nonrecognition of gain or loss in a Sec. 351 transaction.

I:16-23 Corporate formation transactions are either taxable or tax-free events depending on whether the requirements of Sec. 351 are met. Debate the pros

and cons of the following statement: All corporate formations should be treated as taxable events. Teams of two to four persons should conduct the debate. A summary of items for the "pro" and "con" positions should be presented.

I:16-24 a. Brett Nelson transfers a building having a $75,000 FMV and a $30,000 adjusted basis to Gator Corporation. An advantage of the asset transfer under Sec. 351 is that Brett can defer his $45,000 ($75,000 FMV − $30,000 adjusted basis) realized gain. What disadvantages accrue to Gator as a result of the post-transfer aspects of the transaction?

   b. Assume the same facts as in Part a except that the building's FMV is instead $30,000 and its adjusted basis is $75,000. What tax disadvantage results from the transfer as presently structured? Are there any suggestions that you can offer to Brett to improve his tax benefits?

   c. Explain why the basis of gain property that is contributed to a corporation in a Sec. 351 exchange is not equal to its FMV on the date of the exchange. Is the basis of the property that is contributed to the corporation adjusted when gain is recognized by the transferor?

   d. How would your answers to Part a change if Brett Nelson transferred a $25,000 mortgage along with the land and received stock having a value less than the amount of the liability?

I:16-25 Carmen transfers land and a building having a $60,000 adjusted basis and a $100,000 FMV to Bass Corporation in a transaction ostensibly qualifying as tax-free under Sec. 351. Immediately before the exchange, Carmen incurs a $50,000 mortgage on the property. The mortgage is assumed by the corporation, and the mortgage proceeds are used by Carmen to remodel her personal residence.

   a. What are the likely tax consequences of the asset transfer?

   b. What is the rationale for this result?

I:16-26 Sato, Jose, and Satish form a new corporation. Each individual contributes $100,000 in appreciated property and receives a one-third (equity) ownership interest. Jose and Satish also lend the corporation $250,000 cash in exchange for two 30-year notes (debt) bearing annual interest at a below-market rate of 3.5%.

   a. From the corporation's and the shareholders' perspectives, what are the principal advantages of capitalizing with debt as opposed to equity?

   b. What are the tax consequences to Sato, Jose, and Satish if the property transfer meets the requirements of Sec. 351?

   c. What tax consequences to the corporation and its shareholders would ensue if the IRS recharacterizes the debt as equity?

I:16-27 Chang and George, high income taxpayers, are starting a new business that manufactures and sells explosives. They expect the business to sustain $500,000 in losses in its first two years of operation, then gradually generate profits. Given their high income level, the nature of their business, and its projected operating results, what entity form(s) might Chang and George find advantageous, and why?

I:16-28 Under current tax law, a corporation may deduct interest but not dividends paid to shareholders. What potential problems are created by this disparate treatment? Should the law be changed to either disallow the interest deduction or allow a dividends-paid deduction?

I:16-29 Why is it generally preferable to structure the redemption of a shareholder's stock to meet the substantially disproportionate test or the complete termination test rather than the not-essentially-equivalent-to-a-dividend requirement?

I:16-30 Compare the three types of redemptions (i.e., substantially disproportionate, not essentially equivalent to a dividend, and complete termination of shareholder interest) in terms of the following features:

   a. Often permissible, even where percentage stock ownership does not decrease by more than 80%.

   b. Constructive ownership rules may be waived under certain conditions.

   c. Treated as an exchange taxed as a capital gain or loss.

   d. Stock not surrendered in exchange for corporate distribution.

I:16-31 If the requirements for a complete termination of a shareholder's interest are met, should not the substantially disproportionate redemption requirements also be met? What is the major difference between these two requirements?

I:16-32 How does the liquidation of a controlled subsidiary differ from the liquidation of a corporation owned by a single individual? What is the reason for the difference?

I:16-33 A corporate formation can take place tax-free when an individual transfers the assets of a business to a corporation and no boot property is distributed by the corporation to the shareholder. A corporate liquidation, on the other hand, is taxable to both the liquidating corporation and its shareholder(s). Why does the tax law differentiate between the two transactions?

I:16-34 Why is Sec. 1244, which pertains to small business corporation stock, in the tax code? What advantages and disadvantages are afforded to owners of Sec. 1244 stock?

I:16-35 Why is it generally preferable to increase salaries, interest, or rental payments to employee-shareholders in a closely held corporation rather than increase dividends?

I:16-36 What advantages and disadvantages accrue to a corporation and its shareholders of (1) electing C corporation status for the business, or (2) electing S corporation status?

I:16-37 Explain the purpose of Schedule M-3 in corporate income tax reporting. Explain which C corporations must file this form and which C corporations need not file this form.

I:16-38 Besides M-1 and M-2, what other schedules are incorporated in Form 1120, and what do they purport to report? *(Hint: go to www.irs.gov. Retrieve and review the form.)*

ISSUE IDENTIFICATION QUESTIONS

I:16-39 Acorn Corporation is a very profitable closely held corporation that is owned solely by Helen, age 55, who plans to retire in 10 years. Management continuity is a problem because neither the existing employees nor Helen's children are interested in or capable of managing the company. Acorn has never paid a dividend and does not intend to do so in the future because dividends are not deductible by the corporation and would be taxable to the shareholders. Helen does not wish to expand the business and plans to have the corporation reinvest its earnings in securities. What tax issues should Helen consider in the short run? In the long run?

I:16-40 Hugo and Helga each own unincorporated businesses. They plan to form a corporation to which they would transfer all of their business assets and liabilities in exchange for all of the corporation's stock. Hugo's assets have substantially appreciated over time. A transfer of all of his assets and liabilities would result in an excess of liabilities over the adjusted basis of the assets. Helga has substantial unrealized losses on some of her business properties (e.g., land and a building). Her tax accountant has recommended that she sell the properties to a third party or to the corporation to recognize capital losses or Sec. 1231 losses that could be used to offset personal capital or ordinary gains. The sales proceeds then could be invested in the new corporation. What tax issues should Hugo and Helga consider with respect to the asset transfer, the organizational expenditures, the capital structure, and other aspects of the corporate formation?

I:16-41 Eastern Corporation is formed by John and Joy with an initial capitalization of $500,000. Two alternative capitalization plans are being considered: (1) John and Joy, who are unrelated, each would receive $200,000 of 8% 15-year bonds and $50,000 of Eastern stock, or (2) John and Joy each would receive $250,000 of Eastern stock. John's business assets that would be transferred to Eastern have significantly appreciated over time, and John does not want to recognize any gain on the transfer of these assets. Organizational costs of $3,000 are expected to be incurred. What tax issues should John and Joy consider with respect to the asset transfer, the organizational expenditures, the capital structure, and other aspects of the corporate formation?

PROBLEMS

I:16-42 *Capital Gains and Losses.* First Corporation, in its fifth year of operations, realizes the following capital gains and losses in the current year:

LTCG	$20,000
LTCL	(8,000)
STCG	16,000
STCL	(40,000)

Taxable income (exclusive of the capital gains and losses) is $60,000.
a. What is First's net capital gain or loss?
b. What is First's taxable income for the current year?
c. Assuming that the gains and losses reported in the current year are the first capital gains and losses ever reported by the corporation and then that the corporation had reported an excess of capital gains over capital losses in its prior tax years, explain the tax treatment of any unused capital losses

I:16-43 *Capital Loss Carrybacks and Carryovers.* Federal Corporation realizes the following net capital losses in 2010:

STCL	$ 80,000
LTCL	120,000

NLTCGs were incurred in 2007 through 2009 as follows:

2007	$20,000
2008	20,000
2009	60,000

a. What are the amount and character of any capital loss carryback to 2007 through 2009?

b. What treatment should be accorded any unused capital loss amount after the carryback?

c. What is the character of any unused capital loss carryovers?

I:16-44 *Netting of Gains and Losses.* For each of the four independent scenarios below, compute the additional amount of income tax (or tax savings if a loss) that would result from current gains and losses for (a) Able Corporation that is taxed at a 34% marginal tax rate or (b) a sole proprietorship whose ordinary income is taxed at a 35% rate and long-term capital gains, at a 15% rate.

Scenario	LTCG or (LTCL)	STCG or (STCL)	Sec. 1231 Gains	Sec. 1231 Losses
1	$10,000	$ 5,000	$10,000	$ 5,000
2	$10,000	$ 15,000	$20,000	$ 5,000
3	$10,000	$(15,000)	$ –0–	$15,000
4	$20,000	$ 5,000	$10,000	$10,000

I:16-45 *Dividends-Received Deduction.* During the current year, Florida Corporation reports the following results:

Net income from operations	$100,000
Dividend from a 20%-owned corporation (qualifying for the dividends-received deduction)	200,000

a. What is the amount of Florida's dividends-received deduction?

b. How would your answer to Part a change if Florida instead reported a $20,000 loss from operations?

c. How would your answer to Parts a and b change if the dividend income were instead from a 10%-owned corporation and the loss from operations in Part b were instead $70,000?

I:16-46 *Dividends-Received Deduction.* Calculate the dividends-received deduction and taxable income for each independent scenario below. Assume there are no other income or deduction items.

a. Purple Corporation reports $260,000 of gross income from operations and $170,000 of allowable business deductions during the current year. In addition, Purple receives dividends of $200,000 from Blue Corporation. Purple owns 25% of Blue and the dividends qualify for the dividends-received deduction.

b. Yellow Corporation reports $160,000 of gross income from operations and $180,000 of allowable business deductions during the current year. In addition, Yellow receives dividends of $220,000 from Green Corporation. Yellow owns 15% of Green common stock and the dividends qualify for the dividends-received deduction.

I:16-47 *Net Operating Losses.* Alpha Corporation reports $500,000 of gross income from business operations and $625,000 of allowable business deductions. It also received from a domestic corporation $150,000 in dividends for which it is entitled to an 80% dividends-received deduction. What is Alpha's taxable income reported on Form 1120?

I:16-48 *Charitable Contributions.* On May 15 of the current year, the board of directors of Georgia Corporation authorized a $40,000 donation to a qualified charity. The corporation donated the $40,000 to the charity on December 1 of the current year. It made no other charitable contributions during the year. Georgia reports the following results for the current year:

Taxable income (before the dividends-received deduction and charitable contributions)	$250,000
Dividends-received deduction	10,000

a. What amount of charitable contributions is deductible in the current year?
b. How are any excess contributions treated?
c. How would your answer to Part a change if Georgia incurs a $50,000 NOL in the next year that is carried back to the current year?

I:16-49 *Corporate Tax Rates.* Calculate Ajax Corporation's regular tax liability for the following amounts of taxable income:
a. $90,000
b. $300,000
c. $5 million
d. $12 million
e. $17 million
f. $20 million
g. Alternatively, for Parts a, b, and c above, compute Ajax's regular tax liability if it were a personal service corporation.

I:16-50 *Corporate Tax Rates.* In December of the current year, Colorado Corporation considers a sale of certain corporate assets that would result in the recognition of a $50,000 LTCG. Colorado's controller estimates that taxable income for the current year will be $60,000 (excluding the LTCG). She also estimates that taxable income for the following year will be $200,000 (excluding the LTCG).
a. What is Colorado's tax liability for the two years if the assets are sold in the current year?
b. What is Colorado's tax liability for the two years if the assets are sold in the following year?
c. Should Colorado sell the assets in the current year or in the following year? Explain.

I:16-51 *Alternative Minimum Tax.* In an audit of Control Corporation, you were assigned to review the company's current-year tax accrual (e.g., provision for federal income taxes and the related liability). Control was incorporated in 1998. The following tax information is available for your review:

- Taxable income for regular tax purposes is $150,000.
- Depreciation for regular tax purposes is $100,000. Depreciation for AMT purposes is $60,000.
- Gain on the sale of a depreciable property included in taxable income is $30,000. Depreciation for regular tax purposes exceeded that claimed for AMT purposes by $11,000.
- Adjusted current earnings is $370,000.
- No AMT adjustment for the U.S. production activities deduction.

Assume that Control is not eligible for the small corporation AMT exemption.
a. What is the total amount of Control's AMT adjustments for the current year?
b. Calculate the following amounts for Control:
  - Alternative minimum taxable income
  - AMT base
  - Tentative minimum tax
  - Alternative minimum tax
  - Total tax liability

I:16-52 *Accumulated Earnings Tax.* The IRS is auditing Crane Corporation, a manufacturer of widgets, to determine whether the company is liable for the accumulated earnings tax in a prior tax year. Crane is owned by 20 shareholders who are unrelated and was not a personal holding company in the year in question. Crane reported the following results for the current year:

Taxable income	$150,000
Federal income taxes	41,750
Dividends-received deduction	85,000
Dividend paid on June 1	20,000

The accumulated E&P balance on January 1 is $180,000, and the company can justify the retention of the $180,000 of E&P at the beginning of the year plus $80,000 of earnings earned in the current year in terms of meeting its reasonable business needs. In fact, all of the January 1 earnings were retained for the reasonable needs of the business.

a. What is Crane's accumulated taxable income?

b. What is Crane's accumulated earnings tax liability?

c. If Crane potentially owes the accumulated earnings tax, what steps can it take to reduce or eliminate the liability?

I:16-53 *Personal Holding Company Tax.* Delta Corporation is being reorganized as an investment company because its retained earnings have been used for passive investments. The company is owned by three shareholders, and more than 60% of its income is personal holding company income. George, the president of Delta believes that personal holding company status is not detrimental because the company has paid dividends to its shareholders for several years and therefore should not be liable for any penalty tax.

Delta reports the following results for the current year:

Taxable income	$50,000
Federal income tax liability	7,500
Dividends paid	6,000
Dividends-received deduction	80,000

a. Do you agree or disagree with George? Explain.

b. What is the Delta's personal holding company tax liability, if any, for the current year?

c. How could Delta avoid liability for the personal holding company tax?

I:16-54 *Controlled Group.* Eagle and East Corporations are members of a brother-sister controlled group. Eagle's taxable income is $75,000, and East's taxable income is $50,000.

a. What is Eagle and East's total federal income tax liability?

b. What is Eagle and East's total federal income tax liability if they are not members of a controlled group?

I:16-55 *Controlled Group.* Alfred, Barbara, and Cathy own stock in First, Second, and Third Corporations as follows:

Individuals	First	Second	Third
Alfred	40%	40%	40%
Barbara	30%	60%	30%
Cathy	30%	–0–	30%

Which corporations are members of a brother-sister controlled group under the 80%-50% test?

I:16-56 *Corporate Formation.* In the current year, Jack, Karen, Latoya, and Marc transfer the following property to Giant Corporation (an existing corporation), which is owned equally by the four transferors.

- Jack transfers land and a building with a $60,000 adjusted basis and a $100,000 FMV for additional Giant stock having an $80,000 FMV and $20,000 of marketable securities having an adjusted basis of $15,000 in Giant's hands. $10,000 of MACRS straight-line depreciation on the building was claimed by Jack prior to the transfer.

- Karen transfers equipment with a $120,000 adjusted basis and a $200,000 FMV for additional Giant stock having an $80,000 FMV and a $10,000 20-year Giant note. $25,000 of MACRS depreciation on the equipment was claimed by Karen prior to the transfer.

- Latoya transfers inventory with a $70,000 adjusted basis and a $100,000 FMV for additional Giant stock having an $80,000 FMV and $20,000 cash.

- Marc transfers land with a $30,000 adjusted basis and a $100,000 FMV, subject to a $40,000 mortgage, which Giant assumes, for additional Giant stock having a $60,000 FMV.

a. What amount and character of gain or loss does Jack recognize? What is Jack's basis in the Giant stock and the marketable securities? What is Giant's basis in the land and building?

b. What amount and character of gain or loss does Karen recognize? What is Karen's basis in the Giant stock and note? What is Giant's basis in the equipment?

c. What amount and character of gain or loss does Latoya recognize? What is Latoya's basis in the Giant stock? What is Giant's basis in the inventory?

d. What amount and character of gain or loss does Marc recognize? What is Marc's basis in the Giant stock? What is Giant's basis in the land?

e. What amount and character of gain or loss does Giant recognize on the distribution of its stock, note, and other property to its shareholders?

I:16-57 *Corporate Formation.* Gold Corporation receives land from Marty in a transaction that meets the requirements of Sec. 351. Marty's basis in the land was $80,000. The FMV of the land is $200,000. Marty receives $20,000 cash and 80% of Gold stock. Molly transfers inventory with a $50,000 adjusted basis and a $200,000 FMV to Gold in exchange for $200,000 of Gold debt obligations. Molly acquires the remaining 20% of Gold stock for $50,000 in cash. Molly recognizes a $150,000 gain because she received debt obligations of Gold, in addition to the Gold stock.
a. What is Gold's basis in the land?
b. What is Gold's basis in the inventory?
c. Under what circumstances might it be preferable for Sec. 351 *not* to apply?

I:16-58 *Corporate Formations: Transfer of Liabilities.* In a transaction that meets the requirements of Sec. 351, Matt transfers to Hill Corporation land with a $600,000 adjusted basis and a $1,000,000 FMV that was used in his business. The land is subject to an $800,000 mortgage, which Hill assumes. Matt receives 100% of Hill stock.
a. What amount and character of gain or loss are recognized by Matt?
b. What is Matt's basis in the Hill stock?
c. What is Hill's basis in the land?

I:16-59 *Earnings and Profits (E&P).* During the current year, Nevada Corporation distributed $100,000 in cash to its sole shareholder. Because the corporation has a $300,000 accumulated E&P deficit at the beginning of the current year and only $30,000 of taxable income in the current year, Nevada's controller believes that the distribution should be treated as a tax-free return of capital to the shareholder. Your investigation sheds light on the following items that may have an effect on the computation of current E&P:

Federal income tax liability	$ 4,500
Dividends-received deduction	60,000
Excess of MACRS depreciation over	
Alternative Depreciation System depreciation	30,000
Excess charitable contributions	9,000
U.S. production activities deduction	10,000

a. What is Nevada's current E&P?
b. How much (if any) of the $100,000 cash distribution is taxable as a dividend to the sole shareholder?
c. What is the amount of Nevada's accumulated E&P balance (deficit) on the last day of the current year?

I:16-60 *Earnings and Profits (E&P).* North Corporation has $200,000 of accumulated E&P at the beginning of the current year. North distributed $300,000 cash during the current year to its shareholders. The company's operating results for the current year are as follows:

Taxable income	$100,000
Tax-exempt bond interest	10,000
Dividends-received deduction	7,000
Federal income tax liability	22,250
Net capital losses	27,000
U.S. production activities deduction	12,000

a. What is North Corporation's current E&P?
b. How much of the $300,000 cash distribution is taxable as a dividend?
c. What is North's accumulated E&P balance (deficit) at the end of the current year?

I:16-61 *Earnings and Profits (E&P).* At the beginning of the current year Ohio Corporation has a $40,000 accumulated E&P balance and a $73,000 current E&P deficit. The corporation distributes $60,000 cash to its sole shareholder on May 5. The shareholder's tax basis in her Ohio stock at the beginning of the year is $325,000.
a. What amount of the $50,000 distribution is taxable as a dividend (assume a ratable allocation of the deficit)?
b. What are the amount and character of any nondividend distributions to the shareholder?
c. What is the amount of Ohio's accumulated E&P balance (deficit) on the last day of the year?

I:16-62 *Property Distributions.* Old Corporation has liquidity problems but wants to maintain its existing dividend policy. Old distributes investment land to its two shareholders. The land has a $30,000 adjusted basis and a $100,000 FMV. Old has an E&P balance of $300,000 (excluding the effects of the distribution). Nancy receives 50% of the land, and Palm Corporation receives the remaining 50%. Assume no taxable income or loss from current year operations.
a. What distribution amount is taxable to Nancy and Palm?
b. What is the basis of the property to Nancy and Palm?
c. What are the income tax consequences of the distribution to Old?

I:16-63 *Property Distributions.* Without liquidating, Park Corporation distributes equipment with a $70,000 adjusted basis and a $80,000 FMV to Pam. The equipment is subject to a $25,000 mortgage assumed by Pam. Park has $300,000 of E&P (excluding the distribution).
a. How much gain (if any) does Park recognize on the distribution of the equipment?
b. What distribution amount is taxable as a dividend to Pam?
c. What is Pam's basis in the equipment?

I:16-64 *Withdrawing Earnings from a Business.* Galadriel Corporation reports pre-tax earnings of $500,000 during the current year. The corporation wishes to distribute $100,000 to Gabby, its sole owner and CEO, in a manner that will minimize taxes for Galadriel and Gabby. The corporation is subject to the regular corporate tax rates. Gabby's tax rate is a flat 35%. Ignoring FICA employment taxes paid by the corporation and Gabby, compare the after-tax income reported if the $100,000 is paid to Gabby as (1) salary and (2) as a qualifying dividend.

I:16-65 *Stock Redemptions.* Private Corporation redeems some of its stock from Jane, a major shareholder. Before the redemption Jane owns 50 of the 100 outstanding shares, and her daughter Jill owns 40 shares. The remaining ten shares are owned by unrelated individuals. Private redeems for $600,000 in cash 40 of Jane's shares, having a $200,000 basis. Private has $900,000 of current and accumulated E&P. Jane's basis in her remaining ten shares is $50,000.
a. What are the tax consequences of the redemption to Jane?
b. What is Jane's basis in her remaining ten shares after her 40 shares are redeemed?
c. How would your answers to Parts a and b change if Jane and Jill were not related?

I:16-66 *Stock Redemption.* Prime Corporation redeems some of its stock from two of its shareholders on the same date. Frank and his son Sam own 50 and 20 shares, respectively, of the 100 shares outstanding before the redemption. The remaining 30 shares are owned by unrelated individuals. Prime redeems for $50,000 10 of Frank's shares having a $15,000 basis. All of Sam's shares, having a $30,000 basis, are redeemed for $100,000. Sam files an agreement with the IRS that he will acquire no interest in the corporation other than as a creditor for 10 years. Prime has current and accumulated E&P of $200,000.
a. What are the tax consequences of the redemption to Frank and Sam?
b. What are the tax consequences of the redemption to Sam if he does not file the agreement or if he violates the agreement during the 10-year period?

I:16-67 *Corporate Liquidation.* Queen Corporation adopts a plan of complete liquidation on January 1 of the current year. The corporation sells the assets listed below during the current year. This sale is followed by the settling of Queen's liabilities and a single liquidating distribution of $1,200,000 cash on December 12 of the current year to Ahmed (Queen's sole shareholder). Ahmed has a $400,000 basis in his Queen stock, which he has held for seven years. The following facts are relevant:
- Inventory costing $600,000 is sold to customers for $1,000,000.
- Depreciable fixed assets with a $2,000,000 adjusted basis are sold for $3,000,000. Depreciation recapture under Sec. 1245 is $800,000.
- Land held as a capital asset with a $4,000,000 adjusted basis is sold for $5,000,000.

a. What are the tax consequences of the liquidation to Queen?
b. What are the tax consequences to Ahmed upon his receiving the liquidating distribution?
c. How would your answers to Parts a and b change if the assets were instead distributed to Ahmed in exchange for his Queen stock and Ahmed then proceeded to sell the assets for the prices indicated above?

I:16-68 *Corporate Liquidation.* Several years ago, Tampa Corporation acquired 100% of Union Corporation stock for $1,000,000. In the current year, Tampa liquidates Union and

receives all of its assets and liabilities. Tampa continues to operate Union as a division. On the liquidation date, the basis and FMV of Union's assets are $700,000 and $2,500,000, respectively. Union also has $100,000 of liabilities that were owed to third parties and E&P of $125,000 on the liquidation date.

a. How much gain or loss does Union recognize as a result of the liquidation?

b. What is Tampa's basis in the Union assets?

c. What Union tax attributes (if any) carry over to Tampa?

TAX STRATEGY PROBLEMS

I:16-69   Sandra and John, unrelated individuals, own all of Alpha and Beta corporation stock. John owns 60% of Alpha stock and 40% of Beta stock. Sandra owns 40% of Alpha stock and 60% of Beta stock. For five years, Alpha has conducted manufacturing activities and sold machine parts primarily in the eastern United States. Alpha reported $75,000 of operating profits in each of the last two years. Alpha's operating profits are expected to grow to $150,000 during the next five years. Alpha still has $100,000 of NOLs that must be used before it incurs federal income tax liability.

One-fourth of Alpha's output is sold to Beta, which is attempting to establish a market niche for reselling Alpha products in the southwestern United States. In the start-up phase of this effort, Beta incurred $200,000 of NOLs. Under the sales arrangement with Alpha, the best that Beta can hope to do in the short run is break-even.

What suggestions can you offer Sandra and John about the short-term possibility of offsetting Alpha and Beta's NOLs against the profits that Alpha expects to earn and minimizing their overall tax liabilities if both businesses become profitable? Sandra has specifically asked about merging the two companies into a single entity so that the losses of one entity can offset the profits of the other and defer federal income taxes. Sandra indicates that the two companies were created for non-tax reasons. The operating situation has changed, and according to Sandra, now may be the time to consolidate the entities. John is not sure that combining the two businesses is a good idea.

I:16-70   Penny and Rick, equal partners in a partnership, recently attended a business-planning seminar held in their town. While at the seminar they learned about limiting their personal liability by using the corporate form of business association. Penny and Rick's business has incurred product liability because it manufactures replacement parts for motorcycles. The most important information that Penny and Rick acquired from the seminar was the tax and legal advantages of incorporating their partnership business. According to a speaker at the seminar, incorporation would protect Penny and Rick from losing their personal wealth if someone sued them. Following a phone call from the partners to set up an appointment, you have scheduled a meeting with Rick and Penny for this afternoon. In preparation for the meeting you draft a list of points to discuss with the couple. What kinds of tax and non-tax strategies should you include in this list?

I:16-71   Peter Martin owned an equity interest in retail hardware stores for a nationwide chain. The eleven stores operate in a single midwestern state under the name Martin Corporation. Peter has been the chief financial officer of the company for fifteen years. His retirement plans call for him to take his pension from Martin in six months and play golf in sunny Gainesville, Florida. Since Peter's son and daughter will be operating the company, Peter will probably drop by the office to see family and old friends and to provide management advice. Peter will continue to serve on Martin's board of directors. The Martin stock is owned as follows: Peter and his wife Jaclyn, 25%; Peter's son and daughter-in-law, 25%; Peter's daughter and son-in-law, 25%. All six individuals serve on Martin's board of directors, along with six outside directors. The outside directors and Martin employees (other than those listed above) own the remaining 25% of the stock. Peter is thinking about his post-retirement years. He would like to withdraw money from the company, in addition to his pension and board of directors compensation. He would like to redeem some of his stockholdings each year. What advice can you provide Peter about the tax consequences of the redemption(s)?

I:16-72   Gertrude, age 67 and widowed, owns 50 acres of land on the Chattahoochee River that she and her husband purchased for $10,000 when they were newlyweds in 1970. The land is near Atlanta and is now worth at least $1,500,000 if sold undivided. Gertrude is considering selling the land to her wholly owned ABC Corporation for its $1,500,000 market value. Alternatively, Gertrude is considering transferring ownership of the land to ABC in exchange for additional ABC stock.

ABC will subdivide the land and sell it off as 50 one-acre lots with total proceeds of the lot sales expected to be at least $3,000,000. Land development costs will be approximately $300,000 and sales commissions will be 5% of the sales price.

Analyze the tax implications of Gertrude's two choices. Assume that Gertrude's marginal tax rate on ordinary income is 35% and that she has never had capital gains. Assume that ABC would recognize ordinary income on the lot sales taxed at a marginal tax rate of 34%.

TAX FORM/RETURN PREPARATION PROBLEMS

I:16-73 The financial accounting balance sheet for Zane, a retail sales corporation, as of the end of the current year is as follows:

Assets

Cash	$ 50,000
Accounts receivable	20,000
Inventory	10,000
Land	20,000
Buildings (net of $30,000 accumulated depreciation)	100,000
Equipment (net of $50,000 accumulated depreciation)	150,000
Intangibles	60,000
Total assets	$410,000

Liabilities & Owner's Equity

Accounts payable	$ 40,000
Mortgage payable	40,000
Long-term debt	60,000
Capital stock	100,000
Retained earnings	170,000[a]
Total liabilities and stockholders' equity	$410,000

[a]The retained earnings balance at the beginning of the current year was $70,000. Beginning inventory was $15,000. Dividends in the amount of $25,000 were paid.

Using the accrual method Zane reports the following financial accounting operating results for the current year:

Sales	$550,000
Minus: Costs of goods sold	(350,000)
Gross profit	$200,000
Dividend income from a 20%-owned domestic corporation	75,000
Net long-term capital gains	150,000
Total income	$425,000
Expenses:	
Salaries (including officer's salary of $40,000)	$120,000
Repairs	30,000
Bad debts	10,000
State and local taxes	20,000
Amortization	5,000
Contributions	35,000
Depreciation (straight-line)	40,000
Total expenses (before federal income tax expense)	$260,000
Operating profit	$165,000
Minus: Provision for federal income taxes	(40,000)
Net income	$125,000

All dividends qualify for the dividends-received deduction. In addition, the following items should be taken into account:

Current-year estimated tax payments	$15,000
MACRS depreciation for tax purposes	60,000

Prepare a current year Form 1120 (U.S. Corporation Income Tax Return) for Zane. Disregard beginning-of-the-year balance sheet amounts other than retained earnings. Also, leave spaces blank on Form 1120 for information not provided.

I:16-74 Huge Corporation reports the following balance sheet for the current year:

	Beginning of Year	End of Year
Cash	$ 40,000	$ 70,000
Accounts receivable	23,000	21,500
Inventories	26,000	53,000
Marketable securities	30,000	30,000
Investment in 100%-owned subsidiary	100,000	115,000
Depreciable assets	100,000	100,000
Less: Accumulated depreciation	(20,000)	(30,000)
Total assets	$299,000	$359,500
Accounts payable	$ 50,000	$ 80,000
Short-term loans payable	20,000	35,000
Mortgage payable	80,000	79,000
Common stock	1,000	1,000
Additional paid-in capital	49,000	49,000
Retained earnings	99,000	115,500
Total liabilities and stockholders' equity	$299,000	$359,500

Huge reports the following income and expenses for the year:

Sales	$720,000
Purchases	570,000
Dividend from 100%-owned subsidiary	30,000
Dividend from less-than-20%-owned corporation	10,000
Salaries (including officers' salaries of $30,000)	90,000
Repairs	12,000
Contributions	60,000
State and local taxes	7,500
Interest expense	11,000
Financial accounting depreciation	10,000
MACRS depreciation	17,490
Federal income tax expense per books	10,000

In addition, Huge reported an NOL carryover of $12,000 from the preceding year and paid current year estimated taxes of $10,000.

Prepare a current year Form 1120 (U.S. Corporation Income Tax Return) for Huge. Leave spaces blank on Form 1120 for information not provided. Note: You should prepare a schedule of net income per books to complete Line 1 of Schedule M-1.

CASE STUDY PROBLEMS

I:16-75 Frank, Paul, and Sam are considering merging their respective unincorporated businesses into a new C corporation called FPS. Frank would transfer land and a building with a $50,000 adjusted basis and $100,000 FMV to the corporation in exchange for $100,000 of FPS common stock. Paul would transfer inventory with an adjusted basis of $60,000 and $100,000 FMV in exchange for $50,000 of FPS stock and $50,000 of FPS 10-year notes. Sam would contribute equipment with an adjusted basis of $80,000 and $60,000 FMV along with legal services worth $40,000 in exchange for $100,000 of FPS stock.

Prepare a client memo that details the tax consequences of the transactions to FPS, Frank, Paul, and Sam.

I:16-76 Beth, who is married, is the sole shareholder of Pet Store Inc., a C corporation. She also manages the store. She wishes to expand the business, but the corporation needs additional capital for her to do so. Fortunately, she has saved $50,000 cash and plans to contribute it to the corporation. However, she does not know whether to contribute the cash in exchange for additional stock or lend the cash in exchange for a note.

Prepare a client memo that explains the tax consequences and requirements of each alternative so that Beth can make an informed decision.

TAX RESEARCH PROBLEMS

I:16-77 The income tax laws for a particular state depend on the business entity's organizational status. Answer the following four questions using the web site for a particular department of state (for example, Florida's information can be found at http://www.floridasecretaryofstate.com).

a. What business entity forms are permitted in the state selected?

b. Must a business that uses one of the basic business forms (for example, corporation, partnership, or LLC) organized and operating in the state register with a state agency? If so, which agency?

c. Must a business that uses one of the basic business forms that is organized outside of the state (for example, Georgia) but which operates in the state (for example, Florida) register with an agency in the state of organization? In the state in which it operates? In both states?

d. Does the state selected impose an income tax on corporations organized in the state? On foreign corporations (corporations formed outside of the state selected) who conduct part or all of their business in their home state and part in the state selected?

I:16-78 Charlie Corporation acquired 100% of Delta Corporation common stock on July 1 of the current tax year. Prior to the acquisition, Delta supplied Charlie with about 50% of the raw materials and other components used in producing its plastic toys. Delta will continue to be Charlie's major supplier as well as a supplier to other toy makers. Both corporations have been profitable for years and expect to be profitable after the acquisition. Charlie's CEO asks you if the two corporations, filing a single consolidated tax return would be less costly (in terms of both taxes paid and filing fees) than their filing two separate tax returns. How do you respond to this inquiry?

I:16-79 Ted is the sole shareholder of Zero Corporation. Before his retirement from the company, he gave 100 shares of Zero stock to his son. A few months later, Ted sold his remaining 1,900 shares to Zero for $2 million. The company has E&P exceeding $2 million. Ted's basis in his 2,000 shares before the two transfers was $80,000. Ted requested a waiver of the Sec. 318 attribution rules and treated the redemption of Zero stock as a long-term capital gain. Ted also agreed to serve as a consultant to the company. The terms of the agreement are that Ted will be paid as an independent contractor $175 per hour plus expenses. The agreement does not specify a minimum number of hours of services to be provided each month. Three years later the IRS audits Ted's return and argues that the redemption should be treated as a dividend under Sec. 301. Have the Sec. 302(c)(2) requirements that permit a waiver of the family attribution rules been met?

A partial list of research sources is:

- Secs. 302(c)(2) and (b)(3)
- Reg. Sec. 1.302-4
- *Estate of Milton S. Lennard v. CIR*, 61 T.C. 554 (1974)
- *William M. Lynch v. CIR*, 58 AFTR 2d 86-5970, 86-2 USTC ¶9731 (9th Cir., 1986)

I:16-80 Beth in Case Study Problem I:16-76 also wants to know whether she can make a $50,000 capital contribution to the corporation without the corporation's issuing additional shares. If so, should she have the corporation issue the shares or not? Assume that Beth's basis in her stock is $40,000 and that she files a joint return with her husband.

A partial list of research sources is:

- Sec. 1244(d)(1)(B)
- Reg. Secs. 1.1244(c)-1(b) and 1.1244(d)-2(a)
- *Sol Lessinger v. CIR*, 63 AFTR 2d 89-1055, 89-1 USTC ¶9254 (2nd Cir., 1989)
- *James D. Pierce*, 1989 PH T.C. Memo ¶89,647, 58 TCM 865 (1989).

I:16-81 In 2007, Peter purchased 150 shares of Able Manufacturing Corporation stock for $75,000. Able is a C corporation that has 40 shareholders. None of the other 39 shareholders own more than 5% of the 5,000 shares outstanding. No events have occurred that have changed either the number of shares of stock that Peter owns, or Peter's total basis in his shares. Peter is unhappy with Able's management. It is now Spring 2009 and Peter would like to sell part or all of his Able stock and reinvest the proceeds in the stock

of another small corporation. At present, his total unrealized gain is $300,000. Peter was told by his stockbroker that he may be eligible to exclude part or all of his profit on the sale of the Able shares from current taxable income. What advice on reducing the tax cost of the sale can you give him?

A partial list of research sources is:

- Sec. 1(h)
- Sec. 1202
- Sec. 1044
- Sec. 1045
- Sec. 1244

I:16-82 Erin Brinson founded BCD Corporation in 1989 with a contribution of $50,000 cash. The entity has always been a C corporation and Erin has not made any other capital contributions nor has BCD made any distributions. When she retired in 2010, Erin transferred ownership of BCD to her son, Evan, and two other employees. Evan now owns 60% of BCD stock and the two other employees each own 20%. The transaction was consummated by BCD redeeming 90% of Erin's shares for a $2,000,000 note payable over the next 15 years and Evan and the two other employees' buying the remaining 10% for notes totaling $250,000 payable over the next 15 years. All notes bear market rates with interest and principal payable twice a year on a regular basis. Erin owned the building in which BCD operates. As part of this transaction, Erin agreed to a new 5-year lease to BCD at market rental rates. How should the transfers of stock in BCD be taxed? Must Erin take measures to qualify for the most favorable tax treatment?

A partial list of research sources is:

- Sec. 302(b)
- Reg. Sec. 1.302
- Rev. Rul. 77-467, 1977-2 CB 92
- *Hurst,* 124 TC No. 2 (2005)

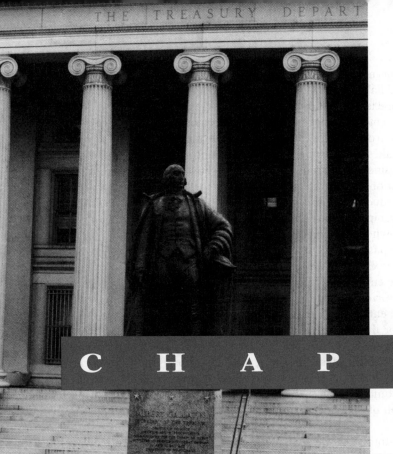

CHAPTER

17

PARTNERSHIPS AND S CORPORATIONS

LEARNING OBJECTIVES

After studying this chapter, you should be able to

▶ 1 Determine the tax implications of a partnership formation

▶ 2 Apply the operating rules for partnerships

▶ 3 Understand the tax implications (to the partnership and its partners) of distributions to partners

▶ 4 Understand the requirements for electing and maintaining S corporation status

▶ 5 Apply the operating rules for S corporations

▶ 6 Apply basis and other special rules to S corporation shareholders

KEY POINT

Pass-through entities (also called flow-through entities) entail taxation only at the ownership level. This single level of taxation is achieved by (1) exempting the entity from taxation; (2) passing income, deductions, losses, and credits through to the owners; and (3) adjusting the basis of the owner's interest in the entity.

Pass-through or conduit business entities, such as partnerships, S corporations, limited liability companies, and limited liability partnerships, have the major advantage of entailing only one level of taxation.[1] These legal organizational forms thus represent an interesting blend of what tax theorists call the entity and aggregate theories of taxation. In some ways, they are treated as entities separate from their owners. For example, the entity files a tax return (for information purposes), makes elections pertaining to accounting periods and methods, and computes the results of business operations. In other ways, however, a pass-through entity is treated as a mere aggregation of its owners. For example, the entity is generally not taxed, and the entity's income, deductions, losses, and credits are allocated to the owners based on their proportionate ownership or some other allocation arrangement. These allocated items then pass through to the owners to be reported in their own tax returns.

Aside from exempting pass-through entities from entity level taxation, the tax law preserves the single level of taxation in another important way: basis adjustments made to the owner's interest in the entity. Each owner obtains an original basis in his or her ownership interest upon acquiring the interest via formation of the entity, purchase of the entity interest, gift of the entity interest, etc. Subsequently, the owner's basis increases if the entity earns income or if the owner contributes additional money or property to the entity. Conversely, the owner's basis decreases if the entity incurs a loss or if the entity distributes money or property to the owner. In short, the owner's basis increases as the entity expands, and the owner's basis decreases as the entity contracts. Without these basis adjustments, the owner could be subject to double taxation upon selling his or her interest or upon the liquidation of the entity.

EXAMPLE I:17-1 ▶ Conduit Company is a pass-through entity with two owners, George and Flo. Each owner has a $10,000 original basis in the entity. In its first year of operations, Conduit earns $30,000, which is allocated $15,000 to each owner. Thus, each owner reports $15,000 in his or her individual tax return even though the entity does not distribute the earnings to the owners. At the beginning of the second year, Flo sells her interest to Fred for $25,000. If Flo did not get an increased basis adjustment for her $15,000 of earnings, she would recognize a $15,000 ($25,000 selling price − $10,000 basis in the entity) gain on the sale of her interest, which taxes her twice on the $15,000. However, both George and Flo do increase their bases to $25,000 ($10,000 original basis + $15,000 share of entity earnings) at the end of the first year. Therefore, when Flo sells her interest for $25,000, she incurs no addition taxable gain ($25,000 selling price − $25,000 basis in the entity = $0 gain). ◀

The next section of this chapter briefly describes the four basic types of flow-through business entities. Afterward, the chapter provides more detail on the tax treatment of partnerships and S corporations.

TYPES OF PASS-THROUGH ENTITIES

PARTNERSHIPS

Of the pass-through business entities, partnerships have been around the longest. The IRC defines a **partnership** as "a syndicate, group, pool, joint venture, or other unincorporated organization" that carries on any business, financial operation, or venture. The definition of a partnership, however, does not include a trust, estate, or corporation.[2] A partner is a member of such syndicate, group, pool, joint venture, or organization, and the partner can be an individual, corporation, trust, or estate. Unlike a corporation, which must file incorporation documents with the state, partnerships require no legal documentation although most states have laws that govern the rights and restrictions of partnerships. Moreover, most states model their laws on the Uniform Partnership Act (UPA) or the

---

[1] Trusts and estates also are conduit entities to some extent in that they are not taxed on income that is distributed. Trusts and estates are not generally used to conduct business activities. Income taxation of trusts and estates is discussed in Chapter C:14 of the *Prentice Hall Federal Taxation of Corporations, Partnerships, Estates, and Trusts* text.

[2] Secs. 761(a) and 7701(a)(2).

Uniform Limited Partnership Act (UPLA). A partnership must have at least two partners but can have an unlimited number beyond two.

A partnership can be either a general partnership or a limited partnership. In a general partnership, each partner has unlimited liability for partnership debts. Thus, these partners are at risk for more than their investment in the partnership. In a limited partnership, at least one partner must be a general partner, and at least one partner must be a limited partner. As in a general partnership, the general partners are liable for all partnership debts, but the limited partners are liable only to the extent of their investment plus any amount they commit to contribute to the partnership if called upon. Moreover, limited partners may not participate in the management of the partnership.

A major document for a partnership is the partnership agreement. In this agreement, the partners set out the terms of how the partnership will operate and how income, deductions, losses, and credits will be allocated to the partners. The partners, therefore, should take great care in drafting this agreement.

A partnership files an annual information return with the IRS. This return, Form 1065 (U.S. Partnership Return of Income), reports the results of the partnership's operations and indicates the separate income, deduction, loss, and credit items that pass through to the partners. A sample Form 1065 appears in Appendix B of the *Comprehensive* and *Corporations, Partnerships, Estates, and Trusts* volumes.

S CORPORATIONS

An **S corporation** is so designated because rules pertaining to this entity are located in Subchapter S of the Internal Revenue Code (IRC). S corporations are corporations that have elected to be treated by the tax laws as pass-through entities. Similar to partnerships, therefore, S corporations are not taxed, and income, deduction, loss, and credit items pass through to the shareholders. These entities, however, still are corporations so that corporate tax rules apply to them unless overridden by the Subchapter S provisions.[4] As with C corporations, the shareholders enjoy limited liability, but S corporations offer less flexibility than do partnerships. For example, the number and type of shareholders are limited, and the shareholders cannot agree to allocate income, deduction, loss, and credit items in a way that differs from their proportionate stock ownership.

To achieve S corporation status, the corporation must file an S election, and its shareholders must consent to that election. An electing S corporation files an information return, Form 1120S (U.S. Income Tax Return for an S Corporation), which reports the results of the corporation's operations and indicates the separate income, deduction, loss, and credit items that pass through to the shareholders. A sample Form 1120S appears in Appendix B of the *Comprehensive* and *Corporations, Partnerships, Estates, and Trusts* volumes.

LIMITED LIABILITY COMPANIES

A qualifying **limited liability company** (LLC) combines the best features of a partnership and a corporation even though it is neither. Specifically, it provides the limited liability protection of a corporation for all the LLC's owners, called members. An LLC can have an unlimited number of members who can be individuals, corporations, estates, or trusts.

As mentioned in Chapter I:16, an LLC may elect to be taxed as either a corporation or a partnership under the check-the-box regulations.[5] Under these Treasury Regulations, an LLC with more than one member is treated as a partnership unless the LLC affirmatively elects to be classified as a corporation. In most cases, LLCs will prefer to be classified as a partnership because of the tax advantages of that organizational form. Assuming the LLC opts for its default partnership classification, it annually files Form 1065 (U.S. Partnership Return of Income). Nevertheless, an LLC is not legally a partnership; it just is treated as one for tax purposes. A single member LLC may choose to be taxed as a corporation or

ADDITIONAL COMMENT

A number of states allow a variation on the limited partnership, called the limited liability limited partnership (LLLP). The LLLP is a partnership formed under a state's limited partnership laws but that can elect under the state's laws to provide the general partners with limited liability.[3]

REAL-WORLD EXAMPLE

S corporation returns will represent about 63% of all corporate tax returns. The total number of S corporations has grown from 736,900 returns filed in 1985 to a projected 4.4 million filed in 2009.

ADDITIONAL COMMENT

The LLC type of entity has been legislatively adopted by all 50 states.

---

[3] For a detailed discussion, see Shop Talk, "Service Firms Practicing as LLLPs: What are the Tax Consequences?," *Journal of Taxation*, August 2005.

[4] Sec. 1371(a)(1).
[5] Reg. Secs. 301.7701-1 through -4.

to be disregarded for tax purposes. If the entity is disregarded, income earned by the single member LLC is generally taxed to its owner under the sole proprietorship rules.

LIMITED LIABILITY PARTNERSHIPS

Many states also have statutes that allow a business to operate as an **limited liability partnership (LLP)**. This partnership form is particularly attractive to professional service partnerships, such as public accounting firms. As a result, many professional firms have adopted the LLP form, primarily to limit legal liability. Under state LLP laws, partners are liable for their own acts and the acts of individuals under their direction. However, LLP partners are not liable for the negligence or misconduct of other partners. Thus, from a liability perspective, an LLP partner is like a limited partner with respect to other partners' acts but like a general partner with respect to his or her own acts.

TAXATION OF PARTNERSHIPS[6]

FORMATION OF A PARTNERSHIP

Upon forming a partnership, the partners often contribute property (e.g., money, business equipment, and inventory previously used in a proprietorship) or services to the partnership. In exchange for this property and/or services, the partners receive an interest in the partnership. For each partner, a **partnership interest** represents an equity interest similar to corporate stock and is a capital asset.

SECTION 721: NONRECOGNITION RULES. Section 721 prevents the recognition of gain or loss upon either the transfer of property in exchange for a partnership interest or subsequent transfers of property by the partners in exchange for a pro rata increase in their partnership interests. Without this nonrecognition provision, gain on a transfer of appreciated property would be recognized, and the partners might not have sufficient liquidity (e.g., cash) to pay the tax. In addition, the transfer of property to the partnership represents a mere change in ownership form, which is not a recognition event under the tax laws. Finally, the depreciation recapture rules do not apply if no gain is recognized under Sec. 721.

The following exceptions to the Sec. 721 nonrecognition rules should be noted:

▶ The Sec. 721 nonrecognition of gain or loss rules do not apply if the partner acts in a capacity other than as partner. For example, if a partner sells property to the partnership in an arm's-length transaction, the sale would be taxable.[7]

▶ If a partner contributes services instead of cash or property in exchange for an unrestricted partnership interest, the fair market value (FMV) of the services is taxed as compensation to the contributing partner because services do not qualify as property.[8]

▶ The contributing partner recognizes gain if liabilities transferred to the partnership exceed the partner's basis in the partnership.[9]

▶ The contributing partner recognizes gain if the partnership would be treated as an investment company had it incorporated under Sec. 351.[10]

BASIS OF A PARTNERSHIP INTEREST. If the Sec. 721 nonrecognition rules apply, Sec. 722 provides a substituted basis rule for determining the basis of a partnership interest. In a simple case where no liabilities exist, the basis of the contributing partner's part-

---

[6] The rules described in this chapter apply generally to partnerships. However, a legislative change enacted in 1997 added special rules for electing large partnerships (those having at least 100 partners). A brief discussion of these rules is provided on pages I:17-17 and I:17-18.

[7] Reg. Sec. 1.721-1(a).

[8] Reg. Sec. 1.721-1(b)(1). In May 2005, the IRS issued proposed regulations which would bring partnership interests issued in exchange for services under Sec. 83 rules. If and when these regulations become final, they will significantly change the taxation of a partnership interest received for services.

[9] (See Example I:17-4 and the discussion of the partnership basis rules.)

[10] Sec. 721(b). The partnership is considered to be an investment company if 80% or more of the transferred assets (excluding cash and nonconvertible debt obligations) consist of marketable stocks or securities. This restriction prevents investors from diversifying their portfolios by creating a partnership through a nontaxable transfer of securities in exchange for a partnership interest.

nership interest equals the sum of money contributed plus the adjusted basis of other property transferred to the partnership.

EXAMPLE I:17-2 ▶ Allen contributes business equipment having a $10,000 FMV and a $4,000 adjusted basis to the ABC Partnership in exchange for a 30% interest in the partnership. The basis of Allen's partnership interest is $4,000 because he recognizes no gain or loss on the asset transfer under Sec. 721. ◀

If a contributing partner renders services to the partnership in exchange for a partnership interest, the contributing partner's basis equals the amount of income recognized from rendering the services (i.e., the FMV of the services).[11] The FMV basis is permitted because the partner recognizes ordinary income equal to the FMV of the services.

EXAMPLE I:17-3 ▶ Angela contributes property having a $10,000 FMV and a $4,000 adjusted basis and renders services valued at $10,000 in exchange for a 60% interest in the ABC Partnership. Section 721 protects Angela from gain recognition on the property transfer. However, Angela recognizes $10,000 of ordinary income for the services rendered. Thus, the basis of Angela's partnership interest equals $14,000 ($4,000 adjusted basis of the property plus the $10,000 FMV of the services). ◀

ADDITIONAL COMMENT

A partner's basis in the partnership interest commonly is called "outside basis."

Section 752 Basis Adjustments. A partner's basis for his or her partnership interest includes the partner's ratable share of partnership liabilities as well as the basis attributable to any property and services contributed to the partnership. In addition, the following rules apply if a partnership assumes a partner's liability or if the partner transfers property to the partnership subject to a liability:

▶ An increase in partnership liabilities is treated as a cash contribution by all partners, which increases their bases by their share of the assumed liabilities.

▶ The partnership's assumption of a partner's liability is treated as a cash distribution to the partner whose liability it assumed, which decreases that partner's basis in the partnership.

EXAMPLE I:17-4 ▶ Brad contributes a building to a newly formed partnership, BCD Partnership, in exchange for a one-third interest in the partnership. The building has a $90,000 FMV, an $80,000 adjusted basis, and is subject to a $60,000 mortgage. The partnership assumes the mortgage but has no other liabilities. Carol and Dale each contribute $30,000 of cash for a one-third interest in the partnership. After the contributions, the partners have the following bases in their partnership interests:

	Brad	Carol	Dale
Adjusted basis of property or amount of cash contributed	$80,000	$30,000	$30,000
Plus: Share of mortgage assumed by the partnership ($60,000 × 1/3 to each)	20,000	20,000	20,000
Minus: Decrease in Brad's personal liabilities	(60,000)	–0–	–0–
Basis in partnership interest	$40,000	$50,000	$50,000 ◀

Under the general rules of Sec. 752, a partner's basis in the partnership interest increases by the partner's share of any changes in the partnership's liabilities during the year. For example, if total partnership liabilities (including accounts and notes payable, mortgages, bank loans, etc.) increase during the year from $100,000 to $200,000, the basis of a partner with a 50% interest in the partnership increases by $50,000 ($100,000 increase in liabilities × 0.50).

Negative Basis Rule. The basis of a partnership interest cannot be negative. Therefore, Sec. 731 requires recognition of gain in situations where a negative basis would otherwise occur.

EXAMPLE I:17-5 ▶ Becky transfers property having a $100,000 FMV and a $25,000 adjusted basis, which is subject to a $60,000 mortgage, in exchange for a one-third interest in the BCD Partnership. The

---

[11] Reg. Sec. 1.722-1. Also, see footnote 8.

partnership owes no other liabilities. Becky, Cindy, and Dan each have a one-third interest in the partnership. The $60,000 reduction in Becky's individual liabilities is treated as a distribution of money. Thus, Becky recognizes a $15,000 gain because the distribution exceeds her $45,000 ($25,000 + $20,000) basis in the partnership interest. Becky's basis in the partnership interest is zero after the distribution. The basis is computed as follows:

Adjusted basis of property transferred		$25,000
Plus:	Becky's share of the mortgage assumed by the partnership ($60,000 × 1/3)	20,000
Basis before deemed distribution		45,000
Minus:	Decrease in Becky's individual liabilities	(60,000)
Becky's basis in the partnership interest (cannot be negative)		$ –0–

The cash deemed distributed in excess of Becky's predistribution basis causes her to recognize a $15,000 ($60,000 − $45,000) gain. Becky reduces her basis to zero by the deemed distribution because her basis in the partnership interest cannot be less than zero. ◄

 STOP & THINK

Question: In Example I:17-5, Becky transferred property subject to a liability exceeding the property's adjusted basis. How does the treatment of excess liabilities in a partnership differ from the treatment when such property is transferred to a corporation?

Solution: In a corporate situation, the shareholder recognizes gain to the extent that total liabilities exceed the total basis of property transferred by that shareholder. Thus, had Becky transferred the same property to a corporation in a Sec. 351 transaction, she would have recognized gain for the entire $35,000 ($60,000 mortgage − $25,000 adjusted basis) excess liability. In a partnership, however, the transferor partner recognizes gain only if the deemed money distribution associated with the liability exceeds the partner's basis in the partnership interest. Thus, in Example I:17-5, Becky recognized only a $15,000 gain. If she had substantial basis in an existing partnership, she would have recognized no gain.

HOLDING PERIOD FOR A PARTNERSHIP INTEREST. If a partner contributes only cash to the partnership in exchange for a partnership interest, the holding period begins the day after the partner acquires the interest. If the partner contributes property, the holding period for the partnership interest generally includes the holding period of the contributed property. However, if the contributed property is other than a capital asset or Sec. 1231 property, the holding period begins on the date the partnership interest is acquired.[12]

EXAMPLE I:17-6 ►

In the current year, Johanna contributes business machinery to the JK Partnership in exchange for a partnership interest. Johanna originally acquired the machinery in 2007. Because the machinery is Sec. 1231 property, Johanna's holding period for her partnership interest begins in 2007 (the date she acquired the machinery). If Johanna had contributed inventory instead of machinery, the holding period would begin the day after the inventory contribution date. ◄

ADDITIONAL COMMENT

When property that has been held for personal use is contributed to a partnership, the basis equals the lesser of the property's FMV or adjusted basis on the contribution date.

BASIS OF PARTNERSHIP ASSETS. Section 723 provides a carryover basis rule for property contributed to the partnership. Generally the partnership's basis in the property is the same as that of the transferor partner, even if the contributing partner recognizes gain. Without this rule, partners could increase the basis of their property for depreciation and subsequent sale purposes merely by contributing appreciated property to a partnership. When the carryover basis rule applies, the partnership's holding period for the property includes the period the property was held by the contributing partner.[13]

EXAMPLE I:17-7 ►

In the current year, Carlos contributes equipment with a $6,000 adjusted basis and an $8,000 FMV to the CDE Partnership and receives a one-third interest in the partnership. Carlos acquired the equipment in 2008. CDE's basis for the equipment is $6,000, its adjusted basis in the hands of the contributing partner. Carlos recognizes no gain due to the Sec. 721 nonrecog-

---

[12] Reg. Sec. 1.1223-1(a).

[13] Sec. 1223(2) and Reg. Sec. 1.723-1.

nition rules. CDE's holding period for the equipment begins in 2008 because it includes Carlos' holding period for the property. ◄

ADDITIONAL COMMENT

A partnership's basis in its assets commonly is called "inside basis."

An individual who contributes property encumbered with a liability to a partnership may have to recognize gain on the transfer if the deemed cash distribution from the partnership's assumption of the liability exceeds the partner's basis in the partnership (see Example I:17-5). The adjusted basis of Becky's partnership interest in Example I:17-5 is reduced by this release from the liability (but not below zero). It is not increased by the gain Becky recognizes, however, because the gain recognition is due to a distribution of money on the release from the liability and not from the contribution of the property to the partnership. For a similar reason, the partnership does not increase its basis in contributed property by the partner's recognized gain.[14]

KEY POINT

For many items, the partnership must maintain separate sets of records for tax purposes, partnership "book" purposes, and financial accounting (GAAP) purposes.

BOOK ACCOUNTING CONSIDERATIONS. Like all publicly traded entities, publicly traded partnerships must produce financial statements prepared in accordance with GAAP. However, one of the most confusing aspects of partnership tax accounting is that Treasury Regulations require the maintenance of another set of accounting "books" based on the requirements of Reg. Sec. 1.704-1(b)(2)(iv). These regulations for properly maintaining partnership capital accounts mandate "book" accounting that is similar (but not identical) to GAAP financial accounting partnership rules. Under these partnership book rules, the carryover basis rules used in taxation do not apply for book accounting. For example, if property is contributed to a partnership, its book value is recorded at the contributed property's FMV while the tax basis is recorded as a carryover. This book accounting treatment in the regulations results in differences between the tax bases and book values of contributed assets. These differences between tax and book values will be important in our study of special allocations (page I:17-8). Just remember that when the text mentions book accounting for partnerships, it is the accounting required by Reg. Sec. 1.704-1(b)(2)(iv) and not financial statements prepared according to GAAP.

EXAMPLE I:17-8 ▶

BOOK-TAX ACCOUNTING COMPARISON

The difference between book value and tax basis also causes GAAP, book, and tax depreciation to differ if a partner contributes depreciable property.

Anwar contributes cash of $30,000 and Beth contributes land having a $30,000 FMV and a $20,000 adjusted basis to the AB Partnership. Each partner receives a 50% interest in the partnership. For book accounting purposes, the cash and land are each recorded at $30,000. For tax purposes, the carryover basis of the land to the partnership is $20,000. The partnership realizes no gain or loss for book accounting purposes if it later sells the land for $30,000. However, the partnership recognizes a $10,000 gain under the tax rules because the land's adjusted basis for tax purposes is only $20,000. The $10,000 precontribution gain must be allocated to Beth. (See the section titled Special Allocations on page I:17-8 for a discussion of precontribution gains and losses.) ◄

Topic Review I:17-1 highlights the nonrecognition of gain or loss provisions and basis rules.

ADDITIONAL COMMENT

For organizational expenditures paid or incurred after September 8, 2008, a partnership is deemed to have made the election to amortize for the tax year the partnership begins business. If the partnership chooses to forgo the deemed election, it can elect to capitalize the expenditures (without amortization) on a timely filed tax return for the tax year the partnership begins business. See Temp. Reg. Sec. 1.709-1T.

ORGANIZATIONAL AND SYNDICATION FEES. A partnership can deduct up to $5,000 of costs of organizing the partnership in the year the partnership begins business. The deduction is limited to the lesser of (1) the amount of organizational expenditures or (2) $5,000, reduced by the amount by which such organizational expenditures exceed $50,000. Any organizational expenditures exceeding the first year deduction can be deducted ratably over the 180 month period beginning with the month the partnership begins business.[15] Organizational expenditures that qualify for this amortization treatment include items such as the attorney's fees for drafting the partnership agreement, the accountant's fees for setting up the financial record system, and filing fees.

The partnership must capitalize expenses attributable to syndicating the partnership. These expenses, however, are *not* amortizable. **Syndication fees** are expenses incurred to promote and market partnership interests (usually associated with tax-sheltered limited partnership interests). Examples of nondeductible syndication fees include brokerage and registration fees, legal fees of the underwriter and issuer, and printing costs associated with the prospectus and promotional materials.

---

[14] Rev. Rul. 84-15, 1984-1 C.B. 158.   [15] These rules are contained in Sec. 709.

Topic Review I:17-1

Section 721 Formations: Nonrecognition of Gain or Loss Rules

▶ Neither the partnership nor the partners recognize gain or loss on the transfer of property to a partnership in exchange for a partnership interest or an increase in a partnership interest.

▶ A partner's basis in his or her partnership interest is adjusted upward for the following items:
Amount of cash contributed to the partnership
Adjusted basis of noncash property contributed
FMV of services contributed
Section 752 adjustment for liabilities

▶ The partnership's basis in transferred property carries over from the transferor partners.

▶ With exceptions pertaining to contributions of cash and ordinary income property, a partner's holding period for his or her partnership interest includes the holding period of the contributed property.

▶ The partnership's holding period in contributed property includes the transferor's holding period.

▶ The nonrecognition rules do not apply to services contributed. The contributing partner recognizes ordinary income equal to the FMV of the services, and the partner's basis in the partnership interest is increased by the amount of income recognized from rendering the services.

▶ The depreciation recapture rules generally do not apply to contributed property. Instead, the depreciation recapture potential carries over to the partnership.

OBJECTIVE 2

Apply the operating rules for partnerships

ADDITIONAL COMMENT

Many states impose an income tax on each nonresident partner's share of income produced by the partnership in that state, which can cause a partner to file several state income tax returns when a partnership conducts business in those states.

ADDITIONAL COMMENT

In general, partnership income or loss is allocated according the partnership agreement, which can be amended any time up to the due date for filing the partnership return.

PARTNERSHIP OPERATIONS

The partnership tax return (Form 1065) provides information regarding the measurement and reporting of income, deductions, losses, and credits that pass through to the partners. Certain separately stated items (e.g., capital gains and losses, charitable contributions, and Sec. 1231 gains and losses) pass through to the partners without losing their identity. Such items must be separately stated because their tax effect depends on the partner's particular tax situation. These items are reported on Schedules K and K-1 of the partnership return. Schedule K reports tax information for the entire partnership, and a separate Schedule K-1 summarizes the results for each partner.

Items that do not have special tax effect are netted at the partnership level and are reported on page 1 of Form 1065. The netting of such items results in partnership ordinary income or ordinary loss, which then is allocated to the partners depending on the profit and loss sharing ratios contained in the partnership agreement. Table I:17-1 contains a list of commonly encountered separately stated items and items that make up partnership ordinary income or loss.

SPECIAL ALLOCATIONS

Section 704 permits partners some latitude in allocating income, deductions, losses, and credits among the individual partners. Special allocations are unique to partnerships and permit flexible arrangements among the partners for sharing specific income and loss items. A partner's distributive share of such items generally is determined by the partnership agreement. However, the special allocation provisions restrict the partners' freedom to shift tax benefits among individual partners. For example, the special allocation must have substantial economic effect (e.g., it cannot be a tax sham). In addition, a special allocation must be made for property contributed by the partners when determining the allocation of depreciation deductions and the amount of gain or loss recognized when the partnership eventually sells the property. Essentially, the allocation of the depreciation deductions and the amount of recognized gain or loss must take into account the difference between the partnership's basis for the contributed property and the property's FMV at the time of the contribution.

EXAMPLE I:17-9 ▶ Clay and Dana formed an equal partnership five years ago. Clay contributed cash of $100,000, and Dana contributed land having a $60,000 adjusted basis and a $100,000 FMV. The partner-

▼ TABLE I:17-1
Segregation of Ordinary Income and Separately Stated Items

Items	Separately Stated Items (Schedules K and K-1)	Partnership Ordinary Income (or Loss) (Page 1 of Form 1065)
Sales minus cost of goods sold (gross profit)		X
Salaries and wage expense		X
Guaranteed payments to partners[a]	X	X
Tax, bad debt, and repair expenses		X
Charitable contributions	X	
Investment income (interest, dividends, etc.) and expense	X	
Foreign income taxes paid or accrued	X	
Specially allocated income, deduction, loss, gain, and credit items that differ from the general profit and loss allocation ratios	X	
Tax-exempt interest income	X	
Capital gains and losses	X	
Section 1245 and Sec. 1250 depreciation recapture		X
Section 1250 gain	X	
Section 1231 gains or losses	X	
Section 179 expensing	X	
Tax credits	X	
Tax preference items	X	

[a]Guaranteed payments appear in both columns because the partnership deducts them to arrive at partnership ordinary income (or loss), and they are reported separately and are taxable to the partner who receives the payments.

ship's basis for the land is $60,000 (Dana's carryover basis). If the partnership sells the land in the current year for $110,000, it recognizes $50,000 ($110,000 − $60,000) of gain. If a special allocation of the gain were not required, Clay and Dana each would be allocated $25,000 of the gain based on their equal profit and loss sharing ratios. The special allocation rules, however, require $45,000 of the gain to be allocated to Dana ($40,000 appreciation accruing before her transfer of property to the partnership plus $5,000, which is one-half of the $10,000 of post-contribution appreciation). The remaining $5,000 of post-contribution gain is allocated to Clay [($110,000 − $100,000) × 0.50]. ◄

WHAT WOULD YOU DO IN THIS SITUATION?

Alex and Alicia plan to form a partnership in the current year with each partner making an equal capital contribution to the partnership. The partnership agreement will specify that the partners share equally in partnership profits and losses. Among other things, the partnership will invest in taxable and tax-exempt bonds. The partners expect the taxable and tax-exempt bonds each to generate $2,500 of interest per year. For the next several years, Alex expects to be in the 15% tax bracket and Alicia expects to be in the top individual tax bracket (35% in 2010). Without a special allocation, each partner would be allocated $1,250 of each type interest. Instead, however, they want a special allocation in the partnership agreement that allocates (1) all $2,500 of taxable interest to Alex plus $187 ($1,250 × 0.15) of tax-exempt interest to compensate him for the additional taxes owed on the extra $1,250 of taxable interest and (2) the remaining $2,313 ($2,500 − $187) of tax-exempt interest to Alicia. Alex and Alicia seek your advice on the propriety of this special allocation. Hint: Prepare a schedule of after-tax interest income to the partners with and without the special allocation.

ALLOCATION OF PARTNERSHIP INCOME, DEDUCTIONS, LOSSES, AND CREDITS TO PARTNERS

If a partner's interest in the partnership changes during the year (e.g., due to the sale of a partnership interest or the entry of a new partner who contributes property to the partnership in exchange for an interest), all the partners must determine their distributive share of the partnership income, deductions, losses, and credits according to their varying interests in the partnership during the year.[16] Retroactive allocations (e.g., an allocation of deductions or losses incurred before admission of a new partner to the partnership) may not be made to new partners admitted during the partnership's tax year.

EXAMPLE I:17-10 ▶ Colleen and Dan are equal partners in the CDE Partnership, which uses the calendar year as its tax year. On December 1 of the current year, Ed contributes $50,000 cash for a one-third interest in the partnership. The partnership reports a $9,000 ordinary loss for the current tax year ending on December 31. The partners must report their shares of the partnership loss based on their varying interests as follows:[17]

Partner		Loss Allocation
Colleen	1/2 × $9,000 × 11/12	$4,125
	1/3 × $9,000 × 1/12	250
	Colleen's share of loss	$4,375
Dan	Same as Colleen	4,375
Ed	1/3 × $9,000 × 1/12	250
	Total allocation of loss	$9,000

Ed's loss is limited to his ratable (one-third) share of the loss incurred after his entry into the partnership, or $250. This result occurs even if the partnership agreement provides that Ed would receive one-third of all losses for the entire year. ◀

BASIS ADJUSTMENTS FOR OPERATING ITEMS

Under Sec. 705, the basis of each partnership interest is adjusted to reflect the partner's share of income and deduction items. This basis adjustment is necessary to ensure the single level of taxation of partnerships. Basis adjustments for income and deduction items are made currently regardless of whether the partners receive an actual distribution from the partnership. In addition, each partner's basis in the partnership interest is adjusted for capital contributions, withdrawals, and changes in liabilities that occur during the year. Each partner's basis is increased by the partner's distributive share of partnership ordinary income and separately stated income and gain items. The basis of the partnership interest is increased whether the income is taxable to the partners or is tax-exempt.[18]

A partner's basis is decreased (but not below zero) by partnership distributions and by the partner's distributive share of partnership ordinary loss, separately stated losses and deductions, and expenditures that are nondeductible in computing partnership ordinary income or loss (e.g., charitable contributions made by the partnership).

Partners also increase their basis by their share of partnership liabilities. That share depends on whether the partnership liabilities are recourse or nonrecourse. A recourse liability is one where the lender has recourse to all partnership assets as well as general partners' other assets for satisfaction of the loan. In other words, the lender has recourse to the general partners, so they have what is called the economic risk of loss. Thus, recourse liabilities are allocated to the partners based on their economic risk of loss. A nonrecourse liability is one where the lender has recourse only to specified partnership property, such as real estate, for satisfaction of the loan. In other words, the lender has no recourse to the

---

[16] Sec. 706(d)(1).
[17] Regulation Sec. 1.706-1(c)(2) provides for alternative allocation methods. The partners may elect to use the interim closing method as an alternative to the pro rata allocation method used in Example I:17-10.

[18] If the partnership includes oil and gas properties, an increase in basis is made for the excess of percentage depletion claimed over the basis of the property subject to depletion, and a reduction in basis is made for the depletion deduction claimed under Sec. 611.

partners. Nonrecourse liabilities are allocated based on the partners' profit sharing percentages.

EXAMPLE I:17-11 ▶ David and Edith form a partnership in the current year and share profits and losses equally. However, David is a general partner, and Edith is a limited partner. Thus, David has all the economic risk of loss for recourse liabilities. The partnership agreement provides for no special allocations. The following transactions occur during the year:

▶ David contributes land having a $60,000 basis and a $100,000 FMV in exchange for his initial partnership interest.

▶ At the end of the year, the partnership has $100,000 of nonrecourse liabilities and $30,000 of recourse liabilities.

▶ The partnership earns $50,000 of ordinary income.

▶ The partnership earns $5,000 of tax-exempt interest income.

▶ The partnership incurs $10,000 of capital losses.

▶ The partnership makes a $15,000 charitable contribution.

▶ The partnership distributes $20,000 in cash to David.

David's year-end basis is determined as follows:

Capital contribution of land (adjusted basis)		$ 60,000
Plus:	Share of partnership nonrecourse liabilities	
	($100,000 × 0.50)	50,000
	Share of partnership recourse liabilities ($30,000 × 1.00)	30,000
	Share of ordinary income ($50,000 × 0.50)	25,000
	Share of tax-exempt interest income ($5,000 × 0.50)	2,500
Minus:	Distribution to David	(20,000)
	Share of charitable contribution ($15,000 × 0.50)	(7,500)
	Share of capital losses ($10,000 × 0.50)	(5,000)
David's basis at the end of the current year		$135,000 ◀

STOP & THINK *Question:* Why do partners increase the basis of their partnership interests by their share of tax-exempt income?

Solution: Increasing the basis ensures that the income will retain its tax-exempt character when the partnership income is subsequently distributed in the form of cash or the partner's interest in the partnership is sold or exchanged.

LIMITATIONS ON LOSSES AND RESTORATION OF BASIS

Although a partner's distributive share of the partnership's ordinary loss and any separately stated losses and deductions passes through to the partner, Sec. 704(d) limits deductibility of the losses to the partner's adjusted basis in his or her partnership interest as determined at the end of the partnership's tax year.[19] All positive and negative adjustments referred to in Example I:17-11 (except the loss) are made before the limitation is considered. If the loss limitation rule did not apply, the partner's interest could have a negative basis. Any unused losses and deductions carry over indefinitely and are allowed in subsequent years when the partner again has a positive basis in his or her partnership interest.

EXAMPLE I:17-12 ▶ Ellen, who has a 50% interest in the EF Partnership, has a $10,000 basis in her partnership interest at the end of 2010 (before deducting her share of losses). The EF Partnership incurs a $50,000 ordinary loss in 2010. Ellen's share of the loss is $25,000 ($50,000 × 0.50), but Ellen can deduct only $10,000 in 2010. The remaining $15,000 of loss carries over to 2011. The deductible loss reduces Ellen's partnership basis to zero at the end of 2010. ◀

---

[19] Two other rules also restrict the deductibility of losses. The at-risk rules contained in Sec. 465 limit loss deductions to the partner's at-risk basis. In addition, Sec. 469 contains passive activity loss rules that disallow virtually all net passive activity losses. These restrictions are discussed in Chapter I:8 of this text and in Chapter C:9 of *Prentice Hall's Federal Taxation: Corporations, Partnerships, Estates, and Trusts.*

EXAMPLE I:17-13 ▶

BOOK-TAX ACCOUNTING COMPARISON

Although a partner's basis in his or her partnership interest may not go below zero, a partner's book capital account (equity) may be negative.

Assume the same facts as in Example I:17-12 except in 2011 Ellen's share of partnership liabilities increases by $5,000, Ellen's share of 2011 ordinary income is $5,000, and Ellen makes a $5,000 additional capital contribution. Ellen's basis increases by a total of $15,000 due to the three items. Therefore, she deducts the $15,000 loss carryover from 2010 in 2011. The deduction reduces Ellen's partnership basis to zero at the end of 2011. A zero tax basis for a partnership interest does not necessarily mean that the interest is worthless. The FMV of the partnership's net assets and accounting book value, nevertheless, may be substantial. ◀

Topic Review I:17-2 summarizes the allocation and basis rules.

TAX STRATEGY TIP

Taxpayers can control to a limited degree when they use partnership and S corporation losses in their individual tax returns. If loss pass-throughs exceed the partner's end-of-year basis in his or her investment, the loss will not be deductible until the partner again has basis in his or her investment. If a taxpayer incurs a loss in the current year and wants to deduct the loss on next year's personal tax return, he or she must make an additional capital contribution after year-end. Alternatively, a shareholder can loan money to his or her S corporation before year-end to ensure having sufficient basis to use the loss currently. A partner can make similar capital contributions. A partnership (but not an S corporation) can control the timing of the loss deductions for its partners through additional borrowings it makes prior to the end of the tax year.

PASSIVE ACTIVITY LOSS LIMITATIONS. The passive activity loss limitations discussed in Chapter I:8 apply to partners who do not materially participate in the business of the partnership. The passive activity loss rules apply at the *partner* level, that is, each partner must determine whether he or she materially participates in the partnership. If a loss is determined to be passive, a partner may not deduct the loss against either earned income or portfolio income (e.g., dividends and interest) but may deduct the loss only against other passive income. These rules are highly significant and play a major role in determining the deductibility of partnership losses by partners.

TRANSACTIONS BETWEEN A PARTNER AND THE PARTNERSHIP

Sometimes a partner may independently engage in transactions with the partnership. For example, a partner may sell property to the partnership rather than make a capital contribution of the property. In such transactions, the partner is treated as an outside independent party.[20] Thus, a partner recognizes gain or loss on the sale of property to the partnership, and the partnership receives a cost basis equal to the amount of consideration paid. Because the partner and the partnership are not truly independent parties, abuse of this provision is possible. For example, the partners might want to recognize losses by selling certain assets at a loss to the partnership while still retaining those assets in the partnership. Alternatively, a partner may wish to sell certain depreciable business assets (Sec. 1231 property) at a gain taxable to the partner at favorable capital gains rates while the partnership receives a stepped-up FMV basis in the assets for depreciation purposes. Section 707(b) forestalls such potential abuses by disallowing losses and by providing ordinary income (rather than capital gain) treatment under the following circumstances:

Topic Review I:17-2

Allocation Rules and Basis Adjustments

▶ When a partner contributes property to a partnership, any unrecognized precontribution gain or loss must be allocated to the contributing partner when the partnership sells the property.

▶ Partnership income, gains, deductions, losses, and credits are allocated to the partners on a daily basis based on each partner's interest in the partnership.

▶ Special allocations of income, gains, deductions, losses, and credits are permitted as long as they have substantial economic effect.

▶ Basis in the partnership interest is increased by the partner's share of ordinary income, separately stated income items, and tax-exempt income. Basis is reduced by a partner's share of ordinary loss, separately stated deductions and losses, and nondeductible expenditures. Basis also is adjusted for capital contributions, distributions, and changes in partnership liabilities. Basis cannot be decreased below zero.

▶ Ordinary losses and separately stated deduction and loss items that exceed a partner's basis carry over indefinitely until the partner again has a positive basis in his or her partnership interest.

---

[20] Rules for transactions taking place between a partner and the partnership are found in Sec. 707.

▶ Losses are disallowed on sales or exchanges between a partner and the partnership if the partner owns more than a 50% interest in the partnership. A loss also is disallowed if a sale or exchange of property occurs between two partnerships in which the same persons own more than a 50% interest. The Sec. 267 constructive ownership rules apply to determine whether the 50% test is met. If the purchaser (i.e., the partner or the partnership) of the property later sells the asset to an outsider, the gain recognized is reduced by the previously disallowed loss.

▶ Gains are treated as ordinary income (rather than capital gains) if the partner owns (directly or indirectly) more than a 50% interest in the partnership and if the exchanged asset is not a capital asset in the transferee's hands.[21] Again, the Sec. 267(b) constructive ownership rules apply.

EXAMPLE I:17-14 ▶ Ira has a 60% interest in the HI Partnership. Ira sells land with a $100,000 adjusted basis to the partnership for its $60,000 FMV. Ira does not recognize the $40,000 ($60,000 − $100,000) loss because Ira owns more than a 50% interest in the partnership. The partnership takes a $60,000 cost basis in the land. If the partnership later sells the land to an outsider for $110,000, the partnership recognizes only $10,000 of gain because the $50,000 ($110,000 − $60,000) realized gain is reduced by Ira's $40,000 previously disallowed loss. ◀

EXAMPLE I:17-15 ▶ Helen has a 90% interest in the HI Partnership. Helen sells a building used in her business with a $60,000 adjusted basis to the HI Partnership for its FMV of $100,000. After the purchase, the partnership continues to use the building in its business activities. Before the sale, Helen had taken straight-line depreciation. Had Helen instead sold the building to an outsider, she would have recognized $40,000 of Sec. 1250 and/or Sec. 1231 gain, which usually receives capital gain treatment. However, Helen's $40,000 gain is treated as ordinary income because she sold the building to a partnership in which she owns a more than 50% interest, and the building is not a capital asset to the partnership. The ordinary income does not qualify for a reduced tax rate, nor can it be used to offset capital losses. HI Partnership takes a $100,000 cost basis in the building. ◀

GUARANTEED PAYMENTS. Even though a partner does not qualify as an employee of the partnership for tax purposes, the partnership agreement may provide for fixed salary payments that are not based on partnership income. Generally, the partnership deducts such payments as guaranteed payments to arrive at partnership ordinary income. They are includible in the partner's gross income in the tax year received. The partnership also can make guaranteed payments in lieu of interest payments on the amount of the partner's capital investment. Such payments are deductible by the partnership to arrive at partnership ordinary income and are includible in the partner's gross income.

EXAMPLE I:17-16 ▶

José owns a 40% interest in the JKL Partnership. The partnership agreement provides that José is to receive a fixed salary of $20,000 plus 10% interest on his average capital balance. The partnership makes no guaranteed payments to the other partners. If his average capital balance for the year is $50,000, the partnership would pay $5,000 (0.10 × $50,000) of interest as a guaranteed payment. If partnership ordinary income is $10,000 before deducting the guaranteed payments, the partnership ordinary loss is $15,000 ($10,000 income − $25,000 of guaranteed payments to José). José reports $25,000 of ordinary income for the year, consisting of the $20,000 salary and the $5,000 interest. He also reports a $6,000 ($15,000 × 0.40) ordinary loss. The other partners in total report a $9,000 ($15,000 × 0.60) ordinary loss. ◀

OBJECTIVE 3

Understand the tax implications (to the partnership and its partners) of distributions to partners

PARTNERSHIP DISTRIBUTIONS

A distribution of cash or property from the partnership to a partner generally is treated as a nontaxable return of capital. This treatment closely parallels the nontaxable consequences resulting from a capital contribution of property made in exchange for a partnership interest under Sec. 721.

A distribution may result in a reduction of a partner's capital interest in the partnership. This type of distribution is called a **nonliquidating distribution**. The partnership may

[21] Gains also are converted to ordinary income if the sale is between two partnerships in which the same persons own directly or indirectly more than a 50% interest in the partnership. In determining the 50% ownership rule, the Sec. 267 constructive ownership rules apply.

wish to liquidate a partner's entire interest due to retirement, death, or other business reasons. These distributions are called **liquidating distributions**. In such cases, the liquidating distribution is treated as a sale or exchange of the partnership interest.

Due to the complex nature of this topic, this chapter includes only an abbreviated coverage of these materials, and the discussion of liquidating distributions is omitted. Chapter C:10 of *Prentice Hall's Federal Taxation: Corporations, Partnerships, Estates, and Trusts* includes detailed coverage of these topics.

NONLIQUIDATING DISTRIBUTIONS. As a general rule, neither the partner nor the partnership recognize gain or loss if the partnership distributes money or other property to the partner.[22] Such nonliquidating distributions usually are treated as nontaxable returns of capital. If the amount of money received by the partner exceeds the partner's basis for the partnership interest, however, the partner recognizes gain to the extent of the excess.[23] If the partnership distributes property other than money (e.g., land and machinery) to the partner, the basis of the partnership interest is reduced by the adjusted basis of the distributed assets. As previously mentioned, neither the partnership nor the distributee partner recognize gain or loss even if the adjusted basis of the distributed property exceeds the partner's basis in his or her partnership interest. In this case, the basis of the property to the partner is reduced to equal the basis of the partnership interest. If the partnership distributes both money and property, the money distribution reduces the basis of the partnership interest before any adjustment for the property distribution.

EXAMPLE I:17-17 ▶ Jane receives a nonliquidating distribution of $10,000 cash from the JK Partnership. At the distribution date, Jane's basis in her partnership interest is $8,000. Of the $10,000 distribution, $8,000 is a nontaxable free return of capital, which reduces Jane's basis to zero. The remaining $2,000 is a capital gain.[24] ◀

EXAMPLE I:17-18 ▶ Jeff receives a nonliquidating distribution of land having a $6,000 adjusted basis and a $10,000 FMV from the JK Partnership. Jeff's predistribution basis in his partnership interest is $8,000. Neither Jeff nor the partnership recognize gain or loss on the distribution. Jeff's basis in the land is $6,000, and his basis in his partnership interest is reduced by $6,000 (the adjusted basis of the property distributed). Thus, following the distribution, Jeff's basis in his partnership interest is $2,000 ($8,000 − $6,000). ◀

EXAMPLE I:17-19 ▶ Jean receives from the JK Partnership a nonliquidating distribution of $5,000 cash plus land having a $6,000 adjusted basis and a $10,000 FMV. Jean's predistribution basis in her partnership interest is $8,000. Her basis initially is reduced by the $5,000 cash distribution to reflect a nontaxable return of capital treatment. The remaining $3,000 basis in her partnership interest is allocated to the land, and neither Jane nor the partnership recognize gain or loss on the distribution. Jean's basis for her partnership interest is zero after the distribution. ◀

Topic Review I:17-3 summarizes the gain or loss recognition rules relating to nonliquidating distributions.

SALE OF A PARTNERSHIP INTEREST

RECOGNITION OF GAIN OR LOSS. A partnership interest is a capital asset similar to a corporate security. It may be sold or exchanged as existing partners retire or withdraw from the business. The remaining partners may acquire the selling partner's interest, or the outgoing partner may sell the interest to an outsider.

Capital gain or loss generally arises from the sale of a partnership interest because the interest is a capital asset in the hands of the selling partner. For most noncorporate part-

---

[22] Sections 731 through 733 contain the partnership distribution rules. Distribution of marketable securities also can trigger gain recognition.

[23] Exceptions apply if unrealized receivables and inventory items, referred to as Sec. 751 assets, remain in the partnership or are distributed to the partner. In such instances, the partnership and/or the partner may recognize gain on the distribution.

[24] A portion of this gain may be converted to ordinary income if Jane's share of any Sec. 751 assets (i.e., unrealized receivables and substantially appreciated inventory items) held by the partnership changes as a result of the cash distribution.

Topic Review I:17-3

Nonliquidating Distributions

▶ Generally, neither the partner nor the partnership recognize gain or loss on a nonliquidating distribution of money or other property. However, if the distributed money exceeds the distributee partner's basis in the partnership interest, the partner recognizes gain on the excess. For this purpose, any release from partnership liabilities is treated as money distributed to the partner.

▶ The partner's basis in the partnership interest is reduced (but not below zero) by the amount of money distributed. If the partnership distributes property other than money, the following two points apply.

- If the adjusted basis of distributed property does not exceed the partner's basis in the partnership interest (after reduction for money distributions), the basis of the distributed property carries over to the partner, and the partner's basis in the partnership interest is reduced by the distributed property's adjusted basis.

- If the adjusted basis of distributed property exceeds the partner's basis in the partnership interest (after reduction for money distributions), the distributed property takes a basis equal to the partner's remaining basis in the partnership interest, and the partner's basis in the partnership interest is reduced to zero.

ners, the long-term capital gain is taxed at a 15% maximum rate (through 2010). In this case, a partnership is viewed as an entity separate and distinct from the partners. However, under Sec. 751, a partner is considered to own a proportionate interest in each partnership asset (i.e., the partnership is viewed as a conduit), which results in part capital gain and part ordinary income treatment depending on the character of the underlying assets.

Under the general rules of Sec. 741, gain or loss is measured by the difference between the amount realized and the selling partner's adjusted basis in the partnership interest. The amount realized includes the partner's share of partnership liabilities from which the partner is released as a result of the sale. The basis of the partnership interest also is adjusted by the selling partner's distributive share of partnership income or loss, which must be computed up to the sale date.

EXAMPLE I:17-20 ▶ On October 1, Jesse sells his interest in the JK Partnership to Paula, an outsider, for $150,000 cash plus release from $30,000 of partnership liabilities. Jesse's basis in his partnership interest is $74,000 before taking into account his distributive share of partnership income for the period ending on the sale date and his share of any increase in partnership liabilities during the same period. For the current year, Jesse's share of the partnership income for the period up to the date of sale is $20,000, and his share of increased partnership liabilities is $6,000. Thus, at the sale date, Jesse's basis in his partnership interest is $100,000 ($74,000 basis on January 1 + $20,000 share of partnership income + $6,000 share of increased partnership liabilities). The amount realized on the sale is $180,000 ($150,000 selling price + $30,000 liability release). Thus, Jesse recognizes an $80,000 gain on the sale, which is capital gain unless ordinary income is triggered under Sec. 751. (See Example I:17-21 for an illustration of Sec. 751 treatment.) ◀

SECTION 751 ORDINARY INCOME TREATMENT. Ordinary income rather than capital gain treatment may result under Sec. 751 if a partnership has unrealized receivables or inventory items when the partner sells a partnership interest. A sale of Sec. 751 assets by the partnership results in ordinary income, which passes through to the partners. Thus, this rule prevents a partner from converting ordinary income into capital gain by selling or liquidating the partnership interest before the partnership sells or collects on the Sec. 751 assets. Section 751 assets include the following:

▶ Inventory items include the traditional definition of inventory plus any other property except capital assets and Sec. 1231 property

▶ Unrealized receivables for services rendered or goods delivered, such as accounts receivable of a cash method partnership (i.e., receivables having a zero basis)

▶ Unrealized receivables also include Sec. 1245 and 1250 depreciation recapture potential (i.e., amounts that would be recaptured as ordinary income if Sec. 1245 or 1250 property were sold by the partnership) or recapture potential arising under another IRC section (for example, Secs. 617(d), 1252, 1254, 1278, or 1283)

EXAMPLE I:17-21 ▶ Joy's basis in her partnership interest is $100,000, and the amount realized on its sale is $180,000, which results in an $80,000 gain. The cash basis partnership has accounts receivable with a zero basis and a $30,000 FMV. Joy's share of these receivables is $10,000. Thus, $10,000 of the amount realized on the sale of the partnership interest is attributed to Joy's share of the accounts receivable. Because her share of the receivables has a zero basis and a $10,000 FMV, $10,000 ($10,000 − $0) of the gain is ordinary income to Joy as though she had sold her share of the receivables. The remaining $70,000 ($80,000 − $10,000) of gain from the sale of Joy's partnership interest is a capital gain. ◀

OTHER SPECIAL TREATMENTS. In addition to Sec. 751 ordinary income treatment, Sec. 1(h) applies various other tax rates on the sale of a partnership interest. First, a 28% rate applies to gain the partner would have recognized had the partnership sold its collectibles and small business (Sec. 1202) stock. Second, a 25% rate applies to unrecaptured Sec. 1250 gain the partner would have recognized had the partnership sold its Sec. 1250 property. These two special rules are in lieu of the 15% rate (in 2010) that generally applies to capital gains of a partner selling his partnership interest. Thus, any gain on the sale of a partnership interest allocable to these items will be taxed at a 25% or 28% tax rate rather than 15%.

OPTIONAL AND MANDATORY BASIS ADJUSTMENTS

Section 754 provides an election that permits a basis adjustment to the assets of a continuing partnership when a partner sells or exchanges a partnership interest or when certain distributions occur. This election, made by the partnership, prevents inequities that might arise because the basis of partnership assets are not adjusted under general partnership tax accounting rules. The election is binding for all future years unless the IRS consents to a revocation of the election. In addition, a partnership may have to make mandatory basis adjustments in certain circumstances even if a Sec. 754 election is not in effect.

EXAMPLE I:17-22 ▶ Jim acquires Antonio's one-third partnership interest in the ABC Partnership for $40,000. The partnership's balance sheet on the sale date includes the following:

	Adjusted Basis	FMV
Assets:		
Cash	$20,000	$ 20,000
Accounts receivable	10,000	10,000
Inventory	15,000	20,000
Depreciable assets	15,000	85,000
Total	$60,000	$135,000
Liabilities	$15,000	$ 15,000
Capital:		
Antonio	15,000	40,000
Beth	15,000	40,000
Carmen	15,000	40,000
Total	$60,000	$135,000

If the partnership has a Sec. 754 election in effect, Jim's optional basis adjustment equals the difference between his basis in the partnership interest of $45,000 ($40,000 amount paid + $5,000 of ABC's liabilities) and his $20,000 ($60,000 × 1/3) share of basis in the underlying partnership assets. Thus, Jim steps up the basis of his share of partnership assets from $20,000 to $45,000. The election does not affect the remaining partners' underlying basis in partnership assets.

The election would be favorable only to Jim because his share of the appreciated partnership assets (inventories and depreciable assets) would be stepped up by $25,000, based on the relative amounts of appreciation for each asset. Jim then would be entitled to additional depreciation deductions on the increased basis of the depreciable assets. In addition, Jim would receive an increased basis for calculating gain on the sale of the inventory. If this election were not in effect and the inventory were sold, Jim would report $1,667 (1/3 × $5,000) gain from the sale of his one-third interest in the inventory even though he paid $6,667 (1/3 × $20,000) for such interest. ◀

Once the election is in effect, its application may be detrimental because a downward adjustment is required if the amount paid for a partnership interest is less than the adjusted basis of the assets (i.e., the assets have declined rather than appreciated in value).

In addition, the IRC contains provisions to prevent shifting of losses using the optional basis adjustment mechanism. Under these rules, the partnership must make a mandatory basis adjustment following a transfer of partnership interest, whether or not the partnership has made a Sec. 754 election, if the partnership's basis in its partnership property is more than $250,000 above the FMV for partnership property (i.e., a built-in loss of $250,000 or more). This rule, and a similar rule related to distributions, are an attempt to prevent taxpayers from transferring losses on partnership property or on property contributed to a partnership.

ELECTING LARGE PARTNERSHIPS

ADDITIONAL COMMENT

Congress enacted the electing large partnership provisions for two basic reasons: (1) to ease the reporting burden of partners who own a relatively small interest in a large partnership and (2) to ease the computer matching effort of the IRS.

Partnerships meeting the definition of a large partnership can elect under Sec. 775 to be treated as an electing large partnership. To qualify, a partnership must satisfy the following four requirements:

▶ Must not be a service partnership

▶ Must not be engaged in commodity trading

▶ Must have at least 100 partners

▶ Must file an election

Section 775(b) defines a service partnership as one in which substantially all the partners perform substantial services in connection with the partnership activities or the partners are retired but in the past performed substantial services in connection with the partnership's activities. For example, a partnership that performs accounting services cannot be an electing large partnership. In addition, the partnership must have 100 or more partners excluding those partners who provide substantial services in connection with the partnership's business activities.

The calculation of an electing large partnership's taxable income includes separately stated income and other income. However, the items separately stated under Sec. 772(a) for an electing large partnership are much different from other partnerships. For example, under Sec. 773(b)(3), miscellaneous itemized deductions for an electing large partnership are combined at the partnership level and subject to a 70% disallowance at the partnership level. After the 70% disallowance, the remaining miscellaneous itemized deductions are combined with other income items and pass through to the partner. Because the miscellaneous itemized deductions are combined with other partnership income, the deductions are not subject to the 2% nondeductible floor at the partner level. Under Sec. 773(b)(2), charitable contributions made by an electing large partnership are subject to a 10% of taxable income limit similar to the limit applying to a C corporation.

Section 773(a)(3) requires an electing large partnership to apply the Sec. 179 expensing deduction limitation at only the entity level instead of at both the partnership and partner levels. Under Sec. 773(a)(4), Sec. 1231 gains and losses are netted at the partnership level. The partnership reports net Sec. 1231 losses with other ordinary taxable income or loss and reports net Sec. 1231 gains with capital gains and losses. The capital gains and losses are netted at the partnership level with only a single, net number reported to the partners. The capital gain or loss is treated as long-term, unless the net is a short-term capital gain, in which case it gets combined with ordinary income. Many of the partnership's tax credits are combined at the partnership level into a single number with the exception of the four credit categories listed below as being separately reported.

The separate items reported to the partners under Sec. 772(a) include:

▶ Taxable income or loss from passive loss limitation activities

▶ Taxable income or loss from other partnership activities

▶ Net capital gain or loss from passive loss limitation activities

▶ Net capital gain or loss from other partnership activities

▶ Tax-exempt interest

▶ Net alternative minimum tax adjustments, which are computed separately for passive loss limitation activities and other activities

▶ Separate credit passthroughs for only the general credits, low income housing credit, rehabilitation credit, and foreign income taxes

▶ Any other item the IRS determines should be separately stated

EXAMPLE I:17-23 ▶ The JLK Partnership elects to be treated as an electing large partnership. The partnership reports the following activities for the current year. It has no passive activities.

Ordinary income	$120,000
Sec. 1231 gain	60,000
Tax-exempt income	12,000
Net long-term capital loss	40,000
Charitable contributions	30,000

JLK Partnership reports the following results to its partners:

Ordinary income	$106,000
Net long-term capital gain	20,000
Tax-exempt income	12,000

The partnership's net Sec. 1231 gain ($60,000) is treated as a long-term capital gain and offsets the net long-term capital loss ($40,000), thereby producing a $20,000 net long-term capital gain. Ordinary income is reduced only by the charitable contribution. However, the 10% contribution deduction limitation restricts the deduction to $14,000 [($120,000 + $20,000) × 0.10]. The remaining $16,000 of contributions carry forward. The partnership's ordinary income is $106,000 ($120,000 − $14,000). ◀

An electing large partnership must provide a Schedule K-1 to its partners on or before March 15 following the close of the partnership tax year without regard to when the partnership tax return is due. Partnerships other than electing large partnerships need only provide the Schedule K-1 by the due date for the partnership's tax return. The March 15 date is different from the April 15 deadline otherwise applied to calendar year partnerships. Unlike other partnerships, an electing large partnership does not terminate for tax purposes when a substantial change in ownership occurs. Instead, an electing large partnership terminates only when the partners cease to conduct any business, financial operation, or venture using the partnership form.

Partners of an electing large partnership must report all items of partnership income, gain, loss, or deduction the same way that the partnership reports the item. Deviations from the required reporting will be "corrected" by the IRS in the same say that a math mistake is corrected. An electing large partnership is subject to special audit rules and will be audited only at the partnership level.

PARTNERSHIP ELECTIONS

TAX YEAR RESTRICTIONS

When a partnership's tax year ends, each partner's distributive share of the partnership income (including guaranteed payments) is reported on each partner's Form 1040 (or Form 1120 for corporate partners). With no restrictions about partnership tax year ends, this rule would allow significant deferral of partnership income. Thus, if a partnership's tax year ends on January 31, 2010, and the partners report on a calendar year ending December 31, partnership income earned from February 1, 2010 through December 31, 2010 (as well as partnership income earned in January 2011) is reported in the partners' 2011 federal income tax returns (filed in 2012). This situation results in an effective 11-month income deferral.

EXAMPLE I:17-24 ▶ Kim is admitted to the ABC Partnership on April 1, 2010. Kim is a calendar year taxpayer who previously was an employee of the partnership from January 1, 2010, until her admission to the partnership. Kim's earnings as an employee for the three-month period are $8,000. She receives monthly distributions of $3,000 for the last nine months of the year that represent draws

against her share of estimated partnership income for the partnership year ending January 31, 2011. Kim's distributive share of the partnership income for the period April 1, 2010, through January 31, 2011, is $60,000. Because distributions to a partner are treated as made on the last day of the partnership's tax year (January 31, 2011) and because the partnership tax year ends after December 31, 2010, Kim's income for 2010 is only $8,000 (her salary as an employee for the first three months of 2010). Kim's reports her $60,000 share of partnership income for the year ending January 31, 2011, on her 2011 tax return. ◄

ADDITIONAL COMMENT

Partnerships having only individual partners usually have calendar tax years. The three-step test most often comes into play when the partnership has one or more fiscal year corporate partners.

To prevent or minimize opportunities for deferring partnership income as illustrated in Example I:17-24, Sec. 706 provides the following requirements on the selection of a tax year by the partnership:

▶ A partnership uses the tax year of the one or more partners who, in aggregate, own a majority interest (more than 50%) in the partnership. This majority interest tax year rule is determined on the first day of the partnership's existing tax year.

▶ If partners having a majority interest in the partnership do not have the same tax year, the partnership uses the same tax year as *all* of its principal partners (a **principal partner** has a 5% or greater interest in the partnership).

▶ If the principal partners do not have the same tax year and no majority of its partners have the same tax year, the partnership uses the tax year that allows the "least aggregate deferral." (See Chapter C:9 of *Prentice Hall's Federal Taxation: Corporations, Partnerships, Estates, and Trusts* for a detailed discussion of this requirement.)

EXAMPLE I:17-25 ▶ ABC Partnership has one corporate partner, Ace Corporation, with a fiscal year-end of March 31. Ace Corporation has a 25% interest in the ABC Partnership. The other partners are individuals with a calendar year for tax purposes, none of whom has a 5% or more interest in the ABC Partnership. ABC Partnership must use a calendar year for tax purposes (the tax year of the individual partners who in aggregate own a 75% majority interest). ◄

SELF-STUDY QUESTION

Ace and Buckeye, corporate partners in the ABC Partnership, have September 30 year-ends. Craig, an individual partner, uses the calendar year. Ace, Buckeye, and Craig have equal one-third interests in the partnership. What tax year must the newly-organized partnership adopt?

ANSWER

It must adopt a September 30 year-end because it must use the tax year of the two partners who own a majority (66⅔%) interest.

The rules given above have three exceptions. First, a partnership with all calendar year partners can adopt or change to a fiscal year if it can convince the IRS that a business purpose exists for the choice. For example, if the partnership owns a ski resort, it probably could make a good case for closing the partnership tax year on May 31, shortly after the ski season ends, rather than on December 31, which is in the middle of the ski season. However, the IRS must agree that a valid business purpose exists for using the fiscal year.

Second, a partnership may adopt or change to a fiscal year-end if the business recognizes 25% or more of its annual gross receipts in the last two months of the fiscal year, with this being the case for three consecutive 12-month periods. Third, a partnership may elect a maximum three-month deferral if it agrees to make a special tax payment each year that approximates the income deferral benefit.[25] The net effect of these rules is to restrict any deferral opportunities for partnerships in choosing their tax year-end.

(See Chapter C:9 of *Prentice Hall's Federal Taxation, Corporations, Partnerships, Estates, and Trusts* for a detailed discussion of partnership tax years.)

CASH METHOD OF ACCOUNTING RESTRICTIONS

A partnership may elect with its first tax return any method of accounting that clearly reflects income. Unlike the tax year election, partnerships may elect an accounting method without regard to the methods used by its partners. The two most commonly used methods are the cash method and the accrual method. Under the cash method, the partnership reports income as received and expenses when actually paid. Under the accrual method, the partnership reports income when earned even if the cash has not yet been received. Similarly, the partnership reports expenses when incurred, not when actually paid.

Congress understands that the cash method does not always reflect the economic realities of a business. However, Congress also concedes that the cash method is much simpler to use than the accrual method. Because of its simplicity, the cash method still is an

---

[25] Secs. 444 and 7519.

option, but Congress has restricted its use. For example, partnerships that have a C corporation for a partner and that have average gross receipts exceeding $5 million during the prior three years are not allowed to use the cash method of accounting.[26] Tax shelters, no matter what their size, may not use the cash method under any circumstances. (See Chapter I:11 for a discussion of permissible accounting methods.)

OBJECTIVE 4

TAXATION OF S CORPORATIONS

Understand the requirements for electing and maintaining S corporation status

QUALIFICATION REQUIREMENTS

To qualify as an S corporation, a business must meet the definition of a small business corporation.[27] To meet this definition, the entity[28]:

▶ Must be a domestic (U.S.) corporation rather than a foreign corporation

▶ Must not be an ineligible corporation[29]

▶ Must not have more than 100 shareholders[30]

▶ Must have only individuals, estates, certain kinds of trusts, and certain kinds of tax-exempt organizations as shareholders

▶ Must not have a nonresident alien as a shareholder

▶ Must issue only one class of stock

All the above requirements must be met for the initial election to be made. Once the corporation makes an S election, the requirements must be met on every day of each tax year the S election is in effect. Otherwise, the election terminates.

ADDITIONAL COMMENT

Some states do not recognize the S election for state income tax purposes, which results in the payment of state income taxes by S corporations.

100-SHAREHOLDER LIMITATION. The S corporation rules place no restriction on the amount of an S corporation's assets or income. Nevertheless, most large, publicly-traded corporations have more than 100 shareholders and therefore are not eligible for S corporation status.

Members of a family count as one shareholder for the 100-shareholder limitation. Members of a family include a common ancestor, the lineal descendants of the common ancestor, and the spouses (or former spouses) of the lineal descendants or common ancestor. The common ancestor must not be more than six generations removed from the youngest shareholder at the time the corporation makes the election. This is a surprisingly large group treated as a single shareholder. For example, if the common ancester marries only once and has two children, and each of his descendants does the same, the generation that is six generations removed from the common ancestor includes 64 direct descendants and their 64 spouses. Also, the common ancestor need not be living at the time of the election. The requirement is only that the group of individuals who are to be treated as one family shareholder must have a common ancestor no more than six generations removed.

SELF-STUDY QUESTION

At any one time, how many different individuals could be shareholders in a single S corporation?

ANSWER

The number could be huge because 100 different families could be shareholders.

EXAMPLE I:17-26 ▶

Adobe Corporation, a qualifying S corporation, has 100 shareholders, including both Brad and Vanessa, who are married and are counted as one shareholder. No other shareholders are members of one family. Brad dies and wills his stock to his two best friends, who do not already own Adobe stock. Before the estate distributes the stock, the estate and Vanessa count as one shareholder, and the S corporation remains qualified under the 100-shareholder limitation. Adobe becomes disqualified as an S corporation when the estate distributes the stock to the two friends because the corporation then has 102 shareholders. ◀

---

[26] Sec. 448(a)(2). Section 448(b) provides exceptions for farming businesses and certain qualified personal service corporations.

[27] These qualification rules are in Sec. 1361.

[28] An S corporation does not have to be a corporation. Under the check-the-box regulations, a noncorporate entity can make an S election, in which case the entity is automatically deemed to have elected to be treated as a corporation under the check-the-box regulations. (See Reg. Secs. 301.7701-1, -2, and -3 that describe the tax consequences of a noncorporate entity electing to be

taxed under the check-the-box regulations.) Most LLCs and partnerships will not make an S election because of the additional benefits available with the more liberal partnership tax rules.

[29] Ineligible corporations include insurance companies, certain financial institutions, U.S. possessions corporations, and Domestic International Sales Corporations.

[30] Members of a single family are counted as one shareholder for tax years beginning after December 31, 2004.

TAX STRATEGY TIP

The lower a shareholder's marginal tax rate is in relation to the C corporation tax rate, the more attractive is the S corporation election.

TYPE OF SHAREHOLDER RESTRICTIONS.   A qualifying shareholder must be an individual (other than a nonresident alien), estate, qualifying trust, or qualifying tax-exempt organization.[31] Thus, a C corporation or a partnership may not own stock in an S corporation. If a C corporation or partnership were permitted to own stock, the 100-shareholder limitation easily could be avoided through indirect ownership of the S corporation stock through another corporation or partnership having many shareholders or partners.

SUBSIDIARIES OF S CORPORATIONS.   Although an S corporation may not have a corporate shareholder, it may own stock of a C corporation. If this stock ownership equals or exceeds 80%, however, the S corporation (parent) and the C corporation (subsidiary) are considered an affiliated group under Sec. 1504. Nevertheless, an S corporation may not file a consolidated tax return with its 80%-owned subsidiaries.[32] In addition, an S corporation may have a Qualified Subchapter S Subsidiary (QSub).[33] The subsidiary is a QSub if the parent S corporation owns 100% of the QSub stock and elects to treat the QSub as such. Under this election, the QSub is not treated as a separate corporation for income tax purposes. Instead, all assets, liabilities, income, deductions, and credits of the QSub are treated as those of the parent S corporation.

ONE CLASS OF STOCK RESTRICTION.   An S corporation can have only one class of stock outstanding. This requirement simplifies problems that otherwise would result from determining how corporate income and losses should be allocated to the shareholders.

TAX STRATEGY TIP

If a corporation needs to issue preferred stock for estate planning reasons (e.g., freezing the value of the stock), the S corporation is not an available choice because the preferred stock is a second class of stock.

The requirement for one class of stock, however, can be troublesome if an S corporation is thinly capitalized (i.e., significant amounts of debt exist in the capital structure) because the debt may in fact be equity and represent a second class of stock. To reduce the uncertainty regarding the second class of stock issue, a safe-harbor rule provides that straight debt shall not be treated as a second class of stock if it meets certain requirements. To qualify as straight debt, the interest rate cannot be contingent on profits,[34] the debt cannot be convertible into stock, and the creditor must be either a person otherwise eligible to be an S corporation shareholder or a person actively and regularly engaged in the business of lending money.

Aside from the debt issue, Treasury Regulations provide that a corporation is treated as having only one class of stock if all outstanding shares of stock confer identical rights to distribution and liquidation proceeds. This test is based on the corporate charter, articles of incorporation, bylaws, applicable state law, and any binding agreements relating to distribution or liquidation proceeds.[35] Nevertheless, shares of common stock can have different voting rights without violating the one-class-of-stock restriction.

EXAMPLE I:17-27 ▶   Dale is the sole owner of an S corporation. For estate tax planning purposes, Dale wishes to make gifts of certain shares of the corporation's stock to his children while still retaining control of the company. A class of S corporation common stock with limited or no voting rights may be issued to Dale in exchange for a capital contribution. Dale can subsequently make gifts of this new stock to his children without disqualifying the S election.   ◀

ELECTION REQUIREMENTS

The corporation files an election for S corporation status, and all shareholders who own stock on the date of the S election must consent to the election.[36] The election and consent are filed with the IRS on Form 2553 (Election by a Small Business Corporation). Shareholders who own stock during any part of the tax year including the election date must consent to the election even if they are not shareholders on the election date. A shareholder who sells his or her stock during the year but before the election will receive an allocation of the S corporation's income or loss for the portion of the election year he or she owned the stock.

---

[31] Qualifying trusts include voting trusts, Sec. 678 grantor trusts, electing small business trusts, and qualified Subchapter S trusts. Qualifying tax-exempt organizations include qualified retirement plan trusts and charitable organizations. (See Chapter C:11 of *Prentice Hall's Federal Taxation: Corporations, Partnerships, Estates, and Trusts* for a discussion of these trusts.)

[32] Sec. 1504(a)(8).

[33] Sec. 1361(b)(3).

[34] The interest rate, however, may vary with the prime rate or a similar factor unrelated to the debtor corporation.

[35] Reg. Sec. 1.1361-1(l).

[36] Election and termination rules are in Sec. 1362.

A corporation may make the election in the tax year preceding the election year or on or before the fifteenth day of the third month of the election year. An election after the fifteenth day of the third month of the election year is treated as made for the next tax year. Once made, the election remains in effect until revoked or terminated.

The tax law, however, provides some relief for improper elections. First, if the corporation misses the deadline for making the S election, the IRS can treat the election as timely if the IRS determines that the corporation had reasonable cause for making the late election. Second, if the election was ineffective because the corporation inadvertently failed to qualify as a small business corporation or because it inadvertently failed to obtain shareholder consents, the IRS can nevertheless honor the election if the corporation and shareholders take steps to correct the deficiency within a reasonable time period.

EXAMPLE I:17-28 ▶ Circle Corporation is a calendar year C corporation. To elect S corporation status for 2010, it must file the election anytime in 2009 or during the period January 1, 2010, through March 15, 2010. If Circle makes the election on March 31, 2010, the corporation remains a C corporation in 2010 and becomes an S corporation in 2011. However, if Circle can show reasonable cause for making the late election, the IRS may allow the election to be effective for 2010. ◀

TERMINATION CONDITIONS

REVOCATION OF S CORPORATION STATUS. A corporation may terminate an S election either voluntarily via a revocation or involuntarily by failing to continue to meet the requirements for a small business corporation (e.g., if on any day in any year the S corporation has more than 100 shareholders or issues a second class of stock). A voluntary revocation requires consents from shareholders owning more than 50% of the corporation's stock.

General Effective Date. Under the general rules, a revocation is effective for the entire tax year if the corporation files a statement on or before the fifteenth day of the third month of the tax year. If the corporation files the revocation after this date (e.g., after March 15 for a calendar year S corporation), the effective date is the first day of the next tax year.

EXAMPLE I:17-29 ▶ Shareholders owning more than 50% of the stock of a qualifying calendar year S corporation consent to a voluntary revocation statement filed by the corporation on March 12, 2010. Because the corporation filed the revocation on or before March 15, it is taxed as a C corporation for all of 2010. If the corporation does not file the revocation until March 16, 2009, it continues to be treated as an S corporation during 2010, and it becomes a C corporation in 2011. ◀

Specified Revocation Date. The law provides an exception when the corporation and its shareholders specify a prospective revocation date. In this case, the revocation takes effect as of the specified date. If the corporation specifies a prospective date other than the first day of a tax year, the revocation results in a short tax year for the final S corporation tax return and a short tax year for the initial C corporation tax return. In this case, the income or loss is allocated between the two short years on a prorated daily basis.[37]

EXAMPLE I:17-30 ▶ Assume the same facts as in Example I:17-29 except the corporation specifies a prospective termination date of July 1, 2010. The revocation is effective as of this date, and the corporation files an S corporation short-period return for the period January 1 through June 30, 2010, and files a C corporation short-period return for the period July 1 through December 31, 2010. The income or loss is prorated to each return on a daily basis. Unless extended, the S corporation return is due September 15, 2010, and the C corporation return is due March 15, 2011. ◀

TAX STRATEGY TIP

S corporations have been around since the 1960s. Limited liability companies (LLC) and limited liability partnerships (LLP) have become quite popular since the mid-1990s. Sometimes, shareholders may want to change their S corporation to an LLC or LLP. Careful planning is essential to avoid unintended results. Changing from an S corporation to an LLC can be costly because the S corporation is liquidated for income tax purposes. Shareholders may recognize substantial gains in addition to legal and accounting costs in making the transition.

KEY POINT

An election to be treated as an S corporation becomes effective only as of the beginning of a tax year, but a termination can become effective before the end of the normal tax year.

---

[37] The first day of the C corporation tax year is the day on which the revocation occurs. Under Sec. 1377(a)(2), a special election may be made to use the interim closing method (i.e., the books are closed as of the termination date) if all affected shareholders consent to this method.

INVOLUNTARY AND INADVERTENT TERMINATIONS. An S corporation may involuntarily lose its special tax status and revert to a C corporation if it fails to meet the small business corporation requirements or if it has excessive amounts of passive (investment) income for each year in a three-year period (i.e., more than 25% of gross receipts).[38] However, if the IRS deems that the termination was inadvertent and the S corporation or its shareholders take the necessary steps within a reasonable time period to restore its small business corporation status, the S corporation status is considered to have been continuously in effect.

EXAMPLE I:17-31 ▶ A calendar year S corporation adds an unqualified shareholder on June 4. The S corporation status terminates on June 3. The corporation files a short-period S corporation tax return for the period January 1 through June 3 and files a C corporation tax return for the period from June 4 through December 31. Income or loss is prorated to the two tax returns on a daily basis. ◀

EXAMPLE I:17-32 ▶ Assume the same facts as in Example I:17-31 except the termination is deemed to be inadvertent, and the violation of shareholder requirements is corrected within a reasonable time period. The S corporation status is considered to have been continuously in effect, and no C corporation tax return is required. A single S corporation tax return will be filed for the year. ◀

ELECTION AFTER TERMINATION. If an S corporation terminates its election either by ceasing to be a small business corporation or by revocation, the corporation may not reelect S corporation status for five years unless the IRS consents to an early reelection.

Topic Review I:17-4 summarizes the S corporation qualification, election, and termination rules.

OBJECTIVE 5

Apply the operating rules for S corporations

S CORPORATION OPERATIONS

Income, gains, losses, deductions, and credits pass through to the S corporation's shareholders in a manner similar to the partnership rules. Some common separately stated items include:

▶ Short-term and long-term capital gains and losses

▶ Sec. 1231 gains and losses

▶ Charitable contributions[39]

▶ Credits

▶ Interest on investment indebtedness

▶ AMT adjustments and tax preference items

▶ Foreign taxes paid or accrued

▶ Dividends and other portfolio income

Table I:17-1, appearing earlier in this chapter, provides a list of comparable items for partnerships. These separately stated items are segregated from the computation of ordinary income (or loss) because each item affects the tax returns of the various shareholders differently, depending on their particular tax situation. The residual income or loss amount (i.e., the amount remaining after removing the separately stated items) represents the S corporation's ordinary income (or loss). Separately stated items and S corporation ordinary income (or loss) pass through to the shareholders as of the last day of the S corporation's tax year.[40] The S corporation computes its ordinary income (or loss) on page 1 of Form 1120S (U.S. Income Tax Return for an S Corporation), and it reports all items on

---

[38] The passive income restrictions apply solely to S corporations that were previously taxed as C corporations in pre-election years and have accumulated Subchapter C earnings and profits from those years on the last day of three consecutive S corporation tax years. Thus, a corporation that elects S corporation status in its initial tax year and continually retains such status is not subject to the restrictions. If the restrictions apply and the S corporation has passive income exceeding 25% of its gross receipts for three consecutive tax years, the S election automatically terminates on the first day of the fourth

tax year. In addition, a penalty tax equal to 35% of the corporation's excess net passive income is imposed during each year of the three-year period.

[39] The IRS has ruled in Rev. Rul. 2000-43, 2000-2 C.B. 333, that charitable contributions made by an S corporation cannot be reported using the accrual method permitted for C corporations under Sec. 170(a)(2).

[40] Sec. 1363. Special rules apply if the S election terminates during the tax year. These rules are beyond the scope of this text.

Topic Review I:17-4

S Corporation Qualification, Election, and Termination Rules

QUALIFICATION REQUIREMENTS

▶ An S corporation must be a domestic corporation.

▶ A maximum of 100 shareholders are allowed. Members of a family count as one shareholder, and each beneficiary of a qualifying trust is a separate shareholder.

▶ Only individuals (citizens or resident aliens), estates, certain kinds of trusts, and certain kinds of tax-exempt organizations can be shareholders. No corporate or general partnership shareholders are permitted.

▶ Only one class of stock generally may be issued and outstanding. Multiple classes of stock can be used if the only difference between the classes is voting rights.

▶ Certain corporations that maintain special tax statuses are ineligible.

▶ If an S corporation has an 80%-or-more-owned subsidiary, it cannot file a consolidated tax return with that subsidiary. Special rules apply to a Qualified Subchapter S Subsidiary (QSub).

ELECTION REQUIREMENTS

▶ All shareholders on the S election date must consent to the election and the corporation must file Form 2553. To be effective for the election year, the corporation must file the S election and consent form on or before the fifteenth day of the third month of the election year. Otherwise, the election is effective for the next tax year.

▶ The IRS can waive the election deadline if the corporation shows reasonable cause for late filing.

▶ The IRS can grant relief for improper elections if they are inadvertent and subsequently corrected.

TERMINATION RULES

▶ To effect a voluntary revocation, shareholders owning more than 50% of the S corporation's stock must consent. The revocation is effective for the entire year if made on or before the fifteenth day of the third month of the tax year. Otherwise, the revocation is effective the first day of the next tax year unless the corporation specifies a prospective revocation.

▶ An involuntary termination occurs if (1) the S corporation fails to meet any of the small business corporation requirements (e.g., it has more than 100 shareholders) or (2) it has excessive passive investment income in a three-year period (assuming the corporation has prior C corporation accumulated E&P). If the IRS deems the involuntary termination to be inadvertent, the S corporation status is considered to have been continuously in effect provided the corporation and shareholders correct the defect.

▶ Aside from the inadvertent termination exception, a corporation may not reelect S corporation status for five years after a termination or revocation.

Schedule K of that return. Then, the corporation prepares a Schedule K-1, which reports to each shareholder his or her share of the S corporation items. The shareholders use the Schedule K-1 information to prepare their individual tax returns (Form 1040).

ADDITIONAL COMMENT

A shareholder of a corporation also can be an employee of the corporation. Payments with respect to the employment status are considered salary whereas payments with respect to owner-ship of stock are treated as corporate distributions.

The tax treatment of some S corporation items is similar to that for C corporations. For example, the S corporation deducts salaries paid to its shareholders in the calculation of ordinary income or loss and not as a separately stated item on Schedule K-1. In addition, S Corporations can elect to deduct up to $5,000 in organizational expenditures in the year in which business begins. The deduction is limited to the lesser of the organizational expenditures or $5,000, reduced by the amount by which such organizational expenditures exceed $50,000. Any excess organizational expenditures may be amortized over 180 months beginning with the month the S Corporation's business begins. S corporations, however, are not entitled to certain other corporate deductions, such as the dividends-received deduction or the net operating loss deduction because dividends and net operating losses pass through to the S corporation's shareholders.

EXAMPLE I:17-33 ▶ Ajax Corporation, an S corporation owned equally by Linda and Hal, reports the following operating results for the current year (a non-leap year):

SELF-STUDY QUESTION

Compare the manner in which income of an S corporation is allocated among the shareholders to the manner in which partnership income is allocated among the partners.

ANSWER

In the case of an S corporation, the income must be allocated based on the percentage of stock owned on a daily basis. Partners have much greater flexibility. The partnership agreement serves as the basis for allocation, with special allocations being permitted. No special allocations are permitted for an S corporation.

Sales	$10,000
Minus: Cost of goods sold	(2,000)
Gross profit	$ 8,000
Plus: Long-term capital gains	3,000
Total income	$11,000
Minus: Administrative expenses	(800)
Repairs	(200)
Sec. 1231 losses	(1,100)
Charitable contributions	(900)
Net income per books	$ 8,000

The S corporation reports these items on its tax return as follows:

	Schedule K			
	Ordinary Income	Separately Stated Items	Linda's K-1	Hal's K-1
Sales	$10,000			
Cost of goods sold	(2,000)			
Administrative expenses	(800)			
Repairs	(200)			
Total ordinary income	$ 7,000		$3,500	$3,500
Long-term capital gains		$3,000	1,500	1,500
Sec. 1231 losses		(1,100)	(550)	(550)
Charitable contributions		(900)	(450)	(450)

Linda and Hal each report $3,500 of ordinary income plus 50% of each separately stated item on their individual tax returns. ◀

Income, gains, losses, deductions, credits, and other separately stated items are allocated to the shareholders based on the number of shares of stock owned on each day of the S corporation's tax year. Thus, if a shareholder sells S corporation stock during the year, ordinary income (or loss) and separately stated items are allocated on a daily basis to the seller and purchaser of the stock.[41]

EXAMPLE I:17-34 ▶ Assume the same facts as in Example I:17-33 except Linda sells her stock to Mark on the 181st day of the tax year. Income through the date of the transfer is allocated to Linda. Thus, Linda reports $1,736 [0.50 × (181 ÷ 365)× $7,000] of the ordinary income and a similar portion of each separately stated item. Mark reports the ordinary income and separately stated items for the remainder of the year. The sale does not affect the way Hal reports his share of the income. ◀

OBJECTIVE 6

Apply basis and other special rules to S corporation shareholders

BASIS ADJUSTMENTS TO S CORPORATION STOCK

Usually, a shareholder's original basis for S corporation stock is either the amount paid for the stock or a substituted basis from a nontaxable transaction (e.g., a Sec. 351 corporate formation).[42] Adjustments subsequently are made for ordinary income (or loss) and separately stated items that pass through to the shareholders, as well as additional capital contributions by shareholders and distributions to shareholders.[43] These basis adjustments apply in the following order: (1) positive adjustments for contributions, S corporation ordinary income, and separately stated income and gain items; (2) negative adjustments for distributions; and (3) negative adjustments for S corporation ordinary loss and separately stated deduction and loss items.

---

[41] If the corporation makes a special election under Sec. 1377(a)(2), the income is allocated according to the accounting methods used by the S corporation (instead of on a daily basis) when a shareholder terminates his or her interest during the tax year.

[42] The death or gift tax basis rules also may be used to determine the initial basis for S corporation stock.

[43] Sec. 1367.

EXAMPLE I:17-35 ▶ During the current year, Juan pays $40,000 for 100 shares of Allied Corporation stock. Allied is a calendar year S corporation. Juan's share of Allied's current year ordinary income is $10,000. In addition, his share of separately stated items includes $4,000 of long-term capital gains and $2,000 of Sec. 1231 losses. Allied also distributes $5,000 cash to Juan during the year. Juan's basis in the S corporation stock on December 31 is computed as follows:

Original basis (cost)		$40,000
Plus:	Share of ordinary income	10,000
	Share of long-term capital gains	4,000
Minus:	Cash distribution to Juan	(5,000)
	Share of Sec. 1231 losses	(2,000)
Basis of stock on December 31		$47,000 ◀

The logic behind these basis adjustments is the same as for partnerships. They prevent double taxation of income or double deductions for losses.

EXAMPLE I:17-36 ▶ Kayla, a 35% bracket taxpayer, plans to form Alpha Corporation by contributing $100,000 in exchange for Alplha stock. Alpha will invest the contributed funds in its business operations. During the next ten years, Kayla expects Alpha to earn $900,000 of ordinary income before taxes. At the end of the ten-year period, Kayla plans to sell her Alpha stock. If Alpha operates as an S corporation, Kayla will recognize $900,000 of pass-through income on which she must pay taxes. So that Kayla will have sufficient cash to pay these taxes, Alpha will distribute $315,000 over the ten-year period. On the other hand, if Alpha operates as a C corporation, it will pay taxes at its 35% tax rate (assumed) and will make no distributions to Kayla. In either case, Alpha's value at the end of ten years will be $685,000 ($100,000 + $900,000 − $315,000). Thus, Kayla will sell the Alpha stock for this amount. The results of each alternative are as follows:

	S Corporation With Stock Basis Adjustments	C Corporation With No Stock Basis Adjustments
Selling price of stock	$ 685,000	$685,000
Original contribution	$ 100,000	$100,000
Kayla's pass-through income	900,000	–0–
Distributions to Kayla	(315,000)	–0–
Adjusted basis of Alpha stock	$ 685,000	$100,000
Gain on sale of stock	$ –0–	$585,000

Thus, the C corporation form, with no stock basis adjustments, results in double taxation, once at the corporate level and again at the shareholder level upon sale of the stock. ◀

S CORPORATION LOSSES AND LIMITATIONS

LIMITATIONS ON LOSS DEDUCTIONS. An ordinary loss and any separately stated loss and deduction items of an S corporation are allocated among the shareholders based on the number of shares of stock owned on each day of the S corporation's tax year.[44] The last day of the S corporation's tax year determines when the shareholders report the loss on their tax return.[45] Most S corporations must use a calendar tax year.

EXAMPLE I:17-37 ▶ Sigma Corporation is an S corporation whose tax year ends on January 31, 2010 because Sigma has a natural business year that ends on that date. All of its shareholders report their taxes using a calendar year. Sigma reports a $100,000 ordinary loss for the 12-month period ending January 31, 2010. The shareholders report this loss on their calendar year 2010 returns. ◀

A shareholder's deduction for ordinary losses and separately stated items cannot exceed his or her basis for the S corporation stock plus the debt basis for any shareholder loans made to the S corporation.[46] A shareholder, however, obtains no debt basis for

---

[44] Sec. 1366(a)(1).
[45] The same rule applies for reporting ordinary income and separately stated income and gain items.
[46] Sec. 1366(d)(1). The deductible loss is treated as a deduction for AGI on an individual shareholder's tax return. S corporation shareholders also are

subject to special limitations on losses and deductions that pass through from the S corporation (e.g., at-risk limitations under Sec. 465 and passive activity losses under Sec. 469). (See Chapter C:11 of *Prentice Hall's Federal Taxation: Corporations, Partnerships, Estates, and Trusts* for a discussion of these additional limitations.)

KEY POINT

An S corporation shareholder gets debt basis, separate from stock basis, for amounts the shareholder lends directly to the corporation, but the shareholder gets no basis for corporate liabilities owed to third parties. This treatment differs from that of partnership liabilities.

corporate-level loans even if he or she guarantees them. The following rules apply in determining the deductibility of ordinary loss and separately stated loss items:

▶ Positive basis adjustments increase stock basis for ordinary income or separately stated income or gain items incurred during the year before ordinary losses, and separately stated losses and deductions reduce stock basis.

▶ The shareholder's deduction for pass-through losses is limited to the sum of (1) stock basis after the above positive adjustments and after distributions but before negative adjustments for losses and deductions and (2) the shareholder's debt basis.[47]

▶ A shareholder's pass-through loss first reduces the shareholder's stock basis (but not below zero).

▶ If the loss exceeds the shareholder's stock basis, the remaining pass-through loss reduces the shareholder's debt basis (but not below zero).

▶ If the loss exceeds both the stock and debt basis, the shareholder carries over the excess loss and deducts it in a subsequent year when the shareholder again has basis in the stock or debt. The carryover period is indefinite but does not transfer to another taxpayer if the shareholder disposes of all his or her stock or if the shareholder dies. Furthermore, if the S election terminates, the loss must be used against any basis of the former S corporation stock by the end of a one-year post-termination transition period.

EXAMPLE I:17-38 ▶

Matt owns 20% of the stock of an S corporation. His stock basis is $18,000 at the end of 2010 after adjustments for separately stated income and gain items. Matt also loans the S corporation $12,000 during 2010. The S corporation incurs a $200,000 ordinary loss in 2010. Matt's share of the ordinary loss is $40,000 (0.20 × $200,000). Matt's deduction and carryover of the unused loss are as follows:

Basis in stock	$18,000
Minus: Ordinary loss applied against stock basis	(18,000)
Basis in stock after ordinary loss	$ –0–
Debt basis in loan	$12,000
Minus: Ordinary loss applied against debt basis	(12,000)
Debt basis in loan after ordinary loss	$ –0–
Share of ordinary loss	$40,000
Minus: Deduction in 2010 ($18,000 + $12,000)	(30,000)
Carryover of ordinary loss to 2011	$10,000 ◀

If a shareholder's basis is insufficient to absorb the entire amount of ordinary loss (and separately stated loss and deduction items), the pass-through of each item is pro rated. For example, if a shareholder's basis is $5,000 and he or she has a $6,000 ordinary loss and a $4,000 capital loss, the total deduction is limited to $5,000. This deduction consists of a $3,000 [($6,000 ÷ $10,000) × $5,000] ordinary loss and a $2,000 [($4,000 ÷ $10,000) × $5,000] capital loss. The shareholder also has a $3,000 ($6,000 − $3,000) ordinary loss carryover and a $2,000 ($4,000 − $2,000) capital loss carryover.

RESTORATION OF BASIS. If a shareholder's debt basis is reduced by a loss deduction, subsequent net increases in a future year initially increase the debt basis until that basis reduction is fully restored. Any excess positive adjustment then increases the shareholder's stock basis.

EXAMPLE I:17-39 ▶

Assume the same facts as in Example I:17-38, and in 2011 the S corporation's ordinary income is $140,000. Matt's share of the income is $28,000 (0.20 × $140,000). The $28,000 of income earned in 2011 permits Matt to deduct the $10,000 ordinary loss carryover from 2010. Matt's net increase is $18,000 ($28,000 − $10,000 loss carryover). Thus, Matt restores debt basis by $12,000, its original amount. The remaining $16,000 of income increases stock basis. Accordingly, stock and debt basis are adjusted as follows:

---

[47] Secs. 1366(d)(1)(A) and 1367(a)(2).

	Stock Basis	Debt Basis
Basis at beginning of year	$ –0–	$ –0–
Plus: Income for the year ($28,000)	16,000	12,000
Minus: Loss carryover from prior year	(10,000)	–0–
Basis at end of year	$ 6,000	$12,000 ◀

If the debt basis is not fully restored, gain results when the corporation repays the loan. If the loan is in the form of a note, the repayment results in a capital gain because the note constitutes a capital asset.[48] However, ordinary income results if the loan is an unsecured advance.[49]

PASSIVE ACTIVITY LOSS LIMITATIONS. S corporation shareholders are subject to the passive activity loss limitations in the same manner as partners. Losses that pass through to a shareholder who does not materially participate in the S corporation's business may not be deducted against that shareholder's other earned income or against portfolio income (e.g., dividends and interest). Such passive losses can offset only other passive activity income. S corporation shareholders who materially participate (i.e., participate on a regular, continuous, and substantial basis) can avoid the passive activity loss limitations. (See Chapter I:8 for a detailed discussion of the passive activity loss limitations rules.)

Topic Review I:17-5 summarizes the basic tax rules for S corporation shareholders.

OTHER S CORPORATION CONSIDERATIONS

ADDITIONAL COMMENT

Another important difference between partnerships and S corporations involves the tax consequences of property distributions. An S corporation recognizes gain if it distributes appreciated property to its shareholders, but a partnership would not recognize such gain. Also, the property's FMV is used for S corporation distributions while the property's adjusted basis is used for partnership distributions.

DISTRIBUTIONS OF CASH AND PROPERTY TO SHAREHOLDERS. A money or property distribution made by an S corporation to its shareholders is treated as a return of capital if the S corporation has no accumulated earnings and profits from pre-S corporation years.[50] As such, the amount of money or FMV of the nonmoney property distributed to a shareholder reduces the basis of the shareholder's S corporation stock. If distributions exceed the shareholder's stock basis, the excess is treated as a capital gain if the stock is a capital asset.[51]

The S corporation recognizes gain (but not loss) if it distributes nonmoney property to its shareholders.[52] The distribution is treated as if the corporation sold the property to the shareholders at its FMV. The gain passes through to the shareholders who increase their stock basis accordingly. The distributed property's FMV then reduces the shareholders' stock bases.

Topic Review I:17-5

Basic Tax Rules for S Corporation Shareholders

- ▶ Ordinary losses and separately stated loss and deduction items are allocated to shareholders on a per share per day basis.

- ▶ The last day of the S corporation's tax year determines the year in which the shareholders report their share of income, gain, deductions, losses, credits, and other separately stated items.

- ▶ Basis cannot be reduced below zero. Positive basis adjustments are made for ordinary income and separately stated income or gain items before basis reductions for distributions, ordinary losses, and separately stated loss and deduction items.

- ▶ Losses initially reduce the shareholder's stock basis (but not below zero). Any excess losses then reduce a shareholder's basis in debt owed by the S corporation to the shareholder.

- ▶ Unused losses are suspended and carried over until the shareholder again has basis to absorb the losses.

- ▶ Net positive basis adjustments in subsequent years initially increase the shareholder's debt basis until fully restored. Any additional positive basis adjustments increase the shareholder's basis in S corporation stock.

[48] Rev. Rul. 64-162, 1964-1 C.B. 304.

[49] Rev. Rul. 68-537, 1968-2 C.B. 372.

[50] The tax consequences of property distributions to an S corporation's shareholders are discussed in Chapter C:11 of *Prentice Hall's Federal Taxation: Corporations, Partnerships, Estates, and Trusts.*

[51] Sec. 1368(b). The S corporation also can have accumulated E&P from a

tax year in which it was taxed as a C corporation. The tax consequences of a distribution made by an S corporation having accumulated E&P are complex. These rules are beyond the scope of this text but are discussed in Chapter C:11 of *Prentice Hall's Federal Taxation: Corporations, Partnerships, Estates, and Trusts.*

[52] Sec. 311(b).

EXAMPLE I:17-40 ▶ Austin Corporation, an S corporation, distributes land (a capital asset) to its sole shareholder Sue. The land has a $10,000 basis and a $90,000 FMV. Prior to the distribution, Sue's stock basis is $200,000. The S corporation recognizes an $80,000 capital gain, which passes through to Sue. Sue increases her Austin stock basis by the $80,000 pass-through gain and decreases it by the $90,000 FMV of the distribution. Thus, after the distribution, her stock basis is $190,000, and her basis in the land is $90,000 (its FMV). ◀

TAX YEAR RESTRICTIONS. S corporations must use a calendar year unless the corporation can establish a business purpose (i.e., a natural business year) for choosing a fiscal year-end.[53] These year-end restrictions prevent shareholders from deferring pass-through income for up to 11 months (e.g., if a January 31 fiscal year-end were permitted). Also, like a partnership, an S corporation may elect a maximum three-month deferral if it agrees to make a special tax payment each year that approximates the deferral benefit.

ADDITIONAL COMMENT

For purposes of calculating which shareholders own more than 2% of the S corporation's outstanding stock, the Sec. 318 attribution rules apply.

TREATMENT OF FRINGE BENEFITS. S corporation shareholders who own more than 2% of the outstanding stock are not eligible for some nontaxable corporate employee fringe benefits, including the following examples:

▶ The group term life insurance exclusion for premiums paid for up to $50,000 coverage (Sec. 79)

▶ The exclusion from income for premiums paid for accident and health insurance and medical reimbursement plans (Secs. 105 and 106)[54]

▶ The exclusion for cafeteria plan benefits (Sec. 125)

▶ Meals and lodging furnished for the convenience of the employer (Sec. 119)

A more-than-2% shareholder includes the fringe benefits listed above in gross income as a guaranteed payment, which is deductible by the S corporation. Amounts received by a shareholder owning 2% or less of the S corporation's stock are excluded from the shareholder's gross income and deductible by the corporation as they would be for an employee of a C corporation.

EXAMPLE I:17-41 ▶ Bass Corporation, an S corporation, pays health insurance and group term life insurance premiums for its employee-owner group, all of whom own more than 2% of the Bass stock. The owner-employees include the premiums in their gross income, and the S corporation deducts the premiums. Employee-shareholders who own more than 2% of the S corporation's stock can deduct 100% of the amount includible in gross income as being paid for medical insurance for themselves, their spouses, and their dependents.[55] The premiums would not be included in the gross income of employees who did not own any Bass stock, or who owned 2% or less of the Bass stock. ◀

Many S corporation fringe benefits are not subject to special treatment for a more-than-2% shareholder. A partial list of such fringe benefits includes:

▶ Stock options

▶ Nonqualified deferred compensation

▶ Compensation for injuries and sickness (Sec. 104)

▶ Educational assistance programs (Sec. 127)

▶ Dependent care assistance programs (Sec. 129)

▶ Certain fringe benefits (Sec. 132)

The employee reports these fringe benefits under the general gross income inclusion rule applicable to the fringe benefit, and the corporation deducts them as ordinary business expenses under Sec. 162.

---

[53] Sec. 1378(b).
[54] Rev. Rul. 91-26, 1991-1 C.B. 184. Rules similar to those applying to more than 2% S corporation shareholders will apply to all partners in a partnership. The payment is deductible by the partnership and includible in the partner's

gross income. Notice 2008-1, 2008-2 I.R.B. 251, eases the for-AGI deductibility of health insurance premiums.
[55] Sec. 162(l)(1) and (5).

NEW TAX ACT

The American Recovery and Reinvestment Act of 2009 provides a reduced recognition period for tax years beginning in 2009 and 2010. For example, a calendar year S corporation recognizes no built-in gains tax in 2009 or 2010 if the seventh year of the recognition period preceded 2009 or 2010. This rule will affect S corporations whose election was effective at the beginning of 2002 or 2003.

CORPORATE TAX ON BUILT-IN GAINS. A 35% corporate tax on built-in gains applies if a corporation that previously was a C corporation elects S corporation status.[56] The built-in gains tax does not apply to a corporation that always has been an S corporation or that elected S corporation status before 1987. A built-in gain exists if the FMV of an asset exceeds its adjusted basis on the day the S election becomes effective. If the corporation sells an asset with a built-in gain within the ten-year recognition period beginning on the effective date for the election, the S corporation pays tax on the built-in gain. Built-in losses existing on the first day of the S election period can reduce built-in gains. Any appreciation on the asset that occurs after conversion from a C corporation to an S corporation is subject to the regular S corporation pass-through rules but is not taxed under the built-in gains tax. Assets acquired after the first day of the S corporation election period also are exempt from the built-in gains tax.

EXAMPLE I:17-42 ▶

KEY POINT

Congress enacted the built-in gains tax to prevent C corporations from avoiding double taxation in a corporate liquidation or asset sale by electing S corporation status immediately before the liquidation or sale.

Beach Corporation, an accrual basis taxpayer, incorporated six years ago and subsequently elected S corporation status beginning January 1 of last year. On January 1 of last year, Beach owned land with a $50,000 basis and a $200,000 FMV. Beach sold the land this year for $225,000. Thus, Beach reports a total gain of $175,000 ($225,000 − $50,000). The first $150,000 of the gain is subject to the built-in gains tax at the corporate level and passes through to the shareholders. The remaining $25,000 of post-conversion appreciation also is subject to the regular S corporation pass-through rules but is not subject to the built-in gains tax. In addition, the built-in gains tax paid by the corporation passes through as a loss to the shareholders. ◀

TAX ON EXCESS NET PASSIVE INCOME. A 35% excess net passive income tax applies when an S corporation has passive investment income for the tax year that exceeds 25% of its gross receipts and, at the close of the tax year, the S corporation has E&P that accumulated while it was a C corporation.[57]

EXAMPLE I:17-43 ▶

Acorn Corporation made an S election last year after having been a C corporation for several years. Acorn has accumulated C corporation E&P at the end of the current year. During the current year, Acorn's excess net passive income is $10,000, comprised of dividends and interest. The excess net passive income tax is $3,500 ($10,000 × 0.35). The tax reduces (on a pro rata basis) the passive income items (e.g., dividends and interest) that pass through to Acorn's shareholders. ◀

 STOP & THINK

Question: Suppose shareholders of an S corporation wanted to convert the business into a limited liability company (LLC). What tax obstacles might they encounter?

Solution: The shareholders would have to liquidate the corporation and recontribute the assets to the LLC. Because the S corporation must comply with general corporate tax rules, the liquidation will cause gain and loss recognition at the corporate level for property distributed (Sec. 336). This gain (loss) will pass through to the shareholders and be taxable (deductible) to them. In addition, the liquidation might trigger the corporate level tax on built-in gains (Sec. 1374). Thus, conversion from an S corporation to an LLC could have adverse tax consequences. Contrast these major tax obstacles with the conversion of a partnership to an LLC. The IRS has ruled that the conversion of a partnership to an LLC is a nontaxable event.[58]

SALE OF S CORPORATION STOCK. If an S corporation shareholder sells his or her stock, he or she recognizes a capital gain. Unlike under the partnership rules discussed earlier, the S corporation shareholder does not have to convert any of the gain to ordinary income as under Sec. 751 or to unrecaptured Sec. 1250 gain under Sec. 1(h). If the S corporation owns collectibles, however, gain attributable to those assets would be subject to the

---

[56] Sec. 1374. This discussion is only a sketch of these complex rules.

[57] Sec. 1375(a). These rules are discussed in greater detail in Chapter C:11 of *Prentice Hall's Federal Taxation: Corporations, Partnerships, Estates, and Trusts.*

[58] Rev. Rul. 95-37, 1995-1 C.B. 130.

28% capital gains tax rate. Aside from this somewhat rare exception, the shareholder's gain would be taxed at the 15% capital gains tax rate if he or she has held the stock for more than one year.

TAX PLANNING CONSIDERATIONS

USE OF OPERATING LOSSES

Often, the decision to select a particular form of business organization involves both tax and nontax issues. For example, owners may prefer the corporate form because of nontax attributes such as limited liability, the relative freedom to transfer ownership interests, and the ability to raise outside equity capital.

In many instances, however, the tax attributes dominate, making the partnership or S corporation form preferable to the C corporation. If the owners expect operating losses in the initial years of operation, they may prefer the partnership (or LLC) form to either the C corporation or the S corporation form of organization. In a C corporation, the operating losses do not benefit the shareholders directly and may be of no benefit if the corporation cannot generate sufficient profits in future years to offset the loss carryovers.[59] In a partnership, the losses pass through to the partners, limited by their basis for the partnership interest. The basis of a partner's interest, however, includes his or her share of partnership liabilities. In contrast, an S corporation's ability to pass through losses is limited to the shareholder's basis in the stock and any shareholder loans to the corporation. Other S corporation liabilities are not included in determining the shareholder's loss limitation. Thus, the partnership (or LLC) form of conducting business may provide its owners a greater opportunity to deduct losses than does the S corporation form.

EXAMPLE I:17-44 ▶ Mary and Marty are considering whether to operate a new business venture as a C corporation, S corporation, LLC, or a partnership. Regardless of the form chosen, Mary and Marty will materially participate in the business. Mary and Marty plan to invest $50,000 of equity and raise an additional $50,000 from outside creditors (e.g., accounts payable and a mortgage). They expect initial losses of $20,000 per year for five years. Three alternatives are available. If they use a C corporation, the corporate losses are not deductible (i.e., the corporation has net operating loss carryovers of $100,000 after the five-year period). If they elect S corporation status, Mary and Marty can deduct only $50,000 because the general corporate debt is not included in their stock basis. The remaining $50,000 loss carries forward indefinitely at the shareholder level unless the shareholders lend $50,000 of additional funds to the corporation (instead of having the corporation borrow these amounts from outside creditors) or make $50,000 of additional capital contributions. If they form a partnership or LLC, Mary and Marty can deduct the full $100,000 of losses because their basis includes their ratable share of the partnership's liabilities.[60] Assuming Mary and Marty have sufficient other sources of income to absorb the losses, the value of these additional deductions in the first five years favors the partnership or LLC form of organization. A nontax factor that might influence the decision is the limited liability protection offered by the corporate or LLC forms. ◀

 STOP & THINK

Question: Paul, a single taxpayer, owns a business that produces $50,000 of annual profits. If the business were incorporated, it could justify retaining all of its earnings and pay little or no dividends. Paul also has $100,000 of taxable income from other sources. Should Paul organize the business as an S corporation or as a C corporation?

Solution: Although many factors would be involved, one important tax factor is that Paul's income from the business would be taxed at a marginal tax rate between 28% and 33% (in 2010) if it is an S corporation because it increases his taxable income to

---

[59] In a C corporation, net operating losses carry back two years (or an extended period if applicable) and forward 20 years. In a newly formed corporation with initial losses, the carryback rules would not apply because the corporation has no income in the carryback years.

[60] Taxpayers also must satisfy the at risk rules of Sec. 465 and the passive activity loss rules of Sec. 469. These topics are discussed in Chapter I:8.

$150,000. In contrast, the C corporation tax rate is 15% on the first $50,000 of taxable income. Thus, the marginal tax rate on the $50,000 is much lower with the C corporation form. Additional taxation would result, however, if Paul withdrew profits as a dividend or recognized a capital gain upon selling his stock or liquidating the corporation. This double taxation penalty has been lessened through 2010 by the 15% maximum dividend and capital gains tax rate.

INCOME SHIFTING AMONG FAMILY MEMBERS

Subject to gift tax rules and restrictions, an attractive tax planning strategy is to shift income from higher tax bracket family members to children or others who are subject to lower tax rates. With an S corporation, parents may gift nonvoting common stock and shift income to their children if the children are not subject to the kiddie tax. Thus, a portion of the S corporation income is taxed to the children even though the parents retain all voting rights for the corporate stock. A partnership interest also may be gifted to other family members. However, the IRS generally does not recognize the family member as a partner where capital (e.g., inventory, plant, and equipment) is a material income-producing factor unless the individual is the real owner of the interest and has dominion and control over it. If property is given to a child subject to the kiddie tax, a 10% or 15% marginal tax rate could apply to the unearned income generated from the property. Should the child's unearned income exceed $1,900 (in 2010), however, it is taxed at the parents' higher tax rate. Therefore, if S corporation stock or a partnership interest is given to a child subject to the kiddie tax, the child's share of S corporation or partnership income will be taxed to the child at the parents' highest marginal tax rate if it exceeds the $1,900 threshold (see Chapter I:2).

With an S corporation or a partnership, family members (e.g., children) can be hired as employees. Thus, income may be shifted to lower tax bracket family members. The kiddie tax rules discussed previously have no effect on earned income even if derived from a parent's business. In a partnership and an S corporation, however, the IRS will reallocate income to reflect the value of the services and capital contributions if the entity pays unreasonable salaries.[61]

EXAMPLE I:17-45 ▶ Paul, the sole owner of an S corporation, gifts 20% of the corporation's stock equally to his children Kelly, age 25, and Joslyn, age 12. The S corporation's ordinary income is $100,000 after deducting a $10,000 salary paid to Paul. If a reasonable salary for Paul's services is $50,000, the IRS may reduce ordinary income by the additional $40,000 of salary to $60,000 ($100,000 − $40,000) and increase Paul's taxable compensation to $50,000. Thus, the share of ordinary income that passes through to the children is reduced from $20,000 (0.20 × $100,000) to $12,000 (0.20 × $60,000). Kelly's $6,000 ([$60,000 × 0.20] × 0.50) of income is taxed at her regular tax rate because she is not subject to the kiddie tax. On the other hand, $4,100 ($6,000 − $1,900) of Joslyn's income is taxed at her parents' marginal tax rate. ◀

ADDITIONAL COMMENT

The Sec. 754 election may be revoked only with the approval of the IRS. The IRS, however, will not approve a revocation if the primary purpose is to avoid stepping down the basis of partnership assets.

OPTIONAL BASIS ADJUSTMENT ELECTION UNDER SEC. 754

A basis adjustment election under Sec. 754 usually is desirable for an incoming partner whose partnership interest cost more than the tax basis of his or her share of partnership assets. The excess amount increases the new partner's basis for his or her interest in the partnership's assets. If the partnership made a Sec. 754 election in a prior year, the election continues in effect and automatically applies to subsequent years. When made, all partners must agree to the election because the partnership makes the election rather than the individual partner.

Therefore, before consummating a sale, an incoming partner should attempt to obtain assurances from the remaining partners that the partnership will make the election in the current year if the election is not already in effect. The partnership makes the election by attaching a statement to a timely filed tax return for the year the transaction occurs. The partnership cannot make a retroactive election for prior years.[62] A Sec. 754 election, how-

---

[61] Secs. 1366(e) and 704(e).   [62] Reg. Sec. 1.754-1(b).

ever, may have adverse effects in subsequent years if the amount paid for a partnership interest is less than the tax basis of partnership assets because the incoming partner must reduce his or her share of basis in partnership assets. However, if the partnership assets have a built-in loss exceeding $250,000, the downward basis adjustment would be mandatory even without the Sec. 754 election. See Chapter C:10 of *Prentice Hall's Federal Taxation of Corporations, Partnerships, Estates, and Trusts* for additional coverage of this topic.

COMPLIANCE AND PROCEDURAL CONSIDERATIONS

PARTNERSHIP FILING REQUIREMENTS AND ELECTIONS

Partnerships must file Form 1065 (U.S. Return of Partnership Income) on or before the fifteenth day of the fourth month following the close of its tax year (by April 15 for a calendar year partnership). The partnership, however, can obtain an automatic five-month extension by filing Form 7004 (Application for Automatic Extension of Time to File Certain Business Income Tax, Information, and Other Returns).[63] The IRS imposes penalties for failure to file a timely or complete partnership return.

PARTNERSHIP ELECTIONS. The partnership makes most elections affecting the computation of partnership income. These elections include:

► Selection of a tax year

► Selection of an overall accounting method

► Inventory valuation method

► Depreciation methods

► Amortization method for organizational expenditures

► Optional basis adjustments under Sec. 754

An election made at the partnership level is binding on all partners.

In addition, each partner also makes certain elections. The common elections falling into this category are the partners' own accounting periods and methods and the election to take a credit or deduction for foreign income taxes.

REPORTING PARTNERSHIP ITEMS ON FORM 1065

A partnership reports ordinary income or loss on page 1 of Form 1065 while Schedule K summarizes all the separately stated items (e.g., capital gains and losses, tax credits, and charitable contributions). Schedule K also includes guaranteed payments made to partners and the partnership's ordinary income or loss, even though reported on page 1. The partnership prepares a separate Schedule K-1 for each partner. The Schedule K-1 reports each partner's share of the Schedule K items, depending on the agreed upon ratio for sharing income, deduction, loss, and credit items. This schedule becomes the primary input for preparing each partner's federal income tax return.

A partnership also must prepare a balance sheet (Schedule L), a reconciliation of income per books with income per tax (Schedule M-1), and an analysis of capital accounts (Schedule M-2). For tax years ending on or after December 31, 2006, a partnership must file Schedule M-3 in lieu of Schedule M-1 if any one of the following conditions holds: (1) the amount of total assets reported in Schedule L exceeds $10 million; (2) the amount of adjusted total assets equals or exceeds $10 million, where adjusted total assets equal the Schedule L amount plus the following items that appear in Schedule M-2: (a) capital distributions made during the year, (b) net book loss for the year, and (c) other

REAL-WORLD EXAMPLE

A partnership reported its capital gain on a sale in one tax year rather than on the installment basis. The partners could not use the installment method because this is a partnership election. *George Rothenberg,* 48 T.C. 369 (1967).

ADDITIONAL COMMENT

Most partnerships having more than ten partners must select a partner to serve as the tax matters partner. This partner will be in charge of administrative matters in the event of a partnership audit.

---

[63] Form 7004 allows five-month extensions for some entities (e.g., a partnership) and six-month extensions for other entities (e.g., C and S corporations).

adjustments; (3) total receipts equal or exceed $35 million; or (4) a reportable entity partner owns at least a 50% interest in the partnership on any day of the tax year, where a reportable entity partner is one that had to file its own Schedule M-3.

S CORPORATION FILING REQUIREMENTS AND ACCOUNTING METHOD ELECTIONS

An S corporation must file its corporate tax return no later than the fifteenth day of the third month following the end of the tax year. The S corporation reports its results on Form 1120S (U.S. Income Tax Return for an S Corporation). An S corporation can obtain an automatic six-month extension of time for filing its tax return by filing Form 7004 (Application for Automatic Extension of Time to File Certain Business Income Tax, Information, and Other Returns).

The S corporation, rather than the shareholders, makes the accounting method elections used to compute ordinary income or loss and the separately stated items. As with a partnership, the corporation makes these elections independently of the accounting method elections made by its shareholders.

REPORTING S CORPORATION ITEMS ON FORM 1120S

Page 1 of Form 1120S summarizes the ordinary income and deduction items for the S corporation. If the corporation owes any tax due to the excess net passive income tax or the built-in gains tax, such amounts also are reported on page 1 of the return. Schedule K lists the separately stated items and ordinary income or losses for the S corporation, S corporation distributions, and selected other items. The corporation prepares a Schedule K-1 for each shareholder reflecting his or her share of the ordinary income (loss) and separately stated items. The Schedule K-1 becomes the basis for preparing each shareholder's federal income tax return. The S corporation also must prepare a balance sheet (Schedule L) and a reconciliation of income per books with income per tax (Schedule M-1). For tax years ending on or after December 31, 2006, an S corporation must file Schedule M-3 in lieu of Schedule M-1 if the amount of total assets reported in Schedule L equals or exceeds $10 million.

COMPARISON OF ALTERNATIVE FORMS OF BUSINESS ORGANIZATIONS

Table I:17-2 provides a comparison of sole proprietorships, partnerships, S corporations, and C corporations. The partnership comments also apply to entities treated as partnerships for tax purposes such as LLCs or LLPs.

PROBLEM MATERIALS

DISCUSSION QUESTIONS

I:17-1 Distinguish between the partnership, S corporation, and C corporation forms regarding the following:
   a. Incidence of taxation on the organization's business income
   b. Taxation of distributions to owners
   c. Application of the conduit and separate entity concepts of taxation
   d. Limitation on number and type of owners.

I:17-2 Explain how the following types of business entities are treated under the check-the-box regulations. What alternative treatments are available other than the default classification?

   a. Corporation
   b. Partnership (general and limited)
   c. Limited liability company (LLC)
   d. Limited liability partnership (LLP)

I:17-3 Anya is considering whether to become a limited partner in a real estate investment partnership by making a $10,000 investment. The limited partnership will generate substantial operating losses for its first five years. What are the tax advantages to Anya if the new entity is treated as a partnership or S corporation instead of taxed as a C corporation? Is the selection of the partnership or S corporation form of doing business a good idea?

▼ **TABLE I:17-2**

Comparison of Alternative Forms of Business Organizations

Attributes	Sole Proprietorship	Partnership	S Corporation	C Corporation
Application of the separate entity versus the conduit (pass-through) concepts.	Single level of taxation. The proprietor is the same person as the individual taxpayer. The sole proprietor reports proprietorship income, gains, deductions, losses, and credits in his or her individual tax return.	Conduit with a single level of taxation. The partnership is not taxed. Instead, its income, gains, deductions, losses, and credits pass through to the partners to be taxed in their tax returns.	Conduit with a single level of taxation. Similar to a partnership in that its income, gains, deductions, losses, and credits pass through to the shareholders to be taxed in their tax returns. In special cases, the S corporation may pay entity level taxes on built-in gains and excess net passive income.	Entity with double taxation. The corporation is taxed at the entity level, and its shareholders are taxed again when they receive dividends, sell their stock, or liquidate the corporation.
Applicable income tax rates	Individual tax rates apply to the proprietorship's income, which is included in the proprietor's total taxable income.	Individual tax rates apply to individual partners; corporate tax rates apply to corporate partners; and estate and trust tax rates apply to fiduciary partners.	Individual tax rates apply to individual shareholders; estate and trust tax rates apply to fiduciary shareholders.	Corporate tax rates apply to a corporation's taxable income. Individual, corporate, or estate and trust tax rates apply to shareholders receiving dividends from the C corporation. Dividend tax rates in 2010 are 15% for individuals generally and 0% for taxpayers having 10% or 15% marginal tax rates. Eligible dividends are those paid by domestic corporations and certain "qualified" foreign corporations.
Ownership restrictions	By definition, a sole proprietorship can have only one owner.	A partnership can have an unlimited number of partners, and these partners can be individuals, corporations, estates, or trusts.	An S corporation can have up to 100 shareholders (with members of a family counting as one). Shareholders are limited to individuals, estates, certain trusts, and certain tax-exempt organizations.	A C corporation can have an unlimited number of shareholders of any type.
Personal liability	The sole proprietor is liable for debts of the proprietorship.	General partners have unlimited liability. Limited partners have liability to the extent of their investment.	Shareholders have limited liability.	Shareholders have limited liability.
Other nontax factors	A sole proprietorship has management continuity problems and may have difficulty raising outside capital.	A partnership has management continuity problems and restrictions on the transfer of partnership interests. It may have difficulty raising outside capital although limited partners, who are pure investors, mitigate this problem.	S corporations have the same characteristics as C corporations. An additional cost may arise if the state income tax law does not recognize the conduit form of taxation and taxes the S corporation as a C corporation.	Along with limited liability, C corporations have continuity of life, centralized management, and free transferability of ownership interests. These factors may outweigh the disadvantages of double taxation.

▼ TABLE I:17-2 (Continued)
Comparison of Alternative Forms of Business Organizations

Attributes	Sole Proprietorship	Partnership	S Corporation	C Corporation
Basis	A sole proprietor has basis in the business's assets but has no basis in the entity.	A partnership has basis in its assets, and its partners have basis in their partnership interests. A partner's basis includes his or her share of partnership liabilities. A partner's basis is adjusted for his or her share of partnership transactions.	An S corporation has basis in its assets. Shareholders have basis in their stock and a separate debt basis in their loans to the corporation. A shareholder's basis does not include corporate level liabilities. A shareholder's stock basis is adjusted for his or her share of corporate transactions. Debt basis is adjusted downward for pass-through losses and increased for restorations.	A C corporation has basis in its assets, and shareholders have basis in their stock. Stock basis is adjusted upward only for additional contributions to the corporation and downward for distributions that exceed the corporation's E&P.
Treatment of losses	No limitations apply to the proprietor's NOLs assuming the at-risk and passive activity loss limitations do not apply. Unused proprietor NOLs carry back two years (or an extended period if applicable) and carry over 20 years.	Partners' pass-through losses are limited to the basis of their partnership interests. At-risk and passive activity loss limitations also may apply.	Shareholders' pass-through losses are limited to their stock and debt basis. At-risk and passive activity loss limitations also may apply.	C corporation losses do not pass through to its shareholders. Unused corporate level NOLs carry back two years (or an extended period if applicable) and carry over 20 years at the corporate level.
Choice of accounting methods	The sole proprietor can elect the cash or accrual method for business items. However, the accrual method for sales and purchases is required if inventory is a material income producing factor.	Partnerships can elect the cash or accrual method unless they are tax shelters or have a C corporation as a partner, in which case they must use the accrual method. Also, the accrual method for sales and purchases is required if inventory is a material income producing factor.	S corporations can elect the cash or accrual method unless they are tax shelters, in which case they must use the accrual method. Also, the accrual method for sales and purchases is required if inventory is a material income producing factor.	C corporations must use the accrual method unless they are personal service corporations or have annual gross receipts less than $5 million, in which case they can elect the cash or accrual method.
Choice of tax year	A sole proprietorship must use the same tax year as the sole proprietor, usually a calendar year.	The tax year is restricted to that of the majority partners, principal partners, or the least aggregate deferral. The partnership can use a fiscal year if it establishes a business purpose (e.g., a natural business cycle). Other special rules allow a tax year resulting in a maximum three-month deferral.	The tax year is restricted to a calendar year unless the corporation establishes a business purpose (e.g., a natural business cycle) for a fiscal year. Other special rules allow a tax year resulting in a maximum three-month deferral.	C corporations can use a calendar year or any fiscal year. Personal service corporations, however, face restrictions similar to those for S corporations.

▼ TABLE I:17-2 (Continued)
Comparison of Alternative Forms of Business Organizations

Attributes	Sole Proprietorship	Partnership	S Corporation	C Corporation
Employment related tax considerations	A sole proprietor is not considered an employee of the business and must pay self-employment taxes on business earnings. Special tax treatment for corporate fringe benefits, such as group term life insurance, are not available to the proprietor.	A partner is not considered an employee of the partnership and must pay self-employment taxes on business earnings. Special tax treatment for corporate fringe benefits, such as group term life insurance, are not available to the partners.	Same as partnerships for shareholders owning more than 2% of the S corporation's stock. S corporation shareholders may be treated as employees, however, for Social Security tax purposes if they receive a salary.	A shareholder-employee may be treated as an employee for Social Security tax and fringe benefits purposes.

I:17-4 Paula transfers two assets to a partnership in separate transactions:
  a. Land with a $60,000 adjusted basis and a $100,000 FMV in exchange for a 20% interest in the partnership
  b. A machine with a $50,000 adjusted basis and a $40,000 FMV. The partnership signs a note for $40,000 as consideration for the exchange.
  Explain whether Paula recognizes gain or loss for either or both of these transactions, and discuss the reason for any difference in tax treatment.

I:17-5 Peggy agrees to act as a broker to arrange debt financing for the PQR Partnership. In exchange, the PQR Partnership offers Peggy, as compensation for the services she rendered, a 10% interest in the partnership having a $50,000 value. Discuss the tax implications of this offer to Peggy and the partnership.

I:17-6 In the current year, Penny contributes machinery to a partnership in exchange for a minority partnership interest. She acquired the machinary five years earlier. It now has a $50,000 adjusted basis and a $90,000 FMV. What are Penny's basis and holding period for the partnership interest? What is the partnership's basis and holding period for the asset? Why are the partnership formation rules structured in their current format?

I:17-7 Compare the Sec. 721 partnership formation rules for a new partnership with the Sec. 351 corporate formation rules for a new C corporation.

I:17-8 How is Mario's basis in his accrual method partnership interest affected by each of the following changes in partnership assets and liabilities (assuming he has a 50% interest in the partnership)?
  a. Mario contributes a building with a $100,000 FMV, and a $70,000 adjusted basis. The building is subject to a $50,000 mortgage, which the partnership assumes.
  b. The partnership's accounts payable increase by $50,000 during the tax year.

  c. The partnership pays off a $40,000 bank note that was outstanding for several years.
  d. The partnership distributes $10,000 cash each to Mario and his partner.

I:17-9 Sally contributes farm machinery with a $150,000 FMV, a $125,000 basis, and a $50,000 note owed to the AB Bank to a new partnership in exchange for a 25% partnership interest. Total partnership liabilities after Sally's contribution are $340,000. What gain or loss do Sally and the partnership recognize on the property contribution to the partnership? What is Sally's basis in her partnership interest? How would your answers to this problem change (if at all) had Sally's asset contribution instead been made to an existing corporation for a 25% stock interest?

I:17-10 Assume the same basic facts as in Problem I:17-9. How would your answer change if the entity is a new corporation with all owners making property contributions? The corporation makes a timely election to be treated as an S corporation beginning with its first year.

I:17-11 What are the tax consequences to a partner who contributes liabilities that exceed the total basis of assets transferred to a new partnership in exchange for a partnership interest? How does your answer change if the same assets and liabilities are instead transferred to form a new C corporation?

I:17-12 Why are certain special partnership income and deduction items (e.g., capital gains and losses and charitable contributions) reported separately on Schedule K rather than being included in ordinary income on page 1 of Form 1065?

I:17-13 What inequities might result if partners were not required to make special allocations for pre-contribution gains and losses on noncash property contributed to a partnership?

I:17-14 Indicate whether a partner's basis in the partnership interest increases, decreases, or is not

affected by the partner's share of the following operating items:

a. Ordinary income
b. Ordinary loss
c. Tax-exempt income
d. Capital loss
e. Capital gain
f. Charitable contribution made by the partnership
g. Distributions of cash to the partners
h. Distributions of appreciated noncash property to the partners
i. Guaranteed payments

I:17-15 Phyllis owns a 30% interest in the PQR Partnership and has a $20,000 basis in her partnership interest (before adjustments for Phyllis's share of current year partnership income or loss). During the current year, the PQR Partnership reports a $100,000 ordinary loss and no change in partnership liabilities. Phyllis materially participates in the business in the current year.

a. What amount of the loss can Phyllis deduct in the current year?
b. What is Phyllis's basis in her partnership interest at the end of the current year?
c. What happens to Phyllis's unused ordinary loss (if any)?
d. What advice can you give Phyllis about reducing the amount of unused loss (if any) that was not deductible in the current year?

I:17-16 Ralph sells an asset to the RST Partnership at a loss. In which of the following situations does he recognize a loss?

a. Ralph owns a 20% direct interest in the partnership, and his son also owns a 20% interest.
b. Ralph owns a 35% direct interest in the partnership, and his daughter also owns a 35% interest.
c. Ralph owns a 35% direct interest in the partnership, and his 100%-owned C corporation also owns a 35% interest.

I:17-17 Jose owns a 60% interest in the JKL Partnership. What are the amount and character of the recognized gain or loss in each of the following situations?

a. Jose sells common stock held as an investment with a $1,000 adjusted basis and a $3,000 FMV to the partnership. Jose held the stock for more than one year as an investment before the sale. The partnership also held the stock as an investment after the sale.
b. Jose sells a parcel of land held for investment purposes with a $10,000 adjusted basis and a $25,000 FMV to the partnership. The land is used in the partnership's business.
c. The partnership sells Jose a building used in its business with a $100,000 adjusted basis and a $60,000 FMV.

I:17-18 Ursula is a 30% partner in the UV Partnership. The partnership agreement states that she shall receive 30% of partnership profits computed before considering guaranteed payments. However, she is not to receive less than $10,000.

a. What is Ursula's income if the partnership earns $60,000? How much of her income is a guaranteed payment?
b. What is Ursula's income if the partnership earns $20,000? How much of her income is a guaranteed payment?

I:17-19 The SJ Partnership, in which Sandy and Jack are equal partners, reported the following income and losses in the current year:

Interest from muncipal bonds	$ 30,000
Interest from corporate bonds	25,000
LTCL from stock sale	20,000
Net income from operations	125,000

How do the partners treat these items?

I:17-20 Explain the circumstances that cause a partner to recognize gain or loss if the partnership distributes money or other property in a nonliquidating partnership distribution.

I:17-21 Explain why a partner who sells his or her interest in the partnership for cash must include his or her share of the partnership liabilities in the amount realized from the sale.

I:17-22 What are the tax consequences to a partner who sells his or her partnership interest if the partnership has Sec. 751 assets (i.e., unrealized receivables or inventory items)? What is the reason for this result?

I:17-23 What is an electing large partnership? What requirements must a partnership meet to make an election to use the simplified reporting rules available to electing large partnerships?

I:17-24 What are the major differences between the reporting of business profits and losses earned by an electing large partnership having 200 partners and a regular partnership having two partners?

I:17-25 What are the primary advantages and disadvantages of using an S corporation instead of a C corporation?

I:17-26 What are the tax consequences to an S corporation and its shareholders if one of the requirements for a small business corporation is not met at some time in a tax year?

I:17-27 An S corporation issues straight debt obligations to its shareholders. Is it possible for the debt to be treated as a second class of stock, which would terminate the S election? Explain.

I:17-28 Andrew sells his Ajax Corporation stock to Angela on March 1. On March 15, Ajax elects S corporation status for the current year. Ajax is a calendar year taxpayer. Which shareholder(s) must consent to the election? Why? Which shareholder(s) receive an allocation of the S corporation's profits? Losses? For what time period is the allocation received by each shareholder?

I:17-29 An S corporation's shareholder wants the corporation to voluntarily revoke the S election. What percentage of the stock interests must agree to the revocation? When is the revocation effective?

I:17-30 Under what conditions will an S corporation involuntarily lose its special tax status and revert to being a C corporation? What remedies are available if the S corporation termination is deemed to be inadvertent?

I:17-31 Indicate whether the following items are reported on the tax return of an S corporation as part of ordinary income (or loss) or as separately stated items:
   a. Repairs
   b. Long-term capital gains
   c. Short-term capital losses
   d. Section 1231 gains
   e. Tax-exempt interest income
   f. Tax credits
   g. Tax preference items
   h. Salary paid to an S corporation shareholder

I:17-32 Explain why the basis of S corporation stock is increased by the stockholder's share of ordinary income and separately stated gain and income items and reduced by the stockholder's share of an ordinary loss and separately stated loss and deduction items.

I:17-33 Anne has a $10,000 basis in her S corporation stock on January 1 of the current year. On March 1 of the current year, Anne lends the corporation $8,000. Her share of the S corporation's ordinary loss for the current year (which has not yet ended) is expected to be $28,000. Anne expects her marginal tax rate to be 15% in the current year. She expects that her marginal tax rate will increase to 35% next year, and she anticipates substantial profits for the S corporation next year. Advise Anne regarding the deductibility of her share of the losses and the desirability of making additional capital contributions or loans to the S corporation in either year.

I:17-34 Allied Corporation, an S corporation, is considering making a distribution of land to its sole shareholder. Allied acquired the land three years ago and used it in its business activities. The land now has a $30,000 adjusted basis and a $130,000 FMV. Allied has been an S corporation since its inception 12 years ago. Explain the tax consequences of the land distribution to the corporation and to the shareholder.

I:17-35 Barry and Bart are considering whether to start a new manufacturing business. Alternative forms of business organization being considered include operating as a partnership, a limited liability company, an S corporation, or a C corporation. Barry and Bart are calendar year taxpayers but would like to use a January 31 year-end for the business to obtain an 11-month income deferral. Discuss the implications and restrictions of operating under each alternative form of business organization being considered.

I:17-36 Assume the same facts as in Problem I:17-35 except Barry and Bart instead are considering the treatment of fringe benefits. Barry and Bart want to provide group term life insurance and accident and health insurance for themselves and their employees and plan to make the premium payments from business funds. Explain any restrictions that apply to each form of business organization.

I:17-37 Explain the circumstances in which an S corporation is subject to taxation at the corporate level.

ISSUE IDENTIFICATION QUESTIONS

I:17-38 Bert and José plan to combine their unincorporated businesses by forming a partnership. Bert has substantially appreciated business assets. Moreover, if he transfers all the business' liabilities and assets, the liabilities will exceed the adjusted basis of the assets but not their FMV. José will render services to the entity in addition to transferring his business assets. What tax issues should Bert and José consider?

I:17-39 Helen and Helga are equal partners in the HH Partnership. However, Helen devotes most of her time managing the business and believes that she should be given additional compensation in the form of a guaranteed payment. Currently, the partnership is operating at a break-even point (i.e., zero ordinary income and no separately stated items of income or loss). The basis of each partner's partnership interest also is negligible. Helen has requested a $40,000 guaranteed payment as compensation for her additional efforts. What tax issues should Helen and Helga consider?

I:17-40 Coastal Corporation has been a C corporation for several years and has substantial earnings and profits. Its tangible business assets are highly appreciated, and the corporation has paid no dividends for several years. The board of directors and its key shareholders are now recommending making an S election, selling the appreciated property, and paying a substantial cash distribution in the initial S corporation tax year. What tax issues should Coastal and its shareholders consider?

PROBLEMS

I:17-41 *Formation of Partnership and Treatment of Liabilities.* Andrea, Robert, and Agatha form the ARA Partnership as equal general partners. Andrea contributes land with a

$20,000 basis and a $40,000 FMV along with cash of $60,000. Andrea has held the land for two years as an investment. Robert contributes equipment with a $50,000 adjusted basis and a $100,000 FMV. Robert has used the equipment in his sole proprietorship for three years and has claimed $40,000 of accelerated depreciation. Agatha contributes accounts receivable from her sole proprietorship with a zero basis and a $45,000 FMV along with cash of $35,000. In addition, Agatha set up the accounting system for the business. She normally would charge $20,000 to do the same job for a client. On the first day of business, the partnership borrows $90,000 (recourse debt) from their bank to begin the business. The partners have equal risk of loss for these liabilities.

a. How much gain, loss, or income must each partner recognize on the formation of the partnership? What is the character of any gain, loss, or income recognized?

b. How much gain, loss, income, or deduction will the ARA Partnership recognize on the formation?

c. What is the partnership's basis in its property on the day the business begins?

d. What is each partner's basis in his or her partnership interest?

I:17-42 *Formation of a Partnership and Treatment of Liabilities.* Bonnie, Carlos, and Dale form the BCD Partnership as equal partners. Bonnie contributes land and a building having a $50,000 adjusted basis and a $200,000 FMV that is subject to a $100,000 mortgage assumed by the partnership. The land and the building originally cost $200,000, with $180,000 allocated to the building and $20,000 allocated to the land. The partnership has claimed $150,000 of straight-line depreciation on the building. Carlos contributes cash of $100,000, and Dale contributes land (a capital asset) having a $200,000 adjusted basis and a $100,000 FMV. All assets have been held for more than one year. Assume the partners have an equal economic risk of loss.

a. What are the amount and character of Bonnie's recognized gain or loss on the transfer?

b. What is Bonnie's basis in her partnership interest?

c. What is Carlos's basis in his partnership interest?

d. What are the amount and character of Dale's recognized gain or loss on the transfer?

e. What is Dale's basis in his partnership interest?

f. What is the partnership's basis for each of the contributed properties?

I:17-43 *Formation of a Partnership and Treatment of Liabilities.* In the current year, Dana transfers to the DE Partnership land and a building having a total $25,000 adjusted basis and an $80,000 FMV. In addition, the property is subject to a $70,000 mortgage. The land and the building cost $100,000 when Dana acquired them in 1988, and Dana has claimed $80,000 of straight-line depreciation on the building. The land and building originally cost $20,000 and $85,000, respectively. Dana, who is active in the management of the partnership, receives a one-half interest in the partnership. Assume the partners' economic risk of loss is equal to their interest in the partnership.

a. What are the amount and character of Dana's recognized gain or loss on the transfer?

b. What is Dana's basis in her partnership interest?

c. When does Dana's holding period for the partnership interest begin?

d. What is the basis of the contributed properties to the DE Partnership?

I:17-44 *Formation of a Partnership and Loss Limitation.* Dan, who is active in the management of the partnership, contributes $10,000 in cash to the newly formed DEF Partnership for a 10% interest in the partnership. The partners transfer no liabilities to the partnership. During the partnership's first year, DEF borrows $75,000 from a bank and is liable for accounts payable amounting to $180,000 at the end of the current year. The DEF Partnership incurs a $400,000 ordinary loss during the current year.

a. How much of the ordinary loss may Dan deduct on his individual tax return?

b. What is Dan's basis in his partnership interest at the end of the current year?

c. How much of the loss (if any) carries over to future years?

I:17-45 *Expenses of Forming a Partnership.* The ABC Partnership, a calendar year entity, is formed and begins business on July 1 of the current year. ABC incurs the following expenditures on the date the partnership is formed:

Legal fees incident to the organization of the partnership	$ 6,000
Printing costs associated with the syndication of the partnership	4,000
Brokerage fees associated with underwriting efforts to sell limited partnership interests	5,000
Legal fees associated with asset transfers by three partners	10,000
Accounting services incurred during the organizational period	3,000

    a. What is the appropriate tax treatment (i.e., capitalization, capitalization subject to amortization, or immediate expensing) for each of these items?

    b. How much amortization should the partnership deduct for the current year?

I:17-46   *Pass-Through of Income and Separately Stated Items.* Damien and Donna are equal partners in the DD Partnership. The passive activity loss and the at-risk rules are not applicable to the partners. The partnership reports the following items on its Schedule K during the current year:

Ordinary loss	$10,000
Long-term capital gains	40,000
Research and experimentation credit	4,000
AMT tax preference items	6,000
Distribution to the partners	25,000

Damien's basis in his partnership interest is $80,000 at the beginning of the current year. The DD Partnership's liabilities increased by $20,000 during the current year.

    a. What amounts should Damien report on his individual tax return as a result of DD Partnership's activities?

    b. What is Damien's basis in his partnership interest after taking into account the Schedule K items?

I:17-47   *Special Allocations on Contributed Property.* Ed contributes land (a capital asset) having a $60,000 adjusted basis and a $100,000 FMV, and Gail contributes $100,000 cash to the EG Partnership. Ed and Gail each receive 50% interests in the partnership. Two years later the partnership sells the land (still a capital asset) for $110,000. What are the amount and character of the EG Partnership's gain or loss? How much of EG's gain or loss is allocated to Ed? To Gail? Are the results equitable?

I:17-48   *Loss Allocations.* Alice and Bruce are equal partners in the calendar year AB Partnership. On November 1 of the current year, Carl joined the partnership by making a $100,000 cash contribution in exchange for a one-third interest. Alice and Bruce's partnership interests are each reduced to one-third. The partners want to provide that Carl will receive a retroactive allocation of one-third of all partnership profits and losses incurred for the entire year. The AB Partnership reports a $90,000 ordinary loss for the tax year ending on December 31. How much of the partnership's loss is allocated to Alice, Bruce, and Carl?

I:17-49   *Basis of a Partnership Interest.* Anita has a one-half interest in the AB Partnership. Anita's basis in her interest at the beginning of the current year is $75,000. During the year, the following events occur:

- Partnership liabilities increase by $50,000.
- Partnership earns $60,000 of ordinary income.
- Partnership recognizes $20,000 of capital losses.
- Partnership incurs $3,000 of nondeductible expenses.
- Partnership earns $10,000 of tax-exempt interest.
- Anita withdraws $15,000 in cash.
- Anita contributes land having a $20,000 adjusted basis and a $100,000 FMV as an additional capital contribution without increasing her interest in the partnership.

    a. What gain (if any) does Anita recognize on the transfer of the land to the partnership?

    b. What is Anita's basis in her partnership interest at the end of the current year?

I:17-50   *Partnership Losses and Basis.* Ken has a one-half interest in the KL Partnership. His basis in the partnership interest at the end of the current year (before deducting his share of partnership losses) is $40,000. His share of the partnership's ordinary loss in the current year is $180,000. Next year, Ken makes a $60,000 additional capital contribution, and the partnership's ordinary income is $100,000. Assume that no change occurs in Ken's partnership interest as a result of the capital contribution and that he materially participates in the business. Partnership liabilities do not change.

    a. How much ordinary loss can Ken deduct in the current year?

    b. What is Ken's basis in his partnership interest at the end of the current year?

    c. How much ordinary income or loss does Ken report next year?

    d. What is Ken's basis in his partnership interest at the end of next year?

    e. How much loss can Ken use in future years? What has to happen to enable him to use the loss?

I:17-51 *Transactions Between the Partners and the Partnership.* Kevin has a 30% interest in the KLM Partnership. Louis (Kevin's son) also has a 30% interest. An individual unrelated to either Kevin or Louis holds the remaining 40% interest. Kevin sells the following assets to the partnership during the year:

- Common stock (a capital asset) having a $10,000 basis and a $25,000 FMV and selling price.
- Land (a Sec. 1231 asset) having a $100,000 adjusted basis and a $60,000 FMV and selling price.
- Machine having a $50,000 adjusted basis and a $70,000 FMV and selling price. The original cost of the machine was $60,000, and Kevin deducted $10,000 in MACRS depreciation before the transfer.

a. What are the amount and character of Kevin's recognized gain or loss on the sale of the common stock? The land? The machine?

b. What gain or loss would the partnership recognize if it sells the land two years later for $90,000?

I:17-52 *Guaranteed Payments.* Laura and Mark are equal partners in the LM Partnership. Laura receives a $35,000 guaranteed payment in the current year and also withdraws $15,000 of her partnership capital in cash. Partnership ordinary income is $100,000 after deducting the guaranteed payments for the current year. What amounts must Laura include in her gross income for the current year?

I:17-53 *Nonliquidating Distributions.* Lynn's basis in her partnership interest is $9,000 when she receives a nonliquidating distribution of $5,000 cash and land having a $6,000 adjusted basis and a $12,000 FMV.

a. What gain or loss does the partnership recognize when making the distribution?

b. What are the amount and character of the income or gain Lynn must recognize on the distribution?

c. What is Lynn's basis in the land?

d. What is Lynn's basis in her partnership interest after the distribution?

I:17-54 *Sale of a Partnership Interest.* The balance sheet of the ABC Partnership at December 31 of the current year is as follows:

	Adjusted Basis	FMV
Assets:		
Cash	$ 10,000	$ 10,000
Accounts receivable	20,000	20,000
Inventory	15,000	21,000
Land, buildings, and machinery	60,000	84,000[a]
Total	$105,000	$135,000
Liabilities and capital:		
Accounts payable	$ 5,000	$ 5,000
Notes payable	10,000	10,000
Allen's capital (⅓)	30,000	40,000
Beth's capital (⅓)	30,000	40,000
Candace's capital (⅓)	30,000	40,000
Total	$105,000	$135,000

[a]Assume that $3,000 would be ordinary income under the depreciation recapture rules and $5,400 would be Sec. 1250 gain if the partnership sold the assets.

All partners have an equal interest in the partnership. Allen sells his partnership interest to an outsider on December 31 of the current year for $40,000. Allen's basis in the partnership interest is $35,000 (which includes Allen's share of partnership liabilities).

a. What amount does Allen realize on the sale?

b. What are the amount and character of Allen's recognized gain or loss on the sale?

I:17-55 *Reporting Partnership Income.* Rita, a calendar year taxpayer, is an employee of the RST Partnership, which has a June 30 year-end. The partnership pays Rita a salary of $2,500 per month for the period January 1 through June 30, 2010. On July 1, she joins the partnership and receives monthly drawings of $2,500 for the 12-month period ending June 30, 2011. The drawings reflect her approximate share of partnership income for the

period July 1, 2010, through June 30, 2011. On June 30, 2011, Rita's share of partnership ordinary income is $40,000.
a. What amount of income does Rita report on her 2010 individual tax return?
b. What amount of income does Rita report on her 2011 individual tax return?
c. Which part (if any) of Rita's income is subject to Social Security taxes?

I:17-56 *Electing Large Partnerships.* JLK Partnership is an electing large partnership with 100 partners. The partnership reports the following operating results from the current year:

Ordinary income	$2,000,000
Net Sec. 1231 gain	250,000
Tax-exempt interest income	100,000
Net long-term capital gain	150,000
Charitable contributions	200,000
Miscellaneous itemized deductions	50,000

None of JLK's activities is passive. During the year, JLK distributed $5,000 to each of its partners.
a. What income, gains, losses, and deductions must the JLK Partnership report to each of its partners?
b. How are the items from Part a reported by JLK's partners?

I:17-57 *S Corporation Terminations.* Which of the following events will cause termination of the S election for a calendar year corporation? When is the termination effective? (Assume all other requirements for an S election are met and that the termination is not inadvertent.)
a. Best Corporation has 100 qualifying S corporation shareholders. Sam dies on October 13, and the estate holds his stock for the rest of the year.
b. Assume the same facts as in Part a except the estate distributes the stock to Sam's child before the end of the tax year. Sam's child did not previously own any Best stock.
c. Best issues nonvoting common stock to Susan's two children during the current year. Susan's children did not previously own any Best stock.
d. Shareholders Susan, Ted, and Tim, who own 60% of the Best stock, file the necessary form on October 1 to revoke the election as of this date. All three shareholders are calendar year taxpayers.

I:17-58 *S Corporation Ordinary Income and Separately Stated Items.* The income statement for Central Corporation, an S corporation, reports the following:

Sales	$260,000
Cost of goods sold	(60,000)
Repair expense	(5,000)
Depreciation expense	(20,000)
Salary expense	(30,000)
Long-term capital losses	(15,000)
Charitable contributions	(5,000)
Sec. 1231 losses	(8,000)
Net income per tax books	$117,000

a. What is Central's ordinary income (or loss) for the year?
b. Which of the above items appear as separately stated items on Schedule K?
c. Carol owns 50% of Central's stock, which has a $75,000 basis (before taking into account any of the items listed above). What is Carol's stock basis after all adjustments for Carol's share of Central's ordinary income or loss and separately stated items?

I:17-59 *Basis of S Corporation Stock.* Cathy is a 40% shareholder of City Corporation. City is a calendar year S corporation. Cathy acquired her stock on January 1 of the current year for $80,000. In the current year, City reports the following results of operations, cash distributions, and salary payments:

Ordinary income allocable to Cathy	$30,000
Salary payments to Cathy	40,000
Long-term capital loss allocable to Cathy	5,000
Cash distributions to Cathy	17,000

a. What is Cathy's stock basis at the end of the current year?
b. What amounts should Cathy include in her individual tax return for the current year?

I:17-60   *S Corporation Losses and Stock Basis.* Chris owns one-third of Coastal Corporation's stock, and he materially participates in the business. Coastal, an S corporation, uses the calendar year as its tax year. On January 1 of the current year, Chris's stock basis is $25,000, and he has a $10,000 loan outstanding to the corporation. In the current year, Coastal reports a $180,000 ordinary loss.
  a. What amount of loss can Chris deduct on his individual tax return?
  b. What is Chris's basis in his stock and debt at December 31?
  c. How much of the loss (if any) carries over to subsequent years?
  d. If Coastal reports ordinary income of $90,000 during the next year, what is Chris's basis in his stock and debt at the end of next year?

I:17-61   *S Corporation Basis for Stock and Debt.* Because of earlier losses, Cindy has a zero basis in her S corporation stock and a zero basis in her $10,000 loan to the corporation. During the current year, Cindy acquires additional shares of the S corporation stock for $8,000, and her share of the S corporation income is $7,000.
  a. What are Cindy's stock and debt bases on December 31?
  b. What are the tax consequences to Cindy if the corporation fully repays her loan (secured by a note) on January 1 of the following year?

I:17-62   *S Corporation Distributions and Stock Basis.* Control Corporation distributes $11,000 cash to shareholder Craig whose stock basis is $8,000 before this year's income or the distribution. Craig's share of ordinary income for the current year is $1,000, and the corporation has no separately stated items. Control always has been an S corporation.
  a. What are the tax consequences of the distribution (i.e., amount and character of income or gain to Control and Craig)?
  b. What is Craig's stock basis at the end of the tax year?

I:17-63   *S Corporation Distributions and Basis of Property.* Compact Corporation, an S corporation, distributes land used in its business to Clay, its sole shareholder. The land has a $75,000 adjusted basis and a $125,000 FMV. Clay assumes a $20,000 mortgage secured by the land distributed to him. Immediately before the distribution, Clay's basis in the Compact stock is $170,000, which includes his share of ordinary income and separately stated items for the current year (other than any gains or losses recognized because of the distribution). Compact always has been an S corporation.
  a. What are the tax consequences of the distribution to Compact and Clay?
  b. What is Clay's basis in the land?
  c. How would your answer to Part a change if the land instead had a $100,000 adjusted basis and a $75,000 FMV?

I:17-64   *S Corporation Fringe Benefits.* Copper Corporation formed two years ago and immediately elected S corporation status. In the current year, the corporation pays the following insurance premiums for its employees:

Group term life insurance for shareholder-employees, all of whom own more than 2% of the stock	$3,000
Accident, health, and medical reimbursement plan insurance premiums for shareholder-employees, all of whom own more than 2% of the stock	5,000
Group term life insurance premiums for employees who are not shareholders	1,000
Accident, health, and medical reimbursement plan insurance premiums for employees who are not shareholders	2,000

  a. What tax consequences result from Copper's payment of the insurance premiums?
  b. What are the tax consequences to the shareholder-employees and to the employees who are not shareholders?

I:17-65   *S Corporation Built-in Gains Tax.* Delta Corporation made an S election on January 1 of the current year. Delta had been a C corporation since its inception in 1982. The corporation has the following operating results during the current year:

Ordinary income	$200,000
Long-term capital gains	130,000

The adjusted basis and FMV of capital assets held on January 1 and sold during the current year were $200,000 and $320,000, respectively, as of the January 1 beginning of the S election period.
  a. Is Delta Corporation subject to the built-in gains tax under Sec. 1374? Explain.

b. What is the corporation's tax liability on the built-in gain (if applicable)?

c. How would your answers to Parts a and b change if Delta Corporation instead had made its S election on January 31, 1986?

COMPREHENSIVE PROBLEM

I:17-66 Charles is a 60% partner in CD Partnership, a calendar year partnership. For 2010, Charles received a Schedule K-1 that reported his share of partnership items as follows:

Partnership ordinary income	$125,000
Tax-exempt income	1,000
Qualified dividend income	3,000
Short-term capital loss	20,000
Sec. 1231 loss	17,000
Charitable contributions	2,000
Cash distribution	60,000
Guaranteed payment	50,000

In addition, Charles and his wife, Charlene, had the following items relating to activities outside the partnership:

Charlene's salary	$80,000
Long-term capital gain	49,000
Interest income from corporate bonds	5,000
Mortgage interest expense	12,000
State income taxes	8,000
Property taxes on home	3,000
Charitable contributions	5,500
Withholding on Charlene's salary	26,000
Estimated tax payments (paid one-fourth on each of the quarterly due dates)	22,000

Charles and Charlene have two dependent children, ages 7 and 9, and file a joint tax return. Calculate the following items for Charles and Charlene:
a. Adjusted gross income (AGI)
b. Taxable income
c. Tax liability
d. Taxes due or refund

TAX STRATEGY PROBLEMS

I:17-67 Joann and Bob, both single taxpayers in their mid-40s, own an employment business. The firm finds temporary employment for students in the college town of Gainesville, Florida. They have operated the business as a two-person equal partnership for five years. Profits have grown in each of the first five years until the partnership earns approximately $260,000 per year after deducting the small $30,000 salaries each is drawing from the business. Bob's parents operate a small grocery store in Nebraska and have successfully used the C corporation form for many years. They have become confused with all the new business forms—limited liability companies, limited liability partnerships, S corporations, etc.—that people have recommended to them. Bob mentions that he has been taking money out of his and Joann's business as distributions. They have come to you for help in determining whether their partnership form of business is the way to operate the business in the future. What strategies can you develop for improving Joann's and Bob's personal and business tax positions?

I:17-68 Peter, Paul, and Mary plan to create a new business that buys, restores, and sells classic cars. The three individuals have been involved in a number of business deals dating back to the 1990s. Each individual has a net worth of at least $2 million. Peter has located an old auto dealership to be the showroom for the classic cars. Paul has restored many classic cars so he has developed the network for purchasing restorable cars. Mary is a well-established promoter of new businesses and is in charge of determining the business plan, selecting the entity form, obtaining the external financing, and hiring the firm's accountant. She also will handle most of the day-to-day management. Mary has narrowed the business entity choice down to a partnership, C or S corporation, or limited liability company. You have talked with Mary about this project at length in three different meetings.

She wants your advice about selecting the appropriate business entity for the business. Prepare a short list of the pros and cons of using each of the four business forms and be prepared to make a final recommendation to Mary at your next meeting with her.

I:17-69 Steve and Erin started a general partnership to do landscaping and sell gardening supplies. Both will work in the business full time and need to withdraw approximately $40,000 a year each to live on. The partnership has purchased substantial capital assets that it will hold until the cash from their sale is needed in the business. For the first five years of operations, the partnership expects to earn approximately $70,000 of ordinary income and $50,000 of long-term capital gain each year before distributions to the two owners. Steve and Erin are single taxpayers and have income from other sources so their partnership earnings will be taxed at a 25% marginal rate. Should the two set up $40,000 guaranteed payments for each, or should they take out the $40,000 as draws from their distributive shares of partnership income?

TAX FORM/RETURN PREPARATION PROBLEMS

I:17-70 The XYZ Partnership reports the following items during 2009:

Sales	$400,000
Cost of goods sold	120,000
Dividends—all qualified	6,000*
Interest income on certificate of deposit held as an investment	2,000
Tax-exempt interest	1,500
Salaries to employees	130,000
Federal employment taxes	9,000
Rental expense	5,000
Guaranteed payments to partners	40,000
Net long-term capital gain	12,000*
Net short-term capital loss	5,000
Repairs	3,000
MACRS depreciation	10,000
Section 1231 losses	8,000
Charitable contributions	3,500
Amortization of organizational expenditures	1,000
Research and experimentation credit	2,500
Cash distributions to partners	20,000

*Eligible to be taxed at a 15% tax rate.

Calculate ordinary income (or loss) by completing page 1 of Form 1065, and complete Schedule K (Partners' Shares of Income, Credits, Deductions, etc.). Leave spaces blank on Form 1065 if information is not provided.

I:17-71 Eagle Corporation, an S corporation, reports the following items during 2009:

Sales	$500,000
Cost of goods sold	150,000
Dividends—all qualified	7,000*
Interest income on certificate of deposit held as an investment	2,500
Tax-exempt interest income	1,200
Employees' salaries (other than officers)	90,000
Federal employment taxes	6,000
Rental expense	8,000
Officers' salaries (all shareholders)	40,000
Net long-term capital gain	8,000*
Net short-term capital loss	10,000
Repairs	2,000
MACRS depreciation	12,000
Section 1231 losses	4,000
Charitable contributions	2,000
Amortization of organizational expenditures	1,000
Research and experimentation credit	3,500
Cash distributions to shareholders	12,000

*Eligible to be taxed at 15% rate.

Calculate ordinary income (or loss) by completing page 1 of Form 1120S, and complete Schedule K (Shareholders' Shares of Income, Credits, Deductions, etc.). Leave spaces blank on Form 1120S if information is not provided.

CASE STUDY PROBLEMS

I:17-72 Peggy, Phil, and Ralph each have unincorporated accounting practices, and they wish to pool their resources and operate as a single business entity. Peggy owns a building that has appreciated in value since she purchased it eight years ago. They intend to use this building for their office. Other than the building, they own office equipment, computer equipment, and furniture, none of which is worth more than book value. They all have substantial outstanding accounts receivable with a zero basis because each individual uses the cash method of accounting. Each individual has substantial amounts of portfolio income (i.e., dividends and interest) earned outside of their business activities. Under the plan, accounts payable with a zero basis from the unincorporated accounting practices would be transferred to the new entity.

Each accountant has two or three employees. They all agree on the importance of providing benefits to their employees, such as group health insurance, group term life insurance, and a retirement plan of some kind. Additionally, they wish to have their staff participate in the profits of the company and have some form of equity interest in the company.

Peggy, Phil, and Ralph use different computerized accounting and billing systems. They also have different documentation requirements for their client files. The computerized accounting records, billing records, and client files will all have to be consolidated from three systems to one system. The conversion will take place over a period of time. For this reason, they anticipate reporting a loss for their first tax year.

Peggy, Phil, and Ralph have agreed that they want to operate as a pass-through entity because they wish to avoid double taxation, and they want to use the losses from the first year immediately. They have come to you for advice. Prepare a client memo comparing the pros and cons of operating the accounting practice as a partnership or an S corporation.

I:17-73 Dan is the partial owner of an S corporation that currently has 100 shareholders. In March of the current year, Dan sold some of his S corporation stock to each of his two adult children. In August, Dan redeemed the stock he sold because he is in the midst of a divorce and was fearful of the consequences associated with giving voting rights for his business to his children. Dan informs you, his tax consultant, of the stock sale and subsequent redemption. You explain to Dan that by selling the stock he created 102 shareholders between the months of March and August and that the S election had been terminated on the day preceding the date on which the corporation first had more than 100 shareholders. Dan tells you that he sees no reason to inform the IRS of the termination because he bought back the stock within the same tax year, and the IRS probably would not discover the event. What are your responsibilities as a CPA under the SSTS rules as mandated by the AICPA concerning the S election termination? (See the *Statements on Standards for Tax Services* in Appendix E for a discussion of these issues.) What advice can you offer Dan concerning reinstatement of the S election under the rules for inadvertent terminations?

TAX RESEARCH PROBLEMS

I:17-74 Sandra is an employee of the Beach Group, an organization active in the Florida real estate industry. Sandra finds real estate property on Miami Beach and subsequently organizes partnerships to acquire and finance the property. Sandra was particularly interested in one building in the Art Deco district that was to be purchased and renovated. She gathered interested investors who formed the Deco Partnership, consisting of two general partners and several limited partners. In exchange for her services in organizing the partnership, Sandra received a 3% limited partnership interest only in the profits of the Deco Partnership. As part of the agreement, the profits interest was transferable only at the discretion of the general partners. Based on the uncertainty in the South Florida real estate industry at the time, the partners could not estimate whether profits or losses would be generated when the renovation was completed in three years. Based on these facts, will Sandra's receipt of the limited partnership interest be a taxable event?

A partial list of research sources is:

- Sec. 721
- Reg. Sec. 1.721-1(a)

- *William G. Campbell v. CIR*, 68 AFTR 2d 91-5425, 91-2 USTC ¶50,420 (8th Cir., 1991)
- *Sol Diamond v. CIR*, 33 AFTR 2d 74-852, 74-1 USTC ¶9306 (7th Cir., 1974)
- Rev. Proc. 93-27, 1993-2 C.B. 343
- Notice 2005-43, 2005-43 C.B. 1221

I:17-75 Chuck, Cindy, and Clay are equal shareholders of Able Corporation common stock. Able was incorporated in the current year. Able elects to be treated as an S corporation starting in its initial year. Chuck, Cindy, and Clay each contributed $10,000 cash to Able in exchange for their common stock. Able borrows $60,000 from a bank, and Chuck, Cindy, and Clay personally guaranteed the corporation's loan. In the current year, Able suffers a $90,000 ordinary loss. How much of the corporation's loss can Chuck, Cindy, and Clay deduct? (Assume the at-risk and passive activity loss limitation rules do not apply.)

A partial list of research sources is:

- Sec. 1366(d)(1)
- *Estate of Daniel Leavitt v. CIR*, 63 AFTR 2d 89-1437, 89-1 USTC ¶9332 (4th Cir., 1989)
- *Edward M. Selfe v. U.S.*, 57 AFTR 2d 86-464, 86-1 USTC ¶9115 (11th Cir., 1986)
- *Dennis E. Bolding v. U.S.*, 80 AFTR 2d 97-5481, 97-2 USTC ¶50,553 (7th Cir., 1997).

I:17-76 In January 2009, Joey contributed investment land he had held two years with a FMV of $6,000 and an adjusted basis of $10,000, and Rachel contributed $6,000 cash to form the Green Partnership as equal general partners. During 2009, the partnership earned ordinary income of $10,000 and made no distributions. On January 1, 2010, while the partnership still held the land, Joey sold his interest in the partnership to Phoebe for $11,000. In April 2010, Green partnership sold for $5,400 the land that Joey contributed. What are the tax consequences of these transactions?

A partial list of research resources includes:

- Sec. 721
- Sec. 704(c)
- Sec. 705
- Sec. 741
- Reg. Sec. 1.704-1(c)

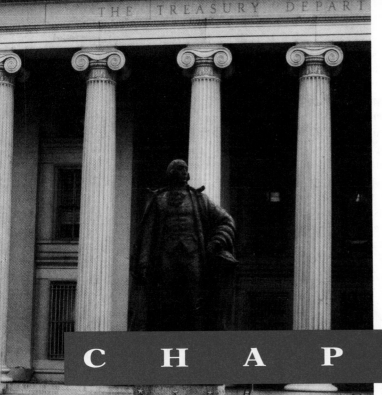

18

C H A P T E R

TAXES AND
INVESTMENT
PLANNING

LEARNING OBJECTIVES

After studying this chapter, you should be able to

1▶ Apply the investment models to various investment alternatives

2▶ Use the investment models to make entity choices

3▶ Use the investment models to make current salary versus deferred compensation decisions

4▶ Understand the role of implicit taxes in investment decisions

CHAPTER OUTLINE

This chapter has been derived from a book originally written by Myron S. Scholes and Mark A. Wolfson and takes what has become known as the Scholes-Wolfson approach to investment strategy.[1] Consequently, the chapter differs significantly from other chapters in this text. First, the chapter does not present details of tax law. Instead, it introduces a conceptual framework for understanding how taxes affect basic investment decisions. Second, the chapter develops and illustrates models for determining the after-tax outcomes of various investment alternatives. Although these models may look strange at first, they become familiar and manageable after some study and practice. Third, the chapter extends the models' application to the flow-through versus C corporation choice and the current salary versus deferred compensation decision. Fourth, the chapter introduces the role of implicit taxes as well as explicit taxes in investment decisions. As demonstrated later, the before-tax rate of return of a tax-favored asset will be reduced by market forces as investors increase their demand for these investments. This reduced rate of return is an implicit tax that investors need to consider when making their decisions.

INVESTMENT MODELS

OBJECTIVE 1

Apply the investment models to various investment alternatives

The investment models described in this chapter fall into four categories depending on how investment earnings are taxed. We refer to these models as follows:

▶ The Current Model—Investment earnings are taxed currently.

▶ The Deferred Model—Investment earnings are taxed at the end of the investment period.

▶ The Exempt Model—Investment earnings are exempt from explicit taxation.

▶ The Pension Model—The initial investment is deductible or excludable from gross income, and investment earnings are taxed at the end of the investment period.

These models in their basic form reflect the following assumptions:

▶ The investment's before-tax rate of return is constant over the investment period.

▶ The investor's marginal tax rate is constant over the investment period.

▶ Investment earnings are reinvested at the same rate of return as earned by the original investment.

▶ The investor knows future rates of returns and tax rates with certainty.

▶ The investor incurs no transaction costs.

KEY POINT

Future values are necessary to compare all amounts at the same point in time. This comparable time frame is critical in evaluating alternative investment opportunities.

The models can be modified, however, to accommodate changes to these assumptions. For example, we later show how to adapt the Current Model for changing tax rates (see Example I:18-5).

For simplicity, this chapter generally uses the following individual marginal tax rates for ordinary income: 40%, 35%, 30%, 25%, and 15%. Although these rates do not conform exactly to current tax rates, they are sufficient to demonstrate the concepts in this chapter. In addition, the chapter assumes either a 15% or 5% capital gains tax rate for transactions not subject to the Sec. 1202 exclusion. For regular C corporations, the chapter uses the following marginal tax rates: 39%, 35%, 34%, 25%, and 15%.

ADDITIONAL COMMENT

Although we use 5%, the capital gains tax rate for taxpayers in the 15% or lower tax brackets will be zero in 2008–2010.

THE CURRENT MODEL

The Current Model gives the future value of an investment having the following characteristics:

▶ Only after-tax dollars are invested.

▶ The earnings on the investment are taxed annually (currently); thus, the reinvested earnings grow at the after-tax rate of return.

---

[1] M. S. Scholes, M. A. Wolfson, M. Erickson, E. L. Maydew, and T. Shevlin, *Taxes and Business Strategy: A Planning Approach,* Fourth Edition (Upper Saddle River, NJ: Pearson Prentice Hall, 2008).

Common examples of investments taxed this way are savings accounts, money market funds, and taxable bonds, if the investor reinvests the after-tax earnings annually.

INVESTMENT WITH NO TAXATION. Before developing the Current Model, however, we first illustrate how an investment grows when compounded annually in a no-tax situation, and we introduce the notions of before-tax dollars and the before-tax rate of return. We then show the relationship between before-tax dollars and after-tax dollars and between before-tax and after-tax rates of return. Finally, we incorporate these concepts into the Current Model.

EXAMPLE I:18-1 ▶ Carla, an individual investor, lives in a land of no taxation and earns $1,000 of salary. She invests this amount in a bond that pays interest at 10% per year and holds the bond for three years, reinvesting the interest annually at the same 10% return. The following schedule details the investment's cash flow over the three years:

(1) Year	(2) Cumulative Investment at Beginning of Year	(3) Interest Income[a]	(4) Cumulative Investment at End of Year[b]
1	$1,000	$100	$1,100
2	1,100	110	1,210
3	1,210	121	1,331

[a]Column 2 × 10%
[b]Column 2 + Column 3

Thus, at the end of three years, the $1,000 original investment accumulates to $1,331. ◀

The three-year accumulation determined in Example I:18-1 also can be calculated as follows: $1,000 (1.1)^3 = $1,331$, which is $1,000 compounded at 10% for three years. Thus, the general form of the compounding formula is:

$$\text{Accumulation} = BT\$(1 + R)^n$$

In this formula, BT$ stands for before-tax dollars invested. For instance, in Example I:18-1, Carla invested the entire $1,000 because taxes did not reduce her salary. Also in the formula, R is the before-tax rate of return (BTROR). Again, this return is a before-tax percentage because, as in Example I:18-1, the interest on the investment is not taxed. Consequently, the investor can reinvest all the interest with nothing siphoned away as taxes. Finally, n equals the number of years the investor holds the investment or, in other words, n represents the investment horizon. Thus, the formula gives the future value (accumulation) of before-tax dollars invested for n years while earning a BTROR equal to R.

THE CURRENT MODEL. Now assume our investor is subject to taxation at marginal tax rate t. In this case, any earned income, such as salary, will be subject to taxes, leaving only after-tax dollars available for investment.

EXAMPLE I:18-2 ▶ Assume the same facts as Example I:18-1 except Carla's $1,000 salary is subject to tax, and her marginal tax rate is 40%. That is, t = 40% or 0.4. In this case, Carla has only $600 to invest. This amount is computed as follows:

TAX STRATEGY TIP

Although this chapter focuses on federal income taxes, a taxpayer must consider all applicable taxes when making investment decisions.

Salary before taxes	$1,000
Minus: Taxes ($1,000 × 0.4)	(400)
After-tax dollars available to invest	$ 600

◀

The $600 amount determined in Example I:18-2 also can be calculated as follows:

$$
\begin{aligned}
\text{After-tax dollars} &= \$1,000 - (\$1,000 \times 0.4) \\
&= \$1,000 (1 - 0.4) \quad \text{(Factoring out the \$1,000 salary)} \\
&= \$1,000 \times 0.6 = \$600
\end{aligned}
$$

In general, then, the relationship between before-tax dollars (BT$) and after-tax dollars (AT$) can be expressed as follows:

$$AT\$ = BT\$(1 - t)$$

Now assume that the interest our investor earns also is taxed at her marginal tax rate. The following example shows the impact on the investor's after-tax cash flows.

EXAMPLE I:18-3 ▶ Carla (from the two previous examples) again earns $1,000 of salary, but because of taxation at 40%, she has only $600 to invest, as shown in Example I:18-2. She invests the $600 in a bond for three years that yields 10% interest per year before taxes. However, in this case, the interest income also is taxed at 40%. The following schedule details the investment's cash flow over the three years:

(1)	(2)	(3) Before-Tax Interest Income[a]	(4) Tax on Interest[b]	(5) After-Tax Interest Income[c]	(6)
Year	Cumulative Investment at Beginning of Year				Cumulative Investment at End of Year[d]
1	$600.00	$60.00	$24.00	$36.00	$636.00
2	636.00	63.60	25.44	38.16	674.16
3	674.16	67.42	26.97	40.45	714.61

[a]Column 2 × 10%
[b]Column 3 × 40%
[c]Column 3 − Column 4
[d]Column 2 + Column 5

◀

In Example I:18-3, after-tax interest in Column 5 for Year 1 also can be calculated as follows:

After-tax interest = $600(0.1) − $600(0.1)(0.4)
             = $600(0.1)(1 − 0.4)   (Factoring out the $600 after-tax salary and the 10% before-tax rate of return)
             = $600(0.1)(0.6)
             = $600(.06) = $36

Thus, although the BTROR is 10%, the after-tax rate of return (ATROR) is only 6%. In general, the relationship between the BTROR and the ATROR can be expressed as follows:

$$r = R(1 - t)$$

As before, R equals the BTROR, and t equals the investor's marginal tax rate. The new variable, r, equals the ATROR, which is easy to remember because taxes reduce big R to little r.

With knowledge of this ATROR, the three-year accumulation in Example I:18-3 also can be calculated as follows: After-tax accumulation (ATA) = $600 $(1.06)^3$ = $714.61, which is $600 compounded at 6% for three years. Thus, the general form of the after-tax compounding formula is:

> The Current Model:
> $$ATA = AT\$(1 + r)^n \text{ or}$$
> $$ATA = AT\$[1 + R(1 - t)]^n$$

Note that, because of current taxation, investments conforming to the Current Model provide no deferral advantages because all earnings are taxed currently. As demonstrated later in this chapter, the other three models reflect certain tax advantages.

EXAMPLE I:18-4 ▶ At the beginning of Year 1, Harry invests $5,000 (AT$) in a money market fund that pays a 5% annual return before taxes. Harry's marginal tax rate is 30%, and he allows all after-tax earnings to remain in the money market fund. That is, he withdraws only enough cash to pay taxes on the fund's annual earnings. The following table shows Harry's after-tax accumulation for various investment horizons. In this table, note that Harry's ATROR equals 3.5%, which is 5% $(1 - 0.30)$. Thus, the Current Model appears as $5,000 $[1 + 0.05 (1 - 0.30)]^n$ or $5,000 $(1.035)^n$.

Investment Horizon (n)	Computation	After-Tax Accumulation
5 years	$5,000 $(1.035)^5$	$5,938.43
10 years	$5,000 $(1.035)^{10}$	$7,052.99
20 years	$5,000 $(1.035)^{20}$	$9,948.94 ◀

Changes to Assumptions. As stated earlier, the Current Model (as well as other models) assumes that R and t are constant over the investment period. However, the model can be modified to accommodate changes to these assumptions. This modification is accomplished by breaking the model into separate components, as demonstrated in the next example.

EXAMPLE I:18-5 ▶ At the beginning of Year 1, Dan invests $5,000 (AT$) in a money market fund that pays a 5% annual return before taxes. He plans to leave the after-tax earnings in the fund for 15 years. Dan expects his marginal tax rate to be 25% over the next five years but expects his tax rate to be 35% for the subsequent ten years. Thus, his ATROR for the first five years equals 3.75%, which is 5% $(1 - 0.25)$. For the remaining ten years, his ATROR equals 3.25%, which is 5% $(1 - 0.35)$. Dan's after-tax accumulation (ATA) after 15 years is calculated as follows:

$$\text{ATA} = \$5,000(1.0375)^5(1.0325)^{10} = \$8,275.82$$

Note that the first part of this calculation, $5,000 $(1.0375)^5$ = $6,010.50, gives the accumulation after the five years during which Dan's tax rate is 25%. This accumulation then continues to grow at the 3.25% ATROR for the remaining ten years as follows: $6,010.50 $(1.0325)^{10}$ = $8,275.82. ◀

THE DEFERRED MODEL

KEY POINT

Deferral is beneficial because the tax dollars not used currently to pay tax can be reinvested to help generate additional earnings.

The Deferred Model gives the future value of an investment having the following characteristics:

▶ Only after-tax dollars are invested (as with the Current Model).

▶ The earnings on the investment are not taxed annually; thus, they grow at the BTROR.

▶ The accumulated earnings are taxed at the end of the investment horizon when the investor cashes out of the investment; thus, taxation of these earnings is deferred.

The traditional nondeductible IRA described in Chapter I:9 is a classic example of the Deferred Model. Recall that, if the taxpayer or the taxpayer's spouse is covered by an employer-sponsored qualified retirement plan and the taxpayer's AGI exceeds a specified amount,[2] the taxpayer may not deduct contributions to a traditional IRA. Moreover, if the taxpayer's AGI exceeds another threshold,[3] the taxpayer may not contribute to a Roth IRA. Nevertheless, a taxpayer precluded from making *deductible* contributions to a traditional IRA or contributions to a Roth IRA still may make *nondeductible* contributions up to $5,000 (in 2010) per year to a traditional IRA. These nondeductible contributions are after-tax dollars.

EXAMPLE I:18-6 ▶ Marsha is in the 35% tax bracket and is ineligible to make deductible or Roth IRA contributions. Nevertheless, she wishes to contribute $5,000 to a traditional nondeductible IRA. She wants to know how much taxable salary she must earn to have $5,000 left for the contribution. Recall that AT$ = BT$(1 − t). Rearranging these terms gives BT$ = AT$/(1 − t). In other words, we can

---

[2] In 2010 for a taxpayer covered by an employer plan, this AGI amount is $109,000 for married filing jointly and $66,000 for other taxpayers except those married filing separately. If the taxpayer is not covered by an employer plan but his or her spouse is covered, the AGI amount is $177,000.

[3] The AGI amount in 2010 is $177,000 for married filing jointly and $120,000 for other taxpayers except those married filing separately.

"gross up" after-tax dollars by dividing after-tax dollars by one minus the tax rate. Accordingly, the before-tax dollars necessary to yield $5,000 after taxes equals $7,692.31, which is $5,000/(1 − 0.35). Thus, Marsha must earn $7,692.31 of salary before taxes. The tax on this amount equals $2,692.31, which is $7,692.31 × 0.35, leaving $5,000 available for contribution to the IRA. ◀

EXAMPLE I:18-7 ▶ Suppose Marsha makes the $5,000 contribution to a traditional nondeductible IRA in the current year and makes no subsequent contributions. Suppose further that investments in the IRA yield 12% per year before taxes and that Marsha allows her investment to accumulate in the IRA for 15 years. At the end of 15 years, she withdraws all amounts from the IRA, at which time her marginal tax rate still is 35%. The following calculation demonstrates one way to determine Marsha's after-tax accumulation in the IRA:

(1) Before-tax accumulation in the IRA [$5,000(1.12)^{15}$]	$27,367.83
(2) Minus: Original contribution	(5,000.00)
(3) Accumulated earnings before taxes	$22,367.83
(4) Times: Tax rate	0.35
(5) Tax on accumulated earnings	$ 7,828.74
(6) After-tax accumulation (Line 1 − Line 5)	$19,539.09 ◀

The calculation in Example I:18-7 also can be formulated as follows:

$$ATA = \$5,000(1.12)^{15} - [\$5,000(1.12)^{15} - \$5,000] \times 0.35$$

The first term, $5,000 $(1.12)^{15}$, gives the total before-tax accumulation; the subtraction in brackets gives the accumulated before-tax earnings; and the multiplication by 35% gives the tax on the accumulated earnings. Subtracting these taxes from the first term gives the total after-tax accumulation. Factoring out the $5,000 investment yields the following expression:

$$ATA = \$5,000\{(1.12)^{15} - [(1.12)^{15} - 1] \times 0.35\}$$

Substituting our general symbols into this expression yields the following model, the component parts of which are shown in Figure I:18-1:

$$ATA = AT\$\{(1 + R)^n - [(1 + R)^n - 1] \times t_n\}$$

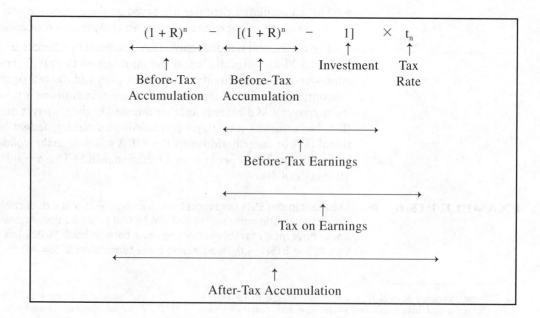

FIGURE I:18-1 ▶ Deferred Model before Algebraic Simplification

The subscript n on the tax rate emphasizes that the rate in Year n applies rather than the rate in the investment year or any intervening year. To make the model easier to use computationally, we can simplify this model algebraically with the following three steps. Multiplying through by t_n yields:

$$ATA = AT\$\{(1 + R)^n - [t_n (1 + R)^n - t_n]\}$$

Carrying the first minus sign through yields:

$$ATA = AT\$[(1 + R)^n - t_n (1 + R)^n + t_n]$$

Factoring out $(1 + R)^n$ yields:

> The Deferred Model:
> $$ATA = AT\$[(1 + R)^n(1 - t_n) + t_n]$$

We call this model the Deferred Model because the tax on investment earnings is deferred until the investor cashes out of the investment. This characteristic causes the Deferred Model investment to outperform the Current Model investment given equal BTRORs and constant tax rates.

EXAMPLE I:18-8 ▶ Phillip can invest $1,000 (AT$) directly in a taxable bond outside an IRA, or he can contribute the $1,000 to a traditional nondeductible IRA and invest in the same bond through the IRA vehicle. In either case, the bond yields an annual 10% BTROR. Phillip's marginal tax rate is 35%, and he expects it to remain so for the entire investment horizon. The two alternatives give the following after-tax accumulations after 20 years:

Bond outside the IRA (Current Model):

$$\$1,000[1 + 0.1(1 - 0.35)]^{20} = \$1,000(1.065)^{20} = \$3,523.65$$

Bond inside the IRA (Deferred Model):

$$\$1,000[(1.1)^{20} \times (1 - 0.35) + 0.35] = \$4,722.87$$

The Deferred Model investment outperforms the Current Model investment because, within the IRA, the interest on the bond grows at the BTROR (10%), with taxation deferred until Year 20. ◀

ANNUALIZED ATROR. As we explained earlier, the ATROR in the Current Model is $r = R (1 - t)$. That is, an investment that fits the Current Model yields this ATROR annually. The annual ATROR is a useful number for comparison to annual ATRORs of other models. However, the annual ATROR of other models, such as the Deferred Model, is not always obvious. Therefore, to determine this comparable number, we compute a variable called the annualized ATROR. The annualized ATROR is the rate of return that would cause a Current Model investment to yield the same accumulation per after-tax dollar invested as does the model under consideration.

For example, we derive the annualized ATROR for the Deferred Model as follows:

$$(1 + r_{ann})^n = [(1 + R)^n(1 - t_n) + t_n]$$

Here, the left-hand side of the equation is the Current Model investment compounding at the annualized ATROR, which we symbolize as r_{ann}. The right-hand side is the Deferred Model with one after-tax dollar invested. Taking the nth root of each side yields:

$$(1 + r_{ann}) = [(1 + R)^n(1 - t_n) + t_n]^{1/n}$$

Subtracting 1 from each side yields:

$$r_{ann} = [(1 + R)^n(1 - t_n) + t_n]^{1/n} - 1$$

The general form for this relationship, which can be used for any model, is:

> Annualized ATROR:
> $$r_{ann} = [\text{Accumulation per AT\$ invested}]^{1/n} - 1$$

EXAMPLE I:18-9 ▶ Consider the same facts as in Example I:18-8. The annualized ATROR for the investment outside the IRA is 6.5%. No additional computation is necessary because the model already is in the Current Model form. The accumulation per AT\$ invested inside the IRA (the Deferred Model) can be determined two ways. First, divide the total accumulation (\$4,722.87) by the \$1,000 (AT\$) invested, which yields 4.72287. Alternatively, compute the accumulation per AT\$ as follows: $[(1.1)^{20}(1 - 0.35) + 0.35] = 4.72287$. The annualized ATROR, then, is computed as follows: $r_{ann} = (4.72287)^{1/20} - 1 = 0.0807128$ or 8.07128%. Thus, on an annualized basis, a 20-year investment outside the IRA (the Current Model) yields 6.5% after taxes, while a 20-year investment inside the IRA (the Deferred Model) yields 8.07128% after taxes. To check this result, simply put the 8.07128% annualized ATROR in the Current Model to see that it yields the same result as did the Deferred Model.

$$\text{ATA} = \$1,000(1.0807128)^{20} = \$1,000(4.72287) = \$4,722.87 \quad ◀$$

CAPITAL ASSETS. The Deferred Model also describes the after-tax growth of a capital asset. For example, suppose a stock grows annually at rate R and does not pay dividends, that is, the stock is strictly a growth stock. In n years, the stock will be worth $(1 + R)^n$. If the investor then sells the stock for its fair market value (FMV), the investor pays tax on the capital gain. Consequently, the tax on the gain is deferred until the investor sells the asset, which reflects the realization principle of taxation. Moreover, the capital gain may be taxed at a preferential tax rate, for example, the 15% maximum rate on long-term capital gains. Thus, when applied to capital assets, the Deferred Model provides two tax advantages: deferral and a preferential tax rate.

When Figure I:18-1 is applied to this situation, the before-tax accumulation represents the selling price at the FMV, and the before-tax earnings represent the capital gain.

EXAMPLE I:18-10 ▶ Brian purchases stock for \$5,000. The stock appreciates (grows) at an 8% rate before taxes. Brian sells the stock ten years later for \$10,794.62, which is $\$5,000(1.08)^{10}$. At the time of sale, his regular tax rate is 40%, but his long-term capital gains tax rate is 15%. One way to calculate Brian's after-tax proceeds is as follows:

(1) Selling price $[\$5,000(1.08)^{10}]$	\$10,794.62
(2) Minus: Original investment (basis)	(5,000.00)
(3) Long-term capital gain	\$ 5,794.62
(4) Times: Long-term capital gains tax rate	0.15
(5) Tax on capital gain	\$ 869.19
(6) After-tax proceeds (Line 1 − Line 5)	\$ 9,925.43

Alternatively, the after-tax proceeds can be determined quickly with the Deferred Model as follows:

$$\text{ATA} = \$5,000 \times [(1.08)^{10}(1 - 0.15) + 0.15] = \$9,925.43 \quad ◀$$

COMPARING CURRENT AND DEFERRED MODELS. As mentioned earlier, a Deferred Model investment always outperforms a Current Model investment if BTRORs are constant over time and equal across models and if tax rates also are constant and equal. However, when these conditions are not present, the models must be compared to determine which is preferable. One way to make this comparison is to set up a spreadsheet of the various alternatives.

EXAMPLE I:18-11 ▶ As in Example I:18-8, assume that Phillip can invest \$1,000 (AT\$) in a taxable bond either outside or inside a traditional nondeductible IRA. The bond yields 10% per year before taxes, and

ADDITIONAL COMMENT

For traditional IRAs, minimum withdrawals must begin when a taxpayer reaches age 70½. Otherwise, the taxpayer faces a 50% penalty on the difference between the minimum required distribution and the actual distribution.

Phillip's marginal tax rate is 35%. Assume also that Phillip will be younger than 59½ when he withdraws the funds from the IRA. As described in Chapter I:9, a taxpayer who withdraws amounts from a traditional IRA before reaching age 59½ generally must pay a 10% penalty tax on the taxable portion of the withdrawal. This penalty, in effect, increases the applicable tax rate in the Deferred Model. Thus, the following models apply (the Deferred Model with no penalty is repeated for comparison):

Bond outside the IRA (Current Model):

$$\$1,000[1 + 0.1(1 - 0.35)]^n = \$1,000(1.065)^n$$

Bond inside the IRA (Deferred Model)—No penalty:

$$\$1,000[(1.1)^n \times (1 - 0.35) + 0.35]$$

Bond inside the IRA (Deferred Model)—With penalty:

$$\$1,000[(1.1)^n \times (1 - 0.45) + 0.45]$$

Notice that the 10% penalty increases the effective tax rate to 45%. Given the 10% penalty, which investment is better, the Current Model or the Deferred Model? The answer depends on the length of the investment horizon. Table I:18-1 schedules the after-tax accumulations and related annualized ATRORs for various investment horizons (n) from one to 20 years.

Before considering the penalty situation, observe the no penalty case. For all values of n above one, the Deferred Model investment produces a greater after-tax accumulation than does the Current Model investment (compare Columns 2 and 3). This result also is apparent in

▼ TABLE I:18-1

Comparison of Current and Deferred Models

(1)	After-Tax Accumulations			Annualized ATRORs[d]		
	(2)	(3)	(4)	(5)	(6)	(7)
		Deferred	Deferred		Deferred	Deferred
	Current	Model	Model	Current	Model	Model
n	Model[a]	No Penalty[b]	with Penalty[c]	Model	No Penalty	with Penalty
1	$1,065	$1,065	$1,055	6.5%	6.500%	5.500%
2	1,134	1,137	1,116	6.5	6.607	5.617
3	1,208	1,215	1,182	6.5	6.711	5.733
4	1,286	1,302	1,255	6.5	6.813	5.848
5	1,370	1,397	1,336	6.5	6.913	5.961
6	1,459	1,502	1,424	6.5	7.009	6.073
7	1,544	1,617	1,522	6.5	7.103	6.182
8	1,655	1,743	1,629	6.5	7.195	6.289
9	1,763	1,883	1,747	6.5	7.283	6.394
10	1,877	2,036	1,876	6.5	7.368	6.497
11	1,999	2,205	2,019	6.5	7.451	6.597
12	2,129	2,390	2,176	6.5	7.531	6.694
13	2,267	2,594	2,349	6.5	7.608	6.789
14	2,415	2,818	2,539	6.5	7.682	6.881
15	2,572	3,065	2,747	6.5	7.753	6.970
16	2,739	3,337	2,977	6.5	7.822	7.057
17	2,917	3,635	3,230	6.5	7.888	7.140
18	3,107	3,964	3,508	6.5	7.952	7.221
19	3,309	4,325	3,814	6.5	8.013	7.299
20	3,524	4,723	4,150	6.5	8.071	7.375

[a]$1,000(1.065)^n$
[b]$\$1,000[(1.1)^n(1 - 0.35) + 0.35]$
[c]$\$1,000[(1.1)^n(1 - 0.45) + 0.45]$
[d]$[(\text{ATA per AT\$})^{1/n} - 1] \times 100$

the annualized ATRORs. For all values of n above one, the Deferred Model investment produces an annualized ATROR greater than 6.5% (compare Columns 5 and 6). Moreover, the greater the n, the greater the annualized ATROR from the Deferred Model investment. This result occurs because tax deferral increases as the investment horizon lengthens. Thus, the longer the deferral, the better the annualized ATROR produced by the Deferred Model investment.

Now compare the Current Model to the Deferred Model with the 10% penalty. For investment horizons up to ten years, the Current Model investment outperforms the Deferred Model investment, while for horizons greater than ten years, the Deferred Model investment beats the Current Model investment (compare Columns 2 and 4). This result can be seen more easily with the annualized ATRORs, where beginning in Year 11, the annualized ATRORs for the Deferred Model investment exceed 6.5% (compare Columns 5 and 7). The Current Model investment is better for short horizons because the applicable tax rate is 35% rather than 45% (rate + penalty). However, after ten years, the deferral benefit of the Deferred Model investment overcomes the penalty's detrimental effect. Thus, if an investor has a long enough investment horizon, a traditional nondeductible IRA subject to the 10% penalty may be the preferred method of accumulating savings, assuming the investor is ineligible for the Roth IRA. ◄

THE EXEMPT MODEL

The Exempt Model gives the future value of an investment having the following characteristics:

▶ Only after-tax dollars are invested (as with the Current and Deferred Models).

▶ Earnings on the investment are exempt from explicit taxation (unlike the Current and Deferred Models).

In fact, the Exempt Model is a special case of either the Current Model or the Deferred Model with the tax rate equal to zero. Consequently, the investment grows at the BTROR and appears as follows:

$$\boxed{\begin{array}{c} \text{The Exempt Model:} \\ \text{ATA} = \text{AT\$}(1 + R)^n \end{array}}$$

State and local government obligations, such as municipal bonds, are classic examples of the Exempt Model. Section 103 excludes interest on these instruments from gross income.

EXAMPLE I:18-12 ▶ Carmen invests $10,000 (AT$) in tax-exempt municipal bonds, which yield 5% per year. She reinvests the interest and holds the bonds for ten years. Thus, the investment accumulates to $16,288.95, which is $10,000 $(1.05)^{10}$. ◄

Other examples of the Exempt Model are the Roth IRA (see Chapter I:9) and the Roth option for Sec. 401(k) and Sec. 403(b) plans. Like the traditional nondeductible IRA, the Roth IRA does not allow a deduction for contributions. However, upon withdrawals, the accumulated earnings are not taxed. We will say more about the Roth IRA after developing the Pension Model.

 STOP & THINK *Question:* Does the Exempt Model imply that no taxation occurs in the tax system for investments of this type?

Solution: No. Taxation occurs because the taxpayer invests after-tax dollars, which means the invested amount comes from some taxable source. If no taxation occurred at all, the model would appear as Accumulation = BT$ $(1 + R)^n$, which is the situation described on page I:18-3 just after Example I:18-1.

THE PENSION MODEL

The Pension Model gives the future value of an investment in a qualified retirement plan having the following characteristics:

▶ Before-tax dollars are invested (unlike the previous three models).

▶ The annual earnings on the investment grow at the BTROR (as with the Deferred and Exempt Models).

▶ The entire accumulation, not just the earnings, is taxed at the end of the investment horizon when the investor cashes out of the plan.

Thus, the Pension Model provides two levels of tax deferral. First, salary or earned income contributed to the plan escapes taxation when contributed but is taxed later upon withdrawal. Second, earnings on the underlying investment are not taxed while in the plan but also are taxed later upon withdrawal. This double deferral contrasts with the Deferral Model, in which only the taxes on investment earnings are deferred.

Deductible IRAs and H.R. 10 plans described in Chapter I:9 are classic examples of the Pension Model. The taxpayer deducts the IRA or H.R. 10 contribution from gross income, the underlying investments grow at before-tax rates of return, and the taxpayer later includes any withdrawals in gross income.

EXAMPLE I:18-13 ▶ Frank, whose marginal tax rate is 35%, earns $1,000 of salary and wishes to contribute this amount to a deductible IRA (Pension Model). He may do so because he can deduct the $1,000 contribution from gross income, leaving the entire $1,000 available for contribution. If, instead, Frank contributes to a traditional nondeductible IRA (Deferred Model) or a Roth IRA (Exempt Model), he can contribute only $650 because he must pay $350 of taxes on the $1,000 salary. Thus, Frank can contribute $1,000 before-tax dollars to a deductible IRA as contrasted with $650 after-tax dollars to a traditional nondeductible IRA or a Roth IRA. ◀

Other examples of the Pension Model include cash or deferred arrangements, commonly known as Sec. 401(k) plans, and tax-deferred annuities, sometimes referred to as Sec. 403(b) plans. Both of these type plans operate through a salary reduction agreement whereby the employee elects to have a specified amount of his or her salary contributed to the plan. The employee excludes the amount of salary contributed to the plan from his or her gross income. However, annual contributions are limited to $16,500 (in 2010).[4] As with IRA and H.R. 10 plans, the underlying investments in Sec. 401(k) and Sec. 403(b) plans grow at before-tax rates of return, and the employee later includes any withdrawals in gross income. Withdrawals before the employee reaches age 59½, however, are subject to a 10% penalty in addition to the tax. Although most employers can offer Sec. 401(k) plans, only educational institutions and certain tax-exempt organizations may provide Sec. 403(b) plans.

Employer-sponsored qualified retirement plans also fit the Pension Model. In this case, the employer makes a deductible contribution on the employee's behalf, and the employee excludes the contribution from gross income. Upon retirement, the employee's retirement payments are fully taxed.

EXAMPLE I:18-14 ▶ Frank in Example I:18-13 makes the $1,000 contribution to a deductible IRA. The investment in the IRA will earn 10% per year before taxes, and Frank will withdraw all accumulated amounts from the IRA after 20 years. He expects his tax rate to be 25% at that time, and he will not be subject to the 10% penalty for early withdrawals. The following calculation demonstrates one way to determine Frank's after-tax accumulation in the IRA:

Before-tax accumulation in the IRA [$1,000(1.1)^{20}]	$6,727.50
Minus: Tax on withdrawn accumulation ($6,727.50 × 0.25)	(1,681.88)
Accumulated earnings after taxes	$5,045.62 ◀

The calculation in Example I:18-14 also can be formulated as follows:

$$ATA = \$1,000(1.1)^{20} - [\$1,000(1.1)^{20}] \times 0.25$$

---

[4] Section 402(g) imposes this dollar limitation. In addition, Sec. 414(v) increases the limitation for taxpayers age 50 or older. This additional catch-up limitation is $5,500 in 2010. Percentage of compensation limitations also apply to contributions to Sec. 401(k) and Sec. 403(b) plans, but these limitations are complex and beyond the scope of this chapter. (See Chapter I:9 and Secs. 403(b) and 415(c).)

Factoring out the before-tax accumulation of $\$1,000(1.1)^{20}$ yields the following expression:

$$ATA = \$1,000(1.1)^{20}(1 - 0.25)$$

Substituting our general symbols into this expression yields:

> The Pension Model:
> $$ATA = BT\$(1 + R)^n(1 - t_n) \text{ or}$$
> $$ATA = AT\$\left[\frac{1}{(1 - t_o)}(1 + R)^n(1 - t_n)\right]$$

Recall that $BT\$ = AT\$/(1 - t)$. That is, before-tax dollars equal after-tax dollars grossed up by one minus the tax rate. Thus, the second form of the Pension Model is equivalent to the first form. The second form, however, has the same format as the other three models: AT$ times a future value formula. This format allows the investor to compare all four models without considering a specific level of investment because each model in this format is stated in terms of the after-tax accumulation per AT$ invested. In these models, t_o is the tax rate in Year 0, and t_n is the tax rate in Year n.

EXAMPLE I:18-15 ▶ Given four options listed below, Beth wants to know the after-tax accumulation and annualized ATROR of each.

▶ Current Model: R = 10%, t = 25%, n = 5

▶ Deferred Model: R = 9%, t_n = 35%, n = 5

▶ Exempt Model: R = 8%, n = 5

▶ Pension Model: R = 10%, t_o = 25%, t_n = 35%, n = 5

The results of the four options are as follows:

Model	Computation	After-Tax Accumulation	Annualized ATROR
Current	$[1 + 0.1(1 - 0.25)]^5$	1.4356	7.50%
Deferred	$(1.09)^5(1 - 0.35) + 0.35$	1.3501	6.19%
Exempt	$(1.08)^5$	1.4693	8.00%
Pension	$[1/(1 - 0.25)](1.1)^5(1 - 0.35)$	1.3958	6.90%

◀

COMPARING EXEMPT AND PENSION MODELS. With equal BTRORs, constant tax rates (i.e., $t_o = t_n$), and no limitation on contributions, the Exempt and Pension Models are equivalent because the $1/(1 - t_o)$ and $(1 - t_n)$ terms cancel out, leaving the Pension Model (second form) to appear as $AT\$(1 + R)^n$. However, if t_o and t_n differ, this equivalency disappears. Thus, the following relationships hold:

▶ If $t_o = t_n$, ATA per Exempt Model = ATA per Pension Model.

▶ If $t_o > t_n$, ATA per Exempt Model < ATA per Pension Model.

▶ If $t_o < t_n$, ATA per Exempt Model > ATA per Pension Model.

EXAMPLE I:18-16 ▶ Consider the following situations:

▶ R = 10%, t_o = 30%, t_n = 30%, n = 10

▶ R = 10%, t_o = 40%, t_n = 30%, n = 10

▶ R = 10%, t_o = 30%, t_n = 40%, n = 10

The after-tax accumulations (ATAs) for the three situations are as follows:

Situation	Exempt Model	Pension Model
t_o = 30%, t_n = 30%	$(1.1)^{10} = 2.5937$	$[1/(1 - 0.30)](1.1)^{10}(1 - 0.30) = 2.5937$
t_o = 40%, t_n = 30%	$(1.1)^{10} = 2.5937$	$[1/(1 - 0.40)](1.1)^{10}(1 - 0.30) = 3.0260$
t_o = 30%, t_n = 40%	$(1.1)^{10} = 2.5937$	$[1/(1 - 0.30)](1.1)^{10}(1 - 0.40) = 2.2232$

◀

DEDUCTIBLE IRA VERSUS ROTH IRA.   The Exempt and Pension models can be used to compare investment in a traditional deductible IRA versus a Roth IRA. If the amount of before-tax dollars available for investment does not exceed the $5,000 limitation (in 2010),[5] the comparative results are similar to those in Example I:18-16.

EXAMPLE I:18-17 ▶

Marcy has $5,000 of salary before taxes available for contribution to either a traditional deductible IRA or a Roth IRA. The underlying investments will earn a 10% BTROR. After ten years, Marcy plans to withdraw the entire accumulation without penalty. If her marginal tax rate is 30% in the contribution year, she can contribute either $5,000 (BT$) to the deductible IRA or $3,500 (AT$) to the Roth IRA. If her marginal tax rate upon withdrawal is 30%, she will have the following after tax accumulations under each alternative:

Roth IRA: $[\$3,500(1.1)^{10}]$	$9,078.10
Deductible IRA: $[\$5,000(1.1)^{10}(1 - 0.30)]$	$9,078.10

TAX STRATEGY TIP

When given a choice between a Roth IRA and a traditional *non*deductible IRA, the taxpayer always should choose the Roth IRA.

Thus, with constant tax rates, the two alternatives yield the same after-tax accumulation.

If Marcy's current tax rate is 40%, and her later tax rate is 30%, the two alternatives yield the following after-tax accumulations:

Roth IRA: $[\$3,000(1.1)^{10}]$	$7,781.23
Deductible IRA: $[\$5,000(1.1)^{10}(1 - 0.30)]$	$9,078.10

Thus, with decreasing tax rates, the deductible IRA yields the better result.

Finally, if Marcy's current tax rate is 30%, and her later tax rate is 40%, the two alternatives yield the following after-tax accumulations:

Roth IRA: $[\$3,500(1.1)^{10}]$	$9,078.10
Deductible IRA: $[\$5,000(1.1)^{10}(1 - 0.4)]$	$7,781.23

Thus, with increasing tax rates, the Roth IRA yields the better result.   ◀

In Example I:18-17, the before-tax dollars available for contribution did not exceed the $5,000 limitation on IRA contributions. However, suppose the taxpayer wishes to compare a $5,000 contribution to a deductible IRA with a $5,000 contribution to a Roth IRA. In this case, the two contributions are not equivalent because the taxpayer makes the contribution to the deductible IRA with before-tax dollars and to the Roth IRA with after-tax dollars. To have $5,000 after-tax dollars available for a Roth IRA contribution, the taxpayer must have $5,000/(1 − t_o) before-tax dollars available for investment. If the taxpayer has this amount available and contributes $5,000 to a deductible IRA, the taxpayer will have some available funds left over for investment outside the deductible IRA.[6]

EXAMPLE I:18-18 ▶

Mark wants to contribute $5,000 to either a deductible IRA or a Roth IRA. His current marginal tax rate is 30%. To contribute $5,000 (AT$) to a Roth IRA, his before-tax dollars available for investment must be $7,142.86, which is computed as BT$ = $5,000/(1 − 0.30). On the other hand, if he contributes $5,000 (BT$) to a deductible IRA, he has $2,142.86 remaining. This $2,142.86 is subject to tax so that, after taxes at 30%, Mark will have $1,500 (AT$) remaining for investment outside the IRA.

A convenient short-cut method to determine the amount remaining for outside investment is to multiply the $5,000 deduction by the tax rate to arrive at the tax savings from the traditional IRA deduction. Specifically, the $5,000 deduction will generate $1,500 of tax savings for outside investment, computed as $5,000 × 0.30 = $1,500. This shortcut, however, works only if the taxpayer considers contributing the maximum amount to the deductible or Roth IRA.   ◀

Given the previous discussion, the deductible IRA versus Roth IRA decision can be framed as follows:

---

[5] This limitation increased to $5,000 for 2008 and thereafter with inflation adjustments after 2008. For taxpayers age 50 or older, the limitations are increased by $1,000 for 2006 and thereafter. For 2010, these limitations remain at $5,000 and $1,000.

[6] Participants in Sec. 401(k) and Sec. 403(b) plans can opt to have their elective deferrals treated as Roth contributions. For a detailed analysis of this decision, (see K. E. Anderson and D. P. Murphy, "The New Roth Option for 401(k) and 403(b) Plans: A Decision Framework," *Journal of Financial Service Professionals*, January 2002, pp. 45–56).

Roth IRA	$\$5,000(1 + R)^n$
Versus	
Deductible IRA	$\$5,000(1 + R)^n(1 - t_n)$
Plus	
Outside Investment	$\$5,000(t_o)[1 + R(1 - t)]^n$

In this framework, $\$5,000(t_o)$ is the tax savings from the traditional IRA deduction, which the taxpayer invests in an investment conforming to the Current Model. If the taxpayer's outside investment conforms to the Deferred Model or some other model, the alternative model can be substituted for the Current Model in this decision framework.

EXAMPLE I:18-19 ▶ Helen wishes to invest $5,000 in either a deductible IRA or a Roth IRA. The underlying investments will earn a 10% BTROR. After ten years, Helen plans to withdraw the entire accumulation without penalty. Her marginal tax rate is 30% in the contribution year, and she expects her marginal tax rate upon withdrawal to be 30%. If she contributes to the deductible IRA, she will invest the tax savings in an investment yielding a 10% BTROR and which is currently taxable at 30%. The alternative investments yield the following results:

Roth IRA [$\$5,000(1.1)^{10}$]	$12,968.71
Deductible IRA [$\$5,000(1.1)^{10}(1 - 0.30)$]	$ 9,078.10
Plus: Outside investment [$\$5,000(0.30)(1.07)^{10}$]	$ 2,950.73
Total	$12,028.83

With constant tax rates, the Roth IRA produces the better result because, with the deductible IRA, part of the investment goes to an outside investment taxed less favorably than the IRA. Note also that, because the $5,000 limitation is after-tax dollars for the Roth IRA but before-tax dollars for the deductible IRA, constant tax rates no longer produce equivalent results.

Suppose instead that Helen expects her tax rate to be 15% when she withdraws the IRA accumulation. In this case, the alternative investments yield the following results:

Roth IRA [$\$5,000(1.1)^{10}$]	$12,968.71
Deductible IRA [$\$5,000(1.1)^{10}(1 - 0.15)$]	$11,023.41
Plus: Outside investment [$\$5,000(0.30)(1.07)^{10}$]	$ 2,950.73
Total	$13,974.14

Thus, with a reduced tax rate in the withdrawal year, the deductible IRA (plus the outside investment) yields the better result. ◀

MULTIPERIOD STRATEGIES

All previous examples assumed a single amount invested for a specified time period. However, suppose an investor wants to invest a certain amount each year over several years. In this case, the investor may optimize his or her after-tax accumulation by investing in one type of investment in early years and another type investment in late years.

EXAMPLE I:18-20 ▶ For the next 15 years, Jack wishes to invest $10,000 (AT$) at the beginning of each year into either nondividend paying stock that increases in value at 8% per year before taxes or a taxable bond that yields 10% per year before taxes. Jack's regular tax rate is 30%, but he pays only 15% on long-term capital gains. Jack wants to know which asset to invest in for each of the 15 years. The following models apply to this situation:

Stock (Deferred Model):

$$\$10,000[(1.08)^n(1 - 0.15) + 0.15]$$

Taxable bond (Current Model):

$$\$10,000[1 + 0.1(1 - 0.30)]^n = \$10,000(1.07)^n$$

Table I:18-2 schedules the alternatives for each year. The stock produces the larger after-tax accumulations for investments made in Years 1 through 9. For Years 10 through 15, however, the taxable bonds outperform the stock. Consequently, Jack should invest in stock for each of

▼ TABLE I:18-2
Multiperiod Investments

(1) Year	(2) n	(3) Amount Invested	(4) Stock[a] (Deferred Model)	(5) Taxable Bond[b] (Current Model)	(6) Greater of Column 4 or 5
1	15	$10,000	$ 28,463	$ 27,590	$ 28,463
2	14	10,000	26,466	25,785	26,466
3	13	10,000	24,617	24,098	24,617
4	12	10,000	22,904	22,522	22,904
5	11	10,000	21,319	21,049	21,319
6	10	10,000	19,851	19,672	19,851
7	9	10,000	18,492	18,385	18,492
8	8	10,000	17,233	17,182	17,233
9	7	10,000	16,068	16,058	16,068
10	6	10,000	14,988	15,007	15,007
11	5	10,000	13,989	14,026	14,026
12	4	10,000	13,064	13,108	13,108
13	3	10,000	12,208	12,250	12,250
14	2	10,000	11,414	11,449	11,449
15	1	10,000	10,680	10,700	10,700
Total ATA with no switching			$271,756	$268,881	
Total ATA with switching strategy					$271,953

[a]$10,000 [(1.08)^n(1 - 0.15) + 0.15]$
[b]$10,000 (1.07)^n$

the first nine years and hold the stock for the rest of the 15-year investment horizon. For the remaining six years, he should invest in taxable bonds. This switching strategy maximizes the total after-tax accumulation compared to investing in either stock or bonds for the entire 15-year period (compare Column 4 and 5 totals to Column 6 total).

The stock outperforms the taxable bonds for the first nine years even though the taxable bonds yield a higher BTROR than does the stock. This result occurs because the deferral benefit outweighs the lower BTROR for long investment horizons. ◀

SUMMARY AND COMPARISON OF BASIC INVESTMENT MODELS

Topic Review I:18-1 summarizes the models along with simple examples. In the examples, each model assumes an investment earning 10% before taxes and assumes a constant 30% tax rate. With these assumptions, the Exempt and Pension Models outperform the Current and Deferred Models, and the Deferred Model outperforms the Current Model.

OTHER APPLICATIONS OF INVESTMENT MODELS

In the previous section of this chapter, we developed four investment models and applied them to currently taxable investments, capital gains assets, tax-exempt bonds, and retirement plans. In this section, we present two additional applications: (1) the flow-through entity versus the C corporation form of business operations and (2) current salary versus deferred compensation.

Topic Review I:18-1

Summary of Investment Models

INVESTMENT MODEL	INITIAL INCOME	INVESTMENT EARNINGS OR CAPITAL GAIN	EXAMPLES[a]	ATA	ATA/AT$	r_{ann}
Current: $AT\$[1 + R(1-t)]^n$ — or — $AT\$(1+r)^n$	Taxed currently	Taxed annually	$\$700(1.07)^5$	$981.79	1.4026[b]	7.00%
Deferred: $AT\$[(1+R)^n(1-t_n) + t_n]$	Taxed currently	Tax deferred	$\$700[(1.1)^5(0.7) + 0.30]$	$999.15	1.4274[c]	7.38%
Exempt: $AT\$(1+R)^n$	Taxed currently	Tax exempt	$\$700(1.1)^5$	$1,127.36	1.6105[d]	10.00%
Pension: $BT\$(1+R)^n(1-t_n)$ — or — $AT\$\left[\dfrac{1}{(1-t_o)}(1+R)^n(1-t_n)\right]$	Tax deferred	Tax deferred	$\$1,000(1.1)^5(0.7)$ — or — $\$700(1/0.7)(1.1)^5(0.7)$	$1,127.36	1.6105[e]	10.00%

Definitions of Variables:

ATA = After-tax accumulation (future value of an investment)
BT$ = Before-tax dollars
AT$ = After-tax dollars
R = Before-tax rate of return (BTROR)
r = After-tax rate of return (ATROR)
r_{ann} = Annualized ATROR
n = Investment horizon
t = Marginal tax rate, generally and for Current Model
t_o = Marginal tax rate in the year of investment (Year 0) for Pension Model
t_n = Marginal tax rate at the end of the investment horizon (Year n) for Deferred and Pension Models

[a]Initial before-tax income (BT$) = $1,000; AT$ = $1,000(0.7) = $700; R = 10%; t = t_o = t_n = 30%; n = 5
[b]Also: $(1.07)^5$ = 1.4026
[c]Also: $(1.1)^5(0.7) + 0.30$ = 1.4274
[d]Also: $(1.1)^5$ = 1.6105
[e]Note that the $1,127.36 after-tax accumulation is divided by $700, not $1,000, because $700 is the after-tax dollar equivalent of $1,000 before taxes.
Also: $(1/0.7)(1.1)^5(0.7)$ = 1.6105

OBJECTIVE 2

Use the investment models to make entity choices

FLOW-THROUGH ENTITY VERSUS C CORPORATION

Chapter I:16 described how the government taxes C corporations and their shareholders, and Chapter I:17 introduced the tax consequences of operating as a flow-through entity (also called a pass-through entity). Flow-through entities include partnerships, limited liability companies (LLCs), limited liability partnerships (LLPs), and S corporations. A flow-through entity's primary characteristic is that income escapes taxation at the entity level and flows through to be taxed at the ownership level. Corporate income, on the other hand, is taxed once at the entity level and again at the owner level. Taxation at the owner level occurs when the corporation distributes its earnings, when the shareholder sells his or her stock, or when the corporation liquidates.

In this section, we show that the Current Model describes a flow-through entity and that a variation of the Deferred Model describes a C corporation. These models can be used to decide which form of business is best from a tax perspective. At first, one might think the flow-through entity is the better form because it avoids double taxation. But, in fact, the better alternative depends on a combination of factors, specifically, rates of returns, the corporate tax rate, the owner's tax rate, and the entity's expected life span (investment horizon).

THE FLOW-THROUGH MODEL. To keep matters simple, we assume an S corporation with only one shareholder. The one-owner assumption allows us to focus on the entity decision without worrying about distributive shares and differential individual tax rates among owners. The model also applies to an S corporation, a partnership, an LLC, or an LLP with more than one owner. In addition, the model applies to a sole proprietorship because that form of business also entails one level of taxation.

ADDITIONAL COMMENT

As the income and deductions flow through to the owners of partnerships and S corporations, they retain their character. For example, ordinary income at the entity level is ordinary income to the owner, and capital gains at the entity level flow through as capital gains.

EXAMPLE I:18-21 ▶ Assume the following facts. Rebecca forms an S corporation by contributing $10,000 to the corporation in exchange for all the corporation's stock. The S corporation invests in assets that produce a 10% BTROR per year. At the end of each year, the S corporation distributes cash to Rebecca equal to the taxes she must pay on the S corporation's flow-through earnings. The corporation reinvests the remaining earnings in its business. Rebecca's tax rate is 40%. Immediately after the end of the second year, the S corporation liquidates, selling the assets and distributing the cash proceeds to Rebecca. Because the corporation reinvested its retained earnings, the total basis of the corporation's assets increased as well. Assuming the FMV of the assets increased similarly, the sale produces no realized gain at the entity level. The following schedule shows the results of these transactions at the entity and owner levels:

	Year 1	Year 2
Entity level:		
Investment at beginning of year	$10,000	$10,600
Plus: Earnings on investment (10% × investment)	1,000	1,060
Minus: Distribution to shareholder (40% × earnings)	(400)	(424)
Investment at end of year	$10,600	$11,236
Owner level:		
Stock basis at beginning of year	$10,000	$10,600
Plus: Increase due to flow-through income	1,000	1,060
Minus: Decrease due to distribution	(400)	(424)
Stock basis at end of year	$10,600	$11,236

Upon liquidation, the S corporation sells the assets and distributes the $11,236 to Rebecca. Because Rebecca's stock basis equals $11,236, she recognizes no additional gain on the liquidation. Thus, after two years, she ends up with $11,236 on a $10,000 original investment. ◀

In Example I:18-21, the S corporation could reinvest only its earnings after paying the shareholder's tax. Thus, the investment grew at a 6% ATROR, which is 10% $(1 - 0.4)$. Consequently, the shareholder's after-tax accumulation also can be calculated as follows: ATA = $\$10,000(1.06)^2 = \$11,236$. From the owner's viewpoint, then, the flow-through entity resembles the Current Model. In general terms, the owner's after-tax accumulation can be expressed as:

> The Flow-Through Model:
> $$ATA = \text{Contribution}[1 + R_f(1 - t_p)]^n$$

In this model, R_f equals the flow-through entity's BTROR, t_p is the owner's marginal tax rate (p is for personal), and n is the investment horizon. Although Example I:18-21 assumes a liquidating distribution at the end of the investment, the same result would have occurred had the owner sold her ownership interest (stock in this case) to another party.

THE C CORPORATION MODEL. Again, to keep matters simple, we assume a C corporation with only one shareholder, and we further assume that the corporation retains all earnings after paying corporate level taxes. That is, the corporation pays no dividends. The model could be modified to reflect annual dividend payments, but such a model becomes extremely complicated and is beyond the scope of this chapter.

EXAMPLE I:18-22 ▶ Assume the same facts as in Example I:18-21 except that Rebecca forms a C corporation instead of an S corporation. In this case, the corporation makes no annual distributions to Rebecca. Instead, the corporation pays its own taxes at a 35% rate and reinvests the after-tax retained earnings. Thus, the shareholder has no owner-level taxes until the corporation liquidates. Rebecca's ordinary tax rate remains 40%, but her capital gains tax rate is 15%. As in Example I:18-21, the sale prior to liquidation produces no realized gain at the entity level. The following schedule shows the results of these transactions at the entity and owner levels:

	Year 1	Year 2
Entity level:		
Investment at beginning of year	$10,000	$10,650
Plus: Earnings on investment (10% × investment)	1,000	1,065
Minus: Corporate taxes (35% × earnings)	(350)	(373)
Investment at end of year	$10,650	$11,342
Owner level:		
Stock basis	$10,000	$10,000
(1) Liquidation proceeds		$11,342
(2) Minus: Stock basis		(10,000)
(3) Capital gain on liquidation		$ 1,342
(4) Times: Long-term capital gains tax rate		0.15
(5) Tax on capital gain		$ 201
(6) After-tax proceeds (Line 1 − Line 5)		$11,141

Because the corporation is a C corporation, Rebecca makes no adjustments to her stock basis, which remains at $10,000. Consequently, she recognizes a capital gain upon liquidation, and after two years she ends up with $11,141 on a $10,000 original investment. ◄

In Example I:18-22, the C corporation was able to reinvest only its after-tax earnings. Thus, at the corporate level, the investment grew at a 6.5% ATROR, which is 10% $(1 − 0.35)$. Consequently, the corporate-level accumulation before distribution to the shareholders can be calculated as follows: $\$10,000[1 + 0.1(1 − 0.35)]^2 = \$10,000(1.065)^2 = \$11,342$. In general terms, this expression is: Contribution$[1 + R_c(1 − t_c)]^n$, or Contribution $[1 + r_c]^n$. This formulation is a variation of the Current Model, where R_c is the corporation's BTROR, r_c is the corporation's ATROR, and t_c is the corporation's marginal tax rate.

Upon liquidation, the shareholder receives the corporate-level accumulation and pays tax at rate t_p on the difference between the distribution and her stock basis. Thus, the shareholder's after-tax accumulation in Example I:18-22 can be formulated as follows:

$$ATA = \$10,000(1.065)^2 − [\$10,000(1.065)^2 − \$10,000] \times 0.15$$

The first term, $\$10,000(1.065)^2$, gives the corporate-level after-tax accumulation; the subtraction in brackets gives the shareholder's liquidation gain before shareholder-level taxes; and the multiplication by 15% gives the tax on the liquidation gain. Subtracting this tax from the first term gives the shareholder's total after-tax accumulation on the investment in the C corporation. Factoring out the $10,000 contribution yields the following expression:

$$ATA = \$10,000\{(1.065)^2 − [(1.065)^2 − 1] \times 0.15\}$$

Substituting our general symbols into this expression yields the following model, which is a variation of the Deferred Model shown earlier in Figure I:18-1:

$$ATA = Contribution\{(1 + r_c)^n − [(1 + r_c)^n − 1] \times t_p\}$$

As done earlier with the Deferred Model, we can simplify this model algebraically to obtain:

> The C Corporation Model:
> $$ATA = Contribution[(1 + r_c)^n(1 − t_p) + t_p]\ or$$
> $$ATA = Contribution\{[1 + R_c(1 − t_c)]^n(1 − t_p) + t_p\}$$

In the first form of this model, the corporation's ATROR (r_c) plays the same role as the BTROR plays in the Deferred Model developed earlier in this chapter. More specifically, in terms used in Example I:18-10, r_c is the appreciation (growth) rate of the shareholder's stock investment, assuming the stock value reflects increases in the corporation's after-tax retained earnings. Thus, the corporation's ATROR functions as the shareholder's BTROR on his or her stock investment. The second form of the C Corporation Model emphasizes that the corporate-level accumulation (the Current Model) is embedded in the shareholder's after-tax accumulation model (the Deferred Model).

COMPARING THE FLOW-THROUGH AND C CORPORATION MODELS. Given these two models, an owner can compare whether operating as a flow-through entity or a C corporation provides the better result.

EXAMPLE I:18-23 ▶ Assume the following facts. Mark forms Wolfson Corporation by contributing $5 million in exchange for the corporation's stock. The corporation expects to earn 18% per year before taxes on this investment. The corporate tax rate is 34%, and Mark's individual tax rate on ordinary income is 40%. Because Wolfson stock qualifies as small business stock under Sec. 1202, any gain recognized on disposition of the stock after a five-year holding period qualifies for a 50% exclusion. The maximum capital gain rate on the included gain is 28% rather than 15%. Thus, Mark's effective rate on the *entire* capital gain is 15% if he holds the stock for five years or less and is 14% if he holds the stock for more than five years (that is, 28% of half the gain is equivalent to 14% of the entire gain). Wolfson can operate either as an S corporation or a C corporation. If the corporation elects S corporation status, each year it will distribute exactly enough cash for Mark to pay taxes on any flow-through income, and it will reinvest the remaining earnings in the business. If the corporation operates as a C corporation, it will make no annual distributions, reinvesting all after-tax earnings in the business. In either case, the corporation will liquidate at the end of the investment horizon. Mark wants to know how long he must operate the corporation to make the C corporation form better than the S corporation form. Table I:18-3 gives Mark's after-tax accumulation for each alternative.

According to Table I:18-3, if Mark decides to operate the corporation for ten years or less, the corporation should make the S corporation election. However, if he plans to operate for more than ten years, the corporation should remain a C corporation. ◀

▼ **TABLE I:18-3**

S Corporation Versus C Corporation

Years of Operation (n)	S Corporation[a]	C Corporation[b]
1	$ 5,540,000	$ 5,504,900
2	6,138,320	6,069,782
3	6,801,259	6,701,772
4	7,535,794	7,408,843
5	8,349,660	8,199,913
6	9,251,424	9,133,021
7	10,250,577	10,134,864
8	11,357,640	11,255,726
9	12,584,265	12,509,746
10	13,943,365	13,912,744
11	15,449,249	15,482,418
12	17,117,768	17,238,570

[a]For all n, ATA = $5,000,000[1 + 0.18(1 − 0.4)]^n
[b]For n = 1 through 5, ATA = $5,000,000\{[1 + 0.18(1 − 0.34)]^n(1 − 0.15) + 0.15\}$
For n > 5, ATA = $5,000,000\{[1 + 0.18(1 − 0.34)]^n(1 − 0.14) + 0.14\}$

STOP & THINK

Question: Assume that a flow-through entity and a C corporation earn the same BTROR, that is, $R_f = R_c$. Given the following comparisons of the corporate tax rate (t_c) and the owner's tax rate (t_p), can you tell from just looking at the two models which entity form is better from a tax perspective?

    Comparison 1: $t_c = t_p$
    Comparison 2: $t_c > t_p$
    Comparison 3: $t_c < t_p$

Solution: In Comparisons 1 and 2, the flow-through entity is always better than the C corporation (given $R_f = R_c$). In Comparison 3, however, the answer is not obvious. Consider the two models:

    Flow-through: $[1 + R_f(1 - t_p)]^n$
    C corporation: $[1 + R_c(1 - t_c)]^n(1 - t_p) + t_p$

Notice that, if $R_f = R_c$ and $t_c = t_p$, the bracketed terms in the two models will be equal, which means the flow-through entity accumulation equals the corporate-level accumulation. The C corporation, however, entails additional taxation at the shareholder level, which is represented by the terms following the bracketed term. This additional tax makes the C corporation worse than the flow-through entity. If $t_c > t_p$, the bracketed term in the C corporation model accumulates to a lesser amount than does the flow-through model, and the shareholder-level tax just makes matters worse. Thus, the flow-through entity again is the preferred form. Finally, if $t_c < t_p$, the bracketed term in the C corporation model accumulates to a greater amount than does the flow-through model, but the shareholder level tax lessens the overall benefit. However, whether the overall effect causes the C corporation to be better than the flow-through entity depends on how much t_p exceeds t_c and on how long the investment horizon (n) is. Thus, the answer is not obvious.

OBJECTIVE 3

Use the investment models to make current salary versus deferred compensation decisions

SUMMARY.   The Flow-Through Model is an application of the Current Model, where taxation occurs only at the owner level. The C Corporation Model is a variation of the Deferred Model, where taxation occurs at both the entity and the owner levels. These models can help the planner decide whether the flow-through entity or the C corporation is the better alternative from a tax perspective. Topic Review I:18-2 summarizes these models.[7]

CURRENT SALARY VERSUS DEFERRED COMPENSATION

Chapter I:9 introduced the characteristics of a nonqualified deferred compensation plan. This arrangement differs from current salary in that the employer's deduction and the employee's inclusion in gross income occur later than with current salary. The key question, then, is whether an employee should choose current salary or deferred compensation. The decision model developed in this section helps answer this question. Because both the employer and the employee are affected by the timing of compensation, the decision model must incorporate these dual effects. Specifically, the model includes the current and future tax rates of the employer and employee as well as the employer's and employee's ATRORs.

THE EMPLOYEE'S POINT OF VIEW.   The employee can choose between current salary in Year 0 or deferred compensation in Year n. If the employee chooses current salary, the employee immediately pays taxes on the salary and invests the after-tax amount at his or her ATROR.[8] If, instead, the employee receives deferred compensation, the employee pays taxes on this compensation in Year n, leaving an after-tax amount of deferred compensation. These two alternatives are comparable because both are stated in terms of future values.

---

[7] For an interesting analysis of the flow-through versus C corporation decision, see D. S. Hulse and T. R. Pope, "The Effect of Income Taxes on the Preference of Organizational Forms for Small Businesses in the United States," *Journal of Small Business Management,* January 1996, pp. 24–35. The article demonstrates the tradeoffs of the two organizational forms using indifference curves based on BTRORs, the investment horizon (n), and tax rates.

[8] The employee also could spend the current salary. However, this current consumption is equivalent to the future consumption available if the employee invests and spends later. In this case, the investment assumption gives the future value of current consumption. Thus, whether the employee actually spends or invests, the investment assumption provides the future value of that decision.

Topic Review I:18-2

Flow-Through and C Corporation Models

Flow-Through Model:
$$ATA = Contribution[1 + R_f(1 - t_p)]^n$$

C Corporation Model:
$$ATA = Contribution[(1 + r_c)^n(1 - t_p) + t_p]$$

or

$$ATA = Contribution\{[1 + R_c(1 - t_c)]^n(1 - t_p) + t_p\}$$

Definitions of Variables:
R_f = Flow-through entity's BTROR
R_c = C corporation's BTROR
t_p = Owner's marginal tax rate
t_c = C corporation's marginal tax rate
r_c = C corporation's ATROR
n = Investment horizon

EXAMPLE I:18-24 ▶ Bruce works for Xeron Corporation and is considering receiving either $10,000 of current salary or $25,000 of deferred compensation in ten years. His current tax rate is 40%, but he expects his tax rate to be 25% ten years from now. Bruce can invest any after-tax current salary at a 10% ATROR. If Bruce receives current salary and invests the after-tax amount, his investment will accumulate as follows:

$$\$10,000(1 - 0.4)(1.1)^{10} = \$15,562$$

Bruce's after-tax salary is $6,000, which grows to $15,562 in ten years if invested at a 10% ATROR. Thus, this calculation, which is an application of the Current Model, gives the future value of Bruce's after-tax current salary. Alternatively, if Bruce receives deferred compensation, his after-tax deferred compensation is calculated as follows:

$$\$25,000(1 - 0.25) = \$18,750$$

In this case, Bruce prefers the deferred compensation alternative because he will have $18,000 in ten years instead of $15,562 under the current salary alternative. ◀

Using general terms, we can state the employee's current salary and deferred compensation alternatives as follows:

$$CSI = BT\$(1 - t_{po})(1 + r_p)^n$$

$$DCI = BT\$(D_n)(1 - t_{pn})$$

In these formulas, CSI stands for current salary income and is the employee's after-tax future value of current salary; DCI stands for deferred compensation income and is the employee's after-tax future value of deferred compensation; and BT$ stands for before-tax current salary. In the second formula, D_n is the amount of deferred compensation received in lieu of $1 currently. Accordingly, BT$ $\times$ D_n gives total deferred compensation before taxes. For example, in Example I:18-24, BT$ = $10,000, and BT$ $\times$ D_n = $25,000. Thus, D_n = 2.50. In other words, Bruce could choose between $1 of current salary or $2.50 of deferred compensation, before taxes. The factor, BT$, converts these per dollar amounts to total dollars of current salary or deferred compensation. The other variables in the formulas are defined as follows:

▶ t_{po} = The employee's marginal tax rate in Year 0
▶ t_{pn} = The employee's marginal tax rate in Year n

> ▶ r_p = The employee's ATROR
> ▶ n = The number of years until the employee receives the deferred compensation

The employee prefers deferred compensation if DCI exceeds CSI. From the previous formulas, this relationship can be expressed as follows:

$$DCI > CSI \text{ or}$$

$$BT\$(D_n)(1 - t_{pn}) > BT\$(1 - t_{po})(1 + r_p)^n$$

Solving the second expression for D_n yields:

$$D_n > \frac{(1 - t_{po})(1 + r_p)^n}{(1 - t_{pn})}$$

The level of D_n that exactly equals the right-hand side of this expression makes the employee indifferent to receiving current salary or deferred compensation. That is, at the indifference level of D_n, the employee's current salary income (CSI) equals the employee's deferred compensation income (DCI). Levels of D_n above the indifference level make deferred compensation more beneficial than current salary to the employee.

EXAMPLE I:18-25 ▶ Assume the same facts as in Example I:18-24. Bruce prefers deferred compensation rather than $1 of current salary if D_n exceeds 2.0750, calculated as follows:

$$D_n > \frac{(1 - 0.4)(1.1)^{10}}{(1 - 0.25)} = 2.0750$$

Therefore, D_n = 2.0750 is Bruce's indifference level, as shown by the following calculation for $1 of current salary:

$$CSI = \$1\,(1 - 0.4)(1.1)^{10} = \$1.5562$$
$$DCI = \$1\,(2.0750)(1 - 0.25) = \$1.5562$$

Given a choice between $10,000 of current salary (BT$) and deferred compensation, Bruce will prefer deferred compensation to current salary if the deferred compensation exceeds $20,750, which is $10,000 × 2.0750. ◀

REAL-WORLD EXAMPLE

Many contracts of professional athletes are structured using deferred compensation arrangements. The current value of the contract usually is publicized in nominal dollars. For example, if the press reports that an athlete signed a $75 million contract for $5 million per year for 15 years, the report is ignoring the time value of money.

THE EMPLOYER'S POINT OF VIEW. The issue from the employer's point of view is whether the employer is willing to pay deferred compensation in lieu of current salary. If the employer pays current salary, the employer takes a business deduction and obtains an immediate tax benefit. The current salary net of the tax benefit is the employer's after-tax salary expense. This after-tax amount must be projected to Year n to be comparable to the alternative deferred compensation expense. We compound the after-tax salary expense at the employer's ATROR because, if the employer does not pay the salary, the employer will have the after-tax amount available for investment in its business. This investment, in turn, grows at the employer's ATROR. Thus, compounding determines the future value of the employer's after-tax salary expense. If instead of paying salary the employer pays deferred compensation, the employer deducts the deferred compensation expense in Year n. The deferred compensation net of the Year n tax benefit is the employer's after-tax deferred compensation expense.

EXAMPLE I:18-26 ▶ Again consider the facts in Example I:18-24, that is, $10,000 of current salary versus $25,000 of deferred compensation in ten years. In addition, the employer's current tax rate is 39%, but the employer expects its tax rate to be 34% ten years from now. The employer's ATROR is 10%. If the employer pays current salary, its after-tax salary expense projected to Year n is calculated as follows:

$$\$10,000(1 - 0.39)(1.1)^{10} = \$15,822$$

Alternatively, the after-tax deferred compensation expense is calculated as follows:

$$\$25,000(1 - 0.34) = \$16,500$$

In this case, the employer's after-tax deferred compensation expense ($16,500) exceeds its after-tax salary expense ($15,822). Consequently, the employer is unwilling to pay Bruce the $25,000 of deferred compensation even though Bruce prefers that alternative. ◄

Using general terms, we can state the employer's current salary and deferred compensation alternatives as follows:

$$CSE = BT\$(1 - t_{co})(1 + r_c)^n$$
$$DCE = BT\$(D_n)(1 - t_{cn})$$

In these formulas, CSE stands for current salary expense and is the employer's after-tax salary expense projected to Year n; DCE stands for deferred compensation expense and is the employer's after-tax deferred compensation expense in Year n; and BT$ stands for before-tax current salary. As before, D_n equals the amount of deferred compensation paid in lieu of $1 currently. Accordingly, $BT\$ \times D_n$ gives total deferred compensation before taxes. The other variables in the formulas are defined as follows:

▶ t_{co} = The employer's marginal tax rate in Year 0
▶ t_{cn} = The employer's marginal tax rate in Year n
▶ r_c = The employer's ATROR
▶ n = The number of years until the employer pays the deferred compensation

The employer will pay deferred compensation only if DCE does not exceed CSE. From the previous formulas, this relationship can be expressed as follows:

$$DCE \leq CSE \text{ or}$$
$$BT\$(D_n)(1 - t_{cn}) \leq BT\$(1 - t_{co})(1 + r_c)^n$$

Solving the second expression for D_n yields:

$$D_n \leq \frac{(1 - t_{co})(1 + r_c)^n}{(1 - t_{cn})}$$

The level of D_n that exactly equals the right-hand side of this expression makes the employer indifferent to paying current salary or deferred compensation. That is, at the indifference level of D_n, the employer's current salary expense (CSE) equals the employer's deferred compensation expense (DCE). Levels of D_n below the indifference level make deferred compensation more beneficial than current salary to the employer.

EXAMPLE I:18-27 ▶ Assume the same facts as in Example I:18-26. Compared to $1 of current salary, the employer will pay deferred compensation only if D_n does not exceed 2.3972, calculated as follows:

$$D_n \leq \frac{(1 - 0.39)(1.1)^{10}}{(1 - 0.34)} = 2.3972$$

Therefore, D_n = 2.3972 is the employer's indifference level, as shown by the following calculation for $1 of current salary:

$$CSE = \$1(1 - 0.39)(1.1)^{10} = \$1.5822$$
$$DCE = \$1(2.3972)(1 - 0.34) = \$1.5822$$

Given a choice between $10,000 of current salary (BT$) and deferred compensation, the employer will pay deferred compensation instead of current salary only if deferred compensation does not exceed $23,972, which is $10,000 × 2.3972. ◄

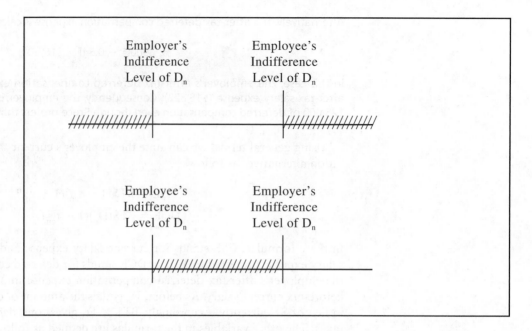

FIGURE I:18-2 ▶ Comparing the Employee's and Employer's Views

COMPARING THE EMPLOYEE'S AND EMPLOYER'S VIEWS. Knowledge of the employee's and employer's acceptable levels of D_n gives the two parties the necessary tools to decide whether deferred compensation is preferable to current salary. Specifically, the employee and employer can apply the following decision rules:

▶ If the employee's indifference level of D_n exceeds the employer's indifference level of D_n, the employee must accept current salary because the employer will not pay the employee's required deferred compensation.

▶ If the employee's indifference level of D_n is less than the employer's indifference level of D_n, the employer can pay deferred compensation up to its indifference level.

Figure I:18-2 shows these decision rules graphically. In both graphs, the shaded portion of the lines indicates the employee's and employer's acceptable levels of D_n. In the top graph, these areas are separated, leaving the middle part of the line empty. This empty region indicates the employee and employer cannot agree on a mutually acceptable level of D_n. In the bottom graph, however, the employee's and employer's acceptable levels of D_n overlap in the middle part of the line. Thus, both parties can accept any level of D_n in this region. For example, in Examples I:18-25 and I:18-27 the parties could agree on deferred compensation between $20,750 and $23,972.

EXAMPLE I:18-28 ▶ Marsha and Todd are employed by Omega Corporation. They want to compare deferred compensation two years from now (n = 2) to $10,000 of current salary. Assume the following tax rates and rates of return:

	Year 0	Year n	ATROR
Marsha	$t_{po} = 0.30$	$t_{pn} = 0.15$	$r_p = 0.10$
Todd	$t_{po} = 0.40$	$t_{pn} = 0.15$	$r_p = 0.10$
Omega Corporation	$t_{co} = 0.39$	$t_{cn} = 0.25$	$r_c = 0.10$

The indifference level of D_n for each party is as follows:

Marsha: $D_n = \dfrac{(1 - 0.30)(1.1)^2}{(1 - 0.15)} = 0.9965$

Todd: $D_n = \dfrac{(1 - 0.4)(1.1)^2}{(1 - 0.15)} = 0.8541$

Omega Corporation: $D_n = \dfrac{(1 - 0.39)(1.1)^2}{(1 - 0.25)} = 0.9841$

Compared to $10,000 of current salary, Omega Corporation will pay no more than $9,841 of deferred compensation. Consequently, Marsha must settle for $10,000 of current salary because she requires more than $9,965 of deferred compensation to make that alternative preferable. This amount exceeds what Omega Corporation is willing to pay as deferred compensation.

Todd, on the other hand, can benefit from a deferred compensation arrangement. He requires deferred compensation exceeding $8,541, and Omega Corporation is willing to pay up to $9,841 of deferred compensation. ◄

We can provide additional insight into the salary versus deferred compensation decision by carrying Example I:18-28 a bit further. If Omega Corporation pays Todd $9,841 of deferred compensation, Omega Corporation incurs the same after-tax expense it would have incurred had it paid $10,000 of current salary. Thus, Omega Corporation remains indifferent, and Todd obtains the full benefit of the deferred compensation arrangement. This outcome can be seen with the following income and expense amounts:

Todd:
$$CSI = \$10,000(1 - 0.4)(1.1)^2 = \$7,260$$
$$DCI = \$10,000(0.9841)(1 - 0.15) = \$8,365$$

Omega Corporation:
$$CSE = \$10,000(1 - 0.39)(1.1)^2 = \$7,381$$
$$DCE = \$10,000(0.9841)(1 - 0.25) = \$7,381$$

Because Omega Corporation pays its indifference level of D_n, its current salary and deferred compensation expenses are equal. Under the deferred compensation arrangement, however, Todd ends up with $8,365 rather than $7,260.

Suppose instead that Omega Corporation pays deferred compensation that makes Todd indifferent. In this case, Todd obtains the same amount of after-tax income as under the salary option, and Omega Corporation obtains the full benefit of the deferred compensation arrangement. This outcome can be seen with the following income and expense amounts:

Todd:
$$CSI = \$10,000(1 - 0.4)(1.1)^2 = \$7,260$$
$$DCI = \$10,000(0.8541)(1 - 0.15) = \$7,260$$

Omega Corporation:
$$CSE = \$10,000(1 - 0.39)(1.1)^2 = \$7,381$$
$$DCE = \$10,000(0.8541)(1 - 0.25) = \$6,406$$

Because Omega Corporation pays Todd's indifference level of D_n, Todd's current salary and deferred compensation income are equal. Under the deferred compensation arrangement, however, Omega Corporation's deferred compensation expense ($6,406) is less than the alternative current salary expense ($7,381).

In each case, one party was made indifferent while the other party benefited from the deferred compensation alternative. However, Omega Corporation also could pay deferred compensation somewhere between the two indifference levels of D_n. The shaded middle region in the bottom graph of Figure I:18-2 depicts this range. For example, suppose Omega Corporation chose $D_n = 0.92$. The following outcomes would occur:

Todd:
$$CSI = \$10,000(1 - 0.4)(1.1)^2 = \$7,260$$
$$DCI = \$10,000(0.92)(1 - 0.15) = \$7,820$$

Omega Corporation:
$$CSE = \$10,000(1 - 0.39)(1.1)^2 = \$7,381$$
$$DCE = \$10,000(0.92)(1 - 0.25) = \$6,900$$

In this case, Todd's deferred compensation income is $7,820 rather than $7,260 of current salary income. In addition, Omega Corporation's deferred compensation expense is $6,900 rather than the $7,381 current salary expense. Thus, both parties are better off with the deferred compensation arrangement than with current salary. However, neither party is as well off had the other party remained indifferent. In short, they share the benefit.

The preceding analysis incorporated tax rates and ATRORs in the decision model for current salary versus deferred compensation. The outcomes in the examples, however, depended only on the differential tax rates across taxpayers and over time because the

ATRORs of the employer and employees were the same. In other situations, the employer's ATROR may differ from that of the employees, further influencing the results.

STOP & THINK

Question: What nontax factors might affect the current salary versus deferred compensation decision, possibly overriding the tax factors?

Solution: In addition to tax factors, the parties must consider their cash-flow requirements. If the employee needs cash now, he or she may be unwilling to defer income despite a better result from the decision model. Similarly, an employer short on current cash may prefer deferred compensation even though the decision model suggests current salary as the better alternative. Deferred compensation also carries some risk. Under nonqualified deferred compensation plans, the employee becomes a general creditor of the employer. Consequently, if the employer runs into financial difficulties later, the employer may not be able to pay the deferred compensation. The employee, therefore, may decide for the safe alternative, current salary, regardless of the decision model outcome. Finally, deferred compensation may lock the employee into continued employment unless the deferred compensation contract makes adequate provision for the employee's severance.

SUMMARY. The decision model developed in this section provides an analytic tool for employees and employers to plan current salary versus deferred compensation arrangements. The model takes into account the tax and ATROR attributes of both parties to the transaction. This approach prevents one party benefiting at the disadvantage of the other and therefore leads to the best overall solution. Topic Review I:18-3 summarizes the decision model.

Topic Review I:18-3

Current Salary Versus Deferred Compensation

EMPLOYEE'S POINT OF VIEW

$$CSI = BT\$(1 - t_{po})(1 + r_p)^n$$
$$DCI = BT\$(D_n)(1 - t_{pn})$$
$$D_n = \frac{(1 - t_{po})(1 + r_p)^n}{(1 - t_{pn})}$$

EMPLOYER'S POINT OF VIEW

$$CSE = BT\$(1 - t_{co})(1 + r_c)^n$$
$$DCE = BT\$(D_n)(1 - t_{cn})$$
$$0D_n = \frac{(1 - t_{co})(1 + r_c)^n}{(1 - t_{cn})}$$

Decision rules:
▶ If the employee's indifference level of D_n exceeds the employer's indifference level of D_n, the employee must accept current salary because the employer will not pay the employee's required deferred compensation.

▶ If the employee's indifference level of D_n is less than the employer's indifference level of D_n, the employer can pay deferred compensation up to its indifference level.

Definitions of Variables:
CSI = Current salary income; employee's after-tax future value of before-tax current salary
DCI = Deferred compensation income; employee's after-tax future value of deferred compensation
CSE = Current salary expense; employer's after-tax salary expense projected to Year n
DCE = Deferred compensation expense; employer's after-tax deferred compensation expense in Year n
$BT\$$ = Before-tax current salary
D_n = Amount of deferred compensation paid in lieu of \$1 of current salary
t_{po} = Employee's marginal tax rate in Year 0
t_{pn} = Employee's marginal tax rate in Year n
r_p = Employee's ATROR
t_{co} = Employer's marginal tax rate in Year 0
t_{cn} = Employer's marginal tax rate in Year n
r_c = Employer's ATROR
n = Number of years until the deferred compensation is paid

IMPLICIT TAXES AND CLIENTELES

OBJECTIVE 4

Understand the role of implicit taxes in investment decisions

Several of the investment vehicles we modeled earlier have certain tax benefits compared to other investments. For example, interest earned on tax-exempt investments, such as state and local bonds, is excluded from gross income. The Exempt Model reflects this tax benefit. As another example, assets that generate long-term capital gains also are tax favored. The taxation of the capital gain is deferred until realization, and then the realized gain may be subject to a preferential tax rate, for example, the 15% maximum tax rate on long-term capital gains. The Deferred Model, when applied to capital gain assets, reflects this preferential taxation. For the sake of simplicity, however, this section focuses on tax-exempt bonds to introduce the concept of implicit taxes and clientele effects.

IMPLICIT TAXES. Consider what happens in the marketplace for tax-favored assets. Given a choice between a fully-taxable investment and a tax-favored investment, investors will prefer the tax-favored investment, assuming the two investments are equally risky. This preference manifests itself as an increased demand for the tax-favored investment, thereby driving up the asset's price. The increased price, in turn, causes the asset's BTROR to decrease. For example, the BTROR on a bond with an unlimited life (a perpetuity) is as follows:

$$BTROR = \frac{Annual\ cash\ flow}{Bond's\ price}$$

If the bond's price increases, the BTROR must decrease.

The difference between the BTRORs of the fully-taxable and tax-favored investments is an implicit tax, which can be expressed as follows:

$$IT = R_b - R_e$$

In this formula, IT stands for implicit tax, R_b is the BTROR on a fully-taxable benchmark investment, and R_e is the BTROR on a tax-favored investment having the same risk level as the benchmark. (Later in this chapter, we will show the problem with comparing investments of unequal risk.) Dividing the implicit tax by the benchmark BTROR (R_b) converts the implicit tax (IT) to an implicit tax *rate* (t_I), expressed as follows:

$$t_I = \frac{R_b - R_e}{R_b}$$

EXAMPLE I:18-29 ▶ Maria invests $1,000 in a taxable bond that yields a 10% BTROR and another $1,000 in a tax-exempt bond that yields a 7.5% BTROR (i.e., R_b = 10%, and R_e = 7.5%). Maria's marginal tax rate is 25% (i.e., t = 25%). The two investments yield the following earnings each year:

	Taxable Bond	Tax-Exempt Bond
Before-tax interest	$100	$75
Minus: Explicit tax on interest	(25)	0
After-tax interest	$ 75	$75

Although the tax-exempt bond is free from explicit taxation, it reflects a 2.5% implicit tax, which is $R_b - R_e$ = 10% − 7.5% = 2.5%. Here, we express the implicit tax as a 2.5% reduction in the BTROR. Stated in dollars, the implicit tax is $1,000 × 0.025 = $25. Thus, Maria incurs a $25 explicit tax on the taxable bond and a $25 implicit tax on the tax-exempt bond. Maria's implicit tax *rate* on the tax-exempt bond is 25%, calculated as follows:

$$t_I = \frac{R_b - R_e}{R_b} = \frac{10\% - 7.5\%}{10\%} = 0.25\ or\ 25\%$$

Thus, Maria incurs a 25% explicit tax *rate* on the taxable bond and a 25% implicit tax *rate* on the tax-exempt bond.

Maria's ATROR on each bond is 7.5%. For the taxable bond, the ATROR is calculated as follows: $r_b = R_b(1 - t) = 10\%(1 - 0.25) = 7.5\%$. For the tax-exempt bond, the ATROR is the same as the BTROR. ◄

REAL-WORLD EXAMPLE

Tax return filings show that high income taxpayers invest in tax-exempt bonds more than do lower income taxpayers. For those returns reporting tax-exempt interest in 2007, taxpayers with AGI over $100,000 reported almost four times as much tax-exempt interest as did taxpayers with AGI under $100,000.

EQUILIBRIUM CONDITION AND CLIENTELES.   The degree to which R_e falls in relation to R_b depends on the marginal investor's tax rate. By definition, marginal investors are indifferent between fully-taxable and tax-favored investments. As marginal investors compete for a tax-favored investment, supply and demand forces drive up its price (and reduce its BTROR) to the point where the ATRORs of the fully-taxable and tax-favored investments are equal. That is, in equilibrium for marginal investors, the ATRORs for investments meet the following condition: $r_b = r_e$. For example, in Example I:18-29, Maria is a marginal investor because $r_b = r_e = 7.5\%$. Thus, Maria is indifferent between the two investments. (Note that, for tax-exempt bonds, $r_e = R_e$.)

In Example I:18-29, Maria incurred a 25% tax rate on each investment, explicit on the fully-taxable bond and implicit on the tax-exempt bond. Thus, Maria did not realize a tax benefit on the tax-exempt bond. In fact, the term *tax-exempt* is a misnomer when implicit taxes are considered. The issuer of the tax-exempt bond, however, received a tax subsidy in the form of a reduced interest rate. Therefore, the transaction works as though Maria paid a tax while the bond issuer received a subsidy.

This result leads to the following question: Can any investor benefit from tax-exempt bonds? In a flat-rate tax system where only one tax rate prevails, the answer is no because all investors are marginal investors. In a progressive tax rate system, however, the answer is yes for an investor whose marginal tax rate exceeds that of the marginal investor. In this situation, investors form natural clienteles for the alternative investments.

EXAMPLE I:18-30 ▶

Assume the same facts as in Example I:18-29, where Maria is the indifferent marginal investor. Consider two other investors, Silvia and Bob. Silvia's tax rate is 40%, and Bob's tax rate is 15%. If Silvia invested in a fully-taxable bond, her ATROR would be as follows: $r_b = 10\%(1 - 0.4) = 6\%$. Consequently, Silvia will prefer the tax-exempt bond that yields a 7.5% ATROR (which also equals its BTROR). Silvia's high tax rate puts her in the clientele for tax-exempt bonds. By investing in the tax-exempt bond, Silvia converts her 40% explicit tax rate into a 25% implicit tax rate, thereby giving her the higher ATROR.

If Bob invests in the fully-taxable bond, his ATROR will be as follows: $r_b = 10\%(1 - 0.15) = 8.5\%$. Thus, Bob prefers the fully-taxable bond because he obtains an 8.5% ATROR rather than 7.5% from the tax-exempt bond. Bob's low tax rate puts him in the clientele for taxable bonds. If he mistakenly invests in the tax-exempt bond, he will convert a 15% explicit tax rate into a 25% implicit tax rate. Therefore, he should avoid the tax-exempt bond. ◄

TAX STRATEGY TIP

Example I:18-30 highlights a key planning concept. Investors must consider the ATRORs of investments in making their investment decisions. Doing so will ensure that all tax effects are accounted for, including implicit as well as explicit taxes.

RISKY ASSETS.   A key requirement for calculating the implicit tax rate on a tax-favored investment is that the risk level be the same as the benchmark investment. The BTROR of a risky asset has two components, the riskless return and a risk premium. This relationship can be formulated as follows:

$$\tilde{R} = R + P$$

In this formula, $\tilde{R}$ is the risky return, R is the riskless return, and P is the risk premium. Investors who invest in risky assets require this premium as an incentive to make the investment. If the benchmark investment is a fully-taxable, riskless bond, the tax-favored investment's BTROR must be adjusted to remove this risk premium to obtain an accurate measure of the implicit tax rate.

EXAMPLE I:18-31 ▶

A tax-exempt bond issued by Troubled City is highly risky and therefore yields a 12% BTROR, which is composed of a 7% riskless return and a 5% risk premium. A riskless benchmark investment yields a 10% BTROR. Computing the implicit tax rate with the 12% return yields the following incorrect (and negative) implicit tax rate:

$$t_I = \frac{R_b - \tilde{R}_e}{R_b} = \frac{10\% - 12\%}{10\%} = -0.2 \text{ or } -20\%$$

The correct implicit tax rate is calculated with the risk-adjusted return as follows:

$$t_I = \frac{R_b - R_e}{R_b} = \frac{10\% - 7\%}{10\%} = 0.30 \text{ or } 30\%$$

◄

SUMMARY. Market forces drive down the BTRORs of tax-favored assets. This reduced return is an implicit tax. Thus, potential tax benefits to a marginal investor are competed away, thereby providing an implicit subsidy to the asset's issuer or seller. Investors whose tax rate exceeds that of the marginal investor, however, still can reap some benefit through the clientele effect. Topic Review I:18-4 summarizes the implicit tax rate formula.

Topic Review I:18-4

Implicit Taxes

Implicit tax:
$$IT = R_b - R_e$$

Implicit tax rate:
$$t_I = \frac{R_b - R_e}{R_b}$$

Equilibrium condition for marginal investor:
$$r_b = r_e.$$

Definitions of Variables:
IT = Implicit tax
t_I = Implicit tax rate
R_b = BTROR on a fully-taxable benchmark investment
R_e = Risk-adjusted BTROR on a tax-favored investment
r_b = ATROR on a fully-taxable benchmark investment
r_e = Risk-adjusted ATROR on a tax-favored investment

PROBLEM MATERIALS

DISCUSSION QUESTIONS

I:18-1 What is the primary distinguishing feature that causes the Current Model, Deferred Model, and Pension Model to differ?

I:18-2 What is an annualized ATROR, and why is it useful?

I:18-3 Why might an investment in a capital asset be preferable to an investment that is fully taxed currently even though the capital asset's BTROR is less than that of the fully-taxable investment?

I:18-4 Suppose a taxpayer is trying to decide between saving outside an IRA or saving through a traditional IRA. If the taxpayer needs the savings before reaching age 59½, should he or she necessarily avoid the IRA because of the 10% early withdrawal penalty? Why or why not? If the taxpayer must make a withdrawal before age 59½, which IRA might be better, the traditional IRA or the Roth IRA?

I:18-5 How does the length of the investment horizon affect the annualized ATROR of an investment conforming to the Deferred Model?

I:18-6 Under what conditions are the Exempt Model and Pension Model equivalent? Under what conditions would one model perform better than the other? How does the $5,000 limitation on deductible and Roth IRA contributions (in 2008) affect the comparison of these two vehicles?

I:18-7 What characteristics of a C corporation cause the shareholder's stock investment to conform to the Deferred Model?

I:18-8 How does the tax treatment of deferred compensation differ from the tax treatment of current salary?

I:18-9 What is the variable, D_n, and why is it important to the current salary versus deferred compensation decision?

I:18-10 Why might the employee and/or employer prefer salary over deferred compensation even in cases where deferred compensation provides the better tax results?

I:18-11 Why might an investment conforming to the Exempt Model have a lower BTROR than would an equivalent-risk investment conforming to the Current Model?

I:18-12 What is an implicit tax, and how does it arise?

I:18-13 What forces cause ATRORs of various investments to be equal for marginal investors?

I:18-14 What is a clientele effect, and what conditions are necessary for it to occur?

I:18-15 An article that appeared in *The Wall Street Journal* several years ago made the following statement:

At the highest federal tax rates . . . dividends and interest from private sector investments are taxed at 39.6% [35% in 2010], capital gains at 28% [15% in 2010], while interest from state and local debt instruments isn't taxed at all.

What problem do you see with the author's statement?

I:18-16 Why would a flat-rate tax system eliminate clientele effects?

I:18-17 Why might the BTROR on a tax-favored investment be higher than the BTROR on a fully-taxable investment even though implicit tax theory says that it should be lower?

I:18-18 We have discussed implicit taxes using tax-exempt bonds as an example, and we have mentioned capital gains assets as another case where implicit taxes might occur. Give one or two other specific tax provisions that might cause implicit taxes to arise. In so doing, explain:

- How the implicit tax is manifested (e.g., increased prices, reduced returns, increased costs, etc.).
- Who "pays" the implicit tax.
- Who "receives" the implicit subsidy.

PROBLEMS

I:18-19 *Tax-Exempt Bond.* Laura, who is in the 35% tax bracket, notices that tax-exempt municipal bonds are yielding a 7% return. What before-tax rate of return on a fully-taxable bond must Laura obtain to make her prefer the taxable bond over the tax-exempt bond?

I:18-20 *After-Tax Rates of Return.* Suppose a bond is taxable for both federal and state purposes. Let R_b = the BTROR on the bond, t_{fed} = the federal tax rate, and t_{st} = the state tax rate. Determine the ATROR (i.e., after federal and state taxes) if:
a. The state tax is *not* deductible for either federal or state purposes.
b. The state tax *is* deductible for federal but not for state purposes.
After algebraic simplification, each answer should take the form: $R_b($ $)$, with the rest of the answer inside the parentheses.

I:18-21 *Investment Models.* David can make a single investment in one of three alternatives. The first investment conforms to the Current Model, the second investment conforms to the Deferred Model, and the third investment conforms to the Pension Model. The investment horizon is seven years, and the BTROR for each alternative is 10%. David will incur no penalties upon withdrawal.
a. Assuming David's tax rate will be 15% for all seven years, what is the accumulation and annualized ATROR for each investment? Which alternative should David choose?
b. Assuming David's tax rate will be 15% for the first six years but will be 25% in the seventh year, what is the accumulation and annualized ATROR for each investment? Which alternative should David choose?

I:18-22 *Investment Models.* Mark is considering investing in either a tax-exempt municipal bond that yields 7% or a nondeductible IRA that contains investments that yield 10% before taxes. (Mark is ineligible to contribute to a Roth IRA.) Mark's current tax rate is 35%, and he plans to make a single investment now with a 15-year investment horizon.
a. Using after-tax accumulations and annualized ATRORs, show that the nondeductible IRA outperforms the municipal bonds assuming Mark's tax rate remains at 35%. Assume no additional penalty upon withdrawal from the IRA.
b. How high would Mark's tax rate have to rise in Year n to make the municipal bond more attractive than the nondeductible IRA? Assume the 7% and 10% BTRORs remain constant over time.

I:18-23   *Investment Models and IRAs.* Brenda has $5,000 of before-tax dollars available for a one-time investment. She is in the 25% bracket and expects to remain in this bracket indefinitely. She can invest directly in a taxable bond yielding 8% before taxes, or she can open an IRA and invest in the bond within the IRA. She knows that she will need the accumulated funds before she reaches age 59½. Thus, if she invests in an IRA, she will incur a 10% penalty on taxable amounts withdrawn from the IRA. Note: The two parts to this problem are best solved using a spreadsheet.

    a. If she invests in an IRA that allows immediate deduction of contributed amounts (i.e., a traditional deductible IRA), how many years must she wait before the IRA is a better vehicle than direct investment in the bond outside the IRA?

    b. How many years must she wait if she invests in a Roth IRA? Reminder: Withdrawals from a Roth IRA first come from contributions and are a nontaxable return of capital. However, if Brenda withdraws the *entire* accumulation before she attains age 59½, the accumulated earnings will be fully taxable and also subject to the 10% early withdrawal penalty. Hence, in this situation, the Roth IRA operates exactly like a traditional nondeductible IRA (the Deferred Model instead of the Exempt Model).

I:18-24   *Investment Planning.* Martha, who is in the 35% tax bracket, has $40,000 of before-tax income with which she wants to make a one-time investment. She wants to put $20,000 of this income in a deductible H.R. 10 plan, and she wants to invest any remaining after-tax income outside the H.R. 10 plan. Assume that Martha has sufficient self-employment income such that her contribution does not exceed the H.R. 10 contribution limit. Two investments are available: (1) a taxable bond yielding a 10% BTROR and (2) a nondividend paying stock that appreciates at a 10% annual rate before taxes. She is considering two alternatives:

    1. Have the H.R. 10 plan invest in the stock, and Martha will invest in the bond outside the H.R. 10 plan.

    2. Have the H.R. 10 plan invest in the bond, and Martha will invest in the stock outside the H.R. 10 plan.

The investment horizon is ten years with tax rates constant over this period. Capital gains upon sale of stock outside the H.R. 10 plan are taxed at 15%. However, if the stock is placed in the H.R. 10 plan, the H.R. 10 plan will sell the stock after ten years and distribute the proceeds to Martha, triggering ordinary income recognition to Martha. Assume no early withdrawal penalties on H.R. 10 plan distributions. Determine the total after-tax accumulation of Alternative 1 and of Alternative 2. Which of the two alternatives should Martha choose?

I:18-25   *Roth IRA Versus Deductible IRA.* Harry wants to contribute either $5,000 (BT$) to a traditional deductible IRA or $5,000 (AT$) to a Roth IRA. His current tax rate is 30% for ordinary income and 15% for capital gains. He expects his IRA investment to earn a 12% BTROR, and he plans to withdraw the IRA accumulation in 25 years, at which time he will be over age 59½. If he contributes to a deductible IRA, he will invest the tax savings from the deduction in a nondividend paying stock that he expects to grow at a 12% BTROR. Harry will sell the stock at the same time he withdraws the IRA accumulation.

    a. Compare the two alternatives assuming that, at the time of withdrawal, Harry's tax rate will be 30% for ordinary income and 15% for capital gains.

    b. Compare the two alternatives assuming that, at the time of withdrawal, Harry's tax rate will be 15% for ordinary income and 5% for capital gains.

I:18-26   *Roth IRA Versus Deductible IRA.* Beth wants to contribute to either a traditional deductible IRA or a Roth IRA. However, she can afford to contribute only $4,200 after-tax dollars to a Roth IRA even though the maximum contribution is $5,000. Alternatively, she can contribute a comparable amount to a deductible IRA plus an outside investment if necessary. (Remember that deductible IRA contributions are made with before-tax dollars and are limited to $5,000.) Beth's current tax rate is 25%, and she expects her tax rate to remain at 25% throughout the investment period. In addition, she expects her IRA investment to earn a 10% BTROR, and she plans to withdraw the IRA accumulation in 30 years, at which time she will be over age 59½. Any outside investment will conform to the Current Model earning a 10% BTROR. Determine the after-tax accumulation from each IRA alternative. Which of the two IRA types will give Beth the greater after-tax accumulation?

I:18-27 *Multiperiod Investment Strategy.* Given the following facts and assumptions, determine what investment strategy Karen should follow to maximize accumulations and how much she will have accumulated at the *beginning* of Year 10 (including her last paycheck).

- Karen's ordinary tax rate is 25%, and her long-term capital gains tax rate is 15%. These rates will remain constant over her investment horizon.
- Karen earns $40,000 per year, which she receives on the first day of each year.
- Karen saves all her income after paying income taxes on her earnings. Taxes are payable immediately upon receiving her paycheck.
- At the beginning of each year, Karen can invest her savings in any of three vehicles:
  1. A money market fund yielding 6% per year before taxes,
  2. A traditional deductible IRA that yields 6% per year before taxes, and/or
  3. Capital assets that grow at 5.21% per year before taxes.
- IRA contributions are limited to $5,000 per year and are deductible up to that amount. Assume this limit applies to all years under consideration.
- At the beginning of Year 10, Karen saves no more income. Instead, she withdraws any IRA and/or money market accumulations and sells her capital assets for their accumulated FMV before taxes. She also receives a $40,000 paycheck at the beginning of Year 10.
- IRA accumulations are taxable immediately upon withdrawal with no additional penalty.
- Ignore itemized deductions, standard deductions, exemptions, etc.

I:18-28 *Proprietorship Versus C Corporation.* Myron has $10,000 to invest in a business. He can either (1) operate as a sole proprietor or (2) form a regular C corporation by contributing the $10,000 in exchange for corporate stock. In either case, the $10,000 will be invested in business assets and will earn a 10% BTROR for the first five years and an 18% BTROR for years six through 15. All after-tax earnings will be reinvested in the business. If Myron uses the corporate form, the corporation will liquidate at the end of the investment horizon. Myron's personal tax rate is 40%; the corporate tax rate is 25%; and the maximum tax rate on capital gains for individuals is 15% (assume no Sec. 1202 50% exclusion for gain on the sale of small business stock). Determine whether Myron should operate as a sole proprietor or form a C corporation if the investment horizon is 15 years. Show the after-tax accumulation and annualized after-tax rate of return for each alternative.

I:18-29 *Flow-Through Versus C Corporation.* Twelve years ago, your client formed a C corporation with a $100,000 investment (contribution). The corporation's BTROR (R_c) has been and will continue to be 10%. The corporate tax rate (t_c) has been and will continue to be 35%. The corporation pays no dividends and reinvests all after-tax earnings in its business. Thus, the corporation's value grows at its ATROR. Your client's marginal ordinary tax rate (t_p) has been 33%, and her capital gains rate has been 15%. Your client expects her ordinary tax rate to drop to 25% at the beginning of this year and stay at that level indefinitely. Her capital gains tax rate will remain at 15%. Assume the corporate stock does not qualify for the Sec. 1202 50% exclusion for gain on the sale of small business stock. Your client wants you to consider three alternatives:
(1) Continue the business in C corporation form for the next 20 years and liquidate at that time (32 years in total).
(2) Liquidate the C corporation at the beginning of this year, invest the after-tax proceeds in a sole proprietorship, and operate as a sole proprietorship for the next 20 years.
(3) Make an S corporation election effective at the beginning of this year, operate as an S corporation for the next 20 years, and liquidate the S corporation at that time (32 years in total).
Regarding Alternatives 2 and 3, the sole proprietorship's or S corporation's BTROR (R_p) also will be 10% for the next 20 years. Earnings from the sole proprietorship or S corporation will be taxed currently at your client's ordinary tax rate, and your client will withdraw just enough from the business to pay her taxes. The remaining after-tax earnings will remain in the business until the end of the investment horizon (20 years from now). Show the results of each alternative along with supporting models and calculations. Which alternative should your client adopt? Ignore the accumulated earnings tax for C corporations.

I:18-30 *Flow-Through Versus C Corporation.* Assume the corporation in Problem I:18-29 had been an S corporation for its first 12 years, during which it distributed just enough cash for the shareholder to pay taxes on the flow-through income. Thus, the S corporation reinvested after-tax income. Now the corporation is considering revoking its S election and operating as a C corporation for the remaining 20 years with no dividend distributions. Show the results of remaining an S corporation versus revoking the election. Also show supporting models and calculations. Which alternative should the corporation adopt? Ignore the accumulated earnings tax for C corporations. How does your answer change if the C corporation's tax rate is 15% instead of 35%?

I:18-31 *S Corporation Versus C Corporation.* Consider the following facts:

$$R_f = R_c = 18\%$$
$$t_c = 34\%$$
$$t_p = 40\% \text{ for ordinary income}$$
$$= 15\% \text{ for capital gains}$$
$$n = 5, 15, \text{ or } 50 \text{ years}$$

Other information:
- The corporation is formed with a $10,000 contribution.
- The corporation pays no dividends.
- Assume the Sec. 1202 50% exclusion for gain on the sale of small business stock does not apply.

a. Using the format below, compare after-tax accumulations for each investment horizon. Should the corporation make the S election for any of these investment horizons?
b. How does your answer change if t_p for ordinary income is 35% instead of 40%?

	Years (n)		
	5	15	50
S corporation ($t_p = 40\%$)			
C corporation			
S corporation ($t_p = 35\%$)			

I:18-32 *Current Salary Versus Deferred Compensation.* Consider Marsha and Todd from Example I:18-28 in the text. Suppose these employees worked for Learned University, a tax-exempt organization, instead of a taxable corporation. The university's BTROR equals its ATROR, i.e., $R_c = r_c = 0.10$. Would the university be willing to pay deferred compensation to either employee? If so, how much? That is, what is the university's indifference level of D_n?

I:18-33 *Current Salary Versus Deferred Compensation.* Consider the following facts:

Variables	Case 1	Case 2	Case 3
BT$	$10,000	$10,000	$10,000
t_{po}	.30	.30	.40
t_{pn}	.40	.40	.30
r_p	.10	.10	.10
t_{co}	.35	.35	.35
t_{cn}	.35	.35	.25
r_c	.15	.20	.10
n	3	3	3

a. Complete the following table for each case:

	Case 1	Case 2	Case 3
Employer's D_n			
Employee's D_n			
Decision (CS or DC?)			
CSI			
DCI (employer indiff.)			

CSE
DCE (employer indiff.)
CSI
DCI (employee indiff.)
CSE
DCE (employee indiff.)

b. Suppose in Case 2 from Part a that the employer and employee negotiate a D_n of 1.62. Compute CSI, DCI, CSE, and DCE with this D_n to show that each party to the deferred compensation contract shares in the tax benefit.

I:18-34 *Current Salary Versus Deferred Compensation.* Sandy will earn a $100,000 bonus that can be split between current and deferred compensation in any of the following ways:

*Current (BT$)**	*Deferred (BT$)**
$100,000	$ –0–
80,000	20,000
60,000	40,000
40,000	60,000
20,000	80,000
–0–	100,000

* The numbers in the above lists are BT$ as in the text formulas. Thus, the numbers in the second column are not BT$ $\times D_n$.

Assume that Sandy is subject to the following progressive tax rate schedule in the current and future years:

Income Range	*Marginal Tax Rate*	*Computation of Tax*
$ 0–20,000	30.0%	$0.30 \times$ TI
20,001–40,000	32.5	$ 6,000 + 0.325($TI $- $20,000)$
40,001–60,000	35.0	$12,500 + 0.35($TI $- $40,000)$
60,001–80,000	37.5	$19,500 + 0.375($TI $- $60,000)$
Over 80,000	40.0	$27,000 + 0.4($TI $- $80,000)$

- Corporate tax rates are as follows: $t_{co} = .35$, $t_{cn} = .34$.
- Rates of return are as follows: $r_c = .08$; $r_p = .07$.
- The length of deferral is five years, i.e., $n = 5$.

a. What is the best way for Sandy to split the $100,000 bonus given a level of D_n that makes the corporation indifferent?

b. Now assume the bonus allocations are not restricted to $20,000 increments. What is the optimal allocation of the current and deferred bonus given the level of D_n that makes the employer indifferent?

I:18-35 *Implicit Tax Rates and Clientele Effects.* Terry's marginal tax rate is 30%. He can invest in a taxable bond yielding 7.5% before taxes. What is the implicit tax rate on a tax-exempt bond of equivalent risk that yields 6%?

a. Which bond should Terry invest in? Why?

b. How would your answer to Part a change if Terry's statutory marginal tax rate were 15%?

I:18-36 *Implicit Tax Rates and Clientele Effects.* Consider three taxpayers who are in the following tax brackets:

Alice	25%
Brad	35%
Camille	40%

The BTROR on a benchmark investment is 10% (i.e., $R_b = 10\%$). Compute the equilibrium BTROR and the implicit tax rate on a tax-exempt bond under each of the following three alternative assumptions.

a. Alice is the marginal investor.

b. Brad is the marginal investor.

c. Camille is the marginal investor.

d. Which taxpayer (Alice, Brad, or Camille) would Camille like to see be the marginal investor? Why?

2009 TAX TABLES AND RATE SCHEDULES

2010 WITHHOLDING TABLES (PARTIAL)

2009 Tax Table

See the instructions for line 44 that begin on page 37 to see if you must use the Tax Table below to figure your tax.

Example. Mr. and Mrs. Brown are filing a joint return. Their taxable income on Form 1040, line 43, is $25,300. First, they find the $25,300–25,350 taxable income line. Next, they find the column for married filing jointly and read down the column. The amount shown where the taxable income line and filing status column meet is $2,964. This is the tax amount they should enter on Form 1040, line 44.

Sample Table

At least	But less than	Single	Married filing jointly *	Married filing separately	Head of a household
			Your tax is—		
25,200	25,250	3,366	2,949	3,366	3,186
25,250	25,300	3,374	2,956	3,374	3,194
25,300	25,350	3,381	(2,964)	3,381	3,201
25,350	25,400	3,389	2,971	3,389	3,209

If line 43 (taxable income) is— At least	But less than	Single	Married filing jointly *	Married filing separately	Head of a household
			Your tax is—		
0	5	0	0	0	0
5	15	1	1	1	1
15	25	2	2	2	2
25	50	4	4	4	4
50	75	6	6	6	6
75	100	9	9	9	9
100	125	11	11	11	11
125	150	14	14	14	14
150	175	16	16	16	16
175	200	19	19	19	19
200	225	21	21	21	21
225	250	24	24	24	24
250	275	26	26	26	26
275	300	29	29	29	29
300	325	31	31	31	31
325	350	34	34	34	34
350	375	36	36	36	36
375	400	39	39	39	39
400	425	41	41	41	41
425	450	44	44	44	44
450	475	46	46	46	46
475	500	49	49	49	49
500	525	51	51	51	51
525	550	54	54	54	54
550	575	56	56	56	56
575	600	59	59	59	59
600	625	61	61	61	61
625	650	64	64	64	64
650	675	66	66	66	66
675	700	69	69	69	69
700	725	71	71	71	71
725	750	74	74	74	74
750	775	76	76	76	76
775	800	79	79	79	79
800	825	81	81	81	81
825	850	84	84	84	84
850	875	86	86	86	86
875	900	89	89	89	89
900	925	91	91	91	91
925	950	94	94	94	94
950	975	96	96	96	96
975	1,000	99	99	99	99

1,000

At least	But less than	Single	Married filing jointly *	Married filing separately	Head of a household
1,000	1,025	101	101	101	101
1,025	1,050	104	104	104	104
1,050	1,075	106	106	106	106
1,075	1,100	109	109	109	109
1,100	1,125	111	111	111	111
1,125	1,150	114	114	114	114
1,150	1,175	116	116	116	116
1,175	1,200	119	119	119	119
1,200	1,225	121	121	121	121
1,225	1,250	124	124	124	124
1,250	1,275	126	126	126	126
1,275	1,300	129	129	129	129

If line 43 (taxable income) is— At least	But less than	Single	Married filing jointly *	Married filing separately	Head of a household
			Your tax is—		
1,300	1,325	131	131	131	131
1,325	1,350	134	134	134	134
1,350	1,375	136	136	136	136
1,375	1,400	139	139	139	139
1,400	1,425	141	141	141	141
1,425	1,450	144	144	144	144
1,450	1,475	146	146	146	146
1,475	1,500	149	149	149	149
1,500	1,525	151	151	151	151
1,525	1,550	154	154	154	154
1,550	1,575	156	156	156	156
1,575	1,600	159	159	159	159
1,600	1,625	161	161	161	161
1,625	1,650	164	164	164	164
1,650	1,675	166	166	166	166
1,675	1,700	169	169	169	169
1,700	1,725	171	171	171	171
1,725	1,750	174	174	174	174
1,750	1,775	176	176	176	176
1,775	1,800	179	179	179	179
1,800	1,825	181	181	181	181
1,825	1,850	184	184	184	184
1,850	1,875	186	186	186	186
1,875	1,900	189	189	189	189
1,900	1,925	191	191	191	191
1,925	1,950	194	194	194	194
1,950	1,975	196	196	196	196
1,975	2,000	199	199	199	199

2,000

At least	But less than	Single	Married filing jointly *	Married filing separately	Head of a household
2,000	2,025	201	201	201	201
2,025	2,050	204	204	204	204
2,050	2,075	206	206	206	206
2,075	2,100	209	209	209	209
2,100	2,125	211	211	211	211
2,125	2,150	214	214	214	214
2,150	2,175	216	216	216	216
2,175	2,200	219	219	219	219
2,200	2,225	221	221	221	221
2,225	2,250	224	224	224	224
2,250	2,275	226	226	226	226
2,275	2,300	229	229	229	229
2,300	2,325	231	231	231	231
2,325	2,350	234	234	234	234
2,350	2,375	236	236	236	236
2,375	2,400	239	239	239	239
2,400	2,425	241	241	241	241
2,425	2,450	244	244	244	244
2,450	2,475	246	246	246	246
2,475	2,500	249	249	249	249
2,500	2,525	251	251	251	251
2,525	2,550	254	254	254	254
2,550	2,575	256	256	256	256
2,575	2,600	259	259	259	259
2,600	2,625	261	261	261	261
2,625	2,650	264	264	264	264
2,650	2,675	266	266	266	266
2,675	2,700	269	269	269	269

If line 43 (taxable income) is— At least	But less than	Single	Married filing jointly *	Married filing separately	Head of a household
			Your tax is—		
2,700	2,725	271	271	271	271
2,725	2,750	274	274	274	274
2,750	2,775	276	276	276	276
2,775	2,800	279	279	279	279
2,800	2,825	281	281	281	281
2,825	2,850	284	284	284	284
2,850	2,875	286	286	286	286
2,875	2,900	289	289	289	289
2,900	2,925	291	291	291	291
2,925	2,950	294	294	294	294
2,950	2,975	296	296	296	296
2,975	3,000	299	299	299	299

3,000

At least	But less than	Single	Married filing jointly *	Married filing separately	Head of a household
3,000	3,050	303	303	303	303
3,050	3,100	308	308	308	308
3,100	3,150	313	313	313	313
3,150	3,200	318	318	318	318
3,200	3,250	323	323	323	323
3,250	3,300	328	328	328	328
3,300	3,350	333	333	333	333
3,350	3,400	338	338	338	338
3,400	3,450	343	343	343	343
3,450	3,500	348	348	348	348
3,500	3,550	353	353	353	353
3,550	3,600	358	358	358	358
3,600	3,650	363	363	363	363
3,650	3,700	368	368	368	368
3,700	3,750	373	373	373	373
3,750	3,800	378	378	378	378
3,800	3,850	383	383	383	383
3,850	3,900	388	388	388	388
3,900	3,950	393	393	393	393
3,950	4,000	398	398	398	398

4,000

At least	But less than	Single	Married filing jointly *	Married filing separately	Head of a household
4,000	4,050	403	403	403	403
4,050	4,100	408	408	408	408
4,100	4,150	413	413	413	413
4,150	4,200	418	418	418	418
4,200	4,250	423	423	423	423
4,250	4,300	428	428	428	428
4,300	4,350	433	433	433	433
4,350	4,400	438	438	438	438
4,400	4,450	443	443	443	443
4,450	4,500	448	448	448	448
4,500	4,550	453	453	453	453
4,550	4,600	458	458	458	458
4,600	4,650	463	463	463	463
4,650	4,700	468	468	468	468
4,700	4,750	473	473	473	473
4,750	4,800	478	478	478	478
4,800	4,850	483	483	483	483
4,850	4,900	488	488	488	488
4,900	4,950	493	493	493	493
4,950	5,000	498	498	498	498

* This column must also be used by a qualifying widow(er).

(Continued on page T-3)

2009 Tax Table– *Continued*

If line 43 (taxable income) is— At least	But less than	And you are— Single	Married filing jointly*	Married filing separately	Head of a house-hold
5,000					
5,000	5,050	503	503	503	503
5,050	5,100	508	508	508	508
5,100	5,150	513	513	513	513
5,150	5,200	518	518	518	518
5,200	5,250	523	523	523	523
5,250	5,300	528	528	528	528
5,300	5,350	533	533	533	533
5,350	5,400	538	538	538	538
5,400	5,450	543	543	543	543
5,450	5,500	548	548	548	548
5,500	5,550	553	553	553	553
5,550	5,600	558	558	558	558
5,600	5,650	563	563	563	563
5,650	5,700	568	568	568	568
5,700	5,750	573	573	573	573
5,750	5,800	578	578	578	578
5,800	5,850	583	583	583	583
5,850	5,900	588	588	588	588
5,900	5,950	593	593	593	593
5,950	6,000	598	598	598	598
6,000					
6,000	6,050	603	603	603	603
6,050	6,100	608	608	608	608
6,100	6,150	613	613	613	613
6,150	6,200	618	618	618	618
6,200	6,250	623	623	623	623
6,250	6,300	628	628	628	628
6,300	6,350	633	633	633	633
6,350	6,400	638	638	638	638
6,400	6,450	643	643	643	643
6,450	6,500	648	648	648	648
6,500	6,550	653	653	653	653
6,550	6,600	658	658	658	658
6,600	6,650	663	663	663	663
6,650	6,700	668	668	668	668
6,700	6,750	673	673	673	673
6,750	6,800	678	678	678	678
6,800	6,850	683	683	683	683
6,850	6,900	688	688	688	688
6,900	6,950	693	693	693	693
6,950	7,000	698	698	698	698
7,000					
7,000	7,050	703	703	703	703
7,050	7,100	708	708	708	708
7,100	7,150	713	713	713	713
7,150	7,200	718	718	718	718
7,200	7,250	723	723	723	723
7,250	7,300	728	728	728	728
7,300	7,350	733	733	733	733
7,350	7,400	738	738	738	738
7,400	7,450	743	743	743	743
7,450	7,500	748	748	748	748
7,500	7,550	753	753	753	753
7,550	7,600	758	758	758	758
7,600	7,650	763	763	763	763
7,650	7,700	768	768	768	768
7,700	7,750	773	773	773	773
7,750	7,800	778	778	778	778
7,800	7,850	783	783	783	783
7,850	7,900	788	788	788	788
7,900	7,950	793	793	793	793
7,950	8,000	798	798	798	798

If line 43 (taxable income) is— At least	But less than	And you are— Single	Married filing jointly*	Married filing separately	Head of a house-hold
8,000					
8,000	8,050	803	803	803	803
8,050	8,100	808	808	808	808
8,100	8,150	813	813	813	813
8,150	8,200	818	818	818	818
8,200	8,250	823	823	823	823
8,250	8,300	828	828	828	828
8,300	8,350	833	833	833	833
8,350	8,400	839	838	839	838
8,400	8,450	846	843	846	843
8,450	8,500	854	848	854	848
8,500	8,550	861	853	861	853
8,550	8,600	869	858	869	858
8,600	8,650	876	863	876	863
8,650	8,700	884	868	884	868
8,700	8,750	891	873	891	873
8,750	8,800	899	878	899	878
8,800	8,850	906	883	906	883
8,850	8,900	914	888	914	888
8,900	8,950	921	893	921	893
8,950	9,000	929	898	929	898
9,000					
9,000	9,050	936	903	936	903
9,050	9,100	944	908	944	908
9,100	9,150	951	913	951	913
9,150	9,200	959	918	959	918
9,200	9,250	966	923	966	923
9,250	9,300	974	928	974	928
9,300	9,350	981	933	981	933
9,350	9,400	989	938	989	938
9,400	9,450	996	943	996	943
9,450	9,500	1,004	948	1,004	948
9,500	9,550	1,011	953	1,011	953
9,550	9,600	1,019	958	1,019	958
9,600	9,650	1,026	963	1,026	963
9,650	9,700	1,034	968	1,034	968
9,700	9,750	1,041	973	1,041	973
9,750	9,800	1,049	978	1,049	978
9,800	9,850	1,056	983	1,056	983
9,850	9,900	1,064	988	1,064	988
9,900	9,950	1,071	993	1,071	993
9,950	10,000	1,079	998	1,079	998
10,000					
10,000	10,050	1,086	1,003	1,086	1,003
10,050	10,100	1,094	1,008	1,094	1,008
10,100	10,150	1,101	1,013	1,101	1,013
10,150	10,200	1,109	1,018	1,109	1,018
10,200	10,250	1,116	1,023	1,116	1,023
10,250	10,300	1,124	1,028	1,124	1,028
10,300	10,350	1,131	1,033	1,131	1,033
10,350	10,400	1,139	1,038	1,139	1,038
10,400	10,450	1,146	1,043	1,146	1,043
10,450	10,500	1,154	1,048	1,154	1,048
10,500	10,550	1,161	1,053	1,161	1,053
10,550	10,600	1,169	1,058	1,169	1,058
10,600	10,650	1,176	1,063	1,176	1,063
10,650	10,700	1,184	1,068	1,184	1,068
10,700	10,750	1,191	1,073	1,191	1,073
10,750	10,800	1,199	1,078	1,199	1,078
10,800	10,850	1,206	1,083	1,206	1,083
10,850	10,900	1,214	1,088	1,214	1,088
10,900	10,950	1,221	1,093	1,221	1,093
10,950	11,000	1,229	1,098	1,229	1,098

If line 43 (taxable income) is— At least	But less than	And you are— Single	Married filing jointly*	Married filing separately	Head of a house-hold
11,000					
11,000	11,050	1,236	1,103	1,236	1,103
11,050	11,100	1,244	1,108	1,244	1,108
11,100	11,150	1,251	1,113	1,251	1,113
11,150	11,200	1,259	1,118	1,259	1,118
11,200	11,250	1,266	1,123	1,266	1,123
11,250	11,300	1,274	1,128	1,274	1,128
11,300	11,350	1,281	1,133	1,281	1,133
11,350	11,400	1,289	1,138	1,289	1,138
11,400	11,450	1,296	1,143	1,296	1,143
11,450	11,500	1,304	1,148	1,304	1,148
11,500	11,550	1,311	1,153	1,311	1,153
11,550	11,600	1,319	1,158	1,319	1,158
11,600	11,650	1,326	1,163	1,326	1,163
11,650	11,700	1,334	1,168	1,334	1,168
11,700	11,750	1,341	1,173	1,341	1,173
11,750	11,800	1,349	1,178	1,349	1,178
11,800	11,850	1,356	1,183	1,356	1,183
11,850	11,900	1,364	1,188	1,364	1,188
11,900	11,950	1,371	1,193	1,371	1,193
11,950	12,000	1,379	1,198	1,379	1,199
12,000					
12,000	12,050	1,386	1,203	1,386	1,206
12,050	12,100	1,394	1,208	1,394	1,214
12,100	12,150	1,401	1,213	1,401	1,221
12,150	12,200	1,409	1,218	1,409	1,229
12,200	12,250	1,416	1,223	1,416	1,236
12,250	12,300	1,424	1,228	1,424	1,244
12,300	12,350	1,431	1,233	1,431	1,251
12,350	12,400	1,439	1,238	1,439	1,259
12,400	12,450	1,446	1,243	1,446	1,266
12,450	12,500	1,454	1,248	1,454	1,274
12,500	12,550	1,461	1,253	1,461	1,281
12,550	12,600	1,469	1,258	1,469	1,289
12,600	12,650	1,476	1,263	1,476	1,296
12,650	12,700	1,484	1,268	1,484	1,304
12,700	12,750	1,491	1,273	1,491	1,311
12,750	12,800	1,499	1,278	1,499	1,319
12,800	12,850	1,506	1,283	1,506	1,326
12,850	12,900	1,514	1,288	1,514	1,334
12,900	12,950	1,521	1,293	1,521	1,341
12,950	13,000	1,529	1,298	1,529	1,349
13,000					
13,000	13,050	1,536	1,303	1,536	1,356
13,050	13,100	1,544	1,308	1,544	1,364
13,100	13,150	1,551	1,313	1,551	1,371
13,150	13,200	1,559	1,318	1,559	1,379
13,200	13,250	1,566	1,323	1,566	1,386
13,250	13,300	1,574	1,328	1,574	1,394
13,300	13,350	1,581	1,333	1,581	1,401
13,350	13,400	1,589	1,338	1,589	1,409
13,400	13,450	1,596	1,343	1,596	1,416
13,450	13,500	1,604	1,348	1,604	1,424
13,500	13,550	1,611	1,353	1,611	1,431
13,550	13,600	1,619	1,358	1,619	1,439
13,600	13,650	1,626	1,363	1,626	1,446
13,650	13,700	1,634	1,368	1,634	1,454
13,700	13,750	1,641	1,373	1,641	1,461
13,750	13,800	1,649	1,378	1,649	1,469
13,800	13,850	1,656	1,383	1,656	1,476
13,850	13,900	1,664	1,388	1,664	1,484
13,900	13,950	1,671	1,393	1,671	1,491
13,950	14,000	1,679	1,398	1,679	1,499

* This column must also be used by a qualifying widow(er).

(Continued on page T-4)

2009 Tax Table– *Continued*

If line 43 (taxable income) is—		And you are—			
At least	But less than	Single	Married filing jointly *	Married filing separately	Head of a household
		Your tax is—			

14,000

At least	But less than	Single	MFJ	MFS	HoH
14,000	14,050	1,686	1,403	1,686	1,506
14,050	14,100	1,694	1,408	1,694	1,514
14,100	14,150	1,701	1,413	1,701	1,521
14,150	14,200	1,709	1,418	1,709	1,529
14,200	14,250	1,716	1,423	1,716	1,536
14,250	14,300	1,724	1,428	1,724	1,544
14,300	14,350	1,731	1,433	1,731	1,551
14,350	14,400	1,739	1,438	1,739	1,559
14,400	14,450	1,746	1,443	1,746	1,566
14,450	14,500	1,754	1,448	1,754	1,574
14,500	14,550	1,761	1,453	1,761	1,581
14,550	14,600	1,769	1,458	1,769	1,589
14,600	14,650	1,776	1,463	1,776	1,596
14,650	14,700	1,784	1,468	1,784	1,604
14,700	14,750	1,791	1,473	1,791	1,611
14,750	14,800	1,799	1,478	1,799	1,619
14,800	14,850	1,806	1,483	1,806	1,626
14,850	14,900	1,814	1,488	1,814	1,634
14,900	14,950	1,821	1,493	1,821	1,641
14,950	15,000	1,829	1,498	1,829	1,649

15,000

At least	But less than	Single	MFJ	MFS	HoH
15,000	15,050	1,836	1,503	1,836	1,656
15,050	15,100	1,844	1,508	1,844	1,664
15,100	15,150	1,851	1,513	1,851	1,671
15,150	15,200	1,859	1,518	1,859	1,679
15,200	15,250	1,866	1,523	1,866	1,686
15,250	15,300	1,874	1,528	1,874	1,694
15,300	15,350	1,881	1,533	1,881	1,701
15,350	15,400	1,889	1,538	1,889	1,709
15,400	15,450	1,896	1,543	1,896	1,716
15,450	15,500	1,904	1,548	1,904	1,724
15,500	15,550	1,911	1,553	1,911	1,731
15,550	15,600	1,919	1,558	1,919	1,739
15,600	15,650	1,926	1,563	1,926	1,746
15,650	15,700	1,934	1,568	1,934	1,754
15,700	15,750	1,941	1,573	1,941	1,761
15,750	15,800	1,949	1,578	1,949	1,769
15,800	15,850	1,956	1,583	1,956	1,776
15,850	15,900	1,964	1,588	1,964	1,784
15,900	15,950	1,971	1,593	1,971	1,791
15,950	16,000	1,979	1,598	1,979	1,799

16,000

At least	But less than	Single	MFJ	MFS	HoH
16,000	16,050	1,986	1,603	1,986	1,806
16,050	16,100	1,994	1,608	1,994	1,814
16,100	16,150	2,001	1,613	2,001	1,821
16,150	16,200	2,009	1,618	2,009	1,829
16,200	16,250	2,016	1,623	2,016	1,836
16,250	16,300	2,024	1,628	2,024	1,844
16,300	16,350	2,031	1,633	2,031	1,851
16,350	16,400	2,039	1,638	2,039	1,859
16,400	16,450	2,046	1,643	2,046	1,866
16,450	16,500	2,054	1,648	2,054	1,874
16,500	16,550	2,061	1,653	2,061	1,881
16,550	16,600	2,069	1,658	2,069	1,889
16,600	16,650	2,076	1,663	2,076	1,896
16,650	16,700	2,084	1,668	2,084	1,904
16,700	16,750	2,091	1,674	2,091	1,911
16,750	16,800	2,099	1,681	2,099	1,919
16,800	16,850	2,106	1,689	2,106	1,926
16,850	16,900	2,114	1,696	2,114	1,934
16,900	16,950	2,121	1,704	2,121	1,941
16,950	17,000	2,129	1,711	2,129	1,949

17,000

At least	But less than	Single	MFJ	MFS	HoH
17,000	17,050	2,136	1,719	2,136	1,956
17,050	17,100	2,144	1,726	2,144	1,964
17,100	17,150	2,151	1,734	2,151	1,971
17,150	17,200	2,159	1,741	2,159	1,979
17,200	17,250	2,166	1,749	2,166	1,986
17,250	17,300	2,174	1,756	2,174	1,994
17,300	17,350	2,181	1,764	2,181	2,001
17,350	17,400	2,189	1,771	2,189	2,009
17,400	17,450	2,196	1,779	2,196	2,016
17,450	17,500	2,204	1,786	2,204	2,024
17,500	17,550	2,211	1,794	2,211	2,031
17,550	17,600	2,219	1,801	2,219	2,039
17,600	17,650	2,226	1,809	2,226	2,046
17,650	17,700	2,234	1,816	2,234	2,054
17,700	17,750	2,241	1,824	2,241	2,061
17,750	17,800	2,249	1,831	2,249	2,069
17,800	17,850	2,256	1,839	2,256	2,076
17,850	17,900	2,264	1,846	2,264	2,084
17,900	17,950	2,271	1,854	2,271	2,091
17,950	18,000	2,279	1,861	2,279	2,099

18,000

At least	But less than	Single	MFJ	MFS	HoH
18,000	18,050	2,286	1,869	2,286	2,106
18,050	18,100	2,294	1,876	2,294	2,114
18,100	18,150	2,301	1,884	2,301	2,121
18,150	18,200	2,309	1,891	2,309	2,129
18,200	18,250	2,316	1,899	2,316	2,136
18,250	18,300	2,324	1,906	2,324	2,144
18,300	18,350	2,331	1,914	2,331	2,151
18,350	18,400	2,339	1,921	2,339	2,159
18,400	18,450	2,346	1,929	2,346	2,166
18,450	18,500	2,354	1,936	2,354	2,174
18,500	18,550	2,361	1,944	2,361	2,181
18,550	18,600	2,369	1,951	2,369	2,189
18,600	18,650	2,376	1,959	2,376	2,196
18,650	18,700	2,384	1,966	2,384	2,204
18,700	18,750	2,391	1,974	2,391	2,211
18,750	18,800	2,399	1,981	2,399	2,219
18,800	18,850	2,406	1,989	2,406	2,226
18,850	18,900	2,414	1,996	2,414	2,234
18,900	18,950	2,421	2,004	2,421	2,241
18,950	19,000	2,429	2,011	2,429	2,249

19,000

At least	But less than	Single	MFJ	MFS	HoH
19,000	19,050	2,436	2,019	2,436	2,256
19,050	19,100	2,444	2,026	2,444	2,264
19,100	19,150	2,451	2,034	2,451	2,271
19,150	19,200	2,459	2,041	2,459	2,279
19,200	19,250	2,466	2,049	2,466	2,286
19,250	19,300	2,474	2,056	2,474	2,294
19,300	19,350	2,481	2,064	2,481	2,301
19,350	19,400	2,489	2,071	2,489	2,309
19,400	19,450	2,496	2,079	2,496	2,316
19,450	19,500	2,504	2,086	2,504	2,324
19,500	19,550	2,511	2,094	2,511	2,331
19,550	19,600	2,519	2,101	2,519	2,339
19,600	19,650	2,526	2,109	2,526	2,346
19,650	19,700	2,534	2,116	2,534	2,354
19,700	19,750	2,541	2,124	2,541	2,361
19,750	19,800	2,549	2,131	2,549	2,369
19,800	19,850	2,556	2,139	2,556	2,376
19,850	19,900	2,564	2,146	2,564	2,384
19,900	19,950	2,571	2,154	2,571	2,391
19,950	20,000	2,579	2,161	2,579	2,399

20,000

At least	But less than	Single	MFJ	MFS	HoH
20,000	20,050	2,586	2,169	2,586	2,406
20,050	20,100	2,594	2,176	2,594	2,414
20,100	20,150	2,601	2,184	2,601	2,421
20,150	20,200	2,609	2,191	2,609	2,429
20,200	20,250	2,616	2,199	2,616	2,436
20,250	20,300	2,624	2,206	2,624	2,444
20,300	20,350	2,631	2,214	2,631	2,451
20,350	20,400	2,639	2,221	2,639	2,459
20,400	20,450	2,646	2,229	2,646	2,466
20,450	20,500	2,654	2,236	2,654	2,474
20,500	20,550	2,661	2,244	2,661	2,481
20,550	20,600	2,669	2,251	2,669	2,489
20,600	20,650	2,676	2,259	2,676	2,496
20,650	20,700	2,684	2,266	2,684	2,504
20,700	20,750	2,691	2,274	2,691	2,511
20,750	20,800	2,699	2,281	2,699	2,519
20,800	20,850	2,706	2,289	2,706	2,526
20,850	20,900	2,714	2,296	2,714	2,534
20,900	20,950	2,721	2,304	2,721	2,541
20,950	21,000	2,729	2,311	2,729	2,549

21,000

At least	But less than	Single	MFJ	MFS	HoH
21,000	21,050	2,736	2,319	2,736	2,556
21,050	21,100	2,744	2,326	2,744	2,564
21,100	21,150	2,751	2,334	2,751	2,571
21,150	21,200	2,759	2,341	2,759	2,579
21,200	21,250	2,766	2,349	2,766	2,586
21,250	21,300	2,774	2,356	2,774	2,594
21,300	21,350	2,781	2,364	2,781	2,601
21,350	21,400	2,789	2,371	2,789	2,609
21,400	21,450	2,796	2,379	2,796	2,616
21,450	21,500	2,804	2,386	2,804	2,624
21,500	21,550	2,811	2,394	2,811	2,631
21,550	21,600	2,819	2,401	2,819	2,639
21,600	21,650	2,826	2,409	2,826	2,646
21,650	21,700	2,834	2,416	2,834	2,654
21,700	21,750	2,841	2,424	2,841	2,661
21,750	21,800	2,849	2,431	2,849	2,669
21,800	21,850	2,856	2,439	2,856	2,676
21,850	21,900	2,864	2,446	2,864	2,684
21,900	21,950	2,871	2,454	2,871	2,691
21,950	22,000	2,879	2,461	2,879	2,699

22,000

At least	But less than	Single	MFJ	MFS	HoH
22,000	22,050	2,886	2,469	2,886	2,706
22,050	22,100	2,894	2,476	2,894	2,714
22,100	22,150	2,901	2,484	2,901	2,721
22,150	22,200	2,909	2,491	2,909	2,729
22,200	22,250	2,916	2,499	2,916	2,736
22,250	22,300	2,924	2,506	2,924	2,744
22,300	22,350	2,931	2,514	2,931	2,751
22,350	22,400	2,939	2,521	2,939	2,759
22,400	22,450	2,946	2,529	2,946	2,766
22,450	22,500	2,954	2,536	2,954	2,774
22,500	22,550	2,961	2,544	2,961	2,781
22,550	22,600	2,969	2,551	2,969	2,789
22,600	22,650	2,976	2,559	2,976	2,796
22,650	22,700	2,984	2,566	2,984	2,804
22,700	22,750	2,991	2,574	2,991	2,811
22,750	22,800	2,999	2,581	2,999	2,819
22,800	22,850	3,006	2,589	3,006	2,826
22,850	22,900	3,014	2,596	3,014	2,834
22,900	22,950	3,021	2,604	3,021	2,841
22,950	23,000	3,029	2,611	3,029	2,849

* This column must also be used by a qualifying widow(er).

(Continued on page T-5)

2009 Tax Table– *Continued*

If line 43 (taxable income) is—		And you are—			
At least	But less than	Single	Married filing jointly *	Married filing separately	Head of a household
		Your tax is—			

23,000

At least	But less than	Single	Married filing jointly	Married filing separately	Head of a household
23,000	23,050	3,036	2,619	3,036	2,856
23,050	23,100	3,044	2,626	3,044	2,864
23,100	23,150	3,051	2,634	3,051	2,871
23,150	23,200	3,059	2,641	3,059	2,879
23,200	23,250	3,066	2,649	3,066	2,886
23,250	23,300	3,074	2,656	3,074	2,894
23,300	23,350	3,081	2,664	3,081	2,901
23,350	23,400	3,089	2,671	3,089	2,909
23,400	23,450	3,096	2,679	3,096	2,916
23,450	23,500	3,104	2,686	3,104	2,924
23,500	23,550	3,111	2,694	3,111	2,931
23,550	23,600	3,119	2,701	3,119	2,939
23,600	23,650	3,126	2,709	3,126	2,946
23,650	23,700	3,134	2,716	3,134	2,954
23,700	23,750	3,141	2,724	3,141	2,961
23,750	23,800	3,149	2,731	3,149	2,969
23,800	23,850	3,156	2,739	3,156	2,976
23,850	23,900	3,164	2,746	3,164	2,984
23,900	23,950	3,171	2,754	3,171	2,991
23,950	24,000	3,179	2,761	3,179	2,999

24,000

At least	But less than	Single	Married filing jointly	Married filing separately	Head of a household
24,000	24,050	3,186	2,769	3,186	3,006
24,050	24,100	3,194	2,776	3,194	3,014
24,100	24,150	3,201	2,784	3,201	3,021
24,150	24,200	3,209	2,791	3,209	3,029
24,200	24,250	3,216	2,799	3,216	3,036
24,250	24,300	3,224	2,806	3,224	3,044
24,300	24,350	3,231	2,814	3,231	3,051
24,350	24,400	3,239	2,821	3,239	3,059
24,400	24,450	3,246	2,829	3,246	3,066
24,450	24,500	3,254	2,836	3,254	3,074
24,500	24,550	3,261	2,844	3,261	3,081
24,550	24,600	3,269	2,851	3,269	3,089
24,600	24,650	3,276	2,859	3,276	3,096
24,650	24,700	3,284	2,866	3,284	3,104
24,700	24,750	3,291	2,874	3,291	3,111
24,750	24,800	3,299	2,881	3,299	3,119
24,800	24,850	3,306	2,889	3,306	3,126
24,850	24,900	3,314	2,896	3,314	3,134
24,900	24,950	3,321	2,904	3,321	3,141
24,950	25,000	3,329	2,911	3,329	3,149

25,000

At least	But less than	Single	Married filing jointly	Married filing separately	Head of a household
25,000	25,050	3,336	2,919	3,336	3,156
25,050	25,100	3,344	2,926	3,344	3,164
25,100	25,150	3,351	2,934	3,351	3,171
25,150	25,200	3,359	2,941	3,359	3,179
25,200	25,250	3,366	2,949	3,366	3,186
25,250	25,300	3,374	2,956	3,374	3,194
25,300	25,350	3,381	2,964	3,381	3,201
25,350	25,400	3,389	2,971	3,389	3,209
25,400	25,450	3,396	2,979	3,396	3,216
25,450	25,500	3,404	2,986	3,404	3,224
25,500	25,550	3,411	2,994	3,411	3,231
25,550	25,600	3,419	3,001	3,419	3,239
25,600	25,650	3,426	3,009	3,426	3,246
25,650	25,700	3,434	3,016	3,434	3,254
25,700	25,750	3,441	3,024	3,441	3,261
25,750	25,800	3,449	3,031	3,449	3,269
25,800	25,850	3,456	3,039	3,456	3,276
25,850	25,900	3,464	3,046	3,464	3,284
25,900	25,950	3,471	3,054	3,471	3,291
25,950	26,000	3,479	3,061	3,479	3,299

26,000

At least	But less than	Single	Married filing jointly	Married filing separately	Head of a household
26,000	26,050	3,486	3,069	3,486	3,306
26,050	26,100	3,494	3,076	3,494	3,314
26,100	26,150	3,501	3,084	3,501	3,321
26,150	26,200	3,509	3,091	3,509	3,329
26,200	26,250	3,516	3,099	3,516	3,336
26,250	26,300	3,524	3,106	3,524	3,344
26,300	26,350	3,531	3,114	3,531	3,351
26,350	26,400	3,539	3,121	3,539	3,359
26,400	26,450	3,546	3,129	3,546	3,366
26,450	26,500	3,554	3,136	3,554	3,374
26,500	26,550	3,561	3,144	3,561	3,381
26,550	26,600	3,569	3,151	3,569	3,389
26,600	26,650	3,576	3,159	3,576	3,396
26,650	26,700	3,584	3,166	3,584	3,404
26,700	26,750	3,591	3,174	3,591	3,411
26,750	26,800	3,599	3,181	3,599	3,419
26,800	26,850	3,606	3,189	3,606	3,426
26,850	26,900	3,614	3,196	3,614	3,434
26,900	26,950	3,621	3,204	3,621	3,441
26,950	27,000	3,629	3,211	3,629	3,449

27,000

At least	But less than	Single	Married filing jointly	Married filing separately	Head of a household
27,000	27,050	3,636	3,219	3,636	3,456
27,050	27,100	3,644	3,226	3,644	3,464
27,100	27,150	3,651	3,234	3,651	3,471
27,150	27,200	3,659	3,241	3,659	3,479
27,200	27,250	3,666	3,249	3,666	3,486
27,250	27,300	3,674	3,256	3,674	3,494
27,300	27,350	3,681	3,264	3,681	3,501
27,350	27,400	3,689	3,271	3,689	3,509
27,400	27,450	3,696	3,279	3,696	3,516
27,450	27,500	3,704	3,286	3,704	3,524
27,500	27,550	3,711	3,294	3,711	3,531
27,550	27,600	3,719	3,301	3,719	3,539
27,600	27,650	3,726	3,309	3,726	3,546
27,650	27,700	3,734	3,316	3,734	3,554
27,700	27,750	3,741	3,324	3,741	3,561
27,750	27,800	3,749	3,331	3,749	3,569
27,800	27,850	3,756	3,339	3,756	3,576
27,850	27,900	3,764	3,346	3,764	3,584
27,900	27,950	3,771	3,354	3,771	3,591
27,950	28,000	3,779	3,361	3,779	3,599

28,000

At least	But less than	Single	Married filing jointly	Married filing separately	Head of a household
28,000	28,050	3,786	3,369	3,786	3,606
28,050	28,100	3,794	3,376	3,794	3,614
28,100	28,150	3,801	3,384	3,801	3,621
28,150	28,200	3,809	3,391	3,809	3,629
28,200	28,250	3,816	3,399	3,816	3,636
28,250	28,300	3,824	3,406	3,824	3,644
28,300	28,350	3,831	3,414	3,831	3,651
28,350	28,400	3,839	3,421	3,839	3,659
28,400	28,450	3,846	3,429	3,846	3,666
28,450	28,500	3,854	3,436	3,854	3,674
28,500	28,550	3,861	3,444	3,861	3,681
28,550	28,600	3,869	3,451	3,869	3,689
28,600	28,650	3,876	3,459	3,876	3,696
28,650	28,700	3,884	3,466	3,884	3,704
28,700	28,750	3,891	3,474	3,891	3,711
28,750	28,800	3,899	3,481	3,899	3,719
28,800	28,850	3,906	3,489	3,906	3,726
28,850	28,900	3,914	3,496	3,914	3,734
28,900	28,950	3,921	3,504	3,921	3,741
28,950	29,000	3,929	3,511	3,929	3,749

29,000

At least	But less than	Single	Married filing jointly	Married filing separately	Head of a household
29,000	29,050	3,936	3,519	3,936	3,756
29,050	29,100	3,944	3,526	3,944	3,764
29,100	29,150	3,951	3,534	3,951	3,771
29,150	29,200	3,959	3,541	3,959	3,779
29,200	29,250	3,966	3,549	3,966	3,786
29,250	29,300	3,974	3,556	3,974	3,794
29,300	29,350	3,981	3,564	3,981	3,801
29,350	29,400	3,989	3,571	3,989	3,809
29,400	29,450	3,996	3,579	3,996	3,816
29,450	29,500	4,004	3,586	4,004	3,824
29,500	29,550	4,011	3,594	4,011	3,831
29,550	29,600	4,019	3,601	4,019	3,839
29,600	29,650	4,026	3,609	4,026	3,846
29,650	29,700	4,034	3,616	4,034	3,854
29,700	29,750	4,041	3,624	4,041	3,861
29,750	29,800	4,049	3,631	4,049	3,869
29,800	29,850	4,056	3,639	4,056	3,876
29,850	29,900	4,064	3,646	4,064	3,884
29,900	29,950	4,071	3,654	4,071	3,891
29,950	30,000	4,079	3,661	4,079	3,899

30,000

At least	But less than	Single	Married filing jointly	Married filing separately	Head of a household
30,000	30,050	4,086	3,669	4,086	3,906
30,050	30,100	4,094	3,676	4,094	3,914
30,100	30,150	4,101	3,684	4,101	3,921
30,150	30,200	4,109	3,691	4,109	3,929
30,200	30,250	4,116	3,699	4,116	3,936
30,250	30,300	4,124	3,706	4,124	3,944
30,300	30,350	4,131	3,714	4,131	3,951
30,350	30,400	4,139	3,721	4,139	3,959
30,400	30,450	4,146	3,729	4,146	3,966
30,450	30,500	4,154	3,736	4,154	3,974
30,500	30,550	4,161	3,744	4,161	3,981
30,550	30,600	4,169	3,751	4,169	3,989
30,600	30,650	4,176	3,759	4,176	3,996
30,650	30,700	4,184	3,766	4,184	4,004
30,700	30,750	4,191	3,774	4,191	4,011
30,750	30,800	4,199	3,781	4,199	4,019
30,800	30,850	4,206	3,789	4,206	4,026
30,850	30,900	4,214	3,796	4,214	4,034
30,900	30,950	4,221	3,804	4,221	4,041
30,950	31,000	4,229	3,811	4,229	4,049

31,000

At least	But less than	Single	Married filing jointly	Married filing separately	Head of a household
31,000	31,050	4,236	3,819	4,236	4,056
31,050	31,100	4,244	3,826	4,244	4,064
31,100	31,150	4,251	3,834	4,251	4,071
31,150	31,200	4,259	3,841	4,259	4,079
31,200	31,250	4,266	3,849	4,266	4,086
31,250	31,300	4,274	3,856	4,274	4,094
31,300	31,350	4,281	3,864	4,281	4,101
31,350	31,400	4,289	3,871	4,289	4,109
31,400	31,450	4,296	3,879	4,296	4,116
31,450	31,500	4,304	3,886	4,304	4,124
31,500	31,550	4,311	3,894	4,311	4,131
31,550	31,600	4,319	3,901	4,319	4,139
31,600	31,650	4,326	3,909	4,326	4,146
31,650	31,700	4,334	3,916	4,334	4,154
31,700	31,750	4,341	3,924	4,341	4,161
31,750	31,800	4,349	3,931	4,349	4,169
31,800	31,850	4,356	3,939	4,356	4,176
31,850	31,900	4,364	3,946	4,364	4,184
31,900	31,950	4,371	3,954	4,371	4,191
31,950	32,000	4,379	3,961	4,379	4,199

* This column must also be used by a qualifying widow(er).

(Continued on page T-6)

2009 Tax Table– Continued

If line 43 (taxable income) is— At least	But less than	Single	Married filing jointly *	Married filing separately	Head of a house-hold
			Your tax is—		

32,000

At least	But less than	Single	Married filing jointly *	Married filing separately	Head of a household
32,000	32,050	4,386	3,969	4,386	4,206
32,050	32,100	4,394	3,976	4,394	4,214
32,100	32,150	4,401	3,984	4,401	4,221
32,150	32,200	4,409	3,991	4,409	4,229
32,200	32,250	4,416	3,999	4,416	4,236
32,250	32,300	4,424	4,006	4,424	4,244
32,300	32,350	4,431	4,014	4,431	4,251
32,350	32,400	4,439	4,021	4,439	4,259
32,400	32,450	4,446	4,029	4,446	4,266
32,450	32,500	4,454	4,036	4,454	4,274
32,500	32,550	4,461	4,044	4,461	4,281
32,550	32,600	4,469	4,051	4,469	4,289
32,600	32,650	4,476	4,059	4,476	4,296
32,650	32,700	4,484	4,066	4,484	4,304
32,700	32,750	4,491	4,074	4,491	4,311
32,750	32,800	4,499	4,081	4,499	4,319
32,800	32,850	4,506	4,089	4,506	4,326
32,850	32,900	4,514	4,096	4,514	4,334
32,900	32,950	4,521	4,104	4,521	4,341
32,950	33,000	4,529	4,111	4,529	4,349

33,000

At least	But less than	Single	Married filing jointly *	Married filing separately	Head of a household
33,000	33,050	4,536	4,119	4,536	4,356
33,050	33,100	4,544	4,126	4,544	4,364
33,100	33,150	4,551	4,134	4,551	4,371
33,150	33,200	4,559	4,141	4,559	4,379
33,200	33,250	4,566	4,149	4,566	4,386
33,250	33,300	4,574	4,156	4,574	4,394
33,300	33,350	4,581	4,164	4,581	4,401
33,350	33,400	4,589	4,171	4,589	4,409
33,400	33,450	4,596	4,179	4,596	4,416
33,450	33,500	4,604	4,186	4,604	4,424
33,500	33,550	4,611	4,194	4,611	4,431
33,550	33,600	4,619	4,201	4,619	4,439
33,600	33,650	4,626	4,209	4,626	4,446
33,650	33,700	4,634	4,216	4,634	4,454
33,700	33,750	4,641	4,224	4,641	4,461
33,750	33,800	4,649	4,231	4,649	4,469
33,800	33,850	4,656	4,239	4,656	4,476
33,850	33,900	4,664	4,246	4,664	4,484
33,900	33,950	4,671	4,254	4,671	4,491
33,950	34,000	4,681	4,261	4,681	4,499

34,000

At least	But less than	Single	Married filing jointly *	Married filing separately	Head of a household
34,000	34,050	4,694	4,269	4,694	4,506
34,050	34,100	4,706	4,276	4,706	4,514
34,100	34,150	4,719	4,284	4,719	4,521
34,150	34,200	4,731	4,291	4,731	4,529
34,200	34,250	4,744	4,299	4,744	4,536
34,250	34,300	4,756	4,306	4,756	4,544
34,300	34,350	4,769	4,314	4,769	4,551
34,350	34,400	4,781	4,321	4,781	4,559
34,400	34,450	4,794	4,329	4,794	4,566
34,450	34,500	4,806	4,336	4,806	4,574
34,500	34,550	4,819	4,344	4,819	4,581
34,550	34,600	4,831	4,351	4,831	4,589
34,600	34,650	4,844	4,359	4,844	4,596
34,650	34,700	4,856	4,366	4,856	4,604
34,700	34,750	4,869	4,374	4,869	4,611
34,750	34,800	4,881	4,381	4,881	4,619
34,800	34,850	4,894	4,389	4,894	4,626
34,850	34,900	4,906	4,396	4,906	4,634
34,900	34,950	4,919	4,404	4,919	4,641
34,950	35,000	4,931	4,411	4,931	4,649

35,000

At least	But less than	Single	Married filing jointly *	Married filing separately	Head of a household
35,000	35,050	4,944	4,419	4,944	4,656
35,050	35,100	4,956	4,426	4,956	4,664
35,100	35,150	4,969	4,434	4,969	4,671
35,150	35,200	4,981	4,441	4,981	4,679
35,200	35,250	4,994	4,449	4,994	4,686
35,250	35,300	5,006	4,456	5,006	4,694
35,300	35,350	5,019	4,464	5,019	4,701
35,350	35,400	5,031	4,471	5,031	4,709
35,400	35,450	5,044	4,479	5,044	4,716
35,450	35,500	5,056	4,486	5,056	4,724
35,500	35,550	5,069	4,494	5,069	4,731
35,550	35,600	5,081	4,501	5,081	4,739
35,600	35,650	5,094	4,509	5,094	4,746
35,650	35,700	5,106	4,516	5,106	4,754
35,700	35,750	5,119	4,524	5,119	4,761
35,750	35,800	5,131	4,531	5,131	4,769
35,800	35,850	5,144	4,539	5,144	4,776
35,850	35,900	5,156	4,546	5,156	4,784
35,900	35,950	5,169	4,554	5,169	4,791
35,950	36,000	5,181	4,561	5,181	4,799

36,000

At least	But less than	Single	Married filing jointly *	Married filing separately	Head of a household
36,000	36,050	5,194	4,569	5,194	4,806
36,050	36,100	5,206	4,576	5,206	4,814
36,100	36,150	5,219	4,584	5,219	4,821
36,150	36,200	5,231	4,591	5,231	4,829
36,200	36,250	5,244	4,599	5,244	4,836
36,250	36,300	5,256	4,606	5,256	4,844
36,300	36,350	5,269	4,614	5,269	4,851
36,350	36,400	5,281	4,621	5,281	4,859
36,400	36,450	5,294	4,629	5,294	4,866
36,450	36,500	5,306	4,636	5,306	4,874
36,500	36,550	5,319	4,644	5,319	4,881
36,550	36,600	5,331	4,651	5,331	4,889
36,600	36,650	5,344	4,659	5,344	4,896
36,650	36,700	5,356	4,666	5,356	4,904
36,700	36,750	5,369	4,674	5,369	4,911
36,750	36,800	5,381	4,681	5,381	4,919
36,800	36,850	5,394	4,689	5,394	4,926
36,850	36,900	5,406	4,696	5,406	4,934
36,900	36,950	5,419	4,704	5,419	4,941
36,950	37,000	5,431	4,711	5,431	4,949

37,000

At least	But less than	Single	Married filing jointly *	Married filing separately	Head of a household
37,000	37,050	5,444	4,719	5,444	4,956
37,050	37,100	5,456	4,726	5,456	4,964
37,100	37,150	5,469	4,734	5,469	4,971
37,150	37,200	5,481	4,741	5,481	4,979
37,200	37,250	5,494	4,749	5,494	4,986
37,250	37,300	5,506	4,756	5,506	4,994
37,300	37,350	5,519	4,764	5,519	5,001
37,350	37,400	5,531	4,771	5,531	5,009
37,400	37,450	5,544	4,779	5,544	5,016
37,450	37,500	5,556	4,786	5,556	5,024
37,500	37,550	5,569	4,794	5,569	5,031
37,550	37,600	5,581	4,801	5,581	5,039
37,600	37,650	5,594	4,809	5,594	5,046
37,650	37,700	5,606	4,816	5,606	5,054
37,700	37,750	5,619	4,824	5,619	5,061
37,750	37,800	5,631	4,831	5,631	5,069
37,800	37,850	5,644	4,839	5,644	5,076
37,850	37,900	5,656	4,846	5,656	5,084
37,900	37,950	5,669	4,854	5,669	5,091
37,950	38,000	5,681	4,861	5,681	5,099

38,000

At least	But less than	Single	Married filing jointly *	Married filing separately	Head of a household
38,000	38,050	5,694	4,869	5,694	5,106
38,050	38,100	5,706	4,876	5,706	5,114
38,100	38,150	5,719	4,884	5,719	5,121
38,150	38,200	5,731	4,891	5,731	5,129
38,200	38,250	5,744	4,899	5,744	5,136
38,250	38,300	5,756	4,906	5,756	5,144
38,300	38,350	5,769	4,914	5,769	5,151
38,350	38,400	5,781	4,921	5,781	5,159
38,400	38,450	5,794	4,929	5,794	5,166
38,450	38,500	5,806	4,936	5,806	5,174
38,500	38,550	5,819	4,944	5,819	5,181
38,550	38,600	5,831	4,951	5,831	5,189
38,600	38,650	5,844	4,959	5,844	5,196
38,650	38,700	5,856	4,966	5,856	5,204
38,700	38,750	5,869	4,974	5,869	5,211
38,750	38,800	5,881	4,981	5,881	5,219
38,800	38,850	5,894	4,989	5,894	5,226
38,850	38,900	5,906	4,996	5,906	5,234
38,900	38,950	5,919	5,004	5,919	5,241
38,950	39,000	5,931	5,011	5,931	5,249

39,000

At least	But less than	Single	Married filing jointly *	Married filing separately	Head of a household
39,000	39,050	5,944	5,019	5,944	5,256
39,050	39,100	5,956	5,026	5,956	5,264
39,100	39,150	5,969	5,034	5,969	5,271
39,150	39,200	5,981	5,041	5,981	5,279
39,200	39,250	5,994	5,049	5,994	5,286
39,250	39,300	6,006	5,056	6,006	5,294
39,300	39,350	6,019	5,064	6,019	5,301
39,350	39,400	6,031	5,071	6,031	5,309
39,400	39,450	6,044	5,079	6,044	5,316
39,450	39,500	6,056	5,086	6,056	5,324
39,500	39,550	6,069	5,094	6,069	5,331
39,550	39,600	6,081	5,101	6,081	5,339
39,600	39,650	6,094	5,109	6,094	5,346
39,650	39,700	6,106	5,116	6,106	5,354
39,700	39,750	6,119	5,124	6,119	5,361
39,750	39,800	6,131	5,131	6,131	5,369
39,800	39,850	6,144	5,139	6,144	5,376
39,850	39,900	6,156	5,146	6,156	5,384
39,900	39,950	6,169	5,154	6,169	5,391
39,950	40,000	6,181	5,161	6,181	5,399

40,000

At least	But less than	Single	Married filing jointly *	Married filing separately	Head of a household
40,000	40,050	6,194	5,169	6,194	5,406
40,050	40,100	6,206	5,176	6,206	5,414
40,100	40,150	6,219	5,184	6,219	5,421
40,150	40,200	6,231	5,191	6,231	5,429
40,200	40,250	6,244	5,199	6,244	5,436
40,250	40,300	6,256	5,206	6,256	5,444
40,300	40,350	6,269	5,214	6,269	5,451
40,350	40,400	6,281	5,221	6,281	5,459
40,400	40,450	6,294	5,229	6,294	5,466
40,450	40,500	6,306	5,236	6,306	5,474
40,500	40,550	6,319	5,244	6,319	5,481
40,550	40,600	6,331	5,251	6,331	5,489
40,600	40,650	6,344	5,259	6,344	5,496
40,650	40,700	6,356	5,266	6,356	5,504
40,700	40,750	6,369	5,274	6,369	5,511
40,750	40,800	6,381	5,281	6,381	5,519
40,800	40,850	6,394	5,289	6,394	5,526
40,850	40,900	6,406	5,296	6,406	5,534
40,900	40,950	6,419	5,304	6,419	5,541
40,950	41,000	6,431	5,311	6,431	5,549

* This column must also be used by a qualifying widow(er).

(Continued on page T-7)

2009 Tax Table– *Continued*

If line 43 (taxable income) is—		And you are—			
At least	But less than	Single	Married filing jointly *	Married filing separately	Head of a household
		Your tax is—			

41,000

At least	But less than	Single	MFJ *	MFS	HoH
41,000	41,050	6,444	5,319	6,444	5,556
41,050	41,100	6,456	5,326	6,456	5,564
41,100	41,150	6,469	5,334	6,469	5,571
41,150	41,200	6,481	5,341	6,481	5,579
41,200	41,250	6,494	5,349	6,494	5,586
41,250	41,300	6,506	5,356	6,506	5,594
41,300	41,350	6,519	5,364	6,519	5,601
41,350	41,400	6,531	5,371	6,531	5,609
41,400	41,450	6,544	5,379	6,544	5,616
41,450	41,500	6,556	5,386	6,556	5,624
41,500	41,550	6,569	5,394	6,569	5,631
41,550	41,600	6,581	5,401	6,581	5,639
41,600	41,650	6,594	5,409	6,594	5,646
41,650	41,700	6,606	5,416	6,606	5,654
41,700	41,750	6,619	5,424	6,619	5,661
41,750	41,800	6,631	5,431	6,631	5,669
41,800	41,850	6,644	5,439	6,644	5,676
41,850	41,900	6,656	5,446	6,656	5,684
41,900	41,950	6,669	5,454	6,669	5,691
41,950	42,000	6,681	5,461	6,681	5,699

42,000

At least	But less than	Single	MFJ *	MFS	HoH
42,000	42,050	6,694	5,469	6,694	5,706
42,050	42,100	6,706	5,476	6,706	5,714
42,100	42,150	6,719	5,484	6,719	5,721
42,150	42,200	6,731	5,491	6,731	5,729
42,200	42,250	6,744	5,499	6,744	5,736
42,250	42,300	6,756	5,506	6,756	5,744
42,300	42,350	6,769	5,514	6,769	5,751
42,350	42,400	6,781	5,521	6,781	5,759
42,400	42,450	6,794	5,529	6,794	5,766
42,450	42,500	6,806	5,536	6,806	5,774
42,500	42,550	6,819	5,544	6,819	5,781
42,550	42,600	6,831	5,551	6,831	5,789
42,600	42,650	6,844	5,559	6,844	5,796
42,650	42,700	6,856	5,566	6,856	5,804
42,700	42,750	6,869	5,574	6,869	5,811
42,750	42,800	6,881	5,581	6,881	5,819
42,800	42,850	6,894	5,589	6,894	5,826
42,850	42,900	6,906	5,596	6,906	5,834
42,900	42,950	6,919	5,604	6,919	5,841
42,950	43,000	6,931	5,611	6,931	5,849

43,000

At least	But less than	Single	MFJ *	MFS	HoH
43,000	43,050	6,944	5,619	6,944	5,856
43,050	43,100	6,956	5,626	6,956	5,864
43,100	43,150	6,969	5,634	6,969	5,871
43,150	43,200	6,981	5,641	6,981	5,879
43,200	43,250	6,994	5,649	6,994	5,886
43,250	43,300	7,006	5,656	7,006	5,894
43,300	43,350	7,019	5,664	7,019	5,901
43,350	43,400	7,031	5,671	7,031	5,909
43,400	43,450	7,044	5,679	7,044	5,916
43,450	43,500	7,056	5,686	7,056	5,924
43,500	43,550	7,069	5,694	7,069	5,931
43,550	43,600	7,081	5,701	7,081	5,939
43,600	43,650	7,094	5,709	7,094	5,946
43,650	43,700	7,106	5,716	7,106	5,954
43,700	43,750	7,119	5,724	7,119	5,961
43,750	43,800	7,131	5,731	7,131	5,969
43,800	43,850	7,144	5,739	7,144	5,976
43,850	43,900	7,156	5,746	7,156	5,984
43,900	43,950	7,169	5,754	7,169	5,991
43,950	44,000	7,181	5,761	7,181	5,999

44,000

At least	But less than	Single	MFJ *	MFS	HoH
44,000	44,050	7,194	5,769	7,194	6,006
44,050	44,100	7,206	5,776	7,206	6,014
44,100	44,150	7,219	5,784	7,219	6,021
44,150	44,200	7,231	5,791	7,231	6,029
44,200	44,250	7,244	5,799	7,244	6,036
44,250	44,300	7,256	5,806	7,256	6,044
44,300	44,350	7,269	5,814	7,269	6,051
44,350	44,400	7,281	5,821	7,281	6,059
44,400	44,450	7,294	5,829	7,294	6,066
44,450	44,500	7,306	5,836	7,306	6,074
44,500	44,550	7,319	5,844	7,319	6,081
44,550	44,600	7,331	5,851	7,331	6,089
44,600	44,650	7,344	5,859	7,344	6,096
44,650	44,700	7,356	5,866	7,356	6,104
44,700	44,750	7,369	5,874	7,369	6,111
44,750	44,800	7,381	5,881	7,381	6,119
44,800	44,850	7,394	5,889	7,394	6,126
44,850	44,900	7,406	5,896	7,406	6,134
44,900	44,950	7,419	5,904	7,419	6,141
44,950	45,000	7,431	5,911	7,431	6,149

45,000

At least	But less than	Single	MFJ *	MFS	HoH
45,000	45,050	7,444	5,919	7,444	6,156
45,050	45,100	7,456	5,926	7,456	6,164
45,100	45,150	7,469	5,934	7,469	6,171
45,150	45,200	7,481	5,941	7,481	6,179
45,200	45,250	7,494	5,949	7,494	6,186
45,250	45,300	7,506	5,956	7,506	6,194
45,300	45,350	7,519	5,964	7,519	6,201
45,350	45,400	7,531	5,971	7,531	6,209
45,400	45,450	7,544	5,979	7,544	6,216
45,450	45,500	7,556	5,986	7,556	6,224
45,500	45,550	7,569	5,994	7,569	6,234
45,550	45,600	7,581	6,001	7,581	6,246
45,600	45,650	7,594	6,009	7,594	6,259
45,650	45,700	7,606	6,016	7,606	6,271
45,700	45,750	7,619	6,024	7,619	6,284
45,750	45,800	7,631	6,031	7,631	6,296
45,800	45,850	7,644	6,039	7,644	6,309
45,850	45,900	7,656	6,046	7,656	6,321
45,900	45,950	7,669	6,054	7,669	6,334
45,950	46,000	7,681	6,061	7,681	6,346

46,000

At least	But less than	Single	MFJ *	MFS	HoH
46,000	46,050	7,694	6,069	7,694	6,359
46,050	46,100	7,706	6,076	7,706	6,371
46,100	46,150	7,719	6,084	7,719	6,384
46,150	46,200	7,731	6,091	7,731	6,396
46,200	46,250	7,744	6,099	7,744	6,409
46,250	46,300	7,756	6,106	7,756	6,421
46,300	46,350	7,769	6,114	7,769	6,434
46,350	46,400	7,781	6,121	7,781	6,446
46,400	46,450	7,794	6,129	7,794	6,459
46,450	46,500	7,806	6,136	7,806	6,471
46,500	46,550	7,819	6,144	7,819	6,484
46,550	46,600	7,831	6,151	7,831	6,496
46,600	46,650	7,844	6,159	7,844	6,509
46,650	46,700	7,856	6,166	7,856	6,521
46,700	46,750	7,869	6,174	7,869	6,534
46,750	46,800	7,881	6,181	7,881	6,546
46,800	46,850	7,894	6,189	7,894	6,559
46,850	46,900	7,906	6,196	7,906	6,571
46,900	46,950	7,919	6,204	7,919	6,584
46,950	47,000	7,931	6,211	7,931	6,596

47,000

At least	But less than	Single	MFJ *	MFS	HoH
47,000	47,050	7,944	6,219	7,944	6,609
47,050	47,100	7,956	6,226	7,956	6,621
47,100	47,150	7,969	6,234	7,969	6,634
47,150	47,200	7,981	6,241	7,981	6,646
47,200	47,250	7,994	6,249	7,994	6,659
47,250	47,300	8,006	6,256	8,006	6,671
47,300	47,350	8,019	6,264	8,019	6,684
47,350	47,400	8,031	6,271	8,031	6,696
47,400	47,450	8,044	6,279	8,044	6,709
47,450	47,500	8,056	6,286	8,056	6,721
47,500	47,550	8,069	6,294	8,069	6,734
47,550	47,600	8,081	6,301	8,081	6,746
47,600	47,650	8,094	6,309	8,094	6,759
47,650	47,700	8,106	6,316	8,106	6,771
47,700	47,750	8,119	6,324	8,119	6,784
47,750	47,800	8,131	6,331	8,131	6,796
47,800	47,850	8,144	6,339	8,144	6,809
47,850	47,900	8,156	6,346	8,156	6,821
47,900	47,950	8,169	6,354	8,169	6,834
47,950	48,000	8,181	6,361	8,181	6,846

48,000

At least	But less than	Single	MFJ *	MFS	HoH
48,000	48,050	8,194	6,369	8,194	6,859
48,050	48,100	8,206	6,376	8,206	6,871
48,100	48,150	8,219	6,384	8,219	6,884
48,150	48,200	8,231	6,391	8,231	6,896
48,200	48,250	8,244	6,399	8,244	6,909
48,250	48,300	8,256	6,406	8,256	6,921
48,300	48,350	8,269	6,414	8,269	6,934
48,350	48,400	8,281	6,421	8,281	6,946
48,400	48,450	8,294	6,429	8,294	6,959
48,450	48,500	8,306	6,436	8,306	6,971
48,500	48,550	8,319	6,444	8,319	6,984
48,550	48,600	8,331	6,451	8,331	6,996
48,600	48,650	8,344	6,459	8,344	7,009
48,650	48,700	8,356	6,466	8,356	7,021
48,700	48,750	8,369	6,474	8,369	7,034
48,750	48,800	8,381	6,481	8,381	7,046
48,800	48,850	8,394	6,489	8,394	7,059
48,850	48,900	8,406	6,496	8,406	7,071
48,900	48,950	8,419	6,504	8,419	7,084
48,950	49,000	8,431	6,511	8,431	7,096

49,000

At least	But less than	Single	MFJ *	MFS	HoH
49,000	49,050	8,444	6,519	8,444	7,109
49,050	49,100	8,456	6,526	8,456	7,121
49,100	49,150	8,469	6,534	8,469	7,134
49,150	49,200	8,481	6,541	8,481	7,146
49,200	49,250	8,494	6,549	8,494	7,159
49,250	49,300	8,506	6,556	8,506	7,171
49,300	49,350	8,519	6,564	8,519	7,184
49,350	49,400	8,531	6,571	8,531	7,196
49,400	49,450	8,544	6,579	8,544	7,209
49,450	49,500	8,556	6,586	8,556	7,221
49,500	49,550	8,569	6,594	8,569	7,234
49,550	49,600	8,581	6,601	8,581	7,246
49,600	49,650	8,594	6,609	8,594	7,259
49,650	49,700	8,606	6,616	8,606	7,271
49,700	49,750	8,619	6,624	8,619	7,284
49,750	49,800	8,631	6,631	8,631	7,296
49,800	49,850	8,644	6,639	8,644	7,309
49,850	49,900	8,656	6,646	8,656	7,321
49,900	49,950	8,669	6,654	8,669	7,334
49,950	50,000	8,681	6,661	8,681	7,346

* This column must also be used by a qualifying widow(er).

(Continued on page T-8)

2009 Tax Table– *Continued*

If line 43 (taxable income) is—		And you are—			
At least	But less than	Single	Married filing jointly *	Married filing separately	Head of a household
		Your tax is—			

50,000

At least	But less than	Single	Married filing jointly	Married filing separately	Head of a household
50,000	50,050	8,694	6,669	8,694	7,359
50,050	50,100	8,706	6,676	8,706	7,371
50,100	50,150	8,719	6,684	8,719	7,384
50,150	50,200	8,731	6,691	8,731	7,396
50,200	50,250	8,744	6,699	8,744	7,409
50,250	50,300	8,756	6,706	8,756	7,421
50,300	50,350	8,769	6,714	8,769	7,434
50,350	50,400	8,781	6,721	8,781	7,446
50,400	50,450	8,794	6,729	8,794	7,459
50,450	50,500	8,806	6,736	8,806	7,471
50,500	50,550	8,819	6,744	8,819	7,484
50,550	50,600	8,831	6,751	8,831	7,496
50,600	50,650	8,844	6,759	8,844	7,509
50,650	50,700	8,856	6,766	8,856	7,521
50,700	50,750	8,869	6,774	8,869	7,534
50,750	50,800	8,881	6,781	8,881	7,546
50,800	50,850	8,894	6,789	8,894	7,559
50,850	50,900	8,906	6,796	8,906	7,571
50,900	50,950	8,919	6,804	8,919	7,584
50,950	51,000	8,931	6,811	8,931	7,596

51,000

At least	But less than	Single	Married filing jointly	Married filing separately	Head of a household
51,000	51,050	8,944	6,819	8,944	7,609
51,050	51,100	8,956	6,826	8,956	7,621
51,100	51,150	8,969	6,834	8,969	7,634
51,150	51,200	8,981	6,841	8,981	7,646
51,200	51,250	8,994	6,849	8,994	7,659
51,250	51,300	9,006	6,856	9,006	7,671
51,300	51,350	9,019	6,864	9,019	7,684
51,350	51,400	9,031	6,871	9,031	7,696
51,400	51,450	9,044	6,879	9,044	7,709
51,450	51,500	9,056	6,886	9,056	7,721
51,500	51,550	9,069	6,894	9,069	7,734
51,550	51,600	9,081	6,901	9,081	7,746
51,600	51,650	9,094	6,909	9,094	7,759
51,650	51,700	9,106	6,916	9,106	7,771
51,700	51,750	9,119	6,924	9,119	7,784
51,750	51,800	9,131	6,931	9,131	7,796
51,800	51,850	9,144	6,939	9,144	7,809
51,850	51,900	9,156	6,946	9,156	7,821
51,900	51,950	9,169	6,954	9,169	7,834
51,950	52,000	9,181	6,961	9,181	7,846

52,000

At least	But less than	Single	Married filing jointly	Married filing separately	Head of a household
52,000	52,050	9,194	6,969	9,194	7,859
52,050	52,100	9,206	6,976	9,206	7,871
52,100	52,150	9,219	6,984	9,219	7,884
52,150	52,200	9,231	6,991	9,231	7,896
52,200	52,250	9,244	6,999	9,244	7,909
52,250	52,300	9,256	7,006	9,256	7,921
52,300	52,350	9,269	7,014	9,269	7,934
52,350	52,400	9,281	7,021	9,281	7,946
52,400	52,450	9,294	7,029	9,294	7,959
52,450	52,500	9,306	7,036	9,306	7,971
52,500	52,550	9,319	7,044	9,319	7,984
52,550	52,600	9,331	7,051	9,331	7,996
52,600	52,650	9,344	7,059	9,344	8,009
52,650	52,700	9,356	7,066	9,356	8,021
52,700	52,750	9,369	7,074	9,369	8,034
52,750	52,800	9,381	7,081	9,381	8,046
52,800	52,850	9,394	7,089	9,394	8,059
52,850	52,900	9,406	7,096	9,406	8,071
52,900	52,950	9,419	7,104	9,419	8,084
52,950	53,000	9,431	7,111	9,431	8,096

53,000

At least	But less than	Single	Married filing jointly	Married filing separately	Head of a household
53,000	53,050	9,444	7,119	9,444	8,109
53,050	53,100	9,456	7,126	9,456	8,121
53,100	53,150	9,469	7,134	9,469	8,134
53,150	53,200	9,481	7,141	9,481	8,146
53,200	53,250	9,494	7,149	9,494	8,159
53,250	53,300	9,506	7,156	9,506	8,171
53,300	53,350	9,519	7,164	9,519	8,184
53,350	53,400	9,531	7,171	9,531	8,196
53,400	53,450	9,544	7,179	9,544	8,209
53,450	53,500	9,556	7,186	9,556	8,221
53,500	53,550	9,569	7,194	9,569	8,234
53,550	53,600	9,581	7,201	9,581	8,246
53,600	53,650	9,594	7,209	9,594	8,259
53,650	53,700	9,606	7,216	9,606	8,271
53,700	53,750	9,619	7,224	9,619	8,284
53,750	53,800	9,631	7,231	9,631	8,296
53,800	53,850	9,644	7,239	9,644	8,309
53,850	53,900	9,656	7,246	9,656	8,321
53,900	53,950	9,669	7,254	9,669	8,334
53,950	54,000	9,681	7,261	9,681	8,346

54,000

At least	But less than	Single	Married filing jointly	Married filing separately	Head of a household
54,000	54,050	9,694	7,269	9,694	8,359
54,050	54,100	9,706	7,276	9,706	8,371
54,100	54,150	9,719	7,284	9,719	8,384
54,150	54,200	9,731	7,291	9,731	8,396
54,200	54,250	9,744	7,299	9,744	8,409
54,250	54,300	9,756	7,306	9,756	8,421
54,300	54,350	9,769	7,314	9,769	8,434
54,350	54,400	9,781	7,321	9,781	8,446
54,400	54,450	9,794	7,329	9,794	8,459
54,450	54,500	9,806	7,336	9,806	8,471
54,500	54,550	9,819	7,344	9,819	8,484
54,550	54,600	9,831	7,351	9,831	8,496
54,600	54,650	9,844	7,359	9,844	8,509
54,650	54,700	9,856	7,366	9,856	8,521
54,700	54,750	9,869	7,374	9,869	8,534
54,750	54,800	9,881	7,381	9,881	8,546
54,800	54,850	9,894	7,389	9,894	8,559
54,850	54,900	9,906	7,396	9,906	8,571
54,900	54,950	9,919	7,404	9,919	8,584
54,950	55,000	9,931	7,411	9,931	8,596

55,000

At least	But less than	Single	Married filing jointly	Married filing separately	Head of a household
55,000	55,050	9,944	7,419	9,944	8,609
55,050	55,100	9,956	7,426	9,956	8,621
55,100	55,150	9,969	7,434	9,969	8,634
55,150	55,200	9,981	7,441	9,981	8,646
55,200	55,250	9,994	7,449	9,994	8,659
55,250	55,300	10,006	7,456	10,006	8,671
55,300	55,350	10,019	7,464	10,019	8,684
55,350	55,400	10,031	7,471	10,031	8,696
55,400	55,450	10,044	7,479	10,044	8,709
55,450	55,500	10,056	7,486	10,056	8,721
55,500	55,550	10,069	7,494	10,069	8,734
55,550	55,600	10,081	7,501	10,081	8,746
55,600	55,650	10,094	7,509	10,094	8,759
55,650	55,700	10,106	7,516	10,106	8,771
55,700	55,750	10,119	7,524	10,119	8,784
55,750	55,800	10,131	7,531	10,131	8,796
55,800	55,850	10,144	7,539	10,144	8,809
55,850	55,900	10,156	7,546	10,156	8,821
55,900	55,950	10,169	7,554	10,169	8,834
55,950	56,000	10,181	7,561	10,181	8,846

56,000

At least	But less than	Single	Married filing jointly	Married filing separately	Head of a household
56,000	56,050	10,194	7,569	10,194	8,859
56,050	56,100	10,206	7,576	10,206	8,871
56,100	56,150	10,219	7,584	10,219	8,884
56,150	56,200	10,231	7,591	10,231	8,896
56,200	56,250	10,244	7,599	10,244	8,909
56,250	56,300	10,256	7,606	10,256	8,921
56,300	56,350	10,269	7,614	10,269	8,934
56,350	56,400	10,281	7,621	10,281	8,946
56,400	56,450	10,294	7,629	10,294	8,959
56,450	56,500	10,306	7,636	10,306	8,971
56,500	56,550	10,319	7,644	10,319	8,984
56,550	56,600	10,331	7,651	10,331	8,996
56,600	56,650	10,344	7,659	10,344	9,009
56,650	56,700	10,356	7,666	10,356	9,021
56,700	56,750	10,369	7,674	10,369	9,034
56,750	56,800	10,381	7,681	10,381	9,046
56,800	56,850	10,394	7,689	10,394	9,059
56,850	56,900	10,406	7,696	10,406	9,071
56,900	56,950	10,419	7,704	10,419	9,084
56,950	57,000	10,431	7,711	10,431	9,096

57,000

At least	But less than	Single	Married filing jointly	Married filing separately	Head of a household
57,000	57,050	10,444	7,719	10,444	9,109
57,050	57,100	10,456	7,726	10,456	9,121
57,100	57,150	10,469	7,734	10,469	9,134
57,150	57,200	10,481	7,741	10,481	9,146
57,200	57,250	10,494	7,749	10,494	9,159
57,250	57,300	10,506	7,756	10,506	9,171
57,300	57,350	10,519	7,764	10,519	9,184
57,350	57,400	10,531	7,771	10,531	9,196
57,400	57,450	10,544	7,779	10,544	9,209
57,450	57,500	10,556	7,786	10,556	9,221
57,500	57,550	10,569	7,794	10,569	9,234
57,550	57,600	10,581	7,801	10,581	9,246
57,600	57,650	10,594	7,809	10,594	9,259
57,650	57,700	10,606	7,816	10,606	9,271
57,700	57,750	10,619	7,824	10,619	9,284
57,750	57,800	10,631	7,831	10,631	9,296
57,800	57,850	10,644	7,839	10,644	9,309
57,850	57,900	10,656	7,846	10,656	9,321
57,900	57,950	10,669	7,854	10,669	9,334
57,950	58,000	10,681	7,861	10,681	9,346

58,000

At least	But less than	Single	Married filing jointly	Married filing separately	Head of a household
58,000	58,050	10,694	7,869	10,694	9,359
58,050	58,100	10,706	7,876	10,706	9,371
58,100	58,150	10,719	7,884	10,719	9,384
58,150	58,200	10,731	7,891	10,731	9,396
58,200	58,250	10,744	7,899	10,744	9,409
58,250	58,300	10,756	7,906	10,756	9,421
58,300	58,350	10,769	7,914	10,769	9,434
58,350	58,400	10,781	7,921	10,781	9,446
58,400	58,450	10,794	7,929	10,794	9,459
58,450	58,500	10,806	7,936	10,806	9,471
58,500	58,550	10,819	7,944	10,819	9,484
58,550	58,600	10,831	7,951	10,831	9,496
58,600	58,650	10,844	7,959	10,844	9,509
58,650	58,700	10,856	7,966	10,856	9,521
58,700	58,750	10,869	7,974	10,869	9,534
58,750	58,800	10,881	7,981	10,881	9,546
58,800	58,850	10,894	7,989	10,894	9,559
58,850	58,900	10,906	7,996	10,906	9,571
58,900	58,950	10,919	8,004	10,919	9,584
58,950	59,000	10,931	8,011	10,931	9,596

* This column must also be used by a qualifying widow(er).

(Continued on page T-9)

2009 Tax Table– *Continued*

If line 43 (taxable income) is—		And you are—			
At least	But less than	Single	Married filing jointly *	Married filing separately	Head of a household
		Your tax is—			

59,000

At least	But less than	Single	Married filing jointly	Married filing separately	Head of a household
59,000	59,050	10,944	8,019	10,944	9,609
59,050	59,100	10,956	8,026	10,956	9,621
59,100	59,150	10,969	8,034	10,969	9,634
59,150	59,200	10,981	8,041	10,981	9,646
59,200	59,250	10,994	8,049	10,994	9,659
59,250	59,300	11,006	8,056	11,006	9,671
59,300	59,350	11,019	8,064	11,019	9,684
59,350	59,400	11,031	8,071	11,031	9,696
59,400	59,450	11,044	8,079	11,044	9,709
59,450	59,500	11,056	8,086	11,056	9,721
59,500	59,550	11,069	8,094	11,069	9,734
59,550	59,600	11,081	8,101	11,081	9,746
59,600	59,650	11,094	8,109	11,094	9,759
59,650	59,700	11,106	8,116	11,106	9,771
59,700	59,750	11,119	8,124	11,119	9,784
59,750	59,800	11,131	8,131	11,131	9,796
59,800	59,850	11,144	8,139	11,144	9,809
59,850	59,900	11,156	8,146	11,156	9,821
59,900	59,950	11,169	8,154	11,169	9,834
59,950	60,000	11,181	8,161	11,181	9,846

60,000

At least	But less than	Single	Married filing jointly	Married filing separately	Head of a household
60,000	60,050	11,194	8,169	11,194	9,859
60,050	60,100	11,206	8,176	11,206	9,871
60,100	60,150	11,219	8,184	11,219	9,884
60,150	60,200	11,231	8,191	11,231	9,896
60,200	60,250	11,244	8,199	11,244	9,909
60,250	60,300	11,256	8,206	11,256	9,921
60,300	60,350	11,269	8,214	11,269	9,934
60,350	60,400	11,281	8,221	11,281	9,946
60,400	60,450	11,294	8,229	11,294	9,959
60,450	60,500	11,306	8,236	11,306	9,971
60,500	60,550	11,319	8,244	11,319	9,984
60,550	60,600	11,331	8,251	11,331	9,996
60,600	60,650	11,344	8,259	11,344	10,009
60,650	60,700	11,356	8,266	11,356	10,021
60,700	60,750	11,369	8,274	11,369	10,034
60,750	60,800	11,381	8,281	11,381	10,046
60,800	60,850	11,394	8,289	11,394	10,059
60,850	60,900	11,406	8,296	11,406	10,071
60,900	60,950	11,419	8,304	11,419	10,084
60,950	61,000	11,431	8,311	11,431	10,096

61,000

At least	But less than	Single	Married filing jointly	Married filing separately	Head of a household
61,000	61,050	11,444	8,319	11,444	10,109
61,050	61,100	11,456	8,326	11,456	10,121
61,100	61,150	11,469	8,334	11,469	10,134
61,150	61,200	11,481	8,341	11,481	10,146
61,200	61,250	11,494	8,349	11,494	10,159
61,250	61,300	11,506	8,356	11,506	10,171
61,300	61,350	11,519	8,364	11,519	10,184
61,350	61,400	11,531	8,371	11,531	10,196
61,400	61,450	11,544	8,379	11,544	10,209
61,450	61,500	11,556	8,386	11,556	10,221
61,500	61,550	11,569	8,394	11,569	10,234
61,550	61,600	11,581	8,401	11,581	10,246
61,600	61,650	11,594	8,409	11,594	10,259
61,650	61,700	11,606	8,416	11,606	10,271
61,700	61,750	11,619	8,424	11,619	10,284
61,750	61,800	11,631	8,431	11,631	10,296
61,800	61,850	11,644	8,439	11,644	10,309
61,850	61,900	11,656	8,446	11,656	10,321
61,900	61,950	11,669	8,454	11,669	10,334
61,950	62,000	11,681	8,461	11,681	10,346

62,000

At least	But less than	Single	Married filing jointly	Married filing separately	Head of a household
62,000	62,050	11,694	8,469	11,694	10,359
62,050	62,100	11,706	8,476	11,706	10,371
62,100	62,150	11,719	8,484	11,719	10,384
62,150	62,200	11,731	8,491	11,731	10,396
62,200	62,250	11,744	8,499	11,744	10,409
62,250	62,300	11,756	8,506	11,756	10,421
62,300	62,350	11,769	8,514	11,769	10,434
62,350	62,400	11,781	8,521	11,781	10,446
62,400	62,450	11,794	8,529	11,794	10,459
62,450	62,500	11,806	8,536	11,806	10,471
62,500	62,550	11,819	8,544	11,819	10,484
62,550	62,600	11,831	8,551	11,831	10,496
62,600	62,650	11,844	8,559	11,844	10,509
62,650	62,700	11,856	8,566	11,856	10,521
62,700	62,750	11,869	8,574	11,869	10,534
62,750	62,800	11,881	8,581	11,881	10,546
62,800	62,850	11,894	8,589	11,894	10,559
62,850	62,900	11,906	8,596	11,906	10,571
62,900	62,950	11,919	8,604	11,919	10,584
62,950	63,000	11,931	8,611	11,931	10,596

63,000

At least	But less than	Single	Married filing jointly	Married filing separately	Head of a household
63,000	63,050	11,944	8,619	11,944	10,609
63,050	63,100	11,956	8,626	11,956	10,621
63,100	63,150	11,969	8,634	11,969	10,634
63,150	63,200	11,981	8,641	11,981	10,646
63,200	63,250	11,994	8,649	11,994	10,659
63,250	63,300	12,006	8,656	12,006	10,671
63,300	63,350	12,019	8,664	12,019	10,684
63,350	63,400	12,031	8,671	12,031	10,696
63,400	63,450	12,044	8,679	12,044	10,709
63,450	63,500	12,056	8,686	12,056	10,721
63,500	63,550	12,069	8,694	12,069	10,734
63,550	63,600	12,081	8,701	12,081	10,746
63,600	63,650	12,094	8,709	12,094	10,759
63,650	63,700	12,106	8,716	12,106	10,771
63,700	63,750	12,119	8,724	12,119	10,784
63,750	63,800	12,131	8,731	12,131	10,796
63,800	63,850	12,144	8,739	12,144	10,809
63,850	63,900	12,156	8,746	12,156	10,821
63,900	63,950	12,169	8,754	12,169	10,834
63,950	64,000	12,181	8,761	12,181	10,846

64,000

At least	But less than	Single	Married filing jointly	Married filing separately	Head of a household
64,000	64,050	12,194	8,769	12,194	10,859
64,050	64,100	12,206	8,776	12,206	10,871
64,100	64,150	12,219	8,784	12,219	10,884
64,150	64,200	12,231	8,791	12,231	10,896
64,200	64,250	12,244	8,799	12,244	10,909
64,250	64,300	12,256	8,806	12,256	10,921
64,300	64,350	12,269	8,814	12,269	10,934
64,350	64,400	12,281	8,821	12,281	10,946
64,400	64,450	12,294	8,829	12,294	10,959
64,450	64,500	12,306	8,836	12,306	10,971
64,500	64,550	12,319	8,844	12,319	10,984
64,550	64,600	12,331	8,851	12,331	10,996
64,600	64,650	12,344	8,859	12,344	11,009
64,650	64,700	12,356	8,866	12,356	11,021
64,700	64,750	12,369	8,874	12,369	11,034
64,750	64,800	12,381	8,881	12,381	11,046
64,800	64,850	12,394	8,889	12,394	11,059
64,850	64,900	12,406	8,896	12,406	11,071
64,900	64,950	12,419	8,904	12,419	11,084
64,950	65,000	12,431	8,911	12,431	11,096

65,000

At least	But less than	Single	Married filing jointly	Married filing separately	Head of a household
65,000	65,050	12,444	8,919	12,444	11,109
65,050	65,100	12,456	8,926	12,456	11,121
65,100	65,150	12,469	8,934	12,469	11,134
65,150	65,200	12,481	8,941	12,481	11,146
65,200	65,250	12,494	8,949	12,494	11,159
65,250	65,300	12,506	8,956	12,506	11,171
65,300	65,350	12,519	8,964	12,519	11,184
65,350	65,400	12,531	8,971	12,531	11,196
65,400	65,450	12,544	8,979	12,544	11,209
65,450	65,500	12,556	8,986	12,556	11,221
65,500	65,550	12,569	8,994	12,569	11,234
65,550	65,600	12,581	9,001	12,581	11,246
65,600	65,650	12,594	9,009	12,594	11,259
65,650	65,700	12,606	9,016	12,606	11,271
65,700	65,750	12,619	9,024	12,619	11,284
65,750	65,800	12,631	9,031	12,631	11,296
65,800	65,850	12,644	9,039	12,644	11,309
65,850	65,900	12,656	9,046	12,656	11,321
65,900	65,950	12,669	9,054	12,669	11,334
65,950	66,000	12,681	9,061	12,681	11,346

66,000

At least	But less than	Single	Married filing jointly	Married filing separately	Head of a household
66,000	66,050	12,694	9,069	12,694	11,359
66,050	66,100	12,706	9,076	12,706	11,371
66,100	66,150	12,719	9,084	12,719	11,384
66,150	66,200	12,731	9,091	12,731	11,396
66,200	66,250	12,744	9,099	12,744	11,409
66,250	66,300	12,756	9,106	12,756	11,421
66,300	66,350	12,769	9,114	12,769	11,434
66,350	66,400	12,781	9,121	12,781	11,446
66,400	66,450	12,794	9,129	12,794	11,459
66,450	66,500	12,806	9,136	12,806	11,471
66,500	66,550	12,819	9,144	12,819	11,484
66,550	66,600	12,831	9,151	12,831	11,496
66,600	66,650	12,844	9,159	12,844	11,509
66,650	66,700	12,856	9,166	12,856	11,521
66,700	66,750	12,869	9,174	12,869	11,534
66,750	66,800	12,881	9,181	12,881	11,546
66,800	66,850	12,894	9,189	12,894	11,559
66,850	66,900	12,906	9,196	12,906	11,571
66,900	66,950	12,919	9,204	12,919	11,584
66,950	67,000	12,931	9,211	12,931	11,596

67,000

At least	But less than	Single	Married filing jointly	Married filing separately	Head of a household
67,000	67,050	12,944	9,219	12,944	11,609
67,050	67,100	12,956	9,226	12,956	11,621
67,100	67,150	12,969	9,234	12,969	11,634
67,150	67,200	12,981	9,241	12,981	11,646
67,200	67,250	12,994	9,249	12,994	11,659
67,250	67,300	13,006	9,256	13,006	11,671
67,300	67,350	13,019	9,264	13,019	11,684
67,350	67,400	13,031	9,271	13,031	11,696
67,400	67,450	13,044	9,279	13,044	11,709
67,450	67,500	13,056	9,286	13,056	11,721
67,500	67,550	13,069	9,294	13,069	11,734
67,550	67,600	13,081	9,301	13,081	11,746
67,600	67,650	13,094	9,309	13,094	11,759
67,650	67,700	13,106	9,316	13,106	11,771
67,700	67,750	13,119	9,324	13,119	11,784
67,750	67,800	13,131	9,331	13,131	11,796
67,800	67,850	13,144	9,339	13,144	11,809
67,850	67,900	13,156	9,346	13,156	11,821
67,900	67,950	13,169	9,356	13,169	11,834
67,950	68,000	13,181	9,369	13,181	11,846

* This column must also be used by a qualifying widow(er).

(Continued on page T-10)

2009 Tax Table– Continued

68,000

At least	But less than	Single	Married filing jointly*	Married filing separately	Head of a household
68,000	68,050	13,194	9,381	13,194	11,859
68,050	68,100	13,206	9,394	13,206	11,871
68,100	68,150	13,219	9,406	13,219	11,884
68,150	68,200	13,231	9,419	13,231	11,896
68,200	68,250	13,244	9,431	13,244	11,909
68,250	68,300	13,256	9,444	13,256	11,921
68,300	68,350	13,269	9,456	13,269	11,934
68,350	68,400	13,281	9,469	13,281	11,946
68,400	68,450	13,294	9,481	13,294	11,959
68,450	68,500	13,306	9,494	13,306	11,971
68,500	68,550	13,319	9,506	13,319	11,984
68,550	68,600	13,331	9,519	13,333	11,996
68,600	68,650	13,344	9,531	13,347	12,009
68,650	68,700	13,356	9,544	13,361	12,021
68,700	68,750	13,369	9,556	13,375	12,034
68,750	68,800	13,381	9,569	13,389	12,046
68,800	68,850	13,394	9,581	13,403	12,059
68,850	68,900	13,406	9,594	13,417	12,071
68,900	68,950	13,419	9,606	13,431	12,084
68,950	69,000	13,431	9,619	13,445	12,096

69,000

At least	But less than	Single	Married filing jointly*	Married filing separately	Head of a household
69,000	69,050	13,444	9,631	13,459	12,109
69,050	69,100	13,456	9,644	13,473	12,121
69,100	69,150	13,469	9,656	13,487	12,134
69,150	69,200	13,481	9,669	13,501	12,146
69,200	69,250	13,494	9,681	13,515	12,159
69,250	69,300	13,506	9,694	13,529	12,171
69,300	69,350	13,519	9,706	13,543	12,184
69,350	69,400	13,531	9,719	13,557	12,196
69,400	69,450	13,544	9,731	13,571	12,209
69,450	69,500	13,556	9,744	13,585	12,221
69,500	69,550	13,569	9,756	13,599	12,234
69,550	69,600	13,581	9,769	13,613	12,246
69,600	69,650	13,594	9,781	13,627	12,259
69,650	69,700	13,606	9,794	13,641	12,271
69,700	69,750	13,619	9,806	13,655	12,284
69,750	69,800	13,631	9,819	13,669	12,296
69,800	69,850	13,644	9,831	13,683	12,309
69,850	69,900	13,656	9,844	13,697	12,321
69,900	69,950	13,669	9,856	13,711	12,334
69,950	70,000	13,681	9,869	13,725	12,346

70,000

At least	But less than	Single	Married filing jointly*	Married filing separately	Head of a household
70,000	70,050	13,694	9,881	13,739	12,359
70,050	70,100	13,706	9,894	13,753	12,371
70,100	70,150	13,719	9,906	13,767	12,384
70,150	70,200	13,731	9,919	13,781	12,396
70,200	70,250	13,744	9,931	13,795	12,409
70,250	70,300	13,756	9,944	13,809	12,421
70,300	70,350	13,769	9,956	13,823	12,434
70,350	70,400	13,781	9,969	13,837	12,446
70,400	70,450	13,794	9,981	13,851	12,459
70,450	70,500	13,806	9,994	13,865	12,471
70,500	70,550	13,819	10,006	13,879	12,484
70,550	70,600	13,831	10,019	13,893	12,496
70,600	70,650	13,844	10,031	13,907	12,509
70,650	70,700	13,856	10,044	13,921	12,521
70,700	70,750	13,869	10,056	13,935	12,534
70,750	70,800	13,881	10,069	13,949	12,546
70,800	70,850	13,894	10,081	13,963	12,559
70,850	70,900	13,906	10,094	13,977	12,571
70,900	70,950	13,919	10,106	13,991	12,584
70,950	71,000	13,931	10,119	14,005	12,596

71,000

At least	But less than	Single	Married filing jointly*	Married filing separately	Head of a household
71,000	71,050	13,944	10,131	14,019	12,609
71,050	71,100	13,956	10,144	14,033	12,621
71,100	71,150	13,969	10,156	14,047	12,634
71,150	71,200	13,981	10,169	14,061	12,646
71,200	71,250	13,994	10,181	14,075	12,659
71,250	71,300	14,006	10,194	14,089	12,671
71,300	71,350	14,019	10,206	14,103	12,684
71,350	71,400	14,031	10,219	14,117	12,696
71,400	71,450	14,044	10,231	14,131	12,709
71,450	71,500	14,056	10,244	14,145	12,721
71,500	71,550	14,069	10,256	14,159	12,734
71,550	71,600	14,081	10,269	14,173	12,746
71,600	71,650	14,094	10,281	14,187	12,759
71,650	71,700	14,106	10,294	14,201	12,771
71,700	71,750	14,119	10,306	14,215	12,784
71,750	71,800	14,131	10,319	14,229	12,796
71,800	71,850	14,144	10,331	14,243	12,809
71,850	71,900	14,156	10,344	14,257	12,821
71,900	71,950	14,169	10,356	14,271	12,834
71,950	72,000	14,181	10,369	14,285	12,846

72,000

At least	But less than	Single	Married filing jointly*	Married filing separately	Head of a household
72,000	72,050	14,194	10,381	14,299	12,859
72,050	72,100	14,206	10,394	14,313	12,871
72,100	72,150	14,219	10,406	14,327	12,884
72,150	72,200	14,231	10,419	14,341	12,896
72,200	72,250	14,244	10,431	14,355	12,909
72,250	72,300	14,256	10,444	14,369	12,921
72,300	72,350	14,269	10,456	14,383	12,934
72,350	72,400	14,281	10,469	14,397	12,946
72,400	72,450	14,294	10,481	14,411	12,959
72,450	72,500	14,306	10,494	14,425	12,971
72,500	72,550	14,319	10,506	14,439	12,984
72,550	72,600	14,331	10,519	14,453	12,996
72,600	72,650	14,344	10,531	14,467	13,009
72,650	72,700	14,356	10,544	14,481	13,021
72,700	72,750	14,369	10,556	14,495	13,034
72,750	72,800	14,381	10,569	14,509	13,046
72,800	72,850	14,394	10,581	14,523	13,059
72,850	72,900	14,406	10,594	14,537	13,071
72,900	72,950	14,419	10,606	14,551	13,084
72,950	73,000	14,431	10,619	14,565	13,096

73,000

At least	But less than	Single	Married filing jointly*	Married filing separately	Head of a household
73,000	73,050	14,444	10,631	14,579	13,109
73,050	73,100	14,456	10,644	14,593	13,121
73,100	73,150	14,469	10,656	14,607	13,134
73,150	73,200	14,481	10,669	14,621	13,146
73,200	73,250	14,494	10,681	14,635	13,159
73,250	73,300	14,506	10,694	14,649	13,171
73,300	73,350	14,519	10,706	14,663	13,184
73,350	73,400	14,531	10,719	14,677	13,196
73,400	73,450	14,544	10,731	14,691	13,209
73,450	73,500	14,556	10,744	14,705	13,221
73,500	73,550	14,569	10,756	14,719	13,234
73,550	73,600	14,581	10,769	14,733	13,246
73,600	73,650	14,594	10,781	14,747	13,259
73,650	73,700	14,606	10,794	14,761	13,271
73,700	73,750	14,619	10,806	14,775	13,284
73,750	73,800	14,631	10,819	14,789	13,296
73,800	73,850	14,644	10,831	14,803	13,309
73,850	73,900	14,656	10,844	14,817	13,321
73,900	73,950	14,669	10,856	14,831	13,334
73,950	74,000	14,681	10,869	14,845	13,346

74,000

At least	But less than	Single	Married filing jointly*	Married filing separately	Head of a household
74,000	74,050	14,694	10,881	14,859	13,359
74,050	74,100	14,706	10,894	14,873	13,371
74,100	74,150	14,719	10,906	14,887	13,384
74,150	74,200	14,731	10,919	14,901	13,396
74,200	74,250	14,744	10,931	14,915	13,409
74,250	74,300	14,756	10,944	14,929	13,421
74,300	74,350	14,769	10,956	14,943	13,434
74,350	74,400	14,781	10,969	14,957	13,446
74,400	74,450	14,794	10,981	14,971	13,459
74,450	74,500	14,806	10,994	14,985	13,471
74,500	74,550	14,819	11,006	14,999	13,484
74,550	74,600	14,831	11,019	15,013	13,496
74,600	74,650	14,844	11,031	15,027	13,509
74,650	74,700	14,856	11,044	15,041	13,521
74,700	74,750	14,869	11,056	15,055	13,534
74,750	74,800	14,881	11,069	15,069	13,546
74,800	74,850	14,894	11,081	15,083	13,559
74,850	74,900	14,906	11,094	15,097	13,571
74,900	74,950	14,919	11,106	15,111	13,584
74,950	75,000	14,931	11,119	15,125	13,596

75,000

At least	But less than	Single	Married filing jointly*	Married filing separately	Head of a household
75,000	75,050	14,944	11,131	15,139	13,609
75,050	75,100	14,956	11,144	15,153	13,621
75,100	75,150	14,969	11,156	15,167	13,634
75,150	75,200	14,981	11,169	15,181	13,646
75,200	75,250	14,994	11,181	15,195	13,659
75,250	75,300	15,006	11,194	15,209	13,671
75,300	75,350	15,019	11,206	15,223	13,684
75,350	75,400	15,031	11,219	15,237	13,696
75,400	75,450	15,044	11,231	15,251	13,709
75,450	75,500	15,056	11,244	15,265	13,721
75,500	75,550	15,069	11,256	15,279	13,734
75,550	75,600	15,081	11,269	15,293	13,746
75,600	75,650	15,094	11,281	15,307	13,759
75,650	75,700	15,106	11,294	15,321	13,771
75,700	75,750	15,119	11,306	15,335	13,784
75,750	75,800	15,131	11,319	15,349	13,796
75,800	75,850	15,144	11,331	15,363	13,809
75,850	75,900	15,156	11,344	15,377	13,821
75,900	75,950	15,169	11,356	15,391	13,834
75,950	76,000	15,181	11,369	15,405	13,846

76,000

At least	But less than	Single	Married filing jointly*	Married filing separately	Head of a household
76,000	76,050	15,194	11,381	15,419	13,859
76,050	76,100	15,206	11,394	15,433	13,871
76,100	76,150	15,219	11,406	15,447	13,884
76,150	76,200	15,231	11,419	15,461	13,896
76,200	76,250	15,244	11,431	15,475	13,909
76,250	76,300	15,256	11,444	15,489	13,921
76,300	76,350	15,269	11,456	15,503	13,934
76,350	76,400	15,281	11,469	15,517	13,946
76,400	76,450	15,294	11,481	15,531	13,959
76,450	76,500	15,306	11,494	15,545	13,971
76,500	76,550	15,319	11,506	15,559	13,984
76,550	76,600	15,331	11,519	15,573	13,996
76,600	76,650	15,344	11,531	15,587	14,009
76,650	76,700	15,356	11,544	15,601	14,021
76,700	76,750	15,369	11,556	15,615	14,034
76,750	76,800	15,381	11,569	15,629	14,046
76,800	76,850	15,394	11,581	15,643	14,059
76,850	76,900	15,406	11,594	15,657	14,071
76,900	76,950	15,419	11,606	15,671	14,084
76,950	77,000	15,431	11,619	15,685	14,096

* This column must also be used by a qualifying widow(er).

(Continued on page T-11)

2009 Tax Table– *Continued*

If line 43 (taxable income) is—		And you are—			
At least	But less than	Single	Married filing jointly *	Married filing separately	Head of a household
		Your tax is—			

77,000

At least	But less than	Single	Married filing jointly	Married filing separately	Head of a household
77,000	77,050	15,444	11,631	15,699	14,109
77,050	77,100	15,456	11,644	15,713	14,121
77,100	77,150	15,469	11,656	15,727	14,134
77,150	77,200	15,481	11,669	15,741	14,146
77,200	77,250	15,494	11,681	15,755	14,159
77,250	77,300	15,506	11,694	15,769	14,171
77,300	77,350	15,519	11,706	15,783	14,184
77,350	77,400	15,531	11,719	15,797	14,196
77,400	77,450	15,544	11,731	15,811	14,209
77,450	77,500	15,556	11,744	15,825	14,221
77,500	77,550	15,569	11,756	15,839	14,234
77,550	77,600	15,581	11,769	15,853	14,246
77,600	77,650	15,594	11,781	15,867	14,259
77,650	77,700	15,606	11,794	15,881	14,271
77,700	77,750	15,619	11,806	15,895	14,284
77,750	77,800	15,631	11,819	15,909	14,296
77,800	77,850	15,644	11,831	15,923	14,309
77,850	77,900	15,656	11,844	15,937	14,321
77,900	77,950	15,669	11,856	15,951	14,334
77,950	78,000	15,681	11,869	15,965	14,346

78,000

At least	But less than	Single	Married filing jointly	Married filing separately	Head of a household
78,000	78,050	15,694	11,881	15,979	14,359
78,050	78,100	15,706	11,894	15,993	14,371
78,100	78,150	15,719	11,906	16,007	14,384
78,150	78,200	15,731	11,919	16,021	14,396
78,200	78,250	15,744	11,931	16,035	14,409
78,250	78,300	15,756	11,944	16,049	14,421
78,300	78,350	15,769	11,956	16,063	14,434
78,350	78,400	15,781	11,969	16,077	14,446
78,400	78,450	15,794	11,981	16,091	14,459
78,450	78,500	15,806	11,994	16,105	14,471
78,500	78,550	15,819	12,006	16,119	14,484
78,550	78,600	15,831	12,019	16,133	14,496
78,600	78,650	15,844	12,031	16,147	14,509
78,650	78,700	15,856	12,044	16,161	14,521
78,700	78,750	15,869	12,056	16,175	14,534
78,750	78,800	15,881	12,069	16,189	14,546
78,800	78,850	15,894	12,081	16,203	14,559
78,850	78,900	15,906	12,094	16,217	14,571
78,900	78,950	15,919	12,106	16,231	14,584
78,950	79,000	15,931	12,119	16,245	14,596

79,000

At least	But less than	Single	Married filing jointly	Married filing separately	Head of a household
79,000	79,050	15,944	12,131	16,259	14,609
79,050	79,100	15,956	12,144	16,273	14,621
79,100	79,150	15,969	12,156	16,287	14,634
79,150	79,200	15,981	12,169	16,301	14,646
79,200	79,250	15,994	12,181	16,315	14,659
79,250	79,300	16,006	12,194	16,329	14,671
79,300	79,350	16,019	12,206	16,343	14,684
79,350	79,400	16,031	12,219	16,357	14,696
79,400	79,450	16,044	12,231	16,371	14,709
79,450	79,500	16,056	12,244	16,385	14,721
79,500	79,550	16,069	12,256	16,399	14,734
79,550	79,600	16,081	12,269	16,413	14,746
79,600	79,650	16,094	12,281	16,427	14,759
79,650	79,700	16,106	12,294	16,441	14,771
79,700	79,750	16,119	12,306	16,455	14,784
79,750	79,800	16,131	12,319	16,469	14,796
79,800	79,850	16,144	12,331	16,483	14,809
79,850	79,900	16,156	12,344	16,497	14,821
79,900	79,950	16,169	12,356	16,511	14,834
79,950	80,000	16,181	12,369	16,525	14,846

80,000

At least	But less than	Single	Married filing jointly	Married filing separately	Head of a household
80,000	80,050	16,194	12,381	16,539	14,859
80,050	80,100	16,206	12,394	16,553	14,871
80,100	80,150	16,219	12,406	16,567	14,884
80,150	80,200	16,231	12,419	16,581	14,896
80,200	80,250	16,244	12,431	16,595	14,909
80,250	80,300	16,256	12,444	16,609	14,921
80,300	80,350	16,269	12,456	16,623	14,934
80,350	80,400	16,281	12,469	16,637	14,946
80,400	80,450	16,294	12,481	16,651	14,959
80,450	80,500	16,306	12,494	16,665	14,971
80,500	80,550	16,319	12,506	16,679	14,984
80,550	80,600	16,331	12,519	16,693	14,996
80,600	80,650	16,344	12,531	16,707	15,009
80,650	80,700	16,356	12,544	16,721	15,021
80,700	80,750	16,369	12,556	16,735	15,034
80,750	80,800	16,381	12,569	16,749	15,046
80,800	80,850	16,394	12,581	16,763	15,059
80,850	80,900	16,406	12,594	16,777	15,071
80,900	80,950	16,419	12,606	16,791	15,084
80,950	81,000	16,431	12,619	16,805	15,096

81,000

At least	But less than	Single	Married filing jointly	Married filing separately	Head of a household
81,000	81,050	16,444	12,631	16,819	15,109
81,050	81,100	16,456	12,644	16,833	15,121
81,100	81,150	16,469	12,656	16,847	15,134
81,150	81,200	16,481	12,669	16,861	15,146
81,200	81,250	16,494	12,681	16,875	15,159
81,250	81,300	16,506	12,694	16,889	15,171
81,300	81,350	16,519	12,706	16,903	15,184
81,350	81,400	16,531	12,719	16,917	15,196
81,400	81,450	16,544	12,731	16,931	15,209
81,450	81,500	16,556	12,744	16,945	15,221
81,500	81,550	16,569	12,756	16,959	15,234
81,550	81,600	16,581	12,769	16,973	15,246
81,600	81,650	16,594	12,781	16,987	15,259
81,650	81,700	16,606	12,794	17,001	15,271
81,700	81,750	16,619	12,806	17,015	15,284
81,750	81,800	16,631	12,819	17,029	15,296
81,800	81,850	16,644	12,831	17,043	15,309
81,850	81,900	16,656	12,844	17,057	15,321
81,900	81,950	16,669	12,856	17,071	15,334
81,950	82,000	16,681	12,869	17,085	15,346

82,000

At least	But less than	Single	Married filing jointly	Married filing separately	Head of a household
82,000	82,050	16,694	12,881	17,099	15,359
82,050	82,100	16,706	12,894	17,113	15,371
82,100	82,150	16,719	12,906	17,127	15,384
82,150	82,200	16,731	12,919	17,141	15,396
82,200	82,250	16,744	12,931	17,155	15,409
82,250	82,300	16,757	12,944	17,169	15,421
82,300	82,350	16,771	12,956	17,183	15,434
82,350	82,400	16,785	12,969	17,197	15,446
82,400	82,450	16,799	12,981	17,211	15,459
82,450	82,500	16,813	12,994	17,225	15,471
82,500	82,550	16,827	13,006	17,239	15,484
82,550	82,600	16,841	13,019	17,253	15,496
82,600	82,650	16,855	13,031	17,267	15,509
82,650	82,700	16,869	13,044	17,281	15,521
82,700	82,750	16,883	13,056	17,295	15,534
82,750	82,800	16,897	13,069	17,309	15,546
82,800	82,850	16,911	13,081	17,323	15,559
82,850	82,900	16,925	13,094	17,337	15,571
82,900	82,950	16,939	13,106	17,351	15,584
82,950	83,000	16,953	13,119	17,365	15,596

83,000

At least	But less than	Single	Married filing jointly	Married filing separately	Head of a household
83,000	83,050	16,967	13,131	17,379	15,609
83,050	83,100	16,981	13,144	17,393	15,621
83,100	83,150	16,995	13,156	17,407	15,634
83,150	83,200	17,009	13,169	17,421	15,646
83,200	83,250	17,023	13,181	17,435	15,659
83,250	83,300	17,037	13,194	17,449	15,671
83,300	83,350	17,051	13,206	17,463	15,684
83,350	83,400	17,065	13,219	17,477	15,696
83,400	83,450	17,079	13,231	17,491	15,709
83,450	83,500	17,093	13,244	17,505	15,721
83,500	83,550	17,107	13,256	17,519	15,734
83,550	83,600	17,121	13,269	17,533	15,746
83,600	83,650	17,135	13,281	17,547	15,759
83,650	83,700	17,149	13,294	17,561	15,771
83,700	83,750	17,163	13,306	17,575	15,784
83,750	83,800	17,177	13,319	17,589	15,796
83,800	83,850	17,191	13,331	17,603	15,809
83,850	83,900	17,205	13,344	17,617	15,821
83,900	83,950	17,219	13,356	17,631	15,834
83,950	84,000	17,233	13,369	17,645	15,846

84,000

At least	But less than	Single	Married filing jointly	Married filing separately	Head of a household
84,000	84,050	17,247	13,381	17,659	15,859
84,050	84,100	17,261	13,394	17,673	15,871
84,100	84,150	17,275	13,406	17,687	15,884
84,150	84,200	17,289	13,419	17,701	15,896
84,200	84,250	17,303	13,431	17,715	15,909
84,250	84,300	17,317	13,444	17,729	15,921
84,300	84,350	17,331	13,456	17,743	15,934
84,350	84,400	17,345	13,469	17,757	15,946
84,400	84,450	17,359	13,481	17,771	15,959
84,450	84,500	17,373	13,494	17,785	15,971
84,500	84,550	17,387	13,506	17,799	15,984
84,550	84,600	17,401	13,519	17,813	15,996
84,600	84,650	17,415	13,531	17,827	16,009
84,650	84,700	17,429	13,544	17,841	16,021
84,700	84,750	17,443	13,556	17,855	16,034
84,750	84,800	17,457	13,569	17,869	16,046
84,800	84,850	17,471	13,581	17,883	16,059
84,850	84,900	17,485	13,594	17,897	16,071
84,900	84,950	17,499	13,606	17,911	16,084
84,950	85,000	17,513	13,619	17,925	16,096

85,000

At least	But less than	Single	Married filing jointly	Married filing separately	Head of a household
85,000	85,050	17,527	13,631	17,939	16,109
85,050	85,100	17,541	13,644	17,953	16,121
85,100	85,150	17,555	13,656	17,967	16,134
85,150	85,200	17,569	13,669	17,981	16,146
85,200	85,250	17,583	13,681	17,995	16,159
85,250	85,300	17,597	13,694	18,009	16,171
85,300	85,350	17,611	13,706	18,023	16,184
85,350	85,400	17,625	13,719	18,037	16,196
85,400	85,450	17,639	13,731	18,051	16,209
85,450	85,500	17,653	13,744	18,065	16,221
85,500	85,550	17,667	13,756	18,079	16,234
85,550	85,600	17,681	13,769	18,093	16,246
85,600	85,650	17,695	13,781	18,107	16,259
85,650	85,700	17,709	13,794	18,121	16,271
85,700	85,750	17,723	13,806	18,135	16,284
85,750	85,800	17,737	13,819	18,149	16,296
85,800	85,850	17,751	13,831	18,163	16,309
85,850	85,900	17,765	13,844	18,177	16,321
85,900	85,950	17,779	13,856	18,191	16,334
85,950	86,000	17,793	13,869	18,205	16,346

* This column must also be used by a qualifying widow(er).

(Continued on page T-12)

If line 43 (taxable income) is—		And you are—			
At least	But less than	Single	Married filing jointly *	Married filing separately	Head of a household
		Your tax is—			

86,000

At least	But less than	Single	Married filing jointly *	Married filing separately	Head of a household
86,000	86,050	17,807	13,881	18,219	16,359
86,050	86,100	17,821	13,894	18,233	16,371
86,100	86,150	17,835	13,906	18,247	16,384
86,150	86,200	17,849	13,919	18,261	16,396
86,200	86,250	17,863	13,931	18,275	16,409
86,250	86,300	17,877	13,944	18,289	16,421
86,300	86,350	17,891	13,956	18,303	16,434
86,350	86,400	17,905	13,969	18,317	16,446
86,400	86,450	17,919	13,981	18,331	16,459
86,450	86,500	17,933	13,994	18,345	16,471
86,500	86,550	17,947	14,006	18,359	16,484
86,550	86,600	17,961	14,019	18,373	16,496
86,600	86,650	17,975	14,031	18,387	16,509
86,650	86,700	17,989	14,044	18,401	16,521
86,700	86,750	18,003	14,056	18,415	16,534
86,750	86,800	18,017	14,069	18,429	16,546
86,800	86,850	18,031	14,081	18,443	16,559
86,850	86,900	18,045	14,094	18,457	16,571
86,900	86,950	18,059	14,106	18,471	16,584
86,950	87,000	18,073	14,119	18,485	16,596

87,000

At least	But less than	Single	Married filing jointly *	Married filing separately	Head of a household
87,000	87,050	18,087	14,131	18,499	16,609
87,050	87,100	18,101	14,144	18,513	16,621
87,100	87,150	18,115	14,156	18,527	16,634
87,150	87,200	18,129	14,169	18,541	16,646
87,200	87,250	18,143	14,181	18,555	16,659
87,250	87,300	18,157	14,194	18,569	16,671
87,300	87,350	18,171	14,206	18,583	16,684
87,350	87,400	18,185	14,219	18,597	16,696
87,400	87,450	18,199	14,231	18,611	16,709
87,450	87,500	18,213	14,244	18,625	16,721
87,500	87,550	18,227	14,256	18,639	16,734
87,550	87,600	18,241	14,269	18,653	16,746
87,600	87,650	18,255	14,281	18,667	16,759
87,650	87,700	18,269	14,294	18,681	16,771
87,700	87,750	18,283	14,306	18,695	16,784
87,750	87,800	18,297	14,319	18,709	16,796
87,800	87,850	18,311	14,331	18,723	16,809
87,850	87,900	18,325	14,344	18,737	16,821
87,900	87,950	18,339	14,356	18,751	16,834
87,950	88,000	18,353	14,369	18,765	16,846

88,000

At least	But less than	Single	Married filing jointly *	Married filing separately	Head of a household
88,000	88,050	18,367	14,381	18,779	16,859
88,050	88,100	18,381	14,394	18,793	16,871
88,100	88,150	18,395	14,406	18,807	16,884
88,150	88,200	18,409	14,419	18,821	16,896
88,200	88,250	18,423	14,431	18,835	16,909
88,250	88,300	18,437	14,444	18,849	16,921
88,300	88,350	18,451	14,456	18,863	16,934
88,350	88,400	18,465	14,469	18,877	16,946
88,400	88,450	18,479	14,481	18,891	16,959
88,450	88,500	18,493	14,494	18,905	16,971
88,500	88,550	18,507	14,506	18,919	16,984
88,550	88,600	18,521	14,519	18,933	16,996
88,600	88,650	18,535	14,531	18,947	17,009
88,650	88,700	18,549	14,544	18,961	17,021
88,700	88,750	18,563	14,556	18,975	17,034
88,750	88,800	18,577	14,569	18,989	17,046
88,800	88,850	18,591	14,581	19,003	17,059
88,850	88,900	18,605	14,594	19,017	17,071
88,900	88,950	18,619	14,606	19,031	17,084
88,950	89,000	18,633	14,619	19,045	17,096

89,000

At least	But less than	Single	Married filing jointly *	Married filing separately	Head of a household
89,000	89,050	18,647	14,631	19,059	17,109
89,050	89,100	18,661	14,644	19,073	17,121
89,100	89,150	18,675	14,656	19,087	17,134
89,150	89,200	18,689	14,669	19,101	17,146
89,200	89,250	18,703	14,681	19,115	17,159
89,250	89,300	18,717	14,694	19,129	17,171
89,300	89,350	18,731	14,706	19,143	17,184
89,350	89,400	18,745	14,719	19,157	17,196
89,400	89,450	18,759	14,731	19,171	17,209
89,450	89,500	18,773	14,744	19,185	17,221
89,500	89,550	18,787	14,756	19,199	17,234
89,550	89,600	18,801	14,769	19,213	17,246
89,600	89,650	18,815	14,781	19,227	17,259
89,650	89,700	18,829	14,794	19,241	17,271
89,700	89,750	18,843	14,806	19,255	17,284
89,750	89,800	18,857	14,819	19,269	17,296
89,800	89,850	18,871	14,831	19,283	17,309
89,850	89,900	18,885	14,844	19,297	17,321
89,900	89,950	18,899	14,856	19,311	17,334
89,950	90,000	18,913	14,869	19,325	17,346

90,000

At least	But less than	Single	Married filing jointly *	Married filing separately	Head of a household
90,000	90,050	18,927	14,881	19,339	17,359
90,050	90,100	18,941	14,894	19,353	17,371
90,100	90,150	18,955	14,906	19,367	17,384
90,150	90,200	18,969	14,919	19,381	17,396
90,200	90,250	18,983	14,931	19,395	17,409
90,250	90,300	18,997	14,944	19,409	17,421
90,300	90,350	19,011	14,956	19,423	17,434
90,350	90,400	19,025	14,969	19,437	17,446
90,400	90,450	19,039	14,981	19,451	17,459
90,450	90,500	19,053	14,994	19,465	17,471
90,500	90,550	19,067	15,006	19,479	17,484
90,550	90,600	19,081	15,019	19,493	17,496
90,600	90,650	19,095	15,031	19,507	17,509
90,650	90,700	19,109	15,044	19,521	17,521
90,700	90,750	19,123	15,056	19,535	17,534
90,750	90,800	19,137	15,069	19,549	17,546
90,800	90,850	19,151	15,081	19,563	17,559
90,850	90,900	19,165	15,094	19,577	17,571
90,900	90,950	19,179	15,106	19,591	17,584
90,950	91,000	19,193	15,119	19,605	17,596

91,000

At least	But less than	Single	Married filing jointly *	Married filing separately	Head of a household
91,000	91,050	19,207	15,131	19,619	17,609
91,050	91,100	19,221	15,144	19,633	17,621
91,100	91,150	19,235	15,156	19,647	17,634
91,150	91,200	19,249	15,169	19,661	17,646
91,200	91,250	19,263	15,181	19,675	17,659
91,250	91,300	19,277	15,194	19,689	17,671
91,300	91,350	19,291	15,206	19,703	17,684
91,350	91,400	19,305	15,219	19,717	17,696
91,400	91,450	19,319	15,231	19,731	17,709
91,450	91,500	19,333	15,244	19,745	17,721
91,500	91,550	19,347	15,256	19,759	17,734
91,550	91,600	19,361	15,269	19,773	17,746
91,600	91,650	19,375	15,281	19,787	17,759
91,650	91,700	19,389	15,294	19,801	17,771
91,700	91,750	19,403	15,306	19,815	17,784
91,750	91,800	19,417	15,319	19,829	17,796
91,800	91,850	19,431	15,331	19,843	17,809
91,850	91,900	19,445	15,344	19,857	17,821
91,900	91,950	19,459	15,356	19,871	17,834
91,950	92,000	19,473	15,369	19,885	17,846

92,000

At least	But less than	Single	Married filing jointly *	Married filing separately	Head of a household
92,000	92,050	19,487	15,381	19,899	17,859
92,050	92,100	19,501	15,394	19,913	17,871
92,100	92,150	19,515	15,406	19,927	17,884
92,150	92,200	19,529	15,419	19,941	17,896
92,200	92,250	19,543	15,431	19,955	17,909
92,250	92,300	19,557	15,444	19,969	17,921
92,300	92,350	19,571	15,456	19,983	17,934
92,350	92,400	19,585	15,469	19,997	17,946
92,400	92,450	19,599	15,481	20,011	17,959
92,450	92,500	19,613	15,494	20,025	17,971
92,500	92,550	19,627	15,506	20,039	17,984
92,550	92,600	19,641	15,519	20,053	17,996
92,600	92,650	19,655	15,531	20,067	18,009
92,650	92,700	19,669	15,544	20,081	18,021
92,700	92,750	19,683	15,556	20,095	18,034
92,750	92,800	19,697	15,569	20,109	18,046
92,800	92,850	19,711	15,581	20,123	18,059
92,850	92,900	19,725	15,594	20,137	18,071
92,900	92,950	19,739	15,606	20,151	18,084
92,950	93,000	19,753	15,619	20,165	18,096

93,000

At least	But less than	Single	Married filing jointly *	Married filing separately	Head of a household
93,000	93,050	19,767	15,631	20,179	18,109
93,050	93,100	19,781	15,644	20,193	18,121
93,100	93,150	19,795	15,656	20,207	18,134
93,150	93,200	19,809	15,669	20,221	18,146
93,200	93,250	19,823	15,681	20,235	18,159
93,250	93,300	19,837	15,694	20,249	18,171
93,300	93,350	19,851	15,706	20,263	18,184
93,350	93,400	19,865	15,719	20,277	18,196
93,400	93,450	19,879	15,731	20,291	18,209
93,450	93,500	19,893	15,744	20,305	18,221
93,500	93,550	19,907	15,756	20,319	18,234
93,550	93,600	19,921	15,769	20,333	18,246
93,600	93,650	19,935	15,781	20,347	18,259
93,650	93,700	19,949	15,794	20,361	18,271
93,700	93,750	19,963	15,806	20,375	18,284
93,750	93,800	19,977	15,819	20,389	18,296
93,800	93,850	19,991	15,831	20,403	18,309
93,850	93,900	20,005	15,844	20,417	18,321
93,900	93,950	20,019	15,856	20,431	18,334
93,950	94,000	20,033	15,869	20,445	18,346

94,000

At least	But less than	Single	Married filing jointly *	Married filing separately	Head of a household
94,000	94,050	20,047	15,881	20,459	18,359
94,050	94,100	20,061	15,894	20,473	18,371
94,100	94,150	20,075	15,906	20,487	18,384
94,150	94,200	20,089	15,919	20,501	18,396
94,200	94,250	20,103	15,931	20,515	18,409
94,250	94,300	20,117	15,944	20,529	18,421
94,300	94,350	20,131	15,956	20,543	18,434
94,350	94,400	20,145	15,969	20,557	18,446
94,400	94,450	20,159	15,981	20,571	18,459
94,450	94,500	20,173	15,994	20,585	18,471
94,500	94,550	20,187	16,006	20,599	18,484
94,550	94,600	20,201	16,019	20,613	18,496
94,600	94,650	20,215	16,031	20,627	18,509
94,650	94,700	20,229	16,044	20,641	18,521
94,700	94,750	20,243	16,056	20,655	18,534
94,750	94,800	20,257	16,069	20,669	18,546
94,800	94,850	20,271	16,081	20,683	18,559
94,850	94,900	20,285	16,094	20,697	18,571
94,900	94,950	20,299	16,106	20,711	18,584
94,950	95,000	20,313	16,119	20,725	18,596

* This column must also be used by a qualifying widow(er).

(Continued on page T-13)

2009 Tax Table– *Continued*

If line 43 (taxable income) is—		And you are—			
At least	But less than	Single	Married filing jointly *	Married filing sepa-rately	Head of a house-hold
		Your tax is—			

95,000

At least	But less than	Single	MFJ	MFS	HoH
95,000	95,050	20,327	16,131	20,739	18,609
95,050	95,100	20,341	16,144	20,753	18,621
95,100	95,150	20,355	16,156	20,767	18,634
95,150	95,200	20,369	16,169	20,781	18,646
95,200	95,250	20,383	16,181	20,795	18,659
95,250	95,300	20,397	16,194	20,809	18,671
95,300	95,350	20,411	16,206	20,823	18,684
95,350	95,400	20,425	16,219	20,837	18,696
95,400	95,450	20,439	16,231	20,851	18,709
95,450	95,500	20,453	16,244	20,865	18,721
95,500	95,550	20,467	16,256	20,879	18,734
95,550	95,600	20,481	16,269	20,893	18,746
95,600	95,650	20,495	16,281	20,907	18,759
95,650	95,700	20,509	16,294	20,921	18,771
95,700	95,750	20,523	16,306	20,935	18,784
95,750	95,800	20,537	16,319	20,949	18,796
95,800	95,850	20,551	16,331	20,963	18,809
95,850	95,900	20,565	16,344	20,977	18,821
95,900	95,950	20,579	16,356	20,991	18,834
95,950	96,000	20,593	16,369	21,005	18,846

96,000

At least	But less than	Single	MFJ	MFS	HoH
96,000	96,050	20,607	16,381	21,019	18,859
96,050	96,100	20,621	16,394	21,033	18,871
96,100	96,150	20,635	16,406	21,047	18,884
96,150	96,200	20,649	16,419	21,061	18,896
96,200	96,250	20,663	16,431	21,075	18,909
96,250	96,300	20,677	16,444	21,089	18,921
96,300	96,350	20,691	16,456	21,103	18,934
96,350	96,400	20,705	16,469	21,117	18,946
96,400	96,450	20,719	16,481	21,131	18,959
96,450	96,500	20,733	16,494	21,145	18,971
96,500	96,550	20,747	16,506	21,159	18,984
96,550	96,600	20,761	16,519	21,173	18,996
96,600	96,650	20,775	16,531	21,187	19,009
96,650	96,700	20,789	16,544	21,201	19,021
96,700	96,750	20,803	16,556	21,215	19,034
96,750	96,800	20,817	16,569	21,229	19,046
96,800	96,850	20,831	16,581	21,243	19,059
96,850	96,900	20,845	16,594	21,257	19,071
96,900	96,950	20,859	16,606	21,271	19,084
96,950	97,000	20,873	16,619	21,285	19,096

If line 43 (taxable income) is—		And you are—			
At least	But less than	Single	Married filing jointly *	Married filing sepa-rately	Head of a house-hold
		Your tax is—			

97,000

At least	But less than	Single	MFJ	MFS	HoH
97,000	97,050	20,887	16,631	21,299	19,109
97,050	97,100	20,901	16,644	21,313	19,121
97,100	97,150	20,915	16,656	21,327	19,134
97,150	97,200	20,929	16,669	21,341	19,146
97,200	97,250	20,943	16,681	21,355	19,159
97,250	97,300	20,957	16,694	21,369	19,171
97,300	97,350	20,971	16,706	21,383	19,184
97,350	97,400	20,985	16,719	21,397	19,196
97,400	97,450	20,999	16,731	21,411	19,209
97,450	97,500	21,013	16,744	21,425	19,221
97,500	97,550	21,027	16,756	21,439	19,234
97,550	97,600	21,041	16,769	21,453	19,246
97,600	97,650	21,055	16,781	21,467	19,259
97,650	97,700	21,069	16,794	21,481	19,271
97,700	97,750	21,083	16,806	21,495	19,284
97,750	97,800	21,097	16,819	21,509	19,296
97,800	97,850	21,111	16,831	21,523	19,309
97,850	97,900	21,125	16,844	21,537	19,321
97,900	97,950	21,139	16,856	21,551	19,334
97,950	98,000	21,153	16,869	21,565	19,346

98,000

At least	But less than	Single	MFJ	MFS	HoH
98,000	98,050	21,167	16,881	21,579	19,359
98,050	98,100	21,181	16,894	21,593	19,371
98,100	98,150	21,195	16,906	21,607	19,384
98,150	98,200	21,209	16,919	21,621	19,396
98,200	98,250	21,223	16,931	21,635	19,409
98,250	98,300	21,237	16,944	21,649	19,421
98,300	98,350	21,251	16,956	21,663	19,434
98,350	98,400	21,265	16,969	21,677	19,446
98,400	98,450	21,279	16,981	21,691	19,459
98,450	98,500	21,293	16,994	21,705	19,471
98,500	98,550	21,307	17,006	21,719	19,484
98,550	98,600	21,321	17,019	21,733	19,496
98,600	98,650	21,335	17,031	21,747	19,509
98,650	98,700	21,349	17,044	21,761	19,521
98,700	98,750	21,363	17,056	21,775	19,534
98,750	98,800	21,377	17,069	21,789	19,546
98,800	98,850	21,391	17,081	21,803	19,559
98,850	98,900	21,405	17,094	21,817	19,571
98,900	98,950	21,419	17,106	21,831	19,584
98,950	99,000	21,433	17,119	21,845	19,596

If line 43 (taxable income) is—		And you are—			
At least	But less than	Single	Married filing jointly *	Married filing sepa-rately	Head of a house-hold
		Your tax is—			

99,000

At least	But less than	Single	MFJ	MFS	HoH
99,000	99,050	21,447	17,131	21,859	19,609
99,050	99,100	21,461	17,144	21,873	19,621
99,100	99,150	21,475	17,156	21,887	19,634
99,150	99,200	21,489	17,169	21,901	19,646
99,200	99,250	21,503	17,181	21,915	19,659
99,250	99,300	21,517	17,194	21,929	19,671
99,300	99,350	21,531	17,206	21,943	19,684
99,350	99,400	21,545	17,219	21,957	19,696
99,400	99,450	21,559	17,231	21,971	19,709
99,450	99,500	21,573	17,244	21,985	19,721
99,500	99,550	21,587	17,256	21,999	19,734
99,550	99,600	21,601	17,269	22,013	19,746
99,600	99,650	21,615	17,281	22,027	19,759
99,650	99,700	21,629	17,294	22,041	19,771
99,700	99,750	21,643	17,306	22,055	19,784
99,750	99,800	21,657	17,319	22,069	19,796
99,800	99,850	21,671	17,331	22,083	19,809
99,850	99,900	21,685	17,344	22,097	19,821
99,900	99,950	21,699	17,356	22,111	19,834
99,950	100,000	21,713	17,369	22,125	19,846

$100,000 or over — use the Tax Computation Worksheet on page 89

* This column must also be used by a qualifying widow(er).

2009 Tax Rate Schedules

The Tax Rate Schedules are shown so you can see the tax rate that applies to all levels of taxable income. Do not use them to figure your tax. Instead, see the instructions for line 44 that begin on page 37.

Schedule X—If your filing status is **Single**

If your taxable income is: Over—	But not over—	The tax is:	of the amount over—
$0	$8,350	---------- 10%	$0
8,350	33,950	$835.00 + 15%	8,350
33,950	82,250	4,675.00 + 25%	33,950
82,250	171,550	16,750.00 + 28%	82,250
171,550	372,950	41,754.00 + 33%	171,550
372,950	----------	108,216.00 + 35%	372,950

Schedule Y-1—If your filing status is **Married filing jointly** or **Qualifying widow(er)**

If your taxable income is: Over—	But not over—	The tax is:	of the amount over—
$0	$16,700	---------- 10%	$0
16,700	67,900	$1,670.00 + 15%	16,700
67,900	137,050	9,350.00 + 25%	67,900
137,050	208,850	26,637.50 + 28%	137,050
208,850	372,950	46,741.50 + 33%	208,850
372,950	----------	100,894.50 + 35%	372,950

Schedule Y-2—If your filing status is **Married filing separately**

If your taxable income is: Over—	But not over—	The tax is:	of the amount over—
$0	$8,350	---------- 10%	$0
8,350	33,950	$835.00 + 15%	8,350
33,950	68,525	4,675.00 + 25%	33,950
68,525	104,425	13,318.75 + 28%	68,525
104,425	186,475	23,370.75 + 33%	104,425
186,475	----------	50,447.25 + 35%	186,475

Schedule Z—If your filing status is **Head of household**

If your taxable income is: Over—	But not over—	The tax is:	of the amount over—
$0	$11,950	---------- 10%	$0
11,950	45,500	$1,195.00 + 15%	11,950
45,500	117,450	6,227.50 + 25%	45,500
117,450	190,200	24,215.00 + 28%	117,450
190,200	372,950	44,585.00 + 33%	190,200
372,950	----------	104,892.50 + 35%	372,950

SINGLE Persons—MONTHLY Payroll Period
(For Wages Paid in 2010)

And the wages are—		And the number of withholding allowances claimed is—										
At least	But less than	0	1	2	3	4	5	6	7	8	9	10
		The amount of income, social security, and Medicare taxes to be withheld is—										
$0	$220	7.65%	7.65%	7.65%	7.65%	7.65%	7.65%	7.65%	7.65%	7.65%	7.65%	7.65%
220	230	17.21	17.21	17.21	17.21	17.21	17.21	17.21	17.21	17.21	17.21	17.21
230	240	17.98	17.98	17.98	17.98	17.98	17.98	17.98	17.98	17.98	17.98	17.98
240	250	18.74	18.74	18.74	18.74	18.74	18.74	18.74	18.74	18.74	18.74	18.74
250	260	19.51	19.51	19.51	19.51	19.51	19.51	19.51	19.51	19.51	19.51	19.51
260	270	20.27	20.27	20.27	20.27	20.27	20.27	20.27	20.27	20.27	20.27	20.27
270	280	21.04	21.04	21.04	21.04	21.04	21.04	21.04	21.04	21.04	21.04	21.04
280	290	21.80	21.80	21.80	21.80	21.80	21.80	21.80	21.80	21.80	21.80	21.80
290	300	22.57	22.57	22.57	22.57	22.57	22.57	22.57	22.57	22.57	22.57	22.57
300	320	23.72	23.72	23.72	23.72	23.72	23.72	23.72	23.72	23.72	23.72	23.72
320	340	25.25	25.25	25.25	25.25	25.25	25.25	25.25	25.25	25.25	25.25	25.25
340	360	26.78	26.78	26.78	26.78	26.78	26.78	26.78	26.78	26.78	26.78	26.78
360	380	28.31	28.31	28.31	28.31	28.31	28.31	28.31	28.31	28.31	28.31	28.31
380	400	29.84	29.84	29.84	29.84	29.84	29.84	29.84	29.84	29.84	29.84	29.84
400	420	31.37	31.37	31.37	31.37	31.37	31.37	31.37	31.37	31.37	31.37	31.37
420	440	32.90	32.90	32.90	32.90	32.90	32.90	32.90	32.90	32.90	32.90	32.90
440	460	34.43	34.43	34.43	34.43	34.43	34.43	34.43	34.43	34.43	34.43	34.43
460	480	35.96	35.96	35.96	35.96	35.96	35.96	35.96	35.96	35.96	35.96	35.96
480	500	37.49	37.49	37.49	37.49	37.49	37.49	37.49	37.49	37.49	37.49	37.49
500	520	40.02	39.02	39.02	39.02	39.02	39.02	39.02	39.02	39.02	39.02	39.02
520	540	43.55	40.55	40.55	40.55	40.55	40.55	40.55	40.55	40.55	40.55	40.55
540	560	47.08	42.08	42.08	42.08	42.08	42.08	42.08	42.08	42.08	42.08	42.08
560	580	50.61	43.61	43.61	43.61	43.61	43.61	43.61	43.61	43.61	43.61	43.61
580	600	54.14	45.14	45.14	45.14	45.14	45.14	45.14	45.14	45.14	45.14	45.14
600	640	59.43	47.43	47.43	47.43	47.43	47.43	47.43	47.43	47.43	47.43	47.43
640	680	66.49	50.49	50.49	50.49	50.49	50.49	50.49	50.49	50.49	50.49	50.49
680	720	73.55	53.55	53.55	53.55	53.55	53.55	53.55	53.55	53.55	53.55	53.55
720	760	80.61	56.61	56.61	56.61	56.61	56.61	56.61	56.61	56.61	56.61	56.61
760	800	87.67	59.67	59.67	59.67	59.67	59.67	59.67	59.67	59.67	59.67	59.67
800	840	94.73	63.73	62.73	62.73	62.73	62.73	62.73	62.73	62.73	62.73	62.73
840	880	101.79	70.79	65.79	65.79	65.79	65.79	65.79	65.79	65.79	65.79	65.79
880	920	109.85	77.85	68.85	68.85	68.85	68.85	68.85	68.85	68.85	68.85	68.85
920	960	118.91	84.91	71.91	71.91	71.91	71.91	71.91	71.91	71.91	71.91	71.91
960	1000	127.97	91.97	74.97	74.97	74.97	74.97	74.97	74.97	74.97	74.97	74.97
1000	1040	137.03	99.03	78.03	78.03	78.03	78.03	78.03	78.03	78.03	78.03	78.03
1040	1080	146.09	106.09	81.09	81.09	81.09	81.09	81.09	81.09	81.09	81.09	81.09
1080	1120	155.15	113.15	84.15	84.15	84.15	84.15	84.15	84.15	84.15	84.15	84.15
1120	1160	164.21	120.21	90.21	87.21	87.21	87.21	87.21	87.21	87.21	87.21	87.21
1160	1200	173.27	128.27	97.27	90.27	90.27	90.27	90.27	90.27	90.27	90.27	90.27
1200	1240	182.33	137.33	104.33	93.33	93.33	93.33	93.33	93.33	93.33	93.33	93.33
1240	1280	191.39	146.39	111.39	96.39	96.39	96.39	96.39	96.39	96.39	96.39	96.39
1280	1320	200.45	155.45	118.45	99.45	99.45	99.45	99.45	99.45	99.45	99.45	99.45
1320	1360	209.51	164.51	125.51	102.51	102.51	102.51	102.51	102.51	102.51	102.51	102.51
1360	1400	218.57	173.57	132.57	105.57	105.57	105.57	105.57	105.57	105.57	105.57	105.57
1400	1440	227.63	182.63	139.63	108.63	108.63	108.63	108.63	108.63	108.63	108.63	108.63
1440	1480	236.69	191.69	146.69	115.69	111.69	111.69	111.69	111.69	111.69	111.69	111.69
1480	1520	245.75	200.75	154.75	122.75	114.75	114.75	114.75	114.75	114.75	114.75	114.75
1520	1560	254.81	209.81	163.81	129.81	117.81	117.81	117.81	117.81	117.81	117.81	117.81
1560	1600	263.87	218.87	172.87	136.87	120.87	120.87	120.87	120.87	120.87	120.87	120.87
1600	1640	272.93	227.93	181.93	143.93	123.93	123.93	123.93	123.93	123.93	123.93	123.93
1640	1680	281.99	236.99	190.99	150.99	126.99	126.99	126.99	126.99	126.99	126.99	126.99
1680	1720	291.05	246.05	200.05	158.05	130.05	130.05	130.05	130.05	130.05	130.05	130.05
1720	1760	300.11	255.11	209.11	165.11	135.11	133.11	133.11	133.11	133.11	133.11	133.11
1760	1800	309.17	264.17	218.17	172.17	142.17	136.17	136.17	136.17	136.17	136.17	136.17
1800	1840	318.23	273.23	227.23	181.23	149.23	139.23	139.23	139.23	139.23	139.23	139.23
1840	1880	327.29	282.29	236.29	190.29	156.29	142.29	142.29	142.29	142.29	142.29	142.29
1880	1920	336.35	291.35	245.35	199.35	163.35	145.35	145.35	145.35	145.35	145.35	145.35
1920	1960	345.41	300.41	254.41	208.41	170.41	148.41	148.41	148.41	148.41	148.41	148.41
1960	2000	354.47	309.47	263.47	217.47	177.47	151.47	151.47	151.47	151.47	151.47	151.47
2000	2040	363.53	318.53	272.53	226.53	184.53	154.53	154.53	154.53	154.53	154.53	154.53
2040	2080	372.59	327.59	281.59	235.59	191.59	161.59	157.59	157.59	157.59	157.59	157.59
2080	2120	381.65	336.65	290.65	244.65	199.65	168.65	160.65	160.65	160.65	160.65	160.65
2120	2160	390.71	345.71	299.71	253.71	208.71	175.71	163.71	163.71	163.71	163.71	163.71
2160	2200	399.77	354.77	308.77	262.77	217.77	182.77	166.77	166.77	166.77	166.77	166.77
2200	2240	408.83	363.83	317.83	271.83	226.83	189.83	169.83	169.83	169.83	169.83	169.83
2240	2280	417.89	372.89	326.89	280.89	235.89	196.89	172.89	172.89	172.89	172.89	172.89
2280	2320	426.95	381.95	335.95	289.95	244.95	203.95	175.95	175.95	175.95	175.95	175.95
2320	2360	436.01	391.01	345.01	299.01	254.01	211.01	180.01	179.01	179.01	179.01	179.01
2360	2400	445.07	400.07	354.07	308.07	263.07	218.07	187.07	182.07	182.07	182.07	182.07
2400	2440	454.13	409.13	363.13	317.13	272.13	226.13	194.13	185.13	185.13	185.13	185.13
2440	2480	463.19	418.19	372.19	326.19	281.19	235.19	201.19	188.19	188.19	188.19	188.19
2480	2520	472.25	427.25	381.25	335.25	290.25	244.25	208.25	191.25	191.25	191.25	191.25
2520	2560	481.31	436.31	390.31	344.31	299.31	253.31	215.31	194.31	194.31	194.31	194.31
2560	2600	490.37	445.37	399.37	353.37	308.37	262.37	222.37	197.37	197.37	197.37	197.37
2600	2640	499.43	454.43	408.43	362.43	317.43	271.43	229.43	200.43	200.43	200.43	200.43

SINGLE Persons—MONTHLY Payroll Period
(For Wages Paid in 2010)

And the wages are—		And the number of withholding allowances claimed is—										
At least	But less than	0	1	2	3	4	5	6	7	8	9	10
		The amount of income, social security, and Medicare taxes to be withheld is—										
$2640	$2680	$508.49	$463.49	$417.49	$371.49	$326.49	$280.49	$236.49	$206.49	$203.49	$203.49	$203.49
2680	2720	517.55	472.55	426.55	380.55	335.55	289.55	243.55	213.55	206.55	206.55	206.55
2720	2760	526.61	481.61	435.61	389.61	344.61	298.61	252.61	220.61	209.61	209.61	209.61
2760	2800	535.67	490.67	444.67	398.67	353.67	307.67	261.67	227.67	212.67	212.67	212.67
2800	2840	544.73	499.73	453.73	407.73	362.73	316.73	270.73	234.73	215.73	215.73	215.73
2840	2880	553.79	508.79	462.79	416.79	371.79	325.79	279.79	241.79	218.79	218.79	218.79
2880	2920	562.85	517.85	471.85	425.85	380.85	334.85	288.85	248.85	221.85	221.85	221.85
2920	2960	571.91	526.91	480.91	434.91	389.91	343.91	297.91	255.91	224.91	224.91	224.91
2960	3000	580.97	535.97	489.97	443.97	398.97	352.97	306.97	262.97	231.97	227.97	227.97
3000	3040	592.03	545.03	499.03	453.03	408.03	362.03	316.03	271.03	239.03	231.03	231.03
3040	3080	605.09	554.09	508.09	462.09	417.09	371.09	325.09	280.09	246.09	234.09	234.09
3080	3120	618.15	563.15	517.15	471.15	426.15	380.15	334.15	289.15	253.15	237.15	237.15
3120	3160	631.21	572.21	526.21	480.21	435.21	389.21	343.21	298.21	260.21	240.21	240.21
3160	3200	644.27	581.27	535.27	489.27	444.27	398.27	352.27	307.27	267.27	243.27	243.27
3200	3240	657.33	590.33	544.33	498.33	453.33	407.33	361.33	316.33	274.33	246.33	246.33
3240	3280	670.39	599.39	553.39	507.39	462.39	416.39	370.39	325.39	281.39	251.39	249.39
3280	3320	683.45	608.45	562.45	516.45	471.45	425.45	379.45	334.45	288.45	258.45	252.45
3320	3360	696.51	620.51	571.51	525.51	480.51	434.51	388.51	343.51	297.51	265.51	255.51
3360	3400	709.57	633.57	580.57	534.57	489.57	443.57	397.57	352.57	306.57	272.57	258.57
3400	3440	722.63	646.63	589.63	543.63	498.63	452.63	406.63	361.63	315.63	279.63	261.63
3440	3480	735.69	659.69	598.69	552.69	507.69	461.69	415.69	370.69	324.69	286.69	264.69
3480	3520	748.75	672.75	607.75	561.75	516.75	470.75	424.75	379.75	333.75	293.75	267.75
3520	3560	761.81	685.81	616.81	570.81	525.81	479.81	433.81	388.81	342.81	300.81	270.81
3560	3600	774.87	698.87	625.87	579.87	534.87	488.87	442.87	397.87	351.87	307.87	276.87
3600	3640	787.93	711.93	635.93	588.93	543.93	497.93	451.93	406.93	360.93	315.93	283.93
3640	3680	800.99	724.99	648.99	597.99	552.99	506.99	460.99	415.99	369.99	324.99	290.99
3680	3720	814.05	738.05	662.05	607.05	562.05	516.05	470.05	425.05	379.05	334.05	298.05
3720	3760	827.11	751.11	675.11	616.11	571.11	525.11	479.11	434.11	388.11	343.11	305.11
3760	3800	840.17	764.17	688.17	625.17	580.17	534.17	488.17	443.17	397.17	352.17	312.17
3800	3840	853.23	777.23	701.23	634.23	589.23	543.23	497.23	452.23	406.23	361.23	319.23
3840	3880	866.29	790.29	714.29	643.29	598.29	552.29	506.29	461.29	415.29	370.29	326.29
3880	3920	879.35	803.35	727.35	652.35	607.35	561.35	515.35	470.35	424.35	379.35	333.35
3920	3960	892.41	816.41	740.41	664.41	616.41	570.41	524.41	479.41	433.41	388.41	342.41
3960	4000	905.47	829.47	753.47	677.47	625.47	579.47	533.47	488.47	442.47	397.47	351.47
4000	4040	918.53	842.53	766.53	690.53	634.53	588.53	542.53	497.53	451.53	406.53	360.53
4040	4080	931.59	855.59	779.59	703.59	643.59	597.59	551.59	506.59	460.59	415.59	369.59
4080	4120	944.65	868.65	792.65	716.65	652.65	606.65	560.65	515.65	469.65	424.65	378.65
4120	4160	957.71	881.71	805.71	729.71	661.71	615.71	569.71	524.71	478.71	433.71	387.71
4160	4200	970.77	894.77	818.77	742.77	670.77	624.77	578.77	533.77	487.77	442.77	396.77
4200	4240	983.83	907.83	831.83	755.83	679.83	633.83	587.83	542.83	496.83	451.83	405.83
4240	4280	996.89	920.89	844.89	768.89	692.89	642.89	596.89	551.89	505.89	460.89	414.89
4280	4320	1009.95	933.95	857.95	781.95	705.95	651.95	605.95	560.95	514.95	469.95	423.95
4320	4360	1023.01	947.01	871.01	795.01	719.01	661.01	615.01	570.01	524.01	479.01	433.01
4360	4400	1036.07	960.07	884.07	808.07	732.07	670.07	624.07	579.07	533.07	488.07	442.07
4400	4440	1049.13	973.13	897.13	821.13	745.13	679.13	633.13	588.13	542.13	497.13	451.13
4440	4480	1062.19	986.19	910.19	834.19	758.19	688.19	642.19	597.19	551.19	506.19	460.19
4480	4520	1075.25	999.25	923.25	847.25	771.25	697.25	651.25	606.25	560.25	515.25	469.25
4520	4560	1088.31	1012.31	936.31	860.31	784.31	708.31	660.31	615.31	569.31	524.31	478.31
4560	4600	1101.37	1025.37	949.37	873.37	797.37	721.37	669.37	624.37	578.37	533.37	487.37
4600	4640	1114.43	1038.43	962.43	886.43	810.43	734.43	678.43	633.43	587.43	542.43	496.43
4640	4680	1127.49	1051.49	975.49	899.49	823.49	747.49	687.49	642.49	596.49	551.49	505.49
4680	4720	1140.55	1064.55	988.55	912.55	836.55	760.55	696.55	651.55	605.55	560.55	514.55
4720	4760	1153.61	1077.61	1001.61	925.61	849.61	773.61	705.61	660.61	614.61	569.61	523.61
4760	4800	1166.67	1090.67	1014.67	938.67	862.67	786.67	714.67	669.67	623.67	578.67	532.67
4800	4840	1179.73	1103.73	1027.73	951.73	875.73	799.73	723.73	678.73	632.73	587.73	541.73
4840	4880	1192.79	1116.79	1040.79	964.79	888.79	812.79	735.79	687.79	641.79	596.79	550.79
4880	4920	1205.85	1129.85	1053.85	977.85	901.85	825.85	748.85	696.85	650.85	605.85	559.85
4920	4960	1218.91	1142.91	1066.91	990.91	914.91	838.91	761.91	705.91	659.91	614.91	568.91
4960	5000	1231.97	1155.97	1079.97	1003.97	927.97	851.97	774.97	714.97	668.97	623.97	577.97
5000	5040	1245.03	1169.03	1093.03	1017.03	941.03	865.03	788.03	724.03	678.03	633.03	587.03

$5040 and over   Do not use this table. See page 46 for instructions.

MARRIED Persons—MONTHLY Payroll Period
(For Wages Paid in 2010)

And the wages are—		And the number of withholding allowances claimed is—										
At least	But less than	0	1	2	3	4	5	6	7	8	9	10
		The amount of income, social security, and Medicare taxes to be withheld is—										
$0	$540	7.65%	7.65%	7.65%	7.65%	7.65%	7.65%	7.65%	7.65%	7.65%	7.65%	7.65%
540	560	42.08	42.08	42.08	42.08	42.08	42.08	42.08	42.08	42.08	42.08	42.08
560	580	43.61	43.61	43.61	43.61	43.61	43.61	43.61	43.61	43.61	43.61	43.61
580	600	45.14	45.14	45.14	45.14	45.14	45.14	45.14	45.14	45.14	45.14	45.14
600	640	47.43	47.43	47.43	47.43	47.43	47.43	47.43	47.43	47.43	47.43	47.43
640	680	50.49	50.49	50.49	50.49	50.49	50.49	50.49	50.49	50.49	50.49	50.49
680	720	53.55	53.55	53.55	53.55	53.55	53.55	53.55	53.55	53.55	53.55	53.55
720	760	56.61	56.61	56.61	56.61	56.61	56.61	56.61	56.61	56.61	56.61	56.61
760	800	59.67	59.67	59.67	59.67	59.67	59.67	59.67	59.67	59.67	59.67	59.67
800	840	62.73	62.73	62.73	62.73	62.73	62.73	62.73	62.73	62.73	62.73	62.73
840	880	65.79	65.79	65.79	65.79	65.79	65.79	65.79	65.79	65.79	65.79	65.79
880	920	68.85	68.85	68.85	68.85	68.85	68.85	68.85	68.85	68.85	68.85	68.85
920	960	71.91	71.91	71.91	71.91	71.91	71.91	71.91	71.91	71.91	71.91	71.91
960	1000	74.97	74.97	74.97	74.97	74.97	74.97	74.97	74.97	74.97	74.97	74.97
1000	1040	78.03	78.03	78.03	78.03	78.03	78.03	78.03	78.03	78.03	78.03	78.03
1040	1080	81.09	81.09	81.09	81.09	81.09	81.09	81.09	81.09	81.09	81.09	81.09
1080	1120	84.15	84.15	84.15	84.15	84.15	84.15	84.15	84.15	84.15	84.15	84.15
1120	1160	87.21	87.21	87.21	87.21	87.21	87.21	87.21	87.21	87.21	87.21	87.21
1160	1200	93.27	90.27	90.27	90.27	90.27	90.27	90.27	90.27	90.27	90.27	90.27
1200	1240	100.33	93.33	93.33	93.33	93.33	93.33	93.33	93.33	93.33	93.33	93.33
1240	1280	107.39	96.39	96.39	96.39	96.39	96.39	96.39	96.39	96.39	96.39	96.39
1280	1320	114.45	99.45	99.45	99.45	99.45	99.45	99.45	99.45	99.45	99.45	99.45
1320	1360	121.51	102.51	102.51	102.51	102.51	102.51	102.51	102.51	102.51	102.51	102.51
1360	1400	128.57	105.57	105.57	105.57	105.57	105.57	105.57	105.57	105.57	105.57	105.57
1400	1440	135.63	108.63	108.63	108.63	108.63	108.63	108.63	108.63	108.63	108.63	108.63
1440	1480	142.69	112.69	111.69	111.69	111.69	111.69	111.69	111.69	111.69	111.69	111.69
1480	1520	149.75	119.75	114.75	114.75	114.75	114.75	114.75	114.75	114.75	114.75	114.75
1520	1560	156.81	126.81	117.81	117.81	117.81	117.81	117.81	117.81	117.81	117.81	117.81
1560	1600	163.87	133.87	120.87	120.87	120.87	120.87	120.87	120.87	120.87	120.87	120.87
1600	1640	170.93	140.93	123.93	123.93	123.93	123.93	123.93	123.93	123.93	123.93	123.93
1640	1680	177.99	147.99	126.99	126.99	126.99	126.99	126.99	126.99	126.99	126.99	126.99
1680	1720	185.05	155.05	130.05	130.05	130.05	130.05	130.05	130.05	130.05	130.05	130.05
1720	1760	192.11	162.11	133.11	133.11	133.11	133.11	133.11	133.11	133.11	133.11	133.11
1760	1800	199.17	169.17	139.17	136.17	136.17	136.17	136.17	136.17	136.17	136.17	136.17
1800	1840	206.23	176.23	146.23	139.23	139.23	139.23	139.23	139.23	139.23	139.23	139.23
1840	1880	213.29	183.29	153.29	142.29	142.29	142.29	142.29	142.29	142.29	142.29	142.29
1880	1920	220.35	190.35	160.35	145.35	145.35	145.35	145.35	145.35	145.35	145.35	145.35
1920	1960	227.41	197.41	167.41	148.41	148.41	148.41	148.41	148.41	148.41	148.41	148.41
1960	2000	234.47	204.47	174.47	151.47	151.47	151.47	151.47	151.47	151.47	151.47	151.47
2000	2040	241.53	211.53	181.53	154.53	154.53	154.53	154.53	154.53	154.53	154.53	154.53
2040	2080	249.59	218.59	188.59	157.59	157.59	157.59	157.59	157.59	157.59	157.59	157.59
2080	2120	258.65	225.65	195.65	164.65	160.65	160.65	160.65	160.65	160.65	160.65	160.65
2120	2160	267.71	232.71	202.71	171.71	163.71	163.71	163.71	163.71	163.71	163.71	163.71
2160	2200	276.77	239.77	209.77	178.77	166.77	166.77	166.77	166.77	166.77	166.77	166.77
2200	2240	285.83	246.83	216.83	185.83	169.83	169.83	169.83	169.83	169.83	169.83	169.83
2240	2280	294.89	253.89	223.89	192.89	172.89	172.89	172.89	172.89	172.89	172.89	172.89
2280	2320	303.95	260.95	230.95	199.95	175.95	175.95	175.95	175.95	175.95	175.95	175.95
2320	2360	313.01	268.01	238.01	207.01	179.01	179.01	179.01	179.01	179.01	179.01	179.01
2360	2400	322.07	277.07	245.07	214.07	184.07	182.07	182.07	182.07	182.07	182.07	182.07
2400	2440	331.13	286.13	252.13	221.13	191.13	185.13	185.13	185.13	185.13	185.13	185.13
2440	2480	340.19	295.19	259.19	228.19	198.19	188.19	188.19	188.19	188.19	188.19	188.19
2480	2520	349.25	304.25	266.25	235.25	205.25	191.25	191.25	191.25	191.25	191.25	191.25
2520	2560	358.31	313.31	273.31	242.31	212.31	194.31	194.31	194.31	194.31	194.31	194.31
2560	2600	367.37	322.37	280.37	249.37	219.37	197.37	197.37	197.37	197.37	197.37	197.37
2600	2640	376.43	331.43	287.43	256.43	226.43	200.43	200.43	200.43	200.43	200.43	200.43
2640	2680	385.49	340.49	294.49	263.49	233.49	203.49	203.49	203.49	203.49	203.49	203.49
2680	2720	394.55	349.55	303.55	270.55	240.55	209.55	206.55	206.55	206.55	206.55	206.55
2720	2760	403.61	358.61	312.61	277.61	247.61	216.61	209.61	209.61	209.61	209.61	209.61
2760	2800	412.67	367.67	321.67	284.67	254.67	223.67	212.67	212.67	212.67	212.67	212.67
2800	2840	421.73	376.73	330.73	291.73	261.73	230.73	215.73	215.73	215.73	215.73	215.73
2840	2880	430.79	385.79	339.79	298.79	268.79	237.79	218.79	218.79	218.79	218.79	218.79
2880	2920	439.85	394.85	348.85	305.85	275.85	244.85	221.85	221.85	221.85	221.85	221.85
2920	2960	448.91	403.91	357.91	312.91	282.91	251.91	224.91	224.91	224.91	224.91	224.91
2960	3000	457.97	412.97	366.97	320.97	289.97	258.97	228.97	227.97	227.97	227.97	227.97
3000	3040	467.03	422.03	376.03	330.03	297.03	266.03	236.03	231.03	231.03	231.03	231.03
3040	3080	476.09	431.09	385.09	339.09	304.09	273.09	243.09	234.09	234.09	234.09	234.09
3080	3120	485.15	440.15	394.15	348.15	311.15	280.15	250.15	237.15	237.15	237.15	237.15
3120	3160	494.21	449.21	403.21	357.21	318.21	287.21	257.21	240.21	240.21	240.21	240.21
3160	3200	503.27	458.27	412.27	366.27	325.27	294.27	264.27	243.27	243.27	243.27	243.27
3200	3240	512.33	467.33	421.33	375.33	332.33	301.33	271.33	246.33	246.33	246.33	246.33
3240	3280	521.39	476.39	430.39	384.39	339.39	308.39	278.39	249.39	249.39	249.39	249.39
3280	3320	530.45	485.45	439.45	393.45	348.45	315.45	285.45	255.45	252.45	252.45	252.45
3320	3360	539.51	494.51	448.51	402.51	357.51	322.51	292.51	262.51	255.51	255.51	255.51
3360	3400	548.57	503.57	457.57	411.57	366.57	329.57	299.57	269.57	258.57	258.57	258.57
3400	3440	557.63	512.63	466.63	420.63	375.63	336.63	306.63	276.63	261.63	261.63	261.63

MARRIED Persons—MONTHLY Payroll Period

(For Wages Paid in 2010)

And the wages are—		And the number of withholding allowances claimed is—										
At least	But less than	0	1	2	3	4	5	6	7	8	9	10
		The amount of income, social security, and Medicare taxes to be withheld is—										
$3440	$3480	$566.69	$521.69	$475.69	$429.69	$384.69	$343.69	$313.69	$283.69	$264.69	$264.69	$264.69
3480	3520	575.75	530.75	484.75	438.75	393.75	350.75	320.75	290.75	267.75	267.75	267.75
3520	3560	584.81	539.81	493.81	447.81	402.81	357.81	327.81	297.81	270.81	270.81	270.81
3560	3600	593.87	548.87	502.87	456.87	411.87	365.87	334.87	304.87	273.87	273.87	273.87
3600	3640	602.93	557.93	511.93	465.93	420.93	374.93	341.93	311.93	280.93	276.93	276.93
3640	3680	611.99	566.99	520.99	474.99	429.99	383.99	348.99	318.99	287.99	279.99	279.99
3680	3720	621.05	576.05	530.05	484.05	439.05	393.05	356.05	326.05	295.05	283.05	283.05
3720	3760	630.11	585.11	539.11	493.11	448.11	402.11	363.11	333.11	302.11	286.11	286.11
3760	3800	639.17	594.17	548.17	502.17	457.17	411.17	370.17	340.17	309.17	289.17	289.17
3800	3840	648.23	603.23	557.23	511.23	466.23	420.23	377.23	347.23	316.23	292.23	292.23
3840	3880	657.29	612.29	566.29	520.29	475.29	429.29	384.29	354.29	323.29	295.29	295.29
3880	3920	666.35	621.35	575.35	529.35	484.35	438.35	393.35	361.35	330.35	300.35	298.35
3920	3960	675.41	630.41	584.41	538.41	493.41	447.41	402.41	368.41	337.41	307.41	301.41
3960	4000	684.47	639.47	593.47	547.47	502.47	456.47	411.47	375.47	344.47	314.47	304.47
4000	4040	693.53	648.53	602.53	556.53	511.53	465.53	420.53	382.53	351.53	321.53	307.53
4040	4080	702.59	657.59	611.59	565.59	520.59	474.59	429.59	389.59	358.59	328.59	310.59
4080	4120	711.65	666.65	620.65	574.65	529.65	483.65	438.65	396.65	365.65	335.65	313.65
4120	4160	720.71	675.71	629.71	583.71	538.71	492.71	447.71	403.71	372.71	342.71	316.71
4160	4200	729.77	684.77	638.77	592.77	547.77	501.77	456.77	410.77	379.77	349.77	319.77
4200	4240	738.83	693.83	647.83	601.83	556.83	510.83	465.83	419.83	386.83	356.83	325.83
4240	4280	747.89	702.89	656.89	610.89	565.89	519.89	474.89	428.89	393.89	363.89	332.89
4280	4320	756.95	711.95	665.95	619.95	574.95	528.95	483.95	437.95	400.95	370.95	339.95
4320	4360	766.01	721.01	675.01	629.01	584.01	538.01	493.01	447.01	408.01	378.01	347.01
4360	4400	775.07	730.07	684.07	638.07	593.07	547.07	502.07	456.07	415.07	385.07	354.07
4400	4440	784.13	739.13	693.13	647.13	602.13	556.13	511.13	465.13	422.13	392.13	361.13
4440	4480	793.19	748.19	702.19	656.19	611.19	565.19	520.19	474.19	429.19	399.19	368.19
4480	4520	802.25	757.25	711.25	665.25	620.25	574.25	529.25	483.25	437.25	406.25	375.25
4520	4560	811.31	766.31	720.31	674.31	629.31	583.31	538.31	492.31	446.31	413.31	382.31
4560	4600	820.37	775.37	729.37	683.37	638.37	592.37	547.37	501.37	455.37	420.37	389.37
4600	4640	829.43	784.43	738.43	692.43	647.43	601.43	556.43	510.43	464.43	427.43	396.43
4640	4680	838.49	793.49	747.49	701.49	656.49	610.49	565.49	519.49	473.49	434.49	403.49
4680	4720	847.55	802.55	756.55	710.55	665.55	619.55	574.55	528.55	482.55	441.55	410.55
4720	4760	856.61	811.61	765.61	719.61	674.61	628.61	583.61	537.61	491.61	448.61	417.61
4760	4800	865.67	820.67	774.67	728.67	683.67	637.67	592.67	546.67	500.67	455.67	424.67
4800	4840	874.73	829.73	783.73	737.73	692.73	646.73	601.73	555.73	509.73	464.73	431.73
4840	4880	883.79	838.79	792.79	746.79	701.79	655.79	610.79	564.79	518.79	473.79	438.79
4880	4920	892.85	847.85	801.85	755.85	710.85	664.85	619.85	573.85	527.85	482.85	445.85
4920	4960	901.91	856.91	810.91	764.91	719.91	673.91	628.91	582.91	536.91	491.91	452.91
4960	5000	910.97	865.97	819.97	773.97	728.97	682.97	637.97	591.97	545.97	500.97	459.97
5000	5040	920.03	875.03	829.03	783.03	738.03	692.03	647.03	601.03	555.03	510.03	467.03
5040	5080	929.09	884.09	838.09	792.09	747.09	701.09	656.09	610.09	564.09	519.09	474.09
5080	5120	938.15	893.15	847.15	801.15	756.15	710.15	665.15	619.15	573.15	528.15	482.15
5120	5160	947.21	902.21	856.21	810.21	765.21	719.21	674.21	628.21	582.21	537.21	491.21
5160	5200	956.27	911.27	865.27	819.27	774.27	728.27	683.27	637.27	591.27	546.27	500.27
5200	5240	965.33	920.33	874.33	828.33	783.33	737.33	692.33	646.33	600.33	555.33	509.33
5240	5280	974.39	929.39	883.39	837.39	792.39	746.39	701.39	655.39	609.39	564.39	518.39
5280	5320	983.45	938.45	892.45	846.45	801.45	755.45	710.45	664.45	618.45	573.45	527.45
5320	5360	992.51	947.51	901.51	855.51	810.51	764.51	719.51	673.51	627.51	582.51	536.51
5360	5400	1001.57	956.57	910.57	864.57	819.57	773.57	728.57	682.57	636.57	591.57	545.57
5400	5440	1010.63	965.63	919.63	873.63	828.63	782.63	737.63	691.63	645.63	600.63	554.63
5440	5480	1019.69	974.69	928.69	882.69	837.69	791.69	746.69	700.69	654.69	609.69	563.69
5480	5520	1028.75	983.75	937.75	891.75	846.75	800.75	755.75	709.75	663.75	618.75	572.75
5520	5560	1037.81	992.81	946.81	900.81	855.81	809.81	764.81	718.81	672.81	627.81	581.81
5560	5600	1046.87	1001.87	955.87	909.87	864.87	818.87	773.87	727.87	681.87	636.87	590.87
5600	5640	1055.93	1010.93	964.93	918.93	873.93	827.93	782.93	736.93	690.93	645.93	599.93
5640	5680	1064.99	1019.99	973.99	927.99	882.99	836.99	791.99	745.99	699.99	654.99	608.99
5680	5720	1074.05	1029.05	983.05	937.05	892.05	846.05	801.05	755.05	709.05	664.05	618.05
5720	5760	1083.11	1038.11	992.11	946.11	901.11	855.11	810.11	764.11	718.11	673.11	627.11
5760	5800	1092.17	1047.17	1001.17	955.17	910.17	864.17	819.17	773.17	727.17	682.17	636.17
5800	5840	1101.23	1056.23	1010.23	964.23	919.23	873.23	828.23	782.23	736.23	691.23	645.23

$5840 and over   Do not use this table. See page 46 for instructions.

APPENDIX A

TAX RESEARCH WORKING PAPER FILE

INDEX TO TAX RESEARCH FILE*

*Most accounting firms maintain a **client file** for each of their clients. Typically, this file contains copies of client letters, memoranda-to-the-file, relevant primary and secondary authorities, and billing information. In our case, the client file for Mercy Hospital would include copies of the following: (1) the December 12 letter to Elizabeth Feghali, (2) the December 9 memorandum-to-the-file, (3) Sec. 119, (4) Reg. Sec. 1.119-1, (5) the *Kowalski* opinion, (6) the *Standard Federal Tax Reporter* annotation, and (7) pertinent billing information.

TAX RESEARCH FILE

As mentioned in Chapter C:1 the tax research process entails six steps.

1. Determine the facts
2. Identify the issues
3. Locate applicable authorities
4. Evaluate these authorities
5. Analyze the facts in terms of applicable authorities
6. Communicate conclusions and recommendations to others.

Let us walk through each of these steps.

Determine the Facts   Assume that we have determined the facts to be as follows:

> *Mercy Hospital maintains a cafeteria on its premises. In addition, it rents space to MacDougal's, a privately owned sandwich shop. The cafeteria closes at 8:00 p.m. MacDougal's is open 24 hours. Mercy provides meal vouchers to each of its 240 medical employees to enable them to remain on call in case of emergency. The vouchers are redeemable either at the cafeteria or at MacDougal's. Although the employees are not required to remain on or near the premises during meal hours, they generally do. Elizabeth Fegali, Mercy's Chief Administrator, has approached you with the following question: Is the value of a meal voucher includible in the employees' gross income?*

At this juncture, be sure you understand the facts before proceeding further. Remember, researching the wrong facts could produce the wrong results.

Identify the Issues   Identifying the issues presupposes a minimum level of proficiency in tax accounting. This proficiency will come with time, effort, and perseverance. The central issue raised by the facts is the taxability of the meal vouchers. A resolution of this issue will hinge on the resolution of other issues raised in the course of the research.

Locate Applicable Authorities   For some students, this step is the most difficult in the research process. It raises the perplexing question, "Where do I begin to look?" The answer depends on the tax resources at one's disposal, as well as one's research preferences. Four rules of thumb apply:

1. *Adopt an approach with which you are comfortable, and that you are confident will produce reliable results.*
2. *Always consult the IRC and other primary authorities.*
3. *Be as thorough as possible, taking into consideration time and billing constraints.*
4. *Make sure that the authorities you consult are current.*

One approach is to conduct a topical search. Begin by consulting the index to the Internal Revenue Code (IRC). Then read the relevant IRC section(s). If the language of the IRC is vague or ambiguous, turn to the Treasury Regulations. Read the relevant regulation section that elaborates or expounds on the IRC provision. If the language of the regulation is confusing or unclear, go to a commercial tax service. Read the relevant tax service paragraphs that explain or analyze the statutory and regulatory provisions. For references to other authorities, browse through the footnotes and annotations of the service. Then, consult these authorities directly. Finally, check the currency of the authorities consulted, with the aid of a citator or status (finding) list.

   If a pertinent court decision or IRS ruling has been called to your attention, consult this authority directly. Alternatively, browse through the status (finding) list of a tax service for references to tax service paragraphs that discuss this authority. Better still, consult a citator or status list for references to court opinions or rulings that cite the authority. If you subscribe to a computerized tax service, conduct a keyword, citation, contents, or topical search. (For a discussion of these types of searches, see the computerized research supplement available for download at *www.prenhall.com/phtax*.) Then, hyperlink to the authorities cited within the text of the documents retrieved. So numerous are the

approaches to tax research that one is virtually free to pick and choose. All that is required of the researcher is a basic level of skill and some imagination.

Let us adopt a topical approach to the issue of the meal vouchers. If we consult an index to the IRC, we are likely to find the heading "Meals and Lodging." Below this heading are likely to be several subheadings, some pertaining to deductions, others to exclusions. Because the voucher issue pertains to an exclusion, let us browse through these subheadings. In so doing, we will notice that most of these subheadings refer to Sec. 119. If we look up this IRC section, we will see the following passage:

Sec. 119. Meals or lodging furnished for the convenience of the employer.

(a) **Meals and lodging furnished to employee, his spouse, and his dependents, pursuant to employment.**
There shall be excluded from gross income of an employee the value of any meals or lodging furnished to him . . . by, or on behalf of his employer for the convenience of the employer, but only if—

    (1) in the case of meals, the meals are furnished on the business premises of the employer . . .

(b) **Special rules.** For purposes of subsection (a)—
    (4) **Meals furnished to employees on business premises where meals of most employees are otherwise excludable.** All meals furnished on the business premises of an employer to such employer's employees shall be treated as furnished for the convenience of the employer if . . . more than half of the employees to whom such meals are furnished on such premises are furnished such meals for the convenience of the employer.

Section 119 appears to be applicable. It deals with meals furnished to an employee on the business premises of the employer. Our case deals with meal vouchers furnished to employees for redemption at employer-maintained and employer-rented-out facilities. But here, additional issues arise. For purposes of Sec. 119, are meal vouchers the same as "meals"? (Do not assume they are.) Are employer-maintained and employer-rented-out facilities the same as "the business premises of the employer"? (Again, do not assume they are.) And what does the IRC mean by "for the convenience of the employer"? Because the IRC offers no guidance in this respect, let us turn to the Treasury Regulations.

The applicable regulation is Reg. Sec. 1.119-1. How do we know this? Because Treasury Regulation section numbers track the IRC section numbers. Regulation Sec. 1.119-1 is the only regulation under Sec. 119. If we browse through this regulation, we will find the following provision:

    (a) Meals . . .
        (2) **Meals furnished without a charge**
            (i) Meals furnished by an employer without charge to the employee will be regarded as furnished for the convenience of the employer if such meals are furnished for a substantial noncompensatory business reason of the employer . . .
            (ii) (a) Meals will be regarded as furnished for a substantial noncompensatory business reason of the employer when the meals are furnished to the employee during his working hours to have the employee available for emergency call during his meal period . . .
    (c) **Business premises of the employer.**
        (1) **In general.** For purposes of this section, the term "business premises of the employer" generally means the place of employment of the employee . . .

Based on a reading of this provision, we might conclude that the hospital meals are furnished "for the convenience of the employer." Why? Because they are furnished for a "substantial noncompensatory business reason of the employer," namely, to have the employees available for emergency call during their meal periods. They also are furnished during the employees' working hours. Moreover, under Sec. 119(b)(4), if more than half the employees satisfy the "for the convenience of the employer" test, all employees will be regarded as satisfying the test. But are the meals furnished on "the business premises of the employer"? Under the regulation, the answer would depend. If the meals are furnished in the hospital cafeteria, they probably are furnished on "the business premises of the employer." The hospital is the place of employment of the medical employees. The cafeteria is part of the hospital. On the other hand, if the meals are furnished at MacDougal's, they probably are not

furnished on "the business premises of the employer." MacDougal's is not the place of employment of the medical employees. Nor is it a part of the hospital. Thus, Reg. Sec. 1.119-1 is enlightening with respect to two statutory terms: "for the convenience of the employer" and "the business premises of the employer." However, it is obscure with respect to the third term, "meals." Because of this obscurity, let us turn to a tax service.

Although the index to CCH's *Standard Federal Tax Reporter* does not list "meal vouchers," it does list "cash allowances in lieu of meals" as a subtopic under Meals and Lodging. Are meal vouchers the same as cash meal allowances?—perhaps so; let us see. Next to the heading "cash allowances in lieu of meals" is a reference to CCH ¶7222.59. If we look up this reference, we will find the following annotation:

¶7222.59 **Meal allowances.**—Cash meal allowances received by an employee (state trooper) from his employer were not excludible from income. *R.J. Kowalski*, SCt, 77-2 USTC ¶9748, 434 US 77.[1]

Here we discover that, in the *Kowalski* case, the U.S. Supreme Court decided that cash meal allowances received by an employee were not excludible from the employee's income. Is the *Kowalski* case similar to our case? It might be. Let us find out. If we turn to paragraph 9748 of the second 1977 volume of *United States Tax Cases*, we will find the text of the *Kowalski* opinion. A synopsis of this opinion is present below.

In the mid-1970s, the State of New Jersey provided cash meal allowances to its state troopers. The state did not require the troopers to use the allowances exclusively for meals. Nor did it require them to consume their meals on its business premises. One trooper, Robert J. Kowalski, failed to report a portion of his allowance on his tax return. The IRS assessed a deficiency, and Kowalski took the IRS to court. In court, Kowalski argued that the meal allowances were excludible, because they were furnished "for the convenience of the employer." The IRS contended that the allowances were taxable because they amounted to compensation. The Supreme Court took up the case and sided with the IRS. The Court held that the Sec. 119 income exclusion does not apply to cash payments; it applies only to meals in kind.[2]

For the sake of illustration, let us assume that Sec. 119, Reg. Sec. 1.119-1, and the *Kowalski* case are the *only* authorities "on point." How should we evaluate them?

Evaluate Authorities Section 119 is the key authority applicable to our case. It supplies the operative rule for resolving the issue of the meal vouchers. It is vague, however, with respect to three terms: "meals," "business premises of the employer," and "for the convenience of the employer." The principal judicial authority is the *Kowalski* case. It provides an official interpretation of the term "meals." Because the U.S. Supreme Court decided *Kowalski*, the case should be assigned considerable weight. The relevant administrative authority is Reg. Sec. 1.119-1. It expounds on the terms "business premises of the employer" and "for the convenience of the employer." Because neither the IRC nor *Kowalski* explain these terms, Reg. Sec. 1.119-1 should be accorded great weight. But what if *Kowalski* had conflicted with Reg. Sec. 1.119-1? Which should be considered more authoritative? As a general rule, high court decisions "trump" the Treasury Regulations (and all IRS pronouncements for that matter). The more recent the decision, the greater its precedential weight. Had there been no Supreme Court decision and a division of appellate authority, equal weight should have been assigned to each of the appellate court decisions.

Analyze the Facts in Terms of Applicable Authorities Analyzing the facts in terms of applicable authorities involves applying the abstraction of the law to the concreteness of the facts. It entails expressing the generalities of the law in terms of the specifics of the facts. In this process, every legal condition must be satisfied for the result implied by the

---

[1] The researcher also might read the main *Standard Federal Tax Reporter* paragraph that discusses meals and lodging furnished by the employer (CCH ¶7222.01). Within this paragraph are likely to be references to other primary authorities.

[2] At this juncture, the researcher should consult a citator to determine whether *Kowalski* is still "good law," and to locate other authorities that cite *Kowalski*.

general rule to ensue. Thus, in our case, the conditions of furnishing "meals," "on the business premises of the employer," and "for the convenience of the employer" must be satisfied for the value of the "meals" to be excluded from the employee's income.

When analyzing the facts in terms of case law, the researcher should always draw an *analogy* between case facts and client facts. Likewise, he or she should always draw a *distinction* between case facts and client facts. Remember, under the rule of precedent, a court deciding the client's case will be bound by the precedent of cases involving *similar* facts and issues. By the same token, it will *not* be bound by the precedent of cases involving *dissimilar* facts and issues.

The most useful vehicle for analyzing client facts is the memorandum-to-the-file (see page A-6). The purpose of this document is threefold: first, it assists the researcher in recollecting transactions long transpired; second, it apprises colleagues and supervisors of the nature of one's research; third, it provides "substantial authority" for the tax treatment of a particular item. Let us analyze the facts of our case by way of a memorandum-to-the-file. Notice the format of this document; it generally tracks the steps in the research process itself.

Communicate Conclusions and Recommendations to Others For three practical reasons, research results always should be communicated to the client *in writing*. First, a written communication can be made after extensive revisions. An oral communication cannot. Second, in a written communication, the researcher can delve into the intricacies of tax law. Often, in an oral communication, he or she cannot. Third, a written communication reinforces an oral understanding. Alternatively, it brings to light an oral misunderstanding.

The written communication usually takes the form of a client letter (see page A-7). The purpose of this letter is two-fold: first, it apprises the client of the results of one's research and, second, it recommends to the client a course of action based on these results. A sample client letter is presented below. Notice the organization of this document; it is similar to that of the memorandum-to-the-file.

Memorandum-to-the-File

Date: December 9, 20X1
From: Rosina Havacek
Re: The taxability of meal vouchers furnished by Mercy Hospital to its medical staff.

Facts

[*State only the facts that are relevant to the Issue(s) and necessary for the Analysis.*] Our client, Mercy Hospital ("Mercy"), provides meal vouchers to its medical employees to enable them to remain on emergency call. The vouchers are redeemable at Mercy's onsite cafeteria and at MacDougal's, a privately owned sandwich shop. MacDougal's rents business space from the hospital. Although Mercy does not require its employees to remain on or near its premises during their meal hours, the employees generally do. Elizabeth Fegali, Mercy's Chief Administrator, has asked us to research whether the value of the meal vouchers is taxable to the employees.

Issues

[*Identify the issue(s) raised by the facts. Be specific.*] The taxability of the meal vouchers depends on three issues: first, whether the meals are furnished "for the convenience of the employer"; second, whether they are furnished "on the business premises of the employer"; and third, whether the vouchers are equivalent to cash.

Applicable Law

[*Discuss those legal principles that both strengthen and weaken the client's case. Because the primary authority for tax law is the IRC, begin with the IRC.*] Section 119 provides that the value of meals is excludible from an employee's income if the meals are furnished for the convenience of, and on the business premises of the employer. [*Discuss how administrative and/or judicial authorities expound on statutory terms.*] Under Reg. Sec. 1.119-1, a meal is furnished "for the convenience of the employer" if it is furnished for a "substantial noncompensatory business reason." A "substantial noncompensatory business reason" includes the need to have the employee available for emergency calls during his or her meal period. Under Sec. 119(b)(4), if more than half the employees satisfy the "for the convenience of the employer" test, all employees will be regarded as satisfying the test. Regulation Sec. 1.119-1 defines "business premises of the employer" as the place of employment of the employee.

[*When discussing court cases, present case facts in such a way as to enable the reader to draw an analogy with client facts.*] A Supreme Court case, *Kowalski v. CIR*, 434 U.S. 77, 77-2 USTC ¶9748, discusses what constitutes "meals" for purposes of Sec. 119. In *Kowalski*, the State of New Jersey furnished cash meal allowances to its state troopers to enable them to eat while on duty. It did not require the troopers to use the allowances exclusively for meals. Nor did it require them to consume their meals on its business premises. One trooper, R.J. Kowalski, excluded the value of his allowances from his income. The IRS disputed this treatment, and Kowalski took the IRS to Court. In Court, Kowalski argued that the allowances were excludible because they were furnished "for the convenience of the employer." The IRS contended that the allowances were taxable because they amounted to compensation. The U.S. Supreme Court took up the case and decided for the IRS. The Court held that the Sec. 119 income exlusion does not apply to payments in cash.

Analysis

[*The analysis should (a) apply applicable law to the facts and (b) address the issue(s). In this section, every proposition should be supported by either authority, logic, or plausible assumptions.*]

Issue 1: The meals provided by Mercy seem to be furnished "for the convenience of the employer." They are furnished to have employees available for emergency call during their meal breaks. This is a "substantial noncompensatory reason" within the meaning of Reg. Sec. 1.119-1.

Issue 2: Although the hospital cafeteria appears to be the "business premises of the employer," MacDougal's does not appear to be. The hospital is the place of employment of the medical employees. MacDougal's is not.

Issue 3: [*In applying case law to the facts, indicate how case facts are similar to/dissimilar from client facts. If the analysis does not support a "yes-no" answer, do not give one.*] Based on the foregoing authorities, it is unclear whether the vouchers are equivalent to cash. On the one hand, they are redeemable only in meals. Thus, they resemble meals-in-kind. On the other hand, they are redeemable at more than one institution. Thus, they resemble cash. Nor is it clear whether a court deciding this case would reach the same conclusion as the Supreme Court did in *Kowalski*. In the latter case, the State of New Jersey provided its meal allowances in the form of cash. It did not require its employees to use the allowances exclusively for meals. Nor did it require them to consume their meals on its business premises. In our case, Mercy provides its meal allowances in the form of vouchers. Thus, it indirectly requires its employees to use the allowances exclusively for meals. On the other hand, it does not require them to consume their meals on its business premises.

Conclusion

[*The conclusion should (a) logically flow from the analysis, and (b) address the issue(s).*] Although it appears that the meals acquired by voucher in the hospital cafeteria are furnished "for the convenience of the employer" and "on the business premises of the employer," it is unclear whether the vouchers are equivalent to cash. If they *are* equivalent to cash, *or* if they are redeemed at MacDougal's, their value is likely to be taxable to the employees. On the other hand, if they are not equivalent to cash, *and* they are redeemed only in the hospital cafeteria, their value is likely to be excludible.

Professional Accounting Associates
2701 First City Plaza
Suite 905
Dallas, Texas 75019

December 12, 20X1

Elizabeth Feghali, Chief Administrator
Mercy Hospital
22650 West Haven Drive
Arlington, Texas 75527

Dear Ms. Feghali:

[*Introduction. Set a cordial tone.*] It was great to see you at last Thursday's football game. If not for that last minute fumble, the Longhorns might have taken the Big 12 Conference championship!

[*Issue/Purpose.*] In our meeting of December 6, you asked us to research whether the value of the meal vouchers that Mercy provides to its medical employees is taxable to the employees. [*Short Answer.*] I regret to inform you that if the vouchers are redeemed at MacDougal's, their value is likely to be taxable to the employees. On the other hand, if the vouchers are redeemed in the hospital cafeteria, their value is likely to be excludible from the employee's income. [*The remainder of the letter should elaborate, support, and qualify this answer.*]

[*Steps taken in deriving conclusion.*] In reaching this conclusion, we consulted relevant provisions of the Internal Revenue Code ("IRC"), applicable Treasury Regulations under the IRC, and a pertinent Supreme Court case. In addition, we reviewed the documents on employee benefits that you submitted to us at our earlier meeting.

[*Facts. State only the facts that are relevant to the issue and necessary for the analysis.*] The facts as we understand them are as follows: Mercy provides meal vouchers to its medical employees to enable them to eat while on emergency call. The vouchers are redeemable either in the hospital cafeteria or at MacDougal's. MacDougal's is a privately owned institution that rents business space from the hospital. Although Mercy's employees are not required to remain on or near the premises during their meal hours, they generally do.

[*Applicable law. State, do not interpret.*] Under the IRC, the value of meals is excludible from an employee's income if two conditions are met: first, the meals are furnished "for the convenience of the employer" and second, they are provided "on the business premises of the employer." Although the IRC does not explain what is meant by "for the convenience of the employer," "business premises of the employer," and "meals," other authorities do. Specifically, the Treasury Regulations define "business premises of the employer" to be the place of employment of the employees. The regulations state that providing meals during work hours to have an employee available for emergency calls is "for the convenience of the employer." Moreover, under the IRC, if more than half the employees satisfy the "for the convenience of the employer" test, all the employees will be regarded as satisfying the test. The Supreme Court has interpreted "meals" to mean food-in-kind. The Court has held that cash allowances do not qualify as "meals."

[*Analysis. Express the generalities of applicable law in terms of the specifics of the facts.*] Clearly, the meals furnished by Mercy are "for the convenience of the employer." They are furnished during the employees' work hours to have the employees available for emergency call. Although the meals provided in the hospital cafeteria appear to be furnished "on the business premises of the employer," the meals provided at MacDougal's do not appear to be. The hospital is the place of employment of the medical employees. MacDougal's is not. What is unclear is whether the meal vouchers are equivalent to food-in-kind. On the one hand, they are redeemable at more than one institution and thus resemble cash allowances. On the other hand, they are redeemable only in meals and thus resemble food-in-kind.

[*Conclusion/Recommendation.*] Because of this lack of clarity, we suggest that you modify your employee benefits plan to allow for the provision of meals-in-kind exclusively in the hospital cafeteria. In this way, you will dispel any doubt that Mercy is furnishing "meals," "for the convenience of the employer," "on the premises of the employer."

[*Closing/Follow Up.*] Please call me at 475-2020 if you have any questions concerning this conclusion. May I suggest that we meet next week to discuss the possibility of revising your employee benefits plan.

[*Circular 230 Disclaimer.*] U.S. Treasury Regulations require us to advise you that, unless otherwise specifically noted, any federal tax advice in this communication (including any attachments, enclosures, or other accompanying materials) was not intended or written to be used, and it cannot be used, by any taxpayer for the purpose of avoiding penalties; furthermore, this communication was not intended or written to support the promotion or marketing of any of the transactions or matters it addresses.

Very truly yours,
Professional Accounting Associates

By: Rosina Havacek, Junior Associate

APPENDIX B

2009 TAX FORMS

Note: Because of the availability of tax forms from many sources, only a limited number of forms are reprinted in this textbook. All federal forms are available from the Internal Revenue Service, either in paper form or from the IRS Web site, http://www.irs.gov.

| SCHEDULE SE
(Form 1040)

Department of the Treasury
Internal Revenue Service (99) | **Self-Employment Tax**

▶ **Attach to Form 1040.**　　▶ **See Instructions for Schedule SE (Form 1040).** | OMB No. 1545-0074

20**09**

Attachment
Sequence No. **17** |

| Name of person with **self-employment** income (as shown on Form 1040) | Social security number of person
with **self-employment** income ▶ |

Who Must File Schedule SE

You must file Schedule SE if:

● You had net earnings from self-employment from **other than** church employee income (line 4 of Short Schedule SE or line 4c of Long Schedule SE) of $400 or more, **or**

● You had church employee income of $108.28 or more. Income from services you performed as a minister or a member of a religious order **is not** church employee income (see page SE-1).

Note. Even if you had a loss or a small amount of income from self-employment, it may be to your benefit to file Schedule SE and use either "optional method" in Part II of Long Schedule SE (see page SE-4).

Exception. If your only self-employment income was from earnings as a minister, member of a religious order, or Christian Science practitioner **and** you filed Form 4361 and received IRS approval not to be taxed on those earnings, **do not** file Schedule SE. Instead, write "Exempt—Form 4361" on Form 1040, line 56.

May I Use Short Schedule SE or Must I Use Long Schedule SE?

Note. Use this flowchart **only if** you must file Schedule SE. If unsure, see *Who Must File Schedule SE,* above.

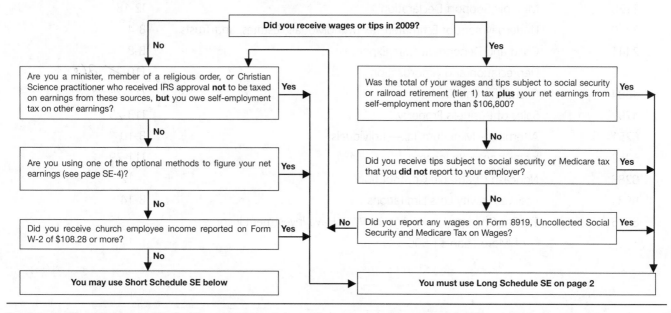

Section A—Short Schedule SE. Caution. Read above to see if you can use Short Schedule SE.

1a	Net farm profit or (loss) from Schedule F, line 36, and farm partnerships, Schedule K-1 (Form 1065), box 14, code A	**1a**	
b	If you received social security retirement or disability benefits, enter the amount of Conservation Reserve Program payments included on Schedule F, line 6b, or listed on Schedule K-1 (Form 1065), box 20, code Y	**1b** (	)
2	Net profit or (loss) from Schedule C, line 31; Schedule C-EZ, line 3; Schedule K-1 (Form 1065), box 14, code A (other than farming); and Schedule K-1 (Form 1065-B), box 9, code J1. Ministers and members of religious orders, see page SE-1 for types of income to report on this line. See page SE-3 for other income to report	**2**	
3	Combine lines 1a, 1b, and 2	**3**	
4	**Net earnings from self-employment.** Multiply line 3 by 92.35% (.9235). If less than $400, **do not** file this schedule; you do not owe self-employment tax . . . . ▶	**4**	
5	**Self-employment tax.** If the amount on line 4 is: ● $106,800 or less, multiply line 4 by 15.3% (.153). Enter the result here and on **Form 1040, line 56.** ● More than $106,800, multiply line 4 by 2.9% (.029). Then, add $13,243.20 to the result. Enter the total here and on **Form 1040, line 56.**	**5**	
6	**Deduction for one-half of self-employment tax.** Multiply line 5 by 50% (.50). Enter the result here and on **Form 1040, line 27**	**6**		

For Paperwork Reduction Act Notice, see Form 1040 instructions.　　　Cat. No. 11358Z　　　**Schedule SE (Form 1040) 2009**

Name of person with **self-employment** income (as shown on Form 1040) | Social security number of person with **self-employment** income ▶

Section B—Long Schedule SE

Part I   **Self-Employment Tax**

Note. If your only income subject to self-employment tax is **church employee income**, skip lines 1 through 4b. Enter -0- on line 4c and go to line 5a. Income from services you performed as a minister or a member of a religious order **is not** church employee income. See page SE-1.

A   If you are a minister, member of a religious order, or Christian Science practitioner **and** you filed Form 4361, but you had $400 or more of **other** net earnings from self-employment, check here and continue with Part I . . . . . . ▶ ☐

1a   Net farm profit or (loss) from Schedule F, line 36, and farm partnerships, Schedule K-1 (Form 1065), box 14, code A. **Note.** Skip lines 1a and 1b if you use the farm optional method (see page SE-4) | **1a** |

  b   If you received social security retirement or disability benefits, enter the amount of Conservation Reserve Program payments included on Schedule F, line 6b, or listed on Schedule K-1 (Form 1065), box 20, code Y | **1b** (|)

2   Net profit or (loss) from Schedule C, line 31; Schedule C-EZ, line 3; Schedule K-1 (Form 1065), box 14, code A (other than farming); and Schedule K-1 (Form 1065-B), box 9, code J1. Ministers and members of religious orders, see page SE-1 for types of income to report on this line. See page SE-3 for other income to report. **Note.** Skip this line if you use the nonfarm optional method (see page SE-4) . . . . | **2** |

3   Combine lines 1a, 1b, and 2 . . . . | **3** |

4a   If line 3 is more than zero, multiply line 3 by 92.35% (.9235). Otherwise, enter amount from line 3 | **4a** |

  b   If you elect one or both of the optional methods, enter the total of lines 15 and 17 here . . | **4b** |

  c   Combine lines 4a and 4b. If less than $400, **stop**; you do not owe self-employment tax. **Exception.** If less than $400 and you had **church employee income**, enter -0- and continue ▶ | **4c** |

5a   Enter your **church employee income** from Form W-2. See page SE-1 for definition of church employee income. . . . . . | **5a** |

  b   Multiply line 5a by 92.35% (.9235). If less than $100, enter -0- . . . . | **5b** |

6   **Net earnings from self-employment.** Add lines 4c and 5b . . . . | **6** |

7   Maximum amount of combined wages and self-employment earnings subject to social security tax or the 6.2% portion of the 7.65% railroad retirement (tier 1) tax for 2009 . . . . . . | **7** | **106,800** 00

8a   Total social security wages and tips (total of boxes 3 and 7 on Form(s) W-2) and railroad retirement (tier 1) compensation. If $106,800 or more, skip lines 8b through 10, and go to line 11 | **8a** |

  b   Unreported tips subject to social security tax (from Form 4137, line 10) | **8b** |

  c   Wages subject to social security tax (from Form 8919, line 10) | **8c** |

  d   Add lines 8a, 8b, and 8c . . . . | **8d** |

9   Subtract line 8d from line 7. If zero or less, enter -0- here and on line 10 and go to line 11 . ▶ | **9** |

10   Multiply the **smaller** of line 6 or line 9 by 12.4% (.124) . . . . | **10** |

11   Multiply line 6 by 2.9% (.029) . . . . | **11** |

12   **Self-employment tax.** Add lines 10 and 11. Enter here and on **Form 1040, line 56.** . . . | **12** |

13   **Deduction for one-half of self-employment tax.** Multiply line 12 by 50% (.50). Enter the result here and on **Form 1040, line 27** . | **13** |

Part II   **Optional Methods To Figure Net Earnings** (see page SE-4)

Farm Optional Method. You may use this method **only** if **(a)** your gross farm income[1] was not more than $6,540, **or (b)** your net farm profits[2] were less than $4,721.

14   Maximum income for optional methods | **14** | **4,360** 00

15   Enter the **smaller** of: two-thirds (²/₃) of gross farm income[1] (not less than zero) **or** $4,360. Also include this amount on line 4b above . . . . | **15** |

Nonfarm Optional Method. You may use this method **only** if **(a)** your net nonfarm profits[3] were less than $4,721 and also less than 72.189% of your gross nonfarm income,[4] **and (b)** you had net earnings from self-employment of at least $400 in 2 of the prior 3 years. **Caution.** You may use this method no more than five times.

16   Subtract line 15 from line 14 . . . . | **16** |

17   Enter the **smaller** of: two-thirds (²/₃) of gross nonfarm income[4] (not less than zero) **or** the amount on line 16. Also include this amount on line 4b above . . . . | **17** |

[1] From Sch. F, line 11, and Sch. K-1 (Form 1065), box 14, code B.

[2] From Sch. F, line 36, and Sch. K-1 (Form 1065), box 14, code A— minus the amount you would have entered on line 1b had you not used the optional method.

[3] From Sch. C, line 31; Sch. C-EZ, line 3; Sch. K-1 (Form 1065), box 14, code A; and Sch. K-1 (Form 1065-B), box 9, code J1.

[4] From Sch. C, line 7; Sch. C-EZ, line 1; Sch. K-1 (Form 1065), box 14, code C; and Sch. K-1 (Form 1065-B), box 9, code J2.

Form **2210**

Department of the Treasury
Internal Revenue Service

Underpayment of
Estimated Tax by Individuals, Estates, and Trusts
▶ See separate instructions.
▶ **Attach to Form 1040, 1040A, 1040NR, 1040NR-EZ, or 1041.**

OMB No. 1545-0140

2009

Attachment
Sequence No. **06**

Name(s) shown on tax return

Identifying number

Do You Have To File Form 2210?

Complete lines 1 through 7 below. Is line 7 less than $1,000? **Yes** ▶	**Do not file Form 2210.** You do not owe a penalty.
↓ **No**	
Complete lines 8 and 9 below. Is line 6 equal to or more than line 9? **Yes** ▶	You do not owe a penalty. **Do not file Form 2210** (but if box **E** in Part II applies, you must file page 1 of Form 2210).
↓ **No**	
You may owe a penalty. Does any box in Part II below apply? **Yes** ▶	You **must** file Form 2210. Does box **B, C,** or **D** in Part II apply?
↓ **No**	**No** / **Yes** ▶ You must figure your penalty.

Do not file Form 2210. You are not required to figure your penalty because the IRS will figure it and send you a bill for any unpaid amount. If you want to figure it, you may use Part III or Part IV as a worksheet and enter your penalty amount on your tax return, but **do not file Form 2210.**

You are **not** required to figure your penalty because the IRS will figure it and send you a bill for any unpaid amount. If you want to figure it, you may use Part III or Part IV as a worksheet and enter your penalty amount on your tax return, but **file only page 1 of Form 2210.**

Part I Required Annual Payment

1	Enter your 2009 tax after credits from Form 1040, line 55 (see instructions if not filing Form 1040)	**1**	
2	Other taxes, including self-employment tax (see page 2 of the instructions)	**2**	
3	Refundable credits. Enter the total of your making work pay and government retiree credits, earned income credit, additional child tax credit, refundable education credit, first-time homebuyer credit, credit for federal tax paid on fuels, refundable credit for prior year minimum tax, and health coverage tax credit	**3** ( )
4	Current year tax. Combine lines 1, 2, and 3. If less than $1,000, **stop;** you do not owe a penalty. **Do not** file Form 2210	**4**	
5	Multiply line 4 by 90% (.90)	5	
6	Withholding taxes. **Do not** include estimated tax payments (see page 3 of the instructions) .	**6**	
7	Subtract line 6 from line 4. If less than $1,000, **stop;** you do not owe a penalty. **Do not** file Form 2210	**7**	
8	Maximum required annual payment based on prior year's tax (see page 3 of the instructions) .	**8**	
9	**Required annual payment.** Enter the **smaller** of line 5 or line 8	**9**	

Next: Is line 9 more than line 6?

☐ **No.** You **do not** owe a penalty. **Do not** file Form 2210 unless box **E** below applies.

☐ **Yes.** You may owe a penalty, but **do not** file Form 2210 unless one or more boxes in Part II below applies.

• If box **B, C,** or **D** applies, you must figure your penalty and file Form 2210.

• If box **A, E,** or **F** applies (but not **B, C,** or **D**) file only page 1 of Form 2210. You are **not** required to figure your penalty; the IRS will figure it and send you a bill for any unpaid amount. If you want to figure your penalty, you may use Part III or IV as a worksheet and enter your penalty on your tax return, but **file only page 1 of Form 2210.**

Part II Reasons for Filing. Check applicable boxes. If none apply, **do not** file Form 2210.

A ☐ You request a **waiver** (see page 2 of the instructions) of your entire penalty. You must check this box and file page 1 of Form 2210, but you are not required to figure your penalty.

B ☐ You request a **waiver** (see page 2 of the instructions) of part of your penalty. You must figure your penalty and waiver amount and file Form 2210.

C ☐ Your income varied during the year and your penalty is reduced or eliminated when figured using the **annualized income installment method.** You must figure the penalty using Schedule AI and file Form 2210.

D ☐ Your penalty is lower when figured by treating the federal income tax withheld from your income as paid on the dates it was actually withheld, instead of in equal amounts on the payment due dates. You must figure your penalty and file Form 2210.

E ☐ You filed or are filing a joint return for either 2008 or 2009, but not for both years, and line 8 above is smaller than line 5 above. You must file page 1 of Form 2210, but you are **not** required to figure your penalty (unless box **B, C,** or **D** applies).

F ☐ You are certifying that more than 50% of the gross income shown on your 2008 tax return is income from a small business (as defined in the instructions) and your adjusted gross income for 2008 is less than $500,000 (less than $250,000 if your 2009 filing status is married filing separately).

For Paperwork Reduction Act Notice, see page 7 of separate instructions.   Cat. No. 11744P   Form **2210** (2009)

Form 2210 (2009)   Page **2**

Part III	**Short Method**

| *Can You Use the Short Method?* | You may use the short method if:
• You made no estimated tax payments (or your only payments were withheld federal income tax), **or**
• You paid the same amount of estimated tax on each of the four payment due dates. |
| *Must You Use the Regular Method?* | You must use the regular method (Part IV) instead of the short method if:
• You made any estimated tax payments late,
• You checked box **C** or **D** in Part II, **or**
• You are filing Form 1040NR or 1040NR-EZ and you did not receive wages as an employee subject to U.S. income tax withholding. |

Note: *If any payment was made earlier than the due date, you may use the short method, but using it may cause you to pay a larger penalty than the regular method. If the payment was only a few days early, the difference is likely to be small.*

10	Enter the amount from Form 2210, line 9	**10**
11	Enter the amount, if any, from Form 2210, line 6 . . . . . . **11**	
12	Enter the total amount, if any, of estimated tax payments you made (see page 3 of the instructions) **12**	
13	Add lines 11 and 12	**13**
14	**Total underpayment for year.** Subtract line 13 from line 10. If zero or less, **stop**; you do not owe a penalty. **Do not file Form 2210 unless you checked box E or F in Part II**	**14**
15	Multiply line 14 by .02660	**15**
16	• If the amount on line 14 was paid **on or after** 4/15/10, enter -0-. • If the amount on line 14 was paid **before** 4/15/10, make the following computation to find the amount to enter on line 16. $$\begin{array}{ccc} \text{Amount on} & & \text{Number of days paid} \\ \text{line 14} & \times & \text{before 4/15/10} & \times & .00011 \end{array}$$	**16**
17	**Penalty.** Subtract line 16 from line 15. Enter the result here and on Form 1040, line 76; Form 1040A, line 49; Form 1040NR, line 71; Form 1040NR-EZ, line 26; or Form 1041, line 26. **Do not file Form 2210 unless you checked a box in Part II** . . . . ▶	**17**

Form **2210** (2009)

Form 2210 (2009)   Page **3**

Part IV   **Regular Method**   (See page 3 of the instructions if you are filing Form 1040NR or 1040NR-EZ.)

Section A—Figure Your Underpayment

		Payment Due Dates			
		(a) 4/15/09	**(b)** 6/15/09	**(c)** 9/15/09	**(d)** 1/15/10
18 Required installments. If box C in Part II applies, enter the amounts from Schedule AI, line 25. Otherwise, enter 25% (.25) of line 9, Form 2210, in each column . . .	**18**				
19 Estimated tax paid and tax withheld (see page 3 of the instructions). For column (a) only, also enter the amount from line 19 on line 23. If line 19 is equal to or more than line 18 for all payment periods, stop here; you do not owe a penalty. **Do not file Form 2210 unless you checked a box in Part II**	**19**				
Complete lines 20 through 26 of one column before going to line 20 of the next column.					
20 Enter the amount, if any, from line 26 in the previous column	**20**				
21 Add lines 19 and 20	**21**				
22 Add the amounts on lines 24 and 25 in the previous column	**22**				
23 Subtract line 22 from line 21. If zero or less, enter -0-. For column (a) only, enter the amount from line 19 . .	**23**				
24 If line 23 is zero, subtract line 21 from line 22. Otherwise, enter -0-	**24**				
25 Underpayment. If line 18 is equal to or more than line 23, subtract line 23 from line 18. Then go to line 20 of the next column. Otherwise, go to line 26 . . . . . . ▶	**25**				
26 Overpayment. If line 23 is more than line 18, subtract line 18 from line 23. Then go to line 20 of the next column.	**26**				

Section B—Figure the Penalty (Complete lines 29 through 30 of one column before going to the next column.)

Note: Only one underpayment rate applies for all underpayments of required installments. To reduce the number of computations, we have removed lines 27 and 28.

April 16, 2009—April 15, 2010		4/15/09	6/15/09	9/15/09	1/15/10
29 Number of days **from** the date shown above line 29 **to** the date the amount on line 25 was paid **or** 4/15/10, whichever is earlier	**29**	Days:	Days:	Days:	Days:
30 Underpayment on line 25 (see page 5 of the instructions) $\times \dfrac{\text{Number of days on line 29}}{365} \times .04$ ▶	**30**	$	$	$	$

31 Penalty. Add the amounts in each column of line 30. Enter the total here and on Form 1040, line 76; Form 1040A, line 49; Form 1040NR, line 71; Form 1040NR-EZ, line 26; or Form 1041, line 26. **Do not file Form 2210 unless you checked a box in Part II** . . . . ▶   **31**

Form **2210** (2009)

Form 2210 (2009)   Page **4**

Schedule AI—Annualized Income Installment Method (See pages 5 through 7 of the instructions.)

Estates and trusts, **do not** use the period ending dates shown to the right. Instead, use the following: 2/28/09, 4/30/09, 7/31/09, and 11/30/09.

		(a) 1/1/09–3/31/09	(b) 1/1/09–5/31/09	(c) 1/1/09–8/31/09	(d) 1/1/09–12/31/09
Part I **Annualized Income Installments**					
1 Enter your adjusted gross income for each period (see instructions). (Estates and trusts, enter your taxable income without your exemption for each period.)	**1**				
2 Annualization amounts. (Estates and trusts, see instructions)	**2**	4	2.4	1.5	1
3 Annualized income. Multiply line 1 by line 2	**3**				
4 If you itemize, enter itemized deductions for the period shown in each column. All others enter -0-, and skip to line 7. **Exception:** Estates and trusts, skip to line 9 and enter amount from line 3	**4**				
5 Annualization amounts	**5**	4	2.4	1.5	1
6 Multiply line 4 by line 5 (see instructions if line 3 is more than $83,400)	**6**				
7 In each column, enter the full amount of your standard deduction from Form 1040, line 40a, or Form 1040A, line 24a. (Form 1040NR or 1040NR-EZ filers, enter -0-. **Exception:** Indian students and business apprentices, see instructions.)	**7**				
8 Enter the **larger** of line 6 or line 7	**8**				
9 Subtract line 8 from line 3	**9**				
10 In each column, multiply $3,650 by the total number of exemptions claimed (see instructions if line 3 is more than $125,100). (Estates, trusts, and Form 1040NR or 1040NR-EZ filers, see instructions.)	**10**				
11 Subtract line 10 from line 9. If zero or less, enter -0-	**11**				
12 Figure your tax on the amount on line 11 (see instructions)	**12**				
13 Self-employment tax from line 34 (complete Part II below).	**13**				
14 Enter other taxes for each payment period (see instructions)	**14**				
15 Total tax. Add lines 12, 13, and 14.	**15**				
16 For each period, enter the same type of credits as allowed on Form 2210, Part I, lines 1 and 3 (see instructions)	**16**				
17 Subtract line 16 from line 15. If zero or less, enter -0-	**17**				
18 Applicable percentage	**18**	22.5%	45%	67.5%	90%
19 Multiply line 17 by line 18	**19**				
Complete lines 20–25 of one column before going to line 20 of the next column.					
20 Enter the total of the amounts in all previous columns of line 25	**20**				
21 Subtract line 20 from line 19. If zero or less, enter -0-	**21**				
22 Enter 25% (.25) of line 9 on page 1 of Form 2210 in each column	**22**				
23 Subtract line 25 of the previous column from line 24 of that column.	**23**				
24 Add lines 22 and 23.	**24**				
25 Enter the **smaller** of line 21 or line 24 here and on Form 2210, line 18 ▶	**25**				
Part II **Annualized Self-Employment Tax** (Form 1040 filers only)					
26 Net earnings from self-employment for the period (see instructions)	**26**				
27 Prorated social security tax limit	**27**	$26,700	$44,500	$71,200	$106,800
28 Enter actual wages for the period subject to social security tax or the 6.2% portion of the 7.65% railroad retirement (tier 1) tax. **Exception:** If you filed Form 4137 or Form 8919, see instructions	**28**				
29 Subtract line 28 from line 27. If zero or less, enter -0-	**29**				
30 Annualization amounts	**30**	0.496	0.2976	0.186	0.124
31 Multiply line 30 by the **smaller** of line 26 or line 29	**31**				
32 Annualization amounts	**32**	0.116	0.0696	0.0435	0.029
33 Multiply line 26 by line 32	**33**				
34 Add lines 31 and 33. Enter here and on line 13 above ▶	**34**				

| Form **2441** | **Child and Dependent Care Expenses** | 1040 1040A 1040NR 2441 | OMB No. 1545-0074 20**09** |

Department of the Treasury
Internal Revenue Service (99)

► Attach to Form 1040, Form 1040A, or Form 1040NR.
► See separate instructions.

Attachment Sequence No. **21**

Name(s) shown on return

Your social security number

Part I — Persons or Organizations Who Provided the Care—You **must** complete this part.
(If you have more than two care providers, see the instructions.)

1

(a) Care provider's name	(b) Address (number, street, apt. no., city, state, and ZIP code)	(c) Identifying number (SSN or EIN)	(d) Amount paid (see instructions)

Did you receive **dependent care benefits?**

No ──────► Complete only Part II below.
Yes ──────► Complete Part III on the back next.

Caution. If the care was provided in your home, you may owe employment taxes. If you do, you cannot file Form 1040A. For details, see the instructions for Form 1040, line 59, or Form 1040NR, line 56.

Part II — Credit for Child and Dependent Care Expenses

2 Information about your **qualifying person(s)**. If you have more than two qualifying persons, see the instructions.

(a) Qualifying person's name		(b) Qualifying person's social security number	(c) **Qualified expenses** you incurred and paid in 2009 for the person listed in column (a)
First	Last		

3 Add the amounts in column (c) of line 2. **Do not** enter more than $3,000 for one qualifying person or $6,000 for two or more persons. If you completed Part III, enter the amount from line 34 . . . . | **3** |

4 Enter your **earned income**. See instructions . . . . | **4** |

5 If married filing jointly, enter your spouse's earned income (if your spouse was a student or was disabled, see the instructions); **all others**, enter the amount from line 4 . . . . | **5** |

6 Enter the **smallest** of line 3, 4, or 5 . . . . | **6** |

7 Enter the amount from Form 1040, line 38; Form 1040A, line 22; or Form 1040NR, line 36. . . . . | **7** |

8 Enter on line 8 the decimal amount shown below that applies to the amount on line 7

If line 7 is:			If line 7 is:		
Over	**But not over**	**Decimal amount is**	**Over**	**But not over**	**Decimal amount is**
$0—15,000		.35	$29,000—31,000		.27
15,000—17,000		.34	31,000—33,000		.26
17,000—19,000		.33	33,000—35,000		.25
19,000—21,000		.32	35,000—37,000		.24
21,000—23,000		.31	37,000—39,000		.23
23,000—25,000		.30	39,000—41,000		.22
25,000—27,000		.29	41,000—43,000		.21
27,000—29,000		.28	43,000—No limit		.20

8 | X . |

9 Multiply line 6 by the decimal amount on line 8. If you paid 2008 expenses in 2009, see the instructions . . . . | **9** |

10 Enter the amount from Form 1040, line 46; Form 1040A, line 28; or Form 1040NR, line 43. . . . . | **10** |

11 Enter the amount from Form 1040, line 47; or Form 1040NR, line 44. Form 1040A filers, enter -0- . . . | **11** |

12 Subtract line 11 from line 10. If zero or less, **stop.** You cannot take the credit . . . . | **12** |

13 **Credit for child and dependent care expenses.** Enter the **smaller** of line 9 or line 12 here and on Form 1040, line 48; Form 1040A, line 29; or Form 1040NR, line 45 . . . . | **13** |

For Paperwork Reduction Act Notice, see page 4 of the instructions.   Cat. No. 11862M   Form **2441** (2009)

Form 2441 (2009)   Page **2**

Part III	**Dependent Care Benefits**		

14 Enter the total amount of **dependent care benefits** you received in 2009. Amounts you received as an employee should be shown in box 10 of your Form(s) W-2. **Do not** include amounts reported as wages in box 1 of Form(s) W-2. If you were self-employed or a partner, include amounts you received under a dependent care assistance program from your sole proprietorship or partnership **14**

15 Enter the amount, if any, you carried over from 2008 and used in 2009 during the grace period. See instructions **15**

16 Enter the amount, if any, you forfeited or carried forward to 2010. See instructions . . . **16** ( )

17 Combine lines 14 through 16. See instructions **17**

18 Enter the total amount of **qualified expenses** incurred in 2009 for the care of the **qualifying person(s)** . . . **18**

19 Enter the **smaller** of line 17 or 18 . . . . **19**

20 Enter your **earned income.** See instructions **20**

21 Enter the amount shown below that applies to you.

  • If married filing jointly, enter your spouse's earned income (if your spouse was a student or was disabled, see the instructions for line 5). } . . . **21**
  • If married filing separately, see instructions.
  • All others, enter the amount from line 20.

22 Enter the **smallest** of line 19, 20, or 21 . . . . . . **22**

23 Enter $5,000 ($2,500 if married filing separately **and** you were required to enter your spouse's earned income on line 21) **23**

24 Are you filing Form 1040A?
  ☐ **Yes.** Skip lines 24 through 27 and go to line 28.
  ☐ **No.** Enter the amount from line 14 that you received from your sole proprietorship or partnership. If you did not receive any such amounts, enter -0- **24**

25 Subtract line 24 from line 17 . . . . **25**

26 Enter the **smaller** of line 22 or 23 . . . . **26**

27 **Deductible benefits.** Enter the **smallest** of line 22, 23, or 24. Also, include this amount on the appropriate line(s) of your return. See instructions **27**

28 **Excluded benefits. Form 1040 and 1040NR filers:** Subtract line 27 from line 26. If zero or less, enter-0-. **Form 1040A filers:** Enter the **smaller** of line 22 or line 23 . . . . . . **28**

29 **Taxable benefits. Form 1040 and 1040NR filers:** Subtract line 28 from line 25. If zero or less, enter -0-. Also, include this amount on Form 1040, line 7; or Form 1040NR, line 8. On the dotted line next to Form 1040, line 7; or Form 1040NR, line 8, enter "DCB." **Form 1040A filers:** Subtract line 28 from line 17. Also, include this amount on Form 1040A, line 7. In the space to the left of line 7, enter "DCB". **29**

To claim the child and dependent care
credit, complete lines 30 through 34 below.

30 Enter $3,000 ($6,000 if two or more qualifying persons) **30**

31 **Form 1040 and 1040NR filers:** Add lines 27 and 28. **Form 1040A filers:** Enter the amount from line 28 . . . . **31**

32 Subtract line 31 from line 30. If zero or less, **stop.** You cannot take the credit. **Exception.** If you paid 2008 expenses in 2009, see the instructions for line 9 . . . . . **32**

33 Complete line 2 on the front of this form. **Do not** include in column (c) any benefits shown on line 31 above. Then, add the amounts in column (c) and enter the total here. **33**

34 Enter the **smaller** of line 32 or 33. Also, enter this amount on line 3 on the front of this form and complete lines 4 through 13 . . . . **34**

Form **2441** (2009)

Form **6251**

Department of the Treasury
Internal Revenue Service (99)

Alternative Minimum Tax—Individuals

▶ See separate instructions.

▶ Attach to Form 1040 or Form 1040NR.

OMB No. 1545-0074

2009

Attachment
Sequence No. **32**

Name(s) shown on Form 1040 or Form 1040NR

Your social security number

Part I	**Alternative Minimum Taxable Income** (See instructions for how to complete each line.)	
1	If filing Schedule A (Form 1040), enter the amount from Form 1040, line 41 (minus any amount on Form 8914, line 6), and go to line 2. Otherwise, enter the amount from Form 1040, line 38 (minus any amount on Form 8914, line 6), and go to line 7. (If less than zero, enter as a negative amount.)	1
2	Medical and dental. Enter the **smaller** of Schedule A (Form 1040), line 4, **or** 2.5% (.025) of Form 1040, line 38. If zero or less, enter -0-	2
3	Taxes from Schedule A (Form 1040), lines 5, 6, and 8	3
4	Enter the home mortgage interest adjustment, if any, from line 6 of the worksheet on page 2 of the instructions	4
5	Miscellaneous deductions from Schedule A (Form 1040), line 27	5
6	If Form 1040, line 38, is over $166,800 (over $83,400 if married filing separately), enter the amount from line 11 of the **Itemized Deductions Worksheet** on page A-11 of the instructions for Schedule A (Form 1040)	6 ( )
7	If filing Schedule L (Form 1040A or 1040), enter as a negative amount the sum of lines 6 and 20 from that schedule	7 ( )
8	Tax refund from Form 1040, line 10 or line 21	8 ( )
9	Investment interest expense (difference between regular tax and AMT)	9
10	Depletion (difference between regular tax and AMT)	10
11	Net operating loss deduction from Form 1040, line 21. Enter as a positive amount	11
12	Alternative tax net operating loss deduction	12 ( )
13	Interest from specified private activity bonds exempt from the regular tax	13
14	Qualified small business stock (7% of gain excluded under section 1202)	14
15	Exercise of incentive stock options (excess of AMT income over regular tax income)	15
16	Estates and trusts (amount from Schedule K-1 (Form 1041), box 12, code A)	16
17	Electing large partnerships (amount from Schedule K-1 (Form 1065-B), box 6)	17
18	Disposition of property (difference between AMT and regular tax gain or loss)	18
19	Depreciation on assets placed in service after 1986 (difference between regular tax and AMT)	19
20	Passive activities (difference between AMT and regular tax income or loss)	20
21	Loss limitations (difference between AMT and regular tax income or loss)	21
22	Circulation costs (difference between regular tax and AMT)	22
23	Long-term contracts (difference between AMT and regular tax income)	23
24	Mining costs (difference between regular tax and AMT)	24
25	Research and experimental costs (difference between regular tax and AMT)	25
26	Income from certain installment sales before January 1, 1987	26 ( )
27	Intangible drilling costs preference	27
28	Other adjustments, including income-based related adjustments	28
29	**Alternative minimum taxable income.** Combine lines 1 through 28. (If married filing separately and line 29 is more than $216,900, see page 8 of the instructions.)	29

Part II	**Alternative Minimum Tax (AMT)**	
30	Exemption. (If you were under age 24 at the end of 2009, see page 8 of the instructions.)	

IF your filing status is . . .	AND line 29 is not over . . .	THEN enter on line 30 . . .	
Single or head of household	$112,500	$46,700	
Married filing jointly or qualifying widow(er)	150,000	70,950	
Married filing separately	75,000	35,475	30

If line 29 is **over** the amount shown above for your filing status, see page 8 of the instructions.

31	Subtract line 30 from line 29. If more than zero, go to line 32. If zero or less, enter -0- here and on lines 34 and 36 and skip the rest of Part II.	31
32	• If you are filing Form 2555 or 2555-EZ, see page 9 of the instructions for the amount to enter. • If you reported capital gain distributions directly on Form 1040, line 13; you reported qualified dividends on Form 1040, line 9b; **or** you had a gain on both lines 15 and 16 of Schedule D (Form 1040) (as refigured for the AMT, if necessary), complete Part III on the back and enter the amount from line 55 here. • All others: If line 31 is $175,000 or less ($87,500 or less if married filing separately), multiply line 31 by 26% (.26). Otherwise, multiply line 31 by 28% (.28) and subtract $3,500 ($1,750 if married filing separately) from the result.	32
33	Alternative minimum tax foreign tax credit (see page 9 of the instructions)	33
34	Tentative minimum tax. Subtract line 33 from line 32	34
35	Tax from Form 1040, line 44 (minus any tax from Form 4972 and any foreign tax credit from Form 1040, line 47). If you used Schedule J to figure your tax, the amount from line 44 of Form 1040 must be refigured without using Schedule J (see page 11 of the instructions)	35
36	**AMT.** Subtract line 35 from line 34. If zero or less, enter -0-. Enter here and on Form 1040, line 45	36

For Paperwork Reduction Act Notice, see page 12 of the instructions.   Cat. No. 13600G   Form **6251** (2009)

Form 6251 (2009)   Page **2**

Part III   Tax Computation Using Maximum Capital Gains Rates

37 Enter the amount from Form 6251, line 31. If you are filing Form 2555 or 2555-EZ, enter the amount from line 3 of the worksheet on page 9 of the instructions . . . . | **37** |

38 Enter the amount from line 6 of the Qualified Dividends and Capital Gain Tax Worksheet in the instructions for Form 1040, line 44, or the amount from line 13 of the Schedule D Tax Worksheet on page D-10 of the instructions for Schedule D (Form 1040), whichever applies (as refigured for the AMT, if necessary) (see page 11 of the instructions). If you are filing Form 2555 or 2555-EZ, see page 11 of the instructions for the amount to enter . . . . | **38** |

39 Enter the amount from Schedule D (Form 1040), line 19 (as refigured for the AMT, if necessary) (see page 11 of the instructions). If you are filing Form 2555 or 2555-EZ, see page 11 of the instructions for the amount to enter . . . . | **39** |

40 If you did not complete a Schedule D Tax Worksheet for the regular tax or the AMT, enter the amount from line 38. Otherwise, add lines 38 and 39, and enter the **smaller** of that result or the amount from line 10 of the Schedule D Tax Worksheet (as refigured for the AMT, if necessary). If you are filing Form 2555 or 2555-EZ, see page 11 of the instructions for the amount to enter . . . . . | **40** |

41 Enter the **smaller** of line 37 or line 40 . . . . | **41** |

42 Subtract line 41 from line 37 . . . . | **42** |

43 If line 42 is $175,000 or less ($87,500 or less if married filing separately), multiply line 42 by 26% (.26). Otherwise, multiply line 42 by 28% (.28) and subtract $3,500 ($1,750 if married filing separately) from the result . . . ▶ | **43** |

44 Enter:
 • $67,900 if married filing jointly or qualifying widow(er),
 • $33,950 if single or married filing separately, or   } . . . . | **44** |
 • $45,500 if head of household.

45 Enter the amount from line 7 of the Qualified Dividends and Capital Gain Tax Worksheet in the instructions for Form 1040, line 44, or the amount from line 14 of the Schedule D Tax Worksheet on page D-10 of the instructions for Schedule D (Form 1040), whichever applies (as figured for the regular tax). If you did not complete either worksheet for the regular tax, enter -0- . . . . | **45** |

46 Subtract line 45 from line 44. If zero or less, enter -0- . . . . | **46** |

47 Enter the **smaller** of line 37 or line 38 . . . . | **47** |

48 Enter the **smaller** of line 46 or line 47 . . . . | **48** |

49 Subtract line 48 from line 47 . . . . | **49** |

50 Multiply line 49 by 15% (.15) . . . . ▶ | **50** |

If line 39 is zero or blank, skip lines 51 and 52 and go to line 53. Otherwise, go to line 51.

51 Subtract line 47 from line 41 . . . . | **51** |

52 Multiply line 51 by 25% (.25) . . . . ▶ | **52** |

53 Add lines 43, 50, and 52 . . . . | **53** |

54 If line 37 is $175,000 or less ($87,500 or less if married filing separately), multiply line 37 by 26% (.26). Otherwise, multiply line 37 by 28% (.28) and subtract $3,500 ($1,750 if married filing separately) from the result . . . . | **54** |

55 Enter the **smaller** of line 53 or line 54 here and on line 32. If you are filing Form 2555 or 2555-EZ, do not enter this amount on line 32. Instead, enter it on line 4 of the worksheet on page 9 of the instructions. . . . . . | **55** |

Form **6251** (2009)

Form **8283**
(Rev. December 2006)
Department of the Treasury
Internal Revenue Service

Noncash Charitable Contributions

▶ Attach to your tax return if you claimed a total deduction
of over $500 for all contributed property.

▶ See separate instructions.

OMB No. 1545-0908

Attachment
Sequence No. **155**

Name(s) shown on your income tax return

Identifying number

Note. Figure the amount of your contribution deduction before completing this form. See your tax return instructions.

Section A. Donated Property of $5,000 or Less and Certain Publicly Traded Securities—List in this section **only** items (or groups of similar items) for which you claimed a deduction of $5,000 or less. Also, list certain publicly traded securities even if the deduction is more than $5,000 (see instructions).

Part I — Information on Donated Property—If you need more space, attach a statement.

1	(a) Name and address of the donee organization	(b) Description of donated property (For a donated vehicle, enter the year, make, model, condition, and mileage, and attach Form 1098-C if required.)
A		
B		
C		
D		
E		

Note. If the amount you claimed as a deduction for an item is $500 or less, you do not have to complete columns (d), (e), and (f).

	(c) Date of the contribution	(d) Date acquired by donor (mo., yr.)	(e) How acquired by donor	(f) Donor's cost or adjusted basis	(g) Fair market value (see instructions)	(h) Method used to determine the fair market value
A						
B						
C						
D						
E						

Part II — Partial Interests and Restricted Use Property—Complete lines 2a through 2e if you gave less than an entire interest in a property listed in Part I. Complete lines 3a through 3c if conditions were placed on a contribution listed in Part I; also attach the required statement (see instructions).

2a Enter the letter from Part I that identifies the property for which you gave less than an entire interest ▶_____ .
If Part II applies to more than one property, attach a separate statement.

b Total amount claimed as a deduction for the property listed in Part I: **(1)** For this tax year ▶_____ .
(2) For any prior tax years ▶_____ .

c Name and address of each organization to which any such contribution was made in a prior year (complete only if different from the donee organization above):

Name of charitable organization (donee)

Address (number, street, and room or suite no.)

City or town, state, and ZIP code

d For tangible property, enter the place where the property is located or kept ▶_____

e Name of any person, other than the donee organization, having actual possession of the property ▶_____

		Yes	No
3a	Is there a restriction, either temporary or permanent, on the donee's right to use or dispose of the donated property?		
b	Did you give to anyone (other than the donee organization or another organization participating with the donee organization in cooperative fundraising) the right to the income from the donated property or to the possession of the property, including the right to vote donated securities, to acquire the property by purchase or otherwise, or to designate the person having such income, possession, or right to acquire?		
c	Is there a restriction limiting the donated property for a particular use?		

For Paperwork Reduction Act Notice, see separate instructions. Cat. No. 62299J Form **8283** (Rev. 12-2006)

Form 8283 (Rev. 12-2006)   Page **2**

Name(s) shown on your income tax return	Identifying number

Section B. Donated Property Over $5,000 (Except Certain Publicly Traded Securities)— List in this section only items (or groups of similar items) for which you claimed a deduction of more than $5,000 per item or group (except contributions of certain publicly traded securities reported in Section A). An appraisal is generally required for property listed in Section B (see instructions).

Part I **Information on Donated Property**—To be completed by the taxpayer and/or the appraiser.

4 Check the box that describes the type of property donated:

☐ Art* (contribution of $20,000 or more)   ☐ Qualified Conservation Contribution   ☐ Equipment

☐ Art* (contribution of less than $20,000)   ☐ Other Real Estate   ☐ Securities

☐ Collectibles**   ☐ Intellectual Property   ☐ Other

*Art includes paintings, sculptures, watercolors, prints, drawings, ceramics, antiques, decorative arts, textiles, carpets, silver, rare manuscripts, historical memorabilia, and other similar objects.

**Collectibles include coins, stamps, books, gems, jewelry, sports memorabilia, dolls, etc., but not art as defined above.

Note. In certain cases, you must attach a qualified appraisal of the property. See instructions.

5	(a) Description of donated property (if you need more space, attach a separate statement)	(b) If tangible property was donated, give a brief summary of the overall physical condition of the property at the time of the gift	(c) Appraised fair market value
A			
B			
C			
D			

| | (d) Date acquired by donor (mo., yr.) | (e) How acquired by donor | (f) Donor's cost or adjusted basis | (g) For bargain sales, enter amount received | See instructions | |
					(h) Amount claimed as a deduction	(i) Average trading price of securities
A						
B						
C						
D						

Part II **Taxpayer (Donor) Statement**—List each item included in Part I above that the appraisal identifies as having a value of $500 or less. See instructions.

I declare that the following item(s) included in Part I above has to the best of my knowledge and belief an appraised value of not more than $500 (per item). Enter identifying letter from Part I and describe the specific item. See instructions. ▶ _____

Signature of taxpayer (donor) ▶   Date ▶

Part III **Declaration of Appraiser**

I declare that I am not the donor, the donee, a party to the transaction in which the donor acquired the property, employed by, or related to any of the foregoing persons, or married to any person who is related to any of the foregoing persons. And, if regularly used by the donor, donee, or party to the transaction, I performed the majority of my appraisals during my tax year for other persons.

Also, I declare that I hold myself out to the public as an appraiser or perform appraisals on a regular basis; and that because of my qualifications as described in the appraisal, I am qualified to make appraisals of the type of property being valued. I certify that the appraisal fees were not based on a percentage of the appraised property value. Furthermore, I understand that a false or fraudulent overstatement of the property value as described in the qualified appraisal or this Form 8283 may subject me to the penalty under section 6701(a) (aiding and abetting the understatement of tax liability). In addition, I understand that a substantial or gross valuation misstatement resulting from the appraisal of the value of the property that I know, or reasonably should know, would be used in connection with a return or claim for refund, may subject me to the penalty under section 6695A. I affirm that I have not been barred from presenting evidence or testimony by the Office of Professional Responsibility.

Sign Here

Signature ▶	Title ▶	Date ▶

Business address (including room or suite no.)	Identifying number
City or town, state, and ZIP code	

Part IV **Donee Acknowledgment**—To be completed by the charitable organization.

This charitable organization acknowledges that it is a qualified organization under section 170(c) and that it received the donated property as described in Section B, Part I, above on the following date ▶ _____

Furthermore, this organization affirms that in the event it sells, exchanges, or otherwise disposes of the property described in Section B, Part I (or any portion thereof) within 3 years after the date of receipt, it will file **Form 8282,** Donee Information Return, with the IRS and give the donor a copy of that form. This acknowledgment does not represent agreement with the claimed fair market value.

Does the organization intend to use the property for an unrelated use? . . . . ▶ ☐ Yes   ☐ No

Name of charitable organization (donee)	Employer identification number
Address (number, street, and room or suite no.)	City or town, state, and ZIP code
Authorized signature	Title	Date

Printed on Recycled Paper   Form **8283** (Rev. 12-2006)

Form 8582

Department of the Treasury
Internal Revenue Service (99)

Passive Activity Loss Limitations

▶ See separate instructions.
▶ Attach to Form 1040 or Form 1041.

OMB No. 1545-1008

2009

Attachment
Sequence No. **88**

Name(s) shown on return

Identifying number

Part I — 2009 Passive Activity Loss

Caution: *Complete Worksheets 1, 2, and 3 on page 2 before completing Part I.*

Rental Real Estate Activities With Active Participation (For the definition of active participation, see **Special Allowance for Rental Real Estate Activities** on page 3 of the instructions.)

1a	Activities with net income (enter the amount from Worksheet 1, column (a))	1a	
b	Activities with net loss (enter the amount from Worksheet 1, column (b))	1b ( )	
c	Prior years unallowed losses (enter the amount from Worksheet 1, column (c))	1c ( )	
d	Combine lines 1a, 1b, and 1c		1d

Commercial Revitalization Deductions From Rental Real Estate Activities

2a	Commercial revitalization deductions from Worksheet 2, column (a) .	2a ( )	
b	Prior year unallowed commercial revitalization deductions from Worksheet 2, column (b)	2b ( )	
c	Add lines 2a and 2b		2c ( )

All Other Passive Activities

3a	Activities with net income (enter the amount from Worksheet 3, column (a))	3a	
b	Activities with net loss (enter the amount from Worksheet 3, column (b))	3b ( )	
c	Prior years unallowed losses (enter the amount from Worksheet 3, column (c))	3c ( )	
d	Combine lines 3a, 3b, and 3c		3d

4 Combine lines 1d, 2c, and 3d. If the result is net income or zero, all losses are allowed, including any prior year unallowed losses entered on line 1c, 2b, or 3c. **Do not** complete Form 8582. Report the losses on the forms and schedules normally used . . . . | **4**

If line 4 is a loss and:
- Line 1d is a loss, go to Part II.
- Line 2c is a loss (and line 1d is zero or more), skip Part II and go to Part III.
- Line 3d is a loss (and lines 1d and 2c are zero or more), skip Parts II and III and go to line 15.

Caution: *If your filing status is married filing separately and you lived with your spouse at any time during the year,* **do not** *complete Part II or Part III. Instead, go to line 15.*

Part II — Special Allowance for Rental Real Estate Activities With Active Participation

Note: *Enter all numbers in Part II as positive amounts. See page 8 of the instructions for an example.*

5	Enter the **smaller** of the loss on line 1d or the loss on line 4	5
6	Enter $150,000. If married filing separately, see page 8	6
7	Enter modified adjusted gross income, but not less than zero (see page 8)	7

Note: *If line 7 is greater than or equal to line 6, skip lines 8 and 9, enter -0- on line 10. Otherwise, go to line 8.*

8	Subtract line 7 from line 6	8
9	Multiply line 8 by 50% (.5). **Do not** enter more than $25,000. If married filing separately, see page 8	9
10	Enter the **smaller** of line 5 or line 9	10

If line 2c is a loss, go to Part III. Otherwise, go to line 15.

Part III — Special Allowance for Commercial Revitalization Deductions From Rental Real Estate Activities

Note: *Enter all numbers in Part III as positive amounts. See the example for Part II on page 8 of the instructions.*

11	Enter $25,000 reduced by the amount, if any, on line 10. If married filing separately, see instructions	11
12	Enter the loss from line 4	12
13	Reduce line 12 by the amount on line 10	13
14	Enter the **smallest** of line 2c (treated as a positive amount), line 11, or line 13	14

Part IV — Total Losses Allowed

15	Add the income, if any, on lines 1a and 3a and enter the total	15
16	**Total losses allowed from all passive activities for 2009.** Add lines 10, 14, and 15. See page 11 of the instructions to find out how to report the losses on your tax return	16

For Paperwork Reduction Act Notice, see page 12 of the instructions.

Cat. No. 63704F

Form **8582** (2009)

Form 8582 (2009)   Page **2**

Caution: *The worksheets must be filed with your tax return. Keep a copy for your records.*

Worksheet 1—For Form 8582, Lines 1a, 1b, and 1c (See pages 7 and 8 of the instructions.)

Name of activity	Current year		Prior years	Overall gain or loss	
	(a) Net income (line 1a)	**(b) Net loss** (line 1b)	**(c) Unallowed loss (line 1c)**	**(d) Gain**	**(e) Loss**
Total. Enter on Form 8582, lines 1a, 1b, and 1c . . . . ▶					

Worksheet 2—For Form 8582, Lines 2a and 2b (See page 8 of the instructions.)

Name of activity	**(a) Current year deductions (line 2a)**	**(b) Prior year unallowed deductions (line 2b)**	**(c) Overall loss**
Total. Enter on Form 8582, lines 2a and 2b . . . . ▶			

Worksheet 3—For Form 8582, Lines 3a, 3b, and 3c (See page 8 of the instructions.)

Name of activity	Current year		Prior years	Overall gain or loss	
	(a) Net income (line 3a)	**(b) Net loss** (line 3b)	**(c) Unallowed loss (line 3c)**	**(d) Gain**	**(e) Loss**
Total. Enter on Form 8582, lines 3a, 3b, and 3c . . . . ▶					

Worksheet 4—Use this worksheet if an amount is shown on Form 8582, line 10 or 14 (See page 9 of the instructions.)

Name of activity	Form or schedule and line number to be reported on (see instructions)	**(a) Loss**	**(b) Ratio**	**(c) Special allowance**	**(d) Subtract column (c) from column (a)**
Total . . . . ▶			1.00		

Worksheet 5—Allocation of Unallowed Losses (See page 9 of the instructions.)

Name of activity	Form or schedule and line number to be reported on (see instructions)	**(a) Loss**	**(b) Ratio**	**(c) Unallowed loss**
Total . . . . ▶			1.00	

Form **8582** (2009)

Worksheet 6—Allowed Losses (See pages 9 and 10 of the instructions.)

Name of activity	Form or schedule and line number to be reported on (see instructions)	(a) Loss	(b) Unallowed loss	(c) Allowed loss
Total . . . . ▶				

Worksheet 7—Activities With Losses Reported on Two or More Forms or Schedules (See page 10 of the instructions.)

Name of activity:	(a)	(b)	(c) Ratio	(d) Unallowed loss	(e) Allowed loss
Form or schedule and line number to be reported on (see instructions): _____					
1a Net loss plus prior year unallowed loss from form or schedule . ▶					
b Net income from form or schedule . . . . ▶					
c Subtract line 1b from line 1a. If zero or less, enter -0- ▶					
Form or schedule and line number to be reported on (see instructions): _____					
1a Net loss plus prior year unallowed loss from form or schedule . ▶					
b Net income from form or schedule . . . . ▶					
c Subtract line 1b from line 1a. If zero or less, enter -0- ▶					
Form or schedule and line number to be reported on (see instructions): _____					
1a Net loss plus prior year unallowed loss from form or schedule . ▶					
b Net income from form or schedule . . . . ▶					
c Subtract line 1b from line 1a. If zero or less, enter -0- ▶					
Total . . . . ▶			1.00		

Form **8582** (2009)

Form **8615**	**Tax for Certain Children Who Have Investment**	OMB No. 1545-0074

Tax for Certain Children Who Have Investment Income of More Than $1,900

► Attach only to the child's Form 1040, Form 1040A, or Form 1040NR.
► See separate instructions.

Department of the Treasury
Internal Revenue Service (99)

2009
Attachment Sequence No. **33**

Child's name shown on return | Child's social security number

Before you begin: If the child, the parent, or any of the parent's other children for whom Form 8615 must be filed must use the Schedule D Tax Worksheet or has income from farming or fishing, see **Pub. 929,** Tax Rules for Children and Dependents. It explains how to figure the child's tax using the **Schedule D Tax Worksheet** or **Schedule J** (Form 1040).

A Parent's name (first, initial, and last). **Caution:** See instructions before completing.

B Parent's social security number

C Parent's filing status (check one):
☐ Single   ☐ Married filing jointly   ☐ Married filing separately   ☐ Head of household   ☐ Qualifying widow(er)

Part I — Child's Net Investment Income

1	Enter the child's investment income (see instructions)	1	
2	If the child **did not** itemize deductions on **Schedule A** (Form 1040 or Form 1040NR), enter $1,900. Otherwise, see instructions	2	
3	Subtract line 2 from line 1. If zero or less, **stop;** do not complete the rest of this form but **do** attach it to the child's return	3	
4	Enter the child's **taxable income** from Form 1040, line 43; Form 1040A, line 27; or Form 1040NR, line 40. If the child files Form 2555 or 2555-EZ, see the instructions	4	
5	Enter the **smaller** of line 3 or line 4. If zero, **stop;** do not complete the rest of this form but **do** attach it to the child's return	5	

Part II — Tentative Tax Based on the Tax Rate of the Parent

6	Enter the parent's **taxable income** from Form 1040, line 43; Form 1040A, line 27; Form 1040EZ, line 6; Form 1040NR, line 40; or Form 1040NR-EZ, line 14. If zero or less, enter -0-. If the parent files Form 2555 or 2555-EZ, see the instructions	6	
7	Enter the total, if any, from Forms 8615, line 5, of **all other** children of the parent named above. **Do not** include the amount from line 5 above	7	
8	Add lines 5, 6, and 7 (see instructions)	8	
9	Enter the tax on the amount on line 8 based on the **parent's** filing status above (see instructions). If the Qualified Dividends and Capital Gain Tax Worksheet, Schedule D Tax Worksheet, or Schedule J (Form 1040) is used to figure the tax, check here ► ☐	9	
10	Enter the parent's tax from Form 1040, line 44; Form 1040A, line 28, minus any alternative minimum tax; Form 1040EZ, line 11; Form 1040NR, line 41; or Form 1040NR-EZ, line 15. **Do not** include any tax from **Form 4972** or **8814** or any tax from recapture of an education credit. If the parent files Form 2555 or 2555-EZ, see the instructions. If the Qualified Dividends and Capital Gain Tax Worksheet, Schedule D Tax Worksheet, or Schedule J (Form 1040) was used to figure the tax, check here ► ☐	10	
11	Subtract line 10 from line 9 and enter the result. If line 7 is blank, also enter this amount on line 13 and go to **Part III**	11	
12a	Add lines 5 and 7	12a	
b	Divide line 5 by line 12a. Enter the result as a decimal (rounded to at least three places)	12b	× .
13	Multiply line 11 by line 12b	13	

Part III — Child's Tax— If lines 4 and 5 above are the same, enter -0- on line 15 and go to line 16.

14	Subtract line 5 from line 4	14	
15	Enter the tax on the amount on line 14 based on the **child's** filing status (see instructions). If the Qualified Dividends and Capital Gain Tax Worksheet, Schedule D Tax Worksheet, or Schedule J (Form 1040) is used to figure the tax, check here ► ☐	15	
16	Add lines 13 and 15	16	
17	Enter the tax on the amount on line 4 based on the **child's** filing status (see instructions). If the Qualified Dividends and Capital Gain Tax Worksheet, Schedule D Tax Worksheet, or Schedule J (Form 1040) is used to figure the tax, check here ► ☐	17	
18	Enter the **larger** of line 16 or line 17 here and on the **child's** Form 1040, line 44; Form 1040A, line 28; or Form 1040NR, line 41. If the child files Form 2555 or 2555-EZ, see the instructions	18	

For Paperwork Reduction Act Notice, see the instructions.   Cat. No. 64113U   Form **8615** (2009)

APPENDIX C

MACRS TABLES

MACRS, ADS and ACRS Depreciation Methods Summary

System	Characteristics	Depreciation Method MACRS	Depreciation Method ADS	Table No.[a] MACRS	Table No.[a] ADS
MACRS & ADS	Personal Property:				
	1. Accounting convention	Half-year or mid-quarter	Half-year or mid-quarter[b]		
	2. Life and method				
	a. 3-year, 5-year, 7-year, 10-year	200% DB or elect straight-line	150% DB or elect straight-line	1, 2, 3, 4, 5	10, 11[c]
	b. 15-year, 20-year	150% DB or elect straight-line	150% DB or elect straight-line[d]	1, 2, 3, 4, 5	
	3. Luxury Automobile Limitations			6	
	Real property:				
	1. Accounting convention	Mid-month	Mid-month		
	2. Life and method				
	a. Residential rental property	27.5 years, straight-line	40 years straight-line	7	12
	b. Nonresidential real property	39 years, straight-line[e]	40 years straight-line	9	12

	Characteristics	ACRS			
ACRS[f]	Personal Property				
	1. Accounting convention	Half-year			
	2. Life and method				
	a. 3-year, 5-year, 10-year, 15-year	150% DB or elect straight-line			
	Real Property				
	1. Accounting convention	First of month or mid-month			
	2. Life				
	a. 15-year property	Placed in service after 12/31/80 and before 3/16/84			
	b. 18-year property	Placed in service after 3/15/84 and before 5/9/85			
	c. 19-year property	Placed in service after 5/8/85 and before 1/1/87			
	3. Method				
	a. All but low-income housing	175% DB or elect straight-line			
	b. Low-income housing property	200% DB or elect straight-line			

[a] All depreciation tables in this appendix are based upon tables contained in Rev. Proc. 87-57, as amended.
[b] General and ADS tables are available for property lives from 2.5–50.0 years using the straight-line method. These tables are contained in Rev. Proc. 87-57 and are only partially reproduced here.
[c] The mid-quarter tables are available in Rev. Proc. 87-57, but are not reproduced here.
[d] Special recovery periods are assigned certain MACRS properties under the alternative depreciation system.
[e] A 31.5-year recovery period applied to nonresidential real property placed in service under the MACRS rules prior to May 13, 1993 (see Table 8).
[f] ACRS was effective for years 1981–1986. ACRS tables are no longer reproduced in this textbook.

▼ TABLE 1

General Depreciation System—MACRS
Personal Property Placed in Service after 12/31/86
Applicable Convention: Half-year
Applicable Depreciation Method: 200 or 150 Percent Declining Balance Switching to Straight Line

If the Recovery Year Is:	And the Recovery Period Is:					
	3-Year	5-Year	7-Year	10-Year	15-Year	20-Year
	The Depreciation Rate Is:					
1	33.33	20.00	14.29	10.00	5.00	3.750
2	44.45	32.00	24.49	18.00	9.50	7.219
3	14.81	19.20	17.49	14.40	8.55	6.677
4	7.41	11.52	12.49	11.52	7.70	6.177
5		11.52	8.93	9.22	6.93	5.713
6		5.76	8.92	7.37	6.23	5.285
7			8.93	6.55	5.90	4.888
8			4.46	6.55	5.90	4.522
9				6.56	5.91	4.462
10				6.55	5.90	4.461
11				3.28	5.91	4.462
12					5.90	4.461
13					5.91	4.462
14					5.90	4.461
15					5.91	4.462
16					2.95	4.461
17						4.462
18						4.461
19						4.462
20						4.461
21						2.231

▼ TABLE 2

General Depreciation System—MACRS
Personal Property Placed in Service after 12/31/86
Applicable Convention: Mid-quarter (Property Placed in Service in First Quarter)
Applicable Depreciation Method: 200 or 150 Percent Declining Balance Switching to Straight Line

If the Recovery Year Is:	And the Recovery Period Is:					
	3-Year	5-Year	7-Year	10-Year	15-Year	20-Year
	The Depreciation Rate Is:					
1	58.33	35.00	25.00	17.50	8.75	6.563
2	27.78	26.00	21.43	16.50	9.13	7.000
3	12.35	15.60	15.31	13.20	8.21	6.482
4	1.54	11.01	10.93	10.56	7.39	5.996
5		11.01	8.75	8.45	6.65	5.546
6		1.38	8.74	6.76	5.99	5.130
7			8.75	6.55	5.90	4.746
8			1.09	6.55	5.91	4.459
9				6.56	5.90	4.459
10				6.55	5.91	4.459
11				0.82	5.90	4.459
12					5.91	4.460
13					5.90	4.459
14					5.91	4.460
15					5.90	4.459
16					0.74	4.460
17						4.459
18						4.460
19						4.459
20						4.460
21						0.557

▼ TABLE 3

General Depreciation System—MACRS
Personal Property Placed in Service after 12/31/86
Applicable Convention: Mid-quarter (Property Placed in Service in Second Quarter)
Applicable Depreciation Method: 200 or 150 Percent Declining Balance Switching to Straight Line

If the Recovery Year Is:	And the Recovery Period Is:					
	3-Year	5-Year	7-Year	10-Year	15-Year	20-Year
	The Depreciation Rate Is:					
1	41.67	25.00	17.85	12.50	6.25	4.688
2	38.89	30.00	23.47	17.50	9.38	7.148
3	14.14	18.00	16.76	14.00	8.44	6.612
4	5.30	11.37	11.97	11.20	7.59	6.116
5		11.37	8.87	8.96	6.83	5.658
6		4.26	8.87	7.17	6.15	5.233
7			8.87	6.55	5.91	4.841
8			3.33	6.55	5.90	4.478
9				6.56	5.91	4.463
10				6.55	5.90	4.463
11				2.46	5.91	4.463
12					5.90	4.463
13					5.91	4.463
14					5.90	4.463
15					5.91	4.462
16					2.21	4.463
17						4.462
18						4.463
19						4.462
20						4.463
21						1.673

▼ TABLE 4

General Depreciation System—MACRS
Personal Property Placed in Service after 12/31/86
Applicable Convention: Mid-quarter (Property Placed in Service in Third Quarter)
Applicable Depreciation Method: 200 or 150 Percent Declining Balance Switching to Straight Line

If the Recovery Year Is:	And the Recovery Period Is:					
	3-Year	5-Year	7-Year	10-Year	15-Year	20-Year
	The Depreciation Rate Is:					
1	25.00	15.00	10.71	7.50	3.75	2.813
2	50.00	34.00	25.51	18.50	9.63	7.289
3	16.67	20.40	18.22	14.80	8.66	6.742
4	8.33	12.24	13.02	11.84	7.80	6.237
5		11.30	9.30	9.47	7.02	5.769
6		7.06	8.85	7.58	6.31	5.336
7			8.86	6.55	5.90	4.936
8			5.53	6.55	5.90	4.566
9				6.56	5.91	4.460
10				6.55	5.90	4.460
11				4.10	5.91	4.460
12					5.90	4.460
13					5.91	4.461
14					5.90	4.460
15					5.91	4.461
16					3.69	4.460
17						4.461
18						4.460
19						4.461
20						4.460
21						2.788

▼ TABLE 5

General Depreciation System—MACRS
Personal Property Placed in Service after 12/31/86
Applicable Convention: Mid-quarter (Property Placed in Service in Fourth Quarter)
Applicable Depreciation Method: 200 or 150 Percent Declining Balance Switching to Straight Line

If the Recovery Year Is:	And the Recovery Period Is:					
	3-Year	5-Year	7-Year	10-Year	15-Year	20-Year
	The Depreciation Rate Is:					
1	8.33	5.00	3.57	2.50	1.25	0.938
2	61.11	38.00	27.55	19.50	9.88	7.430
3	20.37	22.80	19.68	15.60	8.89	6.872
4	10.19	13.68	14.06	12.48	8.00	6.357
5		10.94	10.04	9.98	7.20	5.880
6		9.58	8.73	7.99	6.48	5.439
7			8.73	6.55	5.90	5.031
8			7.64	6.55	5.90	4.654
9				6.56	5.90	4.458
10				6.55	5.91	4.458
11				5.74	5.90	4.458
12					5.91	4.458
13					5.90	4.458
14					5.91	4.458
15					5.90	4.458
16					5.17	4.458
17						4.458
18						4.459
19						4.458
20						4.459
21						3.901

▼ TABLE 6

Luxury Automobile Depreciation Limits

	Year Automobile is Placed in Service[a]						
	2010	2009	2008	2007	2006	2005	2004
Maximum Allowable Depreciation (100% Business Use):							
Year 1	$3,060	$2,960[b]	$2,960[c]	$3,060	$2,960	$2,960	$2,960[d]
Year 2	4,900	4,800	4,800	4,900	4,800	4,700	4,800
Year 3	2,950	2,850	2,850	2,850	2,850	2,850	2,850
Year 4 and Each Succeeding Year	1,775	1,775	1,775	1,775	1,775	1,675	1,675

[a]For years prior to 2004, see the Revenue Procedure for the appropriate year.
[b]$10,960 in Year 1 (2009) if taxpayer claims bonus depreciation.
[c]$10,960 in Year 1 (2008) if taxpayer claimed bonus depreciation.
[d]$10,610 in Year 1 (2004) if taxpayer claimed bonus depreciation.

▼ TABLE 6 (continued)
Truck and Van Depreciation Limits

	Year Truck or Van is Placed in Service[a]						
	2010	2009	2008	2007	2006	2005	2004
Maximum Allowable Depreciation (100% Business Use):							
Year 1	$3,160	$3,060[b]	$3,160[c]	$3,260	$3,260	$3,260	$3,260[d]
Year 2	5,100	4,900	5,100	5,200	5,200	5,200	5,300
Year 3	3,050	2,950	3,050	3,050	3,150	3,150	3,150
Year 4 and Each Succeeding Year	1,875	1,775	1,875	1,875	1,875	1,875	1,875

[a]For years prior to 2004, see the Revenue Procedure for the appropriate year.
[b]$11,060 in Year 1 (2009) if taxpayer claims bonus depreciation.
[c]$11,160 in Year 1 (2008) if taxpayer claimed bonus depreciation.
[d]$10,910 in Year 1 (2004) if taxpayer claimed bonus depreciation.

▼ TABLE 7

General Depreciation System—MACRS
Residential Rental Real Property Placed in Service after 12/31/86
Applicable Recovery Period: 27.5 Years
Applicable Convention: Mid-month
Applicable Depreciation Method: Straight Line

If the Recovery Year Is:	And the Month in the First Recovery Year the Property Is Placed in Service Is:											
	1	2	3	4	5	6	7	8	9	10	11	12
	The Depreciation Rate Is:											
1	3.485	3.182	2.879	2.576	2.273	1.970	1.667	1.364	1.061	0.758	0.455	0.152
2	3.636	3.636	3.636	3.636	3.636	3.636	3.636	3.636	3.636	3.636	3.636	3.636
3	3.636	3.636	3.636	3.636	3.636	3.636	3.636	3.636	3.636	3.636	3.636	3.636
4	3.636	3.636	3.636	3.636	3.636	3.636	3.636	3.636	3.636	3.636	3.636	3.636
5	3.636	3.636	3.636	3.636	3.636	3.636	3.636	3.636	3.636	3.636	3.636	3.636
6	3.636	3.636	3.636	3.636	3.636	3.636	3.636	3.636	3.636	3.636	3.636	3.636
7	3.636	3.636	3.636	3.636	3.636	3.636	3.636	3.636	3.636	3.636	3.636	3.636
8	3.636	3.636	3.636	3.636	3.636	3.636	3.636	3.636	3.636	3.636	3.636	3.636
9	3.636	3.636	3.636	3.636	3.636	3.636	3.636	3.636	3.636	3.636	3.636	3.636
10	3.637	3.637	3.637	3.637	3.637	3.637	3.636	3.636	3.636	3.636	3.636	3.636
11	3.636	3.636	3.636	3.636	3.636	3.636	3.637	3.637	3.637	3.637	3.637	3.637
12	3.637	3.637	3.637	3.637	3.637	3.637	3.636	3.636	3.636	3.636	3.636	3.636
13	3.636	3.636	3.636	3.636	3.636	3.636	3.637	3.637	3.637	3.637	3.637	3.637
14	3.637	3.637	3.637	3.637	3.637	3.637	3.636	3.636	3.636	3.636	3.636	3.636
15	3.636	3.636	3.636	3.636	3.636	3.636	3.637	3.637	3.637	3.637	3.637	3.637
16	3.637	3.637	3.637	3.637	3.637	3.637	3.636	3.636	3.636	3.636	3.636	3.636
17	3.636	3.636	3.636	3.636	3.636	3.636	3.637	3.637	3.637	3.637	3.637	3.637
18	3.637	3.637	3.637	3.637	3.637	3.637	3.636	3.636	3.636	3.636	3.636	3.636
19	3.636	3.636	3.636	3.636	3.636	3.636	3.637	3.637	3.637	3.637	3.637	3.637
20	3.637	3.637	3.637	3.637	3.637	3.637	3.636	3.636	3.636	3.636	3.636	3.636
21	3.636	3.636	3.636	3.636	3.636	3.636	3.637	3.637	3.637	3.637	3.637	3.637
22	3.637	3.637	3.637	3.637	3.637	3.637	3.636	3.636	3.636	3.636	3.636	3.636
23	3.636	3.636	3.636	3.636	3.636	3.636	3.637	3.637	3.637	3.637	3.637	3.637
24	3.637	3.637	3.637	3.637	3.637	3.637	3.636	3.636	3.636	3.636	3.636	3.636
25	3.636	3.636	3.636	3.636	3.636	3.636	3.637	3.637	3.637	3.637	3.637	3.637
26	3.637	3.637	3.637	3.637	3.637	3.637	3.636	3.636	3.636	3.636	3.636	3.636
27	3.636	3.636	3.636	3.636	3.636	3.636	3.637	3.637	3.637	3.637	3.637	3.637
28	1.970	2.273	2.576	2.879	3.182	3.485	3.636	3.636	3.636	3.636	3.636	3.636
29	0.000	0.000	0.000	0.000	0.000	0.000	0.152	0.455	0.758	1.061	1.364	1.667

▼ TABLE 8

General Depreciation System—MACRS
Nonresidential Real Property Placed in Service after 12/31/86 and before 5/13/93
Applicable Recovery Period: 31.5 Years
Applicable Convention: Mid-month
Applicable Depreciation Method: Straight Line

If the Recovery Year Is:	And the Month in the First Recovery Year the Property Is Placed in Service Is:											
	1	2	3	4	5	6	7	8	9	10	11	12
The Depreciation Rate Is:												
1	3.042	2.778	2.513	2.249	1.984	1.720	1.455	1.190	0.926	0.661	0.397	0.132
2	3.175	3.175	3.175	3.175	3.175	3.175	3.175	3.175	3.175	3.175	3.175	3.175
3	3.175	3.175	3.175	3.175	3.175	3.175	3.175	3.175	3.175	3.175	3.175	3.175
4	3.175	3.175	3.175	3.175	3.175	3.175	3.175	3.175	3.175	3.175	3.175	3.175
5	3.175	3.175	3.175	3.175	3.175	3.175	3.175	3.175	3.175	3.175	3.175	3.175
6	3.175	3.175	3.175	3.175	3.175	3.175	3.175	3.175	3.175	3.175	3.175	3.175
7	3.175	3.175	3.175	3.175	3.175	3.175	3.175	3.175	3.175	3.175	3.175	3.175
8	3.175	3.174	3.175	3.174	3.175	3.174	3.175	3.175	3.175	3.175	3.175	3.175
9	3.174	3.175	3.174	3.175	3.174	3.175	3.174	3.175	3.174	3.175	3.174	3.175
10	3.175	3.174	3.175	3.174	3.175	3.174	3.175	3.174	3.175	3.174	3.175	3.174
11	3.174	3.175	3.174	3.175	3.174	3.175	3.174	3.175	3.174	3.175	3.174	3.175
12	3.175	3.174	3.175	3.174	3.175	3.174	3.175	3.174	3.175	3.174	3.175	3.174
13	3.174	3.175	3.174	3.175	3.174	3.175	3.174	3.175	3.174	3.175	3.174	3.175
14	3.175	3.174	3.175	3.174	3.175	3.174	3.175	3.174	3.175	3.174	3.175	3.174
15	3.174	3.175	3.174	3.175	3.174	3.175	3.174	3.175	3.174	3.175	3.174	3.175
16	3.175	3.174	3.175	3.174	3.175	3.174	3.175	3.174	3.175	3.174	3.175	3.174
17	3.174	3.175	3.174	3.175	3.174	3.175	3.174	3.175	3.174	3.175	3.174	3.175
18	3.175	3.174	3.175	3.174	3.175	3.174	3.175	3.174	3.175	3.174	3.175	3.174
19	3.174	3.175	3.174	3.175	3.174	3.175	3.174	3.175	3.174	3.175	3.174	3.175
20	3.175	3.174	3.175	3.174	3.175	3.174	3.175	3.174	3.175	3.174	3.175	3.174
21	3.174	3.175	3.174	3.175	3.174	3.175	3.174	3.175	3.174	3.175	3.174	3.175
22	3.175	3.174	3.175	3.174	3.175	3.174	3.175	3.174	3.175	3.174	3.175	3.174
23	3.174	3.175	3.174	3.175	3.174	3.175	3.174	3.175	3.174	3.175	3.174	3.175
24	3.175	3.174	3.175	3.174	3.175	3.174	3.175	3.174	3.175	3.174	3.175	3.174
25	3.174	3.175	3.174	3.175	3.174	3.175	3.174	3.175	3.174	3.175	3.174	3.175
26	3.175	3.174	3.175	3.174	3.175	3.174	3.175	3.174	3.175	3.174	3.175	3.174
27	3.174	3.175	3.174	3.175	3.174	3.175	3.174	3.175	3.174	3.175	3.174	3.175
28	3.175	3.174	3.175	3.174	3.175	3.174	3.175	3.174	3.175	3.174	3.175	3.174
29	3.174	3.175	3.174	3.175	3.174	3.175	3.174	3.175	3.174	3.175	3.174	3.175
30	3.175	3.174	3.175	3.174	3.175	3.174	3.175	3.174	3.175	3.174	3.175	3.174
31	3.174	3.175	3.174	3.175	3.174	3.175	3.174	3.175	3.174	3.175	3.174	3.175
32	1.720	1.984	2.249	2.513	2.778	3.042	3.175	3.174	3.175	3.174	3.175	3.174
33	0.000	0.000	0.000	0.000	0.000	0.000	0.132	0.397	0.661	0.926	1.190	1.455

▼ TABLE 9

General Depreciation System—MACRS
Nonresidential Real Property Placed in Service after 5/12/93
Applicable Recovery Period: 39 years
Applicable Depreciation Method: Straight Line

If the Recovery Year Is:	And the Month in the First Recovery Year the Property Is Placed in Service Is:											
	1	**2**	**3**	**4**	**5**	**6**	**7**	**8**	**9**	**10**	**11**	**12**
	The Depreciation Rate Is:											
1	2.461	2.247	2.033	1.819	1.605	1.391	1.177	0.963	0.749	0.535	0.321	0.107
2-39	2.564	2.564	2.564	2.564	2.564	2.564	2.564	2.564	2.564	2.564	2.564	2.564
40	0.107	0.321	0.535	0.749	0.963	1.177	1.391	1.605	1.819	2.033	2.247	2.461

▼ TABLE 10

Alternative Depreciation System—MACRS (Partial Table)
Property Placed in Service after 12/31/86
Applicable Convention: Half-year
Applicable Depreciation Method: 150 Percent Declining Balance Switching to Straight Line

If the Recovery Year Is:	And the Recovery Period Is:					
	3	**4**	**5**	**7**	**10**	**12**
	The Depreciation Rate Is:					
1	25.00	18.75	15.00	10.71	7.50	6.25
2	37.50	30.47	25.50	19.13	13.88	11.72
3	25.00	20.31	17.85	15.03	11.79	10.25
4	12.50	20.31	16.66	12.25	10.02	8.97
5		10.16	16.66	12.25	8.74	7.85
6			8.33	12.25	8.74	7.33
7				12.25	8.74	7.33
8				6.13	8.74	7.33
9					8.74	7.33
10					8.74	7.33
11					4.37	7.32
12						7.33
13						3.66

▼ TABLE 11

Alternative Depreciation System—MACRS (Partial Table)
Property Placed in Service after 12/31/86
Applicable Convention: Half-year
Applicable Depreciation Method: Straight Line

If the Recovery Year Is:	And the Recovery Period Is:					
	3	4	5	7	10	12
	The Depreciation Rate Is:					
1	16.67	12.50	10.00	7.14	5.00	4.17
2	33.33	25.00	20.00	14.29	10.00	8.33
3	33.33	25.00	20.00	14.29	10.00	8.33
4	16.67	25.00	20.00	14.28	10.00	8.33
5		12.50	20.00	14.29	10.00	8.33
6			10.00	14.28	10.00	8.33
7				14.29	10.00	8.34
8				7.14	10.00	8.33
9					10.00	8.34
10					10.00	8.33
11					5.00	8.34
12						8.33
13						4.17

▼ TABLE 12

Alternative Depreciation System—MACRS
Real Property Placed into Service after 12/31/86
Applicable Recovery Period: 40 years
Applicable Convention: Mid-month
Applicable Depreciation Method: Straight Line

If the Recovery Year Is:	And the Month in the First Recovery Year the Property Is Placed in Service Is:											
	1	2	3	4	5	6	7	8	9	10	11	12
	The Depreciation Rate Is:											
1	2.396	2.188	1.979	1.771	1.563	1.354	1.146	0.938	0.729	0.521	0.313	0.104
2 to 40	2.500	2.500	2.500	2.500	2.500	2.500	2.500	2.500	2.500	2.500	2.500	2.500
41	0.104	0.312	0.521	0.729	0.937	1.146	1.354	1.562	1.771	1.979	2.187	2.396

▼ TABLE 13

Lease Inclusion Dollar Amounts for Automobiles (Other Than for Trucks, Vans, or Electronic Automobiles) With a Lease Term Beginning in Calendar Year 2009[a]

Fair Market Value of Passenger Automobile		Tax Year During Lease				
Over	Not Over	1st	2nd	3rd	4th	5th and Later
$18,500	$19,000	9	19	28	34	38
19,000	19,500	10	21	32	38	43
19,500	20,000	11	24	36	42	48
20,000	20,500	12	27	39	46	54
20,500	21,000	13	29	43	51	58
21,000	21,500	15	31	47	55	64
21,500	22,000	16	34	50	60	68
22,000	23,000	17	38	56	66	76
23,000	24,000	20	42	64	75	86
24,000	25,000	22	47	71	84	96
25,000	26,000	24	52	78	93	107
26,000	27,000	26	58	85	101	117
27,000	28,000	29	62	93	110	127
28,000	29,000	31	67	100	119	138
29,000	30,000	33	72	108	128	147
30,000	31,000	35	77	115	137	157
31,000	32,000	38	82	122	146	167
32,000	33,000	40	87	129	155	178
33,000	34,000	42	92	137	163	188
34,000	35,000	44	97	144	172	199
35,000	36,000	47	102	151	181	208
36,000	37,000	49	107	159	189	219
37,000	38,000	51	112	166	199	228
38,000	39,000	53	117	173	208	239
39,000	40,000	56	122	180	216	250
40,000	41,000	58	127	188	225	259
41,000	42,000	60	132	195	234	269
42,000	43,000	62	137	203	242	280
43,000	44,000	65	141	210	252	290
44,000	45,000	67	146	218	260	300
45,000	46,000	69	151	225	269	311
46,000	47,000	71	157	232	278	320
47,000	48,000	74	161	240	286	331
48,000	49,000	76	166	247	296	340
49,000	50,000	78	171	255	304	351
50,000	51,000	80	176	262	313	361
51,000	52,000	83	181	269	322	371
52,000	53,000	85	186	276	331	381
53,000	54,000	87	191	284	339	392
54,000	55,000	89	196	291	349	401
55,000	56,000	92	201	298	357	412
56,000	57,000	94	206	306	365	423
57,000	58,000	96	211	313	375	432
58,000	59,000	98	216	320	384	442
59,000	60,000	101	221	327	393	452
60,000	62,000	104	228	339	406	467
62,000	64,000	109	238	353	424	488
64,000	66,000	113	248	368	441	509

[a]Per *Rev. Proc.* 2009-24. The table for 2010 had not been released at the date of the printing.

▼ **TABLE 13ª (continued)**

Fair Market Value of Passenger Automobile		Tax Year During Lease				
Over	Not Over	1st	2nd	3rd	4th	5th and Later
$ 66,000	68,000	118	258	382	459	529
68,000	70,000	122	268	397	476	550
70,000	72,000	127	277	413	493	570
72,000	74,000	131	288	427	511	590
74,000	76,000	136	297	442	529	610
76,000	78,000	140	307	457	546	631
78,000	80,000	145	317	471	564	651
80,000	85,000	152	335	497	595	686
85,000	90,000	164	359	534	639	737
90,000	95,000	175	384	570	683	789
95,000	100,000	186	409	607	727	839
100,000	110,000	203	446	662	793	916
110,000	120,000	226	495	736	881	1,018
120,000	130,000	248	545	809	970	1,119
130,000	140,000	271	594	883	1,058	1,220
140,000	150,000	293	644	956	1,146	1,322
150,000	160,000	316	693	1,030	1,234	1,424
160,000	170,000	338	743	1,103	1,322	1,526
170,000	180,000	361	792	1,177	1,410	1,628
180,000	190,000	383	842	1,250	1,498	1,730
190,000	200,000	406	891	1,324	1,586	1,831
200,000	210,000	428	941	1,397	1,675	1,932
210,000	220,000	451	990	1,471	1,762	2,035
220,000	230,000	473	1,040	1,544	1,851	2,136
230,000	240,000	496	1,089	1,618	1,939	2,238
240,000	and up	518	1,139	1,691	2,027	2,340

ªPer *Rev. Proc.* 2009-24. The table for 2010 had not been released at the date of the printing.

▼ **TABLE 14**

Lease Inclusion Dollar Amounts for Trucks and Vans With a Lease Term Beginning in Calendar Year 2009[a]

Fair Market Value of Truck or Van		Tax Year During Lease				
Over	Not Over	1st	2nd	3rd	4th	5th and Later
$18,500	$19,000	8	17	25	30	35
19,000	19,500	9	19	29	35	40
19,500	20,000	10	22	33	38	45
20,000	20,500	11	25	36	43	50
20,500	21,000	12	27	40	48	55
21,000	21,500	13	30	43	52	60
21,500	22,000	15	32	47	56	66
22,000	23,000	16	36	52	64	72
23,000	24,000	18	41	60	72	83
24,000	25,000	21	45	68	81	93
25,000	26,000	23	50	75	90	103
26,000	27,000	25	56	82	98	114
27,000	28,000	27	61	89	107	124
28,000	29,000	30	65	97	116	134
29,000	30,000	32	70	104	125	144
30,000	31,000	34	75	112	134	154
31,000	32,000	36	80	119	143	164
32,000	33,000	39	85	126	151	175
33,000	34,000	41	90	134	160	184
34,000	35,000	43	95	141	169	195
35,000	36,000	45	100	148	178	205
36,000	37,000	48	105	155	187	215
37,000	38,000	50	110	163	195	226
38,000	39,000	52	115	170	204	236
39,000	40,000	55	120	177	213	246
40,000	41,000	57	125	185	221	256
41,000	42,000	59	130	192	231	266
42,000	43,000	61	135	199	240	276
43,000	44,000	64	139	207	249	286
44,000	45,000	66	144	215	257	296
45,000	46,000	68	149	222	266	307
46,000	47,000	70	155	229	274	317
47,000	48,000	73	159	237	283	327
48,000	49,000	75	164	244	292	338
49,000	50,000	77	169	251	301	348
50,000	51,000	79	174	259	310	357
51,000	52,000	82	179	266	318	368
52,000	53,000	84	184	273	328	378
53,000	54,000	86	189	281	336	388
54,000	55,000	88	194	288	345	399
55,000	56,000	91	199	295	354	408
56,000	57,000	93	204	302	363	419
57,000	58,000	95	209	310	371	429
58,000	59,000	97	214	317	381	439
59,000	60,000	100	219	324	389	450
60,000	62,000	103	226	336	402	465
62,000	64,000	107	236	351	420	485
64,000	66,000	112	246	365	438	505
66,000	68,000	116	256	380	455	526

[a]Per *Rev. Proc.* 2009-24. The table for 2010 had not been released at the date of the printing.

▼ TABLE 14ª (continued)

Fair Market Value of Automobiles		Tax Year During Lease				
Over	Not Over	1st	2nd	3rd	4th	5th and Later
$ 68,000	70,000	121	266	394	473	546
70,000	72,000	125	276	409	491	566
72,000	74,000	130	286	423	509	586
74,000	76,000	134	296	438	526	607
76,000	78,000	139	305	454	543	627
78,000	80,000	143	316	467	561	648
80,000	85,000	151	333	493	592	684
85,000	90,000	163	357	531	635	735
90,000	95,000	174	382	567	680	785
95,000	100,000	185	407	604	724	836
100,000	110,000	202	444	659	790	912
110,000	120,000	225	493	733	878	1,014
120,000	130,000	247	543	806	966	1,116
130,000	140,000	270	592	880	1,054	1,218
140,000	150,000	292	642	953	1,143	1,319
150,000	160,000	315	691	1,027	1,230	1,421
160,000	170,000	337	741	1,100	1,319	1,522
170,000	180,000	360	790	1,174	1,407	1,624
180,000	190,000	382	840	1,247	1,495	1,726
190,000	200,000	405	889	1,321	1,583	1,828
200,000	210,000	427	939	1,394	1,671	1,930
210,000	220,000	450	988	1,468	1,759	2,031
220,000	230,000	472	1,038	1,541	1,847	2,134
230,000	240,000	495	1,087	1,615	1,935	2,235
240,000	and up	517	1,137	1,688	2,024	2,336

ªPer *Rev. Proc.* 2009-24. The table for 2010 had not been released at the date of the printing.

APPENDIX D

GLOSSARY

Ability to pay A concept in taxation that holds that taxpayers be taxed according to their ability to pay such taxes, that is, taxpayers that have sufficient financial resources should pay the tax. This concept is an integral part of vertical equity.

Accelerated Cost Recovery System (ACRS) Established by ERTA in 1981, the ACRS provides an accelerated depreciation and shorter cost-recovery period for real and personal property. The Tax Reform Act of 1986 changed the previously allowed depreciation tables and assigned recovery periods that approach the asset's true economic life. The current depreciation system is referred to as MACRS.

Accounting method The method of determining the taxable year in which income and expenses are reported for tax purposes. Generally, the same method must be used for tax purposes as is used for keeping books and records. The accounting treatment used for any item of income or expense and of specific items (e.g., installment sales and contracts) is included in this term. See also each specific accounting method.

Accounting period The period of time, usually 12 months, used by taxpayers to compute their taxable income. Taxpayers who do not keep records must use a calendar year. Taxpayers who do keep books and records may choose between a calendar year or a fiscal year. The accounting period election is made on the taxpayer's first filed return and cannot be changed without IRS consent. The accounting period may be less than 12 months if it is the taxpayer's first or final return or if the taxpayer is changing accounting periods. Certain restrictions upon the use of a fiscal year apply to partnerships, S corporations, and personal service corporations.

Accountable plan A type of employee reimbursement plan that meets two tests, (1) substantiation, and (2) return of excess reimbursement. Under an accountable plan, reimbursements are excluded from the employee's gross income and the expenses are not deductible by the employee.

Accrual method of accounting Accounting method under which income is reported and expenses are deducted when (1) all events have occurred that fix the taxpayer's right to receive the income and (2) the amount of the item can be determined with reasonable accuracy. Taxpayers with inventories to report must use this method to report sales and purchases.

Accumulated earnings tax This penalty tax is intended to discourage companies from retaining excessive amounts of earnings if the funds are invested in earnings that are unrelated to the business's needs. The current tax rate is 15%.

Acquiescence policy IRS policy of announcing whether it agrees or disagrees with a regular Tax Court decision. Such statements are not issued for every case.

ACRS See Accelerated Cost Recovery System.

Active income Income that is produced by the taxpayer's involvement or participation—wages, salaries, and other business income—is considered active income. It is the opposite of passive income.

Additional depreciation The excess of the actual amount of accelerated depreciation (or cost-recovery deductions under ACRS) over the amount of depreciation that would be deductible under the straight-line method. Such depreciation applies to Section 1250 depreciable real property acquired prior to 1987.

Adjusted current earnings An AMT adjustment item for corporations used to compute the Alternative Minimum Tax. The term is a concept based on the traditional earnings and profits definition found in Sec. 312.

Adjusted gross income (AGI) A measure of taxable income that falls between gross income and taxable income. It is the income amount that is used as the basis for calculating the floor or the ceiling for numerous other tax computations.

Adjusted sales price The amount realized from the sale of a residence less any fixing-up expenses.

AGI See Adjusted gross income.

Alimony Payments made pursuant to divorce or separation or written agreement between spouses subject to conditions specified in the tax law. Alimony payments (as contrasted to property settlements) are deductible for AGI by the payor and are included in the gross income of the recipient.

All events test Rule holding that an accrual basis taxpayer must report an item of income (1) when all events have occurred that fix the taxpayer's right to receive the income and (2) the amount of the item can be determined with reasonable accuracy. This test is not satisfied until economic performance has taken place.

Alternative minimum tax (AMT) Applies to individuals, corporations, and estates and trusts only if the tentative minimum tax (TMT) exceeds the taxpayer's regular tax liability. Most taxpayers are not subject to this tax.

Amount realized The amount realized equals the sum of money plus the fair market value of all other property received from the sale or other disposition of the property less any selling expenses (e.g., commissions, advertising, deed preparation costs, and legal expenses) incurred in connection with the sale.

AMT See Alternative Minimum Tax.

Annual accounting period See Accounting period.

Annuity A series of regular payments that will continue for either a fixed period of time or until the death of the recipient. Pensions are usually paid in this way.

Applicable federal rate The rate determined monthly by the federal government which is based on the rate paid by the government on borrowed funds. The rate varies with the term of the loan. Thus, short-term loans are for a period of under three years, mid-term loans are for over three years and under nine years, and long-term loans are for over nine years.

Asset depreciation range (ADR) system of depreciation Depreciation method allowed for property placed in service before January 1, 1981. This method prescribed useful lives for various classes of assets.

Average tax rate The taxpayer's total tax liability divided by the amount of his taxable income.

Backup withholding A modified withholding system intended to prevent abusive noncompliance situations.

Bad debt Bona fide debt that is uncollectible because it is worthless. Such debts are further characterized as "business bad debts," which give rise to an ordinary deduction, and "nonbusiness bad debts," which are treated as a short-term capital loss. A determination of whether a debt is worthless is

made by reference to all the pertinent evidence (e.g., the debtor's general financial condition and whether the debt is secured by collateral). Such debts are deductible subject to certain requirements.

Bona fide debt A debt that (1) arises from a valid and enforceable obligation to pay a fixed or determinable sum of money and (2) results in a debtor-creditor relationship.

Bonus depreciation Special first year depreciation on qualified property (non-real estate) placed in service after September 10, 2001 and before January 1, 2005 and re-enacted for 2008 and 2009. The bonus depreciation rate was 30% for the period 9/11/01–5/5/03 and 50% for the period 5/6/03–12/31/04 and for the tax years 2008 and 2009.

Boot Cash and nonlike-kind property given to complete an exchange of like-kind property where the property exchanged is not of equal value. Gain on the exchange is limited to the amount of boot received.

Brother-sister controlled group A group of two or more corporations controlled by five or fewer individuals. There are two definitions, a 80%-50% definition and a 50%-only definition. The definition to be used depends on the specific application.

Business bad debt See Bad debt.

Cafeteria plan Employer-financed plan that offers employees the option of choosing cash or statutory nontaxable fringe benefits (other than scholarships, fellowships, and Sec. 132 benefits such as discounts on merchandise). Such plans may not discriminate in favor of highly compensated individuals or their dependents or spouses.

Capital addition See Capital expenditure.

Capital asset This category of assets includes all assets except inventory, notes and accounts receivable, and depreciable property or land used in a trade or business (e.g., property, plant, and machinery).

Capital expenditure An expenditure that adds to the value of, substantially prolongs the useful life of, or adapts the property to a new or different use qualifies as a capital expenditure.

Capital gain Gain realized on the sale or exchange of a capital asset.

Capital gain dividend A distribution by a regulated investment company (i.e., a mutual fund) of capital gains realized from the sale of investments in the fund. Such dividends also include undistributed capital gains allocated to the shareholders.

Capital gain property Property that is contributed to a public charity upon which a long-term capital gain would be recognized if that property was sold at its fair market value.

Capital loss Loss realized on the sale or exchange of a capital asset.

Capital recovery A capital recovery amount is a deduction for depreciation or cost recovery. It is a factor in the determination of a property's adjusted basis.

Cash method of accounting Accounting method that requires the taxpayer to report income for the taxable year in which payments are actually or constructively received. Expenses are reported in the year they are paid. Most individuals and service businesses (i.e., businesses without inventories) use this method. Small businesses with inventories that have gross receipts of less than $1 million may also use the cash method.

Cash receipts and disbursements method of accounting See Cash method of accounting.

Casualty loss Loss that arises from an identifiable event that was sudden, unexpected, or unusual (e.g., fire, storm, shipwreck, other casualty, or theft). Within certain limitations, individuals may deduct such losses from AGI. Business casualty losses are deductible for AGI.

C Corporation Form of business entity that is taxed as a separate tax-paying entity. Its income is subject to an initial tax at the corporate level. Its shareholders are subject to a second tax when dividends are paid from the corporation's earnings and profits. Under certain conditions, S corporation status may be elected for tax purposes. C corporations are sometimes referred to as "regular corporations."

CD See Certificate of deposit.

Charitable contribution deduction Contributions of money or property made to qualified organizations (i.e., public charities and private nonoperating foundations) may be deducted from AGI. The amount of the deduction depends upon (1) the type of charity receiving the contribution, (2) the type of property contributed, and (3) other limitations mandated by the tax law. See also Unrelated use property.

Child tax credit A credit for individual taxpayers of $1,000 per qualifying child. A qualifying child must be a U.S. citizen, under age 17, qualify as the taxpayer's dependent, and be the taxpayer's descendent, stepchild, or foster child.

Closed-fact situation Situation or transaction that has already occurred.

Closely held C corporation For purposes of the at risk rules, a closely held C corporation is defined as a corporation where more than 50% of the stock is owned by five or fewer individuals at any time during the last half of the corporation's taxable year. These individuals may or may not be members of the same family.

Community income In any of the eight community property states, such income consists of the income from the personal efforts, investments, etc. of either spouse. Community income belongs equally to both spouses.

Compensation Payment for personal services. Salaries, wages, fees, commissions, tips, bonuses, and specialized forms of compensation such as director's fees and jury's fees fall into this category. However, certain fringe benefits and some foreign-earned income are not taxed.

Completed contract method of accounting Accounting method for long-term contracts undertaken by smaller companies. Income from the contract is reported in the taxable year in which the contract is completed. The completed contract method is limited to construction contracts undertaken by smaller companies.

Constant interest rate method Used to amortize the original issue discount ratably over the life of the bond, this method determines the amount of interest income by multiplying the interest yield to maturity by the adjusted issue price.

Constructive dividend Distribution that is intended to result in a deduction to the corporation. For example, excessive salary payments to shareholder-employees may be recharacterized as nondeductible dividends to the corporation to the extent that such amounts are not reasonable. The excess amount may be treated as dividend income to the shareholder-employees rather than as compensation provided that certain conditions are met.

Constructive receipt doctrine Rule holding that cash method taxpayers cannot turn their backs on the receipt of income if the funds are unqualifiedly made available.

Constructive stock ownership Shares that are indirectly or deemed to be owned by another shareholder due to related party situations.

Contributory pension plan A qualified pension plan to which employees make voluntary contributions.

Controlled group A controlled group is two or more separately incorporated businesses owned by the same individuals or entities. Such groups may consist of parent-subsidiary corporations, brother-sister corporations, or a combination of both (combined group).

Cost The amount paid for property in cash or the fair market value of the property given in exchange. The costs of acquiring the property and preparing it for use are included in the cost of the property.

Cost depletion method Calculation of the depletion of an asset (e.g., oil and gas properties) under which the asset's adjusted basis is divided by the estimated recoverable units to arrive at a per-unit depletion. This amount is then multiplied by the number of units sold to determine the cost depletion. This method may be alternated with the percentage depletion method as long as the calculation takes that into account.

Current year's exclusion The amount of the annuity payment that is excluded from gross income. This amount is determined by multiplying the exclusion ratio by the amount received during the year.

Customs duties A federal excise tax on imported goods.

Deductions for AGI Expenses one would see on an income statement prepared for financial accounting purposes, for example, compensation paid to employees, repairs to business property, and depreciation expenses. Certain

nonbusiness deductions (e.g., alimony payments, moving expenses, and deductible payments to an individual retirement account (IRA)) are also deductible for AGI.

Deductions from AGI Generally, deductions are allowed for certain personal expenses such as medical deductions and charitable contributions which are referred to as itemized deductions. Alternatively, individuals may deduct the standard deduction. Personal and dependency deductions are also deductions from AGI.

Deferred compensation Methods of compensating employees based upon their current service where the benefits are deferred until future periods (e.g., a pension plan).

Defined benefit pension plan Qualified pension plan which establishes a contribution formula based upon actuarial techniques that are intended to fund a fixed retirement benefit amount. Thus, the amount that will be available at the time of retirement is determined when the contributions are made.

Defined contribution pension plan Qualified pension plan under which a separate account is maintained for each participant and fixed amounts are contributed based upon a specific percentage-of-compensation formula. The retirement benefits are based on the value of the participant's account at the time of retirement. Defined contribution plans for self-employed individuals are referred to as *H.R. 10 plans.*

Dependent care assistance program Employer-financed programs that provide care for an employee's children or other dependents. An employee may exclude up to $5,000 from gross income although the ceiling amount (i.e., $3,000 or $6,000) on the child care credit is reduced by the amount of assistance that is excluded from gross income.

DIF See Discriminate Function System.

Discriminate Function System (DIF) System used by the IRS to select individual returns for audit. This system is intended to identify those tax returns which are most likely to contain errors.

Dividends-received deduction The deduction on dividends received by corporate shareholders that attempts to mitigate the triple taxation that would occur if one corporation paid dividends to a corporate shareholder who, in turn, distributed such amounts to its individual shareholders. Certain restrictions and limitations apply to this deduction.

E&P See Earnings and profits

Earned income credit A refundable credit that encourages lower income individuals to become gainfully employed. The credit is based on the individual's earned income.

Earnings and profits (E&P) A measure of the corporation's ability to pay a dividend from its current and accumulated earnings without an impairment of capital.

Economic performance test Economic performance occurs when the property or services to be provided are actually delivered.

Education expense Subject to certain limitations and restrictions, education expenses are deductible if they are incurred (1) to improve or maintain the individual's existing skills or (2) to meet requirements that are requisite to continued employment or meet the requirements of state law.

Effective tax rate The taxpayer's total tax liability divided by his total economic income.

Electronic Filing The method of filing a tax return with the IRS by electronic means instead of paper forms.

Employee achievement award Award given under circumstances that does not create a likelihood that it is really disguised compensation. It must be in the form of tangible personal property (other than cash) and be valued at no more than $400.

Employee stock ownership plan (ESOP) A qualified stock bonus plan or combined stock bonus plan and money purchase pension plan. ESOP's are funded by contributions of the employer's stock which are held for the employees' benefit.

Employment taxes Social security (FICA) and federal and state unemployment compensation taxes.

Entertainment expense Entertainment expenses (e.g., business meals) that are either directly related to or associated with the active conduct of a trade or business are deductible within certain limitations and restrictions. Directly related expenses are those that (1) derive a business benefit other than goodwill and (2) are incurred in a clear business setting. Expenses that are associated with the business are those that show a clear business purpose (e.g., obtaining new business) and occur on the same day the business is discussed.

ESOP See Employee stock ownership plan.

Estate tax Part of the federal unified transfer tax system, this tax is based upon the total property transfers an individual makes during his lifetime and at death.

Excess depreciation See Additional depreciation.

Exchange A transaction in which one receives a reciprocal transfer of property rather than cash and/or a cash equivalent.

Excise taxes Federal tax on alcohol, gasoline, telephone usage, oil and gas production, etc. State and local governments may impose similar taxes on goods and services.

Exclusion Any item of income that the tax law says is not taxable.

Exclusion ratio The portion of the annuity payment that is excluded from taxation. This amount equals the investment in the contract (its cost) divided by the expected return from the annuity.

Expected return The amount which a taxpayer can expect to receive from an annuity. It is determined by multiplying the amount of the annuity's annual payment by the expected return multiple.

Expected return multiple The number of years that the annuity is expected to continue.

This amount may be a stated term or for the remainder of the taxpayer's life.

Fair market value (FMV) This amount is the price at which property would change hands between a willing buyer and a willing seller where neither party is under any compulsion to buy or sell.

Federal estate tax See estate tax.

Federal Insurance Contributions Act See FICA.

Federal Unemployment Tax Act See FUTA.

FICA Tax withheld through the payment of payroll taxes, FICA is intended to finance social security benefits for individuals who are not self-employed. Employees and employers contribute matching amounts until a federally-set annual earnings ceiling is reached. At that time, no further contributions need be made for that year. No ceiling exists for the hospital insurance (HI) portion of the tax. Self-employed individuals are subject to self-employment tax and currently receive a *for* AGI income tax deduction equal to 50% of their self-employment tax payments.

Field audit procedure Audit procedure generally used by the IRS for corporations or individuals engaged in a trade or business and conducted at either the taxpayer's place of business or his tax advisor's office. Generally, several items on the tax return are examined.

FIFO method of inventory valuation This flow of cost method assumes that the first goods purchased will be the first goods sold. Thus, the ending inventory consists of the last goods purchased.

Fiscal year An annual accounting period that ends on the last day of any month other than December. A fiscal year may be elected by taxpayers that keep books and records, such as businesses.

Flat tax See Proportional tax.

Foreign-earned income An individual's earnings from personal services rendered in a foreign country.

Foreign tax credit Tax credit given to mitigate the possibility of double taxation faced by U.S. taxpayers earning foreign income.

Former passive activity An activity that was formerly considered passive, but which is not considered to be passive with respect to the taxpayer for the current year.

Franchise tax State tax levy sometimes based upon a weighted average formula consisting of net worth, income, and sales.

Functional-use test A test used to determine whether property is considered similar or related in service or use for purposes of involuntary conversions of property under Sec. 1033. The functional-use test requires that the replacement property be functionally the same as the converted property.

FUTA Federal and state unemployment compensation tax.

GAAP See Generally accepted accounting principles.

Gain realized See Realized gain.

General business credit Special credit category consisting of tax credits commonly available to businesses. The more significant credit items are (1) the investment tax credit, (2) the work opportunity credit, (3) the research credit, (4) the low-income housing credit, (5) the empowerment zone employment credit, (6) the disabled access credit.

Generally accepted accounting principles (GAAP) The accounting principles that govern the preparation of financial reports to shareholders. GAAP does not apply to the tax treatment unless the method clearly reflects income. It is used only when the regulations do not specify the treatment of an item or when the regulations provide more than one alternative accounting method.

Gift tax A tax that is imposed upon the donor for transfers that are not supported by full and adequate consideration. A $13,000 annual exclusion is allowed per donee in 2009 and 2010 and $12,000 for 2006–2008. The annual exclusion in 2005 was $11,000.

Goodwill The excess of the purchase price of a business over the fair market value of all identifiable assets acquired.

Gross income All income received in cash, property, or services, from whatever source derived and from which the taxpayer derives a direct economic benefit.

Gross tax For income tax purposes, the amount determined by multiplying taxable income by the appropriate tax rate(s). The gross tax may also be found in the appropriate tax table for the taxpayer's filing status.

Half year convention An assumption with respect to depreciation that assumes that all asset acquisitions and dispositions are made at the midpoint of the tax year.

Health Savings Account Accounts that may be contributed to a fund by eligible individuals to enable such individuals to accumulate funds on a tax-free basis to pay qualified medical expenses. These accounts may only be set up by individuals who are covered under a high-deductible health plan and, within limits, are tax-deductible.

Holding period The length of time an asset is held before it is disposed of. This period is used to determine whether the gain or loss is long- or short-term.

Horizontal equity A concept in taxation that refers to the notion that similarly-situated taxpayers should be treated equally under the tax law.

H.R. 10 Plan Special retirement plan rules applicable to self-employed individuals. Such plans are often referred to as "Keogh plans."

Hybrid method of accounting Accounting method that combines the cash and accrual methods. Under this method, taxpayers can report sales and purchases under the accrual method and other income and expense items under the cash method. See also the cash method of accounting and the accrual method of accounting.

IDCs See Intangible drilling and development costs.

Imputed interest rule This rule reallocates the payments received in an installment sale between interest (fully taxable) and principal (only gain is taxable). To avoid this, the stated interest rate must equal at least 100% of the applicable federal rate as determined monthly according to the rate paid by the government on borrowed funds.

Incentive stock option plan (ISO) Stock option plan that allows executives to receive a proprietary interest in the corporation. The option to participate in this type of plan must be exercised according to certain requirements and must follow certain procedures.

Income The economic concept of income measures the amount an individual can consume during a period and remain as well off at the end of the period as at the beginning. The accounting concept of income is a measure of the income that is realized in a transaction. The tax concept of income is close to the accounting concept. It includes both taxable and nontaxable income from any source. However, it does not include a return of capital.

Incrementalism A concept in taxation that described how the tax law has been changed or modified over the years. Under incrementalism, the tax law is changed on an incremental basis rather than a complete revision basis.

Indeterminate market value If the market value of the property in question cannot be determined by the usual methods, the "open transaction" doctrine may be applied and the tax consequences may be deferred until the transaction is closed. Alternatively, the property may be valued by using the fair market value of the property that is given in the exchange (e.g., the value of the services rendered).

Individual retirement account (IRA) Contribution for AGI that is deductible if (1) neither the taxpayer nor his spouse are active participants in an employer-sponsored retirement plan or (2) certain income limitations are met. Taxpayers who do not meet these requirements may make nondeductible IRA contributions. See also Roth IRA.

Information Release An administrative pronouncement concerning an issue the IRS thinks the general public will be interested in. Such releases are issued in lay terms.

Innocent spouse rule Rule that exempts a spouse from penalty of from liability for the tax if such spouse had no knowledge of nor reason to know about an item of community income.

Installment sale Any disposition of property which involves receiving at least one payment after the close of the taxable year in which the sale occurs.

Installment sale method of accounting Taxpayers may use this method of accounting to reduce the tax burden from gains on the sale of property paid for in installments. Under this method, payment of the tax is deferred until the sale proceeds are collected. This method is not applicable to sales of publicly traded property or to losses.

Intangible drilling and development costs (IDCs) Expenditures made by an operator for wages, fuel, repairs, hauling supplies, and so forth, incident to and necessary for the preparation and drilling of oil and gas wells.

Intangible property Property that does not have physical substance, such as goodwill, patents, stocks and bonds, etc.

Interest The cost charged by a lender for the use of money. For example, finance charges, loan discounts, premiums, loan origination fees, and points paid by a buyer to obtain a mortgage loan are all interest expenses. The deductibility of the expense depends upon the purpose for which the indebtedness was incurred.

Internal Revenue Code The primary legislative source and authority for tax research, planning, and compliance activities.

Internal Revenue Service (IRS) The branch of the Treasury Department that is responsible for administering the federal tax law.

Interpretative Regulations Treasury Regulations that serve to broadly interpret the provisions of the Internal Revenue Code.

Inter vivos gifts Gifts made during the donor's life-time.

Investment expenses All deductions other than interest that are directly connected with the production of investment income.

Investment income Gross income from property held for investment and any net gain attributable to the disposition of such property. See also Net investment income.

Investment interest Interest expense on indebtedness incurred to purchase or carry property held for investment (e.g., income from interest, dividends, annuities, and royalties). Interest expenses incurred from passive activities are not subject to the investment interest limitations and interest incurred to purchase or carry tax-exempt securities is not deductible. Interest incurred from passive activities is subject to the passive activity loss limitation rules.

Involuntary conversion Such a conversion occurs when property is compulsorily converted into money or other property due to theft, seizure, requisition, condemnation, or partial or complete destruction. For example, an involuntary conversion occurs when the government exercises its right of eminent domain.

IRA See Individual retirement account.

IRC See Internal Revenue Code.

IRR See Internal rate of return.

IRS See Internal Revenue Service.

ISO See Incentive stock option.

Itemized deductions Also known as "deductions from AGI," these personal expenditures are allowable for such items as medical expenses, state and local taxes, charitable contributions, unreimbursed employee business expenses, interest on a personal

residence, and casualty and theft losses. There are specific requirements for and limitations on the deductibility of each of these items. In addition, only those taxpayers whose total itemized deductions exceed the standard deduction amount can itemize their deductions. In general, for 2008 and 2009, the total itemized deductions for an individual is reduced by 1% of AGI (2% in 2006 and 2007, 3% in 2005 and earlier years) in excess of specified amounts. No reduction is required for 2010.

Joint income Income from jointly-held property.

Judicial decisions Decisions of a court of law.

Keogh plan Retirement plan for self-employed individuals. This type of plan is also known as an "H.R. 10 plan."

LCM See Lower of cost or market method of inventory valuation.

Legislative Regulations Treasury Regulations issued at the mandate of the Internal Revenue Code. Legislative regulations have a higher degree of authority than interpretative regulations.

Letter Ruling Letter rulings originate from the IRS at the taxpayer's request. They describe how the IRS will treat a proposed transaction. It is only binding on the person requesting the ruling providing the taxpayer completes the transaction as proposed in the ruling. Those of general interest are published as Revenue Rulings.

LIFO method of inventory valuation This method assumes a last-in, first out flow of cost. It results in the lowest taxable income during periods of inflation because it shows the lowest inventory value. Price indexes are used for the valuation. The information in these indexes is grouped into groups (pools) of similar items. See also Simplified LIFO method.

Like class Classes of assets defined by the Regulations that are considered to be property of a like kind for purposes of Sec. 1031. Like class property is tangible personal property that is in the same General Asset Class or the Same Product Class as other property.

Like-kind exchange A direct exchange of like-kind property. The transferred property and the received property must be held for productive use either (1) in a trade or business or (2) as an investment. Nonrecognition of gain or loss is mandatory. Certain like-kind exchanges between related parties are restricted if either party disposes of the property within two years of the exchange.

Like-kind property Property with a similar nature and character. This term does not refer to either the grade or quality of the property.

Limited liability company (LLC) A corporation that is generally taxed under the partnership rules. Although similar to an S corporation,

there is no limit to (1) the number of shareholders, (2) the number of classes of stock, or (3) the types of investments in related entities.

Limited liability partnerships (LLP) LLPs are taxed as partnerships but enjoy limited liability under state partnership laws (i.e., individual partners are liable for their own acts and acts of persons under their direction and control but not for negligence or misconduct by other partners).

Liquidating distribution A distribution that liquidates a partner's entire partnership interest due to retirement, death, or other business reason. Such distributions result in a capital gain or loss to the partner whose interest is liquidated. In a corporate liquidation, the liquidating corporation generally recognizes gains and losses on the distribution of the properties and its shareholders recognize capital gain or loss on the surrender of their stock.

Long-term capital gain (LTCG) Gain realized on the sale or exchange of a capital asset held longer than one year.

Long-term capital loss (LTCL) Loss realized on the sale or exchange of a capital asset held longer than one year.

Long-term contracts Building, manufacturing, installation, and construction contracts that are not completed in the same taxable year in which they are entered into. Service contracts do not qualify as long-term contracts. See also Completed contract method of accounting.

Look-back interest Interest that is assessed on any additional tax that would have been paid if the actual total cost of the contract was used to calculate the tax rather than the estimated cost. Thus, it is applicable to any contract of portion of a contract that is accounted for under either the hybrid or percentage of completion method of accounting.

Lower of cost or market method (LCM) of inventory valuation The valuation method is available to all taxpayers other than those using LIFO valuation. It is applied to each separate item in the inventory.

Marginal tax rate The tax that is applied to an incremental amount of taxable income that is added to the tax base. This rate can be used to measure the tax effect of a proposed transaction. Currently, the highest marginal tax rate for individuals is 35%.

Market value This term refers to replacement cost under the lower of cost or market inventory method. That is, it is the price at which the taxpayer can replace the goods in question. See also Fair market value.

Material participation The level of participation by a taxpayer in an activity that determines whether the activity is either passive or active. If a taxpayer does not meet the material participation requirements, the activity is treated as a passive activity.

Medical expense deduction Unreimbursed medical expenses incurred for medical procedures or treatments that are (1) legal in the locality in which they are performed and

(2) incurred for the purpose of alleviating a physical or mental defect or illness that affects the body's structure or function are deductible from AGI. Out-of-pocket travel costs incurred while en route to a medical facility, certain capital expenditures affecting the sick person, premiums for medical insurance, and in-patient hospital care are also deductible. Certain restrictions and limitations apply to this deduction.

Memorandum decision Decision issued by the Tax Court. They deal with factual variations on matters which were decided in earlier cases.

Method of accounting See Accounting method.

Miscellaneous itemized deductions Certain unreimbursed employee expenses (e.g., required uniforms, travel, entertainment, and so on) fall into this category. Miscellaneous itemized deductions also include certain investment expenses, appraisal fees for charitable contributions and fees for tax return preparation. The nature of the deduction depends on whether the taxpayer is an employee or a self-employed individual.

Modified percentage of completion method A variation of the regular percentage of completion method where an election may be made to defer reporting profit from a long-term contract until at least 10% of the estimated total cost has been incurred.

Moving expense Expenses incurred in relation to employment-related job transfers.

Necessary expense Expense that is deductible under Sec. 162 because it is appropriate and helpful in the taxpayer's business. Such expenses must also qualify as ordinary.

Net investment income The excess of the taxpayer's investment income over his investment expenses. See also Investment income.

Net operating loss (NOL) A net operating loss occurs when business expenses exceed business income for any taxable year. Such losses may be carried back two years or carried forward 20 years to a year in which the taxpayer has taxable income. Loss must be carried back first and must be deducted from years in chronological order.

Net Present Value (NPV) Method used by investment analysts to determine the anticipated return on an investment. This method uses a fixed discount rate to compute the net present value of future cash flows.

NOL See Net operating loss.

Net unearned income The amount of unearned income of a child under age 18 (or under 24 if a full-time student and earned income less than 1/2% of his support) that is taxed at the child's parent's top marginal tax rate.

Nonaccountable plan A type of employee reimbursement plan that does not meet either of the two tests for an accountable plan (see accountable plan). Under a nonaccountable plan, reimbursements are included in the employee's gross income and the expenses are deductible by the employee, subject to the 2% of AGI floor.

Nonbusiness bad debt See Bad debt.

Noncontributory pension plan Only the employer makes contributions to this type of pension plan.

Nonliquidating distribution Distribution that reduces but does not eliminate, a partner's partnership interest. Such distributions are generally treated as tax-free returns of capital.

Nonqualified deferred compensation plan Type of plan used by employer to provide incentives or supplementary retirement benefits for executives. Such plans are not subject to the nondiscrimination and vesting rules.

Nonqualified stock option Stock option that does not meet the requirements for an incentive stock option.

Nonrefundable credit Allowances, such as the dependent child care credit, that have been created for various social, economic, and political reasons. The tax credits in this category do not result from payments made to the government in advance. Thus, they can be deducted from the tax, but they are not payable to the taxpayer in situations where the credit exceeds the tax.

NPV See Net Present Value

Office audit procedure IRS audit of a specific item on an individual's tax return. An office audit takes place at the IRS branch office.

Open-fact situation A situation that has not yet occurred. That is, one for which the facts and events are still controllable and can be planned for.

Ordinary expense An expense that is deductible because it is reasonable in amount and bears a reasonable and proximate relationship to the income-producing activity or property.

Ordinary income property For purposes of the charitable contribution deduction, any property that would result in the recognition of ordinary income if the property were sold. Such property includes inventory, works of art or manuscripts created by the taxpayer, capital assets that have been held for one year or less, and Section 1231 property that results in ordinary income due to depreciation recapture.

Organizational expenditures The amortizable legal, accounting, filing, and other fees incidental to organizing a partnership or a corporation.

Parent-subsidiary controlled group To qualify, a common parent must own at least 80% of the stock of at least one subsidiary corporation and at least 80% of each other component member of the controlled group must be owned by other members of the controlled group.

Partnership Syndicate, group pool, joint venture, or other unincorporateed organization which carries on a business or financial operation or venture.

Partnership interest The capital and/or profits interest in a partnership received in exchange for a contribution of properties or services (e.g., money or business equipment). The nature of a partnership interest is similar to that of corporate stock.

Passive activity To define what constitutes a passive activity for the purpose of applying the passive loss rules, it is necessary to (1) identify what constitutes an activity and (2) determine whether the taxpayer has materially participated in the activity. Temp. Reg. Sec. 1.469-4T contains detailed rules for making these determinations.

Passive income Income from an activity that does not require the taxpayer's material involvement or participation. Thus, income from tax shelters and rental activities fall into the category.

Passive loss Loss generated from a passive activity. Such losses are computed separately. They may be used to offset income from other passive activities, but may not be used to offset either active or portfolio income.

Percentage depletion method Depletion method for assets such as oil and gas that is equal to a specified percentage times the gross income from the property but which may not exceed 100% of the taxable income before depletion is deducted. Lease bonuses, advance royalties, and other amounts payable without regard to production may not be included in the calculation. This method is only available to small oil and gas producers and royalty owners and for certain mineral properties.

Percentage of completion method of accounting Accounting method generally used for long-term contracts under which income is reported in proportion to the amount of work that has been completed in a given year.

Personal exemption A deduction in an amount mandated by Congress. The amount for 2009 and 2010 is $3,650 ($3,500 for 2008) and is adjusted for increases in the cost of living. An additional exemption is allowed for each individual who is a dependent. Personal and dependency exemptions are phased out for high income taxpayers.

Personal holding company (PHC) A closely held corporation (1) that is owned by a five or fewer shareholders who own more than 50% of the corporation's outstanding stock at any time during the last half of its taxable year and (2) whose PHC income equals at least 60% of the corporation's adjusted gross income for the tax year. Certain corporations (e.g., S corporations) are exempt from this definition.

Personal holding company tax This tax is equal to 15% of the undistributed personal holding company income. It is intended to prevent closely held companies from converting an operating company into a nonoperating investment company.

Personal interest All interest other than active business interest, investment interest, interest incurred in a passive activity, qualified residence interest, and interest incurred when paying the estate tax on an installment basis. Personal interest is currently treated as a nondeductible personal expenditure. See also Interest.

Personal property Property that is other than real property, such as equipment.

Personal service corporation (PSC) A regular C corporation whose principal activity is the performance of personal services that are substantially performed by owner-employees who own more than 10% of the value of the corporation's stock.

PHC See Personal holding company.

Portfolio income Dividends, interest, annuities, and royalties not derived in the ordinary course of business. Gains and losses on property that produces portfolio income are included in such income.

Primary cite The highest level official reporter which reports a particular case is called the primary cite.

Principal partner A partner owning 5% or more of the partnership profits and capital interests.

Principal residence The residence that the taxpayer occupies most of the time.

Private activity bond Obligation issued by a state of local government to finance nongovernmental activities (e.g., a sports arena).

Private Letter Ruling See Letter Ruling

Production activities deduction A special deduction for all taxpayers involved in U.S. manufacturing or production activities. The deduction is 3% in 2005 and 2006, 6% in 2007-2009 and 9% in 2010 and thereafter of the lesser of qualified production activities income or taxable income (before the deduction).

Production of income An activity of the taxpayer that is generally related to investment activities or matters connected with the determination of any tax. Deductions related to production of income activities are usually *from AGI*, although is some instances they may be *for AGI*, such as expenses connected with rental property.

Profit-sharing plan A qualified defined benefit plan which may be established in lieu of or in addition to a qualified pension plan. Contributions to a profit-sharing plan are usually based upon profits. Incidental benefits may or may not be included. In addition, the plan must meet certain requirements concerning determination of the amount and timing of the employer's contribution, how the employee wants to receive the employer's contribution, vesting, and forfeitures.

Progressive rate Tax that increases as the taxpayer's taxable income increases. The U.S. income tax is an example of a progressive tax.

Property settlement The division of property between spouses upon their separation or divorce.

Property tax Federal, state, or local tax levied on real and/or personal property (e.g., securities, a personal automobile).

Proportional tax A method of taxation under which the tax rate is the same for all taxpayers

regardless of their income. State and local sales taxes are examples of this form of tax.

Proposed Regulations Issued following changes in the tax law. May or may not be amended after hearings are conducted and comments received. Proposed regulations are not binding on taxpayers.

PSC See Personal service corporation.

Qualified pension plan Pension plan that includes (1) systematic and definite payments made to a pension trust based upon actuarial methods and (2) usually provides for incidental benefits such as disability, or medical insurance benefits.

Qualified plan award Employee achievement awards given under a written plan or program that does not discriminate in favor of highly compensated employees. Such awards must be in the form of tangible personal property other than cash and be worth no more than $1,600.

Qualified residence interest Interest on an indebtedness which is secured by the taxpayer's qualified residence when it is paid or accrued. A taxpayer may have two qualified residences: a principal residence and a residence that he has personally used more than the greater of 14 days or 10% of the rental days during the year.

Qualifying children A child of the taxpayer who meets the four tests of relationship, age abode, and support. A child who meets these tests may be claimed as a dependency exemption by the taxpayer.

Qualifying relative An individual who may be claimed as a dependent if he or she meets the relationship, gross income, and support tests.

Readily ascertainable fair market value The fair market value of nonqualified stock options can be readily ascertained where the option is traded on an established options exchange.

Real property Property that is land or any structure permanently attached to the land, such as buildings.

Realized gain or loss The gain or loss computed by taking the amount realized from a sale of property and subtracting the property's adjusted basis.

Recapture provision A provision requiring recapture of earlier alimony payments as ordinary income by the payor if the payments decline sharply in either the second or third year.

Recovery of basis doctrine Rule that allows taxpayers to recover the basis of an asset without being taxed. Such amounts are considered a return of capital.

Refundable credit See Tax credit.

Regressive tax A form of taxation under which the tax rate decreases as the tax base (e.g., income) increases.

Regular corporation See C corporation.

Regular decision Tax Court decision that is issued on a particular issue for the first time.

Regulation See Treasury Regulation

Replacement property Property that is acquired to replace converted property in order to retain nonrecognition of gain status. Such property must generally be functionally the same as the converted property. For example, a business machine must be replaced with a similar business machine. There are exceptions to this rule: The taxpayer-use test applies to the involuntary conversion of rental property owned by an investor; condemnations of real property held for business or investment use may be replaced by like-kind property.

Residential rental property Property from which at least 80% of the gross rental income is rental from dwelling units. Residential units include manufactured homes that are used for rental purposes, but not hotels, motels, or other establishments for transient use.

Restricted property plan Such plans are used to attract and retain key executives by giving them an ownership interest in the corporation. The income recognition rules contained in Sec. 83 govern this type of plan.

Revenue Amounts received by the taxpayer from any source. It includes both taxable and nontaxable amounts and items that are a return of capital. Although closely related to income or gross income, differences between these items do exist.

Revenue Procedure Issued by the national office of the IRS, Revenue Procedures reflect the IRS' position on compliance relating to tax preparation issues. Revenue Procedures, which are published in the Cumulative Bulletin, have less weight than Treasury Regulations.

Revenue Ruling Issued by the national office of the IRS, Revenue Rulings reflect the IRS's interpretation of a narrow tax issue. Revenue Rulings, which are published in the Cumulative Bulletin, have less weight than the Treasury Regulations.

Roth IRA An IRA in which the contributions are nondeductible, but distributions generally are not subject to tax. Therefore, all earnings in a Roth IRA are not subject to taxation.

Royalties Ordinary income arising from amounts paid for the right to use property that belongs to another and is transferred for valuable consideration (e.g., a patent right where substantially all rights are transferred).

Sale A transaction where one receives cash and/or the equivalent of cash, including the assumption of debt, in exchange for an asset.

Sales tax State or local tax on purchases. Generally, food items and medicines are exempt from such tax.

S corporation Small business corporations may elect S corporation status if they meet the 100-shareholder limitation, the type of shareholder restrictions, and the one class of stock restriction. Taxation of such corporations parallels the tax rules that apply to partnerships.

Secondary cite Citation to secondary source (i.e., unofficial reporter).

Section 401(k) plan Type of plan that is often used to supplement a company's regular qualified pension and profit-sharing plan. Such plans, which generally contain a salary reduction feature, permit the employer to receive either cash or an equivalent contribution to the company's profit-sharing plan. The amount of the contribution is limited.

Section 1231 property Real or depreciable property that is (1) held for more than one year and (2) used in a trade or business. Certain property, such as inventory, U.S. government publications, copyrights, literary, musical, or artistic compositions, and letters, are excluded from this definition.

Section 1245 property Certain property subject to depreciation and, in some cases, amortization. Depreciable personal property such as equipment is Section 1245 property. However, most real property is not.

Section 1250 property Any real property that (1) is not Section 1245 property and (2) is subject to a depreciation allowance.

Security A long-term debt obligation. Long-term is generally defined as 10 years or more.

Self employment tax A tax imposed on self-employed individuals. The SE tax is comprised of the FICA tax (Social Security) of 12.4% on first $106,800 of SE income in 2010 plus the Medicare tax of 2.9% on all SE income.

Separate property All property that is owned before marriage and any gifts or inheritances acquired after marriage are separate property. This distinction depends on the state of residence. However, it is possible even in community property states.

Severance damages Compensation for a decline in the value of the property remaining after part of the taxpayer's property is condemned. The IRS considers such damages analogous to the proceeds from property insurance.

Shifting income The process of transferring income from one family member to another. Methods for shifting income include gifts of stock or bonds to family members who are in lower tax brackets.

Short sale An investment activity where an investor sells a security at its current price and purchases the same security at a future date. A short sale is generally used when the price of a security is expected to decline.

Short-term capital gain (STCG) Gain realized on the sale or exchange of a capital asset held for one year or less.

Short-term capital loss (STCL) Loss realized on the sale or exchange of a capital asset held for one year or less.

Simplified LIFO method This method of inventory valuation allows taxpayers to use a single LIFO pool rather than multiple pools. See also LIFO method.

Small cases procedure When taxes of $50,000 or less are in question for a particular year, the taxpayer may opt to have the case heard by a special commissioner rather than the regular Tax Court. The decision of the commissioner cannot be appealed.

Social security benefits These benefits include (1) the basic monthly retirement and disability benefits paid under social security and (2) tier-one railroad retirement benefits.

Sole proprietorship Form of business entity owned by an individual who reports all items of income, expense, on his individual return on Schedule C.

Specific write-off method of accounting Method of accounting used for bad debts. Under this method, the taxpayer deducts each bad debt individually as it becomes worthless. This is the only allowable accounting method for bad debts arising after 1986.

Splitting income The process of creating additional taxable entities, especially corporations, in order to reduce an individual's effective tax rate.

Standard deduction A floor amount set by Congress to simplify the tax computation. It is used by taxpayers who do not have enough deductions to itemize. The amount of the deduction varies according to the taxpayer's filing status, age, and vision. Taxpayers who use this standard deduction are not required to keep records. See Chapter I:2.

State corporate income tax See Franchise tax.

Statements on Standards for Tax Services (SSTS) Ethical guidelines of the AICPA-Federal Tax Division for CPAs to promote high standards of tax practice.

Statute of Limitations A period of time as provided by law in which a taxpayer's return may not be changed either by the IRS or the taxpayer. The Statute of Limitations is generally three years from the later of the date the tax return is filed or its due date. There is no Statute of Limitations for a fraudulent return.

Stock bonus plan A special type of defined benefit plan under which the employer's stock is contributed to a trust. The stock is then allocated and distributed to the participants. See also Employee stock ownership plan.

Stock dividend A dividend paid in the form of stock in the corporation issuing the dividend.

Stock option plan This category includes incentive stock options and nonqualified Stock option arrangements. Such plans are used to attract and retain key employees.

Substance-over-form doctrine Judicial weighing of a transaction's economic substance more heavily than its legal form.

Surviving spouse A special filing status available to widows and widowers who file a joint return for the year his or her spouse dies and for the following two years. The surviving spouse may not have remarried, must be a U.S. citizen or resident, have qualified to file a joint return for the year, and

must have at least one dependent child living at home during the year.

Syndication fees The nonamortizable fees (e.g., brokerage and registration fees) incurred to promote and market partnership interests. Such fees are generally associated with tax-sheltered limited partnership interests.

Tangible property Property that has physical substance, such as land, buildings, natural resources, equipment, etc.

Tax A mandatory assessment levied under the authority of a political entity for the purpose of raising revenue to be used for public or governmental purposes. Such taxes may be levied by the federal, state, or local government.

Taxable income For individuals, taxable income is adjusted gross income reduced by deductions from adjusted gross income.

Tax base The amount to which the tax rate is applied to determine the tax due. For income tax purposes, the tax base is taxable income.

Tax benefit rule Recovery of an amount in a subsequent year that produced a tax benefit in a prior year and is thus taxable to the recipient.

Tax credit Amount that can be deducted from the gross tax to arrive at the net tax due or refund due. Prepaid amounts, that is, amounts paid to the government during the year, are tax credits. Such prepaid amounts are often referred to as "refundable credits."

Tax Deferred Bonds Bonds on which the interest is not subject to current taxation but is deferred to a future period of time, such as Series EE U.S. Savings Bonds.

Tax Exempt Bonds Bonds on which the interest is completely exempt from federal income taxation, such as state and municipal bonds.

Tax law The tax law is comprised of the Internal Revenue Code, administrative and judicial interpretations, and the committee reports issued by the Congressional committees involved in the legislative process.

Taxpayer Compliance Measurement Program (TCMP) A stratified random sample used to select tax returns for audit. The program is intended to test the extent to which taxpayers are in compliance with the law.

Taxpayer-use test A test used to determine whether property is considered similar or related in service or use for purposes of involuntary conversions of property. This test is used by owner-investors (as opposed to owner-users) of property.

Tax research Search for the best possible solution to a problem involving either a proposed or completed transaction.

Tax shelter Passive activity which may lack economic substance other than creating tax deductions and credits that enable taxpayers to reduce or eliminate the income tax liability from their regular business activities. Section 469 restricts the current use of deductions and credits arising from passive activities.

Tax year See Accounting period.

TCMP See Taxpayer Compliance Measurement Program.

Technical Advice Memorandum Such memoranda are administrative interpretations issued in the form of letter ruling. Taxpayers may request them if they need guidance about the tax treatment of complicated technical matters which are being audited.

Temporary Regulations Temporary Regulations are Treasury Regulations that are issued to provide guidance for taxpayers pending the issuance of the final regulations. They are binding upon taxpayers. Temporary Regulations are also required to be issued as proposed regulations and must expire within three years.

Testamentary gift Transfer of property made at the death of the donor (i.e., bequests, devises, and inheritances).

Theft loss Loss of business, investment, or personal-use property due to crimes such as, but not limited to, larceny, embezzlement, robbery, extortion, blackmail, or kidnapping for ransom. Such losses are deductible from AGI, subject to certain limitations.

Total economic income The amount of the taxpayer's income, including exclusions and deductions from the tax base (e.g., tax-exempt bonds), is categorized as total economic income.

Trade or business A business activity of the taxpayer in which deductions are allowed as *for* AGI deductions.

Transportation expense The deductibility of this type of expense depends upon whether it is trade- or business-related, whether it is related to the production of income, whether the expense is employment related and therefore subject to the 2% nondeductible floor for miscellaneous itemized deductions. Commuting expenses are nondeductible. See also Travel expense.

Travel expense Such expenses include transportation, meals, and lodging incurred in the pursuit of a trade, business, or employment-related activity. There are limitations and restrictions on the deductibility of these expenses. See also Transportation expense.

Treasury bill Short-term (i.e., 90-day) obligation that is issued by the government at a discount from the maturity amount. The difference between the issue price and the maturity amount represents the interest income.

Treasury Regulation The principal administrative source of the federal tax law, these regulations reflect the Treasury's and the IRS's interpretation of the Internal Revenue Code. They may be either legislative or interpretative and they may be issued in either proposed, temporary, or final form.

Unfunded deferred compensation plan This type of plan is used for highly-compensated employees who wish to defer the recognition of income until future periods. Funding is generally accomplished through an escrow account for the employee's benefit.

Uniform Capitalization rules (UNICAP) The requirements under the tax law for determining inventory cost. Under UNICAP certain indirect overhead costs are required to be included in inventory for tax purposes which are generally not included for financial accounting.

Unrelated use property Capital gain property which is also tangible personal property and which is contributed to a public charity for a use that is unrelated to the charity's function. The contribution deduction (from AGI) for such property is equal to the property's fair market value minus the capital gain that would be recognized if the property was sold at that value.

Unreported decision District Court decisions that are not officially reported in the Federal Supplement. Such decisions may be reported in secondary reporters that report only tax-related cases.

U.S. Production Activities Deduction See Production Activities Deduction.

U.S. Treasury Bill See Treasury bill.

Vertical equity A concept in taxation that provides that the incidence of taxation should be borne by taxpayers who have the ability to pay the tax. Taxpayers who are not similarly-situated should be treated differently under the tax law.

Wash sale A wash sale results when the taxpayer (1) sells stock or securities and (2) purchases substantially identical stock or securities within the 61-day period extending from 30 days before the date of sale to 30 days after the date of sale.

Wealth transfer tax A tax imposed upon the value of property transferred during one's lifetime (i.e., a gift tax) or upon the death of the transferor (i.e., an estate tax). The tax is imposed upon the transferor of property or upon the estate.

Writ of certiorari A petition to the U.S. Supreme court to request that the Court agree to hear a case. A writ of certiorari is requested by the party (IRS or taxpayer) that lost at the Court of Appeals level.

Zero coupon bond Bond that is issued at a cost that is substantially less than the current market rate because no interest payments are made. The original issue discount (OID) must be amortized over the term of the bond by investors using the constant rate method. Such bonds offer cash-flow advantages to corporate issuers since no cash outlay for interest is required until the bonds mature.

APPENDIX E

Note: The AICPA released revised Statements on Standards for Tax Services (SSTS) effective on January 1, 2010. These statements are enforceable standards of tax practice for AICPA members. Changes to Statements No. 1 and 7 (formerly No. 8) were substantive in nature. As a result, Interpretations No. 1-1 and 1-2 relating to former Statement No. 1 are currently under revision. The new statements as well as the old statements can be found on the AICPA website at www.aicpa.org.

• AICPA STATEMENTS ON STANDARDS FOR TAX SERVICES NOS. 1–7 (NOVEMBER 2009)

PREFACE

1. Standards are the foundation of a profession. The AICPA aids its members in fulfilling their ethical responsibilities by instituting and maintaining standards against which their professional performance can be measured. Compliance with professional standards of tax practice also reaffirms the public's awareness of the professionalism that is associated with CPAs as well as the AICPA.

2. This publication sets forth enforceable tax practice standards for members of the AICPA, Statements on Standards for Tax Services (SSTSs or statements). These statements apply to all members providing tax services regardless of the jurisdictions in which they practice. Interpretations of these statements may be issued as guidance to assist in understanding and applying the statements. The SSTSs and their interpretations are intended to complement other standards of tax practice, such as Treasury Department Circular No. 230, *Regulations Governing the Practice of Attorneys, Certified Public Accountants, Enrolled Agents, Enrolled Actuaries, Enrolled Retirement Plan Agents, and Appraisers before the Internal Revenue Service*; penalty provisions of the Internal Revenue Code; and state boards of accountancy rules.

3. The SSTSs are written in as simple and objective a manner as possible. However, by their nature, practice standards provide for an appropriate range of behavior and need to be interpreted to address a broad range of personal and professional situations. The SSTSs recognize this need by, in some sections, providing relatively subjective rules and by leaving certain terms undefined. These terms are generally rooted in tax concepts and, therefore, should be readily understood by tax practitioners. Accordingly, enforcement of these rules, as part of the AICPA's Code of Professional Conduct Rule 201, *General Standards*, and Rule 202, *Compliance With Standards* (AICPA, *Professional Standards*, vol. 2, ET sec. 201 par. .01 and ET sec. 202 par. .01),

will be undertaken on a case-by-case basis. Members are expected to comply with them.

HISTORY

4. The SSTSs have their origin in the Statements on Responsibilities in Tax Practice (SRTPs), which provided a body of advisory opinions on good tax practice. The guidelines as originally set forth in the SRTPs became more important than many members had anticipated when the guidelines were issued. The courts, the IRS, state accountancy boards, and other professional organizations recognized and relied on the SRTPs as the appropriate articulation of professional conduct in a CPA's tax practice. The SRTPs became *de facto* enforceable standards of professional practice, because state disciplinary organizations and courts regularly held CPAs accountable for failure to follow the guidelines set forth in the SRTPs.

5. The AICPA's Tax Executive Committee concluded it was appropriate to issue tax practice standards that would become a part of the AICPA's *Professional Standards*. At its July 1999 meeting, the AICPA Board of Directors approved support of the executive committee's initiative and placed the matter on the agenda of the October 1999 meeting of the AICPA's governing Council. On October 19, 1999, Council approved designating the Tax Executive Committee as a standardsetting body, thus authorizing that committee to promulgate standards of tax practice. As a result, the original SSTSs, largely mirroring the SRTPs, were issued in August 2000.

6. The SRTPs were originally issued between 1964 and 1977. The first nine SRTPs and the introduction were promulgated in 1976; the tenth SRTP was issued in 1977. The original SRTPs concerning the CPA's responsibility to sign the tax return (SRTP No. 1, *Signature of Preparers*, and No. 2, *Signature of Reviewer: Assumption of Preparer's Responsibility*) were withdrawn in 1982 after Treasury Department regulations were issued adopting

substantially the same standards for all tax return preparers. The sixth and seventh SRTPs, concerning the responsibility of a CPA who becomes aware of an error, were revised in 1991. The first interpretation of the SRTPs, Interpretation No. 1-1, "Realistic Possibility Standard," was approved in December 1990. The SSTSs and Interpretation No. 1-1, "Realistic Possibility Standard," of SSTS No. 1, *Tax Return Positions*, superseded and replaced the SRTPs and their Interpretation No. 1-1, effective October 31, 2000. Although the number and names of the SSTSs, and the substance of the rules contained in each of them, remained the same as in the SRTPs, the language was revised to both clarify and reflect the enforceable nature of the SSTSs. In addition, because the applicability of these standards is not limited to federal income tax practice (as was the case with the SRTPs), the language was changed to indicate the broader scope. In 2003, in connection with the tax shelter debate, SSTS Interpretation No. 1-2, "Tax Planning," of SSTS No. 1 was issued to clarify a member's responsibilities in connection with tax planning; that interpretation became effective December 31, 2003.

7. When the original SSTSs were issued, an effort was made to keep to a minimum any changes in the language of the SSTSs from that of the predecessor SRTPs. This was done to alleviate concerns regarding the enforceability of standards that differed from the SRTPs under which members had been practicing. Since the issuance of the original SSTSs, members have asked for clarification on certain matters, such as the duplication of the language in SSTS No. 6, *Knowledge of Error: Return Preparation*, and No. 7, *Knowledge of Error: Administrative Proceedings*. Also, certain changes in federal and state tax laws have raised concerns regarding the need to revise SSTS No. 1. As a result, in 2008, the original SSTS Nos. 1–8 were updated, effective January 1, 2010. The original SSTS Nos. 6–7 were combined into the revised SSTS No. 6, *Knowledge of Error: Return Preparation and Administrative Proceedings*. The original SSTS No. 8, *Form and Content of Advice to Taxpayers*, was renumbered SSTS No. 7. In addition, various revisions were made to the language of the original SSTSs.

ONGOING PROCESS

8. The following SSTSs and any interpretations issued thereunder reflect the AICPA's standards of tax practice and delineate members' responsibilities to taxpayers, the public, the government, and the profession. The statements are intended to be part of an ongoing process of articulating standards of tax practice for members. These standards are subject to change as necessary or appropriate to address changes in the tax law or other developments in the tax practice environment.

9. Members are encouraged to assess the adequacy of their practices and procedures for providing tax services in conformity with these standards. This process will vary according to the size of the practice and the nature of tax services performed.

10. The Tax Executive Committee promulgates the SSTSs and their interpretations. Acknowledgment is also due to the

many members who have devoted their time and efforts over the years to developing and revising the AICPA's standards.

STATEMENT ON STANDARDS FOR TAX SERVICES NO. 1, *TAX RETURN POSITIONS*

INTRODUCTION

1. This statement sets forth the applicable standards for members when recommending tax return positions, or preparing or signing tax returns (including amended returns, claims for refund, and information returns) filed with any taxing authority. For purposes of these standards

 a. a *tax return position* is (i) a position reflected on a tax return on which a member has specifically advised a taxpayer or (ii) a position about which a member has knowledge of all material facts and, on the basis of those facts, has concluded whether the position is appropriate.

 b. a *taxpayer* is a client, a member's employer, or any other third-party recipient of tax services.

2. This statement also addresses a member's obligation to advise a taxpayer of relevant tax return disclosure responsibilities and potential penalties.

3. In addition to the AICPA, various taxing authorities, at the federal, state, and local levels, may impose specific reporting and disclosure standards with regard to recommending tax return positions or preparing or signing tax returns.[1] These standards can vary between taxing authorities and by type of tax.

STATEMENT

4. A member should determine and comply with the standards, if any, that are imposed by the applicable taxing authority with respect to recommending a tax return position, or preparing or signing a tax return.

5. If the applicable taxing authority has no written standards with respect to recommending a tax return position or preparing or signing a tax return, or if its standards are lower than the standards set forth in this paragraph, the following standards will apply:

 a. A member should not recommend a tax return position or prepare or sign a tax return taking a position unless the member has a good-faith belief that the position has at least a realistic possibility of being sustained administratively or judicially on its merits if challenged.

 b. Notwithstanding paragraph 5(a), a member may *recommend a tax return position* if the member (i) concludes that there is a reasonable basis for the position and

---

[1] A member should refer to the current version of Internal Revenue Code Section 6694, Understatement of taxpayer's liability by tax return preparer, and other relevant federal, state, and jurisdictional authorities to determine

the reporting and disclosure standards that are applicable to preparers of tax returns.

(ii) advises the taxpayer to appropriately disclose that position. Notwithstanding paragraph 5(a), a member may *prepare or sign a tax return* that reflects a position if (i) the member concludes there is a reasonable basis for the position and (ii) the position is appropriately disclosed.

6. When recommending a tax return position or when preparing or signing a tax return on which a position is taken, a member should, when relevant, advise the taxpayer regarding potential penalty consequences of such tax return position and the opportunity, if any, to avoid such penalties through disclosure.

7. A member should not recommend a tax return position or prepare or sign a tax return reflecting a position that the member knows

   a. exploits the audit selection process of a taxing authority, or
   b. serves as a mere arguing position advanced solely to obtain leverage in a negotiation with a taxing authority.

8. When recommending a tax return position, a member has both the right and the responsibility to be an advocate for the taxpayer with respect to any position satisfying the aforementioned standards.

EXPLANATION

9. The AICPA and various taxing authorities impose specific reporting and disclosure standards with respect to tax return positions and preparing or signing tax returns. In a given situation, the standards, if any, imposed by the applicable taxing authority may be higher or lower than the standards set forth in paragraph 5. A member is to comply with the standards, if any, of the applicable taxing authority; if the applicable taxing authority has no standards or if its standards are lower than the standards set forth in paragraph 5, the standards set forth in paragraph 5 will apply.

10. Our self-assessment tax system can function effectively only if taxpayers file tax returns that are true, correct, and complete. A tax return is prepared based on a taxpayer's representation of facts, and the taxpayer has the final responsibility for positions taken on the return. The standards that apply to a taxpayer may differ from those that apply to a member.

11. In addition to a duty to the taxpayer, a member has a duty to the tax system. However, it is well established that the taxpayer has no obligation to pay more taxes than are legally owed, and a member has a duty to the taxpayer to assist in achieving that result. The standards contained in paragraphs 4–8 recognize a member's responsibilities to both the taxpayer and the tax system.

12. In reaching a conclusion concerning whether a given standard in paragraph 4 or 5 has been satisfied, a member may consider a well-reasoned construction of the applicable statute, well-reasoned articles or treatises, or pronouncements issued by the applicable taxing authority, regardless of whether such sources would be treated as *authority* under Internal Revenue Code Section 6662, *Imposition of accuracy-related penalty on underpayments*, and the regulations thereunder. A position would not fail to meet these standards merely because it is later abandoned for practical or procedural considerations during an administrative hearing or in the litigation process.

13. If a member has a good-faith belief that more than one tax return position meets the standards set forth in paragraphs 4–5, a member's advice concerning alternative acceptable positions may include a discussion of the likelihood that each such position might or might not cause the taxpayer's tax return to be examined and whether the position would be challenged in an examination. In such circumstances, such advice is not a violation of paragraph 7.

14. A member's determination of whether information is appropriately disclosed by the taxpayer should be based on the facts and circumstances of the particular case and the disclosure requirements of the applicable taxing authority. If a member recommending a position, but not engaged to prepare or sign the related tax return, advises the taxpayer concerning appropriate disclosure of the position, then the member shall be deemed to meet the disclosure requirements of these standards.

15. If particular facts and circumstances lead a member to believe that a taxpayer penalty might be asserted, the member should so advise the taxpayer and should discuss with the taxpayer the opportunity, if any, to avoid such penalty by disclosing the position on the tax return. Although a member should advise the taxpayer with respect to disclosure, it is the taxpayer's responsibility to decide whether and how to disclose.

16. For purposes of this statement, preparation of a tax return includes giving advice on events that have occurred at the time the advice is given if the advice is directly relevant to determining the existence, character, or amount of a schedule, entry, or other portion of a tax return.

STATEMENT ON STANDARDS FOR TAX SERVICES NO. 2, ANSWERS TO QUESTIONS ON RETURNS

INTRODUCTION

1. This statement sets forth the applicable standards for members when signing the preparer's declaration on a tax return if one or more questions on the return have not been answered. The term *questions* includes requests for information on the return, in the instructions, or in the regulations, whether or not stated in the form of a question.

STATEMENT

2. A member should make a reasonable effort to obtain from the taxpayer the information necessary to provide appropriate answers to all questions on a tax return before signing as preparer.

EXPLANATION

3. It is recognized that the questions on tax returns are not of uniform importance, and often they are not applicable to the particular taxpayer. Nevertheless, there are at least three reasons why

a member should be satisfied that a reasonable effort has been made to obtain information to provide appropriate answers to the questions on the return that are applicable to a taxpayer:

a. A question may be of importance in determining taxable income or loss, or the tax liability shown on the return, in which circumstance an omission may detract from the quality of the return.

b. A request for information may require a disclosure necessary for a complete return or to avoid penalties.

c. A member often must sign a preparer's declaration stating that the return is true, correct, and complete.

4. Reasonable grounds may exist for omitting an answer to a question applicable to a taxpayer. For example, reasonable grounds may include the following:

a. The information is not readily available and the answer is not significant in terms of taxable income or loss, or the tax liability shown on the return.

b. Genuine uncertainty exists regarding the meaning of the question in relation to the particular return.

c. The answer to the question is voluminous; in such cases, a statement should be made on the return that the data will be supplied upon examination.

5. A member should not omit an answer merely because it might prove disadvantageous to a taxpayer.

6. A member should consider whether the omission of an answer to a question may cause the return to be deemed incomplete or result in penalties.

7. If reasonable grounds exist for omission of an answer to an applicable question, a taxpayer is not required to provide on the return an explanation of the reason for the omission.

STATEMENT ON STANDARDS FOR TAX SERVICES NO. 3, *CERTAIN PROCEDURAL ASPECTS OF PREPARING RETURNS*

INTRODUCTION

1. This statement sets forth the applicable standards for members concerning the obligation to examine or verify certain supporting data or to consider information related to another taxpayer when preparing a taxpayer's tax return.

STATEMENT

2. In preparing or signing a return, a member may in good faith rely, without verification, on information furnished by the taxpayer or by third parties. However, a member should not ignore the implications of information furnished and should make reasonable inquiries if the information furnished appears to be incorrect, incomplete, or inconsistent either on its face or on the basis of other facts known to the member. Further, a member should refer to the taxpayer's returns for one or more prior years whenever feasible.

3. If the tax law or regulations impose a condition with respect to deductibility or other tax treatment of an item, such as taxpayer maintenance of books and records or substantiating documentation to support the reported deduction or tax treatment, a member should make appropriate inquiries to determine to the member's satisfaction whether such condition has been met.

4. When preparing a tax return, a member should consider information actually known to that member from the tax return of another taxpayer if the information is relevant to that tax return and its consideration is necessary to properly prepare that tax return. In using such information, a member should consider any limitations imposed by any law or rule relating to confidentiality.

EXPLANATION

5. The preparer's declaration on a tax return often states that the information contained therein is true, correct, and complete to the best of the preparer's knowledge and belief based on all information known by the preparer. This type of reference should be understood to include information furnished by the taxpayer or by third parties to a member in connection with the preparation of the return.

6. The preparer's declaration does not require a member to examine or verify supporting data; a member may rely on information furnished by the taxpayer unless it appears to be incorrect, incomplete, or inconsistent. However, there is a need to determine by inquiry that a specifically required condition, such as maintaining books and records or substantiating documentation, has been satisfied and to obtain information when the material furnished appears to be incorrect, incomplete, or inconsistent. Although a member has certain responsibilities in exercising due diligence in preparing a return, the taxpayer has the ultimate responsibility for the contents of the return. Thus, if the taxpayer presents unsupported data in the form of lists of tax information, such as dividends and interest received, charitable contributions, and medical expenses, such information may be used in the preparation of a tax return without verification unless it appears to be incorrect, incomplete, or inconsistent either on its face or on the basis of other facts known to a member.

7. Even though there is no requirement to examine underlying documentation, a member should encourage the taxpayer to provide supporting data where appropriate. For example, a member should encourage the taxpayer to submit underlying documents for use in tax return preparation to permit full consideration of income and deductions arising from security transactions and from pass-through entities, such as estates, trusts, partnerships, and S corporations.

8. The source of information provided to a member by a taxpayer for use in preparing the return is often a pass-through entity, such as a limited partnership, in which the taxpayer has an interest but is not involved in management. A member may accept the information provided by the pass-through entity without further inquiry, unless there is reason to believe it is incorrect,

incomplete, or inconsistent, either on its face or on the basis of other facts known to the member. In some instances, it may be appropriate for a member to advise the taxpayer to ascertain the nature and amount of possible exposure to tax deficiencies, interest, and penalties by taxpayer contact with management of the pass-through entity.

9. A member should make use of a taxpayer's returns for one or more prior years in preparing the current return whenever feasible. Reference to prior returns and discussion of prior-year tax determinations with the taxpayer should provide information to determine the taxpayer's general tax status, avoid the omission or duplication of items, and afford a basis for the treatment of similar or related transactions. As with the examination of information supplied for the current year's return, the extent of comparison of the details of income and deduction between years depends on the particular circumstances.

STATEMENT ON STANDARDS FOR TAX SERVICES NO. 4, *USE OF ESTIMATES*

INTRODUCTION

1. This statement sets forth the applicable standards for members when using the taxpayer's estimates in the preparation of a tax return. A member may advise on estimates used in the preparation of a tax return, but the taxpayer has the responsibility to provide the estimated data. Appraisals or valuations are not considered estimates for purposes of this statement.

STATEMENT

2. Unless prohibited by statute or by rule, a member may use the taxpayer's estimates in the preparation of a tax return if it is not practical to obtain exact data and if the member determines that the estimates are reasonable based on the facts and circumstances known to the member. The taxpayer's estimates should be presented in a manner that does not imply greater accuracy than exists.

EXPLANATION

3. Accounting requires the exercise of professional judgment and, in many instances, the use of approximations based on judgment. The application of such accounting judgments, as long as not in conflict with methods set forth by a taxing authority, is acceptable. These judgments are not estimates within the purview of this statement. For example, a federal income tax regulation provides that if all other conditions for accrual are met, the exact amount of income or expense need not be known or ascertained at year end if the amount can be determined with reasonable accuracy.

4. When the taxpayer's records do not accurately reflect information related to small expenditures, accuracy in recording some

data may be difficult to achieve. Therefore, the use of estimates by a taxpayer in determining the amount to be deducted for such items may be appropriate.

5. When records are missing or precise information about a transaction is not available at the time the return must be filed, a member may prepare a tax return using a taxpayer's estimates of the missing data.

6. Estimated amounts should not be presented in a manner that provides a misleading impression about the degree of factual accuracy.

7. Specific disclosure that an estimate is used for an item in the return is not generally required; however, such disclosure should be made in unusual circumstances where nondisclosure might mislead the taxing authority regarding the degree of accuracy of the return as a whole. Some examples of unusual circumstances include the following:

    a. A taxpayer has died or is ill at the time the return must be filed.

    b. A taxpayer has not received a Schedule K-1 for a pass-through entity at the time the tax return is to be filed.

    c. There is litigation pending (for example, a bankruptcy proceeding) that bears on the return.

    d. Fire, computer failure, or natural disaster has destroyed the relevant records.

STATEMENT ON STANDARDS FOR TAX SERVICES NO. 5, *DEPARTURE FROM A POSITION PREVIOUSLY CONCLUDED IN AN ADMINISTRATIVE PROCEEDING OR COURT DECISION*

INTRODUCTION

1. This statement sets forth the applicable standards for members in recommending a tax return position that departs from the position determined in an administrative proceeding or in a court decision with respect to the taxpayer's prior return.

2. For purposes of this statement, *administrative proceeding* includes an examination by a taxing authority or an appeals conference relating to a return or a claim for refund.

3. For purposes of this statement, *court decision* means a decision by any court having jurisdiction over tax matters.

STATEMENT

4. The tax return position with respect to an item as determined in an administrative proceeding or court decision does not restrict a member from recommending a different tax position in a later year's return, unless the taxpayer is bound to a specified treatment

in the later year, such as by a formal closing agreement. Therefore, the member may recommend a tax return position or prepare or sign a tax return that departs from the treatment of an item as concluded in an administrative proceeding or court decision with respect to a prior return of the taxpayer provided the requirements of Statement on Standards for Tax Services (SSTS) No. 1, *Tax Return Positions*, are satisfied.

EXPLANATION

5. If an administrative proceeding or court decision has resulted in a determination concerning a specific tax treatment of an item in a prior year's return, a member will usually recommend this same tax treatment in subsequent years. However, departures from consistent treatment may be justified under such circumstances as the following:

a. Taxing authorities tend to act consistently in the disposition of an item that was the subject of a prior administrative proceeding but generally are not bound to do so. Similarly, a taxpayer is not bound to follow the tax treatment of an item as consented to in an earlier administrative proceeding.

b. The determination in the administrative proceeding or the court's decision may have been caused by a lack of documentation. Supporting data for the later year may be appropriate.

c. A taxpayer may have yielded in the administrative proceeding for settlement purposes or not appealed the court decision, even though the position met the standards in SSTS No. 1.

d. Court decisions, rulings, or other authorities that are more favorable to a taxpayer's current position may have developed since the prior administrative proceeding was concluded or the prior court decision was rendered.

6. The consent in an earlier administrative proceeding and the existence of an unfavorable court decision are factors that the member should consider in evaluating whether the standards in SSTS No. 1 are met.

STATEMENT ON STANDARDS FOR TAX SERVICES NO. 6, *KNOWLEDGE OF ERROR: RETURN PREPARATION AND ADMINISTRATIVE PROCEEDINGS*

INTRODUCTION

1. This statement sets forth the applicable standards for a member who becomes aware of (a) an error in a taxpayer's previously filed tax return; (b) an error in a return that is the subject of an administrative proceeding, such as an examination by a taxing authority or an appeals conference; or (c) a taxpayer's failure to file a required tax return. As used herein, the term *error* includes any position, omission, or method of accounting that, at the time the return is filed, fails to meet the standards set out in Statement on Standards for Tax Services (SSTS) No. 1, *Tax Return Positions*. The term *error* also includes a position taken on a prior year's return that no longer meets these standards due to legislation, judicial decisions, or administrative pronouncements having retroactive effect. However, an error does not include an item that has an insignificant effect on the taxpayer's tax liability. The term *administrative proceeding* does not include a criminal proceeding.

2. This statement applies whether or not the member prepared or signed the return that contains the error.

3. Special considerations may apply when a member has been engaged by legal counsel to provide assistance in a matter relating to the counsel's client.

STATEMENT

4. A member should inform the taxpayer promptly upon becoming aware of an error in a previously filed return, an error in a return that is the subject of an administrative proceeding, or a taxpayer's failure to file a required return. A member also should advise the taxpayer of the potential consequences of the error and recommend the corrective measures to be taken. Such advice and recommendation may be given orally. The member is not allowed to inform the taxing authority without the taxpayer's permission, except when required by law.

5. If a member is requested to prepare the current year's return and the taxpayer has not taken appropriate action to correct an error in a prior year's return, the member should consider whether to withdraw from preparing the return and whether to continue a professional or employment relationship with the taxpayer. If the member does prepare such current year's return, the member should take reasonable steps to ensure that the error is not repeated.

6. If a member is representing a taxpayer in an administrative proceeding with respect to a return that contains an error of which the member is aware, the member should request the taxpayer's agreement to disclose the error to the taxing authority. Lacking such agreement, the member should consider whether to withdraw from representing the taxpayer in the administrative proceeding and whether to continue a professional or employment relationship with the taxpayer.

EXPLANATION

7. While performing services for a taxpayer, a member may become aware of an error in a previously filed return or may become aware that the taxpayer failed to file a required return. The member should advise the taxpayer of the error and the potential consequences, and recommend the measures to be taken. Similarly, when representing the taxpayer before a taxing authority in an administrative proceeding with respect to a return containing an error of which the member is aware, the member should advise the taxpayer to disclose the error to the taxing authority and of the potential consequences of not disclosing the error. Such advice and recommendation may be given orally.

8. It is the taxpayer's responsibility to decide whether to correct the error. If the taxpayer does not correct an error, a member should consider whether to withdraw from the engagement and whether to continue a professional or employment relationship with the taxpayer. Although recognizing that the taxpayer may not be required by statute to correct an error by filing an amended return, a member should consider whether a taxpayer's decision not to file an amended return or otherwise correct an error may predict future behavior that might require termination of the relationship.

9. Once the member has obtained the taxpayer's consent to disclose an error in an administrative proceeding, the disclosure should not be delayed to such a degree that the taxpayer or member might be considered to have failed to act in good faith or to have, in effect, provided misleading information. In any event, disclosure should be made before the conclusion of the administrative proceeding.

10. A conflict between the member's interests and those of the taxpayer may be created by, for example, the potential for violating Code of Professional Conduct Rule 301, *Confidential Client Information* (AICPA, *Professional Standards*, vol. 2, ET sec. 301 par. .01) (relating to the member's confidential client relationship); the tax law and regulations; or laws on privileged communications, as well as by the potential adverse impact on a taxpayer of a member's withdrawal. Therefore, a member should consider consulting with his or her own legal counsel before deciding upon recommendations to the taxpayer and whether to continue a professional or employment relationship with the taxpayer.

11. If a member believes that a taxpayer may face possible exposure to allegations of fraud or other criminal misconduct, the member should advise the taxpayer to consult with an attorney before the taxpayer takes any action.

12. If a member decides to continue a professional or employment relationship with the taxpayer and is requested to prepare a tax return for a year subsequent to that in which the error occurred, the member should take reasonable steps to ensure that the error is not repeated. If the subsequent year's tax return cannot be prepared without perpetuating the error, the member should consider withdrawal from the return preparation. If a member learns that the taxpayer is using an erroneous method of accounting and it is past the due date to request permission to change to a method meeting the standards of SSTS No. 1, the member may sign a tax return for the current year, providing the tax return includes appropriate disclosure of the use of the erroneous method.

13. Whether an error has no more than an insignificant effect on the taxpayer's tax liability is left to the professional judgment of the member based on all the facts and circumstances known to the member. In judging whether an erroneous method of accounting has more than an insignificant effect, a member should consider the method's cumulative effect, as well as its effect on the current year's tax return or the tax return that is the subject of the administrative proceeding.

14. If a member becomes aware of the error while performing services for a taxpayer that do not involve tax return preparation or representation in an administrative proceeding, the member's responsibility is to advise the taxpayer of the existence of the error and to recommend that the error be discussed with the taxpayer's tax return preparer. Such recommendation may be given orally.

STATEMENT ON STANDARDS FOR TAX SERVICES NO. 7, *FORM AND CONTENT OF ADVICE TO TAXPAYERS*

INTRODUCTION

1. This statement sets forth the applicable standards for members concerning certain aspects of providing advice to a taxpayer and considers the circumstances in which a member has a responsibility to communicate with a taxpayer when subsequent developments affect advice previously provided. The statement does not, however, cover a member's responsibilities when the expectation is that the advice rendered is likely to be relied on by parties other than the taxpayer.

STATEMENT

2. A member should use professional judgment to ensure that tax advice provided to a taxpayer reflects competence and appropriately serves the taxpayer's needs. When communicating tax advice to a taxpayer in writing, a member should comply with relevant taxing authorities' standards, if any, applicable to written tax advice. A member should use professional judgment about any need to document oral advice. A member is not required to follow a standard format when communicating or documenting oral advice.

3. A member should assume that tax advice provided to a taxpayer will affect the manner in which the matters or transactions considered would be reported or disclosed on the taxpayer's tax returns. Therefore, for tax advice given to a taxpayer, a member should consider, when relevant (*a*) return reporting and disclosure standards applicable to the related tax return position and (*b*) the potential penalty consequences of the return position. In ascertaining applicable return reporting and disclosure standards, a member should follow the standards in Statement on Standards for Tax Services No. 1, *Tax Return Positions*.

4. A member has no obligation to communicate with a taxpayer when subsequent developments affect advice previously provided with respect to significant matters, except while assisting a taxpayer in implementing procedures or plans associated with the advice provided or when a member undertakes this obligation by specific agreement.

EXPLANATION

5. Tax advice is recognized as a valuable service provided by members. The form of advice may be oral or written and the subject matter may range from routine to complex. Because the range of advice is so extensive and because advice should meet the specific needs of a taxpayer, neither a standard format nor guidelines for communicating or documenting advice to the taxpayer can be established to cover all situations.

6. Although oral advice may serve a taxpayer's needs appropriately in routine matters or in welldefined areas, written

communications are recommended in important, unusual, substantial dollar value, or complicated transactions. The member may use professional judgment about whether, subsequently, to document oral advice.

7. In deciding on the form of advice provided to a taxpayer, a member should exercise professional judgment and should consider such factors as the following:

a. The importance of the transaction and amounts involved

b. The specific or general nature of the taxpayer's inquiry

c. The time available for development and submission of the advice

d. The technical complexity involved

e. The existence of authorities and precedents

f. The tax sophistication of the taxpayer

g. The need to seek other professional advice

h. The type of transaction and whether it is subject to heightened reporting or disclosure requirements

i. The potential penalty consequences of the tax return position for which the advice is rendered

j. Whether any potential applicable penalties can be avoided through disclosure

k. Whether the member intends for the taxpayer to rely upon the advice to avoid potential penalties

8. A member may assist a taxpayer in implementing procedures or plans associated with the advice offered. When providing such assistance, the member should review and revise such advice as warranted by new developments and factors affecting the transaction.

9. Sometimes a member is requested to provide tax advice but does not assist in implementing the plans adopted. Although such developments as legislative or administrative changes or future judicial interpretations may affect the advice previously provided, a member cannot be expected to communicate subsequent developments that affect such advice unless the member undertakes this obligation by specific agreement with the taxpayer.

10. Taxpayers should be informed that (a) the advice reflects professional judgment based upon the member's understanding of the facts, and the law existing as of the date the advice is rendered and (b) subsequent developments could affect previously rendered professional advice. Members may use precautionary language to the effect that their advice is based on facts as stated and authorities that are subject to change.

11. In providing tax advice, a member should be cognizant of applicable confidentiality privileges.

These Statements on Standards for Tax Services were unanimously adopted by the assenting votes of the 17 members of the 18-member Tax Executive Committee who participated in the August 6, 2009, Tax Executive Committee meeting.

Tax Executive Committee (2008–2009)

Alan R. Einhorn, *Chair*	Jeffrey A Porter
Jeffrey R. Hoops, *Immediate Past Chair*	Roby Sawyers
Diane Cornwell	Christopher J. Sokolowski
Eve Elgin	Norman S. Solomon
Andrew D. Gibson	Patricia Thompson
Cherie J. Hennig	Christine Turgeon
Lawrence W. McKoy	Mark Van Deveer
T. Chris Muirhead	Richard P. Weber
Gregory A. Porcaro	Brian T. Whitlock

Tax Practice Responsibilities Committee (2008–2009)

Arthur J. Kip Dellinger, Jr., *Chair*	Douglas Milford
Gregory M. Fowler, *Vice Chair*	Trenton S. Olmstead
Harvey Coustan	Gerald W. Padwe
Todd C. Craft	James W. Sansone
Diane D. Fuller	James H. Schlesser
Jan D. Hayden	Lisa G. Workman
Andrew M. Mattson	

SSTS Revisions Task Force

Conrad M. Davis, *Cochair*	Gregory M. Fowler
Jay M. Levine, *Cochair*	John C. Gardner
Timothy J. Burke, Jr.	Keith R. Lee
Arthur J. Kip Dellinger, Jr.	Mark N. Schneider
Eve Elgin	Gerard H. Schreiber, Jr.
Jeffrey Frishman	J. Edward Swails

AICPA Staff

Thomas P. Ochsenschlager *Vice President—Taxation Tax Division*	Edward S. Karl *Director Tax Division*
	Jean E. Trompeter *Technical Manager Tax Division*

Note: *Statements on Standards for Tax Services are issued by the Tax Executive Committee, the senior technical body of the AICPA designated to promulgate standards of tax practice. Rule 201, General Standards, and Rule 202, Compliance With Standards, of the Code of Professional Conduct (AICPA, Professional Standards, vol. 2, ET sec. 201 par. .01 and ET sec. 202 par. .01), require compliance with these standards.*

INDEX OF CODE SECTIONS

APPENDIX H

INDEX OF GOVERNMENT PROMULGATIONS

APPENDIX I

INDEX OF COURT CASES

NOTES

NOTES

NOTES

NOTES

NOTES

NOTES

NOTES

NOTES

NOTES

NOTES

2010
TAX RATE SCHEDULES

ESTATES AND TRUSTS [§1 (e)]:

If taxable income is:	The tax is:
Not over $2,300	15% of taxable income.
Over $2,300 but not over $5,350	$345.00, plus 25% of the excess over $2,300.
Over $5,350 but not over $8,200	$1,107.50, plus 28% of the excess over $5,350.
Over $8,200 but not over $11,200	$1,905.50, plus 33% of the excess over $8,200.
Over $11,200	$2,895.50, plus 35% of the excess over $11,200.

CORPORATIONS

If Taxable Income Is:		The Tax Is:	
Over—	But Not Over—		Of the Amount Over—
$ 0	$ 50,000	15%	$ 0
50,000	75,000	$ 7,500 + 25%	50,000
75,000	100,000	13,750 + 34%	75,000
100,000	335,000	22,250 + 39%	100,000
335,000	10,000,000	113,900 + 34%	335,000
10,000,000	15,000,000	3,400,000 + 35%	10,000,000
15,000,000	18,333,333	5,150,000 + 38%	15,000,000
18,333,333		6,416,667 + 35%	18,333,333

UNIFIED CREDIT AMOUNT FOR ESTATE AND GIFT TAX

Year of Gift/Year of Death	Amount of Credit	Exemption Equivalent
January through June, 1977	$ 30,000 (6,000)*	$ 120,666 (30,000)*
July through December, 1977	30,000	120,666
1978	34,000	134,000
1979	38,000	147,333
1980	42,500	161,563
1981	47,000	175,625
1982	62,800	225,000
1983	79,300	275,000
1984	96,300	325,000
1985	121,800	400,000
1986	155,800	500,000
1987 through 1997	192,800	600,000
1998	202,050	625,000
1999	211,300	650,000
2000	220,550	675,000
2001	220,550	675,000
2002 and 2003	345,800	1,000,000
2004 and 2005	555,800 (345,800)*	1,500,000 (1,000,000)*
2006, 2007, and 2008	780,800 (345,800)*	2,000,000 (1,000,000)*
2009	1,455,800 (345,800)*	3,500,000 (1,000,000)*
2010	** (330,800)*	** (1,000,000)*
2011***	345,800 (345,800)*	1,000,000 (1,000,000)*

* The numbers in parentheses represent the credit and exemption equivalent amounts for the gift tax. The gift tax credit decreases in 2010 because the top gift tax rate drops to 35% for that year.   ** At the date of publication of this textbook, the estate tax is repealed because Congress did not act by December 31, 2009. Although uncertain, it is expected for Congress to extend the 2009 unified credit amount and the unified transfer tax rates to 2010 on a retroactive basis.   *** Unless Congress acts otherwise, in 2011, the estate and gift tax rules will revert to what they would have been had Congress not enacted the 2001 Act.